THE BABYLONIAN TALMUD

SEDER ṬOHOROTH

NIDDAH

★

KELIM

★

OHOLOTH

★

NEGA'IM

★

PARAH

★

ṬOHOROTH

★

MIḲWAOTH

★

MAKSHIRIN

★

ZABIM

★

ṬEBUL YOM

★

YADAYIM

★

'UḲẒIN

THE BABYLONIAN TALMUD

SEDER ṬOHOROTH

TRANSLATED INTO ENGLISH
WITH NOTES, GLOSSARY AND INDICES
UNDER THE EDITORSHIP OF
RABBI DR I. EPSTEIN
B. A., Ph. D., D. Lit.

INTRODUCTION BY
THE EDITOR

THE SONCINO PRESS
LONDON

FIRST PUBLISHED 1948

PRINTED IN THE NETHERLANDS
BY JOH. ENSCHEDÉ EN ZONEN, HAARLEM

Dedication of the First Edition

THESE VOLUMES OF SEDER ṬOHOROTH ARE DEDICATED

TO THE SACRED MEMORY OF THE

SIX MILLION JEWS

WHO WERE BRUTALLY MURDERED BY THE NAZIS

DURING THE YEARS 1933 TO 1945

THE YEARS DURING WHICH

THESE VOLUMES WERE

BEING COMPILED

PREFATORY NOTE BY THE EDITOR

The Editor desires to state that the translation of the several Tractates, and the notes thereon, are the work of the individual contributors and that he has not attempted to secure general uniformity in style or mode of rendering. He has, nevertheless, revised and supplemented, at his own discretion, their interpretation and elucidation of the original text, and has himself added the footnotes in square brackets containing alternative explanations and matter of historical and geographical interest.

ISIDORE EPSTEIN

NIDDAH

TRANSLATED INTO ENGLISH

WITH NOTES, GLOSSARY

AND INDICES

BY

REV. DR ISRAEL W. SLOTKI, M. A., Litt. D.

CONTENTS

INTRODUCTION TO *SEDER ṬOHOROTH*

BY

THE EDITOR

Ṭohoroth ('Cleannesses')[1], which is the name given to the last of the six 'Orders' into which the Talmud is divided, has for its subject the laws of the 'clean' and 'unclean' in things and persons. These laws constitute a code of levitical purity and are of much more special application than those relating to the 'clean' and 'unclean' food (animals, birds, locusts, fishes), which are discussed and elaborated in the tractate Ḥullin, included in the immediately preceding Order Ḳodashim. Whereas these latter laws are absolute, and are valid for all times and all places, most of those treated in this 'Order' are connected inseparably with the sanctuary, and have no validity apart from it. Even in Temple times many of them did not affect the common man, and unless he was to visit the sanctuary precincts, or come into contact with consecrated food, he need have paid little regard to them. Nor did these laws of 'uncleanness' ever apply outside Palestine; and with the destruction of the Temple they have as a whole fallen into obsolescence even in the Holy Land itself. An exception to this strictly circumscribed character of the laws dealt with in this 'Order' is the law of the menstruant which remains in force to the present day; but even in this case the emphasis here is primarily on the levitical 'uncleanness', rather than on the prohibition of marital relations which this impurity involves.[2]

(1) Generally taken as euphemism for 'uncleanliness', see Z. Frankel, *Darke Ha-Mishnah*, p. 254. (2) Another exception is the prohibition of defilement for the dead imposed on priests which is valid for all times and places. The law of leprosy is also, in a sense, another exception in that its discontinuance since the destruction of the Temple is not due to the absence of the sanctuary but to the lack of authenticated expert priests to whom alone the treatment of this contagion was entrusted. See Maimonides, *Yad, Ṭummeath Ẓaraath*, iii, 4, and *Sefer ha-Ḥinnuk*, 169, 171, 177. The question whether the general laws of 'cleanness' and 'uncleanness' are operative in our time is a matter of controversy between

This connection with the sanctuary makes the Seder Ṭohoroth a fitting sequel to Seder Ḳodashim, which deals principally with the Temple and its sacrificial system and rites.

The 'Order' consists of twelve tractates, arranged according to the separate printed editions of the Mishnah in the following sequence:

(1) KELIM (Vessels):[1] Deals with the rules about the uncleanness of 'vessels' (a term denoting articles of utility of every kind), indicating under which conditions they are unclean, or become susceptible to uncleanness, in accordance with Leviticus XI, 33-35. 30 Chapters.

(2) OHOLOTH (Tents): Treats of the laws concerning the defilement conveyed by a dead body to persons or 'vessels' which happen to be in the same tent or under the same roof with it, as set forth in Numbers, XIX, 14-15. 18 Chapters.

(3) NEGA'IM (Leprosy): Sets forth the rules concerning the treatment of leprosies in men, garments and dwellings in accordance with Leviticus XIII-XIV, and the prescriptions for the leper's purification. 14 Chapters.

(4) PARAH (Heifer): Describes the required properties of the Red Heifer, and the preparation and use of its ashes for the purification of the unclean, according to Numbers XIX. 12 Chapters.

(5) ṬOHOROTH (Cleannesses): Deals with the rules about the uncleanness of food-stuffs and liquids, indicating under what conditions they are rendered unclean through contact with different sources and grades of impurity. 19 Chapters.

(6) MIḲWA'OTH (Pools of Immersion): Gives the requirements for wells and reservoirs in order to render them ritually fit for immersions, and the regulations governing all ritual immersions. 10 Chapters.

(7) NIDDAH (The Menstruant). Details the rules about the legal uncleanness arising from certain conditions in women, such as

the Rabbanites and Karaites, see L. Ginzberg, *Ginze Schechter*, II, pp. 491ff. See also Judah ha-Levi, *Kuzari*, iii, 49.

(1) This tractate was also known under the name 'Ṭohoroth', see J. N. Epstein, *Der gaonäische Kommentar zur Mishnaordnung Teharoth*, Berlin 1915, p. 59 and Berlin 1921; and in *Tarbiz*, XV, pp. 71–134.

those described in Leviticus, XV, 19-31 and XII, 2-8. 10 Chapters.

(8) MAKSHIRIN (Predispositions). Has for its theme the conditions under which foodstuffs become 'predisposed', that is susceptible to uncleanness after having come into contact with liquid (in accordance with Leviticus XI, 34, 38), and enumerates the liquids that make foodstuffs susceptible in this sense. 6 Chapters.

(9) ZABIM (They That Suffer Flux): Treats of the uncleanness of men and women affected with a running issue, according to Leviticus, XV, 2-18. 5 Chapters.

(10) ṬEBUL YOM (Immersed at Day Time): Discusses the character of the uncleanness which, until the setting of the sun, adheres to one who has immersed himself during the day time for his purification (cf. Leviticus XXII, 6f.) 4 Chapters.

(11) YADAYIM (Hands): Treats of the uncleanness of unwashed hands and of their purification. It also includes a discussion on certain books of the Canon of the Bible, and records some controversies between the Sadducees and the Pharisees. 4 Chapters.

(12) 'UḲẒIN (Stalks): Deals with the conditions under which stalks of plants or fruits convey uncleanness to the fruits or plants to which they are attached or *vice versa*. 3 Chapters.

Kelim is well qualified by its contents to serve as a sort of Introduction to the whole of the 'Order'.[1] This alone, quite apart from its length, entitles it to the pride of place as opening tractate in most of the printed editions of the Mishnah. In the Talmud editions, the first place is assigned to Niddah, as being the only tractate within the 'Order' to which there is Gemara extant. Whether there has ever been Gemara to the other tractates is a question which cannot be answered with a definite 'Yes' or 'No'. There is clear evidence in the Talmud that in the days of Raba (299-352 C.E.) the Order Ṭohoroth was studied with the same intensity as the other 'Orders'.[2] Significant in this connection is the mention of ''Uḳẓin', which we are told was discussed in the school of Raba at thirteen sessions;[2] this indicates apparently that the studies covered

(1) See I. Halevy, *Doroth ha-Rishonim*, I (c) 1918, pp. 231-35. (2) See Ta'an. 24*ab*, and Sanh. 106*a*.

the whole of the 'Order' to its very last tractate. Reference is also made in a Berlin MS. to a Palestine Gemara for "Uḳẓin'[1]. On the other hand, Maimonides, who speaks of a Palestine Gemara to Ḳodashim, of which nothing is known to us, declares that 'except for Niddah, there is to be found no Gemara of any kind to Seder Ṭohoroth, neither in the Babylonian nor in the Palestinian version.'[2] It is therefore natural to assume that, while the study of the other 'Orders' was continuous and regular, suffering no break or interruption through the centuries, that of Ṭohoroth was casual and intermittent; and, but for some exceptions, was undertaken in the schools of Palestine and Babylon only in so far as its principles and teachings had a bearing on the subjects of study. This comparative neglect of the 'Order' meant that much of its contents was left unelucidated and unexplained, and that little material beyond that which had already been distributed here and there throughout the other 'Orders', was provided for the Redactors of the Talmud to work up into a separate Gemara.[3]

This neglect was not due to the fact that the subject matter of Ṭohoroth had no relevancy to the times when the edifice of the Talmud was being reared. Had this been the sole explanation there would have been, apart from Ḥullin, no Gemara on Ḳodashim either, seeing that also this 'Order' is devoted to laws which had lost all practical significance. There must have been some deeper reason for this disregard of the study of precepts which were recognised as belonging to the 'essentials of the Torah'[4]. The opinion may be hazarded that it was some vision of the Messianic future which inspired the different attitudes of the schools to Ḳodashim and Ṭohoroth. That vision embraced the restoration of the Temple

(1) See H. L. Strack, *Introduction to the Talmud and Midrash* (English ed.) Philadelphia, 1931 pp. 68 and 266. (2) See Maimonides, *Introduction to Seder Zeraim.* The reference to a 'Talmud Kelim found in "Rome"' מצאו תלמוד כלים בארץ רומא in the Gaonic commentary on Ṭohoroth (see above XIV, n. 1), is not to a Gemara but simply to some lost commentary on the tractate. See J. N. Epstein *op. cit,* 1921, p. 40: תלמוד = פירוש. (3) A Gemara on Kelim and Oholoth consisting of relevant material scattered in the Talmudim and Midrashim has been compiled by Rabbi Gershon Enoch Henech Lainer of Radzin, and published under the name *Sidre Taharah,* Jozefow, 1873, Pietrkow, 1903. (4) Ḥag. 10*a*.

with its sacrificial rites; but whereas the study of Ḳodashim was maintained with all diligence in order to keep the people prepared for the resumption of the Temple service, no similar motive applied to the laws of uncleanness which are treated in Ṭohoroth. They had been rendered obsolete with the destruction of the Temple, and no hope was set on their revival in the future. Not that there was no longing for purity, but Messianism itself spelled purity. The Messianic future, as Jewish teachers conceived it, was one in which, generally speaking, there would be no defilement, no uncleanness, God Himself appearing in His self-manifesting power and redemptive love to cleanse His people from all filthiness and pollution: *'Then I will sprinkle upon you clean water, and ye shall be clean from all your filthiness and from all your idols will I cleanse you'* (Ezekiel XXXVI, 25); *'and I will also cause the unclean spirit to pass out of the land'* (Zechariah, XIII, 2). With the loss of all practical interest which this vision entailed, it was natural for the study of Ṭohoroth to fall into desuetude. There were nevertheless still teachers, particularly of priestly descent,[1] for whom the 'Order' had its fascination, perhaps in satisfaction of a wistful longing for a glory that was past. Preeminent among these was Rabbah bar Naḥmani (d. 339 C.E.) who contributed greatly to the exposition of Ṭohoroth and whose pronouncement on a matter of levitical purity, uttered by him as he was breathing his last, received, according to Talmudic Aggadah, the stamp of Divine approval with the words: 'Happy art thou, O Rabbah bar Naḥmani, whose body is pure and whose soul has departed in purity'.[2] It is thanks to these teachers that the 'disciple of the Torah' may, notwithstanding the absence of Gemara, find his way through the branchings and windings of this 'Order' and through the maze of laws and regulations that compose it.

THE SIGNIFICANCE OF THE LAWS OF 'CLEANNESSES'

The laws of uncleanness elaborated in this 'Order' are based on a number of injunctions found in various places in the Pentateuch, principally in Leviticus Chapters XI-XV. There we find enumerated

(1) See M. Kaplan, *The Redaction of the Babylonian Talmud*, p. 252. (2) See B. M. 86*a*.

a list of things and persons which are deemed unclean in themselves and may communicate uncleanness either directly or sometimes even through an intermediary.

An examination of the sources of uncleanness shows that they are reducible to three categories: (*a*) Death; (*b*) Disease; (*c*) Sexual Functions.

Death: The most potent source of uncleanness is Death. A human corpse or part of it spreads uncleanness, conveying it not only to the person or thing that comes directly or indirectly in contact with it, but even (according to Numbers XIX, 14) to such as happen to be under the same 'tent' or 'cover' as itself. Uncleanness of a minor character also is attached to the carcass of animals, of birds and of certain species of vermin.

Disease. A very high degree of uncleanness is attached to various diseases comprehended under the general term, *Ẓaraath* ('leprosy'), of which there are three types: Leprosy of Men, Leprosy of Houses, and Leprosy of Garments.

Sexual Functions. Sexual functions, whether normal or pathological, carry with them a type of uncleanness varying in severity according to the nature of the affection. Included in this category is the menstruant, and the woman after childbirth.

Each type of uncleanness has its own specific rules defining both its character and the means by which it can be removed.

These laws are the least intelligible in the Torah. The words of the Wise King '*I said, I will get wisdom but it was far from me*' (Eccl. VII. 23), were applied by the Rabbis of the Talmud to the laws of 'cleanness' and 'uncleanness'.[1] Maimonides likewise in the Introduction to his commentary on Ṭohoroth describes the whole subject as 'bristling with difficulties, far from human understanding and one which even the Great Sages of the Mishnah found hard to comprehend.'[2] This may perhaps be the reason that this Order has been designated in the Talmud as '*Da'ath*'[3] ('Knowledge'). While, that is to say, it communicates the knowledge of a body of divine

(1) With special reference to the Red Heifer ordinances, see *Midrash Numbers Rabbah*, xix, 3. (2) See Maimonides' *Introduction to Seder Ṭohoroth.* (3) See Shab. 31*a*.

ordinances, to explain the reason for them is beyond the reach of human wisdom. Yet it was inevitable that the attempt should be made; for it cannot be supposed that these ordinances were devoid of some purpose of vital importance for the life of the Jew. Some there are who would define the object of these laws as mainly hygienic.[1] And indeed when we read the directions for cleanness set forth in the Bible they seem not unlike hygienic orders of a General to soldiers on march, or the rules of a Board of Health. Yet while this will hardly be contested, it cannot be maintained that the hygienic motive is paramount in these laws. The fact that many of the regulations bear no relation whatsoever to hygiene is clear evidence to the contrary. The same criticism applies to other motives which have been suggested, such as taboos and totemism. While these might account for some of the regulations, it is obvious that much of the legislation regarding uncleanness has no connection with these ideas, and they cannot therefore be regarded as the operative reason for it.[2]

More satisfactory is the view of Maimonides,[3] who declared that the object of these regulations was to impose certain limitations and conditions upon Israel's approach to God, which should have the effect of deepening in them the sense of awe and reverence for the majesty of their divine Father and King. It is for this reason, as he points out, that the whole of these laws apply only to relations with the sanctuary and the holy objects connected with it and not to other cases.

This basic principle provides Maimonides with a key to many of the details of the laws of uncleanness and purifications. The source of uncleanness is, in his view, physical dirt and filth. Human corpses, carcasses of animals, birds or creeping things, sexual functions, leprous diseases, are all dirt and filth and accordingly convey uncleanness.

While Maimonides is certainly correct in relating the laws of purity to the sanctuary, his idea of the source of uncleanness does

(1) See I. L. Katzenelsohn, *Talmud and Medizin* (Hebrew), pp. 354,ff. (2) Cf. W. Robertson Smith, *Religion of the Semites*, (2nd ed. 1894) pp. 296. (3) *Guide for the Perplexed*, iii, 47.

not appear adequate. It does not account for the exclusion from the Biblical list of 'uncleannesses' other things that are equally dirty and filthy. There is therefore much to be said in favour of the suggestion that the laws of uncleanness as related to the sanctuary were as a whole instituted to wean Israel away from the then prevalent animal worship and cult of the dead as well as from the sexual perversions that were inseparable from Caananite idolatrous cults.[1] But while there is no reason to doubt that this motive is present in the institution of corpse and carcass uncleanness and the uncleanness of sexual functions, this would still leave most of the laws of uncleanness unexplained.

Many more suggestions in explanation of these laws have been made by Biblical commentators both Jewish and non-Jewish, mediaeval and modern, but notwithstanding the penetration and richness of thought that is to be found in some of them, particularly in those of Naḥmanides, Gersonides and Abrabanel, they cannot be said to satisfy the student. The only correct attitude to adopt in regard to this legislation is that of Maimonides. With all his endeavour to give in his '*Guide*' a rational explanation of these laws, even to their smallest details, he declares categorically in his *Yad ha-Ḥazaḳah* that they are to be treated as divine statutes which baffle human understanding. 'It is clear and obvious', he writes, 'that the regulations concerning uncleanness and cleanness are decrees of the Holy Writ, and do not belong to the subjects which a man can rationally explain. They thus belong to the category of statutes. Similarly the act of immersion to rid oneself of impurity belongs to that class of "statutes" because defilement is not material filth that can be removed by water. It is but a decree of the Holy Writ, and the removal is dependent upon the intention of the heart. On that account the Sages said, "If a man immersed himself without specific intention, it is as though he had not immersed himself at all." Nevertheless there is symbolical significance in this matter. In the same way that a person who directs his heart to self-purification attains cleanness as soon as he immerses although there has been no

(1) See Katzenelsohn, *op. cit.* pp. 365f. and 381ff. On the ancient idolatrous cults referred to, see A. Lods, *Israel*, pp. 227, 243, 409f.

physical change in him, so the person who directs his heart to purify his soul from spiritual impurities, such as inquitous thoughts and evil notions, becomes clean as soon as he determines in his heart to keep apart from these courses, and bathes his soul in the waters of the pure knowledge.'[1]

This attitude follows logically from the belief in Revelation, and any other attitude is *ipso facto* a rejection of the Torah of Israel and of God who is its Author. This does not mean to say that the laws of the Torah are arbitrary, with no purpose and significance. Had this been admitted, Jewish religious thinkers throughout the ages would not have devoted so much of their energies to an inquiry into the specific reasons of the Commandments. But what it does mean is that whilst the laws of the Torah, by the very virtue of their educative character, cannot contain anything which is irrational and which cannot be made to fit into a general framework of reason, and that therefore every attempt to discover their significance is justified, they are nevertheless not reducible altogether to logical concepts; and over and above the reasons that may be adduced there are others that transcend all human thoughts and imagining.

Reverting to the laws of 'cleanness' and 'uncleanness', all that Jewish religious teachers sought to establish in their quest for a meaning of these ordinances was a rationale in accord with the moral and spiritual nature of man which would explain the inclusion of them in the Torah, without however attempting to penetrate into their innermost significance. This, they recognised, was related to a higher order of existence, incomprehensible to our state of human knowledge. Fundamental to their view of life is the close relationship of body and soul, so that what affects the one affects the other. Nor is there anything strange in this conception. In the words of R. Aaron Halevi, 'We may indeed be astonished at this close relationship between body and soul, but we do not know the nature of the soul nor its essence; how then should we know what is good or harmful for it? Just as a doctor can effect no cure without first ascertaining the cause of the malady, so is the reason for some of the commandments bound to elude us so

(1) *Yad, Miḳwa'oth*, xi, 12.

long as we have no complete knowledge of the nature of the soul.'[1]

From this conception it follows that the soul is affected by the uncleanness of the body. The nature of this affection varies in accordance with the source of uncleanness, as determined by the wisdom of the 'Creator of all Souls'. In general, bodily uncleanness has a contaminating influence on the soul, disqualifying the person thus affected from approaching the sanctuary of God. Although no longer valid, the relevant laws have not lost their symbolic significance: the necessity of purity of body, mind and soul in order to gain acceptance with God. Graver in its consequences and in full force to the present day is the law of *Niddah*. The reasons for the *Niddah* ordinances are many and varied. They promote sexual hygiene, physical health, marital continence, respect for womanhood, consecration of married life, and family happiness. But over and above these weighty reasons, they concern the very being of the soul of the Jew. They safeguard the purity of the Jewish soul, without which no true religious moral and spiritual life—individual or corporate—as Judaism conceives it, is attainable.

While the Halachic student will turn to Seder Ṭohoroth in order to satisfy his thirst for knowledge in an important department of Jewish law, and to find intellectual delight in its dialectic, which is of a very high order, the non-Halachic student will be rewarded in his study of the Seder by the discovery of a wealth of material of archaeological, medical and general cultural interest. Of particular value are its deposits of linguistic elements which can supply much of the needs of New Judea for Hebrew norms of expression in keeping with the advance of technology, commerce, science, and modern life in general.

METHOD AND SCOPE

TEXT. The Text for this edition is in the main that of the Wilna Romm Edition. Note has, however, been taken of the most important variants of manuscript and printed editions some of which have been adopted in the main body of the translation, the reason for

(1) *Sefer ha-Ḥinnuk* 159; see I. Epstein, *The Conception of the Commandments of the Torah in Aaron Halevi's Sefer ha-Ḥinnuk*, in 'Essays Presented to J. H. Hertz' pp. 157-8

such preference being generally explained or indicated in the Notes. All the censored passages appear either in the text or in the Notes.

TRANSLATION. The translation aims at reproducing in clear and lucid English the central meaning of the original text. It is true some translators will be found to have been less literal than others, but in checking and controlling *every line* of the work, the Editor has endeavoured not to lose sight of the main aim of the translation. Words and passages not occurring in the original are placed in square brackets.

NOTES. The main purpose of these is to elucidate the translation by making clear the course of the arguments, explaining allusions and technical expressions, thus providing a running commentary on the text. With this in view resort has been made to the standard Hebrew commentators, Rashi, the Tosafists, Asheri, Alfasi, Maimonides, Maharsha, the glosses of BaḤ, Rashal, Strashun, the Wilna Gaon, etc.[1] Advantage has also been taken of the results of modern scholarship, such as represented by the names of Graetz, Bacher, Weiss, Halevy, Levy, Kohut, Jastrow, Obermeyer, Büchler and Klein, and—happily still with us—Krauss, Ginzberg, and Herford among others, in dealing with matters of general cultural interest with which the Talmud teems—historical, geographical, archaeological, philological and social.

GLOSSARY AND INDICES. Each Tractate is equipped with a Glossary wherein recurring technical terms are fully explained, thus obviating the necessity of explaining them afresh each time they appear in the text. To this have been added a Scriptural Index and a General Index of contents.

In the presentation of the tractates the following principles have also been adopted:

(i) The Mishnah and the words of the Mishnah recurring and commented upon in the Gemara are printed in capitals.

(ii) תנן introducing a Mishnah cited in the Gemara, is rendered 'we have learnt'.

(iii) תניא introducing a Baraitha, is rendered 'it has been (or was) taught'.

(1) These names are referred to more fully in the list of Abbreviations at the end of each Tractate.

(iv) תנו רבנן introducing a Tannaitic teaching, is rendered 'Our Rabbis taught'.

(v) Where an Amora cites a Tannaitic teaching the word 'learnt' is used, e.g., תני רב יוסף, 'R. Joseph learnt'.

(vi) The word tanna designating a teacher of the Amoraic period (v. Glos.) is written with a small 't'.

(vii) A distinction is made between . . . הלכה כ referring to a Tannaitic ruling and . . . הלכתא כ which refers to the ruling of an Amora, the former being rendered 'the *halachah* is . . .' and the latter, 'the law is . . .'

(viii) R. stands either for Rabbi designating a Palestinian teacher or Rab designating a Babylonian teacher, except in the case of the frequently recurring Rab Judah where the title 'Rab' has been written in full to distinguish him from the Tanna of the same name.

(ix) רחמנא, lit., 'The Merciful One', has been rendered 'the Divine Law' in cases where the literal rendering may appear somewhat incongruous to the English ear.

(x) Biblical verses appear in italics except for the emphasized word or words in the quotation which appear in Roman characters.

(xi) No particular English version of the Bible is followed, as the Talmud has its own method of exegesis and its own way of understanding Biblical verses which it cites. Where, however, there is a radical departure from the English versions, the rendering of a recognized English version is indicated in the Notes. References to chapter and verse are those of the Massoretic Hebrew text.

(xii) Any answer to a question is preceded by a dash (—), except where the question and the answer form part of one and the same argument.

(xiii) Inverted commas are used sparingly, that is, where they are deemed essential or in dialogues.

(xiv) The archaic second person 'thou', 'thee' etc. is employed only in *Haggadic* passages or where it is necessary to distinguish it from the plural 'you', 'yours', etc.

(xv) The usual English spelling is retained in proper names in vogue like Simeon, Isaac, Akiba, as well as in words like *halachah, Shechinah, shechitah,* etc. which have almost passed into the English language. The transliteration employed for other Hebrew words is given at the end of each tractate.

(xvi) It might also be pointed out for the benefit of the student that the recurring phrases 'Come and hear:' and 'An objection was raised:' or 'He objected:' introduce Tannaitic teachings, the two latter in contradiction, the former either in support or contradiction of a particular view expressed by an Amora.

THANKSGIVING

In presenting this Seder, the Soncino Press is resuming the publication of its English edition of the Babylonian Talmud, interrupted by the hard and bitter years of the world-engulfing and world-devastating war. These were years of unparalleled tragedy for mankind, but for none has the tragedy been so staggering and overwhelming as for the Jewish people. With many Jewries decimated and the flower of their kith and kin annihilated, the Jews stand to-day terribly diminished in numbers and in material and spiritual resources. As they gaze in horror on the universal scene of desolation left by the war, they cannot escape the particularly bewildering shock of the landscape as it affects Jewish life. They look out and see the ruins of many flourishing communities and famous *Torah* centres, which for generations sent forth beams of spiritual and cultural and religious light to Jews throughout the world. It is therefore only fitting on this occasion, for those of us who have been closely connected with this publication and been spared to this day, to utter the traditional שהחינו. We, in a spirit of sincere humility, thank God that to us has been granted the privilege of making a notable and specific contribution to the preservation of the *Torah*, so that it might not be forgotten from Israel, and of continuing the work which can provide a great and stimulating force to this generation in the mighty tasks of spiritual and religious reconstruction that lie ahead.

ACKNOWLEDGEMENTS

I should also like to take this opportunity of expressing my warmest appreciation to the several translators for the learning and industry they have brought to bear upon their work; to Mr. Maurice Simon, M. A., for his helpfulness in many directions; to Mr. Eli Cashdan, M. A., for his valuable assistance, particularly in reading and checking the proofs; and to my dear wife for her help in many ways whilst I was engaged in this work.

Nor must I forget to express my very special thanks to Mr. Jacob Davidson, the Governing Director of the Soncino Press, whose inflexible resolve and dauntless energy enabled him to triumph over all obstacles and difficulties and to resume the publication of this gigantic work.

Nor can I take leave from the reader without a word in affectionate remembrance of the late Chief Rabbi, Dr. J. H. Hertz, who was, alas, not spared to see the completion of the Soncino version of the Talmud. As a patron of Jewish scholarship and learning, the Chief Rabbi took a keen personal interest in this work, as his Forewords to the Orders Neziḳin, Nashim and Mo'ed testifiy. His sponsoring of this publication has indeed been most valuable.

For technical reasons, Seder Ṭohoroth, which is the last of the Sedarim, is published before the two remaining Orders — Zera'im and Ḳodashim. These two Sedarim will shortly be issued and thus bring this great and important task to completion. In the meantime, on behalf of all collaborators and co-workers, associated with me in this publiscation, I offer the time-honoured traditional prayers of the student of the Law as applied to this Seder:

יהי רצון מלפניך ד׳ אלהינו כשם שעזרתנו לסיים סדר טהרות כן תעזרנו להתחיל סדרים אחרים ולסיימם.

'May it be Thy will, O Lord our God, even as Thou hast helped us to complete Seder Ṭohoroth, so to help us to begin the other Sedarim and complete them.'

I. EPSTEIN

Jews' College, London.
5th Tishri, 5708
19th September, 1947.

INTRODUCTION

The Tractate *Niddah*, which comes seventh in the Mishnah editions of the Order of Ṭohoroth, is placed first in the editions of the Talmud, since it is the only Tractate in this order which consists of Gemara as well as Mishnah.

The term *niddah*[1] is applied in Biblical and Rabbinical literature to a woman in menstruation who, by reason of her uncleanness, is subject to certain restrictions during her periods and for a varying number of days subsequently.

The origin of these regulations is Lev. XV, 19ff, which prescribe some general rules concerning *niddah* and *zibah* (v. Glos.). These enactments have been expounded and amplified in accordance with Rabbinical methods of interpretation and tradition, and have been made still more onerous by the strict customs adopted by Jewish women themselves.

The following is a brief summary of the ten chapters of this Tractate:

Chapter I describes the factors that determine the length of the periods of uncleanness in various classes of women, particularly with reference to the retroactive effect of the uncleanness.

Chapter II states the test which establish the beginning of the menstrual period and indicates which colours of discharge are clean and which are unclean.

Chapter III deals with the woman in childbirth, stating under what conditions and for what length of time she is unclean, and determining the period of uncleanness in those cases where the sex of the child cannot be established either because of hermaphroditism or on account of miscarriage or abortion.

Chapter IV is concerned with the condition of uncleanness of non-Jewish women, such as Samaritans, Sadducеans and idolaters, and of women in protracted labour.

(1) נִדָּה (from root נדה or נדד) 'isolation', 'impurity'. A menstruant is 'isolated' from her husband and keeps away from other persons and things because, being in her 'impurity' she renders them ritually unclean if she comes into contact with them.

CHAPTER V deals with the uncleanness of a woman whose child was delivered by a Caesarean section. It indicates also the signs of puberty in both sexes, determining their symptoms and the times of their appearance.

CHAPTER VI gives further details on the signs of puberty in the female. In this connection the rule is evolved that on the appearance of a particular symptom the other are assumed to exist, whereas the converse is not true. This terse rule is illustrated by a number of diverse topics where, likewise, it is seen that one condition or fact implies another, but not *vice versa* (cf. 49*a* ff).

CHAPTER VII discusses the uncleanness of menstrual blood and other impurities. It also states the circumstances and to what extent Samaritans are believed in regard to uncleanness.

CHAPTERS VIII-X indicate the tests to be applied to decide whether a stain is that of menstrual blood or of some other matter; describe the symptoms of the approach of the menstrual period; and deal finally with the condition of uncleanness of the corpse of a menstruant.

This Tractate contains little Haggadic material. Apart from the occasional homiletical interpretations of Biblical verses the following passages are noteworthy: the view that the physical qualities and characteristics of a person are preordained before birth whereas the moral character and spiritual outlook are left to the free choice of man (16*b*); the remarkable experiences of Abba Saul as a grave digger (24*b*); and the folkloristic belief in the blissful condition of the unborn child in the mother's womb (30*b*).

ISRAEL W. SLOTKI

The Indices of this Tractate have been compiled by Dr Judah J. Slotki, M.A.

NIDDAH

CHAPTER I

MISHNAH. [2*a*]. SHAMMAI RULED: FOR ALL WOMEN[1] IT SUFFICES [TO RECKON] THEIR [PERIOD OF UNCLEANNESS FROM THE] TIME [OF THEIR DISCOVERING THE FLOW].[2] HILLEL RULED: [THEIR PERIOD OF UNCLEANNESS IS TO BE RECKONED RETROSPECTIVELY] FROM THE [PREVIOUS] EXAMINATION TO THE [LAST] EXAMINATION,[3] EVEN [IF THE INTERVAL EXTENDED] FOR MANY DAYS. THE SAGES, HOWEVER, RULED: [THE LAW IS] NEITHER IN AGREEMENT WITH THE OPINION OF THE FORMER[4] NOR IN AGREEMENT WITH THAT OF THE LATTER,[5] BUT [THE WOMEN ARE DEEMED TO HAVE BEEN UNCLEAN] DURING [THE PRECEDING] TWENTY-FOUR HOURS[6] WHEN THIS[7] LESSENS THE PERIOD FROM THE [PREVIOUS] EXAMINATION TO THE [LAST] EXAMINATION, AND DURING THE PERIOD FROM THE [PREVIOUS] EXAMINATION TO THE [LAST] EXAMINATION WHEN THIS[8] LESSENS THE PERIOD OF TWENTY-FOUR HOURS.

FOR ANY WOMAN WHO HAS A SETTLED PERIOD IT SUFFICES [TO RECKON HER PERIOD OF UNCLEANNESS FROM] THE TIME

(1) In respect of menstrual uncleanness. (2) It being assumed that up to that moment there was no vestige of blood even in the ante-chamber (cf. Mishnah *infra* 40a). Hence only objects that were touched by the woman after the discovery become ritually unclean. All objects touched prior to that moment remain clean. (3) When she discovered the discharge. If the last, for instance, took place at 5 p.m. on a Thursday and the previous one at 8 a.m. on the preceding Sunday, all objects touched since the Sunday examination are deemed to be ritually unclean because it is assumed that some blood, prevented from leaving the body by the walls of the womb, may have made its way into the ante-chamber immediately after that examination. (4) Shammai, whose ruling is too lenient. (5) Hillel, who is too restrictive, since blood could not well be retained in the ante-chamber for a very long time. (6) *Me'eth le'eth*, lit., 'from time to time'. (7) An interval of more than twenty-four hours having intervened between the two examinations. (8) The two examinations having taken place within twenty-four hours.

SHE DISCOVERS THE FLOW: AND IF A WOMAN USES TESTING-RAGS WHEN[1] SHE HAS MARITAL INTERCOURSE, THIS IS INDEED[2] LIKE AN EXAMINATION WHICH LESSENS EITHER THE PERIOD OF THE [PAST] TWENTY-FOUR HOURS OR THE PERIOD FROM THE [PREVIOUS] EXAMINATION TO THE [LAST] EXAMINATION. HOW [IS ONE TO UNDERSTAND THE RULING THAT][3] 'IT SUFFICES [TO RECKON HER PERIOD OF UNCLEANNESS FROM] THE TIME SHE DISCOVERS THE FLOW'? IF SHE WAS SITTING ON A BED AND WAS OCCUPIED WITH RITUALLY CLEAN OBJECTS[4] AND, HAVING LEFT THEM, OBSERVED A FLOW, SHE IS RITUALLY UNCLEAN WHILE THE OBJECTS[5] REMAIN RITUALLY CLEAN.

ALTHOUGH THEY[6] HAVE LAID DOWN THAT SHE[7] CONVEYS UNCLEANNESS FOR A PERIOD OF TWENTY-FOUR HOURS [RETROSPECTIVELY][8] SHE COUNTS [THE SEVEN DAYS OF HER MENSTRUATION][9] ONLY FROM THE TIME SHE OBSERVED THE FLOW.

GEMARA. What is Shammai's reason?[10]—He is of the opinion that a woman[11] should be presumed to enjoy[12] her usual status, and the status of the woman[13] was one of cleanness.[14] And Hillel?[15]—When is it said that an object is presumed to possess its usual status? Only when the unfavourable condition[16] is not internal;[17] but as regards a woman, [2*b*] since what she observes [is a discharge] from her own body, it cannot be held that she is presumed to have her usual status.

(1) Before and after. (2) Lit., 'behold this'. (3) In the case of 'ANY WOMAN WHO HAS A SETTLED PERIOD' (*supra*). (4) In the preparation, for instance, of foodstuffs. (5) The bed, and the foodstuffs which she handled. (6) The Sages. (7) A woman who had no settled period. (8) From the time she observed the flow. (9) Prescribed in Lev. XV, 19. (10) For his ruling in the first clause of our Mishnah. (11) About whom it is uncertain when her flow began. (12) Lit., 'cause to stand . . . upon'. (13) Spoken of in our Mishnah. (14) Since she was occupied with ritually clean things. (15) How, in view of Shammai's reason, can he maintain his ruling. (16) Which might impair its status. (17) But is due to some external cause. MS.M. adds, 'as, for instance, when it is doubtful whether one did, or did not touch (an unclean object)'.

domain?[1] And should you argue: Is not every doubtful case of ritual uncleanness in a public domain regarded as clean [it could be retorted:] Since [in the case of the bath] there are two unfavourable factors[2] it is regarded as certain uncleanness. R. Simeon, however, holds [that the law of the ritual bath is the same as that of *soṭah* [in this respect]: As the *soṭah* is regarded as clean [where she is suspected of an offence] in a public domain so also here[3] [are all the purifications effected regarded as] clean [if the bath was] in a public domain. If [the inference, however, is made] from the *soṭah*, might it not be argued: It is like the *soṭah* in this respect viz., that as the *soṭah* [if suspected of the offence] in a private domain is regarded as definitely unclean so should also [all purifications effected in this case] be deemed to be definitely unclean [where the bath was] in a private domain?—What a comparison![4] In that case[5] there is some basis for the suspicion,[6] seeing that he[7] had warned her and she had secluded herself with the stranger; what basis for uncleanness,[6] however, is there here?[8]

And if you prefer I might say that this is R. Simeon's reason:[9] He infers the law of the termination of uncleanness[10] from that of the inception of uncleanness;[11] as with the inception of uncleanness if it is doubtful whether an object has or has not touched an uncleanness in a public domain it is deemed to be clean, so also with the termination of uncleanness, if it is doubtful whether an object

(1) Nothing. Hence the Rabbis' ruling that all purifications effected, irrespective of domain, are deemed to be unclean. (2) As pointed out *supra* 2*b*. (3) The case of the ritual bath under discussion. (4) Lit., 'thus, now'. (5) *Soṭah*. (6) Lit., 'there are feet for the thing' (7) Her husband. (8) In the case of the bath. As there is no basis whatever for the assumption that this deficiency occurred before the purifications had been effected it may well be assumed that it occurred afterwards immediately before the bath was measured. It has thus been shown, as R. Ḥanina replied *supra*, that according to R. Simeon all cases of doubtful uncleanness in a private domain where there is no basis for the affirmation of the uncleanness, are regarded as being in suspense. (9) For holding doubtful cases of uncleanness in a public domain to be clean. (10) *Sc.* ritual immersion which takes place when the period of uncleanness is concluded. (11) I.e., uncleanness contracted from coming in contact with an unclean object.

had been duly immersed or not, in a public domain it is deemed to be clean. And the Rabbis?[1] — What an inference![2] There,[3] since the man is in the presumptive status of ritual cleanness, we cannot on account of a doubt transfer him to a state of uncleanness, but here,[4] seeing that the man is in the presumptive status of uncleanness, we cannot on account of a doubt release him from his uncleanness.

Wherein, however, does this[5] essentially differ[6] from the case of an alley of which we learnt: If a dead creeping thing was found in an alley it causes ritual uncleanness retrospectively[7] to such time as one can testify, 'I examined this alley and there was no creeping thing in it',[8] or to such time as it was last swept?[9] — There[10] also, since there are creeping things from the alley itself and also creeping things that make their way into it from the outside world, the case is the same as one that has two unfavourable factors. And if you prefer I might reply,[11] This is Shammai's reason:[12] Because a woman is herself conscious [when she suffers a flow].[13]

(1) How, in view of R. Simeon's inference, could they maintain (v. *supra* 2*b ad fin.*) that 'all purifications . . . whether it was in a public or in a private domain, are unclean'? (2) Lit., 'thus, now'. (3) The case of the inception of uncleanness. (4) In a case of termination of uncleanness. (5) The case of the menstruant in our Mishnah. (6) According to Shammai. (7) To all clean objects that were in the alley prior to its discovery. (8) *Sc.* only clean objects that were in the alley prior to that examination are ritually clean since the examination has established that during that time there was no creeping thing in the alley. (9) *Infra* 56*a*; and no creeping thing was found. The sweeping, which is presumably accompanied by a search for any unclean things, has the same force as a direct examination. Hence (cf. prev. n.) only objects that were in the alley prior to the sweeping are clean while those that were there after the sweeping, since a creeping thing may have fallen into the alley immediately after the sweeping was over, are regarded as unclean. Now seeing that here uncleanness in a doubtful case is caused retrospectively, why does Shammai in our Mishnah restrict the period of uncleanness to the time of THEIR DISCOVERING only? (10) The case of the alley in the Mishnah just cited. (11) To the objection raised against Shammai. (12) For his ruling that menstruants begin their period of uncleanness from the time OF THEIR DISCOVERING OF THE FLOW only and not, as in the case of the alley, retrospectively. (13) As she did not feel any prior to her present discovery it may be safely assumed that previously there had not been any.

And Hillel?[1]—She might have thought that the sensation[2] was that of urine. As to Shammai, is there not [the possibility of suffering a flow while] asleep?[3]—A woman asleep too would[4] awake on account of the pain,[5] as is the case where one feels a discharge of urine.[6] But is there not the case of an imbecile?[7]—Shammai agrees[8] in the case of an imbecile. But did he not state, ALL WOMEN?[9]—[He meant:] All sensible women. Then why did he not merely state WOMEN?[10]—He intended to indicate that the law is not in agreement with R. Eliezer; for R. Eliezer mentioned 'Four classes of women'[11] and no more, hence he[12] informed us [that the law applies to] ALL WOMEN. But is there not the case of stains?[13] Must we then[14] assume that we learnt the Mishnah about stains[15] in disagreement with Shammai?—Abaye replied: Shammai agrees[16] in the case of stains. What is the reason?—Since she was neither handling a slaughtered bird nor was she passing through the butchers' market, whence could that blood have come?[17] And[18] if you prefer I might reply, This is Shammai's reason: If in fact any blood were there[19] it would have flowed out earlier.[20] And Hillel?[21]—The walls of the womb may have held it back.[22]

(1) How, in view of this argument, can he maintain that a menstruant's uncleanness is RECKONED RETROSPECTIVELY? (2) Of the menstrual flow. (3) When the woman is unconscious of it. As this is quite possible, why does not Shammai extend the period of uncleanness retrospectively? (4) In Shammai's opinion. (5) Of the flow. (6) As she did not awake, it may well be presumed that the flow began just before its discovery. (7) Who is incapable of distinguishing the first appearance of a flow. (8) That the period of uncleanness extends retrospectively. (9) Which presumably includes the imbecile also. (10) Omitting 'ALL'. (11) *Infra 7a.* (12) Shammai. (13) Of menstrual blood, which (v. *infra* 56*a*) cause uncleanness retrospectively, though prior to the moment of its discharge the woman was unaware of any flow. (14) Since Shammai does not extend the unclean period retrospectively, maintaining that a woman is invariably aware when her flow first appears. (15) Where it was ruled that a stain causes uncleanness even where the woman had felt no flow whatever. (16) That the menstruant's uncleanness is extended retrospectively. (17) Hence it must be assumed to have come from the woman's menstrual flow. (18) So BaḤ. Cur. edd. omit 'and'. (19) *Sc.* prior to its discovery. (20) As none flowed out it may well be assumed that the flow began only just before it had been discovered. (21) *Sc.* how can he maintain his ruling in view of the argument here advanced for Shammai?

And Shammai?[1]—The walls of the womb do not hold blood back. But what can be said for a woman[2] who[3] uses an absorbent in her marital intercourse?[4]—Abaye replied: Shammai agrees[5] in the case of one who uses an absorbent.[6] Raba replied: An absorbent too [does not affect Shammai's ruling, since] perspiration causes it to shrink.[7] Raba, however, agrees[8] in the case of a tightly packed absorbent.[9]

What, however, is the practical difference between the latter explanations[10] and the former explanation?[11] [3b]—The practical difference between them is the possibility of pointing out an incongruity [between the ruling in our Mishnah and the rulings concerning] the jug, the ritual bath and the alley:[12] According to the former explanation[11] such an incongruity may justifiably be pointed out[12] while according to the latter explanations[10] such an incongruity does not exist. But what practical difference is there [in the case of the latter][10] between the one and the other explanation?—According to Abaye[13] there is the case of the absorbent,[14] and according to Raba[13] there is the case of the absorbent tightly packed.[15]

(22) As, however, it might have made its way to the ante-chamber the period of uncleanness must extend from that time onwards.

(1) Cf. prev. n. but one *mut. mut.* (2) Of the three classes enumerated *infra* 45a. (3) To prevent conception. (4) As the material used would also absorb any menstrual blood, there could be no proof that the discharge did not begin prior to the discovery. How then could Shammai rule that the menstrual uncleanness begins only at 'THE TIME OF THEIR DISCOVERING THE FLOW'? (5) That menstrual uncleanness is reckoned retrospectively. (6) Cf. prev. n. but one. (7) Lit., 'on account of perspiration it inevitably shrinks' and consequently, enables the blood to pass out. As no blood appeared prior to the discovery Shammai may well maintain that the uncleanness does not begin prior to the DISCOVERING OF THE FLOW. (8) With Abaye. (9) Since the blood cannot pass through it. (10) That (*a*) 'a woman feels' and (*b*) 'it would have flowed out earlier' (*supra*). (11) *Supra* 2a, 'a woman should be presumed to enjoy her usual status'. (12) *Supra* 2b and 3a. (13) *Supra* 3a *ad fin.* (14) If the explanation is that 'a woman feels' the period of menstrual uncleanness would begin at the time of the discovery of the blood even where a woman used an absorbent, while if the explanation is that 'it would have flowed out earlier' uncleanness would begin retrospectively since the discharge might have begun earlier but was soaked up by the absorbent. (15) Cf. prev. note.

It was taught in agreement with that explanation that 'if in fact any blood were there it would have flowed out earlier': Hillel said to Shammai, 'Do you not agree that in the case of a basket one corner of which was used for levitically clean objects while in another corner was found[1] a dead creeping thing, the objects that were formerly clean are regarded as unclean retrospectively?'[2] —'Indeed', the other replied. 'Then [Hillel rejoined] what is the difference between the one case and the other?'[3]—'The one[4] [Shammai replied] has a bottom,[5] the other[6] has none.'[7]

Raba stated: Shammai's reason[8] is to avoid[9] neglect of marital life.[10] So it was also taught: Shammai said to Hillel, 'If so,[11] you cause the daughters of Israel the neglect of marital life'.[12]

Now according to him[13] who taught this explanation[14] [it may be objected:] Was it not taught,[15] in agreement with the former explanation,[14] that 'if in fact any blood were there it would have flowed out earlier'?—There[15] it was Hillel who erred. He thought that Shammai's reason was that if any blood had been there it would have flowed out earlier and, therefore, he raised an objection

(1) After the clean objects had been removed from the basket. (2) Lit., 'the former clean are unclean', because it is possible that the creeping thing was in the basket before the objects had been removed and that it consequently imparted uncleanness to the basket from which it was conveyed to the objects. If the creeping thing, it may be added, had been found in the same corner in which the objects were previously kept there could be no question that the latter remain clean, since it may be regarded as certain that they had been removed before the creeping thing had fallen into the basket. For if it had been there earlier it would have been discovered at the time the objects were being removed. (3) *Sc.* why is the uncleanness deemed to be retrospective in the case of the basket and not in that of the menstruant? (4) The basket. (5) Where the creeping thing may well have rested quite unobserved by the person who removed the objects. (6) The menstruant. (7) *Sc.* had any blood found its way to the ante-chamber it would inevitably have flowed out. (8) For his ruling in the first clause of our Mishnah that the uncleanness is not retrospective. (9) Lit., 'on account of'. (10) Lit., 'propagation'. Were it to be assumed that blood can make its way to the vagina even when the woman is unconscious of it, men would abstain from all marital intercourse in order to avoid possible complications of uncleanness. (11) That menstrual uncleanness is to be retrospective (v. our Mishnah). (12) Cf. note 10. (13) Raba. (14) Of Shammai's reason. (15) *Supra*.

against him from the case of the basket,[1] but Shammai answered him, 'My reason is the avoidance of the neglect of marital life; and as regards your erroneous assumption too, in consequence of which you raised an objection from the case of the basket, the latter has a bottom while the former has none.[2]

But according to him who taught[3] the first explanation[4] [it may be objected:] Was it not in fact taught, in agreement with the latter version, that the reason is to avoid the neglect of propagation?—It is this that Hillel in fact said to Shammai, 'Even if you give as your reason that "if in fact any blood were there it would have flowed out earlier," you must nevertheless make a fence[5] for your ruling, for why should this law be different from all the Torah for which a fence is made?' To this the other replied, 'If so,[6] you would cause the daughters of Israel to neglect marital life'.[7] And Hillel?[8]—'Do I [he can reply] speak of marital life?[9] I only speak of levitical cleanness'. And Shammai?[10]—[Restrictions, he holds, must] not [be imposed] even as regards levitical cleanness, since otherwise[11] the man might have scruples[12] and keep away altogether.[13]

(Mnemonic:[14] *Bottom examined covered in a corner.*)

It was stated: If one corner of a basket was used for levitically clean objects and a dead creeping thing was found in another corner, Hezekiah ruled that the objects that were formerly[15] clean

(1) Where it is not assumed (on the analogy of the blood of the menstruant) that if a creeping thing had been there it would have come out together with the objects when the basket had been cleared. (2) Cf. notes *supra*. (3) *Supra*. (4) That Shammai's reason is that if any blood had been in the vagina it would have flowed out earlier. (5) I.e., add some restriction (retrospective uncleanness) in order to avoid possible transgression of the law itself. (6) That menstrual uncleanness is to be retrospective (v. our Mishnah). (7) V. *supra* p. 11 n. 10. (8) How, in view of this reply, could he maintain his ruling. (9) No. He did not say that any marital relations were to be affected. (10) Cf. note 8 *mut. mut.* (11) Lit., 'for if so', were retrospective uncleanness to be imposed. (12) Owing to the possibility of some flow of blood in the vagina. (13) Lit., 'his heart beats him and he separates (from his wife)'. (14) Containing striking words or phrases from each of the four following explanations of the points on which Shammai and Hillel on the one hand and Hezekiah and R. Joḥanan on the other differ. (15) Lit., 'the first'.

remain clean. R. Johanan ruled: The objects that were formerly[1] clean are now regarded as retrospectively unclean. But do not Shammai[2] and Hillel in fact agree[3] in the case of a basket that the objects that were formerly clean are deemed to be retrospectively unclean?[4]—Shammai and Hillel agree[5] only in the case of a basket that had a bottom,[6] while Hezekiah and R. Johanan differ in that of a basket that had no bottom.[7] But if the basket had no bottom what could be R. Johanan's reason?[8]—It had no bottom, but it had[9] a rim.[10] But surely, it was taught:[11] 'If a man drew[12] ten buckets of water one after the other[13] and a creeping thing was found in one of them, this one[14] is unclean and all the others[15] remain clean';[16] and in connection with this Resh Lakish citing R. Jannai stated, 'This[17] was taught only in a case where the bucket had no rim[18] but if it had a rim[19] all the buckets of water are deemed to be unclean.' Now must it be assumed that Hezekiah[20] does not adopt

(1) Lit., 'the first'. (2) So BaH and MS.M. Cur. edd. in parenthesis insert 'Beth'. (3) *Supra*. — MS.M. reads, 'Does not Shammai agree with Hillel'. (4) How then can Hezekiah differ from the unanimous ruling of both? (5) Var. lec. 'Shammai agrees with Hillel' (MS.M.). (6) And the objects were removed through the open top, so that it was quite possible for the creeping thing to be at the time of the removal at the bottom of the basket and thus to have escaped observation. (7) And that was used while it was lying on its side. In such circumstances the objects would be removed by inverting the basket in which case all its contents, including any creeping thing that might have been there, would fall out. (8) For treating the objects as unclean. (9) Near the position of the bottom. (10) Turning inwards, so that the creeping thing might have been caught by it and there remained unobserved. (11) Var. lec., 'we learnt' (BaH citing Toh. IV, 4, which, however, differs slightly from the version here cited). (12) With the same bucket. (13) All of which were poured into one large tank. (14) In which the creeping thing was found. (15) Since no creeping thing was observed to be in them when they were being emptied into the tank. (16) It being assumed that the creeping thing had not fallen into the bucket until it was filled for the last time. (17) That all the others remain clean. (18) Turning inwards so that the creeping thing could not possibly have remained in the bucket when it was tipped over the tank. (19) On which the creeping thing might have been caught and remained unobserved at the time. (20) Who, as explained *supra* in the case of the basket, holds the objects to be clean even where the basket had a rim.

the view of R. Jannai?[1]—[No, since] water[2] glides[3] while fruits[4] do not glide;[5] or else [it may be replied] one is not particular with water[6] but with fruit one is particular.[7] And if you prefer I might reply: Shammai and Hillel agree[8] only in respect of a basket that was not [previously][9] examined[10] [4a] while Hezekiah and R. Johanan differ in the case of a basket that had been examined.[9] One Master[11] holds [the objects to be clean because the basket] surely had been examined,[12] and the other Master[13] [holds them to be unclean, since] it might be assumed that the creeping thing fell in just when the man[14] removed his hand.[15] But [the case of the basket,][16] surely, was taught in the same manner as that of the woman,[17] and is not a woman[18] deemed to be duly examined?[19]—Since the flow of blood from her body is a regular occurrence she is regarded as unexamined.[20] And if you prefer I might reply:[21]

(1) Is it likely, however, that Hezekiah would differ from such an authority? (2) When the bucket is tipped. (3) Hence it is not necessary to incline the bucket at too great an angle when it is being emptied. The creeping thing might, therefore, well have remained within the bucket, held by the rim and unobserved. (4) From a basket. (5) If the basket is only slightly inclined. As it must consequently be turned upside down before all the fruit it contains can be emptied it is quite impossible for the creeping thing to have remained within. If, therefore, one was subsequently found in the basket it may be safely assumed that it fell in after the clean objects had been removed. (6) And does not mind if some of it remains in the bucket. Hence one does not tip the bucket very much, and the creeping thing might consequently have remained within the bucket behind the rim. (7) And turns the bucket upside down in order to get out even the last fruit (cf. prev. n. but one *mut. mut.*). (8) Var. lec. 'Shammai agrees with Hillel' (MS.M.). (9) Before the clean objects were put into it. (10) Hence it cannot be regarded as having a presumptive state of cleanness. (11) Hezekiah. (12) And since at the time it contained no unclean objects a presumptive state of cleanness has been established. (13) R. Johanan. (14) Who conducted the examination. (15) And the clean objects were still in the basket. (16) On which Shammai and Hillel differ. (17) Hillel having asked (*supra 3b*) 'what is the difference between the one case and the other?' (18) Whose duty it is to examine herself every morning and evening. (19) Apparently she is. Hence the basket also, which is in a similar condition (cf. prev. n. but one), must be deemed to be duly examined. Now since it was stated that the objects that were in the basket were regarded as retrospectively unclean an objection arises against Hezekiah. (20) And so also the basket. Hence the justification for Hezekiah's ruling. (21) To the

Shammai and Hillel agree[1] only in respect of a basket that[2] is uncovered,[3] while Hezekiah and R. Joḥanan differ in respect of a covered basket.[4] 'Covered'! Then how [could the creeping thing][5] have fallen into it?—[This is possible when] for instance, the way of using it was by [opening and closing] its cover.[6] But [the case of the basket] surely, was taught in the same manner as that of the woman,[7] and is not a woman[8] in the condition of being covered?[9]—Since the flow of blood from her body is a regular occurrence she is regarded as being in an uncovered condition.[10] And if you prefer I might reply:[11] Shammai and Hillel agree[12] only in respect of the corner of a basket, while Hezekiah and R. Joḥanan differ in that of the corner of a room.[13] But was not a 'basket' spoken of?[14]—It is this that was meant:[14] If a basket was used for clean objects in one corner of a room and, when it was moved into another corner,[15] a creeping thing was found [in it while it was] in that other corner, Hezekiah holds that we do not presume the uncleanness found in one place[16] to apply to another place,[17]

difficulty raised *supra 3b ad fin* on the apparent contradiction between the joint ruling of Shammai and Hillel and the view of Hezekiah.

(1) MS.M. 'Shammai agrees with Hillel'. (2) Though examined. (3) So that the creeping thing might well have fallen in as soon as the examiner has removed his hand. (4) Into which nothing could fall in by accident. Hence the justification for Hezekiah's ruling that the objects are clean. (5) Which was actually found in it. (6) Hezekiah is of the opinion that as long as clean objects are in the basket one is careful to keep it closed in order to prevent any unclean object from falling into it, but when the basket is empty care is no longer exercised and it is quite possible, therefore, for the creeping thing to have fallen in then. R. Joḥanan, however, holds that it is possible for the creeping thing to have fallen in unobserved, even while the clean objects were still in the basket, at a moment when the latter was opened in the ordinary course of use. (7) Hillel having asked (*supra 3b*) 'what is the difference between the one case and the other?' (8) Since no blood from the outside can flow into her body. (9) Cf. *supra* p. 14, n. 19, *mut. mut.* (10) And so also the basket. Hence the justification for Hezekiah's ruling. (11) V. *supra* p. 14, n. 21. (12) MS.M., 'Shammai agrees with Hillel'. (13) This is explained presently. Lit., 'house'. (14) In the statement, *supra 3b ad fin*, under discussion. (15) After the objects had been taken out. (16) If the unclean object was first discovered in the second place. (17) It is rather assumed that the creeping thing fell into the basket when it was

while R. Joḥanan holds that we do presume.[1] But do we[1] apply the rule of presumptive uncleanness? Have we not learnt: 'If a man touched someone in the night and he did not know whether it [was a person who was] alive or [one that was] dead, and in the morning when he got up he found him to be dead, R. Meir declares [the man] clean, but the Sages declare [him] to be unclean because all questions of uncleanness are determined by [the condition of the objects at] the time they are found',[2] and in connection with this it was taught, 'As at the time they are found and in accordance with the place in which they are found'?[3] And should you reply that this[4] holds good only[5] in respect of the law of burning[6] but that in respect of the law of suspense it is well applied,[7] have we not learnt, [it could be retorted,] If a needle[8] was found[9] full of rust or broken[10] it is regarded as clean[11] because all questions of uncleanness are determined by [the condition of the objects at] the time they are found?[12] Now why should this be so?[13] Why should it not rather be assumed that this needle

already in the second place after the objects had been removed from it.

(1) Even in such a case. (2) Lit., 'as the time of their finding', Ṭoh. V, 7. (3) *Sc.* if in the morning the person was found dead in the place where he was touched in the night the man who touched him is unclean, but if he was found dead in a different place he remains clean. Thus it follows that we do not presume uncleanness found in one place to apply to another. How then could R. Joḥanan maintain that the rule is applied even in such a case? (4) That the rule that we do not presume uncleanness found in one place to apply to another. (5) Since the uncleanness is not a matter of certainty. (6) If it was *terumah; sc.* the *terumah* need not be burned on account of the doubtful nature (cf. prev. n.) of its uncleanness. (7) Lit., 'to suspend we suspend', i.e., the uncleanness of the objects thus affected is treated as a matter of doubt, and R. Joḥanan's ruling might be given the same interpretation and may thus be reconciled with that of the Mishnah just cited. (8) That was known to be unclean. (9) In contact with clean objects. (10) Conditions which render it useless as a 'vessel'. Only a proper vessel contracts and conveys uncleanness. (11) I.e., it (cf. prev. n.) conveys no uncleanness whatsoever to the objects with which it was found in contact. (12) Ṭoh. III, 5. Hence it is assumed that the objects and the needle came in contact after the latter had lost the status of 'vessel' when it was no longer able to convey any uncleanness. (13) That the objects should be regarded as absolutely clean and their uncleanness should not be regarded even as doubtful.

was formerly[1] in a sound condition[2] and that it produced the rust just now?[3] Furthermore, have we not learnt: If a burnt creeping thing was found upon olives and so also if a tattered[4] rag[5] was found upon them it is clean,[6] because all [questions of] uncleanness are determined by [the conditions of the objects at] the time they are found?[7] And should you reply that [the uncleanness is determined] in accordance with [the condition of the objects at] the time they are found, irrespective of whether the result is a relaxation[8] or a restriction of the law,[9] only in the place where they[10] are found, but [if the doubt arises] in regard to the place in which they[10] were not found[11] the objects[12] are not to be burned but are nevertheless to be held in suspense,[13] was it not in fact taught,[14] [it could be retorted,] If a loaf of bread was lying on a shelf under which[15] lay an object of a minor degree of uncleanness,[16] [the loaf,][17]

(1) When it first came in contact with the objects under discussion. (2) When it duly conveyed its uncleanness to the objects. (3) Since, however, the assumption is not made and the objects are not subjected either to a certain or to a suspended condition of uncleanness, even, presumably, where there was a change of place, how could R. Johanan maintain, even only in respect of a condition of suspense, that the rule of presumptive uncleanness is applied? (4) *Aliter:* scorched. (5) That was cut off from the unclean garment of a *zab* (v. Glos.). (6) *Sc.* it is assumed that the creeping thing or the rag did not come in contact with the olives until after it had lost its uncleanness (the former by the burning and the latter by becoming tattered or scorched) and was unable to convey any. (7) Ṭoh. IX, 9. Now since the olives are not subjected even to the status of suspended uncleanness (as the categorical rule 'it is clean' implies) it follows that presumptive uncleanness does not apply when there was a change of time and so also, presumably, where there was a change of place. How then could R. Johanan maintain his ruling? (8) As in the case of the needle and the rag (cited from Ṭoh. III, 5 and IX, 9) where the objects are declared clean. (9) Where a man touched some person in the night (cited from Ṭoh. V, 7) in which case the man, according to the Sages, is decidedly unclean. (10) The objects about which the doubt had arisen. (11) I.e., whence the objects have been removed, as is the case with the basket with which R. Johanan was concerned. (12) *Terumah*, for instance. (13) And the same interpretation might also be given to R. Johanan's ruling which would thus be reconciled with the one cited from Ṭoh. IX, 9. (14) V. marg. glos. Cur. edd. 'we learnt'. (15) On the ground. (16) *Middaf.* This is now assumed to be an object (a garment, for instance) which, though not subject to *midras* (v. Glos.)

although if it had fallen down it would have been impossible for it not to touch the unclean object,[1] is clean, because it is assumed that a clean person entered there and removed it,[2] unless one can testify, 'I am certain that no one entered there',[3] in connection with which R. Eleazar stated: This assumption[4] was required only in the case of a sloping shelf?[5]—There[6] the reason[7] is as stated,[8] [4b] 'Because it is assumed that a clean person entered there and removed it'.[9] But why should it not be assumed here also[10] that a raven came and dropped [the creeping thing into the basket]?[11]—In the case of a man who acts[12] with intention such an assumption[13] is made, but in that of a raven which[14] does not act with intention such an assumption[15] is not made. But consider: The loaf[16] is a case of doubtful uncleanness in a private domain. Now is not any case of doubtful uncleanness in a private domain

uncleanness (which could convey uncleanness to both man and vessels) conveys nevertheless uncleanness to foodstuffs and the like, Pentateuchally. (17) Found on the ground away from the unclean object.

(1) Which would have conveyed uncleanness to it. (2) From the shelf, and placed it on the ground where it was found. (3) Tosef. Ṭoh. IV. (4) 'That a clean person entered etc.' (5) From which the loaf is most likely to slide down and fall on the unclean object below. Now, since even in such a case it is not presumed that the loaf fell upon the unclean object and contracted uncleanness before it rolled away to its present position, it follows that the rule of presumptive uncleanness is not applied when two different places are involved. How then could R. Joḥanan rule *supra* (*3b ad fin.*) that presumptive uncleanness is applied even (as in the case of the basket and the creeping thing) where two places are involved? (6) In the Baraitha just cited. (7) Why the rule of presumptive uncleanness is not applied to the loaf. (8) Lit., 'as he learned the reason'. (9) This assumption cannot, of course, be made in the case of the basket, with which R. Joḥanan deals, since the unclean object (the dead creeping thing) was actually found in it, and when it was found it was still in its state of uncleanness. (10) In the case of the basket and the creeping thing. (11) After the clean objects had been removed from it and after it had been moved into its new position. (12) When he removed the loaf from the sloping shelf. (13) That the man entered and moved the loaf to its present safer place. (14) Even if it were to drop the creeping thing into the basket. (15) That the raven dropped the thing after the clean objects had been removed etc. (cf. *supra* n. 11). (16) Since (*a*) it is uncertain whether it touched the unclean object or not and (*b*) it was found within a house.

regarded as unclean?[1]—[The loaf is deemed to be unclean] because it is a thing that possesses no intelligence to answer questions,[2] and any thing that possesses no intelligence to answer questions, irrespective of whether it was in a public or in a private domain, is in any doubtful case of uncleanness regarded as clean.[3] And if you prefer I might reply: Here[4] we are dealing with a Rabbinical uncleanness.[5] A deduction [from the wording][6] also supports this view, for the expression used is '*middaf*'[7] which is analogous to the Scriptural phrase, '*a driven* [niddaf] *leaf*'.[8]

THE SAGES, HOWEVER, RULED: [THE LAW IS] NEITHER IN AGREEMENT WITH THE OPINION OF THE FORMER NOR IN AGREEMENT WITH THAT OF THE LATTER etc. Our Rabbis taught: And the Sages ruled, [The law is] neither in agreement with the opinion of the former nor in agreement with that of the latter, neither [that is] in agreement with the opinion of Shammai who[9] provided no fence for his ruling[10] nor in agreement with the opinion of Hillel who[11] restricted far too much,[12] but [the women are deemed to be unclean] during the preceding twenty-four hours when this lessens the period from the [previous] examination to the [last] examination, and during the period from the [previous]

(1) The answer being in the affirmative, the difficulty arises, why is the loaf deemed to be clean? (2) Lit., 'to be asked', whether it came in contact with the unclean object or not. (3) Because the rule that doubtful uncleanness in a private domain is deemed to be unclean is deduced from that of *soṭah* (v. Glos.) and consequently only rational beings like the *soṭah* herself (who is able to answer whether she was or was not defiled) are subject to the same restrictions. (4) In the case of the loaf. (5) One, for instance, of those enumerated in Ḥag. 18*b* and 20*b*. A doubtful case of Rabbinical uncleanness is regarded as clean even in a private domain. (6) Of the Tosef. Ṭoh. IV cited. (7) Rendered (*supra* 4*a*) 'an object of a minor degree of uncleanness'. (8) Lev. XXVI, 36; the rt. of *niddaf*, and so also that of *middaf* implying something 'light', 'of minor importance', hence a 'minor degree of *or* Rabbinical uncleanness'. (9) Having laid down that the period of uncleanness begins only 'FROM THE TIME OF THEIR DISCOVERING OF THE FLOW'. (10) I.e., made no restriction whatever against the possible infringement of the actual law. (11) Laying down that the period of uncleanness 'IS TO BE RECKONED RETROSPECTIVELY FROM THE PREVIOUS EXAMINATION'. (12) Lit., 'who broke through beyond his measures'.

examination to the [last] examination when this lessens the period of twenty-four hours. '[The women are deemed to be unclean] during the preceding twenty-four hours when this lessens the period from the [previous] examination to the [last] examination'. How is this to be understood? If a woman examined her body on a Sunday[1] and found herself to be clean and then she spent Mon day and Tuesday without holding any examination while on Wednesday she examined herself and found that she was unclean it is not ruled that she should be deemed to be unclean retro spectively from the previous examination to the last examination but only [that she should be deemed to be unclean] during the preceding twenty-four hours. 'And during the period from the [previous] examination to the [last] examination when this lessens the period of twenty-four hours'. How is this to be understood? If the woman examined her body during the first hour of the day and found herself to be clean and then she spent the second and the third hour without holding any examination while in the fourth hour she examined herself and found that she was unclean, it is not ruled that she should be deemed to be unclean retrospectively for a period of twenty-four hours but only during the period from the previous examination to the last examination. But is it not obvious that, since she has examined herself during the first hour and found that she was clean, she is not to be deemed unclean retrospectively for twenty-four hours?[2] — As it was taught, 'during the preceding twenty-four hours when this lessens the period from the [previous] examination to the [last] examination'[3] it also stated,[4] 'during the period from the [previous] examination to the [last] examination when this lessens the period of twenty-four hours'.

Rabbah stated: What is the reason of the Rabbis?[5] Because

(1) Lit., 'on the first of the week'. (2) Of course it is. Why then should such an obvious ruling have to be stated? (3) A ruling that had to be enunciated, since otherwise it could have been argued that the flow began on the Sunday immediately after the examination. (4) As a kind of antithesis. (5) For fixing a twenty-four hours' period of uncleanness. The reason for Hillel's period, 'from examination to examination' (cf. our Mishnah), is quite

a woman well feels herself.[1] Said Abaye to him: If so,[2] [a period of uncleanness from] the time of her observation of the flow should suffice![3] And Rabbah?[4]—He only wished to exercise Abaye's wits.[5] What then is the reason of the Rabbis?[6]—It is one such as that which Rab Judah gave in the name of Samuel: The Sages have ordained for the daughters of Israel that they should examine themselves in the morning and in the evening; 'in the morning', in order to verify the cleanness of objects they handled during the previous night,[7] 'and in the evening' in order to verify the cleanness of objects they handled during the previous day;[8] but this woman,[9] since she did not [regularly] examine her body,[10] has[11] lost one *'onah*.[12] But what could be meant by 'one *'onah*'?[13]—One additional *'onah*.[14] Said R. Papa to Raba: But would you not sometimes find that there are three *'onahs* in twenty-four hours?[15]—

intelligible since the flow may well have begun as soon as the previous examination was concluded, but the twenty-four hours' period appears to have no logical justification whatsoever.

(1) Any flow. Had it begun immediately after the conclusion of her previous examination she would have been aware of it. (2) That a woman is aware of the flow as soon as it begins. (3) It being obvious that the flow began only at that moment, for if it had begun earlier she (cf. prev. n.) would have been aware of the fact. Why then should her period of uncleanness extend backwards for twenty-four hours? An objection against Rabbah. (4) *Sc.*, why did he take up such an untenable position? (5) Lit., 'to sharpen (the mind) of Abaye'. Rabbah advanced the reason merely to afford an opportunity for Abaye, whose guardian and teacher he was, to prove it to be wrong. (6) Cf. p. 20. n. 5. (7) If a woman finds herself on examination to be clean it is thereby verified that all clean objects she handled during the previous night are to be regarded as clean; and should she discover any flow later at the evening examination the doubtful uncleanness would extend only to objects she handled during the day. (8) Cf. prev. n. *mut. mut.* (9) Spoken of in our Mishnah, and in the Baraitha cited. (10) In defiance of the ordinance of the Rabbis. (11) As a penalty. (12) Lit., 'a time' or 'a period' of one day or night, *sc.* her uncleanness begins retrospectively one *'onah* earlier. (13) Seeing that the uncleanness extends backwards for twenty-four hours which represent two *'onahs*. (14) I.e., in addition to the *'onah* immediately preceding the one in which her last examination was held (during which she is in any case unclean owing to the doubt as to when the flow began), she must suffer the penalty of being treated as unclean retrospectively even during the *'onah* that preceded that one. (15) When, for instance, the first examination after a number of days without

The Sages have laid down a uniform limit[1] in order that there shall be no variations in the twenty-four hours' period. And[2] if you prefer I might reply:[3] [the period extends to three *'onahs*] in order that the sinner[4] shall not[5] be at an advantage.[6] What is the practical difference between them?[7]—The practical difference between them is the case of a woman who was the victim of circumstances and in consequence of which she did not hold her examination.[8]

FOR ANY WOMAN WHO HAS A SETTLED PERIOD etc. Must it be conceded that our Mishnah represents the view of R. Dosa and not that of the Rabbis seeing that it was taught:[9] R. Eliezer ruled, For four classes of women it suffices [to reckon the period of their uncleanness from the time they discovered the discharge,] viz., a virgin,[10] a pregnant woman, a woman that gives suck and an old woman; and R. Dosa ruled, For any woman who has a settled period it suffices [to reckon her period of uncleanness from]

an examination took place at midday. If the uncleanness extended backwards for a period of twenty-four hours it would cover (1) the *'onah* of the day of the examination, (2) the *'onah* of the preceding night and (3) the *'onah* of the day preceding that night. Now since the penalty imposed was only one additional *'onah* why should it in this case be increased to two *'onahs*?

(1) Lit., 'made their measures equal', i.e., the period of twenty-four hours has been fixed, irrespective of whether it covers two *'onahs* or three. (2) So BaḤ. Cur. edd. omit. (3) To the objection why in the case mentioned (cf. *supra* p. 21, n. 15) the uncleanness should extend over three *'onahs*. (4) The woman who, not only failed to examine her body regularly in accordance with the ordinance of the Sages but also delayed her last examination from the morning hour to noon. (5) By having her period of uncleanness reduced to less than twenty-four hours. (6) Over one in a similar position who held her examination in the early morning and whose period of uncleanness is extended retrospectively for a full period of twenty-four hours to the previous morning. (7) The two replies offered. (8) According to the first reply she would be subject to uncleanness for a full period of twenty-four hours, while according to the second reply, since in this case she is no sinner, the period would be reduced to two *'onahs* and her uncleanness would be reckoned from the beginning of the previous evening only. (9) What follows, with the exception of R. Dosa's ruling occurs also in the Mishnah *infra* 7a. (10) I.e., one, whether married or unmarried, who suffered a flow for the first time in her life.

the time she discovered the discharge?[1]—It may even be held [that our Mishnah represents the view of] the Rabbis, for the Rabbis differ from R. Dosa only [in respect of a flow] that did not occur at the woman's set time[2] but [in the case of one that did occur] at her set time they might agree with him; and our Mishnah deals with a flow that occurred at the woman's set time and it, therefore, represents the view of both.[3] Thus[4] it follows that R. Dosa maintains his view even where a flow did not occur at the woman's set time. Who then is the author of the following which the Rabbis taught: Though a woman has a settled period her bloodstain[5] is deemed to be unclean retrospectively,[6] for were she to observe a flow when it is not her set time she would be unclean retrospectively for a period of twenty-four hours?[7] Must it be conceded[8] to be the Rabbis only and not R. Dosa?[9]—It may be said to be even R. Dosa; for R. Dosa may disagree with the Rabbis only in the case where the flow occurred at the woman's set time but where it occurred when it was not her set time he agrees with them;[10] and our Mishnah deals with one that occurred at her set time and it is, therefore, in agreement with the opinion of R. Dosa [5*a*] while the Baraitha[11] is in agreement with both.[12] But why should not the final assumption be[13] reversed?[14]—As it is

(1) Now, since the Rabbis elsewhere differ from R. Dosa's ruling, must it be conceded that our Mishnah represents his view only? (2) As the appearance is obviously irregular it may well be suspected that one occurred earlier also. (3) Lit., 'and the words of all', those of the Rabbis as well those of R. Dosa. (4) Since the dispute between R. Dosa and the Rabbis has been limited to a flow that did not occur at the set time. (5) *Sc.* one on a garment of hers. (6) From the time it had been washed. (7) As in this case, despite the woman's settled period, the uncleanness is deemed to be retrospective so it is retrospective in the case of the stain also. (8) Since, from what has been said, it is only the Rabbis who impose retrospective uncleanness in the case of a woman who, though having a settled period, suffered a flow before or after that time. (9) Is it likely, however, that R. Dosa would differ from an anonymous Baraitha? (10) That the uncleanness is retrospective. (11) Just cited, dealing with the bloodstain. (12) Cf. *supra* n. 3. (13) Lit., 'and let him make it stand'. (14) As has been suggested at first, that our Mishnah represents the view of the Rabbis as well as that of R. Dosa while the Baraitha represents only that of the Rabbis.

possible to adopt an explanation that leads to a relaxation of the law[1] and one that leads to a restriction of it[2] we adopt the one that leads to the restriction.

Now it was just taught,[3] 'For were she to observe a flow when it is not her set time she would be unclean retrospectively for a period of twenty-four hours'. [If this[4] is] the reason[5] [it follows] that only in the case of a woman who has a settled period do the Rabbis draw a distinction between her stain and her observation[6] [of a flow],[7] but in the case of the other women[8] concerning whom the Sages ruled that it sufficed for them to reckon their uncleanness from the time they discovered the flow[9] [the extent of the uncleanness of] their stains is like that of their observation of a flow.[10] Now whose view is this?—It is that of R. Ḥanina b. Antigonus; for Rab Judah citing Samuel who had it from R. Ḥanina b. Antigonus stated, In the case of all women their stains cause uncleanness retrospectively but in that of the women[8] concerning whom the Sages ruled that it sufficed for them to reckon their uncleanness from the time they discovered the flow [the extent of the uncleanness of] their stains is like that of their observation of a flow,[10] the exception being a child who has not yet attained the age of the suffering of a flow of whom, though her sheets are soiled with blood,[11] no notice is to be taken.[12] But does R. Ḥanina

(1) As has been previously suggested: That a flow at the set time causes no retrospective uncleanness in accordance with the general opinion, while one occurring at any other time is subject to retrospective uncleanness only in accordance with the view of the Rabbis. (2) The one finally adopted: That a flow at the set time causes retrospective uncleanness according to the Rabbis at least, while one at any other time causes retrospective uncleanness even according to R. Dosa. (3) In the Baraitha *supra 4b ad fin.* (4) 'For were she to observe etc.'. (5) Why a stain causes retrospective uncleanness, *sc.* though a stain cannot be subject to greater restrictions than a discharge it causes uncleanness retrospectively, since a flow that occurred at any time other than the set time also causes retrospective uncleanness. (6) At the set time. (7) *Sc.* while in the latter case the uncleanness is not retrospective in the former, for the reason stated (cf. prev. n.) it is. (8) The four classes, for instance, mentioned *supra 4b* and *infra 7a.* (9) So that in their case the law of retrospective uncleanness never applies. (10) *Sc.* both are not retrospective. (11) It being unknown whether it came from her body

at all uphold[1] the law of the uncleanness of a stain?[2] Was it not taught: In the case of all women their stains are unclean and also in the case of the women concerning whom the Sages ruled that it sufficed for them to reckon their period of uncleanness from the time they discovered the flow their stains are unclean; while R. Ḥanina b. Antigonus ruled, The women concerning whom the Sages ruled that it sufficed for them to reckon their uncleanness from the time they discovered the flow are not subject to the law of uncleanness of the stain? Now does not this mean that they are not subject at all to the law of uncleanness of the stain?[3]—No, it means that they are not subject to the law of the uncleanness of the stain retrospectively but they are well subject to it from now[4] onwards. Does this[5] then imply that the first Tanna[6] is of the opinion that their uncleanness is even retrospective?—Yes; it[7] being the view of R. Meir who restricts the law in respect of stains. For it was taught: In the case of all women their stains are unclean retrospectively and also in the case of the women concerning whom the Sages ruled that it sufficed for them to reckon their period of uncleanness from the time they discovered the flow their stains are unclean retrospectively; so R. Meir. R. Ḥanina b. Antigonus ruled, In the case of the women concerning whom the Sages ruled that it sufficed for them to reckon their period of uncleanness from the time they discovered the flow [the unclean-

or from elsewhere. (12) It being assumed, though the assumption might be most unlikely, that she passed through a butcher's market and soiled her sheets there. In no case is it assumed that the blood came from her own body because the law of uncleanness, as far as stains are concerned, is merely Rabbinical, and in the case of a minor no Rabbinical measure was enacted.

(1) In the case of the four classes of women mentioned. (2) Even after it had been discovered. (3) How then could it be said *supra* that R. Ḥanina does uphold the law of the uncleanness of the stain? (4) The time of discovery. (5) The explanation according to which R. Ḥanina agrees with the first Tanna as regards the uncleanness of stains from the time they are discovered onwards, and that he only differs from him in rejecting their retrospective uncleanness. (6) Whose opinion is stated in the first clause of the Baraitha cited. (7) The first clause (cf. prev. n.).

ness of] their stains is like that of their observation [of their flow]; and a child who has attained the age of suffering a flow is subject to the law of the uncleanness of the stain while one who has not attained that age is not subject to the uncleanness of a stain, and when does she attain the age of suffering a flow? When she attains her maidenhood.[1]

AND IF A WOMAN USES TESTING-RAGS WHEN SHE HAS MARITAL INTERCOURSE etc. Rab Judah citing Samuel ruled: A testing-rag used before[2] marital intercourse does not reduce [the doubtful period[3] of retrospective uncleanness] as an examination. What is the reason?—R. Kaṭṭina replied: Because the woman is in a hurry to do her marital duty.[4] But what matters it even if she is in a hurry to do her marital duty?—Since she is in a hurry to do it she does not insert the testing-rag into depressions and folds.[5]

We learnt: IF A WOMAN USES TESTING-RAGS WHEN SHE HAS MARITAL INTERCOURSE, THIS IS INDEED LIKE AN EXAMINATION. Does not this mean that she uses one before intercourse and one after it?[6]—No, the one as well as the other is used after intercourse but[7] one is for the man[8] and the other is for her; as we learnt: It is the custom of the daughters of Israel when having marital intercourse to use two testing-rags, one for the man and the other for herself.[9] What a comparison![10] If you concede that one is used before intercourse and the other after it one can well understand the necessity for the ruling.[11] As it might have been presumed that on account of her being in a hurry to do her marital duty she does not properly perform her test we were informed that THIS IS INDEED LIKE AN EXAMINATION. If you maintain, how-

(1) The age when she assumes the status of *na'arah* (v. Glos.), i.e., the age when she grows two pubic hairs or (she has no pubic hairs) when she is twelve years and one day old. (2) I.e., only before but not after (cf. relevant note on our Mishnah). (3) Either that of the twenty-four hours or the one between the previous and the last examination. (4) Lit., 'she is in a state of excitement about her house'. (5) The examination, therefore, is not a proper one. (6) Which shows that the test before intercourse, despite R. Kaṭṭina's argument, is deemed to be a proper one. (7) In reply to the objection, why two rags. (8) For wiping. (9) *Infra* 14*a*. (10) Lit., 'that, what'. (11) In our Mishnah, that the test is effective.

ever, that the one testing-rag as well as the other is used after marital intercourse, is not the ruling obvious?[1]—It might have been presumed [that the test should be ineffective][2] on account of the possibility of the appearance of a drop of blood of the size of a mustard seed[3] which semen might cover up,[4] hence we were informed [that such a remote possibility need not be considered]. And if you prefer I might reply: The Rabbis required a woman to perform two tests, one before intercourse and one after it,[5] and in stating 'THIS IS INDEED LIKE AN EXAMINATION' the reference is to the one after the intercourse. But was it not stated, IF A WOMAN USES etc.?[6]—Read: And a woman shall use.[7]

LESSENS EITHER THE PERIOD OF THE PAST TWENTY-FOUR HOURS. Now that you stated that it[8] lessens THE PERIOD OF THE PAST TWENTY-FOUR HOURS[9] [5*b*] was it also necessary to state that it lessens THE PERIOD FROM THE PREVIOUS EXAMINATION TO THE LAST EXAMINATION?[10]—As it might have been presumed that only in the case of the twenty-four hours' period did the Rabbis[11] take into consideration the possible loss of clean things[12] but not in that of the period from the previous examination to the last examination,[13] we were informed [that both periods are equally reduced].

HOW [IS ONE TO UNDERSTAND THE RULING THAT] 'IT SUFFICES [TO RECKON HER PERIOD OF UNCLEANNESS FROM]

(1) And why should an obvious ruling be enunciated? (2) Even though it took place after intercourse. (3) That is sufficient to cause uncleanness. (4) Thus rendering the test useless. (5) Hence the mention of RAGS in the plural. (6) Emphasis on IF which implies that there is no obligation. How then could it be maintained that 'the Rabbis required her etc.'? (7) *Sc.* the clause is to be divided into two separate rulings, (*a*) that a woman shall use two testing-rags, one before intercourse and the other after it and (*b*) the second test is indeed like an examination. (8) The testing-rag examination. (9) Though it is a comparatively long period extending as it does to the previous day. (10) Which is a much shorter one (cf. prev. n.) being confined to the limits of the same day. (11) By enacting that the test is effective and reduces it. (12) Which the woman may have handled during this comparatively long time. (13) A shorter period (cf. *supra* n. 10) during which not many things could have been handled and a much lesser loss is consequently involved.

THE TIME SHE DISCOVERS THE FLOW' etc. What need was there[1] for stating, IF SHE WAS SITTING ON A BED AND WAS OCCUPIED WITH RITUALLY CLEAN OBJECTS, when it should rather have been stated,[2] IF SHE WAS OCCUPIED[3] WITH RITUALLY CLEAN OBJECTS AND HAVING LEFT THEM, OBSERVED A FLOW?—It is this that we were informed:[4] The reason [why the bed is regarded as clean is] because [in the case of that woman][5] it suffices [for her to reckon] her [period of uncleanness from the] time [of her discovery of the flow] but[6] [where the uncleanness extends backwards over] twenty-four hours the bed also is regarded as unclean.[7] This provides support for Ze'iri, for Ze'iri ruled: [A woman[8] during] the twenty-four hours preceding her discovery of a menstrual flow causes bed and seat[9] to convey uncleanness to a man who in turn conveys it to his clothes.[10] But consider: This bed is a thing that has no sense to answer questions,[11] and is not doubtful uncleanness[12] in the case of an object that has no sense to answer questions regarded as clean?[13] Ze'iri explained: [This[14] refers to a case] where her friends were carrying her in the bed so that the latter may be regarded as the hand of her friends.[15]

(1) Lit., 'wherefore to me'. (2) Lit., 'let him teach'. (3) Omitting the apparently superfluous 'WAS SITTING ON A BED'. (4) By the additional words (cf. prev. n.). (5) Who has a settled period. (6) In the case of a woman whose periods were not regular. (7) As the bed of a confirmed menstruant (cf. Lev. XV, 21) which conveys uncleanness to the man that touches it as well as to the clothes he wears though the latter did not come in direct contact with it. (8) Cf. prev. n. but one. (9) On which she lay or sat. (10) Cf. *supra* n. 6. (11) Lit., 'to be asked'. (12) Such as that caused by the woman in question during the twenty-four hours preceding the time she observed the flow. (13) Of course it is, since the law of treating doubtful uncleanness as unclean is deduced from that of the *soṭah* (v. Glos.) who is able to answer questions. (14) The ruling in our Mishnah, which does regard (by implication) the bed on which the woman sat as unclean. (15) The hand, being part of a human being who is well able to answer questions, is justly compared to the *soṭah* whose doubtful uncleanness is regarded as unclean. It is for a similar reason (that things handled by a human being are regarded as his hand), it may be added, that the things the woman handled when sitting on the bed are regarded as unclean even where the bed was resting on the ground, and this explains why the objection *supra* was raised in connection with the bed and not in connection with the things the woman has handled.

Now, however, that R. Joḥanan ruled that in the case of doubtful uncleanness conveyed through a human agency[1] the object in doubt,[2] though lying on the ground, is deemed to be capable of answering questions as if it had been a human being who has the sense to answer questions[3] [this[4] holds good] even though her friends were not carrying her in the bed.

[Reverting to] the [above] text, 'R. Joḥanan ruled: In the case of doubtful uncleanness conveyed through a human agency the object in doubt, though lying on the ground, is deemed to be capable of answering questions as if it had been a human being who has the sense to answer questions'.[5] An objection was raised: If a man was wrapping himself in his cloak while clean or unclean objects were at his side[6] or above his head and it is doubtful whether there was contact[7] or not, they[8] are deemed to be clean,[9] but if it was impossible [for the cloak and the other objects] not to have come in contact they[10] are regarded as unclean. R. Simeon b. Gamaliel ruled: The man is told, 'Do it again'[11] and he does it again.[12] They,[13] however, said to him: No repetition [test[14] is

(1) As in that of the bed and the menstruant during the twenty-four hours preceding the observation of the flow or in that of a dead creeping thing that was carried by a man and a doubt arose as to whether it came in contact with a certain clean object. (2) Since the uncleanness, if any, was brought to it by a human agency. (3) And in a private domain is regarded as unclean. Only when the inanimate object in doubt was near an unclean one that was also inanimate, and no human agency was involved, is it regarded as clean. (4) V. p. 28, n. 14. (5) *Supra* q.v. notes. (6) He being either unclean (in the former case) or clean (in the latter one). (7) Between the cloak and the objects in its vicinity. If there was contact, the cloak that (in the former case) contracted uncleanness from its wearer would convey uncleanness to the clean objects, or the unclean objects (in the latter case) would convey uncleanness to the cloak. (8) The objects in the vicinity (in the former case) and the cloak (in the latter case). (9) Even, it is now assumed, in a private domain, because the cloak as well as the objects in its vicinity are incapable of answering questions. (10) The objects in the vicinity (in the former case) and the cloak (in the latter case). (11) *Sc.* to wrap himself again in his cloak in the same place and position in which he did it first. (12) In this manner it is ascertained whether the cloak and the other objects have or have not come in contact. (13) The Rabbis who disagreed with him. (14) Since it may not exactly reproduce the former conditions.

recognized] in questions of cleanness.[1] Now why [should they[2] be clean][3] seeing that this is a case of uncleanness that is conveyed through a human agency?[4]—This is beside the point,[5] for R. Hoshaia learnt: In a private domain [such a case of] doubtful uncleanness[6] is regarded as unclean, and in a public domain it is regarded as clean.[7]

[Reverting to] the [above] text, 'Ze'iri ruled: [A woman during] the twenty-four hours preceding her discovery of a menstrual flow causes bed and seat to convey uncleanness to a man who in turn conveys it to his clothes'.[8] But, surely, this cannot be correct.[9] For did not Abimi from Be Ḥozai[10] when he came bring with him[11] a Baraitha which stated, 'During the twenty-four hours preceding the discovery of her menstrual flow a woman's bed and seat are [as unclean] as the object she touches', which means, does it not, that as an object she touches does not convey uncleanness to a human being[12] so also does not her bed convey uncleanness to a human being?[13]—Raba retorted: And do you understand this ruling[14] seeing that it [may be refuted by an inference] *a minori ad majus:* If an earthen vessel that was covered with a tight fitting lid, which is protected from uncleanness in a corpse's tent,[15] is yet not so protected [from the uncleanness] of the twenty-four hours preceding the discovery of a menstrual

(1) Tosef. Ṭoh. IV which, however, has the following variation: 'R. Dosa ruled, He is told, "Do it again"... They, however, said to him, No repetition ... R. Simeon b. Gamaliel ruled, He sometimes does it again'. (2) V. p. 29, n. 10. (3) According to the first Tanna. (4) Which according to R. Joḥanan is unclean. (5) Lit., 'outside of that'. (6) One involving conveyance through a human agency. (7) No objection, therefore, may be raised from the Tosef. cited which may be explained to refer to a case in a public domain. (8) *Supra* q.v. notes. (9) Lit., 'I am not'. (10) The Khuzistan. (11) Lit., 'came and brought'. (12) Only a primary uncleanness can do that. An object touched by a menstruant assumes only the status of a first grade of uncleanness which conveys uncleanness to objects but not to a human being. (13) The answer apparently being in the affirmative, the difficulty arises: How could Ze'iri maintain that the woman 'causes bed and seat to convey uncleanness to a man who in turn etc.'? (14) Which seems to reduce the uncleanness of the bed and seat of the menstruant in question to a lower degree than that of earthenware. (15) Only when uncovered does it contract uncleanness (cf. Num. XIX, 15).

flow,[1] is it not logical that the beds and seats [of a menstruant], which are not protected from uncleanness in a corpse's tent, should not be protected from the uncleanness of the twenty-four hours preceding the discovery of a menstrual flow?[2]—But did not Abimi of Be Ḥozai quote a Baraitha?[3]—Read:[4] A woman's bed and seat[5] [6a] are [as unclean] as that which touches the body of the menstruant herself; just as the touching of her body[5] causes the uncleanness of a human being who in turn causes the uncleanness of the clothes he wears[6] so does the touching of her bed or seat[5] cause the uncleanness of a human being who in turn causes the uncleanness of the clothes he wears.

It was taught in agreement with Raba: A woman who observed a bloodstain[7] conveys uncleanness retrospectively.[8] And what are the things to which she conveys the uncleanness?[9] Foodstuffs and drinks,[10] beds and seats,[11] as well as any earthen vessel, even though it was covered with a tightly fitting lid,[12] and her counting[13] is[14] disturbed,[15] and she conveys[16] uncleanness to the man who cohabited with her retrospectively. R. Akiba[17] ruled: She conveys uncleanness to the man who cohabited with her but begins her counting[18] from the time only of her observing a flow. If she observed a flow of blood,[19] she conveys uncleanness retrospectively

(1) If it was touched by the woman during the twenty-four hours (cf. *infra* 6a) (2) As the soundness of this argument cannot be questioned Abimi's ruling is obviously untenable and may well be disregarded. (3) Which is an authoritative utterance. (4) The ruling in the Baraitha. (5) During the twenty-four hours preceding her discovery of a menstrual flow. (6) *Torath kohanim* on Lev. XV, 19. (7) So BaḤ and MS.M. Cur. edd. 'blood'. (8) Cf. prev. n. (Cur. edd. read 'twenty-four hours'), from the time the garment was last washed, it being unknown how soon after this the stain was made. (9) During the period mentioned (cf. prev. n.). (10) Which she touched (cf. foll. n.). (11) On which she lay or sat. (Cur. edd. reverse the order.) (12) Provided the woman shook the vessel and did not merely touch it. (13) Of the 'eleven days' following the seven days of a menstrual period. (14) Cur. edd. 'is not'. (15) So MS.M and Rashi; because it is unknown when the flow actually appeared and the limits of the menstruation period cannot consequently be determined. (16) Cur. edd. 'does not convey'. (17) MS.M inserts R. Akiba's ruling *infra* before 'In either case, however'. (18) Of the seven days of menstruation. (19) So BaḤ and MS.M. Cur. edd., 'stain'.

for twenty-four hours.[1] And what are the things to which she conveys uncleanness?[2] Foodstuffs and drinks,[3] beds and seats[4] as well as any earthen vessel, though it was covered with a tightly fitting lid,[5] her counting[6] is not[7] disturbed and she does not convey[8] uncleanness to the man who cohabited with her.[9] In either case, however,[10] the uncleanness[11] is held in suspense [and any consecrated foodstuffs touched] must neither be eaten nor burned.[12] As to Raba, however,[13] if he heard of the Baraitha,[14] why did he not say [that his ruling is derived from] a Baraitha? And if he did not hear of the Baraitha, whence did he [derive the law for his inference] *a minori ad majus?*—The fact is that he heard of the Baraitha, but[15] were he to derive his ruling from the Baraitha it could have been objected [that the uncleanness[16] is conveyed] either to the man or to his clothes[17] but not to the man as well as to the clothes he wears,[18] hence he had recourse to his inference *a minori ad majus.*[19]

R. Huna ruled: [The retrospective uncleanness during] the twenty-four hours [preceding the observation] of a menstrual flow is conveyed only to hallowed things but not to *terumah*. But if so, should not this law have been mentioned together with those

(1) BaḤ and MS.M. Cur. edd. omit 'for twenty-four hours'. (2) During the period mentioned. (3) Which she touched. (4) On which she lay and sat. (5) Provided the woman shook the vessel and did not merely touch it. (6) Of the 'eleven days' following the seven days of a menstrual period. (7) Cf. Rashi and MS.M. Cur. edd. omit 'not'. (8) So MS.M. Cur. edd., 'she conveys'. (9) Cur. edd. add, 'but begins her counting from the time only of her observing of the flow'. (10) Whether there was only a stain or a flow. (11) During the period mentioned. (12) Thus it has been shown that, in agreement with Raba, the Baraitha tacitly assumes that the beds and seats under discussion convey uncleanness not only to the man who came in contact with them but also to the clothes he wears (cf. Tosaf. Asheri a.l.). (13) Who (*supra* 5*b ad fin.*) took the law of the uncleanness of an earthen vessel for granted and deduced from it that of the bed. (14) That was just cited, in which the law of the earthen vessel is explicitly enunciated. (15) As to the reason why he did not quote it. (16) Of the bed or seat. (17) Whichever of them came in contact with the unclean object. (18) Which did not come in direct contact with the seat or the bed. (19) From an earthenware vessel.

of the other grades [of sanctity]?[1]—Only cases that involve definite uncleanness are enumerated but any in which no definite uncleanness is involved[2] is not mentioned.

An objection was raised: What are the things to which she conveys uncleanness? Foodstuffs and drinks.[3] Does not this[4] mean those that are hallowed as well as those that are *terumah*?—No, only those that are hallowed.[5]

Come and hear: R. Judah ruled [that priestly women must examine their bodies] even after they have concluded a meal[6] of *terumah*;[7] and the point raised, 'Is not the consumed meal a matter of the past?'[8] [And to this] R. Ḥisda replied: This[9] was necessary only for the sake of ensuring the fitness of the remnants before her?[10]—R. Huna reads:[11] 'To burn the remnants that were in her hands',[12] the examination being held immediately after[13] [the meal].[14]

Come and hear: It once happened that Rabbi acted[15] in accord-

(1) In Ḥag. 20*b* where are enumerated the restrictions that are applicable to hallowed things and not to *terumah* and *vice versa*. (2) Such as that of the twenty-four hours' period under discussion where the uncleanness is merely a preventive measure. (3) *Supra*, in the Baraitha last cited. (4) 'Foodstuffs and drinks'. (5) The oil of a meal-offering, for instance, or the wine of libation. (6) Lit., 'at the time of their passing away from eating'. (7) *Infra* 11*a*. (8) Lit., 'what has been, has been', *sc.* what is the use of an examination after the meal has been consumed when nothing can be done even if the woman were to be found unclean. (9) The examination. (10) Should a woman, for instance, discover a flow later in the day the examination after her morning meal would ensure the cleanness of the *terumah* that remained from that meal. Thus it follows that in the absence of an examination the *terumah* would be deemed to be unclean retrospectively. How, then, could R. Huna maintain that the uncleanness is conveyed to hallowed things only? (11) In place of R. Ḥisda's version of R. Judah's meaning. (12) *Sc.* if she finds herself on examination to be unclean the remnants of her meal, since she touched them, are deemed to be unclean and, as unclean *terumah* must be burned. (13) Heb. *Keshi'ur weseth* (v. Rashi). Evthion (Tosaf. Asheri) εὐθέως, 'forthwith' (cf. Jast.). (14) So that it may be taken for granted that the *terumah* she had just handled had come in contact with a confirmed menstruant. Where, however, the woman held no examination immediately after her meal, a subsequent discovery of a place causes no retrospective uncleanness to the *terumah* she handled. (15) In the case of a young woman who did

ance with the ruling of R. Eliezer,[1] and after he reminded him self[2] he observed, 'R. Eliezer deserves to be relied upon [6b] in an emergency'.[3] And the point was raised, What could be the meaning of 'after he reminded himself'? If it be explained, 'After he remembered that the *halachah* was not in agreement with R. Eliezer but in agreement with the Rabbis', [the difficulty would arise:] How could he act according to the former's ruling[4] even in an emergency? Hence,[5] [it means after he recalled] that it was not stated whether the law was in agreement with the one Master or with the other Master, and having recalled that it was not an individual that differed from him[6] but that many differ from him he observed, 'R. Eliezer deserves to be relied upon in an emergency'.[3] Now if it is granted [that retrospective uncleanness applies also] to *terumah*[7] one can well understand the incident[8] since *terumah* was in existence in the days of Rabbi, but if it is maintained [that retrospective uncleanness is applicable only] to hallowed things[9] [the objection would arise:] Were there hallowed things in the days of Rabbi?[10]—[This may be explained] on the lines of a statement of 'Ullah. As 'Ulla stated, 'The Associates'[11] in Galilee[12] keep their things[13] in levitical cleanness';[14] so they may have done it in the days of Rabbi.

Come and hear: It once happened that R. Gamaliel's[15] maid was

not suffer a flow during three consecutive periods (of thirty days each).

(1) That the period of uncleanness is to be reckoned from the discovery of the flow and not retrospectively. The Rabbis who differ from R. Eliezer hold this ruling to apply to an old woman only (whose senility might be assumed to be the cause of the irregularity) but not to a young one (cf. prev. n.). (2) This is discussed presently. (3) *Infra* 9b. Lit., 'in the time of pressure'. For the nature of the emergency cf. Tosaf. contra Rashi. (4) Which is contrary to the *halachah*. (5) Cur. edd. in parenthesis insert 'not'. (6) R. Eliezer. (7) Contrary to the view of R. Huna (*supra* 6a). (8) That occurred in Rabbi's time. (9) As R. Huna laid down (cf. prev. n. but one). (10) Surely not, since the Temple was no longer in existence at that time! (11) *Ḥabraiya* pl. of *ḥaber* (v. Glos.). (12) In their hope and expectation that the Temple might at any moment be rebuilt. (13) Wine, for instance, which was used in the Temple for libation or oil that was used for the meal-offerings. (14) *Sc.* bestow upon them the same care as if they were hallowed things. V. Ḥag., Sonc. ed., p. 157 notes. (15) R. Gamaliel the Elder (Rashb.), prob. R. Gamaliel of Jamnia (Tosaf.).

baking bread loaves of *terumah* and after each[1] she rinsed her hands with water and held an examination. After the last one when she held the examination she found herself to be unclean and she came and asked R. Gamaliel who told her that they were all unclean.[2] 'Master', she said to him, 'did I not hold an examination after each one'?[1] 'If so', he told her, 'the last[3] is unclean[4] while all the others are clean'. At all events was it not here stated, 'bread loaves of *terumah*'?[5]—By *terumah* was meant[6] the bread loaves[7] of a thanksgiving-offering.[8] But how does it come about that the loaves of a thanksgiving-offering[9] should require to be baked?[10]—This is a case where they[11] were set aside[12] while they were being kneaded,[13] this being in line with what R. Ṭobi b. Ḳaṭṭina[14] ruled: 'If a man baked the loaves of a thanksgiving-offering in four loaves[15] he has performed his duty'. [For when] the objection was raised, 'Do we not require forty loaves',[16] [the reply was that] this[17] is just a religious requirement.[18] But, surely, [it was asked,] is it not necessary to separate *terumah*[12] from each?[19] And should you reply that one might break off a piece from each[20] [it could be retorted that:] The All Merciful said, *one*[21] which implies that one must not break off a piece.[12] [To this] it was replied that 'they were set aside

(1) Lit., 'between each one and one'. (2) On account of the twenty-four hours of her retrospective uncleanness. (3) Lit., 'it'. (4) Owing to retrospective uncleanness from the previous examination to the last examination. (5) And yet the law of retrospective uncleanness was applied (cf. prev. n.). How then could R. Huna maintain (*supra* 6a) that it applies only to hallowed things? (6) Lit., 'what *terumah?*' (7) *Sc.* the four loaves (one from each of the four kinds) which are given to the priest and are subject to the restrictions of hallowed things though they are called *terumah* (cf. Lev. VII, 14). (8) Cf. Lev. VII, 11ff. (9) I.e., the four that (cf. prev. n. but one) are given to the priest, which are to be taken from the forty (cf. Men. 76a) baked loaves of the offering. (10) After they have been hallowed by having been given to the priest. (11) The four loaves. (12) For the priest. (13) Hence the baking after they have been hallowed (cf. *supra* n. 10). (14) Var. lec. 'b. R. Ḳisna'. (15) I.e., of the dough of each of the four kinds he made only one loaf instead of the prescribed ten (cf. Men. 76a). (16) How then can four suffice? (17) The number of forty. (18) But no *sine qua non*. (19) Of the four kinds, one from each. (20) Of the four big loaves. (21) Lev. VII, 14, '*and . . . shall offer one*', '*one*' implying a whole one. (Men. 77b.)

while they were being kneaded';[1] so here also[2] it may be explained that they were separated while they were being kneaded.[3]

Come and hear: Another incident took place when R. Gamaliel's maid was sealing wine jars with clay that after each she rinsed her hands with water and held an examination. After the last one when she held the examination and found herself to be unclean she came and asked R. Gamaliel who told her that they were all unclean. 'But, surely', she said to him, 'I held an examination after each one'. 'If so', he told her, 'the last[4] is unclean while all the others are clean'. Now if it is conceded that one incident[5] concerned hallowed things and the other *terumah*, it can be well understood why she asked a second time, but if it is contended that the former as well as the latter concerned hallowed things, why should she have asked him a second time?—[Each] incident occurred with a different maid.[6]

Another version: R. Huna ruled, [The retrospective uncleanness during] the twenty-four hours [preceding the observation] of a menstrual flow is conveyed both to hallowed things and to *terumah*. Whence is this[7] inferred? From its omission in the enumeration of[8] the various grades [of sanctity].[9] Said R. Naḥman to him: Surely, a Tanna[10] recited [that the retrospective uncleanness][11] applies only to hallowed things and not to *terumah*. R. Samuel son of R. Isaac accepted this [teaching][12] from him [and explained it] as applying to common food that was prepared under conditions of hallowed things and not to common food that was prepared in conditions of *terumah*.[13]

(1) One loaf from each kind was set aside for the priest while nine of each were left for the owner, and subsequently each of the four small and the four large (representing nine small) loaves were duly baked. (2) In the case of R. Gamaliel's maid. (3) The maid having been engaged in the baking of the priest's share. (4) Lit., 'it'. (5) Of the two in which the maid figured. (6) Lit., 'it was with two maids'. (7) That the uncleanness mentioned is equally applicable to *terumah* and hallowed things. (8) Lit., 'since he does not teach it at'. (9) Ḥag. 20*b* where the restrictions that apply to hallowed things and not to *terumah* and *vice versa* are enumerated. (10) V. Glos. s.v. (*b*). (11) During the twenty-four hours preceding the observation of a flow. (12) Reported by R. Naḥman in the name of a Tanna. (13) It does not, however, apply to

We learnt elsewhere: If a question of doubtful uncleanness has arisen about a dough[1] before it was rolled[2] it may be prepared in uncleanness,[3] [but if the doubt has arisen] after it had been rolled[4] it must be prepared in cleanness.[5] 'Before it was rolled it may be prepared in uncleanness', because it is common food and it is permitted to cause uncleanness to common food in Ereẓ Israel. 'After it had been rolled it must be prepared in cleanness', because common food that is in a condition of *ṭebel*[6] in respect of the dough-offering is regarded as dough-offering, and it is forbidden to cause uncleanness to the dough-offering. A Tanna taught: [7*a*] Its dough-offering[7] is in a suspended condition[8] and it may neither be eaten nor burned. In respect of what doubt did they[9] give this ruling?[10] In respect of a doubt applicable to the dough-offering.[11] What is meant by 'a doubt applicable to the dough-offering'?—Both Abaye and Raba explained: That one should not assume that the ruling[12] applies only to[13] a case of likely uncleanness[14] such as that of the two paths,[15] for in that case even mere common food contracts uncleanness;[16] but that it applies also in the case

actual *terumah* which is subject to the same restrictions as hallowed things

(1) Lit., 'was produced about it'. (2) So that it was not yet subject to the dough-offering. Only after it had been rolled is a dough regarded as ready and, therefore, subject to the dough-offering. (3) Because owing to its doubtful state of uncleanness it may not be eaten in any case. (4) When it is already subject to the obligation of the offering (cf. prev. n. but one) and when consequently part of it is virtually hallowed. (5) Ḥal. III, 2; since it is forbidden to cause uncleanness to a hallowed thing (cf. Bek. 34*a*) though the dough in question could not in any case be eaten on account of its doubtful condition of uncleanness. (6) V. Glos. (7) Though it was prepared in cleanness. (8) On account of the doubt that had arisen earlier before the offering had been set aside. (9) The Rabbis. (10) That the dough-offering is in a suspended state of uncleanness. (11) And not to common food, *ḥullin* (v. Glos.). This is explained presently. (12) Concerning the uncleanness of the dough. (13) Lit., 'we learnt'. (14) Lit., 'evidences'. (15) One of which was clean and the other unclean, and a person walked through one of them and it is unknown which one it was (Rashi). For a different interpretation cf. Tosaf. (16) And is applicable to common food which is prepared under conditions of levitical purity. Much more then would this uncleanness apply to the common food from which dough-offering must be set aside, and the ruling would be superfluous.

where only 'leaning' might be assumed;[1] for we learnt: If a *zab*[2] and a clean person were unloading an ass or loading it, if the load was heavy[3] [the latter] is unclean; if it was light[4] he is clean and in either case[5] he is regarded as clean[6] [even if he is] of the members of the Synagogue[7] but as unclean[8] in respect of *terumah*,[9] and 'unconsecrated food that is in a condition of *ṭebel* in respect of the dough-offering' is regarded as dough-offering.[10] But have we not learnt:[11] A woman who is a *tebulath yom*[12] may[13] knead her dough and cut off from it its dough-offering[14] and put it on an inverted basket of palm-twigs or on a board,[15] and then[16] bring it close [to the major portion of the dough] and designate it [as dough-offering;[17] this procedure being permitted] because the uncleanness of the dough[18] is only of the third grade,[19] and the third grade is

(1) *Sc.* (cf. next n. but one) where the likelihood of uncleanness is rather remote and not applicable to common food prepared under conditions of levitical purity. (2) V. Glos. (3) Since it is possible that on account of its heavy weight one of the men leaned on the other and was thus shaken by him, 'shaking' (*hesseṭ*) being a means of conveying the uncleanness of a *zab* (cf. Rashi and Tosaf. Asheri). (4) Cf. prev. n. *mut. mut.* (5) Lit., 'and all of them', i.e., even in the case of a heavy load (Rashi); a light load (Tosaf.). (6) Since (*a*) there might have been no shaking at all and (*b*) if there was it could not obviously have been a proper shaking. (7) Who observe levitical cleanness in common food also. (8) Rabbinically. (9) Zabin III, 2. Similarly in the case of the dough-offering under discussion the expression 'a doubt applicable to the dough-offering' means a doubtful uncleanness that does not apply to members of the Synagogue in respect of common food but applies to common food from which the dough-offering has to be taken. (10) Which is in the same category as *terumah* and consequently subject to uncleanness arising from doubtful leaning. (11) So MS.M and marg. n. Cur. edd., 'it was taught'. (12) Fem. of *ṭebul yom* (v. Glos.). (13) Though she, as cleanness could not be completely attained before sunset, is still subject to an uncleanness of the second grade. (14) Without designating it as such, so that it still retains its status of common food. (15) *Sc.* on an object that is not susceptible to ritual uncleanness. Neither the board, nor the basket in its inverted position, has a receptacle, and it is only 'vessels' with proper receptacles that are susceptible to uncleanness. (16) Since the dough-offering when being set aside must be close to the dough for which it is offered. (17) By that time the uncleanness of the woman can no longer be imparted to it since the object on which it rests (cf. prev. n. but one) intervenes. (18) Lit., 'it'; that had been touched by the woman who (v. *supra*) is of the second

regarded as clean in common food.[1] Now if you were to maintain that 'common food that is in a condition of *ṭebel* in respect of the dough-offering is regarded as dough-offering' [the objection would arise:] Did she not in fact convey uncleanness to it?[2]—Said Abaye: In regard to any object,[3] that conveys certain uncleanness to common food, uncleanness has been imposed as a preventive measure, even in a doubtful case, where common food that is in a condition of *ṭebel* in respect of the dough-offering is concerned,[4] but in regard to the woman who is a *tebulath yom*, since she does not convey certain uncleanness to common food,[5] no uncleanness has been imposed as a preventive measure in a doubtful case where common food that is in a condition of *ṭebel* in respect of the dough-offering is concerned.[4] But is there not the case of the retrospective uncleanness of the twenty-four hours [preceding the observation] of a menstrual flow which[6] conveys certain uncleanness to common food and in connection with which, nevertheless, no uncleanness has been imposed as a preventive measure in a case of doubt[7] where common food that is in a condition of *ṭebel* in respect of the dough-offering is concerned;[4] for has not the Master said, 'R. Samuel son of R. Isaac accepted from him this [teaching, and explained it] as applying to common food that was prepared under conditions of hallowed things and not to common food that was prepared in conditions of *terumah*'?[8]—In the former

grade of uncleanness. (19) A clean object touched by an unclean one being always (with some exceptions) subject to a grade of uncleanness that is by one grade lower than the latter.

(1) Ṭ.Y. IV, 2; such as the dough is presumably before the dough-offering had been taken from it. (2) When she first touched it. What then was the use of the entire procedure and precaution after that? (3) Such, e.g., as the load carried by a *zab*. (4) Lit., 'on account of'. (5) A third grade of uncleanness, as stated *supra*, being regarded as clean. (6) During the actual period of the flow. (7) I.e., during the twenty-four hours preceding the observation of the flow when the uncleanness is only doubtful. (8) *Supra 6b ad fin*. 'Common food that was prepared in conditions of *terumah*' being presumably in an analogous position to 'common food that is in a condition of *ṭebel* in respect of the dough-offering' both should be subject to the same restrictions. Why then was the former exempted from the restriction while the latter was subjected to it?

case[1] no *terumah* is kneaded up with the common food[2] but in the latter case *terumah*[3] is kneaded up with the dough.[4] And if you prefer I might reply: Leave out of the question the retrospective uncleanness of the twenty-four hours, since it is merely a Rabbinical measure.

MISHNAH. R. ELIEZER RULED: IN THE CASE OF FOUR CLASSES OF WOMEN IT SUFFICES [FOR THEM TO RECKON] THEIR [PERIOD OF UNCLEANNESS FROM] THE TIME [OF THEIR DISCOVERING OF THE FLOW]: A VIRGIN,[5] A WOMAN IN PREGNANCY,[5] A NURSING WOMAN,[5] AND AN OLD WOMAN.[5] R. JOSHUA SAID: I HAVE ONLY HEARD [THE RULING[6] APPLIED TO] A VIRGIN.[7] [7b] THE HALACHAH, HOWEVER, IS IN AGREEMENT WITH R. ELIEZER.

WHO IS REGARDED AS 'VIRGIN'? ANY WOMAN, EVEN THOUGH SHE IS MARRIED, WHO HAS NEVER YET OBSERVED A FLOW. 'A WOMAN IN PREGNANCY'? ONE WHOSE EMBRYO CAN BE DISCERNED. 'A NURSING WOMAN'? A WOMAN BEFORE SHE HAS WEANED HER CHILD. IF SHE GAVE HER CHILD TO A NURSING WOMAN, IF SHE WEANED IT, OR IF IT DIED, R. MEIR RULED: SHE CONVEYS UNCLEANNESS RETROSPECTIVELY FOR TWENTY-FOUR HOURS;[8] BUT THE SAGES RULED: IT SUFFICES FOR HER[9] [TO RECKON HER PERIOD OF UNCLEANNESS FROM] THE TIME OF HER [OBSERVATION OF THE FLOW]. WHO IS REGARDED AS 'AN OLD WOMAN'? ANY WOMAN OVER WHOM THREE 'ONAHS[10] HAVE PASSED[11] NEAR THE TIME OF HER OLD AGE.[12] R. ELIEZER[13] RULED: FOR ANY WOMAN[14] OVER WHOM HAVE PASSED[11] THREE 'ONAHS IT SUFFICES [TO RECKON

(1) Cf. prev. n. Lit., 'there'. (2) Lit., 'in them'. (3) *Sc.* the dough-offering. (4) The latter must consequently be subject to greater restrictions. (5) This is explained presently. (6) Of R. Eliezer that IT SUFFICES etc. (7) But not to the other three classes. (8) Preceding the time of her observation of the flow. (9) During the twenty-four months after the child's birth throughout which she is expected to suckle it (v. Gemara *infra*). (10) 'Periods'. This is explained in the Gemara *infra*. (11) Without her observing of a flow. (12) This is explained in the Gemara *infra*. (13) Var. lec., 'Eleazar'. (14) Even a young one.

HER PERIOD OF UNCLEANNESS FROM] THE TIME OF HER [OBSERVING OF A FLOW]. R. JOSE RULED: FOR A WOMAN IN PREGNANCY, AND A NURSING WOMAN OVER WHOM THREE 'ONAHS HAVE PASSED[1] IT SUFFICES [TO RECKON THEIR PERIOD OF UNCLEANNESS FROM] THE TIME OF THEIR [OBSERVATION OF THE FLOW].[2]

AND OF WHAT DID THEY[3] SPEAK[4] WHEN THEY LAID DOWN[5] THAT 'IT SUFFICES [FOR THEM TO RECKON] THEIR PERIOD OF UNCLEANNESS FROM THE TIME [OF THEIR DISCOVERING OF THE FLOW]'? OF A FIRST OBSERVATION,[6] BUT AT A SUBSEQUENT OBSERVATION[7] SHE CONVEYS UNCLEANNESS RETROSPECTIVELY FOR A PERIOD OF TWENTY-FOUR HOURS. IF, HOWEVER, SHE SUFFERED THE FIRST FLOW ON ACCOUNT OF AN ACCIDENT[8] IT SUFFICES FOR HER EVEN AT A SUBSEQUENT OBSERVATION [TO RECKON HER UNCLEANNESS FROM] THE TIME OF HER [OBSERVING OF THE FLOW].

GEMARA. It was taught: R. Eliezer said to R. Joshua, 'You have not heard[9] but[10] I have heard; you have only heard one tradition but I have heard many;[11] people do not ask him who has not seen the new moon to come and tender evidence[12] but only him who has seen it.' Throughout the lifetime of[13] R. Eliezer the people acted in accordance with the ruling of R. Joshua, but

(1) Without her observing of a flow. (2) If three consecutive *'onahs*, however, have not passed, there applies the law of retrospective uncleanness, contrary to the view of R. Eliezer and the first Tanna *supra*. (3) The Rabbis, *supra*. (4) So BaḤ. Cur. edd. 'he spoke'. (5) *Supra* in the case of the CLASSES OF WOMEN. This is discussed in the Gemara *infra*. (6) After the three *'onahs* have passed over the virgin, the woman in pregnancy or the old woman. (7) Lit., 'at the second', since her natural proneness to the flow is re-established. (8) So that it cannot be ascribed to the woman's natural disposition (cf. prev. n.). (9) Cf. R. Joshua's statement in our Mishnah. (10) Cf. BaḤ. Cur. edd. omit the *waw*. (11) Reading *harbeh*. Var. lec. *arba'* ('four') *sc.* women, cf. BaḤ. (12) That he has seen it. Such evidence was essential to enable the Great Beth-din in Jerusalem (who regulated the lengths of the months and the fixation of the festival dates) to proclaim the beginning of a new month. (13) Lit., 'all his days'.

after the passing away of R. Eliezer, R. Joshua re-introduced the earlier practice.[1] Why did he[2] not follow R. Eliezer during his lifetime?—Because R. Eliezer was a disciple of Shammai[3] and he[4] felt that if they[5] would act in agreement with his ruling in one matter[6] they[5] would act in agreement with his rulings in other matters also[7] and that out of respect for R. Eliezer no one could interfere[8] with them; but after the passing away of R. Eliezer, when the people[9] could well be interfered with, he[4] re-introduced the original practice.

Rab Judah citing Samuel ruled: The *halachah* is in agreement with R. Eliezer in four cases. One is that which has just been mentioned.[10] The other is that about a woman who was in a hard travail[11] [concerning whom it was stated:] For how long must she be relieved from pain[12] so as to be regarded a *zabah?*[13] Twenty-four

(1) Lit., 'restored the thing to its old (state)', when the practice was in agreement with the view of R. Eliezer. (2) R. Joshua. (3) So R. Tam and Rashb. (*contra* Rashi who, referring to B.M. 59*b*, renders *shamuthi* 'one placed under the ban'). Wherever Beth Hillel differed from Beth Shammai the law (with a very few exceptions) is always in agreement with the former. (4) R. Joshua. (5) Lit., 'we'. (6) I.e., the one mentioned in our Mishnah where the law in fact is in agreement with his view. (7) *Sc.* even in those where the law is in agreement with Beth Hillel. (8) Lit., 'we are not able to prevent'. (9) If they were to follow R. Eliezer in other matters (cf. prev. n. but one) also. (10) Cf. *supra* n. 6. (11) For three days (during the 'eleven days' between the menstrual periods) on each of which there was a discharge of blood. If the discharge was not due to the travail she, having observed the blood on three consecutive days, would be subject to the restrictions of a *zabah;* but if it was due to travail she would be exempt from these restrictions. If a *zabah* she would have to count after childbirth seven days (as a *zabah*) in addition to the number of days prescribed for a woman after childbirth, and she would also have to bring two sacrifices one as a *zabah* and the other as one after childbirth. (12) After the three days mentioned (cf. prev. n.) and before the birth of the child. (13) Retrospectively, on account of the discharges on the three days. If the pain had continued until delivery it would have been obvious that the discharge on the three days mentioned was also due to the same cause, but if it ceased some considerable time before birth it may well be concluded that that discharge had no connection with the childbearing and the woman would consequently come within the category of *zabah* (cf. prev. n. but one).

hours;[1] so R. Eliezer.[2] And the *halachah* is in agreement with his view.[3] And the third[4] is the following: If a *zab* and a *zabah*[5] examined themselves on the first day[6] and found themselves clean and on the seventh day also[7] and found themselves clean, but did not examine themselves during the other days,[8] R. Eliezer ruled: Behold these[9] are in a presumptive condition of cleanness,[10] and R. Joshua ruled: They are entitled [to reckon as clean] only the first day and the seventh day,[11] while R. Akiba ruled: They are entitled [to reckon as clean] the seventh day alone,[12] and it was taught: R. Simeon and R. Jose stated, 'The view of R. Eliezer[13] is more feasible than that of R. Joshua,[14] while that of R. Akiba is more feasible than those of both,[15] but the *halachah* agrees with that of R. Eliezer'.[16] And the fourth is the following.[17] For we have learnt: If the outer sides[18] of vessels were rendered unclean[19] by liquids,[20] R. Eliezer ruled, they convey uncleanness[19] to other

(1) If such a period has intervened it is obvious that the discharge mentioned was in no way due to travail. (2) *Infra* 36b. (3) Though R. Joshua differs from him. (4) Lit., 'and the other'. (5) *Sc.* the same law applies to either. (6) After the flux had ceased. (7) Cf. prev. n. Seven days without any discharge must pass before a *zab* or a *zabah* can attain cleanness. (8) The intermediate five. (9) Since on the first and the last day they were definitely clean. (10) And on performing immersion at the close of the seventh day they became clean. (11) *Sc.* two days only. As the cleanness of the intermediate days is a matter of doubt they must count another five days to make up the prescribed number of seven. In the case of a certain discharge on any of the days all the prescribed seven days must, of course, be counted all over again. (12) *Infra* 68b; since it is possible that there was a discharge on the sixth day, when there was no examination (cf. prev. n. last clause). (13) Who is consistent in disregarding completely the possibility of a discharge on any of the five days that intervened between the first and last clean ones. Cf. following n. (14) Who (cf. prev. n.) is inconsistent, seeing that he assumes the possibility of a discharge during the intermediate days and at the same time allows counting the first day as one of the seven clean days. (15) A possible, like a certain discharge (cf. *supra* n. 11, last clause) on the sixth day might quite reasonably be regarded as sufficient ground for cancelling all the previous days counted, including the first. (16) *Infra* 68b. (17) Lit., 'and the other'. (18) In a case where the insides are not affected (as explained *infra*) lit., 'backs'. (19) Rabbinically (cf. following two notes). (20) Through contracting uncleanness from a dead creeping thing. The latter

liquids[1] but they[2] do not render foodstuffs unfit.[3] 'They convey uncleanness to liquids' even where the latter are common, but they 'do not render foodstuffs unfit', even where the latter are *terumah*. R. Joshua ruled: They convey uncleanness to liquids and also render foodstuffs unfit.[4] Said R. Joshua: This may be inferred *a minori ad majus:* If a *ṭebul yom* who[5] does not convey uncleanness to a common liquid,[6] nevertheless renders foodstuffs of *terumah* unfit how much more then should the outsides of vessels which do convey uncleanness to an unconsecrated liquid render foodstuffs of *terumah* unfit. And R. Eliezer?[7]—The uncleanness of the outsides of vessels[8] is only Rabbinical[9] while that of a *ṭebul yom*[10] is Pentateuchal;[11] and, where it is a question of deducing a Rabbinical from a Pentateuchal law, no inference *a minori ad majus* can be applied.[12] For in accordance with Pentateuchal law no foodstuff conveys uncleanness to a vessel and no liquid conveys uncleanness to a vessel, and it is only the Rabbis that have ordained such uncleanness as a preventive measure against possible laxity in the case of the fluid[13] of a *zab* or a *zabah;*[14] hence it is only in the

being a primary uncleanness causes the liquids to be an uncleanness of the first grade which (though Pentateuchally, since their uncleanness is not a primary one, it cannot, as explained in Pes. 18*a*, convey uncleanness to vessels) renders the vessels unclean Rabbinically. As the uncleanness that is conveyed to vessels by liquids is merely Rabbinical, and as it was desired to make a distinction between Pentateuchal and Rabbinical uncleanness, it was enacted that, in such a case, only the outsides of vessels and not their insides shall contract the uncleanness.

(1) Because liquids are prone to uncleanness. In consequence they contract from the vessels a first grade of uncleanness, the same grade as that of the outer sides of the vessels themselves. (2) Since Pentateuchally (cf. prev. n. but one) they are deemed to be clean. (3) Ṭoh. VIII, 7; much less do they render them unclean. (This is explained presently.) (4) Ṭoh. VIII, 7. (5) Being subject to a secondary grade of uncleanness only (v. following n.). (6) As explained in Pes. 14*b*. (7) How in view of this inference can he maintain his ruling? (8) Contracted from liquids. (9) Cf. *supra* n. 3. (10) In respect of conveying uncleanness to foodstuffs of *terumah*. (11) As deduced from Scripture in Yeb. 74*b*. (12) Since it is obvious that Pentateuchal uncleanness should be subject to greater restrictions. (13) E.g., spittle. (14) Which is a primary uncleanness Pentateuchally (cf. Lev. XV, 8).

case of liquids, which are prone to contract uncleanness, that the Rabbis have enacted a preventive measure, but in that of foodstuffs, since they are not prone to contract uncleanness, the Rabbis enacted no preventive measure. What, however, is the reason for the mention of the outsides of vessels?[1]—Because their restrictions are lighter.[2] For we have learnt: If the outside of a vessel came in contact with unclean liquids,[3] its outside becomes unclean while its inside, its hanger,[4] its rim and its handles remain clean, but if its inside has become unclean all of it is unclean.[5]

But what does Samuel teach us,[6] seeing that in all these cases we learnt that the law [was in agreement with R. Eliezer]? And should you reply that he mainly informed us about the 'outsides of vessels' concerning which we did not learn [elsewhere what the law was], why [it could be retorted] did he not simply state, 'The *halachah* is in agreement with R. Eliezer in the case of the outsides of vessels'?—The fact is that it is this that he informed us:[7] That the *halachah* may not be derived from a theoretical statement.[8]

But are there no more [than the four rulings]?[9] Is there not in fact another, since we have learnt: R. Eliezer ruled, [8*a*] 'A

(1) Lit., 'wherein is the difference . . . that he took up', *sc.* why should not the Mishnah equally speak of the insides of vessels that similarly contracted from liquids Rabbinical uncleanness? (2) Than those that govern the insides of vessels. In the latter case R. Eliezer agrees that *terumah* is rendered invalid. (3) Lit., 'a vessel whose back became unclean by liquids'. (4) Lit., 'its ear'. (5) Kelim XXV, 6. (6) By stating *supra* that 'the *halachah* is in agreement with R. Eliezer in four cases'. (7) By laying down the *halachah* (cf. prev. n.) in the case of rulings where a similar statement was actually embodied in the Mishnah. (8) *Talmud*, lit., 'learning'. All statements as to what is the *halachah* added by a Tanna to a ruling in a Mishnah or a Baraitha must be regarded as a mere opinion or theory which a disciple expressed with reference to a ruling of his master. It is only the carefully considered decisions of the later Amoras that, being based on a minute examination and thorough analysis of their predecessor's views that may be relied upon as authoritative in determining the *halachah* (cf. Rashi). (9) Referred to *supra* by Rab Judah in the name of Samuel, concerning which the *halachah* is in agreement with R. Eliezer.

minor[1] is to be instructed[2] to exercise her right of *mi'un* against him'[3] and in connection with this Rab Judah citing Samuel stated, 'The *halachah* is in agreement with R. Eliezer'?[4]—When Samuel stated 'the *halachah* is in agreement with R. Eliezer in four cases' he referred to rulings in the Order of Ṭoharoth,[5] but in the other Orders there are many such rulings. This[6] also stands to reason, for we learnt: R. Eliezer ruled, 'Also in the case of one who shovels out loaves of bread[7] from an oven and puts them into a basket,[8] the basket causes them to be combined in respect of their liability to the dough-offering',[9] and in connection with this Rab Judah citing Samuel stated, 'The *halachah* is in agreement with R. Eliezer.'[10] This is conclusive. But why is the latter[11] a more valid proof[12] than the former?[13]—Because in the former case R. Eleazar takes up the same standpoint as he,[14] for we learnt: R. Eleazar ruled, The minor is to be instructed[15] to exercise her right of

(1) Who was fatherless and was given in marriage by her mother or brothers (so that her marriage is only Rabbinically valid) and who had a sister that was of age and was married to the minor's husband's brother who died without issue. In accordance with the laws of the levirate marriage the surviving brother must marry the widow, but such marriage cannot take place in this case on account of the prohibition to marry a wife's sister. The minor, furthermore, is now forbidden to live with her husband (whose marriage with her is only Rabbinically valid) on account of the levirate bond between him and her sister (which is Pentateuchal). Rashi speaks here of two 'orphan' sisters, but the Mishnah in Yeb. speaks of 'deaf' sisters. (2) In order to avoid (cf. prev. n.) the difficulties mentioned. (3) Her husband. In virtue of *mi'un* (v. Glos.) she annuls her marriage and sets her husband free to perform the Pentateuchal law of the levirate marriage. Yeb. 109*a*. (4) Yeb. 110*a*. (5) The sixth, and last order of the Talmud in which the tractate of Niddah is included. (6) That Samuel referred to the Order of Ṭoharoth alone. (7) That were made of quantities of dough each of which was never greater than five *ḳab*. Only when dough is no less than five *ḳab* in bulk is it subject to the dough-offering. (8) And in their total they amounted to no less than five *ḳab*. (9) Ḥal. II, 4. (10) Which shows that outside the Order of Ṭoharoth there are other rulings concerning which the *halachah* is in agreement with R. Eliezer. (11) Ḥal. II, 4. (12) In support of the explanation given (cf. n. 10). (13) The ruling cited from Yeb. Lit., 'and what is the strength of that from that?' (14) R. Eliezer. (15) In certain cases enumerated in Yeb. 111*a*.

mi'un against him.[1] But does he[2] take up the same standpoint?[3] Have we not in fact shown[4] that both[5] were required because they are not like one another?[6]—Rather say, Because R. Judah b. Baba takes up the same position as he,[7] for we learnt,[8] 'R. Judah b. Baba testified concerning five things: That minors are urged to exercise their right of *mi'un*,[9] that a woman[10] is allowed to remarry on the evidence of one witness,[11] that a cock was stoned[12] in Jerusalem because it had killed a person,[13] that[14] wine which was only forty days old[15] was poured as a drink-offering upon the altar, and that[14] the continual morning sacrifice was offered[16] [as late as] at the fourth hour [of the day]'.[17] Now does not the expression 'minors'[18] imply[19] the one of which R. Eleazar and the one of which R. Eliezer spoke?[20]—No; by the expression[21] 'minors' minors in general[22] were meant.[23] If so,[24] should it not have been stated, in the case of the woman[25] also, 'women', meaning thereby[26]

(1) Yeb. 111*a*, a ruling that is analogous to that of R. Eliezer in Yeb. 109*a*, and it might have been assumed that only in this case, since R. Eliezer is supported by the authority of R. Eleazar, is the *halachah* in agreement with the former but not in other cases where he has no such support; hence the citation from Ḥal. where the *halachah* is in agreement with R. Eliezer even though his ruling has his own authority alone. (2) R. Eleazar. (3) As R. Eliezer. (4) Yeb. 111*b*. (5) Statements of Samuel, that the *halachah* is in agreement with (*a*) R. Eliezer and (*b*) R. Eleazar. (6) How then could it be suggested here that R. Eleazar's ruling provides support for that of R. Eliezer? (7) R. Eliezer. (8) So MS.M. Cur. edd. 'it was taught'. (9) Cf. notes on the similar ruling of R. Eliezer (cited from Yeb. 109*a supra*). (10) Whose husband left for a country overseas. (11) Who testifies that her husband was dead. (12) In accordance with Ex. XXI, 28 (as expounded in B.Ḳ. 54*b*), though the text speaks only of an ox. (13) It pecked out the brain of a child. (14) Lit., 'and about'. (15) One that is less than forty days old is invalid as 'wine from the vat', which is too new (cf. B. B. 97*a*, Sonc. ed. p. 405). (16) On one occasion, during the Syrian Greek siege of Jerusalem, when no sacrifice could be secured. (17) 'Ed. VI, 1. (18) *Sc.* the use of the plural form. (19) Lit., 'what minors? Not?' etc. (20) The answer being presumably in the affirmative it follows that R. Eliezer's ruling is supported by the authority of R. Judah b. Baba. (21) Lit., 'what'. (22) Of the class spoken of by R. Eleazar. (23) Excluding the one spoken of by R. Eliezer who, consequently, stands unsupported. (24) That the plural form in this context is used to indicate the class. (25) 'That a woman is allowed etc.' (26) Lit., 'and let us say'.

women in general?[1] As in the latter case,[2] however, it was stated 'woman',[3] and in the former 'minors'[4] it may be concluded that the expressions are to be taken literally.[5] This is conclusive.

R. Eleazar[6] also[7] stated, 'The *halachah* is in agreement with R. Eliezer in four things'. But are there no more of such rulings?[8] Have we not in fact learnt, 'R. Eliezer ruled, The minor is to be instructed to exercise her right of *mi'un* against him'[9] and R. Eleazar stated, 'The *halachah* is in agreement with R. Eliezer'?[10] And were you to reply that when R. Eleazar stated, 'The *halachah* is in agreement with R. Eliezer in four things' he referred to the rulings in the Order of Ṭoharoth, but that in the other Orders there are many more such rulings[8] [it could be retorted:] But are there any such? Have we not in fact learnt, 'The rose, henna,[11] lotus[12] and balsam as well as their proceeds are subject to the laws of the Sabbatical year[13] and they and their proceeds are also subject to the law of removal,'[14] in connection with which R. Pedath[15] observed, 'Who taught[16] that balsam is a fruit?[17] R. Eliezer'; and R. Zera replied, 'I see that between[18] you and your father you will cause balsam to be permitted to the world,[19] since you said, "Who taught that balsam is a fruit? R. Eliezer" and your father said, "The *halachah* is in agreement with R. Eliezer in four things".'[20]

(1) Obviously it should. (2) Lit., 'since here' (cf. *supra* p. 47, n. 25). (3) In the sing., though the whole class is included. (4) In the plural. (5) Lit., 'he learns exactly', *sc.* that 'minors' in the plural refers to the two classes of minor, the one dealt with by R. Eleazar and the one spoken of by R. Eliezer. (6) I.e., R. Eleazar b. Pedath who was an Amora. R. Eleazar who laid down the rule of *mi'un* is a Tanna and was b. Shammua'. (7) Like Rab Judah who cited Samuel *supra* 7b. (8) In regard to which the *halachah* is in agreement with R. Eliezer. (9) *Supra* q.v. notes. (10) Yeb. 110a. (11) Or 'cyprus flower'. (12) Or 'gum-mastich'. (13) Shebi. VII, 6; *sc.* during that year they must be treated as *hefker* (v. Glos.) and no trade may be carried on with them. (14) *Sc.* as soon as none of these products respectively remained in the field the owner must remove from his house all that he had previously gathered in. The last quoted part, 'and they . . . removal' is wanting in the Mishnah. (15) The son of R. Eleazar b. Pedath. (16) In the Mishnah cited from Sheb. (17) Were it no fruit it would not have been subject to the laws of the Sabbatical Year. (18) Lit., 'from'. (19) During the Sabbatical Year, i.e., to be exempt from its restrictions. (20) But no more. R. Eliezer's restrictive

Now, if it were so,[1] why did he[2] not reply to him,[3] 'When my father said, "The *halachah* is in agreement with R. Eliezer in four things" he referred only to rulings in the Order of Ṭoharoth but in other Orders there are many more'?[4]—But then,[5] does not the previous difficulty[6] arise?—[In the case of *mi'un*[7] the *halachah* is in agreement with R. Eliezer] because R. Eleazar [b. Shammua'] takes up the same standpoint as he; for we have learnt: R. Eleazar ruled, The minor is to be instructed to exercise her right of *mi'un* against him.[8] But does he[9] take up the same standpoint? Have we not in fact shown that both[10] were required because they are not like one another?[11]—Rather say: Because R. Judah b. Baba takes up the same standpoint as he.[9] But are there no more such rulings?[12]

Have we not in fact learnt: 'R. Akiba ruled, One says it[13] as an independent benediction;[14] R. Eliezer ruled, One includes it in the benediction of thanksgiving';[15] and in connection with this R. Eleazar[16] stated,[17] 'The *halachah* is in agreement with R. Eliezer'?—R. Abba replied: [The *halachah* agrees with him] in that case because he [may have] said it in the name of R. Ḥanina b. Gamaliel, for it was taught: R. Akiba ruled, One says it[18] as an independent benediction;[14] R. Ḥanina b. Gamaliel ruled, One

law concerning balsam, since it is not included in the four, must consequently be against the *halachah* and must, therefore, be disregarded.

(1) That outside the Order of Ṭoharoth there are other rulings of R. Eliezer in agreement with the *halachah*. (2) R. Pedath. (3) R. Zera. (4) And R. Zera's objection would thus have been met. Since R. Pedath, however, gave no such reply it follows that R. Eleazar's statement that 'the *halachah* is in agreement with R. Eliezer in four things' applies to all the Orders of the Talmud. (5) Cf. prev. n. (6) How is it that in the case of *mi'un* (which is not included in the four) the *halachah* is also in agreement with R. Eliezer? (7) Though it is not one of the four (cf. prev. n.). (8) *Supra* q.v. notes. (9) R. Eleazar [b. Shammua']. (10) The rulings of R. Eliezer and R. Eleazar respectively. (11) *Supra* q.v. notes. (12) Concerning which the *halachah* is in agreement with R. Eliezer. (13) The benediction of *habdalah* in the evening service at the conclusion of the Sabbath (cf. *P.B.*, p. 46). (14) *Sc.* it is not to be included in any of the statutory benedictions. (15) Ber. 29*a*, 33*a*. Cf. *P.B.*, p. 51. (16) b. Pedath (cf. *supra*). (17) M. J. Ber. (Tosaf). (18) The benediction of *habdalah* in the evening service at the conclusion of the Sabbath (cf. *P.B.*, p. 46).

includes it in the benediction of thanksgiving. [8b] But was he[1] not much older than he?[2]—Rather say:[3] Because R. Ḥanina b. Gamaliel took up[4] the same line as he. But did he[5] take it up? Was it not in fact taught: On the night of the Day of Atonement[6] one recites in his prayers seven benedictions and makes confession; in the morning[6] one recites seven benedictions and makes confession; during the additional prayer[7] one recites seven benedictions and makes confession; in the afternoon prayer one recites seven benedictions and makes confession; in the concluding prayer[8] one recites seven benedictions and makes confession, and in the evening[9] one recites seven benedictions embodying the substance of the Eighteen;[10] and R. Ḥanina b. Gamaliel in the name of his ancestors ruled: One must recite in his prayers[11] all the eighteen benedictions because it is necessary to include *habdalah*[12] in 'who favourest man with knowledge'?[13]—R. Naḥman b. Isaac replied: He cited it[14] in the name of his ancestors but he himself[15] does not uphold it.

(1) R. Eliezer, a contemporary and brother-in-law of R. Gamaliel the son of Simeon who was one of the 'Ten Royal Martyrs' (Rashi). (2) Ḥanina, who was a son of R. Gamaliel of Jamnia (v. Tosaf.). Now is it likely that an older scholar would quote a tradition on the authority of a younger one? (3) In explanation why the *halachah* is in agreement with R. Eliezer in this particular case. (4) At a later date. Lit., 'stands'. (5) R. Ḥanina. (6) The 'Day' extending over a night and the following day. (7) *Musaf*, which on Sabbaths and festivals is recited after the morning service. (8) *Ne'ilah*, the last prayer before sunset on the Day of Atonement. (9) That follows the solemn day. (10) I.e., instead of all the 'eighteen (now nineteen) benedictions' that are to be recited at ordinary weekday services (cf. *P.B.*, p. 44ff) one recites on this occasion only the first three and the last three benedictions, and inserts between a shortened prayer embracing the salient features of the intermediate ones (cf. *P.B.*, p. 55). (11) Even on the evening mentioned. (12) The prayer added to the service at the conclusion of Sabbaths and festival days (cf. *P.B.*, p. 46). (13) Yoma 87*b*, Pes. 3*a*. Cf. *P.B.*, l.c. In the shortened prayer, where this benediction is reduced to a few words, this cannot be done. Now, since R. Ḥanina here states that *habdalah* is to be included in the benediction 'who favourest etc.' how could it be said *supra* that he adopts the same line as R. Eliezer who requires it to be included in the benediction of thanksgiving? (14) The last quoted ruling. (15) Who is in agreement with R. Eliezer.

Said R. Jeremiah to R. Zera:[1] But do you not yourself hold that he who taught that balsam was a fruit is R. Eliezer, seeing that we have learnt: R. Eliezer ruled, Milk curdled with the sap of *'orlah* is forbidden?[2]—This[3] might be said to agree even with the view of the Rabbis, since they differed from R. Eliezer only in respect of the sap of the tree but in the case of the sap of the fruit they agree with him, for we have learnt: R. Joshua stated, I have explicitly heard that milk curdled with the sap of the leaves or with the sap of the roots is permitted, but if it was curdled with the sap of unripe figs it is forbidden because the latter is regarded as a proper fruit.[4] And if you prefer I might reply: The Rabbis differ from R. Eliezer only in respect of a fruit producing tree but in the case of a tree that does not produce fruit they agree that its sap is regarded as its fruit, for we have learnt: R. Simeon ruled, Balsam is not subject to the laws of the Sabbatical Year[5] and the Sages ruled, Balsam is subject to the laws of the Sabbatical Year because the sap of the tree is regarded as its fruit.[6] Now who are the Sages? Are they not in fact the Rabbis who differ[7] from R. Eliezer?[8]—Thus, a certain elder replied to him, said R. Johanan, 'Who are the "Sages"? R. Eliezer who ruled that its balsam is its fruit'. But if by the 'Sages' R. Eliezer was meant what was the point in speaking of a tree that does not produce fruit seeing that even where a tree produces fruit its sap is regarded as its fruit?—He[9] spoke to them[10] according to the view of the Rabbis. 'According to my view' [he said in effect,] 'even in the case of a fruit

(1) Who objected (*supra* 8a) to R. Pedath's assertion as to the authorship of the ruling on balsam. (2) 'Orlah I, 7; because the sap is considered a fruit to which the prohibitions of *'orlah* apply. Balsam also being a sap, must not the ruling that balsam is a fruit obviously be that of R. Eliezer? (3) The ruling just cited. (4) 'Orlah I, 7. (5) 'Because it is not regarded as a fruit', Sheb. VII, 6. (6) This quotation does not actually occur in the Mishnah cited (cf. prev. n.) but is implied from the ruling of the first Tanna ibid. (7) In the case of other trees. (8) Presumably they are. Thus it follows, as R. Zera submitted, that in the case of balsam the Rabbis are of the same opinion as R. Eliezer and that there is no need, therefore, to attribute to him the ruling which is in agreement with the *halachah*. (9) R. Eliezer. (10) Those who differed from him.

producing tree its sap is regarded as its fruit, but according to your view[1] agree with me at least in this case of a tree that produces no fruit that its sap is its fruit. But the Rabbis told him: No difference is made.[2]

WHO IS REGARDED AS A 'VIRGIN'? ANY WOMAN WHO HAS NOT YET OBSERVED etc. Our Rabbis taught: [If a virgin] married and observed a discharge of blood that was due to the marriage, or if when she bore a child she observed a discharge of blood that was due to the birth, she is still called a 'virgin', because the virgin of whom the Rabbis spoke is one that is a virgin as regards menstrual blood but not one who is so in regard to the blood of virginity.[3] Can this, however, be correct?[4] Has not R. Kahana in fact stated, 'A Tanna taught: There are three kinds of virgin, the human virgin, the soil virgin and the sycamore virgin. The "human virgin" is one that never[5] had any sexual intercourse, the practical issue[6] being her eligibility to marry a High Priest[7] or else her claim to a *kethubah* of two hundred *zuz*;[8] the "virgin soil" is one that had never[5] been cultivated, the practical issue[6] being its designation as "*a rough valley*"[9] or else its legal status as regards purchase and sale;[10] the "virgin sycamore" is one that has never[11] been cut,[12] the practical issue[13] being its legal status as regards purchase and sale[14] or else the permissibility to cut it[12] in the Sabbatical Year, as we have learnt: A virgin sycamore may not be cut in the Sabbatical Year because such cutting is regarded as

(1) Which does not regard the sap of a fruit bearing tree as fruit. (2) Between the two kinds of tree. In neither case can sap be regarded as fruit. (3) Or birth. (4) Lit., 'I am not'. (5) Lit., 'all the time that she (had) not'. (6) Between being regarded as a virgin or not. (7) Cf. Lev. XXI, 13. (8) Only a virgin is entitled to that sum. One who is no virgin is entitled to one hundred *zuz* only. (9) Deut. XXI, 4, in the case where a murdered man was found in a field and his murderers cannot be discovered when a heifer is brought into a rough valley and a prescribed ceremonial is performed (v. ibid. 1ff). (10) If a plot of land has been sold or bought as 'virgin soil' it must be one that has never before been cultivated. (11) Lit., 'all the time that she (had) not'. (12) Since the cutting causes new growth. (13) Between being regarded as a virgin or not. (14) Cf. *supra* n. 10 *mut. mut.*

cultivation'.[1] Now if this[2] were correct why did he[3] not mention this one also?—R. Naḥman b. Isaac replied: He only mentioned such as has no special[4] name[5] but one which bears a special[4] name[6] he does not mention. R. Shesheth son of R. Idi replied: He[7] only mentioned those, the loss of whose virginity[8] is dependent on an act[9] but one the loss of whose virginity[8] is not dependent on an act[10] he does not mention. R. Ḥanina son of R. Iḳa replied: He[7] only mentioned those[8] which do not change[11] into their original condition[12] but one which does change to its original condition[13] he does not mention. Rabina replied: He[14] only mentioned that to which a purchaser is likely to object[15] but that to which a purchaser is not likely to object[16] he does not mention. But do not people object?[17] Was it not in fact taught, 'R. Ḥiyya stated: As leaven is wholesome for the dough so is menstrual blood wholesome for a woman'[18] and it was also taught in the name of R. Meir, 'Every woman who has an abundance of menstrual blood has many children'?[18]—Rather say: He[14] only mentioned that which a purchaser is anxious to acquire[19] but that[20] which a purchaser is not anxious to acquire[21] he does not mention.

(1) Which is forbidden (cf. Lev. XXV, 4); Sheb. IV, 5. (2) That there is also a virginity as regards menstrual blood. (3) R. Kahana who only spoke of three kinds of virgin. (4) Lit., 'attached', 'accompanying'. (5) 'Virgin' alone being sufficient. (6) Such as the 'virgin in respect of menstrual blood' whom 'virgin' alone would not sufficiently describe. (7) R. Kahana who only spoke of three kinds. (8) Lit., 'a thing that'. (9) Such as intercourse, cultivation or cutting. (10) As is the case with a discharge of menstrual blood which is a natural and involuntary process. (11) After intercourse, cultivation and cutting respectively. (12) Lit., 'to its creation', neither the woman nor the soil nor the sycamore can (cf. prev. n.) change into her or its original condition. (13) A woman in old age loses her flow and changes, in this respect, into a condition similar to her original virginity. (14) R. Kahana who only spoke of three kinds. (15) No one who could help it would be likely to marry a non-virgin or to buy land that was already exploited or a sycamore that was cut. (16) One who marries a virgin does not care whether or not she ever had her menstrual flow. (17) Cf. prev. n. (18) Keth. 10*b*. (19) Lit., 'that... jumps on it', people are anxious to marry a virgin, to buy a plot of land that was never before exploited and a sycamore that was never before cut. (20) A virgin who has no menstrual flow. (21) For the reasons indicated by R. Ḥiyya and R. Meir *supra*.

Our Rabbis taught: What is meant by a virgin soil? One which[1] turns up clods[2] and whose earth is not loose. If[1] a potsherd is found in it, it may be known that it had once been cultivated;[3] if flint, it is undoubtedly[4] virgin soil.

'A WOMAN IN PREGNANCY'? ONE WHOSE EMBRYO CAN BE DISCERNED. At what stage[5] is the embryo discernible?—Symmachus citing R. Meir replied: Three months after conception. And though there is no actual proof for this statement there is an allusion[6] to it, for it is said in Scripture, *And it came to pass about three months after*[7] etc. 'An allusion to it' [you say], is not this a text of Scripture and a most reliable[8] proof?—[It can only be regarded as an allusion] because some women[9] give birth after nine months and others after seven months.[10]

Our Rabbis taught: If a woman was[11] in a condition of presumptive pregnancy and after observing a discharge of blood she miscarried an inflated object[12] or any other object which had no vitality[13] she[14] is still deemed to be[15] in the condition of her presumptive pregnancy and it suffices for her to reckon her period of menstrual uncleanness from the time of her observation of the discharge.[16] And though there is no actual proof for this ruling[17] there is an allusion[18] to it, for it is said in Scripture, *We have been with child, we have been in pain, we have as it were brought forth wind.*[19] But why only 'an allusion to it' seeing that the text provides actual[20] proof?—That text was in fact written about males.[21]

(1) On being broken up. (2) That need crushing. (3) How else could the potsherd have found its way into it? (4) Lit., 'behold this'. (5) Lit., 'and how much'. (6) Lit., 'remembrance'. (7) *That it was told . . . she is with child*, Gen. XXXVIII, 24. (8) Lit., 'great'. (9) Lit., 'there is'. (10) And it might have been assumed that the three months of the text (representing a third of nine) applied to the former only while in the case of the latter the stage of recognition begins after $\frac{7}{3} = 2\frac{1}{3}$ months. (11) Lit., 'behold she was'. (12) Lit., 'wind'. (13) Lit., 'existence'. (14) Despite the fact that her pregnancy, as is now evident, was not natural. (15) As regards retrospective uncleanness. (16) Not twenty-four hours retrospectively as is the case with one who is not pregnant. (17) That an inflated object (cf. *supra* n. 12) is regarded as a viable embryo in respect of pregnancy. (18) Lit., 'remembrance'. (19) Emphasis on the last word. Isa. XXVI, 18. Tosef. Nid. I. (20) Lit., 'great'. (21) In whose case conception and birth are mere metaphorical expressions.

I would, however, point out an incongruity: If a woman was in hard labour[1] for two days[2] and on the third day[3] she miscarried an inflated object or any thing that had no vitality, she[4] is regarded as bearing in the condition of a *zabah*.[5] Now if you maintain that such miscarriage is a proper birth [9a] did not the All Merciful [it may be objected] ordain that [a flow of blood in] painful labour immediately before birth[6] is regarded as clean?[7]—R. Papi replied: Leave alone the question of the twenty-four hours retrospective uncleanness[8] which only involves a Rabbinical enactment.[9] R. Papa replied: The actual reason[10] is that the woman[11] feels a heaviness in her head and limbs;[12] well then, here also[13] she feels a heaviness in her head and in her limbs.[14]

R. Jeremiah enquired of R. Zera: What is the ruling[15] where a woman observed a flow and immediately after her pregnancy was discerned? Is she retrospectively unclean because her pregnancy was not known at the time she observed the flow or is she

(1) Accompanied by a flow of blood. (2) During the eleven days in which she is susceptible to the uncleanness of a *zabah* (v. foll. nn.). (3) After a further discharge of blood, so that (cf. prev. n. but one) her bleeding and pain extended over three consecutive days. (4) Since there was no proper birth though she had no relief from her pain between the time of the discharge and the miscarriage. (5) V. Glos. *Sc.* she must count seven days and bring the sacrifice prescribed for a *zabah* before she can attain cleanness. (6) The woman having had no relief from her pain between the appearance of the flow and birth (cf. prev. n. but one). (7) V. *infra* 37b. Why then should the woman here be treated as a *zabah*? (8) With which the first of the apparently contradictory Baraithas deals. (9) And could, therefore, be relaxed even in the case of a pregnancy that ended in a miscarriage. As regards the Pentateuchal uncleanness of a *zabah*, however, a miscarriage of the nature spoken of in the last cited Baraitha cannot be regarded as a proper birth. (10) Why a pregnant woman is to reckon her menstrual uncleanness from the very moment she has observed a discharge and not retrospectively. (11) During her pregnancy. (12) *Sc.* she is suffering from a malady which causes her menstrual flow to disappear. (13) In the case of a pregnancy that ended in a miscarriage spoken of in the first of the Baraithas under discussion. (14) It is obvious, therefore, that she also suffers from the same malady (cf. prev. n. but one) in consequence of which she is entitled to the same privileges (cf. *supra* n. 10). (15) In respect of the twenty-four hours retrospective uncleanness.

not retrospectively unclean since she observed it immediately before she became aware of her pregnancy?—The other replied: The sole reason[1] is that she[2] feels a heaviness in her head and limbs[3] but[4] at the time she observed the flow she felt no heaviness either in her head or in her limbs.[5]

A certain old man asked R. Joḥanan: 'What is the ruling if, when the time of her fixed period had come during the days of her pregnancy and she did not examine herself? I am raising this question on the view of the authority who laid down [that a woman's duty to hold an examination on the arrival of her] fixed periods is an ordinance of the Torah.[6] What is the ruling [I ask]? Must she[7] examine herself since [the duty of holding an examination on the arrival of] the fixed periods is an ordinance of the Torah[6] or is it possible that since[8] her menstrual blood is suspended,[9] she requires no examination'?[10]—The other[11] replied, You have learnt it: R. Meir ruled, If a woman was in a hiding-place[12] when the time of her fixed period arrived and she did not examine herself she is nevertheless clean because fear suspends the menstrual flow.[13] Now the reason is[14] that there was fear, but if there had been no fear and the time of her fixed period had arrived and she did not examine herself she would have been deemed unclean. It is thus clear[15] [that a woman's duty to examine herself at the time of the arrival of her] fixed periods is an ordinance of the Torah and that, nevertheless, since there was fear, her menstrual blood is deemed to be suspended and she requires no exemption; so

(1) V. p. 55, n. 10. (2) During her pregancy. (3) V. p. 55, n. 12. (4) In the case about which R. Jeremiah enquired. (5) She cannot, therefore, be regarded as a pregnant woman, and her uncleanness is retrospective. (6) *Sc.* a traditional *halachah* handed down from the time of Moses (Rashi), so that since the flow may be expected to make its appearance on the regular day, a woman who did not examine herself at such a period, must be regarded as unclean (v. *infra* 16a). (7) If she is to be regarded as clean. (8) During pregnancy. (9) And the regular appearance of her menstrual blood need not be expected. (10) I.e., she is deemed to be clean even if she did not examine herself. (11) R. Joḥanan. (12) In fear of her life. (13) *Infra* 39a. (14) Why in this particular case the woman is regarded as clean. (15) Since in the absence of fear the woman is deemed to be unclean.

also here,[1] since her menstrual blood is suspended she requires no examination.

'A NURSING WOMAN'? A WOMAN BEFORE SHE HAS WEANED etc. Our Rabbis taught: A nursing mother whose child died within twenty-four months[2] is in exactly the same position as all other women[3] and causes retrospective uncleanness for a period of twenty-four hours or from the previous to the last examination. If, therefore,[4] she continued to suck it for four or five years it suffices for her to reckon her period of uncleanness from the time she has observed the flow; so R. Meir. R. Judah, R. Jose and R. Simeon ruled: Only during the twenty-four months[5] does it suffice for women to reckon their uncleanness from the time they have observed a flow.[6] Therefore,[7] even if she suckled it for four or five years she causes uncleanness retrospectively for twenty-four hours or from the previous to the last examination.[8] Now if you will carefully consider [the views just expressed] you will find that[9] according to the view of R. Meir the menstrual blood is decomposed and turns into milk while according to the view of R. Jose, R. Judah and R. Simeon the woman's limbs[10] are disjointed and her natural vigour[11] does not return before the lapse of twenty-four months. Why the necessity for the 'therefore'[12] of R. Meir?[13]—On account of the 'therefore'[14] of R. Jose. But why

(1) The case of the pregnant woman referred to in the old man's enquiry. (2) After birth. This is the normal period a mother is expected to suckle her child. (3) Who are not pregnant or nursing; because the menstrual flow is suspended only on account of its transformation into the mother's milk, but when the child dies and the milk is no longer used the blood changes into its original condition. (4) Since the cleanness of the woman is entirely due to her suckling (cf. prev. n.). (5) Irrespective of whether the child is suckled or not. (6) The suspension of the menstrual blood for twenty-four months being due in their opinion to the physical disturbance caused by the process of child-bearing. (7) Since it is the process of bearing and not the suckling of the child (cf. prev. n.) that causes the suspension of the blood and since that suspension does not continue longer than twenty-four months. (8) Cf. Tosef. Nid. II where, however, 'R. Judah' is omitted. (9) Lit., 'as you will find to say'. (10) When she is in childbirth. (11) Manifested by her menstrual flow. (12) 'If, therefore, she continued etc.' *supra*. (13) *Sc.* since R. Meir ruled that the death of the child causes its mother to resume the status

the necessity for the 'therefore' of R. Jose?[1]—It might have been assumed that R. Jose maintains that[2] there are two [causes];[3] hence we were informed[4] [that he upholds the one cause only].[5] So it was also taught: The menstrual blood[6] is decomposed and turns into milk; so R. Meir. R. Jose stated: Her limbs[7] are disjointed and her natural strength does not return before twenty-four months.[8] R. Elai explained: What is R. Meir's reason?[9] That it is written, *Who can bring a clean thing*[10] *from out of an unclean?*[11] *Is it not the Only One?*[12] And the Rabbis?[13]—R. Joḥanan replied: The reference[14] is to semen which is unclean, while the man who is created from it is clean; and R. Eleazar replied: The reference[14] is to the water of sprinkling[15] in the case of which the man who sprinkles it as well as the man upon whom it is sprinkled is clean while he who touches it is unclean. But is the man who sprinkles it clean? Is it not in fact written, *And he that sprinkleth the water of sprinkling shall wash his clothes?*[16]—What is meant by '*He that sprinkleth*'? He that touches it. But is it not actually written, '*He that sprinkleth*'[16] and also '*He that toucheth*'?[16] Furthermore, is not '*He that sprinkleth*' required to wash his clothes[16] while '*He that toucheth*' is not required to do so?[16]—Rather say: What is meant by '*He that sprinkleth*'? He that carries.[17] Then why was it not written,

of an ordinary non-nursing woman it obviously follows that the main cause of her former exemption from retrospective uncleanness was her suckling of the child, what need then was there to specify an inference (cf. prev. n.) which is all too obvious? (14) 'Therefore, even if she suckled etc.', *supra*.

(1) Cf. prev. n. but one *mut. mut.* (2) For the suspension of the menstrual flow. (3) (*a*) The blood turns into milk and (*b*) the woman's limbs are disjointed On account of (*b*) the woman is exempt from retrospective uncleanness during the twenty-four months following her childbearing, irrespective of whether the child is suckled or not, while on account of (*a*) she should be similarly exempt throughout the time she is suckling the child. (4) By the addition of 'Therefore' (cf. *supra* n. 14). (5) That 'the woman's limbs are disjointed'. (6) Of a nursing woman. (7) Those of a woman in childbirth. (8) Bek. 6*b*. (9) For holding that the menstrual blood turns into milk. (10) Milk. (11) Menstrual blood. (12) Job XIV, 4; E. V. '*not one*'. (13) *Sc.* how do they, who differ from R. Meir, in maintaining that the blood does not turn into milk, explain the text cited? (14) In Job XIV, 4 cited. (15) Cf. Num. XIX, 9. (16) Ibid. 21. (17) The water of sprinkling.

'He that carries'?—We were informed[1] that uncleanness is not contracted unless one carried the minimum quantity prescribed for sprinkling. This is a satisfactory explanation according to him who holds[2] that sprinkling must be performed with a prescribed minimum of the water[3]. What, however, can be said according to him who holds that no prescribed minimum is required?[2]—Even according to him who holds that no prescribed quantity is required the ruling refers only to the quantity applied to the body of the man but as regards that which is in the vessel a prescribed quantity is required; as we have learnt: What must be the quantity of water[3] that it shall suffice for a sprinkling? As much as suffices for both the dipping therein of the tops of the stalks and for the sprinkling.[4] It is, in fact, in view of such laws[5] that Solomon observed, *I said: 'I will get wisdom'; but it was far from me.*[6]

WHO IS REGARDED 'AN OLD WOMAN'? ANY WOMAN OVER WHOM THREE 'ONAHS HAVE PASSED NEAR THE TIME OF HER OLD AGE. What is to be understood by NEAR THE TIME OF HER OLD AGE?—Rab Judah replied: The age when her women friends speak of her as an old woman; and R. Simeon[7] replied: [9b] when people call her mother in her presence[8] and she does not blush. R. Zera and R. Samuel b. Isaac differ:[9] One says, '[When she is called mother] and[10] she does not mind,' and the other says, 'And[10] she does not blush'. What is the practical difference between them?—The practical difference between them is the case of one who blushes but does not mind.

What is the length of an *'onah?*—Resh Laḳish citing R. Judah Nesi'ah[11] replied: A normal *'onah* is thirty days; but Raba, citing R. Ḥisda, replied: Twenty days. In fact, however, there is no difference of opinion between them. One Master[12] reckons both

(1) By the expression, *'He that sprinkleth'* instead of 'he that carries'. (2) Cf. Zeb. 80*a*. (3) The water of sprinkling. (4) Parah XII, 5. (5) Which are apparently paradoxical: The man who sprinkles the water or is sprinkled upon is clean while he who merely touched it is unclean. (6) Eccl. VII, 23. (7) MS.M. adds 'b. Laḳish'. (8) So MS.M. Cur. edd. 'mother, mother'. (9) On what was meant by 'near old age'. (10) Lit., 'all that'. (11) The Prince, Judah II. (12) Resh Laḳish.

the clean and the unclean days[1] while the other Master[2] does not reckon the unclean days.[3]

Our Rabbis taught: If over an old woman have passed three *'onahs*[4] and then she observed a flow, it suffices for her to reckon her period of uncleanness from the time she observed the flow; if another three *'onahs* have passed[4] and then she observed a flow, it again suffices for her to reckon her uncleanness from the time she observed it. If, however, another three *'onahs* have passed[4] and then she observed a flow she is regarded[5] as all other women and causes uncleanness retrospectively for twenty-four hours or from the previous examination to the last examination. This[6] is the case not only[7] where she observed the flow at perfectly regular intervals[8] but even where she observed it at successively decreasing intervals or[9] increasing intervals.[10] [You say,] 'Even[11] where she observed it at successively decreasing intervals'. It thus follows[12] that there is no need to mention that this law[6] applies where she observed the flow at perfectly regular ones. But should not the law be reversed, seeing that where she observes a flow at perfectly regular intervals she thereby establishes for herself a fixed period and it should, therefore, suffice for her to reckon her period of uncleanness from the time she observed the flow? And should

(1) I.e., the interval between one period and another which is thirty days. (2) Raba. (3) Which number ten (seven as menstruant and three as *zabah*) leaving (thirty minus ten are) twenty clean days (Rashi. Cf., however, Tosaf.). (4) Without her observing any flow during all this time. (5) Lit., 'behold she'; since the appearance of the flow for the third time establishes the fact that her menstrual flow had not yet ceased and that only the length of the intervals between its periodic appearances has changed. (6) That after a third appearance the woman's uncleanness begins twenty-four hours retrospectively. (7) Cf. MS.M and marg. n. Cur. edd. 'and it is not necessary (to state)', the word 'necessary' appearing in parenthesis. (8) I.e., if each interval was, for instance, exactly ninety days. (9) Cur. edd. in parenthesis, 'and even'. (10) *Sc.* irrespective of whether (*a*) the first interval extended over ninety-three days, the second over ninety-two and the third only over ninety or (*b*) the first extended over ninety-one days, the second over ninety-two and the third over ninety-three days. (11) Emphasis on this word. (12) Since the expression 'even' is used (cf. prev. n.).

you reply that this[1] represents the view of the Rabbis who differ from R. Dosa in maintaining that even a woman who has a fixed period causes retrospective uncleanness for twenty-four hours,[2] [it could be objected:] Should not the order[3] have been reversed to read as follows: Not only where she observed the flow at successively decreasing intervals or increasing intervals[4] but even where she observed it at perfectly regular ones?[5]—Read: Not only where she observed the flow at successively decreasing intervals or increasing intervals[4] but even where she observed it at perfectly regular ones.[6] And if you prefer I might reply, It is this that was meant: This[7] does not apply where a woman observed the flow at perfectly regular intervals but only where she observed it at successively decreasing or increasing ones. Where, however, she observed it at perfectly regular intervals she thereby establishes for herself a fixed period and it suffices for her to reckon her uncleanness from the time she has observed the flow. And whose view does this represent? That of R. Dosa.[2]

R. ELIEZER RULED: FOR ANY WOMAN OVER WHOM HAVE PASSED etc. It was taught: R. Eliezer said to the Sages, It once happened to a young woman at Haitalu[8] that her menstrual flow was interrupted for three *'onahs*, and when the matter was submitted to the Sages they ruled that it sufficed for her to reckon her uncleanness from the time she observed the flow. They replied: A time of emergency is no proof. What was the emergency?—Some say, It was a time of dearth,[9] while others say, The quantity of foodstuffs the woman had prepared[10] was rather large and the

(1) That the woman is unclean retrospectively even when she has a fixed period. (2) *Supra* 4*b*. (3) Of the Baraitha under discussion. (4) Is her uncleanness retrospective for twenty-four hours. (5) Where it might have been presumed that she has thereby established for herself a fixed period. (6) Cf. prev. n. but one; the ruling representing the view of the Rabbis (*supra* 4*b*). (7) That after a third appearance the woman's uncleanness begins twenty-four hours retrospectively. (8) [Babylonian form for Aitalu, modern Aiterun, N.W. of Kadish. V. S. Klein, *Beiträge*, p. 47.] (9) When a decision to regard all the foodstuffs the woman had touched during the preceding twenty-four hours as unclean would have involved a serious loss and undue hardship. (10) During the preceding twenty-four hours.

Rabbis took into consideration the desirability of avoiding the loss of the levitically clean things.

Our Rabbis taught: It once happened that Rabbi acted in agreement with the ruling of R. Eliezer, and after he reminded himself observed, 'R. Eliezer deserves to be relied upon in an emergency'. What could be the meaning of 'after he reminded himself'? If it be explained: After he reminded himself that the *halachah* was not in agreement with R. Eliezer but in agreement with the Rabbis [the difficulty would arise:] How could he act according to the former's ruling even in an emergency?—The fact is that it was not stated whether the law was in agreement with the one Master or with the other Master. Then what is meant by 'after he reminded himself'?—After he reminded himself that it was not an individual that differed from him but that many differed from him, he observed 'R. Eliezer deserves to be relied upon in an emergency'.

Our Rabbis taught: If a young girl who had not yet attained the age of menstruation[1] observed a discharge, after the first time it suffices for her to reckon her uncleanness from the time she observed it; after the second time also[2] it suffices for her to reckon her uncleanness from the time she observed it, but after the third time[3] she is in the same position as all other women[4] and[5] causes uncleanness retrospectively[6] for twenty-four hours or from her previous examination to her last examination. If subsequently three *'onahs* have passed over her[7] and then she again observed a discharge it suffices for her[8] to reckon her uncleanness from the time she observed it.[9] If another three *'onahs* have passed over her[7]

(1) Lit., 'whose time to see (the menses) has not arrived'. (2) Since presumptive menstruation like any other condition of presumption cannot be established by one occurrence. (3) Since according to Rabbi (with whose view, as shown *infra*, this Baraitha agrees) two occurrences suffice to establish a condition of presumption. (4) Who are in a condition of presumptive menstruation. (5) In accordance with Rabbinic law. (6) As a preventive measure enacted in the case of all such women (cf. prev. n. but one). (7) Without her observing any discharge. (8) Since the complete absence of the flow for three *'onahs* is regarded as the cessation of the flow. (9) In agreement with R. Eliezer (cf. our Mishnah).

and then again she observed a discharge it suffices for her to reckon her uncleanness from the time she observed it. But if another three *'onahs* have passed over her[1] and she again observed a discharge she is in the same position as all other women[2] and causes uncleanness retrospectively for twenty-four hours or from her previous examination to her last one.[3] When, however, a girl had attained the age of menstruation,[4] after the first observation it suffices for her to reckon her uncleanness from the time she observed the discharge, while after the second time she causes uncleanness retrospectively for twenty-four hours or from her previous examination to her last examination.[5] If subsequently three *'onahs* have passed over her[6] and then she again observed a discharge, it suffices for her to reckon her uncleanness from the time she observed it.[7]

The Master said,[8] 'If subsequently three *'onahs* have passed over her and then she again observed a discharge, it suffices for her to reckon her uncleanness from the time she observed it'. [10*a*] What is the ruling where[9] she again observes discharges at the end of subsequent single *'onahs?*[10]—R. Giddal citing Rab replied: After the first time and after the second time it suffices for her to reckon her uncleanness from the time of her observation of the discharge, but after the third time she causes uncleanness retrospectively for twenty-four hours or from her previous examination to her last examination.

(1) Without her observing any discharge. (2) Who are in a condition of presumptive menstruation. (3) Because the appearance of the discharge for the third time proved that her flow had not ceased and that only the intervals between the discharges had been lengthened. (4) This being the case spoken of in our Mishnah: AND OF WHAT DID THEY SPEAK . . . OF A FIRST OBSERVATION. (5) Cf. our Mishnah: BUT AT A SUBSEQUENT OBSERVATION . . . HOURS. (6) Without her observing any discharge. (7) In agreement with R. Eliezer (cf. our Mishnah). (8) *Supra;* in regard to a young girl who had not yet attained the age of menstruation and who observed a discharge at the end of each of three consecutive *'onahs.* (9) After the one discharge at the end of the three *'onahs* respectively. (10) *Sc.* does it suffice for her to reckon her uncleanness from the time she observes the discharge or is her uncleanness to be retrospective? The reasons for and against are discussed in Rashi.

'If another three *'onahs* have passed over her and then again she observed a discharge it suffices for her to reckon her uncleanness from the time she observed it'. What is the ruling where she again observes discharges at the end of single *'onahs?*[1]—R. Kahana citing R. Giddal who had it from Rab replied: After the first time it suffices for her to reckon her uncleanness from the time she observed the discharge but after the second time she causes uncleanness retrospectively for twenty-four hours or from her previous examination to her last examination. Whose view does this[2] represent? That of Rabbi who laid down that if a thing has occurred twice presumption is established.[3] Read then the final clause:[4] 'If subsequently three *'onahs* have passed over her and then she again observed a discharge, it suffices for her to reckon her uncleanness from the time she observed it'. Does not this agree only with the view of R. Eliezer?[5] And should you reply that it in fact represents the view of Rabbi but that in the case of [an interval of three] *'onahs* he holds the same view as R. Eliezer, [it could be retorted]: Does he indeed hold the same view seeing that it was stated, 'After he reminded himself'?[6]—The fact is that it represents the view of R. Eliezer but[7] [in respect of presumption in the case of] menstrual periods he is of the same opinion as Rabbi.[8]

A stain [discovered by one who had not yet reached the age of menstruation] between her first and second [observation of a discharge] is regarded as clean,[9] but as regards one discovered between her second and third observation, Hezekiah ruled: It is unclean, while R. Joḥanan ruled: It is clean. 'Hezekiah ruled: It

(1) V. p. 63, n. 10. (2) The ruling that after the second time she is already in a condition of presumptive menstruation. (3) *Infra* 64a, Keth. 43b, Yeb. 26a. (4) The case of one who 'had attained the age of menstruation'. (5) Who ruled in our Mishnah: FOR ANY WOMAN OVER WHOM HAVE PASSED THREE 'ONAHS IT SUFFICES . . . TO RECKON FROM THE TIME SHE OBSERVED IT. (6) *Supra* 9b q.v., from which it is evident that only after much hesitation and reluctance did he follow R. Eliezer's view. (7) As regards the difficulty of establishing presumption after two occurrences. (8) Who in all cases holds that two occurrences constitute presumption. (9) I.e., it is not deemed to be due to menstrual blood. Cf. *supra* 5a.

is unclean', since, when she observed [a discharge for the third time] she becomes unclean [retrospectively],[1] her stain also[2] causes her to be unclean; 'while R. Johanan ruled: It is clean,' for this reason: Since[3] she was not yet confirmed in the condition of presumptive menstruation[4] she cannot be regarded as unclean on account of her stain. [10b] R. Elai demurred:[5] But what is the difference between this class of woman and a virgin [just married] whose blood is clean?[6]—R. Zera replied: In the case of the latter her secretion[7] is frequent[8] but in that of the former her secretion is not frequent.[9]

'Ulla stated: R. Johanan who had it from R. Simeon b. Jehozadak[10] ruled, 'If a young girl who had not yet attained the age of menstruation observed a discharge, her spittle or her *midras*-uncleanness in the street[11] after a first discharge and after a second discharge is clean,[12] and her stain is also clean'; but I do not know

(1) Which shows that her presumptive menstruation begins after her second discharge. (2) Since it appeared at a period of (cf. prev. n.) presumptive menstruation. (3) At the time the stain was discovered. (4) This condition being established retrospectively only after the appearance of a third discharge. (5) Against Hezekiah. (6) In the case of the latter the blood is assumed to be that of the wound caused by a first intercourse which is exempt from the laws of uncleanness. If on the following day, however, the colour of the discharge changed the woman becomes unclean, but a bloodstain discovered after intercourse (cf. *infra* 60a) is nevertheless clean. Why then should a stain in the former case be unclean on account of the subsequent discharge? (V. Tosaf.). (7) The discharge of the wound (cf. prev. n.). (8) So that there is a double reason why the stain should be regarded as clean. For (*a*) it might be attributed to blood that issued from a foreign body and (*b*) even if it is to be attributed to blood of the woman's own body that blood might have been the secretion of the wound (v. Tosaf.). (9) And if the stain is due to blood that originated from the woman's body it could not be other than menstrual which causes uncleanness. (10) This is not the scholar of the same name mentioned in Sanh. 26a who was spoken of disparagingly in the presence of R. Johanan (R. Tam.). The one here mentioned was a teacher of R. Johanan whose honour the latter would have protected had anything derogatory been said against him in his presence. (11) I.e., if it was discovered in a public place and it is uncertain whether the girl was a menstruant at that time. (12) As presumptive menstruation had not yet been established uncleanness cannot be imposed in a doubtful case (cf. prev. n.).

[whether the last ruling][1] was his own or his Master's.[2] In what practical issue could this matter?—In respect of establishing the ruling[3] to be the view of one authority[3] against two authorities.[4] When Rabin and all the other seafarers came[5] they stated that the ruling was in agreement with the view of R. Simeon b. Jehozadak.

R. Ḥilḳiah b. Ṭobi ruled: In the case of a young girl who had not yet reached the age of menstruation[6] a discharge of menstrual blood, even if it continued[7] throughout all the seven days,[8] is regarded as a single observation.[9] [Since you say,] 'Even[10] if it continued'[7] it follows that there is no necessity to state that the law is so[11] where there was a break.[12] But is not this contrary to reason, seeing that a break would cause the discharge to be like two separate observations?—Rather read: In the case of a young girl who had not yet reached the age of menstruation,[6] a discharge of menstrual blood that[13] continued throughout all the seven days[14] is regarded as a single observation. R. Shimi b. Ḥiyya ruled: Dripping is not like an observation.[15] But does not the woman in fact observe it?[16]—Read: It is not like a continuous discharge but like one broken up.[17] Does this[18] then imply that the con-

(1) Concerning the stain. (2) R. Simeon b. Jehozadak's. (3) Of Hezekiah (*supra* 10*a*). (4) R. Joḥanan and R. Simeon b. Jehozadak; and the law would accordingly be in agreement with the majority. If R. Joḥanan, however, gave the ruling in his own name alone Hezekiah is opposed by one authority only and the law need not necessarily be against him. (5) From Palestine to Babylon. (6) Lit., 'whose time to see (the menses) has not arrived'. (7) Lit., 'she pours'. (8) The normal period of menstruation. (9) *Sc.* until there were two more observations her period of uncleanness does not begin retrospectively but from the time she observes the discharge. (10) Emphasis on this word. (11) That the discharge 'throughout all the seven days is regarded as a single observation'. (12) Though it was followed by a renewal of the discharge. (13) Omitting 'even' (cf. *supra* n. 9) used in the first version *supra*. (14) The normal period of menstruation. (15) Lit., 'one who drips is not like one who sees'. This is now assumed to mean that dripping is not regarded even as a single observation. (16) The dripping. How then can it be maintained that it is not regarded even as one observation (cf. prev. n.)? (17) I.e., like a number of separate observations. By the time the dripping ceases completely the woman is deemed to be in a confirmed condition of presumptive menstruation and any sub-

tinuous discharge[1] was one like[2] a river?[3]—Rather read: It is only like a continuous discharge.[4]

Our Rabbis taught: It is established that the daughters of Israel before reaching the age of puberty are definitely[5] in a condition of presumptive cleanness and the [elder] women need not examine them. When they have reached the age of puberty they are definitely[5] in a condition of presumptive uncleanness and [elder] women must examine them. R. Judah ruled: They must not examine them with their fingers[6] because they might corrupt them,[7] but they dab them with oil within and wipe it off from without and they are thus self examined.[8]

R. JOSE RULED: FOR A WOMAN IN PREGNANCY etc. A Tanna recited in the presence of R. Eleazar, 'R. Jose ruled: As for a woman in pregnancy and a nursing woman over whom three *'onahs* have passed it suffices for her[9] [to reckon her[9] period of uncleanness from] the time of her [observation of the flow]'. 'You', the other remarked, 'began with two[10] and finished with one;[11] do you perchance mean: A pregnant woman who was also[12] a nurse,[13] and this[14] teaches us incidentally the law that [in respect of an interval of three *'onahs*][15] the days of a woman's pregnancy supplement those of her nursing and those of her nursing supple-

sequent discharge causes her uncleanness to be retrospective. (18) The distinction drawn between 'dripping' and a 'continual discharge'.

(1) Since it is regarded as a single observation. (2) Cur. edd. in parenthesis, 'also'. (3) *Sc.* without a stop. But is this likely? No woman surely could survive a discharge of blood that was continuous for seven days. (4) It is regarded as one observation and the girl is not subject to retrospective uncleanness before she has experienced two more menstrual discharges. (5) Lit., 'behold they'. (6) Lit., 'with the hand'. (7) By teaching them unnatural gratification (Jast.). *Aliter:* They might injure them with their nails (Rashi). (8) Since at puberty an application of oil induces the menstrual flow. (9) The use of the sing. for the plural is discussed presently. (10) 'A woman in pregnancy and a nursing woman'. (11) By using the sing. (cf. prev. n. but one). (12) Rendering the *waw* as 'who' instead of 'and'. (13) A woman, for instance, (v. *infra*) who became pregnant while she was still nursing her last-born child. (14) Since the same law applies also to one who is pregnant only. (15) Which exempts a woman from retrospective uncleanness.

ment those of her pregnancy? As it was taught: 'The days of her pregnancy supplement those of her nursing and the days of her nursing supplement those of her pregnancy. In what manner? If there was a break[1] of two *'onahs* during her pregnancy and of one during her nursing, or of two during her nursing and one during her pregnancy, or of one and a half during her pregnancy and one and a half during her nursing, they are all combined into a series of three *'onahs*'.[2] One can well understand the ruling that 'the days of her pregnancy supplement those of her nursing' since this is possible where a woman became pregnant while she was still continuing her nursing. But how is it possible that 'the days of her nursing[3] supplement those of her pregnancy'?[4]—If you wish I might reply: This is possible in the case of a dry birth.[5] And if you prefer I might reply: Menstrual blood is one thing and birth blood is another thing.[6] And if you prefer I might reply: Read the first clause only.[7]

OF WHAT DID THEY SPEAK WHEN THEY LAID DOWN THAT 'IT SUFFICES [FOR THEM TO RECKON] THEIR [PERIOD OF UNCLEANNESS FROM] THE TIME [OF THEIR DISCOVERY OF THE FLOW]'? etc. Rab stated: This[8] refers to all of them,[9] and Samuel stated: This[8] was learnt only in respect of a virgin[10] and an old woman[11] but for pregnant or nursing women[12] it suffices

(1) In the menses. (2) *Infra* 36a. (3) Between which and pregnancy there must be the childbirth and consequent bleeding. (4) Would not the bleeding at childbirth interrupt the bloodless interval of the three *'onahs*? (5) So that there is no bleeding (cf. prev. n. but one) to interrupt the three *'onahs*. (6) I.e., the latter does not in any way interrupt the interval of the former. (7) Lit., 'one', viz., 'the days of her pregnancy supplement those of her nursing', omitting the final clause, 'the days of her nursing . . . pregnancy'. (8) The statement just quoted the conclusion of which is that 'AT A SUBSEQUENT OBSERVATION SHE CONVEYS UNCLEANNESS RETROSPECTIVELY FOR A PERIOD OF TWENTY-FOUR HOURS'. (9) *Sc.* the four classes enumerated earlier in our Mishnah. (10) Who, after two observations, may well be deemed to have reached the age of presumptive menstruation. (11) Who also, since after the interruption she had her menses twice, may be assumed to be reverting to her former status of presumptive menstruation while the interruption might be attributed to a mere delay in the appearance of the discharge. (12) Whose menstrual flow must normally cease and any discharge of blood on whose part, however

for them, throughout all the days of their pregnancy and throughout all the days of their nursing respectively to reckon their uncleanness from the time of their observing a flow. In the same manner R. Simeon b. Laḳish stated: This[1] refers to all of them; while R. Joḥanan stated: This was learnt only in respect of a virgin and an old woman but for pregnant or nursing women it suffices throughout all the days of their pregnancy and throughout all the days of their nursing respectively to reckon their uncleanness from the time of their observing the flow. This dispute[2] is analogous to one between Tannas. [For it was taught]: If pregnant or nursing women were [11*a*] bleeding profusely it suffices for them, throughout all the days of their pregnancy and throughout all the days of their nursing respectively, to reckon their uncleanness from the time of their observing their flow; so R. Meir. R. Jose and R. Judah and R. Simeon, however, ruled: Only after a first observation did [the Sages] rule that it suffices for them[3] to reckon their uncleanness from the time of their observing the flow but after a second observation they cause uncleanness retrospectively for twenty-four hours or from their previous examination to their last examination.

IF, HOWEVER, SHE SUFFERED THE FIRST FLOW etc. R. Huna ruled: If on three occasions she jumped and suffered a flow she[4] has thereby established for herself a fixed period.[5] In what respect?[6] If it be suggested, In respect of certain days,[7] could it not be objected that on any day on which she did not jump she ob-

often that may occur (cf. Tosaf.), can only be regarded as an irregular and passing phase.

(1) For notes on the statements of R. Simeon b. Laḳish and R. Joḥanan cf. those on the statements of Rab and Samuel *supra*. (2) Between the Amoras mentioned regarding a pregnant and a nursing woman. (3) Pregnant and nursing women. (4) Though a flow resulting from a jump is obviously an accident. (5) This is explained presently. (6) Is the period fixed. (7) I.e., if the jump and resulting flow took place, for instance, on three Sundays, every subsequent Sunday is regarded as the fixed day so that even in the absence of a jump, if on examination she discovered a flow, her uncleanness is not retrospective, while if she failed to examine herself she is deemed to be unclean on the presumption that the flow had appeared at the fixed time.

served no flow?[1]—Rather, [the fixation meant is in respect] of jumps.[2] But surely it was taught: 'Any regular discharge established as a result of an accident, even though it had been repeated many times, does not establish a fixed period'. Does not this mean that no fixed period whatsoever[3] is established?—No, it means that no fixed period is established in respect of days alone[4] or jumps alone,[5] but as regards days and jumps jointly[6] a fixed period is well established.[7] But is it not obvious[8] [that no fixed period can be established] in respect of days alone?[9]—R. Ashi replied: [This[10] was necessary in a case] for instance, where the woman jumped on two Sundays and suffered a flow while on a Sabbath[11] she jumped and suffered no flow but on the Sunday following she observed one without jumping. As it might have been presumed that it had now become known retrospectively that[12] it was the day[13] and not the jumping[14] that had caused the flow,[15] we were informed[16] that it was the jump of the previous day[11] that was the cause[17] and that the reason why the woman did not observe it was because the jump was premature.[18]

Another reading:[19] R. Huna ruled: If on three occasions she

(1) Which proves that the day itself is not the fixed period. How then could a Sunday on which she does not jump (cf. prev. n.) be regarded as the fixed period? (2) *Sc.* on any day she jumped she is presumed to be unclean unless on examination she found herself to be clean. (3) Even in respect of jumps. (4) The Sundays, for instance, (cf. *supra*, p. 69, n. 7) on which she did not jump. (5) On any day other than a Sunday. (6) I.e., a Sunday on which she jumped. (7) If she jumped on any Sunday that day is deemed to be her fixed period. (8) Since each discharge was preceded by a jump. (9) The answer being in the affirmative the difficulty arises: What need was there to teach the obvious? (10) The ruling that no fixed period is established in respect of days alone. (11) Saturday. (12) As on the Saturday on which she jumped she suffered no flow while on the Sunday following on which she did not jump she observed one. (13) The Sunday, since it was the third on which she observed a flow. (14) Cf. prev. n. but one. (15) And Sunday might consequently be regarded as her fixed period irrespective of whether she jumped on it or not. (16) By the ruling under discussion (cf. *supra* n. 10). (17) Of the discharge on the Sunday. (18) Lit., 'the time of jumping had not yet arrived'. Her fixed period, therefore, is only a Sunday (not any other day of the week) on which she jumped (and no Sunday on which she did not jump). (19) Cf. nn. on first reading *supra, mut. mut.*

jumped and suffered a flow she has thereby established for herself a fixed period in respect of days but not in respect of jumps. In what circumstances?[1]—R. Ashi replied: If a woman jumped on two Sundays and on each occasion suffered a flow while[2] on one[3] Sunday she suffered one without jumping where it is obvious that it is the day[4] that is the cause.[5]

MISHNAH. ALTHOUGH [THE SAGES] HAVE LAID DOWN THAT [FOR A WOMAN WHO HAS A SETTLED PERIOD] IT SUFFICES TO RECKON HER PERIOD OF UNCLEANNESS FROM THE TIME SHE OBSERVED THE FLOW, SHE MUST NEVERTHELESS EXAMINE HERSELF [REGULARLY],[6] EXCEPT WHERE SHE IS A MENSTRUANT[7] OR[8] IS CONTINUING IN THE BLOOD OF PURIFICATION.[9] SHE[10] MUST ALSO USE TESTING-RAGS WHEN[11] SHE HAS MARITAL INTERCOURSE EXCEPT WHEN SHE CONTINUES IN THE BLOOD OF PURIFICATION[9] OR WHEN SHE IS A VIRGIN[12] WHOSE BLOOD IS CLEAN.[13] AND TWICE [DAILY] MUST SHE[10] EXAMINE HERSELF: IN THE MORNING[14] AND AT THE [EVENING] TWILIGHT,[15] AND ALSO WHEN SHE IS ABOUT[16] TO PERFORM HER MARITAL DUTY.[17] PRIESTLY WOMEN ARE SUBJECT TO AN ADDITIONAL RESTRICTION [IN HAVING TO MAKE EXAMINATION] WHEN THEY ARE ABOUT

(1) Lit., 'how is this to be imagined?' (2) Cur. edd. in parenthesis, 'and on the Sabbath (Saturday) she jumped and did not observe (a flow)'. Cf. Elijah Wilna's glosses. (3) Cur. edd. insert 'another' in parenthesis. (4) In this case the Sunday. (5) Of the discharge. Hence the ruling that a fixed period has been established 'in respect of days'. (6) Morning and evening; in order to make sure that there was no discharge whatsoever. (7) Who, having suffered a flow, is unclean for seven days irrespective of whether she had a flow or not on any of the last six days. (8) After a childbirth. (9) Cf. Lev. XII, 4. The examination would be purposeless since even the appearance of blood would not affect her cleanness. (10) WHO HAS A FIXED PERIOD. (11) Before or after. (12) Newly married. (13) During the first four nights (cf. *supra* n. 9). (14) To make sure that the objects she handled during the previous night are clean. (15) Cf. prev. n. *mut. mut.* (16) Lit., 'passes'. (17) Lit., 'to serve her house'.

TO EAT TERUMAH. R. JUDAH RULED: [THESE MUST EXAMINE THEMSELVES] ALSO AFTER THEY HAVE CONCLUDED A MEAL[1] OF TERUMAH.

GEMARA. EXCEPT WHEN SHE IS A MENSTRUANT, because during the days of her menstruation she needs no examination.[2] This[3] is quite satisfactory according to R. Simeon b. Lakish who ruled, 'A woman may establish for herself a settled period during the days of her *zibah*[4] but not during the days of her menstruation',[5] [since the discarding of an examination would be] well justified.[6] According to R. Johanan, however, who ruled, 'A woman may establish for herself a settled period during the days of her menstruation', why should she not examine herself seeing that it is possible that she had established for herself a settled period?[7]—R. Johanan can answer you: I only spoke of a case where the woman observed the flow issuing[8] from a previously closed source,[9] but I did not speak of one

(1) Lit., 'at the time of their passing away from eating'. (2) Cf. relevant n. on our Mishnah. (3) That no examination is necessary. (4) I.e., during the eleven days between the periods of menstruation. If, for instance, she suffered a menstrual flow on the first day of two consecutive months and also on the fifteenth day (which is one of the eleven days of *zibah*) of the same months, while on the first of the third month she had no menstrual flow and on the fifteenth of that month she again observed a flow she (on account of the three observations on the fifteenth) establishes for herself a settled period on the fifteenth of the subsequent months though the first two observations had taken place during the eleven days of *zibah*. (5) If, for instance, she suffered a flow on the first and on the fifth day of one month and again on the fifth of the two subsequent months no settled period is thereby established for the fifth of the month, because during menstruation, a woman normally bleeds and a recurrent discharge proves no settled habit. (6) Lit., 'beautiful', 'right'. Such an examination could serve no useful purpose whatsoever. It cannot serve the purpose of ascertaining whether she is clean (since she is in any case unclean even in the absence of a discharge) and it cannot serve the purpose of enabling her to establish a settled period (since no settled period can be established during the seven days of menstruation). (7) Cf. prev. n. but one *mut. mut.* (8) On each of the three occasions. (9) If, e.g., the flow made its first appearance (cf. *infra* 39b) on the first day of three consecutive months as well on the twenty-fifth of the second month.

where she observed it issuing[1] from an already open source.[2]

OR IS CONTINUING IN THE BLOOD OF PURIFICATION. It was assumed that the reference is to one who is only desirous of continuing *in the blood of purification*.[3] Now this[4] is quite satisfactory according to Rab who holds that 'it[5] all emanates from the same source which the Torah declared to be unclean [during a certain period][6] and clean [during another period]'[7] [since the discarding of an examination would be] well justified;[8] but according to Levi who holds that 'it[5] emanates from two different sources'[9] why should she not examine herself, seeing that it is possible[10] that the unclean source had not yet ceased to flow?[11]

In this case the first day of each subsequent month is regarded as the settled period, because the first two of the three discharges originated from a closed source (there having been no flow before) while the last (though it appeared after the menstruation had begun on the twenty-fifth of the previous months) is also regarded as originating from a closed source since the discharge on the twenty-fifth which originated from a closed source is deemed to be the commencement of the flow on the first of the following month that followed it.

(1) Even on one of the three occasions. (2) As is the case spoken of in our Mishnah where even the first observation would be made during menstruation where the source is already open. (3) But had not yet commenced then, i.e., a woman after childbirth who concluded the seven unclean days for a male or the fourteen unclean days for a female (cf. Lev. XII, 1, 5). (4) The ruling that no examination is necessary on the seventh or fourteenth day (cf. prev. n.). (5) The blood discharged within forty or eighty days respectively after childbirth (cf. Lev. XII, 1-5). (6) Cf. *supra*, n. 3. (7) The thirty-three days after the seven for a male and the sixty-six days after the fourteen for a female (cf. Lev. XII, 4f). (8) Lit., 'beautiful', 'right'. Such an examination would be purposeless since after the seventh and the fourteenth day respectively the woman would in any case be clean irrespective of whether there was any discharge or not. (9) The unclean source being open during the first seven and fourteen days respectively and after the forty and eighty days respectively when the clean one is closed, while the latter is open during the thirty-three and sixty-six days respectively when the former is closed. (10) Where there was a continuous issue from the unclean period into the clean one (cf. *infra* 35b). (11) Unless there was an examination and it had been ascertained that there was a definite break in the flow at the end of the seven and the fourteen days respectively the woman might still be unclean even though the unclean period prescribed had passed. Why then should no examination be necessary?

—Levi can answer you: This[1] is in agreement with[2] [11b] Beth Shammai who hold that 'it[3] all emanates from the same source'.[4] But would the Tanna teach an anonymous Mishnah[5] in agreement with the view of Beth Shammai?[6]—This is an anonymous ruling that is followed by a divergence of opinion, and wherever an anonymous ruling is followed by a dispute the *halachah* does not agree with the anonymous ruling. And if you prefer I might reply: Was it stated,[7] 'desirous of CONTINUING'?[8] It was only stated, 'CONTINUING'.[9] But if the woman was already 'continuing'[9] what was the purpose of stating the ruling?[10]—It might have been assumed that she should examine herself in case she establishes for herself[11] a settled period, hence we were informed [that no examination is necessary] because no settled period can be established [by the regularity of a discharge from] a clean source for that of an unclean one. This is satisfactory according to Levi who stated that there are two sources,[12] but according to Rab who stated that there was only one source[12] why should she not examine herself seeing that she might have established for herself[11] a settled period?—Even in that case she cannot establish a settled period in the clean days for the unclean ones.

SHE MUST ALSO USE TESTING-RAGS WHEN SHE HAS MARITAL INTERCOURSE etc. We have learnt elsewhere: If a young girl, whose age of menstruation[13] had not yet arrived, married, Beth Shammai ruled: She is allowed[14] four nights,[15] and Beth Hillel

(1) The ruling that the menstruant needs no examination. (2) Lit., 'whose'. (3) The blood discharged within the forty or eighty days respectively after childbirth (cf. Lev. XII, 1-5). (4) *Infra* 35b. (5) Which, as a rule, represents the *halachah*. (6) Whose rulings generally are contrary to the *halachah* which is in agreement with those of Beth Hillel. (7) As has been arbitrarily assumed *supra*. (8) Certainly not. (9) *Sc.* the clean days had already begun. (10) That no examination is necessary. Is it not obvious that an examination in such circumstances could serve no purpose whatsoever? (11) During the period of clean days, by a discharge at regular intervals. (12) *Supra* 11a. (13) Lit., 'her time to see'. (14) After the first intercourse. (15) In which intercourse with her husband is permitted despite the flow of blood, it being assumed that the flow is not due to menstruation (as is the case with one who married after attaining the age of menstruation) but to the wound that had been caused by the first intercourse.

ruled: Until the wound is healed.[1] R. Giddal citing Samuel stated: They[2] learnt this[3] only in the case where bleeding through intercourse had not ceased, though she subsequently observed a discharge that may not have been due to intercourse;[4] but if bleeding through intercourse had ceased[5] and then she observed a discharge[6] she[7] is unclean.[8] If one night has passed without intercourse and then she observed a discharge she is unclean. If the colour of her blood changed[9] she is unclean.

R. Jonah raised an objection:[10] OR WHEN SHE IS A VIRGIN WHOSE BLOOD IS CLEAN [she need not use testing-rags]. But why should she not rather use testing-rags[11] seeing that it is possible that the colour of her blood had changed?—Raba replied, Read the first clause: EXCEPT WHERE SHE IS A MENSTRUANT OR IS CONTINUING IN THE BLOOD OF PURIFICATION, from which it follows that only in those cases no examination is required but that a virgin whose blood is clean does require one.[12] But, then, are not the two rulings[13] mutually contradictory?—The former[14] refers to one who had marital intercourse, where it might well be assumed that the membrum was the cause of the change;[15] while the latter[16] refers to one who had no marital intercourse.[17] So it was also taught: This[18] applies only in the case

(1) Keth. 6a. Cf. prev. two nn. *mut. mut.* (2) Beth Hillel. (3) 'Until the wound is healed'. (4) As intercourse invariably caused the wound to bleed, any discharge of blood before the wound is healed is attributed to the same cause. (5) Even if only on one occasion. (6) Irrespective of whether it occurred during intercourse or at any other time. (7) Since during one intercourse at least there was no bleeding and the wound may consequently be presumed to have been healed. (8) The discharge being attributed to menstruation. (9) From that of the blood at the first intercourse. (10) Against the last ruling, 'If the colour etc.'. (11) Before and after intercourse. (12) As R. Jonah expected. (13) The one referred to by R. Jonah and the inference from the first clause of our Mishnah cited by Raba. (14) Lit., 'here', the ruling referred to by R. Jonah. (15) Lit., 'the attendant (euphemism) disturbed them', so that the test after the intercourse would prove nothing; and since no test is to be made after intercourse none is required before it (v. Rashi). (16) The inference of Raba. (17) And a change of colour would be a clear indication that the wound is healed and the blood is that of menstruation. (18) For notes v. those on R. Giddal's statement *supra*.

where bleeding through intercourse had not ceased, though she subsequently observed a discharge that may not have been due to intercourse, but if bleeding through intercourse had ceased and then she observed a discharge she is unclean. If one night has passed without intercourse and then she observed a discharge she is unclean. If the colour of her blood has changed she is unclean.[1]

TWICE [DAILY] MUST SHE etc. Rab Judah citing Samuel stated: They learnt this[2] only in respect of clean things, but to her husband she is permitted.[3] Is not this[4] obvious, seeing that we learnt, IN THE MORNING?[5]—Rather, if the statement[6] was at all made it was in connection with the final clause: AND[7] ALSO WHEN SHE IS ABOUT TO PERFORM HER MARITAL DUTY; Rab Judah citing Samuel stated, They learnt this only as regards a woman who was handling clean things, who, since it is necessary that she examine herself[8] for the sake of the clean things,[9] must also examine herself[10] for the sake of her husband, but if a woman was not handling clean things she requires no examination. But what new point does he[11] teach us, seeing that we have learnt: All women are in a condition of presumptive cleanness for their husbands?[12]—If the ruling were to be derived from the Mishnah[12] it might have been presumed that the ruling applied only to a woman who had a settled period but that a woman who had no settled period does require examination.[13] But does not our Mishnah[14] deal with one who has a settled period?[15]—Our Mishnah

(1) For notes v. those on R. Giddal's statement *supra*. (2) That there must be an examination (v. our Mishnah). (3) Even without an examination. (4) That the ruling had no reference to the woman's permissibility to her husband. (5) When no marital intercourse is permitted. (6) Of Samuel, 'They learnt this only etc.'. (7) She must examine herself. (8) After intercourse. (9) It being possible that intercourse was the cause of some menstrual discharge. (10) Before intercourse. (11) Samuel, by the statement cited. (12) *Infra* 15a. (13) Hence the necessity for Samuel's ruling that even such a woman requires no examination in respect of her husband. (14) Which begins, ALTHOUGH ... A WOMAN WHO HAS A SETTLED PERIOD and to which Samuel referred. (15) How then could it have been maintained that Samuel applied the law to one who had no settled period?

deals with both one who had a settled period, and one who had no settled period,[1] and it is this that was meant,[2] that although she had a settled period, since she must be examined for the sake of the clean things she handled she must also be examined for the sake of her husband. But did not Samuel state this[3] once, for R. Zera citing R. Abba b. Jeremiah who had it from Samuel stated, 'A woman who had no settled period may not perform marital intercourse before she has examined herself'[4] and it has been explained[4] to refer to one who was engaged in the handling of clean things?[5]—The one statement[6] was inferred from the other.[7] So it was also taught: This[8] applies only to clean things[9] but to her husband she is permitted.[10] This,[11] however, applies only where he left her in a state of presumptive cleanness, but if he left her in one of presumptive uncleanness she remains for ever in her uncleanness until she tells him, 'I am clean'.

[12a] R. Zera enquired of Rab Judah: Should[12] a wife examine herself[13] for her husband?—The other replied: She should not examine herself. But [why should she not] examine herself, seeing that none could be the worse for it?[14]—If [she were to do] so her husband would be uneasy in his mind[15] and he would keep away from her.

R. Abba enquired of R. Huna: Must[16] a woman examine herself immediately [after intercourse] in order to make her husband liable to a sin-offering?[17]—The other replied: Is it at all possible

(1) Since (as has explicitly been stated) the former requires examination it is self-evident that the latter also requires it. (2) By our Mishnah. (3) That even a woman who had no settled period need not be examined as far as her husband is concerned unless she was also in the habit of handling clean things. (4) *Infra* 12b. (5) But not to one who was not so engaged. (6) Cited in the name of Samuel. (7) Samuel himself having made one statement only. (8) That examination is required. (9) *Sc.* to ascertain whether the things the woman has handled are clean. (10) Even without an examination. (11) That to her husband she is permitted even without an examination. (12) Lit., 'what is it (the ruling)'. (13) Before intercourse. (14) Lit., 'and what is there in it'. (15) Lit., 'his heart beats him'. (16) Lit., 'what is it (the ruling)'. (17) Should any trace of blood be found. If any blood is discovered immediately after intercourse the discharge is presumed to have begun before or during intercourse and the man is liable to a sin-offering (cf. *infra* 14a.).

for an examination to take place immediately [after intercourse], seeing that it was taught: 'What is meant by "immediately"? This may be illustrated by the parable of an attendant[1] and the witness[2] who stand at the side of the lintel[3] where the witness enters immediately after the attendant goes out, this being the interval which the Rabbis allowed as regards wiping off[4] but not as regards examination'?[5]—The question rather is whether she must wipe herself.[6] Some there are who say that it was this that he[7] enquired of him:[8] Must a woman examine herself [after intercourse][9] in order to make her husband liable[10] to a suspended guilt-offering?[11]—The other replied: She should not examine herself. But [why should she not] examine herself, seeing that none could be the worse for it?[12]—If [she were to do] so[13] her husband would be uncertain in his mind[14] and he would keep away from her.

AND ALSO WHEN SHE IS ABOUT etc. R. Ammi citing R. Jannai remarked: And this is the test[15] of virtuous women.[16] Said R. Abba b. Memel to R. Ammi: The Tanna learnt MUST,[17] [how then could] you learn 'virtuous women'?[16]—The other replied: Because I maintain that whosoever observes the enactments of the Sages may be described as[18] virtuous.[19] Said Raba: Would then[20] one

(1) Euphemism, 'the membrum'. (2) The testing-rag. The consonants of the Hebrew equivalent may be rendered 'witness' as well as 'testing-rag'. (3) Euphemism. (4) Externally. (5) *Infra* 14b; which requires a longer interval. How then could it happen that an examination should be carried out 'immediately'? (6) Immediately after intercourse, so as to ascertain (cf. *supra* p. 77, n. 17) whether her husband is liable to a sin-offering. (7) R. Abba. (8) R. Huna. (9) After the lapse of the interval defined *supra* as 'immediately'. (10) Should any blood be discovered. (11) Which is incurred in the case of a doubtful transgression. The discovery of blood (cf. prev. n.) is no proof that the discharge began before or during the intercourse as it may have begun after. (12) Lit., 'and what is there in it'. (13) Even if only after intercourse. (14) Lit., 'his heart beats him'. (15) Lit., 'their time' *or* 'testing-rag'. (16) Ordinary women, however, examine themselves only morning and evening (cf. Mishnah *infra* 14a). (17) Implying that every woman is subject to the obligation. (18) Lit., 'is called'. (19) *Sc.* it is the duty of every woman who desires to live in accordance with Rabbinic law to examine herself on each of the occasions specified in our Mishnah. (20) If R. Ammi's submission is correct.

who does not observe the enactments of the Sages merely lose the designation of[1] virtuous man but would not be called wicked? Rather, said Raba, as for virtuous women the testing-rag, with which they have examined themselves before one intercourse, they do not use it before any other intercourse, but those who are not virtuous use it and do not mind.

[Reverting to] the main text,[2] 'R. Zera citing R. Abba b. Jeremiah who had it from Samuel stated: A woman who has no settled period may not perform marital intercourse before she has examined herself'. Said R. Zera to R. Abba b. Jeremiah: Is it[3] only one who has no settled period that must have an examination while a woman who has a settled period requires no examination?[4]—The other replied: A woman who has a settled period must have an examination[5] only when she is awake[6] but not when she is asleep;[7] while a woman who has no settled period must have an examination whether she is awake or asleep. Raba observed: Could he[8] not reply[9] that a woman who had a settled period must be examined[10] in respect of clean things[11] but not in respect of her husband [alone][12] while a woman who had no settled period must have an examination even in respect of her husband [alone]?[13] As, however, he did not give such a reply it may be inferred that Samuel holds the view that in respect of her husband alone[12] a woman[14] needs no examination.[15]

(1) Lit., 'would not be called'. (2) Quoted *supra* 11b *ad fin*. (3) Since Samuel spoke only of a woman 'who has no settled period'. (4) But how could this assumption be upheld in view of our Mishnah which prescribes an examination though it speaks of a woman who had a settled period? (5) Before intercourse is permitted. (6) Because (*a*) as she is then able to handle clean things and would have to be examined for the purpose she must also be examined for the sake of her husband; and (*b*) an examination when one is awake does not involve undue inconvenience. (7) When (*a*) she is unable to handle clean things and (*b*) an examination would mean much inconvenience (cf. prev. n. *mut. mut.*). (8) R. Abba b. Jeremiah. (9) To R. Zera. (10) For the sake of her husband also. (11) *Sc.* if she handled such objects. As she must be examined on account of the latter she must also be examined on account of the former. (12) If she handled no clean things. (13) *Sc.* even if no clean things had been handled by her. (14) Even if she has no settled period. (15) Samuel's statement *supra* that 'a woman . . . may not . . . before she

Our Rabbis taught: The wives of ass-drivers,[1] labourers[2] and people coming from a house of mourning[2] or a house of feasting[3] are in respect of their husbands[4] deemed to be in a state of presumptive cleanness and the latter may, therefore, come and stay with them whether they are asleep or awake. This, however, applies only where the men[5] left the woman in a state of presumptive cleanness but if they left them in a state of presumptive uncleanness each woman is for ever regarded as unclean until she announces to her husband 'I am clean'. But how does Samuel[6] explain this case?[7] If it refers to a woman who has a settled period, does not a difficulty arise from the case where she is awake?[8] And if it refers to one who has no settled period, does not a difficulty arise both from the case where she is awake and from that where she is asleep?[9]—As a matter of fact it refers to one who had a settled period[10] but[11] as the husband had solicited her[12] there can be no more reliable[13] examination than this.[14]

R. Papa asked Raba: May one[15] act in accordance with that

examined herself' refers, therefore, to one who was engaged in the handling of clean things.

(1) *Sc.* people whose occupations take them away from their homes for considerable periods. (2) Cf. prev. n. (3) *Beth ha-mishteh*, usually a wedding feast. (4) When these return home. (5) On departing. (6) Who, according to R. Abba b. Jeremiah, holds that (*a*) one who has a settled period must be examined when awake but not when asleep, while (*b*) one who has no settled period must be examined even when asleep. (7) In the Baraitha just cited. (8) Of course it does. According to this Baraitha no examination is required while according to Samuel (cf. (*a*) note 6) an examination is required. (9) In both cases (even when the woman is awake), no examination is expected, while according to Samuel (cf. (*b*) note 6) an examination must be held even when she is asleep. (10) Hence the ruling that no examination is necessary when she is asleep (cf. note 6). (11) In reply to the objection why no examination is required when she is awake. (12) And she consented. (13) Lit., 'great'. (14) Had she not ascertained beforehand that she was clean she would not have consented. Samuel's ruling, however, which ordains an examination applies only to husbands whose occupations do not take them away from their homes, and not to such (of whom the Baraitha speaks) as returned home after a considerable absence (cf. Tosaf. and Tosaf. Asheri). (15) Lit., 'what is it'.

Baraitha?[1] [12b]—The other replied: Brewer,[2] no; because [otherwise][3] she would become repulsive to him.

R. Kahana stated, 'I asked the women folk of the house of R. Papa and of R. Huna son of R. Joshua, "Do the Rabbis on coming home from the schoolhouse require you to undergo an examination"? And they answered me in the negative'. But why did he[4] not ask[5] the Rabbis themselves?—Because it is possible that they imposed additional restrictions upon themselves.[6]

Our Rabbis taught: A woman who has no settled period is forbidden marital intercourse and is entitled neither to a *kethubah*[7] nor to a usufruct[8] nor to maintenance,[9] nor to her worn-out clothes.[10] Her husband, furthermore, must divorce her and may never marry her again; so R. Meir. R. Ḥanina b. Antigonus ruled: She must use two testing-rags when she has marital intercourse; they render her unfit[11] and they also render her fit.[12] In the name of Abba Ḥanan it was stated: Woe to her husband.[13] 'She is forbidden marital intercourse', because she might[14] cause him moral injury. 'And is entitled neither to a *kethubah*', since she is unfit

(1) Of the ass-drivers etc., i.e., (cf. Tosaf. *contra* Rashi) that no examination is necessary, as far as the husband is concerned, where the woman is half asleep (v. Tosaf. s.v. בין). (2) *Sodani*, reference to R. Papa's occupation. (Cf. B.M. 65*a*). *Aliter:* 'Learned' *or* 'wise man' (v. Rashi). (3) I.e., (cf. Tosaf.) if it had been necessary for the husband to rouse her and to wait until she has collected her thoughts and was in a condition to reply (*contra* Rashi). (4) R. Kahana. (5) What the law was. (6) And this could be ascertained only by enquiring from the women. Had the enquiry been addressed to the Rabbis themselves they might have given the lenient ruling which applied to all, while R. Kahana was anxious to adopt any additional restrictions which the Rabbis may have imposed upon themselves. (7) *Sc.* the fixed amount that is due to her from her husband on divorce or when he dies (v. Glos.). (8) Of the *melog* (v. Glos.) property which she brought to her husband. Her husband is entitled to the usufruct despite the fact that she is deprived of her *kethubah*. (9) *Sc.* if her husband before divorcing her went abroad the court does not authorize her to collect her maintenance expenses from his estate. (10) Though a woman as a rule is entitled to take with her when divorced whatever is left of the clothes she brought to her husband on marriage as *melog* property (cf. Keth. 79*b*). (11) If any blood is observed on them. (12) If they remained clean. (13) This is explained *infra*. (14) Should a discharge occur during intercourse.

for cohabitation she is not entitled to a *kethubah*. 'Nor to usufruct nor to maintenance nor to her worn-out clothes' because the provisions[1] embodied in the agreed terms of a *kethubah* are subject to the same laws as the *kethubah* itself.[2] 'Her husband, furthermore, must divorce her and may never marry her again'. Is not this obvious?[3]—It was necessary in the case where she was subsequently cured.[4] As it might have been presumed that [in such a case] he may remarry her we were informed [that this is forbidden], because it may sometimes happen that having proceeded to marry another man she would be cured and [her first husband] would then say, 'Had I known that to be the case I would not have divorced her even if you had given me a hundred *maneh*', and the *get* would thus be annulled and her children would be bastards.[5]

'In the name of Abba Ḥanan it was stated: Woe to her husband'. Some explain: He said this in opposition to R. Meir,[6] because [Abba Ḥanan maintains that] she must be allowed to collect her *kethubah*. Others there are who explain: He said it in opposition to R. Ḥanina b. Antigonus,[7] because [Abba Ḥanan maintans that intercourse is always forbidden] since thereby she might[8] cause her husband to sin.

Rab Judah citing Samuel stated: The *halachah* is in agreement with R. Ḥanina b. Antigonus. But in what case? If it is one where the woman is engaged in the handling of clean things, has not Samuel [it may be objected] said it once?[9] And if it is one where she was not engaged in the handling of clean things, did he not

(1) Such as are the benefits mentioned. (2) As she cannot claim her *kethubah* she cannot claim these benefits either. (3) Why then should an obvious ruling have to be enunciated? (4) I.e., acquired a settled period. (5) Hence the ruling that he may never again marry her, even if she subsequently acquired a settled period. On the basis of this ruling the husband is duly cautioned when divorce is arranged that his act is definite and final and, consequently, any subsequent plea of his 'Had I known etc.' has no validity whatsoever (cf. Giṭ. 46*a*). (6) Who ruled that she is not entitled to her *kethubah* from her husband. (7) Who holds that if she uses testing-rags she may have intercourse. (8) Were a discharge to occur during intercourse. (9) Cf. *supra* 11*b* *ad fin.* and *infra*.

say [it may again be objected] that as far as her husband is concerned she requires no examination, for did not R. Zera in fact state in the name of R. Abba b. Jeremiah who had it from Samuel, 'A woman who had no settled period may not perform marital intercourse before she examines herself', and it has been explained to refer to one who was engaged in the handling of clean things?[1] — He who taught the one did not teach the other.[2]

(1) *Supra* l.c. (2) It refers indeed to the case where the woman was engaged in handling clean things; but Samuel having given his ruling only once, Rab Judah applied it to the ruling of R. Ḥanina b. Antigonus, while R. Abba quoted it as an independent ruling.

NIDDAH

CHAPTER II

MISHNAH. [13a] EVERY HAND THAT MAKES FREQUENT EXAMINATION IS IN THE CASE OF WOMEN PRAISEWORTHY,[1] BUT IN THE CASE OF MEN IT OUGHT TO BE CUT OFF.[2]

GEMARA. Wherein [in this respect][3] do women differ from men?[4]—Women [in this matter] are not sensitive,[5] hence they are praiseworthy,[1] but in the case of men who are highly sensitive [their hands] ought to be cut off.[2] But, if so,[2] what was the point in saying 'MAKES FREQUENT' [seeing that the same reason[2] applies] also where [the examinations are] infrequent?—When 'MAKES FREQUENT' was mentioned it was intended to refer to women only.[6]

One taught: This[7] applies only to the emission of semen but as regards flux[8] a man also is as praiseworthy as the women;[9] and even in regard to the emission of semen, if he desires to make the examination with a splinter or with a potsherd[10] he may do so. May he not, however, do it with a rag, seeing that it was taught: A man may examine himself with a rag or with any other thing he wishes?—As Abaye stated elsewhere: 'With a thick rag',[10] so also here[11] it may be explained: With a thick rag.[10] And in what

(1) Since both husband and wife are thereby saved either from doubtful uncleanness or from certain transgression. (2) Because of masturbation. (3) FREQUENT EXAMINATION. (4) *Sc.* why is the hand of the former PRAISEWORTHY while that of the latter OUGHT TO BE CUT OFF? (5) I.e., the examination does not unduly excite their passions. (6) Cf. n. 1. (7) The culpability of men who make such examinations. (8) I.e., when a man is suffering from gonorrhoea and is desirous of ascertaining the number of attacks he had (v. next n.). (9) Since it is necessary to ascertain whether the attack occurred only twice or three times. In the former case the man is only unclean while in the latter he must also bring a sacrifice. (10) Avoiding masturbation. (11) In the Baraitha just cited.

connection was Abaye's statement made?—In connection with the following: If a priest, while eating *terumah*, felt a shiver run through his body[1] he takes hold of his membrum[2] and swallows the *terumah*.[3] 'Takes hold'! But has it not been taught: R. Eliezer said, 'Whoever holds his membrum when he makes water is as though he had brought a flood on the world'?[4] To this Abaye replied, 'With a thick rag'.[5] Raba replied: It[6] may even be said to apply to a soft rag for once the semen has been detached the subsequent touch does no longer matter.[7] And Abaye?[8]—He made provision against the possibility of an additional discharge.[9] And Raba?— He does not consider the possibility of any additional discharges. But does he not, seeing that it was taught, 'To what may this[10] be compared? To the putting of a finger upon the eye where, as long as the finger remains on it, the eye continues to tear'?[11] Now Raba?[12]—It is quite uncommon for one to get heated twice in immediate succession.[13]

[Reverting to] the main text: 'R. Eliezer said, Whoever holds his membrum when he makes water is as though he had brought a flood on the world'. But, they said to R. Eliezer, would not the spray bespatter his feet and he would appear to be maimed in his privy parts so that he[14] would be the cause of casting upon his children the reflection of being illegitimate?—It is preferable, he answered them, that a man should be the cause of casting

(1) Lit., 'that his limbs trembled', an indication of the imminent emission of semen. (2) To restrain the emission. Uncleanness does not set in until the semen has actually left the body. (3) *Infra* 40a. (4) Shab. 41a, *infra* 43a. The generation of the flood were guilty of such offences (cf. R.H. 12a). Now how, in view of R. Eliezer's statement, could one be allowed to commit an offence even for the sake of *terumah*? (5) Avoiding masturbation. (6) In the Baraitha just cited. (7) Lit., 'since it was uprooted it was uprooted', no more semen would be emitted despite the heat engendered. (8) Why, in view of Raba's explanation, does he restrict the application to a thick rag only? (9) Of semen. (10) The touching of the membrum after an emission. (11) *Infra* 43a. Lit. 'tears and tears again'. (12) How could he differ from this Baraitha? (13) Lit., 'any being heated and being heated again in its time'. Hence the ruling in the Mishnah *infra* 40a. The Baraitha *infra* 43a, on the other hand, refers to one who practised self-abuse. (14) Being assumed to be incapable of procreation.

upon his children the reflection of being illegitimate than that he should make himself a wicked man, even for a while, before the Omnipresent. Another [Baraitha] taught: R. Eliezer replied to the Sages, It is possible for a man to stand on a raised spot and to make water or to make water in loose earth and thus to avoid making himself wicked, even for a while, before the Omnipresent. Which[1] did he[2] tell them[3] first? If it be suggested that it was the first mentioned statement that he gave them first [is it likely, it may be objected], that after he spoke to them of a prohibition[4] he would merely offer a remedy?[5]—The fact is that it was the last mentioned statement[6] that he gave them first, and when they asked him, 'What is he to do when he can find no raised spot or loose earth', he answered them, 'It is preferable that a man should be the cause of casting upon his children the reflection of being illegitimate than that he should make himself a wicked man, even for a while, before the Omnipresent'.

But why all these precautions?[7]—Because otherwise one might emit semen in vain, and R. Johanan stated: Whosoever emits semen in vain deserves death, for it is said in Scripture, *And the thing which he did*[8] *was evil in the sight of the Lord, and He slew him also.*[9] R. Isaac and R. Ammi said. He[10] is as though he shed blood, for it is said in Scripture, *Ye that inflame yourselves among the terebinths, under every leafy tree, that slay the children in the valleys under the clefts of the rocks;*[11] read not *'that slay'*[12] but 'that press out'.[13] R. Assi said: He[14] is like one who worships idols; for here[11] it is written, *'Under every leafy tree'* and elsewhere[15] it is written, *Upon the high mountains ... and under every leafy tree.*[16]

Rab Judah and Samuel once stood upon the roof of the Synagogue of Shaf-weyathib[17] in Nehardea. Said Rab Judah to Samuel

(1) Of the two statements cited. (2) R. Eliezer. (3) The Sages. (4) Which applies in all cases. (5) Implying that where the remedy is inapplicable the prohibition may be disregarded. (6) Lit., 'that'. (7) Lit., 'and all such, why'. (8) *'He spilled it on the ground'* (Gen. XXXVIII, 9). (9) Gen. XXXVIII, 10. (10) Who emits semen in vain. (11) Isa. LVII, 5. (12) שוחטי. (13) סוחטי interchange of the sibilants *shin* and *sin*. (14) Who emits semen in vain. (15) In reference to idolatry. (16) Deut. XII, 2; an inference by analogy. (17) The name of a man or place, v. Meg. (Sonc. ed.) p. 175, n. 5.

'I must make water'. '*Shinena*',[1] the other replied, 'take hold of your membrum[2] and make the water outside [the roof]'. But how could he[3] do so, seeing that it was taught: R. Eliezer said, Whoever holds his membrum when he makes water is as though he brought a flood on the world?—Abaye replied: He treated this case as that of a reconnoitring troop, concerning which we learnt, 'If a reconnoitring troop has entered a town in time of peace the open wine jars are forbidden[4] and the closed ones are permitted,[5] but in times of war the former as well as the latter are permitted because the troops have no time to offer libations'.[6] Thus it clearly follows that owing to their being in a state of fear they do not think[7] of offering libations, and so also in this case, since he[3] was in a state of fear he would not think of lustful matters. But what fear could there be here?—If you wish I might reply: The fear of the night and of the roof.[8] If you prefer I might reply: The fear of his Master.[9] If you prefer I might say: The fear of the *Shechinah*.[10] If you prefer I might say: The fear of the Lord that was[11] upon him,[12] for Samuel once remarked of him,[3] 'This man is no mortal being'.[13] If you prefer I might say: He was a married man, and concerning such R. Naḥman ruled, 'If a man was married, this is permitted'. If you prefer I might say: It was this that he taught him, viz., that which R. Abba the son of R. Benjamin b. Ḥiyya learnt: But he may support the testicles from below. And if you prefer I might say: It was this that he taught them, viz., that which R. Abbahu stated in the name of R. Joḥanan: It has a limit; from the corona downward [touch]

(1) 'Keen-witted', 'long-toothed' (denoting some facial characteristic) or 'man of iron endurance', cf. B.B. (Sonc. ed.) p. 561, n. 14. (2) To prevent the water from falling on the roof. (3) Rab Judah. (4) Because the troops may have offered them as libation to their idols. (5) It being assumed that the troops who have at their disposal the open jars would not meddle with the closed ones. (6) Keth. 27*a*, A.Z., 70*b*. (7) Lit., 'come'. (8) Standing on its edge in the darkness of the night he is afraid of falling off. (9) Samuel. (10) Which abides in the Synagogue. (11) Always, even when not on a roof or in the darkness of night. (12) So that no impure thoughts would occur to him even at any other time or place. (13) Lit., 'born of woman'.

is permitted [13b] but from the corona upwards[1] it is forbidden.

Rab stated: 'A man who wilfully causes erection should be placed[2] under the ban'. But why did he[3] not say, 'This is forbidden'?—Because the man[4] merely incites his evil inclination against himself.[5] R. Ammi, however, stated: He[4] is called a renegade, because such is the art of the evil inclination: To-day it incites man to do one wrong thing,[6] and to-morrow[7] it incites him to worship idols and he proceeds to worship them.

There are others who read: R. Ammi[8] stated, He who excites himself by lustful thoughts will not be allowed to enter the division of the Holy One, blessed be He. For here it is written, *Was evil in the sight of the Lord,*[9] and elsewhere it is written, *For Thou art not a God that hath pleasure in wickedness; evil shall not sojourn with Thee.*[10]

R.[11] Eleazar stated: Who are referred to[12] in the Scriptural text, *Your hands are full of blood?*[13] Those that commit masturbation with their hands.

It was taught at the school of R. Ishmael, *Thou shalt not commit adultery*[14] implies, Thou shalt not practise masturbation either with hand or with foot.

Our Rabbis taught: 'Proselytes and those that play with children delay the advent of the Messiah'. The statement about proselytes may be understood on the lines of the view of R. Ḥelbo, for R. Ḥelbo said, 'Proselytes are as hard for Israel to endure as a sore',[15] what, however, could be meant by 'those that play with children'?[16] If it be suggested: Those that practise pederasty [it could well be objected]: Are not such people subject to ston-

(1) In the direction of the body. (2) Cf. Tosaf. (3) Rab. (4) Who indulges in the reprehensible practice. (5) The practice, therefore, could only be condemned but not forbidden. (6) Lit., 'tells him: Do so'. (7) Lit., 'and on the morrow'. (8) MS.M., 'Assi'. (9) Gen. XXXVIII, 10. (10) Ps. V, 5, analogy between the two expressions of '*evil*'. Alfasi (Shab. XIV) inserts, 'R. Eleazar said, What is meant by evil shall not sojourn with thee? The evil (minded) man shall not sojourn in Thy dwelling'. (11) So MS.M. and BaḤ. Cur. edd. and Alfasi, 'and R.' (12) Lit., 'what'. (13) Isa. I, 15. (14) Ex. XX, 13. (15) V. Yeb. 47*b*. (16) Who apparently commit no crime at all.

ing?[1] If, however, it be suggested: Those that practise onanism through external contact[2] [it could be objected]: Are not such deserving destruction by flood?[1]—The meaning rather is: Those that marry minors who are not capable of bearing children, for R. Jose[3] stated: The Son of David[4] will not come before all the souls in *Guf*[5] will have been disposed of, since it is said, *For the spirit that enwrappeth itself is from Me, and the souls which I have made.*[6]

BUT IN THE CASE OF MEN IT OUGHT TO BE CUT OFF. The question was raised: Have we here[7] learnt a law or merely an execration? 'Have we here learnt a law' as in the case where R. Huna cut off one's hand;[8] 'or merely an execration'?—Come and hear what was taught: R. Tarfon said, 'If his hand touched the membrum let his hand be cut off upon his belly'. 'But', they said to him,[9] 'would not his belly be split'? 'It is preferable', he replied, 'that his belly shall be split rather than that he should go down into the pit of destruction'.[10] Now if you concede that we have here[11] learnt a law[12] one can well understand why they said, 'Would not his belly be split'; but if you maintain that we have only learnt of an execration,[13] what could be meant by [the question] 'His belly be split'?—What then would you suggest, that we have learnt here a law, would it not suffice, [it may be objected, that the cutting off shall] not be done on his belly?—The fact, however, is that it was this that R. Tarfon meant: Whosoever puts his hand below his belly that hand shall be cut off. They said to R. Tarfon, 'If a thorn stuck in his belly, should he not remove it'? 'No', he replied. 'But [they said] would not his belly be split'?[14] 'It is preferable', he replied, 'that his belly shall be split rather than that he should go down to the pit of destruction'.[10]

(1) They are; while here they are merely described as delaying the advent of the Messiah. (2) Lit., 'by way of limbs'. (3) Var. lec. 'Assi' (Yeb. 62*a*) 'Joseph' (MS.M.). (4) The Messiah. (5) Lit., 'Body', the region inhabited by the souls of the unborn. (6) Isa. LVII, 16. (7) In the expression of 'OUGHT TO BE CUT OFF'. (8) Though the same expression (cf. prev. n.) was used. Sanh. 58*b*. (9) Cur. edd. in parenthesis, 'If a thorn stuck in his belly should he not remove it? He said to them: No'. (10) Gehenna. (11) In the expression of 'OUGHT TO BE CUT OFF'. (12) So that R. Tarfon's statement is to be taken literally. (13) The 'cutting off' being a mere figure of speech. (14) By the thorn.

MISHNAH. IN THE CASE OF A DEAF,[1] AN IMBECILE, A BLIND OR AN INSANE[2] WOMAN, IF OTHER WOMEN OF SOUND SENSES ARE AVAILABLE[3] THEY ATTEND TO HER,[4] AND SHE MAY THEN EAT TERUMAH.

GEMARA. Why should not a DEAF woman make her own examination, seeing that it was taught: Rabbi stated, A deaf woman was living in our neighbourhood and not only[5] did she examine herself but her friends also on observing a discharge would show it to her?[6]—There it was a woman who could speak but not hear while here the reference is to one who can neither speak nor hear; as we have learnt: The deaf person of whom the Sages spoke is always[7] one who can neither hear nor speak.[8]

A BLIND. Why should she not make her own examination and show the testing-rag to her friend?—R. Jose son of R. Ḥanina replied: The 'blind' is no part of the Mishnah.[9]

OR AN INSANE WOMAN. Is not this exactly the same as IMBECILE?[10]—This refers to one whose mind was deranged owing to a disease.

Our Rabbis taught: A priest who is an imbecile may be ritually immersed and then fed with *terumah*[11] in the evening.[12] He must also be watched that he does not fall asleep.[13] If he falls asleep he is deemed unclean[14] and if he does not fall asleep he remains clean. R. Eliezer son of R. Zadok ruled: He should be provided with a leather bag.[15] The Rabbis said to him: 'Would not this cause

(1) I.e., deaf-mute (v. Gemara *infra*). (2) Lit., 'whose mind was deranged'. (3) Lit., 'they have'. (4) Lit., 'they prepare them', i.e., make the necessary examination and supervise the prescribed ritual immersion. (5) Lit., 'it was not enough'. (6) Who was an authority on the subject, in order to obtain her opinion on the colour whether it was that of clean or of unclean blood. (7) Lit., 'in every place'. (8) Ḥag. 2*b*. (9) It is a spurious addition. (10) Apparently it is; why then the repetition? (11) Which is forbidden to an unclean priest. (12) Since after due immersion one attains to cleanness at nightfall. (13) In his sleep under his bedclothes heat might be engendered and this would cause him to emit semen which would render him unclean and, therefore, unfit to eat *terumah*. (14) Cf. prev. n. (15) Which can be examined for traces of semen before any *terumah* is given to him.

heat all the more'? 'According to your view', he replied, 'should an imbecile have no remedy'? 'According to our view', they retorted, 'only if he falls asleep[1] is he deemed unclean but if he does not fall asleep he remains clean, while according to your view there is the possibility that he might discharge a drop of blood of the size of a mustard seed and this would be absorbed in the bag'.[2]

A Tanna taught: It was stated in the name of R. Eleazar, The imbecile is to be provided with a metal bag. Abaye explained: It must be one of copper, as we have learnt:[3] R. Judah ruled, Those buds of hyssop[4] are regarded[5] as if they had been made of copper.[6]

R. Papa remarked: From this[7] it may be inferred that breeches[8] are forbidden. But is it not written in Scripture, *And thou shalt make them linen breeches to cover the flesh of their nakedness?*[9]—That may be explained as it was taught: To what were the breeches of the priests like? They were like the knee breeches of horsemen, reaching upwards to the loins and downwards to the thighs. They also had laces but had no padding either back or front.[10]

Abaye stated: [14a] Camel riders[11] are forbidden to eat *terumah*.[12] So it was also taught: All camel-drivers are wicked,[13] all sailors are righteous,[14] but among the ass-drivers some are wicked and

(1) After immersion and after nightfall. (2) Tosef. Nid. II. As it would thus be lost to sight the priest would be regarded as clean and *terumah* would, as a result, be eaten by one who is in fact unclean; and consequently an offence that is punishable by death (at the hand of God) would unconsciously be committed. (3) MS.M. and marg. n. Cur. edd., 'as it was taught'. (4) Used in connection with the water of purification. (5) When the water is measured to ascertain whether it contained sufficient for a sprinkling (cf. *supra* 9a). (6) Parah XII, 5. *Sc.* as if they did not absorb any water at all; from which it follows, in support of Abaye's explanation, that copper is a non-absorbent. (7) The prohibition of a bag *supra* on account of the heat it engenders. (8) Such as engender heat, v. *infra*. (9) Ex. XXVIII, 42. (10) Hanging loosely round the organ the breeches could engender no heat. (11) Though priests. (12) The friction is apt to engender heat resulting in an emission of semen which renders them unclean and therefore unfit to eat *terumah*. (13) Cf. prev. n. (14) Because, though most of their life is spent on the perilous seas, they nevertheless remain constant in their ancestral faith.

others righteous. Some say: The latter are those who use a saddle[1] and the former are those who use no saddle;[2] while others say: The former are those who ride astraddle[3] and the latter are those who do not ride astraddle.[4]

R. Joshua b. Levi cursed the man who sleeps on his back.[5] But this, surely, is not correct,[6] for did not R. Joseph rule that one lying on his back should not read the *shema'*,[7] from which it follows, does it not, that it is only the *shema'* that he must not read but that he may well sleep in this manner?—As regards sleeping on one's back this is quite proper if one slightly inclines sideways, but as regards the reading of the *shema'* even if one inclines sideways this is forbidden.[8] But did not R. Joḥanan turn slightly on his side and read the *shema'*?—R. Joḥanan was different [from other people] because he was corpulent.[9]

MISHNAH. IT IS THE CUSTOM OF THE DAUGHTERS OF ISRAEL WHEN HAVING MARITAL INTERCOURSE TO USE TWO TESTING-RAGS, ONE FOR THE MAN AND THE OTHER FOR HERSELF,[10] AND VIRTUOUS WOMEN PREPARE ALSO A THIRD RAG WHEREBY TO MAKE THEMSELVES FIT FOR MARITAL DUTY.[11] IF A VESTIGE OF BLOOD IS FOUND ON HIS RAG[12] THEY ARE BOTH UNCLEAN[13] AND ARE ALSO UNDER THE OBLIGATION OF BRINGING A SACRIFICE.[14] IF ANY BLOOD IS FOUND ON HER

(1) When riding. Hence no heat is engendered (v. foll. n.). (2) Cf. prev. n. Contact with the animal's bare back engenders heat, as in the case of the camel-riders who never use a saddle. (3) Which is a cause of friction. (4) Holding both legs on one side. (5) Since this causes erection. (6) Lit., 'I am not'. (7) Cf. *P.B.*, p. 40ff. (8) One must either sit or lie fully on his side. (9) It would have been too great a strain for him to lie on his side. (10) *Supra* 5a q.v. notes. (11) By examining themselves before intercourse. On the difference between the practice of the virtuous and that of the ordinary women cf. *supra* 12a. (12) Even though he made use of it some considerable time after intercourse. (13) Since it is obvious that the blood was due to a menstrual discharge during intercourse. As the woman is unclean the man also is unclean (cf. Lev. XV, 24). (14) For the sin of intercourse during uncleanness.

RAG IMMEDIATELY AFTER THEIR INTERCOURSE THEY ARE BOTH UNCLEAN AND ARE ALSO UNDER THE OBLIGATION OF BRINGING A SACRIFICE. IF, HOWEVER, ANY BLOOD IS FOUND ON HER RAG AFTER A TIME THEY ARE UNCLEAN[1] BY REASON OF DOUBT[2] BUT EXEMPT FROM THE SACRIFICE. WHAT IS MEANT BY 'AFTER A TIME'? WITHIN AN INTERVAL IN WHICH SHE CAN DESCEND FROM THE BED AND WASH HER FACE.[3] BUT [IF BLOOD WAS FOUND SOME TIME] AFTER SUCH AN INTERVAL SHE CAUSES UNCLEANNESS RETROSPECTIVELY[4] FOR A PERIOD OF TWENTY-FOUR HOURS[5] BUT SHE DOES NOT CAUSE THE MAN WHO HAD INTERCOURSE WITH HER TO BE UNCLEAN.[6] R. AKIBA RULED: SHE[7] ALSO CAUSES THE MAN WHO HAD INTERCOURSE WITH HER TO BE UNCLEAN.[8] THE SAGES, HOWEVER, AGREE WITH R. AKIBA THAT ONE WHO OBSERVED A BLOODSTAIN CONVEYS UNCLEANNESS TO THE MAN WHO HAD INTERCOURSE WITH HER.

GEMARA. But[9] why should not the possibility be considered that the blood might be that of a louse?[10]—R. Zera replied that place is presumed to be tested as far as a louse is concerned. There are others, however, who reply: It is too narrow for a louse. What is the practical difference between them?[11]—The practical difference between them is the case where a crushed louse was found.[12]

(1) For seven days. (2) Anything they touched is, therefore, in a suspended state of uncleanness. (3) Euphemism. (4) According to Rabbinic, but not Pentateuchal law. (5) Both to objects and human beings, their uncleanness lasting until the evening. (6) For seven days. He is unclean, however, on the same day until evening in accordance with Rabbinic law (cf. prev. two nn.). (7) On account of the doubt. (8) For seven days (cf. *supra* 6*a*). (9) With reference to the ruling that IF A VESTIGE OF BLOOD IS FOUND ... THEY ARE BOTH UNCLEAN ... AND ARE ALSO UNDER THE OBLIGATION OF BRINGING A SACRIFICE. (10) As this is not impossible the uncleanness should only be one of a doubtful nature, so that if any *terumah* is involved it should not be burned but only kept in suspense, and the sacrifice also should be one for doubtful (*asham talui*) and not one for certain trespass (*asham waddai*). (11) The two replies. (12) On the testing-rag at some distance from the blood mark.

According to the reply[1] that the place is presumed to be tested, this must have come from somewhere else,[2] but according to the reply[1] that the place is too narrow it might be presumed that the attendant[3] has crushed it.[4]

It was stated: If a woman examined herself with a rag that she had previously examined,[5] and then she pressed it against her thigh on which she found blood on the following day, Rab ruled: She[6] is subject to the uncleanness of a menstruant.[7] Said R. Shimi b. Ḥiyya to him: But, surely, you told us, 'She has only to take the possibility[8] into consideration'. It was also stated: Samuel ruled: She is subject to the uncleannes of a menstruant.[7] And so they also ruled at the schoolhouse: She is subject to the uncleanness of a menstruant.

It was stated: If a woman examined herself with a rag which she had not previously examined and having put it into a box she found upon it, on the following day, some blood,[9] R. Joseph stated: Throughout all his lifetime R. Ḥiyya regarded [her] as unclean but in his old age he ruled that [she] was clean. The question was raised: What[10] does he[11] mean: That throughout all his[12] lifetime he regarded [her] as menstrually unclean[13] and in his old age he ruled that [she] was clean as far as menstruation is concerned but unclean on account of the bloodstain,[14] or it is possible that throughout his lifetime he regarded [her] as unclean on account of the stain[14] and in his old age he ruled that [she] was absolutely[15]

(1) Lit., 'that expression which says'. (2) The blood must, therefore, be assumed to be that of menstruation. (3) Euphemism. (4) During intercourse, and the blood may consequently be attributed to it. (5) And ascertained that it was clean. (6) Since the rag was examined by her before use and found to be clean, and the blood that was transferred from it to her thigh must consequently be that of menstruation. (7) *Sc.* her uncleanness is definitely established. It is not regarded as one of a doubtful nature despite the possibility that the blood on her thigh may have come from some object other than the rag. (8) That the blood was that of menstruation. (9) And it is uncertain whether the blood was that of menstruation or of some other source with which the rag may have come in contact before the woman had used it. (10) Lit., 'how'. (11) R. Joseph. (12) R. Ḥiyya's. (13) I.e., certain uncleanness. (14) I.e., uncleanness of a doubtful nature. (15) Lit., 'from nothing'.

clean?—Come and hear what was taught: If a woman examined herself with a rag which she had not previously examined and having put it into a box she found upon it, on the following day, some blood, Rabbi ruled: She is regarded as menstrually unclean,[1] and R. Ḥiyya ruled: She is regarded as unclean on account of the bloodstain.[2] [14b] Said R. Ḥiyya to him: 'Do you not agree that it[3] must be slightly bigger than the size of a bean?'[4] 'Indeed', the other replied. 'If so',[5] the first retorted, 'you also regard it as a stain'.[6] Rabbi, however, holds the opinion that it is necessary for the stain to be slightly bigger than the size of a bean in order to exclude the possibility of its being the blood of a louse, but as soon as this possibility is ruled out the blood must undoubtedly have come from her body. Now did not this occur[7] when he was in his old age but when he was young he regarded it[8] as menstrually unclean?[9] This is conclusive.

Rabbi was commending R. Ḥama b. Bisa to R. Ishmael son of R. Jose as a great man, when the latter said to him, 'If you come across him[10] bring him to me'. When he[11] came he[12] said to him, 'Ask me something'. 'What is the ruling', the other asked, 'if a woman examined herself with a rag which she had not previously examined and having put it into a box she found some blood upon it on the following day?' 'Shall I give you,' the first answered, 'the ruling according to the views of my father[13] or shall I rather give it to you according to the views of Rabbi?'[14] 'Tell me,' the other said, 'the ruling according to Rabbi'. 'Is this the person', R. Ishmael

(1) I.e., certain uncleanness. (2) I.e., uncleanness of a doubtful nature. (3) The bloodmark on the rag. (4) Lit., 'like a bean and more'. If it is smaller it may be presumed to be that of a louse (cf. *infra* 58b). (5) That the stain must be no less than a certain minimum. (6) Cf. *supra* n. 2. Had it been regarded as menstrual blood the smallest speck of it would have sufficed to cause certain uncleanness (cf. *infra* 40a) (7) Lit., 'he stood'. (8) In agreement with Rabbi. (9) Obviously he did, since in his youth he would not have ventured to differ from Rabbi who was his master (Rashi). *Aliter:* In his youth he would not have addressed Rabbi in the second person (cf. B.B. 158b) but as 'the Master' (Tosaf.). (10) Lit., 'when he comes to your hand'. (11) R. Ḥama. (12) R. Ishmael. (13) R. Jose. (14) These views are stated *infra*.

exclaimed, 'of whom it is said that he is a great man! How could one ignore[1] the views of the Master[2] and listen to those of the disciple?[3] R. Ḥama b. Bisa, however, was of the opinion that since Rabbi was the head of the college and the Rabbis were frequently in his company his traditions were more reliable.[4] What is the view of Rabbi [that has just been referred to] and what is that of R. Jose?—R. Adda b. Mattena replied:—

A Tanna taught, Rabbi declares her[5] unclean and R. Jose declares her clean. In connection with this R. Zera stated: When Rabbi declared her unclean he did so in agreement with the ruling of R. Meir, but when R. Jose declared her clean he did so in accordance with his own view. For we learnt:[6] If a woman when attending to her needs[7] observed a discharge of blood, R. Meir ruled: If she was standing at the time she is unclean but if she was sitting she is clean. R. Jose ruled: In either case she is regarded as clean.[8] Said R. Aḥa son of Raba to R. Ashi: But did not R. Jose the son of R. Ḥanina state that when R. Meir ruled that the woman was unclean he did so only on account of the bloodstain,[9] whereas Rabbi regarded her as unclean by reason of menstruation?[10]—The other replied, What we maintain is this: When that ruling[11] was stated it was that the uncleanness was due to menstruation.[12]

IF ANY BLOOD IS FOUND ON HER RAG IMMEDIATELY AFTER HER INTERCOURSE THEY ARE BOTH UNCLEAN etc. Our Rabbis taught:[13] What is meant by 'immediately'? This may be illustrated by the parable of the attendant and the witness who stood at the side of the lintel where the witness enters immediately after the attendant goes out, this being the interval which the Rabbis allowed as regards wiping off,[14] but not as regards an examination.[15]

(1) Lit., 'put down'. (2) R. Jose. (3) Rabbi. (4) Lit., 'sharpened'. (5) The woman referred to in R. Bisa's question. (6) So MS.M. and marg. gl. Cur. edd., 'it was taught'. (7) Making water. (8) Mishnah *infra* 59*b* q.v. notes. (9) I.e., doubtful uncleanness. (10) Certain uncleanness. How then could R. Zera maintain that Rabbi followed the view of R. Meir? (11) Of R. Jose b. Ḥanina. (12) Cf. prev. n. but one *mut. mut.* (13) *Supra* 12*a*, q.v. notes. (14) Externally, which takes place instantly after intercourse. (15) Internally, which must inevitably take place after a longer interval than the one allowed had elapsed. In the former case the uncleanness is certain

IF, HOWEVER, ANY BLOOD IS FOUND ON HER RAG AFTER A TIME etc. A Tanna taught: They[1] do incur the obligation of bringing a suspensive guilt-offering. But what is the reason of our Tanna?[2]—It is essential[3] [that the doubt shall be of the same nature as in the case of the consumption of] one piece of two pieces.[4]

WHAT IS MEANT BY 'AFTER A TIME'? etc. Is not, however, this[5] incongruous with the following: What is meant by 'after a time'? R. Eleazar[6] son of R. Zadok explained: Within an interval in which[7] she can stretch out her hand, put it under the cushion or bolster, take out a testing-rag and make examination with it?[8]—R. Ḥisda replied: By AFTER is meant the interval following this interval.[9] But was it not stated in connection with this,[10] IF, HOWEVER, ANY BLOOD IS FOUND ON HER RAG AFTER A TIME THEY ARE UNCLEAN, BY REASON OF THE DOUBT BUT EXEMPT FROM THE SACRIFICE. WHAT IS MEANT BY 'AFTER A TIME'?

and the sacrifice incurred is a sin-offering, while in the latter case the uncleanness is of a doubtful nature and the sacrifice incurred is a suspensive guilt-offering.

(1) Husband and wife, contrary to the ruling of the Tanna of our Mishnah that they are EXEMPT FROM THE SACRIFICE. (2) Cf. prev. n. (3) If a suspensive guilt-offering is to be incurred. (4) One of which was e.g., permitted fat and the the other was forbidden fat, and it is not known which of the two pieces the person in question had consumed. Only in such a case of doubt is a suspensive guilt-offering incurred (cf. Ker. 17*b*). Where, however, the doubt involves only one object or person (as is the case under discussion where only one woman is concerned) no suspensive guilt-offering can be incurred. (5) The definition of 'AFTER A TIME' (6) So BaḤ. Cur. edd. 'Eliezer'. (7) While still in bed. (8) This interval (cf. prev. n.) being shorter than the one IN WHICH SHE CAN DESCEND FROM THE BED etc., it follows that, according to this Baraitha, during the longer interval the woman does not convey uncleanness to her husband and is only subject to the lesser restrictions of the twenty-four hours' period of retrospective uncleanness. How then are the two rulings to be reconciled? (9) Defined in our Baraitha. Lit., 'after the after'. During the interval as defined in the Baraitha both husband and wife are subject to doubtful uncleanness but after that interval, and during the one defined in our Mishnah, the woman, according to the Rabbis, as stated in the next clause of the Mishnah, does not convey any uncleanness to her husband. (10) The interval defined in our Mishnah.

WITHIN AN INTERVAL IN WHICH SHE CAN DESCEND FROM THE BED AND WASH HER FACE?[1]—It is this that was implied:[2] WHAT IS MEANT BY 'AFTER A TIME'? Within an interval in which she can stretch out her hand, put it under the cushion or bolster, take out a testing-rag and make examination with it; and WITHIN AN INTERVAL IN WHICH SHE CAN DESCEND FROM THE BED AND WASH HER FACE [the question of uncleanness is subject to] a divergence of view between R. Akiba and the Sages. But was it not stated,[3] AFTER SUCH AN INTERVAL?[4]—It is this that was meant: And this is the interval concerning which R. Akiba and the Sages are at variance.

R. Ashi replied: The former and the latter[5] represent the same length of time; when she has the testing-rag in her hand the time is WITHIN AN INTERVAL IN WHICH SHE CAN DESCEND FROM THE BED AND WASH HER FACE, but if she has not the rag in her hand the time is limited to 'within an interval in which she can stretch out her hand, put it under the cushion or bolster, take out a testing-rag and make examination with it'.

An objection was raised: What is meant by 'after a time'? This question was submitted by R. Eleazar son of R. Zadok to the Sages at Usha when he asked them, [15a] 'Are you perchance of the same opinion as R. Akiba that the woman[6] carries uncleanness to the man who had intercourse with her?'[7] 'We', they answered him, 'have not heard his ruling'.[8] 'Thus', he said to them, 'did the Sages at Jamnia enunciate the ruling: If the woman did not delay more than the time in which she can descend from the

(1) Which clearly shows, does it not, that during the interval spoken of in our Mishnah the woman does carry uncleanness to her husband? (2) *Sc.* some words are missing from our Mishnah and are to be regarded as inserted. (3) In connection with the dispute between R. Akiba and the Sages. (4) *Sc.* after the one defined in our Mishnah; from which it follows that during this interval both agree that the woman does carry uncleanness to her husband. (5) The interval defined in our Mishnah and the one defined in the Baraitha. (6) For a period of twenty-four hours retrospectively. (7) This (cf. prev. n.) being the only time limit recognized. (8) *Sc.* his time limit. Consequently they could not possibly have adopted it.

bed and wash her face,[1] this[2] is regarded as 'within the time limit' and both are unclean on account of the doubt,[3] and exempt from bringing a sacrifice but they are subject to the obligation of a suspensive guilt-offering. If she delayed for such a time during which she could descend from the bed and wash her face,[4] this[5] is regarded as being 'after the time'.[6] Similarly if she delayed[7] for twenty-four hours[8] or for a period between her previous and her present examination,[9] the man who had intercourse with her is unclean on account of his contact,[10] but not on account of his intercourse.[11] R. Akiba ruled: He also contracts uncleanness on the ground of his intercourse.[12] R. Judah son of R. Johanan b. Zakkai ruled: Her husband may enter the Temple and burn incense.[13] Now according to R. Ḥisda[14] one can well see why the Rabbis declare the man clean, but according to R. Ashi[15] why do the Rabbis declare him clean? And should you reply that this is a case where she did not have the rag in her hand[16] [it could be retorted:] Should not then[17] a distinction have been made explicitly between the case where the woman had a rag in her hand

(1) *Sc.* the time elapsed was no longer than that during which she can examine herself while still in bed. (2) The discovery of a discharge within that space of time (cf. prev. n.). (3) In agreement with R. Ḥisda *supra.* (4) A period of time which is longer than the former (cf. *supra* n. 1). (5) The discharge discovered after the period mentioned (cf. prev. n.). (6) I.e., 'the interval following this interval' as R. Ḥisda explained (*supra* 14*b*). (7) Longer than the periods mentioned. (8) After intercourse. (9) When the discharge was discovered. (10) With the woman. Such a contact with a menstruant within the twenty-four hours' period only subjects him to one day's uncleanness until nightfall and the uncleanness is only Rabbinical and of an uncertain character. (11) With a menstruant; *sc.* the uncleanness, even in its uncertain character, does not extend over seven days as would have been the case with one who had intercourse with a confirmed menstruant. (12) Cf. prev. n. *mut. mut.* (13) This is explained *infra.* (14) Who explained *supra* that the interval within which SHE CAN DESCEND FROM THE BED is regarded as the 'interval after this interval'. (15) Who maintained *supra* that 'the former and the latter represent the same length of time'. (16) So that after she descended from the bed she spent some more time in taking up the rag. (17) In order to avoid the possible mistake that even within the shorter interval, when the woman had the rag in her hand, the Rabbis hold the man to be clean.

and where she had no rag in her hand?[1]—This is a difficulty.

'R. Judah son of R. Joḥanan b. Zakkai ruled: Her husband may enter the Temple and burn incense'. But why should not a prohibition be imposed[2] on the ground that the man came in contact with a menstruant during the twenty-four hours of her retrospective uncleanness?—He[3] holds the same view as Shammai who ruled: For all women it suffices to reckon their period of uncleanness from the time of their discovering the flow.[4] But should not a prohibition be imposed[2] on the ground that the man has experienced an emission of semen?—This is a case where his intercourse was not consummated.[5]

THE SAGES, HOWEVER, AGREE WITH R. AKIBA THAT ONE WHO OBSERVED A BLOODSTAIN. Rab explained: [She conveys UNCLEANNESS] retrospectively and the ruling is that of R. Meir.[6] Samuel, however, explained: [She conveys UNCLEANNESS] from now[7] onwards and the ruling is that of the Rabbis. 'From now onwards'! Would not this[8] be obvious?—It might have been presumed that, since retrospective uncleanness for a period of twenty-four hours is only a Rabbinical measure and the uncleanness of bloodstains at all times[9] is also only a Rabbinical measure, as during the twenty-four hours' period a woman does not convey uncleanness to the man who had intercourse with her so also in the case of a stain[9] does she not convey uncleanness to the man who had intercourse with her, hence we were informed [that she does convey uncleanness to the man]. Might it not, however, be suggested that the law is so indeed?[10]—[No, since] in the former case there

(1) Of course it should. Since no such distinction, however, is made it is obvious, is it not, that the Rabbis hold the man to be clean even if the discharge was discovered after the interval in which the woman can descend from the bed with the rag in her hand? (2) Lit., 'and let (the prohibition) be inferred'. (3) R. Judah. (4) *Supra* 2*a*. (5) R. Akiba, however, maintains that the first stage of intercourse with a menstruant is regarded as its consummation, and consequently uncleanness is conveyed even in such a case (Rashi). (6) Who in regard to bloodstains adopts (*supra* 5*a* and *infra* 52*b*) the more restrictive view. (7) The time of the discovery of the stain. (8) That the Rabbis agree she conveys uncleanness after the discovery of a stain (cf. prev. n.). (9) Even after discovery. (10) That she does not convey

is no slaughtered ox in your presence[1] but here there is a slaughtered ox in your presence.[2] Resh Lakish also explained in the same way[3] [that uncleanness is conveyed] retrospectively and that the ruling is that of R. Meir. R. Johanan explained: [The uncleanness is conveyed] from now onwards and the ruling is that of the Rabbis.

MISHNAH. ALL WOMEN ARE IN THE CONDITION OF PRESUMPTIVE CLEANNESS FOR THEIR HUSBANDS.[4] FOR THOSE WHO RETURN FROM A JOURNEY THEIR WIVES ARE IN THE CONDITION OF PRESUMPTIVE CLEANNESS.

GEMARA. What need was there[5] to state,[6] THOSE THAT RETURN FROM A JOURNEY?—It might have been presumed that this[7] applies only to a husband who was in the town, since in such a case the woman thinks of her duties[8] and duly examines herself, but not to a husband who was not in town since the question of [marital] duty does not occur to her, hence we were informed [that the law applies to the latter case also]. Resh Lakish in the name of R. Judah Nesi'ah[9] observed: But this[10] applies only where the husband came and found her within her usually clean period.[11] R. Huna observed: This[12] was learnt only of a

uncleanness to the one who had intercourse with her after the discovery of a bloodstain just as she does not render him unclean retrospectively during the twenty-four hours prior to her having observed a discharge.

(1) Metaphor. Within the twenty-four hours prior to her having observed a discharge. (2) *Sc.* the bloodstain had actually been discovered. (3) As Rab *supra.* (4) In respect of intercourse; *sc.* no examination is required for the purpose. It is necessary only for determining the condition of any clean objects the woman may have handled. (5) Lit., 'wherefore to me'. (6) After the ruling in the first clause which applies to all husbands. (7) The ruling in the first clause. (8) Lit., 'she throws upon herself'. (9) The Prince, R. Judah II. (10) The ruling in the final clause. (11) I.e., within thirty days after her last observation of a discharge. After the thirty days, since most women have monthly periods, intercourse must be preceded by an examination. (12) That 'within her usually clean period' no examination is required.

woman who had no settled period, but if she had a settled period intercourse with her is forbidden.[1] Topsy turvy![2] Does not, on the contrary, the reverse stand to reason, since in the case of a woman who has no settled period it might well be assumed that she experienced a discharge, but where she has a settled period [she should be presumed to be clean] since her period was fixed? —Rather, if the statement was at all made it was made in the following terms: R. Huna said, This[3] was learnt only in the case of a woman the time of whose settled period had not arrived[4] but if that time had arrived[4] she is forbidden,[1] for he[5] is of the opinion that [the laws of] settled periods[6] are Pentateuchal. Rabbah b. Bar Ḥana said: Even if the time of her settled period has arrived she is also permitted,[7] for he is of the opinion that [the laws relating to] settled period are only Rabbinical.[8] R. Ashi reported thus: R. Huna said, [15b] This[9] was learnt only of a woman who had no settled period that was determinable by days alone but one that was determinable by both days and leaps, so that since the period depends on some specific act it might well be presumed, that she did not leap and that, therefore, did not observe any discharge. Where, however, she has a settled period that was determinable by the days alone, she must have no intercourse, for he is of the opinion that the restrictions relating to settled periods are Pentateuchal. Rabbah b. Bar Ḥana ruled: Even if she has a settled period that was determined by the days alone, she is permitted intercourse, for he holds the opinion

(1) Unless there was previous examination. (2) Lit., 'towards where' or 'towards the tail' (cf. B.B. (Sonc. ed.) p. 435, n. 17). (3) That 'within her usually clean period' no examination is required. (4) During the husband's absence from town. (5) R. Huna. (6) *Sc.* that when the date of a settled period arrives the woman is presumed to be in a state of doubtful uncleanness. (7) No previous examination being required. (8) *Sc.* the Rabbis required a woman to examine herself when the date of her settled period arrives in order to ascertain whether there was a discharge or not. If, however, her husband was out of town and on his return it was unknown to him whether she did or did not examine herself she is not to be regarded as being in a condition of doubtful uncleanness. (9) That the woman is presumed to be clean even if the date of her settled period had already arrived.

that [the restrictions relating to] settled periods are only Rabbinical.

R. Samuel citing R Johanan ruled: If a woman has a settled period, her husband[1] may[2] calculate the days of that period and[3] come in unto her.[4] Said R. Samuel b. Yeba to R. Abba: Did R. Johanan refer also to a young wife who[5] is too shy to perform immersion?—The other replied: Did then R. Johanan speak of one who had actually[6] observed a discharge? It may [in fact be held] that R. Johanan spoke[7] only of a case where it is doubtful whether or not the woman did observe a discharge and where, [so that] even if some reason could be found for assuming that she did observe one, it may also be assumed that she had since performed immersions,[8] but in a case where it is certain that she had observed a discharge, who could say that she had since performed immersion? And, seeing that it is a question of a doubt[9] being opposed by a certainty[10] [she must be deemed unclean] since a doubt cannot take one out of a certainty. But does it not? Was it not in fact taught: If a *haber*[11] died and left a store-room full of fruits, even if they were only then due to be tithed,[12] they are presumed to have been properly prepared.[13] Now here it is a case of certain *tebel*[14] and there is only the doubt as to whether or not it was tithed, and the doubt nevertheless sets aside the certainty?—No, there it is a case of a certainty against a certainty,

(1) Having been out of town for seven days after that period. (2) On returning home during the days in which she had the opportunity of performing immersion and attain cleanness. (3) Without asking her whether she had made use of her opportunity (cf. prev. n.). (4) On the assumption that she had duly performed immersion and is now clean. (5) Unless urged by her husband. (6) Lit., 'certainly'. (7) That the woman need not be asked. (8) And since R. Johanan's ruling is based on the existence of these doubts there can be no distinction between a younger and an older woman. (9) As to whether there was immersion in consequence of which she would be clean. (10) Of a discharge which renders her unclean. (11) V. Glos. (12) Lit., 'sons of their day'. (13) A.Z. 41b; i.e., that the priestly and levitical dues have been duly set aside for them. (14) V. Glos. Since the fruit had reached a stage when it was liable to the dues (cf. prev. n.).

in agreement with a statement of R. Ḥanina of Ḥozae,[1] for R. Ḥanina of Ḥozae said: It is presumed with a *ḥaber* that he does not allow anything to pass out of his control unless it has been duly prepared. And if you prefer I might say: It is a case of doubt against doubt, since [the man might have acted] in accordance with a suggestion of R. Oshaia, for R. Oshaia said: A man[2] may resort to a device with his produce and store it[3] together with its chaff[4] so that[5] his cattle may eat of it[6] and it is exempt from the tithe.[7]

But does not a doubt set aside a certainty? Surely it has been taught: It once happened that the handmaid of a certain tax-collector in Rimmon[8] threw the body of a premature child into a pit, and a priest[9] came and gazed into it to ascertain whether it was male or female,[10] and when the matter came before the Sages[11] they pronounced him clean because weasels and martens are commonly found there.[12] Now here, surely, it is a certainty that the woman had thrown a premature child into the pit and

(1) A district on the eastern side of the Tigris. (2) Desirous of avoiding tithes. (3) Lit., 'and brings it in'. (4) Only corn that had been winnowed before it was brought into the store-room within the house is liable to tithe. (5) Since it was brought in unwinnowed (cf. prev. n.). (6) Even after its subsequent winnowing. A human being, though permitted to eat it in accordance with Pentateuchal law, may not do so in accordance with a Rabbinic measure. (7) Even Rabbinically. Now since it is possible that the produce was taken to the store-room in accordance with R. Oshaia's suggestion (a case of doubtful *ṭebel*) and it is also possible that it had been duly tithed, we have here a case of doubt against doubt. As a *ḥaber* is presumed not to allow anything to pass out of his hand unless it had been duly prepared the Rabbis in this case waived aside their restriction and allowed a human being also to eat of the produce. (8) A town near Jerusalem. (9) Who was ignorant of the laws of uncleanness (cf. Rashi's fourth interpretation and Tosaf.) and unaware that by bending over the pit just above the embryo he would contract uncleanness. (10) The period of a woman's uncleanness after childbirth is twice as long in the case of the latter as in that of the former (cf. Lev. XII, 2ff). (11) To decide whether the priest contracted uncleanness by bending over the pit and thus 'overshadowing' the dead body. (12) In pits. Tosef. Oh. XVI. These creatures might be presumed to have devoured or dragged away the body so that there was no 'overshadowing' on the part of the priest.

a doubt whether they had dragged it away or not, and yet does not the doubt set aside the certainty?—Do not read, 'Threw the body of a premature child into a pit' but [16*a*] 'a kind of premature child'.[1] But was it not stated, 'To ascertain whether it was male or female'?[2]—It is this that was meant: And a priest came and gazed into it to ascertain whether she had aborted an inflated object or a premature child and, if some ground could be found for assuming that she aborted a premature child, to ascertain whether it was male or female. And if you prefer I might reply: Since weasels and martens are commonly found there they had certainly dragged it away.[3]

An enquiry was addressed to[4] R. Naḥman: [Is the examination at] regular menstrual periods Pentateuchal[5] or only Rabbinical?[6]—The latter replied: Since our colleague Huna citing Rab ruled, If a woman who has a settled period did not make an examination when that period arrived but later on[7] observed a discharge, she must take into consideration the possibility [of a discharge] on the date of the settled period,[8] and also the possibility of [twenty-four hours retrospective uncleanness] on account of her observation.[9] Thus[10] it clearly follows that [the examination at] regular menstrual

(1) *Sc.* it was not certain whether it was a child at all. Hence it is here also a case of doubt against doubt. (2) Implying that it was definitely a child and that the only doubt was as to its sex. (3) Hence it is a case of a certainty against a certainty. (4) Var. lec., 'Raba enquired of' (MS.M. and Asheri). (5) So that if a woman failed to make the examination at the proper time she is deemed to be unclean (on the ground that the discharge had appeared at its usual time) even though she observed no blood when she examined herself some time later (since it might have dropped on the ground and been lost). (6) Hence if she failed to make the examination at the proper time she is regarded as clean. (7) *Sc.* at the first examination after the settled period. (8) If it was due prior to the period of twenty-four hours immediately preceding the observation. Her uncleanness in such a case extends backward to the time of the settled period. (9) If less than twenty-four hours intervened between the time of the settled period and the observation. (10) Since the possibility of a discharge at the time of the settled period is taken into consideration presumably even where no subsequent discharge had been observed. It is now assumed that 'discharge' was mentioned only on account of the second clause, 'the possibility . . . on account of her observation'.

periods is Pentateuchal. There are others who say that he[1] replied thus: The reason then[2] is that she had 'observed a discharge,'[3] but if she had not observed one the possibility[4] need not be taken into consideration. Thus[5] it follows clearly that [the examination at] regular menstrual periods is only Rabbinical.

It was stated: If a woman had a settled period, and when the time of that period arrived she did not make the examination and later she did make one, Rab ruled: If on examination she found that she was unclean she is unclean but if she found that she was clean she remains clean. Samuel, however, ruled, Even if on examination she found herself clean she is deemed unclean, since the guest[6] comes at the usual time. Must it be assumed that they[7] differ on [the question of the necessity for an examination at] regular menstrual periods, one Master[8] holding that it is Pentateuchal[9] and the other Master[10] maintaining that it is only Rabbinical?[11] — R. Zera replied: Both[7] may agree that[12] [the examination at] regular menstrual periods is Pentateuchal, but[13] one ruling[14] refers to a woman who examined herself within the period of the duration of her menstruation[15] while the other[16] refers to a woman who did not examine herself within the period of the duration of her menstruation.[17] R. Naḥman b. Isaac maintained: They[7] differ on the

(1) R. Naḥman. (2) Why 'she must take into consideration ... the date of the settled period'. (3) It being assumed that as she discovered a discharge on examination she might also have discovered one if she had made an examination at the time of her settled period. (4) Cf. prev. n. but one. (5) Since in the absence of an examination she is regarded as clean. (6) Euphemism, *sc.* the regular menstrual discharge. (7) Rab and Samuel. (8) Samuel. (9) Hence the woman's uncleanness in the absence of one. (10) Rab. (11) Cf. prev. n. but one *mut. mut.* But how could this be reconciled with the first version of R. Naḥman *supra* according to which Rab is of the opinion that the examination is Pentateuchal? (12) Lit., 'that all the world'. (13) As to the difficulty raised (v. *supra* n. 11). (14) The last cited. (15) As she nevertheless discovered no discharge, it may safely be assumed that there was none even earlier when the regular menstruation period had begun. (16) The first version of R. Naḥman. (17) But did so later on. As it is quite likely that earlier, during the period of menstruation, there was a discharge, the woman must well be deemed unclean. An old ed. inserts here: 'And there are others who say that one Master spoke of one

very question of [the necessity for an examination at] the regular menstrual periods, one Master[1] holding that it is Pentateuchal[2] while the other Master[3] maintains that it is only Rabbinical.

R. Shesheth observed: [The discussion here] is analogous to that of the following Tannas: [For it was taught:] R. Eliezer[4] ruled, She[5] is to be regarded as menstrually unclean,[6] while R. Joshua[7] ruled: Let her be examined.[8] And these Tannas[9] differ on the same principle as the following Tannas. For it was taught: R. Meir ruled, She[10] is to be regarded as menstrually unclean,[11] while the Sages[7] ruled, Let her be examined.[8] Abaye observed, We also learnt to the same effect. For we learnt: R. Meir ruled, If a woman was in a hiding place[12] when the time of her regular period arrived and she did not examine herself, she is nevertheless clean, because fear suspends the menstrual flow.[13] The reason then[14] is that there was fear, but if there had been no fear she would have been deemed unclean. Thus it clearly follows [that the necessity for an examination at] regular periods is Pentateuchal. May it be assumed that the following Tannas also differ on the same principle? For it was taught: If a woman observed some blood [that might be] due to a wound,[15] even if this occurred during her usual period of menstruation, she is deemed to be clean;[16] so R. Simeon b. Gamaliel.

particular case and the other spoke of another particular case and there is in fact no difference of opinion between them' (v. Maharsha and marginal gloss).

(1) Samuel. (2) Hence the woman's uncleanness in the absence of one. (3) Rab. (4) Maintaining that the examination is Pentateuchal. (5) A woman who failed to make the examination at the time of her regular period. (6) From the time her regular period was due to commence. (7) Holding that the examination is only Rabbinical. (8) Even though her period of menstruation had passed. If on examination she finds herself to be clean she is regarded as clean (despite the possibility of an earlier discharge) and if she finds herself unclean, the uncleanness is retrospective from the time her settled period was due. (9) R. Eliezer and R. Joshua. (10) A woman who failed to make the examination at the time of her regular period. (11) From the time her regular period was due to commence. (12) Sheltering from robbers or raiders. (13) *Infra 39a.* (14) Why she is regarded as clean. (15) In her womb. (16) The blood being attributed to the wound.

Rabbi ruled: If she has a regular period[1] she[2] must take her period into consideration.[3] Now do they not differ on this principle, one Master[4] holding that [the examinations at] the regular periods are Pentateuchal, while the other Master[5] holds that they are only Rabbinical?—Rabina replied: No; both may agree that [the examinations at] the regular periods are only Rabbinical, but it is on the question whether the interior of the uterus is unclean[6] that they differ. R. Simeon b. Gamaliel holds that the woman is clean[7] but the blood[8] is unclean because it comes through the uterus,[9] and Rabbi[10] in effect said to him: If[11] you take into consideration the possibility of her usual menstral flow, the woman also should be unclean,[12] and if[13] you do not take into consideration the possibility of her usual menstrual flow, [the blood also should be clean since] the interior of the uterus[14] is clean.

MISHNAH. BETH SHAMMAI RULED: A WOMAN NEEDS TWO[15] TESTING-RAGS FOR EVERY INTERCOURSE,[16] OR SHE MUST PERFORM IT IN THE LIGHT OF A LAMP.[17] BETH HILLEL RULED: TWO TESTING-RAGS[18] SUFFICE HER FOR THE WHOLE NIGHT.[19]

(1) If she has no regular period Rabbi, for the reason given in prev. n., agrees with R. Simeon b. Gamaliel. (2) If the blood was observed on the day the period was due to commence. (3) *Sc.* she is regarded as unclean, since it is possible that some particle of menstrual blood was mixed up with that of the wound. (4) Rabbi. (5) R. Simeon b. Gamaliel. (6) Lit. 'as to the source, the place thereof is unclean'. And, therefore, capable of imparting uncleanness to any clean blood that passes through it. (7) *Sc.* she is not subject to the major uncleanness of menstruation which extends over seven days. (8) Though coming from a wound. (9) Where it contracts an uncleanness (a 'father of uncleanness') which causes it to impart a one day's uncleanness to a human being, so that any object touched by the woman on that day becomes unclean. (10) Relaxing the law. (11) By regarding the blood as unclean. (12) For seven days, as any other menstruant. (13) Since you exempt the woman from menstrual uncleanness. (14) Lit., 'the source of its place'. (15) Previously unused. (16) One is used before, and the other after and both are preserved until the morning when they are to be examined in daylight. (17) So that the testing-rag may be immediately examined. (18) One of which is used prior to the first intercourse and the other after the last. (19) This being

GEMARA. [16b] Our Rabbis taught: Although [the Sages] have said, 'He who has intercourse in the light of a lamp is contemptible',[1] Beth Shammai ruled: A woman needs two[2] testing-rags for every intercourse[3] or she must perform it in the light of a lamp, but Beth Hillel ruled: Two testing-rags suffice for her for the whole night.

It was taught: Beth Shammai said to Beth Hillel, 'According to your view[4] is there no need to provide against the possibility that she might emit[5] a drop of blood of the size of a mustard seed in the course of the first act and this would be covered up with semen during the second act?'[6] 'But', replied Beth Hillel, 'even according to your view[7] is there no need to provide against the possibility that the spittle,[8] while still in the mouth,[9] was crushed out of existence?'[10] '[We maintain our view',] the former retorted, 'because what is crushed once is not the same as that which is crushed twice'.

It was taught: R. Joshua stated, 'I approve[5] of the view of Beth Shammai'.[7] 'Master', said his disciples to him, 'what an extension [of the restrictions] you have imposed upon us!' 'It is a good thing', he replied, 'that I should impose extensive restrictions upon you in this world in order that your days may be prolonged in the world to come'.

R. Zera remarked: From the words of all these authorities[11] we may infer[12] that a conscientious man should not indulge in intercourse twice in succession.[13] Raba said: One may indulge in

sufficient to determine whether she is menstrually unclean and whether she is to convey uncleanness to any clean object she may have handled. (So Rashi; cf., however, Tosaf. and Tosaf. Asheri for a different interpretation.)

(1) The reason is given *infra*. (2) Previously unused. (3) V. *supra* p. 108, n. 16. (4) That there is no need for a testing-rag after every act. (5) Lit., 'see'. (6) So that the test after that act would not reveal it. (7) That testing-rags must be used after each act. (8) *Sc.* a drop of blood. (9) Euphemism; the uterus; i.e., during the first intercourse. (10) So that the test after that act would not reveal it. (11) Lit., 'all of them', even Beth Hillel who requires only one test after the last act. (12) Since intercourse is presumed to be the possible cause of a discharge. (13) If there was no examination after the first act.

intercourse twice in succession, for that ruling[1] was taught only in respect of clean objects.[2] So it was also taught: This[3] applies only to clean objects[2] but to her husband she is permitted.[4] This,[5] however, applies only where he had left her in a state of presumptive cleanness, but if he left her in a state of presumptive uncleanness she is presumed to be in that state for ever until she tells him, 'I am clean'.

R. Abba citing R. Ḥiyya b. Ashi who had it from Rab ruled: If a woman[6] examined herself with a testing-rag which was subsequently lost she is forbidden intercourse until she had re-examined herself. R. Ela demurred: If it had not been lost[7] would she not[8] have been allowed intercourse even though she is unaware [whether there was or there was not a discharge], why then should she not now also[9] be allowed intercourse?—Raba replied: In the former case her proof is in existence,[10] but in the latter case[9] her proof is not in existence.[11]

R. Joḥanan stated: It is forbidden to perform one's marital duty in the day-time.[12] What is the Scriptural proof? That it is said, *Let the day perish wherein I was born, and the night wherein it*

(1) That each or, at least, the last intercourse must be followed by an examination. (2) *Sc.* to make sure that the woman did not convey to them uncleanness when handling them. As regards intercourse, however, when a woman is in a presumptive state of cleanness no examination is necessary. (3) That each or, at least, the last intercourse must be followed by an examination. (4) Even in the absence of an examination. (5) That as regards her husband no examination is required. (6) At night, before intercourse. (7) Lit., 'it is'. (8) Since the examination of the rags, according to Beth Hillel, is never to take place before the following morning and, even according to Beth Shammai, no lamp is required at night and the examination is equally postponed until the morning whenever two rags are used for each act. (9) Where the rag is lost. (10) And it may well be examined in the morning to ascertain, regarding clean objects the woman had handled, whether she is clean or unclean. As regards intercourse too, should it be found that her uncleanness began prior to the act, she could bring a sin-offering. (11) Were intercourse to be allowed in such a case there would be no possible means of ascertaining the condition of the woman any more than if there had been no examination at all. Hence Rab's prohibition. (12) Cur. edd. insert in parenthesis, 'said R. Hamnuna'. MS.M. reads for 'Hamnuna' 'Huna'.

was said: 'A man-child is brought forth'.[1] The night is thus set aside[2] for conception but the day is not set aside for conception. Resh Laḳish stated: [The proof is] from here: *But he that despiseth His ways*[3] *shall die.*[4] As to Resh Laḳish, how does he expound R. Joḥanan's text?[1]—He requires it for the same exposition as that made by R. Ḥanina b. Papa. For R. Ḥanina b. Papa made the following exposition: The name of the angel who is in charge of conception is *'Night'*, and he takes up a drop and places it in the presence of the Holy One, blessed be He, saying, 'Sovereign of the universe, What shall be the fate of this drop? Shall it produce a strong man or a weak man, a wise man or a fool, a rich man or a poor man?' Whereas 'wicked man' or 'righteous one' he does not mention, in agreement with the view of R. Ḥanina. For R. Ḥanina stated: Everything is in the hands of heaven except the fear of God, as it is said, *And now, Israel, what doth the Lord thy God require of thee, but to fear* etc.[5] And R. Joḥanan?[6]—If that were the only meaning,[7] Scripture should have written,[8] *'A man-child is brought forth'*[9] why then was it stated, *'was brought forth a man-child'?*[10] To indicate that the night[11] is set aside for conception[11] but the day is not set aside for conception. As to R. Joḥanan how does he expound the text of Resh Laḳish?[4]—He requires it for [an application to the same types] as those described in the Book of Ben Sira:[12] 'There are three [types] that I hate, yea, four that I do not love: A Scholar[13] who frequents wine-shops[14] [or, as others say, a scholar that is a gossip],[15] a person who sets up a college in the high parts of a town,[16] one who holds the membrum when making water and one who enters his friend's

(1) Job III, 3. (2) Lit., 'given'. (3) *Sc.* has intercourse at an improper time. (4) Prov. XIX, 16. (5) Deut. X, 12. (6) Since Job III, 3 is required for the exposition of R. Ḥanina, whence does he derive his rulings? (7) Lit., 'if so'. (8) As E.V. in fact renders the Heb. (9) *Sc.* the word *gaber* (male-child) should have preceded *horah* (brought forth). (10) *Horah* (cf. prev. n.) preceding *gaber* and thus standing close to the word 'night'. (11) Cf. prev. n. (12) Cf. Ecclesiasticus XXI, 23. (13) Lit., 'chief'. (14) Lit., 'a house of drinkings'. (15) Cur. edd. in parenthesis insert 'and others say, an excitable scholar'. (16) A manifestation of arrogance.

house suddenly'.[1] R. Joḥanan observed:[2] Even his own house.

R. Simeon b. Yoḥai observed: There are four [types][3] which the Holy One, blessed be He, hates, and as for me, I do not love them: The man who enters his house suddenly and much more so [if he so enters] his friend's house, the man who holds the membrum when he makes water, [17a] the man who when naked makes water in front of his bed, and the man who has intercourse in the presence of any living creature. 'Even', said Rab Judah to Samuel, 'in the presence of mice?' '*Shinena*',[4] the other replied, 'no; but [the reference is to] a house like that of So and so where they have intercourse in the presence of their men-servants and maid-servants.[5] But what was the exposition they made?—*Abide ye here with*[6] *the ass,*[7] implies: People[5] that are like an ass. Rabbah son of R. Huna used to chase away the wasps from his curtained bed.[8] Abaye drove away the flies.[9] Rabba[10] chased away the mosquitoes.[9]

R. Simeon b. Yoḥai stated, There are five things which [cause the man] who does them to forfeit his life and his blood is upon his own head: Eating[11] peeled garlic, a peeled onion or a peeled egg, or drinking diluted liquids that[12] were kept over night; spending a night in a graveyard; removing one's nails and throwing them away in a public thoroughfare; and blood-letting followed immediately by intercourse.

'Eating peeled garlic etc.' Even though they are deposited in a basket and tied up and sealed, an evil spirit rests upon them. This, however, has been said only where their roots or peel did not remain[13] with them, but if their roots or peel remained with them there can be no objection.[14]

(1) It was to types like these that Prov. XIX, 16 alluded. (2) Not only 'his friend's house'. (3) Lit., 'things'. (4) Cf. n. *supra* 13a. (5) Who were heathens. (6) The Heb. equivalent may be read both *'im* (with) and *'am* (a people). (7) Gen. XXII, 5. (8) So Aruch. V. Tosaf. *contra* Rashi. (9) So that no living creature should be near. (10) Var. lec. 'R. Papa' (MS.M and *'En Jacob*). (11) Lit., 'he who eats'. (12) The adjectival clause qualifies all the foodstuffs mentioned. (13) Lit., 'he did not leave'. (14) Lit., 'we have nothing against it'.

'And drinking diluted liquids that were kept over night'. Rab Judah citing Samuel explained: This applies only where they were kept over night in a metal vessel. R. Papa stated: Vessels made of alum crystals are the same in this respect as vessels made of metal. So also said R. Joḥanan: This applies only where they were kept in a metal vessel; and vessels made of alum crystals are the same in this respect as vessels made of metal.

'Spending a night in a graveyard', in order that a spirit of uncleanness may rest upon him.[1] [This should not be done] since in consequence he might sometimes be exposed to danger.

'Removing one's nails and throwing them away in a public thoroughfare'. [This is dangerous] because a pregnant woman passing over them would miscarry. This, however, has been said only of a case where one removes them with a pair of scissors. Furthermore, this has been said only of a case where one removes the nails of both hands and feet. Furthermore, this has been said only in the case where one did not cut anything immediately after cutting them but if something was cut immediately after they were cut there can be no danger.[2] This, however, is not [to be relied upon]. One should be on his guard in all the cases mentioned.[3]

Our Rabbis taught: Three things have been said about the disposal of nails: He who burns them is a pious man, he who buries them is a righteous man, and he who throws them away is a wicked man.[4]

'And blood-letting followed immediately by intercourse'. [This should be avoided] because a Master said: If a man has intercourse immediately after being bled, he will have feeble[5] children; and if intercourse took place after both husband and wife have been bled, they will have children afflicted with *ra'athan*.[6] Rab[7] stated: This has been said only in the case where nothing was

(1) 'To enable him to foretell the future', cf. Sanh. (Sonc. ed.) p. 446. (2) Lit., 'we have nothing against it'. (3) Lit., 'we fear for all the thing'. (4) V. M.Ḳ. 18*a*. (5) Or 'nervous'. (6) *Ra'athan* is one of the skin diseases causing extreme debility and nervous trembling. Cf. Keth. (Sonc. ed.) p. 486f. (7) The parallel passage in Keth. 77*b* has 'R. Papa'.

tasted after the bleeding but if something was tasted after it there can be no harm.[1]

R. Ḥisda ruled: A man is forbidden to perform his marital duty in the day-time, for it is said, *But thou shalt love thy neighbour as thyself*.[2] But what is the proof?—Abaye replied: He might observe something repulsive in her and she would thereby become loathsome to him.

R. Huna said, Israel are holy and do not perform their marital duties in the day-time. Raba said, But in[3] a dark house this is permitted; and a scholar[4] may darken a room with his cloak and perform his marital duty. [But] we have learnt, OR SHE MUST PERFORM IT IN THE LIGHT OF A LAMP?—Read: SHE MUST examine IT IN THE LIGHT OF A LAMP.

Come and hear: Although [the Sages] have said, He who has intercourse in the light of a lamp is loathsome [etc.]?[5]—Read: He who examines his bed[6] in the light of a lamp is loathsome.[7]

Come and hear: And the people of the house of Monobaz[8] did three things, and on account of these they were honourably mentioned: They performed their marital duties in the day-time, they examined their beds with cotton,[9] and they observed the rules of uncleanness and cleanness in the case of snow. At all events, was it not here stated, 'They performed their marital duties in the day-time'?—Read: They examined their beds in the day-time. This may also be supported by logical argument. For if one were to imagine [that the reading is] 'performed their marital duties', would they have been 'honourably mentioned'?—Yes, indeed;[10] because owing to the prevalence[11] of sleep[12] she is likely to become repulsive to him.

(1) Lit., 'we have nothing against it'. (2) Lev. XIX, 18. (3) Lit., 'and if there was'. (4) Who may be relied upon properly to darken the place. (5) V. *supra* 16*b*. Emphasis on the last word, implying that there is no actual prohibition. (6) Euphemism. (7) Since no proper examination can be made in its dim light. (8) King of Adiabene, whose family embraced Judaism. (9) Or 'clean and soft wool', on which the smallest particle of blood could be detected. Lit., 'wool of Parhaba' (probably a geographical name), v. Jast. (10) Lit., 'thus also'. (11) In the night-time. (12) Which numbs the passions.

'They examined their beds with cotton.' This provides support for a ruling of Samuel. For Samuel ruled: The bed[1] may be examined only with cotton tufts or with clean and soft wool. Rab observed: This explains what they said in Palestine[2] on Sabbath eves,[3] when I was there, 'Who requires cotton tufts for his bread',[1] and I did not understand at the time what they meant.

Raba stated: Old flax garments are admirably suited for examination purposes. But can this be correct,[4] seeing that the school of Manasseh taught: The bed[1] may not be examined either with a red rag or with a black one or with flax,[5] but only with cotton tufts or with clean and soft wool?[6]—This is no difficulty, since the latter refers to flax while the former refers to garments of flax. And if you prefer I might reply: Both refer to garments of flax but the latter deals with new ones while the former deals with old ones.[7]

'They observed the rules of uncleanness and cleanness in the case of snow.' We learnt elsewhere: Snow is neither a food nor a drink. Though one intended to use it as food it is not subject to the laws of the uncleanness of foodstuffs,[8] [but if one intended to use it] as a drink it is subject to the laws of the uncleanness of drinks. If a part of it contracted uncleanness all of it does not become unclean,[9] but if a part of it became clean[10] all of it becomes clean. Now is not this self contradictory? You first said, 'If a part of it contracted uncleanness all of it does not become unclean', and then you said, 'If a part of it became clean all of it becomes clean', which implies, does it not, that all of it was previously unclean?[11]—Abaye replied: This is a case, for instance, where it[12]

(1) Euphemism. (2) Lit., 'there'. (3) Fridays. Friday night is the time appointed for scholars. (4) Lit., 'I am not'. (5) Which is not white enough to show up a small speck of blood. (6) An objection against Raba. (7) The more they are washed the more suitable they are for the purpose. (8) Since it is more like a drink than a food. (9) Because each particle of snow is regarded as a separate entity; and only that entity that had directly been touched by the unclean object contracts the uncleanness. (10) By coming in contact with the water of a ritual bath (v. Beẓ. 17*b*). (11) But how is it possible for an uncleanness to have come in contact with all of it? (12) The snow.

was carried across the air-space of an oven,[1] [in which case all the snow is unclean] because the Torah testified concerning an earthen vessel[2] that [17b] even if it was full of mustard seed[3] [all within it is unclean].[4]

MISHNAH. THE SAGES SPOKE OF A WOMAN IN METAPHOR: [THERE IS IN HER] CHAMBER[5] AN ANTE-CHAMBER[6] AND AN UPPER CHAMBER.[7] THE BLOOD OF THE CHAMBER[8] IS UNCLEAN, THAT OF THE UPPER CHAMBER[9] IS CLEAN. IF BLOOD IS FOUND IN THE ANTE-CHAMBER, AND THERE ARISES A DOUBT ABOUT ITS CHARACTER,[10] IT IS DEEMED UNCLEAN, BECAUSE IT IS PRESUMED TO HAVE COME FROM THE SOURCE.[5]

GEMARA. Rami b. Samuel and R. Isaac son of Rab Judah learnt the tractate of Niddah at R. Huna's. Rabba son of R. Huna once found them while they were sitting at their studies and saying: The chamber is within, the ante-chamber is without and the upper chamber is built above them,[11] and a duct communicates between the upper chamber and the ante-chamber.[12] If blood is found anywhere from the duct inwards, and there is any doubt about its character,[10] it is deemed unclean[13] but if it is found anywhere from the duct outwards, and there is a doubt about its character,[10] it is deemed clean.[14] He[15] thereupon proceeded to his

(1) In which there was a dead creeping thing. (2) Such as the oven spoken of. (3) So that only those seeds that are actually round the sides of the oven could possibly come into direct contact with the oven. (4) V. Ḥul. 24*b*. Which proves that, in the case of an earthenware oven, uncleanness is conveyed to objects within it, even though these had not come in direct contact with it. (5) The uterus. (6) Vagina. (7) The urinary bladder (from the point of view of a woman lying on her back). (8) Being menstrual. (9) Being due to some internal wound. (10) *Sc.* whether it originated in the uterus or urinary bladder. (11) Cf. *supra* n. 7. (12) So that blood from the former may trickle down into the latter. (13) Since it is obvious that it came from the chamber. Had it come from the upper chamber it could not in the natural course have made its way backwards to the spot where it was discovered. (14) Because it is presumed to have originated from the upper chamber. (15) Rabbah b. R. Huna.

father and said to him, 'You told them, Master,[1] that "if there is any doubt about its character[2] it is deemed unclean", but have we not learnt: BECAUSE IT IS PRESUMED TO HAVE COME FROM THE SOURCE?'[3] 'I', the other replied, 'meant this: [Blood found anywhere] from the duct inwards is[4] undoubtedly unclean,[5] [but if it was found anywhere] from the duct outwards, it is deemed to be doubtfully unclean'.[6] Said Abaye: Why is[7] it [that if blood is found anywhere] from the duct outwards it is deemed to be doubtfully unclean?[8] Obviously because it is possible that she bowed down and the blood flowed thither from the chamber. [But, then, why in the case where blood is found anywhere] from the duct inwards, is it not also assumed that she might have staggered backwards[9] and the blood originated from the upper chamber?[10] Rather, said Abaye, if you follow possibilities[11] the uncleanness is doubtful in either case[12] and if you follow presumption [blood found anywhere] from the duct inwards is undoubtedly unclean,[13] [but if it was found anywhere] from the duct outwards it is undoubtedly clean.[14]

(1) So MS.M. Cur. edd., 'you told us, Master'. (2) The expression of 'doubt' obviously implying that there was no proof whatsoever that the blood originated in the chamber. (3) Emphasis on PRESUMED. If it is presumed to originate from the source (*sc.* the chamber) the uncleanness could not be described as a matter of 'doubt' but as one of certainty. (4) In agreement with our Mishnah. (5) V. *supra* p. 116, n. 13. (6) It being impossible to decide whether it originated in the chamber or in the upper chamber. (7) Lit., 'what is the difference'. (8) Though, since on that spot it is most likely to have come from the upper chamber, one might well have expected it to be clean. (9) And thus caused the blood to flow inwards. (10) Since this is obviously a possibility the uncleanness should only be a matter of doubt and not, as R. Huna asserted, a certainty. (11) Bending forward or staggering backwards. (12) Whether the blood is found on the one or on the other side of the duct, since in either case two possibilities (cf. prev. n.) may be equally assumed. (13) Since it may well be presumed to have originated in the chamber. Had it originated in the upper chamber it would have made its way to the outer side of the duct only. Our Mishnah's ruling, IT IS DEEMED UNCLEAN etc. may thus refer to such a case. (14) Since in that place it is presumed to have come from the upper chamber, and the possibility of bending forward is disregarded.

R. Ḥiyya taught: Blood found in the ante-chamber[1] renders [the woman] liable [for a sin-offering] if she enters the Sanctuary,[2] and *terumah*[3] must be burnt on its account.[2] R. Ḳaṭṭina, however, ruled: No sin-offering[4] is incurred if she enters the Sanctuary,[5] and *terumah*[3] is not burnt on its account.[5] According to the first alternative[6] which Abaye mentioned, viz., 'If you follow possibilities',[7] support is available for the ruling of R. Ḳaṭṭina[8] but[9] a divergence of view is presented against R. Ḥiyya. According to the second alternative[6] you mentioned, viz., 'If you follow presumption'[10] support is provided for the ruling of R. Ḥiyya[11] [18*a*] but[12] a divergence of view is presented against R. Ḳaṭṭina.[13] According to the ruling of R. Huna[14] neither of them differs from the other,[15] since one[16] might deal with blood found anywhere from the duct inwards while the other[17] might deal with such as was found anywhere from the duct outwards. According to Rami b. Samuel and R. Isaac the son of Rab Judah, however, who ruled, 'From the duct outwards, and there is a doubt about its character, it is deemed clean' and 'from the duct inwards, and there is a doubt about its character, it is deemed unclean', how are these rulings[18] to be explained? Obviously [as referring[19] to blood found] anywhere from the duct inwards.[20] Must it then be assumed[21]

(1) It is explained *infra* on which side of the duct. (2) Because the blood is certainly unclean. (3) That was touched by the woman. (4) Though the entry is forbidden. (5) Since the character of her blood cannot be determined with any degree of certainty. (6) Lit., 'that expression'. (7) *Sc.* that the uncleanness is merely a matter of doubt. (8) Who also regards the uncleanness as doubtful. R. Ḳaṭṭina might thus refer to both cases, where the blood was found on the one, or on the other side of the duct. (9) Since no certain uncleanness is recognized. (10) In accordance with which a distinction is drawn between blood found from the duct inwards or outwards. (11) Whose ruling would thus refer to blood found from the duct inwards. (12) As no doubtful uncleanness is recognized. (13) Who does recognize it (cf. prev. n.). (14) Who told his son that blood on the inward side of the duct is unclean and on its outward side is clean. (15) Neither R. Ḥiyya and R. Ḳaṭṭina differ from each other nor either of them from him. (16) R. Ḥiyya. (17) R. Ḳaṭṭina. (18) Of R. Ḥiyya and R. Ḳaṭṭina. (19) In agreement with R. Ḳaṭṭina. (20) Since blood found on its outward side is deemed to be clean and the woman is not only exempt from a sin-offering if she

that their ruling differs from that of R. Ḥiyya?[1]—This is no difficulty, since one[2] refers to blood found on the floor of the ante-chamber[3] while the others[4] refer to blood found on the roof of the ante-chamber.[5]

R. Joḥanan stated: In three instances[6] did the Sages follow the majority rule[7] and treated them as certainties, viz., the 'source', the 'placenta' and the 'piece'. The 'source'? The case already spoken of.[8] The 'placenta'? Concerning which we have learnt: If a placenta[9] is within a house, the house is unclean;[10] and this is so not because a placenta is regarded as a child but because generally there is no placenta without a child in it.[11] R. Simeon said, The child might have been mashed[12] before it came forth.[13] A 'piece'? For it was taught:[14] If a woman aborted a shaped[15] hand or a shaped foot she[16] is subject to the uncleanness of birth,[17] and there is no need to consider the possibility[18] that it might have come from a shapeless body.[19] But are there[20] no others?[21] Is there not

enters the Sanctuary, but is not even forbidden to enter it. (21) Since in no case do they recognize certain uncleanness.

(1) Who does recognize certain uncleanness. Is it likely, however, that they would both differ from him? (2) R. Ḥiyya, in ruling that the blood is definitely unclean. (3) Which is the natural passage for blood issuing from the chamber. (4) Rami and R. Isaac, who regard the blood as only doubtfully unclean. (5) Which is nearer to the upper chamber. (6) Lit., 'places', where doubts existed. (7) *Sc.* the majority of the respective cases concerning which no doubt exists. (8) In the last clause of our Mishnah, and in the ruling of R. Ḥiyya (*supra* 17*b*), from which it is obvious that, since mostly the blood in question issues from the source, any blood in the ante-chamber is assumed to originate from that source. (9) About which it is unknown whether it did or did not contain a dead embryo. (10) As overshadowing a corpse, though it is unknown (cf. prev. n.) whether the placenta contained one. (11) From which it is obvious that the uncleanness of the placenta is regarded as a certainty by the majority rule, since most placentas contain embryos. (12) And mixed up with the blood of birth which, representing the greater part of the mixture, neutralizes it. (13) *Infra* 26*a*. (14) Cf. marg. gl. Cur. edd., 'we learnt'. (15) Lit., 'cut'. (16) Lit., 'its mother'. (17) And, since it is unknown whether it was that of a male or a female, the restrictions of both are imposed upon her. (18) Which (cf. *infra* 24*a*) would exempt her from the certainty of uncleanness. (19) *Infra* 24*a*, which proves that by the majority rule, the doubtful case is regarded as a certainty because

in fact the case of nine shops[1] concerning which it was taught: If there were nine shops[1] all of which were selling ritually killed meat and one shop that was selling *nebelah*[2] meat and a man bought some meat in one of them and he does not know in which of them he bought it, the meat is forbidden on account of the doubt;[3] but if[4] meat is found,[5] the majority rule is to be followed?[6]—We[7] speak of uncleanness;[8] we do not discuss the question of a prohibition.[9] But is there not the case of the nine [dead] frogs among which there was one [dead] creeping thing[10] and a man touched one of them and he does not know which one it was that he touched, where he is unclean on account of the doubt if this occurred in a private domain,[11] but if it occurred in a public domain such a doubtful case is regarded as clean; and if one[12] was found[13] the majority rule is to be followed?[14]—We[15] deal with the uncleanness of a woman; we do not discuss general questions of uncleanness. But is there not the following case of which R. Joshua b. Levi spoke: If a woman crossed a river [18b] and miscarried[16] in it, she must bring a sacrifice which may be eaten,

the majority of births (which are normal) is followed. (20) Beside the three instances mentioned by R. Joḥanan. (21) Where the majority rule is followed.

(1) In a market in which there were ten such shops. (2) V. Glos. (3) Because the shop with the prohibited meat, being a *fixed* place, has the same status as half the number of all the shops in the market; and, consequently, the majority rule does not apply. (4) On the floor of the market in which the ten shops were situated. (5) So that the meat did not come from a fixed place. (6) V. Ḥul. 95*a*; and, since the majority of the shops sold meat that was ritually killed, the meat found is also regarded as ritually fit. Now since this provides another instance of a doubtful case that, by reason of the majority rule, is regarded as a certainty, why did R. Joḥanan mention three instances only? (7) *Sc.* R. Joḥanan in mentioning the three instances. (8) With which all the three instances deal. (9) To which the last case cited refers. (10) The latter conveys uncleanness but not the former (cf. Lev. XI, 29). (11) Since the creeping thing was in a fixed place which is equal in status to half of all the animals in the place. (12) Of the ten creatures mentioned. (13) *Sc.* the man touched an isolated animal which had no fixed place. (14) Tosef. Ṭoh. VI. As the majority are frogs the man is clean. Now why was not this case of doubtful uncleanness mentioned by R. Joḥanan? (15) *Sc.* R. Joḥanan in mentioning the three instances. (16) In consequence of which it is unknown whether or not the miscarriage was a developed child.

since we follow the majority of women, and the majority of women bear normal children?[1]—We spoke of Tannaitic rulings;[2] we did not discuss reported traditions.[3] But, surely, when Rabin came[4] he stated, 'R. Jose son of R. Ḥanina raised an objection [against R. Joshua b. Levi from a Baraitha dealing with] a forgetful woman,[5] but I do not know what objection it was'.[6] Does not this mean that it[7] presented no objection but rather provided support?[8]—No; it is possible [that he meant that it] neither presented an objection nor provided any support.

What does it[9] exclude?[10] If it be suggested that it[9] was intended to exclude the case[11] where the majority rule is opposed by the rule of presumption[12] so that in such a case *terumah*[13] may not be burnt on its account,[14] surely [it could be retorted] did not R. Joḥanan once say this,[15] for we learnt, 'If a child is found at the side of dough, with a piece of dough in his hand, R. Meir declares the dough clean, but the Sages declare it unclean because it is the nature of a child to slap[16] [dough]';[17] and when it was asked,

(1) *Infra* 29a. Now since her sacrifice, a bird sin-offering (the method of whose killing by pinching would have caused an unconsecrated, or doubtfully consecrated bird to be *nebelah*), may be eaten, it follows that the bird is deemed to be duly consecrated because, by reason of the majority rule, the woman's doubtful birth is regarded as a certain birth of a normal child. Why then did not R. Joḥanan mention this case which concerns a woman's uncleanness? (2) Lit., 'our Mishnah', *sc.* rulings occurring in a Mishnah or a Baraitha. (3) Of Amoras. R. Joshua b. Levi was an Amora. (4) From Palestine to Babylon. (5) Lit., 'mistaken', one who cannot tell the date on which she bore her child. (6) *Infra* 29a. (7) The Baraitha dealing with the forgetful woman. (8) For R. Joshua b. Levi's ruling. Since the answer is presumably in the affirmative the ruling given here in the name of R. Joshua b. Levi has its origin in a Baraitha. Why then, since it is a case of the uncleanness of a woman and is also a Tannaitic ruling, was it not included among those cited *supra* by R. Joḥanan? (9) R. Joḥanan's limitation of the instances *supra* to three. (10) I.e., what other doubtful instance is there that, despite the majority rule, is not treated as a certainty? (11) Of a woman's uncleanness. (12) Lit., 'there is . . . with it'. (13) Being doubtfully unclean. (14) *Sc.* on account of the doubtful uncleanness. (15) Explicitly, in other cases of uncleanness. Why then should he repeat it here by implication? (16) Ṭoh. III, 8. (17) In consequence of which he imparts to it the uncleanness which he is presumed to have contracted from menstrual women who coddle him or

'What is R. Meir's reason' [the answer given was that] he holds the view that though most children slap dough a minority of them do not, and since this dough stands in the presumption of cleanness;[1] you combine the status of the minority[2] with the rule of presumption[3] and the majority rule[4] is impaired,[5] while the Rabbis [regard] the minority as non-existent, and, where the majority rule is opposed by that of presumption, the majority rule takes precedence; and in connection with this Resh Laḳish citing R. Oshaia stated: This is a presumption[6] on the strength of which *terumah* is burnt,[7] while R. Joḥanan stated, This[8] is not a presumption on the strength of which *terumah* is burnt?[9]—It[10] was rather intended to exclude the rule of majority of which R. Judah spoke.[11] For we learnt: If a woman aborted a shapeless object,[12] if there was blood with it she is unclean[13] otherwise she is clean; R. Judah ruled: In either case she is unclean.[14] And in con-

play with him (R. Tam.). *Aliter* (Rashi): 'To dabble in the rubbish heap', where he contracts uncleanness from dead creeping things. His contact with the dough is regarded as a certainty (cf. Tosaf.).

(1) As is any dough, unless the contrary is proved. (2) Of children who do not slap dough and, therefore, cannot impart to it their uncleanness (so according to Tosaf.). *Aliter:* Who do not dabble in the rubbish heap and, therefore, contract no uncleanness (according to Rashi). (3) The dough is presumed to be clean (cf. prev. n. but one). (4) That 'most children slap dough' or 'dabble in the rubbish heap'. (5) By the major force of two to one. (6) *Sc.* that it is a child's nature to slap dough (Rashi). The term 'presumption' is here used loosely and really denotes 'majority'. (7) *Sc.* the majority rule by which it is offered has been given the force of a certainty. (8) Since 'the presumption of uncleanness' is here opposed by 'majority'. (9) Because it has not the force of a certainty. Now, since R. Joḥanan made here this explicit statement on the relative importance of the majority rule and that of presumption, what need was there to repeat it implicitly *supra?* (10) R. Joḥanan's limitation *supra* to three instances. (11) *Sc.* that in that case the uncleanness which is dependent on the majority rule is not regarded as a certainty. It is only one of a doubtful character and, in consequence, *terumah* that is subject to such uncleanness may not be burnt. (12) Lit., 'piece'. (13) As a menstruant. Since the abortion cannot be regarded as a child she is exempt from the uncleanness of childbirth. (14) *Infra* 21a. It is impossible in his opinion for an abortion to be free from all blood, though the latter might sometimes escape attention.

nection with this Rab Judah citing Samuel stated: R. Judah declared the woman unclean only where the shapeless object had the colour of one of the four kinds of blood,[1] but if it had that of any other kinds of blood[2] the woman is clean, while R. Joḥanan stated: [If it had the colour] of one of the four kinds of blood[3] all[4] agree that she is unclean, and if it had that of any other kinds of blood all agree that she is clean; they[5] differ only in the case where she aborted something [19*a*] and she does not know what she has aborted.[6] [In such a case,] R. Judah holds, one must be guided by the nature of most of such shapeless objects, and most such objects have the colour of one of the four kinds of blood, while the Rabbis hold that we do not say that one must be guided by the nature of most such objects.[7]

MISHNAH. FIVE KINDS OF BLOOD IN A WOMAN ARE UNCLEAN: RED, BLACK, A COLOUR LIKE BRIGHT CROCUS, OR LIKE EARTHY WATER OR LIKE DILUTED WINE.[8] BETH SHAMMAI RULED: ALSO A COLOUR LIKE THAT OF FENUGREEK WATER OR THE JUICE OF ROASTED MEAT; BUT BETH HILLEL DECLARE THESE CLEAN. ONE THAT IS YELLOW, AKABIA B. MAHALALEEL DECLARES UNCLEAN AND THE SAGES DECLARE

(1) Described in the Mishnah *infra* 19*a*, as unclean. Black and red blood are here regarded as of the same colour, the latter being a deteriorated form of the former. The Mishnah treating them as two gives the total number of kinds of unclean blood as five. In R. Judah's opinion the colour of unclean blood is proof that the entire mass is a piece of clotted blood. Hence the woman's menstrual uncleanness. The Rabbis, however, do not regard it as blood but as a shapeless piece of flesh. (2) Green or white, for instance. (3) Cf. prev. n. but one. (4) Even the Rabbis. (5) The Rabbis and R. Judah. (6) The object having been lost. (7) Because they do not agree that most such objects have one or other of the colours of the unclean kinds of blood. R. Joḥanan, by his limitation to three (*supra* 18*a*) of the cases in which the majority rule is given the force of a certainty, has implicitly indicated that, in the case dealt with by R. Judah, the uncleanness of the woman, which is entirely dependent on the majority rule, is not one of certainty but one of a doubtful nature. Consequently *terumah* that had been touched by the woman may not be burnt. (8) *Mazug*, wine mixed with water.

CLEAN. R. MEIR SAID: EVEN IF IT DOES NOT CONVEY UNCLEANNESS AS A BLOODSTAIN IT CONVEYS UNCLEANNESS AS A LIQUID.[1] R. JOSE RULED: IT DOES NEITHER THE ONE NOR THE OTHER.[2]

WHAT COLOUR IS REGARDED AS 'RED'? ONE LIKE THE BLOOD OF A WOUND.[1] 'BLACK'? LIKE THE SEDIMENT OF INK; IF IT IS DARKER IT IS UNCLEAN AND IF LIGHTER IT IS CLEAN. 'BRIGHT CROCUS COLOUR'? LIKE THE BRIGHTEST SHADE IN IT.[1] 'A COLOUR LIKE EARTHY WATER'? EARTH FROM THE VALLEY OF BETH KEREM[3] OVER WHICH WATER IS MADE TO FLOAT. 'ONE LIKE DILUTED WINE'? TWO PARTS OF WATER AND ONE OF WINE OF THE WINE OF SHARON.

GEMARA. Whence is it deduced that there is clean discharge of blood in a woman? Is it not possible that all blood that issues from her is unclean?—R. Ḥama b. Joseph citing R. Oshaia[4] replied: Scripture says, *If there arise a matter too hard for thee in judgment, between blood and blood,*[5] which implies between clean blood and unclean blood. But then, would the expression *'between a leprous stroke and a leprous stroke'*[5] also mean between an unclean stroke and a clean one? And should you reply: This is so indeed, [it could be retorted:] Is there at all a leprous stroke that is clean? And should you reply, *'It is all turned white; he is clean'*,[6] [it could be retorted:] That is called a white scurf![7] Consequently it must mean: Between human leprosy and the leprosy of houses and the leprosy of garments, all of which are unclean; why then should it not be said here[5] also that the distinction implied is that between the blood of a menstruant and that of one suffering from gonorrhoea both of which are unclean?[8]—What a comparison! There[9] [the controversy[10] is well justified[11] since] a difference of opinion might arise in the case of human leprosy on the lines of that between

(1) This is explained in the Gemara *infra*. (2) Lit., 'neither so nor so'. (3) V. Nid. III, 4. (4) MS.M., 'Joshua'. (5) Deut. XVII, 8. (6) Lev. XIII, 13. (7) Not a leprous stroke. (8) An objection against R. Oshaia's reply. (9) In the case of leprosy. (10) Implied in Deut. XVII, 8. (11) Though all leprosy is unclean.

R. Joshua and the Rabbis. For we have learnt: If the bright spot[1] preceded the white hair, he[2] is unclean; if the reverse was the case, he is clean. If [the order of appearance is] a matter of doubt he is unclean; but R. Joshua said: It is as though darkened,[3] and in connection with this Rabbah explained: It is as though [the spot] darkened[4] and he is therefore clean.[5] As regards leprosy in houses the point at issue[6] may be the one between R. Eleazar son of R. Simeon and the Rabbis. For we have learnt: R. Eleazar son of R. Simeon ruled: A house never becomes unclean unless the leprosy appears in the size of two beans on two stones,[7] in two walls,[7] at a corner,[8] and it must be two beans in length and one bean in breadth.[9] What is R. Eleazar son of R. Simeon's reason? —It is written[10] *wall*[11] and it is also written *walls*,[12] now what wall is it that is like two walls? Admit that that is a corner.[13] As regards leprosy in garments the divergence of opinion[14] may be the one between R. Jonathan b. Abṭolemos and the Rabbis. For it was taught: R. Jonathan[15] b. Abṭolemos stated, Whence is it deduced that leprosy that is spread over entire garments is clean? Since *ḳaraḥath*[16] and *gabaḥath*[17] are mentioned in respect of garments, and *ḳaraḥath*[18] and *gabuḥath*[19] are also mentioned in the case of human beings, as in the latter case if the leprosy spread over the whole body, he is clean so also in the former case if it spread over the whole garment it is clean.[20] Here,[21] however, if clean blood

(1) In leprosy. Cf. Lev. XIII, 2-4. (2) The man affected. (3) Neg. IV, 11. (4) Cf. *If the plague be dim (or dark)... then the priest shall pronounce him clean* (Lev. XIII, 6). (5) The dispute implied in Deut. XVII, 8, may consequently be analogous to the one between R. Joshua and the Rabbis. (6) Implied in Deut. XVII, 8. (7) The size of one bean on each. (8) Where the walls meet. (9) Neg. XII, 3; so that each stone is covered by leprosy of the size of one bean by one bean, which is the minimum required fcr effecting uncleanness. (10) In respect of leprosy. (11) Lev. XIV, 37. (12) Ibid. (13) The divergence of view implied in Deut. XVII, 8, may consequently be one analogous to that between R. Eleazar son of R. Simeon and the Rabbis. (14) Referred to in Deut. XVII, 8. (15) Var. lec. 'Nathan' (v. Zeb. 49*b*). (16) E.V., *within*, Lev. XIII, 55. (17) E.V., *without*, ibid. (18) E.V., *bald head*, ibid. 42. (19) E.V. *bald forehead*, ibid. (20) Sanh. 87*b*, Zeb. 44*b*. The dispute implied in Deut. XVII, 8, may consequently be the one between R. Jonathan b. Abṭolemos and the Rabbis. (21) In the case of a divergence of view in respect of blood.

does not exist, what could be the point at issue between them?[1] But whence is it inferred that these kinds of blood are clean and the others are unclean?[2]—R. Abbahu replied: Since Scripture says, *And the Moabites saw the water as red as blood,*[3] which indicates that blood is red.[4] Might it not be suggested that only red blood[5] is unclean but no other?[6]—R. Abbahu replied: Scripture says; *Her blood,*[7] *Her blood*[8] implying four kinds.[9] But have we not learnt, FIVE KINDS?—R. Ḥanina replied: Black blood is really red [blood] that had deteriorated.[10] So it was also taught: Black blood is like the sediment of ink; if it is dark it is unclean, and if lighter, even though it has the colour of stibium, it is clean. And black blood is not black originally. It[11] assumes the black colour only after it is discharged, like the blood of a wound which becomes black after it had been discharged from it.

BETH SHAMMAI RULED: ALSO A COLOUR LIKE THAT OF FENUGREEK. But do not Beth Shammai uphold the deduction from, *Her blood,*[7] *her blood*[8] which imply four kinds?[9]—If you wish I may reply that they do not uphold it. And if you prefer I may reply that they do uphold it, but[12] did not R. Ḥanina explain, 'Black blood is really red [blood] that had deteriorated'?[13] Well, here also[14] it may be explained that [the blood][15] had merely deteriorated.

BUT BETH HILLEL DECLARE THESE CLEAN. Is not this ruling identical with that of the first Tanna?[16]—The practical difference between them is [19*b*] the question of suspense.[17]

(1) The authorities in dispute regarding blood referred to in Deut. XVII, 8. Consequently it must be conceded that clean blood also exists. (2) Cf. our Mishnah. (3) II Kings III, 22. (4) As red is the usual colour of blood, all blood which has one of the five colours enumerated in our Mishnah (all of which are shades of red) is unclean. (5) But if so, why does our Mishnah declare the others also to be unclean? (6) One like that of a wound. (7) *Dameha*, the plural form, Lev. XII, 7. (8) Ibid. XX, 18 (cf. prev. n.). (9) Twice two (cf. prev. two notes). (10) The two colours may, therefore, be treated as one. (11) Being originally red. (12) As to the objection from the limitation of the number to five. (13) *Supra.* Of course he did. (14) Blood of the colour of fenugreek. (15) Being originally red. (16) In the first clause of our Mishnah. (17) I.e., whether blood of a colour other than those of the

ONE THAT IS YELLOW, AKABIA B. MAHALALEEL DECLARES UNCLEAN. But does not Akabia uphold the deduction from '*Her blood, her blood*', which imply four kinds?[1]—If you wish I may reply: He does not uphold it. And if you prefer I may reply: He does uphold it; but did not R. Ḥanina explain, 'Black blood is really red [blood] that had deteriorated'? Well, here also it may be explained that [the blood] had merely deteriorated.[1]

AND THE SAGES DECLARE IT CLEAN. Is not this ruling identical with that of the first Tanna?[2]—The practical difference between them is the question of suspense.[3]

R. MEIR SAID: EVEN IF IT DOES NOT CONVEY UNCLEANNESS AS A BLOODSTAIN etc. R. Joḥanan stated: R. Meir took up[4] the line of Akabia b. Mahalaleel and declared it[5] unclean;[6] and it is this that he in effect said to the Rabbis, 'Granted that where a woman finds a yellow bloodstain on her garment you do not regard her as unclean;[7] where she observed a discharge of yellow blood from her body[8] she must be deemed unclean'. If so, instead of saying, EVEN IF IT DOES NOT CONVEY UNCLEANNESS AS A BLOODSTAIN IT CONVEYS UNCLEANNESS AS A LIQUID, should he not have said 'on account of her observation'?[9]—Rather, it is this that he in effect said to them, 'Granted that where the woman observed yellow blood at the outset you do not[10] regard her as unclean;[11] where she observed first red blood[12] and then a yellow discharge the latter also must be deemed unclean,[13]

five enumerated is (*a*) absolutely clean or (*b*) only doubtfully so. Beth Hillel are in agreement with (*a*) and the first Tanna agrees with (*b*).

(1) Cf. nn. on previous paragraph but one. (2) In the first clause of our Mishnah. (3) Cf. prev. n. but one *mut. mut.* (4) Lit., 'descended'. (5) A yellow discharge. (6) As menstrual blood. (7) Being yellow (an unusual colour for blood) it might well be presumed to have originated from some source other than her body. (8) So that its origin is certain. (9) Of an actual discharge. (10) Despite the observation. (11) Because yellow is not the colour of blood; UNCLEANNESS AS A BLOODSTAIN meaning: As other blood whose stain conveys uncleanness. (12) Which causes her to be definitely unclean. (13) *Sc.* in respect of conveying uncleanness to man or object that comes in contact with it.

since it is something like the liquids[1] of a *zab* or a *zabah*'.[2] And the Rabbis?[3]—[An unclean liquid must be] similar to spittle; as spittle is formed in globules when it is discharged so must any other unclean liquid be one that is formed in globules when it is discharged; that liquid[4] is therefore excluded since it is not formed in globules when discharged. If so, do not the Rabbis indeed give R. Meir a most satisfactory answer?[5]—It is rather this that he said to them in effect: 'It[4] should have the status of a liquid in respect of rendering seed susceptible to uncleanness'.[6] And the Rabbis?[7]—[For such a purpose] it is necessary that it shall be like the blood of the slain,[8] which is not the case here. If so, did not the Rabbis indeed answer R. Meir well?[5]—It is rather this that he in effect said to them: 'Deduce this[9] by *gezera shawah;*[10] here[11] it is written, *Thy shoots*[12] *are a park of pomegranates*[13] and elsewhere it is written, *And sendeth*[14] *water upon the fields.*[15] And the Rabbis?[16]—A man may infer a ruling *a minori ad majus* on his own but he may not infer on his own one that is derived from a *gezera shawah*.[17]

R. JOSE RULED: IT DOES NEITHER THE ONE NOR THE OTHER etc. Is not this ruling identical with that of the first Tanna?[18]—It is this that we were informed: Who is the first Tanna? R. Jose; for he who repeats a thing in the name of him who said it brings deliverance into the world.[19]

(1) Spittle, for instance. (2) Which, though they are no blood, convey uncleanness. (3) How, in view of this argument, could they maintain that a yellow discharge is clean in all circumstances? (4) A yellow discharge. (5) How then could R. Meir still maintain his view? (6) Cf. Lev. XI, 38. (7) Cf. *supra* n. 3. (8) Num. XXIII, 24, *sc.* blood on which life depends (cf. Pes. 16*a*). (9) That a yellow discharge renders seed susceptible to uncleanness. (10) V. Glos. (11) In respect of menstrual discharges. (12) *Shelaḥayik* (rt. שלח) euphemism (cf. prev. n.). (13) Cant. IV, 13. (14) *Wesholeaḥ* (rt. שלח). (15) Job V, 10. Analogy between the two words of the same root: As the water referred to in Job renders seed susceptible to uncleanness so does a woman's discharge alluded to in Cant. (16) How can they maintain their view in opposition to the *gezera shawah?* (17) Which must be traditional if it is to be valid. As R. Meir drew the analogy on his own the Rabbis could well disregard it. (18) In the first clause of our Mishnah. Why then the repetition? (19) Cf. Ab. VI, 6.

WHAT COLOUR IS REGARDED AS RED? ONE LIKE THE BLOOD OF A WOUND. What is meant by LIKE THE BLOOD OF A WOUND?—Rab Judah citing Samuel replied: Like the blood of a slaughtered ox.[1] Why then was it not stated, 'Like the blood of slaughtering'?—If it had been stated, 'Like the blood of slaughtering' it might have been presumed to mean like the blood during the entire process of slaughtering,[2] hence we were told, LIKE THE BLOOD OF A WOUND, meaning like that caused by the first stroke of the knife. 'Ulla replied:[3] Like the blood of [a wound inflicted on] a live bird. The question was raised: Does 'live'[4] exclude a slaughtered bird or does it possibly exclude an emaciated one?—This is undecided.[5] Ze'iri citing R. Ḥanina replied:[3] Like the blood of a head louse. An objection was raised: If she[6] killed a louse she may attribute the stain to it.[7] Does not this refer to a louse of any part of the body?—No, to one of her head. Ammi of Wardina[8] citing R. Abbahu replied:[3] Like the blood of the little finger of the hand that was wounded and healed and wounded again. Furthermore, it does not mean that of any person but only that of a young unmarried man. And up to what age?—Up to that of twenty.

An objection was raised: She[6] may attribute it to her son[9] or to her husband.[9] [Now the attribution] to her son is quite reasonable since it is possible [that he was unmarried],[10] but how is this possible in the case of her husband?[11]—R. Naḥman b. Isaac replied: Where, for instance, the woman entered the bridal chamber but had no intercourse.[12] R. Naḥman replied:[13] Like the blood of the arteries.[14]

(1) The true colour of red. Cf. Yoma 56*b*. (2) During which the colours change. (3) To the question *supra*, what is meant by LIKE THE BLOOD OF A WOUND? (4) Heb. *ḥai* (fem. *ḥaiyah*) may mean both 'live' and 'sound', 'healthy'. (5) *Teḳu*. (6) A woman who discovered a bloodstain. (7) *Infra* 58*b*. (8) Place name (cf. 'Er. 49*a*). Wardina or Barada on the eastern bank of the Tigris was two hours distance from the north of Bagdad (cf. 'Er. (Sonc. ed.) p. 340, n. 11). *Aliter:* 'The fragrant (*werad* = rose) Ammi' (çf. Rashi). (9) If either of them was afflicted with a wound. *Infra* 58*b*. (10) And the blood of his wound satisfies, therefore, all the conditions laid down by R. Abbahu. (11) Who must be a married man (cf. prev. n. *mut. mut.*). (12) So that the blood is in reality that of an unmarried man (cf. prev. n. but one). (13) To the ques-

An objection was raised: It once happened that R. Meir attributed it[1] [20a] to collyrium[2] and Rabbi attributed it to the sap of a sycamore.[3] Now did not these cases[4] deal with the question of red blood?[5]—No; with that of other kinds of blood.

Amemar and Mar Zuṭra and R. Ashi once sat before a cupper,[6] and when the first cupping-horn was taken off Amemar he saw it and said to the others, 'The red[7] of which we have learnt[8] is a shade like this'. When the second one was taken off from him, he said to them, 'This has a different shade'. 'One like myself', observed R. Ashi, 'who does not know the difference between the one and the other must not act as an examiner of blood'.

'BLACK? LIKE THE SEDIMENT [OF INK]. Rabbah son of R. Huna stated: The ḤERETH[9] of which the Rabbis spoke[8] is ink. So it was also taught: Black[10] is a colour like *ḥereth* and the 'black' of which the Rabbis spoke[10] is the colour of ink. Then why was it not directly stated, 'Ink'?—If 'ink' had been stated, it might have been presumed to refer to the watery part of the ink,[11] hence we were informed that the colour is like that of the sediment of the ink. The question was raised: Is the reference to liquid, or to dry ink?—Come and hear of [the practice of] R. Ammi who used to split a grain of dry ink and with its aid performed the necessary examination.

Rab Judah citing Samuel ruled: [If a woman's discharge has a colour] like that of black wax, blac ink or a black grape she is

tion, *supra*, what is meant by 'LIKE THE BLOOD OF A WOUND'? (14) *Haḳazah*, lit., 'blood letting'.

(1) A stain. (2) Κολλύριον, a reddish eyesalve, which the woman had handled that day. (3) *Infra* 58*b*. Cf. prev. n. *mut. mut.* (4) From which it follows that colours like that of collyrium or sycamore sap that are not intensely red are regarded as similar to that of menstrual blood. (5) But, if so, how could the authorities (*supra* 19*b*) maintain that menstrual blood is intensely red like that, for instance, of a young unmarried man? (6) For an operation of blood drawing with cupping horns. (7) In respect of menstrual blood. (8) In our Mishnah. (9) Rendered in our Mishnah SEDIMENT OF INK. (10) In respect of a woman's discharge. (11) I.e., the upper part above the sediment. This is not so black as the lower part.

unclean; and it is this that was meant by what we learnt: IF IT IS DARKER IT IS UNCLEAN.

R. Eleazar ruled: [A discharge that has a colour] like that of a black olive, pitch or a raven is clean; and it is this that was alluded to in what we have learnt: IF LIGHTER IT IS CLEAN.

'Ulla explained:[1] One like a Siwa[2] cloak. 'Ulla once visited Pumbeditha when he noticed an Arab merchant who was wearing a black cloak. 'The black of which we have learnt',[3] he told them, 'is a colour like this'. They pulled it off him in bits[4] and paid him for it four hundred *zuz*.

R. Johanan explained:[1] [One of the colour of] those court[5] clothes that are imported from courtiers beyond the sea. This then implies that such clothes are black, but did not R. Jannai address the following request to his sons: 'My children, do not bury me either in black shrouds or white shrouds; "either in black", peradventure I may be worthy [of a place in Paradise] and I would be like a mourner among bridegrooms;[6] "or in white", peradventure I might not be worthy and would be like a bridegroom among mourners;[7] but [bury me] only in court[5] clothes that are imported from countries beyond the sea', which clearly proves, does it not, that these are not black?[8]—This is no difficulty, the latter[9] referring to wrappers,[10] while the former[11] refers to clothes worn[12] at table.[13]

Rab Judah citing Samuel ruled: And all these[14] must be tested only on a white strip of cloth. R. Isaac b. Abudemi ruled: But black blood may be tested on a red strip of cloth. R. Jeremiah of Difti observed: There is really no difference of opinion between them,[15] since the latter speaks only of black blood while the former refers

(1) The unclean black in our Mishnah. (2) A place where dark clothes were manufactured. *Aliter:* Dirty-dark. (3) In our Mishnah. (4) To be preserved as models of the standard black. (5) *Aliter:* bathing attendants. (6) The righteous who are clad in white. (7) The wicked in Gehenna. (8) Is not this then contradictory to R. Johanan's view? (9) Spoken of by R. Jannai. (10) Which are red. (11) R. Johanan's statement. (12) Or 'cloths used'. (13) Which are black. (14) Five kinds of blood (v. our Mishnah). (15) Samuel and R. Isaac b. Abudemi.

to the other kinds of blood. R. Ashi demurred: If so, why did not Samuel say, 'With the exception of black'? Rather, said R. Ashi, they[1] differ on the very question of black itself.

'Ulla ruled: In the case of all these[2] if the discharge is darker[3] it is unclean and if it is lighter[3] it is clean, as is the case with black.[4] Then why did it mention only black?—As it might have been presumed that, since R. Ḥanina stated, 'Black [blood] is really red blood that had deteriorated', it should, therefore, be unclean even if it is lighter, hence we were informed [that IF LIGHTER IT IS CLEAN].

R. Ammi b. Abba ruled: In the case of all these[2] if the discharge is darker[3] it is unclean and if it is lighter it is also unclean, the only exception being black.[5] What then[6] was the use of the standard shade laid down by the Rabbis?—To exclude[7] one that was extremely faint.[8] There are others who read: Rami b. Abba ruled: In the case of all these[9] if the discharge is darker[10] it is clean and if it is lighter it is also clean, the only exception being black;[5] and it is in this case that the Rabbinical standard is of use.

Bar Ḳappara ruled: In the case of all these[9] if the discharge is darker it is unclean and if lighter it is clean, the exception being [the colour of] diluted wine in which a darker shade is clean and a lighter one is also clean. Bar Ḳappara was shown a lighter shade[11] and he declared it clean, and when he was shown a darker shade[11] he also declared it clean. 'How great is the man', exclaimed R. Ḥanina, 'who in practice acts[12] in agreement with his view.'

A COLOUR LIKE BRIGHT CROCUS. A Tanna taught: Fresh crocus and not dry one. One [Baraitha] taught: Like the lower leaf[13] but not like the upper one, and another [Baraitha] taught:

(1) Samuel and R. Isaac b. Abudemi. (2) Five kinds of blood (v. our Mishnah). (3) Than the standard shade. (4) Concerning which the limitations are specifically laid down in our Mishnah. (5) Which IF LIGHTER IT IS CLEAN. (6) In the case of the colours other than black which, as has just been stated, not only a darker, but also a lighter shade is unclean. (7) From uncleanness. (8) Lit., 'lighter of lighter'. Such a shade is clean. (9) Five kinds of blood (v. our Mishnah). (10) Than the standard shade. (11) Of a discharge of the colour of diluted wine. (12) So Maharsha. Cur. edd., 'whose heart'. (13) Of the crocus.

Like the upper leaf but not like the lower one, while a third [Baraitha] taught: Like the upper leaf and much more so like the lower one, and a fourth [Baraitha] taught: Like the lower leaf and much more so like the upper one![1]—Abaye replied: The crocus has three rows of leaves[2] and there are three leaves in each row; keep[3] to the middle row[4] and the middle leaf of that row.[5] When they came before R. Abbahu he told them: What we learnt [about the colour of the crocus refers to such as are still] attached to their clods.[6]

OR LIKE EARTHY WATER. Our Rabbis taught: Like earthy water—one brings fertile soil from the valley of Beth Kerem over which he causes water to float; so R. Meir. R. Judah[7] said: From the valley of Jotapata.[8] R. Jose said: From the valley of Sikni.[9] R. Simeon said: Also from the valley of Gennesaret[10] and similar soil. Another [Baraitha] taught: And like earthy water—one brings fertile soil from the valley of Beth Kerem and over it he causes water to float until it forms a layer as thin as the husk of garlic; and no quantity has been prescribed for the water since none has been prescribed for the earth.[11] The water, furthermore, is not to be examined when it is clean but when turbid. If they become clear they must be stirred up again;[12] and when they are stirred one must not do it with the hand but with a vessel. The question was raised: [Does the expression,] 'One must not do it with the hand but with a vessel' mean that a man must not put

(1) How are the four contradictory statements to be reconciled? (2) One below the other. (3) As the most correct standard for the blood test. (4) Which has the 'lower leaf' as compared with the top row (first Baraitha) and the 'upper leaf' as compared with the lowest row (second Baraitha). V. foll. n. (5) Though the other leaves in that row may also be taken as the standard. The middle leaf is the 'lower one' as compared with the one above it (third Baraitha) and the 'upper one' as compared with the one below it (fourth Baraitha). (6) Of earth. Their colour then is much brighter than that of the detached plant which may not be used as a standard. (7) So MS.M. and Elijah Wilna. Cur. edd., 'Akiba'. (8) A fortress in Galilee. (9) Or Siknin, on the north of Jotapata. (10) In Lower Galilee on the banks of the lake of the same name. (11) The more the earth the more the water and *vice versa*. (12) To mix up the earth with it.

it in his hand and stir it in it but that where it is in a vessel it is quite proper for him to stir it with his hand, or is it possible that the meaning is that one must not stir it with his hand[1] but with an instrument?[2]—Come and hear: When he examines it[3] he must do it in a cup only.[4] But does not the question yet remain: If the examination must be in a cup, wherewith must the stirring be done?—This is undecided.[5]

When they came before Rabba b. Abbuha he told them: What we learnt [about the earth refers to such as is] in its own place.[6]

R. Ḥanina used to break up a piece of potter's clay and thereby performed the examination. R. Ishmael son of R. Jose cursed with croup any other person who adopts such a method [20b] for R. Ḥanina was wise enough;[7] all others are not so wise. R. Joḥanan remarked: The wisdom of R. Ḥanina caused me not to examine any blood, for when I declared any unclean he declared it clean and when I declared it clean he declared it unclean. R. Eleazar remarked: R. Ḥanina's modesty is the cause of my examining blood. [For I felt] if R. Ḥanina who was modest allowed himself to be involved in doubt and examined blood, should not I examine it? R. Zera remarked: The Babylonian coinage was the cause of my refusing to examine blood; for I thought: If I do not understand the coinage system would I understand the nature of blood? This then implies that capability to examine blood depends on an understanding of the coinage; but did not Rabbah in fact understand the coinage system and yet did not understand the qualities of blood?—He was really drawing an inference *a minori ad majus:* If Rabbah who understood the coinage system refused to examine blood, should I[8] examine it?

'Ulla once visited Pumbeditha[9] and when some blood was brought to him for examination he refused to see it. If, he said,

(1) Even when it is in a vessel. (2) The Heb. *Keli* may bear both significations. (3) The earthy water. (4) Which proves that no examination may be performed with the water and the earth in one's hand. (5) *Teḳu* (v. Glos.). (6) Exported earth changes its colour. (7) And was, therefore, capable of using the method. (8) Who do not understand the coinage system. (9) Which was under the jurisdiction of Rab Judah (cf. Sanh. 17b).

R. Eleazar who was the supreme authority in the Land of Israel[1] refused to see blood whenever he visited the place of R. Judah, should I see it?[2] And why was he described as the supreme authority in the Land of Israel?—Because a woman once brought some blood before R. Eleazar when R. Ammi sat in his presence. Having smelt it he[3] told her, 'This is blood of lust'.[4] After she went out R. Ammi joined her and she told him, 'My husband was away on a journey but I felt an intense longing for him'. Thereupon he[5] applied to him[3] the text, *The counsel of the Lord is with them that fear Him.*[6]

Ifra Hormiz,[7] the mother of King Shapur, once sent some blood to Raba when R. Obadiah was sitting in his presence. Having smelt it he said to him, 'This is blood of lust'.[4] 'Come and see', she remarked to her[8] son, 'how wise the Jews are'. 'It is quite possible', he replied, 'that he[9] hit upon it like a blind man on a window'. Thereupon she sent to him[9] sixty different kinds of blood and he identified them all but the last one which was lice blood with which he was not acquainted. Luckily,[10] however, he sent her[11] a comb that exterminates lice. 'O, you Jews', she exclaimed, 'you seem to live in the inner chamber of one's heart'.[12]

Rab Judah stated: 'At first I used to examine blood, but since the mother of my son Isaac told me, "We do not bring the first drop to the Rabbis because it is dirty", I refuse to see it.[13] [An examination, however, for the purpose of distinguishing] between the blood of uncleanness and cleanness[14] I certainly do perform'.[15]

(1) V. Giṭ. 19*b*. (2) Cf. prev. n. (3) R. Eleazar. (4) A discharge due to sexual desire. (5) R. Ammi. (6) Ps. XXV, 14. (7) A gentile woman who observed some of the Jewish ritual (cf. also Zeb. 116*b*). (8) So Emden, Cur. edd. '*his*'. (9) Raba. (10) Lit., 'the matter came to assistance'. (11) As a gift. (12) Nothing is hidden from them. (13) Because the colour changes and though the second drop may be one of clean blood it could not establish a woman's cleanness if the first drop, which she did not present for examination, was one of unclean blood. (14) At the end of the period of cleanness after a childbirth which is the fortieth day for a male and the eightieth for a female (cf. Lev. XII, 1-5). (15) The blood in such circumstances being free from dirt a woman submits for examination the first drop she sees.

Yaltha[1] once brought some blood to Rabbah b. Bar Ḥana who informed her that it was unclean. She then took it to R. Isaac the son of Rab Judah who told her that it was clean. But how could he act in this manner, seeing that is was taught: If a Sage declared [aught] unclean another Sage[2] may not declare it clean; if he forbade anything his colleague may not permit it?[3]—At first he[4] informed her indeed that it was unclean,[5] but when she told him that on every other occasion he[6] declared such blood as clean, but that on the last occasion he had a pain in his eye, he gave her his ruling that it was clean. But are women believed in such circumstances?—Yes, and so it was also taught: A woman[7] is believed when she says, 'I saw a kind of blood like this one[8] but I have lost it.'[9]

The question was raised: What is the law [where a woman says], A kind of blood like this[10] has been declared clean by such and such a Sage?[11]—Come and hear: A woman[7] is believed when she says, 'I saw a kind of blood like this one[8] but I have lost it.'[12] But is not that case[13] different, since the blood is not available?[14]—Come and hear the case of Yaltha: She once brought some blood to Rabbah b. Bar Ḥana who informed her that it was unclean. She then took it[15] to R. Isaac the son of Rab Judah who told her that it was clean. But how could he act in this manner, seeing that it was taught: If a Sage declared [a person or an article] unclean no other Sage[16] may declare it clean etc. And we explained that at first he[4] informed her indeed that it was unclean, but when she told him that on every other occassion he[6] declared such blood as clean but that on that day he had a pain in his eye, he changed his view and gave her his ruling that it was clean.[17] Now

(1) R. Naḥman's wife. (2) Lit., 'his colleague'. (3) Ḥul. 44*b*. (4) R. Isaac. (5) Out of respect for Rabbah b. Bar Ḥana (v. *infra*). (6) Rabbah. (7) Who does not submit the original blood. (8) Which she produces. (9) And if the blood she submits is clean she may be declared clean. (10) Which a friend of hers showed her. (11) May her judgment, it is asked, on the exact similarity of the two kinds be relied upon by her friend or not. (12) Which proves that a woman's judgment in such cases (cf. prev. n.) is relied upon. (13) Just cited. (14) Lit., 'it is not before her'. (15) So BaḤ. Cur. edd. omit the last four words. (16) Lit., 'his colleagues'. (17) *Supra*.

this proves quite clearly, does it not, that a woman is believed?—R. Isaac b. Judah may have relied on his own traditions and experience.[1]

Rabbi once examined some blood at night and declared it unclean but when he examined it in the day time he declared it clean. Then he waited a while and again declared it unclean. 'Woe to me', he said, 'I may have made a mistake'.[2] 'I may have made a mistake'! Has he not in fact made a mistake, seeing that it was taught: A Sage must not say,[3] 'If it had been moist it would undoubtedly have been unclean'; he must rather say, 'The judge must be guided only by what his eyes see'?—At first[4] he presumed it to be definitely unclean, but when he observed in the morning that its colour had changed[5] he said[6] that it was undoubtedly clean but that at night it could not be seen properly. When, however, he observed that the colour had changed again[7] he said, 'It must be unclean blood but the colour is steadily fading away.'

Rabbi examined blood in the light of a lamp. R. Ishmael son of R. Joseph[8] examined it even on a cloudy day between the pillars.[9] R. Ammi b. Samuel ruled: All kinds of blood must be examined only between the sunshine and the shade. R. Naḥman citing Rabbah b. Abbuha ruled: The examination may be performed in the sunshine under the shadow of one's hand.[10]

'ONE LIKE DILUTED WINE'? TWO PARTS etc. A Tanna taught: [21a] Sharon wine[11] [diluted] is regarded[12] as the Carmel wine in its natural undiluted state when it is new[13] R. Isaac b. Abudemi

(1) Not on Yaltha's evidence. The reason why he at first declared the blood as unclean was merely to show his respect to Rabbah b. Bar Ḥana. (2) In finally declaring the blood unclean, since the colour now was of a clean kind. (3) When examining a dry stain. (4) At the night examination. (5) It assumed a lighter shade. (6) So Emden. Cur. edd. in parenthesis 'to him'. (7) To a still lighter shade. (8) MS.M. 'Jose'. (9) Of the schoolhouse where the light was never too bright. (10) Held between the sun and the object. (11) Composed of one part of wine and two parts of water (cf. our Mishnah). (12) In respect of its colour. (13) Lit., 'new and not old'. According to an interpretation of Maimonides and Semag (cf. Maharsha) the Sharon wine, when used in an examination of blood, must first be new and undiluted and then mixed expressly for the purpose of the examination with two parts of water.

ruled: All these[1] must be examined only in a plain Tiberian cup.[2] What is the reason?—Abaye replied: Generally[3] a cup that contains a *log* is made of a *maneh*[4] and one that contains two *log* is made of two hundred *zuz*, but the plain Tiberian cup, even if it contains two *log*, is made of one *maneh*, and since it is so thin [the colour of the wine can] be recognized better [than in any other kind of cup].

(1) Kinds of wine. (2) Which is made of thin and transparent glass. (3) Lit., 'of all the world'. (4) The weight of one hundred *zuz*.

NIDDAH

CHAPTER III

MISHNAH. IF A WOMAN ABORTED A SHAPELESS OBJECT,[1] IF THERE WAS BLOOD WITH IT, SHE IS UNCLEAN,[2] OTHERWISE SHE IS CLEAN.[3] R. JUDAH RULED: IN EITHER CASE SHE IS UNCLEAN.[4]

IF A WOMAN ABORTED AN OBJECT THAT WAS LIKE A RIND, LIKE A HAIR, LIKE EARTH, LIKE RED FLIES, LET HER PUT IT IN WATER AND IF IT DISSOLVES[5] SHE IS UNCLEAN,[2] BUT IF IT DOES NOT SHE IS CLEAN.[6]

IF AN ABORTION WAS IN THE SHAPE OF FISHES, LOCUSTS, OR ANY FORBIDDEN ANIMALS OR CREEPING THINGS, IF THERE WAS BLOOD WITH THEM SHE IS UNCLEAN,[2] OTHERWISE SHE IS CLEAN.[6]

IF AN ABORTION HAD THE SHAPE OF A BEAST, A WILD ANIMAL OR A BIRD, WHETHER CLEAN OR UNCLEAN,[7] IF IT WAS A MALE SHE MUST CONTINUE [IN UNCLEANNESS AND SUBSEQUENT CLEANNESS FOR THE PERIODS PRESCRIBED] FOR A MALE,[8] AND IF IT WAS A FEMALE SHE MUST CONTINUE [IN UNCLEANNESS AND SUBSEQUENT CLEANNESS FOR THE PERIODS PRESCRIBED] FOR A FEMALE,[9] BUT IF THE SEX IS UNKNOWN SHE MUST CONTINUE [IN UNCLEANNESS AND SUBSEQUENT CLEANNESS FOR THE PERIODS PRESCRIBED] FOR BOTH MALE AND FEMALE;[10] SO R. MEIR. THE SAGES, HOW-

(1) Lit., 'piece'. (2) As a menstruant. (3) Because, in the absence of blood, she cannot be regarded as a menstruant, and, since a shapeless object is no proper birth, she cannot be regarded as a woman in childbirth. (4) This is explained in the Gemara *infra.* (5) Into liquid blood. (6) Cf. *supra* n. 3 *mut. mut.* (7) Cf. Lev. XI. (8) Cf. Lev. XII, 2-4. (9) Cf. ibid. 5. (10) *Sc.* she is subject to the restrictions of both: The period of her uncleanness is fourteen days (as for a female) and not seven (as for a male) while the subsequent period of her cleanness terminates on the fortieth day (as for a male) and not on the eightieth (as for a female).

EVER, RULED: ANYTHING THAT HAS NOT THE SHAPE OF A HUMAN BEING CANNOT BE REGARDED AS A HUMAN CHILD.

GEMARA. Rab Judah citing Samuel stated: R. Judah declared the woman[1] unclean only where the object had the colour of one of the four kinds of blood,[2] but if it had that of any of the other kinds of blood[3] she is clean.[4] R. Johanan, however, stated: [If the object had the colour] of one of the four kinds of blood[5] all[6] agree that the woman is unclean and if it had the colour of any of the other kinds of blood all[7] agree that she is clean; they[8] differ only in the case where she aborted something and she does not know what she aborted.[9] [In such a case,] R. Judah holds, one must be guided by the nature of most of shapeless objects, and most shapeless objects have the colour of one of the four kinds of blood, while the Rabbis hold that we do not say, 'most shapeless objects have the colour of one of the four kinds of blood'. But is this correct?[10] Surely when R. Hoshaia arrived from Nehardea he came [to the schoolhouse] and brought with him a Baraitha: If a woman aborted a shapeless object that was red, black, green or white,[11] if there was blood with it, she is unclean, otherwise she is clean. R. Judah ruled: In either case she is unclean. Now does not this present a difficulty against Samuel in one respect and against R. Johanan in two respects? 'Against Samuel in one respect', since Samuel stated, 'R. Judah declared the woman

(1) Who ABORTED A SHAPELESS OBJECT. (2) Described in the Mishnah *supra* 19a as unclean. (Black and red which in the Mishnah are regarded as two different colours and, therefore, bring the total number of unclean colours to five, are here regarded as one colour since the former is but a deterioration of the latter). R. Judah holds that the shapeless object is but a piece of clotted blood. Hence, if its colour is that of unclean blood, the woman, though not in childbirth, must be deemed unclean as a menstruant. (3) White or green, for instance. (4) Since she is neither in childbirth nor a menstruant. (5) Cf. *supra* n. 2. (6) Even the Rabbis. (7) Even R. Judah. (8) The Rabbis and R. Judah (cf. prev. two nn.). (9) The object having been lost. (10) Lit., 'I am not'. (11) The first two are of the unclean colours while the last two are among the clean ones (cf. *supra* 19a).

unclean only where the shapeless object had the colour of one of the four kinds of blood' whereas here 'green and white'[1] were mentioned and R. Judah nevertheless disagrees.[2] And were you to reply that R. Judah differs only in respect of red and black but not in that of green or white [the question would arise:] For whose benefit then was green and white mentioned? If it be suggested: For that of the Rabbis,[3] [it could be retorted:] Since the Rabbis declared the woman clean even in the case of red and black blood,[4] was it any longer necessary to state that the same law applies also to green and white?[1] Must it not then be conceded that these[5] were mentioned for the benefit of R. Judah[6] who, it thus follows, does differ.[7] Furthermore, according to R. Johanan[8] who also stated, '[If it had the colour] of one of the four kinds of blood all agree that she is unclean', [the additional difficulty arises:] Were not red and black also mentioned and the Rabbis nevertheless differ.[9] And should you reply that the Rabbis differ only in regard to green and white but not in that of red and black [the difficulty would arise:] For whose benefit, then, were red and black mentioned? If it be suggested: For that of R. Judah [it could be retorted:] Since green and white are regarded as unclean, was it at all necessary to mention red and black? Must it not then be conceded that these were mentioned for the benefit of the Rabbis who, it follows, do differ?[9]—Rather, explained R. Naḥman b. Isaac: The point at issue between them[10] is the question whether it is possible for the uterus[11] to open[12] without bleeding.[13] They[10]

(1) Which are not of the four unclean kinds. (2) With the Rabbis, maintaining that the woman is unclean. (3) I.e., to indicate that the Rabbis regard the woman in such cases as clean. (4) Which are among the four unclean colours. (5) Green and white. (6) Viz., that even with such colours R. Judah regards the woman as unclean. (7) From the Rabbis. How then could Samuel maintain that in such cases R. Judah regards the woman as clean? (8) Against whom, since he stated that in the case of the other kinds of blood 'all agree that she is clean', the difficulty just pointed out against Samuel equally applies. (9) From R. Judah and declare it clean. (10) R. Judah and the Rabbis. (11) Lit., 'grave'. (12) When an embryo or any other object passes out. (13) Blood of labour. Both R. Judah and the Rabbis regard the shapeless object as a piece of flesh, and not as a mass of congealed blood.

thus differ on the same principle as that on which the following Tannas differ. For it was taught: If a woman was in hard labour for two days[1] and on the third she aborted and[2] does not know what she had aborted[3] [21b] her case is one of doubtful childbirth and doubtful *zibah*, and[4] she must, therefore, bring a sacrifice[5] which may not be eaten.[6] R. Joshua ruled: She must bring a sacrifice and it may be eaten, since it is impossible for the uterus to open without some bleeding.[7]

Another version reads as follows. Rab Judah citing Samuel stated: R. Judah declared the woman unclean only where the object had the colour of one of the four kinds of blood, but if it

Hence whatever its colour the woman cannot be regarded as a menstruant. R. Judah, however, maintains that the uterus never opens without some bleeding though this may sometimes escape observation. The woman is, therefore, unclean on account of the inevitable discharge of the blood of labour even though the object was green or white and no blood whatsoever had been observed. The Rabbis, on the other hand, maintain that the uterus sometimes opens without any accompanying bleeding and the woman is, therefore, clean whenever no discharge is observed.

(1) Within the eleven days' period intervening between the menstrual periods. (2) Besides being uncertain whether the abortion was accompanied by bleeding. (3) *Sc.* whether it was an embryo or a mere lump of flesh. (4) Since it is not known whether (*a*) the abortion was an embryo in consequence of which, whether there was bleeding or not, she is to bring the sacrifice prescribed for a woman in childbirth; or (*b*) a mere lump of flesh, in which case, if there was no bleeding, no such sacrifice is due; or (*c*) there was a discharge of blood with (*b*) in which case (being that of a discharge on three consecutive days) she must bring the sacrifice prescribed for *zibah*. (5) To provide (cf. prev. n.) against the possibility of (*a*) or (*c*). (6) Since it is possible, as explained in note 3 (*b*), that she is neither in the position of one in childbirth nor in that of one in *zibah*, in consequence of which she is not liable to either sacrifice, and the bird that she brought as a sin-offering, having had its head pinched off in accordance with the ritual prescribed for such a sacrifice, is (owing to the possibility that it is no sacrifice at all and that it is, therefore, subject to the rules of slaughter appertaining to unconsecrated animals) thus forbidden to be eaten as the flesh of *nebelah*. (7) So that a sacrifice is due in either case: If she gave birth to an embryo she has to bring the sacrifice prescribed for one in childbirth, and if she merely aborted a lump of flesh, since this was inevitably accompanied by bleeding, she (cf. *supra* n. 4) is regarded as a *zabah* and is liable to bring the one prescribed for *zibah*.

had that of any of the other kinds of blood she is clean. But is this correct? Surely when R. Hoshaia arrived from Nehardea he came [to the schoolhouse] and brought with him a Baraitha: If a woman aborted a shapeless object that was red, black, green or white, if there was blood with it, she is unclean, otherwise she is clean; but R. Judah ruled: In either case she is unclean. Now here red, black, green and white were mentioned and R. Judah nevertheless disagrees.[1] And should you reply that R. Judah differs only in respect of red and black but not in that of green and white [the question would arise]: For[2] whose benefit then was green and white mentioned? If it be suggested: For that of the Rabbis [it could be retorted]: Since the Rabbis declared the woman clean even in the case of red and black blood, was it any longer necessary to state that the same law applies also to green and white? Must it not then be conceded that these were mentioned for the benefit of R. Judah who,[3] it thus follows, does differ?[4]—Rather, said R. Johanan,[5] the point at issue between them is the question whether it is possible for the uterus to open without bleeding.[1] They thus differ on the same principle as that on which the following Tannas differ. For it was taught: If a woman was in hard labour for two days and on the third she aborted and she does not know what she had aborted, her case is one of doubtful childbirth and doubtful *zibah*, and she must, therefore, bring a sacrifice which may not be eaten. R. Joshua ruled: She must bring a sacrifice, and it may be eaten, since it is impossible for the uterus to open without some bleeding.[1]

Our Rabbis taught: If a woman aborted a shapeless object, Symmachus ruled in the name of R. Meir, and R. Simeon b. Menasia likewise gave the same ruling: It must be split, and if there was blood in it the woman is unclean and if there is none in it she is clean. This is in agreement with the Rabbis but also more restrictive than the ruling of the Rabbis. It is 'in agreement with

(1) Cf. notes on prev. version. (2) Cf. BaḤ. (3) Since he ruled, 'In either case she is unclean'. (4) From the Rabbis who declared the woman clean. How then could Samuel maintain that 'if it had that of any of the other kinds of blood she is clean'? (5) Cf. Rashal. Cur. edd. in parenthesis, 'Rab Judah'.

the Rabbis' who ruled that it was possible for the uterus to open without bleeding; but it is 'also more restrictive than the ruling of the Rabbis', since they hold that only where the blood was with it[1] is the woman unclean[2] but not where it was only within it,[3] while Symmachus holds that [the woman is unclean] even if the blood was only within it.[3] Another [Baraitha] taught: If a woman aborted a shapeless object, R. Aḥa ruled: It must be split, and if its interior shows red,[4] the woman is unclean, otherwise she is clean. This is in agreement with Symmachus,[5] but also more restrictive than the ruling of Symmachus.[6] Again another [Baraitha] taught: If a woman aborted a shapeless object, R. Benjamin ruled: It must be split, and if there was a bone in it, its mother is unclean by reason of childbirth.[7] R. Ḥisda explained: This applies only to a white object.[8] So also when a pair [of scholars][9] from Adiabene arrived they came [into the schoolhouse] and brought with them the following Baraitha: If a woman aborted a white shapeless object it must be split and if there was a bone in it the mother is unclean by reason of childbirth.[7]

R. Joḥanan citing R. Simeon b. Yoḥai ruled: If a woman aborted a shapeless object it must be split, and if it contained a quantity of accumulated blood she is unclean, otherwise[10] she is clean. This is in agreement with Symmachus[11] but is also the most lenient of all the previous rulings.[12]

(1) Externally, *sc.* the passing out of the abortion was accompanied by bleeding. (2) Lit., 'yes'. (3) The object. (4) Though it contained no collected blood (5) Who laid down *supra* that blood in the interior of the object causes the same uncleanness as external blood that was discharged with it. (6) He required accumulated blood while here mere redness is regarded as a cause of uncleanness. (7) And she is subject to the restrictions of the laws of the prescribed days of both uncleanness and cleanness. Her period of uncleanness extends over fourteen days (prescribed for the birth of a female, and not seven as for a male) while her period of cleanness terminates on the fortieth day (prescribed for a male and not on the eightieth prescribed for a female). (8) Which is regarded as a kind of flesh. (9) *Zuga*. Var. lec. 'Zuza' and 'Zuwa'. (prop. noun). (10) *Sc.* if the blood is not accumulated in a considerable quantity. (11) Who ruled that blood in the interior is a cause of menstrual uncleanness as external blood. (12) Since according to it blood that is not

R. Jeremiah enquired of R. Zera: What is the ruling where a woman observed a discharge of blood in a tube?[1] Since the All Merciful has said, *In her flesh*[2] He implied: But not in a tube,[3] or is it possible that the text, '*In her flesh*', was required for the deduction that it[4] causes uncleanness within[5] as well as without?[6] —The other replied: The All Merciful said, *In her flesh*[2] implying: But not in a tube; for if the expression '*In her flesh*' had been required for the deduction that it[4] causes uncleanness within as well as without, Scripture should have said, *Her flesh*,[7] why then did it say, '*In her flesh*'? Both rulings may, therefore, be deduced. But did not R. Johanan rule in the name of R. Simeon b. Yohai: If a woman aborted a shapeless object it must be split, and if there was in it a quantity of accumulated blood she is unclean, otherwise she is clean?[8]—What a comparison![9] In that case it is usual for a woman to observe blood in a shapeless abortion,[10] but in this case it is not usual for a woman to observe blood in a tube.[11]

May it be suggested that the question of blood in a tube is a point at issue between Tannas? For it was taught: If a woman aborted a shapeless object, even though it is full of blood, it is only where there was a discharge of blood with it[12] that the woman is unclean; otherwise she is clean. R. Eliezer ruled: '*In her flesh*'[2] implies: But not [where the blood was] within a sac or within any shapeless abortion. (Is not R. Eliezer's ruling identical with that of the first Tanna?[13]—Read: For R. Eliezer ruled, '*In her flesh*'

accumulated (contrary to Symmachus) and a red interior (contrary to R. Aha) are no causes of uncleanness.

(1) That was inserted in the uterus. (2) Lev. XV, 19, dealing with the menstruant. (3) The woman is consequently clean. (4) Menstrual blood. (5) In the vagina after it had left the uterus. (6) *Sc.* when it had completely left the body. In the case of *zibah* and the emission of semen there can be no uncleanness before the discharge had left the body. (7) V. marg. gl. Cur. edd. in parenthesis 'in flesh'. (8) *Supra*. Now if the blood in the abortion causes uncleanness why should not also blood in a tube? (9) Lit., 'thus, now'. (10) It comes, therefore, under the description '*in her flesh*'; hence the woman's uncleanness. (11) Hence R. Zera's ruling that the woman is clean. (12) When it passed out. (13) Obviously it is. Why then should R. Eliezer merely repeat another authority's statement?

implies: But not [where the blood was] within a sac or within any shapeless abortion). But the Sages ruled: This is not menstrual blood but the blood of a shapeless object.[1] Now does not the first Tanna also declare her clean?[2] But the fact is that the difference between them is the case where the abortion was chapped. The first Tanna is of the opinion that *'In her flesh'* implies: But not [where the blood was] in a sac or in a shapeless object,[3] and the same applies also to a tube.[3] This, however, holds good only where it[4] was smooth,[5] but if it was chapped[6] the woman is unclean. What is his reason? It may be described as *'In her flesh'*.[7] Thereupon the Rabbis came to declare: Although it[4] was chapped [the woman is clean since] the discharge is not menstrual but that of the shapeless object.[8] Menstrual blood, however, is undoubtedly a cause of uncleanness[9] even if it was in a tube![10]—Abaye replied: As regards a tube all[11] agree that the woman is clean,[12] [22a] and they only differ in the case of a shapeless object.[13] One Master[14] holds that it is usual for a woman to observe blood in a shapeless object[15] and the Masters[16] hold that it is not usual for a woman to observe blood in such an object.[17] Raba replied that all[18] agreed

(1) The woman is consequently clean. (2) Cf. prev. n. What then is the difference between their respective views? (3) Since in these cases there is an interposition between the woman's body (*'her flesh'*) and the blood. (4) The abortion. (5) So that all the blood within it is completely separated from the woman's body. (6) In consequence of which some of the blood and the woman's body come in direct contact. (7) It being a Pentateuchal ordinance that when the blood was in direct contact with the woman's body uncleanness is caused. (8) As it is not menstrual at all it matters little whether it did, or did not come in contact with the body of the woman who, consequently, is in either case regarded as clean. (9) Since the discharge came from the uterus. (10) It thus follows that R. Zera's view is that of the first Tanna while the Rabbis opposed this view. Is it likely, however, that R. Zera adopted the view of the first Tanna, an individual, when it was opposed by the Rabbis who were in the majority? (11) Even the Rabbis. (12) Since the Scriptural text *'In her flesh'* cannot be applied to it (Rashal). (13) That was chapped. (14) The first Tanna. (15) The woman is, therefore, unclean. Only when the abortion is smooth, and the blood contained within it does not come in contact with the woman's body, the text, *'In her flesh'* cannot, be applied to it. (16) The Rabbis. (17) And if she does

that it is not usual for a woman to observe blood in a shapeless object, but it is on the question whether the woman is clean[1] and the interior of the uterus is unclean[2] that they differ, R. Eliezer being of the opinion that though the woman is clean[3] the blood is unclean since it comes through the uterus,[4] while the Rabbis hold the opinion that the woman is clean and the interior of the uterus is also clean.[5]

Rabba required of R. Huna: What is the ruling where one observed semen on a splinter?[6] Did the Divine Law say, *From him*[7] to indicate that the man is unclean only when it[8] issued naturally from his body but not when it was brought out by means of a splinter, or is it possible that the expression '*from him*' implies [that the man is unclean] only when his uncleanness[8] has come out of his body, in which case [he is unclean] even though that was effected by means of a splinter?—The other replied: You can infer the ruling [from the fact] that the man himself[9] becomes unclean only when the quantity of semen emitted suffices to close up the orifice of the membrum.[10] This then[11] implies that the man[12] is regarded as having touched the semen.[13] But, then, this[14] should

observe any it is no menstrual blood and she consequently remains clean. (18) Even the first Tanna.

(1) Because the blood was not menstrual. (2) And so conveys uncleanness to any blood that passes through it. (3) Because the blood was not menstrual. (4) Cf. prev. n. The blood consequently conveys uncleanness to any object with which it comes in contact and also to the woman herself to the extent that her uncleanness lasts until sunset. (5) So that the blood remains clean even after it had passed through the uterus. (6) After it had been inserted into the membrum. (7) *And if any man's seed of copulation go out from him* (A.V. Lev. XV, 16). (8) The semen. (9) Even where there was a natural discharge of semen. (10) Since the splinter used is inevitably smaller than the orifice, the quantity of semen extracted by it must obviously be less than the prescribed minimum. (11) Since (as in the case of *nebelah* for instance) a minimum has been prescribed, below which semen conveys no uncleanness. (12) Who is deemed unclean on account of the semen. (13) Had the uncleanness been conveyed to him on account of his observation of it, no minimum would have been prescribed, as none was prescribed for menstrual blood (a case of uncleanness through observation) and where the smallest drop of blood suffices to cause uncleanness. (14) The man's contact (cf. prev. nn.) with the semen, as his contact with a dead

not cause [the counting of the clean days] after a *zibah* to be void.[1] Why then was it taught: *This is the law of him that hath an issue,*[2] *and of him from whom the flow of seed*[3] *goeth out,*[4] as *zibah*[5] causes [the counting of the clean days] to be void[6] so does semen?—The other replied: As regards counting again, this is the reason why the previous counting is void: because it is impossible for semen to be emitted[7] without an admixture of some particles of *zibah*.[8] Now then,[9] this should cause the counting of all the seven days[10] to be void,[11] why then was it taught: '*This is the law of him that hath an issue* etc.', as *zibah* causes the clean days to be counted again so does semen? But in case you should assume that as *zibah* causes the counting of all the seven days[10] to be void so does semen also, it was expressly stated, *So that he is unclean thereby;*[4] you can apply to it[12] only that which had been said about it,[13] hence it causes the counting of one day only to be void?[14]—The other[15] replied: It is a decree of Scripture that an absolute *zibah* in which no semen is mixed causes the counting of all seven days to be void, but particles of *zibah* in which semen is mixed cause only the counting of one day[16] to be void.

R. Jose son of R. Ḥanina enquired of R. Eleazar: What is the ruling in the case of dry blood?[17] Did the Divine Law say, *Have an issue*[18] *of her blood*[19] to indicate that it must be actually flowing,[20]

creeping thing, for instance, whose uncleanness also is conveyed through contact.

(1) As is the case where there was such contact with a dead creeping thing. (2) *Sc. zibah.* (3) Semen. (4) Lev. XV, 32. (5) That occurs during the counting of the seven clean days after the termination of a previous *zibah*. (6) And, before ritual cleanness is attained seven clean days must be counted again. (7) During the days following a period of *zibah*. (8) It is the *zibah*, and not the semen, that causes the necessity for a new counting of the seven clean days. (9) Since (cf. prev. n.) the *zibah* is the cause. (10) If the discharge was discovered on the seventh day. (11) As is the case with a discharge of *zibah*. (12) Semen, which causes uncleanness for one day only. (13) *Sc.* (cf. prev. n.) it cannot be expected to cause a recount of seven days when it never causes uncleanness for more than one day. (14) How then could R. Huna maintain that *zibah* is the cause of the recount? (15) R. Huna. (16) The last, on which it was discovered. (17) *Sc.* does it, or does it not convey uncleanness? (18) Lit., 'will flow a flowing' (v. *infra*). (19) Lev. XV, 25. (20) Cf. prev. n. but one.

hence it refers only to fluid blood but not to dry, or is it possible that the expression, *'have an issue of her blood'*[1] was used merely because blood usually flows, but the same law in fact applies to dry blood also?—The other replied: You have learnt it: The blood of a menstruant and the flesh of a corpse convey uncleanness when fresh or when dry.[2] Said he [R. Jose] to him, 'Where the blood was first fresh and then it dried up, I have no question to ask; my question arises only where it was originally dry'.[3] 'This also', the other replied, 'you have learnt: IF A WOMAN ABORTED AN OBJECT THAT WAS LIKE A RIND, LIKE A HAIR, LIKE EARTH, LIKE RED FLIES, LET HER PUT IT IN WATER [22*b*] AND IF IT DISSOLVES SHE IS UNCLEAN.[4] But if so,[5] [should not uncleanness be caused] even if the object was not dissolved?—Rabbah replied: If it is not dissolved it is an independent creature.[6] But is there such a phenomenon?[7]—Yes; and so it was taught: R. Eleazar son of R. Zadok stated, A report of the following two incidents was brought up by my father from Tib'in[8] to Jamnia. It once happened that a woman was aborting objects like pieces of red rind and the people came and asked my father, and my father asked the Sages, and the Sages asked the physicians who explained to them that that woman had an internal sore [the crust] of which she cast out in the shape of the pieces of red rind. [It was ruled that] she should put them in water and if they dissolved she should be declared unclean. And yet another incident occurred when a woman was aborting objects like red hairs, and she came and asked my father, and my father asked the Sages, and the Sages asked the physicians who explained to them that the woman had a wart[9] in her internal organs and that that was the cause of her aborting objects like red hairs.[10]

(1) Lev. XV, 25. (2) *Infra* 54*b*. (3) Sc. the abortion was a piece of dry blood. (4) Because it is regarded as unclean blood though when she first observed the object it was as dry, for instance, as earth. (5) That dry blood also causes uncleanness. (6) And cannot be regarded as congealed blood. (7) An abortion LIKE A RIND OF LIKE A HAIR. (8) In Galilee west of Sepphoris. (9) From which grew hairs. (10) Tosef. Nid. IV.

LET[1] HER PUT IT IN WATER AND IF IT DISSOLVES SHE IS UNCLEAN. Resh Laḳish ruled: And [this must be done] with lukewarm water.[2] So it was also taught: Let her put it in water, viz., in lukewarm water. R. Simeon b. Gamaliel ruled: She [must attempt to] crush it with spittle on her nail. What is the practical difference between them?[3]—Rabina replied: The practical difference between them is [an abortion that can be] crushed by the exercise of pressure.[4]

Elsewhere we have learnt: How long must they[5] be soaked in the lukewarm water?[6] Twenty-four hours.[7] Now in this case,[8] what length of time is required? Do we require a period of twenty-four hours or not?[9] Is it only in regard to a creeping thing and carrion, which are tough, that a twenty-four hours' soaking is required but not in that of blood, which is soft, or is it possible that there is no difference?—This is undecided.[10]

IF AN ABORTION WAS IN THE SHAPE OF FISHES. But why does not R. Judah[11] disagree[12] in this case also?[13]—Resh Laḳish replied: This[14] was indeed learnt as a controversial ruling,[15] and it[14]

(1) Cf. Bomb. ed. Cur. edd. do not indicate that this is a quotation from our Mishnah. (2) Resistance to which is proof that it is no mass of congealed blood. Resistance to cold water alone is no proof that it is not congealed blood, since it is possible that it would dissolve in lukewarm water and the woman, therefore, cannot be declared clean. (3) R. Simeon b. Gamaliel and the first Tanna. (4) But cannot be dissolved by mere immersion in lukewarm water. According to the first Tanna, since lukewarm water cannot dissolve it, it cannot be regarded as blood, while according to R. Simeon b. Gamaliel, since it may be squashed by pressure, it must be regarded as blood. (5) Unclean things such, for instance, as a dead creeping thing and carrion which have become dry. (6) To restore them to their original condition of freshness. These (as stated *infra*) convey uncleanness only when fresh but not when dry. (7) *Infra* 54*b*. (8) RIND, HAIR, EARTH etc. spoken of in our Mishnah. (9) *Sc.* even a lesser period suffices to establish that they are masses of congealed blood. (10) *Teḳu.* (11) Who in an earlier clause of our Mishnah ruled, IN EITHER CASE SHE IS UNCLEAN. (12) With the ruling that, OTHERWISE SHE IS CLEAN. (13) *Sc.* why does he not here also maintain that the woman is unclean in either case? (14) The anonymous ruling under discussion. (15) R. Judah and the Rabbis being in disagreement on it.

represents only the opinion of the Rabbis. R. Joḥanan, however, replied: It[1] may even be said to agree with R. Judah,[2] for R. Judah gave his ruling[3] only there, in the case of a SHAPELESS OBJECT, since it is the nature of blood to congeal and to assume the form of a shapeless object,[4] but [not here,[5] since] it[6] can never assume the form of a creature.[7] According, however, to that version in which R. Joḥanan stated that 'the point at issue between them is the question whether it is possible for the uterus to open without bleedings',[8] should not R. Judah[9] have disagreed in this case also?—He who learnt that version[10] reads here: Both R. Joḥanan and Resh Laḳish replied: This[11] was learnt as a controversial ruling,[12] and it[11] represents only the view of the Rabbis.

IF AN ABORTION HAD THE SHAPE OF A BEAST etc. Rab Judah citing Samuel stated: What is the reason of R. Meir? Since in their case[13] an expression of forming[14] is used as in that of man.[15] Now then, if an abortion was in the likeness of a sea-monster[16] would its mother be unclean by reason of child-birth, since an expression of forming was used in its case as in that of man, it having been said, *And God created*[17] *the great sea-monsters?*[18]—I can answer: An expression of forming[19] may be deduced from another expression of forming[20]

(1) The anonymous ruling under discussion. (2) Who in this case is of the same opinion as the Rabbis. (3) That IN EITHER CASE SHE IS UNCLEAN. (4) Hence his ruling (cf. prev. n.) whenever the object had the colour of one of the four kinds of unclean blood. His ruling is thus entirely independent of the question whether the uterus does or does not open without bleeding. (5) In the case of an abortion of FISHES, LOCUSTS etc. (6) Blood. (7) And since the abortion under discussion did assume the form of a creature, R. Judah agrees with the Rabbis that OTHERWISE SHE IS CLEAN. (8) *Supra* 21*b*. (9) Since the character of the abortion itself is of no consequence. (10) The one just referred to. (11) The anonymous ruling under discussion. (12) R. Judah and the Rabbis being in disagreement on it. (13) Beasts and birds. (14) *And . . . the Lord God formed every beast . . . and every fowl* (Gen. II, 19). (15) *Then the Lord God formed man* (ibid. 7). (16) Which may be classed as a kind of fish. (17) This is now assumed to be analogous to an expression of 'forming'. (18) Gen. I, 21. The answer being presumably in the affirmative, how could our Mishnah rule that IF AN ABORTION WAS IN THE SHAPE OF FISHES . . . SHE IS CLEAN? (19) *And . . . the Lord God formed every beast . . . and every fowl* (Gen. II, 19). (20) *Then the Lord God formed man* (ibid. 7).

but one of creating[1] may not be deduced from one of forming.[2] But where lies the practical difference between the two expressions? Surely the School of R. Ishmael taught: *And the priest shall return*,[3] *and the priest shall come*,[4] 'returning' and 'coming' are the same thing![5] Furthermore, why should not one expression of 'creating'[1] be deduced from another expression of 'creating', it being written, *And God created man in His own image?*[6]—I can answer: '*And ... created*'[6] is required for its own context while '*and ... formed*' is available for deduction, hence it is that the expression of 'forming'[7] may be deducted from the similar one of 'forming'.[2] On the contrary [might it not be submitted that] '*And ... formed*'[2] was required for its own context while '*and ... created*'[6] is available for deduction, hence the expression of 'creating'[1] may be deduced from 'creating'?[6] —The fact is that the expression '*And ... formed*' is available for deduction on the two sides: It is available in the case of man[8] and it is also available in that of beast;[9] but the expression of '*And ... created*' is available for deduction only in the case of man[10] but it is not available for the purpose in that of sea-monsters.[11] But why is it[12] regarded available for deduction in the case of beast? If it be suggested because it is written, *And God made the beast of the earth*[13] and it is also written, *And out of the ground the Lord God formed every beast of the field*,[14] is not a similar expression [it may be retorted] also available for deduction in the case of a sea-monster, since it is written, *And God made ... and every thing that creepeth upon the ground*,[15] and it is also written, *And God created the great sea-*

(1) Used about sea-monsters in Gen. I, 21. (2) *Then the Lord God formed man* (ibid. II, 7). (3) Lev. XIV, 39. (4) Ibid. 44. (5) And an analogy between them may be drawn, though they are derived from different roots, v. Ḥul. 85*a*. Why then should no analogy be drawn between 'forming' and 'creating'? (6) Gen. I, 27. (7) *And ... the Lord God formed every beast ... and every fowl* (Gen. II, 19). (8) Since the expression of 'creating' (Gen. I, 27) has also been used about him. (9) As will be explained presently. (10) Concerning whom there is also the expression of 'forming' (Gen. II, 7). (11) Since Scripture contains no other similar expression about them. (12) The expression of 'forming'. (13) Gen. I, 25; an expression of 'making'. (14) Ibid. II, 19; expression of 'forming'. (15) Ibid. I, 25, an expression of 'making' which presumably includes the sea-monsters.

monsters?[1]—*'Every thing that creepeth'* that was written in the previously mentioned verse refers to those on the dry land. What, however, is the practical difference between an expression that is available for deduction on one side and one that is available for deduction on two sides?[2]—The practical difference is the statement Rab Judah made in the name of Samuel who had it from R. Ishmael:[3] From any *gezerah shawah*[4] neither of whose terms is available for deduction[5] no deduction may be made;[6] if one of the terms is available for the purpose, then according to R. Ishmael, a deduction may be made and no refutation may be offered, while according to the Rabbis deduction may be made[7] but a refutation[8] may be offered; and if both terms are available for deduction, all[9] agree that deduction may be made and no refutation may be offered. As to R. Ishmael, however, what is the practical difference between a *gezerah shawah* one of whose terms only is available for deduction and one both of whose terms are available for the purpose?—The practical difference is that where there is one of which one term only is available for deduction and another both of which both terms are available for deduction we must leave the former [23a] and make the deduction from the latter. And it is for this reason[10] that in the case of beast the All Merciful made both terms available for deduction: In order that no deduction shall be made from one of which one term only is available for deduction.[11]

R. Aḥa son of Raba taught this[12] in the name of R. Eleazar in the direction of leniency. From any *gezerah shawah* none of whose terms is available for deduction, one may make the deduction and one may also offer a refutation; if one of its terms only is available for the purpose, deduction, according to R. Ishmael, may be made

(1) Gen. I, 21, an expression of 'creating' which is superfluous in view of that of 'making' (cf. prev. n.) and, therefore, available for deduction. (2) I.e., why is deduction in the latter case preferable to the former? (3) The last six words apparently require emendation. (4) V. Glos. (5) Lit., 'that is not vacant at all'. (6) Even where no refutation can be offered. (7) If no refutation can be offered against it. (8) If one can be suggested. (9) Even the Rabbis. (10) According to the Rabbis. (11) Since such a *gezerah shawah*, as stated *supra*, could be refuted. (12) The statement cited *supra* by Rab Judah.

and no refutation may be offered, while according to the Rabbis deduction may be made and a refutation may be offered; and if two of its terms are available for deduction, all agree that deduction may be made and no refutation may be offered. But according to the Rabbis[1] what is the practical difference between one whose one term is available for deduction and one none of whose terms is available for deduction?—The practical difference between them is the case where you find a *gezerah shawah* one of whose terms is available for deduction and another none of whose terms is available for the purpose, and neither the one nor the other can be refuted, in such a case we must leave the one neither of whose terms is available and make deduction from the one of which one term is available. But what refutation is there in this case?[2]—One might object:[3] A man is different[4] since he contracts uncleanness[5] even when he is alive.[6]

R. Ḥiyya b. Abba citing R. Joḥanan also stated,[7] This is the reason of R. Meir: Since the expression of 'forming' has been used in its case as in that of man. Said R. Ammi to him: Now then,

(1) Who maintain that whether one, or none of the terms is available for deduction both deduction and refutation are admissible. (2) The analogy (*supra* 22*b*) with man. *Sc.* since, as was explained *supra*, the only reason why deduction is made from a *gezerah shawah* both of whose terms are available for the purpose in preference to one of which one term only is available is the consideration that while the latter can be refuted when a logical refutation is offered the former cannot be refuted even in such a case, it follows that where no refutation can be offered it is immaterial whether the deduction is made from the one or the other. And since R. Meir (*supra* 22*b*) preferred the *gezerah shawah* between man and beast (both of whose terms are available) to that of man and sea-monsters (whose one term only is available) he must have intended to avoid thereby a refutation that had suggested itself to him. Now what was that refutation? (3) Lit., 'because there is (an argument) to refute'. (4) From other creatures. (5) From a dead creeping thing, for instance. (6) Other creatures, however, while alive can never become unclean. It could, therefore, have been argued that man who is subject to the one restriction of uncleanness may also be a cause of uncleanness to his mother when he is born, but any other creature which is not subject to the former restriction is also exempt from the latter. (7) Like Rab Judah, *supra* 22*b*.

If an abortion was in the shape of a mountain would the woman who aborted it[1] be unclean by reason of the birth because it is said, *For, lo, He that formeth*[2] *the mountains and createth the wind?*[3]—The other replied: Does she ever abort a mountain? She can only abort something in the shape of a stone, and that can only be described as a lump.[4] But then, if the abortion was some inflated object would the woman who aborted it[1] be unclean by reason of the birth because the expression of '*creating*' has been used about it as about man, since it is written, *And createth*[5] *the wind?*[3] And should you reply: It[6] is not available for deduction,[7] [it could be retorted:] Since it could have been written, 'Formeth the mountains and the wind', and yet it was written '*And createth the wind*' it may be inferred, may it not, that it[6] was intended to be made available for deduction?—The other replied: An analogy for legal purposes may be drawn between words that occur in the Pentateuch[8] but no analogy may be drawn between words that occur respectively in the Pentateuch and in the post-Pentateuchal books.[9]

Rabbah[10] b. Bar Ḥana citing R. Joḥanan stated, This is the reason of R. Meir: Because [the pupils[11] of] their[12] eyes are similar to those of human beings. Now then, if an abortion was in the likeness of a serpent would the woman who aborted it[1] be unclean on account of the birth since its eye-ball is round like that of a human eye? And should you suggest that the law is so indeed [it could be retorted]: Why then was not the serpent mentioned?[13]—If the serpent had been mentioned[13] it might have been presumed that only in the case of the serpent do the Rabbis disagree with R. Meir, since the expression of 'forming' was not written about it but that in the case of a beast or a wild animal they do not differ

(1) Lit., 'its mother'. (2) An expression of 'forming' like that used of man. (3) Amos IV, 13. (4) To which the term 'mountain' cannot apply. (5) An expression of 'creating' like that used of man. (6) Cf. prev. n. (7) I.e., it is required for its own context. (8) *Torah*, in its restrictive connotation. (9) *Ḳabalah*, lit., 'acceptance', 'tradition' as distinct from *Torah*. (Cf. prev. n.). (10) Cur. edd. in parenthesis 'he said'. (11) V. Rashi and *infra*. (12) Beasts. (13) In our Mishnah, among the shapes of creatures that cause the woman's uncleanness.

from him since the expression of 'forming' had been written about it.[1] But was it not stated in regard to blemishes,[2] 'One whose eyeball is like that of a man'?[3]—This is no difficulty, the one[4] refers to the black of the eye[5] while the other refers to the slit.[6]

R. Jannai stated, This is the reason of R. Meir: Because their[7] eyes are fixed in the front of their heads[8] like those of men. But what about[9] a bird whose eyes are not fixed in the front of its head and R. Meir nevertheless ruled that it is a cause of uncleanness? —Abaye replied: This[10] applies only to the *ḳadia*[11] and the *ḳipufa*.[12] It[10] does not then apply to other birds! An objection was raised: R. Ḥanina b. Gamaliel[13] stated, I approve of the view of R. Meir in regard to beasts and wild animals and that of the Sages in regard to birds. Now what did he mean by 'birds'? If it be suggested: *ḳadia*[11] and *ḳipufa*[12] [the difficulty would arise]: Wherein do beasts and wild animals differ [from other creatures]? [Obviously in that] that their eyes are fixed in front of their heads like those of men. Now are not those of the *ḳadia*[11] and the *ḳipufa*[12] fixed in the same position?[14] Consequently[15] he must have meant other birds. Thus it may be implied, may it not, that R. Meir differs from the Rabbis in regard to the other birds?[16]—Some part is missing[17] and this is the correct reading: R. Ḥanina b. Gamaliel[13] stated, I approve of the view of R. Meir in regard to beasts and wild animals, this applying also to the *ḳadia* and the *ḳipufa*; and that of the Sages

(1) Hence the omission of the serpent. (2) Which disqualify a beast. (3) Bek. 40*a*. Now since such likeness is regarded as a blemish it is obvious that the normal eye of a beast is different from the human one. How then could R. Joḥanan maintain that a beast's eyes are like human eyes? (4) R. Joḥanan's statement. (5) The pupil, which has the same round shape in man and beasts. (6) In which the eye is fixed. This is not so round in the eye of a beast as in the human eye. (7) Beasts'. (8) Lit., 'go before them'. Those of fishes and serpents are fixed in the sides of their heads. (9) Lit., 'and behold'. (10) R. Meir's ruling just cited. (11) Or (as cur. edd.) '*karia*', a species of owls. (12) Also a species of owls. (13) Cf. Tosaf. *supra* 8*b*, s.v. אחוה. Cur. edd. in parenthesis, 'Antigonus'. (14) Of course they are. Consequently they should have been subject to the same law as beasts and wild animals. (15) Since he made them subject to a different law. (16) If he had not differed, there would have been no point in R. Ḥanina's statement, 'I would approve . . . that of the Sages'. (17) In R. Ḥanina's statement.

in regard to other birds; for even R. Meir disagreed with them only in regard to the *ḳadia* and the *ḳipufa*, but in the case of other birds he agrees with them. And so it was also taught: R. Eliezer son of R. Zadok stated: An abortion that had the shape of a beast or a wild animal is, according to the view of R. Meir, regarded as a valid birth, but according to the view of the Sages it is no valid birth; and in the case of birds an examination should take place. Now according to whose view should an examination take place? Obviously[1] according to that of R. Meir who ruled that the law[2] applied[3] to the *ḳadia* and the *ḳipufa* and not to the other birds! R. Aḥa son of R. Iḳa retorted: No; the examination should take place according to the Rabbis who ruled that *ḳadia* and *ḳipufa* are regarded as valid births[3] but not other birds. But wherein does the *ḳadia* or the *ḳipufa* in this respect differ from beasts and wild animals?[4]—In that they have jaws like those of men.[5]

R. Jeremiah enquired of R. Zera: According to R. Meir who ruled: 'A beast that was in a woman's body is a valid birth', what is the law where its father[6] received for it a token of betrothal?[7]—
—In what respect could this[8] ever matter?—In respect of causing its sister to be forbidden.[9] This then presumes[10] that it is viable! But did not Rab Judah citing Rab state: R. Meir gave his ruling[11] only because in the case of its own species[12] it is viable?[13] Said R. Aḥa b. Jacob: 'To such an extent did R. Jeremiah try[14] to make R. Zera laugh; but the latter did not laugh'.[15]

(1) Lit., 'not?' (2) That the birth is regarded as valid. (3) Lit., 'yes'. (4) Who also have their eyes in the sides of their heads. If according to the Rabbis an abortion of the former causes uncleanness why should not also the latter? (5) Which beasts and wild animals have not. (6) Who is entitled to effect the betrothal of his daughter while she is a minor. (7) Which is a valid *ḳinyan* (v. Glos.) in the case of a normal child. (8) Such an absurd betrothal. (9) To marry the man who betrothed it. It is forbidden to marry a wife's sister. (10) Since a wife's sister is forbidden to a man only during the lifetime of his wife. (11) That an abortion of a beast or wild animal is regarded as a valid birth. (12) Beast born from beast or wild animal from wild animal. (13) But not when a woman aborted such creatures. The question of wife's sisters, consequently, could never arise in such a case. What then was the point in R. Jeremiah's peculiar enquiry? (14) By his absurd enquiries. (15) It is forbidden to indulge in laughter in this world (cf. Ber. 31a).

[Reverting to] the [previous] text, 'Rab Judah citing Rab stated: R. Meir gave his ruling only because in the case of its own species it is viable.' Said R. Jeremiah of Difti: [23b] We also learnt the same thing:[1] An abortion in the shape of a beast, wild animal or bird [is regarded as a valid birth];[2] so R. Meir. And the Sages ruled: [It is no valid birth][3] unless it has the features of a human being. But if the abortion was a *sandal*,[4] a placenta or a foetus with some articulated shape, or if a child issued cut up in pieces, the son born after it is regarded as the firstborn in respect of inheritance but he is no firstborn as far as the priest is concerned.[5] Now if one could imagine that such an abortion is viable, would the son born after it be regarded as the firstborn in regard to inheritance?[6] Said Raba: It may well be maintained that it is viable but the case there[7] is different [from what might have been expected][8] since Scripture said, *The first of his mourning*[9] which refers to the one for whom[10] his[11] heart aches, and thus excludes an abortion for which[12] his heart does not ache.[13]

R. Adda b. Ahaba enquired of Abaye: According to R. Meir who ruled that a beast that was in the bowels of a woman is a valid birth, what is the ruling where a human child was in the bowels of a beast?[14]—In what respect does this matter?—In that of permitting it to be eaten.[15] But why can you not solve this question from the following ruling of R. Joḥanan; for R. Joḥanan ruled:

(1) That an abortion of a beast or wild animal is not viable. (2) In regard to the birthright. If a son is born after such an abortion, though he is entitled to a double share in his father's estate (as a firstborn son, since the abortion is not viable) he (unlike an actual firstborn son) need not be redeemed from the priest. The words in square brackets are wanting in the Mishnah Bek. 46a and appear in cur. edd. here in parenthesis. (3) Even (cf. prev. n.) as regards the exemption from redemption of the son born after it. (4) Flat, fish-shaped. (5) Bek. 46a. Cf. *supra* n. 2. (6) Of course not. Since, however, he is so regarded in respect of inheritance it is obvious that an abortion of the nature described is not viable. (7) Inheritance. (8) From its viability. (9) Deut. XXI, 17. E.V., *The first of his strength*. (10) If he dies. (11) The father's. (12) Cf. prev. n. but one. (13) Hence it is that an abortion cannot be treated as 'firstborn' and the privilege is, therefore, passed on to the next child if it is a son. (14) And was discovered after the beast had been slain. (15) Like the beast in which it was found.

If one slaughtered a beast and found in it an object of the shape of a dove it[1] is forbidden to be eaten?[2]—What a comparison! In that case[1] there are neither cloven feet nor hoofs, but in this case, granted that there are no cloven feet, there is at least some thing like a hoof.[3]

THE SAGES, HOWEVER, RULED: ANYTHING THAT HAS NOT etc. R. Jeremiah b. Abba citing Rab stated: All[4] agree that if its body was that of a he-goat and its face that of a human being it is regarded as a human child;[5] if its body was that of a human being and its face that of a he-goat it is no valid birth.[5] They[4] differ only where it had the face of a human being but was so created that one of its eyes was like that of a beast, since R. Meir holds that it[6] need only have some of the features of a human face[7] while the Sages hold that it[6] must have all the features of a human face. They[8] said to R. Jeremiah b. Abba, Was not the reverse taught: R. Meir said, 'It must have all the features of a human face'[9] while the Sages said, 'It need only have some of the features of a human face'?[9]—He answered them: If this was taught so you may well rely on it.[10]

R. Jeremiah b. Abba citing R. Joḥanan ruled:[11] The forehead, the eyebrows, the eyes, the cheeks and the chin must all be present at the same time.[12] Raba, however, citing Ḥasa ruled:[11] The forehead, the eyebrow, the eye, the cheek and the chin must all be present at the same time.[12] These, however,[13] do not differ in principle from one another, since the former ruled according to him who said that[12] 'it must have all the features of a human face',

(1) The dove-like object. (2) Ḥul. 69a. (3) The two cases cannot consequently be compared, and the fanciful question must remain unsolved. (4) R. Meir and the Sages. (5) The face being the determining factor. (6) To be a valid birth. (7) One human eye, therefore, suffices. (8) So Bomb. ed. and marg. gl. Cur. edd. 'he'. (9) For a justification of the rendering cf. Tosaf. (10) Lit., 'it was taught', *sc.* while he was certain that what he reported had behind it the weighty authority of Rab, it was quite legitimate for them, since they had a tradition to the contrary, to follow their own tradition. (11) According to the Rabbis (v. *infra*). (12) If the abortion is to be regarded as a valid birth. (13) R. Joḥanan and Ḥasa, though with the exception of the forehead, the former speaks in the plural and the latter in the singular.

while the latter ruled according to him who stated, 'it need only have some of the features of a human face'.

An objection was raised: By the 'shape of the face' of which the Sages spoke[1] was meant the presence of even only one of the features of the face,[2] except the ear.[3] This shows, does it not, that a single feature suffices?[4]—Abaye replied: That[5] was taught only to indicate what constitutes a hindrance,[6] and it[5] is in agreement with him who stated [that the reading][7] was 'it must have all the features of a human face'. And if you prefer I might say: It[5] is in fact in agreement with him who stated that the reading[7] was 'it need only have one of the features of a human face' but[8] the meaning[9] of 'one'[10] is one of each.[11]

Raba ruled: If a foetus was created with one eye and one thigh, the woman who gives birth to it[12] is unclean[13] if these were on the side,[14] but if they were in the middle[15] she is clean.[16] Raba further ruled: If a child's gullet is perforated[17] his mother is unclean,[18] but if his gullet is closed up[19] she is clean.[20]

Our Rabbis taught: If a woman aborted a stumped body she is not unclean by reason of such a birth. And what is meant by a stumped body?—Rabbi replied: One short of a part which if taken from a live person would cause him to die. And what is the extent of the part that if taken from a live person would cause him to die?—R. Zakkai replied: [24a] To the top of the knee

(1) As a determining factor whether an abortion is a valid birth. (2) One eye or the forehead, for instance. (3) Tosef. Nid. IV. Though the ear has the human shape the abortion is no valid birth if the other features are like those of a beast. (4) To determine that a birth is valid. How then could it be said *supra* that all the features must be human? (5) The Baraitha just cited as an objection. (6) *Sc.* that even the presence of one feature that was not human causes the abortion, according to the Rabbis, to be regarded as an invalid birth. (7) According to the Rabbis. (8) In justification of Ḥasa's ruling. (9) Lit., 'and what (is the meaning of)'. (10) 'One of the features of the face', in the Baraitha cited. (11) Of the double features; as Ḥasa in fact stated. (12) Lit., 'its mother'. (13) As one who bore a normal child. (14) Of the face and body respectively. *sc.* in their normal position. (15) Cf. prev. n. *mut. mut.* (16) Since such an abortion is no valid birth. (17) When it is born. (18) Because, the child being viable, the birth is valid. (19) So that the child is not viable. (20) Such a birth being invalid.

joint.[1] R. Jannai replied: To his lower orifices.[2] R. Joḥanan citing R. Jose b. Joshua replied: To the position of his navel. The point at issue between R. Zakkai and R. Jannai is whether a *ṭrefah*[3] animal[4] can survive.[5] The latter holds that a *ṭrefah* animal can survive[6] while the former holds that it cannot survive.[7] The point at issue between R. Jannai and R. Joḥanan[8] is a ruling of R. Eleazar; for R. Eleazar ruled: If the haunch and its hollow were removed the animal is *nebelah*.[9] R. Papa stated: The dispute[10] refers only to cases where the lower part of the body is affected[11] but if the upper part is affected,[12] even if the missing part is ever so small the woman is clean.[13] So also said R. Giddal in the name of R. Joḥanan: If a woman aborted a foetus whose skull is a shapeless lump she[14] is clean.[13] R. Giddal citing R. Joḥanan further stated: If a woman aborted a foetus shaped like the ramification of a palm-tree[15] she is clean.[13]

It was stated: If a woman aborted a foetus whose face was mashed,[16] R. Joḥanan ruled: She[14] is unclean; and Resh Laḳish ruled: She is clean. R. Joḥanan raised an objection against Resh Laḳish: If a woman aborted a shaped[17] hand or a shaped foot she[14] is subject to the uncleanness of birth[18] and there is no need to consider the possibility[19] that it might have come from a shapeless body.[20] Now if it were so,[21] should it not have been stated, 'The

(1) Inclusive; form the foot upwards. A person cannot live after such an amputation (v. *infra*). (2) Of the intestines and the urethra. Cf. prev. n. second clause. (3) V. Glos. (4) Including man. (5) V. Ḥul 42*a*. (6) Hence his ruling that the birth is valid unless the missing part of the body extended as high as the lower orifices. (7) The birth is consequently invalid even if the missing part extended as far as the knee joint only. (8) Both of whom agree that a fatally wounded animal can survive. (9) V. Glos. Ḥul. 21*a*, 32*b*. (10) On the extent of the missing part of the body that renders a birth invalid and causes the woman to remain clean. (11) Lit., 'from below to above'. (12) Lit., 'from above to below'; if a part of the skull, for instance, is missing. (13) Since such a child is not viable and his birth is no valid one. (14) Lit., 'his mother'. (15) *Sc.* the lower part of his body was shapeless while his limbs branched out from its upper part. (16) But its features were not entirely indistinguishable. (17) Lit., 'cut'. (18) *Sc.* since it is unknown whether the abortion was a male or a female the restrictions of both are imposed upon her. (19) Which would exempt her from the certainty of uncleanness. (20) *Supra* 18*a*, *infra* 28*a*. (21) That,

possibility that it might have come from a shapeless body or from a foetus whose face was mashed'?[1]

R. Papi stated:[2] Where its[3] face was mashed no one[4] disputes the ruling that the woman is unclean. They only differ where its face was entirely covered over,[5] and the statement[6] was made in the reverse order: R. Johanan ruled: His mother is clean; and Resh Lakish ruled: His mother is unclean. Should not then[7] Resh Lakish raise an objection against R. Johanan from that [Baraitha]?[8]—Because the latter could have answered him: 'A stumped body' and 'a foetus whose face was entirely covered over' are identical terms.[9]

The sons of R. Ḥiyya once toured the countryside. When they appeared before their father he asked them, 'Has any case been submitted for your consideration?' 'The case of a foetus whose face was entirely covered over', they told him 'has been submitted to us, and we decided that the woman was unclean'. 'Go back', he said to them, 'and declare as clean that which you have declared unclean. For what did you think?[10] That you are restricting the law;[11] but this is a restriction that results in a relaxation, for thereby[12] you also allow her[13] the days of cleanness'.[14]

as Resh Lakish maintains, the birth of a foetus with a mashed face causes no uncleanness to its mother.

(1) Since both these possibilities would be causes of the woman's cleanness. Why then was only the former possibility mentioned? (2) In accordance with a tradition he received from his teacher (v. Rashi). (3) A foetus'. (4) Not even Resh Lakish. (5) *Sc.* none of the features was distinguishable. (6) Of the dispute. (7) Since it is now R. Johanan who declared the woman clean. (8) From which the latter raised an objection *supra* against the former; thus: Why did not the Baraitha add 'the possibility that it may have come . . . from a foetus whose face was entirely covered over'? (9) Both indicating an abortion none of whose features are distinguishable. This could not be given as a reply in the case of a mashed face where some of the features are not altogether indistinguishable. (10) When declaring the woman unclean. (11) Since it was unknown whether the foetus was male or female the woman, having been declared unclean, would have to remain in her uncleanness for a period of fourteen days (as for a female) and not only for seven days (as for a male). (12) By regarding the abortion as a valid birth. (13) As a woman after childbirth. (14) Which even in the case of a male, are no less than

It was stated: If one aborted a creature that had two backs and two spinal columns, Rab ruled: In the case of a woman it is no valid birth[1] and in that of a beast it is forbidden to be eaten;[2] but Samuel ruled: In the case of a woman it is a valid birth[3] and in that of a beast it is permitted to be eaten.[4] On what principle do they[5] differ?—On that of R. Ḥanin b. Abba; for R. Ḥanin b. Abba stated, '*The cloven*[6] is a creature that has two backs and two spinal columns'.[7] Rab maintains that such a creature exists nowhere in the world, and that when the All Merciful taught Moses about it[8] he must have taught him about one that was still in her dam's bowels, while Samuel maintains that such a creature does exist in the world so that when the All Merciful taught Moses about it[8] he taught him about the species in general,[9] but one that is still in its dam's bowels is well permitted to be eaten.[10] R. Shimi b. Ḥiyya pointed out an objection to Rab: R. Ḥanina b. Antigonus stated, Any [firstling of beasts] that had two backs and two spinal columns is unfit for the Temple service;[11] from which[12] it is obvious, is it not, that it is viable?[13]—'Is it you, Shimi?' the other[14] replied, 'this[15]

thirty-three. Any discharge of blood within this period would consequently be regarded as clean, whereas if the abortion had not been declared to be a valid birth the discharge would have imposed upon the woman the uncleanness of a menstruant.

(1) And she remains, therefore, clean. (2) Even if it was found in the ritually slaughtered body of its dam, and much more so if it was aborted. (3) And the woman is consequently subject to the laws of uncleanness prescribed for one after childbirth. (4) As deduced from Scripture in Ḥul. 69*b*. (5) Rab and Samuel. (6) *Ha-Shesu'ah*, Deut. XIV, 7. (7) Ḥul. 60*b*. (8) That it must not be eaten. (9) Lit., 'in the world'. (10) Wherever the dam is of the clean beasts and was ritually slain. (11) Bek. 43*b*; because these are regarded as blemishes. (12) Since it is only forbidden as a sacrifice and is presumably permitted for consumption in the case of unconsecrated animals. (13) If it had not been viable it could not have been permitted to be eaten. The permissibility to eat the creature, even after it was born, thus raises an objection against both Rab (who ruled that it was always forbidden) and against Samuel (who permitted it only when it was in its dam's bowels). V. Marginal Gloss. Cur. edd. in parenthesis add 'and this is a difficulty against Rab'. (14) Rab, who was his grandfather. (15) R. Ḥanina's ruling from which it follows that a double-backed creature is viable.

refers to a case where its spinal column was only crooked'.[1]

An objection was raised: Among embryos[2] there are some that are forbidden[3] viz., a four monthly embryo among small cattle, and an eight monthly one among large cattle, and one that is younger[4] is equally forbidden. From this is excluded one that had two backs and two spinal columns. Now what is meant by 'is excluded'? Obviously that it[5] is excluded from the category of embryos[6] in that it is forbidden to be eaten even while still in its dam's body?[7]—Rab[8] explains in accordance with his own view, and Samuel[9] explains it in accordance with his view. 'Rab explains in accordance with his own view', thus: A four monthly embryo among small cattle and an eighth monthly one among large cattle, and one that is younger is equally forbidden. This applies only where it saw the light[10] but while it is still in its dam's bowels it is permitted; but from this is excluded one that has two backs and two spinal columns which, even while still in its dam's bowels, is also forbidden. [24b] Samuel also 'explains it in accordance with his view', thus: A four monthly embryo among small cattle, and an eight monthly one among large cattle, and one that is younger is equally forbidden. This, however, applies only to one whose period of pregnancy[11] had not ended, but if the period has ended it is permitted; and from this is excluded one who had two backs and two spinal columns which, even though its period of pregnancy had ended, it is forbidden if

(1) And consequently had the appearance of two backs. Such a creature is viable. (2) Of clean beasts. (3) To be eaten, as *nebelah*, even after their birth. (4) Lit., 'from it and below'. (5) The beast with the two backs and the two spinal columns. (6) Which are permitted if found in their dam's body. (7) How then could Samuel maintain that even while it is in its dam's body it is permitted? (8) Against whom no objection was raised from the last cited Baraitha but who nevertheless finds a difficulty in its present form in reconciling its first and last clauses. As the first clause deals with those who saw the light the last one (double-backed creatures) also deals obviously with one who saw the light. But its permissibility would be contrary to the ruling of Rab. (9) Who has to explain the objection raised against him (cf. prev. n. but one). (10) Lit., 'went out to the air of the world'. (11) Lit., 'its months'.

it saw the light[1] but permitted when still in its dam's body.[2]

A Tanna recited before Rab: As it might have been assumed that if an abortion was a creature with a shapeless body or with a shapeless head its mother is unclean by reason of its birth, it was explicitly stated in Scripture, *If a woman be delivered, and bear a man-child* etc.[3] *And in the eighth day the flesh of his foreskin shall be circumcised* etc.,[4] thus implying[5] that only a child that is fit for the covenant of the eight days[6] [causes uncleanness to his mother] but these[7] are excluded, since they are not fit for the covenant of the eight days. 'And', said Rab to him, 'conclude your statement thus:[8] And one who had two backs and two spinal columns'.

R. Jeremiah b. Abba intended to give a practical decision[9] in agreement with the view of Samuel,[10] but R. Huna said to him: 'What have you in your mind? To impose a restriction?[11] But this is a restriction that results in a relaxation, since you must in consequence[12] allow her also a period of clean blood.[13] Act rather in accordance with the view of Rab, since we have an established rule that in ritual matters the law is in agreement with Rab irrespective of whether this leads to a relaxation or a restriction.

Raba said: It has been stated that a woman may bear[14] at nine months[15] and also at seven months.[15] Can [then] large cattle who bear[16] at nine months also bear[16] at seven months or not?—R. Naḥman b. Isaac replied, Come and hear: 'One that is younger is equally forbidden'.[17] Does not this also refer to the large cattle?[18]—

(1) Not being viable it is forbidden as *nebelah*. (2) As part of that beast which was a clean one and ritually slaughtered. (3) *She shall be unclean*. Lev. XII, 2. (4) Ibid. 3. (5) By the juxtaposition of the texts. (6) The covenant of circumcision. (7) Which are not viable. (8) I.e., insert between 'these' and 'are excluded'. (9) In the case of an abortion without bleeding of a two-backed foetus. (10) That the woman is unclean by reason of the birth which he regards as valid. (11) By treating the woman as unclean. (12) 'Of your regarding the birth as valid'. (13) From the seventh to the fortieth day for a male, and from the fourteenth to the eightieth day for a female. Should there be a discharge of blood within these periods respectively the woman could not be subjected to menstrual uncleanness. (14) A viable child. (15) After conception. (16) Viable young. (17) *Supra* 24a. (18) Mentioned earlier in the

No, it may only refer to the small cattle.[1] What an argument this is! If you grant that the reference[2] was to the large cattle also, one can well see the necessity for it. For it might have been presumed that since [a seven monthly] is viable in the case of a woman it is also viable in that of cattle, we were informed that it is not viable; but if you maintain that reference was made to small cattle only, this would be obvious, for can a three monthly abortion live?[3]—It[4] was necessary: As it might have been presumed that anyone [born within] less than two months [before the conclusion of the normal conception] can survive,[5] hence we were informed that it[6] was not viable.

Rab Judah citing Samuel ruled: If an abortion had the likeness of Lilith[7] its mother is unclean by reason of the birth, for it is a child, but it has wings. So it was also taught: R. Jose stated, It once happened at Simoni[8] that a woman aborted the likeness of Lilith, and when the case came up for a decision before the Sages they ruled that it was a child but that it also had wings. If an abortion had the likeness of a serpent, Ḥanina the son of R. Joshua's brother ruled: Its mother is unclean by reason of the birth. R. Joseph proceeded to report the ruling to R. Gamaliel when the latter sent word [to][9] R. Joshua, 'Take charge of[10] your nephew and come with him to me'. As they were going, Ḥanina's[11] daughter-

Baraitha (*supra* 24a) immediately after the 'small cattle', and in whose case an 'eight monthly' was spoken of. 'One that is younger' would consequently include a seven monthly abortion also who would thus be 'equally forbidden'.

(1) In whose case (cf. prev. n.) only a 'four monthly' abortion was spoken of. The question of a seven monthly abortion cannot, therefore, be solved from this Baraitha. (2) 'One that is younger is equally forbidden'. (3) Of course not; and there would have been no necessity to mention it. (4) The reference to small cattle. (5) *Sc.* as in the case of man and large cattle one born at seven months after conception (two months before the normal period of nine months) is viable (though one born at eight months is not viable) so also in the case of small cattle (though one born at four months is not viable) one born at three months after conception (also two months before the normal period of five months) is viable. (6) A three monthly abortion. (7) A female demon of the night, reputed to have wings and a human face. (8) Semunige in Lower Galilee. (9) So MS.M. Cur. edd. omit. (10) Lit., 'lead'. (11) Curr. edd. in parenthesis insert 'R'.

in-law came out to meet R. Joshua.[1] 'Master', she said to him, 'what is your ruling where an abortion had the likeness of a serpent?' 'Its mother', he replied, 'is clean'. 'But', she retorted, 'was it not in your name that my mother-in-law told me that its mother was unclean?' 'And', he asked her, 'on what ground?' 'Since [she told him] its eye-ball is round like that of a human being'. As a result of her statements R. Joshua recollected his ruling and sent the following message to R. Gamaliel: 'Ḥanina gave his ruling on my authority'.[2] Abaye observed: From this incident it may be learnt that when a scholar gives a ruling he should also indicate his reason so that when he is ever reminded of it he would recollect it.

MISHNAH. IF A WOMAN ABORTED A SAC FULL OF WATER, FULL OF BLOOD, OR FULL OF MATTER OF VARIOUS COLOURS, SHE NEED NOT TAKE INTO CONSIDERATION THE POSSIBILITY OF ITS BEING A VALID BIRTH; BUT IF ITS LIMBS WERE FASHIONED SHE MUST CONTINUE [IN UNCLEANNESS AND SUBSEQUENT CLEANNESS FOR THE PERIODS PRESCRIBED] FOR BOTH MALE AND FEMALE.[3] IF SHE ABORTED A SANDAL OR A PLACENTA SHE MUST ALSO CONTINUE [IN UNCLEANNESS AND CLEANNESS AS] FOR BOTH MALE AND FEMALE.[3]

GEMARA. One can well understand why BLOOD or WATER[4] [constitutes no valid birth, since in this respect] it is of no consequence;[5] but as regards MATTER OF VARIOUS COLOURS,[6] why should not the possibility be taken into consideration that it had originally been a child that was now squashed?—Abaye replied: How much of undiluted wine must the mother of this thing have drunk that her embryo should be squashed within her bowels![7] Raba replied: We have learnt, FULL OF, and if it were the case

(1) So Rashi, Cur. edd. reading 'to meet him' omit 'R. Joshua'. (2) Lit., 'from my mouth'. (3) Cf. Lev. XII, 2-5. (4) In a SAC. (5) Lit., 'nothing'. (6) Being neither water nor blood. (7) Fabulous quantities, of course, which no woman could possibly be suspected of doing. The suggestion that a normal embryo was squashed is, therefore, untenable.

that the embryo had been squashed something would have been missing.[1] R. Adda b. Ahaba replied: We have learnt, MATTER OF VARIOUS COLOURS, and if it were the case that an embryo had been squashed it would all have been reduced to the same colour.

It was taught: Abba Saul stated, I was once a grave-digger[2] when I made a practice of carefully observing the bones of the dead. The bones of one who drinks undiluted wine are burned; those of one who drinks wine excessively diluted are dry;[3] and those of one who drinks wine properly mixed are full of marrow.[4] The bones of a person whose drinking exceeds his eating are burned; those of one whose eating exceeds his drinking are dry,[3] and those of one who eats and drinks in a proper manner are full of marrow.[4]

It was taught: Abba Saul (or, as some say, R. Johanan stated): I was once a grave-digger.[2] On one occasion, when pursuing a deer, I entered the thigh-bone of a corpse, and pursued it for three *parasangs* but did neither reach the deer nor the end of the thigh-bone.[5] When I returned I was told that it was the thigh-bone of Og, King of Bashan.[6]

It was taught: Abba Saul stated, I was once a grave-digger[2] and on one occasion there was opened a cave under me and I stood in the eye-ball of a corpse up to my nose. When I returned I was told that it was the eye of Absalom. And should you suggest that Abba Saul was a dwarf [it may be mentioned that] Abba Saul was the tallest man in his generation, and R. Tarfon reached to his shoulder and that R. Tarfon was the tallest man in his generation and R. Meir reached to his shoulder. R. Meir was the tallest man in his generation and Rabbi reached to his shoulder. Rabbi was the tallest man in his generation and R. Ḥiyya reached to his shoulder, and R. Ḥiyya was the tallest in his generation and Rab reached to his shoulder. Rab was the tallest man in his generation and Rab Judah reached to his shoulder, and Rab Judah was the tallest man in his generation and his waiter Adda reached

(1) From the sac. (2) Lit., 'one who buries the dead'. (3) *Aliter*: Black; *aliter*: Transparent. (4) Lit., 'anointed', 'oiled'. (5) Lit., 'and the thigh-bone did not end'. (6) A Biblical giant (cf. Deut. III, 11).

to his shoulder. [25a] Pushtabna[1] of Pumbeditha reached to[2] half the height of the waiter Adda, while everybody else reached only to the loins of Pushtabna of Pumbeditha.

A question was raised in the presence of Rabbi: What is the ruling where a woman aborted a sac full of flesh? 'I did not hear of such a law', he answered them. 'Thus', announced R. Ishmael son of R. Jose before him, 'said my father: If it was full of blood the woman is unclean as a menstruant, but if it was full of flesh she is unclean as a woman after childbirth'. The other said to him: Had you told us something new in the name of your father we would have listened to you; but now, since his first ruling[3] was given in accordance with the view of an individual, viz., in agreement with Symmachus who cited R. Meir,[4] his second ruling also[5] might be one given in accordance with the view of R. Joshua;[6] but the *halachah* is not in agreement with R. Joshua. For it was taught: If an abortion was a sac with no fashioned limbs, R. Joshua ruled: It[7] is regarded as a valid birth[8] but the Sages ruled, It is no valid birth.[9]

R. Simeon b. Laḳish citing R. Oshaia stated: The dispute[10] refers only to a sac that was turbid[11] but if it was clear[12] all agree that it is no valid birth. R. Joshua b. Levi, however, stated: The dispute[10] refers to the case of a clear sac. The question was raised:[13] Do they differ only in the case of a clear sac but in that of a turbid one all agree that it is a valid birth or is it possible that they differ about the one as well as about the other?—This stands undecided.[14]

An objection was raised: This exposition was made by R. Joshua b. Ḥananiah: *And the Lord God made for Adam and for his wife garments of skins, and clothed them*[15] teaches that the Holy One, blessed be He,

(1) Or (with Aruk) Pashtikna. Cur. edd., Parshtabina. One of the tallest men. (2) Lit., 'stood to him'. (3) A sac filled with blood. (4) Supra 21*b*. (5) On a sac filled with flesh. (6) Also an individual. (7) Even if it was filled with flesh only. (8) And the woman is unclean by reason of childbirth. (9) Cf. prev. two notes. Since the Sages who are the majority differ from R. Joshua the *halachah* cannot be in agreement with his view. (10) Between R. Joshua and the Sages. (11) In which case it may well be assumed that the foetus in it had been crushed. (12) Filled with clear water. (13) On R. Joshua b. Levi's statement. (14) *Teḳu*. (15) Gen. III, 21.

makes no skin for man before[1] he is formed. Thus it is clearly proved that a valid birth[2] depends on the skin irrespective of whether the sac was turbid or clear. Now if you grant[3] that the dispute[4] refers to the case of a clear sac there is full justification for his[5] need for a Scriptural text;[6] but if you maintain[7] that the dispute refers only to a turbid sac,[8] what need was there for a Scriptural text seeing that the reason[9] is a matter of logic? Consequently it may be inferred that the dispute refers also to a clear sac.[10] This is conclusive.

R. Naḥman citing Rabbah b. Abbuha also[11] stated: They[12] differ only in regard to a turbid sac but as regards a clear one all agree that it is no valid birth. Raba raised an objection against R. Naḥman: 'But they ruled: The token of a valid birth[13] in small cattle is a discharge from the womb,[14] in large cattle the placenta,[15] and in a woman the sac or placenta',[16] but, it follows, the abortion of a sac in cattle provides no exemption.[17] Now, if you grant that they[12] differ in the case of a clear sac, one can well see the reason why only a woman whose case Scripture specifically included,[18] was granted exemption in respect of a sac[16] while cattle whose case Scripture did not include no exemption was granted in respect of a sac, but if you maintain that the dispute concerns only a turbid sac consider! [The question of the validity of the birth being dependent] on a logical reason[19] what difference in this respect

(1) Lit., 'but if so', 'unless'. (2) Lit., 'thing'. (3) As R. Joshua b. Levi submitted. (4) Between R. Joshua and the Sages. (5) R. Joshua's. (6) Since by showing that skin alone proves the existence of an embryo he can support his view against that of the Sages. (7) As Resh Lakish does. (8) The reason for his view being not the presence of skin but the possibility that the embryo had been crushed. (9) For being regarded as a valid birth. (10) An objection thus remains against Resh Lakish. (11) Like R. Oshaia. (12) R. Joshua and the Rabbis. (13) In respect of exempting the one born after it from the obligations of 'firstling' or 'first-born son'. (14) After a conception. (15) The young born after such a birth is not regarded as a firstling (16) Bek. 19a. A son born after such an abortion is no 'first-born son'. (17) Of the next born young from the restrictions of a firstling. (18) As deduced *supra* by R. Joshua b. Ḥananiah. (19) And not on a Scriptutal text which specially refers to the human species.

could there be between a woman and cattle?[1]—You think that R. Joshua was quite certain [of the nature of the sac],[2] but the fact is that R. Joshua was rather doubtful on the matter and, therefore, he followed a restrictive course in both cases.[3] [Only the question of the firstborn son] of[4] a woman, which is a mere monetary matter,[5] [did he rule that the abortion of a sac constitutes a valid birth,[6] because] in a case of doubt in monetary matters a lenient course[7] is followed.[8] On the question of the firstling of cattle, however, which involves a ritual prohibition of shearing[9] and of work[10] [he ruled the abortion of a sac to be an invalid birth,[11] because] in case of doubt in a ritual prohibition a restrictive course must be followed; and so also [on the question of the uncleanness] of a woman [the abortion of a sac is deemed to be a valid birth,[12] because] in a case of doubtful uncleanness[13] a restrictive course must be followed. But was he[14] in doubt?[15] Did he not, in fact, quote a Scriptural text?[16]—The ruling is only Rabbinical[17] and the Scriptural text is a mere prop.[18]

Said R. Ḥanina b. Shelemya to Rab: We have[19] the statements of[20] Rabbi,[21] of[20] R. Ishmael son of R. Jose,[22] of R. Oshaia[23] and of

(1) If the foetus may be assumed to have been crushed in the one case why may it not be so assumed in the other? (2) That its abortion constitutes a valid birth. (3) In that of a firstling of cattle and in that of a woman's uncleanness (as will be explained presently). (4) Lit., 'at'. (5) A first-born son must be redeemed by the payment of five *shekels* to the priest. (6) And the son born subsequently is no firstborn, and no redemption money on his behalf need be paid to the priest. (7) In favour of the possessor of the money. (8) The priest, therefore, cannot claim the redemption money (cf. prev. n. but one). (9) Its wool. (10) With the animal. It is forbidden to do any work with a firstling or to shear its wool (cf. Deut. XV, 19). (11) Thus imposing the restrictions of a firstling on the next born young. (12) Which imposes uncleanness upon the woman. (13) Also a ritual matter. (14) R. Joshua. (15) Whether the abortion of a sac is a valid birth. (16) Gen. III, 21, *supra*, in support of his view, which proves that his ruling is Pentateuchal and definite. (17) Based, on account of the doubt, on the principle quoted *supra*. (18) In support of the Rabbinical ruling. (19) *Supra*. (20) Lit., 'that'. (21) Who said (*supra*) 'I did not hear of such a law'. (22) Who said, 'If it was full of flesh she is unclean'. (23) Who said, 'The dispute refers only to a sac that was turbid'.

R. Joshua b. Levi;[1] with whose view does the Master agree?—I maintain, the other replied, that in neither case[2] need she take into consideration the possibility of a valid birth. Samuel, however, ruled: In either case[3] must she consider the possibility of a valid birth.[4] Samuel in this ruling follows his previously expressed view. For R. Dimi when he came[5] stated: Never at Nehardea[6] did they declare [one who aborted] a sac[7] to be clean[8] except in the case of a certain sac that was submitted to Samuel on which a hair that lay on one side could be seen through the other side when he said: If it were in fact an embryo it would not have been so transparent.

BUT IF ITS LIMBS WERE FASHIONED etc. Our Rabbis taught: What is meant by a sac the limbs of which are fashioned? Abba Saul explained: A foetus which in its primary stage resembles a locust,[9] and its two eyes are like two drippings[10] of a fly. R. Ḥiyya taught: They are far removed from one another. Its two nostrils are like two drippings of a fly. R. Ḥiyya taught: They are near one to another. Its mouth is as narrow as a stretched hair,[11] its membrum[12] is of the size of a lentil[13] and in the case of a female [the organ] has the appearance of the longitudinal [slit][14] of a barley grain; but it has no shaped hands or feet.[15] Of such a foetus there is this description in the post-Pentateuchal Scriptures:[16] *Hast thou not poured me out as milk, and curdled me like cheese? Thou hast clothed me with skin and flesh and knit me together with bones and sinews. Thou*

(1) Who said, 'The dispute refers to the case of a clear sac'. (2) Neither in that of a turbid sac nor in that of a clear one. (3) Cf. prev. n. *mut. mut.* (4) *Sc.* she must remain unclean for the prescribed period of childbirth uncleanness, but is not entitled to the privilege of the subsequent period of clean days. (5) From Palestine to Babylon. (6) The principal town under Samuel's jurisdiction. (7) Even if there was no bleeding with the abortion. (8) I.e., to be exempt from the period of uncleanness prescribed for a woman after childbirth. (9) Reading (with R. Ḥan. and R. Tam) *kerashom* (cf. Aruk.) Cur. edd. 'from its head'. (10) Cf. Jast. 'Eyes' (Rashi). (11) Lit., 'stretched as a hair thread'. (12) When sex is distinguishable. (13) The case spoken of in our Mishnah (q.v.) is one of doubtful sex. (14) Cf. the reading of 'En Jacob and *infra* 25*b*. (15) *Sc.* fingers and toes are not yet articulated. (16) Lit., 'acceptance', 'tradition'.

hast granted me life and favour, and Thy providence hath preserved my spirit.[1] It[2] must not be examined in water because water is hard[3] [25b] and disturbs its shape. It must rather be examined in oil because oil is mild and makes it clear. Furthermore, it must be examined in sunlight only. How is it to be examined? 'How is it to be examined' [you ask]! Of course as has just been described.—Rather, wherewith is it to be examined in order to ascertain whether it was male or female?—Abba Saul b. Nashor, as others say, Abba Saul b. Ramash replied: One brings a splinter with a smooth top and moves it [in an upward direction] in that place.[4] If it is caught it will be known that the foetus is a male,[5] and if not it will be known to be a female. R. Naḥman citing Rabbah b. Abbuha stated: This[6] was learnt only of a movement in an upward direction,[5] but if sideways [it is no reliable test, since] it may be assumed [that the obstruction] was caused by the sides of the womb. R. Adda b. Ahaba stated: A Tanna taught, If the foetus was a female the organ has the appearance of the [longitudinal] slit of a barley grain.[7] R. Naḥman demurred: Is it not possible that it[8] is merely the depression between[9] the testes?—Abaye replied: Since the testes themselves are indistinguishable, would the depression between them be distinguishable?[10]

R. Amram stated: A Tanna taught, 'Its[11] two thighs are like two silk threads', and in connection with this R. Amram explained: Like those of the woof;[12] 'and its two arms are like two threads of silk', in connection with which R. Amram explained: Like those of the warp.[12]

Samuel said to Rab Judah: *Shinena*,[13] give no practical decision [on the validity of a birth] unless the embryo has hair [on its

(1) Job X, 10-12. (2) A foetus in the conditions described. (3) Lit., 'strong'. (4) Euphemism. (5) The obstruction being attributed to the membrum. (6) The splinter test. (7) Cf. the reading *supra 25a, ad fin.* The latter reading adds 'slit' which is wanting in the original of the former. (8) The presumed female organ. (9) Lit., 'thread of'. (10) Obviously not. (11) Referring to the foetus in its early stages. (12) The threads of the woof are thicker than those of the warp. (13) Keen witted (rt. שנן, 'to sharpen'); long-toothed (שן, 'tooth'): or man of iron.

head]. But could Samuel have said such a thing, seeing that he ruled, 'In either case must she consider the possibility of a valid birth'?—R. Ammi b. Samuel replied: This was explained to me by the Master Samuel: She must indeed take into consideration the possibility of a valid birth;[1] but she is not allowed the privilege of the clean days[2] unless the embryo had hair [on its head]. This then implies that Samuel was doubtful on the point.[3] But is it not a fact that when a certain sac was submitted to the Master Samuel he said, 'This is forty-one days old', but on calculating the time since the woman had gone to perform her ritual immersion[4] until that day and finding that there were no more than forty days he declared, 'This man[5] must have had marital intercourse during her menstrual period' and having been arrested[6] he confessed?[7]—Samuel was different from other people because his knowledge was exceptional.[8]

IF SHE ABORTED A SANDAL etc. Our Rabbis taught: A *sandal* is like a sea-fish [of the same name].[9] At first it is a normal foetus but later it is crushed. R. Simeon b. Gamaliel said: A *sandal* resembles the tongue of a big ox. In the name of our Masters it was testified: A *sandal*[10] must have the facial features.[11] Rab Judah citing Samuel stated: The *halachah* is that a *sandal*[10] must have the facial features. R. Adda citing R. Joseph who had it from R. Isaac ruled: A *sandal*[10] must have the facial features even if only at the back, this being a case similar to that of a man who slapped his fellow and caused his face to turn backwards.

In the days of R. Jannai it was desired to declare [the mother of] a *sandal* that had no facial features as clean.[12] Said R. Jannai to them:

(1) *Sc.* to remain unclean for fourteen days. (2) After the conclusion of the unclean ones. (3) The stages in the development of a foetus. (4) Following the conclusion of her menstrual period. (5) The husband of the woman. (6) Lit., 'he bound him'. (7) An incident which shows Samuel's remarkable and accurate knowledge of the nature of a foetus. (8) Lit., 'because his strength is great'. Other people, however, whose physiological knowledge is not so great must adopt a cautious course and take into consideration the possibility suggested. (9) Cf. Rashi. (10) If it is to be deemed a valid birth. (11) Tosef. Nid. IV. (12) Regarding it as no valid birth.

You would declare [the mother of newly born] children[1] as clean![2] —But was it not taught, 'In the name of our Masters it was testified: A *sandal*[3] must have the facial features'?[4]—R. Bibi b. Abaye citing R. Johanan replied: It was on the evidence of R. Nehunya[5] that this ruling[6] was learnt.[7] R. Ze'ira observed: R. Bibi was lucky [to be the first] with his reported traditions, for both I and he were sitting in the presence of R. Johanan when he discoursed upon this tradition, but he[8] forestalled me and, reporting it first, gained the advantage.

Why was a *sandal*[9] at all mentioned, seeing that there can be no birth of a *sandal* without that of an embryo with it?[10]—If a female child were to be born with it this would be so indeed,[11] but here we are dealing with one with which a male was born.[12] As it might have been presumed that, since R. Isaac b. Ammi stated, 'If the woman is first to emit the semen she bears a male child and if the male is first to do it she bears a female child', the one[13] is a male as well as the other is a male,[14] hence we were informed [that no such assumption is made, for] it might equally be assumed that both emitted their semen simultaneously so that one might be a male while the other[13] is a female.[15] Another explanation:[16]

(1) A *sandal* being regarded as a valid birth. (2) Contrary to Pentateuchal law. (3) If it is to be deemed a valid birth. (4) Tosef. Nid. IV. (5) An individual authority. (6) Lit., 'teaching', the ruling that a *sandal* that is to be deemed a valid birth must have the facial features. (7) Hence (cf. prev. n. but one) it may well be disregarded. (8) R. Bebai. (9) The law that it causes a woman's uncleanness (cf. our Mishnah). (10) So that the woman would be unclean even in the absence of a *sandal*. (11) There would have been no necessity at all to mention the *sandal* (cf. prev. n. but one), since it could add no uncleanness, whatever its sex: If it is a female it would subject the woman to the very same uncleanness as the female that was born with it, and if it is a male, the period of uncleanness it causes is a lesser one than that of the female. (12) So that if the *sandal* were a female the period of the woman's uncleanness would extend over a longer period. (13) The *sandal*. (14) In consequence of which the woman's uncleanness would be that of a male birth only. (15) Hence the law of the *sandal* which imposes the restrictions of a female birth (fourteen unclean days instead of seven) as well as those of a male birth (thirty-three days of cleanness instead of sixty-six). (16) Which justifies the necessity for the law of *sandal* even where a female was born.

[*Sandal*[1] was mentioned] in order that if a woman bore a female child before sunset and a *sandal* after sunset[2] she must count the beginning of her period of menstruation in accordance with the first birth and in accordance with the second birth.[3]

As regards the *sandal* that we learnt [26a] in the laws of the firstborn,[4] what practical law[5] is thereby taught?[6]—That the son who follows it[7] is regarded as a firstborn son in respect of inheritance[8] but not [in regard to his redemption] from the priest.[9] What practical law is taught by that of the *sandal* of which we learnt in the case of those who incur the penalty of *kareth?*[10]—That if the embryo[11] is born from her side,[12] and the *sandal* from her womb she[13] must bring a sacrifice on account of the *sandal*. But according to R. Simeon who ruled that 'a foetus born from the side constitutes a valid birth',[14] what can be said?[15]—R. Jeremiah replied:

(1) The law that it causes a woman's uncleanness (cf. our Mishnah). (2) The day concluding at sunset, when another day begins, and the *sandal* being thus born a day later than the female child. (3) I.e., the restrictions of both are imposed upon her: As the *sandal* might be a male the eighty-first day from the female birth (if there was a discharge) is regarded as the first day of menstruation though that day is still the eightieth from the *sandal's* birth which in the case of a female is one (the last) of the clean days. The seventh day after the eightieth again is not regarded as the termination of the seven days of menstruation (which began on the eightieth day) since it is possible that the *sandal* was a female whose eightieth day coincided with the eighty-first of the female child and in accordance with which the woman's seven days of menstruation began a day later (the eighty-second day after the first birth) and consequently terminated a day later. (4) Bek. 46*a*. (5) In respect of the child born after it. (6) *Sc.* since the birth of a *sandal* is always accompanied by the birth of an embryo how could the former's presence any more than its absence affect the birthright of a subsequently born son whose status would in any case be determined by that of the embryo. (7) *Sc.* the embryo accompanying it if it was a male and was born after it. (8) He is entitled to a double portion in his deceased father's estate (cf. Deut. XXI, 17). (9) Cf. Num. XVIII, 15-16. (10) *Supra* 7b in respect of the duty of bringing a sacrifice. Cf. *supra* n. 6 *mut. mut.* (11) That accompanied the *sandal*. (12) Extracted by means of the Caesarean cut. (13) Though on account of the embryo, since it was not born from the normal place, she incurs no sacrifice of childbirth. (14) *Infra* 40a; so that a sacrifice is incurred in any case. (15) In reply to the objection: 'What practical law is taught by that of the *sandal*?'

That if a woman bears the child while she is an idolatress and the *sandal* after she has been converted [to Judaism] she[1] must bring a sacrifice on account of the *sandal*.

The following was said by the Rabbis before R. Papa: But are all these answers[2] tenable? Was it not in fact taught, 'When they[3] issue they do so only while clinging to one another'?[4]—R. Papa replied: From this[5] it may be inferred that the embryo clings to the *sandal* at the middle of the latter[6] which lies across the head of the former.[7] Consequently, as regards the law of the firstborn, [the reference is to a case], for instance, where the embryo[8] issued with its head first[9] so that the *sandal*[10] issued first.[11] As regards the law concerning those punishable by *kareth* it is a case where they[12] issued with their feet first so that the embryo was born first.[13] R. Huna b. Taḥlifa citing Raba explained: It may even be said that they[14] cling together side by side, but reverse the previous statement:[15] As regards the law of the firstborn [the reference is to a case] where they[14] issued with their feet first; so that the embryo, being animated hangs on and does

(1) Who incurs no obligation of a sacrifice on account of the child, since she was still an idolatress when it was born. (2) Just given, in reply to the objections as to what practical purpose was served by the law of the *sandal*. (3) *Sandal* and embryo. (4) How then is it possible, for instance, that a woman should be converted between the birth of the child and the birth of the *sandal* which are simultaneous processes or for one to be born by Caesarean section and the other by natural birth? (5) From (*a*) the law relating to those incurring the penalty of *kareth* which presumes the embryo to precede the *sandal* and (*b*) the law of the firstborn wich presumes the *sandal* to precede the embryo and (*c*) the statement that embryo and *sandal* issue while clinging to one another. (6) *Sc*. the head of the embryo is in contact with the centre part of the *sandal*. (7) But does not come in contact with the lower part of its body. (8) The *sandal* and embryo clinging to one another in the manner described. (9) Lit., 'by way of their heads'. (10) Lying across the embryo's head. (11) *Sc*. before the birth of the embryo was consummated. As the *sandal* was the first to issue the embryo cannot be regarded as a firstborn son to be subject to the obligation of redemption from the priest. (12) Clinging to one another in the manner described. (13) Hence the obligation to bring the sacrifice prescribed for a woman in childbirth. (14) *Sandal* and embryo. (15) The one made by R. Papa.

not easily come out; while the *sandal*, not being animated, glides and comes speedily out. As regards the law concerning those subject to the penalty of *kareth* [the reference is to a case] where they issued with their heads first, so that the embryo, being animated is deemed to have consummated its birth as soon as its head came out; while the *sandal* [being inanimated cannot be deemed to have been born] until its greater part came out.

MISHNAH. IF A PLACENTA IS WITHIN A HOUSE, THE HOUSE IS UNCLEAN;[1] NOT BECAUSE A PLACENTA IS A CHILD BUT BECAUSE GENERALLY THERE CAN BE NO PLACENTA WITHOUT A CHILD. R. SIMEON SAID, THE CHILD MIGHT HAVE BEEN MASHED[2] BEFORE IT CAME FORTH.[3]

GEMARA. Our Rabbis taught: The placenta in its first stage resembles a thread of the woof and in its final stage it resembles a lupine. It is hollow like a trumpet; and no placenta is smaller than a handbreadth. R. Simeon b. Gamaliel stated: The placenta resembles the craw of a hen[4] out of which the small bowels issue.[5]

R. Oshaia, the youngest of the fellowship,[6] taught:[7] Five things have a prescribed minimum of a handbreadth, and they are the following. A placenta, a *shofar*, a spine, a *sukkah* wall and a bundle of hyssop. As to the placenta there is the ruling just mentioned.[8] '*Shofar*'?[9] For it was taught: What must be the size of a *shofar?*[10] R. Simeon b. Gamaliel explained: It must be of such a size as can be held in one's hand and be seen at either end, viz.,[11] a handbreath.[12]

(1) As if overshadowed by an actual corpse. (2) And having been mixed up with the blood of childbearing which was the greater quantity became neutralized in it. (3) Hence it can no longer convey any uncleanness. (4) Lit., 'hens'. (5) Tosef. Nid. IV. (6) [*Aliter:* Oshaia Zeira of Haberya, a village in the Hawram district; v. Horowitz, *Palestine* p. 263]. (7) Cf. Bomb. ed. and MS.M. Cur. edd., 'it was taught'. (8) In the citation from Tosef. Nid. IV (9) Cf. MS.M. (10) Ram's horn used on the two days of the New Year festival (cf. Lev. XXIII, 24, Num. XXIX, 1). (11) Cf. Tosaf. Asheri. (12) A handbreadth is equal to the size of four thumbs which equals that of four fingers plus. Hence the prescription that when 'held in one's hand', *sc.*

What is meant by 'spine'? The ruling which R. Parnak laid down in the name of R. Joḥanan: The spine of the *lulab* must be long enough to project a handbreadth above the myrtle.[1] 'The *Sukkah*[2] wall'? As it was taught: Two walls[3] must be proper ones but the third is valid even if it is only one handbreadth wide. 'Hyssop'? As R. Ḥiyya taught: The bundle of hyssop[4] must be a handbreadth long.

R. Ḥanina b. Papa stated: Shila of the village of Tamartha discoursed on three Baraithas and two reported traditions dealing with the prescribed size of a handbreadth. 'Two'[5] [you say]; is it not only one?[6]—Abaye replied, read:[7] R. Ḥiyya stated,[8] 'The bundle of hyssop must be a handbreadth long'. But are there no others?[9] Is there not in fact [the law that an enclosed space of] one handbreadth square and one handbreadth in height, forming a cube[10] conveys uncleanness[11] and constitutes a screen[12] against uncleanness?[13]—We spoke of the size of 'a handbreadth'; we did not speak of 'a handbreadth square'. But is there not the law concerning a stone that projected one handbreadth from an oven[14] or three fingerbreadths from a double stove[15] in which case it serves as a connecting link?[16]—We spoke only of cases where the

with the four fingers, it must 'be seen at either end', i.e., it must slightly project to make up the required size.

(1) With which it is bound to form with the willows the Tabernacles festive wreath (cf. Lev. XXIII, 40). (2) V. Glos. (3) Of a *sukkah* (cf. Lev. XXIII, 42). (4) Cf. Lev. XIV, 4. (5) 'Two reported traditions'. (6) That on the spine of the *lulab* cited in the name of R. Joḥanan. All the others are Baraithas. (7) Instead of 'R. Ḥiyya taught'. (8) As an Amora. R. Ḥiyya lived at the end of the period of the Tannas and the beginning of that of the Amoras. When he 'taught' he was citing a Baraitha but when he 'stated' or 'said' he was speaking only as an Amora. (9) Whose prescribed size is a handbreadth. (10) Thus constituting a '*tent*' of minimum size. (11) By overshadowing. If an unclean object and a clean one were overshadowed by it the latter becomes unclean even though it had not come in direct contact with the former. (12) Where the clean object was above, and the unclean one under such a '*tent*'. (13) Oh. III, 7. (14) So that it can be used as its handle. (15) Cf. prev. n. On the rendering of 'double stove' cf. Tosaf. 26*b*, s.v. בפלוגתא, contra Rashi. (16) Kel. V, 2. Between an object on the stone and the oven or stove. If the object was unclean its uncleanness is

size of less than a handbreadth is invalid, but here the law would apply all the more to such a case where the size is of less than a handbreadth and it is a handle of the oven. But is there not [26b] the law of ovens of the size of one handbreadth?[1] For we learnt:[2] An oven [if it is to be susceptible to uncleanness must] *ab initio*[3] be no less than four handbreadths high, and what remains of it[4] must[5] be no less than four handbreadths high; so R. Meir. But the Sages ruled: This applies only to a big oven but if it is a small one [it is susceptible to uncleanness] *ab initio*, after its manufacture is completed, whatever its size, and what is left of it [remains unclean] if it was the greater part of it.[6] And [to the question] what is meant by 'whatever its size', R. Jannai replied: One handbreadth, since ovens of the height of one handbreadth are made![7] —He[8] did not speak of laws about which a divergence of view exists.[9] Now that you have arrived at this argument that law[10] [it may be explained][11] is also one in dispute, for in the final clause it was stated: R. Judah said, They spoke of the length of a handbreadth only between the oven and the wall.[12] But is there not also *a border of a handbreadth?*[13]—He does not deal with sizes that are prescribed in Scripture. But is there not the ark-cover that was one handbreadth thick?[14]—He[8] does not discuss holy things. But is there not [the following law]: It suffices for a cross-beam[15] to be

conveyed to the oven or stove and if one of the latter was unclean its uncleanness is conveyed to the object.

(1) Used as toys (cf. Rashi and Gold.) (2) Cf. MS.M. Cur. edd., 'for it was taught'. (3) When its manufacture is completed. (4) *Sc.* of a big oven that contracted uncleanness and was then broken. (5) If its uncleanness is to be retained. (6) Kel. V, 1. For a fuller explanation cf. Ḥul. 124*a*. (7) Now why was not this law included among the five enumerated by R. Oshaia *supra*? (8) R. Oshaia. (9) The size of the handbreadth in this case being disputed by R. Meir. (10) About the stone that projected from an oven cited *supra* from Kel. V, 2. (11) As a reason why it was not mentioned by R. Oshaia. (12) Near which the oven is placed. Where a stone is of greater length it prevents the oven from being brought up to the wall and is removed in consequence. Only in such a case is the size restricted to a handbreadth. Where, however, the stone projects on another side, since it would not be removed, it is regarded as a handle. (13) Ex. XXV, 25. (14) Cf. Ex. XXV, 17, as explained in Suk. 4*b*. (15) Placed above the entrance to a

one handbreadth wide?[1]—He[2] does not discuss Rabbinical laws.[3] [He was concerned only] with such as are prescribed in Scripture and in connection with which no sizes[4] have been specified.

R. Isaac b. Samuel b. Martha once sat at his studies before R. Kahana and in the course of the session he observed: Rab Judah citing Rab laid down that throughout the first three days[5] the placenta[6] is attributed to the child,[7] but henceforth the possibility of the birth of a second child[8] must be considered.[9] Said the other to him: But could Rab have said such a thing? Did not Rab in fact state, 'One child is not detained at all after the other [had been born]'?[10] The first remained silent. Said the other to him: Is it not possible that one statement[11] referred to an abortion, while the other[12] referred to a child that was viable?—You, the first[13] answered, have indeed stated Rab's actual rulings, for Rab has explicitly made the following statement: If a woman aborted an embryo and after that she aborted a placenta, if this occurred within three days[14] the placenta is attributed to the embryo, but if it occurred at any subsequent time the possibility of the abortion of a second embryo must be taken into consideration. If, however, she gave birth to a normal child and subsequently aborted a placenta, even if that occurred between that moment and ten days

blind alley in connection with the permissibility of the movement of objects on the Sabbath.

(1) 'Er. 13*b*. (2) R. Oshaia. (3) All the Sabbath laws in connection with an alley are merely Rabbinical. (4) Lit., 'their sizes'. (5) After the birth of a child. (6) That issued after the childbirth. (7) That was born. The days of the woman's uncleanness and cleanness are consequently reckoned from the day of the child's birth and not from the latter day on which the placenta issued. (8) Who was crushed within the placenta and who might have been a female. (9) And the restrictions of a female birth (fourteen unclean days instead of seven, for instance,) are imposed. (10) How then could he have ruled that after three days had passed the placenta might still be attributed to a second child? (11) According to which a second child might be born three or more days after the birth of the first one. (12) 'One child is not detained at all after the other'. (13) Who, thanks to R. Kahana's suggestion, recollected Rab's actual words and as a result was grateful and complimentary (cf. R. Gershom, contra Rashi). (14) After the abortion of the embryo.

later,[1] the possibility of the abortion of a second child[2] need not be considered at all.

Samuel and the disciples of Rab and Rab Judah[3] were once sitting at their studies when R. Joseph the son of R. Menashya of Dewil passed along in great haste. 'There comes towards us', he exclaimed, 'a man whom we can throw down with a piece of straw[4] and he would allow himself to be thrown down and pushed out'.[5] In the meanwhile he approached them. What, said Samuel to him, did Rab rule in regard to a placenta?—Thus, the other replied, said Rab: The placenta may be attributed only to a child that is viable.[6] Samuel then put the question to all the disciples of Rab and they told him the same thing. Thereupon he turned round and looked at Rab Judah with displeasure.[7]

R. Jose b. Saul enquired of Rabbi: What is the law where there was an abortion in the shape of a raven and [this was followed by] a placenta?[8]—The other replied: We can attribute a placenta only to an embryo in whose species[9] the placenta is [one of their organs].[10] What is the law where the placenta is tied to it?[11]—You, the other replied, have asked a question about that which does not exist. He raised an objection against him: If a woman aborted something in the shape of a beast, a wild animal or a bird, and a placenta with them, whenever the placenta is attached to it there is no need to take into consideration the possibility of the existence of a second embryo, but if no placenta is attached to it

(1) Lit., 'from here and onwards'. (2) That may have been crushed in the placenta. (3) Who was a former disciple of Rab and joined Samuel's academy for some time after Rab's death. (4) Lit., 'straw of the wheat'. Metaphor: The man could be upset by the simplest of arguments. *Aliter:* On whom we may throw wheat-chaff, i.e., embarrass with petty questions (Jast.). (5) Cf. prev. n. He would not be able to open his mouth in defence of his views. (6) As suggested *supra* by R. Kahana and confirmed by R. Isaac. (7) He considered it a discourtesy on the part of Rab Judah (cf. *supra* n. 3) not to have informed him earlier of such an important ruling of Rab. (8) Is the placenta, it is asked, attributed to the raven-shaped embryo or is it attributed to a human embryo that may have been crushed in it? (9) Man and beast. (10) Birds are, therefore, excluded. (11) The raven-shaped object.

the possibility of the existence of a second embryo[1] must be considered, and one[2] must [impose on the woman] on account of them[3] [27*a*] the restrictions of the two births;[4] for it is assumed[5] that the foetus of the placenta may have been crushed[6] and that the placenta of the foetus[7] was also crushed.[8] This is indeed a refutation.

Rabbah b. Shila citing R. Mattena who had it from Samuel stated: It once happened that a placenta was attributed to an embryo as late as[9] ten days [after the latter's birth].[10] [The law, however, that it] is to be attributed [to the existing embryo] applies only[11] where the expulsion of the placenta followed the birth of the embryo.[12] Rabbah b. Bar Ḥana citing R. Johanan stated: It once happened that a placenta was attributed to an embryo as late as[13] twenty-three days [after the birth of the latter]. 'You once told us', said R. Joseph to him, 'as late as twenty-four days'. R. Aḥa son of 'Awira citing R. Joḥanan[14] stated: It once happened that the birth of an embryo was delayed for thirty-three days after that of its predecessor. 'You', said R. Joseph to him,

(1) That may have been crushed within the placenta. (2) Lit., 'behold I'. (3) The two embryos. (4) If, for instance, the embryo aborted was a male, the placenta is presumed to contain the crushed embryo of a female, and the woman must, therefore, count fourteen unclean days (as for a female) and not only seven (as prescribed for a male). According to the Rabbis (who do not regard a bird or a beast as a valid birth) the restriction imposed would be to regard neither birth as valid and to deprive the woman in consequence of the advantage of the clean days prescribed for a woman after a childbirth. (5) Lit., 'for I say'. (6) So that the placenta belonged to that foetus and not to the one in existence. (7) That is in existence. (8) And lost. Ḥul. 77*a*. It is thus shown that a placenta is sometimes attached to the foetus. How then could Rabbi maintain (*supra* 26*b ad fin.*) that such a thing 'does not exist'? (9) Lit., 'until'. (10) Despite the long interval between the birth of the embryo and the expulsion of the placenta no assumption was made that the placenta of the embryo in existence was lost and that the placenta in existence belonged to a second embryo that was crushed. (11) Lit., 'and they only said'. (12) If, however, it preceded it the possibility must be taken into consideration that it belonged to another embryo that had been crushed; and consequently the restrictions applying to the two embryos must be imposed. (13) Lit., 'until'. (14) So BaḤ. Cur. edd., 'R. Isaac'.

'have in fact told us thirty-four days.' [Such an incident may be explained] satisfactorily according to him who holds that a woman who bears at nine months does not necessarily complete the full number,[1] since in such circumstances it is possible that the features of one embryo were completed at the end[2] of seven months[3] and those of the other at the beginning[2] of the ninth month,[4] but according to him who maintains that a woman who bears at nine months does complete the full number,[1] what can be said [in explanation of the incident]?[5]—Reverse the statements:[6] Thirty-three days in the case of the placenta[7] and twenty-three days in that of the embryo.[8]

R. Abin b. R. Adda citing R. Menahem of Kefar She'arim or, as some say, Beth She'arim, stated: It once happened that a child was born three months later than its predecessor and lo, both sit before us in the schoolhouse. And who are they?—Judah and Hezekiah the sons of R. Ḥiyya. But did not a Master say that a woman in conception cannot conceive again?[9]—Abaye replied: It was the same drop but it was divided in two sections; the features of one of these were completed at the beginning of the

(1) Of the nine months. *Limekuta'in* (from a rt. meaning 'to lop off'). (2) Within a day or two. (3) In consequence of which it is viable. (4) The eighth month consisting of twenty-nine or thirty days together with the odd days of the seventh and the ninth months (cf. prev. n. but one) making up the interval of thirty-three days. (5) Apparently nothing whatever. If the first was born in the seventh month (even if on the last day) and the second in the ninth month the interval would not be one of thirty-three days but one of no less than two months. If they were both born in the seventh month the interval would inevitably be less than thirty-three days (since a Hebrew month never contains more than thirty days). If again, one was born in the seventh and the other in the eighth month the latter could not be viable, whereas the incident which speaks of a *welad* ('child') and not of *nefel* ('abortion') seems to refer to two viable children. (6) Of R. Joḥanan. (7) The first incident described *supra*. (8) The second of the incidents *supra*. This is quite possible where both embryos were born in the seventh month, since all agree that a child may be viable even if the full number of seven months was not completed. (9) Lit., 'a woman does not conceive and conceive again'. How then was it possible for a child to be born three months after its predecessor.

seventh month and those of the other were completed at the end of the ninth month.

IF A PLACENTA IS WITHIN A HOUSE, THE HOUSE IS UNCLEAN. Our Rabbis taught: If a placenta is in a house, the house is unclean; not because a placenta is a child but because generally there can be no placenta with which there is no child; so R. Meir. R. Jose, R. Judah and R. Simeon regard [the house] as clean. 'Do you not agree', they said to R. Meir, 'that if it had been carried out in a bowl into an outer room it would be clean?' 'Indeed', he replied. 'But why?'[1] 'Because it[2] is no longer in existence'. 'As', they retorted, 'it is not in existence in the outer room so is it not in existence in the inner room'.[3] 'What was mashed once', he replied, 'is not like that which was mashed twice.'[4]

R. Papa once sat behind R. Bubi in the presence of R. Hamnuna and in the course of the session he observed: What is R. Simeon's reason?[5] He is of the opinion that any uncleanness with which anything of a different kind of uncleanness has been mixed is neutralized. Said R. Papa to them: 'Is this also the reason of R. Judah and R. Jose?'[6] They laughed at him. 'Is not this obvious', they said, 'why should there be any difference?'[7]—'Even such a question',[8] said R. Papa, 'a man should submit to his Master[9] and not be content with silence;[10] for it is said, *If thou hast done foolishly*[11] *thou art*[12] *lifting up thyself;*[13] *but*[14] *if thou hast planned devices,*[15] *lay thy hand upon thy mouth.*[16]

(1) Should then the first house be unclean. (2) Having been mashed in the water. (3) Since it was mashed in the placenta. (4) 'There is no comparison between one presumption that the embryo was mashed and two such suppositions (that the placenta of one embryo and the embryo of another placenta were mashed)'. Jast. (5) *Sc.* granted that the embryo was mashed, does not a mashed corpse convey uncleanness? (6) Who are of the same opinion as R. Simeon *supra.* (7) None whatever (cf. prev. n.). (8) Which might cause one to be an object of ridicule. (9) To make sure of his tradition. (10) By relying on his own intelligence. (11) *Sc.* asked what might appear to be a ridiculous question. (12) E.V., *'in'*. (13) One's knowledge is of the highest order and first hand. (14) E.V., *'or'*. (15) In seeking to escape possible ridicule. (16) Prov. XXX, 32; he will not be able to give an authoritative answer when a question on the subject is addressed to him.

R. Simeon[1] follows the view he expressed elsewhere. For it was taught: If some earth fell into a ladleful of corpse-mould [the latter remains] unclean, but R. Simeon holds it to be clean. What is R. Simeon's reason?—Raba[2] replied: 'I met the Rabbis of the schoolhouse while they were sitting at their studies and explaining that[3] it is impossible that [somewhere in the mixture] two particles of earth to one of the corpse-mould should not represent the larger portion, so that[4] something is missing',[5] and I said to them, 'On the contrary! It is impossible that [somewhere in the mixture] two particles of the corpse-mould should not represent a part greater than [27b] one particle of earth,[6] so that[7] the quantity is increased'.[8] The fact, however, is, said Raba,[9] that this is the reason of R. Simeon: Its final stage[10] is treated as its first stage.[11] As in its first stage any other matter[12] becomes its antidote[13] so also in its final stage[10] any other matter[14] becomes its antidote.[13] What is that law?[15]—It was taught: In what circumstances is a corpse subject to the uncleanness of[16] corpse-mould and in what circumstances is a corpse not subject to the uncleanness of corpse-mould? If a corpse was buried naked in a marble sarcophagus or on a stone floor[17] it is one that is subject to the uncleanness of corpse-mould. And in what circumstances is a corpse not subject

(1) In his ruling *supra* that 'Any uncleanness with which anything of a different kind . . . has been mixed is neutralized'. (2) So MS.M. and BaḤ. Cur. edd., 'Rabbah'. (3) Though the earth is much less than the corpse-mould. (4) Since in that part of the mixture, at least, the corpse-mould is neutralized and loses its uncleanness. (5) From the prescribed minimum of a ladleful. The whole mixture is consequently clean. (6) With which they are mixed in that particular section. (7) The earth also becoming unclean on account of the greater part of the corpse-mould with which it is mixed. (8) *We-nafish* (cf. marg. n. and Bomb. ed.) Cur. edd., *we-nafil* (and it falls). (9) So MS.M., Cur. edd. 'Rabbah'. (10) When a corpse is already converted into corpse-mould. (11) When the corpse is buried. (12) That is mixed up with the decaying corpse. (13) Cf. Rashi. *Gingilon* (or *gilgilon*, cf. Tosaf.), lit., 'belt' (cf. cingulum); *sc.* the smallest piece of material buried with a corpse neutralizes the uncleanness of its mould. (14) That mixed with the mould. (15) About the first stage just referred to. (16) Lit., 'which is the corpse that has'. (17) So that there is no foreign matter in the vicinity of the corpse that is likely to be mixed up with its mould.

to the uncleanness of corpse-mould? If it was buried in its shroud,[1] or in a wooden coffin,[2] or on a brick floor[2] it is one that is not subject to the uncleanness of corpse-mould.[3] And [the Sages] spoke of the uncleanness of corpse-mould only in the case of one who died, thus excluding a killed person who[4] is not [subject to this law].[5]

[To turn to] the main text, 'If some earth fell into a ladleful of corpse-mould [the latter remains] unclean, but R. Simeon holds it to be clean. If a ladleful of corpse-mould was scattered in a house the house is unclean,[6] but R. Simeon holds it to be clean'.[7] And both these rulings were required. For if we had been informed of the first one only[8] it might have been presumed that only in that case do the Rabbis maintain their view,[9] since it[10] is collected together but that where it was scattered they agree with R. Simeon, since a succession of incomplete overshadowings[11] is of no consequence.[12] And if we had been informed of the latter only[13] it might have been presumed that only in that case does R. Simeon maintain his view,[14] since a succession of incomplete overshadowings[11] is of no consequence,[15] but that in the former case[16] he agrees with the Rabbis.[9] Hence both were required.

Elsewhere we learnt:[17] A ladleful and more of the earth of a graveyard[18] is unclean,[19] but R. Simeon regards it as clean.[20] What

(1) Which on decaying would naturally be mixed up with the decaying matter of the corpse. (2) Which would moulder (cf. prev. n.). (3) Since the foreign matter that mixes with the decaying matter of the corpse neutralizes it and liberates the corpse-mould from its uncleanness. (4) Being regarded as a defective corpse (cf. Naz. 51*b*) on account of the blood he lost. (5) Tosef. Nid. II, Naz. 51*a*. (6) On account of *ohel* or overshadowing. (7) Oh. III, 2. (8) Earth mixed with corpse-mould. (9) That the mould remains unclean. (10) The corpse-mould. (11) *Sc.* one part of the roof does not overshadow the prescribed minimum of corpse-mould but one part of it overshadows one part of the minimum while another part overshadows another part of it. (12) Lit., 'that one does not make a tent and make a tent again', and the room, therefore, remains clean. (13) Corpse-mould scattered. (14) That the house is clean. (15) Cf. prev. n. but two *mut. mut.* (16) Earth mixed with corpse-mould. (17) V. marg. gl. Cur. edd. 'in another Baraitha it was taught'. (18) Which consists of a mixture of corpse-mould and earth. (19) The reason is explained presently. (20) The reason is given *supra* by Raba.

is the reason of the Rabbis?—Because it is impossible to have 'a ladleful[1] and more' of the earth of a graveyard in which there is not contained a ladleful of corpse-mould.[2]

Now that you have explained that R. Simeon's reason is because 'its final stage is treated as its first stage',[3] what could be his reason in the case of a PLACENTA?[4]—R. Joḥanan replied: Because the law of neutralization in the larger quantity[5] has been applied to it.[6] R. Joḥanan in fact follows here[7] a view he expressed elsewhere. For R. Joḥanan stated: R. Simeon and R. Eliezer b. Jacob laid down the same ruling.[8] R. Simeon laid down the ruling we have just spoken of.[9] R. Eliezer [also laid down the same ruling] for we learnt:[10] R. Eliezer b. Jacob ruled, If a beast[11] of the class of large cattle discharged a clot of blood, this[12] shall be buried[13] and [the beast] is exempt from the law of the firstling;[14] and in connection with this R. Ḥiyya taught: It[12] does not convey uncleanness either through touch or through carriage.[15] But since it conveys no uncleanness either through touch or through carriage[16] why[17] should it be buried?—In order to publish the fact that [the beast] is exempt from the law of the firstling. It thus clearly follows that it[12] is deemed to be a proper embryo,[18] then why did R. Ḥiyya teach, 'It does not convey uncleanness either through touch or through carriage'?—R. Joḥanan replied: Because the law

(1) Lit., 'to fill a ladle'. (2) The required minimum. (3) Cf. prev. n. but two. (4) Where this comparison cannot be made. (5) There is more blood of labour than mashed embryo. (6) Lit., 'they touched it'. As the blood of labour which is the larger quantity is clean, the lesser quantity of the mashed embryo is neutralized in it, and is, therefore, clean. (7) In the answer just given. (8) That a mashed embryo is neutralized in the larger quantity of the blood of labour. (9) An embryo mashed in a placenta causes no uncleanness. (10) Cf. marg. gl. and Bomb. ed. Cur. edd., 'for it was taught'. (11) Which had never before born any young. (12) The clot. (13) It being possible that it contained a mashed firstling which is sacred. (14) Bek. 21*b*; *sc.* its next born young is not regarded as a firstling and need not be given to the priest. (15) Not being regarded as *nebelah* (v. Glos.) the man who touches or carries it remains clean. (16) From which it follows that it is not regarded as an embryo. (17) Since it is consequently no firstling. (18) Had it not had that status the beast would not have been exempt from the law of the firstling.

of neutralization in the larger quantity[1] has been applied to it.[2]

R. Ammi citing R. Johanan stated: R. Simeon, however,[3] agrees that its mother is unclean by reason of childbirth. Said a certain old man to R. Ammi: 'I will explain to you R. Johanan's reason:[4] For Scripture says, *If a woman conceived seed*[5] *and bore a man-child* etc.,[6] which implies: Even if she bore in the same manner only as she *'conceived seed'*[7] she is unclean by reason of childbirth.

Resh Lakish ruled: A sac that was beaten up in its fluid assumes the same status as a corpse whose shape was destroyed.[8] Said R. Johanan to Resh Lakish: Whence do we infer that a corpse whose shape had been destroyed is clean? If it be suggested, From the following statement which R. Shabthai cited in the name of R. Isaac of Magdala or, as others say, R. Isaac of Magdala cited in the name of R. Shabthai, 'If a corpse has been burnt but its shape remained[9] it is unclean. It once happened that on account of such a corpse[10] the big[11] doors[12] were declared unclean[13] [28a] but the small doors[14] were declared clean'; from which you infer that the reason [why the big doors were declared unclean is] because its shape[9] is still intact but had it not been in such a condition they[15] would have been clean; on the contrary [it could be retorted] draw from this the following inference:[16] Only when its shape is intact were the small doors declared clean but otherwise the small doors also are unclean, since everyone of them is fit for

(1) There being more blood of labour than mashed embryo. (2) The mashed embryo is consequently neutralized and is, therefore, clean. (3) Though he ruled in our Mishnah that the house is clean because THE CHILD MIGHT HAVE BEEN MASHED etc. (4) For subjecting the woman to the uncleanness of childbirth even when the embryo is mashed. (5) So according to A.V. and R.V. and the exposition that follows. J.T., *'be delivered'*. (6) Lev. XII, 2. (7) *Sc.* the former was in a fluid state like the latter. (8) *Sc.* burned and scattered. Such human remains convey no uncleanness. (9) I.e., its ashes still kept together so that the body appears whole. (10) Lit., 'for him'. (11) No less than four handbreadths wide. (12) Of the house in which it lay. (13) Since the corpse can be carried intact through them. (14) Less than four handbreadths in width, through which, owing to the availability of larger doors, the corpse would not be carried. (15) The big doors. (16) Lit., 'to that side'.

carrying through it one limb at a time.[1] Said Rabina to R. Ashi: [Do you know] in agreement with whose view R. Joḥanan made his statement?[2] In agreement with that of R. Eliezer. For we learnt: The ashes of burnt corpses, R. Eliezer ruled, [convey uncleanness] if they are a quarter of a *ḳab* in quantity.[3] How is one to imagine a corpse that was burnt but whose shape remained intact?—Abaye replied: In such a case, for instance, as where it was burnt on a leather spread.[4] Raba replied: In such a case, for instance, as where it was burnt on a hard cemented substance.[5] Rabina replied: Where, for instance, it was only charred.[6]

Our Rabbis taught: If a woman aborted a shaped[7] hand or a shaped[8] foot she[9] is subject to the uncleanness of childbirth and there is no need to consider the possibility that it might have come from a shapeless body.[10] Both R. Ḥisda and Rabbah b. R. Huna ruled: She[11] is not allowed the days of cleanness.[12] What is the reason?—It might be assumed that[13] her bearing took place long ago.[14] R. Joseph raised an objection: If a woman aborted an embryo and[15] it is unknown what [was the sex of the embryo] she aborted she must continue [her periods of uncleanness and cleanness as] for both a male child and a female child.[16] Now if it is

(1) From which it would follow that 'a corpse whose shape had been destroyed' is also unclean; contrary to the view of Resh Laḳish (*supra* 27*b*, *ad fin*.). (2) That a corpse whose shape had been destroyed is also unclean (cf. prev. n.). (3) Oh. II, 2. (4) *Ḳatabela*, cf. Καταβολία (Jast.); a skin boiled and hardened which is not consumed when the corpse is burnt (v. Rashi) and moulded in the shape of a human body (Tosaf.) so that the burned remains are kept together. (5) Or 'over the dung on a cemented stable-floor' (Jast.); marble (Rashi); providing a mould for the corpse (cf. prev. n.). (6) In which case the body is kept together without any external aid. (7) Lit., 'cut', *sc*. with fingers well defined. (8) Cf. prev. n. *mut. mut.* (9) Lit., 'his mother'. (10) Which has not the status of a child. (11) Though subject to the uncleanness of a normal birth. (12) Which, in the case of a normal birth, follow the period of uncleanness. (13) Since the embryo was aborted in parts and it is unknown when the birth of the greater part of it occurred. (14) And by the time the hand or foot in question was aborted the prescribed period of uncleanness may have passed. (15) Having been aborted in fractions. (16) *Infra* 29*a*; *sc*. the restrictions of both are imposed upon her.

to be upheld[1] that in any such case[2] it might be assumed that her bearing took place long ago,[3] why[4] was it not also stated, 'and as for menstruation'?[5]—Abaye replied: If 'as for menstruation' had been mentioned it might have been presumed that[6] she brings a sacrifice[7] which[8] may not be eaten; hence we were informed[9] that it may be eaten.[10]

R. Huna ruled: If an embryo put forth its hand and then drew it back its mother is unclean on account of childbirth; for it is said, *And it came to pass, when she bore,*[11] *that one put out a hand.*[12] Rab Judah raised an objection: If an embryo put forth its hand its mother need not consider the possibility of any restriction![13]—R. Naḥman replied: This was explained to me by R. Huna that the woman must indeed consider the possibility [that it is a valid birth],[14] but we do not allow her the privilege of the clean days[15] unless the greater part of the embryo has issued forth. But was it not stated 'Its mother need not consider the possibility of any restriction'?—Abaye replied: Pentateuchally she need not consider the possibility of any restriction, but it is Rabbinically that

(1) Lit., 'it goes up to your mind'. (2) Abortion in parts. (3) Cf. p. 190, n. 14. (4) Since in this case also it is not known when the birth of the greater part of the embryo took place. (5) I.e., the uncleanness should not only extend over fourteen days (prescribed for the birth of a female child) irrespective of whether blood was or was not observed, but even any subsequent discharge of blood, which in the case of a normal birth is clean, should (since her period of clean days may have already passed) be regarded as that of menstruation. (On the mention of male child v. *infra* 30a). (6) Since the ruling that the woman is subject to the restrictions of menstruation implies that it is not certain whether the embryo is, or is not to be regarded as a normal child. (7) Prescribed for a woman after a childbirth. (8) As the embryo possibly may not have the status of a normal child (cf. prev. n. but one). (9) By the omission of 'as for menstruation' which indicates that there is no doubt whatever that the embryo is in this respect regarded as a normal child, and that it was only its sex that was in doubt. (10) As any other valid sacrifice brought by a woman after a childbirth. (11) E. V., *'she travailed'*. (12) Gen. XXXVIII, 28; emphasis on *bore* and *hand* which shows that the issue of a hand alone is described as a 'birth'. (13) How then could R. Huna maintain that a woman in such circumstances is subject to the uncleanness of childbirth? (14) *Sc.* she must continue in the days of uncleanness as after a normal childbirth. (15) That normally follow those of uncleanness.

she must take into consideration the possibility [that it might have constituted a valid birth]. But did he[1] not quote a Scriptural text?[2]—The restriction is Rabbinical, and the Scriptural text is a mere prop.[3]

MISHNAH. IF A WOMAN ABORTED A ṬUMṬUM OR AN ANDROGINOS,[4] SHE MUST CONTINUE [IN HER UNCLEANNESS AND CLEANNESS AS] FOR BOTH A MALE[5] AND A FEMALE.[6] IF SHE GAVE BIRTH TO A ṬUMṬUM AND A MALE, OR TO AN ANDROGINOS AND A MALE, SHE MUST ALSO CONTINUE [IN UNCLEANNESS AND CLEANNESS AS] FOR BOTH A MALE[5] AND A FEMALE.[6] IF SHE HAVE A ṬUMṬUM AND A FEMALE OR AN ANDROGINOS AND A FEMALE, SHE NEED CONTINUE [IN UNCLEANNESS AS] FOR A FEMALE ONLY.[7] IF THE EMBRYO ISSUED IN PIECES[8] OR IN A REVERSED POSITION[9] IT IS DEEMED BORN AS SOON AS ITS GREATER PART ISSUED FORTH. IF IT CAME FORTH IN THE NORMAL WAY [IT IS NOT DEEMED BORN] UNTIL THE GREATER PART OF ITS HEAD ISSUED FORTH. AND WHAT IS MEANT [BY THE ISSUE OF] THE 'GREATER PART OF ITS HEAD'? THE ISSUE[10] OF ITS FOREHEAD.

GEMARA. Now that it has been laid down that for a ṬUMṬUM alone or for an ANDROGINOS alone SHE MUST CONTINUE [IN HER UNCLEANNESS AND CLEANNESS AS] FOR BOTH A MALE AND A FEMALE, why should it again be necessary [to state that the same law applies where she gave birth to] A ṬUMṬUM AND A MALE OR TO AN ANDROGINOS AND A MALE?—This

(1) R. Huna. (2) How then could the restriction be said to be Rabbinical only? (3) *Asmakta.* (4) Hermaphrodite. (5) In respect of the period of cleanness, thirty-three days instead of the sixty-six prescribed for a female birth. (6) Fourteen unclean days instead of the seven prescribed for the birth of a male. (7) Since even if the *ṭumṭum* were a male, the unclean period prescribed for the birth of a male is completely absorbed by the longer one prescribed for the birth of a female (cf. prev. n.); and the same applies also to the clean period (cf. prev. n. but one). (8) Lit., 'cut'. (9) With its feet first. (10) Lit., 'as soon as . . . issued'.

was necessary: As it might have been suggested that since R. Isaac had stated, 'If the woman emits her semen first she bears a male and if the man emits his first she bears a female',[1] it should be assumed that since the one is a male the other[2] also is a male, hence we were informed [that no such assumption is made, since] it might equally be assumed that both[3] emitted their semen simultaneously, the one resulting in a male and the other in a female.[4]

R. Naḥman citing Rab ruled: If a *ṭumṭum* or an *androginos* observed a white,[5] or a red[6] discharge he[7] does not incur the obligation of an offering for entering the Sanctuary[8] nor is *terumah*[9] to be burnt on his account.[10] If he[7] observed a simultaneous discharge of white and red,[11] he incurs indeed no obligation of an offering for entering the Sanctuary[12] but *terumah*[9] must be burnt on his account;[13] for[14] it is said, *Both male and female* [28b] *shall ye put out*,[15] only a confirmed male or a confirmed female [shall ye put out], but not a *ṭumṭum* or an *androginos*. May it be suggested that the following provides support for his[16] view? [For it was taught:] 'If a *ṭumṭum* or an *androginos* observed a white,[17] or a red discharge, he incurs no obligation of an offering for entering the Sanctuary nor is *terumah* to be burnt on his account. If he observed a simultaneous discharge of white and red he incurs indeed no obligation of an offering for entering the Sanctuary but *terumah* must be burnt on his account'. Now is not the reason[18] because it is said,

(1) *Supra* 25*b*. (2) The *ṭumṭum* or the *androginos*. (3) Husband and wife. (4) That other being the *ṭumṭum*. (5) Which resembles semen; a discharge that causes no uncleanness in a woman. (6) Resembling menstrual blood, a discharge that causes no uncleanness in a man. (7) The Heb. uses the plural throughout the passage. (8) Since his uncleanness is a matter of doubt (cf. prev. two notes) and his sacrifice in connection with it would consequently be an unconsecrated beast which is forbidden to be offered on the altar. (9) Which he touched. (10) It must only be kept in suspense owing to the doubtful nature of its uncleanness. (11) So that he is inevitably unclean whatever his sex. (12) For the reason explained presently. (13) Cf. prev. n. but one. (14) This is a reason for the first ruling, why 'he incurs no guilt for entering the Sanctuary'. (15) Num. V, 3, a reference to the sending out of unclean persons from the Sanctuary (v. Rashi). (16) Rab's. (17) For notes v. *supra* on Rab's statement. (18) For the first ruling (cf. *supra* n. 14). Lit., 'what is the reason? Not?'

Both male and female shall ye put out,[1] which implies only a confirmed male and a confirmed female [shall ye put out] but not a *ṭumṭum* or an *androginos?*[2] — 'Ulla replied: No; this may represent the view of[3] R. Eliezer.[4] For we learnt: R. Eliezer stated, [It is written, *If any one touch . . . the carcass of*] *unclean swarming things and . . . it being hidden from him,*[5] one incurs the obligation of an offering only when the unclean swarming thing is hidden from him[6] but no offering is incurred when the Sanctuary is hidden from him.[7] R. Akiba stated, [Scripture says:] *It being hidden from him that he is unclean,*[5] one incurs the obligation of an offering only when it is '*hidden from him that he is unclean*'[6] but no offering is incurred when the Sanctuary is hidden from him.[8] And when it was asked, 'What is the practical difference between them?'[9] Hezekiah replied: The practical difference between them is [the case of a man who is uncertain whether he touched] a dead creeping thing or the carcass of a beast, R. Eliezer[10] holding that it is necessary[11] that a person shall know[12] whether he had contracted uncleanness through a creeping thing or through the carcass of a beast, while R. Akiba[13] maintains that this is not necessary.[14] Now did not R. Eliezer state there[14] that 'it is necessary that a person should

(1) V. p. 193, n. 15. (2) Does this then provide support for Rab's view? (3) Lit., 'this, whose?' (4) Who is of the opinion that no offering in connection with an uncleanness may be brought unless the person affected is fully aware of the actual cause of his uncleanness? Similarly in the case cited, since the actual cause of uncleanness is unknown to the *ṭumṭum* or to the *androginos*, no obligation of an offering is incurred. The Rabbis, however, who differ from R. Eliezer in subjecting one to the obligation of an offering even where the actual cause of the uncleanness is unknown, would equally subject the *ṭumṭum* and the *androginos* to the obligation of an offering in the case cited. As the *halachah* is in agreement with the Rabbis who are in the majority, no authoritative support for Rab's statement is forthcoming from this Baraitha. (5) Lev. V, 2. (6) *Sc.* when entering the Sanctuary the man forgot that he was unclean. (7) *Sc.* he well remembered when entering the Sanctuary that he was unclean but forgot that it was the Sanctuary that he was entering. (8) Shebu. 14*b*. Cf. prev. n. (9) R. Eliezer and R. Akiba. (10) Who explicitly mentioned 'unclean swarming thing'. (11) If an offering is to be incurred. (12) At the time he became unclean. (13) Who merely speaks of uncleanness in general. (14) Shebu. 18*b*.

know whether he contracted uncleanness through a creeping thing or the carcass of a beast'?[1] Well here also[2] it is necessary[3] that the person[4] should know whether he became unclean on account of the white discharge or an account of the red one; but according to R. Akiba who stated that a person incurs the obligation of an offering on account of uncleanness[5] an offering would be incurred here[2] also on account of the uncleanness.[5] But, according to Rab, why is it that they[4] incur no offering for entering the Sanctuary? Because [you say] it is written, *Both male and female shall ye put out,*[6] which implies that only a confirmed male and a confirmed female [must be put out] but not a *ṭumṭum* or an *androginos*. But, if so, *terumah*[7] also should not be burnt, since it is written, *And of them that have an issue, whether it be a man, or a woman,*[8] which implies[9] does it not, that only a confirmed male and a confirmed female [is subject to the restrictions][10] but not a *ṭumṭum* or an *androginos?*[11]—That text[8] is required for an exposition like the one made by R. Isaac; for R. Isaac stated: '*Whether it be a man*'[8] includes[12] a male leper as regards his sources,[13] '*or a woman*'[8] includes a female leper as regards her sources.[14] But is not that text[15] also required [for a deduction that the injunction[16] applies only] to that which may attain cleanness in a ritual bath,[17] thus excluding an earthenware vessel;[18] so R. Jose?[19]—If so[20] the All Merciful

(1) Of course he did. (2) The case of a simultaneous discharge of red and white. (3) If an offering is to be incurred. (4) The *ṭumṭum* or the *androginos*. (5) Though the actual cause of it is unknown to him. (6) Num. V, 3. (7) Which they touched. (8) Lev. XV, 33. (9) As does the expression '*male and female*' in Num. V, 3. (10) Of the laws spoken of in the text. (11) But this is, of course, absurd. (12) Since the expression is not required for the context which spoke previously in general terms in the same verse '*of them that have an issue*'. (13) His mouth, for instance. *Sc.* not only is his body a primary uncleanness but, as the *zab* of which the text explicitly speaks, his spittle also is a primary uncleanness and may, therefore, impart uncleanness of the first grade to man and articles. (14) Cf. prev. n. No further deduction, therefore, can be made from the same expression. (15) Num. V, 3, from which deduttion is made in the Mishnah cited from Shebu. 14*b supra*. (16) To send out from the Temple court. (17) As '*a male and female*' may. (18) Which cannot attain cleanness by immersion. (19) 'Er. 104*b*. How then can Rab deduce his ruling from the very same text? (20) That only the deduction just quoted was to be made.

should have written, 'man'.[1] And should you retort that if the All Merciful had only written 'man' it might have been presumed that a metal vessel need not be sent out[2] [it may be pointed out that this[3] could have been] deduced from *Whatsoever*[4] *is unclean by the dead,*[5] what need then was there for the specification of '*male and female*'? Obviously to deduce the same ruling as Rab did. Might it not then be suggested that the entire text served the same purpose as that to which Rab applied it?[6]—If that were the case[7] it should have been written, 'male and female' why then the expression '*both male and female*'?[8] '*Both*'[9] consequently includes all objects that attain cleanness in a ritual bath. But if so,[10] even if he[11] became unclean through any other cause of uncleanness,[12] he should not be sent out, should he?[13]—Scripture said, '*from*[14] *male*' [implying that the text deals only with] an uncleanness that is discharged from the male.[15] Does, however, any Scriptural expression of '*both male and female*' serve to exclude the *ṭumṭum* and the *androginos*? Surely in the case of valuations it is written, '*The male*',[16] and it was taught: '*The male*'[16] but no *ṭumṭum* or *androginos*. As it might have been presumed that he is not subject to

(1) Heb. *adam*, which would have included both sexes and implied the deduction. (2) And that it is for this reason that Scripture specified '*both male and female*' in order to indicate (by the specific mention of the two sexes) that the deduction must have a reference to a law that applied to both sexes viz., the attainment of cleanness in a ritual bath, so that metal vessels also should be included. (3) The law that an unclean metal vessel must also be sent out of the Temple court. (4) E.V. '*whosoever*'. (5) Num. V, 2, emphasis on the first three words which include metal vessels also. The use of 'man', therefore, would inevitably have excluded earthen vessels. (6) But, if so, whence is the deduction made that the same law applies to all that attain cleanness in a ritual bath? (7) That only Rab's ruling is to be deduced. (8) Lit., 'from male until female'. (9) Heb, '*ad*, lit. 'until'. (10) That, as Rab laid down (*supra* 28*a*), a *ṭumṭum* or an *androginos* who observed a red and a white discharge is exempt from the law requiring an unclean person to be sent out from the Temple court since he is neither a confirmed male nor a confirmed female. (11) A *ṭumṭum* or an *androginos*. (12) By coming in contact with a corpse, for instance. (13) But this surely is contrary to the accepted law. (14) E.V., '*both*'. (15) Thus excluding one contracted from a foreign body. (16) Lev. XXVII, 3.

the valuation of a man but is subject to that of a woman it was explicitly stated. *'The male*[1] ... *And if it be a female'*[2] implying:[3] Only a confirmed male and a confirmed female[4] but no *ṭumṭum* or *androginos*.[5] Is not then the reason [for the exclusion][6] that it was written, *'The male*[1] ... *And if it be a female'*,[2] but from the expression of *'male and female'* alone neither[7] could have been excluded?[8]—That text[9] is required [29a] to indicate a distinction between the valuation of a man and the valuation of a woman.[10]

IF THE EMBRYO ISSUED IN PIECES OR IN A REVERSED CONDITION etc. R. Eleazar ruled: Even if the head was with them;[11] but R. Joḥanan ruled: This[12] was learnt only in a case where the head was not with them but where the head was with them the embryo is deemed born.[13] May it be suggested that they[14] differ on a principle of Samuel for Samuel has laid down: The head[15] does not exempt[16] in the case of miscarriages?[17]—Where it[18] is whole there is no difference of opinion whatever;[19] they only differ in a case where it[18] issued in pieces, one Master[20] holding the opinion that the head is of importance[21] only where the miscarriage is whole but where it is in pieces it is of no importance, while the other Master[22] holds that even where it[18] is in pieces the head is

(1) Cf. prev. n., emphasis on *'the'*. (2) Lev. XXVII, 4, emphasis on *'if'*. (3) By the additional *'the'* and *'if'* (cf. prev. nn.). (4) Are subject to the valuations given. (5) 'Ar 4b. (6) Of the *ṭumṭum* and the *androginos* from the valuations laid down. (7) Cf. prev. n. (8) How then could it be implied *supra* that 'any Scriptural expression of *"both male and female"* serves to exclude the *ṭumṭum* etc.'? (9) *'Male'* and *'female'* in the section of valuations. (10) Hence the necessity for the additional *'the'* and *'if'* which serve the purpose of the deduction. In the text of Num. V, 3, however, the full expression of *'male and female'*, which could well have been condensed to 'man', clearly suggests the deduction made by Rab. (11) With some of the pieces; *sc.* even in such a case the embryo is not deemed born unless ITS GREATER PART ISSUED FORTH. (12) Cf. prev. n. (13) V. marg. gl. Cur. edd. in parenthesis, 'the head exempts'. (14) R. Eleazar and R. Joḥanan. (15) Of a twin, if it was drawn back after it had been put out. (16) The other twin (that was born first) from the duty of redemption (cf. Num. XVIII, 15, 16) even if it was viable. (17) Bek. 46b. Does then R. Eleazar adopt Samuel's principle? (18) The miscarriage. (19) Both R. Eleazar and R. Joḥanan agree that the issue of the head alone suffices to constitute birth. (20) R. Eleazar. (21) Constituting birth. (22) R. Joḥanan.

of importance.[1] There[2] are some who teach this passage as an independent discussion:[3] R. Eleazar ruled, The head[4] has not the status of the greater part of the limbs[5] but R. Joḥanan ruled: The head has the same status as the greater part of the limbs. They thus differ on the validity of Samuel's principle.[6]

We learnt: IF THE EMBRYO ISSUED IN PIECES OR IN A REVERSED POSITION IT IS DEEMED BORN AS SOON AS ITS GREATER PART ISSUED FORTH. Now since 'OR[7] IN A REVERSED POSITION' was specifically stated it follows that 'IN PIECES' refers to one that issued in a normal position,[8] and yet it was stated, IT IS DEEMED BORN AS SOON AS ITS GREATER PART ISSUED. Does not this then present an objection against R. Joḥanan?—R. Joḥanan can answer you: Read, ISSUED IN PIECES and IN A REVERSED POSITION. But was it not stated 'OR'?[9] It is this that was meant: IF THE EMBRYO ISSUED IN PIECES OR whole, but in either case, IN A REVERSED POSITION, IT IS DEEMED BORN AS SOON AS ITS GREATER PART ISSUED FORTH. R. Papa stated, [This[10] is] a matter of dispute between the following Tannas: 'If an embryo issued in pieces or in a reversed position it is deemed born as soon as its greater part issued forth. R. Jose ruled: Only when it issued in the normal way'. What does he[11] mean?—R. Papa replied: It is this that was meant:[12] If the embryo issued in pieces and in a reversed position[13] it is deemed born as soon as its greater part issued forth, but [it follows] if it issued in the normal way[8]

(1) Constituting birth. (2) Cur. edd. in parenthesis add; 'Another reading: The reason then is that it issued in pieces or in a reversed condition but if it issued in the normal manner the (putting out of the) head would have caused exemption. (Thus) both do not uphold Samuel's ruling, for Samuel said, The head does not exempt in the case of miscarriages'. (3) *Sc.* not in connection with our Mishnah. (4) Of a miscarriage. (5) Its issue, therefore, constitutes no birth. (6) R. Eleazar agreeing with Samuel while R. Joḥanan differs from him. According to the former version (which attaches the dispute to our Mishnah) it might be maintained (as has been submitted *supra*) that R. Eleazar also differs from him. (7) Cf. BaḤ. Cur. edd. omit. (8) Head first. (9) How can 'or' be understood as 'and'? (10) R. Joḥanan's ruling. (11) R. Jose. (12) By both the first Tanna and R. Jose. (13) Feet foremost.

the head alone[1] causes exemption.[2] R. Jose ruled: Only where its greater part issued in the normal manner.[3] R. Zebid demurred:[4] Thus it follows[5] that where the embryo issued in a reversed position[6] even the issue of its greater part causes no exemption,[5] but surely, have we not an established rule that the greater part[7] counts as the whole? Rather, said R. Zebid, it is this that was meant:[8] If the embryo issued in pieces and in a reversed position it is deemed born as soon as its greater part issued forth, but [it follows] if it issued in the normal way the head alone causes exemption.[2] R. Jose[9] ruled: Only[10] where it issued in the normal manner in a condition of viability.[11] So it was also taught: If the embryo issued in pieces and[12] in a reversed position it is deemed born as soon as its greater part issued forth, but, it follows, if it issued in the normal way the head alone causes exemption. R. Jose ruled: Only when it issued in the normal manner in a condition of viability. And what is 'the normal manner in a condition of viability'? The issue[13] of the greater part of its head. And what is meant by 'the greater part of its head'? R. Jose[14] said: The issue of its temples. Abba Ḥanan citing R. Joshua said: The issue of its forehead; and some say: The appearance[15] of the corners of its head.[16]

MISHNAH. IF A WOMAN ABORTED AND[17] IT IS UNKNOWN WHAT WAS [THE SEX OF THE EMBRYO] SHE MUST CONTINUE

(1) Even if the body issued in pieces. (2) Cf. n. *supra, sc.* the embryo is deemed to have been born, in agreement with the view of R. Joḥanan. (3) Only then is the embryo deemed to have been born. According to R. Jose the issue of the greater part of the body (but with its feet first) or the lesser part (head first) constitutes no valid birth, since, wherever an embryo issued in pieces, both conditions are essential. (4) Against R. Papa's explanation. (5) Cf. prev. n. but one. (6) Feet foremost. (7) Or 'its majority'. (8) By both the first Tanna and R. Jose. (9) Objecting to the last clause (the inference). (10) Only then does the issue of the head cause exemption. (11) But not where the embryo issued in pieces when it cannot possibly live. In such a case the issue of the head constitutes no valid birth. (12) So MS.M. Cur. edd. in parenthesis 'or'. (13) Lit., 'when it went out'. (14) MS.M., 'Nathan'. (15) Lit., 'since they will appear'. (16) The projection of the head above the neck (Rashi). (17) Being known that the abortion was a child.

[HER PERIODS OF UNCLEANNESS AND CLEANNESS AS] FOR BOTH A MALE CHILD[1] AND A FEMALE CHILD.[2] IF IT IS UNKNOWN WHETHER IT WAS A CHILD OR NOT, SHE MUST CONTINUE [HER PERIODS OF CLEANNESS AND UNCLEANNESS AS] FOR A MALE AND A FEMALE[3] AND AS A MENSTRUANT.[4]

GEMARA. R. Joshua b. Levi ruled: If a woman crossed a river and miscarried in it, she[5] must bring a sacrifice which may be eaten, since we are guided by the nature of[6] the majority of women and the majority of women bear normal children.

We learnt: IF IT IS UNKNOWN WHETHER IT WAS A CHILD OR NOT, SHE MUST CONTINUE [HER PERIODS OF CLEANNESS AND UNCLEANNESS AS] FOR A MALE AND A FEMALE AND AS A MENSTRUANT. But[7] why should she continue as a menstruant. Why should it not be said, 'Be guided by the nature of the majority of women and the majority of women bear normal children'.[8] —Our Mishnah deals with a case where there was no presumption of the existence of an embryo,[9] while R. Joshua b. Levi spoke of one where there was such presumption.

Come and hear: 'If a beast went out[10] full[11] and returned[12] empty, the young that is born subsequently is deemed to be a firstling of a doubtful nature'.[13] But[7] why [should its nature be a matter

(1) In respect of cleanness: Only thirth-three days instead of sixty-six. (2) Fourteen unclean days instead of seven. (3) Cf. prev. two notes. (4) *Sc.* if she observes a discharge of blood even during the 'thirty-three clean' days, she must be regarded as menstrually unclean, since it is possible that the abortion was no child at all in consequence of which she is not entitled to any of the privileges of childbirth. (5) Though the abortion was lost in the water and it is unknown whether it was an embryo or a mere inflated sac. (6) Lit., 'follow'. (7) If R. Joshua b. Levi's argument is tenable. (8) And consequently she ought to be entitled, at least, to the thirty-three clean days prescribed for a male birth (during which she is exempt from all menstrual uncleanness). (9) The rule of the majority is consequently inapplicable. (10) To the pasture. (11) Pregnant. (12) On the same day. (13) Since it is unknown whether it followed the birth of a developed embryo, in which case it is no firstling, or the abortion of an inflated sac, in which case it is a valid firstling. A doubtful firstling may be eaten by its owner after it had contracted a blemish and the priest has no claim upon it.

of doubt]? [Why not] be guided by the majority of beasts and, since the majority of beasts bear normal young, this one also[1] must be an ordinary beast?[2]—Rabina replied, Because it may be said: Most beasts bear young that are exempt from the law of the firstling[3] and a minority of them bear young that are not exempt from the law of the firstling but all that bear secrete,[4] and in the case of this beast, since it did not secrete, the majority rule has been impaired. If, however, all that bear secrete, must not the young, since this beast did not secrete, be a valid firstling?[5]—Rather say: Most of those that bear secrete, and in the case of this beast, since it did not secrete, the majority rule is impaired.

When Rabin came[6] he stated: 'R. Jose b. Ḥanina raised an objection[7] [from a Baraitha dealing with] a forgetful woman,[8] but I do not know what objection it was'. What was it?—It was taught: [29*b*] If a woman who departed in a condition of pregnancy[9] and returned[10] without child[11] spent, within our cognizance,[12] three clean weeks[13] and another ten weeks which were alternately unclean[14] and clean,[15] she may perform her marital duty on the night preceding the thirty-fifth day[16] and she is ordered to undergo ninety-five ritual immersions;[17] so Beth Shammai. But Beth Hillel ruled: Thirty-five immersions.[18] R. Jose son of R. Judah ruled: It

(1) Having thus been born after the birth of a normal one. (2) Not even a doubtful firstling, and its owner should consequently be allowed to eat it even if it had no blemish. (3) Since each beast can only bear one firstling. (4) A day prior to their delivery. (5) Why then was it described as one of a doubtful nature? (6) From Palestine to Babylon. (7) Against R. Joshua b. Levi. (8) Lit., 'erring', a woman who does not remember the time of her delivery; v. *supra* 18*b*. (9) Lit., 'who went out full'. (10) After some considerable time. (11) Lit., 'empty'; and she was unaware when birth took place. (12) Lit., 'and she brought before us'. (13) *Sc.* having arrived in the day-time she experienced no discharge from the moment of her arrival for three weeks. (14) I.e., experiencing a discharge on each of the seven days of the first alternate weeks. (15) I.e., she experienced no discharge on any of the seven days of the second alternate weeks. (16) Of her arrival, viz., the last night of the fifth week. After that night, however, as will be explained presently, no cohabitation can be allowed. (17) One after each period of uncleanness as will be explained presently. (18) Cf. prev. n. *mut. mut.*

suffices if one immersion is performed after the final [period of uncleanness]. Now[1] one can well understand why the woman may not perform her marital duty during the first week,[2] since she might be presumed to have given birth[3] to a male child.[4] During the second week she might be presumed to have given birth[3] to a female child.[5] During the third week she might be presumed to have given birth[3] to a female child while she was in the condition of a *zabah*.[6] But[7] why should she[8] not be permitted to perform her marital duty in the fourth week though she had observed a discharge of blood seeing that it is clean blood?[9] Must it not then be admitted that the reason[10] is because we are not guided here by the majority rule?[11]—What then[12] [is the justification for the statement] 'I do not know what objection it was'?—It might be presumed that her delivery took place a long time ago.[13] But why should she not be allowed to perform her marital

(1) Here begins the 'objection' to which Rabin referred (*supra* 29*a ad fin.*). (2) After her return. 'First week' includes the day of her return. (3) During her absence and immediately before her return. (4) So that everyone of the first seven days might be one of the seven unclean days prescribed for a woman after a male childbirth. (5) The period of uncleanness after whose birth is two weeks (cf. prev. n. *mut. mut.*). (6) I.e., during the 'eleven days' that intervene between the menstrual periods. Since it is possible that she experienced painless discharges on three consecutive days during this period she must, in addition to the fourteen days (cf. prev. n.), wait a period of another seven clean days (irrespective of whether she did, or did not observe any discharge during the fourteen days) before she can attain to cleanness. (7) If R. Joshua b. Levi's rule, that most women bear normal children, is tenable. (8) Who was known to be pregnant before her departure (v. *supra*), and who must, therefore, (cf. prev. n.) be presumed to have given birth to a normal child. (9) Since the fourth week is inevitably excluded from the unclean periods (seven days for a male and fourteen for a female) that follow childbirth, and included in the thirty-three clean days prescribed for a male birth. (10) Why the woman is treated as unclean even during the fourth week. (11) So that there is no presumption of the birth of any child and no consequent allowance of any period of clean blood. How then could R. Joshua b. Levi, contrary to this Baraitha, maintain that in such cases the majority rule is followed? (12) In view of the forceful objection just advanced. (13) And her clean blood period also has terminated long before the fourth week. The Baraitha would consequently present no objection against R. Joshua b. Levi,

duty during the fifth week[1] which[2] is a clean one?—In the case of the fourth week[3] every day might be regarded as being possibly the conclusion of [the clean days prescribed for] a childbirth and the beginning of the period of menstruation, so that the twenty-eighth day itself[4] might be presumed to be the first day of the menstrual period and she must consequently continue [her uncleanness for] seven days in respect of her menstruation.[5] But why should she not be permitted to perform her marital duty on the twenty-first day?[6]—This[7] is in agreement with the view of R. Simeon who ruled: It is forbidden to do so[8] since, thereby, she[9] might be involved in a doubtful uncleanness.[10] But[11] why

since the tenability of his majority rule in no way affects the uncleanness of the fourth week, while, as regards the imposition upon the woman of the obligation of the sacrifice prescribed for one after childbirth, the rule is in fact upheld even in this case.

(1) I.e., on any of its seven days and not only (as laid down *supra*) on the night preceding the last one (the thirty-fifth day). (2) Since the ten weeks were alternately unclean and clean. (3) On every day of which she suffered a discharge. (4) The last day of the fourth week. (5) Which, beginning on the last day of the fourth week, terminates on the sixth day of the fifth week. Hence the permissibility of marital duty (after due ritual immersion) on the night following that day (the one preceding the thirty-fifth day of her return). During the weeks that follow all intercourse would be forbidden, since each alternate 'clean' week might be regarded as the period of seven days that must be allowed to elapse after the *zibah* of the previous 'unclean' week before cleanness is attained. (6) Of her return. This day (the last one of the third week) must inevitably be a clean one. For even if the woman had been delivered on the very day of her return her period of childbirth uncleanness would have terminated (even in the case of a female child) on the fourteenth day, while the seven days following could be counted as the prescribed seven days following a period of *zibah* on the last of which she is permitted to perform ritual immersion at any time of the day and to attain to a state of cleanness (cf. Yoma 6*a*) for the rest of that day. (7) The prohibition of intercourse on the twenty-first day. (8) To have intercourse on the seventh day after the termination of a *zibah* even though ritual immersion had been performed. (9) If she happened to suffer a discharge later in the day after intercourse. (10) Of *zibah*. A discharge on the seventh day following the termination of *zibah* renders void all the previous counting, since the seven clean days must be complete. (11) Since on the twenty-first day she was still clean and her first discharge in the following (fourth) week occurred presumably on the twenty-second day.

should she not be permitted intercourse in the evening?[1]—This is a case where she observed the discharge in the evening.[2] 'And she is ordered to undergo ninety-five ritual immersions': During the first week[3] she is ordered immersion every night, since it might be presumed that she gave birth[4] to a male child.[5] During the second week she is ordered immersion every night,[6] since it might be presumed that she gave birth[7] to a female child;[5] and every day, since it might also be presumed that she gave birth to a male child while she was in a condition of *zibah*.[8] During the third week she is ordered immersion every day, since it might be presumed that she gave birth to a female child while she was in a state of *zibah*;[9] and every night, because Beth Shammai follow the view they expressed elsewhere that one who performed immersion on a long day[10] must again perform immersion [at its conclusion].[11] [30*a*] Consider! How many[12] are the days of cleanness?[13] Sixty-six.[14]

(1) Following the twenty-first day. (2) Cf. prev. n. And similarly in the case of all the alternate unclean weeks the discharges occurred in the evenings. (3) After her return. (4) Seven days previously. (5) So that each day of the first week might possibly be the first one after the termination of the unclean days, and it is a religious duty to perform ritual immersion immediately after the unclean days had terminated. (6) Cf. BaḤ for a different reading. (7) Fourteen days previously. (8) So that each day of the first week counted as the sixth of the clean days after *zibah* which (cf. *supra* n. 5) must be immediately followed (during the day-time of the following day) by ritual immersion. (9) Cf. prev. n. *mut. mut.* (10) The fourteen unclean days (after which the woman performs immersion) and the sixty-six clean days that follow (during which she is forbidden to eat *terumah*) are regarded as one long day on which immersion had been performed and sunset is awaited (sunset being represented by that of the eightieth day after childbirth) to complete and terminate all traces of uncleanness. (11) *Sc.* on the night following the eightieth day and preceding the eighty-first one. As every day of the third week might possibly be the eightieth, immersion must be performed on every night of that week. The same reason could, of course, be given for the necessity for immersion in the previous weeks had there been no other reasons to justify it. (12) On the assumption that the birth was that of a female child. (13) That follow the fourteen days of uncleanness, and the last day of which might be presumed to coincide with any of the days under discussion. (14) So that during the presumed days of cleanness no more than sixty-six immersions can be expected owing to the presumption that each might possibly be the eightieth day.

Deduct[1] the third week[2] in which the woman was required to perform [nightly] immersions[3] there remain sixty minus one. Now, sixty minus one and thirty-five[4] are ninety-four, how then is the number of ninety-five obtained?[5]—R. Jeremiah of Difti replied: This is a case, for instance, where the woman[6] made her appearance before us at twilight,[7] so that[8] we impose upon her an additional immersion.[9] According to Beth Hillel, however, who maintain that one who performed immersion on a long day[10] requires no immersion [at the conclusion][11] how is the number thirty-five obtained?[5]—Twenty-eight, as has been explained,[12] while during the fifth week we require the woman to undergo immersion every night, since[13] it might be assumed [that each day[14] is the] last of the days of her menstruation.[15] What need was there for the mention of ten weeks[16] seeing that eight and a half[17] would suffice?[18]—Since he had to mention half a week he mentioned all of it, and since he had to mention an unclean week[19] he also mentioned a clean one.[20] But are there [not also the additional] immersions[21]

(1) From these sixty-six days. (2) Which comprises the first seven of these. (3) On account of the same possibility that each was the eightieth day (in addition to her daily immersions necessitated by the possibility of her bearing in the condition of *zibah*). (4) Seven during the first week and fourteen during the second as well as during the third week ($7 + 2 \times 14 = 7 + 28 = 35$). (5) Lit., 'what is their doing'. (6) On her return. (7) Of the day preceding the one from which the counting begins. As twilight is a time of doubtful day and doubtful night it cannot be definitely regarded as either. (8) Owing to the doubt. (9) Immediately after her appearance. That day, however, owing to the doubtful nature of twilight (cf. prev. n. but one) cannot be counted among the days and nights under discussion. (10) Cf. p. 204, n. 10. (11) So that in the third week (cf. *supra 29b ad fin.*) only seven immersions are to be performed, and these together with the fourteen of the second week and the seven of the first week only amount to twenty-eight. (12) Cf. prev. n. (13) Owing to her daily discharge during the fourth week. (14) Of the fifth week. (15) Which may have begun on any of the days of the fourth week each of which might have been preceded by the last of the days of cleanness. (16) *Supra 29b ab init.* (17) In addition to the three clean weeks. (18) To make up the number 80: $3 + 8\frac{1}{2}$ weeks $= 11\frac{1}{2}$ weeks $= 11 \times 7 + 3 = 80$ days. (19) The ninth; the first of each pair of alternate weeks, commencing with the first, being assumed (cf. *supra 29b ab init.*) to be an unclean one. (20) The tenth; being second of the last pair. (21) Every day after the fourth week.

due to the possibility of the woman's being a *zabah?*[1] They[2] only count the immersions before intercourse[3] but not those that follow. But according to Beth Shammai who[4] count also the immersions that follow intercourse, why was no mention made of the immersions that are due to the possibility of the woman's being a *zabah?* —They[5] only deal with immersions that are occasioned by childbirth but do not discuss those that are due to *zibah*. Is there then [no mention of the possibility that the woman might have] given birth to a child while she was in a condition of *zibah?*[6]— They do take note of the possibility of a birth in a condition of *zibah*, but no note is taken of *zibah* alone. Why should not the woman perform immersion in the day-time of each of the days of the first week after she appeared before us, seeing that it is possible that her counting[7] ended on that day?[8]—This is in agreement with[9] R. Akiba who ruled: It is required that the counting[7] shall take place within our cognizance.[10] But why should she not perform immersion at the end of the first week?[11]— They do not discuss one day of a week. But why should she not perform immersion on the first day she comes to us, seeing that it is possible that she is awaiting a day for a day?[12]—They deal with a major *zabah*[13] but not with a minor one.[14] Three rulings may thus be inferred: It may be inferred that it was R. Akiba

(1) During the preceding unclean week. Only in the case of the fourth week which has been preceded by clean weeks could no such immersions be expected. (2) Beth Hillel. Lit., 'he'. (3) On the night preceding the thirty-fifth day. (4) Giving the number as ninety-five. (5) Beth Shammai. (6) Of course there is. How then could it be maintained that immersions due to *zibah* are not discussed? (7) Of the seven days of menstruation. (8) Why then was it stated (*supra* 29*b ad fin.*) that she performs immersion in the nights only? (9) Lit., 'this whose?' (10) No valid counting, therefore, is possible before a week had passed from the date of her return. (11) The seventh day after her return, when the counting did take place within our cognizance. (12) A clean day for an unclean one, *sc.* she might be within the period of the eleven days of *zibah* that intervene between the menstrual periods, during which she must perform immersion on the clean day following the one on which she experienced a discharge. (13) The result of discharges on three consecutive days within the eleven days period (cf. prev. n.). (14) Due to a discharge on one or two days only.

who ruled that the counting[1] must take place within our cognizance; and it may be inferred that it was R. Simeon who stated, 'The Sages have truly laid down that it is forbidden to do so since thereby she might be involved in a doubtful uncleanness';[2] and it may also be inferred that it is a religious duty to perform immersion at the proper time.[3] R. Jose son of R. Judah, however, ruled: It suffices if one immersion is performed after the final [period of uncleanness], and we do not uphold the view that it is a religious act to perform immersion at the proper time.[3]

MISHNAH. IF A WOMAN MISCARRIED ON THE FORTIETH DAY,[4] SHE NEED NOT TAKE INTO CONSIDERATION THE POSSIBILITY OF A VALID CHILDBIRTH; BUT IF ON THE FORTY-FIRST DAY,[4] SHE MUST CONTINUE [HER PERIODS OF UNCLEANNESS AND CLEANNESS AS] FOR BOTH A MALE AND A FEMALE[5] AND AS FOR A MENSTRUANT.[6] R. ISHMAEL RULED: [IF SHE MISCARRIED ON] THE FORTY-FIRST DAY[4] SHE CONTINUES [HER PERIODS OF UNCLEANNESS AND CLEANNESS AS] FOR A MALE[7] AND AS FOR A MENSTRUANT, BUT IF ON THE EIGHTY-FIRST DAY SHE MUST CONTINUE [THESE PERIODS AS] FOR A MALE AND A FEMALE AND A MENSTRUANT; BECAUSE A MALE IS FULLY FASHIONED[8] ON THE FORTY-FIRST DAY AND A FEMALE ON THE EIGHTY-FIRST DAY. THE SAGES, HOWEVER, MAINTAIN THAT BOTH THE FASHIONING[9] OF THE MALE AND THE FASHIONING[9] OF THE FEMALE TAKE THE SAME COURSE, EACH LASTING FORTY-ONE DAYS.

(1) Of the seven days of menstruation. (2) *Supra 29b ad fin.* q. v. notes. (3) I.e., at the earliest possible moment. (4) After presumed conception. (5) I.e., since it is possible that the abortion was the embryo of a child either male or female, the restrictions of both are imposed upon her but none of the relaxations of either. (6) It being possible that the embryo was neither male nor female so that there was no valid childbirth. (7) I.e., seven days of uncleanness even if there was no bleeding at the miscarriage. (8) Lit., 'finished'. (9) Lit., 'creation'.

GEMARA. Why was MALE mentioned?[1] If in respect of the days of uncleanness, FEMALE was mentioned;[2] and if in respect of the days of cleanness,[3] [30b] was not menstruant mentioned?[4] —In order that if the woman observed a discharge on the thirty-fourth day[5] and then observed one on the forty-first day[6] she[7] shall remain unclean[8] until the forty-eighth day.[9] And so also in respect [of the possible birth of] a female[10] [the last word had to be mentioned] so that if she observed any blood on the seventy-fourth day and these again on the eighty-first day she shall remain unclean until the eighty-eighth day.[11]

R. ISHMAEL RULED: [IF SHE MISCARRIED ON] THE FORTY-FIRST DAY SHE CONTINUES [HER PERIODS OF UNCLEANNESS AND CLEANNESS AS] FOR A MALE AND AS FOR A MENSTRUANT etc. It was taught: R. Ishmael stated, Scripture prescribed uncleanness[12] and cleanness[13] in respect of a male[14] and it also prescribed uncleanness[15] and cleanness[16] in respect of a female,[17] as

(1) In the ruling, FOR BOTH A MALE AND A FEMALE AND AS FOR A MENSTRUANT. (2) Whose fourteen days of uncleanness obviously absorb the seven unclean days of a male birth. (3) *Sc.* that she is only entitled to the thirty-three clean days of the male and not to the sixty-six days of the female. (4) Whose discharges of blood are invariably unclean whatever the day. (5) When she is held to be unclean on account of possible menstruation, though the day is only $(34 - 7 = 27)$ the twenty-seventh of the thirty-three clean days prescribed for a male birth. (6) Which is the eighth day after the discharge on the thirty-fourth. (7) Despite the previous assumption of menstruation on the thirty-fourth day, which would put the forty-first day outside the seven days of the menstruation period (when the observation of a discharge necessitates the waiting of no more than one single day). (8) Lit., 'damaged'. (9) It being assumed that the miscarriage was a male and that the thirty-fourth day was therefore still within the thirty-three clean days prescribed for a male birth, so that the second discharge on the forty-first day was the first menstrual one after the completion of the thirty-three clean days in consequence of which she must wait another seven days to complete the menstruation period. Her ritual immersion, therefore, cannot take place before $(41 + 7 = 48)$ the forty-eighth day. (10) I.e., the restrictions on account of this possibility imposed in our Mishnah. (11) Cf. prev. nn. *mut. mut.* (12) Seven days (Lev. XII, 2). (13) Thirty-three days (ibid. 4). (14) Making a total of forty days. (15) Fourteen days (Lev. XII, 5). (16) Sixty-six days (ibid.). (17) A total of eighty days.

in the case of the former[1] his fashioning period[2] corresponds to his unclean and clean periods[3] so also in the case of the latter[4] her fashioning period[5] corresponds to her unclean and clean periods.[3] They[6] replied: The duration of the fashioning period cannot be derived from that of uncleanness. Furthermore, they said to R. Ishmael, A story is told of Cleopatra the queen of Alexandria[7] that when her handmaids were sentenced to death by royal decree they[8] were subjected to a test[9] and it was found that both [a male and a female embryo] were fully fashioned on the forty-first day. He replied: I bring you proof from the Torah and you bring proof from some fools! But what was his 'proof from the Torah'? If it was the argument, 'Scripture prescribed uncleanness and cleanness in respect of a male and it also prescribed uncleanness and cleanness in respect of a female etc.', have they not already replied, 'The duration of the fashioning period cannot be derived from that of uncleanness'?—The Scriptural text says, *She bear*,[10] Scripture thus[11] doubles the ante-natal period[12] in the case of a female.[13] But why [should the test spoken of by the Rabbis be described as] 'proof from some fools'?—It might be suggested that the conception of the female preceded that of the male by forty days.[14] And the Rabbis?[15]—They[16] were made to drink[17] a scattering

(1) Lit., 'when it prescribed uncleanness and cleanness in respect of the male'. (2) Forty days. (3) Lit., 'similarly'. (4) Cf. prev. n. but two *mut. mut.* (5) Eighty days. (6) The Rabbis at the schoolhouse. (7) Cur. edd. '*Alexandrus*' (cf. Jast.). The following incident may have its origin in a legend that Cleopatra (68-30 B.C.E.) before committing suicide attempted various forms of execution on her slaves (cf. Golds.). (8) Having forfeited their lives and being at her mercy. (9) Fertilization and subsequent operation. (10) Lev. XII, 5. (11) By the superfluous expression of '*she bear*' the omission of which could in no way have affected the sense of the text. (12) In which the embryo is fashioned. Lit., 'added to her . . . another birth', *sc.* forty days in addition to the forty days during which a male embryo is fashioned. (13) Which proves that the fashioning period of a female embryo is (40 + 40 =) 80 days. (14) And that this was the reason why in the Cleopatra test both were found to be fully fashioned. (15) How could they rely upon such inconclusive evidence? (16) Cleopatra's handmaids. (17) Before they were experimented on.

drug[1] And R. Ishmael?[2]—Some constitution is insusceptible[3] to a drug.[4] Then said R. Ishmael to them:[5] A story is told of Cleopatra the Grecian[6] queen that when her handmaids were sentenced to death under a government order they were subjected to a test and it was found that a male embryo was fully fashioned on the forty-first day[7] and a female embryo on the eighty-first day. They replied: No one adduces proof from fools. What is the reason?[8]—It is possible that the handmaid with the female delayed[9] [intercourse] for forty days and that it was only then that conception occurred.[10] And R. Ishmael?[11]—They were placed in the charge of a warden.[12] And the Rabbis?[13]—There is no guardian against unchastity;[14] and the warden himself might have intercourse with them. But[15] is it not possible that if a surgical operation had been performed on the forty-first day the female embryo also might have been found in a fully fashioned condition like the male?[16]—Abaye replied: They[17] were equal as far as these distinguishing marks were concerned.[18]

THE SAGES, HOWEVER, MAINTAIN THAT BOTH THE FASHIONING OF THE MALE AND THE FASHIONING OF THE FEMALE etc. Is not the ruling of the Sages identical with that of the first Tanna?[19] And should you reply that the object[20] was to indicate

(1) I.e., destroying the semen in the womb. (2) What objection then could he have put forward against the proof of the Rabbis? (3) Lit., 'does not receive'. (4) It was quite possible, therefore, that despite the drug the conception of the female took place forty days prior to that of the male. (5) The Rabbis. (6) Egypt in Cleopatra's reign was under the influence of Greek institutions and Greek culture. (7) After conception. (8) Why the incident cited should not be accepted as proof. MS.M. reads: 'What is the reason why no proof is adduced from fools?' (9) Cf. BaḤ. (10) The 'eighty-first day' was, therefore, in reality the forty-first one. (11) How in view of this possibility can he maintain that the incident provides the required proof? (12) Whose duty it was to prevent all intercourse except on one particular day. (13) How in view of this safeguard could it be suggested that the conception of the female was delayed for forty days? (14) Popular proverb. (15) Since the test in respect of the female took place on the eighty-first day. (16) An objection against R. Ishmael. (17) The male and the female. (18) Those of the male embryo on the fortieth day were like those of the female on the eighty-first. (19) Who earlier in the Mishnah ruled

that the anonymous Mishnah represented the view of the Rabbis because when an individual is opposed by many the *halachah* is in agreement with the many, is not this[1] obvious?[2]—It might have been presumed that R. Ishmael's reason is acceptable since it is also supported by a Scriptural text,[3] hence we were informed[4] [that the *halachah* is in agreement with the Sages].[5]

R. Simlai delivered the following discourse: What does an embryo resemble when it is in the bowels of its mother? Folded writing tablets.[6] Its hands rest on its two temples respectively, its two elbows on its two legs and its two heels against its buttocks. Its head lies between its knees, its mouth is closed and its navel is open, and it eats what its mother eats and drinks what its mother drinks, but produces no excrements because otherwise it might kill its mother. As soon, however, as it sees the light[7] the closed organ[8] opens and the open one[9] closes, for if that had not happened the embryo could not live even one single hour. A light burns above its head and it looks and sees from one end of the world to the other, as it is said, *When his lamp shined above my head, and by His light I walked through darkness.*[10] And do not be astonished at this, for a person sleeping here[11] might see a dream in Spain. And there is no time in which a man enjoys greater happiness than in those days,[12] for it is said, *O that I were as the months of old, as in the days when God watched over me;*[13] now which are *'the days'* that make up *'months'*[14] and do not make up years?

that 'IF ON THE FORTY-FIRST DAY SHE MUST CONTINUE . . . FOR BOTH A MALE AND A FEMALE AND FOR A MENSTRUANT' from which it follows that a female also is fully fashioned on the forty-first day. (20) Of repeating in the name of the Sages an earlier anonymous ruling.

(1) That the anonymous ruling is the view of the Rabbis. (2) Of course it is, since all anonymous rulings generally represent the views of the majority of Sages and the *halachah* is in agreement with them. (3) As quoted by R. Ishmael *supra*. (4) By repeating the anonymous Mishnah in the name of the Sages. (5) Despite R. Ishmael's argument and text. (6) *Pinkas*, cf. πίναξ. (7) Lit., 'went out to the air space of the world'. (8) Its mouth. (9) Navel. (10) Job XXIX, 3. (11) Babylon. (12) Lit., 'and you have no days in which a man dwells in more happiness than in these days'. (13) Job XXIX, 2. (14) Lit., 'in which there are the months' (of bearing).

The months of pregnancy of course.[1] It is also taught all the Torah from beginning to end,[2] for it is said, *And he taught me, and said unto me: 'Let thy heart hold fast my words, keep my commandments and live'*,[3] and it is also said, *When the converse of God was upon my tent.*[4] Why the addition of[5] 'and it is also said'?—In case you might say that it was only the prophet who said that,[6] come and hear '*when the converse of God was upon my tent.*[4] As soon as it sees the light an angel approaches, slaps it on its mouth and causes it to forget all the Torah completely,[2] as it is said, *Sin coucheth at the door.*[7] It does not emerge from there before it is made to take an oath,[8] as it is said, *That unto Me every knee shall bow, every tongue shall swear;*[9] '*That unto Me every knee shall bow*' refers to the day of dying of which it is said, *All they that go down to the dust shall kneel before Him;*[10] '*Every tongue shall swear*' refers to the day of birth of which it is said, *He that hath clean hands, and a pure heart, who hath not taken My name*[11] *in vain, and hath not sworn deceitfully.*[12] What is the nature of the oath that it is made to take? Be righteous, and be never wicked; and even if all the world tells you, 'You are righteous', consider yourself wicked.[13] Always bear in mind[14] that the Holy One, blessed be He, is pure, that his ministers are pure and that the soul which He gave you is pure; if you preserve it in purity, well and good, but if not, I will take it away from you. The school of R. Ishmael taught: This may be compared to the case of a priest who handled over some *terumah* to an *'am ha-areẓ* and told him, 'If you preserve it under conditions of cleanness, well and good, but if not, I will burn it in your presence'. R. Eleazar [31*a*] observed: What is the Scriptural proof?[15] *From my mother's womb Thou art* gozi.[16] What is the proof that '*gozi*'

(1) Lit., 'be saying, these are the months of bearing'. (2) Lit., 'all of it'. (3) Prov. IV, 4. (4) Job XXIX, 4. (5) Lit., 'what'. (6) So that it does not apply to other men. (7) Gen. IV, 7. (8) Its nature is described presently. (9) Isa. XLV, 23. (10) Ps. XXII, 30. (11) So the *ḳre*. The *kethib* is 'his name'. (12) Ps. XXIV, 4. (13) Lit., 'be in your eyes like a wicked man'. (14) Lit., 'be knowing'. (15) That an oath is taken on the day of one's birth. (16) Ps. LXXI, 6; E.V., *Thou art He that took me out of my mother's womb.*

implies 'swearing'?—Because it is written, *Swear* [gozi] *concerning thy naziriteship and cast away.*[1]

R. Eleazar further stated: What does an embryo resemble when it is in its mother's bowels? A nut floating in a bowl of water. Should someone put his finger upon it, it would sink on the one side or on the other.

Our Rabbis taught: During the first three months[2] the embryo occupies the lowest chamber, during the middle ones it occupies the middle chamber and during the last months it occupies the uppermost chamber; and when its time to emerge arrives it turns over and then emerges, and this is the cause of the woman's pains.[3] This also agrees with what was taught:[4] The pains of a female birth are more intense than those of a male birth. R. Eleazar further observed, 'What is the Scriptural proof for this?[5] *When I was made in secret, and curiously wrought in the lowest parts of the earth;*[6] it does not say *'dwelt'* but *'curiously wrought'*.[7] Why are the pains of a female birth greater than those of a male birth?—The female emerges in the position she assumes during intercourse and the male emerges in the position he assumes during intercourse. The former, therefore, turns her face upwards[8] while the latter[9] need not turn his face.

Our Rabbis taught: During the first three months[2] marital intercourse is injurious to the woman and it is also injurious to the child. During the middle ones it is injurious to the woman but beneficial for the child. During the last months it is beneficial for both the woman and the child, since on account of it the child becomes well-formed and of strong vitality.

One taught: He who indulges in marital intercourse on the ninetieth day[2] is as though he had shed blood. But whence could one know this?[10]—Rather, said Abaye, one carries on marital inter-

(1) Jer. VII, 29; E.V., *Cut off thy hair, and cast it away.* (2) Of pregnancy. (3) At a childbirth. (4) So Bomb. ed. Cur. edd. 'we learnt'. (5) That the embryo first occupies the lowest chamber. (6) Ps. CXXXIX, 15. (7) Implying the inception of the embryo; and this is stated to be *'in the lowest parts'*. (8) The turning intensifying the pains. (9) Since the embryo is all the time lying face downwards. (10) When the ninetieth day is.

course in the usual manner and *the Lord preserveth the simple.*[1]

Our Rabbis taught: There are three partners in man, the Holy One, blessed be He, his father and his mother. His father supplies the semen of the white substance out of which are formed the child's bones, sinews, nails, the brain in his head and the white in his eye; his mother supplies the semen of the red substance out of which is formed his skin, flesh, hair, blood[2] and the black of his eye; and the Holy One, blessed be He, gives him the spirit and the breath,[3] beauty of features, eyesight, the power of hearing[4] and the ability to speak[5] and to walk,[6] understanding and discernment. When his time to depart from the world approaches the Holy One, blessed be He, takes away his share and leaves the shares of his father and his mother with them. R. Papa observed: It is this that people have in mind when they say, 'Shake off the salt[7] and cast the flesh to the dog'.[8]

R. Ḥinena b. Papa gave the following exposition: What is the purport of the Scriptural text, *Who doeth great things past finding out; yea, marvellous things without number?*[9] Come and see the contrast between the potency of the Holy One, blessed be He, and that of mortal man.[10] A man might put his things[11] in a skin bottle[12] [whose holes[13] are] tied up and whose orifice is turned upwards and yet it is doubtful whether [the things] would be preserved or not, whereas the Holy One, blessed be He, fashions the embryo in a woman's internal organ that is open and whose orifice is turned downwards and yet it is preserved. Another exposition: If a man puts his things on the scale of a balance, the heavier they are the lower the scale descends, whereas the Holy One, blessed be He,

(1) Ps. CXVI, 6; those who are unable to protect themselves. (2) So MS.M. and Elijah Wilna. Cur. edd. omit. (3) Or 'soul'. (4) Lit., 'of the ear'. (5) Lit., 'of the mouth'. (6) Lit., 'walking of the feet'. (7) Metaph. for the soul, 'the preserver of the human body'. (8) Proverb. The lifeless body is of little more value. (9) Job IX, 10. (10) Lit., 'that not like the measure of . . . is the measure of flesh and blood'. (11) Cf. MS.M. Cur. edd., 'the measure of flesh and blood he puts a thing'. (12) *Ḥemeth*, a skin drawn off the body of the animal in such a manner as not to damage it except for the cuts at the tail and legs. (13) Cf. prev. n.

[fashioned the woman in such a manner that] the heavier the embryo the higher it rises.[1]

R. Jose the Galilean gave the following exposition: What is the purport of the Scriptural text, *I will give thanks unto Thee, for I am fearfully and wonderfully made; wonderful are Thy works; and that my soul knoweth right well?*[2] Come and see the contrast between the potency of the Holy One, blessed be He, and that of mortal man.[3] If a man[4] puts different seeds in a bed each grows in the manner of its own particular species, whereas the Holy One, blessed be He, fashions the embryo in the woman's bowels in such a manner that all[5] grow into one and the same kind. Another exposition: If a dyer puts different ingredients into a boiler they all unite into one colour, whereas the Holy One, blessed be He, fashions the embryo in a woman's bowels in a manner that each element develops in its own natural way.[6]

R. Joseph gave the following exposition: What is the purport of the Scriptural text, *I will give thanks unto Thee, O Lord; for though Thou wast angry with me, Thine anger is turned away, and Thou comfortest me.*[7] The text alludes to[8] two men who set out on a trading expedition when a thorn got into [the foot of] one of them who[9] began to blaspheme and to revile. After a time, however, when he heard that his friend's ship had sunk into the sea he[10] began to laud and praise. Hence it is written, '*Thine anger is turned away, and Thou comfortest me*'. This is indeed in line with what R. Eleazar stated: What is implied by the Scriptural text, *Who doeth wondrous things alone;*[11] *and blessed be His glorious name for ever?*[12] Even the person for whom a miracle is performed[13] is unaware of the miracle.[14]

(1) Beginning in the lowest chamber at conception it rises steadily to the highest, as stated *supra*. (2) Ps. CXXXIX, 14. (3) V. p. 214, n. 10. (4) Cf. MS.M. Cur. edd. add, 'the measure of flesh and blood'. (5) The semen of both parents. (6) The one develops into bones, sinews, nails etc. while the other develops into skin, flesh etc., as stated *supra*. (7) Isa. XII, 1. (8) Lit., 'of what does Scripture speak? Of'. (9) Having been compelled by the accident to interrupt his journey. (10) Being gratified at the turn of events which prevented him from embarking on the disastrous expedition. (11) Emphasis on '*alone*'. E.V., *Who only . . . things*. (12) Ps. LXXII, 18f. (13) Lit., 'master of the miracle'. (14) Only God alone knows it. Cf. prev. n. but two.

R. Ḥanina b. Papa made the following exposition: What is the implication of the Scriptural text, *Thou measurest my going about and my lying down, and art acquainted with all my ways?*[1] It[2] teaches that man is not fashioned from all the drop but only from its purest part. The school of R. Ishmael taught: This is analogous to the action of one who, winnowing[3] in threshing floors, takes up the edible part and leaves the refuse. This is in agreement with an exposition of R. Abbahu. For R. Abbahu pointed out an incongruity: It is written, *For Thou hast winnowed me from*[4] *strength*[5] and it is also written,[6] *The God that girdeth me with strength!*[7] David in effect said to the Holy One, blessed be He, 'Sovereign of the world, Thou hast winnowed me[8] and Thou hast girded me with strength'.

R. Abbahu also gave this exposition: What is the implication of the Scriptural text, *Who hath counted the dust of Jacob, or numbered the stock of Israel?*[9] It teaches that the Holy One, blessed be He, sits and counts the stock of Israel. 'When [He wonders] will appear the drop from which a righteous man could be fashioned'? Moreover, it is for this reason that the eye of the wicked Balaam was blinded. He said, 'Would He who is pure and holy and whose ministers are pure and holy look upon such a thing?' His eye was forthwith blinded, for it is written, *And the saying of the man whose eye is closed.*[14] This is in line with what R. Joḥanan stated: What is the implication of the Scriptural text, *And he lay with her in that night?*[11] It teaches that the Holy One, blessed be He, assisted in that matter. For it is said, *Issaschar is a large-boned ass;*[12] it is the ass[13] that has caused[14] the birth of Issaschar.

R. Isaac citing R. Ammi[15] stated: If the woman emits her semen

(1) Ps. CXXXIX, 3. (2) The expression of *zeritha* ('*Thou measureth*') which coming from the root זרה, may be rendered, 'thou winnowest'. (3) Cf. prev. n. (4) E.V., 'girded me with'. (5) II Sam. XXII, 40. (6) In the corresponding passage. (7) Ps. XVIII, 33. (8) Cf. *supra* n. 2. (9) Num. XXIII, 10. (10) Ibid. XXIV, 3. E.V., '*is opened*'. (11) Gen. XXX, 16; emphasis on הוא. (12) Ibid. XLIX, 14. (13) On which Jacob rode and which stopped at Leah's tent. (14) *Garem* ('*large-boned*') is derived from a root which in Aramaic signifies also 'to cause'. The consonants may be vocalized as *garam. Ḥamor garam*, 'the ass was the cause'. (15) Var. lec. Assi ('En Jacob).

first she bears a male child; if the man emits his semen first she bears a female child; for it is said, *If a woman emits semen*[1] *and bear a man-child.*[2]

Our Rabbis taught: At first it used to be said that 'if the woman emits her semen first she will bear a male, and if the man emits his semen first she will bear a female', but the Sages did not explain the reason, until R. Zadok came and explained it: *These are the sons of Leah, whom she bore unto Jacob in Paddan-aram, with his daughter Dinah,*[3] Scripture thus ascribes the males to the females[4] and the females to the males.[5]

And the sons of Ulam were mighty men of valour, archers; and had many sons, and sons' sons.[6] Now is it within the power of man to increase[7] the number of *'sons and sons' sons'?* But the fact is that because [31b] they contained themselves during intercourse[8] in order that their wives should emit their semen first so that their children shall be males, Scripture attributes to them the same merit as if they had themselves caused the increase of the number of their sons and sons' sons. This explains what R. Kaṭṭina said, 'I could make all my children to be males'. Raba stated: One who desires all his children to be males should cohabit twice in succession.

R. Isaac citing R. Ammi[9] further stated: A woman conceives only immediately before her menstrual period, for it is said, *Behold I was brought forth in iniquity;*[10] but R. Joḥanan stated: A woman conceives only immediately after her ritual immersion, for it is said, *And in cleansing*[11] *did my mother conceive me.*[12] What is the proof that *'ḥeṭ'*[13] bears the meaning of cleansing?—Since it is written *'we-ḥiṭṭe*[14] *the house'*[15] and this is translated,[16] *'And so shall*

(1) E.V., *'be delivered'*. (2) Lev. XII, 2. (3) Gen. XLVI, 15. (4) *'Sons of Leah'*. (5) *'His daughter Dinah'*. (6) I Chron. VIII, 40. (7) The Heb. for *'had many'* is the Hif. of רבה which may be rendered 'cause to increase'. (8) Lit., 'in the belly'. (9) Var. lec. Assi ('En Jacob). (10) Ps. LI, 7. The last word is taken as an allusion to the menstruation period when intercourse is an *'iniquity'* and the prefixed *beth* (*'in'*) is rendered 'near'. (11) E.V., *'sin'*. (12) Ps. LI, 7. (13) The Heb. word here rendered *'cleansing'* (E.V., *'sin'*). (14) Of the same rt. as *ḥeṭ*. (15) Lev. XIV, 52. (16) I.e., by the Targum Onkelos.

he cleanse the house'. And if you prefer I might reply: The proof is derived from the following: *Purge*[1] *me with hyssop and I shall be clean.*[2]

R. Isaac citing R. Ammi further stated: As soon as a male comes into the world peace comes into the world, for it is said, *Send ye a gift*[3] *for the ruler of the land*[4] [and the Hebrew for] male[5] [is composed of the consonants of the words for] 'this is a gift'.[6]

R. Isaac citing[7] R. Ammi further stated: When a male comes into the world his provision comes with him, [the Hebrew for] male [*zakar*, being composed of the consonants of the words for] 'this is provision [*zeh kar*]', for it is written, *And he prepared a great provision* [kera] *for them.*[8] A female has nothing with her, [the Hebrew for] female [*neḳebah*] implying 'she comes with nothing' [*neḳiyyah ba'ah*]. Unless she demands her food nothing is given to her, for it is written, *Demand* [naḳebah][9] *from*[10] *me thy wages and I will give it.*[11]

R. Simeon b. Yoḥai was asked by his disciples: Why did the Torah ordain that a woman after childbirth should bring a sacrifice? He replied: When she kneels in bearing she swears impetuously that she will have no intercourse with her husband. The Torah, therefore, ordained that she should bring a sacrifice. (R. Joseph demurred: Does she not[12] act presumptuously[13] in which case the absolution of the oath[14] depends on her regretting it?[15] Furthermore, she should[16] have brought a sacrifice prescribed for an oath!)[17] And why did the Torah ordain that in the case of a male [the woman is clean] after seven days and in that of a female after fourteen days? [On the birth of a] male with whom all rejoice she regrets her oath after seven days, [but on the birth of a female]

(1) *Teḥaṭe'eni* (cf. prev. n. but one). (2) Ps. LI, 9. (3) *Kar*; E.V. 'lambs'. (4) Isa. XVI, 1. (5) *Zakar*. (6) *Zeh kar*. Gifts foster peace. (7) V. marg. gl. Cur. edd., 'the school of'. (8) II Kings VI, 23. (9) The same consonants as those for female (*neḳebah*). (10) E.V., 'appoint'. (11) Gen. XXX, 28. (12) When swearing. (13) Of course she does. (14) Lit., 'the thing'. (15) It does. Now in such a case it is only a Sage who, after satisfying himself of the sincerity of her plea, may absolve her. A sacrifice, however, has no place here at all. (16) Instead of the sacrifice of a bird prescribed for a woman after a confinement. (17) A lamb or a goat.

about whom everybody is upset she regrets her oath after fourteen days. And why did the Torah ordain circumcision on the eighth day?[1] In order that the guests[2] shall not enjoy themselves[3] while his father and mother are not in the mood for it.[4]

It was taught: R. Meir used to say, Why did the Torah ordain that the uncleanness of menstruation should continue for seven days? Because being in constant contact with his wife[5] [a husband might] develop a loathing towards her. The Torah, therefore, ordained: Let her[6] be unclean for seven days[7] in order that[8] she shall be beloved by her husband as at the time of her first entry into the bridal chamber.

R. Dostai son of R. Jannai was asked by his disciples: Why[9] does a man go in search of a woman and no woman goes in search of a man? This is analogous to the case of a man who lost something. Who goes in search of what? He who lost the thing goes in search of what he lost.[10] And why does the man lie face downwards and the woman face upwards towards the man? He [faces the elements] from which he was created[11] and she [faces the man] from whom she was created.[12] And why is a man easily pacified and a woman is not easily pacified? He [derives his nature] from the place from which he was created[13] and she [derives hers] from the place from which she was created.[14] Why is a woman's voice sweet and a man's voice is not sweet? He [derives his] from the place from which he was created[15] and she [derives hers] from the place from which she was created.[16] Thus it is said, *For sweet is thy voice, and thy countenance is comely.*[17]

(1) After birth, and not on the seventh which is the last day of uncleanness. (2) Lit., 'all.' (3) At the festive meal given in honour of the circumcision. (4) Lit., 'sad', on account of the prohibition of intercourse which remains in force until the conclusion of the seventh day. (5) Lit., 'with her'. (6) Even after the least discharge of blood. (7) When intimate intercourse is forbidden. (8) By being deprived of her intimacy for certain recurrent periods. (9) In matrimony. (10) The rib from which Eve was built was taken from Adam. (11) The earth. (12) Cf. prev. n. but one. (13) Earth, which yields. (14) The unyielding bone of a rib. (15) A beat upon the earth produces no note. (16) A bone can be made to produce certain notes. (17) Cant. II, 14.

NIDDAH

CHAPTER IV

MISHNAH. THE DAUGHTERS OF THE SAMARITANS[1] ARE REGARDED AS MENSTRUANTS FROM THEIR CRADLE;[2] AND THE SAMARITANS IMPART UNCLEANNESS TO A COUCH UNDERNEATH AS TO A COVER ABOVE,[2] SINCE THEY COHABIT WITH MENSTRUANTS BECAUSE [THEIR WIVES] CONTINUE [UNCLEAN FOR SEVEN DAYS] ON ACCOUNT OF A DISCHARGE OF ANY BLOOD.[3] ON ACCOUNT OF THEIR [UNCLEANNESS,][4] HOWEVER, NO OBLIGATION[5] IS INCURRED FOR ENTRANCE INTO THE TEMPLE NOR IS TERUMAH[6] BURNT ON THEIR ACCOUNT, SINCE THEIR UNCLEANNESS[7] IS ONLY OF A DOUBTFUL NATURE.[8]

GEMARA. How is this[9] to be imagined? If they[10] observed a

(1) *Kuthim*, the people of Cutha and other places of Assyria who were transported to Samaria after the destruction of the northern kingdom and who combined their former idol-worship with a belief in the God of Israel (II Kings XVII, 24ff). Their descendants were for a time regarded as suspected Israelites and finally were entirely excluded from the community. (2) This is explained in the Gemara *infra*. (3) Even blood that is clean. Should a discharge of clean blood on one day be followed by one of unclean on the following day, the Samaritan woman would count the seven days of uncleanness from the first day, regarding the second discharge as having occurred within the seven days of menstruation, so that on the eighth day she regards herself as clean, while as a matter of fact her uncleanness began on the second day and continues for seven days, the last of which is the eighth from the first discharge on which she is still menstrually unclean. (4) If a person, for instance, covered himself with the unclean articles mentioned. (5) Of a sacrifice. (6) That came in contact with these articles (cf. prev. n. but one). (7) Though Rabbinically valid as a preventive measure. (8) While a sacrifice and *terumah* are Pentateuchal. A Rabbinical rule can have no force where its observance involves interference with a Pentateuchal ordinance. (9) The first clause of our Mishnah. (10) THE DAUGHTERS OF THE SAMARITANS.

discharge, then[1] even our daughters also [should in such circumstances be regarded as unclean]; and if they[2] have not observed any discharge, their daughters also should not be regarded as unclean, should they?—Raba son of R. Aḥa son of R. Huna citing R. Shesheth replied: Here we are dealing with cases of which nothing definite is known, but since a minority exists that experience discharges, the possibility of such a discharge is taken into consideration. And who is the Tanna that[3] takes a minority into consideration? [32a]—It is R. Meir. For it was taught: A minor, whether male or female, may neither perform, nor submit to *ḥaliẓah*, nor contract levirate marriage; so R. Meir. They[4] said to R. Meir: You spoke well when you ruled that they 'may neither perform, nor submit to *ḥaliẓah*', since in the Pentateuchal section[5] *man*[6] was written, and we draw a comparison between woman and man.[7] What, however, is the reason why they may not contract levirate marriage? He replied: Because a minor male might be found to be a *saris*;[8] a minor female might be found to be incapable of procreation;[9] and thus the law of incest[10] would be violated where no religious act[11] is thereby performed. And the Rabbis?[12]—Follow the majority of minor males and the majority of minors are no *sarisim;* follow the majority of minor females, and the majority of minor females are not incapable of procreation.[13] Might it not be suggested that R. Meir was heard [to take a minority into consideration only where that] minority is frequent; was he, however, heard [to maintain his view in regard to] an infrequent minority?—This also is a frequent minority, for it was taught: R. Jose stated, It happened at 'En Bol[14] that the infant was made

(1) Since menstruation may begin at the earliest stage of life (v. *infra* 32a). (2) THE DAUGHTERS OF THE SAMARITANS. (3) In respect of restriction. (4) The Rabbis who disagreed with him. (5) That deals with *ḥaliẓah*. (6) Deut. XXV, 7; thus excluding the minor. (7) As the latter must be a grown-up *man* so must the former be a grown-up woman. (8) One wanting in generative powers. Only one capable of having a child to *succeed in the name of his brother* (Deut. XXV, 6) is subject to the duty of the levirate marriage. (9) Cf. prev. n. (10) Marriage with a brother's wife. (11) Cf. prev. n. but two. (12) How in view of R. Meir's reason can they maintain their view? (13) Yeb. 61*b*. (14) [Ain Ibl, north west of Safed, v. Klein S., *N.B.* p. 41.]

to undergo ritual immersion[1] before her mother;[2] and Rabbi stated, It once happened at Beth She'arim that the infant was made to undergo ritual immersion[1] before her mother;[2] and R. Joseph stated, It once happened at Pumbeditha that the infant was made to undergo ritual immersion[1] before her mother;[2] One can well understand the incidents spoken of by R. Joseph and Rabbi[3] since [immersion was necessary as a protection for] the *terumah*[4] of Palestine; but why was that necessary[5] in the case spoken of by R. Joseph,[6] seeing that Samuel had laid down: The *terumah* of a country outside the Land of Israel is not forbidden unless [it came in contact] with a person whose uncleanness emanated from his body,[7] and this applies only to eating but not to contact?[8]—Mar Zuṭra replied: This[9] was required only in regard to anointing her with the oil of *terumah;*[10] for it was taught: *And they shall not profane the holy things of the children of Israel, which they set apart unto the Lord*[11] includes[12] one who anoints oneself or drinks.[13] But what need was there for a Scriptural text [for inclusion in the prohibition of] one who drinks, seeing that drinking is included in eating?[14]—Rather [say that the text[11] was intended] to include one who anoints oneself [in the same prohibition] as one who drinks.[15] And if you prefer I might reply, The prohibition[16] is derived from here: *And it is come into his inward parts like water, and like oil into his bones.*[17] But if so[18] should not our daughters also [be unclean from their cradle]?—For us who make a deduction of the use of '*and if a*

(1) To protect any *terumah* which may come in contact with her. (2) Whose immersion is performed on the fourteenth day. That of the menstruant takes place on the seventh. (3) Both of which occurred in Palestinian towns. (4) Which is rendered unfit through contact with a menstruant (cf. prev. n. but two). (5) Lit., 'wherefore to me'. (6) Which occurred in a Babylonian town. (7) A *zab*, for instance, or a menstruant. (8) Bek. 27*a*. (9) The immersion of the infant spoken of by R. Joseph. (10) Anointing being forbidden like eating. (11) Lev. XXII, 15, in the section dealing with persons unclean for *terumah*. (12) In the prohibition. (13) Which proves that anointing is forbidden like eating. (14) Cf. Shebu. 22b; and since eating was forbidden drinking also was obviously forbidden. (15) Reading כשותה instead of ואת השותה. (16) Of anointing. (17) Ps. CIX, 18. (18) That in imposing a restriction a minority also must be taken into consideration.

woman' [1] instead of 'a woman' and [our daughters,] when observing any discharge are kept away,[2] the Rabbis enacted no preventive measure; but as regards the Samaritans[3] who do not make any deduction from the use of *'and if a woman'* [1] instead of 'a woman', and [their daughters] when observing any discharge are not kept away,[2] the Rabbis enacted the preventive measure. What is the exposition of 'a woman', *'and if a woman'?*—It was taught: [If it had been written,][4] 'A woman', I would only know that a woman [is subject to the restrictions of menstrual uncleanness], whence could it be deduced that an infant one day old is also subject to the restrictions of menstruation? Hence it was explicitly stated, *'And if a woman'*.[4] Thus it is evident that in including a child Scripture included even one who is one day old. May not, however, an incongruity be pointed out: [If Scripture had only written,][5] 'the woman' I would only know [that the restriction applies to] a woman, whence could it be derived that a child who is three years and one day old [is equally under the restrictions] in respect of cohabition? Hence it was explicitly stated, *'The woman also'?*[5]—Raba replied: These[6] are traditional laws but the Rabbis tacked them on to Scriptural texts. Which one [can be deduced from] the Scriptural text and which is only a traditional law?[7] If it be suggested that the law relating to an infant one day old is traditional and that the one relating to such as is three years and one day old is deduced from a Scriptural text, is not the text [it may be retorted] written in general terms?[8]—Rather say: The law relating to one who is three years and one day old is traditional and the one derived from the text is that concerning an infant who is one day old. But since the former law is traditional, what was the purpose of

(1) Lev. XV, 19, from which it is inferred *infra* that uncleanness may begin at infancy. (2) From holy things, during the prescribed unclean period. (3) Lit., 'they'. (4) In Lev. XV, 19. (5) Ibid. 18, dealing with uncleanness through cohabitation. (6) The two restrictions under discussion. (7) *Sc.* since Scripture uses the same expression *we-ishah* (rendered *'and if a woman'* in Lev. XV, 19 and *'the woman also'* ibid. 18) in both verses what age exactly was implied? (8) And, since there is no reason why the age of three years and one day should be meant rather than that of two or of four years, the lowest possible age, viz., that of one day, should obviously be the one intended.

the Scriptural text?[1] [32b]—To exclude a man from the uncleanness of a red discharge.[2] But consider the following Baraitha:[3] From the term of *'woman'*[4] I would only infer that a woman [is subject to the restriction of *zibah*], whence, however, could it be deduced that a female child that is ten days old[5] is also subject to the restrictions of *zibah?* Hence it was explicitly stated, *And if a woman.*[4] Now, what need was there for this text,[6] seeing that the law could have been inferred from that of menstruation?[7]—It was necessary. For if the All Merciful had written the law in regard to a menstruant only it might have been presumed that it applied only to the menstruant, since even if she observed a discharge on one day only she must continue unclean for seven days, but not to a *zabah* for whom, if she observed a discharge[8] on one day, it suffices to wait only one day corresponding to it;[9] hence the necessity for the second text. Then why should not the All Merciful write the law in regard to a *zabah* and there would be no need to give it again in regard to a menstruant, since one knows that there can be no *zabah* unless she was previously a menstruant?—That is so indeed. Then what was the need for the Scriptural text?[10]—To exclude a man from the uncleanness of a red discharge.[11] But was he not already once excluded?[12]—One text serves to

(1) *Sc.* why the additional *waw* in *we-ishah*? (2) Of semen (v. *infra*) which is similar in nature to the discharge dealt with in the text under discussion. Only a woman's is subject to uncleanness but not that of a man. (3) Lit., 'and that which was taught'. (4) Lev. XV, 25, dealing with *zibah*. (5) One younger than ten days cannot possibly be subject to this form of uncleanness since one cannot be a confirmed *zabah* before the elapse of seven days of menstruation and three subsequent days on each of which a discharge is observed. (6) Lit., 'wherefore to me'. (7) *Sc.* since, as has been shown *supra*, an infant of one day is subject to the uncleanness of menstruation it naturally follows that on her tenth day (cf. prev. n. but one) she is also subject to that of *zibah*. (8) After the seven days of menstruation. (9) And if she observed a discharge on the second day also, she need only wait one day, after which she is clean. Only a discharge that continued for three consecutive days would subject her to the uncleanness of a confirmed *zabah*. (10) The additional *waw* in the case of the menstruant. (11) The text implying that only a woman is subject to the uncleanness of a red discharge but not a man. (12) *Supra*.

exclude him from the uncleanness of a discharge of red semen and the other from that of blood.

The same law[1] applies also to males. For it was taught:[2] *'A man, a man'*,[3] what need was there for the repetition of *'man'?* To include a male child one day old who also is to be subject to the uncleanness of *zibah;* so R. Judah. R. Ishmael son of R. Joḥanan b. Beroḳa said: This[4] is not necessary, for, surely, Scripture says, *Whether it be a man or a woman*,[5] *'whether it be a man'* implies any one who is man, whether adult or infant; *'or a woman'* implies any one who is a female irrespective of whether she is adult or minor. If so, why was it expressly stated, *'a man, a man'?*[6] The Torah used an ordinary form of speech.[7] Thus it is evident that in including a child Scripture included even an infant one day old. Does not, however, an incongruity arise: [If Scripture had only written][8] *'a man'* I would only know [that the law applied to] a man, whence could it be derived that it also applies to a child who is nine years and one day old? Hence it was explicitly stated, *And a man?*[8]—Raba replied: These[9] are traditional laws but the Rabbis found props for them in Scriptural texts. Which one is only a traditional law and which can be deduced from the Scriptural text? If it be suggested that the law relating to an infant one day old is traditional and that relating to a child who is nine years and one day old is deduced from a Scriptural text, is not the text [it could be objected] written in general terms?[10]—Rather say: The law relating to a child who is nine years and one day old is traditional and the one relating to an infant one day old is derived from the Scriptural text. But, since the former is a traditional law, what was the purpose of the Scriptural text?—To exclude a woman from the uncleanness of a white discharge.

(1) That a child one day old is subject to the uncleanness of a discharge as an adult. (2) 'Ar. 3a. (3) Lev. XV, 2, dealing with the laws of a *zab*. E.V., *'any man'*. (4) The exposition of Lev. XV, 2 (v. prev. n.). (5) Lev. XV, 33. (6) Lev. XV, 2 dealing with the laws of a *zab*. E.V., *'any man'*. (7) Lit., 'spoke as is the language of man'. (8) Lev. XV, 16, in regard to the emission of semen. (9) The law of *zibah* in respect of an infant one day old and the law of the emission of semen in regard to a boy who is nine years and one day old. (10) Cf. *supra* p. 223, n. 8 *mut. mut.*

What need was there for Scripture to write [an additional word[1] and letter][2] as regards males and females respectively?[3]—These were necessary. For if the All Merciful had written the law in respect of males only it might have been presumed that it applied to them alone since they become unclean by [three] observations[4] [on the same day] as by [three observations on three successive] days,[5] but not to females who do not become unclean by [three] observations [on the same day] as by [three observations on three successive] days. And if the All Merciful had written the law in respect of females alone, it might have been presumed to apply to them only, since they become unclean even if a discharge was due to a mishap but not to males who do not become unclean when a discharge is due to a mishap.[6] [The additional letters and words were, therefore,] necessary.

THE SAMARITANS IMPART UNCLEANNESS TO A COUCH UNDERNEATH AS TO A COVER ABOVE. What is meant by A COUCH UNDERNEATH AS A COVER ABOVE? If it be suggested to mean that if there were ten spreads[7] and he sat upon them they all become unclean, is not this [it could be retorted] obvious seeing that he exercised pressure upon them?[8]—The meaning rather is that a couch underneath one who had intercourse with a menstruant is subject to the same law of uncleanness as the cover above a *zab*.[9] As the cover above a *zab* imparts uncleanness to foods and drinks only so does the couch underneath one who had intercourse with a menstruant impart uncleanness to foods and drinks only. Whence is the law concerning the cover above a *zab* deduced?—From the Scriptural text, *And whosoever toucheth any thing that was under him shall be unclean.*[10] For what could be the meaning of '*under him*'? [33a] If it be suggested: Under the *zab* [it could be objected: This][11] is derived from, *And whosoever toucheth his bed.*[12]

(1) *Man.* (2) *Waw* ('and') in *we-ishah.* (3) *Sc.* why could not the same ages of the male and of the female be derived from one another? (4) Of discharges. (5) Cf. B.Ḳ. 24a. (6) *Infra* 36b. (7) One above the other. (8) *Midras* (v. Glos.) is one of the means whereby a *zab* conveys uncleanness. (9) And not as the couch under him which imparts uncleanness to human beings also. (10) Lev. XV, 10. (11) Since it is *midras* (cf. prev. n. but two). (12) Lev. XV, 5.

Consequently it must mean: 'Whosoever toucheth any thing under which the *zab* was';[1] and this is[2] the cover above the *zab*,[3] Scripture[4] segregated it from a grave uncleanness[5] and transferred it to a lighter uncleanness in order to tell you that it imparts uncleanness to foods and drinks only.[6] Might it not be suggested that Scripture segregated it from the grave uncleanness only in order that it shall not impart uncleanness to a man[7] and thereby also impart uncleanness to his clothes, but that it does impart uncleanness to a man[7] or to clothes?[8]—Scripture said: *Shall be unclean*,[9] which implies[10] an uncleanness of a lighter character. And whence is the law concerning the couch beneath one who had intercourse with a menstruant deduced?—From what was taught: *And her impurity be upon him.*[11] As it might have been presumed that he is released from his uncleanness as soon as he is released,[12] it was explicitly stated, *He shall be unclean seven days.*[11] Then why was it explicitly stated, '*And her impurity be upon him*'? As it might have been presumed that he imparts no uncleanness to man or earthenware, it was explicitly stated, '*And her impurity be upon him*',[11] as she imparts uncleanness to man[13] and to earthenware[14] so does he impart uncleanness to man[13] and earthenware.[14] In case it might be suggested:[15] As she causes a couch or a seat to become unclean so as to impart uncleanness to a man and thereby also impart uncleanness to his clothes, so does he also cause his couch and seat

(1) The Heb. *yiheyeh taḥtaw* may be rendered as E.V. '*that was under him*' as well as 'under which he (the *zab*) was'. (2) Lit., 'and what is it'. (3) Cf. Rashal and Rashi. Cur. edd. in parenthesis add: 'And he who carries shall also be unclean; and what is that? What is being carried. What is the reason? It is written: And that which is carried'. (4) By separating the law of touching from that of carrying with the expression of '*shall be unclean*'. (5) Carrying which imparts uncleanness to a person as well as to his clothes. (6) But not to a person. (7) Who touches it. (8) That came in direct contact with it. (9) Lev. XV, 10. (10) Since the washing of garments was not mentioned in that part of the verse. (11) Lev. XV, 24. (12) Lit., 'he shall go up at her foot'. *sc.* if, for instance, on the sixth day of her uncleanness he became unclean through her he should become clean on the following day (which is her seventh day) on which she is released from her uncleanness. (13) And to the clothes he wears. (14) By *heseṭ* (v. Glos.). (15) Lit., 'if'.

to impart uncleanness to man and thereby impart uncleanness to his clothes, it was explicitly stated: *And every bed whereon he lieth shall be unclean.*[1] For[2] it should not have been stated, *'and every bed on which he lieth shall be unclean'*, then why was it written, *'And every bed on which* etc.'? Scripture has, thereby, segregated it from a grave uncleanness[3] and transferred it to a lighter uncleanness, to tell you that it imparts uncleanness to foods and drinks only. R. Aḥai demurred: Might it not be suggested that Scripture had segregated it from a grave uncleanness and transferred it to a lighter uncleanness only in order that it shall not impart uncleanness to a man and thereby also convey it to his clothes, but that it does impart uncleanness to a man[4] or to clothes?[5]—R. Assi replied: Shall be unclean[6] implies[7] an uncleanness of a lighter nature. Might it not be argued: *'And her impurity be upon him'*[1] is a generalization, *'and every bed'*[1] is a specification[8] and, since the scope of a generalization when followed by a specialization already comprehended in it is limited by the thing specified, only[9] a bed and a seat, but no other thing should convey uncleanness?—Abaye replied: *'He shall be unclean for seven days'*[1] makes a break in the context, so that this is a case of a generalization and a specification that are distant from one another and whenever a generalization and a specification are distant from one another the rule of generalization and specification does not apply. Raba replied: The rule[10] in fact does apply, but the expression of *'and every'*[1] is an extension.[11] R. Jacob demurred: Might it not be argued that he[12] is[13] subject to the same uncleanness as she in this respect: As in her case no distinction is made between her touch and her bed

(1) Lev. XV, 24. (2) Since it was written, *'and her impurity be upon him'* and about her it is written, that one who touches her bed must wash his garments. (3) That of the couch of the menstruant which imparts uncleanness to a person as well as to the clothes he wears. (4) Who touches it. (5) That came in direct contact with it. (6) Lev. XV, 10. (7) Since the washing of garments was not mentioned in that part of the verse. (8) Of the same general rule. (9) Lit., 'yes'. (10) Of generalization followed by a specification. (11) Of the general rule. The rule of generalization and specification does not, therefore, apply here. (12) Who cohabits with a menstruant. (13) Since the man and the woman were compared.

as regards the conveyance of uncleanness to a person and to his clothes, thus adopting the stricter course,[1] so also in his case no distinction should be made between his touch and his bed as regards the conveyance of uncleanness to a person and to his clothes, the lenient course being adopted?[2]—Raba replied:[3] '*Upon him*' implies: To put a load upon him.[4]

SINCE THEY COHABIT WITH MENSTRUANTS etc. Do they all[5] cohabit with menstruants?—R. Isaac of Magdala replied: This was learnt about married persons only.

BECAUSE [THEIR WIVES] CONTINUE [UNCLEAN FOR SEVEN DAYS] ON ACCOUNT OF A DISCHARGE OF ANY BLOOD etc. It was taught: R. Meir stated, If they continue [unclean for seven days] on account of a discharge of any blood,[6] is not this[7] rather an important safeguard for them? But the fact is that when they observe a discharge of red blood they treat it as supplementary to a previous discharge of yellow blood.[8] Another explanation: She includes the day on which her discharge ceases[9] in the number of the seven days.[10] Rami b. Ḥama demurred: Why indeed should she not count it,[11] and why should not we also count it,[11] seeing that we have an established rule that part of a day is regarded as the whole of it?—Raba retorted: If so,[12] how could it be possible for an emission of semen to cause the counting[13] after a *zibah* to be void seeing that a part of the day is to be counted as the whole of it?[14]—If one had observed the discharge in the middle of the day

(1) *Sc.* that both the person and his clothes are unclean. (2) Viz., that neither his person nor his clothes contract uncleanness. (3) Var. lec. Scripture said. (4) I.e., in his case too the stricter course must be adopted. (5) *Sc.* married and unmarried men. (6) Whether clean or unclean. (7) The counting of seven days after each discharge whose colour differed from the previous one. (8) Cf. relevant n. on our Mishnah. (9) *Sc.* the third day of three consecutive days (after the termination of her period of menstruation) on each of which she experienced a discharge and in consequence of which she is a confirmed *zabah*. (10) While in the case of a *zabah* the law requires seven full days clear of any discharge whatsoever. (11) As one of the seven clean days. (12) That as regards the counting of the clean days after *zibah* a part of a day could be regarded as the whole of it. (13) Of any one of the seven days (cf. *supra* 22a). (14) And a part of the day presumably remains after the emission.

the law might indeed be so,[1] but here we might be dealing with one who observed the discharge near sunset?[2]—Could it then definitely be assumed that[3] the Scriptural text was written only [in regard to a discharge] near sunset?—Yes; you must indeed allow the text to be so explained, for it[4] forces this interpretation upon itself.

Rami b. Ḥama enquired: If a woman[5] ejected some semen,[6] does she cause her counting[7] after a *zibah* to be void? Is she regarded as one who observed an emission of semen and causes, therefore, the counting[7] to be void [33b] or is she rather regarded as one who merely touched it and, therefore, she does not cause the counting to be void?—Raba replied, His error is as deep as his subtlety: Granted that she causes her counting to be void, how many days could be affected? Should it be suggested that the counting of all the seven days should be void [it could be objected]: Is it not enough that she is treated like the man who had the intercourse with her?[8] Should it be suggested that she should cause the counting of one day to be void [it could be retorted:] Did not the All Merciful say, *And after that she shall be clean*,[9] *'after'* means after all of them, implying that no uncleanness[10] may intervene between them?—But according to your view, how could a *zab* himself cause the counting of one day to be void seeing that the All Merciful said, *He shall number to himself seven days for his cleansing*,[11] which implies that no uncleanness must intervene between them?[12] What then have you to say in reply? That the meaning is that only the uncleanness of *zibah* must not intervene between them;[13]

(1) The remaining part of the day being counted as a full day and the counting of the seven days is in no way interrupted. (2) So that no part of the day remained. (3) Lit., 'and let him arise and say to him to'. (4) In view of the accepted rule that part of a day counts as the whole of it. (5) Who had intercourse during her *zibah*. (6) While she was counting her clean days after her *zibah* had terminated. (7) Of the one day on which the ejection occurred. (8) If a man who was a *zab* emitted semen on one of the seven clean days following a *zibah* he loses that day only. (9) Lev. XV, 28. (10) Even that of one day. (11) Lev. XV, 13. (12) The seven days. How then is he allowed to interrupt his seven days by the exclusion of the day on which he emitted semen? (13) *Sc.* if there was such an intervention,

well, here also it may be explained that the meaning is that only the uncleanness of *zibah* must not intervene between them.[1]

ON ACCOUNT OF THEIR [UNCLEANNESS], HOWEVER, NO OBLIGATION IS INCURRED FOR ENTRANCE INTO THE TEMPLE etc. R. Papa once visited Tuak[2] when he remarked, 'If there lives a scholar in this place I would go and pay him my respects'.[3] 'A scholar lives here', said an old woman to him, 'and his name is R. Samuel and he learns Tannaitic traditions. May it be God's will that you be like him'. 'Since', he thought, 'she blesses me by him I can gather[4] that he is a God[5]-fearing man'. He thereupon visited him when the latter treated him to[6] a bull; and he also treated him to an incongruity[7] between Tannaitic teachings: We have learnt, ON ACCOUNT OF THEIR [UNCLEANNESS], HOWEVER, NO OBLIGATION IS INCURRED FOR ENTRANCE INTO THE TEMPLE NOR IS TERUMAH BURNT ON THEIR ACCOUNT, SINCE THEIR[8] UNCLEANNESS IS ONLY OF A DOUBTFUL NATURE, from which it is evident that *terumah* is not burnt in a case of doubt. But have we not learnt to the contrary: In six doubtful cases of uncleanness is *terumah* burnt [and one of them is] the doubtful uncleanness of the clothes of an *'am ha-arez*?[9]—'May it be God's will', exclaimed R. Papa, 'that this bull shall be eaten in peace:[10] Here[11] we are dealing with the case of a Samaritan who was a *haber*'.[12] 'But would you presume[13] [the other retorted] that a Samaritan who is a *haber* had intercourse with a menstruant?'

all the days counted are void and another seven days must be counted.

(1) The uncleanness of an emission of semen, however, is not regarded as an intervention. (2) Near Naresh, the home of R. Papa not far from Sura, v. Obermeyer, p. 208. (3) Lit., 'I will receive his countenance'. (4) Lit., 'infer from it'. (5) Lit., 'heaven'. (6) Lit., 'cast down for him', *sc.* had it slaughtered to prepare a feast in his honour. (7) Lit., 'cast for him'. (cf. prev. n.). (8) So our Mishnah. The reading here is 'her'. (9) That came in contact with the *terumah*; Toh. IV, 5. As a Samaritan is presumably in the same category why is the *terumah* spoken of in our Mishnah not to be burnt? (10) *Sc.* that the feast shall not be disturbed by his inability to reconcile the apparent contradiction. (11) In our Mishnah. (12) Whose clothes could not be suspected of any uncleanness. (13) Lit., 'make'.

When he left him[1] and came to R. Shimi b. Ashi the latter said to him: Why did you not answer him [that our Mishnah[2] deals] with the case of a Samaritan who, having performed ritual immersion, came up and trod upon the clothes[3] of a *ḥaber* and the clothes[3] of this *ḥaber* then came in contact with *terumah*,[4] so that if [the *terumah* were to be treated as unclean] on account of the uncleanness of the *'am ha-areẓ* [it could be objected]: He has, surely, performed ritual immersion.[5] And if the uncleanness were to be attributed to his likely intercourse with a menstruant [it could be objected]: It is doubtful whether he had his intercourse recently or some time ago.[6] And even if you were to find some ground for assuming that his intercourse took place recently there is still the doubt whether she had completed her period of cleanness for yellow blood or not.[7] This then is a case of double doubt,[8] and no *terumah* may be burnt on account of a doubly doubtful uncleanness. But why should not the uncleanness of the *terumah* be established[9] on account of its contact with the clothes of an *'am ha-areẓ*, a Master having stated: The clothes of an *'am ha-areẓ* are like *midras* uncleanness[10] to Pharisees?[11]—The other replied: This is a case of a naked Samaritan.

MISHNAH. THE DAUGHTERS OF THE SADDUCEES, SO LONG AS THEY ARE IN THE HABIT OF WALKING IN THE PATHS OF THEIR FATHERS, ARE TO BE REGARDED AS SAMARITAN WOMEN. IF THEY LEFT THOSE PATHS[12] TO WALK IN THE PATHS

(1) Rashi: He left his host because he embarassed him. (2) According to which *terumah* is not burnt on account of its contact with a couch that was underneath a Samaritan. (3) *Sc.* the bed clothes, a couch. (4) The *terumah* thus coming in contact with *midras* uncleanness. (5) Whereby his uncleanness came to an end. (6) In the latter case his uncleanness may have terminated before he performed the immersion and he is now clean. (7) It is quite possible that she counted her clean days after a discharge of unclean blood. (8) Lit., 'a doubt of a doubt'. (9) Lit., 'and let it go out for him'. (10) As *midras* conveys uncleanness to man and clothes so do the clothes of an *'am ha-areẓ*. (11) Who were meticulous in the observance of the laws of cleanness, Ḥag. 18*b*. (12) Lit., 'they separated'.

OF ISRAEL, THEY ARE TO BE REGARDED AS ISRAELITISH WOMEN. R. JOSE RULED: THEY ARE ALWAYS REGARDED AS ISRAELITISH WOMEN UNLESS THEY LEAVE THE PATHS OF ISRAEL TO WALK IN THE PATHS OF THEIR FATHERS.

GEMARA. The question was raised: What is the law[1] where their attitude is unknown?[2]—Come and hear: THE DAUGHTERS OF THE SADDUCEES, SO LONG AS THEY ARE IN THE HABIT OF WALKING IN THE PATHS OF THEIR FATHERS, ARE TO BE REGARDED AS SAMARITAN WOMEN; from which it follows that if their attitude is unknown they are like Israelitish women. Read then the final clause: IF THEY LEFT THESE PATHS TO WALK IN THE PATHS OF ISRAEL, THEY ARE TO BE REGARDED AS ISRAELITISH WOMEN; from which it follows that if their attitude is unknown they are like Samaritan women! But the fact is that no inference may be drawn from this [Mishnah].

Come and hear what we have learnt: R. JOSE RULED, THEY ARE ALWAYS REGARDED AS ISRAELITISH WOMEN UNLESS THEY LEAVE THE PATHS OF ISRAEL TO WALK IN THE PATHS OF THEIR FATHERS. Thus it follows that the first Tanna[3] holds that when their attitude is unknown they are to be regarded as Samaritan women. This is conclusive.

Our Rabbis taught: It once happened that a Sadducee was conversing with a High Priest in the market place when some spittle was squirted from his mouth and fell on the clothes of the High Priest. The face of the High Priest[4] turned yellow and he hurried to his[5] wife[6] who assured him that although they were wives of

(1) According to the first Tanna who ruled: IF THEY ARE IN THE HABIT OF WALKING IN THE PATHS OF THEIR FATHERS THEY ARE TO BE REGARDED AS SAMARITAN WOMEN and IF THEY LEFT THESE PATHS for THE PATHS OF ISRAEL THEY ARE TO BE REGARDED AS ISRAELITISH WOMEN. (2) Are they then regarded as Samaritan, or as Israelitish women? (3) Who obviously differs from R. Jose. (4) Who was afraid that the Sadducee may have been unclean owing to intercourse with his menstruant wife and that his spittle consequently conveyed uncleanness to the clothes on which it fell. (5) The Sadducee's. (6) To ascertain whether she observed the laws of menstruation and knew the distinction between clean and unclean blood.

Sadducees they paid homage to the Pharisees and showed their blood to the Sages.[1] R. Jose observed: We[2] know them better than anybody else [and can testify] that they show their menstrual blood to the Sages. There was only one exception, a woman who lived in our neighbourhood who did not show her blood to the Sages but she died. But why was he[3] not concerned about the uncleanness[4] that is occasioned by the spittle of an *'am ha-areẓ?*[5]— Abaye replied: This was a case of a Sadducee who was a *ḥaber.*[6] Said Raba: Is a Sadducee who is a *ḥaber* presumed[7] to have intercourse with a menstruant? Rather, said Raba: [34a] The incident occurred during a festival and the uncleanness of an *'am ha-areẓ*[8] during a festival the Rabbis treated as clean; for it is written, *So all the men of Israel were gathered again against the city, knit together*[9] *as one man,*[10] the text thus treated them all[11] as *ḥaberim.*[12]

MISHNAH. THE BLOOD[13] OF AN IDOLATRESS AND THE CLEAN BLOOD[14] OF A LEPROUS WOMAN, BETH SHAMMAI DECLARE CLEAN[15] AND BETH HILLEL HOLD THAT IT IS LIKE HER SPITTLE OR HER URINE.[16] THE BLOOD OF A WOMAN AFTER CHILDBIRTH WHO DID NOT[17] UNDERGO RITUAL IMMERSION, BETH SHAMMAI RULED, IS LIKE HER SPITTLE OR HER URINE,[16] BUT BETH HILLEL RULED: IT CONVEYS UNCLEANNESS BOTH WHEN WET AND WHEN DRY. THEY[18] AGREE, HOWEVER, THAT

(1) Who gave their decisions in accordance with the rulings of the Pharisees. (2) Who live in their neighbourhood. (3) The High Priest. (4) Lit., 'and let it go out to him'. (5) Even if he is not suspected of intercourse with a menstruant. (6) V. Glos. (7) Lit., 'you make'. (8) Who was no Sadducee and whose wife as a rule properly observed the laws of menstruation. (9) *Ḥaberim,* plural of *ḥaber.* (10) Judges XX, 11. (11) When assembled together, as is also the case on a festival. (12) Cf. prev. n. but two. *Ḥaberim* meticulously observe all the laws of uncleanness. (13) Cf. Lev. XV, 19 and 25. (14) The blood of purification (Lev. XII, 5). (15) This is discussed in the Gemara *infra.* (16) Which conveys uncleanness when wet but not when dry. (17) Seven days after the birth of a male child or fourteen days after that of a female child (cf. Lev. XII, 2, 5). (18) Beth Shammai.

IF SHE GAVE BIRTH WHILE IN ZIBAH, IT CONVEYS UNCLEANNESS BOTH WHEN WET AND WHEN DRY.

GEMARA. But do not Beth Shammai uphold the tradition: *Speak unto the children of Israel, and say unto them, when any man hath an issue,*[1] only the children of Israel convey uncleanness by *zibah* and idolaters do not convey uncleanness by *zibah*, but a preventive measure has been enacted against them that they should be regarded as *zabim* in all respects?[2]—Beth Shammai can answer you:[3] How should it act? It it were to convey uncleanness both when wet and when dry, you would treat it as a Pentateuchal uncleanness.[4] If it were to convey uncleanness only when wet and not when dry, you might also make the same distinction in a Pentateuchal uncleanness.[5] If so, should not the same provision[6] be made in the case of her spittle and her urine also?[7]—Since a distinguishing rule has been laid down in regard to her blood[8] it is sufficiently known that her spittle and her urine are only Rabbinically unclean. And why should no distinguishing rule be laid down in respect of her spittle or her urine while her blood should be ruled to be unclean?—Concerning her spittle and her urine, since they are frequently discharged, the Rabbis have enacted a preventive measure, but concerning her blood which is not frequently discharged the Rabbis have enacted no preventive measure.

Raba ruled: His[9] discharge in *zibah* is unclean[10] even according to Beth Shammai[11] and his discharge of semen is clean even accord-

(1) Lev. XV, 2. (2) Shab. 83*a*; how then could Beth Shammai in our Mishnah declare their blood clean? (3) So Maharsha and old edd. Cur. edd. insert in parenthesis 'that was stated about males, for if about females'. (4) And this might lead to the erroneous assumption that it also causes the burning of *terumah* and other sacred things. (5) That of an Israelite woman. By ruling that it is clean such erroneous conclusions are avoided. (6) To regard it as clean. (7) Since otherwise the same erroneous conclusion might be drawn. (8) By imposing upon it an uncleanness that is less restrictive than that of Pentateuchal uncleanness. (9) An idolater's. (10) Conveying it by contact. (11) Who in our Mishnah relax the law in regard to an idolatrous woman.

ing to Beth Hillel.[1] 'His discharge in *zibah* is unclean even according to Beth Shammai' since a distinguishing rule[2] can be made in connection with the discharge of his semen. 'His discharge of semen is clean even according to Beth Hillel', since the Rabbis have enacted a distinguishing rule[2] in order that *terumah* or other holy things shall not be burnt on its account.[3] But why should not the distinguishing rule be enacted in regard to his discharge in *zibah* while his discharge of semen should be declared unclean?—Concerning his discharge in *zibah* which is not dependent on an act of his the Rabbis have enacted a preventive measure, but concerning a discharge of his semen which does depend on an act of his[4] the Rabbis enacted no preventive measure.

May it be suggested that the following provides support to his[5] ruling: If an idolatress discharged the semen of an Israelite, it is unclean; but if the daughter of an Israelite discharged the semen of an idolater, it is clean.[6] Now does not this mean that it is completely clean?[7]—No; clean Pentateuchally but unclean Rabbinically.

Come and hear: It thus follows[8] that the semen of an Israelite is unclean everywhere, [34b] even in the bowels of an idolatress,[9] while that of an idolater is clean everywhere, even in the bowels of an Israelitish woman, with the exception of any urine of hers that is mixed up with it.[10] And should you argue that here also it is only Pentateuchally clean but unclean Rabbinically, [it could be retorted:] Does then her urine convey uncleanness Pentateuchally?[11] Consequently it may be inferred that it[12] is clean even Rabbinically.[7] This is conclusive.

The Master said, 'The semen of an Israelite is unclean everywhere, even in the bowels of an idolatress'. May you not thereby solve

(1) Cf. prev. n. *mut. mut.* (2) Whereby it is indicated that the uncleanness of an idolater is merely Rabbinical. (3) In the absence of the distinction it might have been presumed that the uncleanness is Pentateuchal and that, therefore, even *terumah* and other holy things must be burnt if they came in contact with it. (4) Sexual excitement. (5) Raba's. (6) Miḳ. VIII, 4. (7) In agreement with Raba. (8) Lit., 'you are found saying'. (9) If she discharged it on a garment. (10) As the idolater's semen is here ruled to be clean everywhere, support is adduced for Raba's ruling. (11) Of course not. Its uncleanness is only Rabbinical. (12) An idolater's semen.

a question of R. Papa; for R. Papa enquired, 'What is the law regarding the semen of an Israelite in the bowels of an idolatress?' [Concerning a discharge] within three days[1] R. Papa raised no questions. His enquiry related only to one after three days.[2] What, he asked, is the law? Is it only in the case of Israelites, who are anxious to observe the commandments, that their bodies engender heat and the semen decomposes[3] but in the case of idolaters, who are not anxious to observe the commandments, their bodies engender no heat and their [semen] therefore does not decompose, or is it possible that on account of their consumption of forbidden animals and reptiles their bodies also engender heat and their semen also decomposes?—This remains undecided.

THE CLEAN BLOOD OF A LEPROUS WOMAN, BETH SHAMMAI etc. What is Beth Hillel's reason?—R. Isaac replied: '*Whether it be a man*'[4] includes[5] a male leper as regards his sources;[6] '*or a woman*'[4] includes[5] a female leper as regards her sources. Now what could be meant by 'her sources'? If it be suggested: Her other sources[7] [the objection could be made that the uncleanness of these] could be inferred from that of the male.[8] The reference consequently must be to [the uncleanness of] her blood,[9] to declare her 'CLEAN BLOOD' unclean. And Beth Shammai?[10]—[The uncleanness of] a female could not be deduced from that of a male, for it can be objected: The position of the male is different[11] since he is also required[12] to uncover his head and to rend his clothes[13] and he is also forbidden cohabitation; [how then could his uncleanness] be

(1) After intercourse. (2) Which in the case of an Israelitish woman is clean. (3) After three days, and in consequence of this it is regarded as clean. (4) Lev. XV, 33. (5) Since the expression is not required for its context that previously in the same verse dealt in general terms '*of him that have an issue*'. (6) His mouth, for instance. *Sc.* not only is his body a primary uncleanness but, as the *zab* of which the text explicitly speaks, his spittle also is a primary uncleanness and may, therefore, impart uncleanness of the first degree to man and articles. (7) Those that do not discharge blood but spittle or urine. (8) As these sources of the male are unclean, so are the similar sources of the female. (9) Which does not apply to the male. (10) How can they maintain their ruling in view of this argument? (11) From that of a female. (12) When leprous. (13) Cf. Lev. XIII, 45.

compared to that of a female[1] who is not [subject to his restrictions]?[2] And Beth Hillel?[3]—The All Merciful could have written down the restrictions in regard to the female and there would have been no need to repeat them in regard to the male; for it could have been argued: If in the case of a female,[1] who is not required to uncover her head or to rend her clothes and who is not forbidden cohabitation either, the All Merciful included her sources[4] how much more then should this be the rule[1] in the case of the male.[5] Now since the text serves no purpose in regard to the male,[6] apply it to the female; and since it can serve no purpose as far as her other sources[7] are concerned,[8] apply it to her blood, to declare her 'CLEAN BLOOD' unclean. And Beth Shammai?[9]—The uncleanness of a male cannot be deduced from that of a female, for it can be objected: The position of a female is different,[10] since she becomes unclean[11] even as a result of a mishap; [how then could her uncleanness] be compared to that of a male who is not [subject to such a restriction]? And Beth Hillel?[9]—The subject dealt with is the position of[12] the leper, how can they raise an objection against it from that of the *zab?*[13] And Beth Shammai?[9]—They raise objections from any form of uncleanness. And if you prefer I might reply that Beth Shammai can answer you: The expression[13] *'whether it be a man'*[14] is required for the following exposition: *'Whether it be a man'* whosoever is a man irrespective of whether he is of age or only a minor.[15] And Beth Hillel?[16]—They derive this ruling from *'This is the law of him that hath an issue'*[17] which implies, whether he be of age or a minor.

(1) When leprous. (2) Cf. Ker. 8*b*. (3) V. p. 237, n. 10. (4) As regards uncleanness. (5) Who is subject to these restrictions. (6) Whose case, as has just been shown, could well have been deduced from that of the female. (7) Those that do not discharge blood but spittle or urine. (8) These having been deduced *supra* from *'or a woman'*. (9) How can they maintain their ruling in view of this argument? (10) From that of a male. (11) In the case of *zibah*. (12) Lit., 'stand at'. (13) Lit., 'that'. (14) Lev. XV, 33. (15) In either case is he subject to the uncleanness of *zibah*. Now since the text is required for this exposition it cannot also serve the purpose for which Beth Hillel seek to employ it. (16) Having used the text for their ruling in our Mishnah whence do they derive this ruling? (17) Lev. XV, 32.

R. Joseph stated: When R. Simeon b. Laḳish discoursed on the *zab* he raised the following question.[1] Does the first observation[2] of a *zab* who was a minor convey uncleanness by contact? The All Merciful having said, *This is the law of him that hath an issue and of him from whom the flow of seed goeth out,*[3] therefore only if his *'flow of seed'* causes uncleanness does his first observation also cause uncleanness, but the minor,[4] since his *'flow of seed'* conveys no uncleanness, his first observation also conveys no uncleanness; or is it possible that it is unclean, since if he observed two discharges the two are combined?[5]—Raba replied, Come and hear: *This is the law of him that have an issue,*[3] implies, whether he is of age or a minor; as in the case of an adult a first observation conveys uncleanness so also in that of a minor a first observation conveys uncleanness.

R. Joseph enquired: Does the blood of a first observation of a leper convey uncleanness by contact? Is the place of the *zibah* a source and, therefore, conveys uncleanness,[6] or is it possible that it is no source and, therefore, conveys no uncleanness?[7]—Raba replied, Come and hear: *His issue is unclean,*[8] this teaches concerning an issue of a *zab* that it is unclean.[9] Now of what kind of person has this been said? If it be suggested: Of one who is only a *zab*[10] [35a] [the difficulty would arise:] If it[11] causes the uncleanness of others,[12] is it not obvious that it causes that of the man himself?[13] It is consequently obvious that this has been said of a *zab* who is a leper.[14] And since a Scriptural text was required to include him in the category of uncleanness after a second observation,[15] it may be inferred that the place of the *zibah* is no source.[16]

(1) Lit., 'enquired thus'. (2) Of a discharge. (3) Lev. XV, 32. (4) Lit., 'that'. (5) Constituting him a confirmed *zab* in respect of the uncleanness of seven days, as an adult *zab*. (6) As the other sources of a leper. (7) Except by contact. (8) Lev. XV, 2, referring (since the root meaning 'issue' is repeated) to a second discharge. (9) And conveys it not only by contact but also by carriage (cf. *infra* 55a). (10) But no leper. (11) The issue of a *zab*. (12) Anything that the *zab* carries is unclean. (13) What need then is there to mention the obvious? (14) To whom, being unclean on account of his leprosy, the inference *a minori ad majus* cannot be applied. (15) Thus implying that a first issue is clean. (16) And, therefore, causes no uncleanness by

Said Rab Judah of Diskarta[1] to Raba: What is the proof?[2] Is it not still possible to maintain that the text deals with one who is only a *zab;*[3] and as to your objection 'If it causes the uncleanness of others, is it not obvious that it causes that of the man himself?' [It can be retorted:] The case of the scapegoat[4] proves [the invalidity of your argument], for it causes uncleanness to others[5] while it is itself clean.[6] Abaye observed: Why did he[7] at all raise such a question, seeing that he himself stated, '*This is the law of him that hath an issue,*[8] implies, whether he is of age or a minor', and since this law[9] has been deduced by him from that text,[8] the expression of '*whether it be a man*'[10] remains free for the purpose of including a leper in regard to his source and '*or a woman*' serves to include a female leper in regard to her sources; and the All Merciful has compared[11] the leper to the confirmed *zab:*[12] As the confirmed *zab* conveys uncleanness through carriage so does the first discharge of a leper convey uncleanness by carriage.

R. Huna ruled: The first observed discharge of a *zab* conveys uncleanness[13] even in the case of a mishap; for it is said, *This is the law of him that hath an issue, and of him from whom the flow of seed goeth out;*[8] as '*the flow of seed*' conveys uncleanness even in the case of a mishap so does the first observed discharge of a *zab* convey uncleanness even in the case of a mishap. Come and hear: If he

carriage. Had it been a source the first discharge would have been unclean and there would have been no need to include in the uncleanness a second one.

(1) [Deskarah, sixteen *parasangs* N.E. of Bagdad, v. Obermeyer, p. 146]. (2) Lit., 'from what'. (3) While the discharge of a leper requires no Scriptural text to tell of its uncleanness since even a first one is unclean by reason of its issue from a leper's source. (4) Cf. Lev. XVI, 5ff. (5) The man who carries it to Azazel (cf. Lev. XVI, 8, 26). (6) As any other live beast. (7) R. Joseph. (8) Lev. XV, 32. (9) The uncleanness of a minor. (10) Lev. XV, 33, from which it was deduced *supra* that the first discharge of a minor is unclean. (11) By including the expression of '*whether it be a man*' (applied to the leper) in the text dealing with the *zab*. (12) One who observed two discharges (for the proof cf. Rashi). (13) Of a light nature: Only by contact and for the duration of one day; and only when it was followed by a second discharge does the person become a confirmed *zab* in respect of the counting of the seven days of uncleanness.

observed a first discharge, he must be examined.[1] Is not this done to determine his[2] uncleanness?[3]—No; in regard to a sacrifice.[4] Come and hear: At the second observation of a discharge he must be examined.[1] Now for what purpose? If it be suggested: For that of a sacrifice but not for that of uncleanness[5] [it could be retorted:] Apply here the Scriptural text *'out of his flesh'*,[6] which implies, but not as a result of a mishap.[7] Consequently it must be for the purpose of uncleanness. And since the final clause refers to an examination in regard to uncleanness must not the first clause also refer to one for uncleanness?[8]—What an argument! Each might refer to an examination for different purposes.[9]

Come and hear: R. Eliezer ruled: Even at the third observation he must be examined on account of the sacrifice.[1] From which it follows, does it not, that the first Tanna requires it[10] on account of the uncleanness?[3]—No; all may require it[10] on account of the sacrifice, but here they[11] differ on the exposition of the *eth*[12] particles. The Rabbis base no exposition on the *eth* particles and R. Eliezer does. 'The Rabbis base no exposition on the *eth* particles': *'He that hath an issue'*[13] represents one discharge, *'his issue'*[14] represents a second one; so far *'for the man'*;[15] while at the third discharge the All Merciful compared him *to the woman*.[16] 'And

(1) Zabim II, 2. (2) Lit., 'what, not to'. (3) By ascertaining whether the discharge was or was not due to a mishap. In the former case it would be deemed clean. An objection against R. Huna. (4) Which must be brought after three observed discharges. In case of a mishap the discharge is not reckoned as one of the three. (5) *Sc.* the major uncleanness. (6) Lev. XV, 2, dealing with one who observed two discharges. (7) How then could it be held that no examination is required for this purpose? (8) Cf. *supra* n. 3. (9) Lit., 'that as it is and that as it is', sc. while the latter examination serves the purposes of ascertaining the person's subjection to uncleanness, the former (as stated *supra*) may serve that of ascertaining whether he is liable to a sacrifice. (10) The examination. (11) R. Eliezer and the first Tanna. (12) Grammatically the sign of the defined accusative. (13) Lev. XV, 33. V. following n. (14) Ibid. E.V., *Of them that have an issue.* (15) Ibid. (E.V., *whether it be a man*). *Sc.* in the case of a mishap it is not subject to uncleanness. (16) Ibid. (E.V. *or a woman*). *Sc.* even in the case of a mishap it is subject to uncleanness (cf. *infra* 36*b*) and also the obligation of a sacrifice.

R. Eliezer does': *'He that hath an issue'*[1] represents one discharge, *'eth'*[2] represents a second one, *'his issue'*[3] represents a third one, while at the fourth discharge the All Merciful compared him *to the woman.*[4]

Come and hear: R. Isaac said, A *zab*, surely, was included in the same law of uncleanness as one who emitted semen,[5] why then was he excluded?[6] In order to relax the law for him in one respect and to restrict it for him in another respect. 'To relax the law for him' in that he does not become unclean in case of a mishap; 'and to restrict it for him' [35*b*] in that he causes a couch and a seat to be unclean.[7] Now when [does this ruling apply]? If it be suggested: When a second discharge was observed [the objection would arise]: How could he then be included in 'the same law of uncleanness as one who emitted semen'? It is consequently obvious [that is was meant to apply] when a first discharge was observed;[8] and yet it was stated, was it not, 'To relax the law for him in that he does not become unclean in case of a mishap'?[9]— But how do you understand this: 'To restrict it for him in that he causes a couch and a seat to be unclean'; is he capable[10] after a first observation to cause a couch and a seat to be unclean? But the fact is that it is this that was meant: 'R. Isaac said, A *zab* after his first observation was surely included in the same law of uncleanness as one who emitted semen, why then was he in the case of a second observation excluded? In order to relax the law for him in one respect and to restrict it for him in another respect. "To relax the law for him" in that he does not become unclean in case of a mishap; "and to restrict it for him" in that he causes a couch and a bed to be unclean'.[11]

(1) Lev. XV, 33. V. *infra* n. 3. (2) Grammatically the sign of the defined accusative. (3) Ibid. E.V., *Of them that have an issue.* (4) Cf. prev. nn. In this case, however, the comparison is restricted to the case of a mishap, viz., if such a discharge occurred after some of the seven days have been counted all the counting is void. Uncleanness sets in after two discharges while a sacrifice is incurred after the third discharge. (5) As will be shown *infra.* (6) In being given a special section to himself. (7) As a 'father of uncleanness'. (8) When (cf. *supra* 34*b ad fin.*) he may well be compared to one who emitted semen. (9) An objection against R. Huna. (10) Lit., 'a son of'. (11) As a 'father of uncleanness'.

R. Huna stated: The discharge of a *zab* resembles the dough water of barley. The discharge of the *zab* issues from dead flesh while semen issues from live flesh. The former is watery and resembles the white of a crushed egg while the latter is viscous and resembles the white of a sound egg.

THE BLOOD OF A WOMAN AFTER CHILDBIRTH WHO DID NOT UNDERGO RITUAL IMMERSION etc. It was taught: Beth Hillel said to Beth Shammai, Do you not agree that if a menstruant who did not undergo ritual immersion observed some blood she is unclean?[1] Said Beth Shammai to them: [This is] no [comparison]. If you apply this law[2] to a menstruant who, even after she had undergone immersion, is unclean if she observed a discharge, would you also apply it to a woman after childbirth who, if she had undergone immersion and then observed a discharge, is clean? The former retorted: The case of one who gave birth during *zibah* proves our case; for if such a woman had undergone ritual immersion[3] and observed a discharge after the counted days she is clean[4] while if she did not undergo immersion and observed a discharge she is unclean. The latter replied: The same law[5] applies,[6] and this is our reply. This then implies that they[7] are in disagreement.[8] But have we not learnt: THEY[7] AGREE, HOWEVER, THAT IF SHE GAVE BIRTH WHILE IN ZIBAH, IT CONVEYS UNCLEANNESS BOTH WHEN WET AND WHEN DRY?—This is no difficulty, since the latter[9] refers to one who already counted the prescribed days while the former[10] refers to one who did not count them.[11]

(1) If they do in this case, why do they differ in that of a WOMAN AFTER CHILDBIRTH? (2) Of uncleanness. (3) After counting the seven clean days in addition to the unclean days of childbirth. (4) Because it is clean blood. (5) That is applicable to a woman after childbirth in the absence of *zibah*. (6) To a childbirth in *zibah*: *sc.* the latter also is clean, if the discharge occurred after the unclean days of childbirth and the seven clean days after *zibah* had been counted, though she had undergone no immersion. (7) Beth Shammai and Beth Hillel. (8) On the uncleanness of one who was in childbirth during *zibah*. (9) The Baraitha. (10) Our Mishnah. (11) *Sc.* the discharge occurred before the lapse of seven clean days after the *zibah*. As she is then still a *zabah* her discharge (unlike that of a woman in childbirth in the absence of *zibah* that is unclean only when wet) is unclean whether wet or dry.

And so it was also taught: If a woman who gave birth during *zibah* had counted the prescribed number of clean days but did not undergo ritual immersion and then observed a discharge, Beth Shammai gave their ruling[1] in accordance with their own view[2] and Beth Hillel ruled in accordance with their own view.[3]

It was stated: Rab said, [the blood discharge[4] emanates[5] from] one and the same source; but it is the Torah that declared it unclean during one period[6] and clean during another.[7] Levi, however, said, It emanates from two different sources. When the unclean one is closed[8] the clean one opens, and when the clean one closes,[9] the unclean one opens. What is the practical difference between them?[10]—The practical difference between them is the case of a continuous discharge from within the seven days into the period following these seven days, or from within the fourteen days into the period after the fourteenth, or from within the forty days to the period after the forty days or from within the eighty days into the period following eighty days. According to Rab the law is to be relaxed in the first case[11] and restricted in the latter;[12] but according to Levi the law is to be restricted in the first case[13] and relaxed in the latter.[14]

(1) Lit., 'went'. (2) Expressed in the case of a childbirth that was free from *zibah*, viz., that even prior to immersion the discharge is clean if the prescribed number of clean days had been duly counted. (3) That cleanness cannot be attained unless there was immersion as well as the due counting of the clean days. (4) After childbirth. (5) During the prescribed unclean and clean days. (6) For seven days after the birth of a male child and for fourteen days after the birth of a female child. (7) For thirty-three days after the seven in the case of the birth of a male and for sixty-six days after the fourteen in the case of the birth of a female. (8) At the end of seven and the fourteen days respectively (cf. prev. n. but one). (9) At the termination (cf. prev. n. but one) of the forty and the eighty days respectively. (10) Rab and Levi. (11) From within the seven and the fourteen days to the respective periods following them. Though the discharge was continuous it becomes clean, in accordance with the ordinance of the Torah, after the seventh and the fourteenth day respectively. (12) From within the forty and the eighty days to the respective periods following them. Cf. prev. n. *mut. mut.* (13) Cf. prev. n. but one. Since the discharge was continuous it must be assumed that the unclean source had not yet closed. (14) Cf. prev. n. *mut. mut.*

An objection was raised: THE BLOOD OF A WOMAN AFTER CHILDBIRTH WHO DID NOT UNDERGO RITUAL IMMERSION, BETH SHAMMAI RULED, IS LIKE HER SPITTLE AND HER URINE, BUT BETH HILLEL RULED: IT CONVEYS UNCLEANNESS BOTH WHEN WET AND WHEN DRY. It was now presumed that this is a case where[1] there was a break.[2] This then is satisfactory according to Rab who said that the discharge emanates from one and the same source,[3] for this reason it conveys uncleanness both when wet and dry.[4] But according to Levi who said that it emanated from two different sources why[5] should it convey uncleanness both when wet and when dry?—Levi can answer you: We are here dealing with the case of a woman whose discharge was continuous.[6] But if the discharge was continuous, what is Beth Shammai's reason?—Beth Shammai are of the opinion that there exists only once source. According to Levi[7] one can quite well see the point that divides Beth Shammai from Beth Hillel;[8] but, according to Rab,[9] what[10] is the point that divides them?[11]—The point that divides them in the question whether[12] both the termination of the prescribed number of days and also ritual immersion are required; Beth Shammai holding that the All Merciful made the cleanness dependent on the days alone while Beth Hillel hold that[13] it is dependent on both the days and immersion.[14]

(1) At the termination of the unclean days. (2) In the continuity of the discharge. (3) And that it is only an ordinance of the Torah that brings about the distinction. (4) As the woman had not yet undergone ritual immersion the source must remain unclean and the discharge continues to convey uncleanness whether it is wet or dry. (5) Since at the termination of the unclean days the clean source opens. (6) *Sc.* there was no break in it when the unclean period had ended, which is an indication that the unclean source had not yet been closed. (7) Who stated that according to Beth Hillel there are two different sources. (8) According to the latter, since the sources are two, and since the unclean one had not yet closed, the discharge must be unclean; while according to the former, since there is only one source and the Torah ordained that after the unclean days prescribed it becomes clean, the discharge must be clean. (9) Who stated that there is only one source. (10) If Beth Hillel uphold this view. (11) Beth Shammai from Beth Hillel, seeing that both agree that there is only one source for the clean and the unclean blood. (12) To enable the woman to attain cleanness. (13) Irrespective of

Come and hear: THEY AGREE, HOWEVER, THAT IF SHE GAVE BIRTH WHILE IN ZIBAH, IT CONVEYS UNCLEANNESS BOTH WHEN WET AND WHEN DRY. It was now assumed that here also[1] it is a case where there was a break.[2] Now, according to Rab who stated that there exists only one source one can quite well see the reason why the discharge conveys UNCLEANNESS BOTH WHEN WET AND WHEN DRY;[3] but according to Levi who stated that the sources are two why does the discharge[4] CONVEY UNCLEANNESS BOTH WHEN WET AND WHEN DRY?[5]—He can answer you: Here also it is a case of a continuous discharge. But if the discharge was continuous, what was the need of stating the law?[6]—It was necessary to state it for the sake of Beth Shammai: Although Beth Shammai maintain that there is only one source and that the All Merciful had ordained the uncleanness to be dependent entirely on the lapse of the prescribed number of days,[7] this applies only to a woman in normal[8] childbirth, the prescribed number of whose unclean days had passed,[9] but not to a woman who gave birth in *zibah* who is required also to count seven clean days.[10]

Come and hear: *Her sickness shall be unclean*[11] includes[12] the man who had intercourse with her;[13] '*her sickness shall be unclean*'[11] in-

whether the discharge was continuous or ceased for a time at the termination of the unclean days. (14) One without the other does not suffice for the attainment of cleanness.

(1) Where, as was explained *supra*, the days prescribed for a childbirth had passed but the seven clean days that are to follow *zibah* had not yet been counted. (2) In the continuity of the discharge, at the conclusion of the unclean period. (3) The reason being that the Torah ordained the blood to be regarded as unclean until the seven clean days that must follow *zibah* had passed. (4) Which after the unclean period emanates from the clean source. (5) *Sc.* while, by reason of its emanating from the source of a *zab*, it is rightly unclean when wet, why should it also be unclean when dry? (6) That it CONVEYS UNCLEANNESS BOTH etc. (7) *Sc.* that the discharge after these unclean days have passed becomes naturally clean. (8) Lit., 'alone'. (9) Lit., 'completed'. (10) After the *zibah*. So long as she had not counted these days she remains subject to the uncleanness of *zibah*. (11) Lev. XII, 2. (12) Since otherwise the text is superfluous after the previous statement '*then she shall be unclean seven days as in the days of impurity*' (ibid.). (13) *Sc.* that he becomes as unclean as she.

cludes[1] the nights;[2] '*her sickness shall she be unclean*'[3] includes[1] a woman who gave birth while in *zibah* who remains in her uncleanness[4] until seven clean days have passed.[5] This[6] is quite intelligible according to Rab who said that there exists only one source, since it is for this reason that she[7] requires seven clean days,[8] [36*a*] but according to Levi, who said that the sources were two, why should it be necessary to count seven days, seeing that the slightest [break][9] should suffice?[10]—It is this that was meant: It is necessary for her that[11] there shall be a slight [break][12] in order that [the following days] shall be counted as her seven clean ones.

Come and hear: The days of her pregnancy supplement those of her nursing,[13] and the days of her nursing supplement those of her pregnancy. In what manner? If there was a break of two *'onahs* during her pregnancy and of one during her nursing, or of two during her nursing and of one during her pregnancy, or of one and a half during her pregnancy and of one and a half during her nursing, they are all combined into a series of three *'onahs*.[14] Now according to Rab who said that there was only one source this ruling is quite justified, for it is for this reason[15] that there must be a break of three *'onahs*,[16] but according to Levi who said that there were two sources why[17] should a break of three *'onahs*

(1) V. p. 246, n. 12. (2) I.e., that the uncleanness is not restricted to the days, though '*days*' only were spoken of in the context. (3) Lev. XII, 2. (4) After all discharge had ceased. (5) *Infra* 37*b*. (6) The last mentioned ruling. (7) To attain cleanness. (8) The discharge emanating from the same source as the unclean blood, the Torah (by its insertion of the superfluous text mentioned) ordained that cleanness cannot be attained before the woman had counted seven clean days. (9) At the termination of the unclean period. (10) For the closing up of the unclean source. As all the blood that is discharged subsequently emanates from the clean source it should suffice for the woman to wait after the unclean period no more than seven days and attain cleanness at their termination, irrespective of whether she observed any discharge during these days or not. (11) At the termination of the unclean period. (12) An indication that the unclean source had been closed. (13). As regards the establishment of a regular period. (14) *Supra* 10*b* q.v. notes. (15) That there is only one source. (16) In the absence of such a break the discharge cannot be regarded as having ceased. (17) Since the blood after the unclean period emanates from the clean source, while the unclean one is closed.

be required, seeing that the slightest [break] should suffice?[1]—It is this that was meant: It is necessary for her that there shall be a slight [break] in order that [the following days] shall be counted for her[2] as three *'onahs*.

Come and hear: Both,[3] however, are of the same opinion that where a woman observed a discharge after her clean blood period[4] it suffices for her to reckon her uncleanness from the time of her observation. Now according to Levi who said that there exist two sources one may well concede this ruling since it is for this reason[5] that[6] it suffices for her to reckon her uncleanness from the time of her observation,[7] but according to Rab who said that there existed only one source, why should it suffice for her to reckon her uncleanness from the time of her observation seeing that[8] she should have become unclean for twenty-four hours retrospectively?—This is a case where there was not time enough.[9] But why should she not be unclean from her previous examination to her last examination?[10]—As there was no interval of twenty-four

(1) Cf. *supra* p. 247, n. 11 *mut. mut.* (2) Even if she observed a discharge. (3) Shammai and Hillel who differ on the question of twenty-four hours retrospective uncleanness. (4) This is now presumed to mean even if a considerable time after, on the eighty-third or ninetieth day after childbirth, for instance. (5) That there exist two sources. (6) The blood from the unclean source having ceased for many days. (7) Which (cf. prev. n.) is rightly regarded as a first discharge after many days from the unclean source. A first discharge in the case of a nursing woman, as in that of another three categories of woman, does not cause any retrospective uncleanness. (8) Since that source has also been discharging during the clean period and the present discharge cannot be regarded as a first one. (9) *Sc.* less than a twenty-four hours interval has elapsed between the end of the clean period and the observation of the discharge. Hence even if the blood discharged had been in the outer chamber twenty-four hours previously the woman (since her blood at that time was still clean) could not be deemed unclean. (10) If, for instance, on examining herself in the morning she observed a discharge, her uncleanness should be retrospective and all objects she handled during the night should be regarded as unclean. The previous answer that 'there was not time enough' cannot be given here, since in such a case there would have been no necessity whatsoever to state, what is so obvious, that in such a case it suffices to reckon the uncleanness from the time of observation.

hours[1] the Rabbis enacted no preventive measure even in regard to uncleanness from the previous examination to the last examination.

Come and hear: If a woman who was in childbirth during *zibah* had counted the prescribed number of clean days but did not undergo ritual immersion, and then observed a discharge, Beth Shammai gave their ruling in accordance with their own view and Beth Hillel ruled in accordance with their own view.[2] Now according to Rab who said that there was only one source this ruling is quite justified, since it is for this reason[3] that[4] the discharge causes uncleanness both when wet and when dry; but according to Levi who said that there were two sources, why[5] does the discharge cause uncleanness both when wet and when dry?—Levi can answer you: I maintain the same view as the Tanna who stated that 'both, however, are of the same opinion'.[6] And if you prefer I might reply that here we are dealing with one whose discharge is continuous. But was it not stated that she had counted?[7]—Here we are dealing with one who gave birth to a female child while in *zibah* and whose discharge ceased during the first week[8] but continued again[9] in the second week,[8] he being of the opinion that the unclean days of childbirth in which no discharge is observed are counted among the clean days of one's *zibah*.[10]

(1) Cf. prev. n. but one. (2) That before ritual immersion the discharge is unclean both when wet and when dry. (3) That there existed only one source. (4) In the absence of ritual immersion. (5) Seeing that the required number of days had been counted and the unclean source must have been stopped. (6) That if there was a discharge after the termination of the clean blood period, even though (as explained *supra*) more than twenty-four hours intervened, it suffices for the woman to be unclean from the time she observed a discharge; which shows that he also holds that there exist two sources. (7) It does. Now, if the flow of blood had not ceased, how could she even begin to count? (8) Of the two unclean weeks prescribed for a woman after the birth of a female. (9) Lit., 'did not cease', 'break off'. (10) Hence the statement that 'she had counted'. As in the second week, however, the discharge began again and continued into the third week, it conveys uncleanness, according to Beth Hillel, both when wet and when dry, since it emanates from an unclean

Rabina said to R. Ashi: R. Shamen of Sikara[1] told us, 'Mar Zuṭra once visited our place when he delivered a discourse in which he laid down: The law is to be restricted in agreement with Rab[2] and it is also to be restricted in agreement with Levi'.[3] R. Ashi stated: The law is in agreement with Rab both in his relaxations[4] and his restrictions.[2] Meremar in his discourse laid down: The law is in agreement with Rab both in his relaxations[4] and restrictions.[2] And the law is in agreement with Rab both in his relaxations[4] and restrictions.[2]

MISHNAH. [36b] A WOMAN IN PROTRACTED LABOUR IS REGARDED AS A MENSTRUANT.[5] IF HAVING BEEN IN LABOUR[6] FOR THREE DAYS OF THE ELEVEN DAYS,[7] SHE WAS RELIEVED FROM HER PAINS FOR TWENTY-FOUR HOURS AND THEN GAVE BIRTH, SHE IS REGARDED AS HAVING GIVEN BIRTH IN A ZIBAH;[8] SO R. ELIEZER. R. JOSHUA RULED: THE RELIEF FROM PAIN[9] MUST HAVE CONTINUED FOR A NIGHT AND A DAY,[10] AS THE NIGHT AND THE DAY OF THE SAB-

source which the Torah did not regard as clean before the prescribed number of days had been counted and immersion had been performed.

(1) On the Tigris near Maḥoza. (2) That if the discharge was continuous from within the clean period into the unclean one following, it conveys uncleanness as if it had emanated from an unclean source. (3) That where a discharge continued from within the unclean days period into the clean one that follows, it is not regarded as clean blood since the continuous discharge is an indication that the unclean source had not yet closed up. (4) That where the discharge continued from within the unclean period into the clean one following, it is regarded as clean after the last unclean day, despite its continuity. (5) This is explained in the Gemara *infra*. (6) And bleeding. (7) That intervene between the menstrual periods and during which a discharge of blood is ordinarily attributed to *zibah*. (8) As the pains ceased before birth it is evident that the previous discharge (cf. prev. n. but one) was not due to the labour but to *zibah*. Had the pains continued until birth all the previous bleeding would have been attributed to that of the labour which is Pentateuchally clean. (9) As result of which the bleeding must be regarded as *zibah* and is not to be attributed to the labour. (10) Not merely for twenty-four hours that began and ended at any time of the day or the night.

BATH.[1] THE RELIEF [SPOKEN OF IS ONE] FROM PAIN, NOT FROM BLEEDING.[2] HOW LONG MAY PROTRACTED LABOUR CONTINUE?[3] R. MEIR RULED: 'EVEN FORTY OR FIFTY DAYS.[4] R. JUDAH RULED: HER [NINTH] MONTH SUFFICES FOR HER.[5] R. JOSE AND R. SIMEON RULED: PROTRACTED LABOUR CANNOT CONTINUE[3] FOR MORE THAN TWO WEEKS.

GEMARA. Is then[6] every woman IN PROTRACTED LABOUR REGARDED AS A MENSTRUANT?[7]—Rab replied: She[8] is deemed to be a menstruant for one day.[9] Samuel, however, ruled: The possibility must be taken into consideration[10] that she might be relieved from her pain,[11] while R. Isaac ruled: A discharge on the part of a woman in labour[12] is of no consequence.[13] But was it not stated, A WOMAN IN PROTRACTED LABOUR IS REGARDED AS

(1) Which begins at sunset of Friday and terminates at that of Saturday. (2) I.e., even if she was bleeding, the relief from pain alone suffices to subject her to the uncleanness of *zibah*. (3) In respect of exempting the woman from *zibah* (cf. *supra* p. 250, n. 8) even if she bled. (4) Prior to childbirth; provided only that there was no period of relief from pain (as defined *supra*) before birth. (5) *Sc.* only blood discharged during that month may be attributed to labour. Should the discharge begin during the 'eleven days' of the previous month and continue for three days she is deemed a *zabah* (on account of the discharge on these three days) even though the bleeding continued throughout the ninth month also. (6) Since our Mishnah seems to lay down a general rule. (7) But this, surely, is absurd. During the eleven days of *zibah* the woman could not be regarded as a MENSTRUANT but as a *zabah*. (8) Even if the discharge in the course of her labour occurred during the eleven days of *zibah*. (9) And on undergoing immersion in the evening she attains to cleanness. A woman who was not in labour, if she had such a discharge, must allow another day (free from any discharge) to pass before she can attain to cleanness. (10) In accordance with Rabbinic law, though Pentateuchally this is not necessary. (11) Before childbirth. As a result it would be evident that the discharge was one of *zibah* and the man cohabiting with the woman would be subject to *kareth* in Pentateuchal law. The woman, like any other who observed a discharge during the eleven days of *zibah*, must consequently remain unclean until another day, that was free from any further discharge, had passed. (12) Even during the 'eleven days' of *zibah*. (13) Sc. it is regarded as the blood of labour and the woman is deemed to be clean even on the same day.

A MENSTRUANT?—Raba replied: During the days of her menstruation[1] SHE[2] IS DEEMED TO BE A MENSTRUANT,[3] but during the days of *zibah*[4] she is clean. And so it was also taught: If a woman is in protracted labour during the days of her menstruation[1] she is deemed to be a menstruant,[2] but if this occurred during the days of her *zibah*[4] she is clean. In what circumstances? If she was in labour for one day and had relief from pain[5] for two days, or if she was in labour for two days and had relief from pain for one day,[5] or if she was relieved from pain[5] and then was again in labour and then was again relieved from pain,[5] such a woman is regarded as having given birth in *zibah;* but if she was relieved from pain for one day and then was in labour for two days, or if she was relieved for two days and then was in labour for one day, or if she was in labour and then was relieved and then was again in labour, such a woman is not regarded as having given birth in *zibah;* the general rule being that where the pains of labour immediately precede[6] birth the woman is not regarded as having given birth in *zibah,* but if release from pain immediately precedes[6] birth the woman[7] must be regarded as having given birth in *zibah.*[8] Hananiah the son of R. Joshua's brother ruled: Provided her pains of labour were experienced[9] on her third day,[10] even though she had relief during the rest of that day, she[11] is not regarded as having given birth in *zibah.* What does the expression 'The general rule' include?—It includes the ruling of Hananiah.

Whence is this[12] deduced?—Our[13] Rabbis taught: *Her blood*[14] refers to blood that is normally discharged,[15] but not to such as is

(1) *Sc.* the period during which a discharge is deemed to be menstrual. (2) Though in labour. (3) The reason is given *infra.* (4) Cf. prev. n. but one *mut. mut.* (5) While still bleeding. (6) Lit., 'near'. (7) Where her discharge continued for three days. (8) The release from pain serving as proof that the previous discharge was not due to childbirth but to *zibah.* (9) Even if only for a short while. (10) Ordinarily it is the discharge on the third day that causes a woman to be a confirmed or major *zabah.* A discharge on not more than one or two days only causes her to be a minor *zabah.* (11) Since on the third day her relief did not extend over the whole night and the whole day. (12) That the blood of labour is clean. (13) Lit., 'for our'. (14) Lev. XV, 25. (15) Lit., 'on account of herself'.

due to childbirth.[1] You say, '[Not to such as is] due to childbirth'; is it not possible that only that blood is excluded[2] which is due to an accident?[1] As it was said, *And if a woman have an issue of her blood,*[3] a discharge that is due to an accident is included;[4] to what then could one apply the limitation of *'her blood'?*[3] Obviously to this: "*Her blood*" refers to blood that is normally discharged but not to such as is due to childbirth'. But[5] what reason do you see for holding the blood of childbirth clean and that which is due to an accident unclean? I hold that which is due to childbirth clean since it is followed by cleanness,[6] but hold that which is due to an accident unclean since it is not followed by cleanness. On the contrary! That which is due to an accident should be held clean since a discharge from a *zab* that is due to an accident is clean?— Now at all events we are dealing with the case of a woman, and we do not find that in the case of a woman blood due to an accident is ever clean. And if you prefer I might reply: What opinion do you hold? Is it to regard a discharge that is due to an accident clean and one that is due to childbirth unclean? Surely you cannot point to any occurrence that is more in the nature of an accident[7] than this.[8] If so,[9] why should it not be said in the case of a menstruant also: *Her issue*[10] refers to an issue that is normally discharged but not to such as is due to childbirth?[11] You say, '[not to such as is due to] childbirth'; is it not possible that only that blood is excluded[2] which is due to an accident?[1] As it was said, *And if a woman have an issue,*[10] a discharge that is due to an accident

(1) The latter being clean. (2) Lit., 'or it is not but'. (3) Lev. XV, 25. (4) Since the text draws no distinctions. (5) Seeing that the text does not specifically mention either the blood of childbirth or that which is due to an accident. (6) The period of unclean blood after a childbirth (seven days for a male and fourteen days for a female) is followed by one of clean blood (thirty-three days for a male and sixty-six days for a female). (7) *Sc.* that is not dependent on the woman's will. (8) If then blood that is due to an accident (cf. prev. n.) is clean that which is due to childbirth must equally be clean. (9) If the deduction just discussed is tenable. (10) Lev. XV, 19, in the section dealing with a menstruant. (11) But if that exposition is upheld how could it be said *supra* that blood of labour discharged during the menstrual period is unclean?

is included;[1] to what then could one apply the limitation of *'her issue'?*[2] Obviously to this: *'Her issue'* refers to an issue that is normally discharged but not to such as is due to childbirth![3]—Resh Laḳish answered: Scripture said, *She shall continue*[4] which implies:[5] You have another continuation which is of the same nature as this one;[6] and which is it?[7] It is that of protracted labour during the days of her *zibah*. Might it not be suggested that this refers to protracted labour during the days of her menstruation?—Rather, said Samuel's father, Scripture said, *Then she shall be unclean two weeks, as in her menstruation,*[8] [implying] but not 'as in her *zibah*', from which it may be inferred that her *zibah* is clean; and which is it?[7] It is that of protracted labour during the days of her *zibah*. Now, however, that it is written, *Then she shall be unclean two weeks as in her menstruation,*[8] what need was there for the expression of *'her blood'?*[9]—If not for the expression *'her blood'* it might have been presumed that the deduction *'as in her menstruation'*[8] and not 'as in her *zibah*' implies that the discharge is clean even where the woman was relieved from pain,[10] hence we were informed[11] [that the discharge is clean only where it is due to childbirth].[12]

Shila b. Abina gave a practical decision in agreement with the view of Rab.[13] When Rab's soul was about to depart to its eternal rest he[14] said to R. Assi, 'Go and restrain him,[15] and if he does not listen to you try to convince him'.[16] The other thought that he was told, 'Put him under the ban'.[17] After Rab's soul came to its eternal

(1) Since the text draws no distinctions. (2) Lev. XV, 19, in the section dealing with a menstruant. (3) V. p. 253, n. 11. (4) Lev. XII, 4, referring to clean blood. (5) Since the expression could well have been omitted without destroying the general meaning of the text. (6) *Sc.* in both cases the discharge is clean. (7) I.e., how could *zibah* be clean? (8) Lev. XII, 5. E.V., *'as in her impurity'*. (9) From which the same deductions, that a discharge of blood that was due to childbirth is clean, was made *supra*. (10) Before the birth of the child. (11) By the additional expression of *'her blood'*. (12) Relief from pain is an indication that the previous discharge was not due to childbirth and is, therefore, unclean. (13) That a woman who was in labour during the eleven days of *zibah* and discharged some blood is unclean for that day (v. *supra*). (14) Having changed his former view. (15) From acting in the same manner. (16) *Garyeh*, lit., 'attract him'. (17) *Gadyeh*, lit., 'cut him off'.

rest he[1] said to him,[2] 'Retract, for Rab has retracted'. 'If', the other retorted, 'he had retracted he would have told me so'.[3] As he[2] did not listen to him[1] the latter put him under the ban. 'Is not the Master', the other[2] asked him, 'afraid of the fire?'[4] 'I', the former replied, 'am Issi b. Judah[5] who is Issi b. Gur-aryeh[6] who is Issi b. Gamaliel who is Issi b. Mahalalel, a brazen mortar[7] over which rust has no power'. 'And I', the other retorted, 'am Shila b. Abina, an iron pestle that breaks the brazen mortar'. Thereupon R. Assi fell ill and they had to put him in hot [blankets] to relieve him from chills and in cold [compresses] to relieve him from heat,[8] and his soul departed to its eternal rest. [37a] Shila proceeded to his wife and said to her, 'Prepare for me my shroud in order that he[1] have no opportunity of going to Rab and saying things about me'. She prepared his shroud for him; and when the soul of Shila came to its eternal rest people saw a myrtle[9] flying from the one bier to the other. 'We may conclude', they said, 'that the Rabbis have been reconciled.'

Raba enquired: Does labour[10] render all previous counting in *zibah*[11] void? Does any discharge that causes uncleanness render all previous counting void and, therefore, this also [does it, since] it causes uncleanness like the days of menstruation; or is it possible that only that which[12] causes the uncleanness of *zibah* that renders all the previous counting void, and this, therefore, [does not do it, since] it is no cause of such uncleanness?—Abaye replied: A *zibah* that is due to an accident provides the answer,[13] for this is no cause of the uncleanness of *zibah*[14] and yet renders all previous counting void.[15] The other retorted: Indeed, this[16] also is a cause

(1) R. Assi. (2) Shila. (3) He was a disciple of Rab. (4) *Sc.* that he would suffer for his high handed action. (5) [He probably meant that his name Assi bore resemblance to that of Assi b. Judah who bore a variety of names, v. Pes., Sonc. ed., p. 585, n. 6.]. (6) Lit., 'lion's whelp' (cf. Gen. XLIX, 9). (7) *Assitha,* play upon 'Assi' or 'Issi'. (8) *Aliter:* They got him hot to relieve him from chills; they got him cold to relieve him from fever (Jast.). (9) It was customary to lay a myrtle on a bier (Rashi). (10) That was accompanied by bleeding. (11) The prescribed seven days. (12) By appearing on three days. (13) Lit., proves'. (14) As was stated *supra.* (15) V. *infra.* (16) *Zibah* that is due to an accident.

of the uncleanness of *zibah*, for we have learnt: If he observed a first discharge he must be examined, if he observed a second discharge he must be examined, but if he observed a third he need not be examined.[1] But according to R. Eliezer who ruled, 'Even after a third discharge he must be examined'[2] would you also maintain that, since it is no cause of the uncleanness of *zibah*, it does not render the previous counting void?—The other replied: According to R. Eliezer the law is so indeed.

Come and hear: R. Eliezer ruled, Even after a third discharge he must be examined, but after a fourth one he need not be examined.[3] Does not this refer to the rendering of previous counting void?[4]—No, to the imposition on that drop of an uncleanness that may be conveyed through carriage.

Come and hear: After a third discharge, R. Eliezer ruled, he must be examined; after a fourth one he need not be examined; and it is in regard to a sacrifice that I said this[5] but not in regard to the rendering void of all previous counting.[6] But the fact is that[7] according to R. Eliezer you may well solve from here that even that which causes no uncleanness of *zibah* renders all previous counting void. What, however, [it is asked], is the solution of the problem according to the Rabbis?—Come and hear what the father of R. Abin learnt: 'What had his *zibah* caused him? Seven days.[8] Hence it renders void the counting of seven days. What had his emission of semen caused him? The [uncleanness of] one day. Hence it renders void the counting of one day'. Now what is meant by 'seven days'? If it be suggested that it causes him to

(1) Zabim II, 2. Thus it is shown that a third discharge, even if it was due to an accident, provided the first two discharges were not due to such a cause, renders a person a confirmed or major *zab*. (2) Zabim l.c., which proves that *zibah* that is due to an accident never causes a person to be a confirmed *zab*. (3) Cf. *supra* 35*a*, Naz. 65*b*. (4) An objection against Raba, who laid down that that which is no cause of the uncleanness of *zibah* does not render void the previous counting. (5) That an examination is necessary. (6) The counting being always void and is in no way dependent on an examination. Now does not this then prove that even that which causes no uncleanness of *zibah* renders the counting void? (7) Contrary to what has been explained before. (8) This is explained presently.

be unclean for seven days, [the objection would arise that] in that case it should have been said: As on account of his *zibah* he is unclean for seven days. Consequently[1] it follows, that only that which causes the uncleanness of *zibah* renders void the counting of the seven days, but that which does not cause the uncleanness of *zibah* does not render void all previous counting. This is conclusive. Abaye stated: We have an accepted tradition that labour does not render void all previous counting in *zibah;* and should you find a Tanna who said that it did render the counting void, that must be R. Eliezer.[2]

It was taught: R. Marinus ruled, A birth does not render void the previous counting after a *zibah.*[3] The question was raised: Is it included in the counting?[4]—Abaye replied: It neither renders void the days that were previously counted[5] nor is it counted in the prescribed days.[5] Raba replied: It does not render void the days counted and it is counted among the prescribed days.[6] Whence, said Raba, do I derive this? From what was taught: *And after that she shall be clean,*[7] *'after'* means after all of them, implying that no uncleanness may intervene between them.[8] Now if you agree that [these days][9] are included one can well see the justification for saying that no uncleanness may intervene between them, but if you contend that these days[9] are not included the birth, surely, would cause a break between them. And Abaye?[10]—He can answer you: The meaning is that the uncleanness of *zibah* shall not intervene between them.[11] Whence, said Raba, do I derive this? From what was taught: *Of her issue,*[7] *'of her issue'*

(1) Since the expression used was 'caused'. (2) Who holds that *zibah* due to an accident, though it causes no *zibah* uncleanness, renders void all previous counting. (3) If the counting was interrupted by a birth it may be continued after the birth had taken place. (4) *Sc.* if the birth took place during the seven days following a *zibah,* and the days following it were free from all discharge, are these days counted as clean ones and make up the required number of seven? (5) The counting must be resumed after the clean days of birth have passed. (6) If the days after birth were free from all discharge. (7) Lev. XV, 28. (8) *Supra* 33b. (9) That follow a birth. (10) How in view of this argument can he maintain his view? (11) That of childbirth does not matter.

implies but not of her leprosy,[1] '*of her issue*' but not of her childbirth.[2] And Abaye?[3]—He can answer you: Deduce once '*Of her issue*[4] but not of her leprosy' and do not deduce again, 'but not of her childbirth'. And Raba?[5]—What an argument is this![6] If you agree that '*of her issue*'[4] implies 'but not of her childbirth' one can well justify the text; for since it was required for the deduction about childbirth, leprosy also was mentioned on account of childbirth; but if you contend that '*of her issue*' implies only 'but not of her leprosy', [the objection would arise] that this could be deduced from *And when he that hath an issue is cleansed of his issue,*[7] which implies '*of his issue*' and not of his leprosy. And Abaye?[3]—One[8] refers to a *zab* and the other to a *zabah,* both being necessary. For if the All Merciful had only written [37b] of a *zab* it might have been presumed to apply to him only, since he does not become unclean through a discharge that is due to an accident, but not to a *zabah* who becomes unclean even through a discharge that is due to an accident. Hence the necessity for the text about the *zabah*. And if the All Merciful had written only of a *zabah,* it might have been presumed to apply only to her, since she does not become unclean through observations [on less than three days] as on [three] days,[9] but not to a *zab* who becomes unclean through [three] observations[10] as [through observations on three] days.[11] Hence both texts were required.

Said Abaye: Whence do I derive this?[12] From what was taught: *Her sickness shall she be unclean,*[13] includes the man who had inter-

(1) *Sc.* as soon as she counted the days prescribed for *zibah* (cf. Lev. XV, 28) she brings the required sacrifice, and attains cleanness from *zibah* irrespective of whether she was or was not still afflicted with leprosy. (2) As soon as she is free from her *zibah* she begins to count the seven days and need not wait until the unclean days of childbirth had passed. It is thus obvious that a birth during the days of *zibah* does not render void the previous counting and that the days following birth are included in the counting. (3) How in view of this argument can he maintain his view? (4) Lev. XV, 28. (5) How can he make two deductions from the same expression? (6) Lit., that, what'. (7) Lev. XV, 13. (8) Of the two texts cited. (9) Only a discharge that made its appearance on three successive days causes her uncleanness. (10) Even on the same day. (11) Cf. B.Ḳ. 24*a*. (12) His ruling *supra* 37*a*. (13) Lev. XII, 2.

course with her; *'her sickness shall she be unclean'* includes the nights;[1] *'her sickness shall she be unclean'* includes a woman who gave birth in *zibah* who is required to continue in her uncleanness until seven clean days have passed. Now does not this mean: Clean from the uncleanness of birth?[2]—No, clean from that of blood.[3]

Abaye further stated, Whence do I derive this?[4] From what was taught: As are the days of her menstruation so are the days of her bearing. As the days of her menstruation are not suitable [for counting as the days] after her *zibah*[5] and they cannot be included in the counting of the prescribed seven days, so also the days following her bearing which[6] are not suitable [for counting as the days] after her *zibah* may not[7] be included in the counting of the seven prescribed days. And Raba?—This is in agreement with[8] R. Eliezer who ruled: It[9] also renders void all previous counting.[10] But may an inference be drawn from the impossible[11] for the possible?[12]—R. Aḥadboy b. Ammi replied: This is the view of R. Eliezer who holds that the possible may be inferred from the impossible.[13] R. Shesheth, however, replied: Scripture has perforce compared them[14] to one another.[15]

There are some who say: R. Aḥadboy b. Ammi citing R. Shesheth

(1) Though the text speaks only of days. (2) *Sc.* that no birth must intervene; from which it follows that if it did intervene the days following it may not be included in the prescribed seven days. (3) Only those days on which a discharge occurred may not be included in the counting, but where the birth was free from bleeding the days following it may well be included. (4) His ruling *supra* 37*a*. (5) Since the *zibah* period follows that of menstruation and not *vice versa*, while a subsequent menstruation period cannot begin before seven clean days have passed after the *zibah* had ceased. (6) Like those of menstruation. (7) If birth took place during the counting. (8) Lit., 'this whose'. (9) Childbirth. (10) From which it is self-evident that the days following it cannot be included in the counting of the seven days. According to the Rabbis, however, whose view Raba follows, birth does not render void all previous counting and the days following it may well be included in the prescribed seven days. (11) Menstruation during *zibah*. (12) Birth, which may well occur during a *zibah* period. (13) Cf. Men. 82*b*. (14) Birth and menstruation. (15) Only a *gezerah shawah* (v. Glos.) may be questioned, but not a comparison made in the Biblical text itself (*hekkesh*) despite any argument that might be raised against it.

replied, This represents the view of R. Eliezer who holds that the possible may be deduced from the impossible; but R. Papa replied: Scripture has perforce compared them to one another.

IF HAVING BEEN IN LABOUR FOR THREE DAYS etc. The question was raised: What is the ruling where she was relieved from both?[1]—R. Ḥisda replied: She is unclean.[2] R. Ḥanina replied: She is clean.[3] R. Ḥanina explained: This may be compared to a king who, when going on a tour, is preceded[4] by his troops and it is known that they are the king's troops.[5] But R. Ḥisda, said: [Immediately before his arrival] he would require even more troops.[6]

We learnt: R. JOSHUA RULED, THE RELIEF FROM PAIN MUST HAVE CONTINUED FOR A NIGHT AND A DAY, AS THE NIGHT AND THE DAY OF THE SABBATH. THE RELIEF [SPOKEN OF IS ONE] FROM PAIN, NOT FROM BLEEDING. The reason then[7] is because [she had relief] FROM PAIN and NOT FROM BLEEDING, but if she had relief from both[1] she is clean. Does not this present an objection against R. Ḥisda?—R. Ḥisda can answer you: There was no need to state that, if she had relief from both, she is unclean, since [metaphorically] the troops completely disappeared; but even where she had relief from pain and not from bleeding where it might have been presumed that as she had not ceased to bleed she has not ceased to labour either and that it was merely stupor that seized her. Hence we were informed [that even in this case she is unclean].

We learnt: IF HAVING BEEN IN LABOUR FOR THREE DAYS OF THE ELEVEN DAYS, SHE WAS RELIEVED FROM HER PAINS FOR TWENTY-FOUR HOURS AND THEN GAVE BIRTH, SHE IS

(1) Pain and bleeding. (2) Since at any rate she had relief from pain it is obvious that the previous bleeding was not due to childbirth. (3) The relief from both is an indication that the bleeding also was due to childbirth. Only where the bleeding continued and the pain ceased is it manifest that the former was not due to the labour. (4) By a day or two. (5) Similarly the pains and bleeding that precede childbirth must be ascribed to it despite the interval (cf. prev. n.) between them. (6) As the bleeding ceased it must be obvious that the childbirth had no connection with it. (7) Why the woman is unclean.

REGARDED AS HAVING GIVEN BIRTH IN ZIBAH. Now, how are we to imagine the circumstances? If it be suggested: As it was stated,[1] [the objection would arise:] What need was there to mention THREE seeing that it suffices[2] if the labour lasted two days and the relief[3] one day? Consequently it must be this that was meant: IF HAVING BEEN IN LABOUR FOR THREE DAYS she was relieved from both,[4] or if having been in labour for two days, SHE WAS RELIEVED FROM HER PAINS FOR TWENTY-FOUR HOURS, SHE IS REGARDED AS HAVING GIVEN BIRTH IN ZIBAH, and this presents, does it not, an objection against R. Ḥanina?—R. Ḥanina can answer you: No; the circumstances may in fact be as stated,[5] but it is this that we were informed, that although the labour continued[6] [for a part only] of the third day and she was relieved from her pains for twenty-four hours[7] she is nevertheless unclean, contrary to the view[8] of R. Ḥanina.[9]

HOW LONG MAY PROTRACTED LABOUR CONTINUE? R. MEIR RULED etc. Now since protracted labour may continue for FIFTY DAYS is there any necessity to mention FORTY?—R. Ḥisda replied: This is no difficulty, the one[10] referring to an ailing woman and the other[11] to a woman in good health.

R. Levi ruled: [The birth of] a child is a cause of the cleanness of those days only in which a woman may normally become a *zabah*,[12] but Rab ruled: Even in the days that are suitable for the counting prescribed for a *zabah*.[13] Said R. Adda b. Ahabah: And

(1) LABOUR FOR THREE DAYS, relief FOR TWENTY-FOUR HOURS, and bleeding all the time. (2) For the woman to be unclean. (3) From pain but not from bleeding. (4) Pain and bleeding. (5) LABOUR FOR THREE DAYS, relief FOR TWENTY-FOUR HOURS, and bleeding all the time. (6) Cf. Rashal. Cur. edd. 'began'. (7) And not for a full night and a full day. (8) Lit., 'to take out'. (9) *Sc.* Hananiah the son of the brother of R. Joshua who stated (*supra* 36b), 'Provided her pains of labour were experienced on her third day . . .she is not regarded as having given birth in *zibah*'. (10) Lit., 'here', the number fifty. (11) Forty. (12) I.e., the eleven days between the menstruation periods. If a birth, however, takes place after these days the woman becomes unclean as a menstruant (as stated *supra*). (13) *Sc.* if labour began during the eleven days of *zibah* not only are these days clean but also the seven days that follow them. Only when the bleeding continued beyond these seven days does the woman become unclean as a menstruant.

according to Rab's view[1] [38a] even the days that are suitable for counting after the previous counting had been rendered void[2] are also clean.[3]

We have learnt: HOW LONG MAY PROTRACTED LABOUR CONTINUE? R. MEIR RULED: EVEN FORTY OR FIFTY DAYS. Now this might quite possibly happen according to Rab on R. Adda b. Ahabah's interpretation,[4] but according to Levi[5] does not this present a difficulty?[6]—Levi can answer you: Was it stated that she was clean throughout all these days?[7] [No; if the birth occurs] in the days of menstruation[8] she is regarded as a menstruant and only when it occurs in the days of her *zibah*[8] is she clean.[9]

Another reading. R. Levi ruled: [The birth of] a child is a cause of cleanness[10] in those days only in which a woman may normally become a major *zabah*.[11] What is the reason? It is written in Scripture,[12] *Her blood many days*.[13] Abba Saul in the name of Rab[14] ruled: Even in the days in which she may normally become a

(1) That even the days following the *zibah* period are clean if the labour began during the *zibah* days. (2) I.e., for ever, since any seven days following a discharge that occurred within any seven days counted after a previous discharge are suitable for counting. (3) Once labour began within the eleven days of *zibah* all subsequent days are clean unless the woman was relieved from her pain for the prescribed period, prior to the birth of the child. (4) Since the counting of the days may sometimes continue for a very long time (cf. prev. n. but one). (5) Who restricts the labour and birth to the eleven days of *zibah*. (6) *Sc.* how is it possible for a woman to be clean when labour is protracted for forty or fifty days? (7) The forty or fifty days. (8) After the protracted labour. (9) The purport of R. Meir's ruling being that there is no obligation to bring a sacrifice or to count the prescribed number of clean days even though labour continued for forty or fifty days; but the woman remains clean only where the birth occurred in the days of *zibah*. If it occurs, however, in the days of menstruation she becomes unclean. (10) Exempting the woman from a sacrifice and from the counting of seven clean days. (11) I.e., where she experienced a discharge on three consecutive days in the course of the eleven days' period. If the discharge, however, appeared only on one day, she need not wait more than one clean day corresponding to the one unclean day. (12) In the text from which it was derived that a birth in *zibah* is a cause of cleanness. (13) Lev. XV, 25, *'many days'* implying a major *zabah* (cf. prev. n. but one). (14) Var. lec. Rabbi (Ronsburg).

minor *zabah*. What is the reason? *Days*[1] and *All the days*[1] are written in the context.[2]

We have learnt: HOW LONG MAY PROTRACTED LABOUR CONTINUE? R. MEIR RULED: EVEN FORTY OR FIFTY DAYS. Does not this present a difficulty against both of them?[3]—Was it stated that she was clean throughout all of them?[4] [No;] if she was in labour during the days of her menstruation she is regarded a menstruant and only where this occurred during the days of her *zibah*[5] is she clean.

It was taught: R. Meir used to say, A woman may sometimes bleed[6] for a hundred and fifty days[7] without becoming a major *zabah*.[8] How? The two days[9] preceding the period of her menstruation,[10] the seven days of menstruation, two days after menstruation,[11] fifty days[12] which childbirth causes to be clean, eighty days[13] prescribed for a female birth,[14] seven days of menstruation[15] and the two days[16] after the menstruation.[17] If so,[18] they[19] said to him, might not a woman bleed all the days of her life and no major *zibah* would occur in them?[20]—He replied: 'What is it that you have in mind? Is it the possibility of frequent abortions? The law of protracted labour[21] does not apply to abortions'.[22]

(1) Lev. XV, 25; instead of *'days'* the text has *'all the days'* and from this is derived (*infra* 73*a*) the law of a minor *zabah*. (2) Cf. *supra* p. 262, n. 12. (3) Rab and Levi both of whom confined the period of cleanness within the eleven days of *zibah*. (4) The forty or fifty days. (5) After the third day according to Levi, and after the first or second one according to Rab. (6) Lit., 'be in protracted labour', labour extending over a part of the period. (7) In succession. (8) Lit., 'and *zibah* does not rise among them'. (9) The last of the eleven days of the *zibah* period. (10) As *zibah* is not established unless a discharge appeared on three consecutive days in the *zibah* period, and as the third day was already one of the menstruation period, none of the days can be counted as one of a major *zibah*. (11) These two days which begin a new *zibah* period are not sufficient to establish a major *zibah* (cf. prev. n. *mut. mut*). (12) Of protracted labour on the part of an ailing woman (cf. *supra* 37*b ad fin*). (13) The child having been born on the day following the (2 + 7 + 2 + 50 =) 61st day. (14) During which there can be no *zibah*. (15) Following the (61 + 80 =) 141st day. (16) V. *supra* n. 11. (17) 2 + 7 + 141 (cf. prev. nn.) = 150. (18) That such a long period may pass without *zibah*. (19) The Rabbis who disagreed with him. (20) Owing to frequent abortions. (21) *Sc.* that childbirth at their termination renders them all clean. (22) Only a viable child confers the privilege.

Our Rabbis taught: A woman may sometimes[1] observe a discharge on a hundred days and yet no major *zibah* would result from it. How? The two days[2] prior to the time of menstruation,[3] the seven days of menstruation, two days after menstruation,[4] eighty days following the birth of a female child,[5] seven days of menstruation and the two days[4] after menstruation. What new law does this[6] teach us?—That the law differs[7] from him who ruled that it was impossible for the uterus to open without some bleeding, [since thereby][8] we were informed that it is possible for the uterus to open without previous bleeding.[9]

R. JUDAH RULED: . . . SUFFICES FOR HER etc. It was taught: R. Judah citing R. Tarfon ruled, Her [ninth] month suffices for her[10] and in this there is one aspect of a relaxation of the law[11] and one of restriction.[12] How? If she was in labour for two days at the end of the eighth month and for one day at the beginning of the ninth month, even though she gave birth to the child at the beginning of the ninth month, she is regarded as having born it in *zibah*;[13] but if she was in labour for one day at the end of the eighth month and for two days at the beginning of the ninth, even though she bore the child at the end of the ninth month,[14] she is not regarded as having given birth in *zibah*.[15] Said R. Adda b. Ahabah: From this[16] it may be inferred that R. Judah holds that

(1) In the absence of protracted labour. (2) The last of the eleven days. (3) V. p. 263, n. 10. (4) V. p. 263, n. 11. (5) During which there can be no *zibah*. (6) Which is self-evident. (7) Lit., 'to exclude'. (8) By implying that a birth on the day following the first two days of the *zibah* period on each of which a discharge was observed, does not cause *zibah*. (9) Had there been bleeding it would have been regarded, in the absence of the pains of labour, as a discharge on the third day (cf. prev. n.) which turns the woman into a confirmed or major *zabah*. (10) Cf. relevant n. on our Mishnah. (11) A month and one day being sometimes regarded as clean. (12) The cleanness sometimes does not extend even to one day. (13) Since the greater part of the duration of the labour (two days out of three) was in the eighth month when labour is no cause of cleanness. (14) During all of which, with the exception of the first two days, she had complete relief from pain. (15) Provided only that there was no bleeding during the time she was free from pain. The reason follows. (16) The ruling that two days of labour in the ninth month are a cause of uncleanness.

it is the *shofar*[1] that is the cause.[2] But could this[3] be right,[4] seeing that Samuel stated: A woman can conceive and bear only on the two hundred and seventy-first day[5] or on the two hundred and seventy-second day[6] or on the two hundred and seventy-third day?[6]—He[7] follows the view of the pious men of old; for it was taught: The pious men of old performed their marital duty on a Wednesday only, in order that their wives[8] should not be led to[9] [38*b*] a desecration of the Sabbath.[10] 'On a Wednesday', but not later?[11]—Read: From Wednesday onwards.[12] Mar Zuṭra stated: What was the reason of the pious men of old?—Because it is written, *And the Lord gave her conception* [herayon],[13] and the numerical value of *herayon*[14] is two hundred and seventy-one.[15]

Mar Zuṭra further stated: Even according to him who holds that a woman who bears at nine months does not give birth before the full number of months has been completed,[16] a woman who bears at seven months may give birth before the full number of months has been completed, for it is stated in Scripture, *And*

(1) The trumpet that announces the beginning of a new month. (2) Of the birth of the child; *sc.* as soon as the ninth month begins the process of bearing begins with it, irrespective of the moment when birth actually took place. Hence all the blood of labour in that month must be attributed to the child, however long the interval of relief may have lasted. (3) That birth should take place at the beginning of the ninth month. (4) Lit., 'I am not'. (5) Full nine months (of thirty days each) plus one day after intercourse. (6) Conception being sometimes delayed one or two days (cf. prev. n.). (7) Samuel, in differing from R. Judah. (8) By bearing on a weekday. 271, 272 and 273 days make up 38 weeks and 5, 6 and 7 days respectively, so that a conception on a Wednesday results in a birth on a Sunday, Monday or Tuesday. (9) Lit., 'come into the hand of', by bearing on the Saturday. (10) Childbirth would necessitate the performance of certain work (e.g., making a fire, boiling hot water) which is otherwise forbidden on the Sabbath. (11) But why not, seeing that conception on a Thursday, Friday or Saturday would equally result in a birth on a weekday? (12) But not on the nights preceding (and ritually belonging to) Sunday, Monday and Tuesday, since conception on any of these might result in a birth on a Sabbath which is the two hundred and seventy-third from a Sunday, the two hundred and seventy-second from a Monday and the two hundred and seventy-first from a Tuesday. (13) Ruth IV, 13. (14) הריון. (15) ה = 5, ר = 200, י = 10, ו = 6, ן = 50. (16) *Limeḳuta'in*, 'incompleted (number)'.

it came to pass, after the cycles of days[1] *that Hannah conceived, and bore a son;*[2] the minimum of *'cycles'*[3] is two,[4] and the minimum of *'days*[3] is two.[5]

R. JOSE AND R. SIMEON RULED: PROTRACTED LABOUR CANNOT CONTINUE FOR MORE THAN TWO WEEKS. Samuel stated: What is the reason of the Rabbis? Because it is written in Scripture, *Then she shall be unclean two weeks, as in her menstruation,*[6] which implies: Only *'as in her menstruation'* but not as in her *zibah;* from which it follows that her *zibah* is clean for[7] *'two weeks'*.

Our Rabbis taught: A woman may sometimes be in labour[8] for twenty-five days and no major *zibah* would intervene.[9] How? Two days preceding her menstruation period;[10] seven days of menstruation, two days following menstruation and the fourteen days which[11] the childbirth causes to be clean. It is impossible, however, for her to be in labour for twenty-six days, where there is no child,[12] without giving birth to it[12] in *zibah*.[13] But if there was no child would not[14] three days suffice?[15]—R. Shesheth replied, Read: Where there is a child. Said Raba to him: But was it not stated 'where there is no child'? Rather, said Raba, it is this that was meant: It is impossible for her to be in labour for twenty-six days, where there is a child, without giving birth to it in *zibah;* and where there is no child but an abortion she is a *zabah* even after three days. What is the reason?—The law of protracted labour[16] does not apply to abortions.

(1) E.V., *When the time was come about.* (2) I Sam. I, 20. (3) The plural number. (4) Each cycle (*tekufah*) consisting of three months (the year being divided into four cycles) and two cycles consisting, therefore, of six months. (5) As the text speaks of Hannah's conception and birth of Samuel it follows that a viable child may be born in the seventh month after the short pregnancy of six months and two days. (6) Lev. XII, 5, E.V., *impurity.* (7) Lit., 'and how much'. (8) Either with or without pains. (9) Prior to birth. (10) For notes v. *supra* 38*a*. (11) According to R. Jose and R. Simeon. (12) This is discussed presently. (13) Since a child causes the cleanness of fourteen days only (that immediately precede its birth), thus leaving twelve days at the beginning of the period of twenty-six days, there remain three days (between the first seven days of menstruation and the last fourteen) in the course of which she becomes a major *zabah.* (14) In the *zabah* period. (15) To render her a major *zabah.* (16) *Sc.* the law that a discharge in such circumstances is clean.

MISHNAH. IF A WOMAN WAS IN PROTRACTED LABOUR DURING THE EIGHTY DAYS[1] PRESCRIBED FOR THE BIRTH OF A FEMALE, ALL KINDS OF BLOOD THAT SHE MAY OBSERVE[2] ARE CLEAN,[3] UNTIL THE CHILD IS BORN, BUT R. ELIEZER HOLDS THEM TO BE UNCLEAN.[4] THEY SAID TO R. ELIEZER: IF IN A CASE WHERE THE LAW WAS RESTRICTED IN REGARD TO BLOOD DISCHARGED IN THE ABSENCE OF PAIN,[5] IT WAS NEVERTHELESS RELAXED.[6] IN REGARD TO BLOOD DISCHARGED DURING PROTRACTED LABOUR, IS THERE NOT EVEN MORE REASON TO RELAX THE LAW[7] IN REGARD TO THE BLOOD OF LABOUR IN A CASE WHERE[8] IT WAS RELAXED[9] EVEN IN REGARD TO A DISCHARGE IN THE ABSENCE OF PAIN?[3] HE REPLIED: IT IS ENOUGH THAT THE CASE INFERRED[10] SHALL BE TREATED IN THE SAME MANNER AS THE ONE[11] FROM WHICH IT IS INFERRED. FOR IN WHAT RESPECT WAS THE LAW RELAXED FOR A WOMAN IN THE LATTER CASE?[12] IN THAT OF THE UNCLEANNESS OF ZIBAH[13] ONLY, WHILE SHE IS STILL SUBJECT TO THE UNCLEANNESS OF THE MENSTRUANT.

GEMARA. Our Rabbis taught: *She shall continue [in the blood of her purification]*,[14] includes a woman who was in protracted labour during the eighty days[1] prescribed for the birth of a female, viz., that all kinds of blood that she may observe are clean, until the

(1) The fourteen unclean and sixty-six clean ones (cf. Lev. XII, 5). (2) During the sixty-six clean days. Within the fourteen days (cf. prev. n.) labour is, of course, impossible. (3) During the sixty-six days the blood is regarded (cf. Lev. XII, 5) as invariably clean. (4) If the birth took place during the period of menstruation. During the sixty-six days (cf. prev. n. but one) she is only free from the uncleanness of *zibah* but not from that of menstruation. (5) A woman who gave birth to a child after she had experienced a discharge without pain on three consecutive days is regarded as having given birth in *zibah*. (6) The woman being exempt from *zibah*. (7) To exempt the woman from all forms of uncleanness. (8) As in the case of a woman who gave birth during the sixty-six clean days (cf. *supra* n. 1). (9) To exempt the woman from all forms of uncleanness. (10) A discharge during labour in the sixty-six days. (11) Protracted labour at any other time. (12) Cf. prev. n. Lit., 'from what did he make it lighter for her'. (13) Cf. *supra* n. 8. (14) Lev. XII, 4.

embryo is born,[1] but R. Eliezer holds them to be unclean. They said to R. Eliezer: If in the case where the law was restricted in regard to blood discharged in the absence of pain before the child was born,[2] it was nevertheless relaxed in regard to blood discharged in the absence of pain after the child was born,[3] is there not even more reason to relax the law in regard to the blood of labour after the child was born[3] in a case where it was relaxed in regard to the blood of labour before the child was born? He replied: It is enough that the case inferred[4] shall be treated in the same manner as the one[5] from which it is inferred. For in what respect was the law relaxed for a woman in the latter case?[5] In that of the uncleanness of *zibah* only, while she is still subject to the uncleanness of the menstruant. They said to him, We would submit to you an objection in a different form: If in the case where the law was restricted in regard to blood discharged in the absence of pain before the child was born,[2] it was nevertheless relaxed in regard to blood discharged at such a time[6] in protracted labour, is there not even more reason that, where the law was relaxed in regard to blood discharged in the absence of pain after the child was born,[7] the law should be relaxed in regard to blood discharged at such a time[6] during protracted labour? He replied: Even if you were to offer objections all day long it must be enough that the case inferred[7] shall be treated in the same manner as the one[5] from which it is inferred. For in what respect was the law relaxed for a woman in the latter case?[5] In that of the uncleanness of *zibah* only, while she is still subject to the uncleanness of the menstruant. Raba observed, R. Eliezer could succesfully have offered the Rabbis the following reply: Did you not explain *Her blood*[8] thus: *'Her blood'* refers to blood that is normally discharged, but not to such as is due to childbirth?[9] Well, here also, it may be explained: *And she shall be cleansed from the fountain of her*

(1) When she becomes unclean by reason of the birth. (2) V. *supra* p. 267, n. 5. (3) During the sixty-six days. (4) Protracted labour after the birth of a previous child. (5) Protracted labour before a birth. (6) Lit., 'which is with it'. (7) A discharge during labour in the sixty-six days. (8) Lev. XV, 25. (9) *Supra* 36b, q.v. notes.

blood,[1] *'her blood'* refers to blood that is normally discharged but not to such as is due to childbirth.[2] But might it not be suggested[3] [that if a discharge occurred] during the days of menstruation she is a menstruant, [while if it occurred] during the days of *zibah* she is clean?—Scripture said, *She shall continue,*[4] which implies: One form of continuation throughout all these days.[5]

MISHNAH. THROUGHOUT ALL THE ELEVEN DAYS[6] A WOMAN IS IN A PRESUMPTIVE STATE OF CLEANNESS.[7] [39a] IF SHE NEGLECTED TO[8] EXAMINE HERSELF, IRRESPECTIVE OF WHETHER THE NEGLECT[9] WAS UNWITTING, UNDER CONSTRAINT OR WILFUL, SHE IS CLEAN. IF THE TIME OF HER REGULAR PERIOD HAS ARRIVED AND SHE FAILED TO EXAMINE HERSELF SHE IS DEFINITELY UNCLEAN.[10] R. MEIR RULED: IF A WOMAN WAS IN A HIDING-PLACE[11] WHEN THE TIME OF HER REGULAR PERIOD ARRIVED AND SHE FAILED TO EXAMINE HERSELF SHE IS DEFINITELY CLEAN, BECAUSE FEAR SUSPENDS THE FLOW OF BLOOD. BUT THE DAYS PRESCRIBED FOR A ZAB OR A ZABAH[12] OR FOR ONE WHO AWAITS DAY AGAINST DAY[13] ARE[14] PRESUMED TO BE UNCLEAN.[15]

GEMARA. In respect of what laws had this[16] to be stated?—Rab Judah replied: In order to lay down that no examination[17] is required.[18] But since it was stated in the final clause, IF SHE NEGLECT-

(1) Lev. XII, 7. (2) Only the former is clean, but not the latter. (3) According to R. Eliezer. (4) Lev. XII, 4. (5) They are either all clean or all unclean. No distinction can, therefore, be made between the periods of *zibah* and menstruation. (6) That follow the seven days' period of menstruation. (7) This is discussed in the Gemara *infra*. (8) Lit., 'she sat and did not'. (9) Lit., 'and she did not examine'. (10) It being presumed that the discharge had made its appearance at the regular time. (11) Taking refuge from raiders or brigands. (12) The seven clean days that must be counted after a confirmed *zibah* before cleanness is attained. (13) One clean day for one unclean one, where the discharge appeared on no more than two days. (14) Though within the ELEVEN DAYS. (15) Unless the contrary was proved by an examination. (16) The first clause of our Mishnah. (17) Morning and evening (cf. *supra* 11a). (18) After the eleven days such examination must be resumed.

ED TO EXAMINE HERSELF,[1] it follows, does it not, that at the outset an examination is required?—The final clause applies to the days of the menstruation period; and it is this that was meant: THROUGHOUT ALL THE ELEVEN DAYS A WOMAN IS IN A PRESUMPTIVE STATE OF CLEANNESS[2] and no examination is necessary, but during the days of her menstruation period[3] an examination[4] is required;[5] but IF SHE NEGLECTED TO EXAMINE HERSELF, IRRESPECTIVE OF WHETHER THE NEGLECT WAS UNWITTING, UNDER CONSTRAINT OR WILFUL, SHE IS CLEAN.[6]

R. Ḥisda replied: This[7] was only required to indicate that R. Meir's ruling that[8] a woman who has no regular period is forbidden marital intercourse,[9] applies only to the days of her menstruation period, but during the days of her *zibah* she enjoys[10] A PRESUMPTIVE STATE OF CLEANNESS. If so,[11] why did R. Meir rule: He must divorce her and never remarry her?[9]—Since it is possible to be tempted[12] to improper conduct during the days of the menstruation period. But since it was stated in the final clause, IF THE TIME OF HER REGULAR PERIOD HAS ARRIVED AND SHE FAILED TO EXAMINE HERSELF, may it not be concluded that we are here dealing with one who had a REGULAR PERIOD?—The Mishnah is defective and the proper reading is this: THROUGHOUT ALL THE ELEVEN DAYS A WOMAN IS IN A PRESUMPTIVE STATE OF CLEANNESS and is, therefore, permitted to her husband, but during the days of her menstruation period she is forbidden to him. This, however, applies only to a woman who has no regular period, but if she has a regular period she is permitted to him and only an examination is necessary. IF SHE NEGLECTED TO EXAMINE HERSELF, IRRESPECTIVE OF WHETHER THE NEGLECT WAS

(1) This presumably referring to the eleven days of the *zibah* period. (2) Since her flow of blood had come to an end during menstruation. (3) Following the conclusion of the eleven days of *zibah*. (4) Morning and evening (cf. *supra* 11*a*). (5) *Ab initio*. (6) Only when THE TIME OF HER REGULAR PERIOD HAS ARRIVED AND SHE FAILED TO EXAMINE HERSELF IS SHE UNCLEAN. (7) The first clause of our Mishnah. (8) Lit., 'but according to R. Meir who said'. (9) *Supra* 12*b*. (10) Lit., 'stands'. (11) That during the eleven days of *zibah* intercourse is permitted. (12) Lit., 'come'.

UNWITTING, UNDER CONSTRAINT OR WILFUL, SHE IS CLEAN. IF THE TIME OF HER REGULAR PERIOD HAS ARRIVED AND SHE FAILED TO EXAMINE HERSELF SHE IS DEFINITELY UNCLEAN. But, since the final clause is the view of R. Meir,[1] the first one is not that of R. Meir, is it?—All the Mishnah represents the view of R. Meir and this is the proper reading: If she was not in a hiding place and the time of her regular period has arrived and she did not examine herself she is unclean, for R. MEIR RULED: IF A WOMAN WAS IN A HIDING PLACE WHEN THE TIME OF HER REGULAR PERIOD ARRIVED AND SHE FAILED TO EXAMINE HERSELF SHE IS CLEAN, BECAUSE FEAR SUSPENDS THE FLOW OF THE BLOOD.

Raba replied: This[2] is to tell that she[3] does not[4] cause twenty-four hours retrospective uncleanness. An objection was raised: A menstruant,[5] a *zabah*,[5] and a woman who awaits day against day[6] or who is in childbirth[7] cause twenty-four hours retrospective uncleanness!—This is indeed a refutation.

R. Huna b. Ḥiyya[8] citing Samuel replied: This[2] is to tell that she cannot establish for herself a regular period during the days of her *zibah*.[9]

R. Joseph[10] remarked: I have not heard this traditional explanation.[11] Said Abaye[12] to him, You yourself have told it to us,[13] and it was in connection with the following that you told it to us: If she was accustomed to observe a flow of menstrual blood on the fifteenth day,[14] and this was changed[15] to the twentieth day,[14]

(1) His name having been given explicitly. (2) The first clause of our Mishnah. (3) As the flow of her blood is suspended. (4) After the first discharge during these days. (5) On the first day of her observing a discharge. (6) Cf. prev. n. After three observations she also would, of course, become a *zabah*. (7) As soon as the uterus opened. (8) Var. lec. Ḥiyyah b. R. Huna (Bomb. ed. and Rashi). (9) Though menstruation began on the same day in three successive months. (10) A disciple of Rab Judah who was the disciple of both Rab and Samuel. (11) Attributed to Samuel. (12) A disciple of R. Joseph who was often reminding his Master of traditions he had forgotten owing to a serious illness (cf. Ned. 41*a*). (13) 'Before your illness'. (14) After undergoing ritual immersion, as will be explained *infra*. (15) Once.

marital intercourse is forbidden[1] on both dates.[2] If this was changed twice to the twentieth day,[3] marital intercourse is again forbidden on both dates. And in connection with this you have told us: Rab Judah citing Samuel explained, This[4] was learnt only [when she was accustomed to observe a flow] on the fifteenth day after her ritual immersion[5] which is the twenty-second day[6] after her observation of her discharge, since on such a day[7] she is already within the days of her menstruation period,[8] but the fifteenth day after her observation, on which she is still within the days of her *zibah* period,[9] cannot be established as a regular period.

R. Papa stated: I recited this tradition before R. Judah of Diskarta [and asked:] Granted that she cannot establish thereby[10] a regular period,[11] must we take into consideration the possibility of such a regular period?[12] The latter remained silent and said nothing at all. Said R. Papa: Let us look into the matter ourselves. [It has been laid down that] if she was accustomed to observe a flow of menstrual blood on the fifteenth day and this was changed to the twentieth day, marital intercourse is forbidden on both

(1) In the next two months. (2) It is forbidden on the fifteenth which is the date of her regular period, and it is also forbidden on the twentieth since it is possible that henceforth that day would become her regular period. If in the third month also she experiences the discharge on the twentieth, she establishes thereby a new regular period and henceforth only the twentieth is forbidden while the fifteenth becomes permitted. (3) V. p. 271, n. 14. (4) That the fifteenth day is regarded as a regular period that cannot be altered unless the discharge appeared three times in three consecutive months respectively on a different date. (5) Which is performed at the conclusion of the seven days' period of menstruation. (6) The seven days of menstruation (cf. prev. n.) plus the fifteen days. (7) Lit., 'for there'. (8) Which begins after eighteen days (i.e., the seven days of menstruation plus the eleven, the days of the *zibah* period) have passed since the first day of the discharge, and continues for seven days. (9) Cf. prev. n. (10) By observing a discharge for three months on the same date during *zibah*. (11) That could not be abolished by less than three observations on a different date in three consecutive months respectively. (12) So that where a woman observed a discharge on the fifteenth day in each of three consecutive months intercourse on that day should be forbidden in the fourth months on the ground that, despite the *zibah* period in which the fifteenth day occurs, a regular period may have been established and the discharge would again appear on that date.

days.[1] [39b] And in connection with this Rab Judah citing Samuel stated: This[2] was learnt only [when she was accustomed to observe a flow] on the fifteenth day after her ritual immersion,[3] which is the twenty-second day[4] after her observation of her discharge, and it was changed to the twenty-seventh day[5] so that when the twenty-second day[6] comes round again she is well within the days of her *zibah* period,[7] and yet it was stated that intercourse was forbidden on both days. It is thus clear that the possibility of a regular period[8] must be taken into consideration.[9] R. Papa is thus[10] of the opinion that the twenty-two days[11] are reckoned from the twenty-second day[12] while the beginning of the menstruation and *zibah* period[13] is reckoned from the twenty-seventh day.[14] Said R. Huna son of R. Joshua to R. Papa: Whence do you draw your ruling? Is it not possible that the twenty-second day also is reckoned from the twenty-seventh day,[15] so that when the twenty-second day comes round again the woman is within the days of her menstruation period?[16] And this[17] is also logical. For if you do not admit this,[17] consider the case of a[18] hen that laid eggs on alternate days[19] and once ceased laying for two days and again laid

(1) *Supra* q.v. notes. (2) V. *supra* p. 272, n. 4. (3) Which is performed at the conclusion of the seven days' period of menstruation. (4) The seven days of menstruation (cf. prev. n.) plus the fifteen days. (5) After her discharge. (6) Since the day on which the discharge should have appeared. (7) There being only (22 − 5 =) 17 days since her last discharge on the twenty-seventh. The seventeenth day, (the last of the seven days of menstruation and the ten of the eleven days of *zibah*) is obviously within the *zibah* period. (8) Even on a day in the *zibah* period. (9) V. *supra* p. 272, n. 12. (10) Since he regards the twenty-second day as one of the days of the *zibah* period. (11) On which intercourse was forbidden. (12) *Sc.* the days on which formerly the discharge usually made its appearance and not from the twenty-seventh day. (13) At the conclusion of the menstruation period, seven days later. (14) The day on which the discharge last appeared. The twenty-second day after the twenty-second is only the seventeenth day after the twenty-seventh (cf. prev. n: but five). (15) On which the discharge last appeared. (16) The twenty-two days consisting of 7 (menstruation) + 11 (*zibah*) + 4 (of the seven of the present menstruation period) days. (17) That the reckoning should begin from the day of the last discharge rather than from the day on which the discharge should have appeared. (18) Lit., '(what about) that'. (19) Lit., 'that lays on a day and holds back on (the next) day' (*bis*).

on the following day. When it reverts to its former habit,[1] does it do so in accordance with the present[2] or in accordance with the past?[3] You have no alternative but to admit that it would do it in accordance with the present.[4] Said R. Papa to him: With reference, however, to what Resh Laḳish ruled, 'A woman may establish for herself a settled period during the days of her *zibah* but not during the days of her menstruation' and to what R. Joḥanan ruled, 'A woman may establish for herself a settled period during the days of her menstruation', is not one to understand this as being a case,[5] for instance, where she observed a discharge on the first day of the month, on the fifth of the month and again on the first of the second month and on the fifth of that month, and finally[6] she observed a discharge on the fifth of the month while on the first of that month she observed none? And yet it was stated that 'a woman may establish for herself a settled period during the days of her menstruation'. It thus clearly follows[7] that we reckon the days from the first day of the month?[8]—No, the other replied, it is this that R. Joḥanan meant: A woman, for instance, who observed a discharge on the first day of the month, on the first day of the next month and on the twenty-fifth of that month, and on the first day of the following month, in which case we presume that[9] she experienced an influx of additional blood.[10]

(1) Laying on alternate days. (2) Lit., 'as before it', i.e., laying on alternate days beginning with the last day (the sixth in the case submitted) refraining on the seventh and laying again on the eighth, and so on. (3) Lit., 'as originally', i.e., alternating with the day on which laying should have taken place (the fifth in the case submitted), thus laying on both the seventh as well as the sixth. (4) Since alternation with the day on which laying should have taken place would only result (cf. prev. n.) in a new disturbance of the regularity (laying on two consecutive days). Similarly, in the case of the woman, a reversion to her regular periods can only be effected by counting the days from the one on which her discharge last appeared, viz., from the twenty-seventh day. (5) Lit., 'how is one to imagine, not?' (6) Lit., 'and now'. (7) Since the fifth day of the month is regarded as of the 'days of her menstruation'. (8) Though on that day no discharge had appeared. From which it follows that the counting of the days begins from the day on which the discharge should have appeared and not from that on which it appeared the last time. (9) The reason why the discharge made its appearance

So also Rabin and all seafarers, when they came,[1] reported the tradition[2] in agreement with the explanation of R. Huna son of R. Joshua.

on the twenty-fifth day of the second month and not on the first day of the following month. (10) And, as a result, the discharge whose regular time of appearance was still the first of the month made its appearance a little earlier. The first day of the month being within seven days from the twenty-fifth of the previous month (on which the discharge appeared) may well be described as within the days of menstruation.

(1) From Palestine to Babylon. (2) Of R. Joḥanan.

NIDDAH

CHAPTER V

MISHNAH. [40*a*] FOR A FOETUS BORN FROM ITS MOTHER'S SIDE[1] THERE IS NO NEED[2] TO SPEND[3] THE PRESCRIBED DAYS OF UNCLEANNESS[4] OR THE DAYS OF CLEANNESS;[5] NOR DOES ONE INCUR ON ITS ACCOUNT THE OBLIGATION TO BRING A SACRIFICE.[6] R. SIMEON RULED: IT IS REGARDED AS A VALID BIRTH. ALL WOMEN ARE SUBJECT TO UNCLEANNESS[7] [IF BLOOD APPEARED] IN THE OUTER CHAMBER,[8] FOR IT IS SAID IN SCRIPTURE, HER ISSUE IN HER FLESH BE BLOOD;[9] BUT A ZAB AND ONE WHO EMITTED SEMEN CONVEY NO UNCLEANNESS UNLESS THE DISCHARGE[10] CAME OUT OF THE BODY. IF A MAN WAS EATING TERUMAH WHEN HE FELT THAT HIS LIMBS SHIVERED,[11] HE TAKES HOLD OF HIS MEMBRUM[12] AND SWALLOWS THE TERUMAH. AND THE DISCHARGES CONVEY UNCLEANNESS, HOWEVER SMALL THE QUANTITY, EVEN IF IT IS ONLY OF THE SIZE OF A MUSTARD SEED OR LESS.

GEMARA. R. Mani b. Paṭṭish stated: What is the Rabbis' reason?[13] Scripture said, *If a woman have conceived seed and born*[14] *a man child,*[15] implying:[16] Only if she bears where she conceives.[17]

(1) By means of the caesarean operation. Lit., 'goes out of a wall'. (2) For its mother. (3) Lit., '(women) do not sit for it'. (4) Seven for a male and fourteen for a female (v. Lev. XII, 2, 5). (5) Thirty-three days after the seven (cf. prev. n.) for a male and sixty-six days after the fourteen for a female (v. Lev. XII, 4f). (6) Prescribed for a woman after childbirth (v. Lev. XII, 6ff). (7) Of menstruation. (8) The vagina; though it did not flow out beyond it. (9) Lev. XV, 19; emphasis on '*in her flesh*' implying: Even if the discharge did not flow out of her body. (10) Lit., 'uncleanness'. (11) A symptom of the imminent discharge of semen. (12) To prevent outflow. (13) For their ruling in the first clause of our Mishnah. (14) So A.V. The A.J.V. reads, '*be delivered and bear*'. (15) Lev. XII, 2, dealing with the laws of cleanness and uncleanness and

And R. Simeon?[1]—That text[2] implies that even if she bore in the same manner only as she conceived[3] she[4] is unclean by reason of childbirth.[5] What, however, is R. Simeon's reason?[6]—Resh Lakish replied: Scripture said, *She bear,*[7] to include[8] A FOETUS BORN FROM ITS MOTHER'S SIDE. And the Rabbis?[9]—That text[7] is required to include[10] a *tumtum*[11] and an hermaphrodite. Since it might have been presumed that as it is written *man child*[12] and *maid child*[13] [the laws in the context apply only to] one who is undoubtedly male or undoubtedly female but not to a *tumtum* or an hermaphrodite, hence we were informed that the law applies to the latter also. And R. Simeon?[14]—He deduces it[15] from a teaching of Bar Liwai; for Bar Liwai taught, *For a son,*[16] implies: For any son, whatsoever his nature; *For a daughter,*[16] for any daughter, whatsoever her nature. And the Rabbis?[17]—They require this text for the deduction that a separate sacrifice is due for each son and for each daughter.[18] And R. Simeon?[14]—He deduced it[15] from the following which a Tanna recited before R. Shesheth: *This is the law for her that beareth*[19] teaches[20] that a woman brings one sacrifice for many children. It might be presumed that she brings only one sacrifice for a birth and for a *zibah* ... But would then one sacrifice suffice for a woman after childbirth who ate blood or for one after

the prescribed sacrifice after childbirth. (16) By the juxtaposition of '*conceived*' and '*born*'. (17) Only then do the laws (cf. prev. n.) apply, but not where a caesarean operation had to be performed.

(1) How in view of this exposition can he differ from the Rabbis? (2) V. p. 276, n. 15. (3) A mashed foetus (cf. *supra* 26a, 27b). (4) Lit., 'his mother'. (5) The Rabbis, however, require no text for this ruling since in their opinion (cf. *supra* 26a) the presence of the placenta alone is a sufficient cause of uncleanness. (6) For his ruling in our Mishnah. (7) *But if she bear a maid-child,* Lev. XII, 5. (8) By the superfluity of the expression, since it would have sufficed to state 'but if a maid-child'. (9) How can they maintain their ruling in view of this exposition? (10) Among those who subject their mothers to the laws prescribed in the context. (11) V. Glos. (12) Lev. XII, 2. (13) Lev. XII, 5. (14) Whence does he deduce the last mentioned law? (15) Cf. prev. n. (16) Lev. XII, 6. (17) What deduction do they make from this text? (18) Though conception of the latter took place before the completion of the clean days of the former. (19) Lev. XII, 7. (20) Since '*beareth*' is not restricted to one child only.

childbirth who ate forbidden fat?—Rather say: It might be presumed that a woman brings only one sacrifice for a birth that took place before the completion of her clean days and for one that took place after their completion.[1] Therefore it was expressly written, '*This*'.[2] And the Rabbis?[3]—Although '*this*'[4] was written it was also necessary to have the text, '*For a son or for a daughter*'.[5] For it might have been presumed that this law[6] applies only to two distinct conceptions[7] but[8] that in the case of a simultaneous conception as, for instance, that of Judah and Hezekiah the sons of R. Ḥiyya,[9] one sacrifice suffices,[10] hence we were informed [that even in such a case separate sacrifices are required for each birth].

R. Joḥanan stated: R. Simeon, however, agrees that in the case of consecrated beasts [the body of the young extracted by means of a caesarean cut] is not sacred.[11] What is the reason? He deduces the expression of 'birth' here[12] from that of 'birth' in the case of the firstling:[13] As in the latter case[14] the reference is to one that *openeth the womb*[15] so here also it is only to one that 'openeth the womb'. But why should not the expression of 'birth' here[12] be deduced from that of 'birth' in the case of a human being:[16] As in

(1) If a child is born after the completion of the eighty days (fourteen unclean and sixty-six clean ones) prescribed for the birth of a female child, the former was obviously born 'before their completion'. (2) Lev. XII, 7, implying, *This* birth alone requires a sacrifice, but an additional birth requires an additional sacrifice. (3) In view of this text what need was there for that of Lev. XII, 6? (4) V. *supra* note 2. (5) Lev. XII, 6. (6) That one birth 'before the completion' of the eighty days and one 'after their completion' require two separate sacrifices. (7) The second one having begun during the eighty days that followed the first, and its birth having occurred after the completion of these days. (8) Cf. Rashal. Cur. edd. in parenthesis insert: 'One of which was an abortion'. (9) The second of whom was born three months after the former (*supra* 27*a*). (10) Lit., 'with one sacrifice it is sufficient for her'. (11) Like other beasts whose blemish preceded their consecration, its value only is consecrated. It may, therefore, be sold, when it loses its sanctity and may be used for shearing or work, while its price is used for the purchase of valid sacrifices. (12) *When a bullock, or a sheep, or a goat, is born* (E.V. *brought forth*) in the context dealing with consecrated beasts (Lev. XXII, 27). (13) *All the firstling males that are born* (Deut. XV, 19). (14) Lit., 'there'. (15) Ex. XXXIV, 19. (16) *If a woman be delivered. and bear a man-child* (Lev. XII, 2).

the latter case[1] a foetus extracted from its mother's side is included[2] so here also the young extracted from its mother's side should be included?—It stands to reason that the deduction should be made from the firstling, since *'the dam'*[3] might also be deduced from *'the dam'*.[4] On the contrary! Should not the deduction be made from the expression used of the human being, since thereby an ordinary birth[5] would be deduced from an ordinary birth?[6]—But the fact is that the deduction was properly to be made from the firstling since in both cases[7] the expression *'dam'*[8] is used, both are sacred beasts and both are subject to the laws of *piggul, nothar*[9] and uncleanness.[10] On the contrary! Should not the deduction be made from the expression used of the human being since both cases[11] are those of ordinary birth,[12] neither is restricted to the male sex,[13] neither[14] is naturally sacred,[15] and neither[16] is a priestly gift?[17]—The former[18] are more in number.[19]

R. Ḥiyya son of R. Huna citing Raba observed, A Baraitha was taught which provides support for the statement of R. Joḥanan:[20] R. Judah stated, *This is the law of the burnt-offering, it is that which goeth up,*[21] behold these[22] are three limitations [40*b*] excluding[23]

(1) Lit., 'there'. (2) As R. Simeon laid down in our Mishnah. (3) *It shall be seven days under the dam* (Lev. XXII, 27) about consecrated beasts. (4) *It shall be with its dam* (Ex. XXII, 29) about the firstling. (5) I.e., a beast that is not a firstling. (6) I.e., a child that is not a firstborn son, the text (Lev. XII, 2) speaking of any child whether a firstborn or not. (7) The consecrated beast and the firstling. (8) Cf. *supra* nn. 3 and 4. (9) On these terms v. Glos. (10) To a human being none of these applies. (11) Those of the child and the consecrated beast. (12) Cf. *supra* nn. 5 and 6. (13) While only a male is subject to the law of a firstling. (14) Unlike the firstling that is sacred from birth. (15) The consecration of the beast is entirely due to a human act. (16) Unlike the firstling which is the priest's due. (17) A peace-offering, for instance, remains the property of its owner. A burnt-offering is completely burnt on the altar. (18) The five points of likeness between the consecrated beast and the firstling. (19) Than the four points of likeness between the beast and a human being. (20) *Supra*, that R. Simeon agrees in the case of consecrated beasts that the body of the young extracted from one by means of a caesarean cut is not sacred. (21) Lev. VI, 2. (22) The expressions, *'this'*, *'it'*, *'which goes up'*. (23) From the scope of the law in the context that once a sacrifice had been placed upon the altar it must never be removed from it.

a sacrifice that was slain in the night, whose blood was poured out,[1] or whose blood was taken outside the hangings,[2] which, even though it was placed upon the altar, must be taken down.[3] R. Simeon stated: From the term *'burnt-offering'*[4] I would only know that the law applied to[5] a valid burnt-offering; whence, however, the inference for including[6] one that was slain in the night, whose blood was poured out,[7] whose blood was taken outside the hangings[2] or was kept overnight, that was taken out,[8] that was unclean, *nothar*,[9] one slain with the intention of eating it later than its permitted time limit or beyond its permitted place limits, whose blood was received or sprinkled by disqualified men,[10] those sacrifices whose blood is to be sprinkled above[11] and was sprinkled below,[11] those whose blood is to be sprinkled below[11] and was sprinkled above,[11] those whose blood is to be applied within[12] and was applied without,[13] and a paschal lamb and a sin-offering that had not been slain as such?[14] Whence, I ask, is the inference? Since it was explicitly said in Scripture, *This is the law of the burnt-offering*,[15] the scope of the law is widened: One law for all that are placed upon the altar, so that once they have been put up they must not be taken down. As one might presume that I also include[6] a beast that covered[16] or was covered,[17] that was set aside[18] for an idolatrous purpose, that was worshipped, the hire of a harlot,

(1) So that the essential service of sprinkling upon the altar could not be performed with it. (2) *Sc.* the enclosure around the Temple that corresponded to the hangings of the court of the Tabernacle of Moses in the wilderness. (3) Only the other disqualified sacrifices, enumerated *infra* in R. Simeon's ruling, must not, according to R. Judah also, be taken down from the altar once they have been put upon it (cf. Zeb. 84*b*). (4) Lev. VI, 2. (5) Lit., 'I have not but'. (6) In the scope of the law. (7) So that the essential service of sprinkling upon the altar could not be performed with it. (8) *Sc.* the flesh of a burnt-offering that was taken out and then brought back and placed upon the altar. (9) Sacrificial meat that was kept beyond the time allowed for its consumption. (10) Priests who had a blemish, for instance. (11) The red line around the altar's sides. (12) *Sc.* the inner altar that was placed within the *Hekal*. (13) On the altar in the Temple court. (14) Lit., 'not for their name', the man intending them at the time to serve respectively as different kinds of sacrifices. (15) Lev. VI, 2, emphasis on '*law*'. (16) A woman. (17) By a man. (18) In a special place.

the price of a dog, *kil'ayim, ṭrefah*[1] and one that had been extracted by means of a caesarean operation, it was explicitly stated, *'This'*.[2] But what reason do you see for including[3] the former and for excluding the latter? [41a] Since Scripture both widened and limited the scope of the law, you might rightly say:[4] I include[3] the former whose disqualification arose within the Sanctuary and exclude the latter whose disqualification did not arise within the Sanctuary.[5] At all events, it was here taught that the young extracted by means of a caesarean operation is not included in the scope of the law;[6] and this refers, does it not, to the young that were so extracted in the case of a consecrated beast?[7]—R. Huna son of R. Nathan replied: No, the reference is to one so extracted in the case of a firstling. But is not the law of the firstling[8] deduced from the expression of *openeth the womb*.[9] What then do you suggest? That the reference is to one of the consecrated beasts? Is not[10] this [it could be retorted] inferred from a deduction of *'the dam'* from *'the dam'*?[11]—What a comparison![12] If you grant that the reference is to a consecrated beast one can well understand the necessity for two Scriptural texts:[13] One[14] to exclude[15] the young of an unconsecrated beast born by way of a caesarean cut and then consecrated, and the other,[16] to exclude[17] the young of a consecrated beast[18] born by way of the caesarean cut,[19] he being of the opinion that the young of consecrated beasts become sacred

(1) On these terms v. Glos. (2) Which implies a limitation. (3) In the scope of the law. (4) By recourse to a process of reasoning. (5) V. Zeb. 27*b*. (6) So that it is obviously not regarded as sacred. (7) In agreement with R. Joḥanan's interpretation of R. Simeon's view. (8) Viz., that a firstling extracted by means of a caesarean cut is not subject to the restrictions and sanctity of a firstling. (9) Ex. XXXIV, 19; emphasis on the last word. Now since it is not sacred it is obviously to be treated like an ordinary beast and must be removed from the altar even after it had been placed upon it; what need then was there to exclude it by the text of Lev. VI, 2. (10) That the one so extracted is not sacred. (11) *Supra* 40*a ad fin*. (12) Lit., 'that, what'. (13) *'This'* and *'the dam'*. (14) *'The dam'*. (15) From sanctity, in consequence of which it must be removed from the altar even after it had been placed on it. (16) *'This'*. (17) From the law that requires a sacrifice that was once upon the altar never to be taken down. (18) Though the dam is sacred. (19) Since the disqualification arose without the Sanctuary.

only after they come into a visible existence,[1] but if you maintain that the reference is to a firstling [the objection would arise:] Is not this[2] deduced from the expression *openeth the womb?*[3] This[4] may also be supported by reason. For 'a beast that covered or was covered, that was set aside for an idolatrous purpose, that was worshipped and *kil'ayim*' were mentioned.[5] Now is the law concerning these deduced from this text?[5] Is it not in fact deduced from a different text:[6] *Of the cattle*[7] excludes[8] a beast that covered or was covered, *Of the herd*[7] excludes[8] a beast that was worshipped, *Of the flock*[7] excludes[8] one that was set aside for an idolatrous purpose, *Or of the flock*[7] excludes[9] one that gores?[10] And, furthermore, is the law concerning *kil'ayim*[11] deduced from here? Is it not in fact deduced from a different text: *When a bullock, or a sheep, or a goat, is brought forth;*[12] '*a bullock*' excludes *kil'ayim*, '*or a goat*' excludes one that[13] only resembles it?[14] But the fact is that two series of texts were required there: One in connection with an unconsecrated beast[15] and the other in connection with a consecrated beast; well then, in this case also two texts were similarly required.

Our Rabbis taught: If a woman was in protracted labour[16] for

(1) *Sc.* on being born, but no earlier; and when the young was born it was already disqualified. Rashi deletes 'he being . . . existence'. (2) V. *supra* p. 281, n. 8. (3) Of course it is. Hence the conclusion that the reference must be to a consecrated beast. (4) That all the disqualifications enumerated *supra*, including the young born by way of the caesarean cut, apply only to consecrated beasts and to their young. (5) *Supra* 40*b*. (6) Lit., 'from there'. (7) Lev. I, 2. (8) '*Of*' implying a limitation. (9) By the use of the redundant '*or*'. (10) And killed a human being. The last three classes (covered, was covered and gores) are such whose status was determined on the evidence of only one witness or their owner. Hence they are only forbidden as sacrifices but permitted for ordinary use; but if their status is determined on the evidence of two witnesses they are forbidden for ordinary use also. (11) In beasts; a cross-breed between a goat and a sheep. (12) Lev. XXII, 27. (13) Being born from a goat and having the appearance of a lamb. (14) The goat. Now, since it follows from these texts that the beasts are not sacred, what need was there for an additional text from which to deduce that even though they have already been put upon the altar they must be taken down from it? (15) Which a man consecrated. (16) Accompanied by bleeding.

three days,[1] but the embryo was born by way of a caesarean cut, she is to be regarded as having given birth in *zibah*.[2] R. Simeon, however,[3] ruled: A woman in such circumstances is not regarded as[4] having given birth in *zibah*. The blood, furthermore, that issues from that place[5] is unclean, but R. Simeon declared it clean. The first clause may be well understood, since R. Simeon follows his known view[6] and the Rabbis follow theirs; on what principle, however, do they differ in the final clause?[7]—Rabina replied: This is a case where, for instance, the embryo was born through the side [41*b*] while the blood issued[8] through the womb; and R. Simeon follows his view[6] while the Rabbis follow theirs.[9] R. Joseph demurred: Firstly, is not then the final clause identical with the first?[10] And, furthermore, 'from that place' means, does it not, the place of birth?[11] Rather, said R. Joseph, this is a case, where, for instance, both the embryo and the blood issued through the side,[12] and the point at issue between them[13] is whether the interior of the uterus is unclean. The Masters hold that the interior of the uterus is unclean,[14] while the Master holds that the interior of the uterus is clean.[15]

(1) During her *zibah* period; the discharge having made its appearance on each of the three days. (2) *Sc.* she is subject to the restrictions of a confirmed or major *zabah*. Only in the case of normal birth is the blood during the labour preceding it exempt from the uncleanness of *zibah*. (3) Being of the opinion (v. our Mishnah) that such a birth is valid. (4) Lit., 'this is not'. (5) This is explained *infra*. (6) Expressed in our Mishnah (cf. prev. n. but two). (7) If the blood issued through the caesarean cut the opinions should have been reversed: According to R. Simeon, who regards the birth as valid, the blood should be unclean while according to the Rabbis it should be clean. (8) During the three days of labour, that preceded the birth. (9) Cf. *supra* no. 2. (10) It is; why then the needless repetition? (11) How then could Rabina explain this as 'the womb'? (12) The clause thus differing from the first one which deals with an issue of blood from the normal place during labour. (13) R. Simeon and the Rabbis. (14) The blood that comes in contact with the uterus causes, therefore, uncleanness for a day until the evening, though, having finally issued through the caesarean cut, it cannot be regarded as a menstrual discharge to subject the woman to an uncleanness of seven days. (15) The blood that issued through the caesarean cut, though it passed through the uterus, is, therefore, regarded as the blood of a mere wound which conveys no un-

Resh Laḳish stated: According to him who holds the blood to be unclean the woman also[1] is unclean[2] and according to him who holds the blood to be clean the woman also is clean. R. Joḥanan, however, stated: Even according to him who holds the blood to be unclean the woman is clean. In this R. Joḥanan follows a view he previously expressed. For R. Joḥanan citing R. Simeon b. Yoḥai stated: Whence is it deduced that a woman is not unclean[3] unless the discharge issues through its normal channel? From Scripture which says, *And if a man shall lie with a woman having her sickness,*[4] *and shall uncover her nakedness—he hath made naked her fountain,*[5] which teaches that a woman is not unclean[3] unless the discharge of her sickness issues through its normal channel.

Resh Laḳish citing R. Judah Nesi'ah[6] ruled: If the uterus[7] became detached and dropped upon the ground the woman is unclean, for it is said, *Because thy filthiness*[8] *was poured out,*[9] *and thy nakedness*[10] *uncovered.*[11] In what respect?[12] If it be suggested: In that of an uncleanness for seven days[3] [the objection would arise:] Did not the All Merciful speak of blood and not of a solid piece? —As a matter of fact the reference is to the uncleanness until evening.[13]

R. Joḥanan ruled: If the uterus produced a discharge that was[14] like two pearl drops[15] the woman is unclean. In what respect? Should it be suggested: In respect of an uncleanness for seven days[3] [it might be objected:] Are there not just five unclean kinds

cleanness. Should the blood issue through the womb, provided there was no relief from pain prior to the birth, the blood, as that of labour, would also, during the *zibah* period, be clean on account of the birth of the child despite its emergence by way of a caesarean cut.

(1) Though the birth was from her side. (2) Seven days, as a menstruant. (3) As a menstruant. (4) *Dawah*, applied to the menstrual discharge. (5) Lev. XX, 18. (6) The Prince, Judah II. (7) Or a part of it. Lit., 'source'. (8) *Neḥushtek*, applied to the uterus. (9) *Sc.* 'dropped upon the ground'. (10) *Erwatek*, synonymous with uncleanness. (11) Ezek. XVI, 36; which shows that a uterus dropped out is as unclean as when it is in its place; hence the uncleanness. (12) Is the uncleanness caused. (13) On account of the woman's external contact with the unclean uterus. (14) Lit., perspired'. (15) White and clear.

of the blood for a woman, and no more?—The fact is that the reference is to the uncleanness until evening.[1] This, however, applies only to two drops but if there was only one drop it may be assumed that it originated elsewhere.[2]

ALL WOMEN ARE SUBJECT TO UNCLEANNESS [IF BLOOD APPEARED] IN THE OUTER CHAMBER. Which is the OUTER CHAMBER?—Resh Lakish replied: All that part which, when a child sits, is exposed. Said R. Johanan to him: Is not that place deemed exposed as regards contact with a dead creeping thing?[3] Rather, said R. Johanan, as far as the glands.[4] The question was raised: Is the region between the glands regarded as internal or as external?—Come and hear what R. Zakkai taught: The region up to the glands and that between the glands is regarded as internal. In a Baraitha it was taught: As far as the threshing-place. What is meant by threshing-place?—Rab Judah replied: The place where the attendant threshes.[5]

Our Rabbis taught: *In her flesh*[6] teaches that she[7] contracts uncleanness internally as externally. But from this text I would only know of the menstruant, whence the deduction that the same law applies to a *zabah?* It was explicitly stated, *Her issue*[8] *in her flesh.*[6] Whence the proof that the same law applies also to one who emitted semen? It was explicitly stated, *Be.*[9] R. Simeon, however, ruled: It is enough that she be subject to the same stringency of uncleanness as the man who had intercourse with her. As he is not subject to uncleanness unless the unclean discharge issued forth, so is she not subject to uncleanness unless her unclean discharge issued forth. But could R. Simeon maintain that 'it is enough that she be subject to the same stringency of uncleanness

(1) The discharge having been in contact with the uterus which is in contact with the woman. (2) Lit., 'came from the world', not from the uterus, and is consequently clean. (3) *Sc.* if the latter came in contact with that place uncleanness is conveyed to the woman though contact with an internal organ conveys no uncleanness. Now since the place is deemed to be exposed, how can Resh Lakish apply to it the expression 'in her flesh' (cf. *infra*) and regard it as internal? (4) Of the vagina. (5) Euphemism. (6) Lev. XV, 19. (7) A menstruant of whom the text speaks. (8) A Heb. word of the same root as *zabah*. (9) *Her issue in her flesh be* etc. (Lev. XV, 19).

as the man who had intercourse with her'? Was it not in fact taught: '*They shall both bathe themselves in water, and be unclean until the even.*[1] What, said R. Simeon, does this[2] come to teach us? If that it applies also to one who came in contact with semen[3] [it could be retorted:] Was it not in fact[4] stated below, *Or from whomsoever [the flow of seed goeth out]*?[5] But [this is the purpose of the text:] Since the uncleanness arises in a concealed region[6] and since an uncleanness in a concealed region is elsewhere ineffective, a special Scriptural ordinance was required[7] [to give it effect in this particular case]'[8]—This is no difficulty: The latter deals with one who received the semen at intercourse,[9] while the former refers to one who ejected it subsequently.[10] 'Ejected'! Should not her uncleanness be due[11] to her preceding intercourse?[12]—This is a case where she had undergone ritual immersion in respect of her intercourse.[13] This then[14] says that for one who had intercourse it suffices to be unclean only until the evening. But did not Raba rule: A woman who had intercourse is forbidden to eat *terumah* for three days since it is impossible that she should not eject some semen during that time?[15]—Here[16] we are dealing with one who

(1) Lev. XV, 18. (2) The repetition of the law of bathing which, as far as the man is concerned, was already stated earlier in Lev. XV, 16. (3) *Sc.* the woman. (4) Lit., 'already'. (5) Lev. XXII, 4, and this was explained (*infra* 43*b*) to apply to a woman who came in external contact with semen virile. Why then the repetition? (6) Of the body, where internal contact with the semen virile takes place. (7) Lit., 'it is'. (8) From which it is evident that, according to R. Simeon, though a man is not subject to an uncleanness arising in an unexposed region of the body, a woman is subject to such an uncleanness. How then could it be maintained that according to R. Simeon 'it is enough that she be subject to the same stringency of uncleanness as the man who had intercourse with her'? (9) Whose uncleanness is due to a special Scriptural ordinance. (10) And for whose uncleanness it is enough to be as stringent as that of the man. (11) Lit., 'let it go out for him'. (12) Cf. prev. n. but two. (13) The ejection having taken place after the immersion. (14) Since, as has been explained, the law subjecting the woman to '*be unclean until the even*' (Lev. XV, 18) applies to one who had intercourse. (15) After three days the semen becomes vapid and conveys uncleanness no longer. Now since during the three days the woman invariably remains unclean, how, according to Raba, could R. Simeon rule that the woman is clean if she had undergone ritual immersion before the three days have passed? (16) In R. Simeon's ruling (cf. prev. n.).

was immersed[1] with her bed.[2] It may thus[3] be inferred that Raba[4] spoke of a woman[5] who went herself on foot and performed immersion, but then is it not possible that she had ejected the semen while she was walking?[6] [42*a*] And should you reply: It is possible that[7] some remained[8] [the objection would arise]: If so, should not the expression used have been:[9] We take into consideration the possibility that some might have remained?—The fact, however, is that according to Raba also this is a case where the woman was immersed with her bed, but there is no difficulty since one ruling[10] deals with a woman who[11] turned over[12] while the other[13] deals with one who[11] did not turn over;[14] and Raba[15] interpreted the Scriptural text in this manner:[16] When Scripture wrote, *They shall both bathe themselves in water and be unclean until the even*,[17] it referred to a woman who did not turn over but one who did turn over is forbidden to eat *terumah* for three days since it is impossible that she should not eject some semen during this time.

R. Samuel b. Bisna enquired of Abaye: 'Is a woman ejecting semen[18] regarded as observing a discharge or as coming in contact with one?[19] The practical issue[20] is the question of rendering[21] any

(1) After intercourse. (2) As she herself did not move her body it is quite possible for her to avoid ejection. (3) Since R. Simeon's rule, according to which the uncleanness terminates at evening, refers only to a woman who was carried in a bed. (4) Who holds the woman to be unclean for three days after intercourse. (5) Lit., 'that when Raba said'. (6) So that her subsequent immersion should render her completely free from both the uncleanness of intercourse and that of the ejection. How then could Raba maintain that she is unclean for three days? (7) Even after the ejection. (8) And that the uncleanness of which Raba spoke is due to this possibility. (9) Instead of the statement, 'it is impossible that she should not eject'. (10) Raba's. (11) After the immersion. (12) Hence 'it is impossible that she etc.'. (13) R. Simeon's. (14) Her uncleanness, therefore, terminates at evening. (15) In his ruling. (16) Lit., 'took his stand on the text and thus he said'. (17) Lev. XV, 18. (18) After she had undergone ritual immersion and was freed thereby from the uncleanness of intercourse to which she was subject (as stated *supra*) under a specific Scriptural ordinance. (19) Externally. Internal contact, being within a concealed region, is (as stated *supra* 41*b*) of no consequence. (20) Between uncleanness through (*a*) observation and (*b*) contact. (21) During the eleven days of *zibah*.

previous counting[1] void,[2] and of conveying uncleanness by means of the smallest quantity[2] and of conveying uncleanness internally as well as externally'.[2] But what is the question?[3] If he[4] heard of the Baraitha[5] [he should have known that] according to the Rabbis she is regarded as observing a discharge while according to R. Simeon she is regarded as coming in contact with one; and if he[4] did not hear of the Baraitha, is it not logical that[6] she should be regarded as coming in contact with one?[7]—Indeed he may well have heard of the Baraitha and, as far as the Rabbis are concerned, he had no question at all;[8] what he did ask concerned only the view of R. Simeon. Furthermore, he had no question[9] as to whether uncleanness is conveyed internally as externally;[10] what he did ask was whether any previous counting is rendered void and whether uncleanness is conveyed by means of the smallest quantity. When [he asked in effect] R. Simeon ruled that 'it is enough that she be subject to the same stringency of uncleanness as the man who had intercourse with her' he meant it only in respect of conveying uncleanness internally as externally[11] but as regards rendering any previous counting void and conveying uncleanness by means of the smallest quantity she is regarded as one observing a discharge, or is it possible that[12] there is no difference?[13] There are others who read: Indeed he[4] may never have

(1) Of the prescribed seven days. (2) Which is the case with an observation but not with contact. (3) Lit., 'what is your desire?' (4) R. Samuel who raised the question. (5) Supra 41*b*, where the Rabbis ruled that the ejection of semen conveys uncleanness internally as well as externally, while R. Simeon ruled that it is enough for the woman to be as unclean as the man who had intercourse with her. For the reading 'Baraitha' cf. Bomb. ed. Cur. edd. 'our Mishnah'. (6) Since the discharge does not originate from the woman's own body. (7) Of course it is. Why then did R. Samuel raise the question at all? (8) Since the Rabbis ruled that uncleanness is conveyed internally as well as externally it is obvious that the woman is regarded as one observing a discharge, and is, therefore, subject all the more to the other restrictions. (9) Even according to R. Simeon. (10) Well knowing that no internal uncleanness is conveyed (cf. *supra* n. 6). (11) *Sc.* as the man is free from internal uncleanness so is she. (12) Since he regarded her only as one coming in contact with a discharge. (13) And she is in all respects to be treated as such.

heard of the Baraitha,[1] but[2] it is this that he asked in effect: Since the All Merciful has considered it proper to impose a restriction[3] at Sinai on those who emitted semen,[4] she must be regarded as one who observed a discharge, or is it possible that no inference may be drawn from Sinai, since it was placed under an anomalous law, seeing that *zabs* and lepers who are elsewhere subject to major restrictions were not subjected by the All Merciful to that restriction?[3]—The other[5] replied: She is regarded as one who has observed a discharge. He[6] then came to Raba[7] and put the question to him. The latter replied: She is regarded as one who observed a discharge. He thereupon came to R. Joseph who also told him: She is regarded as one who observed a discharge. He[6] then returned to Abaye and said to him: 'You all spit the same thing'.[8] 'We', the other replied, 'only gave you the right answer. For when R. Simeon ruled that "it is enough that she be subject to the same stringency of uncleanness as the man who had intercourse with her" it was only in respect of conveying uncleanness internally as externally,[9] but in respect of rendering any previous counting void and in respect of conveying uncleanness by means of the smallest quantity she is regarded as one who observed a discharge.[10]

Our Rabbis taught: A menstruant,[11] a *zabah*,[12] one who awaits a day for a day[12] and a woman after childbirth[13] contract unclean-

(1) V. *supra* p. 288 n. 5. (2) In reply to the objection, 'Is it not logical that she should be regarded as coming in contact with one?' (3) Not to approach the mountain. (4) V. Ex. XIX, 15. '*Come not near a woman*'. This shows that the emission of semen is subject to a higher degree of uncleanness than contact with a dead creeping thing, which did not subject a person to the restriction. (5) Abaye. (6) R. Samuel b. Bisna. (7) Var. lec. Rabbah (BaḤ). (8) Lit., 'spittle', i.e., your opinions are all traceable to the same source. (9) *Sc.* as the man is free from internal uncleanness so is she. (10) Since in the case of the man also (to whose degree of uncleanness hers is compared) any previous counting is rendered void and the smallest quantity conveys uncleanness. (11) After one observation during her menstrual period. (12) Cf. prev. n. *mut. mut.* If this single observation is followed by two other observations the woman is a confirmed *zabah* and must count seven days before she attains to cleanness, but if no other observation followed she only awaits one clean day for the unclean one. (13) This is explained presently.

ness internally[1] as well as externally. Now, the enumeration of three of these cases[2] may well be justified, but how is one to explain the mention of the woman after childbirth? If the birth[3] occurred during her menstruation period she is a menstruant,[4] and if it occurred during her *zibah* period she is a *zabah?*[4]—The mention[5] was necessary only in the case of one who went down[6] to perform ritual immersion in order to pass out thereby from the period of uncleanness to that of cleanness;[7] and this[8] is in agreement with a ruling given by R. Zera citing R. Ḥiyya b. Ashi who had it from Rab: If a woman after childbirth went down[6] to perform ritual immersion in order to pass out thereby from her period of uncleanness to that of cleanness,[7] and some blood was detached from her body,[9] while she was going down,[10] she is unclean,[11] but if it occurred while she was going up, she is clean.[12] Said R. Jeremiah to R. Zera: Why should she be unclean if this occurred 'while she was going down'? Is not the blood merely an absorbed uncleanness?[13]—Go, the other replied, and ask it of R. Abin to whom I have explained the point at the schoolhouse and who

(1) *Sc.* as soon as the discharge made its way into the vagina. (2) Lit., '(almost) all of them'. (3) And the discharge observed. (4) Who was already specifically enumerated among the first three cases. (5) Of the woman after childbirth. (6) After the seven or fourteen days of uncleanness following the birth of a male and a female respectively. (7) The period of thirty-three clean days after the seven, and the sixty-six clean days after the fourteen (cf. prev. n.). (8) The ruling that a woman in such circumstances contracts uncleanness internally. (9) In the vagina, where it remained for a day or two. (10) Since the mere passing of the seven or fourteen days does not restore the woman to cleanness unless immersion had been performed (cf. *supra* 35*b*). When the unclean blood (cf. next n.) is completely discharged from the body a second immersion is required since no cleanness had been attained by the first. (11) While the blood is retained in the vagina, on account of her carriage of, or contact with the detached blood in it. (12) When, owing to the immersion, her clean period had already begun and the blood is clean. It has thus been shown that the Baraitha under discussion is in agreement with the first case, 'while she was going down, she is unclean' of R. Zera. (13) Which (cf. Ḥul. 71*a*) cannot convey uncleanness either through contact or through carriage. Granted that a menstrual, or a *zibah* discharge causes a woman's uncleanness even while it is still absorbed in the vagina (as deduced *supra* from a Scriptural text), how can this blood, which is neither menstrual nor one of *zibah* and which (if it had come in external

nodded to me with his head.[1] He went and asked him [the question], and the latter replied: This was treated like the carcass of a clean bird which[2] conveys uncleanness to garments[3] while it is still passing through the oesophagus.[4] But are the two cases at all similar [42*b*] seeing that in the latter case no uncleanness is conveyed by external contact[5] while here uncleanness would be conveyed when it emerges from the body?[6]—Here also it is a case where the discharge emerged from the body.[7] But if it emerged from the body, what need was there to mention such a case?[8]—It might have been presumed that as the immersion is effective in respect of blood that is internal it is also effective in respect of the other,[9] hence we were informed [that in the latter case the immersion is of no avail]. The difficulty about our cited tradition[10] is well solved; but as regards the woman after childbirth[11] [the difficulty arises again]: If the birth occurred during her menstruation period she is a menstruant, and if it occurred during her *zibah* period she is a *zabah*?[12]—Here we are dealing with the case of a dry birth.[13] But in the case of a dry birth,[14] what point is there in the statement that uncleanness is contracted internally as wel as externally?[15]—The statement is justified in a case for instance,

contact with the woman) could only have caused one day's uncleanness convey to the woman any uncleanness at all while still absorbed?

(1) As a mark of approval. (2) Though it conveys no uncleanness to the garments of the man who comes in contact with it. (3) Those of the man who eats of it. (4) An 'absorbed uncleanness'. (5) Cf. prev. n. but two. (6) From which it is evident that it is rather like other kinds of uncleanness. Why then should it be different from those in conveying uncleanness even while in an absorbed condition? (7) *Sc.* if the blood was detached before the immersion the woman becomes unclean after, but not before its complete emergence. (8) Apparently none, since it is obvious that unclean blood conveys uncleanness when it emerges from the body. (9) That was detached and remained for a time within the vagina. (10) R. Zera's ruling. (11) Included in the Baraitha under discussion, which can now no longer be compared with the ruling of R. Zera. (12) Cf. relevant notes *supra* 42*a ad fin*. (13) And one that was free from bleeding: so that the question of menstrual, or *zibah* blood does not arise. (14) Where there is no detached blood either within or without. (15) How can there be uncleanness in the absence of all blood?

where the embryo put its head out of the ante-chamber;[1] and this[2] is in agreement with R. Oshaia, for R. Oshaia stated, 'This[3] is a preventive measure[4] against the possibility that the embryo might put its head out of the ante-chamber';[5] and this[6] is also in line with the following ruling: A certain person once came before Raba and asked him, 'Is it permissible to perform a circumcision on the Sabbath?' 'This', the other replied, 'is quite in order'. After that person went out Raba considered: Is it likely that this man did not know that it was permissible to perform a circumcision on the Sabbath? He thereupon followed him and said to him, 'Pray tell me all the circumstance of the case'.[7] 'I', the other told him, 'heard the child cry late on the Sabbath eve but it was not born until the Sabbath'. 'This is a case', the first explained to him, 'of a child[8] who put his head out of the ante-chamber[9] and consequently his circumcision[10] is one that does not take place at the proper time,[11] and on account of a circumcision that does not take place at the proper time the Sabbath may not be desecrated.'[12]

The question was raised: Is that region in a woman[13] regarded

(1) And then draw it back (cf. Strashun). Although the head is now within (internal) the woman is unclean as if the embryo had actually been born (external). (2) The ruling that the projection of the head of the embryo without the ante-chamber is regarded as birth. (3) That a midwife is unclean for seven days if she touched a dead embryo before it was extracted, though its mother remains clean until extraction had been effected. (4) Enacted by the Rabbis. Pentateuchally the embryo, being at the time an 'absorbed uncleanness', would convey no uncleanness at all. (5) Ḥul. 72*a*; and the midwife would then touch it when, having touched a corpse, her uncleanness would be Pentateuchal. Thus it follows that according to R. Oshaia the projection of the embryo's head without the ante-chamber is regarded as the actual birth. Similarly in the case under discussion, as soon as the embryo had put its head out of the ante-chamber its mother is subject to the uncleanness of birth as if the birth had taken place. (6) V. *supra* n. 2. (7) Lit., 'how was the body of the incident?' (8) Whose cry could be heard. (9) On the Friday, when he was heard crying. (10) On any day after the following Friday which is the eighth day of his virtual birth. (11) Circumcision being due on the eighth day of birth. (12) The circumcision must, therefore, be postponed until the Sunday. At all events, Raba's ruling shows that the projection of the embryo's head without the ante-chamber is regarded as birth (cf. *supra* n. 2). (13) Euphemism.

as an absorbed place or as a concealed one?—In what respect could this matter?—In the case, for instance, where her friend inserted in her in that region a piece of *nebelah* of the size of an olive. If you say that it is regarded as an absorbed place, this *nebelah* being now an absorbed uncleanness[1] would convey no uncleanness to the woman,[2] but if you say that it is a concealed place, granted that no uncleanness could be conveyed by means of contact[3] uncleanness would be conveyed by means of carriage?[4]—Abaye replied: It is regarded as an absorbed place. Raba replied: It is regarded as a concealed one. Said Raba: Whence do I derive this? From what was taught: Since the uncleanness arises in a concealed region, and since an uncleanness in a concealed region is elsewhere ineffective, a special Scriptural ordinance was required [to give it effect in this particular case].[5] And Abaye?[6]—The meaning[7] is this: There is one reason and there is yet another.[8] In the first place the woman should be clean since the uncleanness is an absorbed one; and, furthermore, even if you were to find some ground for saying that it is a concealed uncleanness and an uncleanness in a concealed region is ineffective, this[9] is a specific Scriptural ordinance.

The question was raised: Is the region through which the *nebelah* of a clean bird conveys uncleanness to a human being[10] regarded as an absorbed place or as a concealed one? In what respect can this matter?—In a case, for instance, where his friend pushed a piece of *nebelah* of the size of an olive into his mouth.[11] If you regard it as an absorbent place, this *nebelah* being now an absorbed uncleanness would convey no uncleanness, but if[12] you say that it

(1) And, therefore, regarded as non-existent. (2) Either through contact or carriage (cf. prev. n.). (3) The uncleanness by contact not applying to a concealed region of the body. (4) Since the woman was carrying the *nebelah*. (5) *Supra* 41b q.v. notes. (6) How can he maintain his view in contradiction to Raba's citation? (7) Of the cited statement. (8) Lit., 'one and more he says'. (9) The woman's uncleanness (cf. *supra* n. 5). (10) *Sc.* the oesophagus. Only by swallowing it does the *nebelah* of a clean bird convey uncleanness to man. (11) So that he himself did not touch it with his hands, (12) Cur. ed. insert the last two words in parenthesis, and marg. n. substitutes 'what would you say'.

is a concealed one, granted that no uncleanness is conveyed by means of contact,[1] uncleanness would be conveyed by means of carriage?[2]—Abaye replied: It is an absorbed place, but Raba replied: It is a concealed one. Whence, said Abaye, do I derive this? From what was taught: As it might have been presumed that the *nebelah* of a beast conveys uncleanness to a person's garments by way of his oesophagus,[3] it was explicitly stated in Scripture, *That which dieth of itself,*[4] *or is torn of beasts, he shall not eat to defile himself therewith,*[5] which implies: Only that[6] which has no other form of uncleanness but that which is conveyed through the eating thereof[6] [conveys uncleanness by way of the oesophagus],[3] but this[7] is excluded since it conveys uncleanness even before one had eaten of it. But why should not this[8] be inferred *a minori ad majus* from the *nebelah* of a clean bird: If the *nebelah* of a clean bird which is not subject to uncleanness externally is subject to uncleanness internally[3] how much more then should this,[7] which is subject to uncleanness externally, be subject to uncleanness internally?—Scripture said, '*therewith*'[5] which implies: Only therewith[9] but not with any other.[7] If so, why was it stated in Scripture, *And he that eateth?*[10] To prescribe for one who touches or carries it the same size as that which was prescribed for one who eats of it: As one who eats of it incurs guilt on consuming the full size of an olive so also one who touches or carries it contracts uncleanness only if it is of the size of an olive.

Raba ruled: A man holding a dead creeping thing in a fold of his body[11] is clean, but if he holds *nebelah* in a fold of his body he is unclean. 'A man holding a dead creeping thing in a fold of his body is clean', since a dead creeping thing conveys uncleanness by means of touch, while a concealed region of the body[11] is not

(1) The uncleanness by contact not applying to a concealed region of the body. (2) The man having carried the *nebelah* in his mouth. (3) *Sc.* by swallowing it. (4) Heb. *nebelah*. (5) Lev. XXII, 8. (6) The *nebelah* of a clean bird. (7) *Nebelah* of a beast. (8) That the *nebelah* of a beast conveys uncleanness by way of the oesophagus. (9) *Sc.* only if a person swallowed the *nebelah* of a clean bird do his garments become unclean. (10) Lev. XI, 40, in respect of the *nebelah* of a beast. (11) Under his arm-pit, for instance.

susceptible to the uncleanness of touch. 'If he holds *nebelah* in a fold of his body he is unclean' for, granted that he contracts no uncleanness through touch, he contracts it, at any rate, through carriage. If a man held a dead creeping thing in the fold of his body[1] and he thus brought it into the air spaces[2] of an oven[3] the latter is unclean. Is not this obvious?[4]—It might have been presumed that the All Merciful said, *Into the inside of which,*[5] implying: [43a] But not the inside of its inside,[6] hence we were informed [that the oven is unclean].[7]

Resh Laḳish ruled: If a reed was held in a fold of the body of a *zab* and he shook therewith a clean person the latter remains clean.[8] If a reed was held in the fold of the body of a clean person and he shook therewith a *zab* the former is unclean.[9] What is the reason?[10] Because Scripture said, *And whomsoever he that hath issue*[11] *toucheth, without having rinsed his hands in water,*[12] and this[13] refers to the shaking of a *zab*, a form of conveyance of uncleanness the like of which we do not find anywhere in all the Torah; and the All Merciful expressed this in the term of touching,[14] in order to tell that shaking and touching must be performed with a part of the body which is like one's hands; as one's hands are exposed[15] so must any other part of the body[16] be exposed.

BUT A ZAB AND ONE WHO EMITTED SEMEN CONVEY NO UNCLEANNESS etc. A ZAB, because it is written in Scripture,

(1) Under his arm-pit, for instance. (2) Without touching its sides. (3) Of earthenware. (4) Apparently it is, since all earthen vessels contract uncleanness from a dead creeping thing within their air spaces though there was no direct contact between it and the creeping thing. (5) E.V., '*whereinto*'; *Every earthen vessel whereinto any of them falleth* (Lev. XI, 33). (6) Inside, for instance, an arm-pit which is inside the oven. (7) The implication, 'but not the inside of its inside' excludes only the case where a creeping thing was within a vessel whose rim and mouth projected above the vessel in which it was contained. (8) The reason is given presently. (9) Since he 'carried' the *zab*. The carrying of a *zab* as the carrying of his couch conveys uncleanness to the carrier (cf. Lev. XV, 10). (10) Why a person who was shaken by a reed held in the fold of the body of a *zab* remains clean. (11) Heb. *zab*. (12) Lev. XV, 11. (13) Since the text cannot refer to direct touch which was already dealt with in Lev. XV, 7. (14) '*Toucheth*'. (15) Lit., 'as there from outside'. (16) If it is to convey uncleanness.

When any man hath an issue out of his flesh,[1] [which implies that no uncleanness is conveyed] unless his issue emerged *'out of his flesh'*; ONE WHO EMITTED SEMEN, because it is written, *And if the flow of seed go out from a man.*[2]

IF A MAN WAS EATING TERUMAH WHEN HE FELT etc. Was it not, however, taught: R. Eliezer stated, whoever holds his membrum when he makes water is as though he had brought a flood on the world?[3]—Abaye replied: One does it with a thick rag.[4] Raba stated: It may even be done with a soft rag, for once the semen has been detached the subsequent touch is of no consequence.[5] And Abaye?[6]—He takes into consideration the possibility of an additional discharge. And Raba?—He does not consider the possibility of an additional discharge. But does he not?[7] Was it not in fact taught: 'To what may this be compared? To the putting of a finger upon the eye when, so long as the finger remains on it, the eye continues to tear'? Now Raba?[8]—It is unusual to get heated twice in immediate succession.[9]

Samuel ruled, Any semen the emission of which is not felt throughout one's body causes no uncleanness. What is the reason? —The All Merciful has said, *The flow of seed,*[10] implying that the text[11] deals only with such as is fit to produce seed. An objection was raised: If a man was troubled with unchaste thoughts in the night and when he rose up he found his flesh heated, he is unclean![12] —R. Huna explained this to apply to a man who dreamt of indulging in sexual intercourse, it being impossible to indulge in the act without experiencing the sensation. Another rendering: Samuel ruled, Any semen which does not shoot forth like an arrow causes

(1) Lev. XV, 2, emphasis on *'out'*. (2) Ibid. 16. Cf. prev. n. (3) *Supra* 13*a*. (4) Which intercepts the warmth of one's hand. (5) Lit., 'since it uprooted it uprooted'. (6) Why, in view of Raba's explanation, does he insist on a thick rag? (7) So with BaḤ. Cur. edd. omit. (8) What has he to say to this? (9) Lit., 'any being heated and being heated again at the time is not usual'. The comparison with the eye holds good only when a discharge was originally due to friction. (10) Lev. XV, 16, emphasis on the last word. (11) *Then he shall . . . . be unclean* (ibid.). (12) Miḳ. VIII, 3; because he might also have emitted some semen. As this would presumably occur without his being aware of it, an objection arises against Samuel.

no uncleanness. What is the practical difference between the latter reading and the former reading?—The practical difference between them is the case where the detachment of the semen was perceived but the emergence was not felt.[1] Now this ruling which was quite obvious to Samuel was a matter of enquiry for Raba. For Raba enquired: What is the law where the detachment of the semen was perceived but its emergence was not felt?[2]—Come and hear: If a man who emitted semen performed immersion[3] before he had made water, his uncleanness is resumed when he makes water![4]—There it is different, since the emergence of most of the semen was perceived. Others have a different reading: Samuel ruled, Any semen which does not shoot forth like an arrow causes no fructification. It is only fructification that it does not cause but it does cause uncleanness, for it is said in Scripture, *If there be among you any man, that is not clean by reason of that which chanceth him*,[5] which implies: Even a chance emission[6] whatever its nature.[7]

Raba enquired: What is the law where an idolater indulged in sexual thoughts,[8] and then[9] he went down and performed ritual immersion?[10] If you were to find some case where we follow the time of detachment[11] [the question would arise], Does this apply only where the law is thereby restricted,[12] but not here[13] where the law would thereby be relaxed,[14] or is it possible that no distinction is made?—This is undecided.

Raba enquired: What is the ruling where the urine of a *zabah*

(1) According to the first reading uncleanness would, and according to the latter reading would not be caused. (2) Is uncleanness thereby conveyed or not? (3) Which frees him from his uncleanness. (4) Mik. VIII, 4 (cur. edd. '3', is an error). Now here there was obviously no perception, and yet uncleanness is nevertheless conveyed. An objection against Samuel. (5) Deut. XXIII, 11, *miḳreh* of the rt. קרה (v. foll. n.). (6) *Ḳeri* of the rt. קרי (cf. prev. n.). (7) Lit., 'in the world'. (8) As a result of which semen had been detached but did not emerge. (9) For the purpose of his conversion to Judaism. (10) Subsequent to which the semen emerged. (11) *Sc.* that, in the case of an Israelite, uncleanness is caused where the detachment was perceived even though the emergence was not felt. (12) Uncleanness is caused. (13) The case of the idolater. (14) Since at the time of the detachment the man was still an idolater and free from the laws of uncleanness.

had been detached from the source[1] and then she went down and performed ritual immersion?[2] If you were to find some case where we follow the time of the detachment [the question would arise], Does this apply only to semen, since it cannot be restrained,[3] but not to her urine which she is able to restrain,[4] or is it possible that no distinction is made?—This is undecided.

Raba enquired: What is the law where the urine of an idolatress[5] who was a *zabah* had been detached [43*b*] from the source, and then she[6] went down and performed ritual immersion? If you were to find a case[7] where we follow the time of the detachment even where the woman can restrain the discharge [the question would arise], Does this apply only to the Israelitish woman who is Pentateuchally unclean but not to an idolatress who was a *zabah*, since she is only Rabbinically unclean,[8] or is it possible that no difference is made between them?—This is undecided.

AND THE DISCHARGES CONVEY UNCLEANNESS HOWEVER SMALL THE QUANTITY. Samuel ruled: [the discharge of] a *zab*[9] must be such a quantity as would stop the orifice of the membrum, for it is said in Scripture, *Or his flesh be stopped from his issue.*[10] But have we not learnt: AND THE DISCHARGES CONVEY UNCLEANNESS, HOWEVER SMALL THE QUANTITY?—He[11] maintains the same view as R. Nathan. For it was taught: R. Nathan citing R. Ishmael ruled, [the discharge of] a *zab*[9] must be such a quantity as would stop the orifice of the membrum; but [the Rabbis] did not agree with him.[12] What is R. Ishmael's reason?—Because Scripture said, *Or his flesh be stopped from his issue.*[10] And the Rabbis?[13]—

(1) Which is a 'father of uncleanness'. (2) Whereby she is freed from her uncleanness; and then she made the water. Is she, it is asked, unclean because at the time of the detachment she was unclean or is she clean because the emergence took place when she was already in a condition of cleanness? (3) In consequence of which detachment must be regarded as virtual emergence. (4) So that the emergence is a separate process which, having taken place after immersion, causes no uncleanness. (5) Which is Rabbinically unclean. (6) For the purpose of her conversion to Judaism. (7) In respect of an Israelitish woman. (8) Cf. *supra* n. 5. (9) If it is to convey uncleanness. (10) Lev. XV, 3. (11) Samuel. (12) Pes. 67*b*. (13) How can they maintain their ruling in view of this text?

That text[1] is required for the inference that the discharge conveys uncleanness only when in a state of fluidity[2] but not when it is dry.[3] And R. Ishmael?[4]—That[5] is inferred from *run*.[6] And the Rabbis?[7]—That text[6] serves the purpose of indicating the number:[8] *His issue*,[1] implies once; *His flesh run*,[1] implies twice; *With his issue*,[1] implies three times; thus it was taught that a *zab* who observed three discharges is under an obligation to bring a sacrifice; *Or his flesh be stopped from his issue, it is his uncleanness*,[1] implies that he is unclean even on account of a part of the number of his issues,[9] this teaches that a *zab* who observed only two discharges conveys uncleanness to his couch and seat. As to R. Ishmael, however,[10] whence does he deduce the number required?[11]—He derives it from an exposition of R. Simai; for it was taught: R. Simai stated, Scripture enumerated two issues and described the man as unclean[12] and it also enumerated three issues and described the man as unclean,[13] how is this to be reconciled? Two observations subject a man to the restrictions of uncleanness, and three observations render him liable to bring a sacrifice. But according to the Rabbis[14] who deduced both numbers from '*This shall be his uncleanness in his issue*',[15] what deduction do they make from the text '*when any man hath an issue out of his flesh*'?[16]—They require it for the deduction that uncleanness does not begin until the discharge emerged from one's flesh. What need, however, was there for '*His issue be unclean*'?[16]—This teaches that the issue itself[17] is unclean.

(1) Lev. XV, 3. (2) Lit., 'wet', when the orifice can '*be stopped*' by it. (3) When it crumbles away and is incapable of adhesion. (4) How, in view of this explanation, can he still maintain his ruling? (5) That a discharge conveys uncleanness only when in a state of fluidity. (6) *Run with his issue* (Lev. XV, 3). (7) How can they maintain their ruling in view of this text? (8) Of issues that determine the various grades of uncleanness. (9) '*From his issues*' (emphasis on '*from*') implying 'a part'. (10) Who requires the expression of '*run with his issue*' for the inference he mentioned *supra*. (11) As just indicated according to the Rabbis. (12) *When any man hath an issue out of his flesh* (Lev. XV, 2), counts as one; *his issue be unclean* (ibid). counts as a second. (13) *This shall be his uncleanness in his issue* (Lev. XV, 3) counts as one; *His flesh run with his issue* (ibid.) counts as a second; *or his flesh be stopped from his issue* (ibid.) counts as a third. (14) Lit., 'him'. (15) *Supra*. (16) Cf. *supra* n. 12. (17) And not only the man who suffered from it.

R. Ḥanilai citing R. Eliezer son of R. Simeon ruled: Semen conveys uncleanness to the man who emitted it,[1] however small its quantity, but as regards the man who touched it its quantity must be of the bulk of a lentil.[2] But did we not learn, AND THE DISCHARGES CONVEY UNCLEANNESS, HOWEVER SMALL THE QUANTITY, which applies, does it not, to the case of one who touched semen?—No, it applies only to one who emitted it.[1]

Come and hear: In one respect the law of semen is more restrictive than that of a dead creeping thing while in another respect the law of a dead creeping thing is more restrictive than that of semen. 'The law of a dead creeping thing is more restrictive' in that no distinction [of age] is made about its uncleanness,[3] which is not the case with semen.[4] 'The law of semen is more restrictive' in that uncleanness is conveyed by its smallest quantity, which is not the case with a creeping thing.[5] Now does not this apply to one who touched the semen?[6]—No, it applies only to one who emitted it.[7] But was it not taught as being on a par with the creeping thing: As the latter is a case of touching so also the former?[6]—R. Adda b. Ahabah replied: The ruling referred to a creeping thing in general[8] and to semen in general.[9] But does a creeping thing convey no uncleanness even when it is of the smallest bulk? Have we not in fact learnt: Members of the body[10] have[11] no prescribed minimum size [and uncleanness is, therefore, conveyed] by less than the size of an olive of corpse,[12] by less than the size of an olive of *nebelah* or by less than the size of a lentil of a dead creeping

(1) Lit., 'to the one who observes'. (2) A lesser quantity, as is the case with a dead creeping thing, conveys no uncleanness. (3) Young and old are equally unclean. (4) The uncleanness on account of an emission of semen being restricted to one who is over nine years of age. (5) Tosef. Kel. I. Cf. *supra* n. 2. (6) But this would present an objection against R. Ḥanilai's ruling. (7) Lit., 'to the one who observes'. (8) Lit., 'the name of' or 'any'. (9) *Sc.* it referred to the form of uncleanness appropriate to each. A dead creeping thing can never convey uncleanness unless its bulk is of the prescribed size, while semen, when it concerns the man who had emitted it, may convey uncleanness, however small its quantity. (10) *Sc.* any part of it which consists of flesh, sinews and bones (v. Bertinoro). (11) In regard to the conveyance of uncleanness. (12) Cf. prev. n. but one.

thing?[1]—It is different with a member of the body[2] since the whole of it takes the place of the size of a lentil; for were any part of it[3] missing,[4] would the member[5] have conveyed any uncleanness?[6] What is meant by the 'distinction in uncleanness' in the case of semen? If it be suggested: The distinction between the semen of an Israelite and that of foreigners [it could be objected]: Is there not in this case also[7] a distinction between a sea-mouse and a land-mouse?[8]—The distinction rather is that between a minor and an adult.[9]

R. Papa stated: This ruling[10] is a point at issue between Tannas:[11] [For it was taught] whence do we derive the inclusion in uncleanness of one who touched semen? From Scripture which explicitly stated, *Or whosoever;*[12] and elsewhere Tannas differ on a relevant point,[13] for there are those who hold that a deduction is carried through in all respects[14] while others hold that a deduction is limited by its original basis.[15] Now according to those who hold that a deduction is carried through in all respects[14] it follows that as a dead creeping thing[16] conveys uncleanness through touch so does semen convey uncleanness by touch and, consequently,[17] as a dead

(1) Oh. I, 7, which shows that a dead creeping thing conveys uncleanness, however small its bulk. (2) V. p. 300, n. 10. (3) Lit., 'a portion'. (4) Cf. *supra* p. 300, n. 10. (5) That was smaller than a lentil. (6) Obviously not; which shows that it is only on account of its importance that the force of conveying uncleanness (as a piece of the prescribed size) was imparted to it. Any other part of the body, however, is subject to the prescribed minimum. (7) That of a creeping thing. (8) Of course there is! A sea-mouse (cf. Ḥul. 126*b*) conveys no uncleanness. (9) No uncleanness is conveyed by that of a child under nine years of age. (10) Of R. Ḥanilai, that semen less in quantity than the bulk of a lentil conveys no uncleanness by means of touch. (11) Lit., 'like Tannas'. (12) This is now presumed to refer to Lev. XXII, 5, which deals with the uncleanness of a creeping thing. (13) Which (as will be shown presently) has a bearing on this deduction. (14) Lit., 'judge from it and (again) from it', i.e., all that applies to the case from which deduction is made is also applicable to the case deduced (15) Lit., 'judge from it and set it in its (original) place', i.e., the rules applicable to the case deduced limit the scope of the deduction. (16) From the law of which that of semen had presumably been deduced (cf. n. 12). (17) Lit., 'and from it', since 'a deduction is carried through in all respects.'

creeping thing conveys uncleanness only when it is of the bulk of a lentil so does semen convey uncleanness only when it is of the bulk of a lentil; while according to him who maintained that a deduction is limited by its original basis[1] it also follows that as a dead creeping thing conveys uncleanness through touch so does semen convey uncleanness through touch, but then, limiting it to its original basis, as semen conveys uncleanness to the man who emitted it, however small its quantity, so does it also convey uncleanness to the man who touched it, however small its quantity.[2] Said[3] R. Huna son of R. Nathan to R. Papa: Whence the proof that the inclusion in uncleanness of one who touched semen is deduced from the expression of '*Or whosoever*' occurring in the context dealing with the creeping thing?[4] Is it not possible that the inclusion is derived from the expression of '*Or from whomsoever the flow of seed goeth out*,[5] and[6] all may be of the opinion that a deduction is to be carried through in all respects?[7] The Tannas[8] were asked.[9] Some recited as R. Papa while others recited in agreement with R. Huna son of R. Nathan.

MISHNAH. A GIRL ONE DAY OLD IS SUBJECT TO THE UNCLEANNESS OF MENSTRUATION. ONE WHO IS TEN DAYS OLD IS SUBJECT TO THE UNCLEANNESS OF ZIBAH. A BOY ONE DAY OLD IS SUBJECT TO THE UNCLEANNESS OF ZIBAH, AND TO THE UNCLEANNESS OF LEPROSY AND THAT OF CORPSE-

(1) V. p. 301, n. 15. (2) It has thus been shown that R. Ḥanilai's ruling is a point at issue between Tannas. Is it likely, however, that R. Ḥanilai would differ from the Tannas who presumably hold a different view? (3) In an attempt to remove the difficulty (cf. prev. n. second clause). (4) Lev. XXII, 5, as presumed by R. Papa *supra*. (5) Lev. XXII, 4. (6) Since the deduction is not made from the contact of the creeping thing. (7) *Sc.* even if all were to uphold this view, uncleanness would nevertheless be conveyed by the touch of the smallest quantity of semen, since the inference is made, not from the uncleanness of the creeping thing but from that of the emission of semen which is conveyed by the smallest quantity. (8) Those who recited Mishnahs and Baraithas at the college; v. Glos. s.v. (*b*). (9) To give a decision as to whether R. Papa or R. Huna was in the right.

UNCLEANNESS; HE SUBJECTS [HIS DECEASED BROTHER'S WIDOW] TO THE DUTY OF LEVIRATE MARRIAGE;[1] HE EXEMPTS [HIS MOTHER] FROM THE LEVIRATE MARRIAGE,[2] HE ENABLES HER[3] TO EAT TERUMAH AND HE ALSO CAUSES HER TO BE DISQUALIFIED FROM EATING TERUMAH;[4] [44a] HE INHERITS AND TRANSMITS;[5] HE WHO KILLS HIM IS GUILTY OF MURDER, AND HE COUNTS TO HIS FATHER, TO HIS MOTHER AND TO ALL HIS RELATIVES AS[5] A FULLY GROWN MAN.[6]

GEMARA. Whence is this ruling[7] deduced?—[From the following]. For our Rabbis taught: From the term *woman*[8] I would only know that the laws[9] are applicable to a grown-up woman, whence, however, the inference that a girl one day old is also subject to the uncleanness of menstruation? Since it was explicitly stated, *And a woman.*[10]

ONE WHO IS TEN DAYS OLD IS SUBJECT TO THE UNCLEANNESS OF ZIBAH. Whence is this ruling deduced? [From the following]. For our Rabbis taught: From the term *woman*[11] I would only know that the laws are applicable to a grown-up woman, whence, however, the inference that a girl who is ten days old is also subject to the uncleanness of *zibah?* Since it was explicitly stated, *And a woman.*[12]

A BOY ONE DAY OLD etc. Whence is this ruling deduced?—[From the following Scriptural text]. For the Rabbis taught: *When any man,*[13] what was the object of stating, '*When any man*'?[14]

(1) Provided he was born prior to his brother's death. (2) If he was born after his father's death though he only lived for a short while. (3) His mother, the daughter of an Israelite, who was married to a priest, though the latter was dead when the child was born. (4) This is now presumed to refer to a priest's daughter who was married to an Israelite who died and was survived by a son one day old (v. *Gemara* infra.) (5) This is explained in the Gemara. (6) Lit., 'bridegroom'. (7) That A GIRL ONE DAY OLD etc. (8) Lev. XV, 19, which deals with the laws of the menstruant. (9) Cf. prev. n. (10) Lev. XV, 19. E.V. *and if a woman.* (11) Cf. prev. n. but two. The exposition now is based on what follows in the Scriptural text: *Her issue . . . be blood.* (12) Cf. prev. two notes. (13) Lev. XV, 2. Lit. '*a man, a man*'. (14) *Sc.* it would have sufficed if one 'man' (cf. prev. n.) had been omitted, the rendering being, 'when a man'.

To include a boy one day old in the restrictions of the uncleanness of *zibah;* so R. Judah. R. Ishmael son of R. Johanan b. Beroka said, This deduction is not necessary, for surely it is stated in Scripture, *And of them that have an issue, whether it be a man or a woman;*[1] '*whether it be a man*' means one of any age, whether adult or minor, '*or a woman*' means one of any age, whether an adult or minor. But if so[2] what need was there to state, '*When any man*'?[3] The Torah employed ordinary phraseology.[4]

[IS SUBJECT TO ...] THE UNCLEANNESS OF LEPROSY, since it is written, *When a man shall have in the skin of his flesh,*[5] implying a man of any age.

[IS SUBJECT TO ...] THAT OF CORPSE-UNCLEANNESS, because it is written, *And upon the persons that were there,*[6] implying a person of any age.

HE SUBJECTS [HIS DECEASED BROTHER'S WIDOW] TO THE DUTY OF LEVIRATE MARRIAGE, for it is written, *If brethren dwell together,*[7] implying brothers who are contemporaries.[8]

HE EXEMPTS [HIS MOTHER] FROM THE LEVIRATE MARRIAGE, for the All Merciful has said, *And have no child,*[7] but this man has one.

HE ENABLES HER TO EAT TERUMAH, for it is written, *And such as are born in his house, they may eat*[9] *of his bread,*[10] read it as, 'Shall cause to eat[11] of his bread'.

AND HE ALSO CAUSES HER TO BE DISQUALIFIED FROM EATING TERUMAH. For the All Merciful has said, *And have no child,*[12] but she has one. But what was the point of speaking of a '*child*' seeing that the same applies even to an embryo, for it is written,[13] *As in her youth,*[12] which excludes[14] one who is pregnant?[15]

(1) Lev. XV, 33. (2) That the law has been enunciated in Lev. XV, 33. (3) Lev. XV, 2. Lit., '*a man, a man*'. (4) Lit., 'spoke in the language of men', who are in the habit of repeating their words. No inference, therefore, may be drawn from the repetition of '*a man*'. (5) Lev. XIII, 2. (6) Num. XIX, 18, in the context dealing with corpse-uncleanness. (7) Deut. XXV, 5, in the context of the law of levirate marriage and *halizah*. (8) Lit., 'who had one (and the same) sitting in the world'. (9) יאכלו, *yokelu* (*kal*). (10) Lev. XXII, 11. (11) יאכילו, *ya'akilu* (*hif.*). (12) Lev. XXII, 13. (13) In the same context. (14) From the privilege of eating *terumah*. (15) *Sc.* if an embryo causes its mother to be disqualified from eating *terumah* it is self-evident

Both texts were required. For if the All Merciful had only written, '*And have no child*' [it might have been presumed that the law[1] applied to that case] because originally there was but one body and now there are two bodies,[2] but that in this case,[3] where there was originally one body and now also there is only one body, it may be held that the woman may eat *terumah*, hence the All Merciful has written, '*As in her youth*'.[4] And if the All Merciful has only written, '*As in her youth*' [it might have been presumed that the law[5] applied to that case alone] since originally the woman's body was empty and now it is a full one, but that in this case,[6] where her body was originally empty and is now also empty, the woman may well eat *terumah*. Hence the necessity for both texts. Now, the Scriptural texts have been well explained, but as regards our Mishnah, why just A BOY ONE DAY OLD, seeing[7] that even an embryo also disqualifies its mother? — R. Shesheth replied: We are here dealing with the case of a priest who had two wives, one who had previously been a divorced woman[8] and the other was not a divorced woman,[9] and he had sons from the latter[10] and one son from the former,[11] so that the latter[12] causes the slaves of his father[13] to be disqualified from eating *terumah*;[14] thus indicating that the law is contrary to the view[15] of R. Jose. He having laid down that an embryo[16] also causes disqualification we were informed that a child does it, what need then was there for the text, '*and have no child*'?

(1) Of disqualification (cf. p. 304, n. 14). (2) Mother and born child. (3) Lit., 'here', that of a pregnant woman. (4) To indicate that even a pregnant woman is disqualified. (5) Of disqualification (cf. *supra* p. 304, n. 14). (6) Where the child was already born. (7) As has just been shown. (8) Whom a priest is forbidden to marry and whose children from a priestly marriage are disqualified priests and are themselves forbidden to eat *terumah* and, of course, have no right to confer the privilege of eating it upon their slaves. (9) And whose sons from her marriage with the priest are qualified priests who also confer upon their slaves the right of eating *terumah*. (10) Cf. prev. n. (11) Cf. *supra* n. 8. (12) After the death of his father, the priest. (13) Whom he and his brothers jointly inherit from their deceased father. (14) On account of his share in them; it being impossible to distinguish which of the slaves are his and which are his brothers'. (15) Lit., 'to bring out'. (16) From a forbidden marriage (cf. *supra* n. 8).

here that only A BOY ONE DAY OLD causes disqualification but not an embryo.[1]

HE INHERITS AND TRANSMITS. From whom does he INHERIT? Obviously from his father; and to whom does he TRANSMIT? Obviously to his paternal brothers;[2] but could not these if they wished inherit from their father and, if they preferred, inherit from him?[3]—R. Shesheth replied: The meaning is, He[4] inherits the estate of his mother to transmit it[5] to his paternal brothers;[6] hence only then when he is ONE DAY OLD but not when he is an embryo. What is the reason?—Because it[7] dies first,[8] and no son may inherit from his mother [44b] in the grave[9] to transmit the inheritance to his paternal brothers. But, surely, this[10] is not so, for was there not a case where an embryo made three convulsive movements?[11]—Mar son of R. Ashi replied: [Those were only reflexive movements] like those of the tail of the lizard which moves convulsively [even after it has been cut off].[12]

Mar son of R. Joseph citing Raba explained: This[13] means to say that he causes a diminution in the portion of the birthright.[14]

Mar son of R. Joseph citing Raba further ruled: A son born

(1) The disqualification spoken of in our Mishnah thus referring to the slaves and not, as has previously been assumed, to the child's mother, the difficulty raised *supra* is now solved. (2) Since only paternal relatives are entitled to inherit one's estate. (3) Of course they could, since the child's estate would in any case revert on his death to his father from whom they would inherit it. What meaning then could be assigned to the law that he TRANSMITS? (4) A BOY ONE DAY OLD. (5) When he dies. (6) Who were born from the same father but not from the same mother. (7) The embryo, when its mother dies. (8) *Sc.* before its mother. (9) *Sc.* after his death. (10) That an embryo dies before its mother. (11) After its mother was dead. (12) But are no signs of life. (13) The law that A BOY ONE DAY OLD ... TRANSMITS. (14) If, for instance, there were two brothers other than the boy in question, and one of them was the firstborn, the estate is divided, not into three portions (two for the ordinary portions of the two brothers and one for the birthright), but into four portions. Each brother, including the young child, receives one such portion and the firstborn receives the additional fourth portion as his birthright. The firstborn thus receives, as the portion of his birthright, a quarter of the estate, and not (as would have been the case if the child were excluded) a third.

after the death of his father causes no diminution in the portion of the birthright.[1] What is the reason?[2] It is required that *They shall have born to him.*[3] Thus[4] it was taught at Sura; but at Pumbeditha it was taught as follows: Mar son of R. Joseph citing Raba ruled, A firstborn son that was born after the death of his father[5] does not receive a double portion. What is the reason? It is necessary that *He shall acknowledge,*[6] and ['*he*',] surely, is not [there to acknowledge]. And the law is in agreement with all those versions which Mar son of R. Joseph cited in the name of Raba.

HE WHO KILLS HIM IS GUILTY OF MURDER, since it is written, *And he that smiteth any man mortally,*[7] implying, whatever the age.[8]

AND HE COUNTS TO HIS FATHER, TO HIS MOTHER AND TO ALL HIS RELATIVES AS A FULLY GROWN MAN. In respect of what law?—R. Papa replied: In respect of that of mourning.

In agreement with whose view [is our Mishnah]?[9] It cannot be, can it, in agreement with[10] R. Simeon b. Gamaliel who ruled: Any human[11] child[12] that survived for thirty days cannot be regarded as a miscarriage,[13] from which it follows that if he had

(1) Though he receives his due portion in the estate. In the case mentioned as an instance in the prev. n. the estate would first be divided into three portions (as if the embryo did not exist) and the firstborn would receive, as his birthright, one of these, which represents a third of the estate. The remaining two thirds would then be divided into three equal shares, each of the three brothers receiving one, i.e., two ninths of the estate. The full portion of the firstborn would accordingly amount to ($\frac{1}{3} + \frac{2}{9} = \frac{5}{9}$) five ninths of the estate, while, where the child was one day old, the firstborn's full portion would only amount to half the estate, i.e., ($\frac{5}{9} - \frac{1}{2} = \frac{1}{18}$) one eighteenth less. (2) That a born child does, and an embryo does not cause a diminution in the portion of the birthright. (3) Deut. XXI, 15, emphasis on 'him', *sc.* while the father is alive. An embryo cannot come within the category of '*have born*'. (4) The version just given. (5) In the case, for instance, where his widow bore twins, or where he was survived by two widows and both bore sons and one of these was the firstborn. (6) Deut. XXI, 17. (7) Lev. XXIV, 17. (8) Lit., 'from any place'. (9) Which, treating an infant one day old in the various laws embodied in it as a grown-up man, obviously assumes him to be viable. (10) Lit., 'that not as'. (11) Opp. to cattle where the period is only eight days. (12) Of doubtful premature birth. (13) Thirty days being a period that suffices to establish the viability of a child.

not lived so long he would have been a doubtful case?[1]—Here[2] we are dealing with the case of a child concerning whom it is established that the months of his pregnancy were duly fulfilled.[3]

MISHNAH. A GIRL OF THE AGE OF THREE YEARS AND ONE DAY MAY BE BETROTHED[4] BY INTERCOURSE; IF THE YABAM[5] HAD INTERCOURSE WITH HER, HE ACQUIRES HER THEREBY;[6] THE GUILT[7] OF ADULTERY[8] MAY BE INCURRED THROUGH HER,[9] AND SHE[10] CAUSES UNCLEANNESS TO THE MAN WHO HAD INTERCOURSE WITH HER SO THAT HE IN TURN CONVEYS UNCLEANNESS TO THAT UPON WHICH HE LIES,[11] AS TO A GARMENT WHICH HAS LAIN UPON [A ZAB].[12] IF SHE WAS MARRIED TO A PRIEST, SHE MAY EAT TERUMAH. IF ANY OF THE INELIGIBLE PERSONS[13] COHABITED WITH HER HE DISQUALIFIES HER FROM THE PRIESTHOOD.[14] IF ANY OF THE FORBIDDEN DEGREES ENUMERATED IN THE TORAH COHABITED WITH HER HE IS TO BE EXECUTED ON HER ACCOUNT, BUT SHE[15] IS EXEMPT [FROM THE PENALTY]. IF ONE WAS YOUNGER THAN THIS AGE INTERCOURSE WITH HER IS LIKE PUTTING A FINGER IN THE EYE.

GEMARA. Our Rabbis taught: A girl of the age of three years

(1) Now since according to our Mishnah a child may be regarded as viable on the first day of its life (cf. p. 307, n. 9) its view must differ from that of R. Simeon b. Gamaliel, must it not? (2) In our Mishnah. (3) Lit., 'whose months have ended'. The child's viability is beyond question even according to R. Simeon b. Gamaliel who (cf. p. 307, n. 12) referred only to a doubtful premature birth. (4) Subject to her father's approval. (5) The brother of her deceased childless husband, whose duty it is to contract the levirate marriage with her. (6) In consequence of which he gains possession of his deceased brother's estate, is entitled if she dies to inherit her own estate and even if he is a priest, he may defile himself to her as to a legally married wife. (7) Punishable by death. (8) Lit., 'on account of the wife of a man'. (9) If, for instance, her father betrothed her to one man and another cohabited with her. (10) When a menstruant. (11) Lit., 'lower couch'. (12) Lit., 'like the upper'. (13) A bastard or a slave, for instance. (14) *Sc.* if she was the daughter of a priest she loses the privilege of eating *terumah*. (15) Being a minor.

may be betrothed by intercourse; so R. Meir. But the Sages say: Only one who is three years and one day old. What is the practical difference between them?—The school of R. Jannai replied: The practical difference between them is the day preceding the first day of the fourth year.[1] R. Johanan, however, replied: The practical difference between them is the rule that thirty days of a year are counted as the full year.[2]

An objection was raised: A girl of the age of three years and even one of the age of two years and one day may be betrothed by intercourse; so R. Meir. But the Sages say: Only one who is three years and one day old. [45a] Now, all is well according to R. Johanan, for just as there is a Tanna[3] who holds[4] that one day of a year is counted as a year so there may also be a Tanna who holds[5] that thirty days of a year are counted as a full year; but, according to R. Jannai,[6] does not this[7] present a difficulty?—This is a difficulty.

IF ONE WAS YOUNGER THAN THIS AGE, INTERCOURSE WITH HER IS LIKE PUTTING A FINGER IN THE EYE. It was asked, Do the features of virginity[8] disappear[9] and reappear again[10] or is it possible that they cannot be completely destroyed until after the third year of her age? In what practical respect could this matter?—In one, for instance, where her husband had intercourse with her before the age of[11] three and found blood, and when he had intercourse after the age of three he found no blood. If you grant that they disappear and reappear again [it might well be

(1) Lit., 'the eve of the beginning of the year'. According to R. Meir she attains the prescribed age on that day while according to the Rabbis she does not attain it until the following day. (2) According to R. Meir the prescribed age is attained as soon as thirty days of the third year have passed, while according to the Rabbis it is not attained until the first day of the fourth year. (3) In the Baraitha just cited. (4) As evidenced by his ruling, 'Even one of the age of two years and one day'. (5) As R. Johanan submitted *supra* according to R. Meir. (6) *Sc.* the school of R. Jannai who submitted *supra* that even R. Meir does not regard the part of the third year as a full year. (7) Cf. prev. n. but two. (8) Of one under three years of age. (9) As a result of intercourse. (10) Lit., 'going do they go and come'. (11) Lit., 'within'.

assumed][1] that[2] there was not sufficient time for their reappearance, but if you maintain that they cannot be destroyed until after the age of three years it would be obvious that[3] a stranger cohabited with her.[4] Now what is your decision?—R. Ḥiyya son of R. Iḳa demurred: But who can tell us that a wound inflicted within the three years is not healed[5] forthwith, seeing it is possible that it is immediately healed and it would thus be obvious[3] that a stranger had cohabited with her?[4] Rather the practical difference is the case, for instance, where her husband had intercourse with her while she was under[6] three years of age and found blood and when he had intercourse after the age of three he also found blood. If you grant that the features disappear and reappear again the blood might well be treated as that of virginity, but if you maintain that they cannot be destroyed until after the age of three years, that[7] must be the blood of menstruation. Now what is your decision?—R. Ḥisda replied, Come and hear: IF ONE WAS YOUNGER THAN THIS AGE, INTERCOURSE WITH HER IS LIKE PUTTING A FINGER IN THE EYE; what need was there to state, 'LIKE PUTTING A FINGER IN THE EYE' instead of merely saying: 'IF ONE WAS YOUNGER THAN THIS AGE, INTERCOURSE WITH HER IS of no consequence'? Does not this then teach us that as the eye tears and tears again so do the features of virginity disappear and reappear again.

Our Rabbis taught: It is related of Justinia[8] the daughter of 'Aseverus son of Antonius that she once appeared before Rabbi 'Master', she said to him, 'at what age may a woman marry?'. 'At the age of three years and one day', he told her. 'And at what age is she capable of conception?' 'At the age of twelve years and one day', he replied. 'I', she said to him, 'married at the age of six and bore a child at the age of seven; alas for the three years

(1) As a reason for the absence of blood. (2) Owing to his continued intercourse. (3) Lit., 'surely', since the husband found no traces of bleeding. (4) After she had attained the age of three. She would consequently be subjected to the disqualifications of a harlot. (5) Lit., 'returns'. (6) Lit., 'within'. (7) The blood found while she was under three. (8) For a different reading and a biographical note v. Golds.

that I have lost at my father's house'. But can a woman conceive at the age of six years? Did not R. Bibi recite in the presence of R. Nahman: Three classes of woman may use an absorbent[1] in their marital intercourse:[2] A minor, and an expectant and a nursing mother. The minor,[3] because otherwise she might become pregnant and die. An expectant mother,[3] because otherwise she might cause her foetus to degenerate into a *sandal*.[4] A nursing mother,[3] because otherwise she might have to wean her child prematurely,[5] and this would result in his death. And what is the age of such a 'minor'?[6] From the age of eleven years and one day to the age of twelve years and one day. One who is under[7] or over this age[8] must carry on her marital intercourse in a normal manner; so R. Meir. But the Sages ruled: The one as well as the other carries on her marital intercourse in a normal manner and mercy[9] will be vouchsafed from heaven, for it is said in Scripture, *The Lord preserveth the simple?*[10]—If you wish I might reply: *Whose flesh is as the flesh of asses.*[11] And if you prefer I might reply: *Whose mouth speaketh falsehood, and their right hand is a right hand of lying.*[12]

Our Rabbis taught: A story is told of a certain woman who came before R. Akiba and said to him, 'Master, intercourse has been forced upon me[13] when I was under[14] three years of age; what is my position towards the priesthood?'[15] 'You are fit for the priesthood',[16] he replied. 'Master', she continued, 'I will give you a comparison; to what may the incident be compared? To a babe

(1) *Muk*, flax or hackled wool. (2) To avoid conception. (3) Is permitted the use of the absorbent. (4) A fish-shaped abortion. Lit., 'flat-fish'. (5) On account of her second conception which causes the deterioration of her breast milk. (6) Of whom it has been said that she is capable of conception but is thereby exposed to fatal consequences. (7) When conception is impossible. (8) When conception involves no danger. (9) To protect them from harm. (10) Ps. CXVI, 6; *sc.* those who are unable to protect themselves. At any rate it was here stated that a minor under eleven years of age is incapable of conception. How then is Justinia's story to be reconciled with this statement? (11) Ezek. XXIII, 20. (12) Ps. CXLIV, 8. (13) By a disqualified person. (14) Lit., 'within'. (15) *Sc.* is she permitted to marry a priest? (16) Cf. prev. n.

whose finger was submerged[1] in honey. The first time and the second time he cries about it, but the third time he sucks it'.[2] 'If so', he replied, 'you are unfit for the priesthood'.[3] Observing that the students were looking at each other,[4] he said to them, 'Why do you find the ruling difficult?'[5] 'Because', they replied, 'as all the Torah is a tradition that was handed to Moses at Sinai so is the law that a girl under the age of three years[6] is fit for the priesthood one that was handed to Moses at Sinai'. R. Akiba too made his statement[7] only for the purpose of exercising the wits of[8] the students.[9]

MISHNAH. IF A BOY OF THE AGE OF NINE YEARS AND ONE DAY COHABITED WITH HIS CHILDLESS BROTHER'S WIDOW, HE[10] ACQUIRES HER THEREBY,[11] BUT[12] HE CANNOT DIVORCE HER UNTIL HE ATTAINS HIS MAJORITY. HE CONTRACTS UNCLEANNESS THROUGH INTERCOURSE WITH A MENSTRUANT AND HE IN TURN CONVEYS THE SAME DEGREE OF UNCLEANNESS TO THAT UPON WHICH HE LIES AS [DOES A ZAB] TO THAT WHICH HAS LAIN UPON HIM.[13] HE[14] DISQUALIFIES A WOMAN FROM THE PRIESTHOOD,[15] BUT[16] CANNOT CONFER UPON ONE[17] THE RIGHT TO EAT TERUMAH.[18] HE RENDERS A BEAST[19] INVALID FOR THE ALTAR, AND IT IS STONED ON HIS

(1) Lit., 'they hid for him'. (2) *Sc.* he ultimately enjoyed the experience. (3) Cf. prev. n. (4) Amazed or perplexed. (5) Lit., 'why is the thing difficult in your eyes'. (6) Who had intercourse. (7) 'If so, you are unfit etc.' (8) Lit., 'to sharpen'. (9) By affording them the opportunity of questioning his ruling. (10) Since his marriage with the widow is Pentateuchally ordained. (11) And in consequence gains possession of his deceased brother's estate, though elsewhere a minor cannot acquire possession. (12) Since his deceased brother's marriage was fully valid and his own bond with the widow is consequently equally valid, while his divorce, being merely that of a minor, has no validity. (13) Lit., 'the lower couch as the upper'. (14) If he is a disqualified person, a bastard, for instance, or a slave. (15) If she was the daughter of a priest she loses her right to the eating of *terumah*. (16) Though a priest. (17) If, for instance, he had intercourse with his childless brother's widow. (18) Though he acquires her as his wife. (19) If he covered it, though his act was seen by one witness only.

ACCOUNT.[1] IF HE HAD INTERCOURSE WITH ANY OF THE FORBIDDEN DEGREES THAT ARE ENUMERATED IN THE TORAH, SHE IS TO BE EXECUTED ON HIS ACCOUNT, THOUGH HE[2] IS EXEMPT FROM PUNISHMENT.

GEMARA. But when HE ATTAINS HIS MAJORITY, is[3] a divorce alone sufficient? Was it not taught: The cohabitation of a boy of nine years[4] of age was given the same validity as that of a *ma'amar*[5] by an adult; as a *ma'amar* by an adult requires[6] a divorce in respect of his *ma'amar* and *ḥaliẓah* in respect of his marital bond so does the cohabitation of a boy of nine years of age[4] require[6] a divorce in respect of his *ma'amar*[7] and *ḥaliẓah* in respect of his marital bond?[8] —Rab replied: It is this that was meant:[9] [45*b*] when HE ATTAINS HIS MAJORITY he shall cohabit with her[10] and give her a divorce.[11]

MISHNAH. THE VOWS OF A GIRL OF THE AGE OF ELEVEN YEARS AND ONE DAY MUST BE EXAMINED;[12] THE VOWS OF ONE WHO IS OF THE AGE OF TWELVE YEARS AND ONE DAY ARE VALID;[13] AND THROUGHOUT THE TWELFTH YEAR THEY ARE TO BE EXAMINED.[12] THE VOWS OF A BOY OF THE AGE OF TWELVE YEARS AND ONE DAY MUST BE EXAMINED;[14] THE VOWS OF ONE WHO IS OF THE AGE OF THIRTEEN YEARS AND ONE DAY ARE VALID; AND THROUGHOUT THE THIRTEENTH YEAR THEY ARE TO BE EXAMINED.[14] PRIOR TO THIS AGE,[15] EVEN THOUGH THEY SAID, 'WE KNOW IN HONOUR OF WHOSE

(1) If his act (cf. prev. n.) was observed by two witnesses. (2) On account of his minority. (3) As our Mishnah seems to imply. (4) And one day. (5) V. Glos. (6) If the parties have agreed upon a divorce. (7) Which corresponds to intercourse which is another form of *ḳinyan* (v. Glos.) Alfasi reads: in respect of his intercourse. (8) How then could it be ruled here that a divorce alone suffices? (9) By our Mishnah. (10) Thus, being of age, affecting valid *ḳinyan* of marriage. (11) Being now in all respects her lawful husband, *ḥaliẓah* is no longer necessary. (12) To ascertain whether the girl was aware of their significance. (13) No examination being necessary. (14) Cf. prev. n. but one, *mut. mut.* (15) The first day of the twelfth year in the case of a girl and the first day of the thirteenth year in that of a boy.

NAME WE HAVE MADE OUR VOW' OR 'IN HONOUR OF WHOSE NAME WE HAVE MADE OUR DEDICATION', THEIR VOW[1] IS NO VALID VOW AND THEIR DEDICATION IS NO VALID DEDICATION. SUBSEQUENT TO THIS AGE,[2] EVEN THOUGH THEY SAID, 'WE DO NOT KNOW IN THE HONOUR OF WHOSE NAME WE HAVE MADE OUR VOW' OR 'IN HONOUR OF WHOSE NAME WE HAVE MADE OUR DEDICATION', THEIR VOW IS A VALID VOW AND THEIR DEDICATION IS A VALID DEDICATION.

GEMARA. But since it was stated, THE VOWS OF A GIRL OF THE AGE OF ELEVEN YEARS AND ONE DAY MUST BE EXAMINED,[1] what need was there for stating, THE VOWS OF ONE WHO IS OF THE AGE OF TWELVE YEARS AND ONE DAY ARE VALID?— It might have been presumed that henceforth they must always be examined,[4] hence we were informed that after the age of twelve years and a day the vows are invariably valid. But since it was stated, THE VOWS OF ONE WHO IS OF THE AGE OF TWELVE YEARS AND ONE DAY ARE VALID,[5] what need was there for stating, AND THROUGHOUT THE TWELFTH YEAR THEY ARE TO BE EXAMINED?[6]—It might have been presumed that, since a Master has laid down that 'Thirty days of a year are counted as a full year', where we examined her vows during a period of thirty days[7] and she knew not how to express their significance,[8] no further examinations[9] should be held[10] hence we were informed that her vows are to be examined all through the twelfth year.

(1) Since they are still minors. (2) Twelve years and a day in the case of a girl and thirteen years and a day in that of a boy when they respectively attain their majority. (3) From which it might well be inferred that at a later age her vows are valid and no examination is necessary. (4) And that the age of eleven years and one day is only the limit below which even an examination does not establish the validity of a vow. (5) And it has previously been stated that from the age of eleven years and one day vows must be examined. (6) A ruling which evidently follows (cf. prev. n.) from the previous statements. (7) The first of the twelfth year. (8) Thus revealing her mental incapacity. (9) During the remaining months of that year. (10) On the assumption that the examinations during the thirty days have established for the rest of that year that her mental state was that of a minor.

Then let the last two cases be stated, THE VOWS OF ONE WHO IS OF THE AGE OF TWELVE YEARS AND ONE DAY ARE VALID, AND THROUGHOUT THE TWELFTH YEAR THEY ARE TO BE EXAMINED, but[1] what was the need for the statement, THE VOWS OF A GIRL OF THE AGE OF ELEVEN YEARS AND ONE DAY MUST BE EXAMINED?—It was required: Since it might have been suggested that as a rule examination was necessary in the twelfth year and unnecessary in the eleventh year, but that where we see that the girl is particularly bright she might also be examined in the eleventh year,[2] we were informed that the period of examination invariably begins at the age of eleven years and one day. What was the need[3] for stating, PRIOR TO THIS AGE and SUBSEQUENT TO THIS AGE?—It might have been presumed that the previous rulings[4] applied only where the children themselves spontaneously say nothing[5] but that where they do assert spontaneous opinion[6] we may rely upon them, hence we were informed that even their own assertions do not affect the age limits.

Our Rabbis taught: These[7] are the rulings of Rabbi. R. Simeon b. Eleazar stated, The age limits that were assigned to the girl apply to the boy while those assigned to the boy apply to the girl.[8] R. Ḥisda stated: What is Rabbi's reason? Because it is written in Scripture, *And the Lord God built*[9] *the rib*[10] which teaches that the Holy One, blessed be He, endowed the woman with more understanding[11] than the man. And the other?[12]—He requires that text[9] for the same deduction as the one made by Resh Laḳish, for Resh Laḳish citing R. Simeon b. Menasya stated, *And the*

(1) In view of the explicit statement that examinations are conducted throughout the twelfth year. (2) And if she shows sufficient mental development her vows are valid even at that early age. (3) In view of the earlier statements. (4) On the limits of minority and majority. (5) *Sc.* they do not claim 'we know' when they are under the age limit or 'we do not know' when they are above the limit. (6) Cf. prev. n. *mut. mut.* (7) The statements on the respective age limits of a boy and a girl, according to which the latter matures earlier than the former. (8) The boy, in his opinion, maturing earlier. (9) *Wa-yiben.* (10) Gen. II, 22. E.V., *And the rib . . . made He.* (11) *Binah,* of a root that is analogous to that of *wa-yiben* (prev. n. but one). (12) R. Simeon b. Eleazar; how in view of this deduction can he maintain his view?

Lord God built the rib which he took from the man into a woman, and he brought her unto the man,[1] teaches that the Holy One, blessed be He, plaited Eve's hair and then brought her to Adam, for in the sea-towns they describe net-work as *binyatha*.[2] But what is R. Simeon b. Eleazar's reason?—R. Samuel son of R. Isaac replied: As a boy frequents the house of his teacher his subtlety[3] develops earlier.[4]

It was asked: Is the intervening period[5] regarded as that of under, or of over age?[6]—In respect of what law could this matter: If in that of vows, it is neither regarded as that of under age nor as that of over age?[7]—Rather in respect of punishments.[8] Now what is the ruling?—Both Rab and R. Ḥanina replied: The intervening period is regarded as that of under age.[9] Both R. Joḥanan and R. Joshua b. Levi replied: The intervening period is regarded as that of over age. Said R. Naḥman b. Isaac: Your mnemonic[10] is: *Now this was the custom in former time in Israel.*[11]

R. Hamnuna raised an objection:[12] SUBSEQUENT TO THIS AGE, EVEN THOUGH THEY SAID, 'WE DO NOT KNOW IN HONOUR OF WHOSE NAME WE HAVE MADE OUR VOW' OR 'IN HONOUR OF WHOSE NAME WE HAVE MADE OUR DEDICATION' THEIR VOW IS A VALID VOW AND THEIR DEDICATION IS A VALID DEDICATION. Thus[13] it follows, does it not, that the intervening period is regarded as that of under age?—Said Raba to him, Read then the first clause: PRIOR TO THIS AGE, EVEN THOUGH

(1) Gen. II, 22. E.V., *And the rib . . . made He.* (2) 'Building'. (3) Or 'shrewdness'. (4) Lit., 'enters into him first'. (5) From the age of eleven years and a day to that of twelve years and a day and from twelve years and a day to thirteen years and a day in the case of a girl and a boy respectively. (6) Lit., 'as before time or as after time'. (7) As stated *supra*. (8) And in the case where the boy or the girl had grown two pubic hairs. In the absence of these, even one of age is exempt from punishments. (9) And exempt from punishment. (10) An aid to the recollection of the respective authorship of the two views just expressed. (11) R. Joshua b. Levi was a Levite, whilst Rab and R. Ḥanina were Israelites; and those who were '*in Israel*' (Israelites) gave '*former time*' which recalls 'before time' ('under age') as their ruling (Tosaf. Asheri). (12) Against R. Joḥanan and R. Joshua b. Levi. (13) Emphasizing SUBSEQUENT.

THEY SAID, 'WE KNEW IN HONOUR OF WHOSE NAME WE HAVE MADE OUR VOW' OR 'IN HONOUR OF WHOSE NAME WE HAVE MADE OUR DEDICATION', THEIR VOW IS NO VALID VOW AND THEIR DEDICATION IS NO VALID DEDICATION. Thus[1] it follows, does it not, that the intervening period is regarded as that of over age?—This, however, is no argument, Raba having laboured under a misapprehension. He thought that R. Hamnuna drew his inference from a Mishnah redundancy,[2] [hence he argued that] instead of drawing an inference from the final clause he might as well have drawn one from the first clause; but this was not the case. R. Hamnuna in fact drew his inference from the very wording[3] of our Mishnah. How [he reasoned] is one to understand the expression of 'SUBSEQUENT TO THAT AGE'? If by that time one had not yet grown two hairs, one would, surely, still be a minor.[4] Consequently it must refer to one who had grown two hairs, [46a] the reason for the ruling[5] being that one was over age, when all requirements[6] were satisfied.[7] Thus it follows, does it not, that the intervening period[8] is regarded as that of under age?[9] A further objection was [also] raised by R. Zera: *When... man... shall clearly utter a vow, the vow of...*[10] What was the purpose of stating *'man'?* To include in the scope of the law a boy of the age of thirteen years and one day whose vows are valid, though he is unable to 'utter clearly'. Now how is this to be understood? If it be suggested that the reference is to a boy who had not yet grown two hairs, [the objection could be raised:] Such a boy would still have the status of a minor.[11] The reference consequently must be to one who had grown two hairs, the reason being that he is thirteen years and one day old, when he is regarded as a *'man'*. Thus[12] it

(1) Emphasis on PRIOR. (2) *Sc.* the apparent superfluity of the rulings PRIOR TO THIS AGE etc. and SUBSEQUENT TO etc. discussed and explained *supra.* (3) Lit., 'from the body'. (4) How then could it be ruled, THEIR VOW IS VALID etc. (5) Cf. prev. n. (6) Age and external marks of puberty. (7) Lit., 'when the thing was completed'. (8) When the prescribed age limit had not yet been reached. (9) An objection against R. Johanan, and R. Joshua b. Levi. (10) Num. VI, 2. (11) How then could his vow be valid? (12) Since the law is applicable only to one who is above the age of thirteen years and a day.

follows, does it not, that the intervening period is regarded as that of under age?[1]—This is indeed a refutation.

R. Naḥman stated, The question[2] is a point at issue between Tannas:[3] [For it was taught:] If a boy of the age of seven years grew two hairs they are attributed to a mole;[4] from the age of nine years to that of twelve years and one day they are also to be attributed to a mole,[4] but R. Jose son of R. Judah ruled: They[5] are a sign of puberty; at the age of thirteen years and one day, all agree that they are a sign of puberty.[6] Now is not this self-contradictory: You said, 'From the age of nine years to that of twelve years and one day they are also to be attributed to a mole', from which it follows that at the actual age of thirteen years they are a sign of puberty; but then it is stated, 'At the age of thirteen years and one day . . . they are a sign of puberty', from which it follows, does it not, that at the actual age of thirteen years they are to be attributed to a mole? Must you not concede then that this question[7] is a point at issue between the Tannas, one Master[8] holding that the intervening period is regarded as that of over age while the other Master maintains that the intervening period is regarded as that of under age?[9]—No; all may agree that the intervening period is regarded as that under age, but both clauses refer to a girl the first[10] supporting the view of Rabbi[11] while the latter[12] represents that of R. Simeon b. Eleazar.[13] And if you prefer I[14] might reply: Both clauses refer to a boy, and the first represents the view of R. Simeon b. Eleazar while the latter represents the

(1) An objection against R. Joḥanan, and R. Joshua b. Levi. (2) To which age the intervening period belongs. (3) Lit., 'as Tannas'. (4) From which hair grows; and they are, therefore, no evidence of puberty. (5) In the latter case, from nine years to twelve years and a day. (6) Ḳid. 16*b*. (7) To which age the intervening period belongs. (8) The first Tanna. (9) Which proves R. Naḥman's contention. (10) According to which the growth of the hairs at the age of thirteen years is sufficient evidence. (11) Who stated *supra* that in the case of a girl the age of thirteen years is regarded as over the prescribed age. (12) From which it is inferred that the growth of hairs at the age of thirteen is attributed to a mole. (13) Who, as stated *supra*, regards a girl at the age of thirteen years as being under the age prescribed. (14) Still maintaining that the intervening period is regarded as that of under age.

view of Rabbi.[1] And if you prefer I[2] might reply: Both clauses are the view of Rabbi, but one[3] refers to a boy while the other[4] refers to a girl. And if you prefer I[2] might say: Both clauses are the view of R. Simeon b. Eleazar, but the one[4] refers to a boy while the other[3] refers to a girl.

'R. Jose son of R. Judah ruled: They are a sign of puberty.' R. Keruspedai son of R. Shabbethai explained: This applies only where they[5] are still on him.[6] So it was also taught: If a boy of the age of nine years and one day had grown two hairs they are to be attributed to a mole; from the age of nine years to that of twelve years and one day, though the hairs are still on him, they are to be attributed to a mole. R. Jose son of R. Judah ruled: They are a sign of puberty.

Raba stated: The law is that the intervening period is regarded as that of under age. R. Samuel b. Zuṭra taught Raba's tradition in the following form:[7] Raba stated, A minor all through her twelfth year may make a declaration of *mi'un*[8] and go away,[9] but from that age upwards she may not make a declaration of *mi'un*[10] but[11] she may not submit to *ḥaliẓah*.[12] Is not this statement, however, self-contradictory? You said, 'she may not make a declaration of *mi'un*' from which it is evident that[13] she is regarded as one of age; but if she is of age why may she not submit to *ḥaliẓah?* And were you to reply that he[14] was in doubt,[15] [it could be retorted:]

(1) V. *supra* 45*b*. (2) Still maintaining that the intervening period is regarded as that of under age. (3) The last clause. (4) The first clause. (5) The two hairs. (6) When he attained his majority. If by that time they have fallen off it is obvious that their growth was merely due to a mole. (7) From which also it may be inferred that the intervening period is regarded as that of under age. (8) V. Glos. (9) And there is no need to consider the possibility that she may have grown two hairs. If any hairs had grown they must be attributed to a mole. It thus follows that the intervening period is regarded as that of under age. (10) Since at this age the possibility must be considered that she may have grown two hairs. (11) If her husband died childless. (12) Because her majority is not yet established. (13) If she has grown two hairs. (14) Raba. (15) Whether a girl at such an age had, or had not grown pubic hairs; and consequently he forbade *mi'un* in case she was already of age and forbade *ḥaliẓah* in case she was still a minor.

Was he in doubt? Did not Raba in fact rule: A minor on attaining the age of majority need not be examined[1] since there is presumption that she has grown the signs of puberty?—This[2] applies only to general cases, but not here where an examination was held and no hairs were found. If so,[3] why should she not be allowed to make a declaration of *mi'un?*—The possibility is taken into consideration that they might have fallen off. This would be a satisfactory explanation according to him who holds that such a possibility is taken into consideration, but what explanation can be offered according to him who holds that such a possibility need not be taken into consideration? Was it not stated: R. Kahana[4] ruled, There is no need to consider the possibility that they may have fallen off and R. Papi ruled, The possibility must be considered?—This[5] applies only to the matter of *ḥaliẓah*,[6] but as regards *mi'un* the possibility is taken into consideration.[7] Thus it follows that according to him who holds that the possibility[8] is taken into consideration she may submit to *ḥaliẓah;* but [it may be objected:] Did he not merely say that the possibility[9] is taken into consideration?[10]—The fact is that this[11] is a case where she was not examined,[12] but the possibility[13] is taken into consideration as regards *ḥaliẓah*,[14] and when Raba stated 'There is presumption' he meant it in regard to *mi'un*,[15] but in regard to *ḥaliẓah*[16] an exami-

(1) For the presence of hairs. (2) Raba's ruling just cited. (3) That an examination has established the absence of hairs. (4) So MS.M. and marg. gl. Cur. edd. 'Papa'. (5) That where no hairs were found there is no need to consider the possibility that they may have fallen off. (6) Since by forbidding it the law is thereby restricted. (7) And *mi'un* is, therefore, forbidden and (cf. prev. n. *mut. mut.*) only a proper divorce can dissolve the marriage. (8) That the hairs may have fallen off. (9) Emphasis on this word. (10) Of course he said. How then can he allow *ḥaliẓah* when the question of majority is still a matter of doubt? (11) Raba's ruling just cited. (12) And as she has attained the age of majority, when she might be presumed to have grown pubic hairs, she must be forbidden *mi'un* and subjected to the restrictions of divorce. (13) That she never grew pubic hairs. (14) And he cannot submit to *ḥaliẓah* in order to be exempt from divorce. Since the law must always be restricted. (15) Cf. prev. n. but two. (16) *Sc.* to allow her to submit to *ḥaliẓah* and be exempt from divorce (cf. prev. n. but one).

nation[1] is a pre-requisite. R. Dimi of Nehardea stated: The law is that the possibility that the hairs may have fallen off is taken into consideration.[2] This,[3] however, applies only where one had betrothed her[4] during the intervening period and cohabited after that period, since a Pentateuchal doubt is thereby involved,[5] but not to the original betrothal alone.[6]

R. Huna ruled: If [a child][7] dedicated some food and then ate it, he[8] is subject to flogging, for it is said in Scripture, *When ... man ... shall clearly utter a vow,*[9] and *He shall not break his word,*[10] which[11] implies that whosoever is able to 'utter clearly'[12] is subject to the prohibition of '*he shall not break his word*'[13] and only he who is not able to 'utter clearly' is not subject to the injunction of '*he shall not break his word*'. R. Huna b. Judah addressed an objection to[14] Raba[15] in support of R. Huna: [46b] Since we find that Scripture has put a minor on a par with an adult[16] as regards a pre-

(1) To establish the presence of hair. (2) Once she has attained the age of majority, though on examination no hairs are found, she may no longer exercise the right of *mi'un*. (3) Cf. prev. n. (4) With the approval of her mother or brothers. (5) Cohabitation, which is a Pentateuchal form of 'acquisition' in marriage, having taken place at an age when she may well be presumed to have attained her majority. (6) That was not followed by cohabitation after the age of majority had been attained. As the betrothal of a minor (if it was not effected through her father) has only Rabbinical sanction, the Rabbis did not insist on the restrictions of a divorce where her majority was in doubt. Where, however, hairs have grown, though betrothal took place during her minority, the Rabbis forbade *mi'un* and insisted on the restrictions of a divorce as a preventive measure against the possibility of allowing *mi'un* to one with whom cohabitation took place after majority had been attained. (7) Who understands the significance of dedications and vows. (8) Though exempt from penalties in other cases. (9) Num. VI, 2, from which it is deduced that a minor approaching manhood (or womanhood), viz., a boy in his thirteenth year (or a girl in her twelfth), provided he (or she) understands the significance of vows and dedications, is regarded as a man (or woman). (10) Num. XXX, 3. (11) By analogy. (12) *Sc.* understands the significance of vows. (13) A negative precept punishable by flogging. (14) Not 'against'. (15) MS.M. and Maharsha delete the last two words the Heb. for which in cur. edd. is enclosed in parenthesis. [The objection is against those who hold *infra* that others who ate it are subject to flagellation but not the child. V. Maharsha]. (16) Cf. *supra* n. 9.

sumptuous oath, a self-imposed prohibition[1] and [the injunction] not to break his word, it might have been presumed that he should also incur the liability of a sacrifice for eating that which he had dedicated, hence it was explicitly stated,[2] *This is the thing.*[3] At any rate, was it not here stated that guilt was incurred for infringing a self-imposed prohibition or [the injunction] not to break one's word?[4]—Read: The prohibition[5] not to break his word.[6] [You say,] 'The prohibition not to break his word'! Whatever your assumption may be [a difficulty arises]. If an intelligent minor[7] approaching manhood is Pentateuchally forbidden to break his word, he should also incur the penalty of flogging;[8] and if an intelligent minor approaching manhood is not Pentateuchally forbidden to do it, there should not be[9] even a mere prohibition?[10]—The prohibition[11] applies to those who are responsible for him.[12] May it then be inferred from this ruling[13] that if a minor eats *nebelah*[14] it is the duty of Beth din to take it away from him?[15]—Here we may be dealing with a case, for instance, where the minor dedicated the food and others[16] ate it.[17] This explanation is quite satisfactory according to him who laid down that if a minor dedicated some food and others[16] ate it the latter are to be flogged, but what can be said in explanation according to

(1) V. Num. XXX, 3. (2) In the same context as the oath and a self-imposed prohibition. (3) Num. XXX, 2, emphasis on '*this*', *sc.* but no other. (4) Evidently it was; but since such a negative precept is punishable by flogging, R. Huna's ruling evidently finds support in the citation. (5) *Issur* instead of *issar* ('bond', self-imposed prohibition). (6) Without incurring a flogging. (7) *Sc.* one understanding the significance of vows and dedications. (8) As in the case of all Pentateuchal prohibitions. (9) Since the Rabbis do not subject minors to preventive measures. (10) *Issur* (cf. prev. n. but three). (11) Spoken of *supra*, which is in fact only Rabbinical. (12) Not to the minor himself (cf. prev. n. but two). (13) According to which those responsible for a minor must prevent him from encroaching even on that which is only Rabbinically forbidden. (14) Symbolic of any religious transgression. (15) But if so why (cf. Yeb. 114*a*) was there a divergence of view on this question? (16) Adults. (17) The original reading, 'prohibition and [the injunction] not to break', may, therefore, be retained and yet no support would be forthcoming for R. Huna since the penalty of flogging does not apply to the minor but to the adults who ate that which he has dedicated.

him who ruled that they were not to be flogged; for it was stated: If a minor dedicated some food and others ate it, R. Kahana ruled, They are not to be flogged, while both R. Joḥanan and Resh Laḳish ruled, They are to be flogged?—The prohibition[1] is[2] merely Rabbinical[3] and the Scriptural text[4] serves as a mere prop.

[Reverting to] the above text, 'If a minor dedicated some food and others ate it, R. Kahana ruled, They are not to be flogged, while both R. Joḥanan and Resh Laḳish ruled, They are to be flogged'. On what principle do they differ?—The Masters[5] are of the opinion that an intelligent minor approaching manhood is under a Pentateuchal obligation[6] while the Master[7] is of the opinion that an intelligent minor approaching manhood is only under a Rabbinical obligation.[6] R. Jeremiah raised an objection: If a fatherless girl[8] made a vow, her husband may disallow it for her. Now if you grant that an intelligent minor approaching manhood is only under a Rabbinical obligation[6] one can well justify the ruling,[9] since the force of a Rabbinical marriage[10] may well annul a Rabbinical vow, but if you maintain that the obligation[6] is Pentateuchal, could [it may be objected] the force of a Rabbinical marriage[11] annul a Pentateuchal vow?—R. Judah citing Samuel replied: Her husband may disallow her vow for her whatever your assumption might be. If the minor's obligation[6] is Rabbinical, the whole matter is a Rabbinical affair; and if the obligation is Pentateuchal, it is a case of a minor who eats *nebelah*[12] where it is not the duty of the Beth din to take it away from him. But would she not be eating, in reliance upon the first disallowance,[13] even when she attains her majority?[14]—Rabbah b. Liwai replied: Her husband disallows her

(1) *Sc.* 'the prohibition not to break his vow'. (2) According to R. Kahana. (3) As was first suggested *supra*. (4) From which deduction was made *supra* 46a *ad fin*. (5) R. Joḥanan and Resh Laḳish. (6) To observe the laws of vows and dedications. (7) R. Kahana. (8) A minor whose marriage was contracted by her mother or brothers. (9) The husband's right by virtue of his marriage with the minor (cf. prev. n.) to disallow her vows. (10) The marriage of a minor contracted in the absence of her father has only Rabbinical sanction. (11) Cf. prev. n. (12) Cf. *supra* p. 322, n. 14. (13) Which has only Rabbinical validity. (14) When she is subject to Pentateuchal prohibitions.

vow for her every now and then.[1] This,[2] however, applies only to one who cohabited with her.[3] But, surely, no husband may disallow vows made prior to marriage?[4]—This[5] is in agreement with R. Phinehas who cited Raba,[6] for R. Phinehas citing Raba stated: Any woman who vows acts in reliance on the opinion of her husband.[7]

Said Abaye, Come and hear: If a minor has not yet grown two hairs, R. Judah ruled, his *terumah* is not[8] valid; while R. Jose ruled, Before reaching the age when his vows are valid[9] his *terumah* is not valid, but after reaching the age when his vows are valid[10] his *terumah* is valid.[11] Assuming[12] that R. Jose is of the opinion that *terumah* at the present time is a Pentateuchal institution, his ruling would be well justified if you grant that an intelligent minor approaching manhood is under a Pentateuchal obligation,[13] since a man under a Pentateuchal obligation may well render fit[14] Pentateuchal *ṭebel*,[15] but if you maintain that he is only under a Rabbinical obligation,[16] could a man under a Rabbinical obligation render fit

(1) Even after she has attained her majority. (2) That the disallowance has Pentateuchal force. (3) After she had attained majority. Cohabitation at that age having the Pentateuchal force of 'acquisition' the marriage which thus has Pentateuchal sanction may well enable the husband to disallow a vow that has Pentateuchal sanction. (4) How then can he disallow here a vow that was made by a minor before her subsequent Pentateuchally valid marriage? (5) The ruling that the husband may disallow the minor's vow though when she comes of age her vow would assume Pentateuchal validity. (6) *Sc.* there is no need to explain, as presumably suggested, that the husband 'disallows the vow every now and then', for even though he only disallowed it during her minority, there is no need to disallow it again when she attains her majority. (7) As the minor was at least Rabbinically married when her vow was made, its validity is entirely dependent on her husband's pleasure. Only where a woman was not married at all at the time her vow was made is her subsequently married husband precluded from disallowing it. (8) In the separate edd. of the Mishnah this word is missing. (9) V. foll. n. (10) *Sc.* an intelligent minor approaching manhood whose vows are to be examined. (11) Ter. I, 3. (12) Lit., 'they (the Rabbis of the college) thought'. (13) In regard to his vows and dedications and consequently also in regard to his *terumah*. (14) By separating *terumah* from it. (15) *Sc.* produce the separation of *terumah* from which is Pentateuchally ordained, v. Glos. (16) As R. Kahana maintains.

Pentateuchal *ṭebel?*[1]—No, R. Jose is of the opinion that *terumah* at the present time is only a Rabbinical institution. But does R. Jose hold that *terumah* at the present time is only Rabbinical? Was it not in fact taught in Seder Olam:[2] *'Which thy fathers possessed and thou shalt possess it,*[3] they had a first,[4] and a second[5] possession[6] but they had no need for a third one';[7] and R. Joḥanan stated, 'Who is the author of Seder Olam? R. Jose?'[8]—R. Jose may well be its compiler[9] but he himself does not uphold this view.[10] This[11] may also be supported by a process of reasoning. For it was taught: A dough[12] that had become subject to the restrictions of *terumah*[13] or became sour through a leaven of *terumah*, [47a] is subject to the obligation of the dough-offering[14] and[15] does not become unfit through contact with a *ṭebul yom;*[16] so R. Meir and R. Judah, but R. Jose and R. Simeon exempt it from the obligation of the dough-offering. Assuming[17] that he who holds that the institution of *terumah*[18] is Pentateuchal also holds that of the dough-offering[18] to be Pentateuchal and that he who holds that *terumah*[18] is Rabbinical also holds the dough-offering[18] to be Rabbinical, the

(1) An objection against R. Kahana. (2) 'Order of the World', a chronological compilation by R. Jose b. Ḥalafta in the first half of the second century. (3) Deut. XXX, 5, repetition of the verb 'to possess'. (4) After the conquest of Joshua. (5) In the days of Ezra. (6) *Sc.* the sanctity of the Land of Israel having ceased with the destruction of the first Temple and the Babylonian exile, a second 'possession' (*sc.* sanctification) was necessary. (7) Since the second sanctification (as the Scriptural text implies) remained for all time. As the land remained sacred the Pentateuchal obligation of *terumah* also obviously remained in force. (8) How then (cf. prev. n.) could it be maintained here that R. Jose holds the institution of *terumah* at the present time to be merely Rabbinical? (9) Lit., 'taught it'. (10) That the second sanctification remained for all time. He may well be of the opinion that it ceased with the destruction of the second Temple and the Roman exile and that *terumah* at the present time is merely a Rabbinical institution. (11) Cf. prev. n. (12) Ordinary and unconsecrated. (13) Where for instance, some *terumah* fell into a dough that was less than a hundred times the quantity of the former. Rabbinically, *terumah* cannot be neutralized unless it was mixed up with unconsecrated commodities that exceeded its quantity a hundredfold. (14) Though *terumah* proper is exempt. (15) Cf. prev. n. *mut. mut.* (16) V. Glos. (17) Lit., 'they thought' (cf. *supra* p. 324, n. 12). (18) At the present time.

ruling would be well justified if you grant that R. Jose[1] is of the opinion that the dough-offering at the present time is only Rabbinical, since the Rabbinic law which subjects the dough to the restrictions of *terumah* may well override the Rabbinical law of the dough-offering, but if you maintain that the institution of the dough-offering[2] is Pentateuchal,[3] could the Rabbinic law which subjects the dough to the restrictions of *terumah* override the institution of the dough-offering which is Pentateuchal?[4]—But is it not possible that R. Jose holds that *terumah* at the present time is a Pentateuchal institution while the dough-offering is only a Rabbinical one, as in fact R. Huna son of R. Joshua stated in a reply?[5] For R. Huna son of R. Joshua stated, I found the Rabbis of the college sitting at their studies and saying, 'Even according to him who holds that *terumah* at the present time is a Rabbinical institution, the dough-offering is a Pentateuchal one, for during the seven years in which they[6] conquered Canaan and during the seven years in which they divided it[7] they were under the obligation of the dough-offering though they were under no obligation to give tithe'; and I told them, 'Even according to him who holds that *terumah* at the present time is Pentateuchal, the dough-offering is only Rabbinical, for it was taught: If Scripture had written, "when you come"[8] it might have been presumed [that the obligation of the dough-offering should come into force] as soon as two or three spies had entered, hence it is said, *In your coming*,[9] I have spoken[10]

(1) Who exempts the dough under discussion from the dough-offering. (2) At the present time. (3) And that, consequently, *terumah* at the present time is also Pentateuchal. (4) Of course not. A Rabbinical enactment could not override a Pentateuchal law. Consequently it must be admitted (as stated *supra* 46b *ad fin.*) that R. Jose holds *terumah* at the present time to be merely a Rabbinical institution. (5) Of course it is possible. Hence the Baraitha cited provides no proof for the contention *supra* that the view that R. Jose holds *terumah* at the present time to be Rabbinical 'may be supported by a process of reasoning'. (6) The Israelites in the days of Joshua. (7) Years that may well be compared to the 'present time'. (8) *Ki thabo'u*, so MS.M. Cur. edd., *bebo'akem*. (9) Num. XV, 18, in the context of the dough-offering; Heb. *beboa'kem*, emphasis on *kem* 'your'. (10) Of the obligation of the dough-offering.

only of the coming of all of you and not of the coming of a portion of you; but when Ezra brought them up not all of them went up with him.'[1]

MISHNAH. THE SAGES SPOKE OF [THE PHYSICAL DEVELOPMENT OF] A WOMAN IN FIGURATIVE SPEECH: AN UNRIPE FIG, A FIG IN ITS EARLY RIPENING STAGE AND A RIPE FIG. SHE IS LIKE 'AN UNRIPE FIG' WHILE SHE IS YET A CHILD; 'A FIG IN ITS EARLY RIPENING STAGE' WHEN SHE IS IN THE AGE OF[2] HER MAIDENHOOD. DURING BOTH THE LATTER AND THE FORMER AGES,[3] THEY[4] RULED, HER FATHER IS ENTITLED TO ANYTHING SHE FINDS AND TO HER HANDIWORK AND TO THE RIGHT OF INVALIDATING HER VOWS. 'A RIPE FIG'—AS SOON AS SHE BECOMES A BOGERETH, AND HER FATHER HAS NO LONGER ANY RIGHT OVER HER.

WHAT ARE THE MARKS [OF A BOGERETH]? R. JOSE THE GALILEAN SAYS: THE APPEARANCE OF[5] THE WRINKLE BENEATH THE BREAST. R. AKIBA SAYS: THE HANGING DOWN OF[6] THE BREASTS. BEN AZZAI SAYS: THE DARKENING OF THE RING AROUND THE NIPPLE. R. JOSE SAYS: [THE DEVELOPMENT OF THE BREAST TO A STAGE] WHEN ONE'S HAND BEING PUT ON THE NIPPLE IT SINKS AND ONLY SLOWLY RISES AGAIN.

GEMARA. SHE IS LIKE 'AN UNRIPE FIG'[7] WHILE SHE IS YET A CHILD, as it is written in Scripture, *The fig-tree putteth forth her green figs.*[8]

'A FIG IN ITS EARLY RIPENING STAGE',[9] WHEN SHE IS

(1) Since that time, therefore, there could be no Pentateuchal obligation; and the dough-offering of the present time must consequently be a mere Rabbinical institution. (2) Lit., 'these are the days of'. (3) Childhood and maidenhood. (4) The Sages. (5) Lit., 'when it rises'. (6) Lit., 'when they incline'. (7) *Paggah* (v. foll. n.). (8) Cant. II, 13, *paggeha*, the noun absolute being *paggah* (with the pron. suff. of the third sing. fem. and the omission of the *dagesh* in the *pe* owing to a preceding *he*) which proves that the term is applied to the earliest stage of growth. (9) *Boḥal* (v. foll. n.).

IN THE AGE OF HER MAIDENHOOD, as we have learnt: Figs [become subject to tithe] as soon as they reach an early stage of ripening[1] and Rabbah b. Bar Ḥana explained this to mean: As soon as their tips grow white. And if you prefer I might say that the meaning[2] is derived from the following: *For my soul became impatient of them, and their soul also loathed*[3] *me.*[4]

'A RIPE FIG',[5] as one would say, 'It has come forth complete.'[6]

WHAT ARE THE MARKS [OF A BOGERETH]? R. JOSE THE GALILEAN SAYS: THE APPEARANCE OF THE WRINKLE. Samuel explained: Not the actual appearance of the wrinkle, but it suffices if, when putting her hands behind her, the wrinkle beneath the breast seems to appear. Samuel[7] examined his slave and paid her four *zuz* compensation for the indignity. Samuel thereby followed his principle, for Samuel stated: *Of them*[8] *may ye make bondmen*[9] *for ever,*[10] I have given them to you for work[11] but not to be subjected to indignities. Samuel assigned his female slaves to individual husbands.[12] R. Naḥman interchanged them.[13] R. Shesheth entrusted them to Arabs[14] but told them 'Be careful to have no intercourse with an Israelite'.

R. JOSE SAYS etc. What is the meaning of *uḳaz?*[15]—Samuel replied: The nipple of the breast.

Our Rabbis taught: What are the marks of *bagruth?* R. Eleazar son of R. Zadok stated, When the breasts begin to shake.[16] R. Joḥanan b. Beroḳa stated, When the top of the nose[17] grows white. But is not a woman when this grows white already old?—Rather

(1) *Misheyibaḥalu,* of the same root as *boḥal.* (2) Of *boḥal.* (3) *Baḥalah,* of the same rt. as *bohal.* (4) Zech. XI, 8; loathing is an early stage in the 'rising' of the food. (5) צמל *Ẓemel.* (6) Phonetic etymology. יצתה מלאה *yaẓetha mele'ah* containing the letters of צמל. (7) In his investigations on the applicability of R. Jose's ruling. (8) Canaanitish slaves. (9) *Ta'abodu,* lit., 'you may cause them to work'. (10) Lev. XXV, 46. (11) Cf. prev. n. but one. (12) Lit., 'he appointed for them', *sc.* he did not allow promiscuous intercourse among his slaves. To each female slave was assigned one particular male slave. (13) Unlike Samuel he did not mind promiscuity among his slaves. (14) Their morality, he held, was not his concern. (15) Rendered *supra* 'nipple'. (16) In walking. *Aliter:* 'to become stiff' (v. Jast.). (17) The central circle of the oblate part of the breast (Jast.),

said R. Ashi, when the top of the nose splits.[1] R. Jose stated, When a ring is formed around the nipple. R. Simeon stated, When the *mons veneris* grows lower. [47*b*] So also did R. Simeon[2] state: The Sages have indicated in [the physical development of] a woman three marks below and corresponding ones above. If, namely, she is like an unripe fig above, it may be taken for granted[3] that she has not yet grown two hairs. If she is above like a fig in its early ripening, it may be taken for granted[3] that she has already grown two hairs. If she is like a ripe fig above it may be taken for granted that the *mons veneris* has grown lower. What is meant by *mons veneris?*—R. Huna replied: There is a rounded eminence above that place,[4] and as the girl grows in age it steadily grows lower.

Rabbi was asked:[5] In agreement with whose view is the *halachah?* He sent word in reply: In agreement with all so as to restrict[6] the law.[7] R. Papa and R. Ḥinena son of R. Iḳa differ. One taught it[8] in connection with this,[9] while the other taught it in connection with the law of the Tyrian courtyard. For we have learnt: Which courtyard[10] imposes the obligations of tithe?[11] R. Simeon[12] ruled: A Tyrian courtyard in which objects are safely kept.[13] (Why is

(1) *Aliter* (Jast.). When the skin of the central circle of the oblate part of the breast appears wrinkled. (2) Cur. edd. in parenthesis add 'b. Yoḥai'. (3) Lit., 'it is known'. (4) Euphemism. (5) With reference to the various views given *supra* on the marks of *bagruth*. (6) *Sc.* whichever of the marks appears the girl is regarded as a *bogereth* and her father has no longer the right to annul her vows. *Aliter:* Even if only the earliest of the marks has appeared she enters a doubtful state of *bagruth* and if her father received on her behalf a token of betrothal from one man and she received a similar token from another she must be properly divorced from both. She must be divorced from the latter in case she is already a *bogereth* when her father's act cannot annul hers; and she must be divorced from the former in case she is not a *bogereth* before all the tokens have appeared. (7) MS.M., Alfasi and Asheri add, 'R. Joḥanan and Sabya say: the *halachah* is in agreement with all of them so as to restrict the law'. (8) Rabbi's reply. (9) The marks of a *bogereth*. (10) So MS.M. and sep. edd. of the Mishnah. Cur. edd. read, 'Tyrian courtyard'. (11) On produce that was brought into it (cf. Beẓah 34*b*). (12) Var. lec. Ishmael (v. separate edd. of the Mishnah). (13) Ma'as. III, 5. Such may be treated for the purpose of tithes as a house and consequently

this described as a Tyrian courtyard?—Rabbah b. Bar Ḥana citing R. Joḥanan replied: Since in Tyre they put a watchman at the door of a courtyard.) R. Akiba ruled: Any courtyard which one may open and another close[1] is exempt from tithe.[2] R. Nehemiah ruled: Any courtyard in which no one is ashamed to eat is subject to tithe.[3] R. Jose ruled: Any courtyard into which people may enter and none is asked, 'What do you want?' is exempt.[2] R. Judah ruled: If there were two courtyards, one within the other, the inner one is subject to tithe[3] while the outer one is exempt.[2] Rabbi was asked: In agreement with whose view is the *halachah?* He replied: The *halachah* is in agreement with all of them so as to restrict the law.[4]

MISHNAH. IF A WOMAN AT THE AGE OF TWENTY DID NOT PRODUCE TWO HAIRS,[5] SHE MUST BRING EVIDENCE THAT SHE IS TWENTY YEARS OF AGE AND SHE BECOMES CONFIRMED AS A WOMAN WHO IS INCAPABLE OF PROCREATION AND NEITHER PERFORMS ḤALIẒAH NOR IS TAKEN IN LEVIRATE MARRIAGE. IF A MAN OF THE AGE OF TWENTY YEARS DID NOT PRODUCE TWO HAIRS,[5] THEY[6] MUST BRING EVIDENCE THAT HE IS TWENTY YEARS OLD AND HE BECOMES CONFIRMED[7] AS A SARIS[8] AND NEITHER SUBMITS TO ḤALIẒAH NOR PERFORMS THE LEVIRATE MARRIAGE; SO BETH HILLEL. BETH SHAMMAI RULED: WITH THE ONE AS WELL AS WITH THE OTHER [THIS TAKES PLACE AT] THE AGE OF EIGHTEEN. R. ELIEZER RULED IN THE CASE OF THE MALE, IN AGREEMENT WITH BETH HILLEL, WHILE IN THAT OF THE FEMALE, IN AGREEMENT WITH BETH SHAMMAI, SINCE A WOMAN MATURES EARLIER THAN A MAN.

it imposes the obligations of tithe on any produce that is brought into it.

(1) *Sc.* there is no one man responsible for both the opening and the closing. (2) *Sc.* produce brought into it does not become subject to tithe, since such a courtyard cannot be regarded as a suitable place for the safe keeping of objects. (3) V. p. 329, n. 11. (4) I.e., if it is in any one of the conditions mentioned it subjects to tithe any produce brought into it. (5) The marks of puberty. (6) The relatives of the widow who desire her to be exempt from the duties of *ḥaliẓah* and the levirate marriage. (7) By a display of the prescribed symptoms. (8) A eunuch.

GEMARA. But I would point out an incongruity: The same law applies whether one is[1] of the age of nine years and one day or whether one is of the age of twenty years but had not produced two hairs![2]—R. Samuel son of R. Isaac citing Rab replied: This law[3] applies only where other symptoms of a *saris*[4] also appeared on him. Raba observed: This[5] may also be arrived at by a deduction. For it was stated, AND HE BECOMES CONFIRMED AS A SARIS.[6] This is conclusive.

Where, however, no other symptoms of a *saris* had developed, how long [is one[7] regarded as a minor]?—R. Ḥiyya taught: Until he has passed middle age.[8] Wherever people come with such a case[9] before R. Ḥiyya,[10] he used to tell them, if the youth was emaciated, 'Let him first be fattened'; and if he was stout, he used to tell them, 'Let him first be made to lose weight';[11] for these symptoms[12] appear[13] sometimes as a result of emaciation and sometimes they appear as a result of stoutness.

Rab stated: It is the law throughout this chapter that age is calculated from one point of time to another point of time;[14] but 'Ulla stated: This is the case only where we have explicitly learnt it.[15] According to 'Ulla all is well since there is a satisfactory reason

(1) Lit., 'it is one (and the same) to me'. (2) Yeb. 96*b*. So long as the pubic hairs have not appeared a person retains the status of a minor. How then is this to be reconciled with our Mishnah which assigns a new legal status at the age of eighteen or twenty? (3) Of our Mishnah (cf. prev. n.). (4) Described in Yeb. 80*b*. (5) That before one is regarded a *saris* other symptoms, besides the absence of pubic hairs, must also have made their appearance. (6) Which implies that other independent symptoms of a *saris* had already developed earlier. (7) If two pubic hairs did not appear. (8) Lit., 'most of his years'. (9) Of one who attained the age of twenty without having grown two hairs. (10) Var. lec. 'Raba' (cf. Yeb. 97*a*). (11) Lit., 'cause him to be lean'. (12) Described in Yeb. 80*b*. (13) The reading in Yeb. 97*a* is 'disappear'. (14) The age of twenty, for instance, is deemed to have been attained at the completion of full twenty years of life and not merely at the beginning of the twentieth calendar year. (15) Lit., 'where we learnt we learnt' etc., *sc*. only where the years and the first day of the year following were specifically mentioned as, for instance, 'three years and one day' (*supra* 44*b*), 'eleven years and one day' (*supra* 45*b*). Where, however, (as in our Mishnah) the years only are given one day of the twentieth

why in one case it was stated[1] 'one day' while in the other this was not stated; but according to Rab, why was not this[2] stated in all cases?[3] Furthermore, it was taught: R. Jose b. Kipper stated in the name of R. Eliezer, If thirty days of the twentieth year have passed it is exactly the same as if the entire year had passed;[4] and so also Rabbi at Lydda ruled, If thirty days of the eighteenth year have passed it is exactly the same as if the entire year had passed.[5] Now one may well agree that there is no difficulty [as regards the contradiction between the ruling] of Rabbi and that of R. Jose b. Kipper, since the former[6] is in agreement with Beth Shammai[7] while the latter[8] is in agreement with Beth Hillel;[7] but does not this[9] present a difficulty against Rab?[10]—This[11] is a question in dispute between Tannas.[12] For it was taught: The year that is mentioned in connection with consecrated things;[13] the year that is mentioned in connection with houses in walled cities;[14] the two years[15] in connection with a field of one's possession;[16] the six years in connection with a Hebrew servant,[17] and so also the years in the age of a son and a daughter[18] are all to be calculated from one point of time to another point of time.[19] Whence do we deduce the duration of the year that was mentioned in connection with consecrated things?—R. Aḥa b. Jacob replied: Scripture said, *A lamb of its*[20] *year*,[21] which implies, Its own year and not a

calendar year is regarded as the whole of that year and the person is deemed to be twenty years of age from that day.

(1) Lit., 'that is it that it was stated here'. (2) 'And one day'. (3) Lit., 'let him teach'. (4) Lit., 'behold it is like the twentieth year in all its matters'. (5) Cf. prev. n. (6) Eighteen years. (7) V. our Mishnah. (8) Twenty years. (9) The view accepted by both authorities cited that the part of a year is regarded as the whole of it. (10) Who stated *supra* that the years must be complete. (11) Whether the part of a year is regarded as the entire one. (12) One of whom, as will be shown presently, holds the same view as Rab. (13) *Sc.* that certain beasts for sacrifices must be one year old. (14) Cf., *If a man sell a dwelling house in a walled city, he may redeem it within a whole year* (Lev. XXV, 29). (15) This is deduced *infra*. (16) Cf. Lev. XXV, 14ff. (17) Cf., *If thou buy a Hebrew servant, six years shall he serve* (Ex. XXI, 2). (18) Which (so it is now presumed) were discussed in our Mishnah. (19) Cf. p. 331, n. 14 *supra*. (20) E.V., '*the first*'. (21) Lev. XII, 6.

calendar year.[1] Whence do we deduce the duration of the year that was mentioned in connection with the houses in walled cities? —Scripture said, *Until the end of his year of sale*[2] which implies, Only *his year of sale* but not a calendar year.[1] Whence do we deduce the duration of the two years in connection with a field of one's possession?—Scripture said, *According unto the number of* [48a] *years of the crops he shall sell unto thee*,[3] which implies[4] that one may sometimes sell three crops in two years.[5] Whence do we deduce the duration of the six years in connection with a Hebrew servant?—Scripture said, *Six years he shall serve, and in the seventh*,[6] which implies that in the seventh [calendar] year also he shall serve.[7] In regard to what law was mention made of 'the years in the age of a son and a daughter'?[8]—R. Giddal citing Rab replied: In regard to valuations.[9] R. Joseph, however, replied: In regard to the ages[10] given in our chapter of 'For a foetus born from its mother's side'.[11] Said Abaye to him,[12] 'Are you in disagreement?'[13] —'No', the other replied, 'he made one statement and I made another statement but there is no essential difference between us'. This is also logically right; for if it could be imagined that there is a radical difference between them and that the one[14] who replied, 'In regard to valuations' does not accept the reply, 'In regard to

(1) Lit., 'the year of the number of the world'. (2) Lev. XXV, 29, E.V., *Within a whole year after it is sold.* (3) Lev. XXV, 15. (4) Since the minimum of '*years*' (plural) is two, and the plural 'crops' denotes all the crops which can be produced in two years. (5) And this is only possible in two complete years, or a full period of twenty-four months, where the sale took place before the produce of the first calendar year had been harvested. In two calendar years there can be no more than two crops. (6) Ex. XXI, 2. (7) But this is possible only if one serves six full years from the date of purchase which took place in the middle of a calendar year. The end of the sixth full year would in such a case coincide with the middle of the seventh calendar year. (8) *Supra* 47b *ad fin.* (9) Which differ with the ages of the persons valued (cf. Lev. XXVII, 2ff). The ruling here serves the purpose of indicating that, even where the Scriptural text provides no clear guidance on the point, the years mentioned throughout the context are full periods each of twelve months duration. (10) Even where 'and a day' does not follow the number of years. (11) *Sc.* the present Chapter V which begins with these words. (12) R. Joseph. (13) With Rab. (14) Rab.

our present chapter'[1] [the difficulty would arise:] Did not Rab in fact state, 'It is the law throughout this chapter that age is calculated from one point of time to another point of time'?[2] But, then, why did not the one[3] who replied, 'In regard to valuations' also add, In regard to our chapter?[4]—[The reference[5] must be to cases] similar to those previously enumerated: As those[6] were recorded in the Scriptures so must these[5] be such as were recorded in the Scriptures.[7] And the other?[8]—[If that were so] it should have been said,[5] instead of 'the age of a son and a daughter', the age of a male and a female.[9]

R. Isaac b. Naḥmani citing R. Eleazar[10] stated: The *halachah* is in agreement with the ruling which R. Jose b. Kipper cited in the name of R. Eliezer.[11] R. Zera observed: May I be worthy to go up[12] and to learn the tradition[13] from the Master's mouth. When he went up[12] he met R. Eleazar and asked him, 'Did you say: The *halachah* is in agreement with R. Jose b. Kipper?'—'What I said was', the other replied, 'that it seemed to be reasonable. For since, throughout the chapter, "one day" was explicitly added[14] while in this case[15] it was not mentioned it may well be inferred that it seems reasonable [that the *halachah* is] in agreement with him'.

(1) Lit., 'for a foetus born from its mother's side' (cf. p. 333, n. 11). (2) *Supra* 47*b*. Of course he did. Consequently it must be admitted that Rab and R. Joseph are essentially of the same opinion. (3) Rab. (4) Lit., 'for a foetus born from its mothers' side' (cf. prev. n. but one). (5) In the expression, 'the years in the age of a son and a daughter' (*supra* 47*b*). (6) Consecrated things, houses in wall cities, etc. (7) Hence his reply that the reference was to valuations (which are also recorded in the Scriptures) though he fully agrees that the same principle applies also to the years in the ages dealt with in the present chapter (which are not Scriptural but merely traditional). (8) R. Joseph; why does he not add, 'In regard to valuation'? (9) Which are the expressions of the Scriptures in the context of valuations (cf. Lev. XXVII, 3f.). (10) R. Eleazar b. Pedath, the famous Palestinian Amora. (11) *Supra* 27*b*. (12) To Palestine (cf. prev. n. but one). (13) Cited by R. Isaac b. Naḥmani. (14) Lit., 'learned', after the number of the years. (15) A man of the age of twenty years (cf. our Mishnah).

NIDDAH

CHAPTER VI

MISHNAH. IF THE LOWER MARK[1] APPEARED BEFORE THE UPPER ONE[2] HAD YET MADE ITS APPEARANCE, SHE MAY PERFORM ḤALIẒAH OR CONTRACT LEVIRATE MARRIAGE.[3] IF THE UPPER MARK[2] APPEARED BEFORE THE LOWER ONE[1] HAD MADE ITS APPEARANCE, THOUGH THIS IS IMPOSSIBLE,[4] R. MEIR RULED, SHE MAY NEITHER PERFORM ḤALIẒAH NOR CONTRACT THE LEVIRATE MARRIAGE; BUT THE SAGES RULED, SHE MAY EITHER PERFORM ḤALIẒAH OR CONTRACT THE LEVIRATE MARRIAGE, BECAUSE THEY MAINTAIN: IT IS POSSIBLE FOR THE LOWER MARK TO APPEAR BEFORE THE UPPER ONE HAD YET MADE ITS APPEARANCE, BUT IT IS IMPOSSIBLE FOR THE UPPER MARK TO APPEAR BEFORE THE LOWER ONE HAD MADE ITS APPEARANCE.[5]

GEMARA. 'THOUGH THIS IS IMPOSSIBLE'! But has it not in fact APPEARED?[6]—'APPEARED', according to R. Meir;[7] 'THOUGH THIS IS IMPOSSIBLE' according to the Rabbis.[8] Why then was it not stated: 'If the upper mark appeared, R. Meir ruled, She may neither perform *ḥaliẓah* nor contract levirate marriage but the Sages ruled, She may either perform *ḥaliẓah* or contract levirate marriage', and I would well have known that their reason is that it is impossible?[9]—If 'THOUGH THIS IS IMPOSSIBLE' had not been

(1) Two pubic hairs. (2) 'A fig in its early ripening' (v. Mishnah *supra* 47a). (3) Because she is deemed to have attained her majority. (4) The apparent contradiction is described in the Gemara *infra*. (5) Though it cannot be discovered the hairs may be presumed to have fallen off. (6) Of course it had; since it was explicitly stated, IF THE UPPER MARK APPEARED BEFORE THE LOWER ONE. (7) Who ruled that SHE MAY NEITHER PERFORM ḤALIẒAH etc., thus regarding her as a minor because, obviously, the upper mark may appear though the lower one had not yet made its appearance. (8) THE SAGES, who in either case (v. our Mishnah) regard her as of age. (9) And this would

stated, It might have been presumed that in most women the lower mark appears first and in that of a minority the upper mark appears first, and that R. Meir[1] is guided by his principle according to which he takes even a minority into consideration,[2] while the Rabbis[3] are guided by their principle according to which they do not take a minority into consideration,[4] and that this[5] applies only to a general case, but where an examination was held and no [lower mark] was found the Rabbis, it might have been assumed, agree with R. Meir[1] since the upper mark has appeared first, hence we were informed that this IS IMPOSSIBLE and that the lower mark[6] had undoubtedly appeared earlier but merely fell off. According to R. Meir[7] one may well justify the Scriptural text, *Thy breasts*[8] *were fashioned, and thy hair*[9] *was grown*,[10] but according to the Rabbis,[11] should not the order have been reversed?[12]—It is this that was meant: As soon as the '*breasts are fashioned*' it is known that '*thy hair was grown*'. According to R. Meir[13] one can well see the justification for the order of the Scriptural text, *When they from Egypt bruised thy breasts*[8] *for the bosom*[9] *of thy youth*,[14] but according to the Rabbis,[11] should not the order have been reversed?[12]—It is this that was meant: As soon as '*thy breasts*' appeared it is known that thy youth[9] had appeared. And if you prefer I might reply: As to the meaning of[15] *shede*,[16] all the clause was written with regard to the breasts; and it is this that the Holy One, blessed

avoid the insertion of the ambiguous clause, 'THOUGH THIS IS IMPOSSIBLE'.

(1) In regarding the girl as a minor. (2) And since a minority have the upper before the lower mark, every girl producing the upper mark alone must be regarded as a minor in case she belonged to the minority. (3) THE SAGES, who in either case (v. our Mishnah) regard her as of age. (4) As soon, therefore, as the upper mark appeared it may be taken for granted that the lower one had appeared previously. (5) The ruling of the Sages, which is dependent on the principle of following the majority. (6) Cf. BaḤ, wanting in cur. edd. (7) Who maintains that the upper mark sometimes appears first. (8) The upper mark. (9) The lower one. (10) Ezek. XVI, 7, since the marks do sometimes appear in this order. (11) Who hold that the upper mark can never appear first. (12) Hair first and breasts afterwards. (13) Who maintains that the upper mark sometimes appears first. (14) Ezek. XXIII, 21. (15) Lit., 'what'. (16) The word rendered *supra* '*bosom*'.

be He, said in effect to Israel: [48*b*] 'Thy breasts were swollen, yet thou didst not repent; yea, thy breasts were dried up, yet thou didst not repent'.[1] All[2] at any rate agree that[3] we rely on the lower mark; whence do we deduce this?—Rab Judah citing Rab replied and so it was taught at the school of R. Ishmael: Scripture said, *When a man or a woman shall commit any sin that men commit,*[4] Scripture[5] compared the '*woman*' to the '*man*' in respect of all the punishments in the Torah; as a man is subject to punishments on the appearance of the one mark[6] so is also a woman subject to punishments on the appearance of the one mark. Might it not be suggested: Either the one or the other?[7]—Like the man: As with the man [the determining factor] is the lower mark and not the upper one so also with the woman it is the lower one that determins majority but not the upper one. So[8] it was also taught: R. Eliezer son of R. Zadok stated, Thus did they explain and promulgate at Jamnia: As soon as the lower mark makes its appearance no attention need any longer be paid to the upper one.

It was taught: R. Simeon b. Gamaliel stated, Among townswomen the lower mark appears earlier because they are in the habit of taking baths; among village women the upper mark appears earlier because they grind with millstones.[9] R. Simeon b. Eleazar stated: Among the daughters of the rich the right hand side develops earlier because it rubs against their scarves;[10] among the daughters of the poor the left side develops earlier because they carry[11] jars of water on them. And if you prefer I might say, Because they carry their brothers on their sides.

(1) Aliter (Jast.) and cf. Rashi's first interpretation: Thy breasts began to develop, yet thou didst not repent, thy breasts were fully developed, yet etc. (2) Lit.,' that all the world'. R. Meir and the Sages. (3) In determining whether a girl is of age. (4) Num. V, 6. (5) By placing the two nouns in juxtaposition. (6) The lower one, which is the only mark he possesses. (7) The analogy between '*man*' and '*woman*' extending only as far as a single mark is concerned, *sc.* that one mark (upper or lower) suffices to establish the majority of a woman as one mark (the lower) establishes the majority of a man. (8) That the lower mark alone is the determining factor. (9) The constant exercise of their arms distends their breasts. (10) Which are worn on the right side. (11) So with a certain reading. Cur. edd. 'draw'.

Our Rabbis taught: The left side develops earlier than the right side. R. Ḥanina the son of the brother of R. Joshua stated: The left side never developed earlier than the right side except in the case of one woman who lived in our neighbourhood whose left side developed earlier than the right one which later regained its normal strength.

Our Rabbis taught: All girls to be examined must be examined by women. So also R. Eliezer entrusted the examination to his wife, and R. Ishmael entrusted it to his mother. R. Judah ruled: Before the period[1] and after the period,[2] women examine them.[3] During the period[4] no woman may examine them, since in doubtful cases[5] no woman is allowed to marry[6] on the evidence of women. R. Simeon ruled, Even during the period[4] women examine them. And a woman may be relied upon when by her evidence the law is restricted but not when it is relaxed thereby. How so? [She may be relied upon when she states: 'The girl] is of age', so that the latter should thereby be denied the right of *mi'un*, or 'She is a minor', so that she should thereby be denied the right of performing *ḥaliẓah;* but she is not trusted when asserting, 'She is a minor', so that she should have the right of exercising *mi'un*, or 'She is of age', so that she should be entitled to perform *ḥaliẓah*.

The Master said, 'R. Judah ruled: Before the period and after the period women examine them'. One can well concede that before the period an examination is required, for should [the same hairs][7]

(1) *Sc.* before the age of eleven years and a day. (2) After the age of twelve years and a day. (3) But, whether they report the presence of hair or their absence, the girls in the former case (a time when hairs are regarded as a mere 'mole') are treated as minors. In the latter case (a time when pubic hairs and maturity may well be expected) the girls are deemed to be of age if the women report the presence of hairs; but even if they report their absence, the girls cannot be treated as minors (since the hairs may have fallen off) and they are consequently deprived of the right of *mi'un* (v. Glos.). (4) From the age of eleven years and one day to that of twelve years and one day, when their status is a matter of doubt and is entirely dependent on the presence or absence of the hairs. (5) Cf. prev. n. In the first two cases (cf. prev. n. but one) a doubt hardly exists. (6) If the women were to report the presence of hairs the girls would have to be allowed to contract levirate marriage. (7) And no others.

be found after the period they would be regarded as a mole;[1] but what need could there be for an examination after the period seeing that Raba has laid down that a minor who has attained the age of her majority need not be examined since there is presumption that she had by that time produced the marks of puberty?—When Raba stated, 'there is presumption', he meant it in respect of *mi'un*,[2] but as regards *ḥaliẓah*[3] an examination is still required.[4] 'During the period no women may examine them', because he is of the opinion [that the presence of hairs] during the period [is a mark of majority] as after the period;[5] but after the period, when Raba's presumption is applicable, we rely upon women who may, therefore, conduct the examination,[4] while during the period, when Raba's presumption is not applicable, we cannot rely upon women, and women, therefore, may not conduct the examination. 'R. Simeon ruled, Even during the period women examine them', for he is of the opinion [that the presence of hairs] during the period [is no more a mark of puberty] than it is before the period; and an examination is, therefore, required so that if [the same hairs][6] should be found after the period they would be regarded as a mole.[7] 'And a woman may be relied upon when by her evidence the law is restricted but not when it is relaxed thereby.' Who taught this?—If you wish I might say: R. Judah, and [the reference is to evidence] during the period.[8] [49*a*] And if you prefer I might say: R. Simeon, and [the reference is to evidence] after

(1) And the girl would still be deemed a minor and denied the right of performing *ḥaliẓah*. (2) *Sc.* to impose the restriction of denying her the right of *mi'un*. (3) I.e., to relax the law by allowing the performance of the rite. (4) A woman's evidence being in such a case relied upon, since a girl at the age mentioned usually has all the marks of puberty. (5) Cur. edd. in parenthesis insert 'like'. (6) And no others. (7) And the girl would still be deemed a minor and denied the right of performing *ḥaliẓah*. (8) His opinion being that hairs discovered during the period are evidence of puberty as are hairs discovered after the period. If the women report the presence of hairs as a result of which the girl is deprived of the right of *mi'un* they are relied upon since the law is thereby restricted. Their evidence, however, is not relied upon as regards entitling her to perform *ḥaliẓah* since thereby the law would be relaxed.

the period,[1] for he does not uphold the principle of Raba's presumption.

BECAUSE THEY MAINTAIN: IT IS POSSIBLE etc. What need again was there for this statement, seeing that it was already taught in the earlier clause? And were you to reply: Because it was desired to lay down an anonymous statement[2] in agreement with the Rabbis [it could be objected:] Is not this obvious, since in a dispute between an individual authority and a number of authorities the *halachah* is in agreement with the majority?—It might have been presumed that R. Meir's reason is more acceptable because Scriptural texts[3] provide support for his view, hence we were informed[4] [that the *halachah* is in agreement with the view of the Rabbis]. And if you prefer I might reply: Because it was desired to state,[5] 'Similarly'.[6]

MISHNAH. SIMILARLY[7] ANY [HOLE IN] AN EARTHEN VESSEL THAT LETS IN A LIQUID[8] WILL[9] LET IT OUT,[10] BUT THERE MAY BE ONE THAT WILL LET IT OUT AND WILL NOT LET IT IN.[11] ANY LIMB[12] THAT GROWS A NAIL HAS ALSO A BONE IN IT,[13] BUT THERE MAY BE ONE THAT HAS A BONE IN IT BUT GROWS NO NAIL.[14] WHATEVER CONTRACTS MIDRAS-UNCLEAN-

(1) And even then women's evidence is accepted only in so far as to impose restrictions (denial of the right of *mi'un*). It is not accepted, however, for the purpose of relaxing the law (allowing the performance of *ḥaliẓah*). (2) Which, as a rule, is the accepted law. (3) From Ezekiel XVI and XXIII (*supra* 48a). (4) By the anonymous statement, BECAUSE THEY MAINTAIN etc. (cf. prev. n. but one). (5) In the next Mishnah. (6) Introducing similar cases where one process follows or is the result of another though the reverse is impossible. (7) Cf. prev. n. (8) In which the vessel stands. (9) If the liquid was within the vessel. (10) A lesser hole in fact being required for the latter process than for the former. (11) Cf. prev. n. *mut. mut.* The legal purpose of this statement is discussed in the Gemara *infra*. (12) *Sc.* a redundant finger. (13) And is, therefore, regarded as a proper limb which (cf. *supra* 43b) conveys uncleanness by overshadowing even though it is smaller than the minimum prescribed for the flesh of a corpse. (14) In such a case, if the limb is a redundant one, the conveyance of uncleanness (cf. prev. n.) is subject to the prescribed minimum.

NESS[1] ALSO CONTRACTS CORPSE-UNCLEANNESS[2] BUT THERE ARE SUCH AS CONTRACT CORPSE UNCLEANNESS[3] AND DO NOT CONTRACT MIDRAS-UNCLEANNESS.[4]

GEMARA. A vessel with a hole THAT LETS IN A LIQUID is unfit for the water of purification[5] and is [even more so] unfit[6] as a defective vessel;[7] one with a hole THAT WILL LET IT OUT[8] is fit for the water of purification[9] but unfit as a defective vessel.[10]

R. Assi stated, It was learnt,[11] The minimum size [of a hole to render] an earthen vessel [unfit for the consecration of the water of purification] is one that will let a liquid in;[12] and one that will let a liquid out[8] was mentioned only in respect of a defective vessel.[10] What is the reason?[13]—Mar Zuṭra son of R. Naḥman replied: Because people do not say,[14] 'Bring a defective vessel for another defective vessel'.[15]

Our Rabbis taught: How is an earthen vessel to be tested in order

(1) Of a *zab*, to be a 'father of uncleanness (v. Glos.). (2) Of the same grade (cf. prev. n.) since whatever object is suitable as *midras* for a *zab* has the status of a 'vessel' and is, therefore, subject to corpse-uncleanness also. (3) Having the status of a vessel in respect of susceptibility to all forms of uncleanness including that of 'father of uncleanness' if it came in contact with a corpse. (4) *Sc.* to become a 'father of uncleanness' through the *midras* of a *zab*. This is further discussed *infra* in the Gemara. (5) Which (cf. Num. XIX, 17) must be consecrated in a sound vessel. (6) To contract uncleanness. (7) Defective vessels which are still suitable for certain uses are, under given conditions, susceptible to uncleanness (cf. Ḥul. 54*b*) but when they have a hole of the nature mentioned they lose even the status of a defective vessel and, like broken sherds, are immune from all forms of uncleanness. (8) But will not let it in, *sc.* a smaller hole. (9) Such a small hole being disregarded in the case of an otherwise sound vessel. (10) Being already defective the smallest hole deprives it altogether of its status (cf. prev. n. but two). (11) *Shonin sc.* as an oral tradition handed down to Moses from Sinai (Rashi). (12) If the hole is smaller the vessel retains in all respects the status of a sound one (cf. Shab. 95*b*.). (13) For the last ruling. (14) When there is a leak in a defective vessel. (15) That the former should receive the leakage from the latter. A defective vessel may be so used under an otherwise sound one, since the latter is not discarded on account of a very small hole. When such a hole, however, occurs in a defective vessel it is completely discarded and, therefore, loses its status (cf. *supra* n. 10).

to ascertain whether its perforation is big enough to admit a liquid or not? One brings a tub full of water and puts the pot[1] into it. If it absorbs any of the liquid, it may be taken for granted that it lets liquids in; and if not, it may be taken for granted that it only lets liquids out. [49b] R. Judah[2] said: One inverts the handles of the pot into the tub[3] and allows water to float over it. If it then absorbs any, it may be taken for granted that it will let liquids in; but if not, it may be taken for granted that it only lets liquids out. Or else, it[4] may be put upon a fire. If the fire stops the leakage it is certain that the pot will only let liquids out; but if not it is certain that it also lets liquids in. R. Jose said: One does not put it upon the actual[5] fire since the fire stops it,[6] but it is put upon embers. If the embers stop it, it is certain that it only lets liquids out, but if not, it is certain that it also lets liquids in. If it drips drop after drop[7] it is certain that it lets liquids in. What is the practical difference between the first Tanna[8] and R. Judah? —'Ulla replied: The practical difference between them is a case of absorption under pressure.[9]

ANY LIMB THAT GROWS A NAIL etc. If it grows a nail[10] it[11] conveys uncleanness[12] by means of touch, carriage and overshadowing. If it contains a bone but grows no nail it conveys uncleanness[13] by means of touch and carriage but does not convey it by means of overshadowing.[14]

R. Hisda stated: The following was said by our great Master,[15] may the Omnipresent be his help. A redundant finger that contains a bone but grows no nail conveys uncleanness[13] by means of touch

(1) That is to be tested. (2) Objecting to the previous test which, since the bottom of the pot is inevitably pressed against the water, would cause the latter to penetrate even through the smallest of holes. (3) Lit., 'into it', while it is still empty. (4) The pot to be tested, with water in it. (5) Lit., 'even not'. (6) Even if the hole is big. (7) This is another test, independent of the former. (8) *Supra* 49a *ad fin*. (9) According to the first Tanna this also is proof that the vessel lets liquids in, while according to R. Judah this is no proof (cf. *supra* n. 2). (10) Though the limb is a redundant one, a sixth finger for instance. (11) Being regarded as a proper limb (cf. relevant n. on our Mishnah). (12) However small its bulk. (13) If the bone is not smaller than a barley-grain. (14) Unless the bulk of the flesh was no less than that of an olive. (15) Rab.

and carriage but does not convey it by means of overshadowing. Rabbah b. Bar Ḥana explained: This is the case only when it[1] is not counted in [the row of the fingers of] the hand.[2]

WHATEVER CONTRACTS MIDRAS-UNCLEANNESS etc. Whatever object is fit for *midras* contracts corpse-uncleanness, but there are such as contract corpse-uncleanness and do not contract *midras*-uncleanness. What is this rule intended to include?—It is intended to include a *se'ah* measure and a *tarkab;*[3] for it was taught: *And he that sitteth on any thing;*[4] as it might have been presumed that if the *zab* inverted a *se'ah* measure and sat upon it or a *tarkab* measure and sat upon it, it shall be unclean,[5] it was explicitly stated, *Whereon he that hath the issue sat,*[4] implying[6] that the text refers only to a thing that is appointed for sitting;[7] but this one[8] is excluded, since people would tell him, 'Get up that we may do our work with it'.[9]

MISHNAH. WHOSOEVER IS FIT TO TRY CAPITAL CASES IS ALSO FIT TO TRY MONETARY SUITS, BUT ONE MAY BE FIT TO TRY MONETARY SUITS AND YET BE UNFIT TO TRY CAPITAL CASES.

GEMARA. Rab Judah stated: This[10] was meant to include a bastard.[11] Have we not, however, learnt this once before: 'All are

(1) Being situated outside the row of the normal fingers. (2) A normal finger, or even a redundant one in the normal row, conveys uncleanness by overshadowing, however small in bulk it may be, as any proper limb. (3) A measure of capacity containing two *kabs; Aliter:* τρικαβος = three *kabs*, or half a *se'ah*, a dry measure. (4) Lev. XV, 6. (5) *Midras*-uncleanness that is conveyed to men and objects which become thereby a 'father of uncleanness'. (6) Emphasis on '*sat*' (v. Ḥag. Sonc. ed., p. 149, n. 2). (7) Such an object only is subject to the major grade of uncleanness (cf. prev. n. but two). (8) An inverted measure. (9) Hence they contract from a *zab* the uncleanness of touch only and this subjects them only to the uncleanness of the first grade, while through contact with a corpse they become a 'father of uncleanness'. (10) The second clause of our Mishnah. (11) Who is a fit person to act as judge in monetary suits but not in capital cases (cf. Sanh. 36b).

eligible to try monetary suits but not all eligible to try capital cases';[1] and when the question was raised, 'What was this intended to include?' Rab Judah replied, 'It was intended to include a bastard'?[2] — One statement was intended to include a proselyte and the other to include a bastard. And both statements were necessary. For if we had been informed of the proselyte only it might have been presumed that it applied to him alone because he is eligible to enter the Assembly[3] but not to a bastard who is not eligible to enter the Assembly.[4] And if we had been informed of the bastard only it might have been presumed to apply to him alone because he issues from an eligible source[5] but not to a proselyte who issues from an ineligible source.[6] Hence the necessity for both rulings.

MISHNAH. WHOSOEVER IS ELIGIBLE TO ACT AS JUDGE IS[7] ELIGIBLE TO ACT AS WITNESS, BUT ONE MAY BE ELIGIBLE TO ACT AS WITNESS AND NOT AS JUDGE.

GEMARA. What [was this[8] intended] to include? — R. Johanan replied: To include one who is blind in one eye;[9] and who is the author? [50a] — R. Meir.[10] For it was taught: R. Meir used to say, What was the purport of the Scriptural text, *According to their word shall every controversy and every leprosy be?*[11] What connection could controversies have with leprosies? But[12] controversies were compared to leprosies, as leprosies must be examined by day, since it is written, *And in the day when . . . appeareth in him,*[13] so must controversies be tried by day; and[14] as leprosies are not to be

(1) Sanh. 32a. (2) That he is fit to adjudicate in indictory cases. Ibid. 36b. Why then the repetition. (3) *Sc.* to marry the daughter of an Israelite. (4) Cf. Deut. XXIII, 3. (5) Lit., 'a fit drop', *sc.* pure Israelite origin. (6) Heathen origin. Cf. prev. n. *mut. mut.* (7) Much more so. (8) The second rule in our Mishnah. (9) Such a person is eligible as witness but not as judge. One blind in both eyes is ineligible even as witness. (10) Who disqualifies a man blind in one eye from acting as judge. (11) Deut. XXI, 5. (12) Owing to juxtaposition. (13) Lev. XIII, 14, emphasis on '*day*'. (E.V. '*whensoever*' for '*in the day when*'). (14) By a further analogy (cf. prev. n. but one).

examined by a blind man,[1] since it is written, *Wherever the priest looketh,*[2] so are controversies not to be tried by a blind man.[1] And[3] leprosies are further compared to controversies: As controversies are not to be tried by relatives, so are leprosies not to be examined by relatives. In case [one were to argue:] 'As controversies must be tried by three men so must leprosies also be examined by three men, this being logically arrived at *a minori ad majus:* If controversies affecting one's wealth must be tried by three men, how much more so matters affecting one's body', it was explicitly stated, *When he shall be brought unto Aaron the priest or unto one of his sons the priests.*[4] Thus you have learnt that even a single[5] priest may examine leprosies.[6]

A certain blind man who lived in the neighbourhood of R. Joḥanan used to try lawsuits and the latter[7] told him nothing against it. But how could he[7] act in this manner, seeing that R. Joḥanan actually stated, 'The *halachah* is in agreement with an anonymous Mishnah', and we have learnt,[8] WHOSOEVER IS ELIGIBLE TO ACT AS JUDGE IS ELIGIBLE TO ACT AS WITNESS, BUT ONE MAY BE ELIGIBLE TO ACT AS WITNESS AND NOT AS JUDGE, and when the question was raised, 'What was this intended to include?' R. Joḥanan replied, 'To include one who is blind in one eye'?[9]—R. Joḥanan found another anonymous Mishnah.[10] For we have learnt, Monetary suits must be tried by day and may be concluded by night.[11] But why should this anonymous Mishnah[12]

(1) Even by one who is blind in one eye only. (2) Lev. XIII, 12 emphasis on the last word. (3) Owing to juxtaposition. (4) Lev. XIII, 2 emphasis on '*Aaron*' and '*one*'. (5) Cf. prev. n. (6) At any rate it follows, as was stated above, that according to R. Meir a blind man (even if in one eye only) is eligible as judge. Our Mishnah, therefore, represents his view. (7) R. Joḥanan. (8) As an anonymous Mishnah. (9) Which clearly shows that according to R. Joḥanan no blind man is eligible to act as judge. Why then did he raise no objection against the blind man's conduct? (10) Which allows a blind man to act as judge. (11) Sanh. 32*a*; which shows that, according to this Mishnah, 'controversies' were not compared to 'leprosies' for though the latter may not be examined by night the trying of the former may well be concluded by night. And since the two were not compared in this respect they were not compared as regards the ineligibility of a blind man either. (12) The latter, cited from Sanh.

be deemed more authoritative than the former?[1]—If you wish I might reply: An anonymous Mishnah which represents the view of a majority[2] is preferable. And if you prefer I might reply: Because it[3] was taught among the laws of legal procedure.[4]

MISHNAH. WHATSOEVER IS SUBJECT TO TITHES IS SUSCEPTIBLE TO FOOD-UNCLEANNESS;[5] BUT THERE IS A KIND OF FOODSTUFF[6] THAT IS SUSCEPTIBLE TO FOOD-UNCLEANNESS AND IS NOT SUBJECT TO TITHES.

GEMARA. What was this[7] intended to include?—To include flesh, fish and eggs.[8]

MISHNAH. WHATSOEVER IS SUBJECT TO THE OBLIGATION OF PE'AH[9] IS ALSO SUBJECT TO THAT OF TITHES; BUT THERE IS A KIND OF PRODUCE WHICH IS SUBJECT TO THE OBLIGATION OF TITHES AND IS NOT SUBJECT TO THAT OF PE'AH.

GEMARA. What was this[7] intended to include?—To include the fig-tree and vegetables, which are not subject to the obligation of *pe'ah.*[10] For we have learnt: They[11] have laid down a general rule concerning *pe'ah.* Whatsoever is a foodstuff, is kept under watch, grows[12] from the ground, is all harvested at the same time, and is

(1) Our Mishnah. Lit., 'and what is the strength of that anonymous etc.' (2) As does the one from Sanh. Our Mishnah, as was explained *supra,* represents the view of R. Meir alone. (3) The latter, cited from Sanh. (4) With which the tractate of Sanh. deals. A law occurring in a tractate that is devoted to similar laws is more reliable than one occurring in a tractate that is mainly devoted to a totally different subject. (5) Since only foodstuffs are subject to tithe. (6) This is presently explained in the Gemara. (7) The second clause of our Mishnah. (8) Only foodstuffs that grow from the ground are subject to tithe. (9) Lit., 'corner'. Cf. *When ye reap the harvest . . . thou shalt not wholly reap the corner of thy field . . . thou shalt leave them for the poor* (Lev. XIX, 9f). (10) But are liable to tithes. (11) The Rabbis. (12) Var. lec. 'draws its nourishment' (v. Tosaf.).

taken in for storage, is subject to *pe'ah*.[1] 'A foodstuff', excludes the after-growths of woad and madder;[2] 'is kept under watch', excludes *hefker*; 'grows[3] from the ground', excludes morils and truffles;[4] 'is all harvested at the same time', excludes the fig-tree;[5] 'and is taken in for storage', excludes vegetables. As regards tithes, however, we have learnt: Whatsoever is a foodstuff, is kept under watch and grows from the ground is subject to the obligation of tithes;[6] whereas 'is all harvested at the same time[7] and is taken in for storage'[8] was not mentioned.[9] But if garlic or onions[10] grew among them[11] they are subject [to *pe'ah*]. For we have learnt: As regards plots of onions between other vegetables, R. Jose ruled, *Pe'ah* must be left from each[12] and the Sages ruled, From one for all.[13]

Rabbah b. Bar Ḥana citing R. Johanan ruled: If endives were originally sown for cattle-food and then [the owner] changed his mind[14] to use them for human food, [50*b*] it is necessary[15] that he should intend them for the purpose[16] after they had been detached; he being of the opinion that intention[16] concerning attached [produce] is no valid intention. Raba observed: We also have learnt a rule to the same effect: Thirteen things have been said about the carrion of a clean bird, (and the following is one of them).[17] It is necessary[18] that it should be intended for food but there is no need for it to be rendered[19] susceptible to uncleanness.[20]

(1) Pe'ah I, 4. (2) Plants used only in dyeing which are unsuitable as food. (3) Var. lec. 'draws its nourishment' (v. Tosaf.). (4) Which are not planted *Aliter:* Which (cf. prev. n.) do not draw their nourishment from the ground. (5) And similar trees whose fruit ripens at different times. (6) Ma'as. I, 1. (7) Which would have excluded the fig-tree and the like. (8) Which would have excluded vegetables. (9) It thus follows that figs and vegetables are liable to tithes though exempt from *pe'ah*. The tithe mentioned is, of course, only Rabbinical, since Pentateuchally only corn, wine and oil are subject to the obligations of tithe. (10) Vegetables that are taken in for storage. (11) The other vegetables. (12) Since the other vegetables form a division between one plot and another. (13) The intervening vegetables being disregarded, Pe'ah III, 4. (14) While they were still attached to the ground. (15) If they are to be rendered susceptible to food-uncleanness as human food. (16) To be used as human food. (17) The bracketed words are not in the cited Mishnah. (18) Cf. prev. n. but one *mut. mut.* (19) By intentionally wetting it. (20) As is

Thus it is clearly evident that[1] an intention concerning a live being is no valid intention; so also here[2] it must be said, that an intention concerning attached [produce][3] is no valid intention.[4] R. Zera said:[5] We are dealing here[6] with a [flying] pigeon that dropped from on high, so that it was not before us[7] to enable one to have any intentions about it.[8] Said Abaye to him:[9] What can be said about the [case of the] hen of Jamnia?[10]—That, the other[9] replied, was a wild cock.[11] They laughed at him: A wild cock is an unclean bird and an unclean bird does not convey uncleanness![12]—'When a great man', Abaye told them, 'said something, do not laugh at him. This was a case of a hen that ran away;[13] and as to the meaning[14] of "wild", it turned wild as far as its master was concerned'.[15] R. Papa said: It was a field-hen.[16] R. Papa thus followed his known view. For R. Papa ruled, A field-cock is forbidden and a field-hen is permitted; and your mnemonic is 'A

the case with other dry foodstuffs which must come in contact with liquids before they can be capable of contracting uncleanness. Ṭoh. I, 1.

(1) Since intention is required when it is already carrion though a live bird is usually intended for food. (2) R. Joḥanan's ruling. (3) Which, analogous to a live animal, is not susceptible to uncleanness. (4) Support is thus adduced for R. Joḥanan's ruling. (5) The cited Mishnah affords no support to R. Joḥanan. (6) The Mishnah of Ṭoh. cited. (7) While it was yet alive. (8) Hence the ruling that 'it is necessary that it should be intended for food' after it was carrion. Where, however, a live animal was intended to be used in due course as food no further intention is necessary after it had been killed. (9) R. Zera. (10) Which (v. *infra*) was in its owner's possession before it died and yet was regarded as a food for the sole reason that the Samaritans living there intended it as such after it was dead. (11) Not usually intended for food. Hence the necessity for intention after its death. (12) Through one's oesophagus, v. Ḥul. 100*b*. Now since the uncleanness of the hen at Jamnia was conveyed through the oesophagus (*sc.* by the swallowing of it) it could not possibly have been a wild cock. (13) Lit., 'rebelled', and thus was not before us while alive and for this reason intention would be necessary after it died. It was one of the young of this hen that dropped at Jamnia and gave rise to the discussion. (14) Lit., 'and what'. (15) Lit., 'from its master'. As the bird in question was consequently a clean one it may well have conveyed uncleanness (as stated) through the oesophagus. (16) Or 'a hen of the marshes', which in his opinion (v. *infra*) is a clean bird.

male Ammonite[1] but not a female Ammonite'. Amemar laid down in his discourse that a field-hen is forbidden.[2] The Rabbis observed that it stamps on its prey[3] when eating it;[4] and it is this bird that is known as *girutha*.[5]

Our Rabbis taught: If a pigeon[6] fell into a winepress[7] and it was intended to pick it up for a Samaritan,[8] it is unclean;[9] but if it was intended for a dog it is clean.[10] R. Johanan b. Nuri[11] ruled, Even if intended for a dog it is unclean.[9] R. Johanan b. Nuri argued: This is arrived at *a minori ad majus*. If it[12] conveys a major uncleanness,[13] though there was no intention,[14] should it not convey a minor uncleanness[15] though there was no intention? They answered him: No; if you maintain your view in the case of a major uncleanness, which never descends to that,[16] would you also maintain it in the case of a minor uncleanness which does descend to that?[16] He replied: the hen of Jamnia proves my contention, for it descends to that and, though there was no intention, it was declared unclean. 'From there', they retorted, 'is your proof? In that place there were Samaritans and it was intended that they shall eat it.' Now with what case are we dealing here? If it be suggested with big cities [the objection would arise]: What need was there for intention, seeing that we have learnt: The carcass of a clean beast anywhere[17] and the carcass of a clean bird and forbidden fat in large towns[18] require neither intention nor to be rendered susceptible.[19] If, how-

(1) Is forbidden to enter the Assembly (cf. Deut. XXIII, 4). (2) As food. (3) In the manner of birds of prey. (4) No clean birds eat in this manner. (5) Presumably the moor-hen. The *giritha* is an unclean bird (cf. Ḥul. 109*b*). (6) A clean bird. (7) Where it got crushed and died, becoming repulsive for eating. (8) To give it to him to eat. (9) Food-uncleanness. It conveys uncleanness to other foodstuffs through contact, without being rendered susceptible. (10) Such an intention being invalid. (11) Holding that no intention is required (v. *infra*). (12) The pigeon. (13) The uncleanness of the person and the clothes worn by him when he ate it. (14) When, for instance, the man was unaware that he was eating that particular pigeon. (15) That of food and drink by means of contact. (16) This is explained presently. (17) Even in a village where there are not many consumers. (18) Where consumers are many and any sort of food finds buyers. (19) 'Uḳ. III, 3; since a clean beast is usually intended for food both in town and in villages while the carcass of a clean bird and forbidden fat would find con-

ever, it is suggested: Of villages, [the difficulty arises:] Is there any authority who maintains that in this case no intention is required, seeing that we have learnt: The carcass of an unclean beast[1] anywhere[2] and the carcass of a clean bird in villages[3] require[4] intention[5] but need not be rendered susceptible?[6]—R. Ze'ira b. Ḥanina replied: We are in fact dealing with an incident in a big city, but[7] the winepress caused it[8] to be objectionable[9] and thus caused the town to be regarded as a village.

'R. Johanan b. Nuri argued: This is arrived at *a minori ad majus*. If it conveys a major uncleanness, though there was no intention, should it not convey a minor uncleanness though there was no intention? They answered him: No; if you maintain your view in the case of a major uncleanness which never descends to that.' What is meant by 'it never descends to that'?—Raba replied: It is this that they[10] in effect said to him,[11] 'No; if you maintain your view [51*a*] in the case of a major uncleanness which never causes an uncleanness of the same grade,[12] would you also maintain it in the case of a minor uncleanness which does cause an uncleanness of the same grade?'[13] Said Abaye to him: [Should not this[14] apply

sumers in large towns only but not in villages (cf. prev. two notes). Intention, therefore, is required in the latter case but not in the former.

(1) Which is not usually eaten. (2) Even in large towns. (3) Where consumers are few. (4) Since they are not usually eaten. (5) To enable them to convey uncleanness. In the case of the former, uncleanness is conveyed even in the absence of intention provided its bulk was no less than that of an olive. The intention, however, avails where the bulk of carcass was less than that of an olive and that of other food was less than the bulk of an egg. In such a case the two quantities combine to form together the prescribed bulk of an egg which contracts uncleanness through contact with a dead creeping thing. (6) Since they would eventually be subject to a major uncleanness. (7) The reason why the Rabbis require intention. (8) The pigeon. (9) So that it is not so very suitable for consumption. (10) The Rabbis. (11) R. Johanan b. Nuri. (12) When a carcass (a 'father of uncleanness'), for instance, imparted uncleanness to a person the latter cannot impart it to another person, since only a 'father of uncleanness' can carry uncleanness to persons. (13) Foodstuffs, for instance, that contracted an uncleanness may (Rabbinically) convey the same uncleanness to other foodstuffs. (14) The view that no intention is necessary.

to the latter] with even more reason: If a major uncleanness, concerning which the law has been relaxed in that it does not cause an uncleanness of the same grade,[1] conveys uncleanness in the absence of intention, how much more then should a minor uncleanness, concerning which the law has been restricted in that it does cause uncleanness of the same grade,[2] convey uncleanness even where there was no intention?—Rather, said R. Shesheth, It is this that they[3] implied: 'No; if you maintain your view[4] in the case of a major uncleanness, which need not be rendered susceptible,[5] would you also maintain it[4] in the case of a minor uncleanness which does require to be rendered susceptible?' But is it required to be rendered susceptible? Have we not in fact learnt:[6] Three[7] things have been said about the carrion of a clean bird,[8] it is necessary that it should be intended for food, it conveys uncleanness through the oesophagus only,[9] and there is no need for it to be rendered susceptible?[10]—Granted that it is not required that a dead creeping thing shall render it susceptible,[11] it is nevertheless necessary that it shall be rendered susceptible[12] by means of water.[13] Why[14] is it not required that a dead creeping thing shall render it susceptible? In agreement with what the school of R. Ishmael taught. But then there should be no need for it to be rendered susceptible by means of water also in agreement with what the school of R. Ishmael taught; for the school of R. Ishmael taught: *Upon any sowing seed which is to be sown*,[15] as seeds[12] which do not eventually contract a major uncleanness[16] must[17] be rendered susceptible so must any other thing which does not eventually

(1) Cf. p. 350, n. 12. (2) V. p. 350, n. 13. (3) The Rabbis. (4) The view that no intention is necessary. (5) A carcass, for instance, is unclean irrespective of whether it had been rendered susceptible by liquids or not. (6) MS.M., 'was it not taught?' (7) In the Mishnah citation *supra* the reading for 'three' is '*thirteen*' (cf. prev. n.) (8) A minor uncleanness. (9) *Sc.* only when it is being swallowed is uncleanness conveyed to the person and to his clothes. (10) Cf. *supra* 50*b* q.v. notes. (11) *Sc.* that it shall cause it to become unclean. (12) Like any other foodstuffs. (13) Only after it had been purposely wetted is it susceptible to uncleanness. (14) Lit., 'wherein the difference?' (15) Lev. XI, 37. (16) *Sc.* they can never convey uncleanness to a person. (17) If they are to contract any uncleanness.

contract a major uncleanness be rendered susceptible; the carcass of a clean bird is excluded, in that it need not be rendered susceptible, since it eventually contracts a major uncleanness?[1]—Rather, replied Raba, or as some say R. Papa, [the reference[2] is to] a major uncleanness in general and to a minor uncleanness in general.[3]

Raba stated: R. Joḥanan,[4] however, agrees in regard to tithe that intention[5] concerning attached [produce] is a valid intention.[6] Raba explained, Whence do I derive this? From what we learnt: Savory,[7] hyssop and calamint[8] that are grown in a courtyard, if they are kept under watch,[9] are subject to tithe.[10] Now how are we to imagine the circumstances?[11] If it be suggested that these herbs were originally sown for human consumption [the difficulty would arise]: Was it at all necessary to enunciate such a law?[12] Consequently the circumstances must be such, must they not, that the herbs were originally sown for cattle food; and yet it was stated, 'if they are kept under watch'[13] they 'are subject to tithe'.[14] R. Ashi retorted: Here[10] we are dealing with a courtyard in which the herbs grew spontaneously[15] so that as a rule they are destined for human consumption, and[16] it is this that was meant: If the courtyard affords protection for the produce it grows[17]

(1) How then could it be maintained that it is 'necessary that it shall be rendered susceptible by means of water'? (2) In the argument of the Rabbis. (3) In the case of the former susceptibility is never required; hence it is that no intention is required either. In the case of the latter susceptibility is usually (though not in the particular case of a bird) required; hence it is that intention also is necessary. (4) Though he stated (*supra* 50*b*) that in regard to uncleanness intention concerning an attached plant is no valid intention. (5) To use the produce as food for men. (6) And it is in consequence subject to tithe. (7) *Satureia Thymbra*. (8) Or 'thyme'. (9) For the purpose, so it is now assumed, of using them for human consumption. (10) Ma'as. III, 9. (11) In which the law mentioned applies. (12) Of course not. The law is too obvious to be stated. (13) For the purpose, so it is now assumed, of using them for human consumption. (14) Which shows that intention regarding the use of attached produce in the case of tithe is valid. (15) *Sc.* they were never intended to be used as cattle food. (16) In reply to the objection: What need was there for enunciating a law that was too obvious? (17) In consequence of which the herbs cannot be regarded as *hefker* (v. Glos.).

the herbs are subject to tithe; otherwise they are exempt.[1]

R. Ashi objected:[2] Whatsoever is subject to tithes is susceptible to food uncleanness.[3] Now if that were so,[4] would there not be the case of these[5] which are liable to tithe[6] and yet[7] do not become susceptible to the uncleanness of food?[8]—The fact is, said Raba, that it is this that was meant: Any species that is liable to tithe is susceptible to food uncleanness. This[9] is also logically sound. For in the final clause[10] it was stated, Whatsoever is subject to the law of the first of the fleece[11] is also subject to that of the priestly gifts[12] but there may be a beast[13] that is subject to the law of the priestly gifts and is not subject to that of the first of the fleece.[14] Now if it were so[15] [the objection would arise]: Is there not also the case of the *ṭerefah* which is subject to the law of the first of the fleece and yet is not subject to that of the priestly gifts?[16]—Rabina retorted: This[17] represents the view of[18] R. Simeon. For it was taught:[19] R. Simeon exempts the *ṭerefah* from the law of the first of the fleece.[20] R. Shimi b. Ashi replied,[21] Come and hear: If a man declared his vineyard *hefker*[22] and, rising early in the morning, he cut its grapes, he is liable[23] to *pereṭ*,[24] *'oleloth*,[25] the forgotten sheaf[26] and *pe'ah*[27]

(1) *Hefker* being exempt from tithe. (2) Against Raba. (3) *Supra* 50*a*. (4) That intention to use attached produce for human consumption is valid enough as regards liability to tithe. (5) Endives sown for the purpose of producing cattle food concerning which the grower changed his mind, while they were still attached to the ground, and decided to use the crop as food for human consumption. (6) Since intention in this respect (cf. prev. n. but one) is valid. (7) Intention regarding attached produce being invalid in respect of susceptibility to uncleanness. (8) How then is Raba's statement to be reconciled with the Mishnah cited? (9) Raba's interpretation just given. (10) The Mishnah *infra* 51*b* which is the continuation of the previous Mishnah. (11) Cf. Deut. XVIII, 4. (12) The shoulder, the two cheeks and the maw given from slaughtered cattle (cf. ibid. 3). (13) An ox or a goat. (14) *Infra* 51*b*. (15) That a general statement like 'whatsoever etc.' includes every individual case. (16) Ḥul. 136*b*. Must it not consequently be admitted, as Raba explained, that by the general rule (cf. prev. n.) the whole species was meant? (17) The Mishnah just cited. (18) Lit., 'that whose? It is'. (19) V. marg. gl. Cur. edd. 'for we learnt'. (20) No proof, therefore, may be adduced from this Mishnah that a general rule refers to the entire species. (21) Justifying Raba's submission (cf. prev. n. but four). (22) V. Glos. (23) For the reason cf. B.Ḳ. 94*a*. (24) Single grapes dropped during the cutting (cf. Lev. XIX, 10)

but[1] is exempt from tithe.[2] But have we not learnt: WHATSOEVER IS SUBJECT TO THE OBLIGATION OF PE'AH IS ALSO SUBJECT TO THAT OF TITHES?[3] Must you not then infer from this[4] that the reference[5] was[6] to the whole species?[7] This is conclusive.

Elsewhere we have learnt:[8] The Sages agree with R. Akiba that if a man sowed dill or mustard seed in two or three different spots he must allow *pe'ah* from each.[9] [51*b*] Now dill, surely, since it is liable to *pe'ah* is also liable[10] to tithe, for we have learnt, WHATSOEVER IS SUBJECT TO THE OBLIGATION OF PE'AH IS ALSO SUBJECT TO THAT OF TITHES; and since it is liable to tithe it is also susceptible to food uncleanness. It is accordingly evident that anything that is used as a flavouring is susceptible to food uncleanness, since dill is used as a flavouring. But is not this incongruous with the following: 'Castus,[11] amomum,[12] and the principal spices, crowfoot, asafoetida, pepper and lozenges of bastard safron may be bought with second tithe money but they are not susceptible to food uncleanness; so R. Akiba. Said R. Joḥanan b. Nuri to him: If they may be bought with second tithe money why are they not susceptible to food uncleanness? And if they are not susceptible,[13] they[14] should not be bought with second tithe money',[15] and in connection with this R. Joḥanan b. Nuri stated, 'A vote was taken and they decided that these are not to be bought with second tithe money and that they are not susceptible to food uncleanness'?[16]—R. Ḥisda replied: When that Mishnah[17] was

which must be left for the poor. (25) 'Gleanings' of the vineyards or a small single bunch of grapes on a single branch which are the portion of the poor (cf. Lev. XIX, 10 and Deut. XXIV, 21). (26) Which had to be left for the poor (cf. Deut. XXIV, 19). (27) V. Glos. Cf. Lev. XIX, 9.

(1) Since the vineyard is *hefker*. (2) Ned. 44*b*. B.Ḳ. 94*a*. (3) How then are the two Tannaitic statements to be reconciled? (4) Cf. prev. n. (5) In the general rule, 'Whatsoever etc.'. (6) Not to each individual case. (7) Of course one must. Raba's submission is thus confirmed. (8) This is quoted here because an objection against it is raised from our Mishnah. (9) Pe'ah III, 2. (10) V. BaḤ. (11) Κοστός, a fragrant root. (12) Cf. ἄμωμον, a spice indigenous to India and Syria. (13) To food uncleanness, which is evidence that they are not regarded as a foodstuff. (14) Since only foodstuffs may be bought with second tithe money. (15) 'Uḳ. III, 5. (16) Now how is this Mishnah (from which it follows that flavouring spices are not susceptible

taught the reference was to dill intended as an ingredient[1] of *kamak*.[2] R. Ashi stated, I submitted the following argument before R. Kahana:[3] Do not say, 'The reference was to dill intended[4] as an ingredient of *kamak*', from which it would follow that generally[5] it is used as flavouring matter,[6] but rather that dill is generally intended as an ingredient of *kamak*.[7] For we have learnt: Dill,[8] as soon as it has imparted some flavour to a dish, is no longer subject to the restrictions of *terumah*[9] and it is no longer susceptible to food uncleanness.[10] From which it follows that before it had imparted any flavour to a dish it is subject to the restrictions of *terumah* and is susceptible to food uncleanness.[11] Now if you were to imagine that as a rule it is used for flavouring[6] [the difficulty would arise]: Even if it had not imparted any flavour to a dish [should it not be free from the restrictions of food since] as a rule it is used for flavouring?[12] Must you not then infer from this[13] that generally it is used as an ingredient of *kamak*?[7] This is conclusive.

MISHNAH. WHATSOEVER IS SUBJECT TO THE LAW OF THE FIRST OF THE FLEECE[14] IS ALSO SUBJECT TO THAT OF THE PRIESTLY GIFTS,[12] BUT THERE MAY BE [A BEAST][16] THAT IS SUBJECT TO THE LAW OF THE PRIESTLY GIFTS AND NOT

to food uncleanness) to be reconciled with the inference drawn *supra* from the Mishnah of Pe'ah III, 2? (17) Of Pe'ah, from which it was inferred that dill is regarded as food.

(1) Not as a mere flavouring. (2) A milk sauce. Such dill is rightly regarded as a foodstuff and is consequently susceptible to food uncleanness. (3) Cur. edd. in parenthesis add, 'he said'. (4) Emphasis on this word. (5) Where the owner's intention has not been expressed. (6) Lit., 'for (the flavouring of) the dish', and should, therefore, be exempt from food uncleanness. (7) And so subject to all the laws of a foodstuff. (8) Of *terumah*. (9) Should the root subsequently fall into a dish of ordinary food no complications would arise. (10) 'Uḳ. III, 4; it being regarded as mere flavouring matter. (11) I.e., it is regarded as food. (12) Of course it should. Why then was its exemption from the restrictions made dependent on the imparting of some flavour to a dish? (13) Cf. prev. n. (14) Cf. Deut. XVIII, 4. (15) *Sc.* the shoulder, the two cheeks and the maw that are due to the priest from slaughtered cattle (cf. Deut. XVIII, 3). (16) An ox or a goat.

TO THAT OF THE FIRST OF THE FLEECE. WHATSOEVER IS SUBJECT TO THE LAW OF REMOVAL[1] IS ALSO SUBJECT TO THE RESTRICTIONS OF THE SABBATICAL YEAR,[2] BUT THERE IS [A KIND OF PRODUCE] THAT IS SUBJECT TO THE RESTRICTIONS OF THE SABBATICAL YEAR[2] AND IS NOT SUBJECT TO THE LAW OF REMOVAL.[1]

GEMARA. As, for instance, the leaves of arum and of miltwaste.[3]

THERE IS A KIND OF PRODUCE THAT IS SUBJECT TO THE RESTRICTIONS OF THE SABBATICAL YEAR AND IS NOT SUBJECT TO THE LAW OF REMOVAL, the root of the arum and the root of miltwaste, since it is written in Scripture, *And for thy cattle and for the beasts that are in thy land, shall all the increase thereof be for food,*[4] as long as '*the beasts*' eat[5] from the field you may feed '*thy cattle*' in the house, but when the produce comes to an end for '*the beasts*' in the field you must bring it to an end for '*thy cattle*' which are in the house; but these,[6] surely, have not come to an end.

MISHNAH. WHATSOEVER[7] HAS SCALES HAS FINS BUT THERE ARE SOME THAT HAVE FINS AND NO SCALES. WHATSOEVER[8] HAS HORNS HAS HOOFS BUT THERE ARE SOME THAT HAVE HOOFS AND NO HORNS.

GEMARA. WHATSOEVER HAS SCALES [etc.] [viz.] a clean fish;[9] THERE ARE SOME THAT HAVE FINS AND NO SCALES, refers to an unclean fish.[10] Now consider: Since we[11] rely on the

(1) In the Sabbatical year. When no produce is left in the field for the beasts the owner must remove all stored produce from his house into the field (cf. Deut. XXVI, 13). (2) Cf. Lev. XXV, 2ff. (3) These and similar products are SUBJECT TO THE LAW OF REMOVAL since (cf. *infra*) their supply is exhausted before the end of the year, and also TO THE RESTRICTIONS OF THE SABBATICAL YEAR. (4) Lev. XXV, 7. (5) *Okeleth* of the same rt. as *le'ekol* (rendered *supra*, '*for food*'). (6) The roots of the herbs mentioned. (7) Among fishes. (8) Among animals. (9) *Sc.* one that may be eaten. (10) Cf. prev. n. *mut. mut.* (11) In determining whether a fish is clean or unclean.

scales,[1] what need then was there for the all Merciful to mention[2] *fins?*[3]—If the All Merciful had not written *fins* it might have been presumed that the written word *kaskeseth*[4] meant[5] fins and that even an unclean fish [is, therefore, permitted]. Hence has the All Merciful written *'fins'* and *'scales'*.[6] But now that the All Merciful has written both *'fins'* and *'scales'*, whence is it deduced that *kaskeseth*[4] means the covering? Because it is written, *And he was clad with a coat of mail.*[7] Then why[8] did not the All Merciful write *kaskeseth*[4] and there would be no need for the mention of *fins?*[9]—R. Abbahu replied and so it was also taught at the school of R. Ishmael: *To make the teaching great and glorious.*[10]

MISHNAH. WHATSOEVER REQUIRES A BENEDICTION AFTER IT REQUIRES ONE BEFORE IT, BUT THERE ARE THINGS THAT REQUIRE A BENEDICTION BEFORE THEM AND NOT AFTER THEM.

GEMARA. [What was the last clause[11] intended] to include?—To include vegetables. But according to R. Isaac who did say a benediction[12] after the eating of vegetables, what was this[11] intended to include?—To include water. But according to R. Papa who said a benediction[12] after he drank water, what was it[11] intended to include?—To include the performance of commandments.[13] But according to the Palestinians[14] who after removing their *tefillin*

(1) As has been stated in our Mishnah, WHATSOEVER HAS SCALES HAS FINS. (2) As one of the marks of a clean fish in Lev. XI, 9ff. (3) Lit., 'fins which the All Merciful has written, wherefore to me'. (4) The word rendered *'scales'*. (5) Lit., 'what *kaskeseth* that is written.' (6) Thus indicating that each is a distinctive mark. (7) *Kaskasim* (of the same rt, as *kaskeseth*). I Sam. XVII, 5. (8) Since the meaning of *kaskeseth* is definitely established and cannot be mistaken for that of fins. (9) Since WHATSOEVER HAS SCALES HAS FINS. (10) Isa. XLII, 21. Even an apparently superfluous word adds to the greatness and glory of the Torah. (11) BUT THERE ARE etc. (12) '... who createst many living beings' (cf. P.B. p. 290). (13) Those, for instance, of *lulab, shofar, zizith* and *tefillin* which require a benediction only before and not after they are performed. (14) Lit., 'the sons of the west'. Palestine lay to the west of Babylon where the discussion took place.

say the benediction of '... who hath sanctified us by his commandments, and hath commanded us to keep his statutes', what does this[1] include?—It includes [52a] fragrant odours.[2]

MISHNAH. IF A GIRL[3] HAS GROWN TWO PUBIC HAIRS SHE[4] MAY EITHER PERFORM ḤALIẒAH OR CONTRACT LEVIRATE MARRIAGE, AND SHE IS UNDER AN OBLIGATION TO PERFORM ALL THE COMMANDMENTS THAT ARE ENUMERATED IN THE TORAH. SO ALSO A BOY, IF HE HAS GROWN TWO PUBIC HAIRS, IS UNDER AN OBLIGATION TO PERFORM ALL THE COMMANDMENTS ENUMERATED IN THE TORAH. HE IS FURTHERMORE LIABLE TO THE PENALTY OF A STUBBORN AND REBELLIOUS SON[5] AS SOON AS HE HAS GROWN TWO HAIRS UNTIL THE TIME WHEN HIS BEARD FORMS A CIRCLE.[6] (THIS REFERS TO THE LOWER, AND NOT TO THE UPPER ONE, BUT[7] THE SAGES USED A EUPHEMISM,)[8] A GIRL WHO HAS GROWN TWO HAIRS[9] MAY NO LONGER EXERCISE THE RIGHT OF MI'UN. R. JUDAH RULED: MI'UN MAY BE EXERCISED UNTIL THE BLACK[10] PREDOMINATES.[11]

GEMARA. But since we have learnt, SHE IS UNDER AN OBLIGATION TO PERFORM ALL THE COMMANDMENTS THAT ARE ENUMERATED IN THE TORAH, what need was there for stating, SHE MAY EITHER PERFORM ḤALIẒAH OR CONTRACT LEVIRATE MARRIAGE?[12]—To exclude a ruling of R. Jose who stated, 'In the Biblical section[13] it is written *man*,[14] but as regards a woman there

(1) BUT THERE ARE etc. (2) Before the smelling of which, but not after, a benediction (cf. P.B. p. 290) is said. (3) Being twelve years and one day old. (4) If her husband died childless. (5) Cf. Deut. XXI, 18ff and Sanh. 68*b*. (6) When he is regarded as an adult who is no longer subject to this law. (7) In speaking in vague terms. (8) Lit., 'spoke in clean language'. (9) Having thus passed out of her minority. (10) The pubic hair. (11) The growth of no more than two hairs does not suffice in his opinion to deprive her of the right of *mi'un* (cf. Gemara *infra*). (12) Which are rites already included in the general rule. (13) Of *ḥaliẓah*. (14) Deut. XXV, 7; '*man*', excluding the woman, implies that only the male must be of age.

is no difference between a major and a minor'.[1] Hence we were informed that[2] if she has grown two hairs she may perform *halizah*,[3] but otherwise she may not. What is the reason? A woman is to be compared to man.[4]

But since it was stated, SO ALSO A BOY, IF HE HAS GROWN TWO PUBIC HAIRS,[5] what need was there for stating, HE IS UNDER AN OBLIGATION TO PERFORM ALL THE COMMANDMENTS ENUMERATED IN THE TORAH? And should you reply: Because it was desired to teach, HE IS FURTHERMORE LIABLE TO THE PENALTY OF A STUBBORN AND REBELLIOUS SON [the objection would arise]: Have we not learnt this once: 'When does one become liable to the penalty of a stubborn and rebellious son? As soon as one grows two hairs until the time the beard forms a circle. (By this was meant the lower, and not the upper one, but the Sages used a euphemism)'?—This is so indeed; only because details were specified about the girl those relating to the boy were also specified.

IF A GIRL HAS GROWN etc. R. Abbahu citing R. Eleazar stated, The *halachah* is in agreement with R. JUDAH. R. Judah, however, agrees that if she was subjected to cohabitation after she had grown two hairs,[6] she may no longer exercise the right of *mi'un*.[7] The colleagues of R. Kahana desired to give a practical decision[8] in agreement with the ruling of R. Judah, although intercourse had taken place, but R. Kahana addressed them as follows: Did not such an incident happen with the daughter of R. Ishmael?[9] She, namely, came to the schoolhouse to exercise the right of *mi'un*

(1) *Sc.* a minor also may perform *halizah*. (2) In the case of a girl also. (3) Lit., 'yes'. (4) Cf. Yeb. 105*b*, B.B. 156*a*. (5) A statement which brings the boy under the same obligations as the girl. (6) So that there was a valid marriage *kinyan* (cf. Kid. 2a) after she had attained her majority. (7) Only where no intercourse had taken place after two hairs have grown does R. Judah maintain his view (cf. relevant n. on our Mishnah). The first Tanna, however, maintains that, even if she allowed only one moment to pass after the growth of two hairs, irrespective of whether intercourse did or did not take place, her right to *mi'un* is lost. (8) Lit., 'to do a deed'. (9) Who, after her father's death, while she was in her minority was given in marriage by her mother.

while her son was riding on her shoulder; and on that day were the views of R. Ishmael mentioned at the schoolhouse; and the Rabbis wept bitterly[1] saying, 'Over a ruling which that righteous man[2] had laid down should his offspring stumble!' For Rab Judah citing Samuel who had it from R. Ishmael stated: *And she be not seized,*[3] [then only][4] is she forbidden,[5] but if she was seized she is permitted. There is, however, another class of woman who is permitted[5] even if she was not seized. And who is that? A woman whose betrothal was a mistaken one,[6] and who, even if her son sits riding on her shoulder, may exercise the right of *mi'un* and go away.[7] Thereupon they took a vote and decided: Up to what age may a girl[8] exercise the right of *mi'un?* Until that at which she grows two hairs. [On hearing this incident] they[9] abstained and did not act as they first intended.[10]

R. Isaac and the disciples of R. Ḥanina gave a practical decision in agreement with R. Judah, though the girl had been subjected to intercourse. R. Shamin b. Abba proceeded to tell it in the presence of R. Joḥanan; R. Joḥanan proceeded to tell it in the presence of R. Judah Nesi'ah[11] and the latter sent a constable[12] who took her away.[13]

R. Ḥisda citing Mar Uḳba stated: The meaning[14] is not that the black must actually predominate but that it shall be such as, when two hairs lie flat, has the appearance[15] of the black predominating over the white.[16] Raba stated: Two hairs that reach from rim to rim.

(1) Lit., 'a great weeping'. For the reading cf. MS.M. Cur. edd. 'and she wept . . . in the schoolhouse and they said'. (2) R. Ishmael. (3) Num. V, 13. E.V. *neither she be taken in the act.* (4) *Sc.* if she did not act under compulsion but willingly. (5) To her husband. (6) If, for instance, a condition was attached to it and the condition remained unfulfilled, or if the marriage was with a minor (in the absence of her father) whose act (even with the consent of her mother) has no validity. In such a case the woman may leave her husband without a letter of divorce and she has the status of a *feme sole* who had never before been married. (7) Since the marriage had no validity. (8) Lit., 'the daughter'. (9) R. Kahana's colleagues. (10) Lit., 'and did not do the deed'. (11) The Prince, Judah II. (12) Or 'a detachment of police'. Lit., 'searcher'. (13) From her second husband who had married her in reliance on her *mi'un*. (14) Of R. Judah's ruling on our Mishnah. (15) Owing to the length of the hairs. (16) The skin.

R. Ḥelbo citing R. Huna stated: The two hairs of which the Rabbis spoke[1] must[2] have follicles at their roots. R. Malkio citing R. Adda b. Ahabah ruled: Follicles suffice even in the absence of hairs. Said R. Ḥanina the son of R. Iḳa: The rulings concerning a spit,[3] bondwomen[4] and follicles[5] were laid down by R. Malkio, but those concerning a forelock,[6] wood-ash[7] and cheese[8] were laid down by R. Malkia. R. Papa, however, stated: If the statement was made on a Mishnah or a Baraitha the author is R. Malkia but if on reported traditions[9] the author is R. Malkio. And the mnemonic[10] is, 'The mathnitha[11] is queen'.[12] What is the practical difference between them?[13]—The practical difference between them is the statement on bondwomen.[14] R. Ashi stated, Mar Zuṭra told me that R. Ḥanina of Sura felt about this the following difficulty: Would not a single Tanna[15] go out of his way to teach[16] us the law of the follicles?—If one[17] had informed us of the law of the follicles it might have been presumed that [puberty is not established] unless there were two hairs in two follicles respectively, hence we

(1) V. our Mishnah. (2) If they are to be taken as a mark of puberty. (3) That has been used on a festival for the roasting of meat, may, by an indirect movement, be made to slip into a corner, though direct movement is forbidden (v. Beẓah 28*b*). (4) Brought by a woman to her husband at her marriage (v. Keth. 59*b*). (5) The law cited here. (6) The law that an Israelite who trims the hairs of a heathen must withdraw his hand at a distance of three fingers' breadth on every side of the forelock (v. A.Z. 29*a*). (7) Forbidden to be spread on a wound because it gives it the appearance of an incised imprint (v. Mak. 21*a*). (8) If made by a heathen is forbidden to be eaten on account of the lard that he smears over it. (9) *Shemathatha*, those not recorded in a Mishnah or a Baraitha. (10) To help one to recollect which of the statements mentioned were made by R. Malkio and R. Malkia respectively. (11) *Mathnitha*, a general term for both Mishnah and Baraitha as opposed to *shemathatha* (cf. prev. n. but one). (12) *Sc.* more authoritative than a reported statement. Malkia (מלכיא) whose name closely resembles מלכתא (queen) is to be associated with the Mishnah and the Baraitha that are designated 'queen'. (13) R. Ḥanina and R. Papa. (14) Which is recorded in a Mishnah. According to R. Papa the comment on it must be that of R. Malkia (cf. prev. n. but one) while according to R. Ḥanina it is one of the rulings attributed to R. Malkio. (15) If follicles alone, in the absence of hairs, sufficed to establish puberty. (16) Anywhere in the Mishnah. (17) Tanna.

were informed[1] that even two hairs in one follicle are sufficient. But is there such a phenomenon?[2] Is it not in fact written in Scripture, *He that would break me with a tempest, and multiply my wounds without cause*[3] in connection with which Raba[4] remarked: Job blasphemed with the mention of tempest and he was answered with a tempest. He 'blasphemed with the mention of tempest', saying to Him, 'Sovereign of the world, perhaps a tempest has passed before Thee, and caused Thee to confuse "Job"[5] with "enemy"?'[6] 'He was answered with a tempest': *Then the Lord answered* [52b] *Job out of the whirlwind, and said*[7] to him, 'Most foolish man,[8] I have created many hairs[9] in a man's head and for every hair I have created a separate follicle, so that two should not suck from the same follicle, for if two were to suck from the same follicle they would impair the sight of man. I did not confuse one follicle with another, would I confuse "Job" and "enemy"?'[10]—This is no difficulty since one[11] refers to the body while the other[12] refers to the head.

Rab Judah citing Samuel ruled: The two hairs of which they spoke [establish puberty] even if one is on the crest and the other on the testes. So it was also taught: The two hairs of which they spoke [establish puberty] even if one grows on her back and the other on her belly, one on the joints of the fingers of her hand and the other on the joints of her toes; so R. Simeon b. Judah of Kefar Akko who cited it in the name of R. Ishmael.[13] But Rab citing R. Assi ruled: Puberty is not established unless two hairs grow in the same spot.

Our Rabbis taught: Up to what age may a girl exercise the right

(1) By the mention of two hairs only. (2) Two hairs in one follicle. (3) Job IX, 17. (4) Var. lec. Rabbah (cf. B.B. 16*a*). (5) איוב (*Iyob*). (6) אויב (*Oyeb*). (7) Job XXXVIII, 1. (8) Lit., 'fool that (you are) in the world'. (9) The Heb. word for tempest, *'se'arah'*, may also be rendered 'hair'. (10) From which it is obvious that two hairs can never grow from the same follicle. How then could it be maintained (*supra* 52*a*) that two hairs may sometimes grow from the same follicle? (11) The case of the hairs mentioned in our Mishnah. (12) The hairs mentioned in connection with Job. (13) The reading to 'ruled' is that of MS.M. Cur. edd. read, 'And the Rabbis [what is their view]? R. Ḥisda replied'. BaḤ substitutes 'Ashi' for 'Ḥisda'.

of *mi'un?* Until she grows two hairs; so R. Meir. R. Judah ruled: Until the black predominates.[1] R. Jose ruled: Until a ring is formed around the nipple. Ben Shelakoth ruled: Until she grows her hair in profusion.[2] In connection with this R. Simeon stated: Ḥanina b. Ḥakinai once met me at Zidon and said to me,[3] 'When you arrive at R. Akiba's ask him "until what age may a girl exercise the right of *mi'un*". If he tells you, "Until she grows two hairs", ask him this: Did not Ben Shelakoth testify in the presence of all of you at Jamnia, "Until she grows her hair in profusion", and you did not say to him a word to the contrary?' When I arrived at R. Akiba's the latter told me, 'I do not know anything about the growing of hair in profusion, and I do not know Ben Shelakoth; a girl may exercise the right of *mi'un* until the age when she grows two hairs'.

MISHNAH. THE TWO HAIRS SPOKEN OF IN REGARD TO THE RED HEIFER[4] AND IN REGARD TO LEPROSY[5] AS WELL AS THOSE SPOKEN OF ANYWHERE ELSE[6] MUST BE LONG ENOUGH FOR THEIR TIPS TO BE BENT TO THEIR ROOTS; SO R. ISHMAEL. R. ELIEZER RULED: LONG ENOUGH TO BE GRASPED BY A FINGER-NAIL. R. AKIBA RULED: LONG ENOUGH TO BE TAKEN OFF WITH SCISSORS.

GEMARA. R. Ḥisda citing Mar Ukba stated: The *halachah* is in agreement with the views of all these in that the law is thereby invariably restricted.[7]

MISHNAH. A WOMAN WHO OBSERVED A BLOOD-STAIN[8]

(1) Cf. relevant n. on our Mishnah. (2) Cf. Tosaf. (3) So MS.M. (4) Cf. A.Z. 24*a* and Parah II, 5. (5) Cf. Neg. I, 5. (6) In regard to the marks of puberty. (7) *Sc.* as soon as the hairs grow to the smallest length mentioned in our Mishnah she is no longer regarded as minor and the right of *mi'un* is denied to her, while *ḥaliẓah* may not be performed until the hairs grew to the maximum of the lengths mentioned, when her majority is beyond all doubt. (8) On her underclothing.

IS IN AN UNSETTLED CONDITION[1] AND MUST[2] TAKE INTO CONSIDERATION THE POSSIBILITY THAT IT WAS DUE TO ZIBAH; SO R. MEIR. BUT THE SAGES RULED: IN THE CASE OF BLOOD-STAINS THERE IS NO [NEED TO CONSIDER THE POSSIBILITY OF THEIR BEING] DUE TO ZIBAH.

GEMARA. Who are THE SAGES?—R. Ḥanina b. Antigonus. For it was taught: R. Ḥanina b. Antigonus ruled, In the case of blood-stains there is no [need to consider the possibility of their being] due to *zibah*, but sometimes blood-stains do lead to *zibah*. How so? If a woman[3] put on three shirts that she had previously examined and then found a blood-stain on each of them, or if she[4] observed a discharge[5] on two days and [a blood-stain on] one shirt,[6] these are the blood-stains that lead to *zibah*. But since in the case of three shirts, where she observed no direct discharge from her body, the possibility of *zibah* is taken into consideration, why was it necessary to mention[7] that of 'two days and one shirt'?—It might have been presumed[8] that in any instance like this[9] the woman brings a sacrifice which may be eaten,[10] hence we were informed [that only the possibility[11] of *zibah* is taken into consideration].[12] Raba observed: In this matter R. Ḥanina b. Antigonus vindicated his case against the Rabbis. For why is it [that when a bloodstain] less than three beans in size is in one spot we

(1) Lit., 'damaged', *sc.* the calculations (that enable her to determine in which days she is liable to menstruation and in which she is susceptible to *zibah*) are upset since she is unable to ascertain when exactly the discharge (of which the blood-stain is the result) had occurred. (2) Under certain circumstances (cf. Gemara *infra*). (3) On three consecutive days respectively during the period in which she is susceptible to *zibah*. (4) In the *zibah* period (cf. prev. n.). (5) An actual flow of blood. (6) That was previously duly examined. (7) That *zibah* must be taken into consideration. (8) If the latter case had not been mentioned. (9) Two actual discharges and one blood-stain. (10) *Sc.* that the sacrifice is deemed to be valid as in the case of certain *zibah*. (11) But not the certainty. (12) So that the sacrifice is of a doubtful nature. As the method of killing that is prescribed for a bird sacrifice renders an unconsecrated bird *nebelah* and forbidden to be eaten, the bird sacrifice offered in this case must (on account of its doubtful nature) be forbidden to be eaten.

do not take into consideration the possibility of *zibah?* [Presumably] because we assume that it is the result of observations on two days.[1] But then why should we not, even if a stain of the size of three beans was in one spot, similarly assume that only to the extent of the size of two and a half beans the discharge was from her body while the rest is the blood of a louse due to the filth?[2]—And the Rabbis?[3]—Since the stain[4] can be divided up into parts of the size of a bean and over for each day[5] we do not ascribe it to any external cause. As to R. Ḥanina b. Antigonus, is it[6] only when a stain of the size of three beans in one spot that we do not take the possibility of *zibah* into consideration, but if it is in three different places[7] the possibility is taken into consideration? But did you not say[8] that this[9] applies only to stains on[10] three shirts,[11] from which it follows that it does not apply to stains[12] in three spots?[13]—He[14] spoke to them on the line of the view of the Rabbis. As far as I am concerned, he said in effect, it[15] applies only to three shirts[11] and not to three spots;[13] but according to your view, agree with me at least that, where she had observed a stain of the size of three beans in one spot, we assume that to the extent of two and a half beans the discharge came from her body while the rest is the blood of a louse due to the filth. And the Rabbis?—Since the stain[16] can be divided up into parts of the size of a little more than a bean for each day,[17] we do not ascribe it to any external cause.

Our Rabbis taught: If a woman observed a blood-stain, if it is big enough[16] to be divided into parts corresponding respectively

(1) While *zibah* cannot be established unless discharges occurred on three consecutive days. (2) Of menstruation; so that (cf. prev. n.) there was no *zibah* at all. (3) How can they maintain their ruling in view of this argument? (4) Being of generous dimensions and rather larger than the size of three beans. (5) So that on each day there may have been a new stain of the size prescribed. (6) As Raba's statement seems to suggest. (7) Though on the same shirt. (8) In the Baraitha *supra*. (9) That the possibility of *zibah* is taken into consideration. (10) Lit., 'yes'. (11) One stain on each. (12) Lit., 'not'. (13) On the same shirt. (14) R. Ḥanina according to Raba's submission. (15) That the possibility of *zibah* is taken into consideration. (16) Being of generous dimensions and rather larger than the size of three beans. (17) So that on each day there may have been a new stain of the size prescribed.

to three beans, each of which being slightly bigger than the size of a bean, she must take into consideration the possibility of *zibah;* otherwise, she need not take this possibility into consideration. R. Judah b. Agra citing R. Jose ruled: In the one case and in the other[1] the possibility must be taken into consideration.[2] [53*a*] Rabbi stated: R. Judah b. Agra's ruling is acceptable where she did not examine[3] and the ruling of the Sages where she did examine. What is meant by 'she did examine' and by 'she did not examine'? —Raba replied: I found the Rabbis of the schoolhouse sitting at their studies and discoursing thus: 'Here[4] we are dealing with the case of a woman who examined herself,[5] but did not examine her shirt;[6] and even her own body was examined by her only at the twilight of R. Judah,[7] while at the twilight of R. Jose[8] she did not examine herself. In such a case, the Rabbis being of the opinion that at the twilight of R. Jose it is already night, [the question of *zibah* does not arise] since she had examined herself at the twilight of R. Judah,[9] and R. Jose follows his own view, he having stated that twilight is a doubtful time'.[10] But I said to him: 'Had her hands

(1) *Sc.* even if the stain was no bigger than the size of two beans. (2) Since it is possible that at least one of the stains was due to a discharge at twilight which counts as two (v. *infra*). (3) This is discussed presently. (4) In the dispute between R. Judah b. Agra and the Rabbis. (5) Each day at twilight. (6) Which was examined for the first time on the third day when a stain of the size of two beans was discovered. As it is thus unknown when the stain was made, the possibility must be taken into consideration that there may have been a discharge at the twilight of each, or at least one, of the two days; and, since a discharge at twilight counts as two (one for the passing and one for the coming day), that she had experienced no less than three discharges on three consecutive days. (7) Which extends after sunset for a time during which one can walk a distance of a thousand cubits. (8) Which lasts no longer than a 'wink of the eye', beginning and ending later than R. Judah's twilight. (9) When she had ascertained that on that day she was clean. Any subsequent discharge at the twilight of R. Jose could only be counted as one for the following day. The total of her discharges cannot consequently have been more than two. (10) Cf. prev. n. but one. As it is possible that there was a discharge at that time (which counts as both possible day and possible night) the woman must be treated as if she experienced two discharges (one on the passing, and one on the incoming day) in addition to

been kept in her eyes[1] throughout the twilight[2] you would[3] have spoken well,[4] but now,[5] is it not possible that she experienced a discharge[6] as soon as she had removed her hands?'[7] They then told me, 'We only spoke of a case where the woman had her hands in her eyes[1] throughout the twilight'.

'Rabbi stated: R. Judah b. Agra's ruling[8] is acceptable where she did not examine'. Now[9] what is meant by 'she did not examine'? If it be suggested that she examined herself in the twilight of R. Judah but did not examine herself in the twilight of R. Jose [the difficulty would arise]: From this[10] it follows that R. Judah holds[11] that even where she examined herself both times,[12] the possibility of *zibah* must be considered; [but why should this be so] seeing that she did examine herself?[13] It is obvious then [that the meaning[14] is] that she did not examine herself either in the twilight of R. Judah or in that of R. Jose;[15] but if she had examined herself in R. Judah's twilight[16] and did not examine herself in R. Jose's[17] there is no need for her to consider the possibility [of *zibah*].[18] It is thus clear that the twilight of R. Jose is according to

the discharge on the other day in question, thus making a total of three discharges.

(1) Euphemism. (2) Of R. Judah. (3) As far as the Rabbis are concerned. (4) Since it would have been definitely established that during the passing day no discharge had occurred. (5) That a general statement was made that the discharge is always ascribed to one day only. (6) During the twilight of R. Judah. (7) And this would count as two. (8) That the possibility of *zibah* is to be considered even where a stain is not big enough to be divided into three parts, each of the prescribed minimum. (9) Since Rabbi stated that only in this case he accepted the ruling of R. Judah b. Agra, it follows that where she did examine herself he does not accept his ruling though R. Judah himself maintains that the possibility of *zibah* must be considered even in the latter case. (10) Since 'no examination' only means the absence of one in R. Jose's twilight though one did take place in R. Judah's twilight. (11) Cf. prev. n. but one. (12) The twilight of R. Judah and the twilight of R. Jose. (13) Making sure that on that day there was no discharge. How then could one subsequent possible discharge in the night be counted as two? (14) Of the expression 'she did not examine'. (15) So that the possibility must be considered that she may have experienced a discharge in R. Judah's twilight. (16) Thus ascertaining that she was clean on that day. (17) Which is regarded as night. (18) Since one discharge in the night cannot possibly be counted as two discharges.

Rabbi[1] regarded as night.[2] Now read the final clause: 'And the ruling of the Sages where she did examine'. What is meant by 'she did examine'? If it be suggested that she examined herself in the twilight of R. Judah but did not examine herself in that of R. Jose,[3] it would follow[4] that the Rabbis are of the opinion that even if she did not examine herself in either[5] there is no need to consider the possibility of *zibah* [but why should this be so] seeing that she did not examine herself?[6] It is obvious then that [the meaning[7] is] that she examined herself both in the twilight of R. Judah and in that of R. Jose, but that if she had examined herself in the twilight of R. Judah and not in that of R. Jose the possibility of *zibah*[8] must be considered.[9] It is thus clear that the twilight of R. Jose is according to Rabbi[10] regarded as doubtful time.[11] Does not this then present a contradiction between two statements of Rabbi?[12]—It is this that he[13] meant: The view of R. Judah b. Agra[14] is acceptable to the Rabbis[15] when she did not examine herself at all either in R. Judah's twilight or

(1) Who on this point disagrees with R. Judah. (2) Cf. prev. n. but two. (3) And it is in this case only that Rabbi stated that the ruling of the Sages is acceptable but, it follows, where she examined herself in neither, though the Rabbis still maintain that the possibility of *zibah* need not be considered he holds that it must be taken into consideration. (4) Cf. prev. n. (5) Lit., 'in the two'. The twilights of R. Judah and R. Jose respectively. (6) In consequence of which she may have experienced a discharge at twilight when the one discharge is counted as two. How then could the possibility of *zibah* be ruled out? (7) Of the expression 'she did examine', in Rabbi's approval of the ruling of the Sages. (8) According to Rabbi who in this case disagrees with the Sages' ruling. (9) It being possible that she experienced a discharge in R. Jose's twilight when one discharge is counted as two. (10) Who on this point disagrees with the Sages. (11) Cf. prev. n. but one. (12) Lit., 'a difficulty of Rabbi on Rabbi'. According to the inference from the first clause R. Jose's twilight is regarded by him as right while according to the inference from the final clause it is doubtful whether it is day or night. (13) Rabbi. (14) That the possibility of a discharge at twilight is to be considered. (15) Not to himself; *sc.* Rabbi did not express any opinion as to what view he accepted and with whom he agreed (as was previously assumed when the contradiction was pointed out) but merely explained the extent and limits of the dispute between the Sages and R. Judah b. Agra.

in that of R. Jose's, for even the Sages differed from him[1] only when she has examined herself in R. Judah's twilight[2] and did not examine herself in that of R. Jose,[3] but where she did not examine herself at all they agree with him.[4] But does not the following show incongruity?[5] [For it was taught:] If a woman observed a blood-stain, the observation being one of a large one,[6] she must take into consideration the possibility of a discharge at twilight,[7] but if the observation was one of a small stain[8] she should not take the possibility into consideration. This is the ruling of R. Judah b. Agra who cited it in the name of R. Jose. Said Rabbi: I heard from him[9] that in both cases must the possibility be taken into consideration; 'and', he said to me, 'it is for this reason: What if she had been a menstruant who did not[10] make sure of her cleanness[11] from the *minḥa* time[12] and onwards, would she not[13] have been regarded as being in a presumptive state of uncleanness?'[14] And his ruling is acceptable to me where she has examined herself. Now what is meant by 'she has examined herself'? If it be suggested that she has examined herself in the twilight of R. Judah and did

(1) In maintaining that the possibility (cf. p. 368, n. 14) may be disregarded. (2) Thus ascertaining that there was no discharge at twilight. (3) Which in their opinion is regarded as night. (4) Cf. p. 368 n. 14. R. Jose, however, who holds his twilight to be a doubtful time, takes into consideration the possibility of a discharge in his twilight which would be regarded as two, one of which must be attributed to the passing, and the other to the incoming day. (5) With what had been said *supra* that according to R. Judah b. Agra it is not certain whether the twilight of R. Jose is night or day. (6) One that can be divided into three stains each of which is slightly bigger than the size of a bean. (7) Which counts as two. (8) *Sc.* one not bigger than a little more than the size of two beans, so that it can only be divided into two stains of the prescribed minimum. (9) R. Jose. (10) On the seventh day after menstruation. (11) Lit., 'separated in cleanness'. (12) Two and a half seasonal hours before nightfall. (13) Though in the morning she made sure of her cleanness. (14) Of course she would, and in consequence she would not be allowed to undergo immersion in the evening. Thus it follows that in the absence of an examination, the possibility of a discharge is considered. Similarly in the case of the stain under discussion, since no examination was held at twilight, the possibility of a discharge that must be counted as two must be taken into consideration.

not examine herself in that of R. Jose, it would follow that R. Judah b. Agra holds that even though she did not examine herself either in the twilight of R. Judah or in that of R. Jose the possibility need not be considered; but why should this be so seeing that she did not examine herself? It must be obvious then that she did examine herself both in the twilight of R. Judah and in that of R. Jose. Thus it follows that R. Judah b. Agra holds that if she examined herself in the twilight of R. Judah and not in that of R. Jose she need not consider the possibility. It is thus clear that the twilight of R. Jose is according to R. Judah b. Agra regarded as night. Does not this then present a contradiction between two rulings of R. Judah b. Agra?[1] In the absence of Rabbi's interpretations[2] there would well be no difficulty, since the former ruling might refer to a case where she has examined herself in R. Judah's twilight and not in that of R. Jose while here it is a case where she has examined herself in R. Jose's twilight as in that of R. Judah's; but with Rabbi's interpretations[3] does not the contradiction arise?—Two Tannas expressed different views as to the opinion of R. Judah b. Agra. The first Tanna holds that the twilight of R. Judah ends first [53*b*] and then begins the twilight of R. Jose,[4] while the second Tanna holds that the twilight of R. Jose is absorbed in that of R. Judah.[5]

Our Rabbis taught: A woman who observes a bloodstain causes uncleanness to herself[6] and to consecrated things retrospectively;[7] so Rabbi. R. Simeon b. Eleazar ruled: She causes uncleanness[8]

(1) According to his first ruling *supra* the twilight of R. Jose is only a doubtful time while according to his present ruling it is definitely night. (2) Both here and *supra*. (3) Which inevitably lead to the conclusion (as stated *supra*) that, according to the first ruling, R. Judah b. Agra holds R. Jose's twilight to be a doubtful time, while according to his second ruling, it is definitely night. (4) Hence it is uncertain whether it still belongs to the day or to the following night. (5) And since in his opinion the examination must extend over all the twilight of the latter it obviously covers also the twilight of the former, so that the examination took place in both twilights. (6) *Sc.* if she was in the process of counting her clean days she must start anew (Tosaf.). (7) To the time the article on which the stain was found had been washed. (8) Retrospectively.

to consecrated things but does not cause uncleanness to herself, since her bloodstain cannot be subject to greater restrictions than her observation.[1] But[2] do we not find that her bloodstain is subject to greater restrictions in regard to consecrated things?—Read rather thus: R. Simeon b. Eleazar ruled; Even to consecrated things she conveys no uncleanness,[3] since her bloodstain should in no case be subject to greater restrictions than her observation.[1]

Our Rabbis taught: If a woman observed first a bloodstain and then[4] she observed a discharge of blood she may for a period of twenty-four hours ascribe her stain to her observation;[5] so Rabbi. R. Simeon b. Eleazar ruled: Only during the same day.[6] Said Rabbi: His view seems more acceptable than mine, since he improves[7] her position while I make it worse. 'He improves it'! Does he not in fact[8] make it worse?—Rabina replied: Reverse the statement.[9] R. Naḥman said: You need not really reverse it, [the meaning being:] Since he improves her position in regard to the laws of *zibah* while I make her position worse as regards the laws of *zibah*.[10]

(1) In the latter case the uncleanness is retrospective for twenty-four hours only, while in the former it would go back to the time the article had been washed. (2) Since R. Simeon b. Eleazar agrees with Rabbi in the case of consecrated things. (3) Retrospectively. (4) Within twenty-four hours. (5) *Sc.* her uncleanness does not extend retrospectively to the time the article had been washed but begins at the time the stain was found. (6) *Sc.* only where the stain was observed on the same day as the discharge of the blood may the former be ascribed to the latter (cf. prev. n.); but if the stain was discovered in the daytime while the blood was not observed until after sunset, though this took place within twenty-four hours, the former cannot be ascribed to the latter. (7) This is discussed presently. (8) By reducing the period of twenty-four hours. (9) Reading, 'my view seems more acceptable etc.'. (10) According to Rabbi who for a period of twenty-four hours ascribes the stain to the observation of the blood the woman is deemed to have been unclean on the day of her observation as well as on the previous day. If, therefore, she were to observe some blood on the next day following she would be regarded as a confirmed *zabah*, while according to R. Simeon who ascribes a stain to blood observed during the same day only the woman would be deemed unclean on one day only and could not become a confirmed *zabah* unless blood was observed on the two following days also (R. Ḥan.).

R. Zera enquired of R. Assi: Do stains[1] necessitate an interval of cleanness[2] or not? The other remained silent, answering him nothing at all. Once he[3] found him[4] as he was sitting at his studies and discoursing as follows: 'She may for twenty-four hours ascribe her stain to her observation. This is the ruling of Rabbi. In connection with this Resh Laḳish explained that it applied only where she has examined herself,[5] while R. Joḥanan explained: Even though she did not examine herself'.[6] 'Thus it follows', he[3] said to him,[4] 'that[7] stains necessitate an interval of cleanness'. 'Yes', the other[4] replied. 'But did I not ask you this question many a time and you gave me no answer at all? It is likely that you recalled the tradition[8] in the rapidity of your reviewing?'[9]—'Yes', the other replied, 'in the rapidity of my reviewing I recalled it'.

MISHNAH. IF A WOMAN OBSERVED A DISCHARGE OF BLOOD ON THE ELEVENTH DAY[10] AT TWILIGHT,[11] AT THE

(1) According to Rabbi who attributes a stain to an observation of blood if the latter took place within twenty-four hours, and does not regard the woman's uncleanness as having begun at the time the article (on which the stain was found) had been washed. (2) *Sc.* must the woman have examined herself between the time the article had been washed and the discovery of the stain? (Tosaf.). (3) R. Zera. (4) R. Assi. (5) Near the time of discovering the stain, within twenty-four hours; but if twenty-four hours have passed between the examination and the discovery of the stain the woman is deemed unclean retrospectively from the time of the examination (Tosaf.). (6) *Sc.* near the examination between which and the discovery of the stain an interval of twenty-four hours had been allowed to pass. Despite this interval the woman's uncleanness is not retrospective since less than twenty-four hours have passed between the time the article had been washed and the discovery on it of the stain. As the uncleanness in such a case is not retrospective to the time of the washing of the article, it is equally not retrospective over the twenty-four hours' period (Tosaf.). Cf. Tosaf. Asheri. (7) According to both Resh Laḳish and R. Joḥanan. (8) Lit., 'it came to thee'. (9) Cf. Jast. (10) After the termination of a menstruation period. Any issue of blood within the eleven days is deemed to be *zibah*. (11) A time which is neither certain day nor certain night, so that it is doubtful whether the issue was one of *zibah* or one of menstruation. If the time were certain day the issue (cf. prev. n.) would be *zibah* and if it were certain night (when a new menstruation period commences) it would be menstrual.

BEGINNING OF A MENSTRUATION PERIOD AND AT THE END OF A MENSTRUATION PERIOD,[1] AT THE BEGINNING OF A ZIBAH PERIOD AND AT THE END OF A ZIBAH PERIOD,[1] ON THE FORTIETH DAY AFTER THE BIRTH OF A MALE[2] OR ON THE EIGHTIETH DAY AFTER THE BIRTH OF A FEMALE,[3] [THE DISCHARGE HAVING BEEN OBSERVED] AT TWILIGHT IN ALL THESE CASES,[4] BEHOLD WOMEN IN SUCH CIRCUMSTANCES[5] ARE IN A STATE OF PERPLEXITY.[6] SAID R. JOSHUA: BEFORE YOU MAKE PROVISION FOR THE FOOLISH WOMEN[7] COME AND MAKE PROVISION FOR THE WISE ONES.[8]

GEMARA. AT THE BEGINNING OF A MENSTRUATION PERIOD AND AT THE END OF A MENSTRUATION PERIOD! Is it[9] not rather the beginning of a menstruation period and the end of a *zibah* period?[10]—R. Ḥisda replied: It is this that was meant: IF A WOMAN OBSERVED A DISCHARGE OF BLOOD ON THE ELEVENTH DAY AT TWILIGHT a time which is THE BEGINNING OF A MENSTRUATION PERIOD AND THE END OF A ZIBAH PERIOD, or on the seventh day of her menstruation when it is THE END OF A MENSTRUATION PERIOD AND THE BEGINNING OF A ZIBAH PERIOD.

SAID R. JOSHUA: BEFORE YOU MAKE PROVISION FOR THE FOOLISH WOMEN etc. But are these [54a] FOOLISH WOMEN?

(1) This is discussed in the Gemara *infra*. (2) All discharges of blood from the eighth to the fortieth day after the birth of a male is regarded as clean and after that begins the menstruation period of seven days followed by the *zibah* one of eleven days. (3) From the fifteenth to the eightieth day after the birth of a female all discharges of blood are clean and after the eightieth day the menstruation period followed by that of *zibah* (cf. prev. n.) begins. (4) Cf. prev. n. but three. (5) Lit., 'these'. (6) Lit., 'erring', as regards the counting of the clean and unclean days prescribed in the various cases mentioned; because they are unable to determine on which of the two days involved they had observed the discharge. (7) Those of the type just mentioned. (8) Women who observed their discharges in the day or the night when no doubt arises. This is further explained in a Baraitha cited *infra*. (9) The twilight of THE ELEVENTH DAY. (10) Since the *zibah* period which began after the seventh day of the menstruation period terminated at the conclusion of the eleventh day when a second menstruation period begins.

Are they not merely IN A STATE OF PERPLEXITY?[1]—Rather read: Women who are in a state of perplexity. For[2] it was taught: [If a woman is alternately] unclean on one day and clean on the next,[3] she may perform her marital duty[4] on the eighth day,[5] the night following being included,[6] and on four nights out of every eighteen days.[7] If, however, she observed any issue in the evening,[8] she performs her marital duty on the eighth day[9] only.[10]

(1) V. *supra* p. 373, n. 6. (2) The following series of rules applies to the WISE ONES of which R. Joshua spoke. (3) *Sc.* is discharging blood every alternate day. (4) If the discharge never occurs in the night. (5) Counting from the one on which her first discharge was observed. On the eighth day her cleanness is established beyond any possible doubt since her unclean period of menstruation terminated with the seventh, and the eighth is one of her alternate clean days. (6) Lit., 'and its night with it', since (cf. prev. n. but one) she never discharges any blood in the night. (7) Again counting from the day of the first discharge (cf. prev. n. but one). As she never discharges on three consecutive days she can never become a major *zabah* (who must allow seven clean days to pass before she can attain cleanness). When she discharges on the ninth day (one of the alternate unclean days) she, as a minor *zabah* (the discharge having taken place within the eleven days of the *zibah* period which began on the eighth), must allow one clean day (the tenth) to pass and may perform her marital duty in the night following it. Observing a discharge on the eleventh day (one of the alternate unclean days) she allows the twelfth day to pass and performs her duty in the night that follows. Similarly she may perform her marital duty on the nights following respectively the fourteenth and the sixteenth. By the time eighteen days have passed with the sunset of the eighteenth day she has, in addition to the eighth day and night following it, the four nights that follow respectively the tenth, twelfth, fourteenth and sixteenth day. The night following the eighteenth day is again one in which performance of marital duty is permitted, but it belongs to the next cycle. On the nineteenth, the seven days of menstruation begin again and the cycle is repeated. (8) Of the alternate unclean days. (9) After her first discharge, *sc.* the day and the night preceding it. On the day she is definitely clean since her discharge does not appear until evening, and in the previous night she is also clean since with the day preceding it (the seventh) her unclean menstruation period had come to an end. (10) During the first seven days she is unclean as a menstruant and in the night following the eighth (one of the alternate unclean nights) she is unclean as a minor *zabah* (the *zibah* period having commenced on the eighth) and must consequently allow one day, the ninth, to pass. On the night following the ninth (another of the alternate unclean nights) she is again unclean as a minor *zabah* and must again allow a day, the tenth, to pass, and so

[If she is alternately] unclean[1] for two days and clean for two days, she may perform her marital duty on the eighth,[2] the twelfth,[3] the sixteenth[4] and the twentieth.[5] But why is she not allowed to perform her marital duty on the nineteenth?[6]—R. Shesheth replied: This[7] proves that the 'gluttony'[8] of which we have learnt[9] is forbidden. R. Ashi[10] replied: Granted that the eleventh day[11] requires no safeguard,[12] the tenth day[13] at any rate does require a safeguard.[14] If she is alternately unclean for three days and clean for three days, she may perform her marital duty on two days[15] and may never

on until the termination of eighteen days when a new cycle of the same number of days begins in which again she is allowed marital duty on the eighth day and the night preceding it only.

(1) The discharge making its appearance (as is also the case in all the following rulings) in the evenings. (2) Which (with the night preceding) is the second of the two alternating clean days and (unlike the first of these two days) follows the immersion on the seventh day of the unclean seven days of the menstruation period. (3) The preceding night included. On the ninth and the tenth (two of the alternating unclean days) she is (since these days are within her *zibah* period) a minor *zabah* and must in consequence allow the eleventh also to pass, performing immersion in the evening of that day and thus attaining cleanness on the twelfth. (4) Including also the night preceding it. On the thirteenth and fourteenth (cf. prev. n. *mut. mut.*) she is a minor *zabah*, the fifteenth is the day she must allow to pass and in the evening of which she performs immersion and attains cleanness by the sixteenth. (5) Cf. prev. n. *mut. mut.* The uncleanness on the twenty-first and twenty-second is already part of a menstruation period and belongs to the next cycle. (6) The day following the eleventh day of the *zibah* period, which (as stated *infra* 72*b*) need not be passed before cleanness is attained. (7) The prohibition of marital intercourse on the nineteenth. (8) Lit., 'glutton'. (9) *Infra* 72*a*: If a woman observed a discharge on the eleventh day of her *zibah* period, and performed immersion on the twelfth, and, after intercourse, again observed a discharge, her husband (who had not the patience to allow the twelfth day to pass) is described by Beth Hillel as a glutton. (10) Maintaining that 'gluttony' is not forbidden. (11) Of the *zibah* period (the eighteenth in the cycle). (12) *Sc.* allowing one clean day to pass after it before cleanness is attained. (13) The seventeenth in the cycle which is also one of the two alternating unclean days. (14) Cf. prev. n. but one. As the day following it (the eleventh of *zibah* or the eighteenth in the cycle) is an unclean one, the next clean day (the nineteenth in the cycle) must be allowed to pass as a safeguard. Hence it is that marital intercourse cannot in this case be permitted before the twentieth. (15) The eleventh and twelfth after her first discharge. On the first

again perform it.[1] If she is alternately unclean for four days and clean for four days she performs her marital duty on one day,[2] and may never again perform it.[3] If she is alternately unclean for five days and clean for five days, she performs her marital duty on three days[4] and may never again perform it.[3] If she is alternately unclean for six days and clean for six days she performs her marital duty on five days[5] and may never again perform it.[3] If she is alternately unclean for seven days and clean for seven days, she may perform her marital duty during a quarter of her lifetime, [seven days][6] out of each twenty-eight days.[7] If she is alternately unclean for eight days and clean for eight days, she may perform her marital duty on fifteen days[8] out of every forty-eight days.[9]

seven days she is unclean as a menstruant, on the eighth and the ninth (two of the alternating three unclean days) being within the eleven days of the *zibah* period, she is unclean as a minor *zabah*, and the tenth must be allowed to pass as a safeguard against these days.

(1) Since after the twelfth day she will never attain cleanness. The thirteenth, fourteenth and fifteenth (three of the alternating three unclean days) will be unclean days within her *zibah* period that subject her to the restrictions of a major *zabah* who cannot attain cleanness before seven clean days have passed, but (owing to these three alternating unclean days) she will never experience a full period of seven clean days. (2) The eighth, the first day after her first unclean menstruation period, which is the last of the second group of four clean days. (3) Cf. prev. n. but one *mut. mut.* (4) The eighth, ninth and tenth (immediately following the first menstruation period) being the last three of the first group of five clean days. (5) The eighth to twelfth. Cf. prev. n. *mut. mut.* (6) That follow the unclean seven days of the menstruation period. (7) Made up as follows: Seven unclean days of menstruation, seven days of cleanness (in which marital intercourse is permitted), seven days of uncleanness in which the woman becomes a major *zabah* and seven days that must be counted after the confirmed *zibah;* and so on with each cycle of twenty-eight days. (8) The tenth to the sixteenth (seven days), the twenty-sixth to the thirty-second (seven days) and the forty-eighth ($7 + 7 + 1 = 15$ days). Cf. foll. n. (9) Composed as follows: Eight unclean days (the last of which being the first of the eleven days of *zibah* turns the woman into a minor *zabah*); one day (the first of the second group of eight days) that must be allowed to pass by a minor *zabah* before cleanness is attained, and seven clean days in which marital intercourse is permitted; two days (the first of the third group of eight days) of *zibah* (being the last two of the eleven days of the first *zibah* period) and six days of the second menstruation period; one day (the first of the fourth group

But is not the number[1] fourteen?[2]—R. Adda b. Isaac replied: This proves that the days of her menstruation in which she observes no discharge[3] are reckoned in the counting[4] prescribed for her *zibah*;[5] for the question was raised: [54b] May the days succeeding childbirth[6] on which the woman observes no discharge[7] be reckoned in the counting prescribed for her *zibah*?[8] R. Kahana replied, Come and hear: If a woman[9] observed a discharge on two days, and on the third day she miscarried but was unaware what she miscarried, behold this is a case of doubtful *zibah* and doubtful birth[10] and[11] she must bring a sacrifice[12] which

of eight days) completing the seventh day of menstruation, and seven days in which marital intercourse is permitted; eight days of uncleanness (the fifth group of eight days during the first three of which she becomes a major *zabah*); seven days (the first of the sixth group) that serve as the number of days prescribed for a major *zabah* and one day (the last of the sixth group and the forty-eighth day in the cycle) in which marital intercourse is permitted.

(1) Lit., 'behold they are', the days on which marital intercourse is permitted. (2) Since the forty-eighth day should be excluded. It is now assumed that in the sixth group of eight days five clean days only are available for the prescribed counting, since the first three days of the group completed a menstruation period that began on the fifth day of the fifth group, and, since seven clean days have not yet passed, the forty-eighth, as the day following it, should be equally forbidden for marital intercourse. (3) As is the case with the first three days of the sixth group in which she was clean. (4) *Sc.* of the seven days. (5) Since the counting thus begins with the first day of the sixth group of eight days it terminates (cf. prev. n.) on the seventh. On the eighth day, the forty-eighth of the cycle, the woman having attained cleanness and undergone immersion on the preceding night, marital intercourse is permitted. (6) Which took place in *zibah* that immediately ceased. (7) But is nevertheless Pentateuchally unclean. (8) So that at the conclusion of seven days, and the due performance of immersion, she is exempt from the restrictions that are imposed upon a *zabah*. (9) During the eleven days of her *zibah* period. (10) Since it is possible that she gave birth to a proper child and that no bleeding accompanied it, in which case it is a valid birth and no *zibah*. It is equally possible that the birth was not that of a proper child and that it was accompanied by a flow of blood, in which case it is a proper *zibah* and no valid birth. It is also possible that the birth was a proper one and that it was accompanied by bleeding in which case it is both a valid birth and a proper *zibah*. It is equally possible that there was neither proper birth nor bleeding so that there was neither *zibah* nor valid birth. (11) Adopting the most restrictive course in

may not be eaten[1] while the days succeeding her childbirth[2] on which she observes no discharge are reckoned in the counting prescribed for her *zibah*.[3] R. Papa retorted: There[4] the case is quite different,[5] since it might be assumed[4] that she gave birth to a male child,[6] so that all the extra seven days that we impose upon her[7] may well be reckoned in the counting prescribed for her *zibah*.[8] Said R. Huna son of R. Joshua to R. Papa: Is there[4] only the doubt of having given birth to a male child, and is there no doubt as to the possibility of the birth of a female child?[9] But the fact is that[10] you may well infer from here that they[11] may be reckoned.[12] This is conclusive.

If a woman is alternately unclean for nine days and clean for nine days she may have marital intercourse on eight days out of every eighteen days.[13] If she is alternately unclean for ten days

order to meet all possible circumstances. (12) In case the birth was a valid one.

(1) Since it is possible that the birth was not valid, that in consequence no sacrifice was required, and that the bird that was mistakenly killed in the manner prescribed for a sacrifice was, therefore, *nebelah*. (2) During the first fourteen days of which, since it is possible that the birth was that of a female, the woman is unclean even though no discharge was observed. (3) To the restrictions of which she is subject on account of the possibility that the miscarriage was accompanied by bleeding. Thus it has been shown that the days succeeding childbirth on which no discharge is observed are reckoned in the counting prescribed for a *zabah*. (4) In the case just cited by R. Kahana where uncertainties exist. (5) From that discussed *supra* 54*a* where no doubtful factor is involved. (6) After the birth of whom a woman is unclean for seven days only. (7) A total of fourteen days as a precaution against the possibility that the birth was that of a female child. (8) Had it, however, been certain that the birth was that of a female child (similar to the certainty *supra* 54a) the days succeeding birth could not be reckoned in the counting prescribed for a *zabah*. (9) Of course there is. The birth of the latter is as possible as the birth of the former and the possibility, therefore, exists that the woman is unclean for fourteen days. (10) Lit., 'but not'. (11) The days succeeding a childbirth during which no discharge is observed. (12) In the seven days prescribed for a *zabah*. (13) In the first group of nine days she is a menstruant during the first seven days and a minor *zabah* on the last two days; and in the second group of nine days she allows the first day to pass (as prescribed for a minor *zabah*) while in the remaining eight days, being fully clean, she is permitted marital intercourse. The same process is repeated in every cycle of eighteen days.

and clean for ten days, the days in which she is permitted marital intercourse are the same in number as the days of her *zibah*.[1] And the same[2] applies to cylces of a hundred[3] and so also to cycles of a thousand.[4]

(1) During the first ten days she is a menstruant for seven days and a *zabah* during the last three days, while during the second group of ten days she counts the prescribed seven days and has three days left in which she is clean and permitted marital intercourse. The three latter days are thus equal in number to the three days of her *zibah*. (2) That the number of days in which marital intercourse is permitted is equal to the number of the days of *zibah*. (3) The woman is menstrual during the first seven days of the first hundred and is a *zabah* during the remaining ninety-three days, while the first seven days of the second hundred are counted as the days prescribed after the *zibah* and in the remaining ninety-three days she is permitted marital intercourse. (4) Cf. prev. n. *mut. mut.*

NIDDAH

CHAPTER VII

MISHNAH. THE BLOOD OF A MENSTRUANT AND THE FLESH OF A CORPSE CONVEY UNCLEANNESS WHEN WET AND WHEN DRY. BUT THE ISSUE, PHLEGM AND SPITTLE OF A ZAB, A DEAD CREEPING THING, A CARCASS AND SEMEN CONVEY UNCLEANNESS WHEN WET BUT NOT WHEN DRY. IF, HOWEVER, ON BEING SOAKED, THEY ARE CAPABLE OF REVERTING TO THEIR ORIGINAL CONDITION THEY CONVEY UNCLEANNESS WHEN WET AND WHEN DRY. AND WHAT IS THE DURATION[1] OF THEIR SOAKING?[2] TWENTY-FOUR HOURS IN LUKEWARM WATER.[3] R. JOSE RULED: IF THE FLESH OF A CORPSE IS DRY, AND ON BEING SOAKED CANNOT REVERT TO ITS ORIGINAL CONDITION, IT IS CLEAN.[4]

GEMARA. Whence are these rulings[5] deduced?—Hezekiah replied: From Scripture which says, *And of her that is sick with her impurity,*[6] her impurity[7] is like herself, as she conveys her uncleanness so does her impurity convey similar uncleanness. Thus we find the law concerning wet blood,[8] whence the deduction concerning dry blood?—R. Isaac replied: Scripture said, *Be,*[9] it shall retain its original force.[10] But might it not be suggested that this[11] applies only to blood that was wet and then dried up; whence, however, the deduction that it applies also to blood that was

(1) *Sc.* the maximum time. (2) To cause them to be regarded as CAPABLE OF REVERTING TO THEIR ORIGINAL CONDITION. (3) But if they do not resume their original freshness unless soaked for a longer time or in warmer water they convey uncleanness when wet only. (4) V. Gemara. (5) That the blood of menstruation conveys uncleanness by contact and carriage. (6) Lev. XV, 33, emphasis on *'her'* and *'impurity'*. (7) *Sc.* menstrual blood. (8) Which is its natural state when discharged from the body. (9) *Her issue . . . be blood* (Lev. XV, 19). (10) Lit., 'in its being it shall be'. (11) Retention of its original force.

originally[1] dry? And, furthermore, with reference to what we have learnt, 'If a woman aborted an object that was like a rind, like earth, like a hair, like red flies, let her put it in water and if it dissolves she is unclean', whence is this[2] deduced?—'*Be*'[3] is an inclusive statement.[4] If [it be argued:] As she causes couch and seat to convey uncleanness to man and to his garments[5] so should her blood also cause couch and garment to convey uncleanness to man and his garments, [it can be retorted:] Is then her blood capable of using a couch or a seat?[6]—But according to your argument[7] [it could also be objected]: Is a leprous stone[8] capable of using a couch or a seat that a text should be required to exclude it?[9] For it was taught, 'It might have been presumed that a leprous stone should cause a couch and a seat to convey uncleanness to man and to his garments, this being arrived at logically, for if a *zab* who does not convey uncleanness by means of entry[10] causes couch and seat to convey uncleanness to man and to his garments, how much more then should a leprous stone, which does convey uncleanness by means of entry,[11] convey uncleanness to couch and seat to convey it to man and his garments, hence it was specifically stated, *He that hath the issue*,[12] implying only '*he that hath the issue*' [is subject to the restriction][13] but not a leprous stone'. Now the reason[14] is that Scripture has excluded it, but if that had not been the case it would have conveyed the uncleanness, would it not?[15]—

(1) *Sc.* when it was discovered. Cf. the cited Mishnah that follows. (2) That subsequent solution renders the originally dry object unclean. (3) *Her issue . . . be blood* (Lev. XV, 19). (4) Covering all the objects mentioned. (5) *Sc.* she does not merely convey to them an uncleanness of a degree next to, and lower than her own but one, that of 'father of uncleanness', which is on a par with hers. Only a 'father of uncleanness' can effect the uncleanness of a man. (6) Of course not. The analogy, therefore, cannot be drawn. (7) That since blood cannot use a couch or a seat it cannot cause it to be a 'father of uncleanness'. (8) Cf. Lev. XIV, 34ff. (9) From the restriction of causing a couch and a seat to become 'fathers of uncleanness'. (10) If a clean person enters with a *zab* into the same house the former does not thereby become unclean. (11) Cf. Lev. XIV, 46. (12) Lev. XV, 4. (13) Of causing couch and seat to convey uncleanness to man and his garments. (14) Why a leprous stone was excluded from the restriction (cf. prev. n.). (15) Though it is not capable of using couch or seat.

A reply may indeed be forthcoming from this very statement,[1] for did you not say, '*He that hath the issue*[2] [is subject to the restriction] but not a leprous stone'? Well here also Scripture said, *Whereon she sitteth,*[3] only she but not her blood. [55a] But might it not be suggested that[4] as she conveys uncleanness to objects under a heavy stone[5] so does her blood also convey uncleanness to objects under a heavy stone?—R. Ashi replied: Scripture said, *And he that beareth those things,*[6] implying[7] an exclusion.[8]

AND THE FLESH OF A CORPSE. Whence is this deduced?—Resh Laḳish replied: Scripture said, *Whatsoever uncleanness he hath,*[9] implying all forms of uncleanness[10] that emanate from him.[11] R. Joḥanan replied: *Or a bone of a man, or a grave,*[12] '*a man*' is[13] on a par with '*a bone*'; as a bone [conveys uncleanness when] dry so does a man.[14] What is the practical difference between them?[15]—The practical difference between them is the case of flesh that[16] crumbles.[17]

An objection was raised: The flesh of a corpse that was crumbled is clean?[18]—There it is a case where it was pulverized and turned into dust.

An objection was raised:[19] Every part of a corpse conveys uncleanness except the teeth, the hair and the nails, but while they are attached [to the corpse] they are all unclean?[20]—R. Adda b. Ahabah replied: It[21] must be exactly like a bone; as a bone was

(1) Lit., 'and from it'. (2) Lev. XV, 4. (3) Lev. XV, 23, emphasis on '*she*'. (4) Lit., 'if'. (5) On which she sits; though her weight can hardly exercise any tangible pressure on the objects (Tosaf.). Lit., 'a stone (used) for closing (a pit)'. V. Shab., Sonc. ed., p. 394, n. 2. (6) Lev. XV, 10, dealing with the couch of a *zab* which (as explained in *Torath Kohanim*) when carried on a heavy stone conveys uncleanness to objects under the stone. (7) Emphasis on '*those*'. (8) *Sc.* only those but not blood. (9) Lev. XXII, 5. (10) Whether wet or dry. (11) Lit., 'separate'. (12) Num. XIX, 16. (13) By analogy. (14) *Sc.* his corpse. (15) R. Joḥanan and Resh Laḳish. (16) Owing to its extreme dryness. (17) While according to Resh Laḳish it would still be unclean since it emanates from a corpse, it would lose its uncleanness according to R. Joḥanan since it is not one solid piece like a bone. (18) An objection against Resh Laḳish. (19) Both against Resh Laḳish and R. Joḥanan. (20) Oh. III, 3. Now teeth are on a par with bones and yet it was stated that when detached from the corpse they are clean (cf. prev. n.). (21) To convey uncleanness.

created simultaneously with it[1] so must every other part[2] be such as was created with it.[3] But are there not the hair and nails that were created with it[1] and they are nevertheless clean?—Rather, said R. Adda b. Ahabah, It[2] must be exactly like a bone; as a bone was created simultaneously with it[1] and when cut[4] does not grow again[5] so must every other part[2] be such as was created with it and when cut[4] does not grow again. The teeth are, therefore, excluded since they were not created with it,[1] and the hair and nails were excluded since, though they were created with it, they[4] grow again. But skin surely [is a part of the body] that[4] grows again, for[6] we have learnt: A skinned animal,[7] R. Meir declares, is ritually fit,[8] and only the Sages declare it to be unfit.[9] And even the Rabbis declare it to be unfit only because in the meantime[10] the air affects it and it would die, but the skin[11] would, as a matter of fact, grow again;[12] and yet have we not learnt: In the case of the following their skins are on a par with their flesh,[13] viz., the skin of a human being?[14]—Surely in connection with this ruling it was stated: 'Ulla said, 'Pentateuchally the skin of a human being is clean, and what is the reason why they ruled it to be unclean? It is a preventive measure against the possibility that a person might use the skins of his father and mother as spreads for an ass.'

Others there are who read: Skin, surely, [is a part of the body] that[15] does not grow again, for[16] we have learnt: And the Sages declare it to be unfit.[17] And even R. Meir declares it to be fit only because its flesh hardens and the animal recovers its health but it does not, as a matter of fact, grow again,[18] and yet did not 'Ulla state, 'Pentateuchally the skin of a man is clean'?—When 'Ulla's

(1) The body. (2) To convey uncleanness. (3) Teeth grow later. (4) Lit., 'its stem'. (5) Lit., 'changes', *sc.* once a bone has been removed no other will grow in its place. (6) So MS.M. and marg. note. Cur. edd., 'and'. (7) One whose skin has worn away owing to scabs or excessive work. (8) For consumption, *sc.* it is not forbidden as *ṭerefah*, since the skin grows again. (9) Ḥul. 54*a*. (10) Before a new skin has grown. (11) Lit., 'its stem'. (12) So that according to R. Adda b. Ahabah the skin should be clean. (13) *Sc.* the former are as unclean as the latter. (14) Ḥul. 122*a*. (15) Lit., 'whose root'. (16) So MS.M. and marg. note. Cur. edd., 'and'. (17) Ḥul. 54*a;* because it does not grow again. (18) The skin should consequently have been unclean.

statement was made it had reference to the final clause[1] only: But all these,[2] if they were dressed or trodden upon sufficiently to render them fit for dressing, are clean[3] with the exception of a human skin.[4] And it was in connection with this ruling that 'Ulla stated, 'Pentateuchally the human skin is clean if it had been dressed; and what is the reason why they ruled it to be unclean? It is a preventive measure against the possibility that a person might use the skins of his father and mother as spreads'. But does not flesh grow again and yet it is unclean?—Mar son of R. Ashi replied: The place of missing flesh becomes a scar.[5]

BUT THE ISSUE. Whence is this[6] deduced?—It was taught: *His issue is unclean,*[7] teaches concerning an issue of a *zab* that it is unclean.[8] But cannot this be arrived at by a process of reasoning: If it[9] causes uncleanness to others[10] would it not, with more reason, cause uncleanness to itself?[11] The case of the scapegoat proves the contrary, since it causes uncleanness to others[12] while it is itself clean. You also should not, therefore, be surprised in this case[13] where, though the issue carries uncleanness to others,[10] it is itself[13] clean. Hence it was specifically stated, '*His issue is unclean*'[7] teaching thereby that the issue is unclean. But might it not be suggested that this[14] applies only to contact [uncleanness] but not to carriage, this being a case similar to that of a dead creeping thing?[15]—R. Bibi b. Abaye replied: There was no need for a Scriptural text as far as contact is concerned, since it[14] is not inferior[16] to semen, [55b] so that if a Scriptural text was required it was only in respect of carriage. But might it not be suggested that by means of carriage it[13] conveys uncleanness to both man and his garments, while by means of contact it conveys uncleanness to man but not to his

(1) Of the Mishnah, beginning 'In the case of the following their skins etc.' cited *supra*. (2) The skins which the Sages ruled to be unclean. (3) Since they have lost all resemblance to flesh. (4) Ḥul. 122*a*, Pes. 46*a*. (5) *Sc.* it does not grow again to its original shape as is the case with hair or nails. (6) That the issue of a *zab* is unclean. (7) Lev. XV, 2. (8) *Supra* 34*b*. (9) The issue. (10) *Sc.* the *zab*. (11) What need then was there for the text of Lev. XV, 2? (12) The man who carries it away (cf. Lev. XVI, 26). (13) *Zibah*. (14) The conveyance of uncleanness by an issue. (15) Which also conveys uncleanness by means of contact but not by carriage. (16) In its uncleanness.

garments, this being a case similar to that of contact with a carcass?[1]—This cannot be entertained, for it was taught: Others[2] say, *Of them that have an issue, whether it be a man, or a woman,*[3] his *'issue'* is compared[4] to himself;[5] as in his case you make no distinction between his contact and his carriage as regards the conveyance of uncleanness to man and to his garments,[6] so also in that of his issue. But now that the law[7] is deduced from *'Of them that have an issue'*,[3] what need is there for *'His issue is unclean'?*[8]—R. Judah of Daskarta[9] replied: It was required; since[10] it might have been presumed that the case of the scapegoat proves the contrary,[11] for it causes uncleanness to others[12] while it itself is clean; and as to the deduction from[13] *'Of them that have an issue'* [it might have been explained that] it serves the purpose of indicating the number,[14] viz., *'issue'*, one; *'his issue'*,[15] two; while after the third issue the All Merciful compared him to the *'woman'*,[16] hence the All Merciful has written, *'His issue is unclean'*. And now that the All Merciful has also written, *'His issue is unclean'*[17] you may apply to the other text[18] this exposition[19] also.

AND SPITTLE. Whence do we deduce [the uncleanness of] spittle?—It was taught *And if he*[20] ... *spit.*[21] As this might be presumed to apply even if the spittle did not touch,[22] it was explicitly stated, *upon him that is clean,*[21] only if it touched him that is clean.[23]

(1) Cf. Lev. XI, 39, 40. (2) *Sc.* R. Meir. (3) Lev. XV, 33. (4) By juxtaposition and analogy. (5) The *zab*. (6) Cf. Lev. XV, 7, 10. The latter verse speaks of the *zab's* couch and seat and applies with greater force to the *zab* himself. (7) That the issue of a *zab* conveys uncleanness by contact and carriage. (8) Lev. XV, 2. (9) Darkarah, 16 *parasangs* N.E. of Bagdad. (10) If the text of Lev. XV, 2, had not been available. (11) Of what is deduced from Lev. XV, 33. (12) The man who carries it away (cf. Lev. XVI, 26). (13) Lit., 'and if on account of'. (14) Lit., 'it is for the number that it came'. (15) E.V., '*of them that have*'. (16) Who becomes unclean even in a case of an accidental issue. After no more than two issues a man does not become unclean unless they were intentional. (17) From which the principle of the uncleanness of an issue is deduced. (18) From which the prescribed number of issues had already been deduced. (19) That no distinction is to be made between contact and carriage. (20) A *zab*. (21) Lev. XV, 8. (22) The clean person in whose direction it was thrown. (23) Only then is he unclean.

Thus I know the law concerning his spittle only,[1] whence could I deduce the uncleanness of his mucus, phlegm and nasal discharge? From the explicit statement, *And*[2] *if he ... spit.*[3]

The Master said, 'As this might be presumed to apply even if the spittle did not touch',[4] but whence could this uncleanness[5] be deduced?—It might have been presumed that the expression of '*spit*' here[3] may be inferred from that of '*spit*'[6] mentioned in the case of a *yebamah*, as there the act[7] is valid though the spittle does not touch [the *yabam*] so is the act[8] valid here also even though the spittle did not touch the clean person, hence we were informed [that actual contact is essential]. But might it not be suggested that this[8] applies only to touch[9] but not to carriage, the law being similar to that of a dead creeping thing?[10]—Resh Laḳish replied: The school of R. Ishmael taught, Scripture said, '*upon that*[11] *which is with the clean*',[3] implying, whatever is in the hand of him that is clean,[12] I have declared it to be unclean to you.[13] But might it not be suggested that by carriage it conveys uncleanness to the man and his garments while by contact it conveys uncleanness to man only but not to his garments, this law being similar to that of the touch of *nebelah?*—Resh Laḳish replied and so it was also taught at the school of R. Ishmael: Scripture said, '*upon that which is with the clean*'[14] implying that that which I have declared to you as clean elsewhere I have declared to you as unclean here, and what is this? It is the touch of *nebelah*.[15] But might it not be suggested that this[16] refers

(1) Lit., 'I have not but'. (2) Emphasis on '*and*' which might well have been omitted. (3) Lev. XV, 8. (4) The clean person in whose direction it was thrown. (5) Cf. prev. n. (6) Deut. XXV, 9. (7) *Ḥaliẓah*. (8) The conveyance of uncleanness by the *zab's* spittle. (9) *Sc.* only if it came in contact with the clean person does it convey uncleanness to him. (10) Which also conveys uncleanness by contact but not through carriage if an object intervened between it and the person. (11) E.V. Upon him that is clean, *sc.* within his hand. (12) *Sc.* even if the spittle has fallen on an object that was merely carried by the clean person, so that the spittle did not come in direct contact with the man. (13) *Sc.* that it conveys uncleanness to the person. (14) Emphasis on '*clean*'. (15) Which causes the uncleanness of the man alone who touched it while his garments remain clean. In the case of the spittle of a *zab*, however, its touch by a clean man conveys uncleanness to his garments also. (16) The deduction just made (cf. MS.M.).

to[1] the carrying of a dead creeping thing?[2]—If that were so, Scripture should have written, 'upon that which is with a man',[3] why then did it write '*upon that which is with the clean*'?[4] Consequently the two deductions may be made.[5]

'And nasal discharge'. What [uncleanness] is [there in a] nasal discharge?[6]—Rab replied: This is the case where it was drawn and discharged through the mouth,[7] since in the circumstances it is impossible for the nasal secretion to be free from particles of spittle. R. Joḥanan, however, stated that it is unclean even if it is drawn and discharged through the nose. It is thus clear that he is of the opinion that the nose is a source,[8] the All Merciful[9] having included it.[10] As to Rab,[11] why should not the tears of a *zab*'s eyes[12] be enumerated?[13] For[14] has not Rab stated, He who wishes to blind his eye shall have it painted by an idolater,[15] and Levi stated, He who wishes to die shall have his eyes painted by an idolater, and in connection with this R. Ḥiyya b. Goria explained, 'What is Rab's reason for not saying "He who wishes to die [etc.]"? Because one might sniff them up and discharge them through the mouth'.[16] Now[17] what is Rab's explanation?[18]—

(1) Cur. edd. 'like'. (2) *Sc.* the garments which remain clean in the case of the carrying of a dead creeping thing are unclean in this case (cf. p. 386, n. 15). Whence, however, the proof that touch in this case is not like the touch of *nebelah* which causes the uncleanness of the man only and not that of his garments? (3) From which (cf. *supra* p. 386, nn. 11 and 12) the deduction ('whatever is in the hand etc.') could well have been made. (4) Emphasis on '*clean*'. (5) Cf. *supra* p. 386, n. 15 (second clause) and *supra* n. 2 (first clause). (6) Seeing that Scripture speaks of spittle only. (7) The uncleanness being due to the spittle. (8) In the case of a *zab* whose sources are unclean. (9) By the use of the expression *ki yaroḳ* (E.V., *if he spit*) which (by change of vowels) may be read as one word, *keroḳ*, 'like spittle', *sc.* any thing that is similar to spittle is subject to the same uncleanness. (10) Among the sources of a *zab*. (11) Who does not regard the nose as a source and attributes the uncleanness of a discharge from it to the particles of spittle that get mixed up with it when it passes through the mouth. (12) Which might also pass through his mouth and collect particles of spittle. (13) Among the unclean discharges. (14) The following is evidence that Rab agrees that tears may be made to pass through the mouth. (15) Who may well be suspected of mixing poisonous drugs in the eye paint. (16) And thus avoid swallowing them. (17) Cf. prev. n. but two. (18) Of the omission of tears

Granted that the poison is discharged,[1] the tears themselves are not so discharged.

Come and hear: 'There are nine fluids of[2] a *zab*. His sweat, foul secretion and excrement are free from all uncleanness of *zibah;* the tears of his eye, the blood of his wound and the milk of a woman convey the uncleanness of liquids[3] if they consist of a minimum quantity of a quarter of a *log;* but his *zibah*, his spittle and his urine[4] convey major uncleanness';[5] but nasal discharge was not mentioned. Now according to Rab[6] one can well see why this was not mentioned, since it was not definite enough to be mentioned, for it is only sometimes that it is discharged through the mouth while at other times it is discharged through the nose;[7] but according to R. Johanan[8] why was it not mentioned?—But according to your view,[9] was his mucus and phlegm[10] mentioned?[11] But the fact is that spittle was mentioned and the same law applies to all other secretions the law of whose uncleanness was derived from the Pentateuchal amplification,[12] and so also here[13] spittle was mentioned and all other secretions the law of whose uncleanness was derived from the amplification are also included. 'The tears of his eye' [is legally a fluid] since it is written in Scripture, *And given them tears to drink in large measure;*[14] 'the blood of his wound', since it is written, *And drink the blood of the slain,*[15] and there is no difference[16] between striking one down outright or striking one down in part;[17] 'the milk of a woman', since it is written, *And she*

of the eye (cf. *supra* p. 387, nn. 11 and 12) from the list of unclean discharges.

(1) Through the mouth. (2) Cf. MS.M. and Bomb. ed. (3) *Sc.* cause the uncleanness of food and drink (as other unclean liquids) but not that of man and garments. (4) Being sources. (5) I.e., that of man and garments. Ker. 13*a*. (6) V. *supra* p. 387, n. 11. (7) When it is free from uncleanness. Hence it could not be included among those discharges that are invariably unclean. (8) Who ruled that it is always unclean, irrespective of the channel through which it passed. (9) That a discharge that is always unclean should have been mentioned among the others. (10) Which are undoubtedly as unclean as his spittle. (11) Of course not. (12) V. *supra* p. 387, n. 9. (13) The Baraitha cited from Ker. 13*a*. (14) Ps. LXXX, 6; emphasis on '*drink*'. (15) Num. XXIII, 24, cf. prev. n. (16) In respect of the blood. (17) Lit., 'what (difference is there) to me (whether) he killed all of him . . . his half'.

opened a bottle of milk, and gave him drink.[1] Whence do we derive the law that 'his urine' [is legally a fluid]?—It was taught: *His issue is unclean, and this*[2] includes his urine in respect of uncleanness. But may not this[3] be arrived at by a logical argument? If spittle, that emanates from a region of cleanness, is unclean how much more so his urine that emanates [56*a*] from an unclean region?[4]—The blood that issues from the orifice of the membrum[5] could prove the contrary, for though it issues from an unclean region it is nevertheless clean; you also need not, therefore, be surprised at this that, though it issues from an unclean region, it should be clean. Hence it was explicitly stated, '*His issue is unclean and this*',[2] to include his urine in respect of uncleanness. Whence is it deduced that the blood that issues from the orifice of the membrum[5] is clean?—From what was taught· It might have been assumed that blood that issues from his[5] mouth or from the orifice of the membrum is unclean,[6] hence it was explicitly stated, *As to his issue it is unclean,*[7] only '*it*' is unclean, but blood that issues from his mouth or from his membrum is not unclean but clean.[8] But might I not reverse the deductions?[9]—R. Johanan citing R. Simeon b. Yohai replied: It[10] must be similar to spittle; as spittle is formed in globules when it is discharged so must any other unclean fluid be one that is formed in globules when it is discharged; blood is, therefore, excluded since it is not formed in globules when it is discharged. But is not a woman's milk formed in globules when it is discharged and the Master nevertheless stated that 'a woman's milk conveys the uncleanness of liquids' which implies: Only[11] the uncleanness of liquids but not major uncleanness?—Rather said R. Johanan citing R. Simeon b. Yohai: It[10] must be similar to spittle, as spittle is formed in globules when discharged but[12] may be re-absorbed,

(1) Judges IV, 19, cf. p. 388, n. 14 (2) Lev. XV, 2f, emphasis on '*and this*', *sc.* and another fluid also is unclean. (3) The uncleanness of urine. (4) Whence actual *zibah* comes. (5) Of a confirmed *zab*. (6) As his spittle and issue respectively are unclean. (7) Lev. XV, 2. (8) Yeb. 105*a*. (9) '*And this*' including blood that issues from his mouth or membrum, and '*as to his issue* etc.' excluding urine. (10) A fluid that is to be included in the same law of uncleanness as spittle. (11) Lit., 'yes'. (12) If it is not ejected.

so must any other unclean fluid be one that is formed in globules when discharged and that[1] may be re-absorbed; blood is, therefore, excluded since it is not formed in globules when it is discharged, and a woman's milk is excluded since, though it is formed in globules when discharged, it cannot be re-absorbed. But why should not deduction be made from the *zab*'s issue: As his issue which is not formed in globules when it is discharged causes uncleanness so does any other fluid?[2]—Raba replied: One cannot make a deduction from his issue, since it also causes uncleanness to others.[3]

A DEAD CREEPING THING. Resh Laḳish ruled: A dead creeping thing that dried up but whose shape was retained is unclean. But have we not learnt that they CONVEY UNCLEANNESS WHEN WET BUT NOT WHEN DRY?—R. Zera replied: This is no difficulty since the former[4] refers to a whole[5] while the latter[6] refers to a part;[7] for it was taught: R. Isaac son of R. Bisna citing R. Simeon b. Yoḥai stated, *In them,*[8] one might presume that it is necessary[9] to touch a whole, hence it was explicitly stated, *Of them.*[10] If only '*Of them*' had been written it might have been presumed that it suffices[9] to touch a part, hence it was explicitly stated '*In them*'.[8] How then are the two to be reconciled? The one[11] refers to a wet creeping thing while the other[12] refers to a dry one. Raba ruled: The lizards of Maḥuza,[13] if their shapes are retained, are unclean.

Resh Laḳish further stated: If a dead creeping thing was burnt while its shape was retained it is unclean. An objection was raised: If a burnt creeping thing was found upon olives and so also if a tattered rag[14] was found upon them they are clean, because all questions of uncleanness are determined by the condition of the

(1) If it is not ejected. (2) Though it is not formed in globules when discharged. (3) *Sc.* the *zab* himself. (4) The ruling of Resh Laḳish. (5) Such is unclean even when dry. (6) Our Mishnah. (7) Cf. MS.M. Cur. edd., 'in all of them . . . in their part'. (8) Lev. XI, 31. E.V. '*them*'. (9) In order to become unclean. (10) Lev. XI, 32; emphasis on '*of*', *sc.* a part. (11) Uncleanness through contact with a part. (12) Requiring contact with a whole. (13) Which are discovered dry. (14) Which is no longer subject to uncleanness.

objects at the time they are found![1]—R. Zera replied: This is no difficulty since the former[2] refers to a whole[3] while the latter[4] refers to a part; for it was taught: R. Isaac son of R. Bisna citing R. Simeon b. Yoḥai stated, *In them*',[5] one might presume that it is necessary[6] to touch a whole, hence it was explicitly stated, *Of them*.[7] If only '*of them*' had been written it might have been presumed that it suffices[6] to touch a part, hence it was explicitly stated, '*in them*'. How then are the two to be reconciled? The one[8] refers to a burnt creeping thing while the other refers to one that is not burnt.

CONVEY UNCLEANNESS WHEN WET. The ISSUE?[9] Because it is written, *His flesh run*.[10] His mucus, PHLEGM AND SPITTLE?[9] Because it is written, *If he that hath the issue spit*[11] implying[12] any fluid like spittle. A DEAD CREEPING THING?[9] The All Merciful said, *When they are dead*,[13] implying when they have the appearance of being dead.[14] SEMEN?[9] Since it must be capable of causing fertilization. A CARCASS?[9] Since it is written, *If . . . die*[15] implying when they have the appearance of being dead.[14]

IF, HOWEVER, ON BEING SOAKED THEY ARE CAPABLE. R. Jeremiah enquired: Is the soaking to be from beginning to end[16] in LUKEWARM WATER,[17] or only at the beginning although it is not so at the end?[18]—Come and hear what was taught: For how long must they be soaked in lukewarm water? Judah b. Naḳosa

(1) Ṭoh. IX, 9; thus the burnt creeping thing, like the tattered rag, is regarded as clean; how then could Resh Laḳish maintain that it is unclean? (2) The ruling of Resh Laḳish. (3) Which is unclean even if burnt. (4) The Mishnah cited. (5) Lev. XI, 31 E.V., '*them*'. (6) In order to become unclean. (7) Lev. XI, 32; emphasis on '*of*', *sc.* a part. (8) Requiring contact with a whole. (9) Conveys uncleanness when wet. (10) Lev. XV, 3. (11) Lev. XV, 8, Heb.; *ki yaroḳ* (v. next note). (12) Since *ki yaroḳ* by change of vowels might be made to read *keroḳ*, 'like spittle'. (13) Lev. XI, 31. (14) *Sc.* while still moist. (15) Lev. XI, 39. (16) *Sc.* throughout the TWENTY-FOUR HOURS. (17) I.e., even if they resume their original moist condition only after soaking in lukewarm water for the full period of twenty-four hours they are unclean. (18) *Sc.* they are regarded as clean if they have not resumed their original condition after being soaked in water that was at first lukewarm and then turned cold, though they would have resumed that condition if they had been soaked all the time in lukewarm water.

replied, For twenty-four hours, being lukewarm at the beginning though not at the end. R. Simeon b. Gamaliel replied, They must be lukewarm throughout the twenty-four hours.

R. JOSE RULED: THE FLESH OF A CORPSE etc. Samuel explained: It IS CLEAN in so far only as not to convey uncleanness if it is of the bulk of an olive, but it does convey the uncleanness of corpse mould.[1] So it was also taught: R. Jose ruled, The flesh of a corpse that is dry and, on being soaked, cannot return to its original condition is clean in so far only as not to convey uncleanness if it is of the bulk of an olive but it is subject to the uncleanness of corpse-mould.[1]

MISHNAH. IF A DEAD CREEPING THING WAS FOUND IN AN ALLEY IT CAUSES UNCLEANNESS RETROSPECTIVELY TO SUCH TIME AS ONE CAN TESTIFY, 'I EXAMINED THIS ALLEY AND THERE WAS NO CREEPING THING IN IT', OR TO SUCH TIME AS IT WAS LAST SWEPT. SO ALSO A BLOODSTAIN, IF IT WAS FOUND ON A SHIRT, CAUSES UNCLEANNESS RETROSPECTIVELY TO SUCH TIME AS ONE CAN TESTIFY, 'I EXAMINED THIS SHIRT AND THERE WAS NO STAIN ON IT' OR TO SUCH TIME AS IT WAS LAST WASHED. AND IT[2] CONVEYS UNCLEANNESS[3] IRRESPECTIVE OF WHETHER IT IS WET OR DRY.[4] R. SIMEON RULED: IF IT IS DRY[4] IT CAUSES UNCLEANNESS RETROSPECTIVELY,[5] BUT IF IT IS WET[4] IT CAUSES UNCLEANNESS ONLY TO A TIME WHEN IT COULD STILL HAVE BEEN WET.[6]

GEMARA. The question was raised: Is the alley TO SUCH TIME AS IT WAS LAST SWEPT in the presumptive state of having

(1) *Sc.* a ladleful of it conveys uncleanness by means of touch, carriage and overshadowing. (2) The dead creeping thing as well as the bloodstain. (3) RETROSPECTIVELY to the times indicated. (4) When discovered. (5) To the times previously indicated, since it is possible that the creeping thing or stain may have been there soon after the alley had been swept or the shirt washed. (6) And not to the times previously indicated if they are earlier. For if it had been there since the earlier times it would have been dry by now.

been duly examined,[1] or is it possible that it is in the presumptive state of having been properly swept?[2] And in what case could this[3] matter?—In that where a person declared that he had swept the alley but did not examine it.[4] If you say that 'it is in the presumptive state of having been duly examined'[1] surely, he had not examined it;[5] but if you say, 'it is in the presumptive state of having been properly swept'[2] surely, at that time[6] it was properly swept.[7] [56*b*] Or also in the case where the creeping thing was found in a hole.[8] If you say that 'it is in the presumptive state of having been duly examined',[1] any one who examines the alley examines also any hole in it;[7] but if you say that 'it is in the presumptive state of having been properly swept',[2] a hole is not usually swept.[9]

SO ALSO A BLOODSTAIN etc. The question was raised: Is the shirt TO SUCH TIME AS IT WAS LAST WASHED in the presumptive state of having been duly examined,[10] or is it possible that it is in the presumptive state of having been properly washed?[11] And in what case could this[12] matter?—In that where a person declared that he had washed the shirt but did not examine it. If you say that 'it is in the presumptive state of having been duly examined', surely, he had not examined it,[13] but if you say that 'it is in the presumptive state of having been properly washed', surely, it had been properly washed.[14] Or also in the case where the stain

(1) By the person who swept it who had thus definitely ascertained that there was no unclean object in it at the time. (2) So that if any unclean object had been there at the time it would have been swept away. (3) The assumption of the former or of the latter. (4) To ascertain whether any unclean object remained after the sweeping. (5) And the uncleanness would be retrospective to the time before the sweeping. (6) Though no examination took place. (7) And no unclean object could have remained. Hence the uncleanness could be retrospective only to the time of the sweeping. (8) And the sweeper made no declaration at all. (9) And the creeping thing may have been lying in that hole long before the alley had been swept (cf. n. 5). (10) At the time it was washed, when it was definitely ascertained that there was then no stain on it. (11) When any stain that may have been on it would have been washed out. (12) Our assumption of the former or of the latter. (13) The uncleanness would, therefore, be restrospective to the time before the washing. (14) And the uncleanness could be retrospective to the time of washing only.

was discovered in a fold.[1] If you say that 'it is in the presumptive state of having been duly examined', anyone engaged in an examination examines also the folds,[2] but if you say that 'it is in the presumptive state of having been properly washed', a stain in a fold may not have been washed out.[3] Now what is the decision?—Come and hear: For it was taught: R. Meir stated, Why did they[4] rule that if a dead creeping thing was found in an alley it causes uncleanness retrospectively to such time as one can testify, 'I examined this alley and there was no creeping thing in it', or to such time as it was last swept?[5] Because there is presumption that the children of Israel examine their alleys at the time they are swept; but if they did not examine them, they impaired its presumptive cleanness retrospectively.[6] And why did they[4] rule that a bloodstain, if found on a shirt, causes uncleanness retrospectively to such time as one can testify, 'I examined this shirt and there was no stain on it', or to such time as it was last washed?[7] Because there is presumption that the daughters of Israel examine their shirts at the time they are washing them; but if they did not examine them, they impair its presumptive cleanness retrospectively.[8] R. Aḥa ruled: Let her[9] wash it again. If its colour fades[10] it may be taken for granted[11] that it was made after the previous washing,[12] but if it does not fade it may be taken for granted[11] that it was made before the previous washing. Rabbi said, A stain after its washing is not like a stain before it had been washed, for the former penetrates into the material while the latter remains clotted on its surface. Thus it may be inferred[13] that[14] there

(1) Lit., 'side', 'border'; and the washer did not make any declaration. (2) V. p. 393, n. 14. (3) V. p. 393, n. 13. (4) The Rabbis. (5) *Sc.* why does not the uncleanness begin prior to the sweeping? (6) To the time prior to the sweeping. (7) *Sc.* why does not the uncleanness begin before the washing? (8) The uncleanness beginning prior to the washing. (9) Who did not examine her shirt when she washed it and subsequently found a bloodstain on it, and it is unknown whether that stain was there before the washing or was made subsequently. (10) As a result of the last washing. (11) Lit., 'it is known'. (12) For if it had been there before the previous washing it would have faded in the course of that washing. Hence the uncleanness is retrospective to the time of the previous washing only. (13) From

is presumption that it was duly examined. This is conclusive.

AND IT CAUSES UNCLEANNESS IRRESPECTIVE OF WHETHER IT IS WET etc. R. Eleazar explained: This[1] was learnt only concerning the dead creeping thing, but a wet bloodstain also causes uncleanness retrospectively,[2] for it might be assumed that it was already dry but water had fallen upon it. But can it not be assumed in the case of a dead creeping thing also that it was already dry but water had fallen upon it?—If that were the case it would have been completely dismembered.[3]

MISHNAH. ALL BLOODSTAINS[4] THAT COME FROM REḲEM[5] ARE CLEAN.[6] R. JUDAH DECLARES THEM UNCLEAN, BECAUSE THE PEOPLE WHO LIVE THERE ARE PROSELYTES[7] THOUGH MISGUIDED.[8] THOSE[9] THAT COME FROM THE HEATHENS[10] ARE CLEAN.[11] THOSE THAT COME FROM ISRAELITES OR FROM SAMARITANS, R. MEIR DECLARES, ARE UNCLEAN, BUT THE SAGES DECLARED THEM CLEAN[12] BECAUSE THEY ARE UNDER NO SUSPICION[12] IN REGARD TO THEIR STAINS.

GEMARA. Since the statement[13] was made categorically[14] it follows, does it not, that it applies even to those from Tarmod?[15]—R. Joḥanan replied: This proves that proselytes may be accepted from Tarmod.[16] But can this be right[17] seeing that both R. Joḥanan

R. Meir's ruling. (14) When nothing to the contrary is definitely known.

(1) R. Simeon b. Gamaliel's ruling. (2) To the time it had last been washed. (3) The assumption can, therefore, be applied to a bloodstain only. (4) On women's garments. (5) V. Yeb., Sonc. ed., p. 88, n. 10. (6) Because no Israelites of pure stock live there. The menstrual blood of heathens is levitically clean. (7) Whose menstrual blood is unclean like that of Israelites proper. (8) *Sc.* though they no longer observed the religious laws of Israel. (9) Bloodstains. (10) *Sc.* from places where no Israelites live. (11) Cf. n. 6. (12) This is discussed in the Gemara *infra.* (13) THOSE THAT CAME FROM THE HEATHENS ARE CLEAN. (14) Lit., 'he decided and teaches'. (15) Whose inhabitants were reputed to have an admixture of Jewish blood. But how could this be reconciled with the law that Jewish menstrual blood is unclean? (16) Palmyra: the inhabitants being regarded in all respects as heathens and

and Sabya ruled, No proselytes may be accepted from Tarmod? And should you reply that R. Johanan only said, 'This',[1] but he himself[2] does not hold this view [it could be retorted]: Did not R. Johanan lay down, 'The *halachah* is in accordance with an anonymous Mishnah'?[3]—It is a question in dispute between Amoras as to what was actually R. Johanan's view.

FROM ISRAELITES etc. As to the Rabbis,[4] if they declare the menstrual blood of Israelites clean, whose do they hold to be unclean?—Some words are missing from our Mishnah, this being the correct reading: FROM ISRAELITES are unclean, FROM SAMARITANS, R. MEIR DECLARES, ARE UNCLEAN, since Samaritans are true proselytes,[5] BUT THE SAGES DECLARED THEM CLEAN because, in their opinion, Samaritans are merely lion-proselytes.[6] If so, instead of saying, BECAUSE THEY ARE UNDER NO SUSPICION IN REGARD TO THEIR STAINS, it should have been said, Because they are lion-proselytes?—The fact rather is that it is this that was meant: FROM ISRAELITES OR FROM SAMARITANS they are unclean, since Samaritans are true proselytes; those that are found in Israelite cities[7] are clean since they are not suspected of leaving their stains exposed, for they rather keep them in privacy; and those that are found[7] in Samaritan cities, R. MEIR DECLARES, ARE UNCLEAN because they are suspected of leaving their stains exposed, BUT THE SAGES DECLARED THEM CLEAN BECAUSE THEY[8] ARE UNDER NO SUSPICION IN REGARD TO THEIR STAINS.

MISHNAH. ALL BLOODSTAINS, WHERESOEVER THEY ARE

not as a mixed breed of bastards from whom no proselytes may be accepted. (17) Lit., 'I am not'.

(1) *Sc.* 'this proves etc.' (2) Maintaining that no proselytes may be accepted from Tadmor. (3) From which, as shown *supra*, it follows that proselytes may be accepted from the Tarmodites. (4) THE SAGES. (5) Whose menstrual blood is, therefore, as unclean as that of a proper Israelite. (6) *Sc.* proselytes who were converted to Judaism not out of religious convictions but out of fear of the lions that attacked them (cf. II Kings XVII, 25). (7) In an open place. (8) Keeping them in privacy.

FOUND,[1] ARE CLEAN, EXCEPT THOSE THAT ARE FOUND INDOORS[2] OR ROUND ABOUT A CHAMBER FOR[3] UNCLEAN WOMEN.[4] A CHAMBER FOR[3] UNCLEAN SAMARITAN WOMEN CONVEYS UNCLEANNESS BY OVERSHADOWING[5] BECAUSE THEY BURY MISCARRIAGES THERE. R. JUDAH STATED, THEY DID NOT BURY THEM BUT THREW THEM AWAY AND THE WILD BEASTS DRAGGED THEM OFF. THEY[6] ARE BELIEVED WHEN THEY DECLARE, 'WE BURIED MISCARRIAGES THERE', OR 'WE DID NOT BURY THEM'. THEY[6] ARE BELIEVED WHEN THEY DECLARE CONCERNING A BEAST WHETHER IT HAD GIVEN BIRTH TO A FIRSTLING[7] OR HAD NOT GIVEN BIRTH TO ONE. THEY[6] ARE BELIEVED WHEN GIVING INFORMATION ON THE MARKING OF GRAVES,[8] BUT THEY ARE NOT BELIEVED EITHER IN REGARD TO OVERHANGING BRANCHES,[9] OR PROTRUDING STONES[9] OR A BETH HA-PERAS.[9] THIS IS THE GENERAL RULE: IN ANY MATTER WHERE THEY ARE UNDER SUSPICION THEY ARE NOT BELIEVED.

GEMARA. [57a] What exposition did they[6] rely upon?[10]— *Thou shalt not remove they neighbour's landmark,*[11] *which they of old time have set, in thine inheritance,*[12] whosoever has an *'inheritance'*[13] has also a *'landmark'*,[11] but whosoever has no inheritance[14] has no landmark.[11]

THEY ARE BELIEVED WHEN THEY SAY, 'WE BURIED...' But,[15] surely, they do not uphold, do they, the exposition of the injunction, *Nor put a stumbling-block before the blind?*[16]—R. Abbahu

(1) In an Israelite locality. (2) Lit., 'in rooms', it being assumed that, since they are kept in privacy, they must be menstrual. (3) Lit., 'a house of'. (4) *Sc.* a chamber used by menstruants. (5) *Sc.* any person who enters into the chamber. (6) Samaritans. (7) So that the next birth is free from the restrictions imposed on a firstling. (8) *Sc.* any place not so marked may be treated as clean. (9) This is explained in the Gemara *infra.* (10) In not burying their miscarriages (v. our Mishnah.). (11) *Sc.* his ancestral grave-yard (Sifri). (12) Deut. XIX, 14. (13) *Sc.* a normal child. (14) A miscarriage. (15) How can they be relied upon? (16) Lev. XIX, 14, which is homiletically applied to the supply of misleading information which leads the unwary into sin. As the Samaritans do not mind misleading in such matters, how could

replied: This[1] is a case where a [Samaritan] priest stood there.[2] But is it not possible that the priest was unclean?[3]—It is a case where he holds *terumah* in his hand.[4] But is it not possible that the *terumah* was unclean?[3]—It is a case where he was eating of it.[5] If so,[6] what was the need of stating it?[7]—It might have been presumed that they are not acquainted with the stages of formation,[8] hence we were informed [that we do rely upon them].[9]

THEY ARE BELIEVED WHEN THEY DECLARE CONCERNING A BEAST etc. But, surely, they do not uphold, the exposition of the injunction, *Nor put a stumbling-block before the blind*, do they?[10]—R. Ḥiyya b. Abba citing R. Joḥanan replied: It is the case of a beast that is shorn and engaged in work.[11] If so, what was the need of stating such a law?[7]—It might have been presumed that they are not acquainted with the nature of a discharge [from the womb],[12] hence we were informed [that they are to be believed].

THEY ARE BELIEVED WHEN GIVING INFORMATION ON THE MARKING OF etc. Although this[13] is only a Rabbinical institution[14] they are careful to observe it, since it is mentioned in Scripture.

their evidence on the cleanness or uncleanness of a place be acted upon?

(1) The law that Samaritans may be relied upon when they declare 'WE DID NOT BURY THEM'. (2) Had there been a grave in that place the priest would not have been there. (3) So that he has nothing to lose by remaining in the unclean place. (4) He would not have held the *terumah* there if the place had been unclean. (5) A certain proof that the *terumah* was clean. Unclean *terumah* is forbidden to a clean, and much more so to an unclean priest. (6) Cf. prev. n. (7) A law that is self-evident. (8) *Sc.* of the embryo; so that a mature one might be mistaken by them for an abortion and, in consequence, they would declare a place to be free from graves when in fact it is not clean. (9) Because they are well capable of distinguishing between an abortion and a normal child. (10) Cf. *supra* p. 397, nn. 15f *mut. mut.* (11) In the case of a firstling both these are forbidden and the Samaritan would not have ventured to shear it or to work with it. (12) Which in the case of small cattle is an indication of a birth that exempts the next from the restrictions of a firstling (cf. Bek. 21*b*); *sc.* they might mistake an ordinary discharge for one of abortion and thus erroneously regard the next birth as free from the restrictions of a firstling. (13) The marking of graves. (14) Which Samaritans usually disregard.

For it is written, *And any seeth a man's bone, then shall he set up a sign by it.*[1]

BUT THEY ARE NOT BELIEVED EITHER IN REGARD TO OVERHANGING BRANCHES etc. 'OVERHANGING BRANCHES', as we have learnt: The following are regarded as overhanging branches. The foliage of a tree that affords a covering over the ground.[2]

PROTRUDING STONES, as we have learnt: Protruding stones that project from a wall.[3]

BETH HA-PERAS. Rab Judah citing Samuel ruled: A man[4] may[5] blow away the earth in a *beth ha-peras*[6] and[7] continue on his way. R. Judah b. Ammi citing Rab Judah ruled: A *beth peras* that had been trodden out is clean.[8] One further taught: If one ploughs a graveyard he forms thereby a *beth ha-peras*.[9] And to what extent does he form it? To that of a full length of a furrow of a hundred cubit [squared, which covers an area of] four *beth se'ah*.[10] R. Jose ruled: Five *beth se'ah*. But are they[11] not believed?[12] Was it not in fact taught, 'Concerning a field in which a grave was lost[13] a Samaritan is believed when he stated, "There is no

(1) Ezek. XXXIX, 15. (2) Oh. VIII, 2. If one of the branches overshadowed a grave, uncleanness is conveyed only to a person under it but not to one under any of the other branches; but when the exact spot of the grave is unknown all the area overshadowed by the foliage is on account of the doubt subject to the same restriction. A Samaritan who is lax in the observance of uncleanness in a doubtful case, is not to be relied upon when he states that the grave was overshadowed by a particular branch or branches and that the others did not overshadow it. (3) Cf. prev. n. *mut. mut.* (4) Who desires to remain clean while making his way through a *beth peras*. (5) Since no flesh of the corpse need be expected, while the bones which the plough crushed (v. *infra*) to fractions convey uncleanness (if they are no smaller than a barley-grain) only by means of touch or carriage. (6) A grave area, v. Ḥag., Sonc. ed., p. 160, n. 1. (7) By thus making sure that his feet would touch no bone. (8) Because the bones are crushed and scattered by the constant treading and no bone of the prescribed minimum bulk (cf. prev. n. but one) remains. (9) *Peras* is derived from a root meaning 'to crush' the bones being crushed by the plough. *Aliter: 'Peras'* means a 'half', the extent of the unclean area being half a furrow in each direction from the grave. *Aliter: 'Peras'* is derived from a root meaning 'to extend', the uncleanness being extended to an area larger than that of the grave. (10) Which means a hundred times a hundred cubits. (11) The Samaritans. (12) About a *beth ha-peras*. (13) And which also, like a

grave there",[1] since he gives his evidence only about the grave itself;[2] concerning a tree whose foliage affords a covering over the ground[3] he is believed when he stated, "There is no grave under it",[4] since he renders evidence only about the grave itself'?[2]—R. Joḥanan replied: This[5] is a case where he walks backward and forward throughout *all* its area.[6] If so,[7] what was the need of stating it?[8]—It might have been presumed that a narrow strip jutted out,[9] hence we were informed that[10] he is believed.[11]

THIS IS THE GENERAL RULE etc. What is the expression THIS IS THE GENERAL RULE intended to include?—To include Sabbath boundaries[12] and wine of libation.[13]

field in which a grave was ploughed, is subject to the uncleanness of a *beth ha-peras* (cf. M.Ḳ. 5*b*).

(1) *Sc.* in any particular spot in the field. (2) Which is subject to Pentateuchal uncleanness which Samaritans observe. As his evidence amounts to an assertion that no Pentateuchal uncleanness is involved in that particular place he may well be relied upon. How then is this to be reconciled with our Mishnah? (3) Cf. *supra* p. 399, n. 2. (4) Under any particular branch. (5) The cited Baraitha according to which a Samaritan is relied upon. (6) Which may well be taken as reliable evidence that there was no grave there. Our Mishnah, however, refers to a case where the Samaritan walks only across a part of the field. As he omits the other part there is reason to suspect that he knows it to contain a grave and that his evidence on the doubtful part of the field is intended to mislead Israelites so that they become subject to an uncleanness in which he himself does not believe. Hence the ruling of our Mishnah. (7) That the Samaritan walked throughout the suspected area. (8) A rule that is self evident. As a grave was known to have been in the field and the Samaritan nevertheless walked through all its area, it must be obvious that he knew that the corpse had been removed. (9) From the field; and that he assumed the grave to be located within that strip. As the rest of the field is still a suspected area the doubtful uncleanness of which Samaritans disregard his evidence aught not to be relied upon. (10) Since he walked across its four sides. (11) The possibility of a narrow strip jutting out not being taken into consideration. (12) Which are a Rabbinical institution. Samaritans who reject it are not trusted when they state where the limit is. (13) *Yen nesek*, wine touched by an idolater and suspected of having been dedicated by him to idolatry. Samaritans do not regard such wine as forbidden and their evidence in such a case cannot, therefore, be trusted.

NIDDAH

CHAPTER VIII

MISHNAH. [57*b*] IF A WOMAN OBSERVED A BLOODSTAIN ON HER BODY,[1] IF IT WAS NEAR THE PUDENDA SHE IS UNCLEAN[2] BUT IF IT WAS NOT NEAR THE PUDENDA SHE REMAINS CLEAN. IF[3] IT WAS ON HER HEEL OR ON THE TIP OF HER GREAT TOE, SHE IS UNCLEAN.[4] ON HER THIGH OR ON HER FEET, IF ON THE INNER SIDE, SHE IS UNCLEAN; IF ON THEIR OUTER SIDE, SHE REMAINS CLEAN; AND IF ON THE FRONT AND BACK SIDES[5] SHE REMAINS CLEAN. IF SHE OBSERVED IT ON HER SHIRT BELOW THE BELT, SHE IS UNCLEAN,[2] BUT IF ABOVE THE BELT, SHE REMAINS CLEAN. IF SHE OBSERVED IT ON THE SLEEVE OF HER SHIRT, SHE IS UNCLEAN IF IT[6] CAN REACH AS LOW AS THE PUDENDA,[2] BUT IF IT CANNOT, SHE REMAINS CLEAN. IF SHE TAKES IT OFF AND COVERS HERSELF WITH IT IN THE NIGHT, SHE IS UNCLEAN WHEREVER THE STAIN IS FOUND,[7] SINCE IT CAN TURN ABOUT.[8] AND THE SAME LAW[9] APPLIES TO A PALLIUM.[10]

GEMARA. Samuel ruled: If a woman examined the ground[11] and after sitting on it, found on it some blood, she remains clean, for it is said, *In her flesh,*[12] implying that she is not unclean unless she feels[13] in her flesh. But the expression[14] *'in her flesh'* is required

(1) Lit., 'flesh'. (2) Since it may be attributed to menstruation. (3) The following illustrates the previous general rule. (4) The reason follows *infra* in the Gemara. (5) Lit., 'and on the sides from here and from here'. (6) The place of the stain. (7) *Sc.* even if it is on a part which when worn cannot reach as low as the pudenda. (8) And the upper part then comes in contact with the lower parts of the body. (9) That she is UNCLEAN WHEREVER THE STAIN IS FOUND. (10) παλλίον a square sheet used as a cloak and as a bed cover. When used as a cover the upper part might well turn about (cf. prev. n. but one). (11) Lit., 'floor of the world'. (12) Lev. XV, 19. (13) The discharge. (14) Lit. 'that'.

for the deduction that she conveys uncleanness within[1] as without?[2]—If so,[3] Scripture could have said, 'In flesh', why then did it say *'in her flesh'?* It may, therefore, be deduced that she is not unclean 'unless she feels[4] in her flesh'. But still, is not the expression required for the deduction, *'In her flesh,* but not within a sac or within a lump of flesh'?[5]—Both deductions may be made from it.

Come and hear: If a woman while attending to her needs[6] observed a discharge of blood, R. Meir ruled: If she was standing at the time she is unclean,[7] but if she was then sitting she remains clean.[8] Now how is one to imagine the circumstance?[9] If she felt the discharge, why should she be clean where she was sitting? Consequently this must be a case where she did not feel a discharge, and yet it was taught, was it not, that she was unclean?[10]—This may in fact be a case where she did feel a discharge but[11] it might be assumed that the feeling was that of the ejection of the urine. When she stands, the urine might well return to the interior of her womb[12] and then carry out some blood with it, but if she sits,[13] she remains clean.

Come and hear: If on a testing rag that was placed under a pillow some blood was found, it is regarded as clean if it[14] was round,[15] but if it was elongated it is unclean. Now how are we to understand the circumstances? If she felt a discharge, why should it be clean when round? Consequently it must be a case where

(1) *Sc.* while the blood is still within her body. (1) *Supra* 21*b* q.v. nn. How then can Samuel's deduction be made from the same expression? (3) That only the latter deduction is to be made. (4) The discharge. (5) *Sc.* if blood is found within any of these abortions, but not on the woman's person, she remains clean (*supra* 21*b*). (6) Making water. (7) Since owing to the narrowness of the passage occasioned by her standing position, her urine may have returned to the interior of her womb whence it gathered up some menstrual blood. (8) *Infra* 59*b*, *supra* 14*a*, the blood being attributed to a wound in the bladder. (9) In which R. Meir's rule applies. (10) An objection against Samuel. (11) As to the reason why she remains clean. (12) Lit., 'source'. (13) A position which does not block the passage. (14) The blood mark. (15) Because it cannot be the result of the test which would produce an elongated patch.

she felt no discharge, and yet it was stated, was it not, that if it was elongated it is unclean?[1]—No, it may in fact be a case where[2] she felt the discharge, but it might be assumed that it was the feeling of the testing rag. Hence if it is elongated it must certainly have issued from her body,[3] but if it is round[4] it is clean.[5]

Come and hear: If a vestige of blood is found on his rag they are both unclean and are also under the obligation of bringing a sacrifice. If any blood is found on her rag immediately after their intercourse they are both unclean and are also under the obligation of bringing a sacrifice. If, however, any blood is found on her rag after a time they are both unclean by reason of the doubt but exempt from the sacrifice.[6] Now how are we to imagine the circumstance? If she has felt a discharge, why should they be exempt from the sacrifice where the blood is found after a time? Must it not then be a case where she did not feel any discharge, and yet it was taught, was it not, that 'if any blood is found on her rag immediately after their intercourse they are both unclean and are also under the obligation of bringing a sacrifice'?[1]—No, she may in fact have felt the discharge, but it might be assumed that it was the feeling of the attendant.[7]

Come and hear: You are thus in a position[8] to say that three forms of doubt appertain to a woman. A bloodstain on her body, concerning which there is doubt whether it is unclean and clean, is regarded as unclean;[9] on her shirt, when it is doubtful whether it is unclean or clean, is regarded as clean;[9] and in regard to the laws of the uncleanness of contact and *heseṭ*[10] you follow the majority. Now what is meant by 'you follow the majority'? Is it not that if on most days she is unclean[11] this is a cause of uncleanness[12] even when she felt no discharge?[1]—No, the meaning

(1) An objection against Samuel. (2) In the course of the test. (3) This being the shape that a blood mark would assume on a testing rag. (4) And, therefore, likely to be the result of some wound. (5) Because it cannot be the result of the test which would produce an elongated patch. (6) Mishnah *supra* 14*a* q.v. notes. (7) Euphemism. (8) Lit., 'thou art found'. (9) This is explained *infra*. (10) V. Glos. (11) Cf. Rashi and Tosaf. for different illustrations of this uncleanness. (22) Lit., 'unclean'.

is that if on most days her observation of the blood is accompanied by a feeling of the discharge she is unclean since it might be assumed that she had felt it this time also but did not pay any attention to it.

The Master said, 'A bloodstain on her body, concerning which there is doubt whether it is unclean or clean, is regarded as unclean; on her shirt, when it is doubtful whether it is unclean or clean, is regarded as clean'. How is one to understand the circumstances? If it[1] was below her belt, why, when on her shirt, is it regarded as clean seeing that we have learnt, BELOW THE BELT, SHE IS UNCLEAN; and if it was above her belt, why, when on her body is it regarded as unclean, seeing that we have learnt that if she observed blood on her body, IF IT WAS NOT NEAR THE PUDENDA, SHE REMAINS CLEAN?—If you wish I could reply that the stain was below the belt; and if you prefer I might reply that it was above the belt. 'If you wish I could reply that the stain was below the belt', in a case, for instance, where she passed through a butchers' market. If the stain was on her body it must have emanated from herself, for if it had emanated from an external source[2] it should have been found on her shirt; but if it is found on her shirt, it must have emanated from an external source,[2] for if it had emanated from herself it should have been found on her body. 'And if you prefer I might reply that it was above her belt', in a case, for instance, where she jumped backwards. If the stain is on her body it must undoubtedly have emanated from herself, for if it had emanated from an external source[2] it should have been found on her shirt; but if it is found on her shirt, it must have emanated from an external source,[2] for if it had emanated from herself, it should have been found on her body. At all events, it was stated, was it not, 'A bloodstain on her body, concerning which there is doubt whether it is unclean or clean, is regarded as clean', presumably even if she did not feel any discharge?[3] Furthermore, we have learnt, IF A WOMAN OBSERVED A BLOODSTAIN ON HER BODY, IF IT WAS NEAR THE PUDENDA, SHE IS UN-

(1) The stain. (2) Lit., 'from the world'. (3) An objection against Samuel.

CLEAN. Does not this imply even where she did not feel any discharge?[1]—R. Jeremiah of Difti replied: Samuel agrees that[2] she is unclean [58a] according to Rabbinic law.[3] R. Ashi[4] replied: Samuel gave his ruling in accordance with the view of R. Nehemiah. For we learnt: R. Nehemiah ruled, Any thing that is not susceptible to uncleanness is not susceptible to stains.[5] According to R. Ashi one can well see the reason why he[6] mentioned 'ground',[7] but according to R. Jeremiah of Difti,[8] what was the point of mentioning 'ground', seeing that even in the case of a cloak[9] the woman is subject to the same law?—This is a case of an implied climax:[10] There is no question [that the woman is clean where she sat on] a cloak since it cannot be thoroughly examined and one may, therefore, well assume [that the stain] emanated from an external source,[11] but even [where she sat on] the ground which can well be thoroughly examined,[11] and where[12] it might justifiably be assumed that it emanated from her body, she is nevertheless regarded as clean.

ON HER HEEL OR ON THE TIP OF HER GREAT TOE, SHE IS UNCLEAN etc. One can well concede that HER HEEL[13] is likely[14] to come in contact with that place,[15] but what is the reason for the

(1) An objection against Samuel. (2) Since it is possible that she was so much pre-occupied at the time of the discharge that she was unconscious of her sensation. (3) The ruling cited in objection to Samuel being also Rabbinical only. Samuel's ruling, however, was concerned with the Pentateuchal law. (4) Maintaining that Samuel's ruling is not at all based on the principle that the woman must feel the discharge. (5) *Infra* 59b, *sc.* a stain found on such an object is no cause of uncleanness to the person in whom it may possibly have originated. As the ground on which the woman sat is not susceptible to uncleanness the woman also, despite the stain found, remains clean. All the rulings cited in objection to Samuel based on the principle of 'feeling', are, therefore, irrelevant. (6) Samuel. (7) Since the ground is not susceptible to uncleanness. (8) Who, as appears from his reply, accepted the view that Samuel based his ruling on the absence of sensation. (9) If, while sitting on it, the woman experienced no sensation of a discharge. (10) Lit., 'there is no question, he implied'. (11) Before the woman sat on it. (12) Since no stain was noticed before she sat down but was found after she rose. (13) When she sits with her legs folded under her body in eastern fashion. (14) Lit., 'does'. (15) Euphemism. Hence the uncleanness.

uncleanness in the case of a stain on THE TIP OF HER GREAT TOE? And should you reply: It might sometimes touch her heel [the objection would arise]: Do we [as regards] uncleanness presume transfer from place to place? Was it not in fact taught: If she[1] had a wound on her neck in a position to which the blood stain might be attributed,[2] she may so attribute it;[3] if it was on her shoulder, in which case she cannot so attribute it,[4] she must not so attribute it; and we do not suggest that it is possible that she had taken it[5] with her hand and transferred it there?[6]—The fact rather is that THE TIP OF HER TOE is in a different category,[7] because [direct dropping of blood] might occur while she is walking. But do we not [as regards] uncleanness presume transfer from place to place? Was it not in fact taught: If it[8] was found on her finger joints,[9] she is unclean, because hands are active.[10] Now what is the reason?[11] Is it not this: That we assume that she had examined herself with one hand[12] and then touched it with her other hand?[13]—No, her hand is different[7] since all of it might come in direct contact[14] [with the menstrual source].

ON HER THIGH OR ON HER FEET, IF ON THEIR INNER SIDE etc. How far[15] ON THEIR INNER SIDE?[16]—The school of R. Jannai

(1) A woman who discovered a bloodstain near her pudenda. (2) *Sc.* if the position of the wound was such that when the woman bends down some blood might drop from it on to the spot where the stain was discovered. (3) And remain clean. (4) Because even when she bends her head low the blood from the shoulder would not fall on the spot (cf. prev. n. but two) where the stain was discovered. (5) The blood from the shoulder wound. (6) How then could it be suggested here that the blood might have been transferred from the heel to the toe? (7) From the shoulder. (8) A bloodstain. (9) On the back of her hand. (10) And might, though the woman was not conscious of the fact, have touched menstrual blood. (11) That blood on the back of the hand (cf. prev. n. but one), which one would not expect to come in contact with the menstrual source, even in the course of an examination, should be regarded as unclean. (12) The palm of which became soiled in the process. (13) Which proves, does it not, that we do presume transfer as regards uncleanness? (14) Lit., 'does that it touches'. (15) From their front and back. (16) *Sc.* at what distance from their front and back is a stain regarded as being on their inner side.

replied: As far as the place of *hebek*.[1] The question was asked: Is the place of the *ḥebeḳ*[2] regarded as the inner, or as the outer side?—Come and hear what R. Ḳaṭṭina learnt: As far as the place of the *ḥebeḳ* and the *ḥebeḳ* itself is regarded as the inner side. R. Ḥiyya son of R. Iwya taught this[3] explicitly: The School of R. Jannai ruled, As far as the place of the *ḥebeḳ* and the *ḥebeḳ* itself is regarded as in the inner side.

R. Jeremiah enquired: What is the ruling[4] where a bloodstain had the shape of a ring, of a straight line of drops,[5] or of a splash of drops,[6] or where it runs across the breadth of her thigh?—Come and hear: 'A bloodstain on her body concerning which there is doubt whether it is unclean or clean, is regarded as unclean'. Now does not 'on her body' imply stains of such shapes?—No, it might only refer to one that is shaped like a stripe.[7]

A woman once found blood on her web. When she came to R. Jannai[8] he told her to experiment by repeating[9] her forward and backward movements.[10] But was it not taught: No repetition [test is recognized] in questions of cleanness?[11]—We say that no repetition test is recognized only[12] where the law would thereby[13] be relaxed, but where it is thereby restricted we do recognize a test of repetition.[14]

IF SHE TAKES IT OFF etc. It was taught: R. Eleazar son of R.

(1) The sinews that connect the thigh and the leg. The part of the leg beneath this junction and the part of the thigh above it are regarded as the INNER SIDE (cf. Rashi and Tosaf. Asheri). *Aliter:* The place where the leg meets the thigh when the woman squats (Aruk); the part of the leg to the place where the (ankle) loop sits (Jast.). (2) *Sc.* the sinews themselves (cf. Rashi and Tosaf. Asheri). *Aliter:* The ankle itself (Jast.). (3) The ruling that was just given in the form of a question and answer. (4) As regards menstrual uncleanness. (5) Cf. Tosaf. and Tosaf. Asheri. (6) Lit., 'drops, drops'. (7) Running downwards, which is the natural shape that may be expected if the blood was menstrual. (8) To enquire whether the stain was to be regarded as menstrual. (9) At the loom. (10) Lit., 'let her go and come'. By repeating the process several times she would be able to ascertain whether the web comes sometimes in contact with the menstrual source. (11) *Supra* 5*b* q.v. notes. (12) Lit., 'when do we say'. (13) By sanctioning the test. (14) Because here, since it was found neither on her body nor shirt, in the absence of evidence we assume her to be clean.

Jose stated, In such a case[1] I gave a ruling in the city of Rome imposing a prohibition,[2] and when I came to the Sages of the South they said to me, 'You have given the right decision'.

Our Rabbis taught: Where a tall woman put on the shirt[3] of a short woman or if a short one put on the shirt[3] of a tall one, if [a blood stain][4] corresponds to the position of the pudenda of the tall one, they are both unclean, but if it does not correspond to it,[5] the tall one is clean while the short one is unclean. Another Baraitha taught: If a woman examined her shirt[6] and then[7] lent it to her friend,[8] she is clean, but her friend may attribute it[9] to her. R. Shesheth explained: This[10] was learnt only in regard to the civil law,[11] but as regards the law of uncleanness the lender is clean while her friend is unclean. [58*b*] But why is this case different from the following where it was taught: If two women were engaged in the preparation of one bird which contained no more than one *sela'* of blood, and then a stain of the size of a *sela'* was found on each, they are both unclean?[12]—There[13] the law is different since there was an additional *sela'*.[14]

Our Rabbis taught: Where a woman put on three shirts[15] that she had previously examined[16] [and then found blood on one of

(1) Lit., 'this thing', a shirt that a woman used at night as a covering (v. our Mishnah). (2) *Sc.* that the blood is regarded as menstrual and that the woman is consequently unclean. (3) Without previously examining it. (4) Discovered subsequently. (5) Not reaching so low. (6) Var. lec., 'herself and her shirt' (v. BaḤ.). (7) Having made sure that it was clean. (8) And subsequently a stain was found on it. (9) The stain. (10) That the borrower may attribute the stain to the lender. (11) *Sc.* the lender, having no valid proof that the shirt was clean when she had lent it to the other, has no legal claim on the other for the cost of washing. (12) *Sc.* as in this case, though one stain could well be attributed to the bird, both women are unclean, so also in the former case, since it is possible that the lender did not properly examine her shirt, both lender and borrower should be unclean. (13) The latter case. (14) Which cannot possibly be attributed to the bird. As the stain of one woman at least must be an unclean one, and since it cannot be ascertained which one it is, uncleanness must be imposed on both women. In the former case, however, where one woman examined the shirt and the other did not, uncleanness may well be imposed on the latter only. (15) One on the top of the other. (16) Lit., 'that are examined to her'.

them], if she is in a position to attribute [the blood to an external source][1] she may do so even though [the blood was found] on the lowest shirt, but if she is not in a position to attribute [it to an external cause][1] she may not do so even though [the blood was found] on the uppermost shirt. How so? If she passed through a butchers' market she may attribute the blood to it even though it was found on the lowest shirt, but if she did not pass through a butchers' market she may not attribute the blood to it even if it was found on the uppermost.

MISHNAH. [A WOMAN] MAY ATTRIBUTE [A BLOODSTAIN] TO ANY [EXTERNAL] CAUSE TO WHICH SHE CAN POSSIBLY ATTRIBUTE IT.[2] IF [FOR INSTANCE] SHE HAD SLAIN A DOMESTIC BEAST, A WILD ANIMAL OR A BIRD, IF SHE WAS HANDLING BLOODSTAINS OR SAT BESIDE THOSE WHO HANDLED THEM, OR IF SHE KILLED A LOUSE, SHE MAY ATTRIBUTE THE BLOODSTAIN TO IT. HOW LARGE A STAIN MAY BE ATTRIBUTED TO A LOUSE?[3] R. ḤANINA B. ANTIGONUS REPLIED: ONE UP TO THE SIZE[4] OF A SPLIT BEAN; [AND IT MAY BE ATTRIBUTED TO A LOUSE] EVEN THOUGH SHE DID NOT KILL IT.[5] SHE MAY ALSO ATTRIBUTE IT TO HER SON OR TO HER HUSBAND.[6] IF SHE HERSELF HAD A WOUND THAT[7] COULD OPEN AGAIN AND BLEED SHE MAY ATTRIBUTE IT TO IT. A WOMAN ONCE CAME TO R. AKIBA AND SAID TO HIM: 'I HAVE OBSERVED A BLOODSTAIN'. 'HAD YOU PERHAPS', HE SAID TO HER, 'A WOUND?' 'YES', SHE REPLIED, 'BUT IT HAS HEALED'. 'IS IT POSSIBLE', HE AGAIN ASKED HER, 'THAT IT COULD OPEN AGAIN AND BLEED?' 'YES', SHE REPLIED; AND R. AKIBA DECLARED HER CLEAN. OBSERVING THAT HIS DISCIPLES LOOKED AT EACH OTHER IN ASTONISHMENT, HE SAID TO THEM, 'WHY DO YOU FIND THIS DIFFICULT, SEEING THAT THE SAGES DID NOT

(1) This is explained presently. (2) And thus regard herself as clean. (3) Lit., 'until how much may she attribute?' (4) This is discussed *infra* in the Gemara. (5) Contrary to the view of the Rabbis. (6) If any of them had a wound. (7) Though it is already dry.

LAY DOWN THE RULE[1] IN ORDER TO IMPOSE RESTRICTIONS BUT RATHER TO RELAX THEM, FOR IT IS SAID IN SCRIPTURE, AND IF A WOMAN HAVE AN ISSUE, AND HER ISSUE IN HER FLESH BE BLOOD,[2] ONLY BLOOD[3] BUT NOT A BLOODSTAIN. IF ON A TESTING RAG THAT WAS PLACED UNDER A PILLOW SOME BLOOD WAS FOUND, IF THE STAIN IS ROUND IT IS CLEAN BUT IF IT IS ELONGATED IT IS UNCLEAN; SO R. ELIEZER SON OF R. ZADOK.

GEMARA. Thus we have here[4] learnt what our Rabbis taught elsewhere: It once happened that R. Meir attributed it to collyrium, and Rabbi attributed it to the sap of a sycamore.[5]

OR SAT. Only where SHE SAT[6] but not [where she believes that] she did not sit.[7] Thus[8] we have here learnt what our Rabbis taught elsewhere: If a woman passed through a butchers' market, and it is a matter of doubt whether any blood was or was not squirted on her she may attribute [any bloodstain on her to a possible contingency]; but if it is doubtful whether she did or did not pass the market she[9] is unclean.[10]

IF SHE KILLED A LOUSE. Only where SHE KILLED[6] but not where she did not kill any. Whose view then does our Mishnah[11] represent?—That of R. Simeon b. Gamaliel. For it was taught: If she killed a louse she may attribute a bloodstain to it, but if she did not kill any she may not so attribute it; so R. Simeon b. Gamaliel. But the Sages ruled: In either case she may attribute the one to the other. Said R. Simeon b. Gamaliel: According to my view there is no limit[12] and according to the view of my colleagues there is no end.[12] 'According to my view there is no limit'

(1) About bloodstains. (2) Lev. XV, 19. (3) Causes uncleanness. (4) In our Mishnah. (5) *Supra* 19*b* f q.v. notes. (6) Does the law apply. Lit., 'yes'. (7) Though it might well be possible that she did sit there without being conscious of the fact (cf. Rashi and Tosaf. Asheri). (8) Since the possibility of an unconscious act is here disregarded. (9) If any bloodstain was found on her. (10) Cf. prev. n. but two *mut. mut.* (11) *Sc.* the anonymous ruling which is contrary to the view of R. Ḥanina b. Antigonus. (12) This is explained presently.

since you could hardly find[1] a woman who could be regarded as clean for her husband, seeing that there is hardly[1] a bed that does not contain ever so many drops of louse blood.[2] 'According to the view of my colleagues there is no end', since there is hardly[1] a woman who could be regarded as unclean for her husband, seeing that there is hardly a sheet on which there are not ever so many drops of blood;[3] but the view of R. Ḥanina b. Antigonus is more feasible than mine and theirs, for he has laid down, 'How large a stain may be attributed to a louse? One not bigger than the size of a split bean',[4] and we rule in agreement with his view.[5] But according to the Rabbis who ruled, SHE MAY ATTRIBUTE,[6] how large may be the stain?[7]—R. Naḥman b. Isaac replied: She may attribute it to a bed-bug even if it is as big as a lupine.[8]

Our Rabbis taught: A[9] bed-bug is of the same length and breadth and the taste of it is like its odour. Whosoever crushes it cannot help[10] smelling it. It was stated to be of 'the same length and breadth' in regard to bloodstains.[11] 'The taste of it is like its odour' has been stated in regard to *terumah*.[12] For we have learnt: 'Or if he tasted the flavour of a bed-bug in his mouth he must spit it out.[13] But how could he know this?[14] Because 'the taste of it is like its odour'. But still, whence could he know this?[15] [Because] 'whosoever crushes it cannot help[10] smelling it'.

R. Ashi ruled: In a town in which there are pigs there is no need to consider the possibility of menstrual bloodstains.[16] R. Naḥman

(1) Lit., 'since you have not'. (2) So that the woman, unless she was certain that she killed one, would always be unclean, however minute the speck of blood. (3) And these can be attributed to lice, however big the stain. (4) Even if she killed nothing; while if it is bigger it is unclean even though a louse was killed. (5) So Elijah Wilna. Cf. MS.M. Cur. edd., 'and we agree with his view'. (6) Even if she is not aware of killing anything. (7) To be regarded as clean. If it is very big it could not obviously be attributed to a louse. (8) Cf. prev. n. (9) Lit., 'this'. (10) Lit., 'a covenant is made for it', *sc.* a protection for its preservation. (11) A stain, though bigger than a split bean, may be regarded as clean if its length is equal to its breadth since it may be attributed to a bug. (12) And the same applies to unconsecrated produce. *Terumah* was mentioned because the Mishnah of Ter. cited happens to deal with *terumah*. (13) Ter. VIII, 2. (14) The taste of vermin. (15) Its odour. (16) Since the pigs, eating all sorts of creeping things and vermin, scatter about their blood.

b. Isaac stated: The condition of[1] Doḳereth[2] is[3] like that of a town in which there are pigs.[4]

HOW LARGE A STAIN MAY BE ATTRIBUTED etc. R. Huna explained: If the stain is equal in size to a split bean it may not be attributed to a louse; if it is smaller in size than a split bean it may be attributed to it. R. Ḥisda, however, explained: If it was of the same size as a split bean it may be attributed to it, but if it was bigger than the size of a split bean it may not be attributed to it. Must it be assumed that they[5] differ on the question whether 'UP TO' is meant to include the terminus,[6] R. Huna[7] holding the opinion that 'up to' does not include the terminus[8] while R. Ḥisda[9] holds that 'up to' is inclusive of the terminus?[10]—R. Huna can answer you: 'Up to' may sometimes include the terminus and sometimes exclude it, but in either case[11] the meaning must be one that leads to a restriction,[12] while R. Ḥisda can answer you: Elsewhere I agree with you[13] that we adopt a meaning that leads to a restriction and not one that leads to a relaxation, but here the meaning must be in agreement with a ruling of R. Abbahu, R. Abbahu having ruled: All prescribed minima of the Sages are intended to impose restrictions, except the prescribed size of a split bean in the case of bloodstains which is intended to relax the law.[14] There are others who give this tradition[15] as an independent statement:[16] R. Huna ruled, A bloodstain of the size of a split

(1) Lit., 'and that of'. (2) Darankat on the Tigris, v. Obermeyer p. 197. (3) Since it had many butchers' shops and swarmed with dung hills and vermin. (4) Cf. prev. n. but three. (5) R. Huna and R. Ḥisda. (6) Lit., 'until and until included'. (7) Who holds that a stain that is equal in size to a split bean may not be attributed to vermin. (8) Which is (cf. our Mishnah) 'THE SIZE OF A SPLIT BEAN'. (9) Who maintains that a stain of the size of a split bean may be attributed to vermin. (10) But if so how could each respectively reconcile his view with (cf. Ḥul. 55a) the cases to the contrary? (11) Lit., 'and here . . . and here'. (12) As in the case of stains here under discussion the law is restricted by excluding the terminus, he justifiably maintains that the stain of the size of a split bean is excluded. (13) Lit., 'In the world I will tell you'. (14) Hence the inclusion of the terminus in the ruling of our Mishnah. (15) The dispute between R. Huna and R. Ḥisda. (16) *Sc.* not as an explanation of our Mishnah.

bean is treated as one bigger than the size of a split bean;[1] while R. Ḥisda ruled, One of the size of a split bean is treated as one that is less than the size of a split bean;[2] but they differ on the interpretation of UP TO here, as has just been explained.[3]

An objection was raised: [59a] If a woman had drops of blood on her body below her belt[4] and drops of blood above it, she may attribute [the former to the blood that is assumed to be the cause of the drops] on the latter[5] up to the size of a split bean. Now does not this[6] mean a stain of the size of a split bean below her belt?[7]—No, a stain of the size of a split bean above the belt.[8]

It was stated: If on the body of a woman[9] was found a stain of the size of a split bean plus some addition,[10] and to that addition clung a louse, R. Ḥanina ruled: She is unclean;[11] and R. Jannai ruled: She is clean.[12] 'R. Ḥanina ruled: She is unclean', since she may attribute a stain to a louse only where the former is of the size of a split bean but not where it is of the size of a split bean plus. 'R. Jannai ruled: She is clean', since this restriction[13] applies only

(1) *Sc.* is regarded as unclean. (2) Is regarded as clean. (3) R. Huna, here as elsewhere, adopting the meaning that leads to a restriction while R. Ḥisda regards the meaning here as an exception in agreement with R. Abbahu's ruling. (4) So Tosaf. and Tosaf. Asheri, (contra Rashi) whose interpretation is here followed. (5) Lit., 'on the upper'. As the drops above the belt may be attributed to blood from a source external to her body so may also the drops below it. (6) The prescribed 'size of a split bean'. (7) But if so, it would follow that only where there are bloodstains above the belt are stains of the size of a split bean below it regarded as originating from the same extraneous source as those above and, therefore, treated as clean, but that where there are no drops of blood above the belt, even a stain of the size of a split bean below it is regarded as unclean. An objection against R. Ḥisda who ruled that a stain of such size is invariably attributed to vermin and is, therefore, clean. (8) *Sc.* so long as the stain above is not smaller than the size of a split bean the stain below, though bigger than the size of a split bean, may be attributed to the same cause as that of the stain above. When the stain below, however, is no bigger than the size of a split bean, it is invariably clean irrespective of whether the body above was or was not stained with drops of blood. (9) Lit., 'upon her'. (10) Lit., 'and more'. (11) It being regarded as due to menstrual blood. (12) *Sc.* it is not attributed to blood of menstruation. (13) That only a stain no bigger than a split bean is attributed to a louse.

where no louse clings to the addition, but where a louse clings to it, it is quite evident that the addition is the blood of a louse, so that only a stain of the size of a split bean remains;[1] and since such a size may elsewhere[2] be attributed to a louse it may also here be so attributed.

R. Jeremiah enquired: What is the ruling where a woman handled some blood of the bulk of a split bean but on her body was found a bloodstain of the size of a split bean and a little more? This question arises according to R. Ḥanina and it also arises according to R. Jannai. 'This question arises according to R. Ḥanina', since R. Ḥanina may have maintained his view there[3] that the woman was unclean, only because she did not handle any blood, but here, where she did handle some, she may well attribute [the stain to an extraneous cause],[4] or is it possible that, even according to R. Jannai who ruled[3] that she was clean, the ruling applies only where a louse clings to the stain, but where no louse clings to it, the stain may not be attributed to it?—Come and hear: If she was handling red stuff she may not attribute to it a black stain; if she was handling a small quantity[5] she may not attribute to it a large stain. Now how is one to imagine the circumstances?[6] Would you not agree that they were of the same nature?[7]—No, this[6] might be a case, for instance, where she handled a quantity of blood of the bulk of a split bean while on her body was found a stain of the size of two split beans and a little more in excess.[8] But if so,[9] what was the need of mentioning it?[10]—It might have been presumed that one takes the part of the stain[11] that may be attributed to the blood of the bird[12] to be in the middle[13] so that there remains

(1) In doubt as to its origin. (2) Where there is no addition to it. (3) In the statement just cited. (4) One part of the stain, to the extent of the size of a bean, might be attributed to the blood of the same quantity that she had previously handled while the remainder might be attributed to some vermin. (5) Of the blood of a bird (cf. *infra*). (6) In the latter case. (7) As the case submitted by R. Jeremiah. Would then a solution be forthcoming from here? (8) As the excess over the size of a split bean amounts to more than a split bean, it cannot possibly be attributed to vermin. Hence the uncleanness. (9) Cf. prev. n. (10) A ruling that is self-evident. (11) The size of one split bean. (12) Cf. *supra* n. 5. (13) Lit., 'take

less than the prescribed minimum on either of its sides,[1] hence we were informed [that the stain cannot be attributed to it[2] at all].

Raba ruled: If one kind of material[3] was found upon a woman[4] she may attribute to it any kind of stain.[5] It was objected: If she was handling red stuff she may not attribute to it a black stain![6]—A case where she had handled the stuff is different.[7] There are some who say: Raba ruled, If a woman was handling one kind of material, she may attribute to it any kinds of stain.[5] It was objected: If she was handling red stuff she may not attribute to it a black stain![8]—When Raba laid down his ruling he referred to a woman who was handling a hen which contains several kinds of blood.

A WOMAN ONCE etc. But was it not taught: Seeing that the Sages did not lay down the rule in order to relax the law but rather to restrict it?[9]—Rabina replied: The meaning is that they did not lay down the rule to relax Pentateuchal laws,[10] but rather to add restrictions to them;[11] but the uncleanness of bloodstains is altogether a Rabbinical enactment.[12]

IF ON A TESTING RAG THAT WAS PLACED. The question was raised: Do the Rabbis differ from R. Eliezer son of R. Zadok or

like the size of a split bean; threw it in the middle' of the stained area.

(1) Lit., 'go here there is no prescribed size (*bis*)'. As the stain is thus smaller than the size prescribed it might have been presumed to be clean. (2) The blood of the bird. (3) Collyrium or sap, for instance, which leaves a stain after it is removed. (4) Lit., 'upon her'. (5) That she subsequently discovers; though the latter is not of the same colour as the material to which it is attributed. (6) How then can Raba maintain that a stain of any colour may be attributed to any stuff that was previously found on the woman? (7) From where, unknown to herself, something had clung to her body. In this latter case, since she was unaware of the particular stuff that clung to her, she may well be presumed to have been unaware also of the presence upon her of the substance from which the stain had originated. In the former case, however, where she had handled a red substance and was fully aware of it no ground for such an assumption exists. (8) Cf. prev. n. but one *mut. mut.* (9) An objection against R. Akiba. (10) Regarding menstruation. (11) *Sc.* by declaring certain stains (which are Pentateuchally clean) to be unclean they have added restrictions to the Pentateuchal laws. (12) Hence wherever it is possible to attribute one to a cause that would exempt it from uncleanness the lenient course must be followed.

not?—Come and hear: A long stain is counted[1] but scattered drops are not combined.[2] Now whose view does this represent? If it be suggested: That of R. Eliezer son of R. Zadok [the difficulty would arise:] Why was there need[3] for the combination, seeing that he ruled that even a stain that was only slightly elongated is unclean. Must we not then conclude that it represents the view of the Rabbis? Thus it follows, does it not, that they differ from his view?—No, this may indeed represent the view of R. Eliezer son of R. Zadok, for he laid down the law[4] in regard to a testing rag[5] but not in regard to a bloodstain.[6]

Come and hear[7] what Rab Judah citing Samuel stated: 'The *halachah* is in agreement with R. Eliezer son of R. Zadok'. Now since the *halachah* had to be declared it follows that they[8] differ from him.[9] This is conclusive.

(1) Lit., 'combined', *sc.* is regarded as compact in respect of the prescribed size of a split bean. (2) Cf. prev. n. *mut. mut.* (3) In the case of a long stain. (4) That even a stain that is only slightly elongated is unclean. (5) An elongated stain on which is obviously the natural shape of one obtained in the course of the test. (6) Which he does not regard as unclean unless it was no less in size than a split bean. (7) In reply to the question whether the Rabbis differ from R. Eliezer son of R. Zadok. (8) The Rabbis. (9) Had they been in agreement with him the question of the *halachah* would not have arisen.

NIDDAH

CHAPTER IX

MISHNAH. [59*b*] IF A WOMAN WHEN ATTENDING TO HER NEEDS[1] OBSERVED AN ISSUE OF BLOOD, R. MEIR RULED: IF SHE WAS STANDING SHE IS UNCLEAN[2] BUT IF SHE WAS SITTING SHE REMAINS CLEAN. R. JOSE RULED: IN EITHER CASE SHE REMAINS CLEAN. IF A MAN AND A WOMAN ATTENDED TO THEIR NEEDS[1] IN THE SAME BOWL AND BLOOD WAS FOUND ON THE WATER, R. JOSE[3] RULED THAT IT WAS CLEAN;[4] WHILE R. SIMEON RULED THAT IT WAS UNCLEAN, SINCE IT IS NOT USUAL FOR A MAN TO DISCHARGE BLOOD, BUT THE PRESUMPTION IS THAT BLOOD ISSUES FROM THE WOMAN.

GEMARA. Wherein does the case where the woman WAS STANDING differ [from that of sitting]? [Obviously] in that we presume that the urine had returned to the source[5] and brought back blood with it. But then, even where SHE WAS SITTING why should it not also be assumed that the urine had returned to the source and brought back blood with it?—Samuel replied: The reference is to a woman who discharges in a gush.[6] But even where a discharge is gushing is it not possible that[7] the blood

(1) Making water. (2) This is discussed in the Gemara *infra*. (3) Who regards the blood as clean even where, as in the first clause, only one doubt is involved, viz., whether the blood originated in the menstrual source or in a wound in the bladder. (4) Since in addition to the doubt mentioned (cf. prev. n.) there is also the one whether the blood issued from the woman or from the man. The necessity for this ruling will be discussed *infra* in the Gemara. (5) Whence the menstrual blood issues. (6) *Sc.* in the natural manner, no strain being involved in the process. Only when a strain is involved (as where the woman is standing or where the discharge is slow) is it likely for the urine to return to the source and to re-issue mixed with blood, but not where the discharge is flowing normally and easily. (7) Though the urine does not return to the source.

issued[1] after the water had ceased to flow?[2]—R. Abba replied. The reference is to a woman who sat on the rim of a bowl, discharging into the bowl, and blood was found within the bowl, [in which case it is obvious] that if the blood had issued after the water had ceased to flow it[3] should have been found on the rim of the bowl.[4] Samuel ruled or, as some say, Rab Judah citing Samuel ruled: The *halachah* is in agreement with R. Jose; and also R. Abba gave a ruling to Ḳala:[5] The *halachah* is in agreement with R. Jose.

IF A MAN AND A WOMAN etc. The question was asked: Where both the man and the woman were standing,[6] what, pray tell me, is the ruling of[7] R. Meir?[8] Did R. Meir maintain his view[9] only where one doubt[10] is involved, but where a double doubt[11] is involved he does not hold the woman to be unclean, or is it possible that there is no difference?—Resh Laḳish replied: His ruling[12] is the same in both. Whence is this[13] inferred?—Since it was not stated:[14] 'R. Meir and R. Jose[15] ruled that she remains clean'. If so,[16] [the difficulty arises:] Now that R. Meir holds the woman to be unclean where a double doubt is involved,[17] was there any need for his ruling[18] where only one doubt is involved?[19]—Yes, in

(1) From the menstrual source, independently of the other discharge. (2) Why then is the woman regarded as clean? (3) Since the discharge of blood is not bow-shaped. (4) As, however, it was found within the bowl it must be assumed to have found its way there together with the water. (5) A person who sought his opinion on the question. (6) When attending to their needs; and blood was found in the bowl. (7) Lit. 'what, to me, said'. (8) Who (v. our Mishnah) regards a woman as unclean if she was standing alone. (9) Cf. prev. n. (10) Whether the blood emanated from the menstrual source or from a wound in the bladder. (11) Lit., 'doubt of a doubt'. Firstly there is the doubt whether the blood emanated from the woman or from the man; and secondly, even if it emanated from the woman, there remains the doubt previously mentioned (cf. prev. n.). (12) That the woman is unclean. (13) Resh Laḳish's statement. (14) In our Mishnah in the case where A MAN AND A WOMAN ATTENDED etc. (15) Instead of the latter name alone. (16) That even in the latter case, where a double doubt is involved (cf. n. 11), R. Meir holds the woman to be unclean. (17) Cf. prev. n. (18) In the first clause of our Mishnah. (19) Apparently not. For if the woman is unclean in the case of a double doubt it is obvious that she is

order to inform you how far reaching is the ruling[1] of R. Jose who laid down that the woman is clean even where only one doubt is involved. But, instead of disputing about such a case involving only one doubt in order to inform you how far reaching is the ruling of R. Jose, why should they not dispute about a case involving a double doubt in order to inform you how far reaching is the ruling of R. Meir?[2]—The power of a lenient view[3] is preferred.[4] R. Joḥanan, however, replied: R. Meir gave his ruling[5] only where one doubt is involved, but where a double doubt is involved[6] he did not maintain his view. But if so,[7] why was it not stated:[8] R. Meir and R. Jose[9] ruled that she remains clean?—This should indeed have been done,[10] but since he had just left R. Jose[11] he also began[12] with R. Jose. As to R. Jose, however, since he holds the woman clean where only one doubt is involved,[13] was there any need for his ruling where a double doubt is involved?[14]—As it might have been presumed that his ruling applied only *ex post facto*[15] but not *ab initio*,[16] we were informed[17] that the ruling applied even *ab initio*. It was taught in agreement with R. Joḥanan: If a man and a woman attended to their needs in the same bowl and blood was found on the water, R. Meir and R. Jose declared it clean and R. Simeon declared it unclean.

unclean in the case of one doubt. Why then was R. Meir's ruling given in the first clause, from which the second cannot be derived, instead of in the second clause from which the first would be self-evident?

(1) Lit., 'the power'. (2) Who even in such a case regards the woman as unclean. (3) As is that of R. Jose who holds the woman to be clean. (4) To that which is more restrictive. While the former must be the result of careful study and conviction the latter may be due to mere indecision and doubt. (5) That the woman is unclean. (6) As in the case of A MAN AND A WOMAN etc. (7) That in the latter case (cf. prev. n.). R. Meir is of the same opinion as R. Jose that the woman is clean. (8) In our Mishnah in the case where A MAN AND A WOMAN ATTENDED etc. (9) Instead of the latter name alone. (10) Lit., 'yes, thus also'. (11) At the conclusion of the preceding clause. (12) The clause under discussion. (13) In the first clause of our Mishnah. (14) Cf. *supra* p. 418, n. 11. (15) Where the woman, for instance, had already handled clean things. (16) *Sc.* if she had not yet come in contact with clean things she is to be ordered to keep away from them. (17) By the additional and apparently superfluous clause.

The question was raised: Where a woman[1] was sitting,[2] what, pray tell me, is the ruling of[3] R. Simeon? Did R. Simeon maintain his view only where she is standing, since her passage is then compressed,[4] but not where she was sitting;[5] or is it possible that there is no difference?—Come and hear what was taught: If she was sitting she may attribute [any discharge of blood to an internal wound], but if she was standing she may not attribute [it to it]; so R. Meir. R. Jose ruled: In either case she may attribute [it to it]. R. Simeon ruled: In either case she may not attribute [it to it].

The question was raised: Where a man and a woman were sitting,[6] what, pray tell me, is the ruling of[3] R. Simeon? Did R. Simeon maintain his view only where the woman was standing, since her passage is then compressed,[7] or where she was sitting, since only one doubt is involved, but not where a double doubt is involved;[8] or is it possible that there is no difference?—Come and hear: Since R. Simeon ruled, THE PRESUMPTION IS THAT BLOOD ISSUES FROM THE WOMAN,[9] no distinction is to be made between an issue when they[10] were standing and one when they were sitting.

MISHNAH. IF SHE LENT HER SHIRT TO A GENTILE WOMAN

(1) Alone. (2) When attending to her needs; and blood was found in the bowl. (3) Lit., 'what, to me, said'. (4) Lit., 'the world is pressed for her'. As a result of the narrowness of the passage blood from the menstrual source might well be presumed to issue together with the returned urine, and since this presumption almost amounts to a certainty there remains no more than one doubt, as to whether the blood emanated from the man or the woman, which well justifies R. Simeon's ruling that the blood is unclean. (5) And the passage allowed of the free movement of the urine. Any blood discharged in this case might well be attributed to a wound in the bladder, and, therefore, regarded as clean. (6) When attending to their needs; and blood was found in the bowl. (7) And the presumption that the blood emanated from the menstrual source is then so strong that, despite the double doubt involved, R. Simeon, disregarding one of the doubts, maintains his view. (8) Whether (*a*) the blood issued from the woman or the man and (*b*) if from the woman whether from the menstrual source or from some internal wound. (9) Which clearly indicates that he never attributes it to the man. (10) The man and the woman.

OR TO A MENSTRUANT SHE MAY ATTRIBUTE A STAIN[1] TO EITHER.[2] IF THREE WOMEN HAD WORN THE SAME SHIRT OR HAD SAT ON THE SAME WOODEN BENCH AND SUBSEQUENTLY BLOOD WAS FOUND ON IT, ALL ARE REGARDED AS UNCLEAN.[3] IF THEY HAD SAT ON A STONE BENCH[4] OR ON THE PROJECTION WITHIN THE COLONNADE OF A BATH HOUSE,[4] R. NEHEMIAH RULES THAT THEY ARE CLEAN;[5] FOR R. NEHEMIAH HAS LAID DOWN: ANY THING THAT IS NOT SUSCEPTIBLE TO UNCLEANNESS IS NOT SUSCEPTIBLE TO STAINS.[6]

GEMARA. Rab explained: The reference[7] is to a GENTILE WOMAN [*60a*] who once experienced a discharge.[8] Whence is this derived? From the fact that she is placed[7] on a par with A MENSTRUANT. As the menstruant is a woman who experienced a discharge[8] so must the GENTILE WOMAN be one who experienced a discharge.[8] R. Shesheth remarked, Rab must have made this statement when he was lying down and about to doze, for it was taught: 'She may attribute it[9] to the gentile woman.[10] R. Meir said, To the gentile woman who is capable of a menstrual discharge'.[11] Now even R. Meir[12] only spoke of one who is 'capable of a menstrual discharge' but did not require one who actually experienced a discharge.[13] Raba retorted: But do you understand

(1) That was found on it after she herself had worn it. (2) Lit., 'on her'; and she remains clean. Such a presumption is permitted since neither the gentile woman nor the menstruant is thereby placed at a disadvantage, the former being free from the restrictions in any case while the latter is already in a state of uncleanness. (3) Since each one might be presumed to have been the cause. (4) Which, unlike a wooden one, is not susceptible to uncleanness. (5) [The same applies to one woman sitting on a stone bench etc. The plural is used here in continuation of the preceding clause. v. Strashun]. (6) *Sc.* no uncleanness of the person is assumed by reason of a stain that was found on it. This is further explained in the Gemara *infra*. (7) In our Mishnah. (8) Lit., 'who sees'. (9) A stain found on her shirt. (10) And thus remain clean. (11) *Sc.* one of mature age. (12) Who seems to be more restrictive than the first Tanna. (13) Much less (cf. prev. n.) would the Rabbis (the first Tanna) require that the gentile woman should be one who actually experienced a discharge once before.

R. Meir to restrict the law?[1] R. Meir in fact relaxes it. For it was taught: 'She may not attribute it[2] to the gentile woman. R. Meir ruled: She may attribute it to her'.[3] But, then, does not a difficulty arise[4] from the former?[5]—Explain thus:[6] Only when she[7] experienced a discharge once before; and R. Meir said, If she is capable of a menstrual discharge even though she never yet experienced one.[8]

Our Rabbis taught: A woman may attribute a stain[9] to another woman[10] who was awaiting a day for a day, if it[11] was the latter's second day,[12] and[13] to a woman[10] who counted seven days[14] before she had performed ritual immersion.[15] Hence she is at an advantage[16] while her friend is at a disadvantage;[17] so R. Simeon b. Gamaliel. Rabbi ruled, She[18] may not so attribute it.[19] Hence both are at a disadvantage. They[20] agree, however, that she may attrib-

(1) More than the Rabbis. V. p. 421, nn. 12, 13. (2) A stain found on her shirt. (3) And since the first Tanna resticts the law he may well uphold also the restriction imposed by Rab. (4) Against the Baraitha cited by Raba from which it is evident that R. Meir is more lenient than the Rabbis. (5) Lit., 'that', the Baraitha cited by R. Shesheth from which it appears that R. Meir is more restrictive. (6) The Baraitha cited by R. Shesheth, according to which the first Tanna ruled that 'she may attribute it to a gentile woman'. (7) The gentile woman. (8) Similarly the Baraitha cited by Raba is to be explained that the first Tanna holds that 'she may not attribute it to the gentile woman' unless the latter had experienced a discharge once before, while R. Meir maintains that it may be attributed to her even if she is only capable of a discharge, though she had not experienced one. Both Baraithas thus give the same rulings in different words, and Rab's view is upheld by that of the first Tanna in each. (9) Found on her underclothing. (10) To whom she had previously lent it. (11) The day on which the latter had worn it. (12) *Sc.* the day during a *zibah* period following the one on which she observed a discharge, though on that day none had been observed. This assumption in favour of the former is permitted (despite the slight disadvantage to the latter of having to wait another day) because of the latter's known condition of uncleanness. (13) For a similar reason (cf. prev. n. second clause). (14) After an established *zibah*. (15) Though the latter would in consequence have to count again a new period of seven days. (16) Lit., 'repaired', 'sound', *sc.* she remains clean. (17) Lit., 'spoilt', 'damaged'; the one having to wait an additional day (cf. *supra* n. 12) and the other to count another seven days (cf. prev. n. but one). (18) Since her attribution would be a disadvantage to her friend. (19) Though she herself would in consequence be regarded as unclean. (20) Rabbi and R. Simeon b. Gamaliel.

ute a stain to a woman who was awaiting a day for a day if it[1] was the latter's first day,[2] and to a woman who was abiding in her clean blood,[3] and to a virgin whose blood is clean.[4] Why was it necessary to state the 'hence' of R. Simeon b. Gamaliel?[5]—On account of the ruling of Rabbi.[6] Why was it necessary to state the 'hence' of Rabbi?[7]—It might have been presumed that only the woman on whom the stain was found shall be at a disadvantage while the other shall not be disadvantaged, hence we were informed that both are at a disadvantage.

R. Ḥisda stated: If a clean and an unclean person walked respectively in two paths one of which was clean and the other unclean,[8] we arrive at the dispute between Rabbi and R. Simeon b. Gamaliel.[9] R. Adda demurred: Rabbi may have maintained his view only[10] there, because both are in similar conditions,[11] but what difference [to the unclean person in this case] could our assumption make?[12]—And R. Ḥisda?[13]—After all[14] she has yet to perform the immersion.[15]

(1) The day on which the latter had worn it. (2) When the assumption that the stain was due to her would impose no additional uncleanness upon her. (3) From the eighth to the fortieth day after the birth of a male child and from the fifteenth to the eightieth after the birth of a female child. Cf. prev. n. (4) Cf. *supra* 10b and prev. n. but one. (5) *Sc.* in view of his specific statement that the stain may be attributed to the other woman who was already in a state of uncleanness, is it not obvious that the former is at an advantage while the latter is at a disadvantage? (6) According to which both women are at a disadvantage. (7) Cf. prev. n. but one *mut. mut.* (8) And it is unknown who walked in which. (9) According to the latter, who ruled that a stain found on a clean woman may be attributed by her to a woman who was known to be unclean while she herself remains clean, it may be here assumed that the clean person walked in the clean path and the unclean walked in the unclean one; while according to Rabbi no such assumption could be allowed and both persons must be regarded as unclean. (10) Lit., 'until here Rabbi only said'. (11) Since even the woman who was hitherto unclean could, by performing immersion, attain cleanness on the day the stain was found. The assumption would consequently place her at an undeserved disadvantage. (12) None; since whatever the assumption he is unclean. As the assumption would not place him under any disadvantage Rabbi in this case may well agree with R. Simeon b. Gamaliel. (13) How in view of this argument could he maintain his statement? (14) Granted the woman could attain to cleanness by immersion. (15) Before

It was stated:[1] R. Jose son of R. Ḥanina ruled, If a clean and an unclean person, and even if a clean, and a doubtfully clean person walked respectively in two paths one of which was unclean and the other clean, it may be assumed, according to the opinion of all,[2] that the unclean path was taken by the doubtfully clean person and the clean path by the clean one.

R. Joḥanan enquired of R. Judah b. Liwai: May a stain[3] be attributed to [another woman[4] who was unclean on account of] a stain? So far as Rabbi's view is concerned the question does not arise; for, since in that case[5] where the woman had observed a discharge from her own body[6] you said [that the other woman's stain] may not be attributed [to her], how much less then may this be done in this case where the stain may have originated from an external cause.[7] The question arises only in connection with the view of R. Simeon b. Gamaliel: Is it only in that case,[5] where the woman had observed a discharge from her own body,[6] that the other woman's stain may be attributed to her, but here, where the stain may have originated from an external cause,[7] she may not so attribute it,[8] or is it possible that no difference is made between the two cases?—The other replied: One may not so attribute it. What is the reason?—Because [there is a tradition that][9] one may not so attribute it.[10]

He pointed out to him the following objection: 'Is it not per-

doing which she is still unclean in all respects. As Rabbi nevertheless rules out the assumption that the stain was due to her, it is obvious that he would equally rule out the assumption that it was the unclean person who walked in the unclean path.

(1) In agreement with R. Adda's view that even according to Rabbi it may be assumed that the clean person walked in the clean path and the unclean person in the unclean one. (2) *Sc.* even according to Rabbi. (3) Found on the under garment of a woman who was known to be clean. (4) Who had previously worn that garment. (5) Discussed *supra*. Lit., 'there'. (6) A case of certain uncleanness. (7) Lit., 'where it came from the world'; a case of doubtful uncleanness. (8) And both women are, therefore, unclean. (9) Since the uncleanness that is due to a stain is merely of a doubtful nature, it being possible that the stain originated from an external cause, and the woman cannot in consequence be regarded as prone to a discharge. (10) And both women are, therefore, unclean.

missible to attribute a stain[1] to [another woman[2] who was unclean on account of] a stain. If a woman[3] had lent her shirt to a gentile woman or to one who continued unclean by reason of a stain, she may attribute it[4] to her'. (But is not this Baraitha self contradictory: In the first clause you stated, 'it is not permissible to attribute' while in the final clause you stated that it was permissible to attribute?—This is no difficulty: The former is the view of Rabbi while the latter is that of R. Simeon b. Gamaliel. There are some who read: The latter as well as the former represents the view of Rabbi, but[5] the latter[6] applies to her first day[7] while the former[8] applies to her second day.[9] R. Ashi replied: The former[10] as well as the latter[6] represents the view of R. Simeon b. Gamaliel and yet there is no difficulty, [60*b*] for the former[10] applies to retrospective uncleanness[11] while the latter[6] applies to future uncleanness.)[12] At all events does not a difficulty arise?[13]—Rabina replied: This is no difficulty for it is this that was meant:[14] If she had lent her shirt to a gentile woman,[15] she who discovered[16]

(1) Found on the under garment of a woman who was known to be clean. (2) Who had previously worn that garment. (3) Who discovered the stain. (4) The stain she discovered. (5) As to the apparent contradiction. (6) 'It is permissible to attribute'. (7) *Sc.* the stain was discovered by the woman on the same day on which the other (to whom the garment had been lent) had found a stain on an under garment of hers which caused her to be unclean on that day and also imposed upon her the restriction of remaining unclean until a second day (a day for a day) had passed. Since she has in any case to lose a second day, the attribution does not cause her any disadvantage. (8) Which does not allow the attribution. (9) When the attribution would place her under a disadvantage by extending her uncleanness to the third day. (10) Which does not allow the attribution. (11) *Sc.* to a case where the owner of the shirt discovered the stain on it before the other to whom she had lent it had discovered the stain on her own under garment. Though the other subsequently discovered the stain, she cannot be regarded as unclean retrospectively (from the time the owner of the shirt had discovered the stain) since at that time she was still in a condition of cleanness (cf. Tosaf. and Tosaf. Asheri, contra Rashi). (12) The stain on the lent shirt having been discovered after the woman who borrowed it had discovered hers (cf. prev. n.). (13) Apparently it does; for since, according to the Baraitha cited, R. Simeon b. Gamaliel allows the attribution how could R. Judah b. Liwai maintain that he does not. (14) By the Baraitha under discussion. (15) Who experienced a discharge. (16) Lit., 'the owner of'.

the stain[1] may attribute it to her.[2] But was it not stated, 'or to one who continued unclean by reason of a stain'?[3]—It is this that was meant: Or to one who continued clean owing to clean blood,[4] she who discovered[5] the stain may attribute it to her.[6]

IF THREE WOMEN HAD WORN etc. FOR R. NEHEMIAH HAS etc. R. Mattenah stated: What is R. Nehemiah's reason? That it is written, *And clean[7] she shall sit upon the ground,*[8] provided she sat on the ground she is clean.[9] R. Huna citing R. Ḥanina stated: R. Nehemiah rules that they are clean if they sat even on the back of an earthenware vessel. But is not this obvious?[10]—It might have been presumed that a restriction shall be imposed on its back as a preventive measure against the possible relaxation of the law in regard to its inside,[11] hence we were informed that on the back of an earthenware vessel they are clean. Abaye stated: R. Nehemiah holds them to be clean if they sat on strips of cloth that were less than three by three fingerbreadths, since such are unsuitable for use either by the poor or the rich.[12]

R. Ḥiyya son of R. Mattenah citing Rab stated in his discourse: The *halachah* is in agreement with R. Nehemiah. Said R. Naḥman to him: Abba[13] learnt, 'A case was once submitted to the Sages and they declared the woman concerned to be unclean' and you state, 'the *halachah* is in agreement with R. Nehemiah'?—What was that case?—The one concerning which it was taught: If two

(1) *Sc.* the Israelitish woman. (2) The gentile, who loses thereby nothing, while the Israelitish woman remains clean. (3) Of course it was. Now if the reference is to the woman who just discovered the stain, how could the expression 'continued' (which implies that the counting of the clean days had already begun) be used? (4) I.e., either to a gentile woman who is free from the restrictions of uncleanness or to an Israelitish woman who for the reason stated is exempt from uncleanness. (5) Lit., 'the owner of'. (6) Since neither would thereby be adversely affected while she remains clean in consequence. (7) E.V., *utterly bereft*. (8) Isa. III, 26. (9) I.e., a stain found on the ground does not render her unclean. (10) Apparently it is, since like a stone bench, the back of an earthenware vessel is not susceptible to uncleanness. (11) Which is susceptible to uncleanness, and a stain on which would in accordance with Rabbinic law subject a woman to uncleanness. (12) And hence unsusceptible to uncleanness. (13) Abba Arika or Rab. 'My father' (Golds.), MS.M., *'ana'* ('I').

women were grinding with a hand mill and blood was found under the inner one,[1] both are unclean.[2] If it was found under the outer one,[3] the outer one is unclean[4] but the inner one remains clean.[5] If it was found between the two, both are unclean.[6] It once happened that blood was found on the edge of a bath,[7] and on an olive leaf while they were making a fire in an oven, and when the case was submitted to the Sages they declared them to be unclean.[8] This[9] is a point at issue between Tannas. For it was taught: R. Jacob[10] ruled that they were unclean and R. Nehemiah ruled that they were clean, and the Sages[11] ruled in agreement with R. Nehemiah.

MISHNAH. IF THREE WOMEN SLEPT IN ONE BED AND BLOOD WAS FOUND UNDER ONE OF THEM, THEY ARE ALL UNCLEAN. IF ONE OF THEM EXAMINED HERSELF AND WAS FOUND TO BE UNCLEAN, SHE ALONE IS UNCLEAN WHILE THE TWO OTHERS ARE CLEAN. THEY MAY ALSO ATTRIBUTE THE BLOOD TO ONE ANOTHER.[12] AND IF THEY WERE NOT LIKELY[13] TO OBSERVE A DISCHARGE,[12] THEY MUST BE REGARDED AS THOUGH THEY WERE LIKELY TO OBSERVE ONE.

GEMARA. Rab Judah citing Rab explained: But this[14] applies

(1) The one nearer to the mill. (2) Since the other who sits behind her would naturally shift her position towards the mill and, assuming sometimes the same position as the inner one, would be as likely as she to be the cause of the stain in that spot. As it is thus uncertain which of the two was the cause both must be regarded as unclean. (3) A position which the inner one would never occupy, the tendency being to come up as close as possible to the mill. (4) Since she may have been the cause of the stain. (5) Cf. prev. n. but one. (6) Because either might have been the cause. (7) Which two women were using. (8) Now an olive leaf is not susceptible to uncleanness and yet the Sages (the majority) ruled that a stain on it causes uncleanness. How then could it be said that the *halachah* agrees with R. Nehemiah who was only an individual? (9) Whether R. Nehemiah is opposed by an individual authority or by a majority. (10) An individual. (11) The majority. (12) This is explained in the Gemara *infra*. (13) Lit., 'suitable'. (14) That IF ONE OF THEM EXAMINED HERSELF . . . SHE ALONE IS UNCLEAN WHILE THE TWO OTHERS ARE CLEAN.

only where she examined herself immediately [after the discovery of the blood].[1] He is of the same opinion as Bar Pada who laid down: Whenever her husband is liable to a sin-offering,[2] her clean things[3] are[4] to be unclean;[5] where her husband is liable to a suspensive guilt-offering,[6] her clean things[7] are regarded as being in a suspended state of uncleanness;[8] and where her husband is exempt,[9] her clean things[10] remain clean. But R. Oshaia[11] ruled: Even where her husband is liable to a sin-offering,[12] her clean things are[13] deemed to be in a suspended state.[14] One can see the reason[15] there, since it might well be assumed that the waiter[16] had caused

(1) If, however, her examination had been delayed the others too are unclean. (2) In the case, for instance, where she discovered menstrual blood immediately after their intercourse, when it is assumed that the discharge had occurred during intercourse. (3) *Terumah*, for instance, which may be eaten only when clean. (4) If she discovered menstrual blood immediately after her contact with them. (5) It being assumed (cf. prev. n. but two) that the discharge occurred while she was still handling the clean things. In such a case the uncleanness is regarded as certain and the things she handled must be burnt. (6) This is the case where she discovered the blood after an interval had elapsed during which she could descend from the bed and wash her genitals it being doubtful whether the discharge had occurred during or after intercourse. (7) If she discovered the blood after such an interval (cf. prev. n.) had passed since she handled them. (8) *Sc.* they may be neither eaten nor burnt. (9) In the case where the longer interval (cf. prev. n. but two) had passed before the blood was discovered, when it is regarded as certain that the discharge occurred after intercourse. (10) If a similar interval (cf. prev. n.) had elapsed between the time she has handled them and the discovery of the blood. (11) Maintaining that even if a discovery of blood was made immediately after she handled the clean things one cannot be sure that the discharge had occurred earlier when she was still handling them. (12) V. *supra* n. 2. (13) On account of the doubt. (14) Thus it follows that our Mishnah which ruled that only the woman who found herself on examination to be unclean is regarded as the cause of the blood while the two others remain clean, upholds the opinion of Bar Pada who, where the examination took place immediately after the clean things had been handled, regards the things as definitely unclean. It must be contrary to the view of R. Oshaia who, even in such a case (an examination after the shortest interval), regards the clean things as being merely in a suspected state. (15) Why it may be assumed that the discharge occurred earlier during intercourse. (16) Euphemism.

the obstruction of the blood; but, in this case,[1] if it were a fact that the blood was there,[2] what could have caused its obstruction?[3] R. Jeremiah observed: As to R. Oshaia's metaphor[4] to what may this be compared? To an old man and a child who were walking together on a road. While they are underway the child restrains his gait,[5] but after they enter the town[6] the child accelerates his pace.[7] Abaye on the other hand observed: As to the metaphor of R. Oshaia, to what may this be compared? To a man who puts his finger on his eye. While the finger is on the eye the tears are held back, but as soon as the finger is removed the tears quickly come forth.[7]

THEY MAY ALSO ATTRIBUTE THE BLOOD TO ONE ANOTHER. Our Rabbis taught: In what manner do they attribute it to one another? If one was a pregnant woman[8] and the other was not pregnant, the former may attribute the blood to the latter. If one was a nursing woman[8] and the other was not a nursing woman, the former may attribute the blood to the latter. If one was an old woman[8] and the other was not an old woman, the former may attribute the blood to the latter. If one was a virgin[9] and the other was no virgin, the former may attribute the blood to the latter. If both were pregnant, nursing, old or virgins — it is [a case like] this concerning which we have learnt, IF THEY WERE NOT LIKELY TO OBSERVE A DISCHARGE, THEY MUST BE REGARDED [61*a*] AS THOUGH THEY WERE LIKELY TO OBSERVE ONE.

(1) The handling of clean things. (2) *Sc.* that the discharge occurred earlier. (3) Obviously nothing. Hence it is only in the case of intercourse (where the assumption is possible) that the husband becomes liable for a sin-offering, but in the case of clean things (where no such assumption is possible) no certain uncleanness may be presumed and only that of a doubtful nature may be imposed upon them Rabbinically for twenty-four hours retrospectively. (4) 'The waiter had caused the obstruction of the blood'. (5) Lit., 'delays to come', waiting for the lead of the old man. (6) When they walk in different directions to their own respective homes. (7) Lit., 'hastens to come'. (8) Who usually loses her menstrual flow. (9) *Sc.* a young woman (whether unmarried or married) who had not yet experienced any menstrual discharge (cf. *supra* 8*b*).

MISHNAH. IF THREE WOMEN SLEPT IN ONE BED, AND BLOOD WAS FOUND UNDER THE MIDDLE ONE, THEY ARE ALL UNCLEAN. IF IT WAS FOUND UNDER THE INNER ONE,[1] THE TWO INNER ONES[2] ARE UNCLEAN WHILE THE OUTER ONE IS CLEAN. IF IT WAS FOUND UNDER THE OUTER ONE,[3] THE TWO OUTER ONES[4] ARE UNCLEAN WHILE THE INNER ONE[5] IS CLEAN. WHEN[6] IS THIS THE CASE?[7] WHEN THEY PASSED[8] BY WAY OF THE FOOT OF THE BED,[9] BUT IF THEY PASSED ACROSS IT,[10] THEY ARE ALL UNCLEAN.[11] IF ONE OF THEM EXAMINED HERSELF AND WAS FOUND CLEAN, SHE REMAINS CLEAN WHILE THE TWO OTHERS ARE UNCLEAN. IF TWO, EXAMINED THEMSELVES AND WERE FOUND TO BE CLEAN THEY REMAIN CLEAN WHILE THE THIRD IS UNCLEAN. IF THE THREE EXAMINED THEMSELVES AND WERE FOUND TO BE CLEAN, THEY ARE ALL UNCLEAN. TO WHAT MAY THIS BE COMPARED? TO AN UNCLEAN HEAP[12] THAT WAS MIXED UP WITH TWO CLEAN HEAPS, WHERE, IF THEY EXAMINED ONE OF THEM AND FOUND IT TO BE CLEAN, IT IS CLEAN WHILE THE TWO OTHERS ARE UNCLEAN; IF THEY EXAMINED TWO OF THE HEAPS AND FOUND THEM TO BE CLEAN, THEY ARE CLEAN WHILE THE THIRD ONE IS UNCLEAN; AND IF THEY EXAMINED THE THREE AND THEY WERE FOUND TO BE CLEAN, THEY ARE ALL UNCLEAN; SO R. MEIR, FOR R. MEIR RULED: ANY OBJECT THAT IS IN A PRESUMPTIVE STATE OF UNCLEANNESS ALWAYS REMAINS UNCLEAN UNTIL IT IS KNOWN TO YOU WHERE THE UNCLEANNESS IS. BUT THE SAGES RULED: ONE

(1) The woman that was nearest to the wall. (2) *Sc.* the one under whom the blood was found (cf. prev. n.) and the middle one. (3) The woman furthest from the wall. (4) The one mentioned and the middle one. (5) The woman that was nearest to the wall. (6) Sep. edd. of the Mishnah read, 'R. Judah said, When'. (7) That IF IT WAS FOUND UNDER THE OUTER ONE . . . THE INNER ONE IS CLEAN. (8) On entering the bed. (9) So that the inner one never passed the spot where the blood was found. (10) Lit., 'the way over it'. The inner two thus passing over the place of the outer one. (11) Even the middle and the inner one, since it is possible that either discharged the blood when she was passing over that spot. (12) One that contained a piece of corpse of the minimum size of an olive.

CONTINUES THE EXAMINATION OF THE HEAP UNTIL ONE REACHES BEDROCK OR VIRGIN SOIL.[1]

GEMARA. Why is it that in the first clause[2] no distinction is made[3] while in the final clause[4] a distinction is made?—R. Ammi replied: The former is a case where the women were interlocked.[5]

IF ONE OF THEM EXAMINED HERSELF etc. What need was there for stating, 'TO WHAT MAY THIS BE COMPARED'?—It is this that R. Meir in effect said to the Rabbis: Why is it that in the case of blood you do not differ from me[6] while in that of a heap you differ?[7]—And the Rabbis?[8]—There [the heap may be regarded as clean] since it might well be assumed that a raven had carried away the piece of corpse, but here, whence[9] could the blood have come?[10]

It was taught: R. Meir stated, It once happened that a sycamore tree at Kefar Saba, held to be in a presumptive state of uncleanness, was examined and no object of uncleanness was found. After a time the wind blew upon it and uprooted it when the skull of a corpse was found stuck in its root.[11] They[12] answered him: 'Do you adduce proof from there? It might be suggested that the examination was not thorough enough'.[13]

It was taught: R. Jose stated, It once happened that a cave at Shiḥin, held to be in a presumptive state of uncleanness, was

(1) And if no uncleanness can be found even there, it may be presumed that the heap is clean. (2) The previous Mishnah, *supra* 60*b*. (3) Between blood found under the middle, the inner or the outer woman. (4) Our Mishnah. (5) As they were so close to each other it is quite possible for the blood of the one to be found under the other. (6) Agreeing that if the three women examined themselves and were found to be clean, they are all unclean. (7) Maintaining that, if the examination was continued down to bedrock or virgin soil and no trace of corpse was found, the heap may be regarded as clean despite the presumptive existence of a piece of corpse in one of the heaps. (8) On what ground do they maintain their view? (9) If all the women are clean. (10) Hence the ruling that they are all unclean. (11) This, in the opinion of R. Meir, proves that an examination that revealed no unclean object is no evidence of cleanness. (12) The Rabbis who disagreed with him. (13) Lit., 'they did not examine all its requirement'.

examined until ground that was as smooth as a finger nail[1] was reached, but no unclean object was found. After a time labourers entered it to shelter from[2] rain, and chopping with their axes found a mortar full of bones.[3] They[4] answered him: 'Do you adduce proof from there? It might be suggested that the examination was not thorough enough'.[5]

It was taught: Abba Saul stated, It once happened that a clod at Beth Horon was held in a presumptive state of uncleanness, and the Sages could not properly examine it because its area was extensive.[6] But there was an old man in the place[7] whose name was R. Joshua b. Hananiah and he said to them, 'Bring me some sheets'. They brought to him sheets and he soaked them in water and then spread them over the clod.[8] The clean area[9] remained dry while the unclean area[10] became moist. And, having examined the latter, they found a large pit full of bones. One taught: That was the pit which Ishmael the son of Nethaniah had filled with slain bodies, as it is written, *Now the pit wherein Ishmael cast all the dead bodies of the men whom he had slain by the hand*[11] *of Gedaliah.*[12] But was it Gedaliah that killed them? Was it not in fact Ishmael that killed them?[13]—But owing to the fact that he[14] should have taken note of the advice of Joḥanan the son of Kareah[15] and did not do so Scripture regards him as though he had killed them.

Raba observed: As to slander, though one should not believe[16] it, one should nevertheless take note of it. There were certain Galileans about whom a rumour was spread that they killed a person. They came to R. Tarfon and said to him, 'Will the Master hide us?' 'How', he replied, 'should I act? Should I not hide you,

(1) *Sc.* that was never cultivated. (2) Lit., 'on account of'. (3) Cf. *supra* p. 431, n. 11 *mut. mut.* (4) The Rabbis who disagreed with him. (5) Lit., 'they did not examine all its requirement'. (6) Lit., 'much'. (7) Lit., 'there'. (8) Lit., 'them'. (9) The soil of which had never been dug and was, therefore, hard and impervious to the moisture from the sheets. (10) Which contained corpses and which, having been dug, consisted of loose earth that absorbed the moisture. (11) E.V., '*side*'. (12) Jer. XLI, 9. (13) Why then was it stated, '*By the hand of Gedaliah*'? (14) Gedaliah. (15) Who told him that Simeon b. Nethaniah wished to kill him. V. Jer. XL, 13ff. (16) Lit., 'accept'.

they[1] would see you.[2] Should I hide you, I would be acting contrary to the statement of the Rabbis,[3] "As to slander, though one should not believe[4] it, one should take note of it".[5] Go you and hide yourselves'.

And the Lord said unto Moses: Fear him not'.[6] Consider: Sihon and Og were brothers, for a Master stated, 'Sihon and Og were the sons of Ahijah the son of Shamḥazai',[7] then why was it that he feared Og while he did not fear Sihon? R. Joḥanan citing R. Simeon b. Yoḥai replied: From the answer that was given[8] to[9] that righteous man[10] you may understand what was in his mind.[11] He thought: Peradventure the merit of our father Abraham will stand him[12] by, for it is said, *And there came one that had escaped, and told Abram the Hebrew,*[13] in connection with which R. Joḥanan explained: This refers to Og who escaped the fate of the generation of the flood.[14]

Our Rabbis taught:[15] If a [woman's] bloodstain was lost in a garment[16] one must apply to it[17] seven substances[18] and thus neutralize it. R. Simeon b. Eleazar ruled: [61*b*] One must examine it in small sections.[19] If semen was lost in it, when new it should be examined with a needle,[20] and when worn out it should be examined in sunlight.[21] One taught: No section need be smaller than three fingerbreadths.

Our Rabbis taught: A garment in which *kil'ayim*[22] was lost[23]

(1) The avengers of the blood. (2) And execute vengeance. (3) Lit., 'surely the Rabbis said'. (4) Lit., 'accept'. (5) And in case the report about you is true, I have no right to shield you. (6) Num. XXI, 34. (7) One of the fallen angels referred to in Gen. VI, 2, 4 as *'sons of God'* or *'Nephilim'*. (8) By God. (9) Lit., 'of'. (10) Moses. (11) Lit., 'heart'. (12) Og. (13) Gen. XIV, 13. (14) Cf. Zeb. 113*b*. (15) The following Baraithas have been suggested to the compiler by the law *supra* concerning heaps in which an unclean object had been lost beyond recovery. (16) By falling, for instance, into water or was soiled with the blood of an animal. (17) Lit., 'causes to pass'. (18) Enumerated in next Mishnah. (19) The size of each section is given presently. (20) Dried up semen offers some resistance to its penetration. (21) When holding up the garment to the light the place of the semen appears darker than the rest of it. A new garment, however, whose texture is close would not show up such a stain even in front of the light. (22) V. Glos. (23) *Sc.* it was known that a thread of wool had been

may not be sold to an idolater,[1] nor may one make of it a pack-saddle for an ass, but it may be made into[2] a shroud for a corpse. R. Joseph observed: This[3] implies that the commandments will be abolished in the Hereafter.[4] Said Abaye (or as some say R. Dimi) to him: But did not R. Manni[5] in the name of R. Jannai state, 'This[3] was learnt only in regard to the time of the lamentations[6] but for burial[7] this is forbidden'?[8]—The other replied: But was it not stated in connection with it, 'R. Joḥanan ruled: Even for burial'? And thereby R. Joḥanan followed his previously expressed view, for R. Joḥanan stated: 'What is the purport of the Scriptural text, *Free*[9] *among the dead?*[10] As soon as a man dies he is free from the commandments'.

Rafram b. Papa citing R. Ḥisda ruled: A garment in which *kil'ayim* was lost may be dyed[11] and[12] it is then permitted to be worn.[13] Said Raba to Rafram b. Papa: Whence does the old man derive this?[14]—The other replied: It is in our Mishnah, for we have learnt, ONE CONTINUES THE EXAMINATION OF THE HEAP UNTIL ONE REACHES BEDROCK; and if it[15] is not there, it is obviously assumed that a raven had carried it away. Here too, dye does not have the same effect on wool and flax and, since no [difference could be] discerned,[16] it may well be assumed [that the compromising threads] had dropped out.

R. Aḥa son of R. Yeba citing Mar Zuṭra ruled: If a man inserted

woven into a garment of flax or a thread of flax into a garment of wool but the thread could not be traced so as to be extracted.

(1) Since he might re-sell it to an Israelite. (2) Lit., 'makes of it'. (3) The permissibility to use *kil'ayim* for a shroud. (4) At the resurrection. Had they remained in force the revived dead (cf. prev. n) would be transgressing the law of *kil'ayim.* (5) Var. lec., Ammi. (6) Lit., 'to lament for him'. (7) Lit., 'to bury him'. (8) How then can R. Joseph derive from this ruling that 'the commandments will be abolished in the Hereafter'? (9) E.V., '*set apart*'. (10) Ps. LXXXVIII, 6. (11) As the colour effect of dye on wool is different from that on flax the one could be distinguished and separated from the other. (12) If the same shade of colour is shown throughout. (13) The assumption being that the threads of the other kind have somehow dropped out of the texture. (14) Cf. prev. n. (15) The unclean object. (16) Even after the dye had been applied.

flaxen threads in his woollen garment and then pulled them out but is not sure whether he pulled them [all] out or not, it is quite proper [for him to wear the garment]. What is the reason?— Pentateuchally, since it is written *sha'aṭnez*[1] the prohibition does not apply unless the material was hackled, spun and woven,[2] but it is only the Rabbis who imposed a prohibition on it,[3] and since the man is not quite sure about the pulling out of the threads the garment is permitted. R. Ashi demurred: Might it not be suggested that it[4] must be either hackled or spun or woven?— The law, however, is in agreement with Mar Zuṭra, because the All Merciful expressed them in one word.[2]

Our Rabbis taught: A dyed garment is susceptible to the uncleanness of a bloodstain. R. Nathan b. Joseph ruled: It is not susceptible to the uncleanness of a stain, for dyed garments were ordained for women only in order to relax the law in regard to their bloodstains. 'Were ordained'! Who[5] ordained them?— Rather read: For dyed garments were permitted to women only in order to relax the law in regard to their bloodstains. 'Were permitted'! Does this then imply that they were once forbidden?— Yes, for we have learnt: At the time of the Vespasian invasion they[6] prohibited the wearing of garlands by bridegrooms and the beating of drums at weddings. They also desired to prohibit dyed garments, but felt that it was better not to do so,[7] in order to relax the law in regard to their bloodstains.

MISHNAH. SEVEN SUBSTANCES MUST BE APPLIED TO A STAIN:[8] TASTELESS SPITTLE,[9] THE LIQUID OF CRUSHED BEANS, URINE, NATRON, LYE [62a], CIMOLIAN EARTH, AND LION'S LEAF. IF ONE IMMERSED IT[10] AND, HAVING HANDLED

(1) Deut. XXII, 11. E.V., *'mingled stuff'*. (2) *Shu'a, ṭawui* and *nuz*, three words Rabbinically assumed to make up the word *sha'aṭnez*. (3) On a material that does not satisfy all the three requirements. (4) A material that is to be forbidden as *kil'ayim*. (5) Lit., 'what'. (6) The Rabbis. (7) Lit., 'they said that was better'. (8) If it is desired to ascertain whether it is blood or dye. (9) This is explained presently. (10) The garment with the suspicious stain.

CLEAN THINGS ON IT, APPLIED TO IT THE SEVEN SUBSTANCES AND THE STAIN DID NOT FADE AWAY IT MUST BE A DYE; AND THE CLEAN THINGS REMAIN CLEAN AND THERE IS NO NEED TO IMMERSE IT[1] AGAIN. IF THE STAIN FADED AWAY OR GREW FAINTER,[2] IT MUST BE A BLOODSTAIN AND THE CLEAN THINGS ARE UNCLEAN AND IT IS NECESSARY[3] TO PERFORM IMMERSION AGAIN.[4] WHAT IS MEANT BY 'TASTELESS SPITTLE'? THAT OF A MAN WHO ON THAT DAY[5] TASTED NOTHING. 'THE LIQUID OF CRUSHED BEANS'? PASTE MADE OF CRUSHED BEANS THAT WERE NATURALLY[6] PEELED OFF. 'URINE'? THIS REFERS TO SUCH AS HAS FERMENTED. ONE MUST SCOUR THE STAIN THREE TIMES WITH EACH OF THE SUBSTANCES. IF THEY WERE NOT APPLIED IN THE PRESCRIBED ORDER, OR IF THE SEVEN SUBSTANCES WERE APPLIED SIMULTANEOUSLY, NOTHING USEFUL HAS THEREBY BEEN DONE.[7]

GEMARA. One taught:[8] The Alexandrian natron and not the Antipatrian one.

BORITH.[9] Rab Judah stated: This means *ahala*.[10] But was it not taught: The *borith* and the *ahal?*[11]—The fact is that *borith* means sulphur. An incongruity was pointed out: They[12] added to them[13] the bulb of ornithogalum[14] and garden-orache,[15] the *borith* and the *ahal*. Now if '*borith*' means sulphur [the objection would arise:] Is it subject to the restrictions of the Sabbatical year, seeing that it was taught:[16] This is the general rule, Whatsoever has a root[17]

(1) The garment with the suspicious stain. (2) As a result of the application of the seven substances. (3) Now that the stain had disappeared. (4) The first immersion when the stain was still on the garment being of no avail. (5) Lit., 'all who'. This is discussed in the Gemara *infra*. (6) *Sc*. not by human hands. (7) Lit., 'he did not do anything'. (8) With reference to NATRON in our Mishnah. (9) Rendered *supra* LYE. (10) An alcalic plant used as soap. (11) *Ahal* and *ahala* being the same, how could Rab Judah maintain that *ahala* is synonymous with *borith* seeing that the latter is placed in juxtaposition with *ahal?* (12) The Rabbis. (13) The fruits that are subject to the restrictions of the Sabbatical year. (14) Or 'Bethlehem-star'. (15) Or 'orach'. (16) V. marg. gl. Cur. edd., 'We learnt'. (17) By means of which it draws its nourishment from the ground.

is subject to the restrictions of the Sabbatical year and whatsoever has no root is not subject to the restrictions of the Sabbatical year?—What then do you suggest: That *borith* means *ahala?* But was it not taught: 'The *borith* and the *ahal'?*[1]—There are two kinds of *ahala.*

KIMONIA.[2] Rab Judah explained: *Shelof-doẓ.*[3]

And *eshlag.*[4] Samuel stated: I enquired of the seamen and they told me that its name was *eshlaga,* that it was to be found between the cracks of pearls and that it was extracted with an iron nail.

IF ONE IMMERSED IT AND, HAVING HANDLED etc. Our Rabbis taught: If one applied to it[5] the seven substances[6] and it did not fade away and then applied to it soap and it disappeared, one's clean things are unclean.[7] But does not soap remove dye also?[8]—Rather read: If one applied to it[5] six of the substances and it did not fade away and when soap had been applied it disappeared, his clean things are unclean, since it is possible that if one had first applied to it the seventh substance it might also have disappeared.[9] Another [Baraitha] taught: If one applied to it[5] the seven substances and it did not fade away but when one applied them a second time it disappeared, one's clean things remain clean.[10] R. Zera stated: This[11] was taught only in regard to clean things that were handled between the first and the second wash;[12] but the clean things that were handled after the second wash[12] are unclean, since the person was particular about it[13] and it had disappeared.[14] [62*b*] Said R. Abba to R. Ashi: Does then

(1) V. p. 436, n. 11. (2) Rendered *supra* CIMOLIAN EARTH. (3) Lit., 'pull out, stick in', the popular name for Cimolian earth. (4) Rendered LION'S LEAF *supra.* (5) A stain on a woman's garment. (6) Enumerated in our Mishnah. (7) Because the disappearance of the stain under the application is evidence that it was one of blood. (8) It does. What proof then is there that the stain was not one of dye? (9) And any stain that disappears under an application of the seven substances can only be a bloodstain. (10) Since the stain must be one of dye. Had it been a bloodstain it would have disappeared after the first application. (11) That 'the clean things remain clean'. (12) *Sc.* the application of the substances. (13) The stain; as is evidenced by his second attempt to remove it. (14) As a result of the second application, which brings it within the category of bloodstains that disappear under the application of the seven substances.

the uncleanness[1] depend on whether one is particular?—Yes, the other replied, for it was taught, 'R. Ḥiyya ruled: To that which is certain menstrual blood one may apply the seven substances and[2] thereby[3] neutralize it'.[4] But why should this be so,[5] seeing that it is menstrual blood? It is obvious then[6] that uncleanness[1] depends[7] on whether one is particular. Here also[8] then uncleanness[1] may depend on whether one is particular.

Elsewhere we learnt: If potsherds which a *zab* has used[9] absorbed liquids and then fell into the air-space of an oven,[10] and the oven[11] was heated, the oven becomes unclean, because the liquid[12] would[13] ultimately emerge.[14] Resh Laḳish stated: This[15] was learnt only in regard to liquids of a minor uncleanness[16] but in the case of liquids of a major uncleanness[17] the oven becomes unclean even though it was not heated.[18] R. Joḥanan stated: Whether the liquids were subject to a minor or a major uncleanness the oven is unclean only if it was heated but not otherwise.[19]

R. Joḥanan raised an objection against Resh Laḳish: IF ONE IMMERSED IT AND, HAVING HANDLED CLEAN THINGS ON IT,

(1) Lit., 'thing'. (2) Though the stain is still slightly visible. (3) Since the application of the substances destroys its natural and original appearance. (4) Since no one minds such a faint stain it becomes clean. (5) Cf. prev. n. (6) From the fact that it is regarded as clean. (7) In this case of R. Ḥiyya. (8) The case *supra* 62*a ad fin*. (9) And thus rendered unclean. (10) Without touching the oven itself. (11) Which was an earthen vessel, that contracts uncleanness through its air-space. (12) Which has contracted uncleanness from the unclean potsherd into which it was absorbed. (13) Owing to the heat of the oven which warms up the potsherds. (14) Into the air-space and thus convey uncleanness to the oven. Cf. Kel. IX, 5, where this Mishnah occurs with some variations. (15) That uncleanness is conveyed to the oven only where it was heated, but if it was not heated the absorbed liquids convey no uncleanness to it. (16) *Sc.* that are not 'father of uncleanness' as for instance, a *zab*'s tears. Since the uncleanness that such liquids convey to a vessel is only Rabbinical the oven remains clean when the liquids are in an absorbed state. (17) Which convey uncleannes to a vessel even according to Pentateuchal law. (18) And no liquid has emerged. Since heat causes it to emerge the liquid cannot be regarded as an absorbed uncleanness. (19) Lit., 'if the oven was heated yes; if not, not', since an absorbed uncleanness (cf. Ḥul. 71*a*) conveys no uncleanness.

APPLIED TO IT THE SEVEN SUBSTANCES AND THE STAIN DID NOT FADE AWAY, IT MUST BE A DYE; AND THE CLEAN THINGS REMAIN CLEAN AND THERE IS NO NEED TO IMMERSE IT AGAIN.[1] The other replied: Leave alone the laws of stains[2] which are merely Rabbinical.[3] But [R. Johanan objected] did not R. Ḥiyya teach, 'To that which is certain menstrual blood one may apply the seven substances and thereby neutralize it'?[4]—The other replied: If Rabbi[5] has not taught[6] it,[7] whence could R. Ḥiyya[8] know it?[9]

R. Joḥanan pointed out another objection against Resh Laḳish: 'If a quarter of a *log* of blood[10] was absorbed in the floor of a house [all[11] that is in] the house becomes unclean,[12] but others say: [All that is in] the house remains clean. These two versions, however, do not essentially differ, since the former refers to vessels that were there originally[13] while the latter refers to vessels that were brought in subsequently.[14] Where blood was absorbed in a garment, and on being washed, a quarter of a *log* of blood would emerge from it, it is unclean, but otherwise it is clean![15]—R. Kahana replied: Here

(1) Now if it be granted (with R. Joḥanan) that an absorbed uncleanness, though it emerges under certain special conditions, is treated as clean, the assumption here that the stain was one of dye and, therefore, clean is well justified; for even though it was blood it would (being absorbed) convey no uncleanness. But if it is maintained (with Resh Laḳish) that even an absorbed uncleanness, wherever it would emerge under certain conditions, conveys uncleanness, how could the law be relaxed in this case where the possibility of blood cannot be ruled out? (2) With which our Mishnah deals. (3) And may be relaxed. Pentateuchally no uncleanness is involved unless blood was found on the woman's body. (4) *Supra* q.v. notes. This shows that even actual blood, if it is in an absorbed state, though it would emerge under an application of soap, is regarded as clean. How then could Resh Laḳish maintain that where the oven was not heated, uncleanness is conveyed by the absorbed liquids? (5) The compiler of the Mishnah. (6) In his authoritative compilation. (7) R. Ḥiyya's ruling. (8) Who was the disciple of Rabbi. (9) It is obvious that he could not. The Baraitha cited must, therefore, be treated as spurious. (10) Of a corpse. (11) That is susceptible to uncleanness. (12) Because the blood of a corpse of the quantity prescribed conveys uncleanness by overshadowing as the corpse itself. (13) Before the blood was absorbed, and thus contracted uncleanness by overshadowing. (14) After the blood had been absorbed, when it conveys uncleanness no longer. (15) Oh. III, 2; though a full quarter

they have learnt some of the more lenient rulings concerning quarters of a *log* [both referring to a mixture of clean and unclean blood]; [and the law of] mixed blood[1] is different[2] since it[3] is only Rabbinical.[4] Resh Lakish raised an objection against R. Johanan: Any absorbed uncleanness that cannot emerge is regarded as clean.[5] Thus it follows, does it not, that if it can emerge it is unclean even though it had not yet emerged?[6]—R. Papa replied: Wherever it[7] cannot emerge[8] and the owner did not mind absorption,[9] all agree that it is regarded as clean. If it can emerge and the owner does mind the absorption, all agree that it is unclean. They only differ where it can emerge but the owner does not mind its absorption. One Master[10] holds the view that since it can emerge [it is unclean], though the owner did not mind its absorption;[11] and the other Master[12] holds that although it can emerge [63*a*] it is unclean only if the owner minds the absorption, but not otherwise.[13]

WHAT IS MEANT BY 'TASTELESS SPITTLE'. One taught:[14] That of a man who tasted nothing since the previous evening. R. Papa intended to explain before Raba [that this bears the same meaning] as when one says that he had tasted nothing in the evening.[15] But Raba[16] pointed out to him: Does it say 'in the evening'?[15] It

of a *log* of blood is absorbed in it. Those two rulings prove that an absorbed uncleanness, though it would emerge under special conditions, is regarded as clean. An objection against Resh Lakish.

(1) *Dam tebusah* (defined *infra* 71*a*) whose uncleanness is doubtful. (2) From blood that is definitely unclean. (3) Even in an unabsorbed condition. (4) Hence the relaxation of the law when it is absorbed. (5) Oh. III, 2. (6) How then could R. Johanan maintain in the case of the potsherd that the oven is unclean only when the liquids emerged? (7) The unclean substance. (8) From the object that absorbed it. (9) MS.M., Maharsha, and some old edd. omit the last eight words. (10) Resh Lakish. (11) Hence his ruling in the case of the potsherd where the liquid would emerge if the oven were heated. (12) R. Johanan. (13) Lit., 'yes; if not, not'. The inference from the Mishnah cited by Resh Lakish, from which it follows that 'if it can emerge it is unclean even though it had not yet emerged', applies to a case where the owner minded the absorption. (14) In explanation of TASTELESS SPITTLE. (15) *Sc.* had nothing to eat since sunset of the previous day. (16) MS.M., Rabina.

only says, 'Since the previous evening',[1] thus excluding only the case of one who got up early[2] and ate.[3] Rabbah b. Bar Ḥana citing R. Joḥanan stated: What is meant by tasteless spittle? [That of a person] who spent half a night in sleep.[4] This then implies that the quality of spittle[5] depends on sleep. But have we not learnt:[6] If a man slept all day his is no tasteless spittle and if he was awake all night it is tasteless spittle?[7]—There[8] it is a case, where one was in a state of drowsiness.[9] What state of drowsiness is hereby to be understood?—R. Ashi replied: Where a man is half asleep and half awake;[10] when addressed he answers but is unable to give any rational reply, and when he is reminded of any thing he can recall it.

One taught: If a man rose up early in the morning and studied his lesson, his is no tasteless spittle.[11] But for how long?[12]—R. Judah b. Shila citing R. Ashi who had it from R. Eleazar replied: For a period during which[13] can be uttered the greater part of one's usual talk in the course of three hours.

THE LIQUID OF CRUSHED BEANS?—PASTE MADE OF CRUSHED BEANS etc. May it be suggested that this[14] provides support for Resh Laḳish; for Resh Laḳish said: There must be tasteless spittle with each of the substances?—It is possible that the heat of one's mouth suffices.[15] Our Mishnah[16] is not in agreement with R. Judah. For it was taught: R. Judah explained,[17]

(1) *Sc.* a part of the night. (2) Before day-break. (3) Since the food sweetens the spittle and causes it to lose its strength. The food, however, that one eats in the early evening before going to bed has no such weakening effect. (4) Lit., 'over whom half a night has passed, and in sleep'. (5) Lit., 'thing'. (6) Emden reads, 'was it not taught'. (7) Which shows that it is the night and not sleep that is the determining factor. (8) The statement, 'If he was awake etc.' (9) Not fully awake. Two conditions are necessary for spittle to be tasteless: Sleep or dozing and night. Sleep in the day-time (after one has had some food which sweetens the spittle) or night without sleep (when the effect of the food has not passed) is not enough. (10) Lit., 'asleep and not asleep, awake and not awake'. (11) Speech also takes away its edge. (12) Must his study have extended. Lit., 'and unto how much?' (13) Lit., 'all'. (14) The ruling in our Mishnah that the beans must be crushed into a paste that is presumably mixed with spittle. (15) To make the paste. Lit., 'avails'. (16) In its definition of the liquid of crushed beans. (17) Cf. prev. n.

Boiling liquid of crushed beans before [*'ober*] salt is put into it.[1] What is the proof that the expression[2] *"ober'* means 'before'?—R. Naḥman b. Isaac replied: Since Scripture says, *Then Ahimaaz ran by way of the plain, and overran* [wa-ya'abor][3] *the Cushite.*[4] Abaye replied, The proof comes from here: *And he himself passed over* ['abar][3] *before them.*[5] And if you prefer I might reply that the proof comes from here: *And their king is passed on* [wa-ya'abor][3] *before them, and the Lord before them.*[6]

URINE? THIS REFERS TO SUCH AS HAS FERMENTED. One taught: What must be the duration of[7] their fermentation? Three days. R. Joḥanan observed, All the standards of the Sages in respect of bloodstains need additional standards to define them:[8] [Is the urine that] of a child or of an old man,[9] of a man or of a woman,[9] covered[9] or uncovered, of the summer season[9] or of the winter season?

ONE MUST SCOUR THE STAIN THREE TIMES. R. Jeremiah enquired: Does the forward and backward movement[10] count as one or is it possible that it counts as two? Now what is the decision?—This stands undecided.[11]

IF THEY WERE NOT APPLIED IS THE PRESCRIBED ORDER. Our Rabbis taught: If the latter[12] were applied before the former,[13] one Baraitha teaches, 'The latter[14] are counted[15] and the former[16] are not counted,'[17] while another [Baraitha] teaches, 'The former are counted and the latter are not counted'![18]—Abaye replied: According to both statements the latter[14] are counted, and the

(1) Since salt would weaken it. (2) Lit., 'that'. (3) Of the same root as "*ober'*. (4) II Sam. XVIII, 23. (5) Gen. XXXIII, 3. (6) Micah II, 13. (7) Lit., 'how long'. (8) Lit., 'a standard to their standard'. (9) This is stronger and more effective. (10) Lit., 'carrying out and bringing in' of the hand in the process of scouring. (11) *Teku;* v. Glos. (12) The last four of the seven substances enumerated in our Mishnah. (13) The first three. (14) *Sc.* those applied last (first mentioned in our Mishnah). (15) Lit., 'went up for him'. (16) *Sc.* the substances (last mentioned in our Mishnah) that were applied first. (17) So that, if the four substances last mentioned in our Mishnah are subsequently applied again, the prescribed order of application is duly complied with. (18) Now how are the two apparently contradictory rulings to be reconciled?

former[1] are not; but 'former'[2] refers to those that are[3] first in the prescribed order[4] though second in the process of application.

MISHNAH. FOR EVERY WOMAN THAT HAS A SETTLED PERIOD IT SUFFICES [TO RECKON HER PERIOD OF UNCLEANNESS FROM] HER SET TIME. AND THESE ARE THE SYMPTOMS OF SETTLED PERIODS: [IF THE WOMAN][5] YAWNS, SNEEZES, FEELS PAIN AT THE TOP OF[6] HER STOMACH OR THE BOTTOM OF HER BOWELS, DISCHARGES,[7] OR IS SEIZED BY A KIND OF SHIVERING, OR ANY OTHER SIMILAR SYMPTOMS.[7] ANY WOMAN WHO ESTABLISHED FOR HERSELF [ONE OF THE SYMPTOMS][5] THREE TIMES MAY BE DEEMED TO HAVE[8] A SETTLED PERIOD.

GEMARA. Have we not learnt once before, 'For any woman who has a settled period it suffices [to reckon her period of uncleanness from] her set time'?[9]—There the reference is to settled periods [that are determined by the number] of days[10] while here the reference is to settled periods [that are determined by conditions] of the body; as it was actually taught, 'The following are the symptoms of settled periods: If a woman yawns, sneezes, feels pain at the top of her stomach or the bottom of her bowels or discharges'. 'Discharges'! Is she not then[11] constantly discharging?[12]—'Ulla son of R. Elai replied: [63*b*] This is a case where she discharges unclean blood as a result of a discharge[13] of clean blood.[14]

OR.. A KIND OF SHIVERING etc. What was the expression, OR ANY OTHER SIMILAR SYMPTOMS, intended to include?—

(1) V. p. 442, n. 16. (2) In the second Baraitha. (3) Lit., 'and what'. (4) In our Mishnah. (5) Before experiencing a menstrual discharge. (6) Lit., 'mouth'. (7) This is discussed in the Gemara. (8) Lit., 'behold this'. (9) Mishnah *supra 2a*. (10) Every fifth or tenth day of the month, for instance. (11) Since every menstrual discharge is preceded by another discharge. (12) And since no symptom precedes the first discharge, which is presumably also an unclean one, how could a settled period ever be established? (13) Lit., 'from the midst'. (14) That is not menstrual, as can be ascertained by an examination of its colour. A settled period is established where menstrual discharge is preceded by one of clean blood, v. *infra*.

Rabbah b. 'Ullah replied: To include a woman who feels a heaviness in her head[1] or a heaviness in her limbs, who shivers or belches. R. Huna b. Ḥiyya citing Samuel observed: Behold [the Sages] have ruled that 'for settled periods [that are determined by the number] of days two [occurrences are required],[2] for settled periods [that are determined by the condition] of the body one occurrence suffices,[3] for settled periods [that are determined by conditions] which the Sages did not enumerate three occurrences are required;[4] But [I do not know] what the expression, 'for settled periods that are determined by conditions which the Sages did not enumerate' intended to include?—R. Joseph replied: To include a woman who feels a heaviness in the head,[1] a heaviness in her limbs, who shivers or belches. Said Abaye to him:[5] What does he teach us thereby,[6] seeing that this is actually a ruling in our Mishnah,[7] Rabbah b. 'Ulla having thus[8] explained it?—Rather, said Abaye, it[6] was intended to include one who ate garlic and observed a discharge, one who ate onions and observed a discharge, and one who chewed pepper and observed a discharge. R. Joseph observed: I have not heard this tradition.[9] Said Abaye to him: You yourself have told it to us, and in was in connection with the following that you told it to us:[10] If a woman was in the habit of observing a discharge on the fifteenth day of the month and this was changed to the twentieth day, intercourse is forbidden to her on both days.[11] If she observed a discharge on three consecutive months[12] on the twentieth day, intercourse on the fifteenth becomes permitted[13] and she establishes the twentieth day as her settled period:

(1) Lit., 'whose head is heavy upon her'. (2) Lit., 'for days two'; *sc.* if the discharge appeared twice on the same day of the month, that day is established as a settled period. (3) To establish a settled period (cf. prev. n. *mut. mut.*). (4) Cf. prev. n. but one *mut. mut.* (5) R. Joseph. (6) By the addition, 'for settled periods... did not enumerate'. (7) OR ANY OTHER SIMILAR etc. (8) As R. Joseph. (9) Just cited in the name of Samuel. (10) R. Joseph, as a result of a serious illness, had lost his memory and had very often to be reminded of the traditions he himself had reported. (11) Lit., 'this and this is forbidden', both the fifteenth (in case her first settled period is re-established) and the twentieth (since this date might form now or become her settled period). (12) Lit., 'three times'. (13) Since a new settled period has been established.

for no woman can establish for herself a settled period unless the discharge had appeared three times on the same date.[1] And in connection with this you told us: Rab Judah citing Samuel stated, This is the view of R. Gamaliel son of Rabbi who cited it in the name of R. Simeon b. Gamaliel,[2] but the Sages ruled: If she observed a discharge once[3] she need not[4] repeat it a second time and a third time. And when we asked you, 'Since you said, "She need not repeat it a second time" was there any need to state that she need not repeat it a third time'? you replied· She need not repeat it a second time in the case of settled periods [that are determined by the condition] of her body and she need not repeat it a third time in the case of settled periods [determined by the number] of days. But why did he not simply say, 'This is the view of R. Simeon b. Gamaliel'?[2]—It is this that Samuel informed us: That R. Gamaliel the son of Rabbi holds the same view as R. Simeon b. Gamaliel.

MISHNAH. IF A WOMAN HAD THE HABIT OF OBSERVING HER MENSTRUAL DISCHARGES AT THE ONSET OF THE SYMPTOMS[5] OF HER SETTLED PERIODS, ALL CLEAN THINGS[6] THAT SHE HANDLED WHILE THE SYMPTOMS WERE IN PROGRESS[7] ARE UNCLEAN; BUT IF SHE HAD THE HABIT OF OBSERVING THEM AT THE END OF THE SYMPTOMS, ALL CLEAN THINGS[6] THAT SHE HANDLED WHILE THE SYMPTOMS LASTED[7] REMAIN CLEAN. R. JOSE RULED: SETTLED PERIODS MAY ALSO BE DETERMINED BY DAYS AND HOURS.[8] IF[9] SHE HAD THE HABIT OF OBSERVING HER MENSTRUAL DISCHARGES AT SUNRISF

(1) Lit., 'until she will fix it three times'. (2) Who holds that presumption cannot be established unless an occurrence was repeated three times (cf. Yeb. 64*b*). (3) On a certain date. (4) In order to establish a settled period. (5) In the condition of her body (cf. prev. Mishnah). (6) *Terumah*, for instance, or any other foodstuffs that may be eaten only when clean. (7) Lit., 'within (the symptoms of) the settled period'. (8) This is explained in the Gemara *infra*. (9) This is a continuation of R. Jose's ruling.

SHE IS FORBIDDEN INTERCOURSE AT SUNRISE ONLY.[1] R. JUDAH RULED: SHE[2] IS PERMITTED IT DURING ALL THAT DAY.[3]

GEMARA. One taught: What[4] did R. Jose mean by 'Settled periods may also be determined by days and hours'? If a woman had the habit of observing her discharge on the twentieth day of the month[5] and at the sixth hour of the day,[6] and the twentieth day arrived and she observed no discharge, she is forbidden intercourse during all the first six hours;[7] so R. Judah. R. Jose, however, permits it until the beginning of the sixth hour[8] but during the sixth hour she must take into consideration [the possibility of a discharge].[9] If the sixth hour has passed and she observed no discharge, she is still forbidden intercourse all that day; so R. Judah. R. Jose, however, permits it from the time of the afternoon service[10] onwards.

IF SHE HAD THE HABIT [etc.]. But was it not taught: R. Judah ruled, She[11] is permitted intercourse all night?[12] — This is no contradiction. The Baraitha deals with the case of[13] one who had the habit of observing the discharge at the beginning of the day[14] while the Mishnah deals with one who had the habit of observing the discharge at the end of the night.[15]

(1) But is permitted it during the preceding night and, if no discharge appeared at sunrise, during all that day also. (2) If no discharge was observed at sunrise. (3) Lit., 'all the day is hers', but, contrary to the view of R. Jose, not the preceding night. (4) Lit., 'how'. (5) Lit., 'from the twentieth day to the twentieth day'. (6) Lit., 'and from six hours to six hours'. (7) Since in his opinion a discharge that usually occurs in the day time causes intercourse to be forbidden all day and one that usually occurs in the night causes it to be forbidden all night. (8) Because the discharge is not due earlier. In his opinion intercourse is forbidden only at the hour the discharge usually occurs, neither earlier nor later. (9) And consequently abstain from intercourse during all that hour. (10) *Sc.* from midday (v. Rashi. Cf., however, Tosaf.). (11) A woman who had the habit of observing her discharge at sunrise. (12) Lit., 'all the night is hers'. How then is this to be reconciled with R. Judah's ruling in our Mishnah that 'SHE IS PERMITTED IT ALL DAY'? (13) Lit., 'that'. (14) Hence intercourse is forbidden in the day time only but not during the preceding night. (15) This being the meaning of the phrase AT SUNRISE in our Mishnah. Intercourse is, therefore, forbidden in the night only but not during the following day.

One [Baraitha] taught: R. Judah forbids intercourse before her settled period, and permits it after the period while another [Baraitha] taught: [R. Judah] forbids it after her settled period and permits it before the period. This,[1] however, represents no difficulty, since the former is a case where she usually observes her discharge at the end of the night while the latter is a case where she usually observes it at the beginning of the day.[2]

Raba stated: The *halachah* is in agreement with R. Judah. But could Raba have said this, seeing that it was taught: *Thus shall ye separate the children of Israel from their uncleanness;*[3] from this, R. Jeremiah[4] observed, follows a warning to the children of Israel that they shall separate from their wives near their periods. And for how long? Raba[5] replied: One *'onah*.[6] Now does not this mean: An additional *'onah?*[7]—No; the same *'onah*. But then, what need is there for the two statements?[8]—Both are required. For, if he had informed us of the former statement only, it might have been presumed that it applied only to the law relating to clean things but not to that relating to a woman's permissibility to her husband. Hence we were informed [of the latter statement]. And if [our information were to be derived] from the latter statement only it might have been presumed that near her settled period an additional *'onah* is required, hence we were informed that only one *'onah* is necessary.

MISHNAH. IF SHE WAS ACCUSTOMED TO OBSERVE A FLOW OF MENSTRUAL BLOOD ON THE FIFTEENTH DAY[9] AND THIS WAS CHANGED[10] TO THE TWENTIETH DAY,[9] MARITAL

(1) Apparent contradiction. (2) Cf. *supra* p. 446, n. 7. (3) Lev. XV, 31. (4) Var. lec. 'Josiah'. Cf. Bomb. ed. and Shebu. 18*b*. (5) Marg. gl. 'Rabbah'. (6) A period. *Sc*. a day or a night. (7) *Sc*. if the discharge occurs during day time the prohibition extends over that day and the previous night, and if it occurs during the night the prohibition extends over that night and the previous day. But, if so, would not this be contradictory to what Raba said here? (8) Of Raba. (9) Of the month. (10) Lit., 'and she changed to be seeing'.

INTERCOURSE IS FORBIDDEN ON BOTH DAYS.[1] IF THIS WAS TWICE CHANGED TO THE TWENTIETH INTERCOURSE IS AGAIN FORBIDDEN ON BOTH DAYS.[1] IF THIS WAS CHANGED THREE TIMES TO THE TWENTIETH DAY, INTERCOURSE IS NOW PERMITTED ON THE FIFTEENTH[2] AND THE TWENTIETH IS ESTABLISHED AS HER SETTLED PERIOD. FOR A WOMAN MAY NOT REGARD HER MENSTRUAL PERIODS AS SETTLED UNLESS THE RECURRENCE HAS BEEN REGULAR THREE TIMES; NOR IS SHE RELEASED FROM THE RESTRICTIONS OF A SETTLED PERIOD UNLESS IT HAS VARIED[3] THREE TIMES.

GEMARA. [64*a*] It was stated: If a woman observed a discharge on the fifteenth day of one month, on the sixteenth of the next month and on the seventeenth of the third month, Rab ruled: She has thereby established for herself a settled period in arithmetical progression,[4] but Samuel ruled: No settled period can be established unless the progression is repeated three times.[5] Must it be conceded that Rab and Samuel differ on the same principle as that on which Rabbi and R. Simeon b. Gamaliel differ? For it was taught: If a woman was married to one man who died and to a second one who also died, she may not be married to a third one; so Rabbi. R. Simeon b. Gamaliel ruled: She may be married to a third but may not be married to a fourth?[6]—No, all[7] may concede that the law is in agreement with R. Simeon b. Gamaliel but it is this principle on which they[8] differ here:

(1) Lit., 'this and this (the fifteenth and the twentieth) are forbidden.' (2) As was the case before that day had been established as a settled period. (3) Lit., 'that it shall be rooted out from her'. (4) Lit., 'in skipping'. The eighteenth day of the fourth month, the nineteenth of the fifth and so on are consequently forbidden days. (5) *Sc.* only if in the intercourse given, the discharge had actually appeared on the eighteenth of the fourth month. The appearance on the fifteenth is not counted since it was the first of the series when the process of progression had not yet been apparent (v. *infra*). (6) Is the case of the husbands, it is asked, analogous to that of the periods, so that Rab's view coincides with that of Rabbi and the view of Samuel with that of R. Simeon b. Gamaliel? But, if so, why should the same principle be discussed twice? (7) Even Rab. (8) Rab and Samuel.

Rab holds that the fifteenth day is included in the number while Samuel holds that the fifteenth, since the observation on it was not in arithmetic progression, is not included in the number.[1]

He raised an objection against him: If a woman had been accustomed to observe her discharge on the fifteenth day[2] and this was changed[3] to the sixteenth, intercourse is forbidden[4] on both days.[5] If this was changed[6] to the seventeenth day, intercourse[7] on the sixteenth is again permitted[8] but on the fifteenth[9] and the seventeenth[10] it is forbidden. If[7] this was changed to the eighteenth intercourse[7] is again permitted on all the former dates;[11] and[12] is forbidden only on the day after[13] the eighteenth and onwards.[14] Now does not this[15] present an objection against Rab?[16]—Rab can answer you: Where a woman was accustomed to observe her discharge on a certain date[17] the law is different.[18]

(1) Cf. prev. n. but three. (2) Of the month. (3) In a subsequent month. (4) In the month following that in which the discharge appeared on the sixteenth. (5) The fifteenth and sixteenth. (6) In the month following that in which the discharge appeared on the sixteenth. (7) In the month following. (8) As a discharge appeared on it once only, the prohibition on it also is abolished by one change. (9) Which was the day of her established settled period. (10) The day on which her discharge was last observed. (11) It is permitted on the sixteenth and seventeenth for the reason given *supra* (prev. n. but two); and on the fifteenth it is permitted because in three consecutive months the discharge appeared on days (sixteenth, seventeenth and eighteenth) other than the fifteenth which, in consequence, can no longer be regarded as the settled period. (12) Since the discharge appeared three times on days that represent an arithmetical progression. (13) Lit., 'from'. (14) *Sc.* on the nineteenth of the next month, the twentieth of the one following it, and so on in arithmetical progression in each succeeding month. (15) From which it is obvious that, since only three occurrences cause the abolition of the old, and the establishment of a new settled period, the first occurrence is not counted. (16) Who ruled that even a change on two dates in arithmetical progression abolishes the old, and establishes a new settled period. (17) As is the case in the Baraitha cited. (18) From that dealt with by Rab. In the former case, the first of the dates under discussion might well be added to the similar dates in the previous months and hence could not be counted as the first in the arithmetical progression. In the case dealt with by Rab, however, either the first of the dates under discussion was one on which the woman observed a discharge for the very first time, or the woman was one who had never before

But as to him who raised the objection, on what possible ground did he raise it?[1]—[He assumed that the case of] one who was accustomed to a settled period had to be stated:[2] As it might have been presumed that since she was accustomed to observe her discharge on a settled date and this was changed, the change is effective[3] even if this[4] occurred only twice, hence we had to be informed [that[5] the change must have recurred three times].

An objection was raised: If she observed a discharge on the twenty-first day of one[6] month, on the twenty-second of the next month and on the twenty-third of the third month, she has thereby established for herself a settled period. If she skipped over[7] to the twenty-fourth[8] day of the month, she has not established for herself a settled period.[9] Does not this[10] present an objection against Samuel?[11]—Samuel can answer you: Here we are dealing with the case of a woman, for instance, who was accustomed to observe her discharge on the twentieth day and this[12] was changed to the twenty-first.[13] An inference from the wording also justifies this view;[14] for the twentieth day was left out[15] and the twenty-first was mentioned.[16] This is conclusive.

had a settled period or one whose settled period was on a day other than the first of those under discussion. The first day, therefore, may well be counted as one of the three days that establish a settled period.

(1) *Sc.* did he not know of the difference between a settled and an unsettled period? (2) Though the same law applies to one who had no settled period. (3) *Sc.* the first date is no longer regarded as a settled period. (4) The change from the date mentioned. (5) If a new settled period is to be established. (6) Lit., 'this'. (7) From the twenty-second. (8) Instead of the twenty-third. (9) Since the difference between the dates of the first and the second month was only one day while that between the second and the third was two days. (10) The first case where three observations, including the first one, establish a settled period. (11) Who maintains that no settled period in arithmetical progression can be established unless the discharge appeared on three dates exclusive of the first. (12) The first discharge mentioned. (13) So that the change actually occurred three times (on the twenty-first, twenty-second and twenty-third) on dates in arithmetical progression exclusive of the first date which was the twentieth. (14) That we are here dealing with a case where the woman 'was accustomed to observe her discharge on the twentieth'. (15) From the three dates given. (16) Had not the woman had the habit of observing her discharge on the twen-

FOR A WOMAN MAY NOT REGARD HER MENSTRUAL PERIOD AS SETTLED UNLESS THE RECURRENCE HAS BEEN REGULAR etc. R. Papa explained: This[1] was said only in regard to the establishment of a settled period,[2] but as regards taking the possibility of a discharge into consideration[3] one occurrence suffices.[4] But what[5] does he[6] teach us, seeing that we have learnt: IF SHE WAS ACCUSTOMED TO OBSERVE A FLOW OF MENSTRUAL BLOOD ON THE FIFTEENTH DAY AND THIS WAS CHANGED TO THE TWENTIETH DAY, MARITAL INTERCOURSE IS FORBIDDEN ON BOTH DAYS?[7]—If the inference had to be made from there,[8] it might have been presumed that the ruling[9] applied only where the woman was still[10] within her menstruation period,[11] but where she is not within her menstruation period[12] she[13] need not consider the possibility of a discharge,[14] hence we were informed[15] [that even in the latter case the possibility of a discharge must be taken into consideration].

NOR IS SHE RELEASED FROM THE RESTRICTIONS OF A

tieth, that date (which is simpler than the twenty-first) would have been taken as an example of the first of the three dates, and the twenty-first and twenty-second would have been taken as examples of the subsequent dates.

(1) That the occurrence must be repeated three times. (2) *Sc.* that the uncleanness should begin just at the time of the period and not earlier; and that the settled period should not be abolished unless a change occurred three times. (3) *Sc.* to treat the date on which a discharge appeared in one month as one on which intercourse is forbidden in the next month. (4) Lit., 'in one time she fears'. If, for instance, she observed a discharge on the fifteenth of one month intercourse is forbidden on the same date in the next month. (5) That we did not know before. (6) R. Papa. (7) A ruling which embodies that of R. Papa. (8) Our Mishnah. (9) As enumerated by R. Papa. (10) When the discharge appeared. (11) As is the case in our Mishnah where the discharge occurred on the fifteenth day after immersion, which is the fourth day (11 days of *zibah* + 4 days of the 7 of menstruation = 15) of a menstruation period. Hence the restriction when the next fifteenth day (also within the menstruation period) arrives. (12) But in the *zibah* period; where, for instance, her discharge appeared on the tenth day after immersion, which is still within the eleven days of a *zibah* period that follows that of the seven days of menstruation. (13) Since the *zibah* period is one during which a discharge is unusual. (14) And intercourse should, therefore, be permitted when the next similar date arrives. (15) By R. Papa.

SETTLED PERIOD etc. R. Papa explained: This, that it is necessary for the change to recur three times before a settled period can be abolished, was said only where a settled period had been established by three regular occurrences, but one that was established by two recurrences only may be abolished by one change. But what[1] does he[2] teach us, seeing that we learnt: A WOMAN MAY NOT REGARD HER MENSTRUAL PERIODS AS SETTLED UNLESS THE RECURRENCE HAS BEEN REGULAR THREE TIMES?[3]—It might have been presumed[4] that one occurence[5] is required for the abolition of one,[6] two[7] for two[8] and three[7] for three,[8] hence we were informed[9] [that even for two occurrences[10] only one[5] is required].[11] It was taught in agreement with R. Papa:[12] If a woman had a habit of observing her menstrual discharge on the twentieth day,[13] and this was changed to the thirtieth, intercourse is forbidden[14] on both days. If the twentieth day[14] arrived and she observed no discharge, she is permitted intercourse until the thirtieth but must consider the possibility of a discharge on the thirtieth day itself.[15] If the thirtieth day arrived and she observed a discharge, the twentieth[14] arrived and she observed none, the thirtieth arrived and she observed none and the twentieth[14] arrived and she observed one, the thirtieth[14] becomes a permitted day[16] [64b] and[14] the twentieth[17] becomes a forbidden one, because the guest[18] comes in his usual time.

(1) That we did not know before. (2) R. Papa. (3) And since this is followed by NOR IS SHE RELEASED . . . UNLESS IT HAS VARIED THREE TIMES it is obvious that the three occurrences for the abolition of a settled period (the latter case) are necessary only where there were three occurrences for its establishment (the first case). What need then was there for R. Papa's ruling? (4) If only our Mishnah were available and not R. Papa's ruling. (5) A change of date (6) Discharge on a certain date. (7) Changes. (8) Discharges on similar dates. (9) By R. Papa. (10) Discharges on similar dates. (11) To release a woman from the restrictions of a settled period. (12) That one change of date suffices to release a woman from the restrictions of a settled period that had been established by two occurrences. (13) Of a month. (14) In the next month. (15) And must consequently abstain from intercourse. (16) Because, though in the course of two months a discharge appeared on it, there was none, in the third one, and one change suffices to release the woman from its restrictions (cf. prev. n. but three). (17) The established settled period which was changed

MISHNAH. WOMEN IN REGARD TO THEIR VIRGINITY ARE LIKE VINES. ONE VINE MAY HAVE RED WINE[1] WHILE ANOTHER HAS BLACK WINE, ONE VINE MAY YIELD MUCH WINE WHILE ANOTHER YIELDS LITTLE.[2] R. JUDAH STATED: EVERY NORMAL VINE YIELDS[3] WINE,[4] AND ONE THAT YIELDS NO WINE IS BUT A DORKETAI.[5]

GEMARA. One taught:[6] A generation cut off.[7] R. Ḥiyya taught: As leaven is wholesome for the dough so is [menstrual] blood wholesome for a woman. One taught in the name of R. Meir: Every woman who has an abundance of [menstrual] blood has many children.

to the thirtieth no more than twice. (The absence of a discharge on the twentieth in the month in which there was none on the thirtieth is not counted as a deviation from the established habit since there was no discharge whatever in that month.) (18) The established period that re-appeared on the twentieth.

(1) Lit., 'there is a vine whose wine is red'. (2) Similarly with the blood of virginity. It may be red or black, much or little. (3) Lit., 'has'. (4) Every normal woman has the blood of virginity. (5) Cf. τρωκτή, a grape that yields no wine and is used for eating only. *Aliter: Dorketai* = *dor kaṭu'a.* This is explained presently. (6) In explanation of DORKETAI. (7) Cf. prev. two notes. A woman who has no blood of virginity cannot have many children.

NIDDAH

CHAPTER X

MISHNAH. IF A YOUNG GIRL, WHOSE AGE OF MENSTRUATION[1] HAS NOT YET ARRIVED, MARRIED, BETH SHAMMAI RULED: SHE IS ALLOWED[2] FOUR NIGHTS,[3] AND BETH HILLEL RULED: UNTIL THE WOUND IS HEALED.[4] IF THE AGE OF HER MENSTRUATION HAS ARRIVED[5] AND SHE MARRIED, BETH SHAMMAI RULED: SHE IS ALLOWED[2] THE FIRST NIGHT, AND BETH HILLEL RULED: FOUR NIGHTS, UNTIL THE EXIT OF THE SABBATH.[6] IF SHE HAD OBSERVED A DISCHARGE WHILE SHE WAS STILL IN HER FATHER'S HOUSE,[7] BETH SHAMMAI RULED: SHE IS ONLY ALLOWED THE OBLIGATORY MARITAL INTERCOURSE,[8] AND BETH HILLEL RULED: ALL THAT[9] NIGHT.

GEMARA. R. Naḥman b. Isaac explained:[10] Even if she already observed a discharge.[11] Whence is this inferred?—Since in the final clause[12] a distinction is drawn between one who did and one who did not observe a discharge it follows that in the case in the first clause no distinction is made between the one and the other.[13] So it was also taught: Beth Hillel ruled: Intercourse is allowed

(1) Lit., 'her time to see'. (2) For marital intercourse. (3) Though blood appeared, it is assumed to be that of injured virginity which, unlike menstrual blood, is clean. (4) This is explained in the Gemara *infra*. (5) But she experienced no discharge. (6) Saturday night. A virgin's marriage takes place usually on a Wednesday, v. Keth. 2*a*. (7) *Sc.* before her marriage. (8) But no more, since the blood may possibly be that of menstruation. (9) The first. (10) The ruling of Beth Hillel in the first clause of our Mishnah. (11) Before marriage, when she was still in her father's house. Even in such a case, since the age of menstruation had not yet arrived, Beth Hillel allow intercourse UNTIL THE WOUND IS HEALED. (12) Dealing with one whose age of menstruation had arrived. (13) Lit., 'no difference whether thus and no difference (whether) thus', *sc.* whether she did or did not observe any menstrual discharge before her marriage.

until the wound is healed irrespective of whether she already[1] did or did not observe a discharge.

UNTIL THE WOUND IS HEALED. For how long?[2]—Rab Judah replied: Rab said, 'So long as it discharges matter', but when I mentioned this in the presence of Samuel the latter said to me, 'I do not know what that "discharging" exactly means; rather explain,[3] So long as spittle is engendered in the mouth[4] on account of intercourse'.[5] How is one to understand the 'discharging' of which Rab spoke?—R. Samuel son of R. Isaac replied, This was explained to me by Rab: If when standing she observes a discharge and when sitting she does not observe one, it may be known that the wound has not healed; if when lying on the ground she observes a discharge and when lying on cushions and bolsters she does not observe one, it may be known that the wound had not healed; and if when lying on any of these she either observes a discharge or does not observe one, it may be known that the wound is healed.

IF THE AGE OF HER MENSTRUATION HAS ARRIVED etc. It was stated: If she had intercourse in the day time,[6] Rab ruled, She has not lost thereby the right to intercourse during the nights, but Levi ruled, She has thereby lost the right to intercourse in the nights. Rab ruled, 'She has not lost thereby the right to intercourse during the nights', because we learnt, UNTIL THE EXIT OF THE SABBATH.[7] 'But Levi ruled, She has thereby lost the right to intercourse in the nights', for the meaning of[8] FOUR NIGHTS mentioned is four *'onahs*.[9] But according to Rab[10] what was the purpose of mentioning FOUR NIGHTS?—We were thereby informed of what is regarded as good manners, viz., that intercourse should take place at night.[11] But according to Levi[12] it

(1) Before her marriage. (2) Is the wound regarded as unhealed. (3) The statement, UNTIL THE WOUND etc. (4) Euphemism. (5) *Sc.* when intercourse is accompanied by bleeding. (6) Lit., 'in the days', the four days following marriage. (7) Implying both the intervening days and the intervening nights. (8) Lit., 'what'. (9) An *'onah* (period) being either a day or a night. (10) Who allows intercourse during both the days and the nights. (11) Lit., 'that the way of . . . in the nights'. (12) Who allows no more than four *'onahs*.

should only have been stated FOUR NIGHTS, what was the purpose of saying, UNTIL THE EXIT OF THE SABBATH?—It is this that we were informed:[1] That it is permitted to perform the first marital intercourse[2] on the Sabbath,[3] in agreement with a ruling of Samuel; for Samuel ruled: It is permissible to enter through a narrow breach[4] on the Sabbath although one causes pebbles to fall.[5]

It was stated: If a man had marital intercourse[6] and found no blood but, having repeated the act,[7] he found blood, R. Ḥanina ruled: The woman is unclean;[8] but R. Assi ruled: She is clean. 'R. Ḥanina ruled: The woman is unclean', for if it were the case that the blood was that of virginity it would have issued on the first occasion. 'But R. Assi ruled: She is clean', because it is possible that something unusual may have happened to her, in accordance with a statement of Samuel; for Samuel stated, 'I could perform a number of acts of intercourse without causing any bleeding'. And the other?[9]—Samuel is different from ordinary people since his capability[10] was great.

Rab stated: A woman who has reached her maturity[11] is[12] allowed[13] all the first night.[14] But this applies only to a woman who had never yet observed a discharge, but if she did observe one she is permitted the obligatory act of intercourse only and no more. An objection was raised: It once happened that Rabbi allowed a woman intercourse on four nights in twelve months.[15]

(1) By the statement mentioned, from which it follows that if intercourse had taken place on two weekday *'onahs* only the night and the day of the Sabbath are also permitted *'onahs*. (2) *Sc.* the one before virginity is finally removed. (3) Though virginity is injured in the process. (4) Euphemism. After the two acts of intercourse the opening is still narrow. (5) Injures virginity. (6) With a virgin, for the first time. (7) Within the following four nights. (8) The blood being deemed to be menstrual. (9) R. Ḥanina. How in view of Samuel's statement can he maintain that the blood must be menstrual? (10) Lit., 'his strength'. (11) *Bogereth*, v. Glos. (12) Even according to Beth Hillel. (13) For intercourse despite the possibility of bleeding. (14) Of her married life. (15) The husband having departed for three months after each of the first three acts of intercourse every one of which has been accompanied by bleeding. Despite the length of time Rabbi regarded the bleeding to be due to virginity.

Now how is one to understand his ruling? If it be suggested that he allowed her all these nights[1] during the period of her minority [65a] the objection would arise: Have we not learnt, UNTIL THE WOUND IS HEALED?[2] If, however, it is suggested that he allowed her all the nights[1] during the period of her *na'aruth*[3] the difficulty would arise: Does *na'aruth* ever extend over twelve months, seeing that Samuel had stated: The period intervening between the commencement of *na'aruth* and maturity is only six months? And should you suggest that the meaning is that the period is not shorter but may be longer[4] it could be retorted: Did he not in fact state 'only'?[5] If, however, it is suggested that he allowed her two nights during the days of her minority and two during her *na'aruth*, the difficulty would arise: Did not R. Ḥinena b. Shelemya once ask Rab, 'what is the ruling where her age of menstruation arrived when she was already under the authority of her husband?' and the other replied: All acts of intercourse which one performs[6] are regarded as one act only and the other[7] make up the four nights?[8] Consequently this must be a case where he allowed her one night during her minority, two nights during her *na'aruth* period and one night during the days of her maturity. Now if you grant that a woman of mature age generally is allowed[9] more than one night[10] one can well see the justification for the ruling;[11] for, as intercourse during minority has the effect of reducing one night[12] during her *na'aruth* period, so intercourse during the *na'aruth* period has the effect of reducing one night[13] during her maturity;[14] but if you maintain[15] that a woman of mature age generally[9] is not allowed more than one night, should

(1) Lit., 'all of them'. (2) Why then 'four nights'? (3) V. Glos. (4) Lit., 'less than this only there is not, but there is more'. (5) He did, thus implying that the period cannot be longer than six months. (6) During her minority. (7) Performed subsequently. (8) Why then did Rabbi allow only two (instead of three) nights during her *na'aruth* period? (9) If she married after attaining the age of maturity. (10) *Sc.* two nights at least. (11) Of Rabbi who allowed, as just explained, one night during the woman's maturity period. (12) Of the four. (13) Of the two (cf. prev. n. but two). (14) Hence Rabbi's ruling (cf. prev. n. but two). (15) As Rab did (*supra* 64b *ad fin.*).

he[1] not have allowed her[2] but one act of the obligatory marital intercourse and no more?[3]—The fact is that he[1] allowed her one night during her minority and three nights during her *na'aruth* period,[4] but[5] it was not as you think[6] that every three months represented a period; every two months rather represented a period.

Menjamin of Saḳsanah was embarking on a journey[7] to the locality of Samuel where he intended to act[8] according to the ruling of Rab,[9] even where the woman had observed a discharge, assuming that Rab drew no distinction between one who did and one who did not observe a discharge, but he died while he was underway. Samuel accordingly applied to Rab[10] the Scriptural text, *There shall no mischief befall the righteous.*[11]

R. Ḥinena b. Shelemya observed: As soon as a person's teeth fall out[12] his means[13] of a livelihood are reduced; for it is said: *And I also have given you cleanness of teeth*[12] *in all your cities, and want of bread in all your places.*[14]

IF SHE OBSERVED A DISCHARGE WHILE SHE WAS STILL etc. Our Rabbis taught: If a girl observed a discharge while she was still in her father's house, Beth Hillel ruled: She is permitted marital intercourse all the night[15] and, moreover, she is allowed a full *'onah*. And how long is a full *'onah?*[16]—R. Simeon b. Gamaliel explained: A night and half a day. But do we require an *'onah* to be so long?[17] Is not [such a requirement] rather incongruous

(1) Rabbi. (2) The woman who, as explained, had been allowed some nights during her minority and *na'aruth* periods. (3) How then could he ignore completely all previous intercourse and allow her a full night? (4) So that the question of maturity does not arise at all. (5) As to the objection, How is it possible for three three-monthly periods to be included in the one six-monthly period of *na'aruth?* (6) Lit., 'do you think?' (7) Lit., 'took and went'. (8) Lit., 'to do a deed'. (9) That one of mature age is allowed all the first night (*supra* 64*b ad fin.*). (10) Whose ruling was misinterpreted by Menjamin. (11) Prov. XII, 21. Rab was spared the mischief that would have ensued if Menjamin had acted in accordance with his erroneous interpretation (cf. prev. n.). (12) Metaph. for old age. (13) Lit., 'his foods'. (14) Amos IV, 6. (15) That follows her marriage. Lit., 'all the night is hers'. (16) A period. (17) Lit., all this'.

with the following: If a person's winepresses or oil-presses were unclean and he desired to prepare his wine and oil respectively[1] in conditions of cleanness, how is he to proceed? He rinses the boards,[2] the twigs[3] and the troughs; [65*b*] and as for the wicker-work, if it is made of willows and hemp it must be scoured, and if of bast or reeds it must remain unused;[4] and for how long must they remain unused? For twelve months. R. Simeon b. Gamaliel ruled: One must leave them from one period of wine-pressing to another[5] and from one period of oil-pressing to another.[5] (But is not this ruling[6] identical with that of the first Tanna?[7]—The practical difference between them arises in the case of early or late ripening fruit.)[8] R. Jose stated: If a person desires to obtain cleanness forthwith he pours over them boiling water or scalds them with olive water. R. Simeon b. Gamaliel citing R. Jose ruled: He puts them under a pipe through which runs a continuous stream of water or in a fountain with flowing water. And for how long? For one *'onah*. (As these provisions were applied to *yen nesek* so were they applied to matters of cleanness. But is not the order[9] reversed, seeing that we are here dealing with the laws of cleanness?—Rather say: As these provisions were applied to matters of cleanness so were they applied to *yen nesek*.) And how long is an *'onah?* R. Ḥiyya b. Abba citing R. Joḥanan replied: Either a day or a night. R. Ḥana She'una or, as some say, R. Ḥana b. She'una citing Rabbah b. Bar Ḥana who had it from R. Joḥanan replied: Half a day and half a night. And in connection with this R. Samuel b. R. Isaac explained: There is no real difference between them,[10] the former referring to the spring and autumn equinoxes[11] and the latter to the summer and winter

(1) Lit., 'to do them'. (2) That are placed on the grapes or the olives. (3) Wherewith the presses are swept and cleaned. (4) Lit., 'causes them to be old'. (5) Presumably twelve months. (6) Of R. Simeon b. Gamaliel. (7) Apparently (cf. prev. n. but one) it is. (8) Where the period intervening between the pressing seasons of two succeeding years is sometimes less, and sometimes more than twelve months. (9) That compares the laws of cleanness to those of *yen nesek* v. Glos. (10) R. Ḥiyya and Rabbah b. Bar Ḥana. (11) Lit., 'in the cycle of Nisan and of Tishri'. When the days and the nights are equal an *'onah* of twelve hours is either a day or a night.

solstices?[1]—Here also, in the case of the menstruant woman,[2] read: Half a day and half a night. But did he not say 'a night and half a day'?—Rather say: Either 'a night' in the spring or autumn equinox or 'half a day and half a night' in the winter or summer solstice. And if you prefer I might reply: The case involving a *kethubah*[3] is different[4] since protracted negotiations take place[5] before it is signed.[6]

Both Rab and Samuel laid down: The *halachah* is that[7] one performs the obligatory marital act and withdraws forthwith. R. Ḥisda raised an objection: It once happened that Rabbi allowed a woman intercourse on four nights in twelve months![8]—Said Rabbah[9] to him: What need have you[10] for repeating the same objection? Rather raise one from our Mishnah?[11]—But he was of the opinion that a practical decision[12] is weightier.[13] At all events,[14] does not a difficulty arise against Rab and Samuel?[15]—They acted in agreement with our Masters; for it was taught: Our Masters decided by a second count of votes[16] that one only performs the obligatory marital act and withdraws forthwith.

'Ulla stated: When R. Joḥanan and Resh Laḳish were engaged in the discussions of the chapter on the 'Young Girl'[17] they carried away from it only what a fox carries away from a ploughed field,[18]

(1) Lit., 'in the cycle of Tammuz and Tebeth'. Since the days and the nights are unequal an *'onah* of twelve hours is half a day and half a night. Now in view of this definition and explanation, how could R. Simeon b. Gamaliel maintain (*supra* 65*a ad fin.*) that an *'onah* is 'a night and half a day'? (2) *Sc.* the case dealt with by R. Simeon b. Gamaliel which bears on the laws of menstruation. (3) Cf. prev. n. mut. mut. (4) From that of cleanness. (5) On its terms. (6) Hence it was necessary to extend the *'onah* to a full night and half a day. (7) Irrespective of whether the girl's age of menstruation has, or has not been reached. (8) *Supra* 64*b*, *ad fin.*; q.v. notes. (9) V. marg. gl. Cur. edd., 'Raba'. (10) So MS.M. Cur. edd., 'I'. (11) Which also allows more than one marital act. (12) As was that of Rabbi. (13) Than a mere theoretical ruling. (14) Whether from Rabbi's decision or from our Mishnah. (15) Who allow no more than one marital act. How could they differ from a Tannaitic ruling? (16) Lit., 'they were counted again'. (17) *Sc.* the present (the tenth) chapter of Niddah, which begins, IF A YOUNG GIRL. (18) I.e., nothing. They completely disregarded its rulings.

and concluded it[1] with this statement: One performs the obligatory marital act and withdraws forthwith. Said R. Abba to R. Ashi: Now then,[2] should a scrupulous man[3] not even finish his act?—The other replied: If that were to be the rule[4] one would be ill at ease[5] and would withdraw altogether.

Our Rabbis taught: But all these women if they[6] were continually discharging blood during[7] the four nights and after the four nights or[8] during the night and after it, must without exception[9] examine themselves;[10] and in the case of all these R. Meir imposes restrictions in agreement with the view of Beth Shammai.[11] In regard, however, to other observations of blood,[12] concerning which a difference of opinion exists between Beth Shammai[13] and Beth Hillel,[14] he is guided[15] by the colour of the blood; for R. Meir ruled: The colours of the various kinds of blood are different from one another. In what manner? Menstrual blood is red, the blood of virginity is not so red; menstrual blood is turbid, the blood of virginity is not turbid; menstrual blood issues from the source, the blood of virginity issues from the sides. R. Isaac son of R. Jose citing R. Joḥanan stated: This is the ruling of R. Meir alone, but the Sages maintain: All the colours of the various kinds of blood are the same.

Our Rabbis taught: A woman who observes a discharge of

(1) In agreement with 'our Masters'. (2) Since one must withdraw immediately after the act, in order to avoid possible blood of menstruation. (3) Lit., 'the master of a soul'. (4) Lit., 'if so'. (5) Lit., 'his heart beats him'. (6) Being in the category of such as observed no discharge while still in their father's homes. (7) Lit., 'from the midst of'. (8) In the case of those who did observe a discharge in the homes of their fathers. (9) Lit., 'all of them'. (10) In order that it may be ascertained (from the colour of the blood) whether the bleeding was due to injured virginity or to menstruation. (11) Thus, a minor is allowed four nights and she must, therefore, examine herself if the bleeding continued beyond the fourth night while a *na'arah* who is allowed one night must examine herself if the bleeding continued after the first night. (12) Where bleeding did not continue after the four nights in the case of the minor or after the first night in that of the *na'arah*. (13) Who hold the blood to be unclean irrespective of whether its colour did, or did not change. (14) Who maintain that the blood is clean even if its colour had changed. (15) In deciding whether the blood is clean or unclean. Lit., 'go'.

blood[1] as a result of marital intercourse may perform her marital duty the first, second and third time. Henceforward,[2] however, she may not perform it until she is divorced [66a] and marries another man.[3] If she was married to another man and again observed a discharge of blood as a result of her marital intercourse, she may perform her marital duty the first, second and third time. Henceforward, however, she may not perform it until she is divorced and marries another man. If she was married to another man and again observed a discharge of blood as a result of her intercourse she may perform her marital duty the first, second and third time. Henceforward, however, she may not perform it unless she first examines herself. How does she examine herself? She inserts a tube within which rests a painting stick to the top of which is attached an absorbent. If blood is found on the top of the absorbent it may be known that it[4] emanated from the source[5] and if no blood is found on the top, it may be known that it[4] emanated from the sides.[6] If, however, she has a wound in that place she may attribute the blood to her wound.[6] If she has a fixed period[7] she may attribute it to her fixed period,[8] but if the nature of the blood of her wound is different from that of the blood of her observation she may not so attribute it. A woman, furthermore, is believed when she says, 'I have a wound in the source from which blood is discharged';[6] so Rabbi.[9] R. Simeon b. Gamaliel ruled: The blood of a wound that is discharged through the source is unclean. Our Masters, however, testified that the blood of a wound that is discharged through the source is clean. What is the point at issue between them?[10]—'Ulla replied: The point at issue between them is the question whether the interior of the uterus is unclean.[11] Would not a tube[12] bruise

(1) Of menstruation. (2) If she observed a discharge three times as a result of intercourse. (3) The reason is explained *infra*. (4) The blood. (5) The uterus; and is unclean. (6) And it is clean. (7) During which intercourse causes her to bleed. (8) And is consequently permitted intercourse at other times without previous examination. (9) This refers to the last ruling only. All the previous rulings in the Baraitha, however, represent the view of R. Simeon. (10) Rabbi and our Masters on the one hand and R. Simeon on the other. (11) Lit., 'the source, its place is unclean'. (12) Presumably a reed.

her?[1]—Samuel replied: The examination is performed with a leaden tube whose edge[2] is bent inwards. But, said Resh Lakish to R. Johanan, why should she not[3] examine herself[4] after the third intercourse with her first husband?[5]—The other replied: Because not all fingers[6] are alike.[7] But, the former said, why should she not[8] have to examine herself[4] after the first intercourse with her third husband?—Because not all ejections[9] are of equal force.[10]

A certain woman once came to Rabbi [with such a complaint].[11] Go, he said to Abdan, and frighten her. As the latter approached and frightened her a clot of blood dropped from her. This woman, Rabbi exclaimed, is now cured. A certain woman [with a similar complaint][11] once came to the Master Samuel. Go, he said to R. Dimi b. Joseph, and frighten her. The latter approached and frightened her but nothing dropped from her. This woman, Samuel pronounced, is one full of blood which she scatters,[12] and any woman who is full of blood which she scatters[12] has no cure. Once there came to R. Johanan a certain woman who, whenever she emerged from her ritual immersion, observed a discharge of blood. It is possible, he said to her, that the gossip of your townspeople[13] has caused the affliction;[14] arrange[15] for your intercourse with him to take place near the river side.[16] There is one who says: He[17] said to her, Reveal your affliction to your friends so that, as they were astounded in one way,[18] they may also be

(1) Why then is she expected to carry out her examination with it? (2) Lit., 'and its mouth'. (3) Instead of being divorced. (4) Before each subsequent intercourse. (5) And thus continue to live with him. (6) Euphemism. (7) *Sc.* the husband might have been the cause. It is preferable, therefore, that she marries another man with whom she can lead a normal life than continue to live with one in an abnormal condition. (8) Since a repetition of the occurrence with three husbands establishes presumption. (9) Lit., 'forces'. (10) Hence it is necessary for the occurrence to be repeated three times with the third husband before presumption is established. (11) Bleeding occasioned by intercourse. (12) As a result of intercourse. (13) *Sc.* their 'evil eye'; jealousy at the affection between her and her husband. (14) Lit., 'went up on thee'. (15) Lit., 'go'. (16) Thus avoiding the town's gossip. (17) R. Johanan. (18) Lit., 'side'; at her husband's affection (cf. prev. n. but four).

astounded in the other.[1] There is also one who says: He[2] said to her, Announce your trouble to your friends so that they may offer prayers for mercy to be vouchsafed to you. For it was taught: *And shall cry, 'Unclean, unclean'*,[3] he must announce his trouble to the public so that they may pray for mercy to be vouchsafed to him. R. Joseph stated: Such an incident once occurred at Pumbeditha and the woman was cured.

R. Joseph citing Rab Judah who had it from Rab stated: Rabbi ordained at Sadoth,[4] If a woman observed a discharge on one day she[5] must wait[6] six days in addition to it.[7] If she observed discharges on two days she[5] must wait[6] six days in addition to these.[8] If she observed a discharge on three days she[5] must wait[6] seven clean days.[9] R. Zera stated: The daughters of Israel have imposed upon themselves the restriction that even if they observe a drop of blood of the size of a mustard seed they wait on account of it seven clean days.

Raba took R. Samuel out for a walk[10] when he discoursed as follows: If a woman[11] was in protracted labour[12] for two days and on the third she miscarried she must wait seven clean days; he being of the opinion that the law relating to protracted labour[13] does not apply to miscarriages and that it is impossible for the uterus[14] to open without bleeding. Said R. Papa to Raba: What is the point in speaking of one who was in protracted labour for two days seeing that the same applies even where there was the

(1) At her affliction. They would in consequence no longer envy her and the influence of their 'evil eye' would disappear. (2) R. Joḥanan. (3) Lev. XIII, 45. (4) A place that was inhabited by unlettered people who were incapable of calculating the dates of the menstrual, and the *zibah* periods. (5) Before she attains cleanness. (6) Lit., 'she shall sit'. (7) *Sc.* seven days, the number prescribed for a menstruant, since (cf. prev. n. but two) it is possible that the discharge occurred during a menstruation period. (8) Since it is possible that the first of the two days was the last of a *zibah* period while the second was the first of a menstruation one. (9) It being possible that the discharge occurred in a period of *zibah*. (10) ארבריה V. Ta'an., (Sonc. ed.), p. 60 n. 5. (11) In her *zibah* period. (12) Accompanied by bleeding. (13) Which regards accompanying bleeding as exempt from uncleanness. (14) Lit., 'the grave'.

minutest discharge, since R. Zera stated, The daughters of Israel have imposed upon themselves the restriction that even where they observe only a drop of blood of the size of a mustard seed they wait on account of it seven clean days?—The other replied: I am speaking to you of a prohibition,[1] and you talk of a custom which applies only where the restriction has been adopted.[2]

(Mnemonic. *Had an offer, natron, in warm water, to perform immersion, folds upon a haven.*)[3] Raba stated: If a woman had an offer of marriage and she accepted it she[4] must allow seven clean days to pass.[5]

Rabina was engaged in preparations for the marriage of his son at R. Ḥanina's.[6] 'Does the Master', the latter said to him, 'intend writing the *kethubah* four days hence?' 'Yes', the other replied; but when the fourth day arrived he waited for another four days and thus caused a delay of seven days after the day in question.[7] 'Why', the first asked, 'all this delay?'[8] 'Does not the Master', the other replied, 'hold the opinion of Raba, Raba having ruled: If a woman had an offer of marriage and she accepted she must allow seven clean days to pass?' 'It is possible', the first suggested, 'that Raba spoke only of one of mature age who is likely to discharge menstrual blood,[9] but did he speak of a minor who is unlikely to discharge menstrual blood?' 'Raba', the other replied, 'has explicitly stated: There is no difference between one of mature age and a minor. For what is the reason why one of mature age is subject to the restriction? Because her passions are excited;[10] well, those of a minor also are excited.

Raba ruled: A woman [66b] must not wash her head either

(1) Which is Pentateuchally applicable to all. (2) Lit., 'where it was restricted it was restricted; where it was not etc.' (3) Words or phrases occurring in the following rulings of Raba. 'Folds' should be inserted before 'to perform' to correspond with the order of the rulings in cur. edd. (4) Since the excitement of the proposal and its acceptance may have produced some menstrual discharge. (5) Before she may regard herself as clean. (6) Var. lec. Ḥabiba (MS.M. and BaḤ.). (7) Lit., 'that day', on which the proposal was made to the girl. (8) Lit., 'what that'. (9) Lit., 'who sees blood'. (10) Lit., 'that she covets'.

with natron or with *ohal.*[1] 'With natron', because it plucks out the hair;[2] and 'with *ohal*' because it causes the hairs to cling to one another.[3]

Amemar also citing Raba ruled: A woman[4] must wash her head in warm water only and she may do it even with such as was warmed by the sun[5] but not with cold water. Why not with cold water?—Because cold water[6] loosens[7] the hair.[8]

Raba further ruled: A man should always give instructions to his household that a woman[9] should wash the folds of her body[10] with water. An objection was raised: It is not necessary for the water[11] to penetrate into the folds of the body[12] or to its concealed parts![13]—Granted that it is not necessary for the water to penetrate,[14] it is necessary nevertheless that it be capable of penetration to every part;[15] in agreement with a ruling of R. Zera. For R. Zera ruled: Wherever proper mingling[16] is possible actual mingling is not essential,[17] but where proper mingling is not possible[18] the actual mingling is indispensable.[19]

Rabin son of R. Adda citing R. Isaac stated: It once happened that a bondmaid of Rabbi performed immersion and when she ascended [from the water] a bone constituting an interposition was found between her teeth, and[20] Rabbi required her to perform a second immersion.[21]

(1) An alcalic plant. So Aruk, Alfasi and Asheri. Cur. edd. 'sand'. (2) Which, remaining on the head, form an interception between the water of the ritual bath and the body. (3) Cf. prev. n. *mut. mut.* (4) Before ritual immersion. (5) For the sequence of the rulings cf. MS.M., BaḤ and Asheri. (6) Cf. BaḤ. (7) *Aliter:* hardens. (8) Cf. prev. n. but five *mut. mut.* (9) Before performing ritual immersion. (10) Her armpits for instance. (11) Of a ritual bath. (12) Lit., 'the house of folds'. (13) How then could Raba maintain that the folds must be washed? (14) Into the folds. (15) Lit., 'a place that is suitable for the entry of the water we require'. (16) Of the flour and the oil of a meal-offering. Perfect mingling is effected with one *log* of oil to sixty *'esronim* of flour in one pan; v. Men. 103*b*. (17) The meal-offering being acceptable even if no mingling took place. (18) If, for instance, the proportions were less than a *log* of oil to sixty *'esronim* of flour. (19) Similarly in the case of ritual immersion, though the water need not penetrate to all parts of the body, the immersion is invalid if owing to dirt or some other interception the water cannot penetrate everywhere. (20) Though it is not necessary for the

Raba further ruled: If a woman performed immersion, and when she ascended [from the water] an object that caused an interposition was found upon her, she need not wash her head or perform immersion again if her immersion was performed immediately after the washing of her head;[1] otherwise, she must wash her head and perform immersion again. There are others who say: If she performed her immersion on the same day on which she washed her head, she need not wash her head or perform immersion again, otherwise she must wash her head and perform immersion again. What is the practical difference between them?[2]—The practical difference between them is the question whether immersion must follow immediately upon the washing of the head,[3] and whether a woman may wash her head during the day and perform her immersion at night.

Raba ruled: A woman may not stand upon an earthenware when she is to perform ritual immersion. R. Kahana intended to say, 'What is the reason? Because a preventive measure has been enacted against the possibility of using[4] bath-houses,[5] but that it is quite proper to stand upon a block of wood'. Said R. Ḥanan of Nehardea to him, 'What is the reason[6] there?[7] Because she is frightened;[8] on a chip of wood she is also frightened'.[8]

R. Samuel b. R. Isaac ruled: A woman shall not perform immersion [67a] in a harbour;[9] although there may be no [mud][10] now[11] it may well be assumed that it had fallen off with the drippings.[12]

water to come in contact with the teeth. (21) In agreement with R. Zera's rule.

(1) It being assumed in such a case that the interposition became attached to the body after the immersion. (2) The two readings. (3) According to the first reading it must. (4) For ritual immersion. (5) Where the benches on which people stand when bathing are made of earth and are thus similar to earthenware. Were a woman to be allowed to stand on earthenware when performing ritual immersion in a ritually valid bath she might assume that ritual immersion is also valid when she stands on an earthen bench in a bath-house. (6) Why a woman must not stand on earthenware. (7) Where immersion is performed in a ritual bath. (8) That she might fall; and in consequence might not perform the immersion in a proper manner. (9) Where mud, stirred up by the incoming and outgoing ships, might cling to her body and constitute an interposition between it and the water. (10) On the woman's body. (11) After she has emerged from the water. (12) *Beridyoni. Aliter:* Into the stream.

Samuel's father made ritual baths for his daughters in the days of Nisan[1] and mats[2] in the days of Tishri.[3]

R. Giddal citing Rab ruled: If a woman gave to her child some cooked food and then performed her ritual immersion and ascended from the water,[4] her immersion has no validity,[5] because, though there may be no food[6] now,[7] it may well be assumed that it had fallen off with the drippings.[8]

Rami b. Abba[9] ruled: Scars[10] constitute no interposition[11] during the first[12] three days;[13] henceforth they constitute an interposition.

Mar Uḳba ruled: Pus within the eye constitutes no interposition when it is moist, but when it is dry it constitutes one. When is it called 'dry'?—From the time it begins to turn yellow.

Samuel ruled: Stibium within the eye constitutes no interposition but on the outside of the eye it constitutes one. If a woman's eyes were twitching it constitutes no interposition even if it is on the outside of the eye.[14]

R. Joḥanan ruled: If a woman[15] opened her eyes too wide[16] or shut them too closely,[17] her immersion has no validity.

(1) When the flowing river, swollen by rainwater, could not be used for the purpose since no ritual immersion may be performed in rainwater that is not collected and stationary. (2) To spread under the feet of the bathers so as to protect them from the river mud which might cling to their feet and constitute an interposition. *Aliter:* He hung up mats on the river shore, to serve as screens for the bathers. *Aliter:* He put up reed tents; v. Ned., (Sonc. ed.), p. 129 notes. (3) When the river contained its normal flow (cf. prev. n. but one *mut. mut.*). (4) With nothing of the food clinging to it. (5) Lit., 'did not go up for her', since it is possible that some of the food clung to her body during the immersion when it constitutes an interposition. (6) On the woman's body. (7) After she has emerged from the water. (8) *Beridyoni. Aliter:* Into the stream. (9) MS.M. Ḥama. (10) Lit., 'the patches of the lancet', 'the marks of the punctures'. (11) In ritual immersion. (12) Lit., 'until' (13) Following the bleeding. Being tender they are regarded as a part of the body. (14) Because the frequent movement of the eye-lids prevents the accumulation of the matter and no interposition can be formed. (15) When performing immersion. (16) Thus forming above the eye a fold that prevents the water from penetrating to every part of that region. (17) Forming a fold below the eye (cf. prev. n.).

Resh Lakish ruled: A woman must perform immersion only when standing in her natural position;[1] as we have learnt:[2] A man[3] is inspected[4] in the same position as when he hoes[5] or[6] gathers olives;[7] and a woman[3] is inspected[4] in the same position as when she weaves[8] or[6] suckles her child.[7]

Rabbah b. R. Huna[9] stated, 'One knotted hair constitutes an interposition,[10] [67*b*] three hairs[11] constitute no interposition;[12] but I do not know the ruling in the case of two'. R. Joḥanan, however, stated, 'We have only this one principle: R. Isaac said, According to traditional law[13] an interposition on its[14] major part[15] to which a man objects constitutes an interposition but one which he does not mind constitutes no interposition; but the Rabbis ruled that an interposition on its[14] greater part shall constitute an interposition, even when the man does not mind it, as a preventive measure against the possibility of allowing an interposition on its major part to which the man does object; and they also ruled that an interposition on its minor part to which a man objects shall constitute an interposition as a preventive measure against the possibility of allowing an interposition on its major part to which a man objects.[16] But why should no prohibition

(1) *Sc.* she must neither press her arms to her body nor her legs or feet to each other, since thereby she prevents the water from reaching parts that are normally exposed; nor need she stretch any natural fold or expose any concealed part to enable the water to reach every part of it, since these regions are normally concealed. (2) Neg. II, 4. (3) Afflicted with leprosy. (4) By the examining priest. (5) *Sc.* if the eruption is high in his arm-pit there is no need for the man to raise his arm higher than he does when hoeing. If, as a result, the priest cannot see it the man must be declared clean. (6) In the case of an eruption in the concealed region of the genitals. (7) When one does not bend too low (cf. prev. n. but one *mut. mut.*). (8) In the case of an eruption in her arm-pit (cf. prev. n. but five *mut. mut*). (9) The reading in the parallel passage in Suk. 6*a* is 'b. Bar Ḥana'. (10) Since it is possible to tie it so closely that no water could penetrate to all its parts. (11) Which cannot be tied very closely. (12) Though they were knotted. (13) *Debar Torah*, lit., 'the word of the (oral) law'. (14) One's hair. (15) When each single hair is knotted. (16) *Sc.* while traditional law restricts a disqualifying interposition to (*a*) its extension over the major part of one's hair and (*b*) the man's objection to it, the Rabbis regard (*a*) without (*b*) or (*b*) without (*a*) also as a disqualifying interposition.

be enacted also against an interposition on its lesser part, to which one does not object, as a preventive measure against the possibility of allowing an interposition over the lesser part to which one does object?[1]—This ruling itself[2] is but a preventive measure, shall we go so far[3] as to institute a preventive measure against the possibility of infringing a preventive measure?[4]

Rab ruled: If a menstruant performs immersion at the proper time[5] she may do it only at night[6] but if she performs it after the proper time[7] she may do it either in the day time or at night.[8] R. Joḥanan ruled: Whether at the proper time or after the proper time a menstruant may perform immersion only at night, on account of the possibility of her daughter's following her lead.[9] Rab, moreover, also withdrew his ruling; for R. Ḥiyya b. Ashi citing Rab laid down: Whether at the proper time or after the proper time[7] a menstruant may perform immersion only at night on account of the possibility of her daughter's following her lead.[9] R. Idi ordained at Narash that immersion shall be performed on the eighth day[10] on account of lions.[11] R. Aḥa b. Jacob issued a similar ordinance at Papunia on account of thieves.[11] Rab Judah did the same at Pumbeditha on account of the cold. Rabbah[12] acted similarly at Maḥoza on account of the guards of the city gates.[13] Said R. Papa[14] to Raba,[15] Consider: At the present time the Rabbis have put all menstruants on the same level as *zabahs*,[16] why then should they not allow them[17] to perform immersion in

(1) Both cases involving a lesser part. (2) The one forbidding an interposition over the lesser part to which one objects. (3) Lit., 'we shall arise'. (4) Certainly not. (5) On the seventh day. (6) Before nightfall the seven prescribed unclean days have not been completed. (7) On the eighth day. (8) Cf. prev. n. but one *mut. mut.* (9) Not knowing the difference between an immersion on the seventh and one on the eighth she, following the example of her mother on an eighth day, would perform immersion in the day time on a seventh also. (10) Instead of the night following the seventh day. (11) That the woman might encounter at night. (12) So with old edd. and Maharsha. Cur. edd., Raba. (13) Who were men of doubtful morality. *Aliter:* Dangerous caverns on the road to the ritual bath. (14) MS.M., Papi. (15) So with Alfasi and Bomb. ed. Cur. edd. insert 'and to Abaye'. (16) Who must allow seven clean days to pass before they can attain cleanness. (17) As in the case of a *zabah*

the daytime of the seventh day?[1]—This cannot be allowed on account of the following ruling of R. Simeon. For it was taught: *After that she shall be clean,*[2] *'after'* means after all of them, implying that no uncleanness may intervene between them; but R. Simeon stated: *After that she shall be clean*[2] implies that after the act[3] she shall[4] be clean, but the Sages have ruled that it was forbidden to do so in case she might thereby land in a doubtful situation.[5]

R. Huna ruled: A woman[6] may wash her head on a Sunday[7] and perform immersion on the following Tuesday,[8] since similarly she[9] is allowed to wash her head[10] on a Friday[11] and undergo immersion on the following Saturday night.[12] A woman may wash her head on a Sunday and undergo immersion on the following Wednesday, since similarly she[13] is allowed to wash her head[14] on a Friday[11] and undergo immersion in the night following a festival that occurred on a Sunday. A woman may wash her head on a Sunday and undergo immersion on the following Thursday, since similarly she may wash her head on a Friday and undergo immersion in the night following the two festival days of the New Year that happened to fall immediately after a Saturday. R. Ḥisda, however, stated: In all these cases[15] we rule as men-

(1) And should one happen to be no *zabah* but a menstruant her uncleanness had in fact terminated seven days earlier. (2) Lev. XV, 28. (3) Of counting the seventh day, even before the day had ended. (4) On performing immersion. (5) Of cleanness. She might have intercourse on that day and experience a discharge subsequently before its termination, in which case her counting as well as her immersion must be deemed invalid, and her intercourse has thus taken place during a period of doubtful cleanness. (6) About to undergo immersion. (7) Lit., 'on the first day of the week'. (8) *Sc.* an interval of a day may be allowed between the washing of her head and her immersion. (9) Whose immersion is due on a Saturday night. (10) An act forbidden on a Saturday which is the Sabbath day. This question is asked on the view that the washing of the head may not be performed on the same night as the immersion, v. *infra*. (11) Lit., 'Sabbath eve'. (12) Lit., 'at the goings out of the Sabbath'. As an interval of one day must inevitably be allowed in this case (cf. prev. nn.) it is also allowed where the interval is merely a matter of the woman's convenience. (13) Whose immersion is due on the termination of a festival day that fell on a Sunday. (14) An act forbidden on a festival day. (15) Where immersion is due on a night that

tioned[1] but we do not draw the inference of 'since similarly'; for where [the avoidance of an interval] is possible an interval must be avoided,[2] and only where this is impossible[3] may an interval be allowed.[4] R. Yemar, however, stated: We may even draw the inferences of 'since similarly'[5] except in the case where a woman is permitted to wash her head on a Sunday and undergo immersion on the following Thursday, for the parallel of the night following the two festival days of the New Year that happened to fall immediately after a Saturday does not hold, since it is possible for the woman to wash her head and undergo immersion in the same night.[6] Meremar in his discourse laid down: The law is in agreement with R. Ḥisda[7] but[8] in accordance with the interpretation of R. Yemar.[9]

The question was raised: May a woman wash her head at night[10]

followed a Sabbath or a festival day on which the washing of one's head is forbidden.

(1) That an interval of a day or more is permitted between the time of the washing of the head and immersion. (2) Lit., 'possible'. (3) As in the cases where the days preceding the nights of immersion are ones on which the washing of the head is forbidden. (4) Lit., 'it is not possible'. (5) *Sc.* an interval may be allowed even on account of a woman's personal convenience, since she is allowed a similar interval when the day preceding the night of her immersion is one on which it is forbidden to wash one's head. (6) The one following the second festival day of the New Year. Had she been allowed to wash her head on the preceding Friday the interval between the washing and the immersion would have been too long; hence it is preferable that the washing be done in the same night as the immersion. As a long interval of three days is not allowed even in such a case, where the washing of the head on the day preceding the night of the immersion is impossible, it cannot be allowed, with much more reason, where the interval is no necessity but a matter of convenience. (7) That 'we do not draw the inference of since similarly' and that, consequently, no interval for the sake of a woman's personal convenience may be allowed between the washing of her head and her immersion. (8) Though R. Ḥisda allows an interval where the day preceding the immersion is one on which labour is forbidden. (9) Who allows the interval only in the first two cases but not in the third case where the immersion is due on the termination of the New Year festival that happened to fall on a Sunday and a Monday. (10) The night in which her immersion is due.

and perform immersion the same night?[1]—Mar Zuṭra forbids this, but R. Ḥinena of Sura permits it. Said R. Adda to R. Ḥinena of Sura:[2] Did not the following incident[3] actually occur[4] to the wife of the exilarch Abba Mari? She having had some quarrel[5] R. Naḥman b. Isaac proceeded to pacify her, and when she said to him, 'What is the hurry now?[6] [68a] There will be time enough to-morrow', he understood what she meant[7] and retorted, 'Are you short of kettles? Are you short of buckets?[8] Are you short of servants?'[9]

Raba delivered the following discourse: A woman may wash her head on the Sabbath eve[10] and perform immersion at the termination of the Sabbath.[11] Said R. Papa to Raba: But did not Rabin send in his letter the message that 'a woman must not wash her head on the Sabbath eve and perform immersion at the termination of the Sabbath'? And, furthermore, is it not surprising to yourself that a woman should be allowed to[12] wash her head in the day time and perform immersion at night seeing that it is required that immersion should follow immediately after the washing of the head, which is not the case here? Raba subsequently appointed an amora[13] in connection with this matter and delivered the following discourse: The statement I made to you is an erroneous one,[14] but in fact it was this that was reported in the name of R. Joḥanan, 'A woman may not wash her head on the Sabbath eve and perform immersion at the termination of the Sabbath'; and, furthermore, it would be surprising that a woman should be allowed to[12] wash her head in the day time and

(1) Is she, it is asked, likely to pay scant attention to the former on account of her hurry to get through with her immersion? (2) Var. lec., R. Adda of Sura to Mar Zuṭra (BaḤ). (3) Which proves that washing the head and immersion may take place the same night. (4) Lit., 'was not thus the incident'. (5) With her husband, as a result of which she refused to perform immersion. (6) At night. (7) Viz., that she had not washed her head before nightfall. (8) *Tashṭeke*. *Aliter:* Bath chairs. *Aliter:* Combs. (9) To bring, and warm up the water. This proves that the washing of the head may take place the same night. (10) Friday. (11) Saturday night. (12) Lit., 'and wonder at yourself how'. (13) To expound and clarify his discourse to the public. (14) Lit., 'they are an error in my hand'.

perform immersion at night seeing that it is required that immersion should closely follow the washing of the head, which would not be the case here. But the law is that a woman may wash her head in the day time and perform immersion at night. And the law is that a woman may wash her head at night only.[1] But does not a contradiction arise between the one law and the other?—There is no contradiction: The former refers to a case where washing in the day time is possible while the latter refers to one where this is impossible.[2]

MISNAH. IF A MENSTRUANT EXAMINED HERSELF ON THE SEVENTH DAY[3] IN THE MORNING AND FOUND HERSELF TO BE CLEAN, AND AT TWILIGHT[4] SHE DID NOT ASCERTAIN HER SEPARATION,[5] AND AFTER SOME DAYS SHE EXAMINED HERSELF AND FOUND THAT SHE WAS UNCLEAN, BEHOLD SHE IS[6] IN A PRESUMPTIVE STATE OF CLEANNESS.[7] IF SHE EXAMINED HERSELF ON THE SEVENTH DAY[8] IN THE MORNING AND FOUND THAT SHE WAS UNCLEAN, AND AT TWILIGHT[9] SHE DID NOT ASCERTAIN HER SEPARATION,[5] AND AFTER A TIME SHE EXAMINED HERSELF AND FOUND THAT SHE WAS CLEAN, BEHOLD SHE IS[6] IN A PRESUMPTIVE STATE OF UNCLEANNESS.[10] SHE[11] CONVEYS, HOWEVER, UNCLEANNESS FOR

(1) *Sc.* immediately before immersion. (2) Where, for instance, immersion is due on a night that follows a Sabbath or a festival day. (3) After her first discharge, *sc.* on the last day of her seven days period of menstruation. (4) When the prescribed menstruation period terminates. (5) Lit., 'she did not separate', *sc.* did not examine herself to make sure of the separation of her clean, from her unclean days. (6) In regard to the days intervening between the seventh and the one on which she found herself unclean. (7) It being assumed that the discharge did not occur before the moment she had discovered it. All clean things which she handled between the time of her immersion (on the night following the seventh day) and the time of her last examination are consequently regarded as clean. (8) After her first discharge, *sc.* on the last day of her seven days' period of menstruation. (9) When the prescribed menstruation period terminates. (10) Since she was known to be unclean on the seventh day and at its twilight she did not ascertain that the discharge had ceased. (11) In the case dealt with in the first clause.

TWENTY-FOUR HOURS RETROSPECTIVELY OR DURING THE TIME BETWEEN THE LAST AND THE PREVIOUS EXAMINATION, BUT IF SHE HAD A SETTLED PERIOD, IT SUFFICES FOR HER TO BE DEEMED UNCLEAN FROM THE TIME OF HER DISCHARGE. R.[1] JUDAH RULED: ANY WOMAN WHO DID NOT,[2] FOLLOWING THE AFTERNOON, ASCERTAIN HER SEPARATION TO A STATE OF CLEANNESS IS REGARDED AS BEING IN A PRESUMPTIVE STATE OF UNCLEANNESS.[3] BUT THE SAGES RULED: EVEN IF SHE EXAMINED HERSELF ON THE SECOND DAY OF HER MENSTRUATION AND FOUND THAT SHE WAS CLEAN, AND AT TWILIGHT SHE DID NOT ASCERTAIN HER SEPARATION, AND AFTER A TIME SHE EXAMINED HERSELF AND FOUND THAT SHE WAS UNCLEAN, SHE IS REGARDED AS BEING IN A PRESUMPTIVE STATE OF CLEANNESS.[4]

GEMARA. It was stated: Rab ruled: She[5] is a certain *zabah*, but Levi ruled: She is a doubtful *zabah*. What do they refer to? If it be suggested: To the first clause [it could be objected]: Was it not stated, BEHOLD SHE IS IN A PRESUMPTIVE STATE OF CLEANNESS? If, on the other hand, they refer[6] to the final clause,[7] one can well see the logic of regarding the woman[8] as a doubtful *zabah*,[9] but why also[10] a certain *zabah* seeing that she has examined herself and found that she was clean?[11]—The fact is that when

(1) V. margl. gl. Cur. edd., 'and R.' (2) On the seventh day. (3) Even though she examined herself earlier in the day and found that she was clean. (4) The examination on the second day being sufficient to establish a presumptive cleanness. (5) This is explained presently. (6) Lit., 'but'. (7) SHE EXAMINED HERSELF ... IN THE MORNING AND FOUND THAT SHE WAS UNCLEAN AND AT TWILIGHT SHE DID NOT ASCERTAIN HER SEPARATION. (8) According to Levi. (9) Since on the seventh day in the morning she was still unclean and since at twilight of that day it was not ascertained that she was clean, it may well be suspected that there was a discharge on the eighth, ninth and tenth in consequence of which she would become a *zabah*. (10) According to Rab. (11) In consequence of which it might justifiably be assumed that as she was now found clean she was also clean previously.

the statements of Rab and Levi were made they were given as independent rulings:[1] If a menstruant examined herself on the seventh day in the morning and found that she was unclean, and at twilight she did not ascertain her separation, and after some days she examined herself and found that she was unclean, Rab ruled: She is a certain *zabah*, but Levi ruled: She is a doubtful *zabah*. 'Rab ruled: She is a certain *zabah*', since she was previously found to be unclean and now also she was found to be unclean, she must be definitely unclean. 'But Levi ruled: She is a doubtful *zabah*', because it might be assumed that the discharge may have been discontinued in the intervening time. [68*b*] Levi also taught the same ruling in a Baraitha: After these days[2] irrespective of whether she examined herself and found that she was clean or whether she examined herself and found that she was unclean, behold she is to be regarded as a doubtful *zabah*.

SHE CONVEYS, HOWEVER, UNCLEANNESS FOR TWENTY-FOUR HOURS RETROSPECTIVELY. Must it be conceded that this[3] represents an objection against a view of Raba, since Raba stated: This[4] tells that[5] a woman during the days of her *zibah* does not[6] cause twenty-four hours retrospective uncleanness?—But was not an objection against Raba raised once before?[7]—It is this that we meant: Must it be conceded that an objection may be raised against Raba from this Mishnah also?—Raba can answer you: When it was stated, SHE CONVEYS, HOWEVER, UNCLEANNESS FOR TWENTY-FOUR HOURS RETROSPECTIVELY, the reference was to the beginning of this chapter, viz., to a girl who observed a discharge while she was still in her father's house.[8]

(1) Not in connection with our Mishnah. (2) Referred to in the second clause of our Mishnah (cf. prev. n. but five). (3) The ruling that if after the passing of her menstruation period a woman found that she was unclean (the first clause in our Mishnah) her uncleanness is retrospective for twenty-four hours (the third clause of our Mishnah which, as explained *supra*, is an interpretation of the first). (4) The first clause of the second Mishnah *supra* 38*b*: Throughout all the eleven days a woman is in a presumptive state of cleanness. (5) Since during the *zibah* period the menstrual flow is suspended. (6) After the first discharge. (7) Of course it was, *supra* 39*a* where the objection remained unsolved. (8) *Supra* 64*b*. In such a case Beth Hillel ruled that intercourse is per-

As it might have been presumed that, since clean days intervened, the discharge should be regarded as one at the beginning of her menstruation and she[1] should in consequence convey no retrospective uncleanness for twenty-four hours, hence we were informed [that she does].

BUT IF SHE HAS A SETTLED PERIOD. Must it be conceded that this[2] presents an objection against the view of R. Huna b. Ḥiyya cited in the name of Samuel, since R. Huna b. Ḥiyya citing Samuel stated: This[3] tells that a woman cannot establish for herself a regular period[4] during the days of her *zibah*?—R. Huna b. Ḥiyya can answer you: When we ruled that 'a woman cannot establish for herself a regular period during the days of her *zibah*' we meant that it is not necessary for her[5] to have a change of period three times for the purpose of abolishing a settled period because we maintain that her blood is suspended; and, since her blood is suspended, IT SUFFICES FOR HER TO BE DEEMED UNCLEAN FROM THE TIME OF HER DISCHARGE.

R. JUDAH RULED. It was taught: They said to R. Judah, Had her hands been lying in her eyes[6] throughout twilight you would have spoken well, but now, since it might be assumed that she experienced a discharge as soon as she removed her hands, what practical difference is there between the case where she ascertained her separation to a state of cleanness on the seventh day following the afternoon and that where she has ascertained her separation

mitted all night, and to this our Mishnah adds that if the woman found subsequently that she was unclean, her uncleanness is retrospective for twenty-four hours.

(1) As a virgin who experienced a discharge for the first time. (2) That IF SHE HAS A SETTLED PERIOD and she observed a discharge at that period in the days of her *zibah*, IT SUFFICES FOR HER TO BE DEEMED UNCLEAN FROM THE TIME OF HER DISCHARGE. It is now assumed that this ruling of our Mishnah referred to the case where AFTER SOME DAYS (viz., after the termination of the menstruation period and during one of *zibah*) SHE EXAMINED HERSELF AND FOUND THAT SHE WAS UNCLEAN. (3) The first clause of the second Mishnah *supra* 38b: Throughout all the eleven days a woman is in a presumptive state of cleanness. (4) Though menstruation began on the same date in three consecutive months. (5) In the days of her *zibah*. (6) Euphemism.

to a state of cleanness on the first day? 'On the first day'! Is there any authority who holds such a view?[1]—Yes; and so it was taught: Rabbi stated, 'I once asked R. Jose and R. Simeon when they were underway: What is the law where a menstruant examined herself on the seventh day in the morning and found that she was clean, and at twilight she did not ascertain her separation,[2] and after some days she examined herself and found that she was unclean? And they replied:[3] Behold such a woman is in a presumptive state of cleanness. What, I asked, is the law where she examined herself on the sixth, fifth, fourth, third or second? And they replied: There is no difference. As regards an examination on the first day I did not ask, but it was a mistake on my part that I did not ask. For is she not on all these days in a state of presumptive uncleanness and yet as soon as the discharge ceased it is deemed to have completely ceased, so also in regard to the first day as soon as the discharge ceased it may be deemed to have ceased completely'.[4] What view, however, did he[5] hold at first?[6]—[That the woman is unclean] since there is[7] the presumption of an open source.

MISHNAH. IF A ZAB AND A ZABAH[8] EXAMINED THEMSELVES ON THE FIRST DAY[9] AND FOUND THEMSELVES CLEAN AND ON THE SEVENTH DAY[9] ALSO AND FOUND THEMSELVES CLEAN, BUT DID NOT EXAMINE THEMSELVES DURING THE OTHER, INTERVENING, DAYS, R. ELIEZER RULED: BEHOLD THESE ARE IN A PRESUMPTIVE CONDITION OF CLEANNESS. R. JOSHUA RULED: THEY ARE ENTITLED [TO RECKON AS

(1) That an examination whereby uncleanness was established on the first day has the same validity as one on the seventh day. (2) From her state of uncleanness to that of cleanness. (3) Lit., 'they said to me' (Emden). Cur. edd. 'they said to him'. (4) A question as to the first day might consequently have elicited the same reply as the one concerning the other days mentioned. (5) Rabbi. (6) When he was reluctant to put the question to them. (7) On the first day. (8) Whose discharge has ceased. (9) Of the prescribed seven days.

CLEAN] ONLY THE FIRST DAY AND THE SEVENTH DAY. R. AKIBA RULED: THEY ARE ENTITLED TO RECKON AS CLEAN THE SEVENTH DAY ALONE.[1]

GEMARA. It was taught: Said R. Eliezer to R. Joshua, According to your view[2] you would be counting with interruptions; but did not the Torah state, *After that she shall be clean,*[3] *'after'* meaning 'after all of them', implying that no uncleanness may intervene between them?[4]—Said R. Joshua to him: But do you not agree that a *zab* who[5] observed an emission of semen[6] or a nazirite who[7] walked under overshadowing branches or mural projections[8] counts with interruptions though the Torah said,[9] *But the former days shall be void?*[10]—And R. Eliezer?[11]—All is well there[12] since the All Merciful has said,[13] *So that he is unclean thereby,*[14] implying that it renders void one day only.[15] And if the imposition of a restriction[16] be suggested, on account of the possibility of mistaking one uncleanness for another,[17] it could be retorted: A *zab* would not be mistaken for one who emitted semen. All is also well[18] with a nazirite who walked under overshadowing

(1) Since it is possible that during the intervening days they have experienced a discharge which caused the counting of the previous days to be null and void. (2) That the first and the seventh days are counted. (3) Lev. XV, 28. (4) How then could the five days that are presumably unclean be allowed to intervene? (5) While he was counting, after the termination of his *zibah*, the prescribed number of seven days. (6) Which renders him unclean for one day while on the following day he resumes his counting from the interrupted number. (7) While counting the thirty days prescribed for him. (8) Under which lay parts of a corpse. As the branches and the projections have the character of a doubtful 'tent' the nazirite is subject to uncleanness for one day only, and on the following one he continues his interrupted counting. (9) Where a longer uncleanness interrupted the counting. (10) Num. VI, 12. (11) How in view of this argument of R. Joshua can he maintain his ruling? (12) The case of a *zab* who emitted semen where an interrupted counting is allowed. (13) About such an uncleanness. (14) Lev. XV, 32, emphasis on the last word. (15) Lit., 'its day'. (16) That interrupted counting should not be allowed. (17) And, as a result, such interrupted counting would also be allowed in the case of a discharge of *zibah*. (18) With the permission for interrupted counting.

branches or mural projections, since Pentateuchally it is necessary[1] that the [overshadowing] tent shall be a proper one and it is only the Rabbis who enacted the ruling[2] as a preventive measure, and no one would mistake a Rabbinic law for a Pentateuchal one; but here,[3] if we were to take into consideration the possibility of a doubtful observation,[4] one might mistake this case for one of a certain observation.[5]

It was taught: R. Jose and R. Simeon stated, The view of R. Eliezer is more feasible than that of R. Joshua, and the view of R. Akiba is more acceptable than those of all of them, but the *halachah* is in agreement with R. Eliezer.

The question was raised: If a *zab* or a *zabah* examined themselves on the first day[6] and on the eighth day[7] and found that they were clean while on the other days they did not examine themselves, [69a] what is the law according to R. Eliezer.[8] Is it necessary[9] that an examination should take place both at the beginning and at the end of the prescribed days[10] [hence this case is excluded][11] since there was one at the beginning only[12] but not at the end,[13] or is it possible that an examination at the beginning[12] suffices although there was none at the end?[13]—Rab replied: The law is the same in either case,[14] an examination at the beginning sufficing although there was none at the end. R. Ḥanina, however, replied: It is necessary[9] that there be an examination

(1) If corpse uncleanness is to be conveyed by overshadowing. (2) That even an imperfect 'tent' conveyed uncleanness for one day. (3) The case discussed by R. Eliezer and R. Joshua. (4) On the days on which no examination took place; and, in consequence, those days would not be counted. (5) And, assuming that on the uncounted days the woman was definitely unclean, one would also allow interrupted counting in the case of the intervention of a certain uncleanness. (6) Of the seven that must be counted after a *zibah* before cleanness is attained. (7) Cf. prev. n. The eighth day is the one that follows the period of the seven prescribed days in which obviously it is not included. (8) Who, in the case of an examination on the first and the seventh, regards all the seven days as clean. (9) If the seven days are to be regarded as clean. (10) Lit., 'their beginning and their end'. (11) And the days are regarded as unclean. (12) On the first of the seven days. (13) On the seventh day, the examination having taken place on the eighth. (14) Lit., 'it it', the seven days are regarded as clean in both cases.

both at the beginning and at the end[1] [hence this case is excluded] since there was one at the beginning only but not at the end.

An objection was raised: But both hold the same opinion,[2] where a *zab* and a *zabah* examined themselves on the first day and on the eighth day and found themselves clean, that they may count the eighth day only as clean.[3] Now who are referred to in the expression 'both hold the same opinion'? Is it not R. Eliezer and R. Joshua?[4]—No; R. Joshua and R. Akiba.[5]

R. Shesheth citing R. Jeremiah b. Abba who had it from Rab stated: If a menstruant has ascertained her separation to a state of cleanness on her third day,[6] she may count it in the number of the seven clean days.[7] 'A menstruant'! What need has she for counting?[8]—Rather read: If a *zabah* has ascertained her separation to a state of cleanness on her third day,[6] she may count it in the number of the seven clean days.[7] Said R. Shesheth to R. Jeremiah b. Abba: Did then Rab pronounce his ruling in agreement with the view of the Samaritans who ruled that the day on which a woman ceases to have her discharge may be counted by her in the number of the prescribed seven days?[9]—When Rab spoke he meant: Exclusive of the third day.[10] But if 'exclusive of the third day' is not the ruling obvious?—The ruling was necessary only in a case, for instance, where the woman[11] did not examine herself until the seventh day,[12] so that[13] we were informed there[14]

(1) Lit., 'their beginning and their end'. (2) Lit., 'and equal'. (3) Lit., 'that they have only the eighth day'. (4) Who agree in this case with R. Akiba though they differ from him where the examination took place on the first and the seventh. How then could Rab maintain his view on the ruling of R. Eliezer? (5) But R. Eliezer maintains, as Rab stated, that since the examination on the first day proved the person to be clean all the seven days also are regarded as clean. (6) Since her discharge first appeared. (7) *Sc.* the clean days may begin to be counted from that day. (8) None, since a menstruant becomes clean after seven days irrespective of whether these were clean or not. (9) *Supra* 33a. (10) The counting beginning from the following day. (11) Though her discharge ceased on the third day. (12) So that the beginning of the counting was not in a condition of ascertained cleanness. (13) Rab adopting two relaxations of the law. (14) Where Rab stated that R. Eliezer holds the woman clean if she examined herself on the first and the eighth.

that an examination at the beginning[1] suffices although there was none at the end,[2] while here[3] we were informed that an examination at the end[2] suffices[4] even though there was none at the beginning.[1] As it might have been presumed that only where there was an examination at the beginning,[1] though there was none at the end,[2] do we assume [the days to be clean], because we regard them as remaining in their presumptive state,[5] but not where the examination was held at their conclusion[2] and[6] not at their beginning,[1] hence we were informed [that in either case the days are regarded as clean]. But can this[7] be correct seeing that[8] when Rabin came[9] he stated, 'R. Jose b. Ḥanina raised an objection [from a Baraitha dealing with] a forgetful[10] woman but I do not know what his objection was', and[11] we have an established rule that during the first week of her appearance before us we require her to undergo immersion in the nights[12] but we do not require her to undergo immersion in the day time. Now if it could be entertained that it is not necessary that the days[13] be counted in our presence, she[14] should have been made to undergo immersion in the day time also, since it is possible that she gave birth during a *zibah* period and had completed the counting on that day. Must it not consequently be inferred from the ruling that it is necessary for the counting to take place in our presence?[15] —But have we not explained this ruling to be in agreement with the view of R. Akiba who ruled that it was necessary for the counting to take place in our presence?[16]—And whence do you

(1) On the first day. (2) On the seventh. (3) In the last cited ruling of Rab. (4) To justify the assumption that all the six preceding days were also clean. (5) Which, owing to the examination, was known to be one of cleanness. (6) Lit., 'although'. (7) Rab's ruling that it is not necessary to make sure that each of the seven days individually has been a clean one. (8) Lit., 'I am not, for surely'. (9) From Palestine to Babylon. (10) Lit., 'erring'. (11) So with BaḤ. Cur. edd. 'for'. (12) Since of each night it might be said that it is the one following the seventh day of the period of uncleanness prescribed after the birth of a male child. (13) Following *zibah*. (14) Since a *zabah* undergoes immersion on her seventh clean day. (15) Apparently it must; and thus an objection arises against Rab. (16) And, since the Rabbis differ from R. Akiba, Rab may follow their view.

infer that according to the Rabbis it is not necessary for the counting to take place in our presence?—From what was taught:[1] 'If a forgetful[2] woman stated, "I observed some uncleanness on a certain day",[3] she[4] is expected to undergo nine immersions, seven[5] in respect of menstruation[6] and two[7] in respect of *zibah*.[8] If she states, "I observed some uncleanness at twilight", she is to undergo eleven immersions'. 'Eleven'! For what purpose?[9]—R. Jeremiah of Difti replied: This is a case, for instance, where the woman[10] actually appeared before us at twilight,[11] so that provision has to be made for[12] eight immersions in respect of menstruation[13] and for three in respect of *zibah*.[14] 'If she states, "I

(1) V. marg. glos. Cur. edd., 'for we learnt'. (2) Lit., 'erring'. (3) But she is unable to say whether it happened on the same, or on any other day, or whether that day was one of the days of her menstruation or of her *zibah*. (4) In order to perform the precept of immersion at the proper time and at the earliest possible moment. (5) On the following seven nights, if she arrived in the day time. (6) V. *supra* p. 482, n. 12. (7) In the day time. (8) On the first day of her arrival she must undergo immersion since it is possible that the previous day was one of her *zibah* period and her discharge appeared that day (a woman who experienced a discharge on one of the days of her *zibah* period awaits one day, viz., the following one, and on that day she undergoes immersion in the day time). On the second day of her arrival she again undergoes immersion for a similar reason, since it is possible that the day on which her discharge had appeared was not the previous one but the day of her arrival. On the third day no immersion is necessary since it is certain that on the second there was no discharge. (9) *Sc.* why should more immersions be required in this case, where she states that her discharge took place at twilight, than in the former where she does not specify the time of day. (10) Who did not merely state during the day that her discharge took place at twilight. (11) And stated that her discharge occurred either earlier or possibly at that very moment when it is doubtful whether it was day or night. (12) Lit., 'and they are'. (13) In addition to the seven immersions as in the former case (beginning on the night that followed the twilight at which she arrived) there must be one on the eighth night because it is possible that her discharge took place actually at the twilight of her arrival which was part of the following night, so that the menstruation period did not terminate until the seven following days have passed and her cleanness is attained by her immersion on the last, which is the eighth night after her arrival. (14) She performs the first two immersions for the same reason as in the former case, since it is possible that her discharge in *zibah* took place on the

observed no discharge whatsoever", she is to undergo fifteen immersions'.[1] Raba observed: 'This kind of law that is a negation of all reason[2] is in vogue at Galḥi where there is a law that one who owns a bull must feed the town's cattle one day while one who owns no bull must feed them on two days. Once they had occasion to deal with[3] an orphan the son of a widow. Having been entrusted with the bulls [to feed] he proceeded to kill them, saying to the people, "He who owned a bull shall receive one hide and he who owned no bull shall receive two hides". "What", they said to him, "is this that you say?" "The conclusion of this process", he answered them, "follows the same principle as the beginning of the process. Was it not the case with the beginning of this process that one who owned nothing was better off? Well, at the conclusion of the process too, one who owned nothing is better off". Here also: If where a woman states, "I observed a discharge", it suffices for her to undergo either nine immersions or eleven immersions,[4] should it be necessary for her, where she states, "I observed no discharge whatsoever", to undergo fifteen immersions?'—Rather read thus: If she states, 'I observed a discharge and I do not know how long it continued[5] and whether I observed it during a menstruation period or a *zibah* one', she is to undergo fifteen immersions. For if she appeared before us in the day time we allow her seven days in respect of menstruation[4] [69*b*] and eight in respect of *zibah*;[6] and if she appeared before

day prior to her arrival (so that immersion must be performed immediately at the twilight when she arrived) or on that day (so that immersion has to be performed on the following day). She must also undergo immersion on the third day since it is possible that the discharge occurred at the twilight at which she arrived and that that time was a part of the night, so that she was unclean on the day following, and having waited the second day she becomes clean on the third when the immersion is performed.

(1) This is discussed presently. (2) Lit., 'this law that is no law'. (3) Lit., 'it happened to them'. (4) As explained *supra*. (5) *Sc.* whether it appeared on one day only or on three days. (6) Because each of the eight days might be the last of the seven clean days that followed a *zibah* discharge that had extended over three days. No immersion is necessary on the ninth day because even if the very day of the woman's arrival had been the last of

us at night we allow her eight in respect of menstruation[1] and seven in respect of *zibah*.[2] But does not menstruation require eight days?[3]—Rather say: In either case[4] seven in respect of menstruation and eight in respect of *zibah*. But if she appeared at night, does she not require[3] eight in respect of menstruation?[5]—In respect of *zibah* where the number of immersions is fixed, since it does not vary whether she appeared before us in the day time or at night, [the eighth immersion] was counted, but in respect of menstruation where the number is not fixed, for only where she appeared before us at night does she require eight immersions while if she appeared before us in the day time she does not require eight [the eighth immersion] was not counted. Now, if it could be entertained that it is necessary for all the counting to take place in our presence, what need is there[6] for all these immersions?[7] Should she not rather count the seven days and then undergo immersion?[8] Consequently it may be inferred from here that[9] it is the Rabbis[10] who hold that it is not necessary for the counting to take place in our presence.[11] Said R. Aḥa son of R. Joseph to R. Ashi, Have we not had recourse to explanations of this ruling?[12] Explain it then in the following manner and read thus: If a woman states, 'I counted[13] and know not how many days I counted and whether I counted them during the period

the three days on which her *zibah* discharge had been making its appearance, seven clean days have elapsed since that day.

(1) On the first night of her arrival and on the following six nights immersion is necessary because each might be the night following the seventh day, while on the eighth immersion is required on account of the possibility of the discharge having appeared on the very of night of her arrival which caused the day following to be regarded as the first of the prescribed seven days of menstruation. (2) This is discussed presently. (3) As explained *supra*. (4) Whether the woman arrived at night or in the day time. (5) Of course she does. (6) In respect of *zibah*. (7) That the woman is expected to perform in the day time. (8) But not before; since even if her seven clean days have terminated she, owing to her neglect of examining herself, is not fit for immersion. (9) As submitted *supra* 69a. (10) Who differ from R. Akiba. (11) And Rab in his ruling *supra* follows their view. (12) We had; since in the absence of explanations it bristles with difficulties. (13) *Sc*. she examined herself on certain days and ascertained that she was then clean.

of menstruation or during that of *zibah'*, she is to undergo fifteen immersions.[1] But if she stated, 'I counted and know not how many days I counted', it is at any rate impossible that she should not have counted one day, at least, is she then not short of one immersion?[2] Rather read: If she states, 'I know not whether I did or did not count'.[3]

MISHNAH. IF A ZAB, A ZABAH, A MENSTRUANT, A WOMAN AFTER CHILDBIRTH OR A LEPER HAVE DIED [THEIR CORPSES] CONVEY UNCLEANNESS BY CARRIAGE[4] UNTIL THE FLESH HAS DECAYED. IF AN IDOLATER HAS DIED HE CONVEYS NO UNCLEANNESS.[5] BETH SHAMMAI RULED: ALL WOMEN DIE AS MENSTRUANTS;[4] BUT BETH HILLEL RULED: A WOMAN[6] CANNOT BE REGARDED AS A MENSTRUANT UNLESS SHE DIED WHILE SHE WAS IN MENSTRUATION.

GEMARA. What is the meaning of BY CARRIAGE? If it be suggested: By actual carriage, [the objection would arise:] Does not in fact every corpse convey uncleanness by carriage?[7]—Rather say that BY CARRIAGE means[8] through a heavy[9] stone,[10] for[11] it is written, *And a stone was brought, and laid*[12] *upon the mouth of the den.*[13] What is the reason?[14]—Rab replied: This[15] is a preventive

(1) As explained *supra.* (2) Obviously she is; why then was the number given fifteen and not fourteen? (3) So that it is possible that she did not count even one clean day. (4) This is discussed in the Gemara *infra.* (5) Lit., 'clean from causing uncleanness'. (6) Who died. (7) Of course it does; why then did our Mishnah restrict it to the classes specified? (8) Lit., 'but what by carriage'. (9) *Mesamma,* lit., 'closing' (cf. foll. n.). (10) One used for closing up a pit. If the corpse lay on such a heavy stone, and certain objects rested under it, the latter contract the uncleanness though the weight of the corpse can hardly be perceptible. (11) The following explains the etymology of *mesamma* ('heavy'). (12) *Wesumath,* a word of a sound similar to *mesamma* (v. prev. n. but two). (13) Dan. VI, 18. (14) Why the corpses enumerated in our Mishnah convey uncleanness through the stone mentioned while others do not. (15) The enactment that the corpses enumerated in our Mishnah shall convey uncleanness even through a heavy stone.

measure against the case where they[1] swoon.[2] One taught: In the name of R. Eliezer it was stated, This possibility must be taken into consideration until his stomach bursts.

IF AN IDOLATER HAS DIED etc. It was taught: Rabbi stated, On what ground did they rule that if an idolater has died he conveys no uncleanness by carriage? Because his uncleanness when alive[3] is not Pentateuchal but Rabbinical.

Our Rabbis taught: Twelve questions did the Alexandrians address to R. Joshua b. Hananiah.[4] Three were of a scientific nature,[5] three were matters of *aggada*, three were mere nonsense and three were matters of conduct.[6]

'Three were of a scientific nature': If a *zab*, a *zabah*, a menstruant, a woman after childbirth or a leper have died, how long do their corpses convey uncleanness by carriage? He replied: Until the flesh has decayed. Is the daughter of a woman that was divorced and remarried by her first husband[7] allowed to marry a priest? Do we say that this might be inferred *a minori ad majus*: If the son of a widow who was married to a High Priest, who is not forbidden to all,[8] is nevertheless tainted,[9] how much more so the offspring of her[10] who is forbidden to all;[11] or is it possible to refute the argument, thus: The case of a widow married to a High Priest is different because she herself is profaned?[12] He replied: [70a]

(1) The persons mentioned. (2) As such persons when alive, if they sit on such a stone, convey uncleanness to objects under it in accordance with Pentateuchal law, a Rabbinic enactment has imposed a similar restriction when they are dead in case they might be merely in a swoon and mistaken for a corpse. Were the objects to be deemed clean in the case of a corpse they might erroneously be deemed clean even when the person is alive. (3) Through *zibah*, for instance. (4) V. marg. glos. and Bomb. ed. Cur. edd., 'Ḥinena'. (5) *Halachah*. (6) Lit., 'the way of the earth', worldly affairs. (7) After she had been married and divorced by a second husband. Such a marriage is forbidden according to Deut. XXIV, 1-4. (8) A widow being forbidden to a High Priest only (v. Lev. XXI, 14). (9) Though not actually a bastard he would be, if of priestly stock, disqualified from the priesthood. (10) A remarried divorcee after she had been married and divorced by another man. (11) Non-priests as well as priests. (12) If the High Priest to whom she was unlawfully married dies she may not marry even a common priest, and if she was a priest's daughter she is henceforth forbidden to eat *terumah*. No

She is an abomination,[1] but her children are no abomination. If the sacrifices of two lepers were mixed up and after the sacrifice of one of them was offered[2] one of them died, what is to be done about the other?[3] He replied: He assigns[4] his possessions to others so that he becomes a poor man and then[5] brings a bird sin-offering which may be brought[6] even in a case of doubt. But is there not also a guilt-offering?[7]—Samuel replied: This[8] applies only where his guilt-offering had been duly offered.[9] R. Shesheth observed: A great man like Samuel should say such a thing! In agreement with whose view [could his answer[10] have been given]? If in agreement with that of R. Judah,[11] [the difficulty arises:] Did he not state that[12] the guilt-offering[13] determines a person's status,[14] so that since the guilt-offering determined for him[15] a status of wealth he could no longer bring a sin-offering in

such restrictions are imposed on the woman who was remarried after her divorcement.

(1) Deut. XXIV, 4, dealing with a remarried divorcee. Emphasis on '*she*'. (2) It being unknown whose sacrifice it was. (3) The survivor. *Sc.* how is he to attain cleanness? He cannot bring the second sacrifice, since it may possibly be the one that belonged to the dead man and a sin-offering whose owner is dead may not be offered upon the altar; and he cannot bring a new sacrifice, since it is possible that the one that was already offered was his so that he is now exempt from bringing any other sacrifice and the new one he would bring would have no sanctity and, as an unconsecrated animal, is forbidden to be brought into the Temple court. (4) Lit., 'writes'. (5) Exercising the privilege of the poor. (6) Into the Temple. (7) Which a leper, whether rich or poor, must bring. Of course there is. Now since the sacrifice (presumably both the sin- and the guilt-offerings) were mixed up, how can he bring an animal as a guilt-offering in a case of doubt? (8) R. Joshua's ruling. (9) Before the other leper died. (10) 'Where his guilt-offering had been duly offered'. (11) Who, holding that a guilt-offering may not be brought conditionally, could find no remedy for the leper if his guilt-offering had not been offered up before. (12) Cf. marg. n., Rashi and Bomb. ed. Cur. edd., 'for he said'. (13) The first of the three sacrifices which a leper must bring at the termination of his uncleanness. (14) *Sc.* if at that time he was rich or poor his other two sacrifices must be those prescribed for a rich or poor man respectively, irrespective of whether at the time he brings the latter his condition has changed from wealth to poverty of from poverty to wealth. (15) Lit., 'for itself', dative of advantage.

the state of poverty? For we have learnt, 'If a leper brought the sacrifice of a poor man[1] and then[2] became rich or if he brought that of a rich man[3] and became poor, all depends[4] on[5] the sin-offering;[6] so R. Simeon. R.[7] Judah ruled: All depends on the guilt-offering.[8] R. Eliezer b. Jacob ruled: All depends on the birds'.[9] And if [Samuel has given his answer] in agreement with the view of R. Simeon who ruled that the sin-offering[10] determines the man's status,[11] why should he not bring another sacrifice[12] even where the guilt-offering had not been offered,[13] for, surely, we have heard R. Simeon say, 'Let him bring one and make his stipulation'; for it was taught: R. Simeon ruled,[14] On the morrow[15] he brings his guilt-offering and its *log*[16] with it, places it at the Nikanor gate[17] and pronounces over it the following stipulation: If he is a leper, behold his guilt-offering and its *log*[16] with it, and if he is not, let this guilt-offering be a freewill peace-offering. Now this guilt-offering[18] is [70*b*] to be slain[19] in the north[20] and is subject to the requirements of application[19] to the thumbs,[21] leaning,[22] drink-offerings, waving[23] and the presentation of the breast and shoulder to the priest.[23] It may also be eaten by the priestly males on the same day and the following night;[19] but

(1) A bird. (2) Before bringing his burnt-offering, the last of the prescribed sacrifices. (3) A ewe-lamb. (4) As regards the burnt-offering. (5) Lit., 'follows'. (6) Cf. p. 488, n. 15 *mut. mut.* (7) V. marg. n. Cur. edd. 'and R.' (8) Cf. p. 488, n. 15. (9) Which the leper brings seven days before the ritual cutting of his hair. His financial condition at that time determines whether the sacrifices he is to bring later are to be those of a rich man or of a poor man. (10) And not the guilt-offering. (11) So that even though the guilt-offering was brought when the man was rich he may still bring a poor man's sin-offering if he subsequently became poor. (12) As a conditional guilt-offering (v. *infra*). (13) And the adoption of this procedure would remove the necessity for Samuel to limit the case *supra* to one who had already brought his guilt-offering. (14) In the case of a doubtful leprosy. (15) The day following immersion on which the sacrifices have to be brought. (16) Of oil. (17) Of the Temple court. A leper is not permitted to enter into the court. (18) Being subject to the requirements of both guilt-offerings and peace-offerings. (19) As a guilt-offering. (20) Of the altar. (21) Cf. Lev. XIV, 17. (22) As a peace-offering (cf. Lev. III, 2). (23) As peace-offerings.

the Sages did not agree with R. Simeon because[1] one might[2] cause holy things[3] to be brought into the place of disqualified sacrifices.[4]—Samuel may hold the same view as R. Simeon in one respect[5] while differing from him in another.[6]

'Three were matters of *aggada*': One verse says, *For I have no pleasure in the death of him that dieth*,[7] but another verse says, *Because the Lord would slay them?*[8]—The former refers to those who are penitents while the latter refers to those who are not penitent. One verse says, *Who regardeth not persons*,[9] *nor taketh reward*,[10] but another verse says, *The Lord lift up His countenance upon thee?*[11]—The former refers to the time before sentence is passed while the latter refers to the time after the sentence has been passed. One verse says, *For the Lord hath chosen Zion*,[12] but another verse says, *For this city*[13] *hath been to Me a provocation of Mine anger and of My fury from the day that they built it even unto this day?*[14]—The former applied to the time before Solomon married the daughter of Pharaoh while the latter applied to the time after Solomon married the daughter of Pharaoh.

'Three were mere nonsense': Does the wife of Lot[15] convey uncleanness? He replied: A corpse conveys uncleanness but no pillar of salt conveys uncleanness. Does the son of the Shunamite[16] convey uncleanness?[17] He replied: A corpse conveys uncleanness but no live person conveys uncleanness. Will the dead in the

(1) By restricting the time of consumption to a day and a night. (2) If some of the sacrificial meat remained after the day and the night (cf. prev. n.) have passed. (3) *Sc.* this sacrifice which, in case the man was no leper, is a peace-offering that may be eaten on two days. (4) Lit., 'the house of disqualification', the enclosure where disqualified sacrificial meat was burnt. Now since Samuel follows R. Simeon and the latter allows a conditional sacrifice why was it necessary for the former to explain (*supra* 70*a*) that the guilt-offering had been offered while the man was rich? (5) That the guilt-offering of a leper does not determine his financial condition in regard to his other two sacrifices. (6) Maintaining, contrary to R. Simeon's view, that a guilt-offering may not be offered up conditionally. (7) Ezek. XVIII, 32. (8) I Sam. II, 25. (9) Heb. *lo yissa panim*, lit., 'shall not lift up the countenance'. (10) Deut. X, 17. (11) Num. VI, 26. (12) Ps. CXXXII, 13. (13) Zion. (14) Jer. XXXII, 31. (15) Who became a pillar of salt (Gen. XIX, 26.). (16) Whom Elisha restored to life (II Kings IV, 35). (17) As if he were still dead.

hereafter[1] require to be sprinkled upon[2] on the third and the seventh[3] or will they not require it? He replied: When they will be resurrected we shall go into the matter.[4] Others say: When our Master Moses will come with them.

'Three were concerned with matters of conduct': What must a man do that he may become wise? He replied: Let him engage much in study[5] and a little in business. Did not many, they said, do so and it was of no avail to them?—Rather, let them pray for mercy from Him to whom is the wisdom, for it is said, *For the Lord giveth wisdom, out of His mouth cometh knowledge and discernment.*[6] R. Ḥiyya taught: This[7] may be compared to the action of a mortal king who prepared for his servants a banquet but to his friends he sent from that which he had before himself. What then[8] does he[9] teach us?[10]—That one without the other[11] does not suffice. What must a man do that he may become rich? He replied: Let him engage much in business[12] and deal honestly. Did not many, they said to him, do so but it was of no avail to them?—Rather, let him pray for mercy from Him to whom are the riches, for it is said, *Mine is the silver, and Mine the gold.*[13] What then[14] does he[15] teach us?[16]—That one without the other[17] does not suffice. What must a man do that he may have male children? He replied: He shall marry a wife that is worthy of him [71*a*] and conduct himself in modesty[18] at the time of marital intercourse. Did not many, they said to him, act in this manner but it did not avail them?—Rather, let him pray for mercy from Him to whom are the children,

(1) At the resurrection. (2) As is the case with one who was in contact with a corpse. (3) Of the seven days that are to be counted after one had contracted corpse uncleanness. (4) Lit., 'we shall be wise about them'. (5) Lit., 'in sitting (in the schoolhouse)'. (6) Prov. II, 6. (7) The knowledge that is given 'out of His mouth'. (8) Seeing that one has in any case to pray for mercy. (9) Samuel who stated, 'Let him engage much' etc. (10) *Sc.* what is the use of study if mercy from heaven must in any case be sought? (11) Study without prayer and *vice-versa.* (12) 'Engage ... business' is deleted by Elijah Wilna. (13) Hag. II, 8. (14) Seeing that one has in any case to pray for mercy. (15) Samuel who stated, 'Let him engage much' etc. (16) Cf. prev. n. but five *mut. mut.* (17) Honest dealing without prayer and *vice versa.* (18) Cf. Rashi. Lit., 'and sanctify himself'.

for it is said, *Lo, children are a heritage of the Lord; the fruit of the womb is a reward.*[1] What then[2] does he teach us? That one without the other does dot suffice. What is exactly meant by '*the fruit of the womb is a reward*'?—R. Ḥama son of R. Ḥanina replied: As a reward for containing oneself during intercourse in the womb, in order that one's wife may emit the semen first, the Holy One, blessed be He, gives one the reward of the fruit of the womb.

BETH SHAMMAI RULED etc. What is Beth Shammai's reason? If it be suggested: Because it is written, *And the queen was exceedingly pained,*[3] and Rab explained, 'This teaches that she had experienced a menstrual discharge', so that here also,[4] owing to the fright of the angel of death, she experiences a discharge [it could be retorted]: Have we not in fact learnt that fear causes blood to disappear?[5]—This is no difficulty since fear[5] detains it while sudden fright[6] loosens it. But [then what of] that which was taught,[7] 'Beth Shammai stated: All men die as *zabs* and Beth Hillel stated: No dying man is deemed to be a *zab* unless he died when he was actually one', why[8] should not one apply here[9] the text, *Out of his flesh*[10] but not on account of a mishap?[11]—Beth Shammai's reason is rather as it was taught: Formerly they were wont to subject to ritual immersion all utensils that had been used by dying menstruants,[12] but as living menstruants felt ashamed in consequence[13] it was enacted that utensils used by all dying women should be subject to immersion,[14] out of a deference to the living menstruants. Formerly they were wont to subject to ritual immer-

(1) Ps. CXXVII, 3. (2) Seeing that one has in any case to pray for mercy. (3) Est. IV, 4. (4) The case of dying women spoken of in our Mishnah. (5) *Supra* 39a, Soṭ. 20b. (6) As was the case with Esther or with a dying woman who sees the angel of death. (7) So MS.M. Cur. edd., 'we have learnt'. (8) According to Beth Shammai, if in their opinion the discharge is due to the fright of the angel of death. (9) The discharge of a dying man. (10) Lev. XV, 2; only in that case is the man unclean. (11) In which case he is clean; and since a discharge that is due to the fright of the angel of death is evidently a mishap, why should the man be unclean? (12) Since uncleanness is conveyed from the person to the utensils. (13) For being differentiated from all other women even when dying. (14) Even though they did not come in contact with them after death.

sion utensils used by dying *zabs*,[1] but as living *zabs* felt ashamed in consequence it was enacted that utensils used by all dying men[2] should be subject to ritual immersion, out of deference to the living *zabs*.[3]

MISHNAH. IF A WOMAN DIED AND A QUARTER OF A LOG OF BLOOD ISSUED FROM HER, IT[4] CONVEYS UNCLEANNESS AS A BLOODSTAIN[5] AND IT[6] ALSO CONVEYS UNCLEANNESS BY OVERSHADOWING.[7] R. JUDAH RULED: IT DOES NOT CONVEY UNCLEANNESS AS A STAIN, SINCE IT WAS DETACHED AFTER SHE HAD DIED.[8] R. JUDAH, HOWEVER, AGREES THAT WHERE A WOMAN SITTING ON THE TRAVAILING STOOL DIED AND A QUARTER OF A LOG OF BLOOD ISSUED FROM HER, IT[9] CONVEYS UNCLEANNESS AS A BLOODSTAIN.[5] R. JOSE RULED: HENCE[9] IT CONVEYS NO UNCLEANNESS BY OVERSHADOWING.[10]

GEMARA. Does it then follow[11] that the first Tanna[12] holds that even though blood was detached after she died[13] it conveys uncleanness as a bloodstain?[14]—Ze'iri[15] replied: The difference between them[16] is[17] the question whether the interior of the uterus is unclean.[18]

(1) V. p. 492, n. 12. (2) V. p. 492, n. 14. (3) Tosef. Nid. IX, M.Ḳ. 27b; from which it follows that the reason for the uncleanness of the utensils any dying person had used is a Rabbinical enactment instituted in deference to the feeling of living menstruants and *zabs*. This reason is also that of Beth Shammai in our Mishnah. (4) *Sc*. the minutest drop of the blood. (5) Of a menstrual discharge. As the blood of a corpse it could convey no uncleanness unless it consisted of no less a quantity than a quarter of a *log*. (6) If all the quarter-*log* is accumulated. (7) As the blood of a corpse. (8) When menstrual uncleanness does not apply. (9) Since it was detached while the woman was still alive. (10) Only a corpse or the prescribed minimum of a part of it conveys uncleanness in this manner. (11) From R. Judah's ruling. (12) From whom R. Judah obviously differs. (13) When menstrual uncleanness does not apply. (14) But on what ground could such a view be justified?. (15) So MS.M. Cur. edd. in parenthesis add, 'R.' (16) R. Judah and the first Tanna. (17) Not the point whether the blood is menstrual or not. (18) According to the first Tanna it is unclean, hence the uncleanness of the

R. JUDAH, HOWEVER, AGREES. Does it then follow that the first Tanna[1] holds that it conveys uncleanness by overshadowing also?[2]—Rab Judah replied: The difference between them[3] is[4] the question of mingled blood;[5] for it was taught: What is meant by 'mingled blood'?[6] R. Eleazar son of R. Judah explained: If blood issued from a slain man both while he was still alive and when he was dead and it is doubtful whether [a full quarter of a *log*] issued while he was still alive or when he was already dead or whether it partly issued while he was alive and partly while he was dead, such is mingled blood.[6] But the Sages[7] ruled: In a private domain such a case of doubt is unclean while in a public domain such a case of doubt is clean. What then is meant by 'mingled blood'?[6] If a quarter of a *log* of blood issued from a slain man both while he was still alive and when he was dead and the flow had not yet ceased[8] and[9] it is doubtful whether the greater part[10] issued

blood that was within it when the woman was alive though when it emerged the woman was dead and no longer subject to the uncleanness of menstruation. According to R. Judah it is clean.

(1) With whom R. Judah agrees only on the one point mentioned. Rashi and Meharsha read 'R. Jose' for 'the first Tanna'. (2) But how could uncleanness be conveyed in this manner, seeing that the blood issued when the woman was still alive? (3) R. Judah and the first Tanna. (4) Not, as has been assumed, the question whether the blood is subject to corpse uncleanness. (5) *Sc.* the blood of a corpse mingled with that of a living person. According to R. Judah, since it is doubtful whether all the blood was detached while the woman was still alive or whether part of it was detached after she died, it is regarded as mingled blood which Rabbinically conveys uncleanness by overshadowing (though Pentateuchally it cannot do so unless the prescribed minimum had been detached after death), while the first Tanna (or R. Jose according to Rashi and Meharsha) maintains that, since the woman was in travail, all the blood that issued may be presumed to have been detached while she was alive so that the question of mingled blood does not arise. (6) The corpse uncleanness of which is Rabbinic, and is conveyed by overshadowing. (7) Maintaining that in such a case, since one must take into account the possibility that all the quarter of a *log* may have issued after death, a possible Pentateuchal uncleanness is involved. (8) So that it is yet possible for the quantity of blood to increase to the prescribed minimum of a quarter of a *log*. Where the flow ceased, so that it is certain that the blood issuing after death will never make up the prescribed minimum, not even a Rabbinical prohi-

while he was alive and the lesser part when he was dead or whether the lesser part issued while he was alive and the greater part when he was dead, such is mingled blood.[1] R. Judah ruled: The blood of a slain man, from whom a quarter of a *log* of blood issued while he was lying in a bed with his blood dripping into a hole, is unclean, because the drop of death is mingled with it, but the Sages hold it to be clean[2] because[3] [71b] each single drop[4] is detached from the other.[5] But did not the Rabbis speak well to R. Judah?[6]—R. Judah follows his own principle, for he laid down that no blood can neutralize other blood.[7] R. Simeon ruled: If the blood of a man crucified upon the beam was flowing slowly[8] to the ground, and a quarter of a *log* of blood was found under him, it is unclean.[9] R. Judah declared it clean, since it might be held[10] that the drop of death remained on the beam. But why should not R. Judah say to himself[11] 'Since it might be held[10] that the drop of death remained on the bed'?—[The case of blood] in a bed is different[12] since it percolates.[13]

MISHNAH. FORMERLY IT WAS RULED: A WOMAN WHO

bition is imposed (cf. Tosaf. Asheri). (9) Though it is certain that a full quarter of a *log* of blood did not issue after death. (10) Of the quarter.

(1) V. p. 494, n. 6. (2) Even if the greater part issued after his death. (3) Since the blood did not emerge in a continuous flow but in single drops. (4) Lit., 'first first'. (5) And so soon as it drops into the hole it becomes neutralized in the clean blood that issued while the man was still alive. Only where the flow of the blood is continuous and the man lies on the ground, so that there is no mingling of the two kinds of blood, is corpse uncleanness imposed by the Rabbis where the greater part issued after death. (6) They did. How then (cf. prev. n.) can R. Judah maintain his view? (7) V. Zeb. 78a. (8) In a continuous stream. Had it been falling in drops each drop would have been neutralized as it fell into the clean blood that issued earlier while the man was still alive. (9) Since the blood that issued after death and that could not be neutralized (cf. prev. n.) is subject to corpse uncleanness. (10) Lit., 'because I say'. (11) In the case of his previous ruling about a slain man lying in a bed (*supra* 71a *ad fin.*) where R. Judah ruled that the blood is unclean. (12) From that on the beam. (13) Through the bed to the ground.

ABIDES IN CLEAN BLOOD[1] MAY POUR OUT[2] WATER[3] FOR [WASHING OF] THE PASCHAL LAMB.[4] SUBSEQUENTLY THEY CHANGED THEIR VIEW: IN RESPECT OF CONSECRATED FOOD SHE IS LIKE ONE WHO CAME IN CONTACT WITH A PERSON THAT WAS SUBJECT TO CORPSE UNCLEANNESS.[5] THIS ACCORDING TO THE VIEW OF BETH HILLEL. BETH SHAMMAI RULED: EVEN AS ONE WHO IS SUBJECT TO CORPSE UNCLEANNESS.[6]

GEMARA. 'SHE MAY POUR OUT' only, but may not touch it.[7] It is thus evident[8] that unconsecrated foodstuffs prepared in conditions of holiness[9] are treated as holy. But then read the final clause: SUBSEQUENTLY THEY CHANGED THEIR VIEW: IN RESPECT OF CONSECRATED FOOD SHE IS LIKE ONE WHO CAME IN CONTACT WITH A PERSON THAT WAS SUBJECT TO CORPSE UNCLEANNESS. Thus only[10] IN RESPECT OF CONSECRATED FOOD but not in respect of unconsecrated food.[11] It is thus evident, is it not, that unconsecrated foodstuffs prepared in conditions of holiness[9] are not treated as holy?—Who is the author of our Mishnah?[12] It is Abba Saul; for it was taught: Abba Saul ruled, A *ṭebul yom* is unclean in the first grade in respect of

(1) *Sc.* from the eighth to the fortieth, and from the fifteenth to the eightieth day after the birth of a male and female child respectively (cf. Lev. XII, 2ff). (2) Lit., 'was pouring out'. (3) From one vessel into another, the water itself not being touched by her (v. next n. final clause). (4) *Sc.* she is subject to the second grade of uncleanness like a *ṭebul yom* (v. Glos.), since her immersion was performed at the end of the seven, and the fourteen days respectively, and the sunset prior to the first day of her complete cleanness will not occur before the fortieth and eightieth day respectively. One who is subject to second grade of uncleanness conveys a third grade of uncleanness to foodstuffs only but not to vessels. (5) *Sc.* her uncleanness in this respect is of the first grade. In regard to unconsecrated things, however, she is still subject to the second grade of uncleanness only. (6) Who is a 'father of uncleanness' and conveys an uncleanness of the first grade to vessels also. (7) The water. (8) Since she may not touch the water itself. (9) As in the case of the water under discussion which was being prepared for the washing of the paschal lamb. (10) Lit., 'yes'. (11) So that the woman may touch the water itself. (12) *Sc.* of the final clause.

consecrated food to cause two further grades of uncleanness[1] and one grade of disqualification.[2]

MISHNAH. BUT THEY[3] AGREE THAT SHE[4] MAY EAT[5] SECOND TITHE; SHE MAY SET ASIDE HER[6] DOUGH-OFFERING,[7] BRING IT NEAR[8] TO THE DOUGH[9] AND DESIGNATE IT AS SUCH;[10] AND THAT IF ANY OF HER SPITTLE OR OF THE BLOOD OF HER PURIFICATION[11] FELL ON A LOAF OF TERUMAH THE LATTER REMAINS CLEAN. BETH SHAMMAI RULED: SHE REQUIRES IMMERSION AT THE END [OF HER DAYS OF PURIFICATION],[12] AND BETH HILLEL RULED: SHE REQUIRES NO IMMERSION AT THE END.

GEMARA. Because[13] a Master ruled: If a person performed immersion and came up [from his bathing] he may[14] eat of second tithe.

SHE MAY SET ASIDE HER DOUGH-OFFERING. For unconsecrated dough that is *tebel*[15] in respect of the dough-offering[16] is not treated like the dough-offering.[17]

BRING IT NEAR. Because a Master stated: It is a religious duty to set aside the offering from dough that is in close proximity to that for which it is set aside.

(1) The consecrated food that comes in contact with him is unclean in the second grade and that which comes in contact with this food is unclean in the third grade. (2) If *terumah*, for instance, came in contact with the food that is unclean in the third grade (cf. prev. n.) it becomes disqualified but cannot convey any uncleanness to other foodstuffs. (3) Beth Shammai and Beth Hillel. (4) Cf. prev. Mishnah. (5) Like a *tebul yom*. (6) Lit., 'for herself'. (7) Before she designates it as such. (8) In the vessel in which she has put it. (9) Since the dough-offering must be close to the dough for which it is taken when it is named as the offering for it. (10) After which, of course, she must not touch it (cf. prev. n. but one). (11) Cf. *supra* p. 496, n. 1. (12) After the fortieth and eightieth day respectively. (13) A reason for the first ruling in our Mishnah. (14) Even before sunset. (15) V. Glos. (16) *Sc.* from which the dough-offering had not been taken. (17) A *tebul yom* (as one subject to the second grade of uncleanness) cannot, therefore, impart any uncleanness to it.

AND DESIGNATE IT AS SUCH. Since it might have been presumed that this should be forbidden as a preventive measure against the possibility of her touching the dough[1] from the outside,[2] we were informed [that this is permitted].

AND IF ANY OF HER SPITTLE . . . FELL. For we have learnt: The liquid [issues] of a *tebul yom*[3] are like the liquids that he touches, neither of them conveying uncleanness. The exception is the liquid issue of a *zab*[4] which is a father of uncleanness.

BETH SHAMMAI. What is the point at issue between them?[5]— R. Ḳaṭṭina replied: The point at issue between them is the necessity for immersion[6] at the end of a long day.[7]

MISHNAH. IF A WOMAN OBSERVED A DISCHARGE ON THE ELEVENTH DAY[8] AND PERFORMED IMMERSION IN THE EVENING AND THEN HAD MARITAL INTERCOURSE, BETH SHAMMAI RULED: THEY[9] CONVEY UNCLEANNESS[10] TO COUCH AND SEAT[11] AND THEY ARE LIABLE TO A SACRIFICE,[12] [72a] BUT BETH HILLEL[13] RULED: THEY[9] ARE EXEMPT FROM THE SACRIFICE.[14] IF SHE PERFORMED IMMERSION ON THE NEXT

(1) Lit., 'it', after it had been designated as dough offering. (2) *Sc.* she might put her hand across the sides of the vessel in which the dough-offering is kept, and so impart uncleanness to the offering. (3) 'The liquids that issue from him' is added in cur. edd., in parenthesis. (4) The passage from here to the end of the sentence is deleted by Elijah Wilna. (5) Beth Shammai and Beth Hillel. (6) If earlier in that day immersion had already been performed. (7) That terminated a period of uncleanness. The forty as well as the eighty days (cf. *supra* p. 496, n. 1) are regarded as one long day in the course of which (on the seventh and the fourteenth day respectively) immersion had already been performed. (8) *Sc.* the last day of a *zibah* period which is followed by the first day of the next menstruation period. (9) The woman and her husband. (10) As a woman under the obligation of allowing a clean day to pass after a day of uncleanness and as the man who had intercourse with such a woman respectively. (11) I.e., to any object on which they lie or sit, which in turn conveys uncleanness to foodstuffs and drinks. (12) Prescribed for a woman and a man who had intercourse in such circumstances (cf. prev. n. but one). (13) Maintaining that a woman who observed a discharge on the eleventh day of her *zibah* period need not allow a clean day to pass before cleanness can be established. (14) But, in accordance with a Rabbinical enactment, are subject to uncleanness, as

DAY[1] AND THEN HAD MARITAL INTERCOURSE AND AFTER THAT OBSERVED A DISCHARGE, BETH SHAMMAI RULED: THEY[2] CONVEY UNCLEANNESS[3] TO COUCH AND SEAT[4] AND ARE EXEMPT FROM THE SACRIFICE,[5] BUT BETH HILLEL RULED: SUCH A PERSON[6] IS A GLUTTON.[7] THEY[8] AGREE, HOWEVER, THAT, WHERE A WOMAN OBSERVED A DISCHARGE DURING THE ELEVEN DAYS[9] AND PERFORMED IMMERSION IN THE EVENING AND THEN HAD INTERCOURSE, BOTH[10] CONVEY UNCLEANNESS TO COUCH AND SEAT[11] AND ARE LIABLE TO A SACRIFICE.[12] IF SHE PERFORMED IMMERSION ON THE NEXT DAY[13] AND THEN HAD INTERCOURSE, SUCH AN ACT IS IMPROPER[14] CONDUCT,[15] BUT THE UNCLEANNESS OF THEIR TOUCH AND THEIR LIABILITY TO A SACRIFICE ON ACCOUNT OF THEIR INTERCOURSE ARE IN SUSPENSE.[16]

a preventive measure against a discharge during the eleven days (other than the last) in which case the uncleanness is Pentateuchal unless a portion at least of the following day had passed in cleanness.

(1) The day following the *zibah* period (which is the first day of that of menstruation), a portion of that day having passed in cleanness. (2) The woman and her husband. (3) Rabbinically as a preventive measure (cf. p. 498, n. 14). (4) V. p. 498, n. 11. (5) Since a portion of the day at least, has passed in cleanness. The discharge observed later in the day has no bearing on *zibah* since that day belonged to the menstruation period. (6) Lit., 'behold this', the person who is in such a hurry as not to allow even one clean day to pass after a *zibah* discharge. (7) Sexually. Such hurry is indecent, since it might lead one to act similarly in the case of a discharge in the intermediate days of the *zibah* period when a Pentateuchal prohibition might be infringed. The uncleanness of *zibah*, however, does not apply. (8) Beth Shammai and Beth Hillel. (9) Other than the last. (10) Husband and wife. (11) Though no discharge appeared on the following day. (12) Since, as a minor *zabah* (one who experienced a discharge on one of the days of a *zibah* period) she must allow one clean day to pass before she can regard herself as clean. (13) So that a part of the day at least had passed in cleanness. (14) Lit., 'bad'. (15) Because a discharge that might possibly occur later in the day would continue and extend the uncleanness of the previous day and render the immersion invalid. (16) Until the evening. If later in the day she experienced a discharge their touch conveys the uncleanness of *zibah* and they are liable to bring the prescribed sacrifice; but if no discharge appeared the touch conveys no uncleanness and no liability to a sacrifice is incurred.

GEMARA. Our Rabbis taught: And both[1] agree[2] that if a woman performs immersion at night after a *zibah*[3] the immersion is invalid, for both agree that if a woman who observed a discharge during the eleven days[3] and performed immersion in the evening and then had intercourse she conveys uncleanness to couch and seat and both are liable to a sacrifice. They[1] only differ where a discharge occurred on the eleventh day in which case Beth Shammai ruled: They[4] convey uncleanness to couch and seat and are liable to a sacrifice, and Beth Hillel exempt them from the sacrifice. Said Beth Shammai to Beth Hillel: Why should in this respect the eleventh day differ from one of the intermediate of the eleven days; seeing that the former is like the latter in regard to uncleanness, why should it not also be like it in regard to the sacrifice? Beth Hillel answered Beth Shammai: No; if you ruled that a sacrifice is due after a discharge in the intermediate of the eleven days because the following day[5] combines with it in regard to *zibah*, would you also maintain the same ruling in regard to the eleventh day which[6] is not followed by one that we could combine with it in regard to *zibah?* Said Beth Shammai to them: You must be consistent;[7] if the one is like the other in regard to uncleanness it should also be like it in regard to the sacrifice, and if it is not like it in regard to the sacrifice it should not be like it in regard to uncleanness either. Said Beth Hillel to them: If we impose upon a man[8] uncleanness in order to restrict the law[9] we cannot on that ground impose upon him the obligation of a sacrifice which might[10] lead to a relaxation of the law.[11] And, furthermore, you stand refuted[12] out of your own rulings. For, since you rule

(1) Beth Shammai and Beth Hillel. (2) Though Beth Hillel hold that, where a discharge appeared on the eleventh day and immersion was performed in the evening, intercourse in that night does not involve the bringing of a sacrifice. (3) *Sc*. on any day other than the eleventh. (4) Husband and wife. (5) Which is also one of the days of the *zibah* period. (6) Being the last of the *zibah* days and followed by the first of those of menstruation. (7) Lit., 'make your measures equal'. (8) Lit., 'we brought him'. (9) Rabbinically. (10) In case the sacrifice is not obligatory. (11) Offering on the altar an unconsecrated beast. (12) *Noshekin*, lit., 'you bite'. Golds. suggests the reading *mushabin*, 'you are answered'.

that if she performed immersion on the next day and having had intercourse she observed a discharge, uncleanness is conveyed to couch and seat and she is exempt from a sacrifice, you also must be consistent.[1] If the one is like the other in regard to uncleanness it should also be like it in regard to the sacrifice and if it is not like it in regard to the sacrifice it should not be like it in regard to uncleanness either. The fact, however, is that they are like one another only where the law is thereby restricted but not where it would thereby be relaxed; well, here also, they are like one another where the law is thereby restricted but not where it is thereby relaxed.

R. Huna stated: Couches and seats[2] which she occupies on the second day[3] are held to be unclean[4] by Beth Shammai even though she performed immersion[5] and even though she observed no discharge.[5] What is the reason?—Because if she had observed a discharge she would have been unclean,[6] she is therefore now[7] also unclean.[4] Said R. Joseph: What new law does he[8] teach us,[9] seeing that we have learnt, IF SHE PERFORMED IMMERSION ON THE NEXT DAY[10] AND THEN HAD MARITAL INTERCOURSE AND AFTER THAT OBSERVED A DISCHARGE, BETH SHAMMAI RULED: THEY[11] CONVEY UNCLEANNESS TO COUCH AND SEAT[12] AND ARE[11] EXEMPT FROM THE SACRIFICE?[13] R. Kahana objected:[14]

(1) Lit., 'make your measures equal'. (2) So MS.M. and Rashi. Cur. edd. 'her couch and seat'. (3) *Sc.* the day following one of the intermediate days of the *zibah* period on which she experienced a discharge. (4) Rabbinically. (5) On the second day. (6) Retrospectively, in accordance with Pentateuchal law, since the discharge on the second day is joined to that on the first to constitute a continuous *zibah*. (7) As a preventive measure. (8) R. Huna. (9) By his statement. (10) The day following the eleventh of a *zibah* period, which is the first of the following menstruation period, and a discharge on which cannot be treated as a continuation of the *zibah* discharge of the previous day. (11) Cur. edd. use here the fem. sing. (12) In cur. edd., the plural is here used. (13) Now, since a discharge on the twelfth day cannot be treated as a continuation of that on the eleventh (cf. prev. n. but two) and since it does not invalidate the immersion on that day, that discharge, as far as *zibah* is concerned, might well be regarded as if it had never occurred. The case is consequently similar to that of R. Huna where a discharge on an intermediate day in the *zibah* period was followed by a day on which none had occurred. As in the

Where she observed a discharge[1] the case is different.[2] Said R. Joseph: But what matters it that she observed a discharge[3] seeing that it is one of menstruation?[4]—Abaye answered R. Joseph: R. Kahana[5] had this difficulty: Where the woman did observe a discharge one can well see the reason why uncleanness has been imposed since[6] an observation of menstruation had to be declared unclean as a preventive measure against the possibility of an observation of a discharge of *zibah*, but where one observed no discharge[7] what possibility was there to be provided against? And, furthermore, we have learnt:[8] If a man observed one discharge of *zibah*, Beth Shammai ruled: He is like a woman who waits a day for a day[9] and Beth Hillel ruled: Like a man who emitted semen,[10] [72b] and it was taught:[11] If a man[12] caused the

Mishnah, where the second discharge occurred on the twelfth, uncleanness has been imposed Rabbinically as a preventive measure against the possibility of a second discharge occurring on the eleventh so also in the case of R. Huna uncleanness must be imposed where no discharge occurred on the second day as a preventive measure against the possibility of a discharge occurring on the second day. What need then was there for R. Huna to make a statement which is implicit in the ruling of our Mishnah? (14) Against R. Huna.

(1) The case dealt with in our Mishnah though that discharge could not be attributed to *zibah*. (2) From one where there was no discharge at all. How then could R. Huna maintain his statement? (3) The case in our Mishnah. (4) Which cannot be attributed to *zibah*; and consequently (cf. p. 501, n. 13) might be regarded (as in the case of R. Huna) as if no discharge had taken place. What then is the basis of R. Kahana's objection? (5) Who advanced the opinion that 'where she observed a discharge the case is different'. (6) The ruling concerning one discharge being likely to be misunderstood for that of another discharge. (7) And since the absence of a discharge is not likely to be misunderstood for a discharge. (8) Contrary to the view of R. Huna. (9) *Sc.* who must allow one clean day to pass for every day on which she experienced a discharge before she may be regarded as clean. As the uncleanness of the touch of such a woman on the second day after she performed immersion is left in suspense to provide against the possibility of a discharge appearing later in the day, so must also be the uncleanness of such a person if after experiencing the discharge he performed immersion. If, e.g., he touches tithe its uncleanness must remain in suspense in case he observes a second discharge which would continue his former *zibah*. (10) *Sc.* he is clean in regard to tithe immediately after his immersion. At all events it was here stated that, according to Beth Shammai, a woman

shaking of the [first] observed discharge, Beth Shammai ruled: The man must be held in suspense,[1] and Beth Hillel declared him clean.[2] As to couches and seats occupied between a first and a second discharge, Beth Shammai hold them in suspense and Beth Hillel declare them clean. Now in the first clause it was stated, 'If a man observed one discharge of *zibah*, Beth Shammai ruled: He is like a woman who waits a day for a day', from which it is evident, is it not, that in the case of a woman who waits a day for a day the uncleanness is held in suspense?[3]—Do not read, 'A woman who waits a day for a day' but read: Like a man who had intercourse with one who waits a day for a day.[4] But why is it that he[5] does not convey uncleanness to couch and seat,[6] while she does convey uncleanness to them?[7]—About him, since he does not usually bleed, the Rabbis enacted no preventive measure,[8] but in her case, since she does usually bleed, the Rabbis enacted a preventive measure. But[9] why is it that she conveys uncleanness to couch and seat and does not convey uncleanness to the man who had intercourse with her?—To couch and seat which are in common use she conveys uncleanness but to the man who had intercourse, which in such circumstances is an unusual occurrence, no uncleanness is conveyed.

We learnt, IF SHE PERFORMED IMMERSION ON THE NEXT

who waits a day for a day is on a par with a man who experienced a first discharge of *zibah*. (11) Regarding a *zab* who experienced one discharge. (12) Who was clean.

(1) Until evening. If the *zab* experienced a second discharge on that day he becomes a confirmed *zab* retrospectively and the man who shook the discharge becomes unclean. (2) As is the case with one who caused the shaking of semen who remains clean. (3) And if she experiences no second discharge she is clean. (4) Because R. Huna agrees in the case of the man that, if the intercourse took place on the second day after the woman's immersion, the question of his uncleanness must be held in suspense and that before a second discharge appears he is even Rabbinically free from certain uncleanness. (5) The man who had the intercourse. (6) Which he alone occupied. (7) To couch and seat that have been occupied by her. (8) That, even where the woman observed no discharge after their intercourse, he shall convey uncleanness to couch and seat. (9) Since a preventive measure was enacted in her case on account of her tendency to bleed.

DAY AND THEN HAD INTERCOURSE, SUCH AN ACT IS IMPROPER CONDUCT, BUT THE UNCLEANNESS OF THEIR TOUCH AND THEIR LIABILITY TO A SACRIFICE ON ACCOUNT OF THEIR INTERCOURSE ARE IN SUSPENSE. Does not this represent the general view?[1]—No, it is only the view of Beth Hillel. For it was taught: Said R. Judah to Beth Hillel: Do you then call such an act improper conduct, seeing that this man only intended to have intercourse with a menstruant?—'A menstruant'! How could such an idea be entertained?—Rather read: To have intercourse with a *zabah*. 'A *zabah*'! How could this idea be entertained?—Rather read: To have intercourse with one who waits a day for a day.

It was stated: As to the tenth day,[2] R. Joḥanan ruled, The tenth is on a par with the ninth; as the ninth[3] must be followed[4] by observation[5] so must the tenth[6] be followed by observation.[7] Resh Laḳish ruled: The tenth is on a par with the eleventh; as the eleventh[8] need not be followed by observation[9] so the tenth need not be followed by observation.

Some there are who teach this[10] in connection with the following. R. Eleazar b. 'Azariah said to R. Akiba, Even if you were all day to draw inferences from[11] the repetition of '*with oil*'[12] I would not

(1) Even that of Beth Shammai who accordingly hold that on the day following a discharge during the intermediate days of the *zibah* period the woman's touch causes only a suspended uncleanness. An objection thus arises against R. Huna who maintained that according to Beth Shammai couch and seat in such circumstances are held to be unclean. (2) *Sc.* a first discharge on the tenth day of the *zibah* period. Such a discharge can never develop into a major *zibah* (by being repeated on three consecutive days) since the tenth day is followed by one day only of the *zibah* period (the eleventh) the twelfth being the first of the next menstruation period. (3) Since a discharge on it may develop (if it is repeated on the tenth and the eleventh) into a major *zibah*. (4) Lit., 'requires'. (5) On the next day. (6) If it was the first day in the *zibah* period on which a discharge appeared. (7) On the eleventh; though a repeated discharge on the latter day would not constitute a major *zibah*. (8) Which is the last day of the *zibah* period. (9) According to Beth Hillel the day following being one of menstruation. (10) The dispute between R. Joḥanan and Resh Laḳish. (11) Lit., 'increase', i.e., to regard every Scriptural mention of '*with oil*', in connection with the thanksgiving-offering, as implying an addition to the

listen to you, the fact being that the prescribed quantities of half a *log* of oil for a thanksgiving-offering, and a quarter of a *log* of wine for a nazirite, and the eleven days that intervene between one menstruation period and the next are the *halachah* of Moses handed down from Sinai. What is the '*halachah*' referred to?— R. Joḥanan replied: The one *halachah* applicable to the eleventh day.[1] Resh Laḳish replied: The *halachahs*[2] applicable to the eleventh day. 'R. Joḥanan replied: The one *halachah* applicable to the eleventh day' i.e., the eleventh day[3] only need not be followed[4] by a day of observation[5] but for the other days[6] it[7] does serve as a day of observation. But 'Resh Laḳish replied: The *halachahs* applicable to the eleventh day', i.e., neither need the eleventh be followed by one of observation nor does it serve as one of observation for the tenth.[8] But are these[9] *halachahs?* Are they not in fact derived from Scriptural texts? For it was taught: As it might have been presumed that if a woman observes a discharge on three consecutive days at the beginning of a menstruation period she shall be a *zabah*,[10] and that the text[11] '*If a woman have an issue and her issue in her flesh be blood*'[12] applies[13] to one who observed a discharge on one day only[14] it was, therefore, explicitly stated, [73a] *Not in the time of her menstruation*,[15] implying,[16] close to the time of her menstruation.[17] Thus I only know

quantity specified. Any two additions imply a reduction (cf. Zeb. 82*a*, 89*a*). (12) Lit., '*with oil, with oil*,' (cf. Rashal and BaḤ).

(1) Of a *zibah* period. (2) Two. (3) If a discharge was observed on it. (4) As any other of the eleven days must. (5) Since the next day is the first of the menstruation period. (6) The tenth. (7) The eleventh. (8) This is the Pentateuchal law. Rabbinically, however, even the eleventh day must be followed by one of observation before the woman may be regarded as clean. (9) The rules regarding the eleventh day. (10) Requiring a count of seven days after the third, and a sacrifice at the end of the counting. (11) Lit., 'and what do I establish', *sc*, what is derived from. (12) Lev. XV, 19, which implies that neither the counting of seven days nor any sacrifice is required. (13) Cf. prev. n. but one. (14) Cf. Rashal. Cur. edd. in parenthesis, 'but she who observes on three days at the beginning shall be a *zabah*'. (15) Lev. XV, 25. E.V., '*of her impurity*'. (16) Cur. edd. in parenthesis, 'beyond the time of her menstruation'. (17) *Sc.* the three consecutive days on which a discharge appears and which subject the woman to the restrictions of a major *zabah*

about[1] the three days that immediately follow[2] the period of her menstruation, whence is it deduced that the same restrictions apply where the three days are separated from the period of her menstruation by one day? It was explicitly stated, *Or if she have an issue.*[3] Thus I only know about an interval of one day, whence is it deduced that the restrictions extend [where the day or the days on which the discharge appeared were] separated [from the menstruation period] by two, three, four, five, six, seven, eight, nine or ten days? You may reason thus: As we find in the case of the fourth day[4] that[5] it is suitable for the counting[6] and[7] is also appropriate as one for *zibah*[8] so may I also introduce[9] the tenth day[10] since it is both suitable for the prescribed counting[11] and appropriate as one for *zibah.*[12] But whence is it it deduced that the eleventh day[13] is also included?[14] It was explicitly stated, *Not in the time of her menstruation.*[15] Might I also[16] include[14] the twelfth day?[4] You must admit that this cannot be done.[17] But what reason do you see for including[14] the eleventh and for excluding the twelfth? I include the eleventh since it is suitable for being counted [as one of the seven clean days following the one[18] that is deduced[19] from] *'or if she have an issue'*[20] and I exclude

must be close to (not within) the seven days of the menstruation period, viz., the first three days of the period of *zibah.*

(1) Lit., 'and I have not but'. (2) Lit., 'near to'. (3) Lev. XV, 25. (4) After the menstruation period. (5) Where the discharge appeared on the first three days following menstruation and then ceased. (6) Of the prescribed seven days beginning with it. (7) As has just been deduced from Lev. XV, 25: *Or if she have an issue.* (8) If the discharge first appeared on the second day following menstruation and was repeated on the third and fourth. (9) Under the *zibah* restrictions. (10) And, much more so, the other days enumerated. (11) Where the discharge appeared on the first three days after menstruation. (12) If the discharge occurred on it as well as on the preceding two days. (13) Which, if the discharge appeared on the first three days, cannot be counted among the seven days prescribed. (14) In the restrictions, so that if a discharge appeared on it and on the preceding two days *zibah* is established. (15) Lev. XV, 25. E.V. *'of her impurity'.* (16) As a deduction from the text just cited. (17) A discharge on the twelfth being regarded as one of menstruation that cannot be added to the *zibah.* (18) The fourth day. (19) *Supra.* (20) The seven days following a discharge on the fourth terminating on the eleventh.

the twelfth since it is not suitable for being counted as one of the seven clean days following the one that is deduced from *'or if she have an issue'*.[1] But so far I only know that *zibah*[2] is established after a discharge on[3] three days, whence is it deduced that the restrictions apply to a discharge on two days? It was explicitly stated, *Days.*[4] Whence the deduction that the same applies also to a discharge on one day? It was explicitly stated, *All the days.*[4] *'Unclean'*,[4] implies that she conveys uncleanness to the man who had intercourse with her like a menstruant. *'She'*,[4] implies that only she conveys uncleanness to the man who had intercourse with her but that the *zab* conveys no uncleanness to the woman with whom he had intercourse. But is there not an argument [*a minori ad majus*]: If she, who does not contract uncleanness on account of observation[5] as on account of days,[6] does convey uncleanness to the man who had intercourse with her, is there not more reason that the man who does contract uncleanness on account of observation as on account of days[7] should convey uncleanness to the woman with whom he had intercourse? It was expressly stated, *'she'*,[4] implying that only she conveys uncleanness to the man who had intercourse with her but that a *zab* does not convey uncleanness to the woman with whom he had intercourse. But whence is it deduced that he conveys uncleanness to couch and seat? It was expressly stated, *As the bed of her menstruation.*[8] From this,[8] however, I would only know the case of a man who experienced a discharge on three days, whence the deduction that the restrictions apply to a discharge on two days? It was explicitly stated, *'Days'*. But whence the deduction that the same applies to a discharge on one day? It was stated,

(1) It being the first day of menstruation. (2) That conveys uncleanness to couch and seat. (3) Lit., 'and I have not but'. (4) Lev. XV, 25. (5) If, e.g., she experienced three discharges on one day she is not regarded as a major *zabah* (v. foll. n.) to incur the obligation of a sacrifice. (6) A discharge that appeared on three consecutive days confirms a woman as a major *zabah* (cf. prev. n.). (7) A man is confirmed as a *zab* irrespective of whether he observed three discharges on three consecutive days respectively or all the three discharges on the same day (cf. B.Ḳ. 24*a*). (8) Lev. XV, 26.

'All the days'. And whence do we infer that the woman must count one day to correspond to one day?[1] It was stated, *She shall be.*[2] As it might have been presumed that she should count seven days after a discharge has appeared on two days only, this being arrived at by the following argument, 'If the man who does not count one day to correspond to one day[3] counts seven days after a discharge on two days, how much more reason is there that she who does count one day to correspond to one day[1] should count seven days after a discharge on two days', it was explicitly stated, *She shall be,*[2] implying that she counts one day only. It is thus evident,[4] is it not, that these[5] are derived from Scriptural texts?[6]—According to R. Akiba they are derived from Scriptural texts, but according to R. Eleazar b. 'Azariah they are traditional *halachahs*.

Said R. Shemaiah[7] to R. Abba:[8] Might it be suggested that on account of a discharge in the day time[9] a woman is a *zabah*, and that on account of one in the night[10] she is a menstruant?—For your sake,[11] the other replied, Scripture stated, *By*[12] *the time of her menstruation,*[13] implying[14] a discharge close to the time of her menstruation. Now which is a discharge that is close to the time of

(1) *Sc.* if she experienced a discharge on one day she must allow one clean day to pass before she may be regarded as clean. (2) Lit., 'shall be to her', Lev. XV, 25. (3) After one discharge on one day he performs immersion in the evening and resumes his cleanness. (4) The argument begun on 72*b ad fin.* is now resumed and concluded. (5) The laws regarding the intervals between the menstruation periods, viz., that each interval extends over eleven days; that a discharge on three consecutive days of these eleven subjects the woman to the restrictions of a major *zabah;* that after a discharge on only one or two of these days no more than one clean day need be allowed to pass; that after the eleven days' period the menstruation period begins, and that a discharge on the first of these causes the woman to be unclean on that day and on the following six days. (6) How then could it be stated *supra* that these laws were *halachahs?* (7) Var. lec., Isaiah (Yalḳut). (8) Var. lec., Raba (MS.M.). (9) Since the text from which the laws of *zibah* are derived (Lev. XV, 25) speaks of *days.* (10) When (cf. prev. n.) she cannot be regarded a *zabah.* (11) *Sc.* in order to avert the possibility of his deduction. (12) *'Al,* E.V. *'beyond'.* (13) Lev. XV, 25. E.V. *'her impurity'.* (14) By the use of *'al* (*'by'*).

her menstruation? One that occurred in the night;[1] and yet Scripture called her a *zabah*.[2]

The Tanna debe Eliyahu[3] [teaches]: Whoever repeats[4] *halachahs* every day may rest assured that he will be a denizen of the world to come, for it is said, Halikoth—*the world is his*;[5] read not *halikoth*[6] but *halakoth*.[7]

(1) Since the menstruation period comes to an end at the sunset of the seventh day. (2) The verb rendered by *'have an issue'* (Lev. XV, 25) being derived from the same root as *zabah*. (3) A treatise bearing this name is mentioned in Keth., (Sonc. ed.,) p. 680, n. 2 (4) Or 'learns'. (5) Hab. III, 6. E.V. *'his goings are of old'*. (6) *'Goings out'*. (7) Or *'halachahs'* (the Mishnah, Baraitha, and the oral laws that were handed down through Moses from Sinai). If a man studies these *'halachahs, the world* (to come) *is his'*.

GLOSSARY

INDEX OF SCRIPTURAL REFERENCES

GENERAL INDEX

TRANSLITERATION OF HEBREW LETTERS

ABBREVIATIONS

GLOSSARY

AB. The fifth month of the Jewish calendar, corresponding approximately to July or August.

ABBA. Father. A title given to many Rabbis of the Talmud as a mark of affection or honour.

'ABODAH ZARAH. Idolatry; lit., 'strange service'.

ADAR. The name of the twelfth month of the Jewish Calendar, corresponding approximately to February or March.

ADRAKTA. A court document authorizing the creditor to trace out the debtor's property for the purpose of distraint.

AGGADAH (Lit., 'tale', 'lesson'); the name given to those sections of Rabbinic literature which contain homiletic expositions of the Bible, stories, legends, folk-lore, anecdotes or maxims. Opposed to *halachah*, q.v.

ALIF. The first letter of the Hebrew alphabet, with numerical value 1.

AMARḲAL, according to the interpretation given by R. Ḥisda in Horayoth 13*a*, the word is composed of *amar* and *kola*, lit., 'who said (i.e. directs) all things'. One of the Temple trustees whose duty it was to supervise the work of the cashiers.

'AM HA-AREẒ pl. *'amme ha-areẓ*, (lit., 'people of the land', 'country people'); the name given in Rabbinic literature to (*a*) a person who through ignorance was careless in the observance of the laws of Levitical purity and of those relating to the priestly and Levitical gifts. In this sense opposed to *ḥaber*, q.v.; (*b*) an illiterate or uncultured man, as opposed to *ṭalmid ḥakam*, q.v.

'AMIDAH (Lit., 'standing'); the Eighteen Benedictions (seven on Sabbaths and Festivals) which the worshipper always recites in a standing posture.

AMORA. 'Speaker', 'interpreter'; originally denoted the interpreter who attended upon the public preacher or lecturer for the purpose of expounding at length and in popular style the heads of the discourse given to him by the latter. Subsequently (pl. Amoraim) the name given to the Rabbinic authorities responsible for the Gemara, as opposed to the Mishnah or Baraitha (v. Tanna).

ANINUTH. The state of being an *onan*, q.v.

'ARAKIN; vows to donate a person's valuation to the Temple, v. Lev. XXVII, 1ff.

'AREB. A surety who agrees to pay in case the borrower fails to meet his obligation. (Cf. ḲABBELAN.)

ARIS. A tenant farmer, who pays a fixed percentage of the crops in rent.

ARUS. The technical term for a husband of a betrothed woman, when *erusin* (q.v.) has taken place; v. ARUSAH.

ARUSAH. A betrothed woman after *erusin* (q.v.); v. ARUS.

ASHAM TALUI (*asham* 'a guilt-offering', *talui* 'hung', 'suspended'), the offering which is to be brought by one who is in doubt as to the transgression committed. V. Lev. V, 17-19.

ASHAM WADDAI (v. ASHAM TALUI; *waddai* 'certainty'), the guilt-offering incumbent upon one who is certain of having committed a sinful act that has to be atoned for by a guilt-offering.

ASHERAH. The biblical name given to a tree or pole which was the object of idolatrous worship.

ASMAKTA. 'Reliance'; (*a*) Biblical text adduced to give some slight support or provide a mnemonic for a law enacted by the Rabbis; (*b*) an assurance that one will pay or forfeit something in case of the non-fulfilment of a certain condition which, however, he is confident that he will fulfil.

ASUFI (Lit., 'one gathered in'); a foundling, a child, gathered in from the street, whose father or mother is unknown.

'AYIN. The sixteenth letter of the Hebrew alphabet, with numerical value 70.

BA'AL ḲERI. One unclean through nocturnal pollution.

BARAITHA (Lit., 'outside'); a teaching or a tradition of the Tannaim that has been excluded from the Mishnah and incorporated in a later collection compiled by R. Ḥiyya and R. Oshaiah, generally introduced by 'Our Rabbis taught', or, 'It has been taught'.

BATH ḲOL (Lit., 'daughter of a voice'); (*a*) a reverberating sound; (*b*) a voice descending from heaven (cf. Dan. IV, 28) to offer guidance in human affairs, and regarded as a lower grade of prophecy.

BERERAH (Lit., 'choice'); the selection retrospectively of one object rather than another as having been designated by a term equally applicable to both.

BETH AB (*Beth* 'house' and *Ab* 'father') 'family', one of the six family divisions into which each of the eight major divisions of the priests and Levites (*mishmar*, q.v.) was subdivided for the purpose of the Temple service.

BETH DIN (Lit., 'house of law or judgment'); a gathering of three or more learned men acting as a Jewish court of law.

BETH HAMIDRASH. House of study; the college or academy where the study of the Torah was carried on under the guidance of a Rabbinical authority.

BETH KOR. An area in which a *kor* of seed may be sown.

BETH PERAS. An area (of a square *peras* = half the length of a furrow) regarded as unclean owing to crushed bones scattered in it from a ploughed grave.

BETH SE'AH. An area in which a *se'ah* of seed may be sown.

BIKKURIM. The first ripe fruits which had to be brought to the Temple in Jerusalem, Deut. XXV, 1ff.

BINYAN AB (Lit., 'constructing of a family'); a norm of interpretation denoting that a certain Biblical passage is regarded as having laid the foundation of a family, because it *is* the *principal passage* from which is derived the explanation to passages which are similar to it.

BOGERETH. A girl from the age of twelve and a half years plus one day onwards.

CUTHEAN. A member of the sect of Samaritans by whom Northern Israel was repopulated after the dispersal of the ten tribes.

DANḲA. (*a*) The sixth of a *denar;* (*b*) a sixth in general.

DAYYO (Lit., 'it is sufficient'); the legal maxim, 'it is sufficient for the object *to* which an analogy is drawn to be on the same footing as that *from* which it is drawn,' even though, were the analogy to be applied strictly, it would be treated with greater rigour.

DEMAI (Lit., 'dubious', 'suspicious'); produce concerning which there is a doubt as to whether the rules relating to the priestly and Levitical dues and ritual cleanness and uncleanness were strictly observed. Any produce bought from *'am ha-areẓ* (q.v.), unless the contrary is known, is treated as *demai;* and *terumah gedolah* and *terumah* (q.v.) of the tithe must be separated from it.

DENAR. *Denarius*, a silver or gold coin, the former being worth one twenty-fourth (according to others one twenty-fifth) of the latter.

DEYOMAD. A corner-piece constructed from two boards placed at right-angles to each other or a block cut into such a shape.

DUCHAN. A raised platform on which the Levites stood when chanting Psalms in divine service.

DUPONDIUM. A Roman coin of the value of two *issars*.

ELUL. The sixth month of the Jewish Calendar, corresponding to August or September.

EMURIM (Lit., 'the consecrated parts'); the parts of a sacrifice which were to be burnt on the altar.

'ERUB (Lit., 'mixture'); a quantity of food, enough for two meals, placed (*a*) 2000 cubits from the town boundary, so as to extend the Sabbath limit by that distance; (*b*) in a room or in a court-yard to enable all the residents to carry to and fro in the court-yard on Sabbath.

'ERUB TABSHILIN (Lit., 'mixture of dishes'); a dish prepared on the eve of a Festival immediately preceding Sabbath enabling the preparing of food on the Festival for the Sabbath.

ERUSIN (Lit., 'betrothal'); a formal betrothal, which cannot be annulled without a bill of divorce.

ETHROG. A fruit of the citrus family used with the palm leaves, myrtle and willows on the Festival of Tabernacles. Cf. Lev. XXIII, 40.

EXEDRA. A covered way leading up to the house, open at both sides.

GADOL. An adult male, over thirteen years of age.

GEMARA (Lit., 'completion 'or 'learning'). The traditions, discussions and rulings of the Amoras, based mainly on the Mishnah and forming (*a*) the Babylonian Talmud and (*b*) the Palestinian Talmud.

GEMATRIA. The numerical value of letters used as a basis of homiletical interpretation.

GEṬ. A deed or legal document; when used without further specification denotes generally a writ of divorce.

GEZERAH SHAWAH (Lit., 'equal cut'); the application to one subject of a rule already known to apply to another, on the strength of a common expression used in connection with both in the Scriptures.

GRIVA. A dry measure equal to one *se'ah*. (q.v.)

GUD AḤITH (Lit., 'pull and bring down'); a legal fiction that a wall or any other partition may in certain circumstances be deemed to reach the ground though an air-space in fact intervenes.

HABDALAH (Lit., 'separation'); the blessing (usually made over wine) by which the Sabbath or any other holy day is ushered out.

ḤABER. 'Fellow', 'associate', opp. to *'am ha-areẓ* (q.v.); one scrupulous in the observance of the law, particularly in relation to ritual cleanness and the separation of the priestly and Levitical dues.

ḤABUT (From a root meaning 'to strike' or 'press down'); a legal fiction that an inclined projection may be regarded as horizontal, and stretching downwards to the spot required (cf. LABUD).

ḤADASH ('new'); the new cereal crops, which may not be eaten before the waving of the 'sheaf' (*'omer*); v. Lev. XXIII, 10-14.

ḤAFINAH. The priest's taking handfuls of incense, v. Lev. XVI, 12.

HAFTARAH (Lit., 'leave-taking'); a section from the Prophetical books recited after the reading from the Pentateuch on Sabbaths and Holy Days.

HAGBAHAH (Lit., 'a lifting'); a legal form of acquisition consisting in the lifting up of the object to be acquired.

HAKANAH. 'Preparation' for use on the Sabbath or Festival; used as a technical term with reference to והכינו, Ex. XVI, 5.

HALACHAH (Lit., 'step', 'guidance'), (*a*) the final decision of the Rabbis, whether based on tradition or argument, on disputed rules of conduct; (*b*) those sections of Rabbinic literature which deal with legal questions, as opposed to the *Aggadah*.

ḤALAL, ḤALALAH. The issue of an interdicted priestly union.

ḤALIFIN. 'Exchange'; a legal form of acquisition effected by handing to the seller an object in nominal exchange for the object bought (V. KINYAN SUDAR).

ḤALIẒAH (Lit., 'drawing off'); the ceremony of taking off the shoe of the brother of a husband who has died childless. (V. Deut. XXV, 5-9.)

ḤALLAH. The portion of the dough which belongs to the priest (v. Num. XV, 20f); in the Diaspora this is not given to the priest but burnt.

HALLEL (Lit., 'Praise'); Psalms CXIII–CXVIII, recited in the morning service on New Moons and Festivals.

ḤALUẒAH. A woman who has performed *ḥalizah* (q.v.).

ḤANUKAH. The Festival of Dedication (frequently designated the Feast of Lights); a minor eight days' festival, from the 25th of Kislev to the 2nd or 3rd of Tebeth, in commemoration of the rededication of the Temple in 165 B.C.E. after its desecration by Antiochus Epiphanes.

ḤAROSETH. A mixture of apples, nuts and wine, so made as to resemble mortar, into which the bitter herbs are dipped on the first two nights of Passover.

ḤASID ('pious'). A pious man; at one time possibly a designation of a member of a particularly pious and strictly observant sect.

HAZA'AH. The sprinkling of the blood of sacrifices, and of the water of purification, upon the unclean.

ḤAZAḲAH (Lit., 'taking hold'); a legal term denoting (*a*) presumptive title based on the occupier's undisturbed possession during a fixed legal period, in cases where a claim to ownership cannot be established by other legal evidence; usucaption; (*b*) taking possession (of landed property) by means of a formal act of acquisition, e.g., digging, fencing.

HEDYOT (From Gr. ἰδιωτής); (*a*) a commoner or layman, as opposed to a king or High Priest; (*b*) an ignorant or ill-mannered man; (*c*) untrained, as opposed to a skilled worker; (*d*) private writings, as opposed to biblical books.

HEFḲER. Property which has no owner: a renunciation of ownership in favour of all and sundry. When used in reference to a court of law, it denotes an act of transfer of property from one person to another, in virtue of the power of the court to declare property ownerless, after which it can assign it to another.

HEKAL. The holy temple, especially the hall containing the golden altar etc. in contradistinction to the Holy of Holies.

HEḲDESH. Any object consecrated to the Sanctuary.

HEḲḲESH. Analogy, proving that the law in respect of one thing applies also to another, either because both have some feature in common or there is a Biblical intimation to the effect.

ḤELEB. The portion of the fat of a permitted domestic animal which may not be eaten; in sacrifices that fat was burnt upon the altar.

ḤEREM, pl. *ḥaramim* ('devoted'). Property devoted to the use of the priests or the Temple; when used in vows it denotes that benefit shall be prohibited from the person or things so designated.

HESSEṬ (Lit., 'shaking'); levitical uncleanness caused through the vibration of an unclean object.

HIN. Measure of capacity equal to three *ḳabs* or twelve *logs*.

HOMER. Equal to a *ḳor* or thirty *se'ahs*.

ḤULLIN (Lit., 'profane'); ordinary unhallowed food, as opposed to *terumah*, q.v.; unconsecrated animals, as opposed to *heḳdesh*, q.v.

ḤUPPAH (Lit., 'canopy'). The bridal chamber; the entrance of a bride into the bridal chamber, whereby the marriage was completed; v. *ḳiddushin*.

'ISḲA (Lit., 'occupation', 'business', 'merchandise'); a business arrangement whereby one invests money with a trader, who trades therewith on their joint behalf. To avoid the prohibition of usury, the investor took a greater share of the risk than of the profit, e.g. he received either half of the profit but bore two-thirds of the loss, or a third of the profit but bore half the loss.

ISSAR. A small Roman coin.

ḲAB. Measure of capacity equal to four *logs* or one sixth of a *se'ah*.

ḲABBELAN. 'Receiver'; a surety who receives money from the lender to convey to the borrower and who thus becomes liable to pay the debt whenever called upon by the lender, even though the borrower has not been first approached. Also any surety who accepts such liability. (V. also 'AREB.)

ḲABU'A. That which is stationed in a definite place; hence a technical term for a doubt arising in respect of that which is so stationed.

KALLAH. Name given to an assembly at which the law was expounded to scholars, as well as to the half-yearly assemblies of the Babylonian Academies.

ḲAL WA-ḤOMER (Lit., 'light and heavy'); an argument, or proof of a contention, *a minori* or *a fortiori*.

KARETH. 'Cutting off'; divine punishment for a number of sins for which no human penalty is specified. Sudden death is described as '*kareth* of days', premature death at sixty as '*kareth* of years'.

KARMELITH. An area which is neither a public nor a private domain, and which is subject to special laws in respect of the Sabbath and the legal acquisition of objects that happen to be within its limits.

ḲARPAF or ḲARPIF (Lit., 'an enclosure'); an area enclosed for the storage of wood or similar purposes, outside a settlement.

ḲENAS. A fine or penalty (as distinct from actual monetary loss caused), to be paid by certain classes of wrongdoers, e.g., a seducer.

KETHUBAH (Lit., 'a written [document]'); (*a*) a wife's marriage settlement which she is entitled to recover on her being divorced or on the death of her husband. The minimum settlement for a virgin is two hundred *zuz*, and for a widow remarrying one hundred *zuz*; (*b*) the marriage contract specifying the mutual obligations between husband and wife and containing the amount of the endowment and any other special financial obligations assumed by the husband.

ḲIDDUSH (Lit., 'sanctification'); the blessing (usually made over wine) by which the Sabbath or any other holy day is ushered in.

ḲIDDUSHIN (Lit., 'sanctification'); (*a*) the act of affiancing or betrothal; (*b*) the money or article given to effect the betrothal.

KIL'AYIM (Lit., 'junction of diverse kinds'); the prohibition either (*a*) of seeds or plants for sowing; (*b*) of animals for propagation; and (*c*) of material containing wool and linen for wearing (v. Lev. XIX, 19, Deut. XXII, 9ff).

ḲINYAN. 'Acquisition'; the legal acquisition of either landed or movable property. (V. ḲINYAN SUDAR.)

ḲINYAN SUDAR (Lit., 'acquisition of a scarf'); a legal form of acquisition of objects or of confirming agreements, executed by the handing of a scarf (or any other article) on the part of one of the contracting parties to the other, or on that of the witnesses to the agreement, as a symbol that the object itself has been transferred or the obligation assumed.

KOFER (Lit., 'atonement'); the indemnity paid by the owner of an ox which has gored a man to death (v. Ex. XXI, 30).

KOHANIM. Plural of *Kohen*, Priest, Aaronide.

KOHEN. A priest, a descendant of Aaron (v. Lev. XXI, XXII).

ḲONAM. (A substitute for *ḳorban*); an expression used in taking a vow of abstinence.

KOR. A measure of capacity = thirty *se'ahs* (q.v.).

KORBAN. An expression used in taking a vow of abstinence.

ḲORTOB. A sixty-fourth of a *log*.

KUTAḤ. A preserve or relish made of bread crusts and sour milk.

LABUD (Lit., 'joined'). A legal fiction whereby a horizontal gap of certain prescribed dimensions is deemed to be closed up (cf. ḤABUṬ).

LAGIN. A vessel larger in size than a cup (*kos*) and smaller than the jar (*kad*).

LEVIRATE MARRIAGE. The marriage between a man and the widow of his dead brother who has died childless. (V. ḤALIẒAH.)

LITRA. (*a*) a measure of capacity equal to half a *log*, q.v.; (*b*) the weight of one pound, the Roman *libra*.

LOG. A liquid measure equal to a quarter of a *ḳab* (q.v.), or the space occupied by six eggs, c. 549 cubic centimetres.

LULAB. The palm-branch used in the ceremony of the Feast of Tabernacles (v. Lev. XXIII, 40).

MA'AH. The smallest current silver coin, weighing sixteen barleycorns, equal in value to two *dupondia*, a sixth of the silver *denar* or *zuz*.

MA'AMAD pl. MA'AMADOTH (lit., 'station'); a group of lay Israelites who participated in the Temple service as representatives of the public.

MA'AMAR (Lit., 'saying', 'declaration'); the formal betrothal, instituted by the Rabbis, of the *yebamah* (q.v.) by the levir. This is accompanied either by the gift of money or by a deed.

MADDIR. He who vows that his neighbour should not benefit from him; his neighbour is then called the *muddar*.

MAKKATH MARDUTH (Lit., 'stripes for rebellion'); lashes inflicted for disobedience the number of which being left to the discretion of the court in contradistinction to the 40 (39) lashes ordained by the Bible.

MAḲOM (Lit., 'place'); a name of God, who is so called because 'He is the place of His universe'.

MAMZER. A child born from a union prohibited under penalty of death or *kareth*.

MANEH. One hundred *zuz*. The *maneh* was a weight in gold or silver equal to fifty holy, or a hundred common *shekels*.

MAẒẒAH. Unleavened bread (in the form of fairly thin wafers) eaten during Passover.

MEGILLAH (Lit., 'Scroll'); a term commonly applied to the Book of Esther.

MEGILLATH TA'ANITH (Lit., 'Scroll of Fasting'); a list compiled some time before the destruction of the Temple, of days on which it was forbidden to fast, with the reasons in each case.

ME'ILAH. Illegal or improper use of consecrated objects (v. Lev. V, 15ff).

MELIḲAH (Lit., 'wringing'); the wringing off of the head of the burnt-offering of a bird, v. Lev. I, 15.

MEMA'ENETH (Lit., 'she who refuses'); a woman who exercises the right of *mi'un*, q.v.

MESHIKAH (Lit., 'pulling'); one of the legal modes of acquiring a movable object which the buyer performs by drawing the object into his—though not exclusive—possession.

MESIRAH (Lit., 'delivery' or 'harnessing'); a form of legal acquisition which is executed by the buyer's performance of some act, resembling harnessing in the case of a beast, or in the case of other heavy objects by obtaining actual delivery.

MESITH (Lit., 'seducer'); one who entices another to idolatry (v. Deut. XIII, 7ff).

METH MIẒWAH (Lit., 'a dead [body] which is a commandment'); a corpse lying unattended with nobody to arrange for its burial. The duty of burying it devolves upon whomsoever discovers it, even if he be a Nazirite or a High Priest.

MEZUZAH (Lit., 'doorpost'); a small case containing certain passages from the Scripture affixed to the post of a door (v. Deut. VI, 9).

MIDRAS (Lit., 'treading', 'place of treading'). It denotes uncleanness of the first degree ('Father of uncleanness') contracted by an object on which a gonorrhoeist (more exactly those mentioned in Lev. XII, 2; XV, 2, 25) sits, lies, rides or leans against. Any object fit for, and usually used as a seat, cover, etc. is susceptible to *midras* uncleanness.

MIGGO (Lit., 'from the content of'); an argument that a statement should be accepted because a stronger statement to the same effect could have been made without fear of contradiction.

MIḲWEH (Lit., 'a gathering [of water]'); a ritual bath containing not less than forty *se'ahs* of water.

MIL (= *mille*); a Roman mile, 2.000 cubits.

MIN pl. *minim*, (lit., 'kind', 'species'); (*a*) a heretic, esp. (*b*) a member of the sect of the early Jewish Christians.

MINḤAH. The afternoon service, about two and a half hours before nightfall.

MINUTH. Heresy, the belief in more than one Power, especially Judeo-Christianity.

MISHMAR (rt. SHaMaR, 'to keep'), a guard of priests and Levites representing one of the eight divisions which carried on the Temple services in rotation. The *mishmar* again was subdivided into smaller groups each being designated *beth ab*, q.v.

MISHNAH (rt. SHaNaH, 'to learn', 'to repeat'), (*a*) the collection of the statements, discussions and Biblical interpretations of the Tannaim in the form edited by R. Judah the Patriarch c. 200; (*b*) similar minor collections by previous editors; (*c*) a single clause or paragraph the author of which was a Tanna.

MI'UN (Lit., 'refusal'); a declaration by a fatherless girl who has been married off by her mother or brothers under age, that she does not wish to live with her husband. Such a declaration made by her in the presence of a Beth din secures her freedom without the requirement of a *Geṭ*.

MODA'AH (Lit., 'a notification'); a legal term for an affidavit made by a man that a sale or gift which he is about to execute is being forced on him against his will, and that he intends, when opportunity arises, to take legal steps to annul it.

MU'AD (Lit., 'forewarned'); applied to an ox (or any other animal) that has gored or done injury on three successive occasions, so that the owner thus stands 'forewarned' and is liable to pay in full for any damage that has been done by his beast.

MUDDAR; v. MADDIR.

MUFLA, lit., 'separated', 'distinguished', the expert of the court, who instructs the members on legal points that are submitted for his consideration and report.

MUKAN (Lit., 'prepared', 'set in readiness'); a term describing an object as being in a state of preparedness and fitness before a Festival for use as may become desirable on the Festival.

MUḲẒEH (Lit., 'set aside'); that which may not be used or handled on the Sabbath or Festivals, though its use does not constitute actual labour.

MULUG or MELOG (Lit., 'plucking' or 'milking'); denotes property which belongs to the wife and of which the husband has only the usufruct without any rights to the capital, or responsibility for its loss or deterioration.

MUMḤE. 'Skilled', 'qualified', 'experienced'; a scholar well qualified by his attainments to deal with matters of law, such, e.g., as the remission of vows.

MUSAF (Lit., 'addition'); the additional *'Amidah* recited during the morning service on Sabbaths and Holy Days.

NA'ARAH. A girl between the ages of twelve years and one day and twelve and a half years plus one day.

NA'ARUTH. The state of being a *na'arah*, q.v.

NASI. Chief, Patriarch; the chief of the Great Sanhedrin in Jerusalem; after its abolition, the head of Palestinian Jewry.

NATHIN (rt. NaTHaN 'to give'), a descendant of the Gibeonites who deceived Joshua (v. Josh. IX, 3ff) and, when their identity was discovered, were made (lit., 'given', v. ibid. v. 27) into hewers of wood and drawers of water for the congregation and the altar. V. also Ezra II, 43ff, VIII, 20, Neh. III, 26 and 1 Chron. IX, 2, wherein *Nethinim*, the plural of *Nathin* occurs.

NAZIR. One who has taken a nazirite vow (to abstain from wine and let the hair grow long; v. Num. VI).

NEBELAH (pl. *nebeloth*); an animal slaughtered in any manner other than that prescribed by Jewish ritual law; the least deviation therefrom, e.g., if the knife has the slightest notch, renders the animal *nebelah*.

NE'ILAH. The concluding service of the Day of Atonement.

NESU'AH. A married woman after home-taking (*nissu'in*, q.v.), whereby the marriage is completed in the sense that cohabitation is permitted; opposed to *arusah*, q.v., with whom cohabitation is yet prohibited.

NETHINAH. A descendant of the Gibeonites (Josh. IX) with whom Israelites were not allowed to intermarry. An illegitimate was debarred under the law of Deut. XXIII, 3, E.V. 2.

NEZIRAH. A female NAZIR.

NEZIROTH. Vows of naziriteship.

NEZIRUTH. The state of a nazirite after binding himself with a vow.

NIDDAH. A woman in the period of her menstruation.

NISAN. The first month of the year in the Jewish calendar, corresponding to March or April.

NISSU'IN. The ceremony of home-taking, which completes the marriage.

NOLAD (Lit., 'it is born'); an object that made its first appearance or became available for use on the Sabbath or on any other holy day and the handling of which is forbidden in the days mentioned (cf. MUḲẒEH).

NOTHAR ('left over'); portions of sacrifices left over after the prescribed time within which they must be eaten.

OHEL (Lit., 'tent'); technical name for the uncleanness conveyed by a dead human body, or part of it, to men or utensils which are under the same tent or roof.

'OMER (Lit., 'sheaf'); the sheaf of barley offered on the sixteenth of Nisan, before which the new cereals of that year were forbidden for use (v. Lev. XXIII, 10).

ONAN. A mourner while his dead relative is awaiting burial; opposite to *abel*, a mourner from the time of burial for a period of seven or thirty days.

'ORLAH ('uncircumcised'); applied to newly-planted trees for a period of three years during which their fruits must not be eaten (v. Lev. XIX, 23ff).

PARASANG. A Persian mile, about 4000 yards.

PE'AH ('corner'); the corner of a field that is being reaped, which must be left for the poor (v. Lev. XIX, 9ff).

PERAS (Lit., 'part'); half a loaf of the size of a third of a *ḳab*, q.v.

PERUṬAH. The smallest copper coin, equal to one-eighth of an *issar* or one-sixteenth of a *dupondium*.

PIGGUL (Lit., 'abhorred'); flesh of the sacrifice which the officiating priest has formed the intention of eating at an improper time. V. Lev. VII, 18.

PROSBUL. Perhaps from προσβολή, or an abbreviation of πρὸς βουλῇ or βουλευτῶν; a form of declaration before the Beth din by means of which a creditor, provided he possessed some landed property, could secure exemption from the laws of Sabbatical release (v. Deut. XV, 2) and thus retain his right to the collection of his debts after the Sabbatical year had elapsed.

PUNDION, v. DUPONDIUM.

PURIM. A festival held on the fourteenth or fifteenth day of Adar in commemoration of the delivery of the Jews of Persia through Mordecai and Esther from the destruction designed against them by Haman.

RESH GALUTHA. Head of the Exile, the title of the official head of Babylonian and Persian Jewry.

RESHUTH HARABBIM. 'Domain of the many'; the domain or territory belonging to, or used by, the public; public roads, as opposed to *reshuth hayyaḥid*.

RESHUTH HAYYAḤID. 'Domain of the individual'; private premises, as opposed to *reshuth harabbim*.

RIS. The seventh part of a mil.

ROHITNI (Lit., 'a carpenter's plane'); an instrument for cropping close the hair of the beard.

SANHEDRIN (συνέδριον); the council of state and supreme tribunal of the Jewish people during the century or more preceding the fall of the Second Temple. It consisted of seventy-one members, and was presided over by the High Priest. A minor court (for judicial purposes only) consisting of twenty-three members was known as the 'Small Sanhedrin'.

SANṬER (Apparently = Lat. '*senator*'); according to the Talmudic interpretation, (*a*) a recorder, a slave appointed by the town to answer enquiries respecting the boundaries of fields; or (*b*) a stretch of fields adjoining the town. According to others, a guardsman or sentry.

SARIS. A castrate; one who is physically unable to beget child.

SE'AH. Measure of capacity, equal to six *ḳabs*.

SEGAN. The title given to the Deputy High Priest.

SELA'. Coin, equal to four *denarii* (one sacred, or two common, *shekels*).

SHAḤARITH (Lit., 'morning time'); the morning service.

SHAMTA (Lit., 'desolation'); a ban, or excommunication.

SHEBUTH (Lit., 'cessation'); an act forbidden by the Rabbis to be performed on the Sabbath.

SHECHINAH (Lit., 'abiding [of God]' 'Divine presence'); the spirit of the Omnipresent as manifested on earth.

SHECHITAH. Ritual slaughter, without which an animal is not fit for food.

SHEKEL. Coin or weight, equal to two *denarii* or ten *ma'ah* (q.v.). The sacred *shekel* was worth twenty *ma'ah* or *gerah* (cf. Ex. XXX, 13), twice the value of the common *shekel*.

SHEMA' (Lit., 'hear'); the biblical verse, '*Hear, Israel*' etc. (Deut. VI, 4); also the three sections (Deut. VI, 5-9; Deut. XI, 13-20; and Num. XV, 37-41) which are recited after this verse in the morning and evening prayers.

SHEMA'TA. Something heard from the lips of an eminent person; a reported topic.

SHEMIṬṬAH, pl. SHEMIṬṬIN. Every seventh year, which is the Sabbatical year or the year of release.

SHEREẒ. Unclean reptile (including rodents).

SHEṬAR. A deed (v. GEṬ), a writ.

SHETUḲI (Lit., 'silenced'); a child who knows who his mother is but not his father.

SHIDDUKIN. The arrangements and negotiations prior to betrothal.

SHITTUF (from a root meaning 'association', 'partnership'). An association for the purposes of the Sabbath law of the residents of an alley into a partnership by contributing their shares to a prescribed quantity of food, which is deposited in one of the courts of the alley, and whereby they are regarded as a united body, each of whom is allowed free access to his neighbours.

SHOFAR (Lit., 'ram's horn'); a horn used as a trumpet for military and religious purposes, particularly in the service of the New Year and at the conclusion of the Day of Atonement.

SHOMERETH YABAM (Lit., 'waiting for the *yabam*'); a childless widow awaiting the brother of her deceased husband to marry her or free her by means of *ḥaliẓah* (q.v.).

SHOSBIN. A groomsman, who in addition to acting as best man or companion to the groom, also brought him presents.

SHUM. 'Appraisement'; the term used to designate a dowry in which goods are brought instead of cash.

SIFRA. A legal Rabbinical commentary on Leviticus.

SIVAN. The third month of the Jewish Calendar corresponding to May or June.

SOBEB. A sort of gallery around the altar where the priests would walk.

SOFER (pl. *soferim*); (*a*) scribe, title of the pre-Tannaitic teachers, beginning with Ezra (v. Ezra VII, 11); (*b*) teacher; esp. the authorities on Jewish law who preceded the Tannaim.

SOṬAH. A married woman suspected of infidelity who has been formally warned by her husband.

SUKKAH. 'Booth'; esp. the festive booth for Tabernacles (Lev. XXIII, 34ff), the roof of which must be made of something that grows from the ground such as reeds, branches or leaves of a prescribed size, quantity and quality.

SUKKOTH. The Festival of Tabernacles during the eight days of which (seven in Palestine) all Israel must dwell in booths. (V. Lev. XXIII, 34, 42f.)

TALLITH. A garment, cloak, esp. the four-cornered shawl with fringes (*ẓiẓith*) at each corner, worn during the recital of certain prayers.

TALMID ḤAKAM (Lit., 'disciple of the wise'); scholar, student of the Torah.

TALMUD (Lit., 'teaching', 'learning') applies (*a*) to the Gemara (q.v.) or (*b*) generally to the Mishnah and Gemara combined.

TAM 'Perfect', (lit., 'innocuous' opp. to *mu'ad*, q.v.); applied to an animal that did injury not more than twice. Its owner, not having been forewarned, pays only for half the damage.

TAMAD. An inferior kind of wine or vinegar produced by keeping stalks and skins of pressed grapes in water, or by pouring water into lees.

TAMID. The continual or daily burnt-offering, sacrificed every morning and evening.

TAMUN (Lit., 'hidden'); articles hidden in a heap which catches fire.

TAMUZ. The fourth month of the Jewish Calendar, corresponding to June or July.

TARḲAB. A measure containing two *ḳabs* (q.v.).

TANNA (Lit., 'one who repeats' or 'teaches'); (*a*) a Rabbi quoted in the Mishnah or Baraitha (q.v.); (*b*) in the Amoraic period, a scholar whose special task was to memorize and recite Baraithas in the presence of expounding teachers.

ṬEBEL. Produce, already at the stage of liability to the levitical and priestly dues (v. *Terumah*), before these have been separated.

ṬEBILLAH. The act of taking a ritual bath in a *miḳweh*, q.v.

ṬEBUL YOM (Lit., 'bathed during the day'); a person who has bathed to cleanse himself at the end of the period of his defilement, but who must wait until sunset to regain his ritual purity (Lev. XXII, 7).

TEFILLIN. Phylacteries; small cases containing passages from the Scripture and affixed to the forehead and arm during the recital of morning prayers, in accordance with Deut. VI, 8.

TEḲI'AH (Lit., 'blowing'); the plain blast made with the *Shofar*.

TEḤUM. The boundary beyond which one must not walk on the Sabbath, which is 2.000 cubits without the town limits; this can be extended by another 2.000 cubits by means of an *'erub*, q.v.

TEḲO or TEḲU (imperf. of 'to stand'), 'let it stand'; an expression occurring at the end of an enquiry when no definite answer is obtainable. Others consider it to be a combination of the initials of תשבי יתרץ קושיות ואיבעיות (Elijah the Tishbite will solve all difficulties and enquiries).

TEḲUFAH (Lit., 'circuit', 'cycle'). The year is divided into four cycles called *Teḳufoth;* the *Teḳufah* of Nisan (Vernal Equinox); Tammuz (Summer Solstice); Tishri (Autumn Equinox); Tebeth (Winter Solstice). The term *Teḳufah* is also applied to the season itself.

TERU'AH (Lit., 'shout'); the tremolo blast made with the *Shofar*.

TERUMAH. 'That which is lifted or separated'; the heave-offering given from the yields of the yearly harvests, from certain sacrifices, and from the *shekels* collected in a special chamber in the Temple (*terumath ha-lishkah*). *Terumah gedolah* (great offering): the first levy on the produce of the year given to the priest, (v. Num. XVIII, 8ff). Its quantity varied according to the generosity of the owner, who could give one-fortieth, one-fiftieth, or one-sixtieth of his harvest. *Terumath ma'aser* (heave-offering of the tithe): the heave-offering given to the priest by the Levite from the tithes he receives, (v. Num. XVIII, 25ff).

TISHRI. The seventh month of the Jewish calendar, corresponding to September or October.

TORAH (Lit., 'teaching', 'learning', 'instruction'); (*a*) the Pentateuch (Written Law); (*b*) the Mishnah (Oral Law); (*c*) the whole body of Jewish religious literature.

ṬREFA or ṬEREFA (Lit., 'torn'); (*a*) an animal torn by a wild beast; (*b*) any animal suffering from a serious organic disease, whose meat is forbidden even if it has been ritually slaughtered.

ṬUMṬUM. A person whose sex cannot be determined.

'UKLA. One of the smaller measures of capicity and standards of weight equal to $^1/_{32}$ (others $^1/_{20}$) of a *ḳab*, q.v.

YABAM. The brother of a married man who dies childless; the widow is called YEBAMAH, v. ḤALIẒAH.

YEBAMAH. A brother's childless widow. V. Deut. XXV, 5-10.

YEN NESEK (Lit., 'wine of libation'); wine forbidden to the Jew because it has been handed by an idolator who may have dedicated it as an offering to his deity.

YEẒER HARA' (Lit., 'formation of evil'); (*a*) the evil inclination of man; (*b*) the tempter, Satan and the Angel of Death.

YIBBUM. Levirate marriage with a brother's childless widow (v. Deut. XXV, 5-10).

YIḤUD (Lit., 'privacy'); the prohibition instituted by the Rabbis against the private association of the sexes.

ZAB, (fem. ZABAH). The biblical term for a person who has experienced seminal emission (Lev. XV, 2).

ZAR (Lit., 'stranger'); an Israelite, as opposed to a priest, who may not eat of *terumah* or perform certain acts in connection with sacrifices.

ZARAH. A co-wife, a married woman in relation to the other wives of her husband.

ẒEDAḲAH. (*a*) righteousness, equity; (*b*) charity, almsgiving.

ZEḲUḲAH. The widow who is tied by the levirate bond to her deceased husband's brother.

ẒEROROTH (Lit., 'pebbels'); pebbles or clods kicked up by an ox in walking and capable of doing damage.

ZIḲAH. The levirate bond.

ZIMMUN (rt. *ZaMaN* in Pi'el, 'to designate', 'to summon'), the ceremonial consisting of responses in answer to the summons or invitation of the leader when three men or more who partook of a common meal join together in the recital of the Grace after the meal. The responses with the prescribed variations for a company of ten or more, and for a meal in the house of a mourner, are given in full in Singer's *P.B.*, p. 279.

ẒIẒITH. The biblical name of the fringe which is attached to each of the four corners of the garment (Num. XV, 38).

ZOMEM p. *zomemim*, a witness giving false evidence and who is thus subject to the law of retaliation. Cf. Deut. XIX, 19.

ZONAH. A harlot, i.e. a woman who has intercourse with a man forbidden to her on all grounds save those specifically applying to priests; in the latter case she is a ḤALALAH.

ẒON BARZEL (Lit., 'property of the iron sheep'); which the wife makes over to the husband from her dowry, on condition that the husband is responsible to her for its full money value, whether he makes a profit or a loss on the transaction.

ZUZ. A coin of the value of a *denarius*, six *ma'ah*, or twelve *dupondia*.

SCRIPTURAL REFERENCES

NUMBERS

SCRIPTURAL REFERENCES

SCRIPTURAL REFERENCES

GENERAL INDEX*

* An Index of Rabbinical Names will be provided in the special Index Volume to be published on completion of the translation of the entire Talmud.

D

E

N

O

TRANSLITERATION OF HEBREW LETTERS

א (in middle of word)	= '
ב	= b
ו	= w
ח	= ḥ
ט	= ṭ
כ	= k
ע	= '
פ	= f
צ	= ẓ
ק	= ḳ
ת	= th

Full particulars regarding the method and scope of the translation are given in the Editor's Introduction.

ABBREVIATIONS

Alfasi	R. Isaac b. Jacob Alfasi (1013-1103).
Aruk	Talmudic Dictionary by R. Nathan b. Jeḥiel of Rome (d. 1106).
Asheri	R. Asher b. Jeḥiel (1250-1327).
A.Z.	'Abodah Zarah.
b.	ben, bar: son of.
B.B.	Baba Bathra.
BaḤ.	Bayith Ḥadash, Glosses by R. Joel b. Samuel Sirkes (1561-1640).
Bek.	Bekoroth.
Ber.	Berakoth.
B.Ḳ.	Baba Ḳamma.
B.M.	Baba Meẓi'a.
Cur. ed(d).	Current edition(s).
D.S.	*Diḳduḳe Soferim* by R. Rabbinowicz.
'Ed.	'Eduyyoth.
E.J.	*Encyclopaedia Judaica.*
'Er.	'Erubin.
E.V.	English Version.
Giṭ.	Giṭṭin.
Glos.	Glossary.
Ḥag.	Ḥagigah.
Hor.	Horayoth.
Ḥul.	Ḥullin.
J.E.	*Jewish Encyclopedia.*
J.T.	Jerusalem Talmud.
Jast.	M. Jastrow's Dictionary of the Targumim, the Talmud Bible and Yerushalmi, and the Midrashic Literature.
Keth.	Kethuboth.
Ḳid.	Ḳiddushin.
Ma'as.	Ma'asroth.
Mak.	Makkoth.
Meg.	Megillah.
Men.	Menaḥoth.
MGWJ.	*Monatsschrift für Geschichte und Wissenschaft des Judentums.*
M.Sh.	Ma'aser Sheni.
MS.M.	Munich Codex of the Talmud.
Naz.	Nazir.
Ned.	Nedarim.
Nid.	Niddah.
Obermeyer	Obermeyer J., *Die Landschaft Babylonien.*
P.B.	*The authorized Daily Prayer Book,* S. Singer.

Pes.	Pesaḥim.
R.	Rab, Rabban, Rabbenu, Rabbi.
Rashal	Notes and Glosses on the Talmud by R. Solomon Luria (d. 1573).
Rashi	Commentary of R. Isaac Yiẓḥaḳi (d. 1105).
R.H.	Rosh Hashannah.
R.V.	Revised version of the Bible.
Sanh.	Sanhedrin.
Shab.	Shabbath.
Sheḳ.	Sheḳalim.
Sonc. ed.	English Translation of the Babylonian Talmud, Soncino Press, London.
Soṭ.	Soṭah.
Suk.	Sukkah.
TA.	*Talmudische Archäologie*, by S. Krauss.
Ta'an.	Ta'anith.
Ter.	Terumoth.
Tosaf.	Tosafoth.
Tosef.	Tosefta.
Wilna Gaon	Notes by Elijah of Wilna (1720-1797) in the Wilna editions of the Talmud.
Yeb.	Yebamoth.
Zeb.	Zebaḥim.

THE MISHNAHS

TRANSLATED INTO ENGLISH

WITH NOTES, GLOSSARY

AND INDICES

BY

REV. DR ISRAEL W. SLOTKI, M. A. Litt. D.

RABBI M. H. SEGAL, M. A.

RABBI DR S. M. LEHRMAN, M. A., PH. D.

DR ISIDORE FISHMAN, PH. D., M. A.

REV. H. BORNSTEIN, B. A.

CONTENTS

KELIM

TRANSLATED INTO ENGLISH

WITH NOTES

BY

Rev. Dr Israel W. SLOTKI, M. A., Litt. D.

INTRODUCTION

Kelim,[1] the first tractate of the Order of Ṭohoroth, is concerned with the laws of levitical cleanness and uncleanness as they affect utensils, garments, instruments and weapons as well as any other articles of utility that come under the designation of *Kelim.*[1]

CHAPTER I describes in ascending order of restriction or holiness (*a*) the primary degrees ('fathers') of uncleanness, (*b*) ten degrees of uncleanness that emanate from man and (*c*) ten degrees of holiness.

CHAPTER II lays down rules on the levitical cleanness and uncleanness of wooden, leather, bone and glass utensils.

CHAPTERS III and IV define the size of a hole or a breach that renders a vessel insusceptible to uncleanness.

CHAPTER V indicates, in respect of susceptibility to, and freedom from uncleanness, the respective sizes of a baking-oven, a double stove and their component parts, as well as the stages in their manufacture at which they may for this purpose be regarded as finished articles.

CHAPTER VI describes a class of improvised stoves that are susceptible to uncleanness.

CHAPTER VII lays down the conditions under which a fire-basket of householders and the hob of a stove are rendered insusceptible to uncleanness.

CHAPTER VIII gives the laws of uncleanness as they affect the air-space of an earthenware oven.

CHAPTER IX deals with an uncleanness that is absorbed or concealed.

CHAPTER X enumerates the kinds of vessel that afford protection against uncleanness whenever they are covered with a tightly fitting lid, and describes the materials wherewith such tight-fitting may be effected.

CHAPTERS XI—XIV deal with the laws of susceptibility to, and freedom from uncleanness as they affect metal vessels.

(1) כֵּלִים plural of כְּלִי, vessel, utensil etc. in fact any article in use.

Chapters XV–XVI resume and amplify the subject of Chapter II.

Chapter XVII gives the extent of damage that frees a vessel from uncleanness, defines a number of standard measures, and lays down some general rules as to what objects are invariably clean or unclean.

Chapters XVIII–XIX lay down rules for measuring size and capacity in simple and composite articles.

Chapter XX classifies articles, damaged and undamaged, that are subject either to *midras* (v. Glos.) uncleanness or only to corpse uncleanness.

Chapter XXI teaches what parts of an object do or do not convey uncleanness as the object itself.

Chapter XXII tells what missing parts do or do not cause an object to lose its susceptibility to one or other of the various forms of uncleanness.

Chapter XXIII enumerates the parts of damaged objects that respectively remain or become free from uncleanness, and deals with the uncleanness of objects that are used for riding or sitting upon, and shows the practical differences between the two classes.

Chapter XXIV contains a series of groups of three in each of which the first is susceptible to *midras* uncleanness, the second only to corpse uncleanness, while the third is free from all uncleanness.

Chapter XXV lays down the different laws that govern the uncleanness of the outer and inner sides of objects.

Chapter XXVI is concerned mainly with objects that consist of component parts, and with the act of intention as a cause of uncleanness or cleanness.

Chapters XXVII–XXVIII enumerate the causes and indicate the minima and change in usage that affect the cleanness and uncleanness of certain objects, and also draw a distinction between articles belonging to different classes according to their owner's means, age and calling.

Chapter XXIX states which parts of articles and which whole

articles that are stitched together are regarded as connectives, and indicates the limit and extent in respect of uncleanness and sprinkling respectively.

CHAPTER XXX is devoted to the laws of cleanness and uncleanness as they affect glassware.

ISRAEL W. SLOTKI

KELIM

CHAPTER I

MISHNAH 1. THE FATHERS OF UNCLEANNESS[1] ARE A [DEAD] CREEPING THING,[2] SEMEN VIRILE, [AN ISRAELITE] WHO HAS CONTRACTED CORPSE UNCLEANNESS, A LEPER DURING THE DAYS OF HIS COUNTING[3] AND THE WATERS OF PURIFICATION[4] WHOSE QUANTITY IS LESS THAN THE MINIMUM PRESCRIBED FOR SPRINKLING.[5] BEHOLD, THESE CONVEY UNCLEANNESS TO MEN AND VESSELS BY CONTACT AND TO EARTHENWARE BY PRESENCE WITHIN THEIR AIR-SPACE,[6] BUT[7] THEY CANNOT CONVEY UNCLEANNESS BY CARRIAGE.

MISHNAH 2. ON A HIGHER PLANE[8] THAN THESE[9] ARE CARRION AND WATERS OF PURIFICATION WHOSE QUANTITY IS SUFFICIENT TO BE SPRINKLED, FOR THESE CONVEY UNCLEANNESS TO MAN BY CARRIAGE,[10] SO THAT HE IN TURN[11] CONVEYS UNCLEANNESS TO CLOTHING BY CONTACT.[12] CLOTHING, HOWEVER,[13] IS FREE FROM UNCLEANNESS WHERE THERE WAS[14] CONTACT ALONE.[15]

(1) *Sc.* those that convey uncleanness to both men and vessels. An 'offspring of uncleanness' conveys uncleanness to foodstuffs and liquids but not to men and vessels. (2) Any of the eight classes enumerated in Lev. XI, 29f. (3) V. Lev. XIV, 8f. (4) V. Num. XIX. (5) V. Parah XII, 5. (6) Even if there was no contact with the vessel. Through the external side of such a vessel, however, no uncleanness can be conveyed even by direct contact. (7) In the absence of direct contact with them. (8) In the intensity of uncleanness. (9) The 'fathers of uncleanness' enumerated in the previous Mishnah. (10) Even in the absence of direct contact between them and the man. (11) While he is still carrying one of the uncleannesses mentioned. (12) With any part of his body. (13) Though it came in contact with the unclean man. (14) Between the man and the 'father of uncleanness'. (15) Only where the man was carrying the 'father of uncleanness' at the time he came in contact with the clothing is uncleanness conveyed to the latter.

MISHNAH 3. ON A HIGHER PLANE[1] IS THE MAN WHO HAD INTERCOURSE WITH A MENSTRUANT, FOR HE CONVEYS TO THAT ON WHICH HE LIES[2] THE SAME UNCLEANNESS AS [A ZAB[3] CONVEYS] TO THAT[4] WHICH LIES ABOVE HIM.[5] ON A HIGHER PLANE[1] THAN THESE ARE THE ISSUE OF A ZAB, HIS SPITTLE, HIS SEMEN AND HIS URINE, AND THE BLOOD OF A MENSTRUANT, FOR THEY CONVEY UNCLEANNESS[6] BOTH BY CONTACT AND BY CARRIAGE.[7] ON A HIGHER PLANE[1] THAN THESE IS AN OBJECT ON WHICH ONE CAN RIDE,[8] FOR IT CONVEYS UNCLEANNESS EVEN WHEN IT LIES UNDER A HEAVY STONE.[9] ON A HIGHER PLANE[1] THAN THE OBJECT ON WHICH ONE CAN RIDE IS THAT ON WHICH ONE CAN LIE, FOR IN THE LATTER CASE UNCLEANNESS[10] IS CONVEYED BY CONTACT AS BY CARRIAGE.[11] ON A HIGHER PLANE[1] THAN THE OBJECT ON WHICH ONE CAN LIE IS THE ZAB, FOR A ZAB CONVEYS UNCLEANNESS TO THE OBJECT ON WHICH HE LIES[12] WHILE THE OBJECT ON WHICH HE LIES[13] CANNOT CONVEY THE SAME UNCLEANNESS[8] TO THAT UPON WHICH IT LIES.[14]

MISHNAH 4. ON A HIGHER PLANE[1] THAN THE ZAB IS THE ZABAH,[15] FOR SHE CONVEYS UNCLEANNESS[16] TO THE

(1) In the intensity of uncleanness. (2) Lit., 'the lower couch'. (3) A male who has a flux. (4) Whether he came in direct contact with it or not. (5) *Sc.* the former like the latter is subject only to the first grade of uncleanness. That on which a *zab* lies becomes a 'father of uncleanness'. (6) To clothes or vessels (other than earthenware). (7) *Sc.* not only by the latter but also by the former. (8) So Maim. Lit., 'a riding seat'. (9) On which the *zab* sat; though, owing to the heavy weight of the stone, the *zab's* weight could make no appreciable impression on the object. The unclean riding object under the stone has uncleanness conveyed to it by the *zab* sitting on the stone and conveys uncleanness to any clean person who sits upon the stone, v. Tosaf. Y. Ṭ. (10) To the person and the clothes he wears. (11) In the former case uncleanness is conveyed through carriage only. (12) Causing it to be a 'father of uncleanness'. (13) Even after it contracted the uncleanness of the *zab* (cf. prev. n.). (14) The latter contracting a first grade of uncleanness only. (15) A woman who has a flux. (16) Of *zibah* (a 'father of uncleanness').

MAN WHO HAS INTERCOURSE WITH HER.[1] ON A HIGHER PLANE THAN THE ZABAH IS THE LEPER, FOR HE CONVEYS UNCLEANNESS[2] BY ENTERING INTO A HOUSE.[3] ON A HIGHER PLANE THAN THE LEPER IS A BONE[4] OF THE SIZE OF A BARLEY GRAIN, FOR IT[5] CONVEYS AN UNCLEANNESS OF SEVEN DAYS. MORE RESTRICTIVE THAN ALL THESE IS A CORPSE, FOR IT CONVEYS UNCLEANNESS BY OHEL[6] WHEREBY ALL THE OTHERS CONVEY NO UNCLEANNESS.[7]

MISHNAH 5. TEN GRADES OF UNCLEANNESS[8] EMANATE FROM MEN: A MAN[9] BEFORE THE OFFERING OF HIS OBLIGATORY SACRIFICES[10] IS FORBIDDEN TO EAT HOLY THINGS BUT PERMITTED TO EAT TERUMAH AND [SECOND] TITHE. IF HE IS[11] A ṬEBUL YOM[12] HE IS FORBIDDEN TO EAT HOLY THINGS AND TERUMAH BUT PERMITTED THE EATING OF [SECOND] TITHE. IF HE[11] EMITTED SEMEN[13] HE IS FORBIDDEN TO EAT ANY OF THE THREE. IF HE[11] HAD INTERCOURSE WITH A MENSTRUANT HE CONVEYS THE SAME UNCLEANNESS TO THAT ON WHICH HE LIES AS [A ZAB CONVEYS] TO THAT WHICH LIES ABOVE HIM.[14] IF HE IS[11] A ZAB WHO HAS OBSERVED TWO DISCHARGES HE CONVEYS UNCLEANNESS TO THAT ON WHICH HE LIES OR SITS AND IS REQUIRED TO UNDERGO IMMERSION

(1) A *zab*, however, by intercourse, conveys to a woman a minor form of uncleanness which lasts until sunset only. (2) To men and vessels. (3) If they (cf. prev. n.) were under the same roof. (4) Of a corpse. (5) Unlike the former where uncleanness terminates at sunset. (6) 'Overshadowing' (v. Glos.). Irrespective of (*a*) whether, for instance, the whole body of the clean person was within the *ohel* (tent) or only a part of it, and (*b*) whether there was a partition in the *ohel* between the corpse and the clean person or not, and (*c*) whether or not the corpse or the clean person was stationary or moving. (7) Even a leper conveys uncleanness by *ohel* only where (*a*) his entire body was within it, (*b*) there was no partition between the leper and the clean person and (*c*) the leper was not on the move. (8) One more restrictive than the other. (9) Such as a confirmed leper or a *zab*, or a *zabah*, whose restoration to cleanness depends on the offering of the prescribed sacrifice. (10) Lit., 'lacking atonement'. (11) Lit., 'he returned to be'. (12) One who immersed himself on the selfsame day (v. Glos.). (13) Lit., 'master (or subject) of a mishap'. (14) Cf. *supra* p. 8, n. 4.

IN RUNNING WATER,[1] BUT IS EXEMPT FROM THE SACRIFICE.[2] IF HE OBSERVED THREE DISCHARGES HE MUST BRING THE SACRIFICE.[3] IF HE[4] IS A LEPER THAT WAS ONLY SHUT UP[5] HE CONVEYS UNCLEANNESS[6] BY ENTRY[7] BUT IS EXEMPT FROM LOOSENING HIS HAIR,[8] FROM RENDING HIS CLOTHES,[8] FROM SHAVING[9] AND FROM THE BIRDS OFFERING;[10] BUT IF HE WAS A CONFIRMED LEPER[11] HE IS LIABLE TO ALL THESE. IF A LIMB ON WHICH THERE WAS NOT THE PROPER QUANTITY OF FLESH[12] WAS SEVERED FROM A PERSON, IT CONVEYS UNCLEANNESS BY CONTACT AND BY CARRIAGE BUT NOT BY OHEL; BUT IF IT BEARS THE PROPER QUANTITY OF FLESH IT CONVEYS UNCLEANNESS BY CONTACT, BY CARRIAGE AND BY OHEL. A 'PROPER QUANTITY OF FLESH' IS SUCH AS IS CAPABLE OF HEALING. R. JUDAH EXPLAINED: IF IN ONE PLACE IT[13] HAS FLESH SUFFICIENT TO SURROUND IT[13] WITH [THE THICKNESS OF] A THREAD OF THE WOOF[14] IT IS CAPABLE OF HEALING.

MISHNAH 6. THERE ARE TEN GRADES OF HOLINESS: THE LAND OF ISRAEL IS HOLIER THAN ALL OTHER LANDS. AND WHAT IS THE NATURE OF ITS HOLINESS? THAT FROM IT ARE BROUGHT THE 'OMER,[15] THE FIRSTFRUITS[16] AND THE TWO LOAVES,[17] WHICH MAY NOT BE BROUGHT FROM ANY OF THE OTHER LANDS.

MISHNAH 7. CITIES[18] THAT ARE WALLED[19] ARE HOLIER,[20] FOR LEPERS MUST BE SENT OUT OF THEM AND A CORPSE, THOUGH IT MAY BE CARRIED ABOUT WITHIN THEM AS LONG

(1) Unlike the others whose immersion may be performed in a ritual bath of standing water. (2) Prescribed only for a *zab* who experienced three discharges (v. *infra*). (3) Cf. prev. n. (4) V. p. 9, n. 11. (5) V. Lev. XIII, 4f. (6) To men and objects in a house. (7) Into that house. (8) V. Lev. XIII, 45. (9) V. Lev. XIV, 8. (10) V. Lev. XIV, 4. (11) One whom the priest declared to be unclean. (12) As prescribed *infra*. (13) The limb. (14) Which is twice as thick as that of the warp. (15) V. Lev. XXIII, 10f. (16) V. Deut. XXVI, 2ff. (17) V. Lev. XXIII, 17. (18) In the Land of Israel. (19) Since the time of Joshua the son of Nun. (20) Than the other parts of the Land.

AS IT IS DESIRED,[1] MAY NOT BE BROUGHT BACK ONCE IT HAS BEEN TAKEN OUT.

MISHNAH 8. THE AREA WITHIN THE WALL[2] IS HOLIER, FOR IT IS THERE[3] THAT HOLY THINGS OF A MINOR DEGREE AND SECOND TITHE MAY BE EATEN. THE TEMPLE MOUNT[4] IS HOLIER, FOR NEITHER ZABS NOR ZABAHS NOR MENSTRUANTS NOR WOMEN AFTER CHILDBIRTH MAY ENTER IT. THE RAMPART[5] IS HOLIER, FOR NEITHER IDOLATERS NOR ONE WHO CONTRACTED CORPSE UNCLEANNESS MAY ENTER IT. THE COURT OF WOMEN[6] IS HOLIER, FOR NO ṬEBUL YOM[7] MAY ENTER IT, THOUGH NO SIN-OFFERING IS THEREBY INCURRED. THE COURT OF THE ISRAELITES[8] IS HOLIER, FOR A MAN WHO HAS NOT YET OFFERED HIS OBLIGATORY SACRIFICES[9] MAY NOT ENTER IT, AND IF HE ENTERS HE INCURS THEREBY A SIN-OFFERING. THE COURT OF THE PRIESTS[10] IS HOLIER, FOR NO ISRAELITES MAY ENTER IT EXCEPT WHEN THEY ARE REQUIRED TO DO SO[11] IN CONNECTION WITH THE LAYING ON OF HANDS,[12] SLAYING OR WAVING.[13]

MISHNAH 9. THE AREA BETWEEN THE ULAM[14] AND THE ALTAR IS HOLIER,[15] FOR MEN AFFLICTED WITH BLEMISHES OR WITH A WILD GROWTH OF HAIR MAY NOT ENTER IT. THE HEKAL IS HOLIER, FOR NO ONE WHOSE HANDS OR FEET ARE UNWASHED MAY ENTER IT. THE HOLY OF HOLIES IS HOLIER, FOR ONLY THE HIGH PRIEST, ON THE DAY OF ATONEMENT, AT

(1) In connection with its funeral or burial arrangements. (2) Of Jerusalem. (3) And not without the wall. (4) An area of five hundred by five hundred cubits in which the Temple buildings were situated. (5) The *Ḥel*. A causeway ten cubits wide surrounding the inner precincts of the Temple (cf. Mid. II, 3). (6) Situated within the Rampart. (7) V. Glos. (8) This was situated within the Court of the Women from which it was approached by an ascent of fifteen steps (cf. Mid. II, 5). (9) Cf. *supra* p. 9, n. 9. (10) Cf. Mid. II, 6. (11) Lit., 'their requirements'. (12) On a sacrifice (v. Lev. III, 2). (13) Cf. Lev. VII, 30. (14) The Porch, the Hall leading into the *Hekal*, the Sanctuary. (15) In accordance with Pentateuchal (Maim.) or only Rabbinical (v. Bert. and L.) law.

THE SERVICE,[1] MAY ENTER IT.[2] R. JOSE STATED: IN FIVE RESPECTS IS THE AREA BETWEEN THE ULAM AND THE ALTAR ON A PAR WITH THE HEKAL, FOR THOSE AFFLICTED WITH BLEMISHES OR WITH A WILD GROWTH OF HAIR, OR WHO HAVE DRUNK WINE OR WHOSE HANDS OR FEET ARE UNWASHED MAY NOT ENTER THERE,[3] AND THE PEOPLE MUST KEEP AWAY FROM THE AREA BETWEEN THE ULAM AND THE ALTAR[4] WHEN THE INCENSE IS BEING BURNED.[5]

(1) In the Temple. (2) Four times: To burn incense, to sprinkle the blood of the bullock, to sprinkle the blood of the he-goat and to take out the spoon and the pan; v. Lev. XVI, 2ff. (3) Except when necessary in connection with the Temple services (L.). (4) And, much more so, from the *Hekal*. (5) In the Holy of Holies or on the golden altar.

KELIM

CHAPTER II

MISHNAH 1. VESSELS OF WOOD, VESSELS OF LEATHER, VESSELS OF BONE OR VESSELS OF GLASS THAT ARE FLAT ARE CLEAN[1] AND THOSE THAT FORM A RECEPTACLE ARE UNCLEAN.[2] IF THEY WERE BROKEN THEY BECOME CLEAN[1] AGAIN. IF ONE REMADE THEM INTO VESSELS THEY ARE SUSCEPTIBLE TO UNCLEANNESS HENCEFORTH.[3] EARTHEN VESSELS AND VESSELS OF ALUM-CRYSTALS ARE ON A PAR IN RESPECT OF UNCLEANNESS: THEY CONTRACT AND CONVEY[4] UNCLEANNESS THROUGH THEIR AIR-SPACE,[5] THEY CONTRACT UNCLEANNESS[6] THROUGH THEIR [CONCAVE] BOTTOMS BUT NOT[7] THROUGH THEIR BACKS;[8] AND WHEN BROKEN[9] THEY BECOME CLEAN.[1]

MISHNAH 2. AS REGARDS THE SMALLEST EARTHEN VESSELS, AND THE BOTTOMS AND SIDES [OF THE LARGER BUT BROKEN VESSELS] THAT CAN STAND[10] UNSUPPORTED,[11] THE PRESCRIBED SIZE[12] IS A CAPACITY TO HOLD OIL SUFFICIENT FOR THE ANOINTING OF A LITTLE FINGER OF A CHILD IF[13] THEIR FORMER CAPACITY[14] WAS THAT OF[15] A LOG. IF[13] THEIR FORMER CAPACITY[14] WAS FROM ONE LOG TO A SE'AH THEIR PRESENT CAPACITY[12] MUST BE A QUARTER OF A LOG; IF IT WAS[14] FROM A SE'AH TO TWO SE'AH IT MUST BE[16] HALF

(1) *Sc.* they are not susceptible to uncleanness. (2) Cf. prev. n. *mut. mut.* (3) They do not, however, resume their former uncleanness as metal vessels do. (4) To foodstuffs and liquids. (5) Even in the absence of contact with the vessel. (6) By contact; but not through their air-space. (7) Even if there was contact between the vessel and the uncleanness. (8) Their outer flat or convex sides. (9) But not by immersion as is the case with vessels made of other materials. (10) When filled with liquid. (11) Without shedding their contents. (12) That renders them susceptible to uncleanness. (13) In the case of broken vessels. (14) While they were whole. (15) Lit., 'and until'. (16) If it is to be susceptible to uncleanness.

A LOG; IF[1] FROM TWO SE'AH TO THREE SE'AH OR AS MUCH AS FIVE SE'AH IT MUST BE[2] A LOG; SO R. ISHMAEL. R. AKIBA STATED: I DO NOT PRESCRIBE ANY SIZE FOR THE UNBROKEN VESSELS,[3] BUT[4] THIS IS THE RULE: AS REGARDS THE SMALLEST EARTHEN VESSELS, AND THE BOTTOMS AND SIDES [OF LARGER BUT BROKEN ONES] THAT CAN STAND[5] UNSUPPORTED,[6] THE PRESCRIBED SIZE[7] IS A CAPACITY TO HOLD ENOUGH OIL TO ANOINT THE LITTLE FINGER OF A CHILD. [THIS SIZE IS PRESCRIBED FOR POTS] THAT ARE NOT BIGGER THAN[8] THE SMALL COOKING-POTS. FOR SMALL COOKING-POTS AND FOR THOSE BETWEEN THESE AND THE LYDDA JARS THE PRESCRIBED CAPACITY[7] IS A QUARTER OF A LOG. FOR THOSE WHICH HAVE A SIZE BETWEEN THAT OF LYDDA JARS AND THE BETHLEHEM JARS THE CAPACITY[7] MUST BE THAT OF HALF A LOG. FOR THOSE BETWEEN THE BETHLEHEM JARS AND LARGE STONE JARS THE CAPACITY[7] MUST BE THAT OF A LOG. R. JOḤANAN B. ZAKKAI RULED: THE PRESCRIBED CAPACITY[7] FOR THE FRAGMENTS OF LARGE STONE JARS IS TWO LOGS, AND THAT FOR THE BOTTOMS OF BROKEN GALILEAN CRUSES AND SMALL JARS IS ANY WHATSOEVER, BUT THE FRAGMENTS OF THEIR SIDES ARE IN NO CASE SUSCEPTIBLE TO UNCLEANNESS.

MISHNAH 3. THE FOLLOWING[9] ARE NOT SUSCEPTIBLE TO UNCLEANNESS AMONG EARTHEN VESSELS: A TRAY WITHOUT A RIM, A FIRE-PAN WITH BROKEN SIDES, A TUBE FOR ROASTING CORN, GUTTERS EVEN IF THEY ARE BENT[10] AND EVEN IF THEY HAVE[11] SOME FORM OF RECEPTACLE,[12] A BASKET-COVER[13] THAT WAS TURNED INTO A BREAD-BASKET,[10] A

(1) V. p. 13, n. 14. (2) V. p. 13, n. 16. (3) Lit., 'in them'. (4) The susceptibility to uncleanness being determined by the shape and place of origin of the vessel. (5) V. p. 13, n. 10. (6) V. p. 13, n. 11. (7) V. p. 13, n. 12. (8) V. p. 13, n. 15. (9) Having no proper concave receptacle. (10) Because the receptacle is an imperfect one. (11) As a result of excavation by constantly dripping water. (12) Since the cavity was not made for the purpose of serving as such. (13) Shaped somewhat in the form

PITCHER[1] THAT HAS BEEN ADAPTED[2] AS A COVER FOR GRAPES,[3] A JAR[1] FOR SWIMMERS,[4] A SMALL JAR[1] FIXED TO THE SIDES OF A LADLE,[5] A BED, A STOOL, A BENCH, A TABLE, A SHIP,[6] AND AN EARTHEN LAMP, BEHOLD THESE ARE INSUSCEPTIBLE TO UNCLEANNESS. THE FOLLOWING IS A GENERAL RULE:[7] ANY AMONG EARTHEN VESSELS THAT HAS NO INNER PART IS NOT SUSCEPTIBLE TO UNCLEANNESS ON ITS OUTER SIDES.[8]

MISHNAH 4. A LANTERN THAT HAS A RECEPTACLE FOR OIL IS SUSCEPTIBLE TO UNCLEANNESS, BUT ONE THAT HAS NONE IS INSUSCEPTIBLE. A POTTER'S MOULD ON WHICH ONE BEGINS TO SHAPE THE CLAY IS INSUSCEPTIBLE TO UNCLEANNESS,[9] BUT THAT ON WHICH ONE FINISHES IT IS SUSCEPTIBLE.[10] A FUNNEL FOR HOME USE[11] IS INSUSCEPTIBLE TO UNCLEANNESS,[9] BUT THAT OF PEDLARS IS SUSCEPTIBLE BECAUSE[12] IT ALSO SERVES AS A MEASURE;[13] SO R. JUDAH B. BATHYRA. R. AKIBA SAID: BECAUSE ONE PUTS IT ON ITS SIDE[14] SO AS TO LET THE BUYER SMELL IT.[15]

MISHNAH 5. THE COVERS OF WINE JARS AND OIL JARS

of a receptacle but not originally intended to hold anything within it.

(1) Though it has a proper receptacle. (2) By some alteration in its shape. (3) In consequence of which it is no longer used as a receptacle. (4) Being permanently stopped up on both sides it can no longer be regarded as having a proper receptacle (cf. prev. n.). (5) To serve as its handle so as to facilitate its use (cf. *supra* n. 3). (6) A ship's insusceptibility to uncleanness, despite its shape and use as a receptacle, is a Pentateuchal ordinance. (7) That has some, though only an indirect, bearing on the preceding laws. (8) Only when it has an inner part may uncleanness be imparted to its outer sides. The inner part of an earthen vessel contracts uncleanness through its inner air-space only. It can never contract uncleanness through its outer sides. (9) Because it has no receptacle. (10) Since it has a receptacle. (11) Lit., 'of householders'. (12) By closing up the narrower hole of the funnel with a finger when filling it and removing the finger when holding the funnel over the buyer's utensil. (13) And may, therefore, be regarded as a proper receptacle. (14) To take up some of the liquid. (15) A funnel is consequently susceptible to uncleanness even if it contains less than any known measure. According

AND THE COVERS OF PAPYRUS[1] JARS[2] ARE INSUSCEPTIBLE TO UNCLEANNESS, BUT IF THEY WERE ADAPTED FOR USE AS RECEPTACLES THEY ARE SUSCEPTIBLE. THE COVER OF A STEW-POT IS NOT SUSCEPTIBLE TO UNCLEANNESS WHEN IT HAS A HOLE[3] OR A POINTED TOP,[4] BUT IF IT HAS NEITHER HOLE NOR POINTED TOP IT IS SUSCEPTIBLE BECAUSE SHE[5] DRAINS THE VEGETABLES INTO IT. R. ELIEZER B. ZADOK SAID: BECAUSE SHE TURNS OUT THE CONTENTS [OF THE POT] ON TO IT.

MISHNAH 6. IF A DAMAGED JAR[6] WAS FOUND IN A FURNACE,[7] BEFORE ITS MANUFACTURE WAS COMPLETE[8] IT IS NOT SUSCEPTIBLE TO UNCLEANNESS,[9] BUT IF AFTER ITS MANUFACTURE WAS COMPLETE[10] IT IS SUSCEPTIBLE.[11] AS TO A SPRINKLER,[12] R. ELIEZER B. ZADOK HOLDS IT TO BE INSUSCEPTIBLE TO UNCLEANNESS; BUT R. JOSE HOLDS IT TO BE SUSCEPTIBLE BECAUSE IT LETS THE LIQUID OUT IN DROPS ONLY.[13]

MISHNAH 7. THE FOLLOWING AMONG EARTHEN VESSELS ARE SUSCEPTIBLE TO UNCLEANNESS: A TRAY WITH A RIM, AN UNBROKEN FIRE-PAN, AND A TRAY MADE UP OF[14] DISHES. IF ONE OF THEM[15] CONTRACTED UNCLEANNESS FROM A

to the first Tanna, however, only when a funnel is capable of containing a known measure is it susceptible to uncleanness.

(1) *Neyaroth*. Some regard this word as a place name. (2) Var. lec., 'and the papyrus (covers of jars)'. (3) In consequence of which it cannot be used as a receptacle. (4) Which prevents it from being inverted and placed with its cavity upwards (cf. prev. n.). (5) *Sc.* the housewife. (6) *Gastra*, γαστήρ; v. *infra* IV, 2-3. (7) In which earthen vessels are baked. (8) So that the defect occurred before the jar assumed the status of a 'vessel'. (9) Since only 'vessels' are susceptible. (10) Cf. n. 8 *mut. mut.* (11) Because it is used as a receptacle for drops falling from a jar. (12) Consisting of a perforated sieve-like receptacle in which the liquid is held by the closing up with the finger of a hole above. (13) Such small holes do not allow a liquid to be taken in, and it is only the bigger kind of holes that destroy the status of a vessel. (14) Lit., 'full'. (15) The dishes in the last mentioned tray.

[DEAD] CREEPING THING[1] THEY DO NOT ALL BECOME UNCLEAN, BUT IF THE TRAY HAD A RIM THAT PROJECTED ABOVE THE RIMS OF THE DISHES AND ONE OF THEM[2] CONTRACTED UNCLEANNESS ALL ARE RENDERED UNCLEAN.[3] SIMILARLY WITH AN EARTHEN SPICE-POT[4] AND A DOUBLE INK-POT.[5] BUT IF ONE CONTAINER OF A WOODEN SPICE-BOX[4] CONTRACTED UNCLEANNESS FROM A LIQUID,[6] THE OTHER IS NOT RENDERED UNCLEAN.[7] R. JOḤANAN B. NURI RULED: ITS THICKNESS[8] IS DEEMED TO BE DIVIDED[9] AND THAT SIDE WHICH SERVES THE UNCLEAN ONE IS UNCLEAN WHILE THAT WHICH SERVES THE CLEAN ONE REMAINS CLEAN. IF ITS RIM PROJECTS ABOVE THE OTHERS AND ONE OF THEM[10] CONTRACTED UNCLEANNESS THE OTHER ALSO IS RENDERED UNCLEAN.

MISHNAH 8. A TORCH[11] IS SUSCEPTIBLE TO UNCLEANNESS,[12] AND THE RESERVOIR[13] OF A LAMP CONTRACTS UNCLEANNESS[14] THROUGH ITS AIR-SPACE.[15] THE COMB[16] OF A COOLER,[17] R. ELIEZER RULED, IS NOT SUSCEPTIBLE TO UNCLEANNESS,[18] BUT THE SAGES RULED THAT IT WAS SUSCEPTIBLE.[19]

(1) And much more so from liquids. (2) V. p. 16, n. 15. (3) Since the creeping thing, when it is in the air-space of any of the dishes, is also within the air-space of the rim of the tray which encompasses all its constituents. (4) That was made up of several containers. (5) In their cases too the uncleanness of one container or pot does not affect the others unless a rim running round the whole contrivance projects above the rims of the constituents. (6) Only a liquid. In the case of a dead creeping thing the entire contrivance becomes unclean. (7) Since the uncleanness of the one container could be conveyed to the other only, by way of the adjoining sides, and the uncleanness of liquids cannot be conveyed, even Rabbinically, through the outside of a vessel. (8) Of the side which separates the clean from the unclean container. (9) Where one of them only came in contact with unclean liquids. (10) The constituent containers. (11) Consisting of an earthen bowl fixed to a pole and filled with wicks and oil. (12) Though on account of its pointed bottom (which fits into the pole) it cannot stand unsupported. (13) Lit., 'the house of its sinking'. (14) As any other earthen vessel that is shaped as a receptacle. (15) Though it does not serve as a proper receptacle for the lamp which is only partly inserted into it. (16) Projections around the rim in the shape of the teeth of a comb. (17) Made of earthenware. (18) *Sc.* an uncleanness on the comb is not regarded as one within the air-space of the cooler. (19) Cf. prev. n. *mut. mut.*

KELIM

CHAPTER III

MISHNAH I. THE SIZE OF A HOLE THAT RENDERS AN EARTHEN VESSEL CLEAN[1] IS THE FOLLOWING: IF THE VESSEL WAS USED FOR FOODSTUFFS THE HOLE MUST BE BIG ENOUGH FOR OLIVES [TO FALL THROUGH],[2] IF IT WAS USED FOR LIQUIDS IT SUFFICES FOR THE HOLE TO BE BIG ENOUGH FOR LIQUIDS [TO BE ADMITTED THROUGH IT],[3] AND IF IT WAS USED FOR BOTH IT IS SUBJECTED TO THE GREATER RESTRICTION, VIZ., THAT THE HOLE MUST BE BIG ENOUGH FOR OLIVES [TO FALL THROUGH].[4]

MISHNAH 2. AS REGARDS A JAR THE SIZE OF THE HOLE[5] MUST BE SUCH THAT A DRIED FIG [WILL FALL THROUGH];[4] SO R. SIMEON. R. JUDAH SAID: WALNUTS.[6] R. MEIR SAID: OLIVES.[6] THE SIZE OF A HOLE[5] IN A STEW-POT OR A COOKING POT MUST BE SUCH THAT OLIVES [WILL FALL THROUGH]; IN A CRUSE AND A PITCHER, SUCH THAT OIL [WILL PENETRATE THROUGH IT];[7] AND IN A COOLER, SUCH THAT WATER [WILL PENETRATE THROUGH IT].[7] R. SIMEON RULED: THE SIZE OF THE HOLE IN THE CASE OF ALL THREE GROUPS[8] MUST BE SUCH THAT SEED [WILL FALL THROUGH IT]. IN A LAMP THE SIZE OF THE HOLE[5] MUST BE SUCH THAT OIL [WILL PENETRATE THROUGH IT].[7] R. ELIEZER SAID: SUCH THAT

(1) If (*a*) it was previously unclean; and if it was clean (*b*) insusceptible to all future uncleanness. (2) If it was smaller, the vessel (cf. prev. n.) remains (*a*) unclean or (*b*) susceptible to future uncleanness, since it can still be used for foodstuffs. Only a vessel that can no longer serve its former purpose is exempt from all uncleanness. (3) When the vessel is placed in a liquid. Such a hole is bigger than one which only allows a liquid within the vessel to flow out. (4) Cf. n. 2 *mut. mut.* (5) That renders the vessel (*a*) clean or (*b*) insusceptible to uncleanness. (6) A smaller size than the previous one. (7) Cf. *supra* n. 3 *mut. mut.* (8) Stew-pot and cooking pot; cruse and pitcher; and cooler.

A SMALL PERUṬAH [WILL DROP OUT THROUGH IT].[1] A LAMP[2] WHOSE NOZZLE HAS BEEN REMOVED IS CLEAN;[3] AND ONE MADE OF EARTH[4] WHOSE NOZZLE HAS BEEN BURNT BY THE WICK IS ALSO CLEAN.[3]

MISHNAH 3. IF A JAR[5] THAT HAD A HOLE[6] WAS MENDED WITH PITCH[7] AND THEN WAS BROKEN AGAIN,[8] IF THE FRAGMENT THAT WAS MENDED WITH THE PITCH CAN CONTAIN A QUARTER OF A LOG[9] IT IS UNCLEAN, SINCE THE DESIGNATION OF VESSEL HAS NEVER CEASED TO BE APPLIED TO IT. IF A POTSHERD HAD A HOLE THAT WAS MENDED WITH PITCH, IT IS CLEAN THOUGH IT CAN CONTAIN A QUARTER OF A LOG, BECAUSE THE DESIGNATION OF VESSEL HAS CEASED TO BE APPLIED TO IT.

MISHNAH 4. IF A JAR WAS CRACKED[10] BUT[11] WAS LINED WITH CATTLE DUNG, ALTHOUGH THE POTSHERDS WOULD FALL APART WERE THE DUNG TO BE REMOVED,[12] IT IS UNCLEAN,[13] BECAUSE[14] IT NEVER CEASED TO BEAR THE NAME OF VESSEL. IF IT WAS BROKEN[15] AND SOME OF ITS SHERDS WERE STUCK TOGETHER AGAIN,[16] OR IF SOME POTTER'S CLAY WAS BROUGHT FOR THE PURPOSE[17] FROM ELSEWHERE, AND[18] IT WAS ALSO LINED WITH CATTLE DUNG, EVEN THOUGH THE POTSHERDS HOLD TOGETHER WHEN THE DUNG IS REMOVED,

(1) A bigger size than the previous one. (2) Of baked earthenware. (3) V. p. 18, n. 1. (4) That was unbaked. (5) Whose capacity was from one *log* to a *se'ah*. (6) Of the prescribed size (cf. prev. Mishnah) and in consequence of which the jar becomes clean. (7) The jar thus resuming the status of a vessel and the susceptibility to uncleanness. (8) Into fragments. (9) And can also stand unsupported. (10) To such an extent that, were it to be moved about while half a *ḳab* of dried figs were in it, it would collapse. (11) In order to keep its parts together. (12) So that the mainstay of the jar is the cattle dung which is insusceptible to uncleanness. (13) If it was unclean before; and if it was clean it is susceptible to uncleanness. (14) Though cracked. (15) Its potsherds falling apart. (16) With any adhesive substance. (17) Of sticking the potsherds together. (18) To provide further strength.

IT IS CLEAN,[1] BECAUSE IT[2] CEASED TO BEAR THE NAME OF VESSEL. IF IT[3] CONTAINED ONE SHERD THAT COULD HOLD[4] A QUARTER OF A LOG,[5] ALL ITS[3] PARTS[6] CONTRACT UNCLEANNESS BY CONTACT,[7] BUT THAT SHERD[8] CONTRACTS UNCLEANNESS THROUGH ITS AIR-SPACE.

MISHNAH 5. IF A SOUND VESSEL WAS LINED, R. MEIR AND R. SIMEON RULED: THE LINING[9] CONTRACTS UNCLEANNESS;[10] BUT THE SAGES RULED: A LINING OVER A SOUND VESSEL IS INSUSCEPTIBLE TO UNCLEANNESS,[11] AND ONLY ONE OVER A CRACKED VESSEL IS SUSCEPTIBLE.[12] AND THE SAME DISPUTE[13] APPLIES TO THE HOOP[14] OF A PUMPKIN SHELL.[15]

MISHNAH 6. AS TO SCUTCHGRASS WHEREWITH THE LARGEST JARS[16] ARE LINED, ANY ONE THAT TOUCHES IT[17] BECOMES UNCLEAN.[18] THE PLUG OF A JAR[19] IS NOT REGARDED AS CONNECTED.[20] THAT[21] WHICH TOUCHES THE LINING OF AN OVEN[22] IS UNCLEAN.[23]

(1) Cf. p. 19 n. 3 *mut. mut.* (2) When it was broken in pieces. (3) The reconstructed vessel. (4) Independently of the others. (5) Of liquids. (6) Which may be regarded as a handle to the biggest part. (7) But not through their air-space, since a handle contracts uncleanness through contact only. (8) That can hold a quarter of a *log*. Lit., 'and opposite it'. (9) Which is now a part of the vessel. (10) If the vessel contracted any through its air-space. Foodstuffs and liquids that come in contact with such a lining consequently contract uncleanness. (11) Since the parts of the vessel are held together without the aid of the lining the latter cannot be regarded as an integral part of the former. (12) Cf. prev. n. *mut. mut.* (13) Between R. Meir and R. Simeon on the one hand and the Sages on the other. (14) Made of wood or iron. (15) Which, when dry and hollow, was used for the drawing of water. The hoop in relation to the pumpkin is in the same position as the lining in relation to the vessel. (16) *Pitesin*, sing. *pitos* cf. πίθος. (17) When the jar is unclean. (18) Even according to the Rabbis (cf. prev. Mishnah). As the lining serves the purpose of preventing leakage of the wine it must be regarded as an integral part of the jar that is subject to the same uncleanness as the jar itself. (19) Since it is movable. (20) With the jar. If one contracted an uncleanness it does not convey it to the other. (21) Foodstuffs. (22) That was unclean. (23) As the lining helps to preserve the heat of the oven it is regarded as an integral part of it.

MISHNAH 7. IF A CAULDRON[1] WAS LINED WITH MORTAR AND WITH POTTER'S CLAY, THAT WHICH TOUCHES THE MORTAR IS UNCLEAN[2] BUT THAT WHICH TOUCHES THE POTTER'S CLAY[3] IS CLEAN.[4] IF A KETTLE[5] WAS PUNCTURED AND THE HOLE WAS STOPPED WITH PITCH, R. JOSE RULES THAT IT IS CLEAN SINCE IT CANNOT HOLD HOT WATER[6] AS COLD.[7] THE SAME RULING HE ALSO GAVE[8] CONCERNING VESSELS MADE OF PITCH. IF COPPER VESSELS WERE LINED WITH PITCH THE LINING[9] IS CLEAN,[10] BUT IF THEY ARE USED FOR WINE[11] IT IS UNCLEAN.[12]

MISHNAH 8. IF A JAR WAS PERFORATED AND THE HOLE WAS STOPPED UP WITH MORE PITCH[13] THAN WAS NECESSARY, THAT[14] WHICH TOUCHES THE NEEDED PORTION IS UNCLEAN, BUT THAT WHICH TOUCHES THE UNNEEDED PORTION[15] IS CLEAN. IF PITCH DRIPPED UPON A JAR,[16] WHAT TOUCHES THE FORMER[17] REMAINS CLEAN. IF A WOODEN OR EARTHEN FUNNEL WAS STOPPED UP WITH PITCH, R. ELEAZAR B. AZARIAH RULES THAT IT IS UNCLEAN.[18] R. AKIBA RULES THAT IT IS UNCLEAN WHERE IT IS OF WOOD[19] AND CLEAN WHERE IT IS OF EARTHENWARE.[20] R. JOSE RULES THAT BOTH ARE CLEAN.[21]

(1) V. p. 20, n. 22. (2) Since the mortar adheres thoroughly to the cauldron it is regarded as part of it and consequently contracts its uncleanness. (3) Which crumbles and falls away. (4) Cf. n. 2 *mut. mut.* (5) Which, unlike the cauldron mentioned before, is not used for the boiling of water. (6) Which would melt the pitch. (7) Much more so does this apply to a cauldron which is placed over a fire. (8) For a similar reason. (9) Since it is likely to be removed. (10) Even where the vessels have contracted an uncleanness. (11) Which is not kept hot. (12) Because the lining is regarded as a part of the vessel. (13) In thickness or extent. (14) Foodstuffs or drinks. (15) Lit., 'more than its need'. (16) That was unclean. (17) Though it was only a drop and might have been presumed to lose itself in the identity of the jar. (18) Since it can now hold liquids. (19) To which pitch thoroughly adheres. (20) From which the pitch falls away. (21) A funnel in his opinion cannot be regarded as a proper receptacle even if it was stopped up.

KELIM

CHAPTER IV

MISHNAH 1. A POTSHERD[1] THAT CANNOT STAND UNSUPPORTED ON ACCOUNT OF ITS HANDLE,[2] OR A POTSHERD WHOSE BOTTOM IS POINTED AND THAT POINT CAUSES IT TO OVERBALANCE, IS CLEAN.[3] IF THE HANDLE WAS REMOVED OR THE POINT WAS BROKEN OFF IT IS STILL CLEAN.[4] R. JUDAH RULES THAT IT IS UNCLEAN.[5] IF A JAR WAS BROKEN[6] BUT IS STILL CAPABLE OF HOLDING SOMETHING IN ITS SIDES, OR IF IT WAS SPLIT INTO A KIND OF TWO TROUGHS, R. JUDAH DECLARES IT CLEAN[3] BUT THE SAGES DECLARE IT TO BE UNCLEAN.[5]

MISHNAH 2. IF A JAR WAS CRACKED AND CANNOT BE MOVED ABOUT WITH HALF A ḲAB OF DRIED FIGS IN IT, IT IS CLEAN.[7] IF A DAMAGED VESSEL[8] WAS CRACKED AND IT CANNOT HOLD ANY LIQUID, EVEN THOUGH IT CAN HOLD FOODSTUFFS, IT IS CLEAN,[3] SINCE ONE REMNANT[9] IS NOT USED FOR THE SAKE OF ANOTHER REMNANT.[10]

MISHNAH 3. WHAT IS MEANT BY A 'DAMAGED VESSEL'?[11]

(1) Broken from a vessel. (2) Lit., 'ear'; *sc.* the handle of the vessel (that happened to be attached to the sherd in question) which overbalances it. (3) If it was previously unclean. If it was clean it is insusceptible to future uncleanness. (4) Because once a damaged earthen vessel becomes clean it remains so for all time. (5) Cf. n. 3 *mut. mut.* (6) In its bottom. (7) Since it is regarded as a broken vessel. (8) *Gasṭra,* v. *supra* II, 6, n. 6. (9) A damaged vessel is a 'remnant' of a sound one. (10) *Sc.* though one might well use a damaged vessel ('a remnant') for the purpose of collecting a liquid dripping from a tiny crack in an otherwise sound vessel (which is no remnant and one does not like to discard on account of so slight a crack) no one would so use a damaged vessel ('a remnant') when a crack occurs in a vessel that is already broken or seriously damaged (which is also 'a remnant'). (11) Which

ONE WHOSE HANDLES WERE REMOVED.[1] IF SHARP ENDS PROJECTED FROM IT,[2] ANY PART OF IT WHICH CAN CONTAIN OLIVES[3] CONTRACTS UNCLEANNESS BY CONTACT, WHILE ANY UNCLEANNESS OPPOSITE AN END[4] CONVEYS UNCLEANNESS TO THE VESSEL THROUGH ITS AIR-SPACE, BUT ANY PART OF IT WHICH CANNOT CONTAIN OLIVES[5] CONTRACTS UNCLEANNESS BY CONTACT, WHILE AN UNCLEANNESS OPPOSITE AN END[4] DOES NOT CONVEY UNCLEANNESS TO THE VESSEL THROUGH ITS AIR-SPACE. IF IT[6] WAS LEANING ON ITS SIDE[7] LIKE A KIND OF CATHEDRA,[8] ANY PART OF IT WHICH CAN CONTAIN OLIVES[3] CONTRACTS UNCLEANNESS BY CONTACT, WHILE ANY UNCLEANNESS OPPOSITE AN END CONVEYS UNCLEANNESS TO THE VESSEL THROUGH ITS AIR-SPACE, BUT ANY PART OF IT WHICH CANNOT CONTAIN OLIVES[5] CONTRACTS UNCLEANNESS BY CONTACT, WHILE AN UNCLEANNESS OPPOSITE AN END DOES NOT CONVEY UNCLEANNESS TO THE VESSEL THROUGH ITS AIR-SPACE.[9] BOWLS WITH KORFIAN[10] [BOTTOMS][11] AND CUPS WITH ZIDONIAN[10] BOTTOMS,[12] ALTHOUGH THEY CANNOT STAND UNSUPPORTED, ARE SUSCEPTIBLE TO UNCLEANNESS, BECAUSE THEY WERE ORIGINALLY FASHIONED IN THIS MANNER.

MISHNAH 4. AS REGARDS AN EARTHEN VESSEL THAT HAS THREE RIMS, IF THE INNERMOST ONE PROJECTS ABOVE THE OTHERS ALL OUTSIDE IT IS NOT SUSCEPTIBLE TO UN-

is rendered clean by the smallest hole that allows a liquid within it to flow out though the hole is not big enough to allow an olive to pass through it; cf. prev. Mishnah.

(1) Though it is otherwise sound. (2) At the top where it was broken. (3) *Sc.* where the sharp ends are to that extent close together. (4) Cf. L. (5) Cf. n. 3 *mut. mut.* (6) A vessel half of which was broken away. (7) Being incapable of standing on its bottom. (8) *καθέδρα*, a seat with a back; and that back had sharp broken ends. (9) The point in this law is that, though the broken vessel cannot stand on its bottom (cf. n. 7), it is nevertheless on a par with the damaged one spoken of previously. (10) Place name. *Aliter:* 'pointed'. (11) Which are pointed. Lit., 'the bottoms of the Karfians'. (12) Cf. prev. n. Lit., 'the bottoms of the Zidonian cups'.

CLEANNESS;[1] IF THE OUTERMOST ONE PROJECTS ABOVE THE OTHERS ALL WITHIN IT IS SUSCEPTIBLE TO UNCLEANNESS;[2] AND IF THE MIDDLE ONE PROJECTS ABOVE THE OTHERS, THAT WHICH IS WITHIN IT IS SUSCEPTIBLE TO UNCLEANNESS,[2] WHILE THAT WHICH IS WITHOUT IT IS NOT SUSCEPTIBLE TO UNCLEANNESS.[1] IF THEY[3] WERE EQUAL IN HEIGHT, R. JUDAH RULED: THE MIDDLE ONE IS DEEMED TO BE DIVIDED.[4] BUT THE SAGES RULED: ALL[5] IS INSUSCEPTIBLE TO UNCLEANNESS.[1] WHEN[6] DO EARTHEN VESSELS BECOME SUSCEPTIBLE TO UNCLEANNESS? AS SOON AS THEY ARE BAKED IN THE FURNACE, THAT BEING THE COMPLETION OF THEIR MANUFACTURE.[7]

(1) Because it is regarded as the outside of the vessel which is not susceptible to uncleanness. (2) As the inside of the vessel. (3) The three rims. (4) In its thickness, so that the outer part of it as well as all that is without it is regarded as the outside of the vessel and is insusceptible to uncleanness while its inner part and all within it is regarded as the inside of the vessel and is susceptible to uncleanness. (5) That is without the innermost rim (Elijah Wilna). (6) In the course of their manufacture. (7) Though they have not yet passed the process of polishing.

KELIM

CHAPTER V

MISHNAH 1. THE ORIGINAL HEIGHT OF A BAKING-OVEN[1] MUST BE NO LESS THAN FOUR HANDBREADTHS[2] AND WHAT IS LEFT OF IT[3] FOUR HANDBREADTHS;[4] SO R. MEIR. BUT THE SAGES RULED: THIS APPLIES ONLY TO A LARGE OVEN BUT IN THE CASE OF A SMALL ONE[1] ANY HEIGHT SUFFICES FOR ITS ORIGINAL BUILD[5] AND[3] THE GREATER PART OF THIS FOR WHAT IS LEFT OF IT.[4] [SUSCEPTIBILITY TO UNCLEANNESS[6] BEGINS] AS SOON AS THE OVEN'S MANUFACTURE IS COMPLETED.[7] WHAT IS REGARDED AS THE COMPLETION OF ITS MANUFACTURE? WHEN IT IS HEATED TO A DEGREE THAT SUFFICES FOR THE BAKING OF SPONGY CAKES.[8] R. JUDAH[9] RULED: WHEN A NEW OVEN[10] HAS BEEN HEATED TO A DEGREE THAT SUFFICED FOR THE BAKING OF SPONGY CAKES IN AN OLD ONE.[11]

MISHNAH 2. AS REGARDS A DOUBLE STOVE[12] ITS ORIGINAL HEIGHT[13] MUST BE NO LESS THAN THREE FINGER-

(1) If it is to be susceptible to uncleanness. (2) Baking-ovens were made of clay in the shape of a truncated cone, the wider side being attached with clay to the ground which constituted its bottom. Though such an oven has no bottom of its own it is regarded as a vessel and is susceptible to uncleanness if it conforms to the conditions laid down in our Mishnah. (3) After it had contracted an uncleanness and was broken. (4) If a lesser height remained it is clean. (5) Since it is only used as a child's toy. (6) In the case of either oven. (7) But not earlier. (8) These require less heat than cakes made of stiffer dough. (9) Restricting the Law. (10) Which needs more heating than an old one. (11) Though it would not be sufficient for baking them in the new oven. (12) A kind of box-shaped earthen vessel, hollow within and having two holes on top. The fire is kept within, while the cooking utensils are set over the holes or, sometimes, inside direct on the coals. (13) If the stove is to be susceptible to uncleanness.

BREADTHS AND WHAT IS LEFT OF IT[1] THREE FINGERBREADTHS.[2] [ITS SUSCEPTIBILITY TO UNCLEANNESS BEGINS] AS SOON AS ITS MANUFACTURE IS COMPLETED.[3] WHAT IS REGARDED AS THE COMPLETION OF ITS MANUFACTURE? WHEN IT IS HEATED TO A DEGREE THAT SUFFICES FOR THE COOKING ON IT OF THE LIGHTEST OF EGGS WHEN BROKEN AND PUT IN A SAUCEPAN. AS REGARDS A SINGLE STOVE,[4] IF IT WAS MADE FOR BAKING ITS PRESCRIBED SIZE[5] IS THE SAME AS THAT FOR A BAKING-OVEN,[6] AND IF IT WAS MADE FOR COOKING ITS PRESCRIBED SIZE[5] IS THE SAME AS THAT FOR A DOUBLE STOVE.[7] A STONE THAT PROJECTS ONE HANDBREADTH FROM A BAKING-OVEN[8] OR THREE FINGERBREADTHS FROM A DOUBLE STOVE[7] IS CONSIDERED A CONNECTION.[9] FOR ONE THAT PROJECTS FROM A SINGLE STOVE, IF THE LATTER WAS MADE FOR BAKING, THE PRESCRIBED SIZE[10] IS THE SAME AS THAT FOR A BAKING-OVEN, AND IF IT IS MADE FOR COOKING THE PRESCRIBED SIZE IS THE SAME AS THAT FOR A DOUBLE STOVE. SAID R. JUDAH: THEY[11] SPOKE OF A 'HANDBREADTH'[12] ONLY WHERE THE PROJECTION WAS BETWEEN THE OVEN[13] AND A WALL.[14] IF TWO OVENS WERE ADJACENT TO ONE ANOTHER[15] ONE HANDBREADTH[10] IS AL-

(1) After it had contracted an uncleanness and was broken. (2) If a lesser height remained it is clean. (3) But not earlier. (4) *Sc.* a stove (cf. p. 25 n. 12) with one hole. (5) And degree of heating. (6) *Supra* Mishnah 1, q.v. (7) *Supra.* (8) In which case the stone may be regarded as a handle of the oven. If it was longer it cannot be so regarded because it would most likely be cut away. (9) *Sc.* if the oven or stove contracted an uncleanness it is passed on to the stone; and if an object of uncleanness came in contact with the stone the oven or stove also contracts it. (10) Of the stone. (11) The Rabbis whose ruling has just been cited. (12) In the case of an oven; and of 'three fingerbreadths' in that of a double stove. *Sc.* that the projection is considered a connection only where it is not longer than a handbreadth and three fingerbreadths respectively. (13) Or double stove (cf. prev. n.). (14) In such a case a longer projection would most likely be cut off in order that the oven should not be too far removed from the wall. Where, however, the stone projected in another direction it is not likely to be cut off and may well be regarded as a handle, and, therefore, as a proper connection. (15) And a stone joined them together.

LOWED TO THE ONE AND ANOTHER[1] TO THE OTHER WHILE THE REMAINDER[2] REMAINS CLEAN.[3]

MISHNAH 3. THE CROWN[4] OF A DOUBLE STOVE IS CLEAN.[5] AS TO THE FENDER AROUND AN OVEN, WHEN IT IS FOUR HANDBREADTHS HIGH IT CONTRACTS UNCLEANNESS BY CONTACT AND THROUGH ITS AIR-SPACE,[6] BUT IF IT WAS LOWER IT IS CLEAN.[7] IF IT[8] WAS JOINED TO IT,[9] EVEN IF ONLY BY THREE STONES,[10] IT IS UNCLEAN.[11] THE SOCKETS [ON THE STOVE][12] FOR THE OIL CRUSE, THE SPICE-POT, AND THE LAMP CONTRACT UNCLEANNESS BY CONTACT[13] BUT NOT THROUGH THEIR AIR-SPACE;[14] SO R. MEIR. R. ISHMAEL[15] RULES THAT THEY ARE CLEAN.[16]

MISHNAH 4. AN OVEN THAT WAS HEATED FROM WITHOUT,[17] OR ONE THAT WAS HEATED[18] WITHOUT THE OWNER'S KNOWLEDGE, OR ONE THAT WAS HEATED WHILE STILL IN THE CRAFTSMAN'S HOUSE[19] IS SUSCEPTIBLE TO UNCLEANNESS. IT ONCE HAPPENED THAT A FIRE BROKE OUT AMONG THE

(1) On the other side of the stone nearest to the other oven. (2) The length of stone between the two handbreadths which (cf. foll. n.) cannot be regarded as a handle to either oven. (3) In agreement with the first Tanna and contrary to the view of R. Judah. (4) A kind of detachable rim around the top of a stove which helps to preserve its heat. (5) Even where the stove had contracted an uncleanness; because it is not considered a proper connection. (6) If a dead creeping thing was suspended within its air-space the oven also becomes unclean. (7) Since it is not considered a proper connection. (8) The fender. (9) The oven. (10) *Sc.* by an imperfect connection (cf. Bert.). *Aliter:* Joined on three sides but not on the fourth (L.). (11) Because it is regarded as a proper connection. (12) On the top. (13) Whether the uncleanness came in contact with any of them or with the stove all become unclean. (14) *Sc.* an uncleanness suspended within the air-space of one of these or of the oven imparts no uncleanness to any of the others, though the uncleanness is imparted to that in whose air-space it was suspended. (15) Var. lec. 'Simeon' *or* 'and R. Simeon'. (16) Always, even where there was contact with one of them. Only that one is unclean that came in contact with the uncleanness. (17) Lit., 'from its back'. (18) Within. (19) *Sc.* before its manufacture was completed.

OVENS OF KEFAR SIGNAH,[1] AND WHEN THE CASE WAS BROUGHT UP AT JABNEH RABBAN GAMALIEL RULED THAT THEY WERE UNCLEAN.[2]

MISHNAH 5. THE CHIMNEY-PIECE[3] ON A HOUSEHOLDER'S OVEN IS CLEAN,[4] BUT THAT OF BAKERS IS UNCLEAN BECAUSE ONE RESTS ON IT THE ROASTING SPIT.[5] R. JOḤANAN HA-SANDELAR[6] SAID: BECAUSE ONE BAKES ON IT WHEN PRESSED [FOR SPACE].[5] SIMILARLY THE RIM[3] OF A BOILER USED BY OLIVE SEETHERS IS SUSCEPTIBLE TO UNCLEANNESS,[7] BUT THAT OF ONE USED BY DYERS[8] IS NOT SUSCEPTIBLE.

MISHNAH 6. IF AN OVEN WAS HALF FILLED WITH EARTH,[9] THE PART FROM THE EARTH DOWNWARDS CONTRACTS UNCLEANNESS BY CONTACT ONLY[10] WHILE THE PART FROM THE EARTH UPWARDS CONTRACTS UNCLEANNESS FROM ITS AIR-SPACE ALSO.[11] IF AN OVEN WAS PLACED OVER THE MOUTH OF A CISTERN OR OVER THAT OF A CELLAR AND A STONE WAS INSERTED AT ITS SIDE,[12] R. JUDAH RULED: IF WHEN HEATED BELOW[13] IT BECOMES ALSO HEATED ABOVE[14] IT[15] IS SUSCEPTIBLE TO UNCLEANNESS.[16] BUT THE SAGES RULED:

(1) In Galilee. (2) The fire was regarded by him as that of a furnace the baking in which is the completion of their manufacture. (3) Lit., 'addition', 'attachment'. (4) Even where the oven is unclean, because it is not considered a connection. (5) So that it forms an integral part of the oven. (6) The Sandal-maker. (7) Because they make use of the rim also. (8) Who do not use the rim. (9) So that its lower half had no longer any cavity as an air-space. (10) If a dead creeping thing was embedded within the earth but did not touch the sides of the oven no uncleanness is imparted. (11) And the uncleanness extends over the entire oven (L.) *or* only to that part which is above the earth (Bert.). (12) Lit., 'there', between the oven and the wall to lessen the space and thus to keep the oven in position. (13) From the cistern or cellar. (14) The heat passing up through the bottom of the oven. (15) The oven, on being heated for the first time (which constitutes the completion of its manufacture). (16) For then it is deemed as joined to the ground and susceptible to uncleanness according to Lev. XI, 35 in the normal way (cf. *supra* Mishnah 1). If the oven, however, can be heated from above only the heating from below does not render it susceptible to uncleanness.

SINCE IT WAS HEATED, NO MATTER HOW,[1] IT IS SUSCEPTIBLE TO UNCLEANNESS.[2]

MISHNAH 7. IF AN OVEN CONTRACTED UNCLEANNESS HOW IS IT TO BE CLEANSED? IT MUST BE DIVIDED INTO THREE PARTS[3] AND THE PLASTERING[4] MUST BE SCRAPED OFF SO THAT [THE OVEN] TOUCHES THE GROUND.[5] R. MEIR RULED: IT IS NOT NECESSARY TO SCRAPE OFF THE PLASTERING NOR IS IT NECESSARY FOR [THE OVEN] TO TOUCH THE GROUND, BUT IT[6] NEED ONLY BE REDUCED WITHIN[7] TO A HEIGHT OF LESS THAN FOUR HANDBREADTHS. R. SIMEON RULED: IT[8] MUST ALSO BE MOVED [FROM ITS POSITION]. IF IT WAS DIVIDED INTO TWO PARTS, ONE LARGE AND THE OTHER SMALL, THE LARGER REMAINS UNCLEAN AND THE SMALLER BECOMES CLEAN. IF IT WAS DIVIDED INTO THREE PARTS ONE OF WHICH WAS AS BIG AS THE OTHER TWO TOGETHER, THE BIG ONE REMAINS UNCLEAN AND THE TWO SMALL ONES BECOME CLEAN.

MISHNAH 8. IF AN OVEN WAS CUT UP BREADTHWISE INTO RINGS THAT ARE EACH LESS THAN FOUR HANDBREADTHS IN HEIGHT, IT IS CLEAN. IF IT WAS SUBSEQUENTLY[9] PLASTERED OVER WITH CLAY, IT BECOMES SUSCEPTIBLE TO UNCLEANNESS WHEN[10] IT IS HEATED TO A DEGREE THAT SUFFICES FOR THE BAKING OF SPONGY CAKES. IF THE PLASTERING WAS REMOVED,[11] AND SAND OR GRAVEL WAS PUT BETWEEN IT AND THE OVEN SIDES—OF SUCH AN OVEN IT HAS BEEN SAID, 'A MENSTRUANT AS WELL AS A CLEAN WOMAN MAY BAKE IN IT AND IT REMAINS CLEAN'.[12]

(1) Even if it is entirely detached from the ground. (2) The divergence of view between R. Judah and the Sages whether or not the oven to become susceptible to uncleanness must be attached to the ground depends on the interpretation of the Pentateuchal expression in Lev. XI, 35. (3) Being cut perpendicularly. (4) Which attaches the oven to the ground. (5) So Maim. (6) The plastering. (7) Within the oven. (8) The oven, *sc.* each of the three parts into which it is divided. (9) The rings having been set up again and the oven resumed its original shape. (10) Like a new oven (*supra* Mishnah 1). (11) From the sides of the oven. (12) Since it is

MISHNAH 9. IF AN OVEN CAME IN SECTIONS[1] FROM THE CRAFTSMAN'S HOUSE AND HOOPS WERE PREPARED FOR IT AND PUT UPON IT[2] WHILE IT WAS CLEAN, AND WHEN[3] IT CONTRACTED AN UNCLEANNESS ITS HOOPS WERE REMOVED, IT IS AGAIN CLEAN.[4] EVEN IF THEY ARE PUT ON AGAIN THE OVEN REMAINS CLEAN.[5] IF, HOWEVER, IT WAS[6] PLASTERED WITH CLAY, IT BECOMES SUSCEPTIBLE TO UNCLEANNESS AND THERE IS NO NEED TO HEAT IT SINCE IT[7] WAS ONCE HEATED.

MISHNAH 10. IF AN OVEN WAS CUT UP[8] INTO RINGS, AND SAND WAS INSERTED BETWEEN EACH PAIR OF RINGS,[9] R. ELIEZER RULES: IT IS CLEAN;[10] BUT THE SAGES RULE: IT IS UNCLEAN.[11] SUCH AN OVEN IS KNOWN AS THE OVEN OF AKNAI.[12] AS REGARDS THE ARABIAN POTS, WHICH ARE HOLES DUG IN THE GROUND AND PLASTERED WITH CLAY, IF THE PLASTERING CAN STAND OF ITSELF IT IS SUSCEPTIBLE TO UNCLEANNESS;[13] OTHERWISE IT IS NOT SUSCEPTIBLE. AND THIS KIND OF OVEN IS KNOWN AS THE OVEN OF BEN DINAI.[14]

MISHNAH 11. AN OVEN OF STONE OR OF METAL IS CLEAN,[15] BUT THE LATTER IS UNCLEAN AS A METAL VESSEL.[16]

insusceptible to uncleanness on account of the sand or gravel which prevents the plaster from adhering to the re-set oven.

(1) Lit., 'cut'. (2) To hold the sections together. (3) Subsequently. (4) Since the sections are no longer held together the oven must be regarded as a broken one that is not susceptible to uncleanness. (5) Because it is no longer considered a whole vessel. Only when the new sections come for the first time from the craftsman's house do the hoops unite them into one whole. (6) After the sections were re-set. (7) When it came in sections from the craftsman. (8) Breadthwise. (9) And plastered over. (10) Because the sand is deemed to break up the oven into isolated fragments. (11) Since the plaster over the sand joins the rings into one whole. (12) Probably the name of a manufacturer of this kind of oven; v. B.M. 59*a*. (13) After it had been duly heated to the prescribed degree. (14) The name of a person (a robber) who designed or made this kind of oven; v. Soṭ. 47*a*, and Josephus, *Ant*. XX, 6, 1. (15) The former is not even susceptible to uncleanness while the latter is cleansed by ritual immersion. Neither contracts uncleanness through its air-space. (16) So that if it is not attached to the ground it contracts uncleanness from

IF A HOLE WAS MADE IN IT, OR IF IT WAS DAMAGED OR CRACKED, AND IT WAS PROVIDED WITH A LINING OF PLASTER OR WITH A RIM OF CLAY, IT IS UNCLEAN.[1] WHAT MUST BE THE SIZE OF THE HOLE?[2] IT MUST BE BIG ENOUGH FOR THE FLAME TO COME THROUGH. THE SAME APPLIES ALSO TO A STOVE. A STOVE OF STONE OR OF METAL IS CLEAN,[3] BUT THE LATTER IS UNCLEAN AS A METAL VESSEL.[4] IF A HOLE WAS MADE IN IT OR IF IT WAS DAMAGED OR CRACKED BUT WAS PROVIDED WITH PROPS[5] IT IS UNCLEAN. IF IT WAS LINED WITH CLAY, WHETHER INSIDE OR OUTSIDE, IT REMAINS CLEAN. R. JUDAH RULED: IF [THE LINING WAS] INSIDE IT IS UNCLEAN BUT IF OUTSIDE IT REMAINS CLEAN.

its outside and it may also become a 'father of the father of uncleanness.

(1) *Sc.* it is susceptible to uncleanness like an oven made of clay. (2) For an oven to be regarded as broken and clean. (3) V. p. 30, n. 15. (4) V. p. 30, n. 16. (5) Three clay props on the top of the stove on which the cooking pot is set (Elijah Wilna).

KELIM

CHAPTER VI

MISHNAH 1. IF THREE PROPS[1] WERE PUT UPON THE GROUND[2] AND JOINED TOGETHER WITH CLAY[3] SO THAT A POT COULD BE SET ON THEM, [THE STRUCTURE] IS SUSCEPTIBLE TO UNCLEANNESS.[4] IF THREE NAILS WERE FIXED IN THE GROUND[2] SO THAT A POT COULD BE SET ON THEM, EVEN THOUGH A PLACE WAS MADE ON THE TOP[5] WHEREON A POT COULD REST, [THE STRUCTURE] IS INSUSCEPTIBLE TO UNCLEANNESS.[6] IF ONE MADE A STOVE OF TWO STONES, JOINING THEM TOGETHER WITH CLAY, IT IS SUSCEPTIBLE TO UNCLEANNESS.[4] R. JUDAH RULES THAT IT IS INSUSCEPTIBLE TO UNCLEANNESS,[7] UNLESS A THIRD STONE IS ADDED OR [THE STRUCTURE] IS PLACED NEAR A WALL.[8] IF ONE STONE WAS JOINED TO THE OTHER WITH CLAY AND THE THIRD WAS NOT JOINED TO IT WITH CLAY, [THE STRUCTURE] IS INSUSCEPTIBLE TO UNCLEANNESS.[9]

MISHNAH 2. A STONE[10] ON WHICH A POT IS SET, [RESTING IT ON IT] AND ON AN OVEN, OR ON A DOUBLE STOVE, OR ON A STOVE,[11] IS SUSCEPTIBLE TO UNCLEANNESS. IF THE POT RESTED ON THE STONE[10] AND ON ANOTHER STONE,[12] ON A ROCK[13] OR ON A WALL,[14] [SUCH STOVE] IS INSUSCEPTIBLE TO

(1) Of clay. (2) In a tripod arrangement. (3) To form a stand. (4) *Sc.* like an earthen vessel it contracts uncleanness through its air-space. (5) *Sc.* each nail was provided at its top with a coating of clay (Tosaf. Y.Ṭ.). (6) Like a metal vessel that is fixed to the ground. (7) Because on two stones a pot cannot properly be set. (8) On which one side of the pot could be supported. (9) According to R. Judah (cf. n. 7). (10) That was fixed to the ground with clay. (11) The pot being supported both on the stone and on one of these earthen vessels. (12) That was not fixed to the ground. (13) In its primordial condition. (14) All of which are insusceptible to uncleanness.

UNCLEANNESS;[1] AND SUCH[2] WAS THE STOVE OF THE NAZIRITES IN JERUSALEM[3] WHICH WAS SET UP AGAINST A ROCK. AS REGARDS THE STOVE OF THE BUTCHERS,[4] WHENEVER THE STONES ARE PLACED SIDE BY SIDE,[5] IF ONE OF THE STOVES CONTRACTED UNCLEANNESS ALL THE OTHERS DO NOT BECOME UNCLEAN.[6]

MISHNAH 3. IF ONE MADE OF THREE STONES TWO STOVES[7] AND ONE OF THE OUTER ONES CONTRACTED AN UNCLEANNESS THE HALF OF THE MIDDLE ONE THAT SERVES THE UNCLEAN ONE[8] IS UNCLEAN BUT THE HALF OF IT THAT SERVES THE CLEAN ONE REMAINS CLEAN. IF THE CLEAN ONE WAS REMOVED, THE MIDDLE ONE IS REGARDED AS COMPLETELY TRANSFERRED TO THE UNCLEAN ONE.[9] IF THE UNCLEAN ONE WAS REMOVED, THE MIDDLE ONE IS REGARDED AS COMPLETELY TRANSFERRED TO THE CLEAN ONE. SHOULD THE TWO OUTER ONES CONTRACT UNCLEANNESS, IF THE MIDDLE STONE WAS LARGE EACH OUTER STONE IS ALLOWED SUCH A PART OF IT AS SUFFICES FOR THE SUPPORT OF A POT[8] AND THE REMAINDER IS CLEAN. BUT IF IT WAS SMALL ALL OF IT IS UNCLEAN. SHOULD THE MIDDLE STONE BE REMOVED, IF A BIG KETTLE CAN BE SET ON THE TWO OUTER STONES[10] THEY ARE UNCLEAN. IF THE MIDDLE STONE IS RESTORED ALL BECOMES CLEAN AGAIN.[11] IF IT WAS PLASTERED WITH CLAY[12] IT BECOMES SUSCEPTIBLE TO UNCLEANNESS

(1) Because to such a stove the prescription *shall be broken in pieces* (Lev. XI, 35) does not apply. (2) A stone fixed to the ground. (3) On which they cooked their peace-offerings (cf. Mid. II, 5). (4) Who sold cooked meat and used a stove for the purpose. (5) Each one being fixed to the ground with clay but separated from the others, and each pair serving as one stove on which a cooking pot could rest. (6) Since each stove may be regarded as an isolated entity. (7) The cooking pots resting on either of the outer stones and the adjacent part of the middle one. (8) Cf. prev. n. (9) And it becomes unclean. (10) I.e., if their distance from one another was not so great as to prevent the opposite sides of the kettle from resting on the two stones respectively. (11) The stone restored being deemed to have broken the larger stove in two. (12) And thus fixed to the ground.

WHEN[1] IT IS HEATED TO A DEGREE THAT SUFFICES FOR THE COOKING OF AN EGG.[2]

MISHNAH 4. IF TWO STONES WERE MADE INTO A STOVE AND THEY CONTRACTED AN UNCLEANNESS, AND A STONE WAS SET UP NEAR THE OUTER SIDE[3] OF THE ONE AND ANOTHER STONE NEAR THE OUTER SIDE OF THE OTHER,[4] [THE INNER HALF] OF EACH [INNER STONES][5] REMAINS UNCLEAN[6] WHILE [THE OUTER] HALF OF EACH [OF THESE STONES][7] IS CLEAN. IF THE CLEAN STONES[8] ARE REMOVED THE OTHERS[9] REVERT TO THEIR UNCLEANNESS.

(1) Like a new oven. (2) As explained *supra* V, 2. (3) Lit., 'from here'. (4) The four stones now forming three stoves. (5) Which serves as part of the middle stove. (6) As it was originally. (7) Which is now forming a new stove with the outer stone adjacent to it. (8) The outer ones that have been added to the original stove. (9) The two stones that constituted the original stove.

KELIM

CHAPTER VII

MISHNAH 1. IF A DOMESTIC[1] FIRE-BASKET[2] WAS HOLLOWED OUT[3] TO A DEPTH OF LESS THAN THREE HANDBREADTHS,[4] IT REMAINS SUSCEPTIBLE TO UNCLEANNESS, BECAUSE WHEN IT IS HEATED FROM BELOW[3] A POT ABOVE WOULD STILL BOIL. IF, HOWEVER, IT WAS HOLLOWED OUT[3] TO A LOWER DEPTH IT IS INSUSCEPTIBLE TO UNCLEANNESS.[5] IF SUBSEQUENTLY A STONE OR GRAVEL WAS PUT INTO IT,[6] IT IS STILL INSUSCEPTIBLE TO UNCLEANNESS.[7] IF IT WAS PLASTERED OVER[8] WITH CLAY, IT MAY CONTRACT UNCLEANNESS HENCEFORWARD.[9] THIS WAS R. JUDAH'S REPLY[10] IN CONNECTION WITH THE OVEN THAT WAS PLACED OVER THE MOUTH OF A CISTERN OR OVER THAT OF A CELLAR.[11]

MISHNAH 2. A HOB[12] THAT HAS A RECEPTACLE FOR POTS[13] IS CLEAN AS A STOVE[14] BUT UNCLEAN AS A RECEP-

(1) Lit., 'of householders'. (2) κάλαθος. A movable earthen stove, open above (where the pot is set) and closed below with a thick bottom (on which the coals rest). (3) In its bottom. (4) Lowering by so much the level of the fire. (5) Because, on account of the distance of the fire from its top, it can no longer be used as a stove. (6) To fill up the hollowed part. (7) Since a movable object cannot be regarded as a valid part of the stove. (8) Above the stone or gravel. (9) Cf. n. 7 *mut. mut.* (10) To the Sages who differed from him (*supra* V, 6). (11) As here it is essential that the heat below shall suffice for the boiling of a pot above so, R. Judah maintained, it is also essential there. (12) *Dakon* or (with MS.M.) *Dikon*, a projection from a stove (triangular in shape, the base of which and the stove have a common side) on which pots are placed to keep them warm. *Aliter:* An oblong chest filled with hot ashes on the top of which are holes for pots. (13) Cf. prev. n. (14) *Sc.* it is (*a*) insusceptible to uncleanness if it was fixed to the ground and (*b*) though the stove contracted an uncleanness the hob remains clean.

TACLE.[1] AS TO ITS[2] SIDES,[3] WHATEVER TOUCHES THEM DOES NOT BECOME UNCLEAN AS IF THE HOB HAD BEEN A STOVE,[4] BUT AS REGARDS ITS WIDE SIDE,[5] R. MEIR HOLDS IT TO BE CLEAN[6] WHILE R. JUDAH HOLDS IT TO BE UNCLEAN.[7] THE SAME LAW[8] APPLIES ALSO WHERE A BASKET WAS INVERTED AND A STOVE WAS PUT UPON IT.[9]

MISHNAH 3. IF A DOUBLE STOVE WAS SPLIT INTO TWO PARTS LONGITUDINALLY IT BECOMES INSUSCEPTIBLE TO UNCLEANNES,[10] BUT IF CROSSWISE[11] IT REMAINS SUSCEPTIBLE TO UNCLEANNESS. IF A SINGLE STOVE WAS SPLIT INTO TWO PARTS, WHETHER LONGITUDINALLY OR CROSSWISE, IT BECOMES INSUSCEPTIBLE TO UNCLEANNESS.[12] AS TO THE FENDER AROUND A STOVE,[13] WHENEVER IT[14] IS THREE FINGERBREADTHS HIGH IT CONTRACTS UNCLEANNESS BY CONTACT AND ALSO THROUGH ITS AIR-SPACE, BUT IF IT IS LESS IT CONTRACTS UNCLEANNESS THROUGH CONTACT AND NOT THROUGH ITS AIR-SPACE.[15] HOW[16] IS THE AIR-SPACE[17] DETERMINED?[18] R. ISHMAEL SAYS: A SPIT[19] IS INCLINED FROM ABOVE[20] DOWN-

(1) *Sc.* if it was detached from the ground it becomes susceptible to uncleanness like any other earthen vessel. (2) The hob's. (3) That are not common to it and the stove. (4) Even though the stove was unclean at the time. (5) That which is common to it and the stove. (6) Because, in his opinion, even the wide side is not wholly regarded as a part of the stove, their common side being considered as a mere stone intervening between two stoves which is deemed to be divided into two halves, that facing the hob remaining clean. (7) *Sc.* if an uncleanness touched the hob it is as unclean as if the stove itself had been touched. (8) That is applicable to the hob. (9) The part of the basket that projects round about the oven and on which pots are placed to keep them warm, are subject to the same laws as the hob. (10) Since neither part is capable of holding a pot. (11) So that each stove is still capable of holding a pot on the unbroken hole on its top. (12) Cf. n. 10. *mut. mut.* (13) Lit., 'court', a flat foundation of clay with a rim around it. (14) Cf. prev. n. (15) Since it is only regarded as a 'handle' of the stove. (16) In the case where the rim of the fender is three fingerbreadths high. (17) Of the fender. (18) In view of the fact that the stove is much higher than the rim of the fender. (19) Or a similar rod. (20) From the edge of the stove.

WARDS[1] AND ALL BELOW IT[2] IS THE AIR-SPACE[3] THROUGH WHICH UNCLEANNESS IS IMPARTED. R. ELIEZER B. JACOB RULED: IF THE STOVE CONTRACTED UNCLEANNESS THE FENDER[4] ALSO BECOMES UNCLEAN, BUT IF THE FENDER CONTRACTS UNCLEANNESS THE STOVE DOES NOT BECOME UNCLEAN.

MISHNAH 4. IF THE FENDER WAS DETACHED FROM THE STOVE, WHENEVER IT WAS THREE FINGERBREADTHS HIGH IT CONTRACTS UNCLEANNESS BY CONTACT AND THROUGH ITS AIR-SPACE, BUT IF IT WAS LOWER OR IF THE FENDER WAS FLAT[5] IT IS CLEAN.[6] IF THREE PROPS[7] ON A STOVE WERE THREE FINGERBREADTHS HIGH, THEY CONTRACT UNCLEANNESS BY CONTACT AND THROUGH THEIR AIR-SPACE. IF THEY WERE LOWER THEY CONTRACT UNCLEANNESS ALL THE MORE,[8] EVEN WHERE THEY WERE FOUR IN NUMBER.[9]

MISHNAH 5. IF ONE OF THEM[10] WAS REMOVED, THE REMAINING ONES CONTRACT UNCLEANNESS BY CONTACT BUT NOT THROUGH THEIR AIR-SPACE;[11] SO R. MEIR. R. SIMEON RULES THAT THEY REMAIN CLEAN. IF ORIGINALLY ONLY TWO PROPS WERE MADE, ONE OPPOSITE THE OTHER,[12] THEY CONTRACT UNCLEANNESS BY CONTACT AND THROUGH THEIR AIR-SPACE; SO R. MEIR. R. SIMEON RULES THAT THEY ARE CLEAN. IF THEY WERE MORE THAN THREE FINGERBREADTHS HIGH, THE PARTS THAT ARE THREE FINGERBREADTHS HIGH AND DOWNWARDS[13] CONTRACT UNCLEANNESS BY CONTACT AND THROUGH THEIR AIR-SPACE BUT THE PARTS THAT ARE

(1) To the rim of the fender. (2) Lit., 'and opposite it'. (3) V. p. 36, n. 17. (4) Which is merely an adjunct to it. (5) Lit., 'smooth', *sc.* there was no rim at all. (6) Though the stove was unclean; since it was completely detached from it. (7) Of clay on which pots are set. (8) Since they are definitely a part of the stove. (9) When one of them is superfluous, since a pot could well be set on three props. (10) Of the three props spoken of in the previous Mishnah. (11) Since they are regarded as a mere 'handle' of the stove. (12) So that the two, being capable of supporting a pot, are in the same condition as two stones of which a stove was made (v. *supra* VI, 1). (13) Towards the stove.

MORE THAN THREE FINGERBREADTHS HIGH CONTRACT UNCLEANNES BY CONTACT AND NOT THROUGH THEIR AIR-SPACE; SO R. MEIR. R. SIMEON RULES THAT THEY[1] ARE CLEAN. IF THEY WERE WITHDRAWN FROM THE RIM,[2] THE PARTS WHICH ARE WITHIN THREE FINGERBREADTHS[2] CONTRACT UNCLEANNESS BY CONTACT AND THROUGH THEIR AIR-SPACE, AND THOSE PARTS THAT ARE REMOVED MORE THAN THREE FINGERBREADTHS[2] CONTRACT UNCLEANNESS BY CONTACT BUT NOT THROUGH THEIR AIR-SPACE; SO R. MEIR. R. SIMEON RULES THAT THEY ARE CLEAN.

MISHNAH 6. HOW IS THEIR AIR-SPACE[3] MEASURED?[4] R. SIMEON B. GAMALIEL SAYS: THE MEASURING-ROD[5] IS PLACED BETWEEN THEM,[6] AND ANY PART THAT IS OUTSIDE THE MEASURING-ROD IS CLEAN WHILE ANY PART INSIDE THE MEASURING-ROD, INCLUDING THE PLACE OF THE MEASURING-ROD ITSELF, IS UNCLEAN.

(1) The parts that are more than three fingerbreadths high. *Aliter:* The entire height of the props. (2) Of the stove or (with another commentary) the mouth of the stove, the props having been bent outwards. (3) Lit., 'them', the props (v. prev. Mishnah). (4) *Sc.* how is it determined which air-space is within the parts of the props that are 'within three fingerbreadths'. (5) With which the three fingerbreadths have been measured. (6) Each pair of props in turn, at a distance of three fingerbreadths (cf. n. 2).

KELIM

CHAPTER VIII

MISHNAH 1. IF WITHIN AN OVEN[1] A PARTITION OF BOARDS OR HANGINGS[2] WAS PUT UP AND A [DEAD] CREEPING THING WAS FOUND IN ONE COMPARTMENT ALL THE OVEN BECOMES UNCLEAN.[3] IF A HIVE THAT WAS BROKEN THROUGH[4] AND ITS GAP WAS STOPPED UP WITH STRAW[5] WAS SUSPENDED WITHIN THE AIR-SPACE OF AN OVEN[6] WHILE A [DEAD] CREEPING THING WAS WITHIN IT, THE OVEN BECOMES UNCLEAN.[7] IF A [DEAD] CREEPING THING WAS WITHIN THE OVEN, ANY FOODSTUFFS WITHIN THE HIVE BECOME UNCLEAN;[8] BUT R. ELIEZER RULES THAT THEY ARE CLEAN. R. ELIEZER ARGUED: IF SUCH A HIVE AFFORDS PROTECTION IN THE CASE OF A CORPSE[9] WHICH IS SUBJECT TO THE GREATER RESTRICTIONS,[10] SHOULD IT NOT AFFORD PROTECTION IN THE CASE OF AN EARTHENWARE WHICH IS SUBJECT TO LIGHTER RESTRICTIONS?[10] THEY ANSWERED HIM: IF IT AFFORDS PROTECTION IN THE CASE OF CORPSE UNCLEANNESS (THOUGH IT IS SUBJECT TO GREATER RESTRICTIONS) ON ACCOUNT OF THE FACT THAT TENTS MAY BE DULY DIVIDED,[11] SHOULD IT ALSO

(1) Of earthenware. (2) Dividing it up from top to bottom. (3) The partition being completely disregarded. (4) In consequence of which it ceased to be a valid vessel. (5) And much more so if it was not stopped up (cf. prev. n.). (6) Though its mouth was above that of the oven. (7) Only where a dead creeping thing was within a sound vessel in the oven does the vessel protect the oven from the uncleanness within it. (8) Having lost the status of a vessel (cf. *supra* n. 4) it cannot prevent uncleanness from penetrating either from itself into the oven or *vice versa*. (9) No corpse uncleanness in a house can penetrate such a hive to any foodstuffs that it contains. (10) Corpse uncleanness extends, for instance, over seven days and affects both men and vessels while that of an earthenware can be imparted to foodstuffs and liquids only. (11) A partition in a tent or a house prevents any corpse uncleanness in that tent or house from penetrating through it into the other part.

AFFORD PROTECTION IN THE CASE OF AN EARTHENWARE (THOUGH IT IS SUBJECT TO LIGHTER RESTRICTIONS) WHERE TENTS CANNOT BE USEFULLY DIVIDED?[1]

MISHNAH 2. IF A HIVE WAS IN A SOUND CONDITION, AND SO TOO IN THE CASE OF A HAMPER OR A SKIN-BOTTLE, AND A [DEAD] CREEPING THING WAS WITHIN IT[2] THE OVEN REMAINS CLEAN.[3] IF THE [DEAD] CREEPING THING WAS IN THE OVEN, ANY FOODSTUFFS IN THE HIVE REMAIN CLEAN.[3] IF IT[4] WAS PERFORATED, A VESSEL THAT IS USED FOR FOODSTUFFS MUST[5] HAVE A HOLE THAT IS LARGE ENOUGH FOR OLIVES TO FALL THROUGH, IF IT IS USED FOR LIQUIDS THE HOLE MUST BE LARGE ENOUGH FOR LIQUIDS TO PASS INTO IT,[6] AND IF IT IS USED FOR EITHER IT IS SUBJECTED TO THE GREATER RESTRICTION, VIZ., THE HOLE NEED ONLY BE LARGE ENOUGH FOR LIQUIDS TO PASS INTO IT.[7]

MISHNAH 3. IF A COLANDER[8] PLACED OVER THE MOUTH OF AN OVEN WAS SLIGHTLY SINKING INTO IT,[9] AND IT HAD NO RIMS,[10] AND A [DEAD] CREEPING THING WAS IN IT, THE OVEN BECOMES UNCLEAN, AND IF THE CREEPING THING WAS IN THE OVEN, FOODSTUFFS IN THE COLANDER BECOME UNCLEAN, SINCE ONLY VESSELS[11] AFFORD PROTECTION AGAINST AN UNCLEANNESS IN AN EARTHEN VESSEL.[12] IF A

(1) No partition (as stated *supra* n. 3 in the case of the oven) affords protection in an earthenware. (2) While it was suspended within an oven with its mouth above, or on a level with, but not lower than, that of the oven. (3) Because the uncleanness cannot penetrate through a sound vessel either into another vessel or from another vessel into it (cf. prev. n.). (4) The hive, the hamper or the skin bottle that with foodstuffs in it was suspended in the oven that contained a dead creeping thing. (5) If it is to lose the status of vessel and allow the uncleanness in the oven to penetrate through it. (6) It is not enough if it only allows liquids to pass out. (7) Even such a small hole destroys the status of the vessel and the uncleanness penetrates through it. (8) A tablet with perforations made of earthenware. *Aliter:* An earthenware slab with no cavity that is used for kneading. (9) Though its upper surface was above the mouth of the oven. (10) In consequence of which it cannot be regarded as a valid 'vessel'. (11) Cf. prev. n. (12) In which they are put.

JAR THAT WAS FULL OF CLEAN LIQUIDS[1] WAS PLACED BENEATH THE BOTTOM OF AN OVEN, AND A [DEAD] CREEPING THING WAS IN THE OVEN, THE JAR AND THE LIQUIDS REMAIN CLEAN.[2] IF IT[3] WAS INVERTED, WITH ITS MOUTH PROJECTING INTO THE AIR-SPACE OF THE OVEN, AND A DEAD CREEPING THING WAS IN THE OVEN, THE LIQUID THAT CLINGS TO[4] THE BOTTOM OF THE JAR REMAINS CLEAN.[5]

MISHNAH 4. IF A POT WAS PLACED IN AN OVEN AND A [DEAD] CREEPING THING WAS IN THE OVEN, THE POT REMAINS CLEAN SINCE NO EARTHEN VESSEL[6] IMPARTS UNCLEANNESS TO VESSELS. IF IT[7] CONTAINED DRIPPING LIQUID, THE LATTER CONTRACTS UNCLEANNESS AND THE POT ALSO BECOMES UNCLEAN.[8] THIS[9] MIGHT WELL SAY,[10] 'THAT[11] WHICH MADE YOU UNCLEAN DID NOT MAKE ME UNCLEAN, BUT YOU HAVE MADE ME UNCLEAN'.

MISHNAH 5. IF A COCK THAT SWALLOWED A CREEPING THING FELL[12] WITHIN THE AIR-SPACE OF AN OVEN, THE OVEN REMAINS CLEAN;[13] BUT IF THE COCK DIED,[14] THE OVEN BECOMES UNCLEAN.[15] IF A [DEAD] CREEPING THING WAS FOUND IN AN OVEN, ANY BREAD IN IT CONTRACTS A SECOND GRADE OF UNCLEANNESS SINCE THE OVEN[16] IS OF THE FIRST GRADE.[17]

(1) Much more so if it was full of foodstuffs, which, unlike liquids, can never impart uncleanness to a vessel. (2) Even though the open bottom of the oven projected into the jar. (3) The jar. (4) Lit., 'moistens'. (5) Since it is without the cavity of the oven; nor does the jar contract uncleanness since no vessel contracts uncleanness through the air-space of an earthen vessel. (6) Such as the oven in question. (7) The pot. (8) Through its contact with the liquids. (9) The pot. (10) To the liquid. (11) The oven. (12) Alive. (13) As if the creeping thing within the body of the cock had been within a tightly closed vessel. (14) And its carcass fell within the air-space of the oven before the creeping thing could be digested, viz., within twenty-four hours from the time it had been swallowed. (15) A carcass cannot be regarded as a tightly closed vessel and the dead creeping thing is thus virtually within the air-space of the oven. (16) Which contracted its uncleanness from the dead creeping thing that is a 'father of uncleanness'. (17) And a first grade imparts only a second grade of uncleanness.

MISHNAH 6. IF A LEAVEN POT[1] THAT HAD A TIGHTLY FITTING LID[2] WAS PUT WITHIN AN OVEN, AND THERE WAS SOME LEAVEN AND A [DEAD] CREEPING THING WITHIN THE POT, BUT THERE WAS A PARTITION[3] BETWEEN THEM,[4] THE OVEN IS UNCLEAN[5] BUT THE LEAVEN[6] IS CLEAN. BUT IF IT[7] WAS AN OLIVE'S BULK OF CORPSE,[8] BOTH THE OVEN AND THE HOUSE[9] BECOME UNCLEAN,[10] BUT THE LEAVEN[6] REMAINS CLEAN. IF, HOWEVER, THERE WAS IN THE PARTITION[3] AN APERTURE ONE HANDBREADTH SQUARE,[11] ALL[12] BECOME UNCLEAN.

MISHNAH 7. IF A [DEAD] CREEPING THING WAS FOUND IN THE OUTLET[13] OF AN OVEN OR OF A DOUBLE STOVE OR OF A SINGLE STOVE OUTSIDE THE INNER EDGE,[14] IT[15] REMAINS CLEAN.[16] IF IT[15] WAS IN THE OPEN AIR,[17] EVEN THOUGH AN OLIVE'S BULK OF CORPSE WAS FOUND IN THE OUTLET, IT[15] REMAINS CLEAN.[18] IF, HOWEVER, THERE WAS IN THE OUTLET AN OPENING OF ONE HANDBREADTH,[19] ALL[20] BECOME UNCLEAN.[11]

MISHNAH 8. IF A [DEAD] CREEPING THING WAS FOUND IN THE APERTURE[21] THROUGH WHICH WOOD IS PUT IN, R.

(1) Of earthenware. (2) Which affords protection against uncleanness to any thing within it; v. *infra* X, 2. (3) Dividing up the pot from top to bottom into two compartments. (4) The creeping thing and the leaven. (5) On account of the dead creeping thing. A tightly fitting lid only prevents the ingress, but not the egress of an uncleanness. (6) Which in its compartment is protected by the tightly fitting lid. (7) The unclean object in one of the compartments of the leaven pot. (8) Instead of a creeping thing. (9) By *ohel* (v. Glos.). (10) From the corpse. (11) The minimum size of an opening that affords passage to corpse uncleanness. (12) Even the leaven. (13) Lit., 'eye', a hole for the admission of air or the escape of smoke. (14) Of the outlet. (15) The oven etc. (16) Since the outlet, which is usually closed when the oven etc. is used (to preserve the heat), is not regarded as an integral part of the vessel. (17) Where the law of *ohel* does not apply. (18) Since the uncleanness cannot penetrate through the outlet which is smaller than the prescribed minimum. (19) In length, breadth and height. (20) The outlet and the oven etc. (21) Of a stove.

JUDAH RULED: IF IT[1] WAS WITHIN THE OUTER EDGE OF THE APERTURE THE STOVE BECOMES UNCLEAN.[2] BUT THE SAGES RULED: IF IT[1] WAS WITHOUT THE INNER EDGE THE OVEN REMAINS CLEAN.[3] R. JOSE RULED: IF IT[1] WAS FOUND BENEATH THE SPOT WHERE THE POT IS SET, INWARDS, THE STOVE BECOMES UNCLEAN, BUT IF BENEATH THE SPOT WHERE THE POT IS SET, OUTWARDS, IT REMAINS CLEAN. IF IT[1] WAS FOUND ON THE PLACE[4] WHERE THE BATH-KEEPER[5] SITS, OR WHERE THE DYER SITS, OR WHERE THE OLIVE SEETHERS SIT, THE STOVE REMAINS CLEAN. THE STOVE BECOMES UNCLEAN[6] ONLY WHEN THE CREEPING THING IS FOUND WITHIN AND BEYOND THAT OPENING WHICH IS BLOCKED UP BY THE POT.[7]

MISHNAH 9. A PIT[8] WHICH HAS A PLACE ON WHICH A POT MAY BE SET IS UNCLEAN;[9] AND SO ALSO AN OVEN OF GLASS-BLOWERS, IF IT HAS A PLACE ON WHICH A POT MAY BE SET, IS UNCLEAN.[9] THE FURNACE OF LIME-BURNERS, OR OF GLAZIERS, OR OF POTTERS IS CLEAN. A LARGE SIZED BAKING-OVEN[10], IF IT HAS A RIM,[11] IS UNCLEAN.[12] R. JUDAH RULED:[13] IF IT HAS A PERFORATED ROOF.[14] R. GAMALIEL RULED:[13] IF IT HAS A BORDER.[15]

(1) The creeping thing. (2) Because the thickness of the oven sides is regarded as the inside of the oven. (3) The thickness of the sides being regarded by them as the outside of the oven (cf. prev. n.). (4) On a stove. (5) Or 'attendant'. (6) Through its air-space. (7) By contact, however, uncleanness is conveyed whatever the spot on which the creeping thing fell. (8) *Bor*, a hole in the ground lined with clay in a manner that the lining can stand of itself, such as the oven of Ben Dinai (*supra* V, 10). Var. lec., *Kur*. 'a crucible'. (9) *Sc.* it is susceptible to uncleanness. (10) Made of clay and having a door in its side. (11) So that it is not attached to the ground and can be moved about. (12) If, however, it has no rim, so that it is fixed to the ground, it is clean. (13) It is unclean. (14) στεγη. *Aliter:* An outlet for the smoke. *Aliter:* Mouldings. In either of these cases the oven would not be attached to the ground and, being movable, is susceptible to uncleanness. Only an oven whose opening is at its top is susceptible to uncleanness even when attached to the ground. (15) Cf. prev. n. *mut. mut.*

MISHNAH 10. IF A MAN WHO CAME IN CONTACT WITH ONE WHO HAS CONTRACTED CORPSE UNCLEANNESS[1] HAD FOODSTUFFS OR LIQUIDS IN HIS MOUTH AND HE PUT HIS HEAD INTO THE AIR-SPACE OF AN OVEN THAT WAS CLEAN, THEY[2] CAUSE THE OVEN TO BE UNCLEAN.[3] IF A MAN WHO WAS CLEAN HAD FOODSTUFFS OR LIQUIDS IN HIS MOUTH AND HE PUT HIS HEAD INTO THE AIR-SPACE OF AN OVEN THAT WAS UNCLEAN, THEY[4] BECOME UNCLEAN.[5] IF A MAN WAS EATING A PRESSED FIG[6] WITH SOILED HANDS[7] AND HE PUT HIS HAND INTO HIS MOUTH TO REMOVE A SMALL STONE,[8] R. MEIR DECLARES THE FIG TO BE UNCLEAN[9] AND R. JUDAH REGARDS IT AS CLEAN.[10] R. JOSE RULED: IF HE[11] TURNED IT OVER[12] THE FIG IS UNCLEAN[9] BUT IF HE DID NOT TURN IT OVER[12] THE FIG REMAINS CLEAN.[13] IF THE MAN HAD A PONDION[14] IN HIS MOUTH, R. JOSE RULED: IF HE KEPT IT THERE TO RELIEVE HIS THIRST IT BECOMES UNCLEAN.[15]

(1) So that he contracted an uncleanness of the first grade. A corpse is the 'father of the father of uncleanness', the man who contracted corpse uncleanness becomes a 'father of uncleanness', and the man who came in contact with him contracts an uncleanness of the first grade. (2) The liquids that become unclean by contact with the man. (3) This is a Rabbinical ordinance applicable to liquids only. In the absence of liquids an oven or any other vessel can contract uncleanness from a 'father of uncleanness' only. (4) The liquids, despite their concealed condition in the closed mouth of the man. (5) A closed mouth is not regarded as a vessel with a tightly fitting cover (cf. *infra* X, 1). (6) Of *terumah*. (7) *Sc.* 'unwashed'. These are subject to the second grade of uncleanness and consequently convey the third grade of uncleanness to the *terumah* with which they come in contact. (8) And so touched the fig with his moistened hand. (9) Because the spittle (a liquid) by moistening the fig rendered it susceptible to uncleanness. The hands that are unclean in the second grade convey to the spittle an uncleanness of the first grade (since whatever conveys uncleanness to *terumah* causes liquids to be unclean in the first grade) and the spittle conveys to the *terumah* an uncleanness of the second grade. (10) Spittle while in one's mouth, he maintains, is deemed to be a part of the body and cannot, therefore, be regarded as a liquid that renders food susceptible to uncleanness. (11) With the spittle in his mouth. (12) In his mouth. (13) Cf. 'Er. 99*a* where the names of R. Judah and R. Jose are transposed. (14) A coin = 16 *perutahs*. (15) Since the spittle that is generated on account of the coin

MISHNAH 11. IF MILK THAT DRIPPED FROM A WOMAN'S BREASTS[1] FELL INTO THE AIR-SPACE OF AN OVEN, THE OVEN BECOMES UNCLEAN,[2] SINCE A LIQUID[3] CONVEYS UNCLEANNESS IRRESPECTIVE OF WHETHER [ITS PRESENCE] IS ACCEPTABLE OR NOT ACCEPTABLE. IF SHE[4] WAS SWEEPING IT[5] OUT WHEN A THORN PRICKED HER AND SHE BLED, OR IF SHE BURNT HERSELF AND PUT HER FINGER INTO HER MOUTH, THE OVEN BECOMES UNCLEAN.[6]

is regarded as a liquid which renders the fig susceptible to uncleanness.

(1) While she was unclean. (2) Though the milk dropped against the woman's wish. (3) That is unclean, as is the milk which contracted uncleanness. (4) Being clean. (5) The oven. (6) From the spittle or the blood which is a liquid and which, contracting uncleanness from the woman's unwashed hands, becomes unclean in the first grade (as stated *supra*) and renders the oven unclean in the second grade.

KELIM

CHAPTER IX

MISHNAH 1. IF A NEEDLE[1] OR A RING[1] WAS FOUND [EMBEDDED] IN THE BOTTOM OF AN OVEN,[2] AND IT[3] WAS VISIBLE BUT DID NOT PROJECT,[4] THE OVEN IS UNCLEAN IF, WHEN IN BAKING, THE DOUGH WOULD TOUCH IT.[5] OF WHAT KIND OF 'DOUGH' DID THEY[6] SPEAK? OF ONE OF MEDIUM CONSISTENCY.[7] IF IT[5] WAS[3] FOUND IN THE PLASTERING OF THE OVEN[8] AND THE LATTER HAD A TIGHTLY FITTING COVER, IT[3] IS UNCLEAN WHERE THE OVEN IS UNCLEAN[9] AND CLEAN WHERE THE OVEN IS CLEAN.[10] IF IT[3] WAS FOUND IN THE [CLAY] STOPPER OF A JAR, IT IS UNCLEAN[11] IF IT WAS AT ITS SIDES,[12] AND CLEAN IF IT WAS OPPOSITE THE JAR'S

(1) Which has come in contact with a corpse, becoming thereby a 'father of uncleanness' and thus imparting in turn to earthenware an uncleanness of the first grade (Bert.). (2) *Sc.* in the ground on which the oven is fixed. (3) The Heb. here as throughout the Mishnah is in the plural. (4) Into the air-space of the oven. (5) The needle or the ring. Since this very slight projection is actually within the air-space of the oven, uncleanness is duly imparted. This, however, applies only where the oven was put in its position after the object had been embedded in the ground. If the oven was there first, the object, by falling through the oven's air-space to its bottom, imparts uncleanness to the oven even before it reached its bottom. (6) The Rabbis of this Mishnah. (7) One that is neither too soft (which would run into the smallest crevices) nor too hard (which would not cling to the oven's sides). (8) Which joins the oven to the ground; and both the oven and the metal object were clean, but were with a corpse under the same roof. (9) *Sc.* where the cover was not properly tight and fitting. (10) *Sc.* where the cover was tightly fitting. The needle or the ring, being embedded in the plastering, loses its independent existence and, being deemed to constitute an integral part of the oven, shares its fate; otherwise as metal vessels they would not be protected by a tightly-fitting cover. (11) By overshadowing (cf. *supra* n. 8). (12) I.e., the part of the stopper that was not opposite the mouth of the jar. (The plug was cone-shaped and thrust its narrow end down into the jar's mouth.) Since the clay in that part of the stopper

MOUTH.[1] THOUGH IT[2] WAS VISIBLE FROM WITHIN, BUT DID NOT PROJECT INTO THE AIR-SPACE OF THE JAR[3] IT IS CLEAN. IF IT[2] WAS SUNK INTO [THE AIR-SPACE OF THE JAR] BUT THERE WAS UNDER IT[4] SOME CLAY, THOUGH THIN AS GARLIC PEEL, IT IS CLEAN.[5]

MISHNAH 2. IF A JAR[6] THAT WAS FULL OF CLEAN LIQUIDS, WITH A SIPHON[7] WITHIN IT, HAD A TIGHTLY FITTING COVER AND WAS PUT IN A TENT[8] IN WHICH THERE WAS A CORPSE, BETH SHAMMAI RULED: BOTH THE JAR AND THE LIQUIDS ARE CLEAN[9] BUT THE SIPHON[7] IS UNCLEAN,[10] AND BETH HILLEL RULED: THE SIPHON ALSO IS CLEAN. SUBSEQUENTLY[11] BETH HILLEL, CHANGING THEIR VIEW, RULED IN AGREEMENT WITH THAT OF BETH SHAMMAI.

MISHNAH 3. IF A DEAD CREEPING THING WAS FOUND BENEATH THE BOTTOM OF AN OVEN,[12] THE OVEN REMAINS

serves no purpose it is deemed to be non-existent and the needle or ring receives no protection from the tightly fitting cover and is thus exposed to the uncleanness of the corpse under the same roof.

(1) And the cover was tightly fitting (cf. p. 46, n. 12 *mut. mut.*). (2) V. p. 46, n. 3. (3) Being completely sunk into the stopper. (4) Between it and the air-space of the jar. (5) Since it loses its identity in the stopper. (6) Of earthenware, belonging to an *'am ha-areẓ* (v. Glos.). (7) Of metal. (8) I.e., under the same roof. (9) *Sc.* the *'am ha-areẓ* may continue to use them, no restriction of uncleanness as a precaution against their use by a *ḥaber* (v. Glos.) having been imposed upon them, since no *ḥaber* would ever borrow from an *'am ha-areẓ* an earthenware or a liquid which cannot attain cleanness through immersion in a ritual bath. (10) As it can attain cleanness by immersion in a ritual bath, a *ḥaber* might sometimes borrow it and, being unaware that it was under the same roof as a corpse (which renders it unclean for seven days, on the third and seventh of which sprinkling is required), would treat it as an ordinary metal utensil of an *'am ha-areẓ* which becomes clean on the same day after ritual immersion and sunset. A tightly fitting cover affords protection to earthenware, foodstuffs and liquids only, but not to metal vessels. (11) Having learned of Beth Shammai's reason as just explained; v. 'Ed. I, 14. (12) *Sc.* embedded in the ground on which the oven is fixed and which serves as its bottom.

CLEAN, FOR I PRESUME[1] THAT IT FELL[2] WHILE IT WAS STILL ALIVE[3] AND THAT IT DIED ONLY NOW.[4] IF A NEEDLE OR A RING[5] WAS FOUND BENEATH THE BOTTOM OF AN OVEN,[6] THE OVEN REMAINS CLEAN, FOR IT MAY BE PRESUMED THAT THEY WERE THERE BEFORE THE OVEN ARRIVED. IF IT[7] WAS FOUND IN THE WOOD ASHES,[8] THE OVEN IS UNCLEAN SINCE ONE HAS NO GROUND ON WHICH TO BASE AN ASSUMPTION OF CLEANNESS.[9]

MISHNAH 4. IF A SPONGE HAD ABSORBED UNCLEAN LIQUIDS AND ITS OUTER SURFACE BECAME DRY AND IT FELL INTO THE AIR-SPACE OF AN OVEN, THE OVEN BECOMES UNCLEAN, FOR THE LIQUID[10] WOULD ULTIMATELY EMERGE. AND THE SAME APPLIES TO A PIECE OF TURNIP[11] OR REED GRASS.[11] R. SIMEON RULES: THE OVEN IS CLEAN IN BOTH THESE CASES.

MISHNAH 5. IF POTSHERDS THAT HAD BEEN USED FOR UNCLEAN LIQUIDS FELL INTO THE AIR-SPACE OF AN OVEN, AND THE OVEN WAS HEATED, IT BECOMES UNCLEAN, FOR THE LIQUID[12] WOULD[13] ULTIMATELY EMERGE.[14] AND THE SAME APPLIES TO FRESH OLIVE PEAT; BUT IF IT WAS OLD,[15] THE OVEN REMAINS CLEAN. IF, HOWEVER, IT WAS KNOWN THAT LIQUID EMERGES, EVEN AFTER THE LAPSE OF THREE YEARS,[16] THE OVEN BECOMES UNCLEAN.

(1) Even where the creeping thing is in a condition indicating recent death and cannot be presumed to have been buried in the ground before the oven was brought there. (2) Through the air-space of the oven. (3) So that no uncleanness could be conveyed to the oven through its air-space at that time. (4) When it was no longer within the oven. (5) Which comes under the category of metal vessels which, when found by chance, are Rabbinically unclean. (6) *Sc.* embedded in the ground on which the oven is fixed and which serves as its bottom. (7) The needle or the ring. (8) Which are within the air-space of the oven. (9) Lit., 'for he has not (a peg) to hang on'. (10) That is now absorbed. (11) That absorbed unclean liquids and was dry on its surface etc. (12) That is now absorbed. (13) As a result of the heating. (14) Hence the uncleanness even in a case where one does not mind its emergence. Where one does mind it, uncleanness is conveyed even before the oven had been heated. (15) *Sc.* older than twelve months. (16) *Sc.* the peat was more than three years old.

MISHNAH 6. IF OLIVE PEAT OR GRAPE SKINS HAD BEEN PREPARED IN CONDITIONS OF CLEANNESS, AND UNCLEAN PERSONS TROD UPON THEM AND, AS A RESULT,[1] LIQUID EMERGED FROM THEM, THEY REMAIN CLEAN,[2] SINCE THEY HAD ORIGINALLY BEEN PREPARED IN CONDITIONS OF CLEANNESS.[3] IF A SPINDLE HOOK WAS SUNK[4] INTO THE SPINDLE, OR THE IRON POINT INTO THE OX GOAD, OR A RING INTO A BRICK, AND ALL THESE[5] WERE CLEAN, AND THEN THEY WERE BROUGHT INTO A TENT[6] IN WHICH WAS A CORPSE, THEY[7] BECOME UNCLEAN.[8] IF A ZAB CAUSED THEM TO SHAKE[9] THEY BECOME UNCLEAN.[10] IF THEY THEN FELL INTO THE AIR-SPACE OF A CLEAN OVEN, THEY CAUSE IT TO BE UNCLEAN.[10] IF A LOAF OF TERUMAH CAME IN CONTACT WITH THEM, IT REMAINS CLEAN.[11]

MISHNAH 7. IF A COLANDER[12] WAS FIXED OVER THE MOUTH OF AN OVEN, FORMING A TIGHTLY FITTING COVER, AND A SPLIT APPEARED BETWEEN THE OVEN AND THE COLANDER, THE MINIMUM SIZE[13] IS THAT OF THE CIRCUMFERENCE[14] OF THE TIP OF AN OX GOAD THAT CANNOT ACTUALLY ENTER IT.[15] R. JUDAH RULED: IT MUST BE ONE INTO WHICH THE TIP

(1) Cf. L. Lit., 'and after that'. (2) They themselves, as dry refuse, cannot contract any uncleanness from the unclean persons, while the liquid, since it was neither intentionally pressed out nor was it acceptable, cannot render them susceptible. (3) Had they not been prepared in such conditions the liquid that then emerged and was acceptable would have become unclean and on emerging after they had been re-absorbed they would obviously be unclean liquids. (4) Completely. (5) Metal objects. (6) *Sc.* under the same roof. (7) Though completely absorbed. (8) Since such an absorption, unlike that within an earthen vessel with a tightly fitting cover, affords no protection against uncleanness. (9) Though he did not touch them. (10) Cf. n. 8 *mut. mut.* (11) As the metal object cannot be extracted without breaking the wood or clay in which it is embedded the latter cannot be regarded as a valid receptacle and, therefore, constitute an interposition between the unclean metal and the loaf. (12) V. *supra* VIII, 3. (13) Of the split that would cause the colander to be no longer regarded as a tightly fitting cover. (14) Lit., 'fulness of'. (15) *Sc.* it must be no less but need not be more than the actual circumference of the tip, which is one third of a handbreadth in diameter.

CAN ENTER.[1] IF A SPLIT APPEARED IN THE COLANDER, THE MINIMUM SIZE[2] IS THE CIRCUMFERENCE OF THE TIP OF AN OX GOAD THAT CAN ENTER IT.[1] R. JUDAH RULED: EVEN IF IT CANNOT ENTER.[3] IF THE SPLIT WAS CURVED[4] IT MUST NOT BE REGARDED AS STRAIGHT,[5] BUT INVARIABLY THE MINIMUM SIZE MUST BE THE CIRCUMFERENCE OF THE TIP OF AN OX GOAD THAT CAN ACTUALLY ENTER.[1]

MISHNAH 8. IF A HOLE APPEARED IN THE SEALED OUTLET[6] OF AN OVEN, THE MINIMUM SIZE[7] MUST BE THAT OF THE CIRCUMFERENCE OF A BURNING SPINDLE STAFF THAT CAN ENTER IT AND COME OUT.[8] R. JUDAH RULED: ONE THAT IS NOT BURNING.[9] IF THE HOLE APPEARED AT ITS[10] SIDE, THE MINIMUM SIZE[7] MUST BE THAT OF THE CIRCUMFERENCE OF A SPINDLE STAFF THAT CAN ENTER AND COME OUT WHILE IT IS NOT BURNING.[9] R. JUDAH RULED: WHILE BURNING.[11] R. SIMEON RULED: IF THE HOLE IS IN THE MIDDLE[10] ITS SIZE MUST BE SUCH THAT A SPINDLE STAFF CAN ENTER IT, BUT IF IT WAS AT THE SIDE IT NEED ONLY BE SUCH AS THE SPINDLE STAFF CANNOT ACTUALLY ENTER. AND SO HE USED TO RULE CONCERNING THE STOPPER OF A JAR IN WHICH A HOLE APPEARED: THE PRESCRIBED SIZE[7] IS THE CIRCUMFERENCE[12] OF THE SECOND KNOT IN AN OAT STALK, BUT IF THE HOLE WAS IN THE MIDDLE THE STALK SHOULD BE ABLE TO ENTER, AND IF AT THE SIDE IT NEED NOT BE ABLE TO ENTER. SO HE USED ALSO TO RULE CONCERNING LARGE STONE JARS IN THE STOPPERS OF WHICH APPEARED A HOLE. THE PRESCRIBED SIZE[2] IS THE CIRCUMFERENCE OF THE SECOND KNOT IN A REED, BUT IF THE HOLE WAS IN THE MIDDLE[13] THE REED MUST

(1) I.e., the split must be slightly bigger than the circumference of the tip. (2) V. p. 49, n. 13. (3) V. p. 49, n. 15. (4) In its passage from the upper to the inner surface so that the tip of an ox goad cannot pass through it (cf. T.Y.Ṭ.). (5) Lit., 'long'. (6) Lit., 'from its eye'. (7) Of the hole (cf. p. 49, n. 13). (8) *Sc.* considerably bigger than the spindle staff. (9) It need be only slightly bigger (cf. prev. n.). (10) The outlet's. (11) *Sc.* considerably bigger than the spindle staffs. (12) Lit., 'fulness of'. (13) Of the stopper.

BE ABLE TO ENTER IT, AND IF IT WAS AT THE SIDE THE REED NEED NOT BE ABLE TO ENTER IT. THIS, HOWEVER, APPLIES ONLY WHERE THE JARS WERE MADE TO STORE WINE,[1] BUT IF THEY WERE MADE TO STORE OTHER LIQUIDS, EVEN THOUGH THE HOLE WAS EVER SO SMALL,[2] THEY CONTRACT UNCLEANNESS.[3] THIS, FURTHERMORE, APPLIES ONLY WHERE THE HOLES WERE NOT MADE INTENTIONALLY,[4] BUT IF THEY WERE MADE INTENTIONALLY, EVEN THOUGH THEY WERE EVER SO SMALL,[5] [THE JARS] CONTRACT UNCLEANNESS.[6] IF A HOLE APPEARED IN THE VESSEL ITSELF, ITS PRESCRIBED SIZE[7] IS AS FOLLOWS: IF THE VESSEL WAS USED FOR FOODSTUFFS, [THE HOLE MUST BE ONE] THROUGH WHICH OLIVES CAN FALL OUT; IF FOR LIQUIDS, ONE THAT ADMITS LIQUIDS; IF FOR EITHER, THE GREATER RESTRICTION IS IMPOSED, VIZ., THERE MUST BE A TIGHTLY FITTING COVER AND [THE SIZE OF THE HOLE[7] NEED ONLY BE] ONE THAT ADMITS A LIQUID.

(1) In which case they would be continued in use after a small hole had appeared. (2) Provided only that it admits a liquid in which it is placed. (3) *Sc.* the hole deprives the contents from the protection against uncleanness which a tightly fitting cover affords. (4) Lit., 'by the hands of man'. (5) Provided only that they admit a liquid in which the jar is placed. (6) *Sc.* the hole deprives the contents from the protection against uncleanness which a tightly fitting cover affords. (7) That deprives the contents of the vessel from the protection afforded by a tightly fitting cover.

KELIM

CHAPTER X

MISHNAH 1. THE FOLLOWING VESSELS[1] PROTECT THEIR CONTENTS[2] WHEN THEY HAVE A TIGHTLY FITTING COVER:[3] THOSE MADE OF CATTLE DUNG, OF STONE, OF CLAY,[4] OF EARTHENWARE,[5] OF ALUM-CRYSTAL, OF THE BONES OF A FISH OR OF ITS SKIN, OR OF THE BONES OF ANY ANIMAL OF THE SEA OR OF ITS SKIN, AND SUCH WOODEN VESSELS AS[6] ARE ALWAYS CLEAN. THESE AFFORD PROTECTION WHETHER THE COVERS CLOSE THEIR MOUTHS OR THEIR SIDES,[7] WHETHER THEY STAND ON THEIR BOTTOMS OR LEAN ON THEIR SIDES. IF THEY WERE INVERTED WITH THEIR MOUTHS DOWNWARDS THEY[8] AFFORD PROTECTION TO ALL THAT IS BENEATH THEM TO THE NETHERMOST DEEP. R. ELIEZER RULES THAT THIS[9] IS UNCLEAN. THESE[10] PROTECT EVERYTHING, EXCEPT THAT AN EARTHEN VESSEL AFFORDS PROTECTION ONLY TO FOODSTUFFS, LIQUIDS AND EARTHEN VESSELS.[11]

MISHNAH 2. WHEREWITH MAY A VESSEL BE TIGHTLY COVERED?[12] WITH LIME OR GYPSUM, PITCH OR WAX, MUD OR EXCREMENT, CRUDE CLAY OR POTTER'S CLAY, OR ANY SUBSTANCE THAT IS USED FOR PLASTERING. ONE MAY NOT MAKE A TIGHTLY FITTING COVER[12] WITH TIN OR WITH LEAD BECAUSE THOUGH IT IS A COVERING, IT IS NOT TIGHTLY FITTING.

(1) Since they are not susceptible to uncleanness even Rabbinically. (2) Against corpse uncleanness under the same roof. (3) V. Num. XIX, 15. (4) That was unburnt in the furnace. (5) Duly burnt. (6) On account of their huge size, holding no less than forty *se'ah* (cf. *infra* XV, 1). (7) If an aperture was there. (8) If they were duly attached with clay to the ground. (9) Anything under an inverted vessel. (10) All the vessels enumerated, if they were provided with a tightly fitting cover. (11) Within it. Objects that can attain cleanness by ritual immersion are not protected (cf. *supra* IX, 2, notes). (12) That its contents be thereby protected in accordance with Num. XIX, 15.

ONE MAY NOT MAKE A TIGHTLY FITTING COVER[1] WITH SWOLLEN FIG-CAKES[2] OR WITH DOUGH THAT WAS KNEADED WITH FRUIT JUICE,[2] SINCE[3] IT MIGHT[4] CAUSE IT TO BECOME UNFIT.[5] IF, HOWEVER, A TIGHTLY FITTING COVER HAD BEEN MADE OF IT[6] PROTECTION FROM UNCLEANNESS IS AFFORDED.[7]

MISHNAH 3. A STOPPER OF A JAR THAT IS LOOSE BUT DOES NOT FALL OUT, R. JUDAH RULED, AFFORDS PROTECTION;[8] BUT THE SAGES RULED: IT DOES NOT AFFORD PROTECTION. IF ITS FINGER-HOLD[9] WAS SUNK WITHIN THE JAR AND A DEAD CREEPING THING WAS IN IT,[10] THE JAR BECOMES UNCLEAN,[11] AND IF THE CREEPING THING WAS IN THE JAR, ANY FOODSTUFFS IN IT[10] BECOME UNCLEAN.[12]

MISHNAH 4. IF A BALL OR COIL OF REED GRASS WAS PLACED OVER THE MOUTH OF A JAR, AND ONLY ITS SIDES[13] WERE PLASTERED, NO PROTECTION IS AFFORDED UNLESS IT WAS ALSO PLASTERED ABOVE[14] OR[15] BELOW.[14] THE SAME LAW APPLIES TO A PATCH OF CLOTH.[16] IF THE STOPPER WAS ONE OF PAPER[17] OR LEATHER[18] AND BOUND[19] WITH A CORD,

(1) V. p. 52, n. 12. (2) Though if it had never been moistened it is insusceptible to uncleanness. (3) Should any liquid fall upon it it would be susceptible to uncleanness, and consequently unclean once it is overshadowed by a corpse. (4) On contracting an uncleanness. (5) To afford protection as a tightly fitting cover. Such a cover must be one that would remain clean in all circumstances. (6) Any of the foodstuffs mentioned. (7) So long as the cover has not become susceptible to uncleanness. (8) Like a tightly fitting cover. (9) A depression in a stopper wherein the fingers are inserted to facilitate the drawing out of the stopper. (10) The finger-hold. (11) The stopper being regarded as one with the jar. (12) Since the stopper cannot be considered a valid vessel that affords protection to its contents. (13) Where they came in contact with the jar. (14) To stop up the air-spaces in the ball or coil. (15) Cf. L. (16) That was less than three by three finger-breadths in size (and, therefore, insusceptible to uncleanness) and rolled up in a ball to serve as a stopper. (17) Papyrus, which is not susceptible to uncleanness. (18) Of a size that is less than the prescribed minimum for susceptibility to uncleanness. (19) Round the jar.

PROTECTION IS AFFORDED IF IT WAS PLASTERED AT THE SIDES ONLY.[1]

MISHNAH 5. IF [THE EARTHENWARE OF] A JAR[2] HAD SCALED OFF WHILE ITS PITCH [LINING][3] REMAINED INTACT,[4] AND SO ALSO IF POTS OF FISH BRINE WERE STOPPED UP WITH GYPSUM AT A LEVEL WITH THE BRIM,[5] R. JUDAH RULED: THEY AFFORD NO PROTECTION; BUT THE SAGES RULED: THEY AFFORD PROTECTION.[6]

MISHNAH 6. IF A JAR HAD A HOLE IN IT AND WINE LEES BLOCKED IT UP, THEY AFFORD PROTECTION.[7] IF IT WAS STOPPED UP WITH A VINE SHOOT [IT AFFORDS NO PROTECTION] UNLESS IT WAS PLASTERED AT THE SIDES.[8] IF THERE WERE[9] TWO VINE SHOOTS, [NO PROTECTION IS AFFORDED] UNLESS THEY WERE PLASTERED AT THE SIDES[8] AND ALSO BETWEEN THE ONE SHOOT AND THE OTHER. IF A BOARD[10] IS PLACED OVER THE MOUTH OF AN OVEN,[11] PROTECTION IS AFFORDED IF IT WAS PLASTERED AT THE SIDES.[8] IF THERE WERE TWO BOARDS NO PROTECTION IS AFFORDED UNLESS THESE ARE PLASTERED AT THE SIDES[8] AND ALSO BETWEEN THE ONE BOARD AND THE OTHER. IF, HOWEVER, THEY[12] WERE FASTENED TOGETHER WITH PEGS OR JOINTS THERE IS NO NEED FOR THEM TO BE PLASTERED IN THE MIDDLE.

(1) Since, unlike a ball of reed-grass or cloth, neither paper nor leather contains holes large enough for an uncleanness to penetrate through them. (2) That had a tightly fitting cover. (3) On which the cover rests. (4) Lit., 'stands'. (5) Cf. L. (6) The point at issue is the interpretation of *'alaw* (*'upon it'*) in Num. XIX, 15. According to R. Judah the word is to be taken literally and the stopper must, therefore, rest *'upon'* the edge of the vessel, while according to the Sages it is not to be taken literally and the stopper may, therefore, rest slightly above (on the pitch) or on a level with the brim of the vessel. (7) Though the lees are only on a level with the hole, in agreement with the Sages *supra*. (8) Where the stopper meets the jar. (9) In the hole, serving as a stopper. (10) Which is a 'flat vessel' that is not susceptible to uncleanness (Bert.) or 'no vessel at all' (L.). (11) Of earthenware. (12) The two boards.

MISHNAH 7. IF[1] AN OLD OVEN[2] WAS WITHIN A NEW ONE[3] AND A COLANDER[4] RESTED OVER THE MOUTH OF THE OLD OVEN[5] IN A MANNER THAT IF THE OLD ONE WERE TO BE REMOVED THE COLANDER WOULD DROP,[6] ALL BECOME UNCLEAN;[7] BUT IF IT WOULD NOT DROP,[8] ALL REMAIN CLEAN.[9] IF A NEW OVEN WAS WITHIN AN OLD ONE AND A COLANDER RESTED ON THE MOUTH OF THE OLD OVEN, AND THERE WAS NOT A HANDBREADTH OF SPACE BETWEEN THE NEW OVEN AND THE COLANDER,[10] ALL THE CONTENTS OF THE NEW ONE REMAIN CLEAN.[9]

MISHNAH 8. IF [EARTHEN] SAUCEPANS WERE PLACED ONE WITHIN THE OTHER BUT THEIR RIMS WERE ON THE SAME LEVEL, AND THERE WAS A [DEAD] CREEPING THING IN THE UPPERMOST ONE OR IN THE LOWEST ONE, THAT PAN ALONE[11] BECOMES UNCLEAN BUT ALL THE OTHERS REMAIN CLEAN.[12] IF [THEY WERE PERFORATED] TO THE EXTENT OF ADMITTING[13]

(1) Under the same roof as a corpse. (2) That had been duly heated and was consequently susceptible to uncleanness. (3) Which, not having been yet properly heated, is insusceptible to uncleanness and may, therefore, serve as a protection for the old one. (4) That was not 'tightly fitting', not having been joined with plaster to the oven. (5) Closing at the same time the mouth of the new one also, the brims of both having been on the same level. (6) *Sc.* if the colander was entirely supported by the old oven and was just filling up the mouth of the new one. (7) From the corpse's uncleanness; because the old oven had no tightly fitting cover (cf. *supra* n. 4) and the new one (since the colander rests entirely on the old one) is not sufficiently closed to afford the protection of a vessel with a tightly fitting cover. (8) The colander having rested partly on the new oven. (9) Because the new oven, which has not yet been properly heated, is not regarded as a valid vessel that cannot afford protection without a tightly fitting cover. Any cover, even one that is not tightly fitting, serves it as a proper covering to constitute it a valid partition between the uncleanness and the old oven. (10) Cf. *supra* n. 4 *mut. mut.* (11) In which the unclean object was found. (12) Not only are the saucepans clean, (because a vessel does not contract uncleanness through the air-space of another earthen vessel) but even foodstuffs or liquids in them remain clean (since it is only to and from the inside of an exposed vessel that uncleanness is conveyed but not to or from the inside of one that is within another vessel). (13) From their outsides.

A LIQUID,[1] AND THE CREEPING THING WAS IN THE UPPERMOST ONE, ALL BECOME UNCLEAN;[2] BUT IF IT WAS IN THE LOWEST ONE, THAT ALONE IS UNCLEAN WHILE ALL THE OTHERS REMAIN CLEAN.[3] IF[4] THE CREEPING THING WAS IN THE UPPERMOST ONE AND THE LOWEST PROJECTED ABOVE IT,[5] BOTH[6] BECOME UNCLEAN.[7] IF THE CREEPING THING WAS IN THE UPPERMOST ONE AND THE LOWEST PROJECTED ABOVE IT,[5] ANY OF THE INTERVENING ONES THAT CONTAINED DRIPPING LIQUID BECOMES[8] UNCLEAN.[9]

(1) In which they are placed. (2) Two restrictions are here imposed: In regard to itself the saucepan is still considered a valid vessel because the hole in it is not big enough for olives to fall through, and it is consequently susceptible to uncleanness; while in relation to the saucepans in which it stands it is considered (on account of the small hole in it) to have lost the status of vessel and thus to be virtually non-existent and incapable of preventing the uncleanness from spreading to the insides of the other saucepans. (3) Since a vessel cannot contract uncleanness from the air-space of an earthen vessel. (4) In the case of undamaged saucepans. (5) The brim of the latter being higher than that of the former. (6) Lit., 'it and the lowest'. (7) The uppermost is unclean because it contained the creeping thing and the lowest is unclean because on account of its projection above the other, the uncleanness is deemed virtually to be contained directly within itself. The intervening saucepans remain clean as explained *supra* n. 3. (8) Since they are all sound vessels. (9) From the liquid which contracted its uncleanness from the lowest saucepan (cf. n. 7).

KELIM

CHAPTER XI

MISHNAH 1. METAL VESSELS, WHETHER THEY ARE FLAT OR FORM A RECEPTACLE, ARE SUSCEPTIBLE TO UNCLEANNESS. ON BEING BROKEN THEY BECOME CLEAN.[1] IF THEY WERE RE-MADE INTO VESSELS THEY REVERT[2] TO THEIR FORMER UNCLEANNESS. RABBAN SIMEON B. GAMALIEL RULED: THIS[3] DOES NOT APPLY TO EVERY FORM OF UNCLEANNESS BUT ONLY TO THAT CONTRACTED FROM A CORPSE.

MISHNAH 2. EVERY METAL VESSEL[4] THAT HAS A NAME OF ITS OWN[5] IS SUSCEPTIBLE TO UNCLEANNESS, EXCEPTING A DOOR, A BOLT, A LOCK, A SOCKET UNDER A HINGE, A HINGE, A CLAPPER, AND THE [THRESHOLD] GROOVE UNDER A DOOR POST, SINCE THESE ARE INTENDED TO BE ATTACHED TO THE GROUND.[6]

MISHNAH 3. IF VESSELS ARE MADE FROM IRON ORE, FROM SMELTED IRON, FROM THE HOOP[7] OF A WHEEL, FROM SHEETS,[7] FROM PLATING,[7] FROM THE BASES, RIMS OR HANDLES OF VESSELS, FROM CHIPPINGS OR FILINGS, THEY ARE CLEAN.[1] R. JOḤANAN B. NURI RULED: THIS[8] APPLIES ALSO TO THOSE MADE OF SHATTERED VESSELS. [VESSELS THAT ARE MADE] OF FRAGMENTS OF VESSELS, FROM SMALL WARE, OR FROM NAILS THAT WERE KNOWN TO HAVE BEEN MADE FROM VESSELS, ARE UNCLEAN.[9] [IF THEY WERE MADE] FROM

(1) Even if they have been formerly unclean. (2) Rabbinically, though not Pentateuchally. (3) The reversion to uncleanness. (4) Though it does not form a receptacle. (5) *Sc.* is not merely a part of another vessel. (6) Hence they are insusceptible to uncleanness even before they have been attached. (7) Of metal. (8) The insusceptibility to uncleanness. (9) Since the material may have formed a part of an unclean vessel

ORDINARY NAILS,[1] BETH SHAMMAI RULE THAT THEY ARE UNCLEAN,[2] AND BETH HILLEL[3] RULE THAT THEY ARE CLEAN.

MISHNAH 4. IF UNCLEAN IRON[4] WAS SMELTED TOGETHER WITH CLEAN IRON AND THE GREATER PART WAS FROM THE UNCLEAN ONE, [THE VESSEL MADE OF THE COMPOSITION] IS UNCLEAN;[5] BUT IF THE GREATER PART WAS FROM THE CLEAN IRON THE VESSEL IS CLEAN. IF EACH REPRESENTED A HALF IT IS UNCLEAN.[5] THE SAME LAW ALSO APPLIES TO A MIXTURE OF CEMENT[6] AND CATTLE DUNG.[7] A DOOR BOLT[8] IS SUSCEPTIBLE TO UNCLEANNESS, BUT [ONE OF WOOD] THAT IS ONLY PLATED WITH METAL IS NOT SUSCEPTIBLE TO UNCLEANNESS.[9] THE CLUTCH AND THE CROSSPIECE [OF A LOCK] ARE SUSCEPTIBLE TO UNCLEANNESS. AS REGARDS A DOOR-BOLT, R. JOSHUA RULED: IT MAY BE DRAWN OFF ONE DOOR AND[10] HUNG ON ANOTHER ON THE SABBATH. R. TARFON RULED: IT IS LIKE ALL OTHER VESSELS AND MAY BE CARRIED ABOUT IN A COURTYARD.

MISHNAH 5. THE SCORPION [-SHAPED] BIT OF A BRIDLE IS SUSCEPTIBLE TO UNCLEANNESS, BUT THE CHEEK-PIECES ARE CLEAN.[11] R. ELIEZER RULES THAT THE CHEEK-PIECES ARE SUSCEPTIBLE TO UNCLEANNESS, AND THE SAGES HOLD THAT THE SCORPION BIT ALONE IS SUSCEPTIBLE TO UN-

whose uncleanness is revived when the material is made into a new one.

(1) About which it is unknown whether they were made from old vessels or from unshaped iron. (2) As a preventive measure. They may possibly have been made from a vessel. (3) Holding that no preventive measure is necessary in this case. (4) *Sc.* one that was known to have formed a part of an old vessel. (5) The former uncleanness passes on to the new vessel. (6) A vessel of which is susceptible to uncleanness as earthenware. (7) Vessels from which are insusceptible to uncleanness. (8) Of metal, which is sometimes used as a pestle. (9) Since the metal plating is a mere attachment, the main part of the bolt being wood which is insusceptible to uncleanness. (10) Dragging it on, without removing it from the ground. Not being a valid vessel, it is forbidden to be carried from place to place on the Sabbath. (11) Serving as mere ornaments they are not susceptible to uncleanness.

CLEANNESS, BUT WHILE THEY[1] ARE JOINED TOGETHER THE WHOLE IS SUSCEPTIBLE TO UNCLEANNESS.

MISHNAH 6. A METAL SPINDLE-KNOB, R. AKIBA DECLARES TO BE SUSCEPTIBLE TO UNCLEANNESS BUT THE SAGES DECLARE IT INSUSCEPTIBLE.[2] IF IT[3] WAS ONLY PLATED [WITH METAL] IT IS CLEAN.[4] A SPINDLE, A DISTAFF, A ROD, A DOUBLE FLUTE AND A PIPE ARE SUSCEPTIBLE TO UNCLEANNESS IF THEY ARE OF METAL, BUT IF THEY ARE ONLY PLATED [WITH METAL] THEY ARE CLEAN. IF A DOUBLE FLUTE HAS A RECEPTACLE FOR THE WINGS[5] IT IS SUSCEPTIBLE TO UNCLEANNESS IN EITHER CASE.[6]

MISHNAH 7. A CURVED HORN[7] IS SUSCEPTIBLE TO UNCLEANNESS[8] AND A STRAIGHT ONE[9] IS CLEAN. IF ITS MOUTHPIECE WAS OF METAL IT[10] IS UNCLEAN. ITS WIDE SIDE[11] R. TARFON DECLARES TO BE SUSCEPTIBLE TO UNCLEANNESS AND THE SAGES DECLARE IT CLEAN. WHILE THEY ARE JOINED TOGETHER THE WHOLE INSTRUMENT IS SUSCEPTIBLE TO UNCLEANNESS. SIMILARLY THE BRANCHES OF A CANDLESTICK ARE CLEAN AND THE CUPS AND THE BASE ARE SUSCEPTIBLE TO UNCLEANNESS, BUT WHILE THEY ARE JOINED TOGETHER THE WHOLE CANDLESTICK IS SUSCEPTIBLE TO UNCLEANNESS.

MISHNAH 8. A HELMET IS SUSCEPTIBLE TO UNCLEANNESS AND THE CHEEK-PIECES ARE CLEAN, BUT IF THE LATTER HAVE A RECEPTACLE FOR WATER[12] THEY ARE SUSCEPTIBLE TO UNCLEANNESS. ALL WEAPONS OF WAR ARE SUSCEPTIBLE

(1) The bit, the bridle and the cheek-pieces. (2) Since the knob has no independent name or existence it is like a piece of metal that serves a flat piece of wood which is insusceptible to uncleanness. (3) The knob. (4) Even according to R. Akiba. (5) A bagpipe. (6) Whether it is made of metal, or only plated with it. (7) A musical pipe made up of links of horn. (8) Since it may be regarded as having a receptacle. (9) Which forms no receptacle. (10) Even a straight horn. (11) If made of metal. (12) From which one drinks in the course of a battle.

TO UNCLEANNESS: A JAVELIN, A SPEAR-HEAD, GREAVES, AND BREASTPLATE ARE SUSCEPTIBLE TO UNCLEANNESS. ALL WOMEN'S ORNAMENTS ARE SUSCEPTIBLE TO UNCLEANNESS: A GOLDEN CITY,[1] A NECKLACE, EAR-RINGS, FINGER-RINGS (WHETHER THE RING IS WITH A SEAL OR WITHOUT ONE) AND NOSE-RINGS. IF A NECKLACE HAS METAL BEADS ON A THREAD OF FLAX OR WOOL AND THE THREAD BROKE, THE BEADS ARE STILL SUSCEPTIBLE TO UNCLEANNESS, SINCE EACH ONE IS A VESSEL IN ITSELF. IF THE THREAD WAS OF METAL AND THE BEADS WERE OF PRECIOUS STONES OR PEARLS OR GLASS, AND THE BEADS WERE BROKEN WHILE THE THREAD ALONE REMAINED, IT IS STILL SUSCEPTIBLE TO UNCLEANNESS. THE REMNANT OF A NECKLACE LONG ENOUGH FOR THE NECK OF A LITTLE GIRL, IS SUSCEPTIBLE TO UNCLEANNESS. R. ELIEZER RULED: EVEN IF ONLY ONE RING REMAINED IT IS UNCLEAN, SINCE IT ALSO IS HUNG AROUND THE NECK.

MISHNAH 9. IF AN EAR-RING WAS SHAPED LIKE A POT[2] AT ITS BOTTOM AND LIKE A LENTIL AT THE TOP AND THE SECTIONS FELL APART, THE POT-SHAPED SECTION[3] IS SUSCEPTIBLE TO UNCLEANNESS AS A RECEPTACLE, WHILE THE LENTIL SHAPED SECTION IS SUSCEPTIBLE TO UNCLEANNESS IN ITSELF.[4] THE HOOKLET[5] IS CLEAN. IF THE SECTIONS OF AN EAR-RING THAT WAS IN THE SHAPE OF A CLUSTER OF GRAPES FELL APART, THEY[3] ARE CLEAN.

(1) A golden tiara shaped like, or engraven with the city of Jerusalem. (2) Wide and hollow. (3) Which can no longer be worn as an ornament. (4) As an ornament, since it is still worn as such. (5) Of an ear-ring.

KELIM

CHAPTER XII

MISHNAH 1. A FINGER-RING FOR A MAN IS[1] SUSCEPTIBLE TO UNCLEANNESS. A RING FOR CATTLE OR FOR VESSELS AND ALL OTHER RINGS ARE CLEAN.[2] A BEAM[3] FOR ARROWS IS SUSCEPTIBLE TO UNCLEANNESS,[4] BUT ONE FOR PRISONERS[5] IS CLEAN.[6] A NECK-IRON[7] IS SUSCEPTIBLE TO UNCLEANNESS. A CHAIN THAT HAS A LOCK-PIECE IS SUSCEPTIBLE TO UNCLEANNESS,[8] BUT ONE USED FOR TYING ON CATTLE IS CLEAN. THE CHAIN OF WHOLESALE PROVISION DEALERS[9] IS SUSCEPTIBLE TO UNCLEANNESS,[8] BUT THAT OF HOUSEHOLDERS[10] IS CLEAN.[11] R. JOSE EXPLAINED: THIS APPLIES ONLY WHERE[12] IT[13] CONSISTS OF ONE LINK, BUT IF IT CONSISTED OF TWO LINKS OR IF IT HAD A SLUG [-SHAPED] PIECE AT ITS END[14] IT IS SUSCEPTIBLE TO UNCLEANNESS.[15]

MISHNAH 2. THE BEAM OF THE WOOL-COMBERS' BALANCE IS SUSCEPTIBLE TO UNCLEANNESS[16] ON ACCOUNT OF THE HOOKS;[17] AND THAT OF THE HOUSEHOLDER, IF IT HAS HOOKS IS ALSO SUSCEPTIBLE TO UNCLEANNESS. THE LADING HOOKS OF PORTERS ARE CLEAN BUT THOSE OF PEDLARS[18]

(1) Like any other ornaments worn by men. (2) Only ornaments for men are susceptible to uncleanness. (3) Plated with iron and used as a target. (4) Cf. *supra* XI, 8. (5) Used as a foot-stock. (6) Since it is immovable. (7) Which is carried about when the prisoner moves from place to place, and is, therefore, considered a 'vessel'. (8) Being regarded as a vessel. (9) Attached by one end to the wall, and by the other to a measure or weight. (10) A mere ornament. (11) Only ornaments for men are susceptible to uncleanness. (12) Lit., 'when, at the time'. (13) The chain of householders. (14) Lit., 'top'; by which the chain is attached to the wall or door. (15) Being then regarded as a vessel. (16) Though it was made of wood. (17) Which are metal and susceptible to uncleanness. (18) Or spice dealers.

ARE SUSCEPTIBLE TO UNCLEANNESS.[1] R. JUDAH RULED: IN THE CASE OF THAT OF THE PEDLARS THE HOOK THAT IS IN FRONT IS SUSCEPTIBLE TO UNCLEANNESS[1] BUT THAT WHICH IS BEHIND IS CLEAN.[2] THE HOOK OF A BED-FRAME IS SUSCEPTIBLE TO UNCLEANNESS BUT THAT OF BED POLES[3] IS CLEAN. [THE HOOK OF] A CHEST IS SUSCEPTIBLE TO UNCLEANNESS BUT THAT OF A FISH TRAP IS CLEAN. THAT OF A TABLE IS SUSCEPTIBLE TO UNCLEANNESS BUT THAT OF A WOODEN CANDLESTICK IS CLEAN. THIS IS THE RULE: ANY HOOK THAT IS ATTACHED TO A SUSCEPTIBLE VESSEL[4] IS SUSCEPTIBLE TO UNCLEANNESS, BUT ONE THAT IS ATTACHED TO A VESSEL THAT IS INSUSCEPTIBLE TO UNCLEANNESS IS CLEAN. ALL THESE, HOWEVER, ARE BY THEMSELVES[5] CLEAN.[6]

MISHNAH 3. THE METAL COVER OF A BASKET OF HOUSEHOLDERS, RABBAN GAMALIEL DECLARES, IS SUSCEPTIBLE TO UNCLEANNESS,[1] AND THE SAGES HOLD THAT IT IS CLEAN;[7] BUT THAT OF PHYSICIANS[8] IS SUSCEPTIBLE TO UNCLEANNESS. THE DOOR[9] OF A CUPBOARD OF HOUSEHOLDERS IS CLEAN BUT THAT OF PHYSICIANS[10] IS SUSCEPTIBLE TO UNCLEANNESS. TONGS[11] ARE SUSCEPTIBLE TO UNCLEANNESS BUT FIRE-BARS ARE CLEAN. THE SCORPION [-SHAPED] HOOK IN AN OLIVE-PRESS IS SUSCEPTIBLE TO UNCLEANNESS BUT THE HOOKS FOR THE WALLS[12] ARE CLEAN.[13]

MISHNAH 4. A BLOOD-LETTERS' LANCET IS SUSCEPTIBLE TO UNCLEANNESS BUT [THE STYLE] OF A SUNDIAL IS CLEAN. R. ZADOK RULES THAT IT IS SUSCEPTIBLE TO UNCLEANNESS. A WEAVER'S PIN IS SUSCEPTIBLE TO UNCLEANNESS; THE

(1) Because it forms a receptacle. (2) Since its receptacle is not used. (3) Fixed at the head and at the foot of the bed. (4) One that is susceptible to uncleanness. (5) *Sc.* when detached from the vessel. (6) Since they are not independent vessels but mere parts of others. (7) Because a cover cannot be considered a vessel. (8) Which is used as a receptacle for medicinal drugs. (9) Of metal. (10) On which medical instruments are hung. (11) Wherewith smelters hold the crucible over the fire. (12) Since they are attached to a permanent building structure. (13) Even before they have been attached.

CHEST OF A GRIST-DEALER, R. ZADOK RULES, IS SUSCEPTIBLE TO UNCLEANNESS, BUT THE SAGES RULE THAT IT IS CLEAN. IF ITS WAGON WAS MADE OF METAL IT IS SUSCEPTIBLE TO UNCLEANNESS.

MISHNAH 5. IF A NAIL[1] WAS ADAPTED TO OPEN OR TO SHUT A LOCK IT IS SUSCEPTIBLE TO UNCLEANNESS, BUT ONE THAT IS ONLY USED AS A SAFEGUARD[2] IS CLEAN. IF A NAIL WAS ADAPTED TO OPEN A JAR, R. AKIBA RULES THAT IT IS SUSCEPTIBLE TO UNCLEANNESS, AND THE SAGES RULE THAT IT IS CLEAN UNLESS IT WAS FORGED ANEW. A MONEY-CHANGER'S NAIL[3] IS CLEAN,[4] BUT R. ZADOK RULED THAT IT IS SUSCEPTIBLE TO UNCLEANNESS.[5] THERE ARE THREE THINGS WHICH R. ZADOK HOLDS TO BE SUSCEPTIBLE TO UNCLEANNESS AND THE SAGES HOLD CLEAN: THE NAIL OF A MONEY-CHANGER, THE CHEST OF A GRIST-DEALER AND THE STYLE OF A SUNDIAL. R. ZADOK RULES THAT THESE ARE SUSCEPTIBLE TO UNCLEANNESS AND THE SAGES RULE THAT THEY ARE CLEAN.

MISHNAH 6. THERE ARE FOUR THINGS WHICH RABBAN GAMALIEL DECLARES TO BE SUSCEPTIBLE TO UNCLEANNESS, AND THE SAGES DECLARE CLEAN: THE METAL COVER OF A BASKET OF HOUSEHOLDERS, THE HANGER OF A STRIGIL, UNFINISHED METAL VESSELS, AND AN EARTHEN SLAB[6] THAT WAS BROKEN INTO TWO EQUAL PARTS. THE SAGES, HOWEVER, AGREE WITH RABBAN GAMALIEL THAT WHERE A SLAB WAS BROKEN INTO TWO PARTS, ONE LARGE AND THE OTHER SMALL, THE LARGER IS SUSCEPTIBLE TO UNCLEANNESS AND THE SMALLER IS CLEAN.

MISHNAH 7. IF A DENAR THAT HAD BEEN INVALIDATED[7]

(1) Which is insusceptible to uncleanness. (2) To detect whether anybody had entered the house. (3) Whereby his shop's shutters (or his balances) are supported. (4) Not intended to be moved about it cannot be considered a vessel. (5) Since sometimes, when repairs are needed, it is moved from its position. (6) Having a rim. (7) Or 'became defective'.

WAS FASHIONED FOR HANGING AROUND A YOUNG GIRL'S NECK IT IS SUSCEPTIBLE TO UNCLEANNESS. SO, TOO, IF A SELA' THAT HAD BEEN INVALIDATED WAS ADAPTED FOR USE AS A WEIGHT, IT IS SUSCEPTIBLE TO UNCLEANNESS. HOW MUCH MAY IT[1] DEPRECIATE WHILE ONE IS STILL PERMITTED TO KEEP IT? AS MUCH AS TWO DENARS.[2] IF ITS VALUE IS LESS IT MUST BE CUT UP.[3]

MISHNAH 8. A PENKNIFE, A WRITING PEN, A PLUMMET, A WEIGHT, PRESSING PLATES, A MEASURING-ROD, AND A MEASURING-TABLE ARE SUSCEPTIBLE TO UNCLEANNESS. ALL UNFINISHED WOODEN VESSELS ALSO ARE SUSCEPTIBLE TO UNCLEANNESS, EXCEPTING THOSE MADE OF BOXWOOD.[4] R. JUDAH RULED: ONE MADE OF AN OLIVE-TREE BRANCH IS ALSO CLEAN UNLESS IT WAS FIRST HEATED.[5]

(1) A *sela'*. (2) *Sc.* half a *sela'* or fifty per cent. (3) To prevent unscrupulous people from passing it on as a good coin. (4) Whose bark is very thick. Only after the bark has been removed by polishing can the vessel be considered finished. (5) To extract its moisture. Cf. prev. n. *mut. mut.*

KELIM

CHAPTER XIII

MISHNAH 1. THE SWORD, KNIFE, DAGGER, SPEAR, HAND-SICKLE, HARVEST-SICKLE, CLIPPER,[1] AND BARBERS' SCISSORS, EVEN THOUGH THEIR COMPONENT PARTS WERE SEPARATED, ARE SUSCEPTIBLE TO UNCLEANNESS. R. JOSE RULED: THE PART THAT IS NEAR THE HAND[2] IS SUSCEPTIBLE TO UNCLEANNESS, BUT THAT WHICH IS NEAR THE TOP[3] IS CLEAN. IF THE TWO PARTS OF SHEARS WERE SEPARATED R. JUDAH RULES THAT THEY ARE STILL SUSCEPTIBLE TO UNCLEANNESS[4] BUT THE SAGES RULE THAT THEY ARE CLEAN.

MISHNAH 2. A SHOVEL-FORK[5] WHOSE SHOVEL[6] HAS BEEN REMOVED IS STILL SUSCEPTIBLE TO UNCLEANNESS ON ACCOUNT OF ITS FORK;[7] IF ITS FORK HAS BEEN REMOVED IT IS STILL SUSCEPTIBLE ON ACCOUNT OF ITS SHOVEL. A KOHLSTICK[8] WHOSE [EAR-] SPOON IS MISSING IS STILL SUSCEPTIBLE TO UNCLEANNESS ON ACCOUNT OF ITS POINT; IF ITS POINT WAS MISSING IT IS STILL SUSCEPTIBLE ON ACCOUNT OF ITS [EAR-] SPOON. A STYLUS WHOSE WRITING POINT IS MISSING IS STILL SUSCEPTIBLE TO UNCLEANNESS ON ACCOUNT OF ITS ERASER;[9] IF ITS ERASER IS MISSING IT IS SUSCEPTIBLE ON ACCOUNT OF ITS WRITING POINT. A SOUP-LADLE[10] WHOSE SPOON IS LOST IS STILL SUSCEPTIBLE TO

(1) Or 'razor'. (2) Since it is used in holding the instrument. (3) Which, owing to its proximity to the blade and the danger of cutting one's hand, is never used when the instrument is handled. (4) Since each part can still be used. (5) An instrument having at one end a fork, wherewith meat or bread is taken out from an oven, and at its other end a flat disk to shovel coals or ashes. (6) Lit., 'spoon'. (7) Lit., 'tooth'. (8) Having at one end a point wherewith stibium is applied to the eyelids (to blacken them) while its other end is wider and is used to clean out the ears. (9) Its flat end wherewith the wax written upon is smoothed over. (10) Having at one end a spoon and at the other a fork.

UNCLEANNESS ON ACCOUNT OF ITS FORK; IF ITS FORK IS LOST IT IS STILL SUSCEPTIBLE ON ACCOUNT OF ITS SPOON. SO ALSO IS THE LAW IN REGARD TO THE PRONG OF A MATTOCK.[1] THE MINIMUM SIZE[2] FOR ALL THESE INSTRUMENTS IS ONE THAT WOULD SUFFICE FOR THE DUE PERFORMANCE OF THEIR USUAL WORK.

MISHNAH 3. A COULTER THAT IS DAMAGED[3] REMAINS SUSCEPTIBLE TO UNCLEANNESS UNTIL ITS GREATER PART IS LOST, BUT IF ITS SHAFT-SOCKET IS BROKEN IT IS CLEAN. A HATCHET-HEAD WHOSE CUTTING EDGE IS LOST REMAINS SUSCEPTIBLE TO UNCLEANNESS ON ACCOUNT OF ITS SPLITTING EDGE; IF ITS SPLITTING EDGE IS LOST IT REMAINS SUSCEPTIBLE ON ACCOUNT OF ITS CUTTING EDGE. IF ITS SHAFT-SOCKET IS BROKEN IT IS CLEAN.

MISHNAH 4. A SHOVEL WHOSE BLADE WAS MISSING IS STILL SUSCEPTIBLE TO UNCLEANNESS, SINCE IT IS STILL LIKE A HAMMER; SO R. MEIR. BUT THE SAGES RULE THAT IT IS CLEAN. A SAW WHOSE TEETH ARE MISSING ONE IN EVERY TWO[4] IS CLEAN, BUT IF AN HASIṬ[5] LENGTH OF CONSECUTIVE TEETH[6] REMAINED IT IS SUSCEPTIBLE TO UNCLEANNESS. AN ADZE, SCALPEL, PLANE, OR DRILL THAT WAS DAMAGED REMAINS SUSCEPTIBLE TO UNCLEANNESS, BUT IF ITS SHARP EDGE WAS MISSING IT IS CLEAN. IN ALL THESE CASES, HOWEVER, IF AN INSTRUMENT WAS SPLIT INTO TWO PARTS BOTH REMAIN SUSCEPTIBLE TO UNCLEANNESS, EXCEPTING THE DRILL. THE BLOCK OF A PLANE BY ITSELF[7] IS CLEAN.

(1) One end of which is used for digging and the other for crushing rubble. If one end is lost the instrument is still susceptible to uncleanness on account of the use of its other end. (2) Of what must remain if it is still to be unclean or susceptible to uncleanness. (3) On the side of its cutting edge. (4) No three consecutive teeth remaining. Lit., 'one from between (two)'. (5) The distance between the tips of the thumb and the forefinger when outstretched; according to Maim. the distance between the outstretched fore and middle fingers. (6) Lit., 'in one place'. (7) Having lest the blade.

MISHNAH 5. A NEEDLE WHOSE EYE OR POINT WAS MISSING IS CLEAN. IF IT WAS SUBSEQUENTLY ADAPTED AS A STRETCHING-PIN IT IS SUSCEPTIBLE TO UNCLEANNESS. A PACK-NEEDLE WHOSE EYE WAS MISSING IS STILL SUSCEPTIBLE TO UNCLEANNESS SINCE ONE WRITES WITH IT.[1] IF ITS POINT WAS MISSING IT IS CLEAN. A STRETCHING-PIN IS IN EITHER CASE[2] SUSCEPTIBLE TO UNCLEANNESS. A NEEDLE THAT HAS BECOME RUSTY IS CLEAN IF THIS HINDERS IT FROM SEWING, BUT OTHERWISE IT REMAINS SUSCEPTIBLE TO UNCLEANNESS. A HOOK THAT WAS STRAIGHTENED OUT IS CLEAN. IF IT IS BENT BACK IT RESUMES ITS SUSCEPTIBILITY TO UNCLEANNESS.

MISHNAH 6. WOOD THAT SERVES [AS A SUBSIDIARY PART OF] A METAL VESSEL IS SUSCEPTIBLE TO UNCLEANNESS BUT METAL THAT SERVES AS A SUBSIDIARY PART OF A WOODEN VESSEL IS CLEAN. FOR INSTANCE,[3] IF A LOCK IS OF WOOD AND ITS CLUTCHES ARE OF METAL, EVEN IF ONLY ONE OF THEM IS SO, IT IS SUSCEPTIBLE TO UNCLEANNESS; BUT IF THE LOCK IS OF METAL AND ITS CLUTCHES ARE OF WOOD, IT IS CLEAN. IF A RING WAS OF METAL AND ITS SEAL OF CORAL, IT IS SUSCEPTIBLE TO UNCLEANNESS, BUT IF THE RING WAS OF CORAL AND ITS SEAL OF METAL, IT IS CLEAN. THE TOOTH IN THE PLATE OF A LOCK OR IN A KEY IS SUSCEPTIBLE TO UNCLEANNESS BY ITSELF.[4]

MISHNAH 7. IF ASHKELON GRAPPLING-IRONS WERE BROKEN BUT THEIR HOOKS REMAINED, THEY REMAIN SUSCEPTIBLE TO UNCLEANNESS. IF A PITCH-FORK, WINNOWING-FAN, OR RAKE (AND THE SAME APPLIES TO A HAIR[5]-COMB) LOST ONE OF ITS TEETH[6] AND IT WAS REPLACED BY ONE OF METAL, IT IS SUSCEPTIBLE TO UNCLEANNESS. AND CONCERNING ALL THESE R. JOSHUA REMARKED: THE SCRIBES

(1) On a wax tablet. (2) Whether its eye or point is missing. (3) Lit., 'how'. (4) Since it can be used independently. (5) Lit., 'head'. (6) Which are of wood.

HAVE HERE INTRODUCED A NEW PRINCIPLE OF LAW,[1] AND I HAVE NO EXPLANATION TO OFFER.[2]

MISHNAH 8. IF THE TEETH OF A FLAX-COMB WERE MISSING BUT TWO REMAINED, IT IS STILL SUSCEPTIBLE TO UNCLEANNESS. IF ONLY ONE, HOWEVER, REMAINED IT IS CLEAN. AS REGARDS ALL THE TEETH[3] EACH ONE INDIVIDUALLY[4] IS SUSCEPTIBLE TO UNCLEANNESS. IF OF A WOOL-COMB ONE TOOTH OUT OF EVERY TWO IS MISSING[5] IT IS CLEAN. IF THREE CONSECUTIVE TEETH[6] REMAINED, IT REMAINS SUSCEPTIBLE TO UNCLEANNESS. IF THE OUTERMOST TOOTH[7] WAS ONE OF THEM, THE COMB IS CLEAN. IF TWO TEETH WERE REMOVED FROM THE COMB AND MADE INTO A PAIR OF FORCEPS, THEY ARE SUSCEPTIBLE TO UNCLEANNESS. EVEN IF ONLY ONE WAS REMOVED BUT IT WAS ADAPTED TO BE USED FOR A LAMP OR AS A STRETCHING-PIN, IT IS SUSCEPTIBLE TO UNCLEANNESS.

(1) Since, as flat wooden vessels, the instruments mentioned should be exempt from uncleanness. (2) Lit., 'I do not know what to answer (when asked for an explanation'). (3) Lit., 'and they all'. (4) Since it can be used then for writing on a wax tablet, as *supra* 5. (5) No three consecutive teeth remaining. Lit., 'one from between (two)'. (6) Lit., 'in one place'. (7) At the end of the row of teeth, which is wider than the others and, therefore, unsuitable for combing.

KELIM

CHAPTER XIV

MISHNAH 1. WHAT IS THE MINIMUM SIZE[1] OF METAL VESSELS?[2] A BUCKET MUST BE OF SUCH A SIZE AS ONE CAN DRAW WATER WITH; A KETTLE MUST BE SUCH AS WATER CAN BE HEATED IN IT; A BOILER, SUCH AS CAN HOLD SELA'S; A CAULDRON, SUCH AS CAN HOLD JUGS; JUGS, SUCH AS CAN HOLD PERUṬAHS; WINE-MEASURES, SUCH AS CAN MEASURE WINE; AND OIL-MEASURES, SUCH AS CAN MEASURE OIL. R. ELIEZER RULED: THE SIZE PRESCRIBED FOR ALL THESE IS A CAPABILITY TO HOLD PERUṬAHS. R. AKIBA RULED: A VESSEL THAT LACKS TRIMMING[3] IS SUSCEPTIBLE TO UNCLEANNESS, BUT ONE THAT LACKS POLISHING IS[4] CLEAN.[5]

MISHNAH 2. A STAFF[6] TO THE END OF WHICH IS ATTACHED A METAL KNOB IN THE SHAPE OF A CHESTNUT BUR IS SUSCEPTIBLE TO UNCLEANNESS.[7] IF THE STAFF WAS STUDDED WITH NAILS IT IS ALSO UNCLEAN. R. SIMEON RULED: THIS APPLIES ONLY WHERE THREE ROWS[8] WERE PUT IN. IN ALL CASES, HOWEVER, WHERE THEY ARE PUT IN FOR ORNAMENTATION THE STAFF IS CLEAN.[9] IF A TUBE[10] WAS ATTACHED TO ITS END, AND SO ALSO IN THE CASE OF A DOOR,[11] IT IS CLEAN.[12] IF IT[13] WAS ONCE AN INDEPENDENT VESSEL AND THEN IT WAS FIXED TO THE STAFF, IT REMAINS

(1) That is still susceptible to, or retains its former uncleanness. (2) When they were broken. (3) Var lec., 'its cover'. (4) Like all 'unshaped' vessels. (5) Whereas the latter work requires special skill, the former can be done by the householder. (6) Of wood. (7) The wooden part being subsidiary to the metal knob the entire staff is subject to the restrictions of a metal vessel. (8) Of nails. (9) Since the metal ornamentation is only subsidiary to the wooden staff. (10) Of metal. (11) Where such a tube serves as a pivot. (12) Since the metal ornamentation is only subsidiary to the wooden object. (13) The metal tube.

SUSCEPTIBLE TO UNCLEANNESS.[1] WHEN DOES IT ATTAIN CLEANNESS? BETH SHAMMAI RULED: WHEN IT IS DAMAGED; AND BETH HILLEL RULED: WHEN IT IS JOINED ON.[2]

MISHNAH 3. THE AUGER OF A BUILDER AND THE PICK OF A CARPENTER ARE SUSCEPTIBLE TO UNCLEANNESS.[3] TENT-PEGS AND SURVEYORS' PEGS ARE SUSCEPTIBLE TO UNCLEANNESS.[4] A SURVEYOR'S CHAIN IS SUSCEPTIBLE TO UNCLEANNESS, BUT ONE USED FOR FAGGOTS[5] IS CLEAN.[6] THE CHAIN OF A BIG BUCKET [IS SUSCEPTIBLE TO UNCLEANNESS TO A LENGTH OF] FOUR HANDBREADTHS,[7] AND THAT OF A SMALL ONE [TO A LENGTH OF] TEN HANDBREADTHS.[7] A BLACKSMITH'S JACK IS SUSCEPTIBLE TO UNCLEANNESS. A SAW[8] THE TEETH OF WHICH WERE INSERTED[9] IN A HOLE[10] IS UNCLEAN,[11] BUT IF THEY WERE TURNED FROM BELOW UPWARDS[12] IT IS CLEAN.[13] ALL COVERS ARE CLEAN[14] EXCEPT THAT OF A BOILER.[15]

MISHNAH 4. THE PARTS OF A WAGON THAT ARE SUSCEPTIBLE TO UNCLEANNESS ARE THE FOLLOWING: THE METAL YOKE,[16] THE CROSS-BAR, THE SIDE-PIECES THAT HOLD THE STRAPS, THE IRON BAR UNDER THE NECKS OF THE CATTLE,

(1) Its new use does not deprive it of its former status of a vessel. (2) To the staff, with nails. (3) Since their wooden handles are merely subsidiary to the metal parts. (4) Though they are inserted in the ground they are not regarded as fixed to it, since they are there only temporarily. (5) To bind them together. (6) Since, like other metal objects that are subsidiary to wooden ones, it is insusceptible to uncleanness. (7) From the bucket; since such a length is used when the bucket is handled. (8) That was unclean. (9) To serve as a door jamb. (10) Of a door, the teeth turning outwards. (11) Lying in a position that might injure passers-by it is not likely to remain there long and cannot consequently be regarded as a fixture in the ground. (12) And sunk in the lintel. (13) Since it is regarded as a permanent fixture in the ground (cf. prev. n. *mut. mut.*). Alternative rendering: A saw in which the teeth are set in sockets is susceptible, but if they were put in upside down it is not susceptible (Danby according to Maimonides). (14) Because they are not used by themselves. (15) Which, independently of the boiler, is also used by itself. (16) Above the necks of the drawing horses or oxen.

THE POLE-PIN, THE METAL GIRTH, THE TRAYS, THE CLAPPER, THE HOOK, AND ANY NAIL THAT HOLDS ANY OF ITS PARTS TOGETHER.

MISHNAH 5. THE CLEAN PARTS OF A WAGON ARE THE FOLLOWING: THE YOKE[1] THAT IS ONLY PLATED [WITH METAL], SIDE-PIECES MADE FOR MERE ORNAMENTATION, TUBES THAT GIVE OUT A NOISE,[2] THE LEAD AT THE SIDE OF THE NECKS OF THE CATTLE, THE RIM OF THE WHEEL, THE PLATES[3] AND MOUNTINGS,[3] AND ALL OTHER NAILS.[4] ALL THESE ARE CLEAN. METAL SHOES OF CATTLE ARE SUSCEPTIBLE TO UNCLEANNESS AND THOSE MADE OF CORK ARE CLEAN. WHEN DOES A SWORD BECOME SUSCEPTIBLE TO UNCLEANNESS? WHEN IT HAS BEEN POLISHED. AND A KNIFE? WHEN IT HAS BEEN SHARPENED.

MISHNAH 6. A METAL BASKET-COVER[5] WHICH WAS TURNED INTO A MIRROR IS, R. JUDAH RULES, CLEAN;[6] AND THE SAGES RULE THAT IT IS SUSCEPTIBLE TO UNCLEANNESS.[7] A BROKEN MIRROR, IF IT DOES NOT REFLECT THE GREATER PART OF THE FACE, IS CLEAN.

MISHNAH 7. METAL VESSELS MAY REMAIN UNCLEAN[8] AND BECOME CLEAN[9] EVEN WHEN BROKEN;[10] SO R. ELIEZER. R. JOSHUA RULED: THEY CAN BE MADE CLEAN ONLY WHEN THEY ARE WHOLE.[11] IF THEY WERE SPRINKLED UPON[12] AND

(1) V. p. 70, n. 16. (2) To drive on the cattle. (3) Of metal. (4) Which serve as mere ornamentation. (5) For domestic use which (cf. *supra* XII, 6) is (in agreement with the Sages) clean. (6) Because its conversion into a mirror does not alter its former status of cleanness. (7) A mirror, they hold, has the status of a valid vessel. (8) If they were unclean before they were broken and were re-made into proper vessels after they were broken. If they came in contact with a man or a vessel while in their broken condition, uncleanness is conveyed retrospectively after they have been re-made (cf. L.). (9) If the prescribed sprinkling had been performed while they were broken. (10) Though they were afterwards re-made into proper vessels (Elijah Wilna). (11) Cur. edd. insert, 'how', which is deleted by Elijah Wilna. (12) For

ON THE SAME DAY THEY WERE BROKEN AND THEN THEY WERE RECAST[1] AND SPRINKLED UPON ON THE SAME DAY, THEY ARE CLEAN;[2] SO R. ELIEZER. R. JOSHUA RULED: THERE CAN BE NO EFFECTIVE SPRINKLING EARLIER THAN ON THE THIRD[3] AND THE SEVENTH DAY[4] RESPECTIVELY.

MISHNAH 8. A KNEE-SHAPED KEY THAT WAS BROKEN OFF AT THE KNEE[5] IS CLEAN.[6] R. JUDAH RULES THAT IT IS UNCLEAN BECAUSE ONE CAN OPEN WITH IT FROM WITHIN.[7] A GAMMA-SHAPED KEY,[8] HOWEVER, THAT WAS BROKEN OFF AT ITS SHORTER[9] ARM[10] IS CLEAN.[11] IF IT[12] RETAINED THE TEETH AND THE GAPS IT REMAINS UNCLEAN. IF THE TEETH WERE MISSING IT IS STILL UNCLEAN ON ACCOUNT OF THE GAPS; IF THE GAPS WERE BLOCKED UP IT IS UNCLEAN ON ACCOUNT OF THE TEETH. IF THE TEETH WERE MISSING AND THE GAPS WERE BLOCKED UP, OR IF THEY WERE MERGED INTO ONE ANOTHER,[13] THE KEY BECOMES CLEAN. IF IN A MUSTARD-STRAINER[14] THREE HOLES IN ITS BOTTOM WERE MERGED INTO ONE ANOTHER THE STRAINER BECOMES CLEAN;[6] BUT A METAL MILL-FUNNEL[15] IS[16] UNCLEAN.[17]

the first time, on the third day, in accordance with Num. XIX, 17ff.

(1) And made into proper vessels. (2) As if they had been duly sprinkled upon on the seventh day. Their broken condition that intervened between their first and their second sprinkling is deemed to be equivalent to the interval of the three days that must elapse between the usual first sprinkling on the third day and the second one on the seventh. (3) For the first sprinkling. (4) For the second. (5) *Sc.* the part that is inserted in the lock was partly broken off. (6) Since it can no longer serve its original purpose. (7) Where a shorter length of key (cf. n. 5) would also reach the lock. (8) In which the arm that is inserted in the lock is much shorter than in the knee-shaped key. (9) Lit., 'its gamma'. (10) *Sc.* the part that is inserted in the lock was partly broken off. (11) Even according to R. Judah, since owing to its shortness (cf. n. 8) it can no longer be used at all. (12) The part that remained. (13) The teeth having been bent into the gaps. (14) That was unclean. (15) Although it has no bottom at all. (16) In a similar condition. (17) As a valid vessel, since it bears an independent name.

KELIM

CHAPTER XV

MISHNAH 1. OF[1] VESSELS OF WOOD, LEATHER, BONE OR GLASS THOSE THAT ARE FLAT ARE CLEAN[2] AND THOSE THAT FORM A RECEPTACLE ARE SUSCEPTIBLE TO UNCLEANNESS. IF THEY ARE BROKEN THEY BECOME CLEAN AGAIN. IF ONE REMADE THEM INTO VESSELS THEY ARE SUSCEPTIBLE TO UNCLEANNESS HENCEFORTH.[1] A CHEST, A BOX, A CUPBOARD, A STRAW BASKET,[3] A REED BASKET,[3] OR THE TANK OF AN ALEXANDRIAN SHIP,[4] THAT HAVE FLAT BOTTOMS AND CONTAIN A MINIMUM OF FORTY SE'AH IN LIQUID MEASURE WHICH REPRESENT TWO KOR IN DRY MEASURE, ARE CLEAN.[5] ALL OTHER VESSELS, HOWEVER, WHETHER THEY CONTAIN THE MINIMUM[6] OR DO NOT CONTAIN IT, ARE SUSCEPTIBLE TO UNCLEANNESS;[7] SO R. MEIR. R. JUDAH RULED: THE TUB OF A WAGON, THE FOOD CHESTS OF KINGS, THE TANNERS' TROUGH, THE TANK OF A SMALL SHIP, AND AN ARK,[8] EVEN THOUGH THEY CONTAIN THE MINIMUM,[6] ARE SUSCEPTIBLE TO UNCLEANNESS, SINCE THEY ARE INVARIABLY INTENDED TO BE MOVED ABOUT WITH THEIR CONTENTS. AS TO ALL OTHER VESSELS, THOSE THAT CONTAIN THE MINIMUM[6] ARE CLEAN AND THOSE THAT CANNOT CONTAIN IT ARE SUSCEPTIBLE TO UNCLEANNESS. THE ONLY PRACTICAL DIFFERENCE BETWEEN THE RULING OF R. MEIR[9] AND THAT OF R.

(1) For notes v. *supra* II, 1. (2) Pentateuchally. Some of these are Rabbinically unclean. (3) Which is subject to the law applicable to wooden vessels. (4) Name given to large ships that serve for long distances. (5) Being heavy they are not moved about when full as when empty and, having flat bottoms, they come under the category of stationary wooden vessels which are insusceptible to uncleanness. (6) Of forty *se'ah*. (7) Since they are moved about when full as when empty. (8) Or large chest. *Aliter:* coffin. (9) Who enumerated the vessels that are clean and gave a general ruling that all others are susceptible to uncleanness.

JUDAH[1] IS THE RULING CONCERNING A DOMESTIC BAKING TROUGH.[2]

MISHNAH 2. BAKERS' BAKING-BOARDS ARE SUSCEPTIBLE TO UNCLEANNESS.[3] THOSE IN DOMESTIC USE[4] ARE CLEAN, BUT IF THEY WERE COLOURED RED OR SAFFRON THEY ARE SUSCEPTIBLE TO UNCLEANNESS. IF A BAKERS' SHELF[5] WAS FIXED TO A WALL, R. ELIEZER RULES THAT IT IS CLEAN[6] AND THE SAGES RULE THAT IT IS SUSCEPTIBLE TO UNCLEANNESS.[7] THE BAKERS' FRAME[8] IS SUSCEPTIBLE TO UNCLEANNESS BUT ONE IN DOMESTIC USE IS CLEAN. IF A RIM WAS MADE ON ITS FOUR SIDES IT IS SUSCEPTIBLE TO UNCLEANNESS, BUT IF ONE SIDE WAS OPEN IT IS CLEAN. R. SIMEON RULED: IF IT WAS SO SHAPED THAT ONE CAN CUT THE DOUGH UPON IT, IT IS SUSCEPTIBLE TO UNCLEANNESS.[9] A ROLLING-PIN IS SIMILARLY SUSCEPTIBLE TO UNCLEANNESS.[10]

MISHNAH 3. THE CONTAINER OF THE FLOUR-DEALERS' SIFTER IS SUSCEPTIBLE TO UNCLEANNESS, BUT THE DOMESTIC ONE[11] IS CLEAN. R. JUDAH RULED: ALSO ONE THAT IS USED BY A HAIRDRESSER IS SUSCEPTIBLE TO UNCLEANNESS AS A SEAT,[12] SINCE GIRLS SIT IN IT WHEN THEIR HAIR IS DRESSED.

MISHNAH 4. ALL HANGERS[13] ARE SUSCEPTIBLE TO UNCLEANNESS, EXCEPTING THOSE OF A SIFTER AND A RIDDLE

(1) Who mentioned those that are susceptible to uncleanness, ruling that all the others are clean. (2) Which neither mentioned. According to the former it is susceptible to uncleanness while according to the latter it is clean. (3) Rabbinically; since, despite their flat shape, they have the form of a vessel. (4) Since they have not the shape of a vessel (cf. prev. n.). (5) Of metal. (6) As any 'vessel' that is fixed to the ground. (7) Once it had the status of a vessel the fixing of it to a wall cannot deprive it of that status unless it was damaged (cf. *supra* XIV, 2). (8) Or 'small trough'. (9) Even though it had no rim. (10) Rabbinically; because flat vessels that serve men and their needs are susceptible to uncleanness. In this case the vessels are of service to the man and to his dough. (11) Which has no proper receptacle. (12) If a *zab* sat on it. (13) Being adjuncts to vessels.

THAT ARE FOR DOMESTIC USE;[1] SO R. MEIR. BUT THE SAGES RULED: ALL HANGERS ARE CLEAN, EXCEPTING THOSE OF A SIFTER OF FLOUR-DEALERS, OF A RIDDLE USED IN THRESHING-FLOORS, OF A HAND-SICKLE AND OF AN EXCISEMAN'S STAFF, SINCE THEY AFFORD AID WHEN THE INSTRUMENT IS IN USE.[2] THIS IS THE GENERAL RULE: [A HANGER] THAT IS INTENDED TO AFFORD AID WHEN THE INSTRUMENT IS IN USE IS SUSCEPTIBLE TO UNCLEANNESS AND ONE INTENDED TO SERVE ONLY AS A HANGER IS CLEAN.

MISHNAH 5. THE GRIST-DEALERS' SHOVEL IS SUSCEPTIBLE TO UNCLEANNESS[3] BUT THE ONE USED IN GRAIN STORES[4] IS CLEAN. THE ONE USED IN WINE-PRESSES IS SUSCEPTIBLE TO UNCLEANNESS[3] BUT THAT USED IN THRESHING-FLOORS[4] IS CLEAN. THIS IS THE GENERAL RULE: [A SHOVEL] THAT IS INTENDED TO HOLD ANYTHING IS SUSCEPTIBLE TO UNCLEANNESS BUT ONE INTENDED ONLY TO HEAP STUFF TOGETHER IS CLEAN.

MISHNAH 6. ORDINARY HARPS[5] ARE SUSCEPTIBLE TO UNCLEANNESS,[6] BUT THE HARPS OF THE SONS OF LEVI[7] ARE CLEAN.[8] ALL LIQUIDS[9] ARE SUSCEPTIBLE TO UNCLEANNESS, BUT THE LIQUIDS[10] IN THE SHAMBLES[11] ARE CLEAN. ALL BOOKS[12] CONVEY UNCLEANNESS TO THE HANDS,[13] EXCEPTING

(1) Since these hangers are not always attached to the vessels mentioned. (2) When fatigued from work one's hand is put on the hanger to facilitate the handling of the instrument. (3) Because it forms a receptacle. (4) Which has no proper receptacle. (5) Lit., 'harps of song'. (6) On account of the receptacle beneath their strings wherein one places any coins collected from the audience. (7) Used in the Temple. (8) Since the receptacles in these harps are not intended to contain any objects. (9) *Sc.* blood, water, dew, wine, oil, milk and honey. (10) Water and blood. (11) Of the Temple, v. 'Ed. VIII, 4. (12) Or 'scrolls', of Scripture. (13) That touched them. This is a Rabbinical measure to prevent holy books from being placed near foodstuffs where mice that attack the food would also destroy them. By the enactment that hands that touch the books contract a second grade of uncleanness any *terumah* that would come in contact with such hands would become unclean, and care would, therefore, be taken to

THE SCROLL OF THE TEMPLE COURT.[1] A WOODEN TOY HORSE[2] IS CLEAN.[3] THE LUTE, THE NIKṬIMON[4] AND THE DRUM ARE SUSCEPTIBLE TO UNCLEANNESS. R. JUDAH RULED: THE DRUM IS UNCLEAN AS A SEAT[5] SINCE THE WAILING WOMAN SITS ON IT. A WEASEL-TRAP IS SUSCEPTIBLE TO UNCLEANNESS,[6] BUT A MOUSE-TRAP[7] IS CLEAN.

keep *terumah* (and similarly unconsecrated food) away from the books; v. Yad. IV, 5.

(1) In which the High Priest read on the Day of Atonement. Being very highly esteemed there is no likelihood of its ever being put together with foodstuffs. Var. lec., 'the scroll of Ezra'. (2) *Aliter:* The wooden arm of a harp. (3) *Sc.* it is not subject to *midras* uncleanness since it is not intended for riding upon. One merely pretends to sit on the horse while in reality it is dragged along, the so-called rider merely walking or running. (4) A musical instrument. *Aliter:* 'a mask', v. Shab. 66*b*. (5) If a *zab* sat on it. (6) Because it has a receptacle for the animal whose skin is of use. (7) Which has no receptacle (cf. prev. n.), its only purpose being to crush the mouse. Even if it has a receptacle it is disregarded since a mouse serves no useful purpose.

KELIM

CHAPTER XVI

MISHNAH 1. ANY WOODEN VESSEL THAT WAS BROKEN INTO TWO PARTS[1] BECOMES CLEAN,[2] EXCEPTING A FOLDING TABLE,[3] A DISH WITH COMPARTMENTS FOR [DIFFERENT KINDS OF] FOOD,[4] AND A DOMESTIC FOOTSTOOL.[5] R. JUDAH RULED: A DOUBLE DISH[3] AND A BABYLONIAN TRAY ARE SUBJECT TO THE SAME LAW.[6] AT WHAT STAGE[7] DO WOODEN VESSELS BEGIN TO BE SUSCEPTIBLE TO UNCLEANNESS? A BED AND A COT, AFTER THEY ARE RUBBED OVER WITH FISH-SKIN.[8] IF THE OWNER DETERMINED NOT TO RUB THEM OVER THEY ARE SUSCEPTIBLE TO UNCLEANNESS [FORTHWITH].[9] R. MEIR RULED: A BED BECOMES SUSCEPTIBLE TO UNCLEANNESS AS SOON AS THREE ROWS OF MESHES HAVE BEEN KNITTED IN IT.

MISHNAH 2. WOODEN BASKETS [BECOME SUSCEPTIBLE TO UNCLEANNESS] AS SOON AS THEIR RIMS ARE BOUND ROUND AND THEIR ROUGH ENDS ARE SMOOTHED OFF; BUT THOSE THAT ARE MADE OF PALM-BRANCHES [BECOME SUSCEPTIBLE TO UNCLEANNESS] EVEN THOUGH THEIR ENDS WERE NOT SMOOTHED OFF ON THE INSIDE, SINCE THEY ARE ALLOWED TO REMAIN IN THIS CONDITION. A BASKET [OF REED-GRASS[10] BECOMES SUSCEPTIBLE TO UNCLEANNESS] AS SOON AS ITS RIM IS BOUND AROUND IT, ITS ROUGH ENDS ARE SMOOTHED OFF, AND ITS HANGER IS FINISHED. A CASE OF WICKERWORK FOR FLAGONS OR FOR CUPS [IS SUSCEPTIBLE TO UNCLEAN-

(1) While it was unclean. (2) And also insusceptible to future uncleanness. (3) Consisting of two sound and independent parts. (4) Cf. prev. n. (5) Made up of sections. (6) Viz., though they were broken into two parts they remain unclean. (7) In their manufacture. (8) Which gives them their smooth surface. (9) Even though their surface is rough. (10) *Aliter:* Of fruit.

NESS] EVEN IF THE ROUGH ENDS WERE NOT SMOOTHED OFF ON THE INSIDE, SINCE THESE ARE ALLOWED TO REMAIN IN THIS CONDITION.

MISHNAH 3. SMALL REED BASKETS AND WOMEN'S WORK BASKETS [ARE SUSCEPTIBLE TO UNCLEANNESS] AS SOON AS THEIR RIMS ARE BOUND ROUND AND THEIR ROUGH ENDS SMOOTHED OFF; LARGE REED BASKETS AND LARGE HAMPERS, AS SOON AS TWO CIRCLING BANDS HAVE BEEN MADE ROUND THEIR WIDE SIDES; THE CONTAINER OF A SIFTER OR A SIEVE AND A CUP OF THE BALANCES, AS SOON AS ONE CIRCLING BAND HAS BEEN MADE ROUND THEIR WIDE SIDES; A WILLOW[1] BASKET, AS SOON AS TWO TWISTS HAVE BEEN MADE AROUND ITS WIDE SIDES; AND A RUSH[2] BASKET,[3] AS SOON AS ONE TWIST HAS BEEN MADE ROUND IT.

MISHNAH 4. AT WHAT STAGE[4] DO LEATHER VESSELS BECOME SUSCEPTIBLE TO UNCLEANNESS? A SHEPHERD'S BAG, AS SOON AS ITS HEM HAS BEEN STITCHED, ITS ROUGH ENDS TRIMMED AND ITS THONGS SEWN ON. R. JUDAH RULED: SO SOON AS ITS EARS[5] HAVE BEEN SEWN ON. A LEATHER APRON[6] [BECOMES SUSCEPTIBLE TO UNCLEANNESS] AS SOON AS ITS HEM HAS BEEN STITCHED, ITS ROUGH ENDS TRIMMED AND ITS STRINGS SEWN ON. R. JUDAH RULED: AS SOON AS ITS LOOPS HAVE BEEN SEWN ON. A LEATHER BED COVER[7] [BECOMES SUSCEPTIBLE] AS SOON AS ITS HEM HAS BEEN STITCHED AND ITS ROUGH ENDS TRIMMED. R. JUDAH RULED: AS SOON AS ITS THONGS HAVE BEEN SEWN ON. A LEATHER CUSHION OR MATTRESS[8] [BECOMES SUSCEPTIBLE] AS SOON AS ITS HEM HAS BEEN STITCHED AND ITS ROUGH ENDS TRIMMED. R. JUDAH RULED: SO SOON AS IT HAS BEEN SEWN UP AND LESS THAN FIVE HANDBREADTHS REMAINED OPEN.[9]

(1) Cf. Danby. (2) Or 'cork'. (3) Which is not so deep as the basket previously mentioned. (4) In their manufacture. (5) The flaps by which it is carried. (6) *Scortea*, or 'leather coat', 'leather table cover', 'leather bed sheet'. (7) Or 'leather table cover'. (8) Or 'bolster'. (9) To admit the packing.

MISHNAH 5. A WILLOW BASKET[1] IS SUSCEPTIBLE TO UNCLEANNESS BUT A THORN BASKET[2] IS CLEAN.[3] MATS[4] MADE OF LEAVES ARE CLEAN, BUT THOSE MADE OF TWIGS ARE SUSCEPTIBLE TO UNCLEANNESS. THE WICKER WRAPPING [IN WHICH DATES ARE LEFT][5] AND INTO WHICH THEY CAN BE EASILY PUT[6] AND FROM WHICH THEY CAN EASILY BE TAKEN OUT[6] IS SUSCEPTIBLE TO UNCLEANNESS, BUT IF THIS CANNOT BE DONE WITHOUT TEARING IT OR UNDOING IT, IT IS CLEAN.

MISHNAH 6. THE LEATHER GLOVE[7] OF WINNOWERS, TRAVELLERS, OR FLAX WORKERS IS SUSCEPTIBLE TO UNCLEANNESS;[8] BUT THE ONE FOR DYERS OR BLACKSMITHS[9] IS CLEAN. R. JOSE RULED: THE SAME LAW APPLIES ALSO TO THE GLOVE[7] OF GRIST DEALERS. THIS IS THE GENERAL RULE: THAT WHICH IS MADE FOR HOLDING ANYTHING IS SUSCEPTIBLE TO UNCLEANNESS, BUT THAT WHICH ONLY AFFORDS PROTECTION AGAINST PERSPIRATION IS CLEAN.

MISHNAH 7. THE DUNG BAG OF A BULLOCK[10] AND ITS MUZZLE, A BEE-SMOKER, AND A FAN ARE CLEAN.[11] THE COVER OF A CASKET IS SUSCEPTIBLE TO UNCLEANNESS; THE COVER OF A CLOTHES-CHEST IS CLEAN. THE COVER OF A BOX, THE COVER OF A BASKET, A CARPENTER'S VICE, A CUSHION[12] UNDER A BOX[13] OR ITS ARCHED COVER,[14] A READING-DESK FOR A BOOK, A BOLT-SOCKET, A LOCK-SOCKET, A MEZUZAH CASE, A LYRE CASE, A VIOLIN CASE, THE BLOCK OF THE TURBAN-MAKERS, A WOODEN MUSICAL TOY HORSE, THE CLAPPERS

(1) In which figs or dates are kept. *Aliter:* A fig *or* date basket. (2) For rubbish. *Aliter:* Provision basket. (3) Because it is much too large to be carried about and consequently is not considered a vessel. (4) *Aliter:* Little fruit baskets. (5) Until they are ripened. (6) Without tearing the wrapper. (7) Or 'head gear', or 'apron', or 'overall'. (8) Since it forms a 'receptacle' for the dust or chaff. (9) Which forms no receptacle, its purpose being merely to absorb the man's perspiration. (10) For receiving its excrements while at work. (11) Since they have not the shape of a 'vessel'. (12) Var. lec., a chair. (13) To protect it from dampness. (14) To protect the chest against rain.

OF A WAILING WOMAN, A POOR MAN'S PARASOL,[1] BED STRUTS, A TEFILLIN MOULD, AND THE CLOAK-MAKER'S BLOCK—ALL THESE ARE CLEAN. THIS, SAID R. JOSE, IS THE GENERAL RULE: ALL OBJECTS[2] THAT SERVE AS A PROTECTION TO OBJECTS THAT A MAN USES, BOTH WHEN THE LATTER ARE IN USE AND WHEN THEY ARE NOT IN USE,[3] ARE SUSCEPTIBLE TO UNCLEANNESS; BUT THOSE THAT SERVE THEM AS A PROTECTION ONLY WHEN THE LATTER ARE IN USE ARE CLEAN.[4]

MISHNAH 8. THE SHEATH OF A SWORD, A KNIFE OR A DAGGER, THE CASE FOR SCISSORS, OR SHEARS OR A RAZOR, THE CASE OF KOHL-STICKS AND THE KOHL-BOX, THE STYLUS CASE, THE INKPOT CASE,[5] THE TABLET CASE, THE LEATHER-APRON,[6] A QUIVER AND A JAVELIN CASE[7]—ALL THESE ARE SUSCEPTIBLE TO UNCLEANNESS. THE CASE FOR A DOUBLE FLUTE IS SUSCEPTIBLE TO UNCLEANNESS IF THE INSTRUMENT IS PUT IN FROM ABOVE,[8] BUT IF IT IS PUT IN FROM THE SIDE, IT[9] IS CLEAN. A CASE FOR PIPES, R. JUDAH RULES, IS CLEAN BECAUSE THESE ARE PUT IN FROM THE SIDE.[10] THE COVERING OF A CLUB, A BOW OR A SPEAR IS CLEAN. THIS IS THE GENERAL RULE: THAT WHICH SERVES AS A CASE IS SUSCEPTIBLE TO UNCLEANNESS, BUT THAT WHICH IS MERELY A COVERING IS CLEAN.

(1) Or 'the poor man's collecting-bag'. (2) Though they are flat and form no receptacle. (3) As, for instance, a cover or a book's case. (4) If they are flat. Those that are concave and thus form a receptacle are in either case susceptible to uncleanness. (5) Or 'a box with many compartments'. (6) Or 'leather coat', or 'leather table-cover'. (7) Or 'catapult'. (8) *Sc.* when the case is long and forms a proper receptacle. (9) Since it can only be regarded as a mere cover. (10) Cf. prev. n.

KELIM

CHAPTER XVII

MISHNAH 1. ALL [WOODEN] VESSELS[1] THAT BELONG TO HOUSEHOLDERS[2] [BECOME CLEAN IF THERE APPEARED IN THEM HOLES OF] THE SIZE OF POMEGRANATES.[3] R. ELIEZER RULED: [THE SIZE OF THE HOLE DEPENDS] ON THE USE TO WHICH A VESSEL IS PUT.[4] GARDENERS' VEGETABLE BASKETS [BECOME CLEAN IF THE HOLES IN THEM ARE OF] THE SIZE OF BUNDLES OF VEGETABLES;[5] BASKETS OF HOUSEHOLDERS [BECOME CLEAN IF] THE SIZE [OF THE HOLES WILL ADMIT] BUNDLES OF STRAW [TO DROP THROUGH]; THOSE OF BATH-KEEPERS, IF BUNDLES OF SHAVINGS [WILL DROP THROUGH]. R. JOSHUA RULED: [THE SIZE][6] IN THE CASE OF ALL THESE IS THAT OF POMEGRANATES.[3]

MISHNAH 2. A SKIN BOTTLE [BECOMES CLEAN IF THE HOLES IN IT ARE OF] A SIZE THROUGH WHICH WARP-CLEWS[7] [WILL DROP OUT]. IF [WOOF-CLEWS ARE USUALLY KEPT IN IT AND NOW][8] IT CANNOT HOLD WARP-CLEWS BUT CAN STILL HOLD[9] WOOF ONES[10] IT REMAINS UNCLEAN.[11] A DISH HOLDER[12] THAT CANNOT HOLD DISHES BUT[13] CAN STILL HOLD TRAYS REMAINS UNCLEAN.[11] A CHAMBER-POT[14] THAT CANNOT HOLD LIQUIDS BUT CAN STILL HOLD EXCREMENTS REMAINS UN-

(1) Which have contracted an uncleanness. (2) Those belonging to craftsmen become clean even if only smaller holes have appeared (v. *infra*). (3) *Sc.* holes big enough for pomegranates to fall through. (4) Lit., 'in what they are'. If big objects are kept in it the hole must be big enough to allow such objects to drop through; and if the objects are small, holes corresponding to their size suffice to render the vessel clean. (5) *Sc.* that such bundles will drop through them. (6) That renders a vessel clean. (7) Which are smaller than woof-clews. (8) Cf. L. (9) Lit., 'although'. (10) Which are bigger than warp-clews (cf. *supra* n. 7). (11) Because it can still serve its original purpose. (12) Used for trays. (13) Lit., 'although'. (14) For excrements.

CLEAN.[1] R. GAMALIEL RULES THAT THE LAST MENTIONED POT IS CLEAN SINCE PEOPLE DO NOT USUALLY KEEP ONE THAT IS IN SUCH A CONDITION.

MISHNAH 3. BREAD-BASKETS [ATTAIN CLEANNESS IF] THE SIZE [OF THEIR HOLES IS SUCH] THAT LOAVES OF BREAD [WOULD FALL THROUGH]. FRAMES FOR HANGINGS, THOUGH REEDS WERE FASTENED TO THEM FROM THE BOTTOM UPWARDS TO STRENGTHEN THEM, ARE CLEAN.[2] IF TO SUCH A FRAME HANDLES OF ANY KIND WERE FIXED IT IS UNCLEAN. R. SIMEON RULED: IF IT CANNOT BE LIFTED UP BY THESE HANDLES[3] IT IS CLEAN.

MISHNAH 4. THE POMEGRANATES OF WHICH THE RABBIS HAVE SPOKEN[4] ARE THREE ATTACHED TO ONE ANOTHER.[5] R. SIMEON B. GAMALIEL RULED: IN A SIFTER OR A SIEVE [THE SIZE OF THE HOLE MUST BE SUCH THAT A POMEGRANATE WILL DROP OUT] WHEN ONE TAKES IT[6] UP AND WALKS ABOUT WITH IT;[7] IN A HAMPER IT MUST BE SUCH [AS WOULD ALLOW A POMEGRANATE] TO FALL THROUGH WHILE A MAN HANGS THE HAMPER BEHIND HIM;[8] AND AS REGARDS ALL OTHER VESSELS WHICH[9] CANNOT HOLD POMEGRANATES AS, FOR INSTANCE, THE QUARTER ḲAB MEASURE AND THE HALF QUARTER ḲAB MEASURE, AND SMALL BASKETS, THE SIZE [OF THEIR HOLES MUST BE] SUCH AS WOULD EXTEND OVER THE GREATER PART OF THEM; SO R. MEIR. R. SIMEON RULED: [THE HOLE IS MEASURED] WITH OLIVES.[10] IF THEIR SIDES

(1) V. p. 81, n. 11. (2) Since they are flat objects that have not the shape of a vessel. (3) On account of their frail texture or weak connection with the frame. (4) *Supra* Mishnah 1. (5) A hole through which one of such three pomegranates would drop must be bigger than one through which a single pomegranate would drop (Tosaf. Y.Ṭ.). (6) The sifter or the sieve. (7) A smaller hole than one through which the fruit could drop out without the shaking of the vessel. (8) Across his shoulders (cf. prev. n. *mut. mut.*). (9) Owing to their small capacity. (10) If it is one through which olives can pass, the vessel, though it can still hold bigger sized fruit, becomes clean.

WERE BROKEN[1] [THE SIZE OF THEIR HOLE MUST BE] SUCH AS OLIVES WOULD DROP THROUGH. IF THEY ARE WORN AWAY THE SIZE [OF THEIR HOLES] MUST BE SUCH AS WOULD ALLOW THE OBJECTS WHICH ARE USUALLY KEPT IN THEM [TO DROP THROUGH].[2]

MISHNAH 5. THE POMEGRANATE OF WHICH THEY HAVE SPOKEN[3] REFERS TO ONE THAT IS NEITHER SMALL NOR BIG BUT OF MODERATE SIZE. AND FOR WHAT PURPOSE[4] WERE THE POMEGRANATES OF BADDAN[5] MENTIONED?[6] THAT WHATEVER THEIR QUANTITY THEY[7] CAUSE [OTHER POMEGRANATES][8] TO BE FORBIDDEN; SO R. MEIR. R. JOḤANAN B. NURI SAID: THAT THEY ARE TO BE USED AS A MEASURE FOR HOLES IN VESSELS.[9] R. AKIBA SAID: THEY WERE MENTIONED FOR BOTH REASONS: THAT THEY ARE TO BE USED AS A MEASURE FOR HOLES IN VESSELS[2] AND THAT WHATEVER THEIR QUANTITY THEY CAUSE [OTHER POMEGRANATES][8] TO BE FORBIDDEN. R. JOSE[10] SAID: THE POMEGRANATES OF BADDAN AND THE LEEKS OF GEBA[11] WERE MENTIONED ONLY TO INDICATE THAT THEY MUST BE TITHED EVERYWHERE AS BEING CERTAINLY UNTITHED.[12]

MISHNAH 6. THE SIZE OF AN EGG WHICH THEY PRESCRIBED[13] IS THAT OF ONE THAT IS NEITHER BIG NOR SMALL BUT OF MODERATE SIZE. R. JUDAH RULED: THE LARGEST AND THE SMALLEST[14] MUST BE BROUGHT AND PUT IN WATER

(1) The holes previously spoken of were those in the bottom of a vessel. (2) 'The size (is determined) by what they are', i.e., by the character of the vessels. *Aliter:* They are regarded as vessels as long as they hold any object. (3) *Supra* Mishnah 1. (4) In connection with prescribed sizes. (5) In Samaria. (6) Cf. 'Or. III, 7. (7) If they are *'orlah* or otherwise forbidden. (8) With which they are mixed. (9) *Sc.* wherever a pomegranate is given in connection with the prescribed size of a hole that renders a vessel clean a pomegranate of Baddan is meant. (10) Var. lec., Judah. (11) In Samaria. (12) Since they are the products of Samaritan localities and the Samaritans are known to disregard the laws of tithe. (13) In connection with the uncleanness of foodstuffs. (14) Of eggs.

AND THE DISPLACED WATER IS THEN DIVIDED.[1] SAID R. JOSE: BUT WHO CAN TELL ME WHICH IS THE LARGEST AND WHICH IS THE SMALLEST?[2] ALL RATHER DEPENDS ON THE OBSERVER'S ESTIMATE.

MISHNAH 7. THE SIZE OF A DRIED FIG WHICH THEY PRESCRIBED[3] IS THAT OF ONE THAT IS NEITHER LARGE NOR SMALL BUT OF MODERATE SIZE. R. JUDAH STATED: THE BIGGEST[4] IN THE LAND OF ISRAEL IS LIKE ONE OF MODERATE SIZE IN OTHER LANDS.

MISHNAH 8. THE SIZE OF AN OLIVE WHICH THEY PRESCRIBED[5] IS THAT OF ONE THAT IS NEITHER LARGE NOR SMALL BUT OF A MODERATE SIZE, VIZ., ONE THAT IS FIT FOR STORAGE.[6] THE SIZE OF A BARLEYCORN WHICH THEY PRESCRIBED[7] IS THAT OF ONE THAT IS NEITHER LARGE NOR SMALL BUT OF MODERATE SIZE, VIZ., THE KIND THAT GROWS IN THE WILDERNESS. THE SEIZE OF THE LENTIL WHICH THEY PRESCRIBED[8] IS THAT OF ONE THAT IS NEITHER LARGE NOR SMALL BUT OF MODERATE SIZE, VIZ., THE EGYPTIAN KIND. 'ANY[9] MOVABLE OBJECT CONVEYS UNCLEANNESS[10] IF IT IS OF THE THICKNESS OF AN OX GOAD', REFERS TO ONE THAT IS NEITHER LARGE NOR SMALL BUT OF MODERATE SIZE. WHAT IS MEANT BY 'ONE OF MODERATE SIZE'? ONE WHOSE CIRCUMFERENCE IS JUST A HANDBREADTH.

MISHNAH 9. THE STANDARD OF THE CUBIT WHICH THEY

(1) To obtain the size of the average egg. (2) *Sc.* there might somewhere be eggs that are much bigger or much smaller than any egg that can be obtained in one's locality. (3) In connection with carrying on the Sabbath (cf. Shab. VII, 4, 'Er. VII, 8). (4) Var. lec. (Wilna, 1907, Berlin 1862), 'smallest'. (5) Frequently (cf. Ber. 39*a*, Ḥal. I, 2). (6) *Aliter:* Of a specially good quality. *Aliter:* An olive that retains its oil. *Aliter:* Whose oil is collected like wine in the grape. (7) Cf. *supra* I, 4; 'Ed. VI, 3. (8) Cf. Oh. I, 7; Miḳ. VI, 7. (9) A citation from Oh. XVI, 1, which is presently explained. (10) To the man that carries it (Bert.); from place to place which it overshadows (L.).

PRESCRIBED[1] IS ONE OF THE MODERATE SIZE.[2] THERE WERE TWO STANDARD CUBITS IN THE PALACE OF SHUSHAN,[3] ONE IN THE NORTH-EASTERN CORNER AND THE OTHER IN THE SOUTH-EASTERN CORNER. THE ONE IN THE NORTH-EASTERN CORNER EXCEEDED[4] THAT OF MOSES[5] BY HALF A FINGER-BREADTH, WHILE THE ONE IN THE SOUTH-EASTERN CORNER EXCEEDED[4] THE OTHER BY HALF A FINGERBREADTH, SO THAT THE LATTER EXCEEDED THAT OF MOSES BY A FINGER-BREADTH. BUT WHY DID THEY PRESCRIBE A LARGER AND A SMALLER CUBIT? ONLY FOR THIS REASON: THAT THE CRAFTS-MEN[6] MIGHT TAKE THEIR ORDERS ACCORDING TO THE SMALLER CUBIT AND RETURN THEIR FINISHED WORK ACCORDING TO THE LARGER CUBIT,[7] SO THAT THEY MIGHT NOT BE GUILTY OF ANY POSSIBLE MAL-APPROPRIATION.[8]

MISHNAH 10. R. MEIR STATED: ALL CUBITS[9] WERE OF THE MODERATE LENGTH[2] EXCEPT THAT FOR THE GOLDEN ALTAR, THE HORNS,[10] THE CIRCUIT[10] AND THE BASE.[10] R. JUDAH STATED: THE CUBIT USED FOR THE BUILDING[11] WAS ONE OF SIX HANDBREADTHS AND THAT FOR THE VESSELS ONE OF FIVE HANDBREADTHS.

MISHNAH 11. SOMETIMES, HOWEVER, THEY PRESCRIBED A SMALLER MEASURE: THE LIQUID AND DRY MEASURES[11] WERE PRESCRIBED TO BE OF THE ITALIAN STANDARD WHICH IS THE ONE THAT WAS USED IN THE WILDERNESS.[12] SOMETIMES,

(1) For various ritual measurements (cf. 'Er. I, 1; Suk. I, 1; Oh. XVI, 3). (2) Six handbreadths. The larger cubit measured six and a sixth handbreadths, while the smaller one measured only five handbreadths. (3) A mural sculpture above the eastern gate of the Temple (cf. Mid. I, 3) representing that palace (cf. Est. I, 2). (4) In length. (5) The cubit of six handbreadths which he used in the wilderness in the construction of the Tabernacle and its furniture. (6) Engaged in Temple work. (7) Thus making sure that they neither appropriated any material that belonged to the Temple nor received payment for labour they had not performed. (8) Cf. prev. n. (9) Used in the Temple. (10) Of the brazen altar. These were measured by the smaller cubit of five handbreadths. (11) Of the Temple. (12) By Moses.

AGAIN,[1] THEY PRESCRIBED A MEASURE THAT VARIED ACCORDING TO THE INDIVIDUAL CONCERNED, AS IS THE CASE OF ONE WHO TAKES THE HANDFUL OF A MEAL-OFFERING,[2] ONE WHO TAKES BOTH HANDS FULL OF INCENSE,[3] ONE WHO DRINKS A MOUTHFUL ON THE DAY OF ATONEMENT,[4] AND THE PREPARATION OF FOOD FOR TWO MEALS IN CONNECTION WITH AN 'ERUB,[5] THE QUANTITY BEING THE FOOD ONE EATS ON WEEKDAYS AND NOT ON THE SABBATH;[6] SO R. MEIR. R. JUDAH RULED: AS ON THE SABBATH AND NOT AS ON WEEKDAYS.[7] AND BOTH INTENDED TO GIVE THE MORE LENIENT RULING.[8] R. SIMEON RULED:[9] TWO THIRDS OF A LOAF, THREE OF WHICH ARE MADE OF A ḲAB.[10] R. JOḤANAN B. BEROḲA RULED:[9] NOT LESS THAN A LOAF THAT IS PURCHASED FOR A DUPONDIUM WHEN THE PRICE OF WHEAT IS FOUR SE'AH FOR A SELA'.[11]

MISHNAH 12. AND SOMETIMES[12] THEY PRESCRIBED A LARGE MEASURE: 'A LADLEFUL OF CORPSE MOULD'[13] REFERS TO THE BIG LADLE OF PHYSICIANS; THE 'SPLIT BEAN' IN THE CASE OF LEPROSY[14] REFERS TO THE CILICIAN KIND; 'ONE WHO EATS ON THE DAY OF ATONEMENT A QUANTITY OF THE

(1) When the thing measured was not a vessel but a part of the human body. (2) Cf. Lev. II, 2. (3) Cf. Lev. XVI, 12. (4) When drinking is forbidden (cf. Yoma VIII, 2). (5) Cf. 'Er. VIII, 2. (6) When more is eaten than on the working days of the week. (7) Holding that on weekdays more is eaten in each meal than on Sabbath when three meals are prescribed. (8) *Sc.* to reduce the prescribed size of the *'erub* (cf. 'Er., Sonc. ed., p. 576, n. 3). (9) In determining the quantity of bread required for two meals. (10) Of wheat. Thus two ninths of a *ḳab* suffice for two meals. When three loaves are made from a *ḳab* $\frac{2}{3}$ of each loaf $= \frac{1}{3} \times \frac{2}{3} = \frac{2}{9}$ *ḳab*. (11) As four *se'ah* are equal to 4×6 *ḳab* $= 24 \times 2 = 48$ half-*ḳab*, and as a *sela'* contains 4 *denars* $= 4 \times 6$ *ma'ah* $= 4 \times 6 \times 2 = 48$ *dupondia*, each loaf must weigh half a *ḳab*; but as the shopkeeper who buys at the price mentioned ($\frac{1}{2}$ a *ḳab* for a *dupondium*) sells at a higher price, allowing himself a profit of fifty per cent of the purchase price, he sells for each *dupondium* $\frac{1}{2}$ of a half a *ḳab* — $\frac{1}{4}$ of a *ḳab*. Each loaf, therefore, weighs $\frac{1}{4}$ of a *ḳab*. Cf. 'Er., Sonc. ed., pp. 576-578 and notes. (12) Cf. prev. Mishnah *ab init.* (13) A citation from Oh. II, 1. (14) Cf. Neg. VI, 1.

BULK OF A LARGE DATE',[1] REFERS TO THE SIZE OF ITSELF AND ITS STONE; IN THE CASE OF SKINS OF WINE AND OIL [THE HOLES][2] MUST BE AS BIG AS THEIR LARGE STOPPER; IN THE CASE OF A LIGHT HOLE THAT WAS NOT MADE BY MAN'S HANDS[3] THE PRESCRIBED SIZE OF WHICH[4] IS THAT OF A LARGE FIST, THE REFERENCE IS TO THE FIST OF BEN BAṬIAḤ[5] (R. JOSE STATED: AND IT IS AS BIG AS A LARGE HUMAN HEAD), AND IN THE CASE OF ONE[6] MADE BY MAN'S HANDS THE PRESCRIBED SIZE[4] IS THAT OF THE LARGE DRILL IN THE TEMPLE CHAMBER WHICH IS THE SIZE OF THE ITALIAN DUPONDIUM OR THE NERONIAN SELA'[7] OR LIKE THE HOLE IN A YOKE.

MISHNAH 13. ALL THAT LIVE IN THE SEA ARE[8] CLEAN,[9] EXCEPT THE SEA-DOG BECAUSE IT SEEKS REFUGE[10] ON DRY LAND; SO R. AKIBA. IF ONE MADE VESSELS FROM WHAT GROWS IN THE SEA AND JOINED TO THEM ANYTHING THAT GROWS ON LAND, EVEN IF ONLY A THREAD OR A CORD, PROVIDED IT IS SUSCEPTIBLE TO UNCLEANNESS, THEY ARE UNCLEAN.

MISHNAH 14. THE LAWS OF UNCLEANNESS CAN APPLY TO WHAT WAS CREATED ON THE FIRST DAY.[11] THERE CAN BE NO UNCLEANNESS IN WHAT WAS CREATED ON THE SECOND DAY.[12] TO WHAT WAS CREATED ON THE THIRD DAY[13] THE LAWS OF UNCLEANNESS CAN APPLY.[14] NO UNCLEANNESS APPLIES TO WHAT WAS CREATED ON THE FOURTH DAY[15] AND ON THE

(1) Is culpable (Yoma VIII, 2). (2) That render them insusceptible to uncleanness. (3) Oh. XIII, 1. (4) That would enable uncleanness to spread through it from one room into another. (5) A Palestinian giant in the time of the destruction of the Temple; v. Lam. Rab. I, 5. (6) A light-hole. (7) A *sela'* named after the Emperor Nero. (8) Unlike animals on land. (9) Even when dead. Hence vessels made of their skins are insusceptible to uncleanness. (10) Lit., 'flees'. (11) The earth (Gen. I, 1). Earthen vessels are subject to the laws of uncleanness. (12) The heavens (Gen. I, 6f). (13) The trees and plants (Gen. I, 11f). (14) Wooden vessels are subject to uncleanness. (15) The luminaries (Gen. I, 14ff).

FIFTH DAY,[1] EXCEPT[2] TO THE WING OF THE VULTURE OR AN OSTRICH-EGG THAT IS PLATED.[3] R. JOḤANAN B. NURI OBJECTED: WHY SHOULD THE WING OF A VULTURE BE DIFFERENT FROM ALL OTHER WINGS? TO ALL THAT WAS CREATED ON THE SIXTH DAY[4] THE LAWS OF UNCLEANNESS CAN APPLY.[5]

MISHNAH 15. IF ONE MADE A RECEPTACLE, WHATEVER ITS SIZE,[6] IT IS SUSCEPTIBLE TO UNCLEANNESS. IF ONE MADE A COUCH OR A BED, WHATEVER ITS SIZE,[7] IT IS SUSCEPTIBLE TO UNCLEANNESS. IF ONE MADE A PURSE FROM UNTANNED HIDE OR FROM PAPYRUS, IT IS SUSCEPTIBLE TO UNCLEANNESS. A POMEGRANATE, AN ACORN AND A NUT WHICH CHILDREN HOLLOWED OUT TO MEASURE DUST THEREWITH OR FASHIONED THEM INTO A PAIR OF SCALES, ARE SUSCEPTIBLE TO UNCLEANNESS, SINCE IN THE CASE OF CHILDREN AN ACT[8] IS VALID THOUGH AN INTENTION IS NOT.[9]

MISHNAH 16. THE BEAM OF A BALANCE AND A STRIKE THAT CONTAIN A RECEPTACLE FOR METAL,[10] A CARRYING-YOKE THAT HAS A RECEPTACLE FOR MONEY,[11] A BEGGAR'S CANE THAT HAS A RECEPTACLE FOR WATER,[12] AND A STICK THAT HAS A RECEPTACLE FOR A MEZUZAH AND FOR PEARLS[13]

(1) Birds and fishes (Gen. I, 20ff). (2) According to Rabbinic Law, though not Pentateuchally. (3) With metal. It is not clear whether this refers to both wing and egg or to the latter only. (4) Land animals and man (Gen. I, 24ff). (5) To animals and men when dead, and to the latter under certain circumstances even when alive. (6) Lit., 'in every place (case)'. *Sc.* however little its capacity may be. (7) Even if one can only lean on it. (8) As in the cases mentioned. (9) If they only intended to turn the fruits mentioned into receptacles their intention is disregarded. (10) By secretly inserting the metal into the beam the scales can be made to turn either in favour of the seller or in that of the buyer. Similarly with the strike, when the metal is inserted the strike levels the measure much lower and benefits the seller. By removing the metal the strike exerts less pressure and the benefit is the buyer's. (11) In which the carrier stealthily throws the money he received for his labour and claims a second payment. (12) From which he drinks or into which he secretly pours any wine or oil he is able to steal. (13) A device to evade customs duties.

ARE SUSCEPTIBLE TO UNCLEANNESS. ABOUT ALL THESE R. JOḤANAN B. ZAKKAI REMARKED: 'WOE TO ME IF I SHOULD SPEAK OF THEM; WOE TO ME IF I SHOULD NOT SPEAK'.[1]

MISHNAH 17. THE BASE OF THE GOLDSMITHS' ANVIL[2] IS SUSCEPTIBLE TO UNCLEANNESS, BUT THAT OF THE BLACKSMITHS[3] IS CLEAN. A WHET-BOARD WHICH HAS A RECEPTACLE FOR OIL IS SUSCEPTIBLE TO UNCLEANNESS, BUT ONE THAT HAS NONE IS CLEAN. A WRITING-TABLET THAT HAS A RECEPTACLE FOR WAX IS SUSCEPTIBLE TO UNCLEANNESS, BUT ONE THAT HAS NONE IS CLEAN. A STRAW MAT OR A TUBE OF STRAW, R. AKIBA RULES, IS SUSCEPTIBLE TO UNCLEANNESS,[4] BUT R. JOḤANAN B. NURI RULES THAT IS IT CLEAN. R. SIMEON RULED: THE HOLLOW STALK OF COLOCYNTH[5] IS SUBJECT TO THE SAME LAW.[6] A MAT OF REEDS OR RUSHES IS CLEAN. A REED-TUBE THAT WAS CUT FOR HOLDING ANYTHING REMAINS CLEAN UNTIL ALL THE PITH HAS BEEN REMOVED.

(1) Cf. B.B. 89*b*: 'Should I speak of them, knaves might learn them; and should I not speak, the knaves might say, "the scholars are unacquainted with our practice", and will deceive us still more'. (2) In which chippings of gold are collected. (3) Whose function is not the collection of the chippings of metal but the protection of the blacksmith from the falling sparks. (4) Though the capacity of either is very little. (5) Or 'wild cucumbers' or 'small bitter water melons'. (6) As the tube of straw (cf. n. 4).

KELIM

CHAPTER XVIII

MISHNAH 1. A WOODEN CHEST,[1] BETH SHAMMAI RULED, IS MEASURED[2] ON THE INSIDE[3] AND BETH HILLEL RULE: ON THE OUTSIDE.[4] BOTH, HOWEVER, AGREE THAT THE THICKNESS OF THE LEGS AND THE THICKNESS OF THE RIM ARE NOT INCLUDED IN THE MEASUREMENT. R. JOSE STATED: BOTH AGREE THAT THE THICKNESS OF THE LEGS AND THE THICKNESS OF THE RIM ARE INCLUDED IN THE MEASUREMENT, BUT THE SPACE BETWEEN THEM[5] IS NOT INCLUDED. R. SIMEON SHEZURI RULED: IF THE LEGS ARE ONE HANDBREADTH HIGH THE SPACE BETWEEN THEM[5] IS NOT INCLUDED IN THE MEASUREMENT, OTHERWISE[6] IT IS INCLUDED.

MISHNAH 2. ITS[7] CARRIAGE,[8] IF IT CAN BE SLIPPED OFF, IS NOT REGARDED AS A CONNECTIVE,[9] NOR IS IT INCLUDED IN ITS MEASUREMENT,[10] NOR DOES IT AFFORD PROTECTION TOGETHER WITH IT IN THE TENT OF A CORPSE,[11] NOR MAY IT BE DRAWN ALONG ON THE SABBATH IF IT CONTAINED MONEY.[12] IF, HOWEVER, IT CANNOT BE SLIPPED OFF, IT IS

(1) Which (cf. *supra* XV, 1) is insusceptible to uncleanness if it has a capacity of no less than forty *se'ah*. (2) To ascertain its capacity. (3) Since the walls cannot be included in the capacity of the chest. (4) The main reason for the uncleanness being the heavy weight of the chest, the walls also, which add to its weight may be included. (5) Between the legs and between the bottom of the chest and the ground. (6) Lit., 'and if not', if the height of the legs was less than a handbreadth. (7) The chest's (cf. prev. Mishnah *ab init.*). (8) Lit., 'machine', a contrivance under a chest to facilitate movement from place to place. (9) And the chest and the carriage are independently susceptible or insusceptible to uncleanness. (10) To supplement the prescribed minimum of forty *se'ah*. (11) Only vessels within the chest (provided its capacity is forty *se'ah* and its cover is tightly fitting) are protected from the uncleanness, but not those within the carriage since the latter is itself susceptible to uncleanness. (12) Being an independent object it becomes a base to

REGARDED AS A CONNECTIVE, IT IS INCLUDED IN ITS MEASUREMENT, IT AFFORDS PROTECTION TOGETHER WITH IT IN THE TENT OF A CORPSE, AND IT MAY BE DRAWN ALONG ON THE SABBATH EVEN IF IT CONTAINS MONEY. ITS[1] ARCHED TOP, IF IT IS FIXED, IS A CONNECTIVE AND IS MEASURED WITH IT, BUT IF IT IS NOT FIXED IT IS NO CONNECTIVE AND IS NOT MEASURED WITH IT. HOW IS IT[2] MEASURED? AS AN OX-HEAD.[3] R. JUDAH RULED: IF IT[1] CANNOT STAND BY ITSELF[4] IT IS CLEAN.[5]

MISHNAH 3. IF ONE OF THE LEGS WAS MISSING FROM A CHEST, A BOX OR A CUPBOARD, EVEN THOUGH IT IS STILL CAPABLE OF HOLDING [OBJECTS],[6] IT IS CLEAN, SINCE IT CANNOT[7] HOLD THEM IN THE USUAL MANNER;[8] BUT R. JOSE RULED: IT IS SUSCEPTIBLE TO UNCLEANNESS. THE POLES OF A BED, ITS BASE, AND [ITS] WRAPPER[9] ARE CLEAN.[10] ONLY THE BED ITSELF AND ITS FRAME ARE SUSCEPTIBLE TO UNCLEANNESS. THE BED FRAMES OF THE SONS OF LEVI,[11] HOWEVER, ARE CLEAN.[12]

MISHNAH 4. A BED FRAME THAT WAS PUT ON PROPS,[13] R. MEIR AND R. JUDAH RULE, IS SUSCEPTIBLE TO UNCLEANNESS BUT R. JOSE AND R. SIMEON RULE THAT IT IS CLEAN.

the money and, therefore, forbidden like it to be moved about on the Sabbath (cf. Shab. XXI, 2).

(1) The chest's (cf. prev. Mishnah *ab init.*). (2) The arched top that was fixed. (3) *Sc.* straight lines are drawn from the highest point in the arched cover to the vertical sides of the chest and all the space contained between the arch of the cover and the lines is included in the measurement. (4) But requires support. (5) Even if its capacity is less than forty *se'ah*. (6) *Sc.* no hole was made in the vessel. (7) Var lec., 'and that which cannot . . . manner R. Jose . . . unclean'. (8) It being necessary to prop it up. (9) Or 'its covering', denoting any bed decorations (Maim.). (10) Even if they are made of metal. (11) Who take them on their journey when going to Jerusalem to serve their turn in the Temple. (12) Because they are easily detachable and quite independent of the bed. (13) Lit., 'tongues', *sc.* it did not rest on the bed legs themselves.

R. JOSE ARGUED: WHEREIN DOES THIS[1] DIFFER FROM THE BED FRAMES OF THE SONS OF LEVI WHICH ARE CLEAN?[2]

MISHNAH 5. IF A BED THAT HAD CONTRACTED MIDRAS UNCLEANNESS LOST A SHORT SIDE AND TWO LEGS IT STILL REMAINS UNCLEAN,[3] BUT IF A LONG SIDE AND TWO LEGS WERE LOST IT BECOMES CLEAN. R. NEHEMIA RULED: IT IS UNCLEAN. IF TWO PROPS AT OPPOSITE CORNERS WERE CUT OFF, OR IF TWO LEGS AT OPPOSITE CORNERS WERE CUT OFF,[4] OR IF THE BED[5] WAS REDUCED TO A LEVEL OF LESS THAN A HANDBREADTH,[6] IT BECOMES CLEAN.

MISHNAH 6. IF A BED HAD CONTRACTED MIDRAS UNCLEANNESS AND A LONG SIDE OF IT WAS BROKEN AND THEN IT WAS REPAIRED, IT STILL RETAINS ITS MIDRAS UNCLEANNESS; BUT IF THE SECOND SIDE WAS ALSO BROKEN,[7] THOUGH IT WAS ALSO REPAIRED, IT BECOMES FREE FROM MIDRAS UNCLEANNESS BUT IS UNCLEAN FROM CONTACT WITH MIDRAS UNCLEANNESS.[8] IF BEFORE ONE COULD MANAGE TO REPAIR THE FIRST SIDE THE SECOND ONE WAS BROKEN THE BED BECOMES CLEAN.

MISHNAH 7. IF A [BED] LEG THAT HAD CONTRACTED MIDRAS UNCLEANNESS WAS JOINED TO A BED, ALL THE BED CONTRACTS MIDRAS UNCLEANNESS. IF IT WAS SUBSEQUENTLY TAKEN OFF, IT RETAINS ITS MIDRAS UNCLEANNESS WHILE THE BED IS UNCLEAN FROM CONTACT WITH MIDRAS. IF A BED LEG THAT WAS SUBJECT TO A SEVEN-DAY UNCLEANNESS[9] WAS JOINED TO A BED, ALL THE BED CONTRACTS SEVEN-DAY UNCLEANNESS. IF IT WAS SUBSEQUENTLY TAKEN

(1) Which is easily detachable. (2) V. p. 91, n. 12. (3) Since it is still useable as a couch. (4) Var lec., 'to the extent of a handbreadth square.' (5) By cutting away parts of each of its four legs. (6) From the ground. (7) Even if this happened after the first one was already repaired. (8) Since it came in contact with the bed that was suffering *midras* uncleanness. (9) Having been in contact with a vessel that contracted corpse uncleanness (cf. Oh. I, 2).

OFF IT REMAINS SUBJECT TO SEVEN-DAY UNCLEANNESS WHILE THE BED IS ONLY SUBJECT TO EVENING-UNCLEANNESS.[1] IF A LEG THAT WAS SUBJECT TO EVENING UNCLEANNESS WAS JOINED TO A BED, ALL THE BED CONTRACTS EVENING UNCLEANNESS. IF IT WAS SUBSEQUENTLY TAKEN OFF IT IS STILL SUBJECT TO EVENING UNCLEANNESS WHILE THE BED BECOMES CLEAN.[2] THE SAME LAW APPLIES ALSO TO THE PRONG OF A MATTOCK.[3]

MISHNAH 8. A PHYLACTERY[4] IS REGARDED AS CONSISTING OF FOUR VESSELS. IF THE FIRST COMPARTMENT WAS UNLOOSED[5] AND THEN IT WAS MENDED IT RETAINS ITS CORPSE UNCLEANNESS. SO IS IT ALSO THE CASE WITH THE SECOND AND THE THIRD.[6] IF THE FOURTH WAS UNLOOSED[7] IT BECOMES FREE FROM CORPSE UNCLEANNESS BUT IS STILL UNCLEAN FROM CONTACT WITH CORPSE UNCLEANNESS.[8] IF SUBSEQUENTLY THE FIRST COMPARTMENT WAS AGAIN UNLOOSED AND MENDED IT REMAINS UNCLEAN FROM CONTACT.[9] SO ALSO IN THE CASE OF THE SECOND COMPARTMENT.[10] IF THE THIRD COMPARTMENT WAS SUBSEQUENTLY UNLOOSED AND MENDED IT BECOMES CLEAN, SINCE THE FOURTH IS UNCLEAN FROM CONTACT,[11] AND WHAT IS UNCLEAN FROM CONTACT CANNOT CONVEY UNCLEANNESS BY CONTACT.

(1) *Sc.* it is unclean until sunset only. (2) Since the leg (which was subject only to a derived uncleanness) cannot impart any uncleanness to the bed which, as a 'vessel', can contract uncleanness from a 'father of uncleanness' only. (3) Which stand respectively in the same relationship as the leg and the bed. (4) *Sc. Tefillah*, sing. of *tefillin* (v. Glos.). Of the head, which consists of four compartments. (5) After the phylactery had contracted corpse uncleanness. (6) If either was unloosed and then mended it retains its corpse uncleanness. (7) So that none of the original compartments remained intact. (8) Since it came in contact with the other compartments which are subject to corpse uncleanness which is a 'father of uncleanness'. (9) With the second which is still a 'father fo uncleanness'. (10) Since it came in contact with the third which, like the second, was still a 'father of uncleanness' (cf. prev. n.). (11) With the third which was a 'father of uncleanness' before it was unloosed and mended the second time.

MISHNAH 9. A BED THE HALF OF WHICH IS STOLEN OR LOST, OR ONE WHICH BROTHERS OR JOINT OWNERS DIVIDED BETWEEN THEMSELVES, BECOMES CLEAN.[1] IF IT WAS RESTORED[2] IT IS SUSCEPTIBLE TO UNCLEANNESS HENCEFORTH.[3] A BED MAY CONTRACT UNCLEANNESS AND BE RENDERED CLEAN[4] ONLY WHEN ALL ITS PARTS ARE BOUND TOGETHER; SO R. ELIEZER. BUT THE SAGES RULED: IT CAN CONTRACT UNCLEANNESS AND BE RENDERED CLEAN[4] EVEN IN SINGLE PARTS.[5]

(1) Since the two parts are not likely ever to be joined again. (2) The two parts again forming one whole. (3) But free from all former uncleanness. (4) By immersion in a ritual bath and/or by ritual sprinkling. (5) Provided it was intended to bind them together again.

KELIM

CHAPTER XIX

MISHNAH 1. IF A MAN DISMANTLED A BED IN ORDER THAT HE MIGHT IMMERSE IT,[1] ANY ONE WHO TOUCHES THE ROPES[2] REMAINS CLEAN.[3] WHEN[4] DOES THE ROPE[5] BEGIN TO CONSTITUTE A CONNECTIVE WITH THE BED? AS SOON AS THREE ROWS OF MESHES OF IT HAVE BEEN KNOTTED.[6] AND [IF ANOTHER ROPE WAS TIED TO THIS ONE] ANY PERSON WHO TOUCHES IT FROM THE KNOT INWARDS BECOMES UNCLEAN; BUT IF FROM THE KNOT OUTWARDS HE REMAINS CLEAN. AS TO THE LOOSE ENDS OF THE KNOT, ANY ONE THAT TOUCHES THAT PART WHICH IS NEEDED FOR IT[7] BECOMES UNCLEAN AND HOW MUCH IS NEEDED FOR IT?[7] R. JUDAH STATED: THREE FINGERBREADTHS.

MISHNAH 2. A ROPE THAT HANGS OVER FROM [THE NETTING OF] A BED[8] IS CLEAN[9] IF IT IS SHORTER THAN FIVE HANDBREADTHS, BUT UNCLEAN IF IT IS FROM FIVE TO TEN HANDBREADTHS LONG, WHILE THAT PART WHICH IS OVER THE TEN HANDBREADTHS IS CLEAN; FOR IT IS ONLY WITH THE FORMER[10] THAT PASCHAL LAMBS WERE TIED[11] AND BEDS SUSPENDED.[12]

(1) In agreement with the Sages in the previous Mishnah. (2) That make up the netting in the bed frame. (3) Even though the bed was a 'father of uncleanness' from which a man contracts an uncleanness of the first grade. The ropes do not constitute a part of the bed after the latter had been dismantled. (4) In the case of a new bed. (5) Cf. n. 2. (6) Though the rope is much longer all of it is unclean since one part contracts uncleanness from the other. (7) The knot, *sc.* the part without which the knot would be undone. (8) After the required netting in the frame had been duly completed. (9) Even when the bed is unclean. (10) Lit., 'for with it', with the part of the rope that was from five to ten handbreadths long. (11) To the bed's legs. A ceremonial that preceded the offering of the lamb. (12) When, for instance, they were to be immersed in a ritual bath.

MISHNAH 3. IF A PART OF A BED-GIRTH HANGS OVER, IT IS UNCLEAN[1] WHATEVER ITS LENGTH;[2] SO R. MEIR. R. JOSE RULED: ONLY THAT WHICH IS SHORTER THAN TEN HANDBREADTHS.[3] THE REMNANT OF A BED-GIRTH[4] REMAINS UNCLEAN IF THE LENGTH IS NO LESS THAN SEVEN HANDBREADTHS FROM WHICH AN ASS'S GIRTH CAN BE MADE.[5]

MISHNAH 4. IF A ZAB WAS CARRIED ON A BED AND ON ITS GIRTH,[6] THE LATTER[7] CAUSES AN UNCLEANNESS OF TWO GRADES[8] AND AN UNFITNESS[9] OF ONE GRADE;[10] SO R. MEIR. R. JOSE RULED: IF A ZAB WAS CARRIED ON A BED AND ON ITS GIRTH[6] THE PART THAT IS SHORTER THAN TEN HANDBREADTHS CAUSES AN UNCLEANNESS OF TWO GRADES[8] AND AN UNFITNESS[9] OF ONE GRADE,[10] BUT THAT WHICH IS OVER THE TEN HANDBREADTHS[11] CAUSES ONLY AN UNCLEANNESS OF ONE GRADE[12] AND AN UNFITNESS[9] OF ONE GRADE.[10] IF HE WAS CARRIED ON THE BED-GIRTH, [ON THE OVERHANGING PART] THAT WAS SHORTER THAN TEN HANDBREADTHS, IT BECOMES UNCLEAN,[13] BUT IF ON THE PART THAT WAS LONGER THAN TEN HANDBREADTHS IT REMAINS CLEAN.[14]

(1) If the bed was unclean. (2) It being invariably regarded as a connective with the bed. (3) That which is longer cannot be regarded as a connective and, therefore, remains clean. (4) That was worn away. (5) A lesser length, which is entirely useless, becomes clean. (6) *Sc.* while the girth was around the bed, though the girth did not come in direct contact with the *zab*. (7) Which, like the bed, becomes a 'father of uncleanness'. (8) *Sc.* the object that touches it contracts an uncleanness of the first grade, and any foodstuffs that touch this object contract one of the second grade. (9) In the case of *terumah*. The term 'unfit' in connection with uncleanness denotes that the uncleanness contracted cannot be carried to a further remove. (10) The third. Any *terumah* that comes in contact with a second grade of uncleanness becomes 'unfit' as having contracted a third grade of uncleanness. (11) Which cannot be treated as a connective with the bed and which, as being in contact with a 'father of uncleanness', is subject only to a first grade of uncleanness. (12) *Sc.* a second grade. (13) Because it is regarded as part of the bed. (14) Cf. prev. n. According to another reading the uncleanness and cleanness apply to the bed.

MISHNAH 5. IF AROUND A BED THAT HAD CONTRACTED MIDRAS UNCLEANNESS ONE WRAPPED A BED-GIRTH, THE WHOLE BECOMES SUBJECT TO MIDRAS UNCLEANNESS; IF IT WAS SUBSEQUENTLY REMOVED, THE BED REMAINS SUBJECT TO MIDRAS UNCLEANNESS BUT THE BED-GIRTH IS UNCLEAN ONLY FROM CONTACT WITH MIDRAS. IF THE BED WAS SUBJECT TO A SEVEN-DAY UNCLEANNESS AND A BED-GIRTH WAS SUBSEQUENTLY WRAPPED AROUND IT, THE WHOLE BECOMES SUBJECT TO A SEVEN-DAY UNCLEANNESS; IF IT WAS REMOVED, THE BED REMAINS SUBJECT TO A SEVEN-DAY UNCLEANNESS BUT THE BED-GIRTH IS SUBJECT ONLY TO EVENING UNCLEANNESS. IF THE BED WAS SUBJECT TO EVENING UNCLEANNESS AND AROUND IT WAS SUBSEQUENTLY WRAPPED A BED-GIRTH, THE WHOLE BECOMES SUBJECT TO EVENING UNCLEANNESS; IF IT WAS REMOVED, THE BED REMAINS SUBJECT TO EVENING UNCLEANNESS BUT THE BED-GIRTH BECOMES CLEAN.

MISHNAH 6. IF A BED-GIRTH WAS WRAPPED AROUND A BED AND A CORPSE TOUCHED THEM, THEY ARE SUBJECT TO A SEVEN-DAY UNCLEANNESS;[1] IF THEY ARE TAKEN APART THEY[2] ARE STILL SUBJECT TO A SEVEN-DAY UNCLEANNESS. IF A [DEAD] CREEPING THING TOUCHED THEM THEY ARE SUBJECT TO AN EVENING UNCLEANNESS; IF THEY ARE TAKEN APART THEY[2] ARE STILL SUBJECT TO EVENING UNCLEANNESS. IF FROM A BED[3] THE TWO LONGER SIDES WERE REMOVED[4] AND TWO NEW ONES WERE PREPARED FOR IT BUT THE ORIGINAL SOCKETS WERE NOT CHANGED, IF THE NEW SIDES WERE BROKEN THE BED[3] RETAINS ITS UNCLEANNESS,[5] BUT IF THE OLD ONES WERE BROKEN IT BECOMES CLEAN, SINCE[6] ALL DEPENDS ON THE OLD ONES.[7]

(1) Even according to R. Jose. Only in regard to *midras* uncleanness does he dispute the connection of the girth with the bed. (2) Since neither can in consequence be regarded as broken. (3) That was unclean. (4) But they were still useable and capable of restoration to the bed. (5) Since the old sides can still be restored (cf. prev. n.). (6) The new sides having changed the bed's entire character from old to new. (7) Cf. prev. two notes.

MISHNAH 7. A BOX WHOSE OPENING IS AT THE TOP IS SUSCEPTIBLE TO CORPSE UNCLEANNESS.[1] IF IT WAS DAMAGED ABOVE IT IS STILL SUSCEPTIBLE TO CORPSE UNCLEANNESS. IF IT WAS DAMAGED BELOW, IT[2] BECOMES CLEAN. THE COMPARTMENTS[3] WITHIN IT REMAIN UNCLEAN AND ARE NOT REGARDED AS A CONNECTIVE WITH IT.[4]

MISHNAH 8. IF A SHEPHERD'S BAG[5] WAS DAMAGED, THE POCKET WITHIN IT RETAINS ITS UNCLEANNESS AND IS NOT REGARDED AS A CONNECTIVE WITH IT. IF THE TESTICLE BAGS IN A SKIN[6] SERVE ALSO[7] AS RECEPTACLES[8] AND THEY WERE DAMAGED, THEY BECOME CLEAN,[9] SINCE THEY[10] WILL NO LONGER SERVE THEIR ORIGINAL PURPOSE.[11]

MISHNAH 9. A BOX WHOSE OPENING IS AT THE SIDE IS SUSCEPTIBLE TO BOTH MIDRAS UNCLEANNESS[12] AND CORPSE UNCLEANNESS. R. JOSE STATED: WHEN DOES THIS APPLY? WHEN IT IS LESS THAN TEN HANDBREADTHS IN HEIGHT[13] OR WHEN IT HAS NOT A RIM ONE HANDBREADTH DEEP.[12] IF IT WAS DAMAGED ABOVE IT IS STILL SUSCEPTIBLE TO CORPSE UNCLEANNESS.[14] IF IT WAS DAMAGED BELOW, R. MEIR RULES THAT IT IS SUSCEPTIBLE TO UNCLEANNESS,[15] BUT THE SAGES RULE THAT IT IS CLEAN BECAUSE WHERE THE PRIMARY FUNCTION[16] CEASES[17] THE SECONDARY ONE[18] ALSO CEASES.

(1) Though, owing to its unsuitability as a seat, it is free from *midras* uncleanness. (2) As a broken vessel. (3) Or 'drawers', that were undamaged. (4) Cf. *supra* II, 7. (5) V. p. 97, n. 3. (6) E.g. of a sheep. (7) Lit., 'with it', with the skin. (8) *Sc.* they also are filled when the liquid is poured into the skin. (9) Though independently of the skin they can still hold some liquid. (10) Not being capable of receiving the liquid from the skin. (11) Lit., 'they do not receive in their usual way'. (12) Since one can sit on it without interfering with its normal uses. (13) Because then one can conveniently sit on it. (14) But not to that of *midras*, since it can no longer be used as a seat. (15) *Midras* uncleanness; since it is still possible to sit on it. (16) To serve as a receptacle. (17) On account of the damage below. (18) That of being used as a seat.

MISHNAH 10. A DUNG-BASKET THAT WAS SO DAMAGED[1] THAT IT WILL NOT HOLD POMEGRANATES, R. MEIR RULES, IS STILL SUSCEPTIBLE TO UNCLEANNESS,[2] BUT THE SAGES RULE THAT IT IS CLEAN BECAUSE WHERE THE PRIMARY FUNCTION[3] CEASES THE SECONDARY ONE[4] ALSO CEASES.

(1) After it had contracted uncleanness. (2) *Midras* uncleanness; since it is still possible to sit on it. (3) V. p. 98, n. 16. (4) V. p. 98, n. 18.

KELIM

CHAPTER XX

MISHNAH 1. BOLSTERS, PILLOWS, SACKS AND PACKING CASES THAT WERE DAMAGED[1] ARE STILL SUSCEPTIBLE TO MIDRAS UNCLEANNESS.[2] A FODDER-BAG THAT CAN HOLD FOUR ḲAB, A SHEPHERD'S BAG THAT CAN HOLD FIVE ḲAB, A TRAVELLING BAG THAT CAN HOLD A SE'AH, A SKIN THAT CAN HOLD SEVEN ḲAB (R. JUDAH RULED: ALSO A SPICE-BAG AND A FOOD WALLET THAT CAN HOLD THE SMALLEST QUANTITY) ARE STILL SUSCEPTIBLE TO MIDRAS UNCLEANNESS.[3] IF ANY OF THEM, HOWEVER, WAS DAMAGED IT BECOMES CLEAN, SINCE WHERE THE PRIMARY FUNCTION[4] CEASES[5] THE SECONDARY FUNCTION[6] ALSO CEASES.

MISHNAH 2. A BAGPIPE IS NOT SUSCEPTIBLE TO MIDRAS UNCLEANNESS.[7] A TROUGH FOR MIXING MORTAR, BETH SHAMMAI RULE, IS SUSCEPTIBLE TO MIDRAS UNCLEANNESS[8], AND BETH HILLEL RULE THAT IT IS SUSCEPTIBLE TO CORPSE UNCLEANNESS ONLY.[9] IF A TROUGH OF A CAPACITY FROM TWO LOG TO NINE ḲAB IS SPLIT, IT BECOMES SUSCEPTIBLE TO MIDRAS UNCLEANNESS.[10] IF IT WAS LEFT IN THE RAIN AND IT SWELLED[11] IT IS SUSCEPTIBLE TO CORPSE UNCLEANNESS ALONE.[12] [IF IT WAS LEFT OUT] DURING THE EAST WIND

(1) So that they can no longer be used as receptacles. (2) Because they can still be used as seats which was one of their original functions. (3) Since they can be used as seats without interfering in any way with their functions as receptacles. (4) To serve as receptacles. (5) On account of the damage. (6) Their use as seats. (7) Even if one sat or lay on it; since it is not intended for such use. (8) Since labourers sometimes sit on it. (9) It is free from *midras* since most people would not sit on such a muddy trough. (10) If, however, its capacity was smaller it is exempt. (11) So that the split was closed up and the trough was again suitable for its original use. (12) It is exempt from *midras* since, owing to its suitability for its original use, one would not be allowed to sit on it.

AND IT SPLIT, IT IS SUSCEPTIBLE TO MIDRAS UNCLEANNESS.[1] IN THIS RESPECT THE LAW IS MORE RESTRICTED IN THE CASE OF REMNANTS OF WOODEN VESSELS THAN IN [THAT OF SUCH VESSELS] IN THEIR ORIGINAL CONDITION.[2] IT IS ALSO MORE RESTRICTED IN REGARD TO THE REMNANTS OF WICKER VESSELS THAN [TO SUCH VESSELS] AS ARE IN THEIR ORIGINAL CONDITION, FOR WHEN THEY ARE IN THEIR ORIGINAL CONDITION THEY ARE INSUSCEPTIBLE TO UNCLEANNESS UNTIL THEIR RIM IS FINISHED, BUT AFTER THEIR RIM HAS BEEN FINISHED, EVEN THOUGH THEIR EDGES FELL AWAY LEAVING ONLY THE SLIGHTEST TRACE OF THEM, THEY ARE UNCLEAN.

MISHNAH 3. IF A STICK WAS USED[3] AS A HAFT FOR A HATCHET, IT[4] IS REGARDED AS A CONNECTIVE[5] FOR UNCLEANNESS AT THE TIME OF USE. A YARN WINDER IS REGARDED AS A CONNECTIVE[6] FOR UNCLEANNESS AT THE TIME OF ITS USE. IF IT WAS FIXED TO A POLE IT IS SUSCEPTIBLE TO UNCLEANNESS,[7] BUT THE LATTER CANNOT BE REGARDED AS A CONNECTIVE WITH IT. IF THE POLE ITSELF WAS[8] CONVERTED INTO A YARN WINDER, ONLY THAT PART[9] WHICH IS NEEDED FOR USE IS SUSCEPTIBLE TO UNCLEANNESS. A SEAT THAT WAS FIXED TO THE POLE IS SUSCEPTIBLE TO UNCLEANNESS, BUT THE LATTER IS NOT REGARDED AS A CONNECTIVE WITH IT. IF THE POLE WAS TURNED INTO A SEAT, ONLY THE PLACE OF THE SEAT IS SUSCEPTIBLE TO UNCLEANNESS. A SEAT THAT WAS FIXED TO THE BEAM OF AN OLIVE-PRESS IS SUSCEPTIBLE TO UNCLEANNESS, BUT THE LATTER IS NO CONNECTIVE WITH IT. IF THE END OF A BEAM WAS TURNED INTO A SEAT IT REMAINS CLEAN, BECAUSE

(1) Because it is no longer used for its original purpose and might well be used as a seat. (2) The former are free from *midras* while the latter are susceptible to it. (3) Occasionally. (4) Though it is a flat wooden vessel which elsewhere is insusceptible to uncleanness. (5) With the hatchet. (6) With the metal cross-pieces which are temporarily attached to it. (7) Even when not in use, since in that case the metal cross-pieces remain permanently fixed. (8) By fixing the metal ends directly on it. (9) Of the pole.

PEOPLE WOULD TELL HIM,[1] 'GET UP AND LET US DO OUR WORK'.[2]

MISHNAH 4. IF A LARGE TROUGH WAS SO DAMAGED THAT IT COULD NO LONGER HOLD POMEGRANATES AND IT WAS ADAPTED AS A SEAT, R. AKIBA RULES THAT IT BECOMES SUSCEPTIBLE TO UNCLEANNESS, BUT THE SAGES RULE THAT IT REMAINS CLEAN UNLESS ITS ROUGH PARTS HAVE BEEN SMOOTHED.[3] IF IT WAS TURNED INTO A CRIB FOR CATTLE, EVEN IF IT WAS FIXED TO A WALL, IT IS SUSCEPTIBLE TO UNCLEANNESS.[4]

MISHNAH 5. A BLOCK[5] THAT WAS FIXED TO A COURSE OF A WALL, WHETHER IT WAS ONLY FIXED AND NOT BUILT UPON OR BUILT UPON AND NOT FIXED, IS SUSCEPTIBLE TO UNCLEANNESS.[6] IF IT WAS FIXED AND ALSO BUILT UPON, IT[7] IS CLEAN.[8] MATTING THAT WAS SPREAD OVER THE ROOF-BEAMS,[9] WHETHER IT WAS FIXED AND NO PLASTERWORK WAS LAID OVER IT OR WHETHER PLASTERWORK WAS LAID OVER IT AND IT WAS NOT FIXED, IT IS SUSCEPTIBLE TO UNCLEANNESS.[10] IF IT WAS FIXED AND PLASTERWORK WAS LAID OVER IT, IT IS CLEAN.[8] A DISH THAT WAS FIXED TO A CHEST, BOX OR CUPBOARD IN SUCH A MANNER AS TO HOLD ITS CONTENTS IN THE USUAL WAY[11] IS SUSCEPTIBLE TO UNCLEANNESS,[10] BUT IF IT WAS IN A MANNER THAT IT CANNOT HOLD IT IN THE USUAL WAY[12] IT IS CLEAN.[8]

(1) Who would sit on it. (2) For which a beam is intended. (3) *Sc.* the adaptation was accomplished by a specific act and not by mere intention. (4) Of a corpse or dead creeping thing, like a movable vessel. Only a vessel that was originally intended to be fixed to the ground (even before it was fixed) and one that is used only when fixed to the ground is insusceptible to uncleanness. (5) Of wood or any other material that is suitable for the making of a seat. (6) Of *midras*, if a *zab* sat even only on the structure above the block; because it can easily revert to its former use. (7) As a part of the wall. (8) As any 'vessel' that is permanently fixed to a building and is regarded as a part of the ground. (9) Of a top floor. (10) Cf. *supra* n. 6 *mut. mut.* (11) *Sc.* with its bottom downwards. (12) With its bottom upwards.

MISHNAH 6. IF A SHEET THAT WAS SUSCEPTIBLE TO THE UNCLEANNESS OF MIDRAS WAS MADE INTO A CURTAIN,[1] IT BECOMES INSUSCEPTIBLE TO MIDRAS UNCLEANNESS BUT[2] IS SUSCEPTIBLE TO CORPSE UNCLEANNESS. WHEN DOES IT BECOME INSUSCEPTIBLE TO UNCLEANNESS?[3] BETH SHAMMAI RULED: WHEN IT HAS BEEN CUT UP.[4] BETH HILLEL RULED: WHEN THE LOOPS HAVE BEEN TIED TO IT. R. AKIBA RULED: WHEN IT HAS BEEN FIXED.[5]

MISHNAH 7. A MAT[6] PROVIDED WITH REEDS THAT STRETCHED LENGTHWISE IS INSUSCEPTIBLE TO UNCLEANNESS;[7] BUT THE SAGES RULE: ONLY IF THEY LAY IN THE SHAPE OF [THE GREEK LETTER] CHI.[8] IF THEY WERE LAID ALONG ITS WIDTH AND THERE WAS A DISTANCE OF LESS THAN FOUR HANDBREADTHS[9] BETWEEN ANY TWO REEDS, IT IS INSUSCEPTIBLE TO UNCLEANNESS.[7] IF IT WAS DIVIDED ALONG ITS WIDTH, R. JUDAH RULES THAT IS CLEAN.[10] SO ALSO, WHERE THE END KNOTS[11] ARE UNTIED, IT IS CLEAN.[10] IF IT WAS DIVIDED ALONG ITS LENGTH[12] BUT THREE END-KNOTS REMAINED INTACT ACROSS A STRETCH OF SIX HANDBREADTHS,[13] IT IS SUSCEPTIBLE TO UNCLEANNESS. WHEN DOES A MAT BECOME SUSCEPTIBLE TO UNCLEANNESS? WHEN ITS ROUGH ENDS ARE TRIMMED, THIS BEING THE COMPLETION OF ITS MANUFACTURE.

(1) Which is not used as a seat. (2) Since it might still be used as a wrapper and must in consequence be regarded as a 'vessel'. (3) Of *midras*. (4) To the size required for the curtain; var. lec., 'sewn up', 'joined'. (5) In its position as a curtain. (6) Which is sometimes strengthened by the insertion of reeds across its width, at distances of four handbreadths from each other. (7) Of *midras;* because reeds in the position mentioned render the mat unsuitable for lying upon. (8) *Sc.* crosswise. If they only stretch lengthwise one can still use the mat by lying between the reeds, and it is, therefore, susceptible to uncleanness. (9) Cf. n. 7. (10) Since it would no longer be used as a mat. It would rather be discarded. (11) Which keep the plaiting together. (12) So that the reeds running along its width were broken. (13) The minimum size of a mat.

KELIM

CHAPTER XXI

MISHNAH 1. A MAN WHO TOUCHES THE UPPER BEAM,[1] THE LOWER BEAM,[1] THE HEDDLES, THE SLEY, THE THREAD THAT IS DRAWN[2] OVER PURPLE MATERIAL,[3] OR A SPOOL WHICH IS NOT TO BE SHOT BACK,[4] REMAINS CLEAN.[5] IF HE TOUCHES THE WOOF, THE STANDING WARP,[6] THE DOUBLE THREAD THAT IS DRAWN OVER PURPLE MATERIAL[7] OR A SPOOL WHICH IS TO BE SHOT BACK,[4] HE BECOMES UNCLEAN.[8] IF A MAN TOUCHES THE WOOL THAT IS ON THE DISTAFF, OR ON THE SPOOL, HE REMAINS CLEAN. IF HE TOUCHES THE SPINNER BEFORE IT WAS LAID BARE[9] HE BECOMES UNCLEAN, BUT IF HE TOUCHES IT AFTER IT WAS LAID BARE[10] HE REMAINS CLEAN.

MISHNAH 2. IF A MAN TOUCHED THE YOKE,[11] THE CROSSBAR, THE COLLAR-PIECE, OR THE THICK ROPES,[12] EVEN AT THE TIME THEY ARE USED, HE REMAINS CLEAN.[13] IF HE TOUCHED THE TAIL PIECE, KNEE OR HANDLE,[12] HE BECOMES UNCLEAN. IF HE TOUCHED THE METAL RINGS,[12] THE GUIDES,[12] OR THE FLANKS,[12] HE BECOMES UNCLEAN. R. JUDAH RULES THAT HE REMAINS CLEAN IF HE TOUCHED THE

(1) Of a loom in which a piece of material that was partially woven had contracted corpse uncleanness. (2) Temporarily. (3) For its protection from dirt. (4) In the web on the loom. (5) Because none of the objects mentioned can be regarded as a connective with the material and, therefore, cannot contract its uncleanness. (6) Before it was woven. (7) And which is to be woven into the material. (8) Since all the objects enumerated are connectives with the material and, therefore, contract uncleanness from it. (9) When it is regarded as a part of the spindle and subject to its uncleanness. (10) Cf. prev. n. *mut. mut.* (11) Of the wagon. (12) Of a plough. (13) Even if the ploughshare is unclean; because the objects enumerated are not regarded as connections with it.

GUIDES, SINCE THEY ONLY SERVE TO INCREASE THE SOIL.[1]

MISHNAH 3. IF A MAN TOUCHED THE HANDLE OF A SAW[2] AT EITHER END[3] HE BECOMES UNCLEAN;[4] BUT IF HE TOUCHED ITS STRING,[5] CORD,[5] CROSS-PIECE OR SIDE-PIECES, A CARPENTER'S PRESS,[6] OR THE BOW-HANDLE OF A BOW-DRILL,[7] HE REMAINS CLEAN.[8] R. JUDAH RULED: ALSO HE WHO TOUCHES THE FRAME OF A LARGE SAW[2] REMAINS CLEAN. IF A MAN TOUCHED THE BOW-STRING[9] OR THE BOW, EVEN THOUGH IT WAS STRETCHED, HE REMAINS CLEAN.[10] A MOLE-TRAP IS CLEAN.[11] R. JUDAH RULED: WHILE IT IS SET THE SEPARATE PARTS ARE [REGARDED AS] CONNECTED.

(1) And are not concerned with the main process of ploughing. Var. lec., 'to break up the soil'. (2) Whose blade was unclean. (3) Of the saw. (4) Since the handle at either end is regarded as a part of the instrument and subject to its uncleanness. (5) Which joins the two handles and strengthens the saw. (6) Whose metal part is unclean. (7) The bow-shaped handle of a borer. (8) Because the parts enumerated are not regarded as connectives. (9) Of a bow. (10) Because these are not regarded as connectives of the arrow and are not affected by its uncleanness. (11) The wooden part remains clean even if the metal part was unclean.

KELIM

CHAPTER XXII

MISHNAH 1. IF A TABLE[1] OR A SIDE-BOARD[2] WAS DAMAGED OR COVERED WITH MARBLE[3] BUT ROOM[4] WAS LEFT ON IT WHERE CUPS COULD BE SET, IT REMAINS UNCLEAN. R. JUDAH RULED: THERE MUST BE ROOM ENOUGH[5] FOR PIECES OF FOOD.[6]

MISHNAH 2. A TABLE[7] ONE OF WHOSE LEGS WAS LOST BECOMES CLEAN.[8] IF A SECOND LEG WAS LOST IT IS STILL CLEAN. BUT IF A THIRD WAS LOST[9] IT BECOMES UNCLEAN WHERE THE OWNER HAS THE INTENTION OF USING IT.[10] R. JOSE RULED: NO INTENTION IS NECESSARY.[11] THE SAME LAW APPLIES ALSO TO THE SIDE-BOARD.[12]

MISHNAH 3. A BENCH[13] ONE OF WHOSE LEGS WAS LOST BECOMES CLEAN.[14] IF ITS SECOND LEG ALSO WAS LOST IT[15] IS STILL CLEAN. IF, HOWEVER, IT[15] WAS ONE HANDBREADTH HIGH[16] IT REMAINS UNCLEAN. A FOOTSTOOL[17] ONE OF WHOSE

(1) That was unclean. (2) *Delphim*, a three-legged side table on which food is placed. (3) Which, as a stone vessel, should not be susceptible to uncleanness. (4) Undamaged and uncovered with marble respectively. (5) If the table or side-board is to remain unclean. (6) Which are of direct service to man. It is not enough that there is room for cups alone which only serve objects that serve man. (7) That was three-legged and unclean. (8) Since it can no longer serve its original purpose. (9) So that, having no legs at all, it can be used as a low table. (10) In its present condition. (11) The fact that it can be used (cf. *supra* n. 9) is sufficient to subject it to uncleanness. (12) If all its legs were missing. (13) That has two wide legs, one at each end of a board that is used as a seat and is unclean. (14) Since the bench, being lop-sided, can no longer be used as a seat. (15) The board (cf. n. 13). (16) Either on account of its thickness, though it rests on the ground, or on account of the remnants of its legs which are one handbreadth high. (17) Cf. *supra* n. 13 *mut. mut.*

LEGS WAS LOST REMAINS UNCLEAN;[1] AND THE SAME LAW APPLIES TO THE STOOL IN FRONT OF A CATHEDRA.[2]

MISHNAH 4. IF A BRIDE'S STOOL LOST ITS SEATBOARDS,[3] BETH SHAMMAI RULE THAT IT IS STILL SUSCEPTIBLE TO UNCLEANNESS,[4] AND BETH HILLEL RULE THAT IT IS CLEAN.[5] SHAMMAI RULED: EVEN THE FRAME OF THE STOOL[6] IS SUSCEPTIBLE TO UNCLEANNESS. IF A STOOL WAS FIXED TO A BAKING-TROUGH,[7] BETH SHAMMAI RULE THAT IT[8] IS SUSCEPTIBLE TO UNCLEANNESS.[9] AND BETH HILLEL RULE THAT IT IS CLEAN.[10] SHAMMAI RULED: EVEN ONE[11] MADE OUT OF IT[12] IS SUSCEPTIBLE TO UNCLEANNESS.[9]

MISHNAH 5. IF THE SEAT BOARDS[13] OF A STOOL DID NOT PROJECT[14] AND THEY WERE REMOVED, IT[15] IS STILL SUSCEPTIBLE TO UNCLEANNESS, FOR IT IS USUAL[16] TO TURN IT ON ITS SIDE AND TO SIT ON IT.

MISHNAH 6. IF THE MIDDLE SEAT BOARD OF A STOOL WAS LOST BUT THE OUTER ONES[17] REMAINED IT IS STILL SUSCEPTIBLE TO UNCLEANNESS. IF THE OUTER ONES[17] WERE LOST AND THE MIDDLE SEAT BOARD REMAINED IT IS ALSO SUSCEPTIBLE TO UNCLEANNESS. R. SIMEON RULED: ONLY IF IT[18] WAS A HANDBREADTH WIDE.[19]

MISHNAH 7. IF THE TWO ADJACENT SEAT BOARDS OF A STOOL WERE LOST, R. AKIBA RULED, IT IS SUSCEPTIBLE TO

(1) Since it can still be used for its original purpose. (2) A chair with back. (3) Lit., 'its coverings'. (4) V. foll. n. (5) Because, though it may still be used as a seat, it is not useable as a bride's stool. (6) That never had a proper seat. (7) Which is not susceptible to *midras* uncleanness since its main use is not for sitting. (8) The stool. (9) Because its identity is not merged in the trough. (10) Cf. prev. n. *mut. mut.* (11) A stool. (12) The troughs, *sc.* a stool that never had a separate existence. (13) These were three in number; v. next Mishnah. (14) Beyond its sides. (15) *Sc.* the stool. (16) Owing to the absence of the projections. (17) *Sc.* its sides. (18) The centre seat board. (19) If it was not so wide it is insusceptible to uncleanness.

UNCLEANNESS; AND THE SAGES RULE THAT IT IS CLEAN. SAID R. JUDAH: ALSO IF THE SEAT BOARDS OF A BRIDE'S STOOL WERE LOST,[1] THOUGH THE RECEPTACLE UNDER REMAINED,[2] IT IS CLEAN, SINCE WHERE THE PRIMARY FUNCTION HAS CEASED[1] THE SECONDARY ONE[3] ALSO CEASES.

MISHNAH 8. A CHEST[4] WHOSE TOP PART[5] WAS LOST IS STILL SUSCEPTIBLE TO UNCLEANNESS ON ACCOUNT OF ITS BOTTOM; IF ITS BOTTOM WAS LOST IT IS STILL SUSCEPTIBLE TO UNCLEANNESS ON ACCOUNT OF ITS TOP PART.[6] IF BOTH THE TOP PART AND THE BOTTOM WERE LOST, R. JUDAH RULES THAT IT IS SUSCEPTIBLE TO UNCLEANNESS ON ACCOUNT OF ITS SIDES,[7] AND THE SAGES RULE THAT IT IS CLEAN. A STONE-CUTTER'S SEAT[8] IS SUBJECT TO MIDRAS UNCLEANNESS.[9]

MISHNAH 9. IF A [WOODEN] BLOCK WAS PAINTED RED OR SAFFRON, OR WAS POLISHED, R. AKIBA RULES THAT IT IS SUSCEPTIBLE TO UNCLEANNESS,[10] BUT THE SAGES[11] RULE THAT IT REMAINS CLEAN UNLESS IT WAS HOLLOWED OUT.[12] A SMALL BASKET OR A BIG ONE THAT WAS FILLED WITH STRAW OR FLOCKING REMAINS CLEAN[13] IF IT WAS PREPARED AS A SEAT;[14] BUT IF IT WAS PLAITED OVER WITH REED-GRASS OR WITH A CORD[15] IT BECOMES SUSCEPTIBLE TO UNCLEANNESS.[16]

MISHNAH 10. A NIGHT STOOL[17] IS SUBJECT TO BOTH

(1) So that it was no longer useable as a seat. (2) The receptacle under the seat boards of a bride's stool for the reception of things. (3) Its use as a receptacle. (4) Containing less than forty *se'ah*, which is consequently susceptible to uncleanness. (5) Its cover. (6) Which also forms a kind of receptacle. (7) On which one can sit. (8) A small block of wood on which he sits when engaged in his work. (9) As a proper seat. (10) Since it may be used as a seat. (11) Regarding it as a mere block of wood. (12) To provide it with a seat. (13) *Sc.* it is not susceptible to *midras* uncleanness. (14) Since most people do not use it as a seat his eccentric act must be disregarded. (15) To prevent the straw or the flocking from falling out. (16) *Sc.* to *midras* uncleanness, since it might well be used as a seat. (17) Having a square iron frame and a leather seat.

MIDRAS AND CORPSE UNCLEANNESS. IF THE LEATHER SEAT WAS SUNDERED,[1] THE LEATHER[2] IS SUBJECT TO MIDRAS UNCLEANNESS AND THE IRON[3] IS SUBJECT ONLY TO CORPSE UNCLEANNESS. A TRIPOD STOOL WHOSE COVER IS OF LEATHER IS SUBJECT TO BOTH MIDRAS AND CORPSE UNCLEANNESS. IF IT WAS TAKEN APART, THE LEATHER[2] IS SUBJECT TO MIDRAS UNCLEANNESS WHILE THE TRIPOD[4] IS ALTOGETHER CLEAN. A BATH-HOUSE BENCH[5] THAT HAS TWO WOODEN LEGS IS[6] SUSCEPTIBLE TO UNCLEANNESS.[7] IF ONE LEG WAS OF WOOD AND THE OTHER OF STONE IT[8] IS CLEAN. IF BOARDS IN A BATH-HOUSE WERE JOINED TOGETHER,[9] R. AKIBA RULES THAT THEY ARE SUSCEPTIBLE TO [MIDRAS] UNCLEANNESS;[10] BUT THE SAGES RULE THAT THEY ARE CLEAN, SINCE THEY ARE MADE ONLY FOR THE WATER TO FLOW UNDER THEM.[11] A FUMIGATION-CAGE THAT CONTAINS A RECEPTACLE FOR GARMENTS IS SUSCEPTIBLE TO UNCLEANNESS,[12] BUT ONE THAT IS MADE LIKE A BEE-HIVE[13] IS CLEAN.

(1) From the iron frame. (2) Which can still be used as a seat. (3) Which can be used for various purposes other than that of sitting. (4) Since it has no receptacle to be regarded as a vessel and since, on account of its smallness, it is useless as a seat. (5) Of stone. (6) On account of its wooden legs. (7) Of *midras*. (8) The bench. (9) *Aliter:* planed. (10) Because they are used for sitting on. (11) But not for sitting purposes. (12) Though its bottom is perforated with holes larger than the size of a pomegranate. (13) Without a bottom.

KELIM

CHAPTER XXIII

MISHNAH 1. IF A BALL, A SHOE-LAST, AN AMULET OR TEFILLIN[1] WERE TORN,[2] HE THAT TOUCHES THEM BECOMES UNCLEAN,[3] BUT HE THAT TOUCHES THEIR CONTENTS[4] REMAINS CLEAN. IF A SADDLE WAS TORN,[2] HE THAT TOUCHES ITS CONTENTS[5] BECOMES UNCLEAN, BECAUSE THE STITCHING JOINS THEM.[6]

MISHNAH 2. THE FOLLOWING ARE SUSCEPTIBLE TO UNCLEANNESS[7] AS OBJECTS THAT ARE FIT FOR RIDING UPON:[8] AN ASHKELON GIRTH, A MEDIAN MORTAR,[9] A CAMEL'S PACK-SADDLE, AND A HORSE-CLOTH.[10] R. JOSE RULED: A HORSE-CLOTH[10] IS ALSO SUSCEPTIBLE TO UNCLEANNESS[7] AS A SEAT,[11] SINCE PEOPLE STAND ON IT[12] IN THE ARENA;[13] BUT A SADDLE OF A FEMALE CAMEL IS SUSCEPTIBLE TO UNCLEANNESS.[14]

MISHNAH 3. WHAT IS THE PRACTICAL DIFFERENCE BETWEEN [THE UNCLEANNESS AS AN OBJECT USED FOR] RIDING UPON AND [AS ONE USED FOR] SITTING UPON? IN THE CASE OF THE FORMER THE EFFECT OF CONTACT WITH IT[15]

(1) All these are leather objects, filled either with some stuffing or (as in the case of the last two) with parchment rolls. (2) At the seams, after contracting corpse uncleanness. (3) Since only their seams were torn they are still useable as receptacles. (4) Which, not being joined to them, cannot be regarded as connectives. (5) Not only he who touches its leather case (cf. n. 3 *mut. mut.* (6) The contents and the casing, to form one object. (7) Of *midras.* (8) Lit., 'riding object'. (9) Or 'saddle'. (10) Or 'saddle-cushion'. (11) But not as an object fit for riding upon. (12) Which in the case of a *zab* is equivalent to sitting. (13) *Campus.* (14) As an object that is used for riding upon, the ruling being that of R. Jose. *Aliter:* As a seat, according to the first Tanna. (15) On the part of a clean person.

IS DIFFERENT FROM THE EFFECT OF CARRYING IT,[1] BUT IN THE CASE OF THE LATTER THERE IS NO DIFFERENCE BETWEEN THE EFFECT OF COMING IN CONTACT WITH IT OR CARRYING IT.[2] THE PACK-FRAME OF AN ASS ON WHICH A ZAB HAS SAT REMAINS CLEAN;[3] BUT IF THE SIZE OF THE SPACES[4] HAS BEEN CHANGED[5] OR IF THEY HAVE BEEN BROKEN ONE INTO ANOTHER[5] IT IS SUSCEPTIBLE TO UNCLEANNESS.[6]

MISHNAH 4. THE BIER, THE MATTRESS AND THE PILLOW OF A CORPSE ARE SUSCEPTIBLE TO THE UNCLEANNESS OF MIDRAS.[7] A BRIDE'S STOOL, A MIDWIFE'S TRAVAILING STOOL, AND A FULLER'S STOOL ON WHICH HE PILES[8] THE CLOTHES, R. JOSE RULED, CANNOT BE REGARDED AS A SEAT.[9]

MISHNAH 5. A FISHING NET IS SUSCEPTIBLE TO UNCLEANNESS ON ACCOUNT OF ITS BAG.[10] NETS, SNARES, BIRD-TRAPS, SLINGS AND FISHERMEN'S[11] SKEINS ARE SUSCEPTIBLE TO UNCLEANNESS.[12] A FISH-TRAP, A BIRD-BASKET AND A BIRD-CAGE ARE NOT SUSCEPTIBLE TO UNCLEANNESS.

(1) One who carries it causes, while still carrying it, the uncleanness of clothes and vessels while one who only comes in contact with it conveys uncleanness to foodstuffs alone. (2) Both convey uncleanness to clothes and vessels. (3) Since it is not usual for people to sit on it. (4) Lit., 'holes'. (5) To facilitate the sitting on it. (6) As a 'seat' because it may be regarded as a proper seat. (7) Since the mourning women sit on them while lamenting the dead. (8) *Aliter:* Folds and presses. (9) That is subject to *midras* uncleanness. These objects, being reserved for special uses, cannot properly serve as a *zab's* seat even if he did sit on them. (10) In its lower parts, which is closely woven and has the status of a garment. (11) Lit., 'makers of water locks (for fishing purposes)'. (12) Of a corpse or a dead creeping thing; not to that of *midras*.

KELIM

CHAPTER XXIV

MISHNAH 1. THREE[1] DIFFERENT LAWS[2] ARE APPLICABLE TO SHIELDS: THE BENT SHIELD[3] IS SUSCEPTIBLE TO MIDRAS UNCLEANNESS;[4] THE SHIELD WITH WHICH COMBATANTS PLAY IN THE ARENA IS SUSCEPTIBLE TO CORPSE UNCLEANNESS;[5] AND THE TOY-SHIELD OF THE ARABS[6] IS FREE FROM ALL UNCLEANNESS.

MISHNAH 2. THREE DIFFERENT LAWS ARE APPLICABLE TO WAGONS: ONE MADE LIKE A CATHEDRA[7] IS SUSCEPTIBLE TO MIDRAS UNCLEANNESS;[4] ONE MADE LIKE A BED IS SUSCEPTIBLE TO CORPSE UNCLEANNESS;[5] AND ONE FOR [THE TRANSPORT OF] STONES IS FREE FROM ALL UNCLEANNESS.

MISHNAH 3. THREE DIFFERENT LAWS ARE APPLICABLE TO BAKING-TROUGHS: IF A BAKING-TROUGH OF A CAPACITY FROM TWO LOG TO NINE ḲAB WAS SPLIT[8] IT IS SUSCEPTIBLE TO MIDRAS UNCLEANNESS; IF IT WAS WHOLE IT IS SUSCEP-

(1) Lit., 'there are three shields'. The general principles underlying the laws throughout this chapter are the following: An object that is normally used for lying, sitting or leaning upon is susceptible to *midras* uncleanness. An earthenware is excluded since it cannot attain cleanness through immersion. A mat, though it cannot attain cleanness through immersion, is (by an inference from a Pentateuchal amplification) susceptible to *midras* uncleanness provided it had not been reduced to less than six by six handbreadths. An object that is not intended for lying upon is susceptible to corpse uncleanness unless it cannot be regarded as a proper vessel when it is free from all uncleanness. (2) Cf. Bert. (3) Which protects the warrior on three sides, and which in a war is used by him for lying upon. (4) And much more so to corpse uncleanness. (5) And much more so to that of a dead creeping thing and *nebelah*, but not to that of *midras*. (6) Used for the entertainment of children. (7) A chair with back. (8) So that it can no longer be used as a baking trough.

TIBLE TO CORPSE UNCLEANNESS; AND IF IT HOLDS THE PRESCRIBED MEASURE[1] IT IS FREE FROM ALL UNCLEANNESS.

MISHNAH 4. THREE DIFFERENT LAWS APPLY TO BOXES: A BOX WHOSE OPENING IS AT THE SIDES[2] IS SUSCEPTIBLE TO MIDRAS UNCLEANNESS; IF IT IS ON THE TOP IT IS SUSCEPTIBLE TO CORPSE UNCLEANNESS;[3] AND IF IT HOLDS THE PRESCRIBED MEASURE[1] IT IS FREE FROM ALL UNCLEANNESS.

MISHNAH 5. THREE DIFFERENT LAWS ARE APPLICABLE TO LEATHER COVERS:[4] THAT OF BARBERS IS SUSCEPTIBLE TO MIDRAS UNCLEANNESS;[5] THAT ON WHICH PEOPLE EAT IS SUSCEPTIBLE TO CORPSE UNCLEANNESS; AND THAT FOR [SPREADING[6] OUT] OLIVES IS FREE FROM ALL UNCLEANNESS.[7]

MISHNAH 6. THREE DIFFERENT LAWS ARE APPLICABLE TO BASES: ONE WHICH LIES BEFORE A BED OR BEFORE A SCRIVENER[8] IS SUSCEPTIBLE TO MIDRAS UNCLEANNESS; ONE FOR A SIDE-BOARD IS SUSCEPTIBLE TO CORPSE UNCLEANNESS; AND ONE FOR A CUPBOARD IS FREE FROM ALL UNCLEANNESS.

MISHNAH 7. THREE DIFFERENT LAWS APPLY TO WRITING TABLETS: THAT OF PAPYRUS[9] IS SUSCEPTIBLE TO MIDRAS UNCLEANNESS; THAT WHICH HAD A RECEPTACLE FOR WAX IS SUSCEPTIBLE TO CORPSE UNCLEANNESS; AND THAT WHICH IS POLISHED IS FREE FROM ALL UNCLEANNESS.

MISHNAH 8. THREE DIFFERENT LAWS APPLY TO BEDS: ONE THAT IS USED FOR LYING UPON IS SUSCEPTIBLE TO MIDRAS UNCLEANNESS; ONE USED BY GLASS MAKERS[10] IS

(1) Forty *se'ah* of liquid. (2) Thus being capable of use as a seat as well as for its normal use. (3) V. p. 112, n. 5. (4) Or 'cases'. (5) Since they sit on it. (6) Or 'pressing'. (7) Because it is not a vessel used for objects that serve men. (8) Which is used as a seat. (9) Which is big and suitable for sitting upon. (10) For the placing of their wares.

SUSCEPTIBLE TO CORPSE UNCLEANNESS; AND ONE USED BY HARNESS MAKERS IS FREE FROM ALL UNCLEANNESS.

MISHNAH 9. THREE DIFFERENT LAWS APPLY TO REFUSE BASKETS: ONE FOR DUNG[1] IS SUSCEPTIBLE TO MIDRAS UNCLEANNESS; ONE FOR STRAW IS SUSCEPTIBLE TO CORPSE UNCLEANNESS; AND A CAMEL'S ROPE BAG[2] IS FREE FROM ALL UNCLEANNESS.

MISHNAH 10. THREE DIFFERENT LAWS APPLY TO MATS: ONE USED FOR SITTING UPON IS SUSCEPTIBLE TO MIDRAS UNCLEANNESS; ONE USED BY DYERS[3] IS SUSCEPTIBLE TO CORPSE UNCLEANNESS; AND ONE USED IN WINE-PRESSES IS FREE FROM ALL UNCLEANNESS.

MISHNAH 11. THREE DIFFERENT LAWS APPLY TO WATER SKINS AND THREE DIFFERENT LAWS APPLY TO SHEPHERDS' WALLETS: THOSE THAT CAN HOLD THE PRESCRIBED QUANTITY[4] ARE SUSCEPTIBLE TO MIDRAS UNCLEANNESS; THOSE THAT CANNOT HOLD THE PRESCRIBED QUANTITY ARE SUSCEPTIBLE TO CORPSE UNCLEANNESS; AND THOSE MADE OF FISH SKIN ARE FREE FROM ALL UNCLEANNESS.[5]

MISHNAH 12. THREE DIFFERENT LAWS APPLY TO HIDES: THAT WHICH IS USED AS A RUG[6] IS SUSCEPTIBLE TO MIDRAS UNCLEANNESS; THAT WHICH IS USED AS A WRAPPER FOR VESSELS[7] IS SUSCEPTIBLE TO CORPSE UNCLEANNESS; AND THAT WHICH IS INTENDED FOR STRAPS AND SANDALS IS FREE FROM ALL UNCLEANNESS.[8]

MISHNAH 13. THREE DIFFERENT LAWS APPLY TO

(1) V. 113, n. 9. (2) Which has big holes and is unsuitable either for sitting upon or for any other human use. (3) For wrapping up the articles that are to be dyed. (4) *Supra* XX, 1; and much more so if they can hold more. (5) Cf. *supra* XVII, 13. (6) To sit on. (7) Knives, for instance. (8) Since its manufacture is not yet completed. Finished straps and sandals, however, are susceptible to uncleanness.

SHEETS: ONE USED FOR LYING UPON IS SUSCEPTIBLE TO MIDRAS UNCLEANNESS; ONE USED AS A CURTAIN IS SUSCEPTIBLE TO CORPSE UNCLEANNESS; AND ONE USED AS A MURAL DECORATION[1] IS FREE FROM ALL UNCLEANNESS.

MISHNAH 14. THREE DIFFERENT LAWS APPLY TO NAPKINS: THAT FOR THE HANDS IS SUSCEPTIBLE TO MIDRAS UNCLEANNESS;[2] THAT FOR BOOKS[3] IS SUSCEPTIBLE TO CORPSE UNCLEANNESS;[4] AND THAT WHICH IS USED AS A SHROUD AS WELL AS THAT USED FOR THE HARPS OF THE LEVITES IS FREE FROM ALL UNCLEANNESS.

MISHNAH 15. THREE DIFFERENT LAWS APPLY TO LEATHERN GLOVES: THOSE USED BY THE HUNTERS OF ANIMALS AND BIRDS ARE SUSCEPTIBLE TO MIDRAS UNCLEANNESS; THOSE USED BY LOCUST-CUTTERS ARE SUSCEPTIBLE TO CORPSE UNCLEANNESS; AND THOSE USED BY FRUIT-PICKERS[5] ARE FREE FROM ALL UNCLEANNESS.

MISHNAH 16. THREE DIFFERENT LAWS APPLY TO HEADNETS: A GIRL'S IS SUSCEPTIBLE TO MIDRAS UNCLEANNESS; AN OLD WOMAN'S IS SUSCEPTIBLE TO CORPSE UNCLEANNESS; AND A HARLOT'S[6] IS FREE FROM ALL UNCLEANNESS.

MISHNAH 17. THREE DIFFERENT LAWS APPLY TO STORE-BASKETS: IF A WORN-OUT BASKET IS PATCHED ON TO A SOUND ONE,[7] ALL IS DETERMINED BY THE SOUND ONE;[8] IF A SMALL BASKET IS PATCHED ON TO A LARGE ONE[9] ALL IS

(1) Lit., 'of figures' or 'forms', one on which ornamental figures are painted which, being used to decorate a wall, is deemed to be a part of it. (2) Since it is also used sometimes as a rest for the head when lying down. (3) Used as a cover. (4) Because it is folded in the shape of a receptacle. (5) *Aliter:* Those that dry figs. Var. lec., those that gather thorns. (6) Lit., 'that goes out'. (7) To strengthen it. (8) If the latter is clean the combination is clean; and if it is unclean, the combination also becomes unclean. (9) Irrespective of whether both were worn out or sound.

DETERMINED BY THE LARGE ONE;[1] IF THEY ARE EQUAL ALL IS DETERMINED BY THE INNER ONE.[1] R. SIMEON RULED: IF THE CUP OF A BALANCE[2] WAS PATCHED ON TO THE BOTTOM OF A BOILER ON THE INSIDE, THE LATTER BECOMES UNCLEAN; BUT IF ON THE OUTSIDE IT REMAINS CLEAN. IF IT WAS PATCHED ON TO THE SIDE, WHETHER ON THE INSIDE OR THE OUTSIDE, THE LATTER REMAINS CLEAN.

(1) V. p. 115, n. 8. (2) That was unclean.

KELIM

CHAPTER XXV

MISHNAH 1. ALL VESSELS ARE SUBJECT[1] TO DIFFERENT LAWS[2] IN REGARD TO THEIR OUTER AND INNER SIDES RESPECTIVELY,[3] AS, FOR INSTANCE, CUSHIONS, BOLSTERS, SACKS AND PACKING-BAGS;[4] SO R. JUDAH. R. MEIR RULED: ANY ARTICLE THAT HAS HANGERS[5] IS SUBJECT TO DIFFERENT LAWS IN ITS OUTER AND INNER SIDES RESPECTIVELY,[6] BUT ONE THAT HAS NO HANGERS[7] IS NOT SUBJECT TO DIFFERENT LAWS IN REGARD TO OUTER AND INNER SIDES.[8] A TABLE AND A SIDE-BOARD[9] ARE SUBJECT TO DIFFERENT LAWS IN REGARD TO THEIR OUTER AND INNER SIDES RESPECTIVELY;[3] SO R. JUDAH. R. MEIR RULED: THEY ARE NOT SUBJECT TO THE LENIENT LAW IN REGARD TO THEIR OUTER SIDES.[8] THE SAME LAW ALSO APPLIES TO A RIMLESS TRAY.

MISHNAH 2. AN OX-GOAD[10] IS SUBJECT[1] TO DIFFERENT LAWS[2] IN ITS OUTER AND INNER PARTS RESPECTIVELY,[3] [THE FORMER BEING THAT SECTION OF THE SHAFT THAT LIES

(1) In respect to uncleanness contracted from liquids, which in the case of vessels is only Rabbinical. (2) In order to distinguish the Rabbinical uncleanness from that which is Pentateuchal. (3) If the inner side of a vessel contracted uncleanness from a liquid the outside also becomes unclean, but if the outer side contracted uncleanness the inner side remains clean. (4) Though each of these objects can be turned inside out when its outer side becomes its inner one and *vice versa*. (5) Which distinguished its outer, from its inner side. (6) Since (cf. prev. n.) the outer side can never become an inner one. (7) So that the outer may become an inner side. (8) The outer side or part being subject to the same restriction as the inner one. (9) Cf. n. 4 *mut. mut.* (10) Consisting of a wooden shaft of the thickness of a third of a handbreadth at the one end of which is a broad blade for cutting away roots, and at its opposite end is a pointed piece of metal wherewith the animal is goaded on when ploughing.

BETWEEN] SEVEN HANDBREADTHS FROM THE BROAD BLADE[1] AND FOUR HANDBREADTHS FROM THE POINT;[1] SO R. JUDAH. R. MEIR RULED: IT IS NOT [SUBJECT TO SUCH DISTINCTION],[2] THE FOUR AND THE SEVEN HANDBREADTHS HAVING BEEN MENTIONED ONLY IN REGARD TO ITS REMNANTS.[3]

MISHNAH 3. MEASURES OF WINE OR OIL, A SOUP-LADLE, A MUSTARD-STRAINER AND A WINE-FILTER ARE SUBJECT[4] TO DIFFERENT LAWS IN REGARD TO THEIR OUTER AND INNER SIDES RESPECTIVELY;[5] SO R. MEIR. R. JUDAH RULED: THEY ARE NOT [SUBJECT TO THESE DISTINCTIONS].[6] R. SIMEON RULED: THEY ARE [SUBJECT TO DIFFERENT LAWS], FOR IF THEIR OUTER PARTS CONTRACTED UNCLEANNESS THEIR INNER PARTS REMAIN CLEAN;[7] THOUGH[8] IMMERSION[9] IS REQUIRED.

MISHNAH 4. IF [IN A MEASURE CONSISTING OF] A QUARTER [OF A LOG] AND HALF A QUARTER [OF A LOG][10] THE QUARTER MEASURE CONTRACTED UNCLEANNESS THE HALF-QUARTER MEASURE DOES NOT BECOME UNCLEAN, AND IF THE HALF-QUARTER CONTRACTED UNCLEANNESS THE QUARTER DOES NOT BECOME UNCLEAN. THE STUDENTS ARGUED BEFORE R. AKIBA:[11] SINCE THE HALF-QUARTER MEASURE IS THE OUTER PART OF THE QUARTER MEASURE, SHOULD NOT THE OUTER SIDE OF THE VESSEL WHOSE INNER SIDE CON-

(1) Cf. p. 117, n. 10. (2) But the outer side or part is subject to the same restriction as the inner one (3) *Sc.* if an ox-goad was broken and so much as seven handbreadths from the shaft remained with the broad blade, or four handbreadths of it remained with the pointed end, it is still susceptible to uncleanness. (4) V. p. 117, n. 1. (5) V. p. 117, n. 3. (6) But, having a kind of receptacle at the back, their outer and inner sides are independent of each other and the uncleanness of the one does not affect the other. (7) In agreement with R. Meir. (8) Contrary to R. Meir's view. (9) Of the vessel whose outer part contracted an uncleanness. (10) The receptacle proper of the utensil measuring a quarter *log*, and its concave bottom a half quarter; or the double measure consisting of two receptacles side by side like a double inkpot. (11) Against the first ruling.

TRACTED UNCLEANNESS BECOME UNCLEAN? HE ANSWERED THEM: DOES IT[1] THEN BELONG TO THE CLASS THAT TAKES PRECEDENCE?[2] IT IS EQUALLY POSSIBLE THAT THE QUARTER IS TO BE REGARDED AS THE OUTER SIDE OF THE HALF QUARTER AND, SURELY, THE INNER SIDE OF A VESSEL DOES NOT BECOME UNCLEAN IF THE OUTER SIDE CONTRACTED UNCLEANNESS.

MISHNAH 5. IF THE QUARTER[3] CONTRACTED UNCLEANNESS, THE QUARTER AND ITS OUTER SIDE ARE UNCLEAN;[4] BUT THE HALF QUARTER AND ITS OUTER SIDE REMAIN CLEAN.[5] IF THE HALF QUARTER CONTRACTED UNCLEANNESS, THE HALF QUARTER AND ITS OUTER SIDE ARE UNCLEAN,[5] BUT THE QUARTER AND ITS OUTER SIDE REMAIN CLEAN. IF THE OUTER SIDE OF THE QUARTER CONTRACTED UNCLEANNESS, THE OUTER SIDE OF THE HALF QUARTER REMAINS CLEAN. SO R. MEIR. BUT THE SAGES RULED: THE OUTER SIDE CANNOT BE DIVIDED.[6] WHEN HOWEVER IMMERSION IS PERFORMED[7] THE WHOLE OF THE VESSEL MUST BE IMMERSED.

MISHNAH 6. IF ON THE BASES, RIMS, HANGERS OR HANDLES OF VESSELS THAT HAVE A RECEPTACLE UNCLEAN LIQUID FELL, ONE MERELY DRIES THEM AND THEY REMAIN CLEAN. BUT [IF UNCLEAN LIQUID FELL] ON A PART OF ANY OTHER VESSEL (WHICH CANNOT HOLD POMEGRANATES)[8] IN WHICH NO DISTINCTION IS MADE[9] BETWEEN ITS OUTER AND INNER SIDES,[10] THE WHOLE BECOMES UNCLEAN. IF THE OUTER

(1) The quarter *log*. (2) To be regarded in consequence as the inner side of the utensil. *Aliter:* 'This question has been asked already by an earlier group of students who received the reply that follows'. (3) Cf. prev. Mishnah and nn. (4) Except the outer side of its bottom, which is the inner side of the half quarter, that remains clean. (5) Cf. prev. n. *mut. mut.* (6) *Sc.* if the part of the side that belongs to the quarter contracted uncleanness the part of the side belonging to the half quarter is also unclean and *vice versa*. (7) In the case dealt with in the first clause. (8) Cf. *supra* XVII, 8. (9) In respect to uncleanness contracted from liquids, which in the case of vessels is only Rabbinical. (10) Cf. Mishnah I and nn. *supra*.

SIDE OF A VESSEL CONTRACTED UNCLEANNESS FROM A LIQUID, ONLY ITS OUTER SIDE IS UNCLEAN BUT ITS INNER SIDE, RIM, HANGER AND HANDLES REMAIN CLEAN. IF ITS INNER SIDE CONTRACTED UNCLEANNESS THE WHOLE IS UNCLEAN.

MISHNAH 7. ALL VESSELS ARE[1] SUBJECT TO DIFFERENT LAWS[2] IN REGARD TO THEIR OUTER AND INNER SIDES RESPECTIVELY[3] AND ALSO IN REGARD TO THE PART BY WHICH THEY ARE HELD.[4] R. TARFON RULED: THIS[5] APPLIES ONLY TO A LARGE WOODEN BAKING TROUGH. R. AKIBA RULED: IT APPLIES ALSO TO CUPS. R. MEIR RULED: IT APPLIES ONLY TO UNCLEAN AND CLEAN[6] HANDS. R. JOSE STATED: THEY SPOKE ONLY OF CLEAN HANDS.[6]

MISHNAH 8. IN WHAT MANNER?[7] IF ONE'S HANDS WERE CLEAN AND THE OUTER SIDE OF A CUP WAS UNCLEAN, A MAN MAY HOLD IT BY ITS HOLDING-PLACE AND NEED HAVE NO SCRUPLES LEST HIS HANDS HAVE CONTRACTED UNCLEANNESS FROM THE OUTER SIDE OF THE CUP. IF[8] HE WAS DRINKING FROM A CUP WHOSE OUTER SIDE WAS UNCLEAN HE NEED HAVE NO SCRUPLES LEST THE LIQUID IN HIS MOUTH CONTRACTED UNCLEANNESS FROM THE OUTER SIDE OF THE CUP AND THAT IT THEN[9] CONVEYED UNCLEANNESS TO THE CUP. IF A KETTLE[10] WAS BOILING ONE NEED HAVE NO SCRUPLES LEST LIQUID SHOULD ISSUE FROM IT AND TOUCH ITS OUTER SIDE AND RETURN AGAIN WITHIN IT.

MISHNAH 9. HOLY VESSELS ARE NOT SUBJECT TO DIF-

(1) V. p. 119, n. 9. (2) In order to distinguish the Rabbinical uncleanness from that which is Pentateuchal. (3) V. *supra*, p, 117, n. 3. (4) *Sc.* if the outer side contracted uncleanness this part remains clean and *vice versa*, v. Ḥag. 22*b*. (5) Cf. prev. n. (6) This is explained in the following Mishnah. (7) Cf. prev. n. (8) The following is an independent ruling, having no bearing on the question with which our Mishnah began. (9) From its inner side. (10) Whose outer side was unclean.

FERENT LAWS[1] IN REGARD TO THEIR OUTER AND INNER SIDES OR IN REGARD TO THE PART BY WHICH THEY ARE HELD,[2] NOR MAY VESSELS THAT ARE WITHIN ONE ANOTHER BE IMMERSED[3] IF THEY ARE TO BE USED FOR HALLOWED THINGS.[4] ALL VESSELS BECOME SUSCEPTIBLE TO UNCLEANNESS BY MERE INTENTION,[5] BUT THEY CANNOT BE RENDERED INSUSCEPTIBLE EXCEPT BY A CHANGE-EFFECTING ACT;[6] FOR AN ACT[7] DISANNULS AN EARLIER ACT AS WELL AS AN EARLIER INTENTION, WHILE AN INTENTION ANNULS NEITHER AN EARLIER ACT NOR AN EARLIER INTENTION.

(1) In respect to uncleanness contracted from liquids, which in the case of vessels is only Rabbinical. (2) *Sc.* whichever part contracted uncleanness the entire vessel is unclean. (3) After an uncleanness. (4) Because the weight of the inner vessels upon the outer one may prevent the access of the water to all its parts. (5) A ring, for instance, which is used for an animal (and is not susceptible to uncleanness) becomes susceptible if it was intended to be used for a man. (6) Cf. prev. n. *mut. mut.* (7) That is change-effecting.

KELIM

CHAPTER XXVI

MISHNAH 1. THE SANDAL OF IMKI[1] AND A LACED-UP BAG[2] (R. JUDAH RULED: ALSO AN EGYPTIAN BASKET;[3] R. SIMEON B. GAMALIEL RULED: THE SAME LAW APPLIES ALSO TO A LAODICEAN SANDAL)[2] CAN BE MADE SUSCEPTIBLE TO UNCLEANNESS[4] AND AGAIN BE MADE INSUSCEPTIBLE[5] WITHOUT THE AID OF A CRAFTSMAN. SAID R. JOSE: 'BUT CANNOT ALL VESSELS BE MADE SUSCEPTIBLE TO UNCLEANNESS AND BE RENDERED INSUSCEPTIBLE WITHOUT THE AID OF A CRAFTSMAN?[6] BUT THESE, EVEN WHEN THEY ARE UNLACED, ARE SUSCEPTIBLE TO UNCLEANNESS SINCE A LAYMAN IS ABLE TO RESTORE THEM'.[7] THEY[8] SPOKE ONLY OF AN EGYPTIAN BASKET[3] WHICH EVEN A CRAFTSMAN CANNOT [EASILY][9] RESTORE.

MISHNAH 2. A LACED-UP BAG WHOSE LACES WERE REMOVED[10] IS STILL SUSCEPTIBLE TO UNCLEANNESS; BUT IF IT WAS MADE FLAT[11] IT BECOMES INSUSCEPTIBLE TO UNCLEANNESS. IF A STRIP OF LINING HAS BEEN PUT ON IT BELOW,[12] IT REMAINS SUSCEPTIBLE. IF A BAG WAS WITHIN ANOTHER BAG AND ONE OF THEM CONTRACTED UNCLEANNESS FROM

(1) From Kefar Imḳi or Amiku, north-east of Acre. *Aliter:* 'Worn in valleys'. (2) These objects are flat (and, therefore, insusceptible to uncleanness), but they can be laced or sewn up to form a kind of receptacle which is susceptible to uncleanness. (3) *Aliter:* A basket of palm-twigs. (4) By being laced or sewn up. (5) By unlacing or unsewing them. (6) Of course they can. What then is the difference between these and the others? (7) To their laced condition. (8) The Sages in laying down that when unlaced it is clean. (9) V. Shab. 58*b* and 83*b*. (10) From the loops, but are still suspended from the bag. *Aliter:* (according to R. Judah) Whose laces are missing. (11) Thus forming no receptacle. (12) So that a receptacle remains even when the bag is made flat.

A LIQUID, THE OTHER DOES NOT BECOME UNCLEAN.[1] A PEARL POUCH IS SUSCEPTIBLE TO UNCLEANNESS. AS TO A MONEY POUCH, R. ELIEZER RULES THAT IT IS SUSCEPTIBLE TO UNCLEANNESS, AND THE SAGES RULE THAT IT IS INSUSCEPTIBLE.[2]

MISHNAH 3. THE HAND-COVER OF THORN-PICKERS[3] IS INSUSCEPTIBLE TO UNCLEANNESS.[4] A BELT[5] AND LEG GUARDS[5] ARE SUSCEPTIBLE TO UNCLEANNESS. SLEEVES[5] ARE SUSCEPTIBLE TO UNCLEANNESS BUT LEGGINGS[5] ARE NOT SUSCEPTIBLE. ANY FINGER-STALL IS INSUSCEPTIBLE TO UNCLEANNESS EXCEPT THAT OF FRUIT[6]-PICKERS, SINCE THE LATTER HOLDS THE SUMACH BERRIES.[7] IF IT[8] WAS TORN, IT IS INSUSCEPTIBLE TO UNCLEANNESS, PROVIDED IT CANNOT HOLD THE GREATER PART OF A SUMACH BERRY.

MISHNAH 4. A SANDAL[9] ONE OF WHOSE STRAPS WAS TORN OFF BUT WAS MENDED AGAIN, RETAINS ITS MIDRAS UNCLEANNESS.[10] IF A SECOND STRAP WAS TORN OFF, THOUGH IT WAS MENDED AGAIN, IT[11] BECOMES FREE FROM MIDRAS UNCLEANNESS BUT IS UNCLEAN FROM CONTACT WITH MIDRAS.[10] IF THE SECOND STRAP WAS TORN OFF BEFORE THE FIRST COULD BE MENDED, IT[11] BECOMES CLEAN.[10] IF ITS HEEL WAS TORN OFF, OR IF ITS TOE-PIECE WAS REMOVED, OR IF IT[11] WAS TORN IN TWO, IT[11] BECOMES CLEAN.[12] A HEELLESS SLIPPER[5] THAT WAS TORN ANYWHERE BECOMES CLEAN. A SHOE THAT WAS DAMAGED BECOMES CLEAN IF IT CANNOT

(1) The uncleanness that vessels contract from liquids being only Rabbinical, the law has been relaxed. In the case of a Pentateuchal uncleanness the one bag causes the uncleanness of the other. (2) Since it is continually opened to take money out, it is not regarded as a valid receptacle. (3) A flat piece of leather which covers the palm of the hand and protects it against the thorns. (4) Since it forms no receptacle. (5) Made of leather. (6) Or 'thorn'. (7) Thus forming a receptacle. (8) The latter. (9) That contracted *midras* uncleanness. (10) Cf. nn. *supra* XVIII, 6. (11) The sandal. (12) From its former uncleanness. It is, however, susceptible to future uncleanness.

CONTAIN THE GREATER PART OF THE FOOT. A SHOE THAT IS STILL ON THE LAST, R. ELIEZER RULES, IS INSUSCEPTIBLE TO UNCLEANNESS,[1] BUT THE SAGES RULE THAT IT IS SUSCEPTIBLE. ALL WATER SKINS WHOSE HOLES[2] HAVE BEEN TIED UP ARE INSUSCEPTIBLE TO UNCLEANNESS,[3] EXCEPT THOSE OF THE ARABS.[4] R. MEIR RULES: IF THEY ARE TIED UP FOR A WHILE, THEY ARE CLEAN; BUT IF THEY ARE TIED WITH A PERMANENT KNOT[5] THEY ARE UNCLEAN. R. JOSE RULED: ALL TIED UP WATER SKINS[6] ARE CLEAN.

MISHNAH 5. THE FOLLOWING HIDES ARE SUSCEPTIBLE TO MIDRAS UNCLEANNESS: A HIDE WHICH IS INTENDED FOR USE AS A RUG,[7] A HIDE USED AS A TANNER'S APRON, A HIDE USED AS THE LOWER COVERING OF A BED, A HIDE USED AS AN APRON BY AN ASS-DRIVER,[8] BY A FLAX-WORKER, BY A PORTER OR BY A PHYSICIAN,[9] A HIDE USED FOR A COT, A HIDE PUT OVER A CHILD'S HEART,[10] A HIDE OF A CUSHION OR A BOLSTER. ALL THESE ARE SUSCEPTIBLE TO MIDRAS UNCLEANNESS. A HIDE FOR WRAPPING UP COMBED WOOL AND A HIDE WORN BY A WOOL-COMBER, R. ELIEZER RULES, IS SUSCEPTIBLE TO MIDRAS, BUT THE SAGES RULE THAT IT IS SUSCEPTIBLE TO CORPSE UNCLEANNESS ONLY.[11]

MISHNAH 6. A BAG[12] OR WRAPPER[12] FOR GARMENTS IS SUSCEPTIBLE TO MIDRAS. A BAG OR WRAPPER FOR PURPLE WOOL, BETH SHAMMAI RULE, IS SUSCEPTIBLE TO MIDRAS, BUT BETH HILLEL RULE THAT[13] IT IS ONLY SUSCEPTIBLE TO CORPSE UNCLEANNESS.[14] IF A HIDE IS USED AS A COVERING

(1) Since its manufacture has not yet been completed. (2) That appeared in them after they had contracted an uncleanness and that have rendered them clean. (3) Since the knots may be easily undone. (4) Whose knots cannot be easily undone. (5) Cf. prev. n. *mut. mut.* (6) Even if the knot was permanent. (7) To sit upon. V. nn. *supra* XXIV, 12. (8) Var. lec., 'a hide of (to protect) an ass.' (9) As a protection against the spurting of blood. (10) To protect it against the bite of a cat. (11) But not to that of *midras*. (12) Of leather. (13) Since, on account of the high value of the purple, ft would not be used as a seat. (14) But not to *midras*.

FOR VESSELS IT IS NOT SUSCEPTIBLE TO UNCLEANNESS, BUT IF IT IS USED AS A COVERING FOR WEIGHTS[1] IT IS SUSCEPTIBLE. R. JOSE IN THE NAME OF HIS FATHER RULES THAT IT IS INSUSCEPTIBLE.

MISHNAH 7. WHENEVER NO ACT IS LACKING[2] INTENTION[3] ALONE[4] CAUSES AN ARTICLE TO BE SUSCEPTIBLE TO UNCLEANNESS, BUT WHEREVER AN ACT IS LACKING[2] INTENTION[3] ALONE DOES NOT RENDER IT SUSCEPTIBLE TO UNCLEANNESS, EXCEPT FUR SKINS.[5]

MISHNAH 8. THE HIDES OF A HOUSEHOLDER BECOME SUSCEPTIBLE TO UNCLEANNESS BY INTENTION,[6] BUT THOSE THAT BELONG TO A TANNER[7] DO NOT BECOME SUSCEPTIBLE BY MERE INTENTION. THOSE TAKEN BY A THIEF[8] BECOME SUSCEPTIBLE BY INTENTION,[9] BUT THOSE TAKEN BY A ROBBER[10] DO NOT BECOME SUSCEPTIBLE BY MERE INTENTION.[11] R. SIMEON STATED: THE RULE IS TO BE REVERSED; THOSE TAKEN BY A ROBBER[12] BECOME SUSCEPTIBLE BY MERE INTENTION, BUT THOSE TAKEN BY A THIEF[13] DO NOT BECOME SUSCEPTIBLE BY INTENTION, SINCE IN THE LATTER CASE THE OWNER DOES NOT ABANDON THE HOPE FOR RECOVERY.[14]

MISHNAH 9. IF A HIDE HAD CONTRACTED MIDRAS

(1) Which cause a depression and give it the shape of a receptacle. (2) To complete its manufacture. (3) To use it for a particular purpose. (4) Even before it was actually used. (5) Which become susceptible to uncleanness by mere intention to use them, even before they have been trimmed, since they can be used without any trimming. (6) To use them; even before actual use. (7) Who, before manufature is completed, might change his mind. (8) Since the owner, not knowing the thief, abandons all hope of recovery. (9) Of the thief who steals secretly. As the owner abandoned hope the thief is regarded as the legal owner. (10) Who steals openly and is known to the owner who, in consequence, does not abandon the hope for recovery. (11) Of the robber who (cf. prev. n.) cannot be regarded as legal owner. (12) Who is much stronger than a thief and recovery from whom is impossible. (13) A weaker man from whom recovery of the article is quite possible. (14) Cf. prev. n.

UNCLEANNESS AND ITS OWNER THEN INTENDED IT TO BE USED FOR STRAPS OR SANDALS[1] IT BECOMES CLEAN AS SOON AS HE PUT THE KNIFE INTO IT; SO R. JUDAH. BUT THE SAGES RULED: IT DOES NOT BECOME CLEAN UNTIL HE HAS REDUCED ITS SIZE TO LESS THAN FIVE HANDBREADTHS. R. ELIEZER SON OF R. ZADOK RULED: EVEN IF ONE MADE A NAPKIN FROM THE HIDE[2] IT[3] REMAINS UNCLEAN,[4] BUT IF FROM A BOLSTER IT BECOMES CLEAN.[5]

(1) Cf. *supra* XXIV, 12. (2) That had contracted *midras* uncleanness. (3) Since it may be regarded as a small rug on which one can sit. (4) Since the change is but slight. (5) Though it is susceptible to future uncleanness.

KELIM

CHAPTER XXVII

MISHNAH 1. CLOTH IS SUSCEPTIBLE TO[1] FIVE FORMS[2] OF UNCLEANNESS; SACKING[3] IS SUSCEPTIBLE TO[1] FOUR; LEATHER TO[1] THREE; WOOD TO TWO; AND AN EARTHEN VESSEL TO ONE. AN EARTHEN VESSEL[4] IS SUSCEPTIBLE TO UNCLEANNESS [ONLY] AS A RECEPTACLE.[5] ANY EARTHEN VESSEL THAT HAS NO INNER PART IS NOT SUSCEPTIBLE TO UNCLEANNESS FROM[6] ITS OUTER PART.[7] WOOD IS SUBJECT TO AN ADDITIONAL FORM OF UNCLEANNESS IN THAT IT IS ALSO SUSCEPTIBLE TO UNCLEANNESS[8] AS A SEAT.[9] SIMILARLY A TABLET WHICH HAS NO RIM IS SUSCEPTIBLE TO UNCLEANNESS IF IT IS A WOODEN OBJECT AND INSUSCEPTIBLE IF IT IS AN EARTHEN ONE. LEATHER IS SUSCEPTIBLE TO AN ADDITIONAL FORM OF UNCLEANNESS IN THAT IT IS ALSO SUSCEPTIBLE TO THE UNCLEANNESS OF OHEL.[10] SACKING HAS AN ADDITIONAL FORM OF UNCLEANNESS IN THAT IT IS SUSCEPTIBLE TO UNCLEANNESS AS WOVEN WORK.[11] CLOTH HAS AN ADDITIONAL FORM OF UNCLEANNESS IN THAT IT IS SUSCEPTIBLE TO UNCLEANNESS WHEN IT IS ONLY THREE BY THREE FINGERBREADTHS.[12]

MISHNAH 2. CLOTH IS SUSCEPTIBLE TO UNCLEANNESS

(1) Lit., 'on account of'. (2) Lit., 'names'. (3) Made of goats' hair and the like. (4) Here begins the illustration of the general statements just made. (5) However small it might be. Otherwise it is not susceptible to any form of uncleanness. (6) Lit., 'it has not'. (7) Even though its bottom is concave. (8) Even though it forms no receptacle. (9) On which a *zab* might sit. It must, however, have no less an area than three handbreadths square. (10) Whereby, if it forms the *ohel*, it becomes a 'father of uncleanness', however small its size (Elijah Wilna and L. contra Bert.). (11) However small its size might be; provided there was no intention to extend the texture. If it was intended to extend it the size must be no less than four handbreadths square. (12) Even if it was not woven.

OF MIDRAS WHEN IT IS[1] THREE HANDBREADTHS SQUARE, AND TO CORPSE UNCLEANNESS[2] WHEN IT IS THREE FINGER-BREADTHS SQUARE.[3] SACKING WHEN IT IS FOUR HAND-BREADTHS SQUARE, LEATHER FIVE HANDBREADTHS SQUARE AND MATTING SIX HANDBREADTHS SQUARE ARE EQUALLY SUSCEPTIBLE TO BOTH MIDRAS AND CORPSE UNCLEANNESS. R. MEIR RULED: WHAT REMAINS OF SACKING IS SUSCEPTIBLE TO UNCLEANNESS IF IT IS FOUR HANDBREADTHS, BUT WHEN IN ITS FIRST CONDITION IT BECOMES SUSCEPTIBLE ONLY AFTER ITS MANUFACTURE IS COMPLETED.

MISHNAH 3. IF ONE MADE UP A PIECE OF MATERIAL FROM TWO HANDBREADTHS OF CLOTH AND ONE OF SACKING, OR OF THREE OF SACKING AND ONE OF LEATHER, OR FOUR OF LEATHER AND ONE OF MATTING, IT IS NOT SUSCEPTIBLE TO UNCLEANNESS.[4] IF, HOWEVER, THE PIECE OF MATERIAL WAS MADE UP OF FIVE HANDBREADTHS OF MATTING AND ONE OF LEATHER, OR FOUR OF LEATHER AND ONE OF SACKING, OR THREE OF SACKING AND ONE OF CLOTH, IT IS SUSCEPTIBLE TO UNCLEANNESS. THIS IS THE GENERAL RULE: IF THE MATERIAL ADDED IS SUBJECT TO GREATER RESTRICTIONS[5] IT[6] IS SUSCEPTIBLE TO UNCLEANNESS,[7] BUT IF THE MATERIAL ADDED WAS SUBJECT TO LESSER RESTRICTIONS[8] IT[6] IS NOT SUSCEPTIBLE.[9]

(1) Lit., 'on account of'. (2) And also to any uncleanness other than *midras*. (3) This, however, applies only to the remnant of a cloth made of wool or flax. For one made of other materials a remnant having a minimum of three hand-breadths square is required even in the case of corpse uncleanness. New cloth is susceptible to all forms of uncleanness other than *midras* whatever its size. (4) Of *midras*. If, however, the piece of material came in contact with corpse uncleanness it remains clean if the contact was with the sacking only (since it is smaller than the prescribed minimum), but if the contact was with the cloth, only the sacking remains clean while the cloth contracts the uncleanness. (5) Than the material to which it was added. (6) The piece of combined materials. (7) Since the latter may well make up the minimum prescribed for the former. (8) Than the material to which it was added. (9) Because the latter whose prescribed minimum is greater cannot be effective when the total area of the material is less than that minimum.

MISHNAH 4. IF FROM ANY OF THESE[1] A PIECE ONE HANDBREADTH SQUARE WAS CUT OFF[2] IT IS SUSCEPTIBLE TO UNCLEANNNESS.[3] [IF A PIECE] ONE HANDBREADTH SQUARE[2] [WAS CUT OFF] FROM THE BOTTOM OF A BASKET IT IS SUSCEPTIBLE TO UNCLEANNESS.[3] [IF IT WAS CUT] FROM THE SIDES OF THE BASKET, R. SIMEON RULES THAT IT IS NOT SUSCEPTIBLE TO UNCLEANNESS, BUT THE SAGES RULE THAT WHEREVER A SQUARE HANDBREADTH IS CUT OFF[4] IT IS SUSCEPTIBLE TO UNCLEANNESS.

MISHNAH 5. WORN-OUT PIECES OF A SIFTER OR A SIEVE THAT WERE ADAPTED FOR USE AS A SEAT, R. AKIBA RULES ARE SUSCEPTIBLE TO UNCLEANNESS, BUT THE SAGES RULE THAT THEY ARE NOT SUSCEPTIBLE UNLESS THEIR ROUGH ENDS WERE CUT OFF.[5] A CHILD'S STOOL THAT HAS LEGS, EVEN THOUGH IT IS LESS THAN A HANDBREADTH HIGH, IS SUSCEPTIBLE TO UNCLEANNESS.[6] A CHILD'S SHIRT, R. ELIEZER RULES, IS SUSCEPTIBLE TO UNCLEANNESS HOWEVER SMALL IT MAY BE; BUT THE SAGES RULED: IT IS SUSCEPTIBLE ONLY IF IT IS OF THE PRESCRIBED SIZE[7] AND MEASURED WHEN DOUBLED.[8]

MISHNAH 6. THE FOLLOWING ARE MEASURED[9] WHEN DOUBLED:[8] SOCKS, LONG STOCKINGS, DRAWERS, A CAP AND A MONEY-BELT. AS REGARDS A PATCH SEWN ON THE HEM,[10] IF IT WAS UNDOUBLED[11] IT IS MEASURED UNDOUBLED,[12] BUT

(1) Four materials mentioned in the previous Mishnah. (2) For use as a seat. (If it was cut off for the purpose of lying upon, the minimum area for susceptibility to uncleanness is three handbreadths). (3) As a seat (cf. prev. n.). (4) Even if from the sides of a basket. (5) To render them fit for a seat. (6) An adult's stool must be no less than one handbreadth high if it is to be susceptible to uncleanness. (7) As laid down *supra* Mishnah 2. (8) So as to allow the prescribed length of material both for the front and the back. (9) To ascertain whether they are of the prescribed size of three fingerbreadths square in respect of corpse uncleanness or three handbreadths square in respect of *midras*. (10) Around the neck. (11) Having been patched on one side of the hem only. (12) The prescribed size being the one in Mishnah 2 *supra*.

IF IT WAS DOUBLED IT IS MEASURED WHEN DOUBLED.[1]

MISHNAH 7. IF A PIECE OF CLOTH WAS WOVEN TO THE EXTENT OF THREE [HANDBREADTHS] SQUARE, WHEN IT CONTRACTED MIDRAS UNCLEANNESS, AND AFTER THE ENTIRE PIECE WAS COMPLETED ONE REMOVED[2] A SINGLE THREAD FROM THE ORIGINAL PART,[3] IT[4] IS RELEASED FROM MIDRAS UNCLEANNESS BUT[5] IS STILL UNCLEAN FROM CONTACT WITH MIDRAS UNCLEANNESS. IF A THREAD WAS REMOVED FROM THE ORIGINAL PART[3] AND THEN ALL THE CLOTH WAS FINISHED, IT[6] IS STILL UNCLEAN FROM CONTACT WITH MIDRAS UNCLEANNESS.

MISHNAH 8. SIMILARLY[7] IF A PIECE OF CLOTH WAS WOVEN TO THE EXTENT OF THREE [FINGERBREADTHS] SQUARE, WHEN IT CONTRACTED CORPSE UNCLEANNESS, AND AFTER THE ENTIRE PIECE WAS FINISHED ONE REMOVED[8] A SINGLE THREAD FROM ITS ORIGINAL PART,[9] IT[4] IS RELEASED FROM CORPSE UNCLEANNESS[10] BUT[11] IS STILL UNCLEAN FROM CONTACT WITH CORPSE UNCLEANNESS. IF A THREAD WAS REMOVED FROM THE ORIGINAL PART[9] AND THEN ALL THE CLOTH WAS FINISHED IT REMAINS CLEAN; FOR THE SAGES HAVE RULED: IF A PIECE OF THREE [FINGERBREADTHS] SQUARE IS LESSENED IT BECOMES CLEAN,[12] BUT IF ONE OF THREE HANDBREADTHS SQUARE IS LESSENED, EVEN THOUGH IT IS RELEASED FROM MIDRAS, IT IS STILL SUSCEPTIBLE TO ALL OTHER FORMS OF UNCLEANNESS.

(1) The length required being twice the size prescribed (cf. p. 129 n. 8). (2) Var. lec. inserts here 'the cloth, all the cloth is susceptible to *midras;* if one removed'. (3) The three handbreadths square which have contracted the *midras* uncleanness. (4) The entire cloth. (5) Since it was in contact with *midras* uncleanness. (6) As a connective. (7) Cf. prev. Mishnah. (8) Var. lec. inserts here 'the cloth, all the cloth is susceptible to corpse uncleanness; if one removed'. (9) The three fingerbreadths square which have contracted corpse uncleanness. (10) Since less than the prescribed minimum remained. (11) Having come in close contact with corpse uncleanness. (12) Since it can no longer serve any useful purpose.

MISHNAH 9. IF A SHEET THAT HAD CONTRACTED MIDRAS UNCLEANNESS WAS MADE[1] INTO A CURTAIN, IT IS RELEASED FROM MIDRAS UNCLEANNESS BUT IS STILL UNCLEAN FROM CONTACT WITH MIDRAS UNCLEANNESS. SAID R. JOSE: BUT WHAT MIDRAS UNCLEANNESS HAS THIS[2] TOUCHED![3] ONLY IF A ZAB HAD TOUCHED IT[4] IS IT UNCLEAN FROM CONTACT WITH A ZAB.

MISHNAH 10. IF A PIECE OF CLOTH THREE [HANDBREADTHS] SQUARE[5] WAS DIVIDED,[6] IT IS RELEASED FROM THE MIDRAS UNCLEANNESS BUT IS STILL UNCLEAN FROM CONTACT WITH MIDRAS UNCLEANNESS. SAID R. JOSE: BUT WHAT MIDRAS UNCLEANNESS HAS THIS TOUCHED![7] ONLY IF A ZAB HAD TOUCHED IT IS IT UNCLEAN FROM CONTACT WITH A ZAB.

MISHNAH 11. IF A PIECE OF CLOTH THREE [HANDBREADTHS] SQUARE [WAS FOUND] ON A RUBBISH HEAP IT MUST[8] BE BOTH SOUND AND CAPABLE OF WRAPPING UP SALT;[9] BUT [IF IT WAS FOUND] IN THE HOUSE IT NEED ONLY BE[10] EITHER SOUND OR CAPABLE OF WRAPPING UP SALT. HOW MUCH SALT MUST IT BE CAPABLE OF WRAPPING UP? A QUARTER OF A ḲAB. R. JUDAH STATED: THIS REFERS TO FINE SALT; BUT THE SAGES STATED: IT REFERS TO COARSE SALT. BOTH INTENDED TO RELAX THE LAW.[11] R. SIMEON RULED: THE LAW CONCERNING A PIECE OF CLOTH THREE [HANDBREADTHS] SQUARE ON A RUBBISH HEAP IS THE SAME

(1) By some adaptation which effected a change in it (cf. *supra* XX, 6.). (2) The curtain. (3) Obviously none, since the previous uncleanness of the sheet has disappeared with its change into a curtain. Hence it should be free from all uncleanness. (4) The curtain (Bert.), the sheet (L.). (5) That has contracted *midras* uncleanness. (6) And each part was smaller than the prescribed minimum. (7) Cf. *supra* n. 3 *mut. mut.* (8) Ii it is to be susceptible to *midras* uncleanness. (9) *Sc.* the texture must be closely woven. (10) If it is to be susceptible to *midras* uncleanness. (11) R. Judah insists on a closely woven texture which can hold fine salt, while the Sages insist on a sound material which can wrap up coarse salt.

AS THAT FOR A PIECE OF CLOTH THAT WAS THREE [FINGERBREADTHS] SQUARE IN A HOUSE.[1]

MISHNAH 12. [A PIECE OF CLOTH] THREE [HANDBREADTHS] SQUARE THAT WAS TORN[2] BECOMES INSUSCEPTIBLE TO UNCLEANNESS IF ON BEING PUT ON A STOOL ONE'S FLESH[3] WOULD[4] TOUCH THE STOOL; OTHERWISE IT REMAINS SUSCEPTIBLE TO UNCLEANNESS. [A PIECE OF CLOTH] THREE [FINGERBREADTHS] SQUARE ONE THREAD OF WHICH WAS WORN AWAY, OR ON WHICH A KNOT WAS FOUND, OR IN WHICH TWO THREADS RAN ALONGSIDE EACH OTHER, IS NOT SUSCEPTIBLE TO UNCLEANNESS. [A PIECE OF CLOTH] THREE [FINGERBREADTHS] SQUARE THAT WAS CAST ON THE RUBBISH HEAP BECOMES INSUSCEPTIBLE TO UNCLEANNESS. IF IT WAS TAKEN BACK AGAIN IT BECOMES SUSCEPTIBLE TO UNCLEANNESS. THROWING IT AWAY INVARIABLY RENDERS IT INSUSCEPTIBLE TO UNCLEANNESS AND TAKING IT BACK AGAIN RENDERS IT SUSCEPTIBLE TO UNCLEANNESS,[5] EXCEPT WHEN IT IS OF PURPLE OR FINE CRIMSON.[6] R. ELIEZER RULED: A PATCH OF NEW CLOTH IS ALSO SUBJECT TO THE SAME LAW. R. SIMEON RULED: ALL THESE MATERIALS[7] BECOME INSUSCEPTIBLE;[8] AND THE LATTER[9] HAVE BEEN MENTIONED [AS DISTINGUISHABLE FROM OTHERS] ONLY IN CONNECTION WITH THE RETURN OF LOST PROPERTY.[10]

(1) Both being susceptible to corpse, but not to *midras* uncleanness. (2) But the parts were not completely severed. (3) That of the man who sits on it. (4) Owing to the width of the tear. (5) Irrespective of the number of times this may have been repeated. (6) Being valuable materials they remain susceptible to uncleanness even when thrown on the rubbish heap. (7) Even the last mentioned. (8) If thrown on the rubbish heap. (9) Purple and fine crimson. (10) Being of greater value than other materials the finding of them even on a rubbish heap must be duly announced in order to afford the loser an opportunity of claiming them; v. B.M. II, 1.

KELIM

CHAPTER XXVIII

MISHNAH 1. [A PIECE OF CLOTH] THREE [FINGER-BREADTHS] SQUARE THAT[1] WAS STUFFED INTO A BALL OR WAS ITSELF MADE INTO A BALL BECOMES CLEAN.[2] BUT [A PIECE OF CLOTH] THREE [HANDBREADTHS] SQUARE THAT[3] WAS STUFFED INTO A BALL REMAINS UNCLEAN.[4] IF THE LATTER[3] WAS ITSELF MADE INTO A BALL IT BECOMES CLEAN[5] BECAUSE THE SEWING REDUCES ITS SIZE.

MISHNAH 2. [A PIECE OF CLOTH] LESS THAN THREE [HANDBREADTHS] SQUARE THAT WAS ADAPTED FOR THE PURPOSE OF STOPPING UP A HOLE IN A BATH HOUSE,[6] OF EMPTYING A COOKING-POT[7] OR OF WIPING WITH IT THE MILL STONES, WHETHER IT WAS OR WAS NOT KEPT IN READINESS FOR ANY SUCH USE,[8] IS SUSCEPTIBLE TO UNCLEANNESS; SO R. ELIEZER. R. JOSHUA RULED: WHETHER IT WAS OR WAS NOT KEPT IN READINESS IT IS NOT SUSCEPTIBLE TO UNCLEANNESS. R. AKIBA RULED: IF IT WAS KEPT IN READINESS IT IS SUSCEPTIBLE, AND IF IT WAS NOT KEPT IN READINESS IT IS NOT SUSCEPTIBLE.

MISHNAH 3. IF A PLASTER IS MADE OF CLOTH OR LEATHER IT IS NOT SUSCEPTIBLE TO UNCLEANNESS.[9] A[10]

(1) Having contracted corpse uncleanness. (2) Since it lost the status of cloth by becoming a ball or part of a ball. (3) After contracting *midras* uncleanness. (4) Owing to its comparatively large size its identity cannot be merged into that of the ball. (5) From *midras* uncleanness, but not from any other. *Aliter:* From all uncleanness (Rabad). (6) To prevent the escape of heat. (7) By holding it with the rag. (8) It was hung up on a nail to be ready for use, v. Shab. 29*b*. (9) Since the greasy substances with which it is smeared render it unfit for sitting on or for any other use. (10) Some edd. in parenthesis read, 'R. Jose ruled: On leather it is insusceptible to uncleanness'.

POULTICE IS INSUSCEPTIBLE TO UNCLEANNESS IF IT IS ON CLOTH,[1] BUT IF ON LEATHER IT IS SUSCEPTIBLE.[2] RABBAN SIMEON B. GAMALIEL RULED: EVEN IT IF WAS ON CLOTH THE LATTER REMAIN SUSCEPTIBLE TO UNCLEANNESS BECAUSE THE FORMER[3] CAN BE SHAKEN OFF.[4]

MISHNAH 4. SCROLL WRAPPERS, WHETHER THEY ARE ORNAMENTED WITH [EMBROIDERED] FIGURES OR NOT, ARE SUSCEPTIBLE TO UNCLEANNESS ACCORDING TO THE VIEW OF BETH SHAMMAI. BETH HILLEL RULED: THOSE THAT ARE ORNAMENTED WITH FIGURES ARE INSUSCEPTIBLE TO UNCLEANNESS,[5] BUT THOSE THAT ARE NOT ORNAMENTED ARE SUSCEPTIBLE. RABBAN GAMALIEL RULED: BOTH THE FORMER AND THE LATTER ARE INSUSCEPTIBLE.

MISHNAH 5. IF A HEAD-WRAP THAT[6] HAD CONTRACTED MIDRAS UNCLEANNESS WAS WRAPPED AROUND A SCROLL, IT IS RELEASED FROM MIDRAS UNCLEANNESS[7] BUT REMAINS SUSCEPTIBLE TO CORPSE UNCLEANNESS. A SKIN[8] THAT WAS MADE INTO A RUG[9] OR A LEATHER RUG THAT WAS MADE INTO A SKIN[8] BECOMES CLEAN.[10] A SKIN[8] THAT WAS MADE INTO A [SHEPHERD'S] WALLET OR A [SHEPHERD'S] WALLET THAT WAS MADE INTO A SKIN; OR A CUSHION COVER THAT WAS MADE INTO A SHEET OR A SHEET THAT WAS MADE INTO A

(1) Since the greasy substances with which it is smeared render it unfit for sitting on or for any other use. (2) Because leather can be used even after a poultice has been on it. (3) The ingredients of the poultice when they dry up. (4) From the cloth which in consequence can again be used. (5) Since the embroidered figures are sufficient evidence that the wrapper was intended for the ornamentation only and not for any man's personal use, v. *supra* XVI, *ad finem*. (6) Being suitable to sit upon; cf. *supra* XXIV, 16. (7) If it was set aside for exclusive use with the scroll. (8) Intended for the holding of liquids. (9) By being cut open and spread out for the purpose of sitting on it. (10) *Sc.* it is released from any *midras* uncleanness it may have contracted, because the adaptation is regarded as the breaking up of the former vessel. It remains, however, susceptible to future *midras* uncleanness.

CUSHION COVER; OR A BOLSTER COVER THAT WAS MADE INTO A PLAIN SHEET OR A PLAIN SHEET THAT WAS MADE INTO A BOLSTER COVER, REMAINS UNCLEAN. THIS IS THE GENERAL RULE: ANY OBJECT THAT HAS BEEN CHANGED INTO ONE OF THE SAME CLASS[1] REMAINS UNCLEAN, BUT IF INTO ONE OF ANOTHER CLASS IT BECOMES CLEAN.

MISHNAH 6. IF A PATCH[2] WAS SEWN ON TO A BASKET,[3] THE LATTER[4] CONVEYS[5] ONE GRADE OF UNCLEANNESS[6] AND[7] ONE OF UNFITNESS.[8] IF IT WAS SEVERED FROM THE BASKET, THE LATTER CONVEYS ONE GRADE OF UNCLEANNESS AND ONE OF UNFITNESS, BUT THE PATCH[9] BECOMES CLEAN.[10] IF IT WAS SEWN ON TO CLOTH[11] THE LATTER[12] CONVEYS TWO GRADES OF UNCLEANNESS[13] AND ONE OF UNFITNESS.[7] IF IT WAS SEVERED FROM THE CLOTH, THE LATTER[14] CONVEYS[5] ONE GRADE OF UNCLEANNESS[6] AND[7] ONE OF UNFITNESS, WHILE THE PATCH CONVEYS TWO GRADES OF UNCLEANNESS AND ONE OF UNFITNESS.[15] THE SAME LAW[16] APPLIES ALSO WHERE A PATCH WAS SEWN ON TO SACKING OR LEATHER; SO R. MEIR. R. SIMEON RULES THAT THEY[17] ARE CLEAN.[18]

(1) Lit., 'to his name'; a skin and a wallet, for instance. are used for similar purposes and so also is a cushion cover and a sheet. (2) That contracted *midras* uncleanness. (3) Which, not being suitable for *midras*, cannot contract such an uncleanness. (4) As a first grade of uncleanness owing to its contact with the patch that was (before it was sewn on to it) suffering from *midras* uncleanness. (5) To foodstuffs. (6) Rendering them unclean in the second grade. (7) If the second grade came in contact with *terumah*. (8) I.e., the uncleanness is not carried over to a further remove. (9) As any other part that is severed from the basket. (10) If it was not intended for sitting on. If it was so intended it is again susceptible in the future to *midras* uncleanness. (11) Which is itself susceptible to *midras*. (12) The cloth as well as the patch on it, since the use of the patch has not been changed to one of a different class, having first been a piece of cloth and being now again part of a piece of cloth. (13) Being a 'father of uncleanness' it causes a first grade of uncleanness which, in turn, causes a second grade. (14) V. *supra* n. 3. (15) As laid down *supra* XVIII, 7. (16) That is applicable to a patch on cloth. (17) Sacking and leather. (18) Since they are not of the same kind of material as the patch they

R. JOSE RULED: IF IT WAS SEWN ON LEATHER IT BECOMES CLEAN; BUT IF ON SACKING IT REMAINS UNCLEAN, SINCE THE LATTER IS A WOVEN MATERIAL.[1]

MISHNAH 7. THE PRESCRIBED MINIMUM OF THREE [FINGERBREADTHS] SQUARE OF WHICH THEY HAVE SPOKEN[2] IS EXCLUSIVE OF THE HEM; SO R. SIMEON. BUT THE SAGES RULED: EXACTLY THREE [FINGERBREADTHS] SQUARE.[3] IF A PATCH[4] WAS SEWN ON TO A CLOTH BY ONE SIDE ONLY,[5] IT CANNOT BE REGARDED AS A CONNECTIVE.[6] IF IT WAS SEWN ON BY TWO OPPOSITE SIDES, IT IS A CONNECTIVE.[7] IF IT WAS SEWN ON IN THE SHAPE OF A GAMMA,[8] R. AKIBA RULES THAT THE CLOTH IS UNCLEAN, BUT THE SAGES RULE THAT IT IS CLEAN. R. JUDAH STATED: THIS[9] APPLIES ONLY TO A CLOAK,[10] BUT IN THE CASE OF A SHIRT[11] THE PATCH IS REGARDED AS A CONNECTIVE IF IT WAS SEWN ON ONLY BY ITS UPPER SIDE,[12] BUT IF BY ITS LOWER SIDE IT IS NO CONNECTIVE.[8]

MISHNAH 8. POOR MEN'S CLOTHES, THOUGH MADE UP OF PIECES NONE OF WHICH MEASURES THREE [FINGERBREADTHS] SQUARE, ARE SUSCEPTIBLE TO MIDRAS UNCLEANNESS.[13] IF A CLOAK BEGAN TO BE TORN, AS SOON AS ITS GREATER PART IS AFFECTED [THE FRAGMENTS] ARE

are to be treated under the law that applies to a basket on which a patch was sewn.

(1) And is thus of the same kind as the patch. (2) In regard to cloth that came in contact with a dead creeping thing or carrion, or that was leprous. (3) Inclusive of the hem. (4) That was three handbreadths square and had contracted *midras* uncleanness. (5) The other three sides remaining unsewn and detached from the cloth. (6) And the larger cloth remains clean. (7) Cf. prev. n. *mut. mut.* (8) *Sc.* by two adjacent sides. (9) That if the patch was sewn on by one side only it is no connective. (10) Which may also be put on upside down so that the patch falls back and exposes the tear. (11) Which cannot be worn upside down. (12) Since in this case the patch always remains in position and covers up the tear. (13) Because the garment as a whole measures no less than three handbreadths square.

NOT REGARDED AS JOINED.[1] EXCEPTIONALLY THICK OR THIN MATERIALS[2] ARE NOT GOVERNED BY THE PRESCRIBED MINIMUM OF THREE [FINGERBREADTHS] SQUARE.[3]

MISHNAH 9. A PORTER'S PAD[4] IS SUSCEPTIBLE TO MIDRAS UNCLEANNESS. A WINE FILTER[5] IS NOT SUSCEPTIBLE TO UNCLEANNESS AS A SEAT.[6] AN OLD WOMAN'S HAIR-NET[7] IS SUSCEPTIBLE TO UNCLEANNESS AS A SEAT.[8] A HARLOT'S SHIRT WHICH IS WOVEN LIKE NET WORK IS NOT SUSCEPTIBLE TO UNCLEANNESS.[9] A GARMENT MADE OF A FISHING NET IS NOT SUSCEPTIBLE TO UNCLEANNESS;[9] BUT ONE MADE OF ITS NETWORK BAG IS SUSCEPTIBLE. R. ELIEZER B. JACOB RULED: EVEN IF A GARMENT IS MADE OUT OF A FISHING NET BUT IS MADE DOUBLE IT IS SUSCEPTIBLE TO UNCLEANNESS.[10]

MISHNAH 10. A HAIR-NET THAT ONE BEGAN TO MAKE FROM ITS HEM REMAINS INSUSCEPTIBLE TO UNCLEANNESS UNTIL ITS BOTTOM SECTION IS FINISHED; AND IF ONE BEGAN FROM ITS BOTTOM SECTION, IT REMAINS INSUSCEPTIBLE TO UNCLEANNESS UNTIL ITS HEM IS FINISHED. ITS HEAD BAND IS SUSCEPTIBLE TO UNCLEANNESS IN ITSELF.[11] ITS STRINGS ARE SUSCEPTIBLE TO UNCLEANNESS AS CONNECTIVES.[12] A HAIR-NET THAT IS TORN BECOMES INSUSCEPTIBLE TO UNCLEANNESS IF IT CANNOT CONTAIN THE GREATER PART OF THE HAIR.

(1) If one of them, e.g., contracts an uncleanness the other remains clean. (2) Felt or silk, for instance. (3) Their prescribed minimum in regard to corpse uncleanness being three handbreadths square, as pieces of lesser size cannot in their case be put to any use. (4) Used as a protection for his shoulders or back. (5) Made of a textile. (6) Being soiled with lees no one is likely to sit on it. (7) That is also in regular use for sitting upon. (8) If, however, it is not intended for sitting upon it is not susceptible. (9) Of *midras;* though one can sit on it. As, owing to its holes, it is not suitable for its primary function (a proper article of dress) it loses also its secondary function (seat). (10) Because the doubling prevents the exposure of the body, and the garment can be properly worn. (11) Since it can be removed from one hair-net to another. (12) If the net contracts uncleanness the strings are equally affected, and *vice versa.*

KELIM

CHAPTER XXIX

MISHNAH 1. THE FRINGES[1] OF A SHEET, A SCARF, A HEAD-WRAP AND A FELT CAP ARE REGARDED AS CONNECTIVES[2] UP TO A LENGTH OF SIX FINGERBREADTHS;[3] THOSE OF AN UNDERGARMENT UP TO TEN [FINGERBREADTHS]. THE FRINGES OF A THICK CLOAK, A VEIL, A SHIRT, OR A LIGHT CLOAK ARE REGARDED AS CONNECTIVES UP TO A LENGTH OF THREE FINGERBREADTHS. THE FRINGES[1] OF AN OLD WOMAN'S HEAD-WRAP, OF THE FACE WRAPS OF THE ARABS, OF THE CILICIAN GOAT'S-HAIR CLOTH, OF A MONEY-BELT, OF A TURBAN OR OF A CURTAIN ARE REGARDED AS CONNECTIVES WHATSOEVER THEIR LENGTH MAY BE.

MISHNAH 2. THREE WOOLLEN BOLSTER-COVERS,[4] SIX LINEN ONES,[4] THREE SHEETS,[4] TWELVE HANDKERCHIEFS,[4] TWO ARM-CLOTHS,[4] ONE SHIRT,[5] ONE CLOAK,[5] OR ONE WINTER-CLOAK,[5] ARE REGARDED AS CONNECTIVES IN RESPECT OF BOTH UNCLEANNESS[6] AND SPRINKLING.[7] IF THEY EXCEED THIS NUMBER THEY ARE REGARDED AS CONNECTIVES IN RESPECT OF UNCLEANNESS[6] BUT NOT IN RESPECT OF SPRINKLING.[8] R. JOSE RULED. NOT EVEN IN RESPECT OF UNCLEANNESS.[9]

(1) *Sc.* the lose threads of the warp hanging from the ends of the garments enumerated. (2) So that where the fringe contracted uncleanness the main garment also contracts it, and *vice versa.* (3) Beyond this length the fringes are insusceptible to uncleanness and, therefore, they neither convey to, nor contract from the garment any uncleanness. (4) That were stitched together by the fuller or kept together in the weaving by the threads of the warp. (5) However large it may be. (6) If one of them contracted it, all become unclean. (7) At the conclusion of a period of uncleanness. If only one of them was sprinkled upon (cf. Num. XIX, 18) all become clean. (8) Cf. prev. n. *mut. mut.* Only the one that was sprinkled upon becomes clean. (9) *Sc.* they are always treated as separate and independent units.

MISHNAH 3. THE CORD OF [THE COMMON] PLUMMET[1] IS REGARDED AS A CONNECTIVE[2] UP TO A LENGTH OF TWELVE [CUBITS];[3] THAT OF THE CARPENTERS' PLUMMET, UP TO EIGHTEEN [CUBITS];[3] AND THAT OF THE BUILDERS' PLUMMET[4] UP TO FIFTY CUBITS. THE PARTS THAT EXCEED THESE LENGTHS, EVEN IF IT WAS DESIRED TO RETAIN THEM,[5] REMAIN INSUSCEPTIBLE TO UNCLEANNESS.[6] THE CORD OF THE PLUMMET OF PLASTERERS OR MOULDERS IS REGARDED AS A CONNECTIVE WHATSOEVER ITS LENGTH.

MISHNAH 4. THE CORD OF THE BALANCES OF GOLDSMITHS[7] OR THE WEIGHERS OF FINE PURPLE IS REGARDED AS A CONNECTIVE UP TO A LENGTH OF THREE FINGERBREADTHS;[8] THE SHAFT OF AN AXE BEHIND THE GRIP, UP TO A LENGTH OF THREE FINGERBREADTHS.[6] R. JOSE RULED: IF THE LENGTH BEHIND THE GRIP IS NO LESS THAN ONE HANDBREADTH THE ENTIRE SHAFT IS INSUSCEPTIBLE TO UNCLEANNESS.[9]

MISHNAH 5. THE CORD OF THE BALANCES OF SHOPKEEPERS[7] OR HOUSEHOLDERS IS REGARDED AS A CONNECTIVE UP TO A LENGTH OF ONE HANDBREADTH;[8] THE SHAFT OF AN AXE IN FRONT OF THE GRIP, UP TO ONE HANDBREADTH; THE PROJECTION[10] OF THE SHAFT OF A PAIR OF COMPASSES, UP TO ONE HANDBREADTH; THAT OF THE SHAFT OF THE STONE-MASONS' CHISEL, ONE HANDBREADTH.

MISHNAH 6. THE CORD OF THE BALANCES OF WOOL-

(1) Used in the construction of small buildings. (2) With the plummet. If the plummet contracted uncleanness only the length of line given also becomes unclean; but if uncleanness touches any part beyond this length, the main portion of the plummet remains clean. (3) *Aliter:* Handbreadths. (4) Used in the construction of big buildings. (5) For practical use. (6) Since only that part which is essential for ordinary use may be regarded as a connective. (7) Whereby the beam is suspended or held. (8) If the balance contracted uncleanness that length of cord also becomes unclean. (9) Since such a shaft renders the axe useless for work and would eventually be entirely discarded. (10) Lit., 'remnants'.

DEALERS[1] OR OF GLASS-WEIGHERS IS REGARDED AS A CONNECTIVE UP TO A LENGTH OF TWO HANDBREADTHS; THE SHAFT OF A MILLSTONE CHISEL, UP TO A LENGTH OF TWO HANDBREADTHS; THE SHAFT OF THE BATTLE-AXE OF THE LEGIONS, UP TO A LENGTH OF TWO HANDBREADTHS; THE SHAFT OF THE GOLDSMITHS' HAMMER, UP TO A LENGTH OF TWO HANDBREADTHS; AND THAT OF THE BLACKSMITHS' HAMMER, UP TO THREE HANDBREADTHS.

MISHNAH 7. THE REMNANT OF THE SHAFT OF AN OX-GOAD[2] AT ITS UPPER END[3] IS REGARDED AS A CONNECTIVE TO A LENGTH OF FOUR [HANDBREADTHS];[4] THE SHAFT OF A SPADE, TO A LENGTH OF FOUR [HANDBREADTHS]; THE SHAFT OF A WEEDING-SPADE, TO FIVE HANDBREADTHS; THE SHAFT OF A SMALL HAMMER, TO FIVE HANDBREADTHS; THAT OF A COMMON HAMMER, TO SIX HANDBREADTHS; THE SHAFT OF AN AXE USED FOR SPLITTING WOOD OR OF ONE USED FOR DIGGING, TO SIX [HANDBREADTHS]; AND THE SHAFT OF THE STONE-TRIMMERS' AXE, UP TO SIX HANDBREADTHS.

MISHNAH 8. THE REMNANT OF THE SHAFT OF AN OX GOAD[2] AT ITS LOWER END[5] IS REGARDED AS A CONNECTIVE TO A LENGTH OF SEVEN HANDBREADTHS; THE SHAFT OF THE TROWEL OF HOUSEHOLDERS—BETH SHAMMAI RULED: TO A LENGTH OF SEVEN [HANDBREADTHS], AND BETH HILLEL RULED: TO ONE OF EIGHT [HANDBREADTHS]; THAT OF THE PLASTERERS—BETH SHAMMAI RULED: NINE [HANDBREADTHS] AND BETH HILLEL RULED: TEN [HANDBREADTHS]. ANY PARTS EXCEEDING THESE LENGTHS, IF IT WAS DESIRED TO RETAIN IT, IS ALSO SUSCEPTIBLE TO UNCLEANNESS.[6] THE SHAFTS OF FIRE INSTRUMENTS[7] ARE SUSCEPTIBLE TO UNCLEANNESS WHATSOEVER THEIR LENGTH.

(1) Whereby the beam is suspended or held. (2) That was broken. (3) The part adjacent to the pointed end of the goad (cf. *supra* XXV, 2). (4) Beyond that and beyond seven handbreadths from the broad blade the shaft is insusceptible to all uncleanness. (5) That part that is adjacent to the broad blade (cf. n. 3). (6) As a connective. (7) A spit, for instance.

KELIM

CHAPTER XXX

MISHNAH 1. AMONG GLASS-WARE THOSE THAT ARE FLAT ARE NOT SUSCEPTIBLE TO UNCLEANNESS AND THOSE THAT FORM RECEPTACLES ARE SUSCEPTIBLE.[1] AFTER THEY ARE BROKEN THEY BECOME CLEAN;[2] AND IF ONE AGAIN MADE UTENSILS OF THEM THEY BECOME HENCEFORTH SUSCEPTIBLE TO UNCLEANNESS. A GLASS TRAY OR A FLAT DISH IS NOT SUSCEPTIBLE TO UNCLEANNESS. IF THEY HAVE A RIM THEY ARE SUSCEPTIBLE. THE CONCAVE BOTTOM OF A GLASS[3] BOWL OR PLATE[3] WHICH WAS ADAPTED FOR USE REMAINS INSUSCEPTIBLE TO UNCLEANNESS.[4] IF THEY WERE POLISHED OR SCRAPED WITH A FILE THEY BECOME SUSCEPTIBLE TO UNCLEANNESS.[5]

MISHNAH 2. A MIRROR IS INSUSCEPTIBLE TO UNCLEANNESS. A TRAY[6] THAT WAS MADE INTO A MIRROR REMAINS SUSCEPTIBLE, BUT IF IT WAS ORIGINALLY MADE TO SERVE AS A MIRROR[7] IT IS INSUSCEPTIBLE.[8] A SPOON[6] THAT IS LAID ON A TABLE IS SUSCEPTIBLE TO UNCLEANNESS IF IT CAN HOLD ANYTHING WHATSOEVER; BUT IF IT CANNOT DO SO,[9] R. AKIBA RULES THAT IT IS SUSCEPTIBLE,[10] AND R. JOḤANAN B. NURI RULES THAT IT IS INSUSCEPTIBLE.[11]

MISHNAH 3. A CUP[6] THE GREATER PART OF WHICH IS BROKEN OFF IS INSUSCEPTIBLE TO UNCLEANNESS. IF IT

(1) Cf. *supra* II, 1; XV, 1. (2) Even where they were formerly unclean. (3) That was broken. (4) Since the rough edges of the broken sides constitute a source of danger. (5) Cf. prev. n. *mut. mut.* (6) Of glass. (7) Even though it had a receptacle. (8) Since the receptacle was not intended to hold anything. (9) When its bottom, for instance, is concave. (10) Because this is the manner of its use. (11) As it cannot hold anything it cannot be regarded as a valid receptacle.

WAS BROKEN IN THREE PLACES[1] EXTENDING OVER ITS GREATER PART IT IS ALSO INSUSCEPTIBLE TO UNCLEANNESS. R. SIMEON RULED: IF IT LETS THE GREATER PART OF THE WATER LEAK OUT IT IS INSUSCEPTIBLE TO UNCLEANNESS. IF A HOLE APPEARED IN IT AND IT WAS MENDED WITH TIN OR PITCH IT IS STILL INSUSCEPTIBLE TO UNCLEANNESS.[2] R. JOSE RULED: IF WITH TIN[3] IT IS SUSCEPTIBLE TO UNCLEANNESS, BUT IF WITH PITCH IT IS INSUSCEPTIBLE.

MISHNAH 4. A SMALL FLASK WHOSE NECK[4] WAS REMOVED REMAINS SUSCEPTIBLE TO UNCLEANNESS,[5] BUT A LARGE ONE WHOSE NECK WAS REMOVED BECOMES INSUSCEPTIBLE.[6] ONE OF SPIKENARD OIL WHOSE NECK[4] WAS REMOVED BECOMES INSUSCEPTIBLE TO UNCLEANNESS, SINCE IT[7] SCRATCHES THE HAND. LARGE FLAGONS[8] WHOSE NECKS WERE REMOVED REMAIN SUSCEPTIBLE TO UNCLEANNESS, SINCE THEY ARE ADAPTED FOR THE USE OF HOLDING PICKLED FOODSTUFFS. A GLASS MILL-FUNNEL IS CLEAN.[9]

R. JOSE OBSERVED: 'BLESSED ART THOU, O KELIM; FOR, THOUGH THOU DIDST ENTER WITH UNCLEANNESS,[10] THOU ART GONE FORTH IN CLEANNESS'.[11]

מסכת כלים

הדרן עלך

והדרך עלן

(1) Var. lec., 'a third'. (2) Because neither sticks for long to glass. (3) Being a metal. (4) Lit., 'mouth'. (5) Since it can be easily carried on one hand without risk of injury it continues to be used as a receptacle for liquids. (6) Having to be carried with both hands there is the danger of receiving a cut from the broken edges in consequence of which the flask is unuseable. (7) By being carried, owing to the smallness of its size, within the hollow of one hand. (8) V. p. 141, n. 6. (9) *Sc.* insusceptible to uncleanness. Being open at the bottom it forms no valid receptacle. (10) 'FATHERS OF UNCLEANNESS' (*supra* I, 1). (11) 'MILL-FUNNEL IS CLEAN', the last ruling in the tractate. A moral lesson to man to endeavour to achieve purity of life before his time comes to depart from this world.

OHOLOTH

TRANSLATED INTO ENGLISH

WITH NOTES

BY

REV. H. BORNSTEIN, B.A.

INTRODUCTION

Oholoth, or Ahiloth ('Tents') deals mainly with those laws of ritual uncleanness deriving from Num. XIX, 14–16, which states that all objects overshadowed by a tent which contains a corpse are rendered unclean. The Sages expounding this section formulated a series of laws of overshadowing which was treated as a means of conveying uncleanness, similar to the processes of contact and carriage discussed in Kelim.

As the rites of purification fell to a great extent into abeyance after the destruction of the Second Temple, most of the laws of uncleanness treated of in this tractate lost their practical importance. In common therefore with all the other tractates of the Order, except Niddah, Oholoth is not provided with a Gemara. The rules of overshadowing contained therein, however, have still some application to-day, as members of the priestly tribe are enjoined to avoid defilement thereby.

The following is a brief summary of the contents as they apply to the main topic.

CHAPTER I. This does not deal with the theme of the tractate but contains various general rules concerning the transmission of the different degrees of uncleanness.

CHAPTER II introduces the subject by enumerating those things which originate an uncleanness capable of being conveyed by overshadowing. These include not only the corpse but also stated portions thereof. The minimum sizes of these portions are given. Several laws concerning the conveyance of uncleanness by contact and carriage are also given.

CHAPTER III discusses the problem arising when the aforesaid minimum sizes are divided. It also enunciates the rule that this uncleanness can emerge from the 'tent' through an aperture whose every dimension exceeds one handbreadth.

CHAPTER IV gives examples of the principle that it is the nature of uncleanness to issue forth into the open and not to enter a confined space.

CHAPTER V enumerates certain articles which can block up an aperture leading from one 'tent' to another and can thus form valid screens against uncleanness in conjunction with 'tent' walls.

CHAPTER VI deals with objects that can form 'tents' but not screens. Human beings and movable articles come into this category. The treatment of objects inside the wall or ceiling of a 'tent' is also discussed.

CHAPTER VII states that uncleannes lying in a confined space of less than one cubic handbreadth constitutes a closed grave whose effect is felt in all directions. A passage destined to be used for the removal of a corpse becomes immediately unclean and thereby enables all other exits to remain clean.

CHAPTER VIII gives a catalogue of objects of varying efficacy for conveying uncleanness and screening against it, this depending upon their own susceptibility.

CHAPTER IX illustrates the preceding by enumerating the laws appertaining to a wooden bee-hive placed in various positions.

CHAPTER X discusses the effect upon the laws of overshadowing a hatchway communicating between a room and an upper storey.

CHAPTER XI. A 'tent' may be divided through a split in its roof and the parts may be subsequently recombined through various agencies.

CHAPTER XII states the capacity for conveying uncleanness of boards, beams and columns in various positions.

CHAPTER XIII. The possibility of light holes serving as exits for uncleanness is discussed and also the minimum sizes of such apertures.

CHAPTER XIV states the position of wall projections with regard to the conveyance of uncleanness through overshadowing.

CHAPTER XV and CHAPTER XVI, 1 and 2 give examples of the conveyance of uncleanness by solid and other bodies.

CHAPTER XVI (2-end) deals with the nature of places suspected as having been used as graveyards.

CHAPTER XVII discusses the laws appertaining to the formation of a *beth peras* or grave-area, through the ploughing up of a grave.

CHAPTER XVIII gives various rules concerning a *beth peras*, three kinds of which are distinguished. It also states how such an area can be decontaminated. The laws of heathen dwellings are given and a discussion reported on the ritual cleanness of sundry towns and districts. The tractate concludes with a list of ten places to which the laws of heathen dwellings did not apply.

Oholoth contains information of the Rabbinic interest in many other studies to which they addressed themselves in the course of their elaboration of the rules of uncleanness. Their acquaintance with anatomy is exemplified by the catalogue of the 248 limbs of the human body (I, 8). An exceedingly important question of obstetrics is discussed in Chapter V, where other occurrences at childbirth are also mentioned. Reference to the surgeon's trepan is made in II, 3. Attention was paid to the behaviour of the blood flow at the time of death (III, 5), and note was taken of the products of the decomposition of a corpse (II, 1). An observation on the digestive rate of animals is quoted in XI, 7. Mathematics was also invoked to assist in the determination of questions of uncleanness and a somewhat crude solution of an involved computation is given in XII, 7.

Canon Danby's *'The Mishnah'* (which contains as Appendix IV the 'Rules of Uncleanness' by the Gaon of Vilna) and the German translation (Itzkowski-Kanel edition) have occasionally been consulted in the preparation of this work.

H. BORNSTEIN

OHOLOTH

CHAPTER I

MISHNAH I. [SOMETIMES] TWO [SERIES OF OBJECTS CAN] BE DEFILED THROUGH A CORPSE,[1] ONE BEING DEFILED WITH A SEVEN [DAYS'] DEFILEMENT AND ONE BEING DEFILED WITH A DEFILEMENT [LASTING TILL THE] EVENING.[2] [SOMETIMES] THREE [SERIES CAN] BE DEFILED THROUGH A CORPSE, TWO BEING DEFILED WITH A SEVEN [DAYS'] DEFILEMENT AND ONE WITH A DEFILEMENT [LASTING TILL THE] EVENING. [SOMETIMES] FOUR [SERIES CAN] BE DEFILED THROUGH A CORPSE, THREE BEING DEFILED WITH A SEVEN [DAYS'] DEFILEMENT AND ONE WITH A DEFILEMENT [LASTING TILL THE] EVENING. HOW [IS THE CASE OF] TWO [SERIES TO BE PRESENTED]? A PERSON WHO TOUCHES A CORPSE IS DEFILED WITH A SEVEN [DAYS'] DEFILEMENT AND A PERSON WHO TOUCHES HIM IS DEFILED WITH A DEFILEMENT [LASTING TILL THE] EVENING.[3]

MISHNAH 2. HOW [IS THE CASE OF] THREE [SERIES TO BE PRESENTED]? VESSELS TOUCHING A CORPSE[4] AND [OTHER]

1) In concatenation, the first series of objects being defiled directly by the corpse, the second by the first after this has ceased to be in contact with the corpse, and so on. (2) These two periods of defilement are mentioned in Num. XIX, 11 and 22. (3) A corpse possesses the highest power of defiling, being regarded as the originating source, the 'father of fathers' of defilement (אבי אבות הטומאה). It can confer a generating defilement 'a father of defilement' (אב הטומאה) on objects with which it comes into connection. Both these degrees of defilement require a cleansing period of seven days and hence are sometimes referred to as טומאת שבעה. The generating defilement can, in turn, confer a generated defilement (ולד הטומאה) of the first grade (ראשון לטומאה). This requires a cleansing period lasting only till sundown and hence is referred to as טומאת ערב. In our case, the first person acquires a generating defilement from the corpse and the second person a generated defilement from the first. (4) Vessels, apart from those of earthenware, (according to a special rule deduced from Num. XIX, 16 in Naz. 53b) acquire the same degree of defilement as the

VESSELS [TOUCHING THESE] VESSELS ARE DEFILED WITH A SEVEN [DAYS'] DEFILEMENT, THE THIRD [SERIES], WHETHER [CONSISTING OF] PERSONS OR VESSELS, IS DEFILED WITH A DEFILEMENT [LASTING TILL THE] EVENING.

MISHNAH 3. HOW [IS THE CASE OF] FOUR [SERIES TO BE PRESENTED]? VESSELS TOUCHING A CORPSE, A PERSON [TOUCHING THESE] VESSELS, AND [OTHER] VESSELS [TOUCHING THIS] PERSON,[1] ARE DEFILED WITH A SEVEN [DAYS'] DEFILEMENT. THE FOURTH [SERIES], WHETHER [CONSISTING OF] PERSONS OR VESSELS, IS DEFILED WITH A DEFILEMENT [LASTING TILL THE] EVENING. R. AKIBA SAID: I HAVE [A CASE OF] A FIFTH SERIES, [IF] A PEG[2] WAS FIXED IN A TENT, THE TENT,[3] THE PEG,[4] A PERSON TOUCHING THE PEG[5] AND VESSELS [TOUCHING] THE PERSON[6] ARE DEFILED WITH A SEVEN [DAYS'] DEFILEMENT. THE FIFTH [SERIES], WHETHER [CONSISTING OF] PERSONS OR VESSELS, IS DEFILED WITH A DEFILEMENT [LASTING TILL THE] EVENING. [THE SAGES] SAID TO HIM: THE TENT IS NOT RECKONED.[7]

MISHNAH 4. [BOTH] PERSONS AND VESSELS CAN BE DEFILED THROUGH A CORPSE.[8] A GREATER STRINGENCY [APPLIES IN SOME CASES] TO PERSONS THAN TO VESSELS AND [IN OTHER CASES] TO VESSELS THAN TO PERSONS; FOR WITH

source which defiles them; v. 'Ed., Sonc. ed., p. 10, n. 1. Here the first series becomes אבי אבות הטומאה and the second אב הטומאה and not until the third series do we get ולד הטומאה.

(1) These latter vessels become אב הטומאה through contact with the preceding person who has that degree of defilement. (2) שפוד Lit., 'a metal spit', explained by Bert. as a tent-peg and by Maim. as a tent-pole. (3) In which there is a corpse. The tent, if made of wool or flax, becomes אבי אבות הטומאה. (4) Also אבי אבות הטומאה even that portion of it outside the tent, because the peg is overshadowed by a tent containing a corpse. (5) He becomes a 'father of defilement'. (6) These too become like the source from which they contracted uncleanness, i.e., 'fathers of defilement'. (7) The peg, being in the tent containing a corpse, is to be regarded as acquiring its defilement, not from the tent, but directly from the corpse. Thus there are four series only. (8) This Mishnah summarizes the result of the three previous Mishnahs.

VESSELS [THERE CAN BE] THREE [SERIES OF DEFILEMENT],[1] WHEREAS WITH PERSONS [THERE CAN BE ONLY] TWO.[2] A GREATER STRINGENCY APPLIES TO PERSONS, FOR WHENEVER THEY FORM AN INTERMEDIATE [SERIES] THERE CAN BE FOUR [SERIES],[3] WHEREAS WHEN THEY DO NOT FORM AN INTERMEDIATE [SERIES] THERE CAN BE [ONLY] THREE.

MISHNAH 5. [BOTH] PERSONS AND GARMENTS CAN BE DEFILED BY A ZAB.[4] A GREATER STRINGENCY [APPLIES IN SOME CASES] TO PERSONS THAN TO GARMENTS AND [IN OTHER CASES] TO GARMENTS THAN TO PERSONS; FOR A PERSON WHO TOUCHES A ZAB CAN DEFILE GARMENTS,[5] WHEREAS GARMENTS THAT TOUCH A ZAB[6] CANNOT DEFILE [OTHER] GARMENTS. A GREATER STRINGENCY [APPLIES] TO GARMENTS, INASMUCH AS GARMENTS WHICH FORM THE SUPPORT OF A ZAB CAN DEFILE PERSONS,[7] WHEREAS A PERSON WHO FORMS THE SUPPORT OF A ZAB CANNOT DEFILE[8] [OTHER] PERSONS.

MISHNAH 6. A PERSON CANNOT DEFILE [AS A CORPSE] UNTIL HIS SOUL IS GONE FORTH, SO THAT EVEN IF HE HAS HIS ARTERIES SEVERED OR EVEN IF HE IS IN HIS LAST AGONIES HE[9] [STILL] MAKES LEVIRATE MARRIAGE OBLIGATORY[10] AND

(1) V. p. 149, n. 2. (2) V. p. 149, n. 1 end. (3) V. p. 149, n. 3. (4) A person who has a flux. The laws of a *zab* are given in Lev. XV, 1-15. As a 'father of defilement' he defiles persons (v. 7) and vessels (v. 12) by contact and other means. (5) I.e., the garments he is wearing when he touches the *zab*, according to an explicit statement in Lev XV, 7. (6) Becoming thereby 'generated defilement', they cannot confer defilement on other garments, since no garments can acquire defilement of a lesser grade than the first. (7) Lev. XV, 10. Garments upon which a *zab* rides can defile persons, i.e., they are אב. This applies to any garments upon which a *zab* is supported, i.e., upon which he stands, sits or lies, by which he is balanced or against which he leans, v. Zab II, 4. This is called *midras* (pressure-) defilement. (8) They themselves are only 'generated defilement'. (9) Even though he is manifestly dying, he is still not accounted a corpse and unclean, but living and possessing the full legal implications of a living man as in the four following cases. (10) On his childless brother's widow (v. Deut. XXV, 5). Until he actually passes away, or grants her *ḥaliẓah* (v. Deut. XXV, 9), she cannot marry another person.

LIBERATES FROM LEVIRATE MARRIAGE,[1] QUALIFIES [HIS MOTHER][2] FOR EATING TERUMAH[3] AND DISQUALIFIES [HIS MOTHER][4] FROM EATING TERUMAH. SIMILARLY IN THE CASE OF CATTLE OR WILD ANIMALS, THEY CANNOT DEFILE UNTIL THEIR SOUL IS GONE FORTH. IF THEIR HEADS HAVE BEEN CUT OFF, EVEN THOUGH THEY ARE MOVING CONVULSIVELY, THEY ARE UNCLEAN;[5] [MOVING, THAT IS TO SAY,] LIKE A LIZARD'S TAIL, WHICH MOVES CONVULSIVELY.

MISHNAH 7. MEMBERS[6] [OF THE BODY] HAVE NO [RESTRICTION AS TO] SIZE: EVEN LESS THAN AN OLIVE-SIZED PORTION OF A CORPSE, OR LESS THAN AN OLIVE-SIZED PORTION OF CARRION, OR LESS THAN A LENTIL-SIZED PORTION OF A REPTILE CAN DEFILE,[7] [EACH AFTER THE MANNER OF] THEIR RESPECTIVE DEFILEMENTS.[8]

MISHNAH 8. THERE ARE TWO HUNDRED AND FORTY-EIGHT MEMBERS IN A HUMAN BODY: THIRTY IN THE FOOT, [THAT IS] SIX TO EVERY TOE,[9] TEN IN THE ANKLE, TWO IN THE SHIN, FIVE IN THE KNEE, ONE IN THE THIGH, THREE IN THE HIP,[10] ELEVEN RIBS, THIRTY IN THE HAND, [THAT IS] SIX TO EVERY FINGER, TWO IN THE FORE-ARM, TWO IN THE ELBOW, ONE IN THE UPPER ARM AND FOUR IN THE SHOULDER, [THUS MAKING] ONE HUNDRED AND ONE ON THE ONE SIDE

(1) If he is the sole son, he can liberate his widowed mother from the obligation of marrying her *levir*. (2) If she, being herself the daughter of a non-priest, is the widow of a priest, since she may continue to eat *terumah* as long as she has a son (a priest). (3) Heave-offering, permitted to be eaten only by priests and their families. (4) If she, being the daughter of a priest, is the widow of a non-priest, since she is precluded from returning to her father's house to eat *terumah* as long as she has a son (a non-priest). (5) The movement is not a sign of life. (6) A unit part of the body having flesh, sinew and bone. (7) If these portions form complete members (v. p. 153, n. 4). (8) A member of a corpse by contact, carriage and overshadowing (v. p. 153, n. 4), that of carrion by contact and carriage (v. Kel. I, 2) and of a dead reptile by contact only (v. Kel. I, 1). (9) Reckoning from the ankle to the tip of the toe and in the case of the hand, from the wrist to the finger tips. (10) Socket of the hip bone.

[OF THE BODY] AND ONE HUNDRED AND ONE ON THE OTHER; THEN EIGHTEEN VERTEBRAE IN THE SPINE, NINE [MEMBERS] IN THE HEAD, EIGHT IN THE NECK, SIX IN THE KEY OF THE HEART,[1] AND FIVE IN THE GENITALS. EACH ONE [OF THESE MEMBERS] CAN DEFILE BY CONTACT, CARRIAGE OR OVERSHADOWING. WHEN IS THIS SO? WHEN THEY HAVE UPON THEM [THEIR] APPROPRIATE FLESH,[2] BUT IF THEY HAVE NOT [THEIR] APPROPRIATE FLESH UPON THEM, THEY[3] CAN DEFILE BY CONTACT AND CARRIAGE BUT CANNOT DEFILE[4] BY OVERSHADOWING.[5]

(1) The chest, so called according to Maim. because by its movements it causes the lungs to breathe upon the heart, opening the way for fresh air. (2) Defined (Kel. I, 5) as sufficient to form the basis of a growth of healing flesh if the member were part of a living organism. (3) But not members of a dead animal or reptile, which, if they have not sufficient flesh upon them, are clean. (4) For defilement by overshadowing, either a whole corpse or a whole member of a corpse is required (deduced from Num. XIX, 14, v. Maim.). (5) For a detailed account of the criticism to which this Mishnah has been subjected from a medical point of view and for an anatomical commentary on the terminology v. Katzenelsohn, I. L. *Talmud und Medizin* (Berlin 1928) pp. 234-303. On p. 257 he states, 'The Rabbinical numeration accords exactly with the number of bones in a seventeen year old male'. That the anatomical knowledge of the Rabbis was based on practical experiments by dissection is known from Bek. 45*a*: 'The disciples of R. Ishmael dissected the body of a prostitute who had been condemned to death by the government. By examination they found two hundred and fifty-two members'. Four were deducted as being found in the female but not in the male body, thus obtaining the figure 248. V. also *J.E.* VIII, p. 410 and Preuss, *Biblische u. Talmudische Medizin*, pp. 66f., who criticizes Katzenelsohn's views.

OHOLOTH

CHAPTER II

MISHNAH 1. THESE THINGS DEFILE[1] BY OVERSHADOWING: A CORPSE,[2] AN OLIVE-SIZED [PORTION OF FLESH] OF A CORPSE, AN OLIVE-SIZED [PORTION] OF NEẒEL,[3] A LADLEFUL[4] OF CORPSE-MOULD,[5] THE SPINE OR THE SKULL,[6] [ANY] MEMBER OF A CORPSE, OR [ANY] MEMBER [SEVERED] FROM A LIVING PERSON, A QUARTER[7] [OF A ḲAB] OF BONES COMPRISING THE STRUCTURAL MAJORITY[8] OR NUMERICAL MAJORITY, THE STRUCTURAL MAJORITY OR NUMERICAL MAJORITY [OF THE BONES] OF A CORPSE EVEN THOUGH THEY DO NOT AMOUNT TO A QUARTER [OF A ḲAB]; [ALL THESE] ARE UNCLEAN. HOW MANY [BONES] FORM THE NUMERICAL MAJORITY? ONE HUNDRED AND TWENTY-FIVE.

MISHNAH 2. [THE FOLLOWING LIKEWISE DEFILE:] A QUARTER[9] [OF A LOG] OF BLOOD,[10] A QUARTER [OF A LOG] OF MIXED BLOOD[11] FROM ONE CORPSE. R. AKIBA SAYS: EVEN FROM TWO CORPSES.[12] [WITH REGARD TO] THE BLOOD OF A CHILD THAT HAS COMPLETELY FLOWED FORTH, R. AKIBA

(1) Cf. Naz. VII, 2. (2) Explained in Naz. 50*a* as being that of an abortion, of less than olive-size. (3) Possibly from *nazal*, 'to melt'; explained in Naz. 50*a* as 'the flesh of a corpse that has coagulated, and liquid secretions from a corpse that has been heated and has congealed'. (4) *Tarwad;* Syrian 'large spoon or ladle'. 'Aruch on Kel. XVII, 12: 'the large ladle of physicians'. (5) Dust known to have originated solely from a corpse, e.g., dust from a corpse buried naked in a marble coffin (v. Naz. 51*a*). (6) Either of these, even if they had not their appropriate flesh. They are recognisably part of a human skeleton (Bert.). (7) One *ḳab* = four *logs* = twenty-four eggs, roughly equivalent to two litres. (8) Bones which make up the greater part of the skeleton's structure e.g., two shin bones and a thigh bone (Bek. 45*a*). (9) One *log* (cf. Lev. XIV, 10) = six eggs, roughly equivalent to half a litre. (10) That has flowed forth after death. (11) That has flowed forth partly before and partly after death (v. III, 5). (12) For the reasons of the dispute between R. Akiba and the Sages v. Ḥul. 72*a*.

SAYS: [IT DEFILES] BE IT OF ANY QUANTITY SOEVER,[1] BUT THE SAGES SAY: [THERE MUST BE] A QUARTER [OF A LOG].[2] [WITH REGARD TO] AN OLIVE-SIZED [PORTION] OF [CORPSE] WORMS WHETHER ALIVE OR DEAD, R. ELIEZER DECLARES [IT] UNCLEAN, LIKE THE FLESH [WHENCE IT COMES], BUT THE SAGES DECLARE [IT] CLEAN. [WITH REGARD TO] THE ASHES OF CREMATED PERSONS, R. ELIEZER DECLARES ITS [MINIMUM] QUANTITY [FOR DEFILEMENT TO BE] A QUARTER [OF A ḲAB], BUT THE SAGES DECLARE [THEM TO BE] CLEAN. A LADLEFUL AND [A LITTLE] MORE[3] OF GRAVE-DUST[4] IS UNCLEAN. R. SIMEON DECLARES [IT TO BE] CLEAN. A LADLEFUL OF CORPSE-MOULD KNEADED WITH WATER IS NOT [REGARDED AS] JOINED [INTO ONE MASS] FOR [THE PURPOSES OF] DEFILEMENT.[5]

MISHNAH 3. THE FOLLOWING DEFILE BY CONTACT AND CARRIAGE BUT NOT BY OVERSHADOWING: A BONE OF BARLEY-CORN SIZE,[6] EARTH FROM A FOREIGN COUNTRY,[7] A BETH PERAS,[8] A MEMBER OF A CORPSE, OR A MEMBER [SEVERED] FROM A LIVING PERSON WHICH HAS NO LONGER ITS APPROPRIATE FLESH, A SPINE OR A SKULL WHICH IS DEFICIENT.

(1) Making the case of blood analogous to that of bones, the majority of the skeleton defiling whatever size it be (v. *supra* 9). (2) Because one cannot tell, as one can in the case of bones, when the whole amount is present. (3) According to the text in most Mishnah editions. But the text printed in the Vilna editions of the Talmud read: 'A ladleful of corpse-mould and some grave-dust'. V. Nid. 27*b* where the same disputants differ over a case of a ladleful of corpse-mould and some (ordinary) dust. (4) Dust, mixed with blood and cadaverous secretions, from a marble coffin. A ladleful and more of this dust is presumed to contain a ladleful of mould. (5) So that if only a part of this ladleful were overshadowed, it could not convey tent-defilement. Human agency cannot effect a connection for defilement (v. *infra* III, 4). (6) Katzenelsohn (op. cit., p. 234, n. 1) suggests that this size may have been chosen because the *ossa sesamoidea*, the smallest human bones, are of barley-corn size. (7) Clods of foreign earth brought in to Palestine were decreed unclean by Jose b. Jo'ezer and Jose b. Joḥanan (Shab. 15*a*; v. also Naz. 54*b*). (8) A grave-area; a field into which human bones have been ploughed (v. *infra* XVIII, 1ff.). *Peras* according to Bert. from the root meaning 'to break' and according to Maim. from the meaning 'to spread' (viz., the area of uncleanness).

HOW MUCH IS [CONSIDERED] A DEFICIENCY IN THE SPINE? BETH SHAMMAI SAY: TWO VERTEBRAE, BUT BETH HILLEL SAY: EVEN ONE VERTEBRA. AND IN THE SKULL? BETH SHAMMAI SAY: [THE SIZE OF A] HOLE [MADE] BY A DRILL, BUT BETH HILLEL SAY: AS MUCH AS IF IT WERE TAKEN FROM A LIVING PERSON, HE WOULD DIE.[1] OF WHAT DRILL DID THEY SPEAK? OF THE SMALL ONE [USED] BY PHYSICIANS.[2] [THIS] IS THE OPINION OF R. MEIR, BUT THE SAGES SAY: OF THE LARGE ONE IN THE TEMPLE-CHAMBER.[3]

MISHNAH 4. THE COVERING STONE[4] AND THE BUTTRESSING[5] STONE [OF A GRAVE] DEFILE BY CONTACT AND OVERSHADOWING[6] BUT NOT BY CARRIAGE.[7] R. ELIEZER SAYS: THEY DO DEFILE BY CARRIAGE. R. JOSHUA SAYS: IF THERE IS GRAVE DUST BENEATH THEM, THEY DEFILE BY CARRIAGE, BUT IF NOT THEY DO NOT DEFILE BY CARRIAGE. WHAT IS THE 'BUTTRESSING STONE'? THAT UPON WHICH THE COVERING STONE IS SUPPORTED. THE STONE THAT SERVES AS BUTTRESS TO THE BUTTRESSING STONE, HOWEVER, IS CLEAN.

MISHNAH 5. THESE ARE CLEAN IF THEY ARE DEFICIENT:[8] AN OLIVE-SIZED [PORTION] OF A CORPSE, AN OLIVE-SIZED

(1) Explained in Bek. 37*b* as a portion the size of a *sela*' (a silver coin worth approx. four shillings). (2) The trepan. (3) An instrument making a hole the size of a *dupondium* (Roman penny); v. Kel. XVII, 12. (4) *Golel*. Maim. (in comment. on the M.) 'the stone (or wooden board etc.) covering a grave'. Rashi (on Keth. 4*b*) 'the cover of a coffin'. Perhaps from גלל 'to roll', hence a stone too heavy for lifting and needing to be rolled into position. Cf. אבן גלל Ezra V, 8. (5) *Dofek*, from root 'to strike, knock against', hence 'frame against which the *golel* knocks'. Preuss however (op. cit. p. 609) explains *golel* as the great rolling stone blocking the entrance to a cave tomb and *dofek* as the wedge holding it in position. (6) The grave is expressly included with the corpse in Num. XIX, 16 for defilement by contact, in the passage following the one giving rules for defilement by overshadowing. (7) Defilement by carriage is not taught in Scripture directly in connection with a corpse but is derived by the Rabbis *a fortiori* from carrion (v. Sifre on Num. XIX, 16). The Rabbis applied it to a corpse but not to the grave-stones. R. Eliezer here applies it even to the grave-stones. (8) I.e., if they fall short of the prescribed measure.

[PORTION] OF NEẒEL, A LADLEFUL OF CORPSE-MOULD, A QUARTER [OF A LOG] OF BLOOD, BONE OF THE SIZE OF A BARLEY-CORN, AND A MEMBER [SEVERED] FROM A LIVING PERSON, THE BONE OF WHICH [MEMBER] IS DEFICIENT.

MISHNAH 6. A BACKBONE OR A SKULL [MADE UP FROM THE BONES] OF TWO CORPSES, A QUARTER [OF A LOG] OF BLOOD FROM TWO CORPSES, A QUARTER [OF A ḲAB] OF BONES FROM TWO CORPSES, A MEMBER OF A CORPSE FROM TWO CORPSES, AND A MEMBER [SEVERED] FROM A LIVING PERSON, [SUCH A MEMBER BEING MADE UP] FROM TWO PERSONS, THESE R. AKIBA DECLARES UNCLEAN BUT THE SAGES DECLARE CLEAN.

MISHNAH 7. A BONE THE SIZE OF A BARLEY-CORN THAT IS DIVIDED INTO TWO, R. AKIBA DECLARES UNCLEAN BUT R. JOḤANAN B. NURI DECLARES CLEAN. R. JOḤANAN B. NURI SAID: THEY DID NOT SAY 'BONES' THE SIZE OF A BARLEY-CORN, BUT 'BONE' THE SIZE OF A BARLEY-CORN. A QUARTER [OF A ḲAB] OF BONES CRUSHED SO FINE THAT THERE IS NOT A SINGLE [BONE] OF BARLEY-CORN SIZE, R. SIMEON DECLARES CLEAN BUT THE SAGES UNCLEAN. A MEMBER [SEVERED] FROM A LIVING PERSON, WHICH [MEMBER] HAS BEEN DIVIDED INTO TWO IS CLEAN. R. JOSE DECLARES [IT] UNCLEAN; BUT HE AGREES THAT IF IT IS TAKEN FROM THE LIVING PERSON BY HALVES IT IS CLEAN.[1]

(1) Because the member has never been of the size to acquire uncleanness

OHOLOTH

CHAPTER III

MISHNAH 1. [WITH REGARD TO] ALL[1] OBJECTS DEFILING BY OVERSHADOWING,[2] IF THEY[3] WERE DIVIDED AND BROUGHT INTO A HOUSE, R. DOSA B. HARKINAS DECLARES CLEAN [WHATSOEVER IS IN THE HOUSE],[4] BUT THE SAGES DECLARE [IT] UNCLEAN. HOW [IS THIS DIFFERENCE OF OPINION TO BE UNDERSTOOD]? IF [A PERSON] TOUCHES TWO [PORTIONS] OF CARRION,[5] EACH OF THE SIZE OF HALF AN OLIVE, OR CARRIES THEM, OR, IN THE CASE OF A CORPSE, IF HE TOUCHES [A PORTION] OF THE SIZE OF HALF AN OLIVE AND OVERSHADOWS [ANOTHER PORTION] OF THE SIZE OF HALF AN OLIVE, OR IF HE TOUCHES [A PORTION] OF THE SIZE OF HALF AN OLIVE AND [ANOTHER PORTION] OF THE SIZE OF HALF AN OLIVE OVERSHADOWS HIM, OR IF HE OVERSHADOWS TWO [PORTIONS, EACH] OF THE SIZE OF HALF AN OLIVE, OR IF HE OVERSHADOWS [A PORTION] OF THE SIZE OF HALF AN OLIVE AND [ANOTHER PORTION] OF THE SIZE OF HALF AN OLIVE OVERSHADOWS HIM, R. DOSA B. HARKINAS DECLARES HIM CLEAN, AND THE SAGES DECLARE HIM UNCLEAN. BUT IF HE TOUCHES [A PORTION] OF THE SIZE OF HALF AN OLIVE AND [HAS] ANOTHER OBJECT[6] OVERSHADOWING HIM AND [ANOTHER PORTION] OF THE SIZE OF HALF AN OLIVE, OR IF HE OVERSHADOWS [A PORTION] OF THE SIZE OF HALF AN OLIVE AND [HAS] ANOTHER OBJECT OVERSHADOWING HIM AND [ANOTHER PORTION] OF THE SIZE OF HALF AN OLIVE, HE IS CLEAN.[7] (R. MEIR SAID: EVEN HERE R. DOSA B. HARKINAS DECLARES

(1) Cf. 'Ed. III, 1. (2) Mentioned *supra* II, 1f. (3) I.e., a portion of the minimum quantity for defilement. (4) In their divided state they cannot combine to convey defilement by overshadowing. (5) The dispute apparently also included defilement by carrion. (6) A board, etc. (7) Even according to the Sages. The reason is discussed in Ḥul. 125*b*.

HIM CLEAN AND THE SAGES DECLARE HIM UNCLEAN. EVERY [CASE] IS UNCLEAN[1] EXCEPT [A CASE OF] CONTACT [COMBINED] WITH CARRIAGE OR OF CARRIAGE [COMBINED] WITH OVERSHADOWING). THIS IS THE GENERAL PRINCIPLE:[2] EVERY OBJECT [WHOSE DEFILEMENT] PROCEEDS FROM ONE CAUSE[3] IS UNCLEAN, FROM TWO CAUSES IS CLEAN.

MISHNAH 2. IF A LADLEFUL OF CORPSE-MOULD WAS SCATTERED ABOUT IN A HOUSE, THE HOUSE IS UNCLEAN[4] BUT R. SIMEON DECLARES IT CLEAN.[5] IF A QUARTER [OF A LOG] OF BLOOD WAS ABSORBED IN [THE GROUND] OF A HOUSE, THE HOUSE IS CLEAN. [IN THE CASE OF] IT BEING ABSORBED BY A GARMENT, IF THIS IS WASHED AND A QUARTER [OF A LOG] OF BLOOD EMERGES FROM IT,[6] IT IS UNCLEAN,[7] IF NOT, IT IS CLEAN,[8] SINCE ANYTHING ABSORBED THAT CANNOT EMERGE IS CLEAN.[9]

MISHNAH 3. [IN THE CASE OF] IT[10] BEING POURED OUT IN THE OPEN AIR, IF THE PLACE [WHERE IT FELL] WAS AN INCLINE AND [A PERSON] OVERSHADOWED PART OF IT, HE

(1) R. Meir, continuing his exposition of the opinion of the Sages. According to him they hold that two quantities may combine to form the minimum quantity in any mixed case of contact and overshadowing (regarded as one and the same cause), but not in any other mixed case arising from two causes. (2) Resuming the view of the first Tanna interrupted by the exposition of R. Meir. (3) The object is being affected by two portions which together form the minimum quantity, and which both defile through the same cause, either contact, carriage or overshadowing. (4) The scattered portions are regarded as combining. (5) Maintaining that since it presumably is now mixed with the dust of the house, it is just like that corpse-mould originating from a mixture of corpse matter and noncadaverous dust which does not defile (v. *supra* II, 1, n. 5). (6) This fact is ascertained by mingling a quarter of a *log* of blood with a quantity of water equal to that used in washing the garment and comparing the colours of the two mixtures (Bert.). (7) And renders the house in which it is brought unclean by overshadowing. (8) In so far as it does not render the house unclean. (9) V. Nid. 62*b*. (10) A quarter *log* of blood from a corpse.

[REMAINS] CLEAN.[1] IF IT WAS A CAVITY,[2] OR IF THE BLOOD CONGEALED,[3] HE [BECOMES] UNCLEAN. IF IT WERE POURED OUT ON A THRESHOLD WHICH INCLINED EITHER INWARDS OR OUTWARDS AND THE HOUSE OVERSHADOWED IT,[4] [THE HOUSE] IS CLEAN.[1] IF THERE WAS A CAVITY,[5] OR IF IT CONGEALED, [THE HOUSE BECOMES] UNCLEAN. EVERYTHING APPERTAINING TO A CORPSE IS UNCLEAN EXCEPT THE TEETH, HAIR AND NAILS;[6] BUT WHEN THEY ARE JOINED [TO THE CORPSE], THEY ARE ALL UNCLEAN.

MISHNAH 4. HOW IS THIS[7] [TO BE ILLUSTRATED]? IF THE CORPSE WERE OUTSIDE AND ITS HAIR INSIDE, THE HOUSE IS UNCLEAN. [WITH REGARD TO] A BONE WHICH HAD UPON IT AN OLIVE-SIZED PORTION OF FLESH, IF ONE BROUGHT PART OF IT WITHIN, SO THAT THE HOUSE WAS OVERSHADOWING IT, [THE HOUSE] IS UNCLEAN.[8] [WITH REGARD TO] TWO BONES WHICH HAD UPON THEM TWO PORTIONS[9] OF FLESH, [EACH] OF THE SIZE OF HALF AN OLIVE, IF ONE BROUGHT PART OF THEM WITHIN SO THAT THE HOUSE WAS OVERSHADOWING THEM, [THE HOUSE] IS UNCLEAN. BUT IF [THE PIECES OF FLESH] WERE FIXED IN POSITION BY HUMAN AGENCY, THE HOUSE IS CLEAN, SINCE CONNECTIONS EFFECTED BY HUMAN AGENCY ARE NOT [REGARDED AS BEING] CONNECTED.[10]

MISHNAH 5. WHAT IS 'MIXED BLOOD'?[11] THE BLOOD OF A CORPSE OF WHICH AN EIGHTH [OF A LOG] ISSUED DURING

(1) The incline cannot be regarded as a connective, holding the full quarter of a *log* together. (2) The equivalent word in Arabic means 'swamp', 'gathering together of waters'. (3) Even on an incline. (4) I.e., part of it. (5) In the threshold. (6) Either because they change their substance continually or because they did not exist at the time the person was created. (7) The last fact mentioned in the previous Mishnah. (8) The bone forms the 'handle' (יד) for the flesh in transmitting uncleanness; v. 'Uḳ. I, 1. (9) One portion upon each bone. (10) Hence the bone, in this last instance, cannot be considered as forming the 'handle' for the flesh in transmitting uncleanness. (11) Referred to in *supra* II, 2.

LIFETIME AND AN EIGHTH AFTER DEATH. THIS IS THE OPINION OF R. AKIBA. R. ISHMAEL SAYS: [WE MUST IMAGINE] A QUARTER [OF A LOG TO HAVE ISSUED] DURING LIFETIME AND A QUARTER AFTER DEATH, [THEN IT IS] A QUARTER TAKEN FROM BOTH OF THESE. R. ELEAZAR SON OF R. JUDAH[1] SAYS: BOTH OF THESE[2] ARE AS WATER. WHAT THEN IS 'MIXED BLOOD'? IT IS THAT OF A CRUCIFIED PERSON WHOSE BLOOD IS STREAMING FORTH AND UNDER WHOM IS FOUND A QUARTER [OF A LOG] OF BLOOD. IT IS UNCLEAN.[3] THAT, HOWEVER, OF A CORPSE WHOSE BLOOD DRIPS FORTH AND UNDER WHOM IS FOUND A QUARTER [OF A LOG] OF BLOOD, IS CLEAN.[4] R. JUDAH SAYS: NOT SO, BUT THAT WHICH STREAMS FORTH IS CLEAN[5] AND THAT WHICH DRIPS FORTH[6] IS UNCLEAN.

MISHNAH 6. FOR AN OLIVE-SIZED PORTION OF A CORPSE, AN OPENING [IN THE ROOM IN WHICH IT IS FOUND] OF ONE HANDBREADTH [SQUARE], AND FOR A [WHOLE] CORPSE, AN OPENING OF FOUR HANDBREADTHS [SQUARE, SUFFICES] TO PREVENT THE UNCLEANNESS FROM [SPREADING TO THE OTHER] OPENINGS;[7] BUT FOR ALLOWING THE UNCLEANNESS TO COME FORTH,[8] AN OPENING OF ONE HANDBREADTH

(1) Sometimes known as R. Eleazar of Bertotha (v. Ab. III, 7). (2) Definitions of 'mixed blood' according to R. Akiba and R. Ishmael. (3) Such blood, streaming forth continually, is regarded as containing that drop issuing forth at the moment of death and also as containing at least half its bulk of unclean blood, issued after death. (4) Each drop of unclean cadaverous blood is regarded as being neutralised as it falls into the greater bulk of non-cadaverous blood. (5) Since it is regarded as possible that the drop of blood issuing from the crucified man at the moment of death did not fall into the quarter of a *log* but remained on the cross (Bert.). (6) The slow rate at which the blood issues proving that it is cadaverous (Maim.). The question is discussed in Nid. 71*a*. V. also Preuss (op. cit.) p. 242. (7) As explained *infra* VII, 3, corpse uncleanness through overshadowing extends beyond the room to the doors thereof, and even if they are closed, to the objects beneath their lintels, because it is assumed that the corpse is due to be removed through any one of them. Where, however, it is known that a definite exit will be used, that exit alone becomes unclean and all the rest, provided the doors be closed, remain clean. The Mishnah gives the minimum size of such an exit. (8) And proceed to an adjacent space.

[SQUARE SUFFICES].[1] [A PORTION] GREATER THAN THE SIZE OF AN OLIVE IS RECKONED AS A [WHOLE] CORPSE. R. JOSE SAYS: [ONLY][2] THE SPINE AND THE SKULL ARE RECKONED AS A [WHOLE] CORPSE.

MISHNAH 7. [AN OBJECT] ONE HANDBREADTH SQUARE[3] [STANDING] ONE HANDBREADTH HIGH[4] CAN BRING UNCLEANNESS[5] AND SCREEN[6] FROM UNCLEANNESS. HOW DOES IT [SCREEN]?[7] IN THE CASE OF AN ARCHED-UP[8] DRAIN BENEATH A HOUSE, IF THERE WAS A SPACE OF A HANDBREADTH WIDE[9] THEREIN AND ITS OUTLET[10] WAS A HANDBREADTH WIDE, WHEN THERE IS UNCLEANNESS[11] INSIDE IT, THE HOUSE REMAINS CLEAN;[12] AND WHEN THERE IS UNCLEANNESS IN THE HOUSE, THAT WHICH IS WITHIN [THE DRAIN] REMAINS CLEAN, FOR THE MANNER OF THE UNCLEANNESS IS TO GO OUT AND NO TO GO IN. IF THERE WAS A SPACE OF ONE HANDBREADTH WIDE THEREIN BUT ITS OUTLET WAS NOT ONE HANDBREADTH WIDE, WHEN THERE IS UNCLEANNESS THEREIN, THE HOUSE BECOMES UNCLEAN;[13] BUT WHEN THERE IS UNCLEANNESS IN THE HOUSE, THAT WHICH IS WITHIN IT REMAINS CLEAN, FOR THE MANNER OF THE UNCLEANNESS IS TO GO OUT[14] AND NOT TO GO IN.[15] IF THERE WAS NOT A SPACE OF ONE HANDBREADTH WIDE THEREIN AND ITS OUTLET WAS NOT

(1) Even for a whole corpse. (2) So Wilna Gaon. (3) At least one handbreadth in length and breadth. (4) Above the uncleanness. (5) To other objects in the same space. (6) The object forming the roof protects other things above it from being defiled. If, however, the roof is less than one handbreadth high, the uncleanness will cleave its way upward and downward (v. *infra* VI, 6). (7) So Bert. and most comm., the screening effect being the novel aspect that needs illustrating. (8) קמור The word is akin to Gr. καμάρα and Latin *camera*, 'a vaulted space'. (9) I.e., a space one handbreadth cube. (10) Carrying the waste out into the street. (11) An olive-sized portion of a corpse, a greater quantity necessitating an outlet of four handbreadths. (12) Since the uncleanness proceeds by the outlet into the street. The drain, by being of the stipulated size, thus screens the house from uncleanness. (13) There being no outlet for the uncleanness, the drain becomes a 'closed grave' whose uncleanness cleaves upwards and downwards. (14) To the street. (15) To the drain.

ONE HANDBREADTH WIDE,[1] WHEN THERE IS UNCLEANNESS WITHIN IT, THE HOUSE BECOMES UNCLEAN; AND WHEN THERE IS UNCLEANNESS IN THE HOUSE, IT [ALSO] BECOMES UNCLEAN. IT IS ONE [AND THE SAME IF THE SPACE IS] A CAVITY EXCAVATED BY WATER OR BY VERMIN OR IF IT HAD BEEN EATEN OUT BY A SALINE SUBSTANCE; AND SIMILARLY [IF IT IS IN] A ROW[2] OF STONES OR A PILE[3] OF BEAMS. R. JUDAH SAYS: ANY 'TENT' NOT MADE BY HUMAN AGENCY[4] IS NOT CONSIDERED A 'TENT'. BUT HE AGREES THAT CREVICES AND CRAGS [CAN BE CONSIDERED AS 'TENTS'].

(1) The dimensions of the outlet in this case are really immaterial, the drain in any case being reckoned as part of the ground of the house. (2) מרבך. The word occurs in the quotation from this Mishnah in Suk. 20*b* as מדבך which is, no doubt, from the same root as נדבך, Ezra VI, 4. The root דבך may possibly be the same as דבק 'to join together', hence a 'course of stones'. If one stone falls out a shelter can be formed. (3) סואר (also found as סוור). Explained in 'Aruch from the cognate Arabic as 'pile'. Possibly from a root similar to 'to collect'. (4) The reason of R. Judah's statement is given in Suk. 21*a*. He considers that 'tent' should be similar in manner to the '*Tent of Meeting*', the tabernacle of the wilderness, made by human agency.

OHOLOTH

CHAPTER IV

MISHNAH 1. [WITH REGARD TO] A CUPBOARD[1] STANDING IN THE OPEN AIR, IF THERE IS UNCLEANNESS WITHIN IT, VESSELS IN THE [NICHES[2] IN THE] THICKNESS [OF ITS WALLS] REMAIN CLEAN.[3] IF THERE IS UNCLEANNESS IN [THE NICHES IN] ITS THICKNESS, VESSELS INSIDE [THE CUPBOARD] REMAIN CLEAN. R. JOSE SAYS: HALF AND HALF.[4] WHEN IT IS STANDING INSIDE A HOUSE, IF THERE IS UNCLEANNESS INSIDE [THE CUPBOARD], THE HOUSE BECOMES UNCLEAN;[5] IF THERE IS UNCLEANNESS IN THE HOUSE, THAT WHICH IS WITHIN [THE CUPBOARD] REMAINS CLEAN,[6] FOR THE MANNER OF UNCLEANNESS IS TO GO OUT[7] AND NOT TO GO IN.[8] [WITH REGARD TO] VESSELS WHICH ARE BETWEEN [THE CUPBOARD] AND THE GROUND, OR BETWEEN IT AND THE WALL, OR BETWEEN IT AND THE ROOF-BEAMS, IF THERE IS A SPACE OF ONE CUBIC HANDBREADTH THERE, THEY BECOME UNCLEAN[9] BUT IF NOT THEY REMAIN CLEAN.[10] IF THERE IS UNCLEANNESS THERE,[11] THE HOUSE BECOMES UNCLEAN.[12]

(1) Of wood, with a cubic content of forty *se'ahs*. According to Kel. XV, 1 such a cupboard cannot receive uncleanness. (2) These niches, of less than a cubic handbreadth in size, go right through the thickness of the walls and open inwards and outwards. (3) The niches are reckoned as pertaining to the open air. (4) The outside half of the niche is reckoned as pertaining to the open air and the inside half to the cupboard. (5) Even if the cupboard doors are closed because the uncleanness must eventually proceed into the house. (6) If the cupboard doors are closed. (7) From the cupboard to the house. (8) From the house to the cupboard. (9) When there is a corpse in the house. (10) The uncleanness not being able to penetrate. (11) The space being less than a cubic handbreadth. (12) The cupboard, though forming a 'tent' within a 'tent', cannot prevent the uncleanness from escaping, just as a sealed cover cannot do it (cf. Kel. VIII, 6).

MISHNAH 2. [WITH REGARD TO] A DRAWER OF THE CUPBOARD, WHICH IS OF ONE CUBIC HANDBREADTH, BUT WHOSE OUTLET IS NOT A SQUARE HANDBREADTH IN SIZE, IF THERE IS UNCLEANNESS THEREIN, THE HOUSE BECOMES UNCLEAN; BUT IF THERE IS UNCLEANNESS IN THE HOUSE, THAT WHICH IS WITHIN [THE DRAWER] REMAINS CLEAN, FOR THE MANNER OF UNCLEANNESS IS TO GO OUT AND NOT TO GO IN. R. JOSE DECLARES [THE HOUSE][1] CLEAN, SINCE HE CAN REMOVE [THE UNCLEANNESS] BY HALVES[2] OR BURN IT WHERE IT STANDS.[3]

MISHNAH 3. [IN THE CASE WHERE] THE CUPBOARD IS STANDING IN THE DOORWAY AND IS OPENED OUTWARD, IF THERE IS UNCLEANNESS THEREIN, THE HOUSE REMAINS CLEAN. IF THERE IS UNCLEANNESS IN THE HOUSE, THAT WHICH IS WITHIN [THE CUPBOARD] BECOMES UNCLEAN,[4] FOR THE MANNER OF UNCLEANNESS IS TO GO OUT AND NOT TO GO IN. IF ITS WHEELED BASE[5] PROTRUDED THREE FINGERBREADTHS BEHIND IT[6] AND THERE WAS UNCLEANNESS THEREIN[7] UNDER THE ROOF-BEAMS, THE HOUSE REMAINS CLEAN.[8] WHEN DOES THIS RULING APPLY? WHEN THERE IS A SPACE THEREIN OF ONE CUBIC HANDBREADTH,[9] WHEN IT IS NOT DETACHABLE,[10] AND WHEN THE CUPBOARD IS OF THE STIPULATED SIZE.[11]

(1) In the former case. (2) So that the uncleanness going forth would be of less than the prescribed minimum size. (3) So that the uncleanness would never go out. (4) The text in Ḥul. 125*b* apparently followed by Bert. reads: 'clean'. This reading regards the uncleanness as going out of the house and missing the cupboard. The reading in this Mishnah is explained by Tosaf. Y.Ṭ. as applying to the case where the cupboard occupies almost the whole of the doorway. The uncleanness being unable to emerge, has to force its way through the cupboard walls. (5) מוכני. Gr. μηχανή, machine (v. Kel. XVIII, 2). (6) I.e., as the cupboard was standing in the doorway. (7) In a container in the base. (8) The base is regarded as belonging to the cupboard. (9) The uncleanness is then not in a confined space and cannot cleave upwards. (10) The base forms part of the cupboard. (11) Forty *se'ahs*, v. Mishnah I, n. 1.

OHOLOTH

CHAPTER V

MISHNAH 1. [WITH REGARD TO] AN OVEN WHICH STOOD IN A HOUSE, WITH ITS OUTLET[1] CURVED TO THE OUTSIDE [OF THE HOUSE], IF CORPSE-BEARERS OVERSHADOWED IT,[2] BETH SHAMMAI SAY: ALL BECOMES UNCLEAN.[3] BETH HILLEL SAY: THE OVEN BECOMES UNCLEAN, BUT THE HOUSE REMAINS CLEAN. R. AKIBA SAYS: EVEN THE OVEN REMAINS CLEAN.[4]

MISHNAH 2. [WITH REGARD TO] A HATCHWAY[5] BETWEEN THE HOUSE AND THE UPPER STOREY, IF THERE WAS A POT PLACED OVER IT AND THIS WAS PERFORATED [BY A HOLE OF SUFFICIENT SIZE] TO ADMIT LIQUID,[6] BETH SHAMMAI SAY: ALL BECOMES UNCLEAN.[7] BETH HILLEL SAY: THE POT BECOMES UNCLEAN[8] BUT THE UPPER STOREY REMAINS CLEAN. R. AKIBA SAYS: ALL REMAINS CLEAN.

MISHNAH 3. IF [THE POT][9] WAS WHOLE, BETH HILLEL SAY: IT PROTECTS ALL [FROM UNCLEANNESS]. BETH SHAMMAI SAY: IT PROTECTS ONLY FOOD, DRINK AND EARTHENWARE VESSELS.[10]

(1) Of one handbreadth square (v. Kel. VIII, 7). The reference is to an earthenware pot. (2) With the corpse. (3) The uncleanness penetrating the house by way of the outlet. (4) Since only the outlet was overshadowed, not the oven itself. (5) Of one handbreadth square. (6) For the prescribed test to determine this fact, v. Nid. 49*a*. (7) When there is a corpse in the house. The earthenware pot, because it is defective, is considered on its own and not as a continuation of the roof of the house. It cannot protect its own contents from uncleanness since it no longer has the equivalent of a tightly fitting lid between itself and the defiling source. Hence it cannot protect the objects in the upper storey. (8) A precautionary measure of the Sages, but really it is clean and therefore can protect the upper storey. (9) This Mishnah deals with the case of a pot belonging to an *'am ha-arez*, a person negligent of Rabbinic law (Bert.). V. 'Ed. I, 14, Sonc. ed., p. 8, for the full argument. (10) These objects,

BETH HILLEL RETRACTED AND TAUGHT AS BETH SHAMMAI.

MISHNAH 4. [WITH REGARD TO] A FLAGON,[1] FULL OF LIQUID, THE FLAGON IS DEFILED WITH A DEFILEMENT OF SEVEN [DAYS' DURATION] BUT THE LIQUID REMAINS CLEAN.[2] BUT IF ONE POURED IT OUT INTO ANOTHER VESSEL,[3] IT BECOMES UNCLEAN.[4] IF A WOMAN WAS KNEADING [IN THE UPPER STOREY] AT A TROUGH, THE WOMAN AND THE TROUGH BECOME UNCLEAN, BUT THE DOUGH REMAINS CLEAN. BUT IF ONE TURNED IT OUT INTO ANOTHER VESSEL, IT BECOMES UNCLEAN. BETH HILLEL RETRACTED AND TAUGHT AS BETH SHAMMAI.[5]

MISHNAH 5. IF [LYING OVER THE HATCHWAY] THERE WERE VESSELS OF [BAKED] ORDURE,[6] VESSELS OF STONE, OR VESSELS OF [UNBAKED] EARTH,[7] ALL [IN THE UPPER STOREY] REMAINS CLEAN. IF IT WAS A VESSEL KNOWN TO BE CLEAN FOR HOLY THINGS OR FOR [THE WATER OF] PURIFICATION,[8] ALL REMAINS CLEAN,[9] EVERYONE[10] BEING TRUSTED WITH [REGARD TO MATTERS OF] PURIFICATION;[11] FOR CLEAN VESSELS AND EARTHENWARE VESSELS THAT ARE [KNOWN TO BE] CLEAN[12] PROTECT IN ASSOCIATION WITH THE WALLS OF 'TENTS'.[13]

if they belonged to an *'am ha-areẓ* would not, in any case, be used by a *ḥaber*, a scrupulous observer of Rabbinic law, without due precaution. Other vessels, however, might be used unless they were definitely declared unclean.

(1) 'Flagon', here of metal or wood. The flagon is in the upper storey, with the pot set over the hatchway. (2) Being protected by the pot, according to Beth Shammai in *supra* 3. (3) Of wood or metal, in the upper storey, which had thus already suffered corpse uncleanness. (4) Food and drink are only protected when they are in their original container. (5) V. 'Ed. I, 14. (6) גללים 'Aruch and Bert. 'cattle dung', but Rashi (on Shab. 16*b*) 'marble'. (7) All these vessels being insusceptible to uncleanness and affording protection to everything, even wood or metal vessels. (8) Cf. Par. V, 1; Num. XIX, 17. It was the water used for compounding the ashes of the red heifer. (9) Cf. n. 7. (10) Even an *'am ha-areẓ*. (11) Cf. Par. V, 1. (12) Such as those mentioned in this Mishnah. (13) As in the case of the pot over the hatchway. No such protection can, however, be afforded by these vessels on their own as is explained in the next Mishnah.

MISHNAH 6. How [IS THE CASE TO BE IMAGINED]? IF THERE WAS A CISTERN OR A CELLAR[1] IN A HOUSE[2] AND AN OLIVE-BASKET[3] WAS PLACED OVER IT, [THE CONTENTS OF THE CISTERN OR CELLAR] REMAIN CLEAN. BUT IF IT WAS A WELL [WITH ITS UPPER EDGE] LEVEL [WITH THE GROUND], OR A DEFICIENT[4] BEEHIVE, UPON WHICH THE OLIVE-BASKET WAS PLACED, [THE CONTENTS] BECOME UNCLEAN.[5] IF IT WAS A SMOOTH BOARD OR A KNEADING BOARD[6] WITHOUT RIMS, [THE CONTENTS] REMAIN CLEAN.[7] FOR VESSELS CANNOT PROTECT ALONG WITH WALLS OF SHELTERS UNLESS THEY THEMSELVES HAVE WALLS. HOW MUCH MUST THE WALL BE? A HANDBREADTH. IF THERE WAS HALF A HANDBREADTH ON ONE AND HALF A HANDBREADTH ON THE OTHER,[8] IT IS NOT [CONSIDERED] A WALL, AS THERE MUST BE A WHOLE HANDBREADTH ON ONE OBJECT.

MISHNAH 7. JUST AS THEY[9] PROTECT INSIDE [A 'TENT'] SO DO THEY PROTECT OUTSIDE. HOW SO? IN THE CASE OF AN OLIVE-BASKET SUPPORTED ON PEGS[10] ON THE OUTSIDE [OF A 'TENT'], IF THERE WAS UNCLEANNESS BENEATH IT, VESSELS IN THE OLIVE-BASKET REMAIN CLEAN.[11] BUT IF IT WAS [NEXT TO] THE WALL OF A COURTYARD OR OF A GARDEN, IT DOES NOT AFFORD PROTECTION.[12] [IN THE CASE OF] A

(1) A cistern or chamber with walls of masonry situated beneath a house. Both cistern and cellar have walls projecting at least one handbreadth above the floor. (2) In which there is a corpse. (3) A large basket in which olives were placed in order to become soft. Having a capacity of more than forty *se'ahs*, it is insusceptible to uncleanness, cf. Kel. XV, 1. (4) A beehive of more than forty *se'ahs'* capacity which had been broken and had not been stopped up with straw or the like. Var. lec., 'open', i.e., at both ends. (5) In neither case are there any walls that could be associated with the walls of the olive-basket to protect from the uncleanness. (6) So Bert. Maim.: a perforated board, colander. (7) Not being regarded as vessels, they require no 'tent' walls with which to be associated. (8) I.e., half a handbreadth on the vessel and half on the projecting wall. (9) Vessels in association with 'tent' walls. (10) The basket standing one handbreadth above the ground. (11) The basket touching the wall of the 'tent' is associated with it to protect its own contents. (12) The walls not being themselves made to serve as 'tent' walls.

BEAM[1] PLACED ACROSS FROM ONE WALL TO ANOTHER,[2] WITH A POT HANGING FROM IT,[3] IF THERE WAS UNCLEANNESS BENEATH IT,[4] R. AKIBA DECLARES THE VESSELS INSIDE IT TO BE CLEAN,[5] BUT THE SAGES DECLARE THEM UNCLEAN.[6]

(1) One handbreadth broad, one handbreadth above the ground. (2) In the open air. (3) At a distance from the beam of less than a handbreadth. (4) The beam. (5) Just as in a room, where uncleanness is not able to penetrate into a space of less than a handbreadth. (6) The pot, not being directly associated with the walls of any 'tent', cannot protect its own contents.

OHOLOTH

CHAPTER VI

MISHNAH 1. BOTH PERSONS AND VESSELS CAN FORM[1] 'TENTS' TO BRING UNCLEANNESS, BUT NOT TO [PROTECT OBJECTS SO THAT THEY] REMAIN CLEAN.[2] HOW [CAN THIS BE ILLUSTRATED]? [BY THE CASE OF] FOUR PERSONS CARRYING[3] A BLOCK OF STONE.[4] IF THERE IS UNCLEANNESS BENEATH IT, VESSELS UPON IT BECOME UNCLEAN.[5] IF THERE IS UNCLEANNESS UPON IT, VESSELS BENEATH IT BECOME UNCLEAN. R. ELIEZER DECLARES THEM CLEAN.[6] [IN THE CASE OF THE LARGE STONE] BEING PLACED UPON FOUR VESSELS, EVEN IF THEY BE VESSELS OF [BAKED] ORDURE, VESSELS OF STONE, OR VESSELS [UNBAKED] OF EARTH,[7] IF THERE IS UNCLEANNESS BENEATH [THE STONE], VESSELS UPON IT BECOME UNCLEAN. IF THERE IS UNCLEANNESS BENEATH IT, VESSELS UPON IT BECOME UNCLEAN. [IN THE CASE OF THE LARGE STONE] BEING PLACED ON FOUR STONES OR ON ANY LIVING CREATURE, IF THERE IS UNCLEANNESS BENEATH IT, VESSELS UPON IT REMAIN CLEAN.[8] IF THERE IS UNCLEANNESS UPON IT VESSELS BENEATH IT REMAIN CLEAN.

MISHNAH 2. IN THE CASE WHERE THE CORPSE-BEARERS

(1) Either by they themselves overshadowing or else by supporting a 'tent' as explained further in this Mishnah. (2) As can clean vessels in association with the walls of 'tents' (v. *supra* V, 5). (3) In the open air. (4) נדבך. Bert. renders the word here 'a large and broad stone'. The reading adopted by the 'Aruch, however, is rendered 'bier'. If this reading is adopted, it is of course understood that there is no corpse on the bier. (5) The stone overshadows all beneath it, causing all to be unclean, but cannot act as a 'tent' to prevent anything upon it from acquiring uncleanness from the source beneath. (6) In both cases (so Bert.), R. Eliezer regarding persons and vessels as forming 'tents', valid for all purposes. (7) These vessels are insusceptible to uncleanness but are too small (less than forty *se'ahs*) to afford protection. (8) The stones

WERE PASSING ALONG A PORTICO[1] AND ONE OF THEM[2] SHUT A DOOR[3] AND[4] LOCKED IT WITH A KEY, IF THE DOOR CAN REMAIN IN ITS POSITION ON ITS OWN,[5] [THE CONTENTS OF THE HOUSE][6] REMAIN CLEAN, BUT IF NOT, THEY BECOME UNCLEAN. SIMILARLY [IN THE CASE OF] A BARREL[7] OF DRIED FIGS OR A BASKET OF STRAW[8] PLACED IN A WINDOW,[9] IF THE DRIED FIGS OR THE STRAW CAN REMAIN IN THEIR POSITION ON THEIR OWN, [THE CONTENTS OF THE ROOM] REMAIN CLEAN, BUT IF NOT THEY BECOME UNCLEAN. [IN THE CASE OF] A HOUSE PARTITIONED OFF BY WINE-JARS, WHICH HAD BEEN PLASTERED WITH CLAY,[10] IF THE CLAY CAN REMAIN IN ITS POSITION ON ITS OWN, [THE SPACE PARTITIONED OFF] REMAINS CLEAN, BUT IF NOT, IT BECOMES UNCLEAN.

MISHNAH 3. A WALL SERVING A HOUSE IS TREATED BY HALVES. HOW SO? [IN THE CASE OF] A WALL LOOKING TOWARDS AN OPEN SPACE, HAVING UNCLEANNESS WITHIN IT, IF THIS IS IN THE INWARD HALF, THE HOUSE BECOMES UNCLEAN, BUT WHAT IS ABOVE [THE WALL][11] REMAINS CLEAN.[12] IF IT IS IN THE OUTWARD HALF, THE HOUSE REMAINS CLEAN, BUT WHAT IS ABOVE [THE WALL] BECOMES UNCLEAN.[13] IF IT IS EXACTLY IN THE MIDDLE, THE HOUSE BECOMES UNCLEAN, AND AS FOR WHAT IS ABOVE, R. MEIR DECLARES IT UNCLEAN,

not being vessels, they serve as valid sides of a 'tent' for all purposes. (1) *Exedra*, a covered walk in front of a house. (2) Of those who followed in the procession (Bert.). (3) Leading directly from the portico to a house. (4) L. suggests 'or', the man either keeping the door closed by his own weight or with a key. (5) Without support of the key, or (L.) of the man. (6) To which the door gives access. (7) Of earthenware, with its mouth turned outwards. (8) These foods, being spoiled beyond all possibility of edible value even for cattle are, of their own, insusceptible to uncleanness (Bert.). (9) Not less than one handbreadth square and communicating between a clean and unclean space. (10) There being uncleanness on one side of the partition. (11) Even if directly above the uncleanness. (12) The uncleanness being considered as belonging for all purposes to the house alone and not as 'compressed', with powers of cleaving upwards and downwards. (13) As compressed uncleanness cleaves upwards.

BUT THE SAGES CLEAN.[1] R. JUDAH SAYS: THE WHOLE OF THE WALL[2] APPERTAINS TO THE HOUSE.

MISHNAH 4. [IN THE CASE OF] A WALL BETWEEN TWO HOUSES, IF THERE IS UNCLEANNESS WITHIN IT, THE HOUSE NEARER TO THE UNCLEANNESS IS UNCLEAN, AND THE HOUSE NEARER TO THE CLEAN PART IS CLEAN. IF [THE UNCLEANNESS] IS IN THE MIDDLE, BOTH ARE UNCLEAN. IF THERE IS UNCLEANNESS IN ONE OF THE [HOUSES] AND THERE ARE VESSELS IN [THE THICKNESS OF] THE WALL, THOSE IN THE HALF NEARER THE UNCLEANNESS ARE UNCLEAN, THOSE IN THE HALF NEARER THE CLEAN [HOUSE] ARE CLEAN, AND THOSE IN THE MIDDLE ARE UNCLEAN. [WITH REGARD TO THE] PLASTER-WORK BETWEEN THE HOUSE AND THE UPPER STOREY, IF THERE IS UNCLEANNESS THEREIN IN THE LOWER HALF, THE HOUSE [BELOW] IS UNCLEAN AND THE UPPER STOREY IS CLEAN; IF IT IS IN THE UPPER HALF, THE UPPER STOREY IS UNCLEAN AND THE HOUSE IS CLEAN; BUT IF IT IS IN THE MIDDLE, BOTH ARE UNCLEAN. IF THERE IS UNCLEANNESS IN EITHER [THE HOUSE OR THE UPPER STOREY] AND THERE ARE VESSELS INSIDE THE PAVEMENT, THOSE IN THE HALF NEARER THE UNCLEANNESS ARE UNCLEAN, AND THOSE IN THE HALF NEARER THE CLEAN [SPACE] ARE CLEAN. IF THEY ARE IN THE MIDDLE, THEY ARE UNCLEAN. R. JUDAH SAYS: ALL THE PLASTER-WORK [IS RECKONED] TO APPERTAIN TO THE UPPER STOREY.

MISHNAH 5. [IN THE CASE OF] UNCLEANNESS AMONG THE ROOF-BEAMS, [WITH A COVERING] BENEATH IT THIN AS GARLIC-SKIN,[3] IF THERE IS A SPACE WITHIN[4] OF A CUBIC HANDBREADTH, EVERYTHING BECOMES UNCLEAN.[5] IF THERE

(1) Whereas R. Meir considers the wall to appertain both to the house and to the open space, the Sages hold that it belongs entirely to the house. (2) Even the half towards the open space. (3) Preventing the uncleanness from being visible within the house (v. Kel. IX, 1). (4) Where the uncleanness is. (5) The space becomes a 'closed grave' defiling all its surroundings, in this case both the house and the upper storey.

IS NOT A SPACE OF A CUBIC HANDBREADTH, THE UNCLEANNESS IS CONSIDERED PLUGGED UP.[1] IF THE UNCLEANNESS WAS VISIBLE WITHIN THE HOUSE, IN EITHER CASE THE HOUSE BECOMES UNCLEAN.

MISHNAH 6. A HOUSE SERVING [TO FORM] A WALL[2] IS SUBJECT TO THE PRINCIPLE OF GARLIC-SKIN. HOW SO? [IN THE CASE OF] A WALL BETWEEN TWO TOMB-NICHES OR TWO CAVERNS, IF THERE IS UNCLEANNESS IN THESE SPACES AND IN THE WALLS ARE VESSELS, OVER WHICH THERE IS A COVERING THIN AS GARLIC-SKIN, THEY REMAIN CLEAN. IF THE UNCLEANNESS IS IN THE WALL AND THE VESSELS ARE IN THE SPACE, AND THERE IS A COVERING THIN AS GARLIC-SKIN OVER THE UNCLEANNESS, THEY REMAIN CLEAN. IF THERE IS UNCLEANNESS BENEATH A PILLAR, THE UNCLEANNESS[3] CLEAVES UPWARDS AND DOWNWARDS.

MISHNAH 7. VESSELS BENEATH THE CAPITAL[4] [OF A PILLAR] REMAIN CLEAN.[5] R. JOḤANAN B. NURI DECLARES THEM UNCLEAN. [IN THE CASE OF] THE UNCLEANNESS AND THE VESSELS BEING [TOGETHER] BENEATH THE CAPITAL, IF THERE IS A SPACE OF ONE CUBIC HANDBREADTH THERE, [THE VESSELS] BECOME UNCLEAN; IF NOT, THEY REMAIN CLEAN.[6] [IN THE CASE OF] TWO WALL-CUPBOARDS,[7] ONE BESIDE THE OTHER, OR ONE ABOVE THE OTHER,[8] IF ONE OF THEM WERE OPENED, BOTH IT AND THE HOUSE BECOME

(1) Compressed uncleanness, cleaving upwards and downwards. (2) I.e., the wall has been formed by the excavation of two adjacent houses or caves. (3) Being compressed beneath the pillar in this vault (cf. *supra* III, 7, n. 6). (4) Lit., 'flower', hence applied to the flower-like decoration on the capital of a pillar. (5) Even when there is 'compressed' uncleanness beneath another part of the capital, since this kind of uncleanness does not spread sidewards. (6) Less than one handbreadth being insufficient to convey uncleanness by overshadowing. (7) פרדסקים, Aramaic 'wall-cupboard'. Perhaps some form from Gk. πύργος 'a tower', hence 'tower-like structure'. (8) With uncleanness beneath one of them. Each has a content of less than a cubic handbreadth (L.), a space of greater size constituting a closed grave. (V. Mishnah 5, n. 5).

UNCLEAN, BUT ITS COMPANION REMAINS CLEAN.[1] THE WALL-CUPBOARDS ARE CONSIDERED[2] AS IF PLUGGED UP,[3] AND ARE SUBJECT TO THE PRINCIPLE OF HALVES[4] FOR CONVEYING UNCLEANNESS INTO THE HOUSE.

(1) The uncleanness is not considered as 'compressed' but follows the law of uncleanness in a wall. When the companion cupboard is closed, it cannot receive the uncleanness. (2) When they are closed. (3) Forming part of the solid wall. (4) When the uncleanness lies beneath them (v. Mishnah 3).

OHOLOTH

CHAPTER VII

MISHNAH 1. IF THERE IS UNCLEANNESS IN A WALL [IN A FREE] SPACE OF ONE CUBIC HANDBREADTH, ALL UPPER STOREYS ABOVE IT, EVEN IF THERE ARE TEN OF THEM,[1] ARE UNCLEAN.[2] IF THERE WAS A SINGLE UPPER STOREY [BUILT] OVER TWO HOUSES,[3] THAT ONE BECOMES UNCLEAN BUT ALL UPPER STOREYS ABOVE IT REMAIN CLEAN.[4] [IN A] BEACH-[5] WALL, UNCLEANNESS CLEAVES UPWARDS AND DOWNWARDS.[6] [WITH REGARD TO] A SOLID TOMB MONUMENT,[7] A PERSON WHO TOUCHES IT FROM THE SIDE REMAINS CLEAN, SINCE [ITS] UNCLEANNESS CLEAVES UPWARDS AND DOWNWARDS.[8] BUT IF THERE WAS A [FREE] SPACE OF A CUBIC HANDBEADTH IN THE PLACE WHERE THE UNCLEANNESS WAS, A PERSON TOUCHING IT ANYWHERE BECOMES UNCLEAN, BECAUSE IT IS LIKE A CLOSED GRAVE. IF BOOTHS WERE PLACED ADJACENT TO [THE MONUMENT] THEY BECOME UNCLEAN.[9] R. JUDAH DECLARES THEM CLEAN.[10]

MISHNAH 2. ALL SLOPING [PARTS] OF 'TENTS' ARE RECKONED AS 'TENTS'.[11] [IN THE CASE OF] A 'TENT' [WHOSE

(1) All connected with this wall by having their floor beams fixed into it. (2) The wall is regarded as a closed grave, defiling all around. (3) And this unclean wall between the two houses supports the upper storey. (4) The first upper storey affording them complete protection. (5) שוניית Bert.: a wall built in the place to which the sea comes in rough weather levelling out all free (hollow) spaces. Var. lec. (followed by L.) is שנית, 'rock'. (6) The wall is regarded as part of the earth, in which no uncleanness is ever treated as a 'closed grave'. According to var. lec., the reason is because the principle of 'free space' applies only to a wall made by human agency (Wilna Gaon). (7) Lit., 'resting place', i.e., tomb (cf. Shek. II, 5). (8) Like compressed uncleanness and not like a closed grave. (9) Being regarded as 'tents' over corpses. (10) Since they are placed against the sides. (11) I.e., spaces under the sloping sides are considered as part of the 'tent' itself.

SIDES] SLOPED DOWNWARDS AND FINISHED OFF [WITH A ROOF][1] OF ONE FINGERBREADTH, IF THERE IS UNCLEANNESS IN THE 'TENT',[2] VESSELS BENEATH THE SLOPE BECOME UNCLEAN. IF THERE IS UNCLEANNESS BENEATH THE SLOPE, VESSELS IN THE 'TENT' BECOME UNCLEAN. IF THERE HAD BEEN[3] UNCLEANNESS WITHIN, A PERSON WHO TOUCHES [THE 'TENT'] FROM THE INSIDE ACQUIRES A SEVEN [DAYS'] DEFILEMENT,[4] BUT FROM THE OUTSIDE, A DEFILEMENT [LASTING TILL] EVENING.[5] IF THERE HAD BEEN UNCLEANNESS OUTSIDE, A PERSON WHO TOUCHES THE 'TENT' FROM THE OUTSIDE ACQUIRES A SEVEN [DAYS'] DEFILEMENT, BUT FROM THE INSIDE, A DEFILEMENT [LASTING TILL] EVENING. IF THERE WAS [A PORTION OF UNCLEANNESS] OF THE SIZE OF HALF AN OLIVE [TOUCHING IT] FROM WITHIN AND HALF AN OLIVE FROM WITHOUT,[6] A PERSON WHO TOUCHES [THE 'TENT'] EITHER FROM WITHIN OR WITHOUT ACQUIRES A DEFILEMENT [LASTING TILL] EVENING.[7] IF A PART [OF THE 'TENT' SIDE] TRAILED ALONG THE GROUND, WHEN THERE IS UNCLEANNESS BENEATH OR ABOVE [THIS PART], THE UNCLEANNESS [THEREOF] CLEAVES UPWARDS AND DOWNWARDS. [IN THE CASE OF] A 'TENT' ERECTED IN AN UPPER STOREY, WITH A PORTION [OF ITS SIDE] TRAILING OVER THE HATCHWAY BETWEEN THE HOUSE AND THE UPPER STOREY, R. JOSE SAYS: IT PROTECTS.[8] R. SIMEON SAYS: IT DOES NOT PROTECT

(1) So Bert. Cf. Shab. 138*b* where it is implied that the minimum size for the roof of a 'tent' must be a handbreadth. In spite of this rule, for the purpose of conveying uncleanness, a smaller size does not prevent this 'tent' from being constituted. (2) I.e., under the roof. (3) In the past. However the uncleanness was not present when the 'tent' was touched. (4) The inner side and the outer side of the 'tent' being reckoned as two vessels (Bert.). The inner side, having come into contact with the corpse, acquires its degree of uncleanness, אבי אבות הטומאה (cf. *supra* I, 2 n. 4) and confers both upon the person and the outer side of the 'tent' a generating defilement. (5) The outer side conferring a generated defilement on the person touching it. (6) In which case the 'tent' acquires a seven days' defilement, the two half olives combining on the view of the Sages, *supra* III, 1. (7) The sides, in relation to those who touch them, being regarded as two vessels. (8) Although it is formed of a substance which is susceptible to uncleanness because it is part of a 'tent'.

UNLESS IT BE STRETCHED OUT AFTER THE USUAL MANNER OF ERECTING 'TENTS'.

MISHNAH 3. IF A CORPSE IS IN A HOUSE IN WHICH THERE ARE MANY DOORS, THEY ALL BECOME UNCLEAN.[1] IF ONE OF THEM WAS OPENED, THAT ONE BECOMES UNCLEAN BUT ALL THE REST REMAIN CLEAN. IF IT WAS INTENDED TO CARRY OUT THE CORPSE THROUGH ONE OF THEM OR THROUGH A WINDOW OF FOUR HANDBREADTHS SQUARE, THAT PROTECTS ALL THE OTHER DOORS.[2] BETH SHAMMAI SAY: THE INTENTION MUST HAVE BEEN FORMED BEFORE THE PERSON DIED.[3] BETH HILLEL SAY: EVEN AFTER HE DIED.[4] IF [A DOOR] WAS BLOCKED UP AND IT WAS DECIDED TO OPEN IT, BETH SHAMMAI SAY: [IT IS EFFECTIVE][5] AS SOON AS [A SPACE] FOUR HANDBREADTHS SQUARE HAS BEEN OPENED UP. BETH HILLEL SAY: AS SOON AS [THE PROCESS] HAS BEGUN. THEY AGREE, HOWEVER, THAT WHEN MAKING AN OPENING FOR THE FIRST TIME, FOUR HANDBREADTHS MUST BE OPENED UP.

MISHNAH 4. IF A WOMAN WAS IN HARD TRAVAIL AND WAS CARRIED FROM ONE HOUSE TO ANOTHER,[6] THE FIRST HOUSE BECOMES UNCLEAN BECAUSE OF DOUBT[7] AND THE SECOND OF A CERTAINTY. R. JUDAH SAID: WHEN IS THIS SO? WHEN SHE IS CARRIED OUT [SUPPORTED] BY THE ARMPITS, BUT IF SHE WAS ABLE TO WALK, THE FIRST HOUSE REMAINS CLEAN, FOR AFTER THE 'TOMB'[8] HAS BEEN OPENED THERE IS NO POSSIBILITY OF WALKING. STILLBORN CHILDREN ARE NOT [DEEMED TO HAVE] OPENED THE 'TOMB' UNTIL THEY PRESENT A HEAD ROUNDED LIKE A SPINDLE-KNOB.[9]

(1) V. *supra* III, 6, n. 7. (2) That are closed. Henceforth objects placed underneath them do not become unclean. (3) After which, only a positive action can avail to afford protection from uncleanness. (4) Nevertheless, vessels already in position at the time of death remain unclean. (5) To protect other doors. V. Preuss op. cit. p. 458. (6) And gave birth there to a dead child. V. also Preuss p. 136. (7) Perhaps the womb had opened there and the child's head had protruded. (8) I.e., the opening of the womb. (9) Cf. Bek. 22*a*.

MISHNAH 5. IF [AT THE BIRTH OF TWINS] THE FIRST PROCEEDED FORTH DEAD AND THE SECOND ALIVE, THE [LIVE ONE] IS CLEAN.[1] IF THE FIRST WAS ALIVE AND THE SECOND DEAD, THE [LIVE CHILD] IS UNCLEAN.[2] R. MEIR SAYS: IF THEY WERE IN ONE MEMBRANE, [THE LIVE CHILD] IS UNCLEAN,[3] BUT IF THERE WERE TWO MEMBRANES, IT REMAINS CLEAN.[4]

MISHNAH 6. IF A WOMAN IS IN HARD TRAVAIL, ONE CUTS UP THE CHILD IN HER WOMB AND BRINGS IT FORTH MEMBER BY MEMBER, BECAUSE HER LIFE COMES BEFORE THAT OF [THE CHILD]. BUT IF THE GREATER PART HAS PROCEEDED FORTH, ONE MAY NOT TOUCH IT, FOR ONE MAY NOT SET ASIDE ONE PERSON'S LIFE FOR THAT OF ANOTHER.[5]

(1) It the dead child had been removed from the house. Uncleanness cannot be contracted in the womb. (2) Having passed through an opening through which uncleanness is due to pass. (3) Since it presumably touched the dead child outside the womb. On the membrane (שפיר) v. Preuss p. 456. (4) On the theory that the dead child does not defile until it is out of the womb. (5) On this principle v. Preuss p. 607.

OHOLOTH

CHAPTER VIII

MISHNAH 1. SOME THINGS FORM A PASSAGE[1] FOR UNCLEANNESS AND [ALSO] A SCREEN [AGAINST IT]; [SOME] FORM A PASSAGE FOR UNCLEANNESS BUT NOT A SCREEN; [SOME] FORM A SCREEN BUT NOT A PASSAGE; [AND SOME] FORM NEITHER A PASSAGE NOR A SCREEN. THE FOLLOWING FORM [BOTH] A PASSAGE AND A SCREEN: A CHEST,[2] A BOX, A CUPBOARD, A BEEHIVE OF STRAW, A BEEHIVE OF REEDS, OR THE WATER-TANK OF AN ALEXANDRIAN[3] SHIP, SUCH OF WHICH [OBJECTS] HAVE [FLAT] BOTTOMS[4] AND A CONTENT OF [AT LEAST] FORTY SE'AHS[5] LIQUID MEASURE OR TWO KORS[6] DRY MEASURE.[7] [FURTHER] A CURTAIN, A LEATHERN APRON,[8] A LEATHERN UNDERCOVER,[9] A SHEET, A MATTING UNDERLAY[10] OR A MAT[11] WHEN MADE INTO 'TENTS';[12] A HERD OF CATTLE,[13]

(1) Cf. *supra* III, 7. (2) Heb. *Shiddah*. This word is frequently found (cf. Shab. 120*a*, Naz. 55*a* etc.) in connection with *tebah* and *migdal*, the two words rendered here 'box' and 'cupboard'. Hence it probably means something similar to them. Kel. XVIII, 1 and 2 contains a description of certain parts of a '*shiddah*' from which Rashi (on Shab. 44*a*) infers that it is a wheeled cart used for carrying people. Bert. and L. describe it as a larger version of *tebah*. 'Aruch suggests the word is possibly derived from late Gk. σέδα, a chair. Perhaps it means a 'wheeled box chair'. (3) Grain ships going from Alexandria to Rome. (4) So that they can rest in stable equilibrium. (5) One *se'ah* = six *kabs*, roughly twelve litres. (6) Cf. 'Uk. V, 2. One *kor* = thirty *se'ahs*, roughly three hundred ninety-three litres = nearly eleven bushels. (7) These dimensions are given in connection with the above vessels in Kel. XV, 1, where it is explained that vessels of such a size are insusceptible to uncleanness. (8) Lat. *scortea*, 'a leathern article'. Bert., 'workman's apron'; Maim., 'bedcover'. (9) Gk. καταβολή, something 'thrown over' the bed, as an undercover. (10) Cf. Kel. XXIV, 10; XXVII, 2; B.K. 25*b*. Perhaps from נפץ 'to spread'. (11) מחצלת. Cf. Kel. XVII, 17; XX, 7. 'Aruch quotes the cognate Arabic meaning 'slender twigs' from which mats are woven. (12) These articles, of their own, are susceptible to uncleanness. When forming 'tents', however, they can convey and screen in the normal manner. (13) Standing in one place, packed tightly together (Bert.).

UNCLEAN OR CLEAN, PACKS[1] OF WILD ANIMALS OR BIRDS, A RESTING BIRD,[2] A [SHADY] PLACE THAT [A WOMAN] MAKES FOR HER SON AMONGST THE EARS OF CORN; THE IRIS,[3] THE IVY,[4] ASS HERBS,[5] GREEK GOURDS[6] AND CLEAN FOODSTUFFS.[7] R. JOḤANAN B. NURI DID NOT AGREE WITH REGARD TO CLEAN FOODSTUFFS EXCEPT IN THE CASE OF A CAKE OF DRIED FIGS.[8]

MISHNAH 2. [FURTHER,] PROJECTING CANOPIES,[9] BALCONIES,[10] DOVE-COTES, CREVICES AND CRAGS,[11] GROTTOES,[12] [OVERHANGING] PINNACLES, INTERLACED BOUGHS AND PROTRUDING STONES SUCH AS ARE CAPABLE OF SUSTAINING THIN PLASTERWORK; ACCORDING TO R. MEIR. BUT THE SAGES SAY A MEDIUM PLASTERWORK. THE FOLLOWING IS A CASE OF 'INTERLACED BOUGHS': A TREE WHICH THROWS SHADE OVER THE GROUND. 'PROTRUDING STONES' ARE [STONES] THAT PROJECT FROM A WALL.

MISHNAH 3. THE FOLLOWING FORM A PASSAGE BUT NOT A SCREEN: A CHEST, A BOX, A CUPBOARD, A BEEHIVE OF STRAW, A BEEHIVE OF REEDS, OR THE WATERTANK OF AN

(1) מכונות Maim. 'packs'. The word is usually taken to mean 'habitation' and here might well be rendered 'stalls', 'coops' (Jast.). The context, however, suggests a parallel with 'herd of cattle'. (2) According to Bert., a captive bird, tied to the place. (3) Cf. Kil. V, 8. (4) Cf. Kil. l.c. (5) ירקות חמור a kind of wild gourd, '*cucumis agrestis*'. (6) All the above-mentioned plants are regarded as having broad leaves (Bert.), or as being evergreen (L.). Moreover the reference is to such as are still connected with the soil, so that they form a suitable 'tent' and are insusceptible to uncleanness. (7) I.e., such as are insusceptible to uncleanness, not having come in contact with any liquid of the seven kinds, v. Maksh. VI, 4. (8) Which he regards as the only foods likely to be used as a shelter. (9) *Zizin*. 'Aruch quotes the cognate Arabic root meaning 'to project'. Cf. B.B. III, 6 and also Oh. XIV, 1 for the distinction between this and the following word. (10) גזריות. A similar word, גזוטרא (Mid. II, 5; Shab. 96*a* etc.) is taken by 'Aruch from Gk. ἐξώστρα 'gallery'. Our word may be a Hebraized form of this word. (11) V. *supra* III end. (12) נהרים corrected by 'Aruch to נחרים, quoting cognate Arabic 'grotto'. Maim.: from גהר 'to stretch' (I. Kings XVIII, 42) hence 'projecting rock'. Bert.: 'light-holes'.

ALEXANDRIAN SHIP, SUCH OF WHICH [OBJECTS] HAVE NOT [FLAT] BOTTOMS OR HAVE NOT A CONTENT OF FORTY SE'AHS LIQUID MEASURE OR TWO KORS DRY MEASURE.[1] [FURTHER,] A CURTAIN, A LEATHERN APRON, A LEATHERN UNDERCOVER, A SHEET, A MATTING UNDERLAY OR A MAT WHEN NOT MADE INTO 'TENTS',[1] CATTLE OR WILD ANIMALS WHEN THEY ARE DEAD, AND FOODSTUFFS THAT ARE [LIABLE TO BECOME] UNCLEAN.[2] IN ADDITION TO THESE, A MILL [WORKED BY] MAN-POWER.[3]

MISHNAH 4. THE FOLLOWING FORM A SCREEN BUT NOT A PASSAGE: A LOOM [WITH A WEB] SPREAD OUT,[4] THE ROPE-WORK OF A BED, REFUSE BASKETS,[5] AND WINDOW-LATTICES.[6]

MISHNAH 5. THE FOLLOWING FORM NEITHER A PASSAGE NOR A SCREEN: SEEDS, PLANTS [STILL] ATTACHED TO THE SOIL, EXCEPT FOR THE PLANTS MENTIONED ABOVE,[7] A LUMP[8] OF HAIL, SNOW, FROST, ICE AND SALT. [FURTHER ANYTHING] THAT HOPS FROM ONE PLACE TO ANOTHER, OR LEAPS FROM ONE PLACE TO ANOTHER, A FLYING BIRD, A LOOSELY-FLAPPING GARMENT,[9] OR A SHIP FLOATING [FREELY] ON THE WATER. IF THE SHIP WERE TIED WITH SOMETHING THAT CAN KEEP IT STEADY, OR A STONE WERE [PLACED SO AS] TO HOLD DOWN THE GARMENT, THEY CAN FORM A PASSAGE FOR THE UNCLEANNESS. R. JOSE SAYS: A HOUSE ON A SHIP CANNOT FORM A PASSAGE FOR UNCLEANNESS.[10]

MISHNAH 6. IF TWO JARS CONTAINING TWO PORTIONS

(1) Thereby being susceptible to uncleanness. (2) Through the process mentioned in Maksh. VI, 4. (3) Not by animal power. A portable mill is susceptible to uncleanness. (4) The web, consisting of the warp threads alone, spread over a hatchway. (5) Cf. Kel. XXIV, 9. 'Aruch connects the word with זבל 'dung'. (6) All the articles in this Mishnah have holes in their structure. These holes, however, are less than one square handbreadth in area and therefore form valid screens (cf. Rashi on Ḥul. 125*b*). (7) V. *supra* I end. (8) Lit., 'a stone'. (9) Flying loose through the air. (10) If it sheltered over a corpse in the sea and vessels on the ship (L.).

[ONE IN EACH] OF A CORPSE OF THE SIZE OF HALF AN OLIVE, AND SEALED WITH TIGHTLY FITTING LIDS[1] WERE LYING IN A HOUSE, THEY REMAIN CLEAN,[2] BUT THE HOUSE BECOMES UNCLEAN.[3] IF ONE OF THEM WAS OPENED, THAT [JAR] AND THE HOUSE BECOME UNCLEAN, BUT ITS COMPANION REMAINS CLEAN. A SIMILAR RULE APPLIES TO TWO ROOMS THAT OPEN INTO A HOUSE.[4]

(1) The tightly fitting lid (Num. XIX, 15) forms a screen for an earthenware jar. (2) Each containing only half an olive's bulk of a corpse. (3) Since it contains an olive-sized portion of a corpse, a tightly fitting lid, while it serves as a screen for what is contained in an earthenware jar, does not prevent any uncleanness in the vessel from penetrating beyond it and defiling what is outside; v. Kel. VIII, 6. (4) If two sealed rooms each contain a portion of a corpse of half an olive size, they remain clean, but the house through which the uncleanness must pass becomes unclean.

OHOLOTH

CHAPTER IX

MISHNAH 1. WITH REGARD TO A BEEHIVE[1] [LYING] IN THE DOORWAY[2] WITH ITS MOUTH [POINTING] OUTSIDE, IF AN OLIVE-SIZED [PORTION] OF A CORPSE WERE PLACED BELOW THAT [PART OF THE HIVE] WHICH IS OUTSIDE [THE HOUSE], EVERYTHING DIRECTLY[3] BELOW OR ABOVE THAT OLIVE-SIZED [PORTION] BECOMES UNCLEAN;[4] BUT EVERYTHING THAT IS NOT DIRECTLY [BELOW OR ABOVE] THAT OLIVE-SIZED [PORTION], OR THAT IS WITHIN [THE HIVE][5] OR WITHIN THE HOUSE, REMAINS CLEAN. [IF THE UNCLEANNESS IS] WITHIN THE HOUSE, NOTHING BECOMES UNCLEAN EXCEPT THAT WHICH IS WITHIN THE HOUSE.[6] [IF THE UNCLEANNESS IS] WITHIN [THE HIVE] EVERYTHING BECOMES UNCLEAN.[7]

MISHNAH 2. [IN THE CASE OF THE HIVE] BEING ONE HANDBREADTH HIGH OFF THE GROUND, IF THERE IS UNCLEANNESS BELOW IT OR IN THE HOUSE OR ABOVE IT, EVERYTHING BECOMES UNCLEAN[8] EXCEPT THAT WHICH IS WITHIN [THE HIVE]. [IF THE UNCLEANNESS IS] WITHIN THE HIVE EVERYTHING BECOMES UNCLEAN.

(1) A wooden cylinder open at one end (its mouth) for the collection of honey, and perforated at the closed end to give ingress to the bees. It is less than forty *se'ahs* in content and therefore is to be considered a vessel and not a valid 'tent' on its own; but the fact that it has perforations renders it insusceptible to uncleanness (L.). (2) Part inside and part outside the house. (3) In a vertical line. (4) Being a vessel, the hive can afford no protection (*supra* VI, 1). (5) Being insusceptible to uncleanness, the hive can protect its own contents. (6) The contents of the hive remain clean, the uncleanness not entering by the perforations, regarded as being loosely stopped up. (7) The uncleanness going out by the perforations. (8) A 'tent' is thereby formed and the uncleanness is carried into the house.

MISHNAH 3. WHEN DO THESE RULES APPLY? WHEN [THE HIVE RETAINS THE STATUS OF] A VESSEL AND IS PERFORATED.[1] [IN THE CASE OF ITS] BEING DEFECTIVE, ALTHOUGH [ITS DEFICIENCY MAY BE] STOPPED UP WITH STRAW[2] OR BLOCKED UP[3] (WHAT IS [CONSIDERED] 'BLOCKED UP?' ANYTHING WHICH HAS NO [LONGER AN OPENING OF] ONE HANDBREADTH [SQUARE] IN ONE PLACE), IF AN OLIVE-SIZED [PORTION] OF A CORPSE IS PLACED BELOW IT, [EVERYTHING] DIRECTLY [BELOW THE PORTION] TO THE NETHERMOST DEEP BECOMES UNCLEAN;[4] [IF PLACED] ABOVE [THE HIVE EVERYTHING] DIRECTLY ABOVE TO THE SKY BECOMES UNCLEAN. [IF THE UNCLEANNESS IS] IN THE HOUSE, NOTHING BECOMES UNCLEAN EXCEPT THE HOUSE. [IF THE UNCLEANNESS IS] WITHIN [THE HIVE], NOTHING BECOMES UNCLEAN EXCEPT THAT WHICH IS WITHIN [THE HIVE].

MISHNAH 4. [IN THE CASE OF SUCH A HIVE] BEING [PLACED] ONE HANDBREADTH HIGH OFF THE GROUND, IF THERE IS UNCLEANNESS BELOW IT OR IN THE HOUSE, [THE SPACE] BELOW IT AND THE HOUSE BECOME UNCLEAN,[5] BUT [THE SPACE] ABOVE AND WITHIN REMAINS CLEAN.[6] [IF THE UNCLEANNESS IS] WITHIN, NOTHING IS UNCLEAN EXCEPT WHAT IS WITHIN; IF ABOVE [THE HIVE], WHAT IS DIRECTLY ABOVE UP TO THE SKY BECOMES UNCLEAN.

(1) מחלחלת. Some commentators, basing their interpretation of these words on Kel. X, 3, render 'lying loosely in the doorway'. But there seem to be two qualities required here. Firstly the hive must be a useable vessel and not defective. Secondly, it must have perforations that are free and not blocked up. L. and Bert. both render 'perforated'. (2) The straw cannot restore it to the status of a vessel. (3) אפוצה. Some commentators, taking this word to be the opposite of מחלחלת, and basing their interpretation on a passage in J. Pes. I, 27*c* (where these two words appear as contrasts) render 'fixed tightly in the entrance'. 'Aruch from Arabic 'to compress', whence Bert. 'with the perforations blocked up'. (4) But all else remains clean. Not being a vessel, the hive can protect. (5) The uncleanness being transferred from one space to another. (6) The hive protecting.

MISHNAH 5. WHEN DO THESE RULES APPLY? WHEN THE MOUTH [OF THE HIVE IS POINTING] OUTWARDS. IN THE CASE OF THE MOUTH [POINTING] INWARDS, IF AN OLIVE-SIZED PORTION OF THE CORPSE IS PLACED BELOW OR ABOVE [THAT PART OF THE HIVE WHICH IS] OUTSIDE, EVERYTHING DIRECTLY BELOW OR ABOVE[1] THAT OLIVE-SIZED PORTION BECOMES UNCLEAN, AND EVERYTHING NOT DIRECTLY [BELOW OR ABOVE IT], AND WHAT IS WITHIN [THE HIVE] AND THE HOUSE, REMAINS CLEAN. [IF THE UNCLEANNESS IS] WITHIN THE HIVE OR THE HOUSE, EVERYTHING BECOMES UNCLEAN.[2]

MISHNAH 6. [IN THE CASE OF THE HIVE IN THIS POSITION] BEING ONE HANDBREADTH HIGH OFF THE GROUND, IF THE UNCLEANNESS IS BELOW IT OR IN THE HOUSE OR WITHIN [THE HIVE] OR ABOVE IT, EVERYTHING BECOMES UNCLEAN.

MISHNAH 7. WHEN DO THESE RULES APPLY? WHEN [THE HIVE RETAINS THE STATUS OF] A VESSEL AND IS PERFORATED. [IN THE CASE OF ITS] BEING DEFECTIVE, ALTHOUGH [ITS DEFICIENCY MAY BE] STOPPED UP WITH STRAW OR BLOCKED UP (WHAT IS CONSIDERED BLOCKED UP? ANYTHING WHICH HAS NO [LONGER AN OPENING OF] ONE HANDBREADTH [SQUARE] IN ONE PLACE), IF AN OLIVE-SIZED [PORTION] OF A CORPSE IS PLACED BELOW IT, [EVERYTHING] DIRECTLY [BELOW THE PORTION] TO THE NETHERMOST DEEP BECOMES UNCLEAN; [IF PLACED] ABOVE [THE HIVE, EVERYTHING] DIRECTLY [ABOVE] TO THE SKY BECOMES UNCLEAN. [IF THE UNCLEANNESS IS PLACED] WITHIN [THE HIVE] OR IN THE HOUSE, EVERYTHING BECOMES UNCLEAN.[3]

MISHNAH 8. [IN THE CASE OF SUCH A HIVE IN THIS POSITION] BEING ONE HANDBREADTH HIGH OFF THE GROUND,

(1) Some texts add 'or within (the hive)'. (2) Even within the hive, the uncleanness entering its mouth. (3) Only in this respect does this Mishnah differ from Mishnah 3.

IF THERE IS UNCLEANNESS BELOW IT OR IN THE HOUSE OR WITHIN [THE HIVE], EVERYTHING[1] BECOMES UNCLEAN EXCEPT WHAT IS ABOVE IT. IF THE UNCLEANNESS IS ABOVE IT, [EVERYTHING] DIRECTLY [ABOVE] TO THE SKY BECOMES UNCLEAN.

MISHNAH 9. [IN THE CASE WHEN THE HIVE] OCCUPIES ALL THE HOUSE AND THERE WAS NOT A SPACE OF A HANDBREADTH BETWEEN IT[2] AND THE ROOF BEAMS, IF THERE IS UNCLEANNESS WITHIN [THE HIVE], THE HOUSE BECOMES UNCLEAN; BUT IF THERE IS UNCLEANNESS IN THE HOUSE, WHAT IS WITHIN [THE HIVE] REMAINS CLEAN, FOR THE MANNER OF THE UNCLEANNESS IS TO GO OUT AND NOT TO GO IN.[3] [THIS APPLIES] WHETHER [THE HIVE] IS STANDING UPRIGHT, OR LYING ON ITS SIDE, WHETHER THERE IS ONE [HIVE] OR TWO.[4]

MISHNAH 10. [IN THE CASE WHERE THE NON-DEFECTIVE HIVE] WAS STANDING UPRIGHT IN THE DOORWAY AND THERE WAS NOT A SPACE OF ONE HANDBREADTH BETWEEN IT AND THE LINTEL, IF THERE IS UNCLEANNESS WITHIN IT, THE HOUSE REMAINS CLEAN; BUT IF THERE IS UNCLEANNESS IN THE HOUSE, WHAT IS WITHIN [THE HIVE] BECOMES UNCLEAN,[5] FOR THE MANNER OF THE UNCLEANNESS IS TO GO OUT AND NOT TO GO IN.[6]

MISHNAH 11. [IN THE CASE WHERE] IT[7] WAS LYING ON ITS SIDE IN THE OPEN AIR, IF AN OLIVE-SIZED [PORTION] OF A CORPSE WAS PLACED BELOW IT OR ABOVE IT, EVERYTHING DIRECTLY BELOW OR ABOVE THE OLIVE-SIZED [PORTION] BECOMES UNCLEAN; BUT EVERYTHING THAT IS NOT DIRECTLY BELOW OR ABOVE, AND WHAT IS WITHIN [THE HIVE] REMAINS

(1) Cf. Mishnah 5 end n. 2. (2) The hive is regarded as resting on its bottom so that there is not a handbreadth's space between the mouth and the roof beams. (3) Cf. *supra* III, 7. (4) The one standing on top of the other. (5) Var. lec., clean. V. Rashi. (6) For this reason if the uncleanness is within the hive the house is clean. (7) The unbroken hive.

CLEAN. [IF THE UNCLEANNESS IS] WITHIN [THE HIVE] EVERYTHING BECOMES UNCLEAN.

MISHNAH 12. [IN THE CASE WHERE THIS HIVE IN THE OPEN AIR] WAS ONE HANDBREADTH HIGH OFF THE GROUND, IF THERE IS UNCLEANNESS BELOW IT OR ABOVE IT, EVERYTHING BECOMES UNCLEAN EXCEPT WHAT IS WITHIN THE HIVE]. [IF THE UNCLEANNESS IS] WITHIN, EVERYTHING BECOMES UNCLEAN. WHEN DO THESE RULES APPLY? WHEN [THE HIVE RETAINS THE STATUS OF] A VESSEL. [IN THE CASE OF ITS] BEING DEFECTIVE, ALTHOUGH [ITS DEFICIENCY MAY BE] STOPPED UP WITH STRAW, OR ACCORDING TO THE SAGES,[1] [IN THE CASE OF IT] CONTAINING FORTY SE'AHS, IF AN OLIVE-SIZED [PORTION] OF A CORPSE WERE PLACED BELOW IT, [EVERYTHING] DIRECTLY [BELOW] UNTO THE NETHERMOST DEEP BECOMES UNCLEAN; ABOVE IT, [EVERYTHING] DIRECTLY ABOVE TO THE SKY BECOMES UNCLEAN. [IF THE UNCLEANNESS IS] WITHIN [THE HIVE], NOTHING IS UNCLEAN EXCEPT THAT WHICH IS WITHIN. [IN THE CASE WHERE] IT WAS ONE HANDBREADTH HIGH OFF THE GROUND, IF THERE WAS UNCLEANNESS BELOW IT, WHAT IS BELOW BECOMES UNCLEAN;[2] [IF THE UNCLEANNESS] WAS WITHIN IT, WHAT IS WITHIN BECOMES UNCLEAN; ABOVE IT, [EVERYTHING] DIRECTLY [ABOVE] TO THE SKY BECOMES UNCLEAN.

MISHNAH 13. [IN THE CASE WHERE] IT WAS RESTING ON ITS BOTTOM AND [RETAINED THE STATUS OF] A VESSEL, IF THERE IS UNCLEANNESS BELOW IT, WITHIN IT OR ABOVE IT,[3] THE UNCLEANNESS CLEAVES UPWARDS AND DOWNWARDS.[4] [IN THE CASE WHERE] IT WAS ONE HANDBREADTH HIGH OFF

(1) Who maintain, as against R. Meir (v. Tosef. Kel. pt. II, V, 1) that certain articles when they are of the size of forty *se'ahs*, no longer retain the status of a vessel, but take on that of a 'tent'. V. also Kel. XV, 1. (2) All below, the object acting as a 'tent'. (3) Above the opening. (4) Even when the uncleanness is within, since the open mouth is in direct communication with the air above.

THE GROUND OR COVERED[1] OR INVERTED [SO AS TO STAND] UPON ITS MOUTH, IF THERE IS UNCLEANNESS BELOW IT, WITHIN IT OR ABOVE IT, EVERYTHING BECOMES UNCLEAN.

MISHNAH 14. WHEN DO THESE RULES APPLY? WHEN [THE HIVE RETAINS THE STATUS OF] A VESSEL. [IN THE CASE OF ITS] BEING DEFECTIVE, ALTHOUGH [THE DEFICIENCY MAY BE] STOPPED UP WITH STRAW, OR ACCORDING TO THE SAGES, [IN THE CASE OF IT] CONTAINING FORTY SE'AHS, IF THE UNCLEANNESS IS BELOW IT, WITHIN IT OR ABOVE IT, THE UNCLEANNESS CLEAVES UPWARDS AND DOWNWARDS. R. ELIEZER AND R. SIMEON SAY: UNCLEANNESS CAN NEITHER ASCEND INTO [THE DEFECTIVE HIVE] NOR DESCEND FROM IT.[2] [IN THE CASE WHERE] IT WAS ONE HANDBREADTH HIGH OFF THE GROUND, IF THERE IS UNCLEANNESS BELOW IT, WHAT IS BELOW BECOMES UNCLEAN; WITHIN IT OR ABOVE IT, [EVERYTHING] DIRECTLY [ABOVE] IT TO THE SKY BECOMES UNCLEAN.

MISHNAH 15. WITH REGARD TO A COFFIN[3] WHICH IS BROAD BELOW AND NARROW ABOVE, AND HAD A CORPSE WITHIN, A PERSON TOUCHING IT BELOW[4] REMAINS CLEAN; BUT ABOVE, BECOMES UNCLEAN.[5] IF IT IS BROAD ABOVE AND NARROW BELOW, A PERSON TOUCHING IT ANYWHERE BECOMES UNCLEAN. IF IT WAS THE SAME [ABOVE AND BELOW], A PERSON TOUCHING IT ANYWHERE BECOMES UNCLEAN. THIS IS THE OPINION OF R. ELIEZER, BUT R. JOSHUA SAYS: A HANDBREADTH AND MORE[6] BELOW IS CLEAN,[7] BUT FROM THAT HANDBREADTH UPWARDS IS UNCLEAN. IF IT IS MADE

(1) With another vessel, which cannot protect what is within the hive from uncleanness. (2) Being defective, it can, in their opinion, afford protection. (3) Excavated from the living rock. (4) I.e., touching a portion of the rock not directly beneath the inner wall-surface of the tomb but outside it. Not immediately supporting the covering stone (*supra* II, 4) it is clean, being reckoned part of the ordinary rock. (5) Touching the covering stone. (6) Measured from the lower base of the hollow of the coffin. (7) Being reckoned part of the ordinary rock.

LIKE A CLOTHES-CHEST,[1] A PERSON TOUCHING IT ANYWHERE BECOMES UNCLEAN. IF IT WAS MADE LIKE A CASE,[2] A PERSON TOUCHING IT ANYWHERE AT THE PLACE WHERE IT OPENS, REMAINS CLEAN.

MISHNAH 16. [WITH REGARD TO] A JAR[3] RESTING ON ITS BOTTOM IN THE OPEN AIR, IF AN OLIVE-SIZED [PORTION] OF A CORPSE IS PLACED BENEATH IT OR WITHIN IT DIRECTLY [ABOVE] ITS BOTTOM, THE UNCLEANNESS CLEAVES UPWARDS AND DOWNWARDS,[4] AND THE JAR BECOMES UNCLEAN.[5] [IF THE UNCLEANNESS IS] OUTSIDE BELOW THE SIDE, THE UNCLEANNESS CLEAVES UPWARDS AND DOWNWARDS,[6] BUT THE JAR REMAINS CLEAN.[7] [IN THE CASE WHERE THE UNCLEANNESS IS] WITHIN [THE JAR] AND BENEATH THE SIDES,[8] IF THERE IS WITHIN THE [CAVITY OF] THE SIDES A SPACE OF A CUBIC HANDBREADTH EVERYTHING[9] [WITHIN THE CAVITY] BECOMES UNCLEAN, BUT WHAT LIES DIRECTLY [BELOW] THE MOUTH REMAINS CLEAN. IF THERE IS NOT [A SPACE OF A CUBIC HANDBREADTH], THE UNCLEANNESS CLEAVES UPWARDS AND DOWNWARDS. WHEN DO THESE RULES APPLY? WHEN THE JAR IS CLEAN.[10] [IN THE CASE WHERE IT WAS CAPABLE OF BECOMING] UNCLEAN,[11] OR WAS ONE HANDBREADTH HIGH OFF THE GROUND,[12] OR COVERED,[13] OR

(1) 'A box' (cf. Kel. XVI, 7). The cover lies over the thickness of the sides (Bert.). (2) גלוסקום perhaps from γλωσσόκομον (the LXX rendering for ארון II Chron. XXIV, 8) 'a case'. The cover sinks in within the sides, not touching their thicknesses. It therefore resembles the first case in our Mishnah (Bert.). (3) Made of a substance insusceptible to uncleanness. It is narrow above and below, bulging in the middle. (4) Cf. Mishnah 13, n. 4. (5) I.e., what is within the jar in a direct line with the uncleanness. (6) In a direct line. There is not a space of one cubic handbreadth below the bulge of the jar, hence the uncleanness is compressed. (7) Being insusceptible to uncleanness from the outside. (8) I.e., in the cavity formed by the bulge. (9) Reckoned a 'tent'. (10) Insusceptible to uncleanness. (11) And consequently unable to serve as a screen to protect the contents in the jar where the uncleanness is outside beneath the bulge. (12) In this case the jar forms a 'tent' which conveys uncleanness and does not serve as a screen (v. *supra* VI, 1), spreading consequently the uncleanness in every case to the

INVERTED [SO AS TO STAND] ON ITS MOUTH,[1] IF THERE IS UNCLEANNESS BENEATH IT, WITHIN IT OR ABOVE IT, EVERYTHING BECOMES UNCLEAN.[2]

jar and its contents. (13) Whilst they would not affect the case where the uncleanness was outside under the bulge of the jar, where it was placed beneath the jar or within it directly above its bottom or beneath the sides, the contents of the jar become unclean because a tightly fitting cover does not serve as a screen against compressed uncleanness (v. Kel. X, 2), with the result that the cover itself forms a 'tent' defiling the contents of the jar.

(1) Cf. previous note *mut. mut.* (2) The cases vary in detail (L.). V. nn. 11-13.

OHOLOTH

CHAPTER X

MISHNAH 1. [WITH REGARD TO] A HATCHWAY IN A HOUSE,[1] WHICH [HATCHWAY] HAS AN OPENING OF A [SQUARE] HANDBREADTH, IF THERE IS UNCLEANNESS IN THE HOUSE,[2] WHAT IS DIRECTLY [BELOW] THE HATCHWAY REMAINS CLEAN.[3] IF THE UNCLEANNESS IS DIRECTLY [BELOW] THE HATCHWAY, THE HOUSE REMAINS CLEAN. IF THE UNCLEANNESS IS EITHER IN THE HOUSE OR DIRECTLY [BELOW] THE HATCHWAY, AND A PERSON PLACED HIS FOOT ABOVE [THE HATCHWAY], HE HAS COMBINED[4] [WITH THE ROOF TO BRING] UNCLEANNESS. IF PART OF THE UNCLEANNESS IS IN THE ROOM AND PART OF IT DIRECTLY [BELOW] THE HATCHWAY,[5] THE HOUSE BECOMES UNCLEAN AND WHAT IS DIRECTLY [AGAINST] THE UNCLEANNESS BECOMES UNCLEAN.[6]

MISHNAH 2. [IN THE CASE WHERE] THE HATCHWAY HAS NOT AN OPENING OF A [SQUARE] HANDBREADTH, IF THERE IS UNCLEANNESS IN THE HOUSE, WHAT IS DIRECTLY [BELOW] THE HATCHWAY REMAINS CLEAN. IF THE UNCLEANNESS IS DIRECTLY [BELOW] THE HATCHWAY, THE HOUSE REMAINS CLEAN.[7] [IN THE CASE WHERE] THE UNCLEANNESS IS IN THE HOUSE, IF HE PLACED HIS LEG ABOVE [THE HATCHWAY], HE REMAINS CLEAN.[8] [IN THE CASE WHERE] THE UNCLEANNESS

(1) In the roof, giving access to the open air. (2) Under the roof away from the hatchway. (3) Not being overshadowed. (4) Cf. *supra* VI, 1. The man's foot has combined with the roof to form a 'tent' for the uncleanness and everything in the room, even what is directly below the hatchway, is unclean. (5) Although the whole does not exceed an olive's bulk, so that neither part has sufficient to convey uncleanness. (6) Since vessels overshadowing but a portion of the prescribed minimum of uncleanness present (cf. *supra* III, 4) become unclean. (7) These rules are the same as in Mishnah 1. (8) No uncleanness escapes through a hole less than a square handbreadth in area (Tosef.

IS DIRECTLY [BELOW] THE HATCHWAY, IF HE PLACED HIS LEG ABOVE IT, R. MEIR DECLARES [HIM] UNCLEAN, BUT THE SAGES SAY: IF THE UNCLEANNESS WAS [IN POSITION] BEFORE HIS LEG, HE BECOMES UNCLEAN,[1] BUT IF HIS LEG WAS [IN POSITION] BEFORE THE UNCLEANNESS, HE REMAINS CLEAN.[2] R. SIMEON SAYS: [IN THE CASE WHERE] TWO [MEN'S] LEGS, ONE ABOVE THE OTHER, WERE [IN POSITION] BEFORE THE UNCLEANNESS, IF THE FIRST PERSON WITHDREW HIS LEG AND THE OTHER PERSON'S LEG WAS STILL THERE, [THE SECOND] REMAINS CLEAN, BECAUSE THE FIRST PERSON'S LEG WAS [IN POSITION] BEFORE THE UNCLEANNESS.[3]

MISHNAH 3. IF PART OF THE UNCLEANNESS IS IN THE HOUSE AND PART DIRECTLY [BELOW] THE HATCHWAY,[4] THE HOUSE BECOMES UNCLEAN, AND WHAT IS DIRECTLY [ABOVE] THE UNCLEANNESS BECOMES UNCLEAN.[5] THIS IS THE OPINION OF R. MEIR. R. JUDAH SAYS: THE HOUSE BECOMES UNCLEAN BUT WHAT IS DIRECTLY [ABOVE] THE UNCLEANNESS REMAINS CLEAN.[6] R. JOSE SAYS: IF THERE IS SUFFICIENT[7] OF THE UNCLEANNESS FOR IT TO BE DIVIDED SO THAT [ONE PART] DEFILES THE HOUSE AND [THE OTHER PART] DEFILES WHAT IS DIRECTLY [ABOVE] THE UNCLEANNESS,[8] [BOTH SPACES] BECOME UNCLEAN; IF NOT, THE HOUSE BECOMES UNCLEAN BUT WHAT IS DIRECTLY [ABOVE] THE UNCLEANNESS REMAINS CLEAN.

MISHNAH 4. [IN THE CASE OF] MANY HATCHWAYS, ONE

XI, 7) but all the house becomes unclean as in Mishnah 1 by combination of foot with roof.

(1) Because it overshadowed uncleanness. (2) Because his leg had already combined to form a complete 'tent' before the uncleanness had come, and the latter cannot escape now through a hole of less than a square handbreadth in a valid 'tent'. (3) He is not regarded as coming into position after the uncleanness. (4) Of less than a square handbreadth in size. (5) V. Mishnah 1, n. 6. (6) Any continuation of a portion of uncleanness not being able to defile through an opening of less than a handbreadth. (7) I.e., a minimum of twice the size of an olive. (8) Though they are not so divided in fact.

ABOVE THE OTHER,[1] HAVING AN OPENING OF ONE HANDBREADTH [SQUARE], IF THERE IS UNCLEANNESS IN THE HOUSE,[2] WHAT IS DIRECTLY [BELOW] THE HATCHWAYS REMAINS CLEAN. IF THE UNCLEANNESS IS DIRECTLY [BELOW] THE HATCHWAYS, THE HOUSE REMAINS CLEAN. [IN THE CASE] WHERE THE UNCLEANNESS IS EITHER IN THE HOUSE OR DIRECTLY [BELOW] THE HATCHWAYS, IF AN ARTICLE SUSCEPTIBLE TO UNCLEANNESS WERE PLACED EITHER IN THE UPPER OR THE LOWER [HATCHWAY], ALL BECOMES UNCLEAN.[3] IF THE ARTICLE IS INSUSCEPTIBLE TO UNCLEANNESS, WHAT IS BELOW BECOMES UNCLEAN,[4] BUT WHAT IS ABOVE REMAINS CLEAN.[5]

MISHNAH 5. [IN THE CASE] WHERE THE HATCHWAYS HAVE NOT AN OPENING OF A SQUARE HANDBREADTH, IF THERE IS UNCLEANNESS IN THE HOUSE, WHAT IS DIRECTLY [BELOW] THE HATCHWAYS REMAINS CLEAN. IF THERE IS UNCLEANNESS DIRECTLY [BELOW] THE HATCHWAYS, THE HOUSE REMAINS CLEAN. [IN THE CASE] WHERE THE UNCLEANNESS IS IN THE HOUSE,[6] IF AN ARTICLE WHETHER SUSCEPTIBLE TO UNCLEANNESS OR INSUSCEPTIBLE TO UNCLEANNESS WAS PLACED EITHER IN THE UPPER OR THE LOWER [HATCHWAY], NOTHING BECOMES UNCLEAN EXCEPT THE LOWER STOREY.[7] [IN THE CASE] WHERE THE UNCLEANNESS IS DIRECTLY [BELOW] THE HATCHWAYS, IF AN ARTICLE SUSCEPTIBLE TO UNCLEANNESS WERE PLACED EITHER IN THE UPPER OR LOWER [HATCHWAY], EVERYTHING BECOMES

(1) One in the ceiling of the ground floor and the other in the roof, vertically above the first. (2) Not under the hatchways. (3) Including whatever is in the house, the article placed over the hatchway forming a 'tent' overshadowing all. Even if the article was only in the lower hatchway the upper storey would become unclean, seeing that the article is susceptible to uncleanness and cannot therefore screen the upper storey, and hence is regarded as being in the upper hatchway (Bert.). (4) Being overshadowed by the article. (5) It forms a valid screen.. (6) In the lower storey. (7) The uncleanness being unable to escape through an opening of less than a square handbreadth.

UNCLEAN.[1] IF THE ARTICLE IS INSUSCEPTIBLE TO UNCLEANNESS, WHETHER [IT IS PLACED] IN THE UPPER OR LOWER [HATCHWAY], NOTHING BECOMES UNCLEAN EXCEPT THE LOWER STOREY.[2]

MISHNAH 6. [WITH REGARD TO] A HATCHWAY IN A HOUSE WITH A POT SO PLACED BELOW IT THAT, IF IT WAS RAISED, ITS RIMS WOULD NOT TOUCH THE [EDGES OF THE] HATCHWAY, IF THERE IS UNCLEANNESS BELOW, WITHIN OR ABOVE [THE POT], THE UNCLEANNESS CLEAVES UPWARDS AND DOWNWARDS.[3] [IN THE CASE] WHERE [THE POT] WAS ONE HANDBREADTH HIGH OFF THE GROUND, IF THERE IS UNCLEANNESS BELOW IT OR IN THE HOUSE, WHAT IS BELOW IT AND IN THE HOUSE BECOMES UNCLEAN,[4] BUT WHAT IS WITHIN [THE POT] OR ABOVE IT, REMAINS CLEAN.[5] [IF THE UNCLEANNESS IS] WITHIN OR ABOVE [THE POT], EVERYTHING BECOMES UNCLEAN.[6]

MISHNAH 7. [IN THE CASE WHERE THE POT WAS] SO PLACED ON THE SIDE OF THE THRESHOLD[7] SO THAT IF IT WAS RAISED IT WOULD TOUCH THE LINTEL OVER A [SPACE OF A SQUARE] HANDBREADTH,[8] IF THERE IS UNCLEANNESS BELOW, WITHIN OR ABOVE [THE POT], THE UNCLEANNESS CLEAVES UPWARDS AND DOWNWARDS. [IN THE CASE] WHERE IT WAS ONE HANDBREADTH HIGH OFF THE GROUND, IF THERE IS UNCLEANNESS BELOW IT OR IN THE HOUSE, WHAT

(1) As in Mishnah 4. (2) Where the uncleanness is, the article screening. (3) Even penetrating the earthenware pot which normally cannot be defiled from its outside. (4) Since the pot combines with the roof and brings the uncleanness by overshadowing. (5) The pot screening in conjunction with the walls of the house (cf. *supra* V, 5). (6) I.e., the pot, which consequently cannot serve as a screen, and hence all else in the house as in Mishnah 4. (7) I.e., on the outer side of the house where also the uncleanness was. (8) It is a case where the pot was wider below and getting narrower towards the opening, so that when it is raised the opening would be entirely outside the lintel, whereas the bottom part would still be covering the lintel over the space of a handbreadth.

IS BELOW IT AND IN THE HOUSE BECOMES UNCLEAN. IF THE UNCLEANNESS IS WITHIN OR ABOVE [THE POT], EVERYTHING BECOMES UNCLEAN.[1] [IN THE CASE WHERE THE POT] IF RAISED WOULD NOT TOUCH THE LINTEL OVER A [SPACE OF A SQUARE] HANDBREADTH, OR IS JOINED TO THE LINTEL,[2] IF THERE IS UNCLEANNESS BELOW IT, NOTHING IS UNCLEAN EXCEPT WHAT IS BELOW [THE POT].[3]

(1) As in Mishnah 6, n. 4. (2) In such a manner as not to touch a handbreadth of the lintel. (3) Since there is no handbreadth under the lintel the uncleanness does not pass into the house and consequently what is within and above the pot is clean.

OHOLOTH

CHAPTER XI

MISHNAH 1. [WITH REGARD TO] A HOUSE, [WHOSE ROOF] HAS BEEN SPLIT [INTO TWO],[1] IF THERE IS UNCLEANNESS IN THE OUTER [PART],[2] VESSELS IN THE INNER [PART] REMAIN CLEAN.[3] IF THE UNCLEANNESS IS IN THE INNER [PART], VESSELS IN THE OUTER [PART ARE DECLARED CLEAN], ACCORDING TO BETH SHAMMAI, WHEN THE SPLIT IS FOUR HANDBREADTHS WIDE;[4] BUT BETH HILLEL SAY: [WHEN THE SPLIT IS OF] ANY SIZE.[5] R. JOSE SAYS IN THE NAME OF BETH HILLEL: [WHEN IT IS] ONE HANDBREADTH WIDE.

MISHNAH 2. [WITH REGARD TO] A PORTICO WHICH HAS BEEN SPLIT [INTO TWO], IF THERE IS UNCLEANNESS ON THE ONE SIDE,[6] VESSELS ON THE OTHER SIDE REMAIN CLEAN.[7] IF A PERSON PLACED HIS LEG OR A REED ABOVE [THE SPLIT],[8] HE HAS COMBINED [WITH THE ROOF TO BRING THE] UNCLEANNESS.[9] IF HE PLACED THE REED ON THE GROUND,[10] IT DOES NOT FORM A PASSAGE FOR THE UNCLEANNESS, [NOR CAN IT DO SO] UNTIL IT IS ONE HANDBREADTH OFF THE GROUND.[11]

MISHNAH 3. A THICK WOOLLEN BLANKET OR A THICK WOODEN BLOCK[12] CANNOT FORM A PASSAGE FOR UNCLEANNESS[13] UNLESS THEY ARE ONE HANDBREADTH HIGH OFF THE

(1) Two separate 'tents' thus being formed. (2) Nearer the exit of the house. (3) Because the uncleanness goes out by the exit and not into the inner portion, however narrow the split. (4) The uncleanness can be taken out through the wide split. (5) Subject to a minimum thickness of a plumb-line (Tosef.). (6) Of the split. (7) Cf. n. 3 *mut. mut.* (8) Either in the case of the house or portico. (9) Cf. *supra* X, 1. (10) Directly below the split. (11) And thus forming a common 'tent' with the roof connecting both parts of the house. (12) כופת from כפת 'to invert', a wooden block used as a low seat. (13) Even though one handbreadth high and placed directly below the split.

GROUND. IF [GARMENTS] ARE FOLDED ONE ABOVE THE OTHER THEY CANNOT FORM A PASSAGE FOR THE UNCLEANNESS UNLESS THE UPPERMOST IS ONE HANDBREADTH HIGH OFF THE GROUND.[1] IF A PERSON WERE PLACED THERE,[2] BETH SHAMMAI SAY: HE CANNOT FORM A PASSAGE FOR THE UNCLEANNESS. BUT BETH HILLEL SAY: A MAN IS HOLLOW AND HIS UPPERMOST SURFACE FORMS A PASSAGE FOR THE UNCLEANNESS.

MISHNAH 4. IF A PERSON WAS LOOKING OUT OF A WINDOW AND OVERSHADOWED A FUNERAL PROCESSION,[3] BETH SHAMMAI SAY: HE DOES NOT FORM A PASSAGE FOR THE UNCLEANNESS.[4] BUT BETH HILLEL SAY: HE DOES FORM A PASSAGE FOR THE UNCLEANNESS. THEY AGREE THAT IF HE WAS DRESSED IN HIS CLOTHES OR IF THERE WERE TWO PERSONS, ONE ABOVE THE OTHER, THESE[5] FORM A PASSAGE FOR THE UNCLEANNESS.[6]

MISHNAH 5. [IN THE CASE] WHERE THE PERSON WAS LYING ON THE THRESHOLD AND THE FUNERAL PROCESSION OVERSHADOWED HIM,[7] BETH SHAMMAI SAY: HE DOES NOT FORM A PASSAGE FOR THE UNCLEANNESS.[8] BUT BETH HILLEL SAY: HE DOES FORM A PASSAGE FOR THE UNCLEANNESS.

MISHNAH 6. [IN THE CASE] WHERE THE UNCLEANNESS WAS IN THE HOUSE AND CLEAN PERSONS OVERSHADOWED HIM,[9] BETH SHAMMAI DECLARE THEM CLEAN, BUT BETH HILLEL DECLARE THEM UNCLEAN.[10]

(1) Rather: they form a passage for the uncleanness if only the uppermost is one handbreadth high from the ground (Wilna Gaon). (2) Directly under the object. V. 'Ed. IV, 12. (3) And the corpse. (4) *Sc.* into the house from which he was looking out, because he is not one handbreadth high above the sill. Beth Shammai differ from Beth Hillel and do not regard the man as being hollow, and his body forms a partition between the corpse and the house. (5) The garments or the upper person. (6) Since these are one handbreadth above the sill. (7) And the corpse. (8) To bring it into the house, as in Mishnah 4. (9) The person described in Mishnah 5. (10) Each school in accordance with its respective view in Mishnahs 4 and 5.

MISHNAH 7. [WITH REGARD TO] A DOG WHICH HAD EATEN THE FLESH OF A CORPSE, HAD [SUBSEQUENTLY] DIED[1] AND WAS LYING OVER THE THRESHOLD, R. MEIR SAYS: IF ITS NECK HAS A THICKNESS OF ONE HANDBREADTH IT CAN FORM A PASSAGE FOR THE UNCLEANNESS, BUT IF NOT, IT CANNOT FORM A PASSAGE FOR THE UNCLEANNESS. R. JOSE SAYS: WE [EXAMINE TO] SEE WHERE THE UNCLEANNESS IS. [IF IT LIES FROM BENEATH] THE LINTEL INWARDS, THE HOUSE BECOMES UNCLEAN; [FROM BENEATH] THE LINTEL OUTWARDS, THE HOUSE REMAINS CLEAN. R. ELIEZER SAYS: IF ITS MOUTH [POINTS] INWARDS, THE HOUSE REMAINS CLEAN; IF ITS MOUTH [POINTS] OUTWARDS, THE HOUSE BECOMES UNCLEAN, SINCE THE UNCLEANNESS PROCEEDS FORTH THROUGH ITS HINDER PARTS. R. JUDAH B. BATHYRA SAYS: WHETHER THE ONE [CONDITION] OR THE OTHER [APPLIES], THE HOUSE BECOMES UNCLEAN.[2] HOW LONG SHOULD [THE UNCLEANNESS] HAVE REMAINED IN ITS ENTRAILS?[3] THREE WHOLE DAYS.[4] [IN THE CASE OF THE UNCLEANNESS BEING IN THE ENTRAILS] OF FISHES OR BIRDS, AS LONG AS [IT TAKES FOR THE UNCLEANNESS] TO FALL IN THE FIRE AND BE CONSUMED; SO R. SIMEON. R. JUDAH B. BATHYRA SAYS: IN THE CASE OF FISHES OR BIRDS, TWENTY-FOUR HOURS.

MISHNAH 8. WITH REGARD TO A CELLAR[5] IN A HOUSE,[6] WITH A CANDLESTICK [STANDING] THEREIN WHOSE CALYX[7] PROTRUDES[8] AND [SUPPORTS] AN OLIVE-BASKET SO PLACED THAT IF THE CANDLESTICK IS TAKEN AWAY THE OLIVE-BASKET WOULD STILL REMAIN OVER THE MOUTH OF THE CELLAR,[9] BETH SHAMMAI SAY: THE CELLAR REMAINS CLEAN[10]

(1) If the dog was alive, any uncleanness that it had swallowed would not defile (v. Ḥul. 71*b*). (2) For notes on this Mishnah v. Ḥul., Sonc. ed., p. 126*a*. (3) Before the dog died so that it would have time to be digested. (4) V. Shab. 155*b* for a Talmudic statement based upon this observation. (5) חרות The same word as רות *supra* V, 6. (6) In which there is a corpse. (7) פרח Cf. Kel. XI, 7. The flower-shaped structure which holds the lamp. (8) Into the house. (9) I.e., it would not fall down into the cellar. (10) Being protected by the olive-basket.

BUT THE CANDLESTICK BECOMES UNCLEAN.[1] BETH HILLEL SAY: THE CANDLESTICK ALSO REMAINS CLEAN. BUT THEY AGREE THAT IF THE OLIVE-BASKET WOULD FALL [INTO THE CELLAR] IF THE CANDLESTICK WAS TAKEN AWAY, ALL WOULD BECOME UNCLEAN.

MISHNAH 9. VESSELS [THAT ARE] BETWEEN THE RIMS OF THE OLIVE-BASKET[2] AND THE RIMS OF THE CELLAR, EVEN TO THE NETHERMOST DEEP,[3] REMAIN CLEAN.[4] IF THERE IS UNCLEANNESS IN THE CELLAR, THE HOUSE BECOMES UNCLEAN.[5] IF THERE IS UNCLEANNESS IN THE HOUSE, VESSELS IN THE WALLS OF THE CELLAR[6] REMAIN CLEAN, IF THE PLACE WHERE THEY ARE HAS A CONTENT OF ONE CUBIC HANDBREADTH;[7] IF NOT, THEY BECOME UNCLEAN. IF THE WALLS OF THE CELLAR ARE WIDER [APART][8] THAN THOSE OF THE HOUSE, IN EITHER CASE THE VESSELS REMAIN CLEAN.[9]

(1) Being made of metal and protruding into the house. (2) That was not supported by the candlestick. (3) I.e., even those in the ground. (4) The basket affording protection, otherwise the corpse uncleanness in the house would spread to the vessels in the ground of the cellar, v. *infra* XV, 5. (5) Cf. *supra* IV, 1. (6) I.e., those parts which are not covered by the basket, the basket being round, whereas the cellar is square, so that the corners of the opening of the latter remain uncovered. (7) V. *supra* III, 7. (8) So that the cellar walls are not the continuation of the walls of the house. (9) In this case the walls of the cellar are not regarded at all as part of the house.

OHOLOTH

CHAPTER XII

MISHNAH 1. [WITH REGARD TO] A BOARD PLACED OVER THE MOUTH OF A NEW[1] OVEN,[2] OVERLAPPING IT ON ALL SIDES TO THE EXTENT OF A HANDBREADTH, IF THERE IS UNCLEANNESS BENEATH [THE BOARD], VESSELS ABOVE IT REMAIN CLEAN; IF THERE IS UNCLEANNESS ABOVE IT, VESSELS BENEATH IT REMAIN CLEAN.[3] IN THE CASE OF AN OLD OVEN, THEY BECOME UNCLEAN.[4] R. JOḤANAN B. NURI DECLARES THEM CLEAN.[5] [IN THE CASE WHERE THE BOARD] IS PLACED OVER THE MOUTH OF TWO [OLD] OVENS, IF THERE IS UNCLEANNESS BETWEEN THEM, THEY BECOME UNCLEAN. R. JOḤANAN B. NURI DECLARES THEM CLEAN.

MISHNAH 2. [WITH REGARD TO] A COLANDER[6] PLACED[7] OVER THE MOUTH OF AN OVEN, [SO THAT THIS IS] CLOSED WITH A SEALED LID,[8] IF THERE IS UNCLEANNESS BELOW OR ABOVE IT, EVERYTHING BECOMES UNCLEAN; BUT WHAT IS DIRECTLY [ABOVE] THE AIR-SPACE OF THE OVEN REMAINS CLEAN.[9] IF THERE IS UNCLEANNESS DIRECTLY [ABOVE] THE AIR-SPACE OF THE OVEN, EVERYTHING DIRECTLY ABOVE IT EVEN TO THE SKY BECOMES UNCLEAN.

MISHNAH 3. [IN THE CASE WHERE] THE BOARD PLACED

(1) One not yet kindled (v. Kel. V, 1). It is not reckoned a vessel and is insusceptible to uncleanness; hence it can protect against uncleanness. (2) Standing in the open air, (3) The board and new oven serving as a screen. (4) Heated ovens are vessels susceptible to uncleanness and hence (v. *supra* VI, 1) serve as 'tents' to bring uncleanness, but not to protect against it. (5) Ovens differing, in his opinion, from other vessels in respect of the law laid down in VI, 1, being completely attached to the ground. (6) Cf. *supra* V, 6. (7) In the same position as the board in Mishnah 1. (8) As in Kel. IX, 7. (9) Since the air-space itself remains clean because of the sealed lid.

OVER THE MOUTH OF AN OLD OVEN PROJECTS FROM EITHER [END] TO THE EXTENT OF ONE HANDBREADTH BUT NOT FROM THE SIDES, IF THERE IS UNCLEANNESS UNDER ONE END [OF THE BOARD], VESSELS [UNDER] THE OTHER END REMAIN CLEAN.[1] R. JOSE DECLARES THEM UNCLEAN.[2] A BATH[3] DOES NOT FORM A PASSAGE FOR UNCLEANNESS.[4] IF THERE WAS A BRACKET[5] IN IT, R. ELIEZER SAYS: IT [STILL] DOES NOT FORM A PASSAGE FOR THE UNCLEANNESS. R. JOSHUA SAYS: THE BATH IS REGARDED AS NOT BEING THERE, AND THE BRACKET ABOVE FORMS A PASSAGE FOR THE UNCLEANNESS.

MISHNAH 4. [WITH REGARD TO] THE SHOE[6] OF A CRADLE,[7] FOR WHICH A HOLE HAD BEEN MADE [IN THE CEILING TO BRING IT] INTO THE HOUSE [BELOW],[8] IF [THE HOLE] IS ONE HANDBREADTH SQUARE, EVERYTHING[9] BECOMES UNCLEAN;[10] BUT IF IT WAS NOT [ONE HANDBREADTH SQUARE], ITS [UNCLEANNESS] IS COMPUTED AS ONE RECKONS WITH [CASES OF CONTACT WITH] A CORPSE.[11]

MISHNAH 5. [WITH REGARD TO] THE ROOF BEAMS[12] OF THE HOUSE AND OF THE UPPER STOREY WHICH HAVE NO CEILING-WORK UPON THEM AND ARE IN A LINE, [THE UPPER ONES EXACTLY ABOVE THE LOWER], IF THERE IS UNCLEANNESS BENEATH ONE OF THEM, ALL BENEATH THAT ONE BECOMES

(1) The board affording no passage for the uncleanness and the oven serving as partition between the two 'tents' formed by each projection. (2) In his view the oven forms no partition. (3) Attached to the ground, בטמה. Some readings have אבטמה. 'Aruch gives a cognate Arabic root meaning 'a bath' or 'sill', whence Bert. renders 'bath' and Maim. 'windowsill'. (4) If there is a board placed over it projecting at both ends. (5) זיז, found also in *supra* VIII, 2 meaning 'wall-projection'. The bracket overlies the whole length of the bath and the board is over the bracket. (6) סנדל 'sandal', explained as metal shoe placed under the cradle legs for protection or adornment. (7) Placed in the upper storey. (8) Where there is a corpse. (9) In the upper storey. Var. lec.: it forms a passage for the uncleanness. (10) The shoe affording no protection. (11) The shoe and cradle acquiring seven-day uncleanness, and the child in it uncleanness lasting till evening (v. *supra* I, 2). (12) Each of one handbreadth in width.

UNCLEAN. IF IT IS BETWEEN A LOWER AND AN UPPER [BEAM], WHAT IS BETWEEN THEM BECOMES UNCLEAN. IF IT IS ABOVE THE UPPER [ROOF BEAMS], WHAT IS DIRECTLY ABOVE TO THE SKY BECOMES UNCLEAN. [IN THE CASE] WHERE THE UPPER [ROOF BEAMS] WERE [OVER THE GAPS] BETWEEN THE LOWER [ROOF BEAMS],[1] IF THERE IS UNCLEANNESS BENEATH ONE OF THEM, WHAT IS BENEATH ALL OF THEM BECOMES UNCLEAN; IF ABOVE THEM, WHAT IS DIRECTLY ABOVE TO THE SKY BECOMES UNCLEAN.

MISHNAH 6. [WITH REGARD TO] A BEAM WHICH IS PLACED ACROSS FROM ONE WALL TO ANOTHER AND WHICH HAS UNCLEANNESS BENEATH IT, IF IT IS ONE HANDBREADTH WIDE, IT CONVEYS THE UNCLEANNESS TO ALL BENEATH IT; IF IT IS NOT [ONE HANDBREADTH WIDE], THE UNCLEANNESS CLEAVES UPWARDS AND DOWNWARDS. HOW MUCH MUST ITS CIRCUMFERENCE BE SO THAT ITS WIDTH SHOULD BE ONE HANDBREADTH? IF IT IS ROUND, ITS CIRCUMFERENCE MUST BE THREE HANDBREADTHS; IF SQUARE, FOUR HANDBREADTHS, SINCE A SQUARE HAS A [CIRCUMFERENCE] ONE QUARTER GREATER THAN [THAT OF] A CIRCLE.[2]

MISHNAH 7. [WITH REGARD TO] A PILLAR LYING [ON ITS SIDE] IN THE OPEN AIR, IF ITS CIRCUMFERENCE IS TWENTY-FOUR HANDBREADTHS, IT FORMS A PASSAGE FOR UNCLEANNESS FOR ALL BENEATH ITS SIDE;[3] BUT IF IT IS NOT, THE UNCLEANNESS CLEAVES UPWARDS AND DOWNWARDS.

(1) And were of the same size as those gaps. (2) Of a diameter equal to the side of the square. The circumference of the square is four handbreadths and of the circle, three, using the simplified calculation employed in the Talmud here and elsewhere ('Er. I, 5; Suk. 7*b*). (3) Such a pillar has, according to the Rabbinic reckoning, a diameter of eight handbreadths. When a circle of this size is inscribed in a square, there is sufficient space in the corners between the circle and the square to inscribe a smaller square with a side of one handbreadth. Therefore under a pillar of these dimensions a space of one cubic handbreadth, the minimum size of a shelter for uncleanness, can be found. Mathematically computed, the side

MISHNAH 8. IF AN OLIVE-SIZED PORTION OF A CORPSE ADHERES TO THE THRESHOLD,[1] R. ELIEZER DECLARES THE HOUSE UNCLEAN. R. JOSHUA DECLARES IT CLEAN. IF IT WAS PLACED BENEATH THE THRESHOLD, THE [CASE] IS JUDGED BY THE HALF [IN WHICH THE UNCLEANNESS IS].[2] IF IT IS ADHERING TO THE LINTEL, THE HOUSE BECOMES UNCLEAN. R. JOSE DECLARES IT CLEAN. IF IT WAS IN THE HOUSE, A PERSON TOUCHING THE LINTEL BECOMES UNCLEAN.[3] [AS FOR] A PERSON TOUCHING THE THRESHOLD, R. ELIEZER DECLARES HIM UNCLEAN. R. JOSHUA SAYS: [IF HE TOUCHES IT AT A POINT] BELOW A HANDBREADTH [FROM THE UPPER SURFACE], HE REMAINS CLEAN; ABOVE THAT HANDBREADTH HE BECOMES UNCLEAN.[4]

of the smaller square inscribed in the corner between a circle and the circumscribed square has a relation to the side of the larger square of $1 : 4 + {}^2/_2$. The circle thus has a circumference $\pi\ (4 + {}^2/_2)$ times the side of the smaller square. If that side was one handbreadth, the circumference would be approximately twenty-one and a half handbreadths. The measurement in our Mishnah is thus slightly too large. V. figure given by Hoffmann (Itzkowski-Kanel ed. Mishnah VI, 1 p. 210).

(1) Outside the door jamb and not under the lintel. (2) Only the inner half of the threshold being reckoned with the inside of the house. (3) Cf. *supra* VII, 3. (4) Cf. *supra* IX, 15.

OHOLOTH

CHAPTER XIII

MISHNAH 1. [WITH REGARD TO] A LIGHT HOLE NEWLY MADE, ITS MINIMUM SIZE[1] IS THAT OF A HOLE MADE BY THE LARGE DRILL OF THE TEMPLE CHAMBER.[2] [IN THE CASE OF] THE RESIDUE OF A LIGHT-HOLE,[3] [THE SIZE IS] TWO FINGER-BREADTHS HIGH BY A THUMBBREADTH BROAD. THE FOLLOWING IS CONSIDERED A RESIDUE OF A LIGHT-HOLE: A WINDOW THAT A PERSON HAD BLOCKED UP BUT HAD NOT BEEN ABLE TO FINISH. [IN THE CASE OF A HOLE] BORED BY WATER, OR BY REPTILES, OR EATEN AWAY BY SALTPETRE, THE MINIMUM SIZE IS THAT OF A FIST.[4] IF THE HOLE HAD BEEN INTENDED FOR [DOMESTIC] USE, ITS MINIMUM SIZE IS ONE HAND-BREADTH SQUARE; FOR LIGHTING, ITS MINIMUM SIZE IS THAT OF A HOLE MADE BY THE DRILL. THE HOLES IN GRATING[5] OR LATTICE-WORK[6] MAY BE JOINED TOGETHER TO FORM [AN OPENING] THE SIZE OF A HOLE MADE BY THE DRILL, ACCORDING TO THE OPINION OF BETH SHAMMAI. BETH HILLEL SAY: [NOTHING CAN BE RECKONED] UNLESS THERE IS A HOLE OF THE SIZE MADE BY THE DRILL IN ONE PLACE. [THE FOREGOING SIZES APPLY] FOR PURPOSES OF ALLOWING THE UNCLEANNESS TO COME IN OR TO GO OUT.[7] R. SIMEON SAYS: ONLY FOR ALLOWING THE UN-CLEANNESS TO COME IN; BUT FOR ALLOWING THE UN-CLEANNESS TO GO OUT [THE MINIMUM SIZE] IS ONE HAND-BREADTH SQUARE.

(1) For giving passage to the uncleanness. (2) V. *supra* II, 3. (3) Already made but partially blocked. (4) Of a giant called Ben Batiaḥ (Kel. XVII, 12). (5) V. *supra* VIII, 4. Such as are used for the doors of food safes (Bert.). (6) רפפות, from the root רפף 'to shake', hence 'loosely-moving shutters'. (Tosef. XIV, 3, those of summer houses). (7) Some commentators refer the case of going out to that in *supra* VII, 3.

MISHNAH 2. [WITH REGARD TO] A WINDOW MADE FOR LETTING IN AIR, ITS MINIMUM SIZE IS THAT OF A HOLE MADE BY THE DRILL. IF A HOUSE WAS BUILT OUTSIDE IT, ITS MINIMUM SIZE BECOMES ONE HANDBREADTH SQUARE. IF THE ROOF[1] WAS PLACED AT THE HEIGHT OF THE MIDDLE OF THE WINDOW, THE MINIMUM SIZE OF THE LOWER PART IS ONE HANDBREADTH SQUARE AND OF THE UPPER PART THAT OF A HOLE MADE BY THE DRILL.

MISHNAH 3. [WITH REGARD TO] A HOLE IN THE DOOR, ITS MINIMUM SIZE IS THAT OF A FIST. THIS IS THE OPINION OF R. AKIBA. R. TARFON SAYS: ONE HANDBREADTH SQUARE. IF THE CARPENTER HAD LEFT A SPACE AT THE BOTTOM OR THE TOP [OF THE DOOR], OR IF ONE HAD SHUT [THE DOOR] BUT NOT CLOSED IT TIGHTLY,[2] OR IF THE WIND BLEW IT OPEN, THE MINIMUM SIZE IS THAT OF A FIST.

MISHNAH 4. IF A PLACE[3] WAS MADE FOR A ROD, A STAVE,[4] OR A LAMP, THE MINIMUM SIZE IS WHATEVER IS NEEDFUL, ACCORDING TO THE OPINION OF BETH SHAMMAI. BETH HILLEL SAY: ONE HANDBREADTH SQUARE. [IF IT WAS MADE] FOR A PEEP-HOLE,[5] FOR SPEAKING THROUGH TO HIS FELLOW, OR FOR [DOMESTIC] USE, THE MINIMUM SIZE IS ONE HANDBREADTH SQUARE.

MISHNAH 5. THE FOLLOWING [OBJECTS SERVE TO] REDUCE [THE AREA OF A SQUARE] HANDBREADTH:[6] [A PORTION] OF LESS THAN AN OLIVE-SIZE OF FLESH [OF A CORPSE] REDUCES [THE OPENING FOR UNCLEANNESS THAT IS] CAUSED BY A QUARTER OF A ḲAB OF BONES[7] [FROM A CORPSE]; [A

(1) Of the adjacent house. (2) מירקה, from מרק 'to finish'. (3) I.e., a hole. (4) The staff with which the weaver beats together the newly spun woof-threads. (5) לזון את עיניו 'to feast his eyes', i.e., to allow of a look-out. Preuss, however, p. 329, translates 'to nourish the eyes', i.e., to effect a cure on them. (6) Making the opening too small to allow passage for the uncleanness. (7) But not for an olive-sized portion of flesh, in

PORTION] OF LESS THAN A BARLEY-CORN SIZE OF BONE REDUCES [THE OPENING FOR UNCLEANNESS THAT IS] CAUSED BY AN OLIVE-SIZED PORTION OF FLESH; LESS THAN AN OLIVE-SIZED PORTION OF A CORPSE,[1] LESS THAN AN OLIVE-SIZED PORTION OF CARRION, LESS THAN A LENTIL-SIZED PORTION OF REPTILE, LESS THAN AN EGG-SIZED PORTION OF FOOD, A PLANT GROWING AGAINST THE WINDOW,[2] A COBWEB[3] HAVING SUBSTANCE, THE CARCASE OF A CLEAN BIRD THAT HAD NOT BEEN INTENDED [FOR FOOD],[4] AND THE CARCASE OF AN UNCLEAN BIRD THAT HAD BEEN INTENDED [FOR FOOD] BUT HAD NOT BEEN RENDERED SUSCEPTIBLE [TO UNCLEANNESS], OR WHICH HAD BEEN RENDERED SUSCEPTIBLE [TO UNCLEANNESS] BUT HAD NOT BEEN INTENDED [FOR FOOD].[5]

MISHNAH 8. THE FOLLOWING CANNOT REDUCE [THE AFORESAID AREA]: BONE CANNOT REDUCE [THE AREA] FOR [OTHER] BONES;[6] NOR [CORPSE] FLESH FOR [OTHER] FLESH; NOR AN OLIVE-SIZED [PORTION] OF A CORPSE, NOR AN OLIVE-SIZED PORTION OF CARRION, NOR A LENTIL-SIZED PORTION OF REPTILE, NOR AN EGG-SIZED PORTION OF FOOD, NOR A PLANT GROWING IN THE WINDOWS,[7] NOR A COBWEB HAVING NO SUBSTANCE, NOR THE CARCASE OF A CLEAN BIRD WHICH HAD BEEN INTENDED [FOR FOOD], NOR THE CARCASE OF AN UNCLEAN BIRD WHICH HAD BEEN INTENDED [FOR FOOD] AND HAD BEEN RENDERED SUSCEPTIBLE TO UNCLEANNESS,

which case the two portions would combine to convey the uncleanness.

(1) This has already been mentioned, but is repeated here to teach that it reduces the opening in respect of all things enumerated in II, 1-2, as conveying uncleanness by overshadowing. (2) But planted some little distance away (according to L. three handbreadths away). (3) כביי 'Aruch quotes a cognate Arabic word meaning 'spider's web' (so Bert.). In Kel. XVII, 17 the same word, as is shown by the context, means 'reed-pith'. (4) And is therefore not yet susceptible to uncleanness. The laws concerning a clean bird are detailed in Ṭoh. I, 1. (5) Unclean birds require both conditions to be fulfilled, intention for food and predisposition by moisture (Maksh.) as in Ṭoh. I, 3. (6) V. *supra* 5, n. 7. (7) In a part where such a growth is undesirable and would ultimately be removed (Bert.).

NOR WARP AND WOOF THREADS SMITTEN WITH PLAGUE,[1] NOR A BRICK FROM A BETH PERAS.[2] [THIS LAST IS] THE OPINION OF R. MEIR,[3] BUT THE SAGES SAY: THE BRICK CAN REDUCE, BECAUSE THE DUST [OF THE BETH PERAS] IS CLEAN.[4] THIS IS THE GENERAL RULE: WHAT IS CLEAN REDUCES [THE AREA], AND WHAT IS UNCLEAN DOES NOT REDUCE IT.

(1) Which are unclean (Neg. XI, 8). (2) V. *supra* II, 3; *infra* XVII, 1. (3) He holds that such bricks are unclean. (4) When the original clod has been broken up.

OHOLOTH

CHAPTER XIV

MISHNAH 1. A CANOPY[1] FORMS A PASSAGE FOR THE UNCLEANNESS,[2] BE IT OF WHATSOEVER WIDTH;[3] BUT A BALCONY OR ROUNDED [PROJECTION[4] ONLY] WHEN THEY ARE ONE HANDBREADTH WIDE. WHAT IS A CANOPY? THAT [PROJECTION] WHOSE [MAIN] SURFACE FACES DOWNWARDS, WHILE A BALCONY HAS ITS [MAIN] SURFACE FACING UPWARDS. IN WHAT [CIRCUMSTANCES] WAS IT SAID THAT A CANOPY FORMED A PASSAGE FOR UNCLEANNESS BE IT OF WHATSOEVER WIDTH? WITH REGARD TO A CANOPY WHICH IS THREE COURSES,[5] OR TWELVE HANDBREADTHS, ABOVE THE DOORWAY. WHEN HIGHER THAN THAT, IF FORMS A PASSAGE FOR UNCLEANNESS ONLY IF IT IS ONE HANDBREADTH WIDE. CORNICES[6] AND CARVINGS FORM A PASSAGE FOR THE UNCLEANNESS WHEN THEY ARE ONE HANDBREADTH WIDE.

MISHNAH 2. A CANOPY THAT IS ABOVE A DOORWAY FORMS A PASSAGE FOR THE UNCLEANNESS WHEN IT IS ONE HANDBREADTH WIDE;[7] IF ABOVE A WINDOW TWO FINGERBREADTHS HIGH OR THE SIZE OF A HOLE MADE BY A DRILL,[8] WHEN OF ANY WIDTH WHATSOEVER. R. JOSE SAYS: WHEN OF EQUAL SIZE [TO THE PARTICULAR WINDOW].

(1) V. *supra* VIII, 2, n. 9. Here it seems to be a kind of ornamental moulding going round the house. (2) Beneath it, transferring it to the house. (3) Since it is joined to the house (L.). (4) גבלית. The cognate Arabic word means 'hill'. The Tosef. XIV explains it as a balcony rounded off at both ends. The word may be similar to גבן 'humpy'. (5) *Sc.* of bricks. נדבך. Cf. *supra* VI, 1, n. 4. (6) עטרות, ornaments in the shape of a crown (*corona*, hence 'cornice') above doorways and windows. (7) This rule seems to contradict that in the previous Mishnah. Bert. explains this case to apply when the door is closed; L. when the canopy extends over the doorway alone. (8) V. *supra* XIII, 1.

MISHNAH 3. A ROD ABOVE A DOORWAY,[1] EVEN IF ONE HUNDRED CUBITS HIGHER,[2] FORMS A PASSAGE FOR THE UNCLEANNESS WHEN IT IS OF ANY WIDTH. THIS IS THE OPINION OF R. JOSHUA. R. JOḤANAN B. NURI SAYS: LET NOT THIS CASE BE MORE STRINGENT THAN THAT OF A CANOPY.

MISHNAH 4. [IN THE CASE OF] A CANOPY[3] GOING ALL ROUND THE HOUSE, OCCUPYING SPACE ABOVE THE DOORWAY TO THE EXTENT OF [BUT] THREE FINGERBREADTHS, IF THERE IS UNCLEANNESS IN THE HOUSE, VESSELS BENEATH [THE CANOPY] BECOME UNCLEAN.[4] IF THE UNCLEANNESS IS BENEATH [THE CANOPY], R. ELIEZER DECLARES THE HOUSE UNCLEAN,[5] BUT R. JOSHUA DECLARES IT CLEAN. A SIMILAR [RULE APPLIES] TO A COURTYARD SURROUNDED BY A PORTICO.[6]

MISHNAH 5. [WITH REGARD TO] TWO CANOPIES, ONE [DIRECTLY] ABOVE THE OTHER, HAVING [EACH] A WIDTH OF ONE HANDBREADTH AND THERE BEING A SPACE OF ONE HANDBREADTH BETWEEN THEM, IF THERE IS UNCLEANNESS BENEATH THEM,[7] WHAT IS BENEATH THEM BECOMES UNCLEAN; IF IT IS BETWEEN THEM, WHAT IS BETWEEN THEM BECOMES UNCLEAN; ABOVE THEM,[8] EVERYTHING DIRECTLY [ABOVE] TO THE SKY BECOMES UNCLEAN. [IN THE CASE WHERE] THE UPPER [CANOPY] OVERLAPPED THE LOWER TO THE EXTENT OF ONE HANDBREADTH, IF THERE IS UNCLEANNESS BENEATH OR BETWEEN THEM, WHAT IS BENEATH AND BETWEEN THEM BECOMES UNCLEAN;[9] IF IT IS ABOVE THEM, WHAT IS DIRECTLY

(1) Placed parallel to the top of the entrance. (2) In contradistinction to a canopy where there is the limit of twelve handbreadths. (3) One handbreadth wide (Bert.). (4) Rendered so by the ultimately emerging uncleanness. (5) Because of the stringency of the laws applying to canopies of even less than a handbreadth in width (Bert.). (6) Whose roofed portion extends for three fingerbreadths over the door of a house in the courtyard. (7) Beneath the lower canopy, and so elsewhere. (8) Above the upper canopy, and so elsewhere. (9) The overlapping combining the upper and lower canopies to form a passage for the uncleanness.

[ABOVE] TO THE SKY BECOMES UNCLEAN. [IN THE CASE WHERE] THE UPPER [CANOPY] OVERLAPPED THE LOWER TO AN EXTENT OF LESS THAN A HANDBREADTH, IF THERE IS UNCLEANNESS BENEATH THEM, WHAT IS BENEATH AND BETWEEN THEM BECOMES UNCLEAN; IF IT IS BETWEEN THEM OR BENEATH THE OVERLAPPING [PART], R. ELIEZER SAYS: WHAT IS BENEATH THEM AND BETWEEN THEM BECOMES UNCLEAN. R. JOSHUA SAYS: WHAT IS BETWEEN THEM AND BENEATH THE OVERLAPPING [PART] BECOMES UNCLEAN, BUT WHAT IS BENEATH [THE LOWER ONE] REMAINS CLEAN.

MISHNAH 6. [IN THE CASE WHERE] THEY HAD A WIDTH OF A HANDBREADTH BUT THERE WAS NOT A SPACE OF A HANDBREADTH BETWEEN THEM, IF THERE IS UNCLEANNESS BENEATH THEM, WHAT IS BENEATH BECOMES UNCLEAN; IF IT IS BETWEEN THEM[1] OR ABOVE THEM, EVERYTHING DIRECTLY [ABOVE] TO THE SKY BECOMES UNCLEAN.[2]

MISHNAH 7. [IN THE CASE WHERE] THEY DID NOT HAVE A WIDTH OF A HANDBREADTH, WHETHER THERE IS A SPACE OF A HANDBREADTH BETWEEN THEM OR WHETHER THERE IS NOT, IF THERE IS UNCLEANNESS BENEATH, BETWEEN OR ABOVE THEM, THE UNCLEANNESS CLEAVES UPWARDS AND DOWNWARDS. A SIMILAR [RULE APPLIES] TO TWO CURTAINS,[3] [THE LOWER ONE OF WHICH IS] ONE HANDBREADTH HIGH OFF THE GROUND.[4]

(1) Being in a space of less than a cubic handbreadth, the uncleanness cleaves upwards and downwards. (2) A variant followed by Bert. reads as follows: (In the case where) the canopies had a width of a handbreadth but the spaces were not a handbreadth wide, if there is uncleanness beneath or between them, what is beneath or between them becomes unclean; if it is above, what is directly (above) to the sky becomes unclean. The spaces referred to are those between the canopies and between the lower canopy and the ground. The lower canopy, since there is not a space of a handbreadth below or above it, is treated as non-existent. (3) Stretched horizontally. (4) The upper curtain being one handbreadth above the lower.

OHOLOTH

CHAPTER XV

MISHNAH 1. A THICK WOOLLEN BLANKET OR A THICK WOODEN BLOCK DO NOT FORM A PASSAGE FOR UNCLEANNESS UNLESS THEY ARE ONE HANDBREADTH HIGH OFF THE GROUND. IF [THE GARMENTS] ARE FOLDED ONE ABOVE THE OTHER THEY DO NOT FORM A PASSAGE FOR THE UNCLEANNESS UNLESS THE UPPERMOST IS ONE HANDBREADTH HIGH OFF THE GROUND.[1] TABLETS OF WOOD [PLACED] ONE ABOVE THE OTHER DO NOT FORM A PASSAGE FOR THE UNCLEANNESS UNLESS THE UPPERMOST IS ONE HANDBREADTH HIGH OFF THE GROUND; BUT IF THEY WERE OF MARBLE, THE UNCLEANNESS[2] CLEAVES UPWARDS AND DOWNWARDS.[3]

MISHNAH 2. [WITH REGARD TO] WOODEN TABLETS TOUCHING EACH OTHER AT THEIR CORNERS,[4] AND ONE HANDBREADTH HIGH OFF THE GROUND, IF THERE IS UNCLEANNESS BENEATH ONE OF THEM, [A PERSON] TOUCHING THE SECOND [TABLET][5] BECOMES DEFILED WITH A SEVEN-DAY DEFILEMENT. VESSELS UNDER THE FIRST [TABLET] BECOME UNCLEAN; BUT THOSE UNDER THE SECOND REMAIN CLEAN.[6] A TABLE CANNOT FORM A PASSAGE FOR UNCLEANNESS UNLESS IT CONTAINS A SQUARE[7] OF ONE HANDBREADTH.

(1) Repeated from *supra* XI, 3. (2) Beneath them. (3) The uncleanness under the marble tablets being regarded as compressed, though the upper is more than a handbreadth high off the ground. (4) But to the extent of less than a handbreadth. (5) Which has contracted אבי אבות הטומאה from direct contact with the 'tent' over the uncleanness (v. *supra* I, 1, n. 3; 3, n. 3). (6) The uncleanness can only be conveyed from the first by contact, not by overshadowing, as the connection between the two tablets is less than one square handbreadth in area. (7) Explained by L. as the minimum area of a square that can be inscribed in a circular table.

MISHNAH 3. [WITH REGARD TO] JARS STANDING ON THEIR BOTTOMS OR LYING ON THEIR SIDES IN THE OPEN AIR AND TOUCHING ONE ANOTHER TO THE EXTENT OF A HANDBREADTH,[1] IF THERE IS UNCLEANNESS BENEATH ONE OF THEM, THE UNCLEANNESS CLEAVES UPWARDS AND DOWNWARDS.[2] WHEN DOES THIS RULE APPLY? WHEN THE [JARS] ARE CLEAN.[3] BUT IN THE CASE WHERE THEY WERE UNCLEAN[4] OR ONE HANDBREADTH HIGH OFF THE GROUND, IF THERE IS UNCLEANNESS BENEATH ONE OF THEM, WHAT IS BENEATH ALL BECOMES UNCLEAN.

MISHNAH 4. [WITH REGARD TO] A HOUSE,[5] PARTITIONED OFF BY BOARDS OR CURTAINS FROM THE SIDES OR FROM THE ROOF BEAMS,[6] IF THERE IS UNCLEANNESS IN THE HOUSE, VESSELS BEYOND THE PARTITION REMAIN CLEAN.[7] IF THERE IS UNCLEANNESS BEYOND THE PARTITION, VESSELS IN THE HOUSE BECOME UNCLEAN.[8] [WITH REGARD TO] THE VESSELS BEYOND THE PARTITION,[9] IF THERE IS A SPACE OF A [CUBIC] HANDBREADTH THERE, THEY BECOME UNCLEAN, BUT IF NOT, THEY REMAIN CLEAN.[10]

MISHNAH 5. [IN THE CASE WHERE] IT WAS PARTITIONED OFF FROM THE FLOOR, IF THERE IS UNCLEANNESS BENEATH THE PARTITION, VESSELS IN THE HOUSE BECOME UNCLEAN.[11] [IN THE CASE WHERE] THE UNCLEANNESS IS IN THE HOUSE, VESSELS BENEATH THE PARTITION, IF THERE IS A SPACE

(1) This proviso is mentioned on account of the final clause. (2) Being regarded as 'compressed'. (3) And are therefore treated like marble tablets. (4) Since unclean vessels cannot serve as a screen they are treated like wooden tablets, and the upper parts of the vessels touching each other (as stated) form a 'tent' to spread the uncleanness to all vessels. (5) Consisting of a single room. (6) I.e., vertically or horizontally. (7) The partition serving as a screen, cf. *supra* VI, 2. (8) Through the emerging uncleanness, since a partition like a closely fitted cover can afford protection only against the entrance of uncleanness; but it does not prevent its egress, v. Kel. VIII, 6. (9) In which was the uncleanness. (10) The uncleanness cleaving upwards and downwards only. (11) V. n. 8, and *supra* III, 7.

THERE OF ONE CUBIC HANDBREADTH, REMAIN CLEAN; BUT IF NOT, THEY BECOME UNCLEAN, SINCE THE FLOOR OF THE HOUSE IS RECKONED AS THE HOUSE EVEN TO THE NETHERMOST DEEP.

MISHNAH 6. [WITH REGARD TO] A HOUSE FILLED WITH STRAW, WITHOUT A SPACE OF A HANDBREADTH [BEING LEFT] BETWEEN [THE STRAW] AND THE ROOF BEAMS, IF THERE IS UNCLEANNESS WITHIN [THE STRAW], VESSELS AT THE EXIT[1] BECOME UNCLEAN.[2] [IN THE CASE WHERE] THE UNCLEANNESS WAS OUTSIDE,[3] THE VESSELS WITHIN, IF THEY ARE IN A SPACE OF A CUBIC HANDBREADTH, REMAIN CLEAN, BUT IF NOT THEY BECOME UNCLEAN.[4] IF THERE IS A SPACE OF A HANDBREADTH BETWEEN THE STRAW AND THE ROOF BEAMS, IN EITHER CASE THE VESSELS BECOME UNCLEAN.[5]

MISHNAH 7. [WITH REGARD TO] A HOUSE FILLED WITH EARTH[6] OR PEBBLES WHICH HAD BEEN DEEMED VALUELESS,[7] OR SIMILARLY A HEAP OF PRODUCE OR A MOUND OF PEBBLES EVEN AS ACHAN'S MOUND,[8] EVEN IF THE UNCLEANNESS IS BY THE SIDE OF THE VESSELS, THE UNCLEANNESS CLEAVES UPWARDS AND DOWNWARDS.[9]

MISHNAH 8. [WITH REGARD TO] THE FORECOURT OF A TOMB, A PERSON STANDING THEREIN REMAINS CLEAN AS LONG AS THERE IS A SPACE OF FOUR CUBITS SQUARE, ACCORDING TO THE OPINION OF BETH SHAMMAI. BETH HILLEL SAY: FOUR HANDBREADTHS [IS THE MINIMUM SIZE]. [WITH REGARD TO] A ROOF BEAM WHICH HAD BEEN USED AS A COVER-

(1) The space left free near the exit. (2) As in Mishnah 4 where the vessels in the house become unclean through the uncleanness in the part partitioned off. (3) I.e., in the above-mentioned free space. (4) As is the case with the vessels beyond the partition where the uncleanness was in the house. (5) In this case the straw is regarded not as a partition but as contents of the house and not able to offer protection. (6) Var. lec., straw. (7) Lit., 'and he abandoned it'. (8) V. Josh. VII, 26. (9) And the vessels remain clean.

ING STONE[1] FOR A TOMB, WHETHER IT IS STANDING UPRIGHT[2] OR LYING ON ITS SIDE, NOTHING BECOMES UNCLEAN EXCEPT WHAT IS OPPOSITE THE OPENING OF THE GRAVE. IF THE END [OF THE BEAM] WERE MADE THE COVERING STONE OF A GRAVE, ONLY [THAT PART] UP TO FOUR HANDBREADTHS [FROM THE GRAVE] BECOMES UNCLEAN. [THIS APPLIES] WHEN [THE BEAM] IS GOING TO BE CUT. R. JUDAH SAYS: ALL THE BEAM IS REGARDED AS BEING ONE.

MISHNAH 9. [WITH REGARD TO] A JAR FULL OF CLEAN LIQUID AND SEALED WITH A TIGHTLY FITTING LID,[3] WHICH HAD BEEN MADE THE COVERING STONE OF A TOMB, A PERSON TOUCHING IT CONTRACTS SEVEN-DAY UNCLEANNESS BUT THE JAR AND THE LIQUID REMAIN CLEAN.[4] [IN THE CASE OF] A BEAST[5] THAT HAD BEEN USED AS A COVERING STONE, A PERSON TOUCHING IT CONTRACTS SEVEN-DAY UNCLEANNESS. R. MEIR SAYS: NOTHING POSSESSING THE BREATH OF LIFE CAN CONVEY UNCLEANNESS ON ACCOUNT OF [ITS BEING USED AS] A COVERING STONE.[6]

MISHNAH 10. IF A PERSON TOUCHES A CORPSE AND [SUBSEQUENTLY][7] TOUCHES VESSELS, OR OVERSHADOWS A CORPSE AND [SUBSEQUENTLY][7] TOUCHES VESSELS, THESE BECOME UNCLEAN. IF HE OVERSHADOWS A CORPSE AND OVERSHADOWS VESSELS,[8] OR TOUCHES A CORPSE AND OVERSHADOWS VESSELS,[8] THESE REMAIN CLEAN. IF HIS HAND HAS A SURFACE OF A HANDBREADTH SQUARE, THEY BECOME UNCLEAN. [WITH REGARD TO] TWO HOUSES CONTAINING TWO PORTIONS OF CORPSE-FLESH OF HALF AN OLIVE SIZE [ONE IN EACH], IF A PERSON STRETCHED BOTH HIS HANDS

(1) V. *supra* II, 4, n. 4. (2) I.e., sloping, its lower end resting on the tomb and the upper leaning on some other object. (3) V. Kel. X, 2. (4) An earthen jar being insusceptible to uncleanness on its outer surface and its contents being protected by the tightly fitting lid. (5) A live one, tied to its place. (6) Agreeing with his decision in 'Er. I, 7. (7) L. (8) Even at the same time, as long as the same part of the body is not performing the two actions (L.).

INTO THEM, AND HIS HANDS WERE EACH ONE HANDBREADTH SQUARE, HE CONVEYS THE UNCLEANNESS;[1] BUT IF [THEY WERE] NOT [ONE HANDBREADTH SQUARE], HE DOES NOT CONVEY THE UNCLEANNESS.

(1) Into both houses, since he joins the two portions into one.

OHOLOTH

CHAPTER XVI

MISHNAH 1. ALL MOVABLE THINGS FORM A PASSAGE FOR THE UNCLEANNESS[1] WHEN THEY ARE OF THE THICKNESS OF AN OX-GOAD.[2] R. TARFON SAID: MAY I [SEE THE] RUIN[3] OF MY SONS IF THIS IS [NOT] A RUINED HALACHAH[4] WHICH SOMEONE [DEDUCED FROM THE FOLLOWING CASE WHICH HE HAD] HEARD AND MISUNDERSTOOD. A FARMER WAS PASSING BY AND OVER HIS SHOULDER WAS AN OX-GOAD, ONE END OF WHICH OVERSHADOWED A GRAVE. HE WAS DECLARED UNCLEAN ON ACCOUNT [OF CARRYING] VESSELS THAT WERE OVERSHADOWING A CORPSE.[5] R. AKIBA SAID: I CAN AMEND [THE HALACHAH] SO THAT THE WORDS OF THE SAGES CAN EXIST [AS THEY ARE]: ALL MOVABLE THINGS FORM A PASSAGE FOR THE UNCLEANNESS TO COME UPON A PERSON CARRYING THEM, WHEN THEY ARE OF THE THICKNESS OF AN OX-GOAD; UPON THEMSELVES, WHEN THEY ARE OF WHATSOEVER THICKNESS;[6] AND UPON OTHER MEN OR VESSELS [WHICH THEY OVERSHADOW], WHEN THEY ARE ONE HANDBREADTH WIDE.[7]

MISHNAH 2. HOW [CAN THIS RULE BE ILLUSTRATED]?

(1) By acting as temporary 'tents'. (2) Defined as having a *circumference* of one handbreadth, which is less than the minimum handbreadth in width required with immovable things (Bert.). (3) אקפח 'to destroy', 'cut off'. The phrase, the equivalent of 'May I bury my sons', was a common one of R. Tarfon's. V. B.M. 85*a*. (4) Rule. (5) Which vessels rendered the bearer unclean through carriage. But the person reporting the *halachah* at the beginning of the Mishnah thought (wrongly according to R. Tarfon) that the man was deemed unclean because he had been overshadowed by a goad simultaneously overshadowing a corpse. (6) No standard being fixed for the defilement of objects which themselves form a 'tent'. (7) For further notes v. Shab. Sonc. ed., p. 16*b*.

[BY THE CASE OF] A SPINDLE[1] FIXED INTO THE WALL, WITH [A PORTION OF CORPSE FLESH] OF HALF AN OLIVE-SIZE ABOVE IT AND [A PORTION OF CORPSE FLESH] OF HALF AN OLIVE-SIZE BELOW IT. EVEN THOUGH ONE [PORTION] IS NOT DIRECTLY [ABOVE] THE OTHER, [THE SPINDLE] BECOMES UNCLEAN.[2] HENCE IT IS FOUND THAT [A MOVABLE OBJECT] FORMS A PASSAGE FOR THE UNCLEANNESS TO COME UPON ITSELF WHATSOEVER ITS THICKNESS. IF A POT SELLER PASSES BY A GRAVE WHEN HE HAS ON HIS SHOULDER HIS CARRYING-YOKE,[3] ONE END OF WHICH OVERSHADOWS A GRAVE, VESSELS ON THE OTHER SIDE REMAIN CLEAN. IF THE YOKE IS ONE HANDBREADTH WIDE, THEY BECOME UNCLEAN.[4]

MOUNDS WHICH ARE NEAR TO A CITY OR TO A ROAD, WHETHER THEY ARE NEW OR OLD, ARE UNCLEAN.[5] [AS FOR THOSE THAT ARE] AFAR OFF, NEW ONES ARE CLEAN BUT OLD ONES ARE UNCLEAN.[6] WHICH [MOUND IS ACCOUNTED] NEAR? ONE FIFTY CUBITS [AFAR OFF]. AND OLD? ONE SIXTY YEARS OLD. [THIS IS] THE OPINION OF R. MEIR. R. JUDAH SAYS: 'NEAR' [MEANS] THERE IS NONE NEARER THAN IT, AND 'OLD' [MEANS] THAT NO ONE REMEMBERS [WHEN IT WAS MADE].

MISHNAH 3. IF ONE FINDS[7] A CORPSE UNEXPECTEDLY[8] LYING IN ITS NATURAL POSITION,[9] HE MAY REMOVE IT ALONG WITH THE [BLOOD-] SATURATED EARTH[10] [ROUND ABOUT].[11]

(1) כוש Jast. 'something hollow', 'reed', cf. כוס כיס. Here 'spindle', cf. Kel. IX, 6. Its size is less than a handbreadth. (2) Both combine to form an olive's bulk according to the view of the Sages, *supra* III, 1. (3) סל. Probably, as Kel. XVII, 16. אסל from Gk. ασιλλα 'a carrying-yoke'. (4) The carrying-yoke forming a 'tent' overshadowing the vessels on both sides. (5) Since they may have been used for the secret burial of abortions. (6) Since they may have been near when newly made. (7) Whilst ploughing the field. This Mishnah occurs in Naz. 64*b*, Sonc. ed., p. 244, where it is discussed in the ensuing Gemara. V. loc. cit. for notes; v. also B.B. 101*b*. (8) בתחלה Lit., 'in the first place'. I.e., without knowing before that there was a corpse lying there. The word is missing in the version of B.B. loc. cit. (9) Showing that there had been a normal burial. (10) Cf. *supra* III, 5. (11) The field being thereby restored to a state of cleanliness.

IF HE FINDS TWO, HE MAY REMOVE THEM ALONG WITH THE [BLOOD-] SATURATED EARTH [ROUND ABOUT]. [IN THE CASE WHERE] HE FINDS THREE, IF THERE IS A SPACE OF FROM FOUR TO EIGHT CUBITS BETWEEN THE FIRST AND THE LAST, THAT IS, THE SPACE OF A BIER AND ITS BEARERS,[1] THEN IT MUST BE ACCOUNTED A GRAVEYARD,[2] AND HE MUST SEARCH [THE GROUND] FOR TWENTY CUBITS[3] FROM THAT POINT. IF HE FOUND [ANOTHER CORPSE] AT THE END OF THOSE TWENTY CUBITS, HE MUST SEARCH FOR A FURTHER TWENTY CUBITS FROM THAT PLACE, SINCE THERE ARE ALREADY GROUNDS FOR BELIEF[4] [THAT THIS IS A GRAVEYARD], IN SPITE OF THE FACT THAT IF HE HAD FOUND THIS [LONE GRAVE] IN THE FIRST CASE, HE COULD HAVE REMOVED IT WITH THE [BLOOD-] SATURATED EARTH [ROUND ABOUT].

MISHNAH 4. HE WHO SEARCHES[5] MUST DO SO OVER A SQUARE CUBIT AND THEN LEAVE A CUBIT, [DIGGING DOWN][6] UNTIL HE REACHES ROCK OR VIRGIN SOIL. [A PRIEST][7] CARRYING OUT EARTH FROM A PLACE OF UNCLEANNESS MAY EAT OF HIS TERUMAH,[8] BUT IF HE IS CLEARING AWAY A RUIN,[9] HE MAY NOT EAT OF HIS TERUMAH.

MISHNAH 5. IF HE WAS SEARCHING AND CAME TO A RIVER BED, A POOL[10] OR A PUBLIC ROAD, HE MAY DISCONTINUE [HIS SEARCH]. [WITH REGARD TO] A FIELD WHERE MEN HAVE BEEN SLAIN, THE BONES MAY BE GATHERED TOGETHER ONE BY ONE, AND ALL [THE AREA] MAY BE ACCOUNTED CLEAN.[11]

(1) This explanation of the distance is missing from Naz. loc. cit. but appears in the B.B. version. The size of the intervening space is evidence of a regular graveyard. (2) The graves must then not be disturbed. (3) The reason for this size is given in B.B. (4) Lit., 'the matter has legs'. (5) The prescribed area. (6) So Bert. (7) Who may, in the case of emergency, occupy himself with such work. (8) דמעו Ex. XXII, 28. The word is referred by Rabbinic commentators to *terumah*. V. Rashi ad loc. דמע 'tear', 'liquor'. (9) Of a house that has fallen on a man, who may have died. (10) שלולית 'pool'. V. B.K. 61*a* for the possible meanings and suggested derivations of this word. (11) No account being taken of blood-saturated earth either in this or the succeeding cases.

IF A PERSON IS REMOVING A GRAVE FROM HIS FIELD, HE MAY GATHER TOGETHER THE BONES ONE BY ONE, AND ALL MAY BE ACCOUNTED CLEAN. [WITH REGARD TO] A PIT INTO WHICH ABORTIONS OR PEOPLE THAT HAD BEEN SLAIN USED TO BE THROWN, THE BONES MAY BE GATHERED TOGETHER ONE BY ONE, AND ALL MAY BE ACCOUNTED CLEAN. R. SIMEON SAYS: IF IN THE FIRST PLACE IT HAD BEEN PREPARED AS A GRAVE, THERE IS [THE QUESTION OF BLOOD-] SATURATED EARTH [TO BE CONSIDERED].

OHOLOTH

CHAPTER XVII

MISHNAH 1. IF A GRAVE IS PLOUGHED [INTO A FIELD] THIS MAKES IT A BETH PERAS.[1] TO WHAT EXTENT IS IT SO MADE? FOR THE LENGTH OF A FURROW OF A HUNDRED CUBITS,[2] [THAT IS TO SAY, OVER] AN AREA OF FOUR SE'AHS.[3] R. JOSE SAYS: AN AREA OF FIVE [SE'AHS]. [THIS[4] APPLIES WHEN THE PLOUGH IS DRIVEN] ON A DOWNWARD SLOPE;[5] BUT WHEN ON AN UPWARD SLOPE, A QUARTER [OF A ḲAB] OF VETCH SEED SHOULD BE PLACED ON THE KNEE[6] OF THE PLOUGH,[7] AND THE SPACE UNTIL WHERE [THE LAST] THREE VETCHES GROW NEXT TO EACH OTHER[8] IS MADE INTO A BETH PERAS. R. JOSE SAYS: [A BETH PERAS IS ONLY MADE BY A PLOUGH GOING] DOWNWARDS BUT NOT UPWARDS.

MISHNAH 2. IF A PERSON WAS PLOUGHING[9] AND STRUCK AGAINST A ROCK OR A FENCE, OR IF HE SHOOK THE PLOUGH-SHARE,[10] [ONLY] TO THAT PLACE IS THE BETH PERAS FORMED. R. ELIEZER SAYS: ONE BETH PERAS CAN FORM ANOTHER BETH PERAS.[11] R. JOSHUA SAYS: SOMETIMES IT CAN, BUT AT

(1) V *supra* II, 3, n. 8. (2) Each way, length and breadth. So Bert. but Tosef XVII, 1 has 'in every direction'. The plough is presumed to carry bones with it to that extent. (3) In which four *se'ahs* of seed can be sown. According to 'Er. 23*b*, the tabernacle area, one hundred cubits by fifty, could be sown by two *se'ahs*. One *se'ah*=six *ḳabs* (v. *supra* II, 1, n. 7). (4) Area of four *se'ahs*. (5) Or on the level (Bert.), the bones in these cases being likely to be carried the full distance. (6) בורך. V. Kel. XXI, 2. A knee-shaped receptacle in the plough sometimee used for containing seed which is gradually shaken out in decreasing number on to the field by the movement of the implement. (7) Which is then driven upwards. (8) I.e., where no more than three had fallen together out of the knee, thus indicating that practically all the seeds (and hence also bones) have been shaken off. (9) Over a grave. (10) So as to free it of soil. All these processes tend to remove any bones that may have been attached to the plough. (11) If one begins to plough from a point within the original area.

OTHER TIMES IT CANNOT. HOW SO? IF HE PLOUGHED FOR HALF A FURROW'S LENGTH[1] AND THEN RETURNED AND PLOUGHED A [FURTHER] HALF, OR SIMILARLY [IF HE PLOUGHED] TO THE SIDE, HE MAKES A BETH PERAS. IF HE PLOUGHED A FULL FURROW'S LENGTH AND THEN RETURNED AND PLOUGHED FROM THAT POINT BEYOND, HE DOES NOT MAKE THIS[2] A BETH PERAS.

MISHNAH 3. IF A PERSON PLOUGHS FROM A QUARRY,[3] OR FROM A HEAP OF BONES,[4] OR FROM A FIELD IN WHICH A GRAVE HAD BEEN LOST,[5] OR IN WHICH A GRAVE WAS SUBSEQUENTLY FOUND,[6] OR IF HE PLOUGHS A FIELD WHICH WAS NOT HIS OWN,[7] OR IF A GENTILE PLOUGHED, THIS DOES NOT MAKE IT A BETH PERAS; FOR THE RULE OF BETH PERAS DOES NOT APPLY [EVEN] TO SAMARITANS.

MISHNAH 4. [IN THE CASE WHERE] THERE WAS A BETH PERAS ABOVE A CLEAN FIELD, IF RAIN WASHED DOWN SOIL FROM THE BETH PERAS TO THE CLEAN FIELD, EVEN WHERE THIS WAS REDDISH AND THE [OTHER SOIL] TURNED IT WHITE, OR WHERE THIS WAS WHITE AND THE OTHER TURNED IT RED,[8] THIS DOES NOT MAKE IT A BETH PERAS.[9]

MISHNAH 5. [WITH REGARD TO] A FIELD IN WHICH A GRAVE HAD BEEN LOST, AND IN WHICH A HOUSE HAD BEEN BUILT WITH AN UPPER STOREY ABOVE IT, IF THE DOOR OF THE UPPER ROOM WAS DIRECTLY ABOVE THE DOOR OF THE HOUSE, THE UPPER STOREY REMAINS CLEAN;[10] BUT IF NOT

(1) Fifty cubits. (2) Outer portion. (3) מלטמיא Possibly Gk. λατομία 'quarry', presumably one containing bones. Bert. מלא טמיא '(pit) filled with bones'. (4) Treated leniently because of the unlikelihood of such a procedure. (5) Doubt existing as to whether any bones have actually been touched and even then, as to whether they have been scattered. (6) He acted unwittingly. (7) And therefore which he cannot render unclean by any doubtful action. (8) Proving definitely that soil had been transferred. (9) The land of a *Beth Peras* applies only to solid soil not to washed down soil. (10) Even if the grave is under the entrance, the uncleanness proceeds into the house and not to the upper storey.

THE UPPER STOREY BECOMES UNCLEAN.[1] [WITH REGARD TO] SOIL FROM A BETH PERAS, OR SOIL FROM A FOREIGN COUNTRY[2] THAT CAME IN WITH VEGETABLES, [SCATTERED PARTICLES ARE REGARDED AS] COMBINING TOGETHER [TO FORM A PORTION] THE SIZE OF A PACKING-BAG[3] SEAL.[4] THIS IS THE OPINION OF R. ELIEZER; BUT THE SAGES SAY: THERE MUST BE ONE PORTION OF THE SIZE OF A PACKING-BAG SEAL. R. JUDAH SAYS: IT HAPPENED ONCE THAT LETTERS CAME FROM OVERSEAS FOR THE SONS OF THE HIGH PRIESTS[5] AND THEY HAD ON THEM ABOUT A SE'AH OR TWO SE'AHS OF SEALS,[6] BUT THE SAGES DID NOT HAVE ANY SCRUPLES ON ACCOUNT OF UNCLEANNESS.[7]

(1) The grave might possibly be directly under the entrance. (2) Cf. *supra* II, 3, n. 7. (3) מרצופין 'packing-bags', from רצף 'to pack', 'pave'. It is mentioned in connection with shipping in B.B. V, 1, and may well have been the common Levantine trade term for the object. As such it was possibly adopted by the Greeks as μάρσιττος. (Lat. *marsupium*, Eng. marsupial). (4) The minimum size for uncleanness for a clod. (5) Cf. Keth. XIII, 1. (6) *Sc.* of clay. (7) No single seal attaining the minimum size.

OHOLOTH

CHAPTER XVIII

MISHNAH 1. HOW CAN THE GRAPES OF A BETH PERAS BE GATHERED?[1] THE MEN AND THE VESSELS MUST BE SPRINKLED [ONCE][2] AND THEN A SECOND TIME.[3] THEREUPON THEY GATHER THE GRAPES AND TAKE THEM OUT OF THE BETH PERAS. OTHERS[4] THEN RECEIVE [THE GRAPES] AND TAKE THEM TO THE WINEPRESS.[5] IF THE LATTER SET [OF PERSONS] CAME INTO CONTACT WITH THE FORMER, THEY BECOME UNCLEAN. THIS IS ACCORDING TO THE OPINION OF BETH HILLEL. BETH SHAMMAI SAY: [THE GATHERER] MUST HOLD THE SICKLE WITH BAST,[6] OR MUST CUT OFF THE GRAPES WITH A SHARP FLINT,[7] LETTING [THE GRAPES FALL] INTO AN OLIVE-BASKET,[8] AND THEN HE TAKES [THEM] TO THE WINEPRESS.[9] R. JOSE SAID: WHEN DO THESE RULES APPLY? [ONLY] IN THE CASE OF A VINEYARD WHICH SUBSEQUENTLY BECAME A BETH PERAS; BUT A PERSON WHO PLANTS [VINES] IN A

(1) So that they remain clean and can be used for making wine without rendering it unclean by virtue of the law of Lev. XI, 38. (2) On the third day (Num. XIX, 18f), notice of the gathering having been given. (3) The sprinkling serves as a precaution, reminding the gatherers of the laws of uncleanness appertaining to a *Beth Peras* and thereby preventing carelessness. Although the grapes have been rendered susceptible to uncleanness by virtue of the gathering (v. Shab. 14*a*), they are not affected by the uncleanness of *Beth Peras* which is only Rabbinical, and the method whereby they have been rendered susceptible also being only Rabbinical. (4) Who did not enter the *Beth Peras*. (5) Once taken to the winepress they become susceptible to uncleanness by virtue of Biblical law, and to such the uncleanness of *Beth Peras* applies, hence they must be taken to the winepress by others. (6) סיב 'fibre', 'palm-bast'. (perhaps from סאב 'to be hairy'). Bast is insusceptible to uncleanness and therefore protects the sickle and hence also the grapes against uncleanness. (7) Insusceptible to uncleanness. (8) Cf. *supra* V, 6. (9) Having taken these precautions, he will be reminded of the laws of a *Beth Peras* even whilst in the winepress.

BETH PERAS MUST SELL [THE GRAPES] IN THE MARKET.[1]

MISHNAH 2. THERE ARE THREE [KINDS OF] BETH PERAS:[2] A FIELD INTO WHICH A GRAVE HAS BEEN PLOUGHED MAY BE PLANTED WITH ANY KIND OF PLANT,[3] BUT MUST NOT BE SOWN WITH ANY KIND OF SEED,[4] EXCEPT WITH SEED [YIELDING PRODUCE] WHICH IS REAPED. IF [SUCH PRODUCE] WERE PLUCKED, THE THRESHING-FLOOR MUST BE PILED UP IN [THE FIELD] ITSELF,[5] AND THE [GRAIN] SIFTED THROUGH TWO SIEVES.[6] THIS IS THE OPINION OF R. MEIR. BUT THE SAGES SAY: GRAIN [MUST BE SIFTED] THROUGH TWO SIEVES, BUT PULSE THROUGH THREE SIEVES.[7] THE STUBBLE AND THE STALKS MUST BE BURNED.[8] [SUCH A FIELD] CONVEYS UNCLEANNESS BY CONTACT AND CARRIAGE BUT DOES NOT CONVEY UNCLEANNESS BY OVERSHADOWING.[9]

MISHNAH 3. A FIELD IN WHICH A GRAVE HAS BEEN LOST[10] MAY BE SOWN WITH ANY KIND OF SEED,[11] BUT MUST NOT BE PLANTED WITH ANY KIND OF PLANT,[12] NOR MAY ANY TREES BE PERMITTED TO REMAIN THERE EXCEPT SHADE-TREES WHICH DO NOT PRODUCE FRUIT.[13] [SUCH A FIELD] CONVEYS

(1) As a penalty he is not allowed to use the methods enabling wine to be made. (2) Enumerated respectively in Mishnahs 2, 3 and 4. (3) Because its fruit cannot become unclean, as the law of overshadowing does not apply to such a field (v. end of Mishnah). (4) The roots of such plants are sometimes pulled out with the produce and they may have been in contact with a portion of bone. (5) So as not to spread the uncleanness abroad. (6) To detect any portion of bone. (7) More earth being found in association with this type of produce. (8) On the field. (9) The field owes its uncleanness to the possible presence of a barleycorn-sized portion of bone and therefore has the same laws as that object (v. *supra* II, 3). (10) The exact location of the grave being unknown. This is the second type of *Beth Peras*. (11) Because the roots could not reach as far as the grave (Maim). Tosef. XVIII, 11, however, has the reading, in the name of R. Judah, 'may *not* be sown', and this is read also in our Mishnah by Bert. and others. (12) Because the roots would reach to the grave (Maim.). Bert.: Otherwise people might be attracted to the field and thus contract defilement by overshadowing. (13) Such may be planted at the outset (Bert.).

UNCLEANNESS BY CONTACT, CARRIAGE AND OVERSHADOWING.

MISHNAH 4. A MOURNERS' FIELD[1] MAY NEITHER BE PLANTED NOR SOWN,[2] BUT ITS EARTH IS REGARDED AS CLEAN AND OVENS MAY BE MADE OF IT FOR HOLY USE.[3] [WITH REGARD TO THE FIRST[4] CASE OF A BETH PERAS] BETH SHAMMAI AND BETH HILLEL AGREE THAT IT IS EXAMINED[5] FOR ONE WHO WOULD PERFORM THE PASCHAL SACRIFICE,[6] BUT IS NOT EXAMINED FOR ONE WHO WOULD EAT TERUMAH.[7] [WITH REGARD TO A] NAZIRITE,[8] BETH SHAMMAI SAY: IT IS EXAMINED,[9] BUT BETH HILLEL SAY: IT IS NOT EXAMINED.[10] HOW IS IT EXAMINED? THE EARTH THAT IS ABLE TO BE MOVED IS TAKEN,[11] PLACED INTO A SIEVE WITH FINE MESHES, AND CRUMBLED. IF A BONE OF BARLEY-CORN SIZE IS FOUND THERE [THE PERSON PASSING THROUGH THE FIELD] IS DEEMED UNCLEAN.

MISHNAH 5. HOW IS A BETH PERAS[12] RENDERED CLEAN? [SOIL TO A DEPTH OF] THREE HANDBREADTHS[13] IS REMOVED FROM IT, OR[14] [SOIL TO A HEIGHT OF] THREE HANDBREADTHS IS PLACED UPON IT. IF FROM THE ONE HALF [SOIL TO A DEPTH OF] THREE HANDBREADTHS WAS REMOVED, AND

(1) שדה בוכין Lit., 'field of those who bewail'. This is the third type of *Beth Peras*. It is explained in M.Ḳ. 5*b* as a field in which final leave is taken of the departed before the burial. It was close to the cemetery. Tosef. XVII, 12 reads כוכין, 'tomb niches'. (2) Because the owner has given up hope of ever using the field again, and it now becomes common property, v. M.Ḳ. loc. cit. Maim. explains the prohibition as a precaution lest a corpse may possibly be concealed therein, since it is in proximity to the cemetery. (3) The field differs in this respect from the two former types. (4) So Bert. (5) To determine whether it is unclean or not. (6) Who must definitely be clean (Num. IX, 6). (7) The neglect to eat *terumah* is not as grave as in the case of the paschal lamb. (8) Who passed through such a field. (9) B. Sh. afford the Nazirite an opportunity of having himself declared clean. (10) The Nazirite is considered unclean and must perform the rites prescribed in Num. VI, 9-12. (11) I.e., loose earth. (12) Of the first type. (13) The depth to which a ploughshare penetrates (cf. B.B. II, 12). (14) Some texts prefix 'Rabbi (Judah the Patriarch) says'.

UPON THE OTHER HALF [SOIL TO A HEIGHT OF] THREE HANDBREADTHS WAS PLACED, IT BECOMES CLEAN. R. SIMEON SAYS: EVEN IF ONE HANDBREADTH AND A HALF WAS REMOVED[1] AND ONE HANDBREADTH AND A HALF FROM ANOTHER PLACE WAS PLACED UPON IT, IT BECOMES CLEAN. IF A BETH PERAS IS PAVED WITH STONES THAT CANNOT [EASILY] BE MOVED, IT BECOMES CLEAN. R. SIMEON SAYS: EVEN IF [THE SOIL OF] A BETH PERAS IS BROKEN UP IT BECOMES CLEAN.

MISHNAH 6. A PERSON WHO WALKS THROUGH A BETH PERAS[2] ON STONES THAT CANNOT [EASILY] BE MOVED, OR [WHO RIDES] ON A MAN OR BEAST WHOSE STRENGTH IS GREAT, REMAINS CLEAN; [BUT IF HE WALKS] ON STONES THAT CAN [EASILY] BE MOVED, OR [RIDES] UPON A MAN OR BEAST WHOSE STRENGTH IS SMALL,[3] HE BECOMES UNCLEAN.[4] A PERSON WHO TRAVELS IN THE LAND OF THE GENTILES OVER MOUNTAINS OR ROCKS, BECOMES UNCLEAN;[5] BUT IF [HE TRAVELS] BY THE SEA OR ALONG THE STRAND,[6] HE REMAINS CLEAN. WHAT IS [MEANT BY] 'THE STRAND'? ANY PLACE TO WHICH THE SEA RISES WHEN IT IS STORMY.

MISHNAH 7. IF ONE BUYS A FIELD IN SYRIA NEAR TO THE LAND OF ISRAEL, IF IT CAN BE ENTERED IN CLEANNESS,[7] IT IS DEEMED CLEAN AND IS SUBJECT TO [THE LAWS OF] TITHES AND SABBATICAL YEAR [PRODUCE];[8] BUT IF IT CANNOT BE ENTERED IN CLEANNESS, IT [IS DEEMED] UNCLEAN, ALTHOUGH IT IS STILL SUBJECT TO [THE LAWS OF] TITHES AND SABBATICAL YEAR [PRODUCE].[9] THE DWELLING-PLACES OF HEATHENS[10] ARE UNCLEAN.[11] HOW LONG MUST [THE HEATHEN]

(1) From the surface of the whole field. (2) Of the first type. (3) As defined in B.M. 105*b*. (4) By his own weight he may have moved a bone. (5) Earth from the neighbouring regions may have collected there and it is unclean (*supra* II, 3). (6) שונית V. *supra* VII, 1. Possibly from שן 'rock'. (7) No gentile land intervening. (8) It is considered part of the Land of Israel. (9) The laws of Sabbatical year produce applied in Syria (v. Tosef. Kel. B.Ḳ. I, 5). (10) כנענים. I.e., heathens living in the Land of Israel. (11) Because of the heathen practice of burying abortions in their houses (Bert.).

HAVE REMAINED IN [THE DWELLING-PLACES] FOR THEM TO REQUIRE EXAMINATION? FORTY DAYS,[1] EVEN IF THERE WAS NO WOMAN WITH HIM. IF, HOWEVER, A SLAVE[2] OR [AN ISRAELITE] WOMAN WATCHED OVER [THE DWELLING-PLACE], IT DOES NOT REQUIRE EXAMINATION.

MISHNAH 8. WHAT DO THEY EXAMINE? DEEP DRAINS AND EVIL-SMELLING WATERS. BETH SHAMMAI SAY: EVEN ASH-HEAPS AND CRUMBLED EARTH.[3] BETH HILLEL SAY: ANY PLACE WHERE A PIG OR A WEASEL[4] CAN GO REQUIRES NO EXAMINATION.[5]

MISHNAH 9. COLONNADES[6] ARE NOT [SUBJECT TO THE LAWS] OF HEATHEN DWELLING-PLACES.[7] R. SIMEON B. GAMALIEL SAYS: A HEATHEN CITY[8] THAT HAS BEEN DESTROYED IS NOT [SUBJECT TO THE LAWS] OF HEATHEN DWELLING-PLACES. THE EAST [SIDE] OF CAESAREA[9] AND THE WEST [SIDE] OF CAESAREA[10] ARE GRAVEYARDS. THE [NATURE OF THE] EAST [SIDE] OF ACRE WAS DOUBTFUL,[11] BUT THE SAGES DECLARED IT CLEAN. RABBI AND HIS LAW COURT VOTED [TO DECIDE] ABOUT ḲENI[12] AND DECLARED IT CLEAN.

MISHNAH 10. [THE FOLLOWING] TEN PLACES ARE NOT [SUBJECT TO THE LAWS] OF HEATHEN DWELLING-PLACES:

(1) The time of the formation of the child in the womb. V. Nid. III, 7. (2) Of an Israelite. (3) The crumbling may be an indication of a burial. (4) חולדה. Bert. reads instead ברדלס ('hyena' or 'marten') which is found together with חולדה in the Tosef. XVI, 13. (5) The animals would have discovered and devoured the uncleanness. (6) אצטונית. From Gk. στοά, 'colonnade'. (7) As no abortions are likely to be buried there. (8) Situated in the Land of Israel. (9) Maritima, the Roman capital of Palestine. (10) קסרין. In a variant version קסריון, the district of Caesarea (Phillipi), in the north of Palestine, near the headwaters of the Jordan. It was a less important city than C. Maritima, hence the diminutive form. (11) According to one opinion as to whether it was on Israelite territory (cf. Giṭ. I, 1), and to another as to whether it was a graveyard. (12) Neubauer's *Géographie du Talmud* p. 276 suggests an identification with Wady Kanah (in Samaria). Perhaps Cana (of Galilee), five miles from Sepphoris, the seat of Rabbi's court.

ARABS' TENTS,[1] FIELD-HUTS, LEAN-TO SHEDS, FRUIT-SHELTERS,[2] SUMMER SHELTERS,[3] A GATE-HOUSE, THE OPEN SPACES OF A COURTYARD, A BATH-HOUSE, AN ARMOURY[4] AND THE PLACE WHERE THE LEGIONS [CAMP].[5]

מסכת אהלות
הדרן עלך
והדרך עלן
תורה אור

(1) Of the nomadic Bedouin who move their tents from one place to another. The place on which they stand is only temporarily occupied. (2) According to Bert. a field-shelter in which the fruit was kept in order to guard it from rain (v. Ma'as. III, 7 where the word is found along with the other agricultural buildings mentioned here). (3) אלקטיות. 'Aruch quotes Aramaic קיטא 'summer'. Bert. describes the structure as one which has a roof but no walls. (4) Lit., 'the place of the arrows'. (5) All these places are only temporarily occupied and hence no fear is entertained lest abortion had been buried in them.

NEGA'IM

TRANSLATED INTO ENGLISH

WITH NOTES

BY

REV. DR ISRAEL W. SLOTKI, M. A., Litt. D.

INTRODUCTION

The Tractate Nega'im[1] develops and amplifies the rules for the diagnosis, isolation and purification of plagues or leprosy signs in men, garments and houses laid down in general terms in Leviticus XIII and XIV.

The colours and shades of the various symptoms of leprosy are defined in Chapter I. The leprosy known as the white spot; the times when leprosy signs may be inspected; the posture of the sufferer when inspection takes place and the kind of person qualified to carry out the inspection are the subjects of Chapter II.

The classes that are subject to the uncleanness of leprosy; the procedure to be followed when an inspection is made by a non-priest; and the symptoms and periods of uncleanness in the case of all leprosy signs are dealt with in Chapter III.

In Chapter IV contrasts are drawn between the conditions that cause the cleanness or uncleanness of the several leprosy signs, and rules are enunciated for determining the uncleanness of leprosy in which different symptoms appear simultaneously or in succession and one of them disappears first; and also of those in which one symptom increases while the other decreases.

Conditions of doubt in leprosy signs and symptoms that disappear and reappear again in the same or in a changed form are the subjects of Chapter V. The minimum sizes of leprosy signs and their symptoms that are to be certified unclean are given in Chapter VI, which also enumerates the limbs and other parts of the body that are altogether immune from the uncleanness of one or other of the leprosy signs.

A number of cases where bright spots are clean are given in Chapter VII, which also discusses those whose colour changed or whose other symptoms underwent a natural or forcible change during the inspection or at a subsequent stage.

(1) נְגָעִים plural of נֶגַע, 'plague', 'leprosy'.

The cleanness and uncleanness of cases where the leprosy covers one's entire body are discussed in CHAPTER VIII; the leprosy known as boil and burning is dealt with in CHAPTER IX, and that known as scall in CHAPTER X.

The leprosy of garments is the subject of CHAPTER XI; while that of houses is discussed in CHAPTERS XII and XIII.

The ceremonial of the cleansing of the leper, his shaving, sprinkling and sacrifices are described in CHAPTER XIV.

I. W. SLOTKI

NEGA'IM

CHAPTER I

MISHNAH 1. THE COLOURS OF LEPROSY SIGNS[1] ARE TWO[2] WHICH, IN FACT, ARE[3] FOUR.[4] THE BRIGHT SPOT IS BRIGHT WHITE LIKE SNOW; SECONDARY TO IT IS THE LEPROSY SIGN AS WHITE AS THE LIME OF THE TEMPLE.[5] THE RISING IS AS WHITE AS THE SKIN OF AN EGG; SECONDARY TO IT IS THE LEPROSY SIGN AS WHITE AS WOOL.[6] SO R. MEIR. BUT THE SAGES RULED: THE RISING IS AS WHITE AS WHITE WOOL AND SECONDARY TO IT IS THE LEPROSY SIGN AS WHITE AS THE SKIN OF AN EGG.[7]

MISHNAH 2. THE VARIEGATION[8] OF THE SNOW-LIKE WHITENESS[9] IS LIKE WINE MINGLED WITH SNOW.[10] THE VARIEGATION[8] OF THE LIME-LIKE WHITENESS IS LIKE BLOOD[11] MINGLED WITH MILK.[12] SO R. ISHMAEL. R. AKIBA RULED: THE REDDISHNESS[13] IN EITHER OF THEM IS LIKE WINE MINGLED WITH WATER, ONLY THAT IN THE SNOW-LIKE WHITENESS THE COLOUR IS BRIGHT WHILE IN THAT OF LIME-LIKE WHITENESS IT IS DULLER.

(1) V. Lev. XIII-XIV on which the laws in this tractate are based. (2) Viz., those of the *bright spot* and the *rising* (Lev. XIII, 2). (3) By the addition of another two colours derived by a Rabbinical deduction from *sappaḥath* (ibid.) which signifies 'attachment', 'addition' (E.V. *scab*). (4) One secondary colour added to each of the two mentioned (cf. *supra* n. 2). (5) Cf. Mid. III, 4. (6) Of a lamb one day old that was duly washed. (7) Which is the dullest of the four shades of white mentioned. Whiter than the skin of an egg is white wool, whiter than the wool is the lime of the Temple, and whiter than the lime is snow. (8) With red. Lit., 'mixture'. (9) Which (cf. Lev. XIII, 19) is another colour of leprosy. (10) In the proportion of one of wine to two of snow. (11) Var. lec. 'wine' (12) One of blood to two of milk. (13) *Sc.* the variegation spoken of *supra* (cf. n. 8).

MISHNAH 3. THESE[1] FOUR COLOURS[2] ARE COMBINED WITH EACH OTHER[3] IN RESPECT OF DECLARING A SIGN FREE FROM UNCLEANNESS, OF CERTIFYING[4] IT AS UNCLEAN, OR OF CAUSING IT TO BE SHUT UP.[5] 'OF CAUSING IT TO BE SHUT UP',[6] WHEN IT[7] CONTINUED UNCHANGED[8] BY THE END OF THE FIRST WEEK;[9] 'OF DECLARING A SIGN FREE FROM UNCLEANNESS', WHEN IT[7] CONTINUED UNCHANGED[8] BY THE END OF THE SECOND WEEK;[10] 'OF CERTIFYING IT AS UNCLEAN', WHEN IT[7] HAD PRODUCED QUICK FLESH OR WHITE HAIR IN THE BEGINNING,[11] BY THE END OF THE FIRST WEEK,[12] BY THE END OF THE SECOND WEEK[12] OR AFTER IT HAD BEEN DECLARED FREE [FROM UNCLEANNESS]. [OR AGAIN] 'OF CERTIFYING IT AS UNCLEAN', WHEN A SPREADING HAS ARISEN IN IT BY THE END OF THE FIRST WEEK,[12] BY THE END OF THE SECOND WEEK,[12] OR AFTER IT HAD BEEN DECLARED FREE FROM UNCLEANNESS; [ALSO] 'OF CERTIFYING IT AS UNCLEAN', WHEN ALL ONE'S SKIN TURNED WHITE AFTER THE SIGN[13] HAD BEEN DECLARED FREE FROM UNCLEANNESS; 'OF DECLARING A SIGN FREE FROM UNCLEANNESS' ALSO, WHEN ALL THE SKIN TURNED WHITE AFTER THE SIGN HAD BEEN CERTIFIED UNCLEAN OR AFTER IT HAD BEEN SHUT UP. THESE[14] ARE THE COLOURS OF LEPROSY SIGNS WHEREON DEPEND ALL DECISIONS CONCERNING LEPROSY SIGNS.[15]

(1) Var. lec. '(some) of these' (cf. Bert. and L.). (2) Cf. *supra* Mishnah 1. (3) To make up the prescribed minimum of the size of a split bean. (4) Lit., 'to determine'. (5) Cf. Lev. XIII, 4. (6) For a second week (cf. *infra* n. 9). (7) Lit., 'that which'. (8) In size and colour. (9) Since its appearance. The colours are similarly combined on its first appearance when it is to be shut up for a week. (10) If, for instance, a bright spot of the size of two split beans was shut up and found at the end of the second week to have the colour of the bright spot extending over an area of the size of one split bean and that of rising over the other, the two colours are regarded as combined and the sign is deemed to be unchanged. (11) When it was first shown to the priest. (12) Since it was shut up. (13) Having continued unchanged for two weeks. (14) The four colours and their variegations enumerated *supra*. (15) On the human body.

MISHNAH 4. R. ḤANINA, THE SEGAN[1] OF THE PRIESTS, RULED: THE COLOURS OF LEPROSY SIGNS ARE SIXTEEN.[2] R. DOSA B. HARKINAS RULED: THE COLOURS OF LEPROSY SIGNS ARE THIRTY-SIX.[3] AKABIAH B. MAHALALEEL RULED SEVENTY-TWO.[4] R. ḤANINA, THE SEGAN OF THE PRIESTS, RULED: LEPROSY SIGNS MAY NOT BE INSPECTED FOR THE FIRST TIME ON A SUNDAY,[5] SINCE THE END OF THAT WEEK[6] WILL FALL ON THE SABBATH;[7] NOR ON A MONDAY, SINCE THE END OF THE SECOND WEEK[8] WILL FALL ON THE SABBATH; NOR ON A TUESDAY, IN THE CASE OF HOUSES, SINCE THE END OF THE THIRD WEEK WILL FALL ON THE SABBATH.[9] R. AKIBA RULED: THEY MAY BE INSPECTED AT ALL TIMES, AND IF THE TIME FOR THE SECOND INSPECTION[10] FALLS ON A SABBATH IT IS POSTPONED TO THE SUNDAY; AND THIS PROCEDURE LEADS SOMETIMES TO A RELAXATION OF THE LAW[11] AND SOMETIMES TO RESTRICTIONS.[11]

MISHNAH 5. HOW DOES IT[12] LEAD TO A RELAXATION OF

(1) Deputy High Priest, and chief of the priests; v. Glos. (2) Viz., the four simple colours given *supra* (Mishnah 1), the three colours obtained by the combination of that of the bright spot with each of the other three, the one colour which is a combination of lime and the skin of an egg, and another eight colours consisting of the variegations of each of these eight. Some texts omit the entire sentence from 'R. Ḥanina' to 'sixteen'. (3) The four simple colours and their four variegations in the leprosy signs of the skin, the eight corresponding colours of the boil and the burn, the eight leprosy signs on the baldness of the scalp and the forehead, the eight of the scall, two of greenishness and reddishness in garments and similar two in houses. (4) The thirty-six colours enumerated in the previous note, (when a leprosy sign makes its first appearance) and another thirty-six corresponding colours when a leprosy sign has been shut up for a week or two weeks in the case of men or for three weeks in the case of houses. (5) Lit., 'after the Sabbath'. (6) During the seven days of which the leprosy sign might have to be shut up. (7) On which no leprosy signs are examined. (8) The second period of seven days which begins on the following Sunday, that day being counted both as the last day of the first week and as the first day of the second week. (9) Cf. prev. n. *mut. mut.* (10) The seventh day after the first inspection. (11) As will be explained in the Mishnah following. (12) Cf. the final clause of the prev. Mishnah.

THE LAW? IF THE LEPROSY SIGN HAD[1] WHITE HAIRS[2] AND[3] THESE WHITE HAIRS DISAPPEARED;[4] IF THEY WERE WHITE[2] AND THEN[3] TURNED BLACK; IF ONE HAIR WAS WHITE AND THE OTHER BLACK, AND[3] BOTH TURNED BLACK;[5] IF THEY WERE LONG[2] AND THEN[3] THEY BECAME SHORT;[4] IF[1] ONE WAS LONG AND THE OTHER SHORT AND[3] BOTH BECAME SHORT;[5] IF[3] A BOIL ADJOINED BOTH HAIRS[6] OR ONE OF THEM;[6] IF THE BOIL ENCOMPASSED[3] BOTH HAIRS OR ONE OF THEM,[7] OR IF THEY WERE[3] SEPARATED FROM EACH OTHER BY A BOIL, THE QUICK FLESH OF A BOIL, A BURNING, OR THE QUICK FLESH OF A BURNING, OR A TETTER;[7] IF IT HAD[1] QUICK FLESH[2] AND THIS QUICK FLESH DISAPPEARED;[3] IF IT WAS[3] FOUR SIDED[8] AND THEN[3] BECAME ROUND[9] OR LONG;[9] IF IT[10] WAS[1] ENCOMPASSED[11] AND THEN[3] SHIFTED TO THE SIDE; IF IT WAS[1] UNITED[12] AND THEN[3] IT WAS DISPERSED, OR A BOIL APPEARED[3] AND MADE ITS WAY INTO IT;[10] IF IT WAS[3] ENCOMPASSED, PARTED OR LESSENED BY A BOIL, THE QUICK FLESH OF A BOIL, A BURNING, THE QUICK FLESH OF A BURNING, OR A TETTER; IF IT HAD[1] A SPREADING AND THEN[3] THE SPREADING DISAPPEARED; IF THE FIRST SIGN ITSELF DISAPPEARED OR WAS SO LESSENED THAT BOTH[13] ARE LESS THAN THE SIZE OF A SPLIT BEAN; OR IF A BOIL, THE QUICK FLESH OF A BOIL, A BURNING, THE QUICK FLESH OF A BURNING, OR A TETTER, FORMED A DIVISION BETWEEN THE FIRST SIGN AND THE SPREADING—BEHOLD THESE LEAD TO A RELAXATION OF THE LAW.

(1) On the Sabbath when the second inspection (after the first period of seven days) was due. (2) Which are a sign of uncleanness. (3) On the Sunday when the inspection took place. (4) Thus exempting the man from the sacrifices and shaving. (5) This instance seems purposeless, since the leprosy sign is clean in either case. (6) Which is no sign of uncleanness; while on the Sabbath when the inspection was due the hairs were within the leprosy sign and constituted uncleanness. (7) Cf. prev. n. *mut. mut.* (8) And just of the size of a split bean which is the minimum prescribed for an unclean leprosy sign. (9) Which, being of the minimum size (cf. prev. n.), is no sign of uncleanness. (10) The quick flesh. (11) By the bright spot. (12) Which is a sign of uncleanness. (13) The first sign and the spreading.

MISHNAH 6. HOW DOES IT[1] LEAD TO RESTRICTIONS? IF THE LEPROSY SIGN HAD[2] NO WHITE HAIRS[3] AND THEN[4] WHITE HAIRS APPEARED;[5] IF THEY WERE[2] BLACK[3] AND THEN[4] TURNED WHITE;[5] IF[2] ONE HAIR WAS BLACK AND THE OTHER WHITE AND BOTH TURNED[4] WHITE;[5] IF THEY WERE[2] SHORT[3] AND THEY BECAME[4] LONG;[5] IF[2] ONE WAS SHORT AND THE OTHER LONG AND BOTH BECAME[4] LONG;[5] IF[2] A BOIL ADJOINED BOTH HAIRS OR ONE OF THEM,[3] IF[2] A BOIL ENCOMPASSED BOTH HAIRS OR ONE OF THEM[3] OR IF[2] THEY WERE PARTED FROM ONE ANOTHER BY A BOIL, THE QUICK FLESH OF A BOIL, A BURNING, OR THE QUICK FLESH OF A BURNING, OR A TETTER, AND THEN[4] THEY DISAPPEARED;[5] IF[2] IT HAD NO QUICK FLESH[3] AND THEN QUICK FLESH APPEARED;[5] IF IT WAS[2] ROUND OR LONG[3] AND THEN[4] BECAME FOUR SIDED;[5] IF IT WAS[2] AT THE SIDE[3] AND THEN[4] IT BECAME ENCOMPASSED;[5] IF IT WAS[2] DISPERSED[3] AND THEN[4] IT BECAME UNITED[5] OR A BOIL APPEARED[4] AND MADE ITS WAY INTO IT;[5] IF IT WAS[2] ENCOMPASSED,[5] PARTED OR LESSENED BY A BOIL, THE QUICK FLESH OF A BOIL, A BURNING, THE QUICK FLESH OF A BURNING OR A TETTER,[3] AND THEN[4] THEY DISAPPEARED;[5] IF[2] IT HAD NO SPREADING[3] AND THEN[4] A SPREADING APPEARED;[5] IF A BOIL, THE QUICK FLESH OF A BOIL, A BURNING, THE QUICK FLESH OF A BURNING, OR A TETTER FORMED A DIVISION[2] BETWEEN THE FIRST SIGN AND THE SPREADING[3] AND THEN[4] THEY DISAPPEARED[5]—BEHOLD THESE LEAD TO RESTRICTIONS.

(1) Cf. Mishnah 4. (2) V. p. 236, n. 1. (3) Which is a sign of cleanness. (4) V. p. 236, n. 11. (5) V. p. 236, n. 12.

NEGA'IM

CHAPTER II

MISHNAH I. THE BRIGHT SPOT IN A GERMAN[1] APPEARS AS DULL WHITE,[2] AND THE DULL WHITE ONE IN AN ETHIOPIAN[3] APPEARS AS BRIGHT WHITE.[4] R. ISHMAEL[5] STATED: 'THE CHILDREN OF ISRAEL[6] (MAY I BE AN ATONEMENT FOR THEM!)[7] ARE LIKE BOXWOOD, NEITHER BLACK NOR WHITE BUT OF AN INTERMEDIATE SHADE'.[8] R. AKIBA STATED: PAINTERS HAVE MATERIALS WHEREWITH THEY PORTRAY FIGURES IN BLACK, IN WHITE, AND IN AN INTERMEDIATE SHADE; LET, THEREFORE, A PAINT OF AN INTERMEDIATE SHADE BE BROUGHT AND APPLIED ROUND THE LEPROSY SIGN FROM WITHOUT, AND IT WILL THEN APPEAR AS ON A SKIN OF INTERMEDIATE SHADE. R. JUDAH RULED: IN DETERMINING THE COLOURS OF LEPROSY SIGNS THE LAW IS TO BE RELAXED BUT NEVER TO BE RESTRICTED; LET, THEREFORE, THE LEPROSY SIGN OF THE GERMAN BE INSPECTED ON THE COLOUR OF HIS OWN BODY[9] SO THAT[10] THE LAW IS THEREBY RELAXED, AND LET THAT OF THE ETHIOPIAN BE INSPECTED AS IF IT WERE ON THE INTERMEDIATE SHADE[11] SO THAT[10] THE LAW IS THEREBY ALSO RELAXED. THE SAGES, HOWEVER, RULED: THE ONE AS WELL AS THE OTHER IS TO BE TREATED AS IF

(1) Whose skin is bright white. (2) Hence it must be pronounced clean. (3) Who is dark. (4) And must be shut up; each case being determined according to the individual concerned. (5) Differing from the ruling just enunciated. (6) With whose leprosy signs the law is concerned. (7) An expression of love and homage. 'May I be the victim making atonement for any punishment that may have to come upon them'. (8) A leprosy sign is, therefore, to be determined by its appearance on such an intermediate shade. (9) Which causes the leprosy sign to appear dull white. (10) He being as a result pronounced clean. (11) As a result of which the leprosy sign would appear duller than on his own dark skin.

THE LEPROSY SIGN WERE ON THE INTERMEDIATE SHADE.[1]

MISHNAH 2. LEPROSY SIGNS MAY NOT BE INSPECTED IN THE EARLY MORNING OR IN THE EVENING, NOR WITHIN A HOUSE, NOR ON A CLOUDY DAY, BECAUSE THEN THE DULL WHITE APPEARS LIKE BRIGHT WHITE; NOR MAY IT BE INSPECTED AT NOON, BECAUSE THEN THE BRIGHT WHITE APPEARS LIKE DULL WHITE. WHEN ARE THEY TO BE INSPECTED? DURING THE THIRD, FOURTH, FIFTH,[2] EIGHTH OR NINTH HOUR;[3] SO R. MEIR. R. JUDAH RULED: DURING THE FOURTH, FIFTH, EIGHTH OR NINTH HOUR.[3]

MISHNAH 3. A PRIEST WHO IS BLIND IN ONE EYE OR THE LIGHT OF WHOSE EYES IS DIM MAY NOT INSPECT LEPROSY SIGNS; FOR IT IS WRITTEN, AS FAR AS APPEARETH IN THE EYES OF THE PRIEST.[4] IN A DARK HOUSE[5] ONE MAY NOT OPEN UP WINDOWS IN ORDER TO INSPECT ITS LEPROSY SIGN.[6]

MISHNAH 4. IN WHAT POSTURE IS A LEPROSY SIGN TO BE INSPECTED? A MAN IS INSPECTED IN THE POSTURE OF ONE THAT HOES[7] AND ONE THAT GATHERS OLIVES;[7] AND A WOMAN IN THAT OF ONE WHO ROLLS OUT DOUGH[8] AND[9] ONE WHO SUCKLES HER CHILD, AND ONE THAT WEAVES AT AN UPRIGHT LOOM[10] IF THE LEPROSY SIGN WAS WITHIN THE RIGHT ARMPIT. R. JUDAH RULED: ALSO IN THE POSTURE OF ONE THAT SPINS FLAX[11] IF IT WAS WITHIN THE LEFT ARMPIT. THE SAME POSTURE THAT A MAN ADOPTS[5] IN THE CASE OF

(1) Though this, in the case of a German, would result in a restriction. (2) Some texts add 'seventh'. (3) Of the day, beginning with sunrise, each hour being equal to one twelfth of the day. (4) Lev. XIII, 12, emphasis on '*appeareth*' and '*eyes*' (5) One that had no windows. (6) Cf. Lev. XIV, 34ff. (7) In such a position he exposes some of the concealed parts of his body while others still remain concealed. Only a leprosy on the latter is deemed to be 'concealed' and, therefore, clean. (7) Cf. prev. n. *mut. mut.* (8) If the leprosy sign is under the breast. (9) When the right arm is raised. (10) Who raises her left arm. (11) Lit., 'as he is seen'.

HIS LEPROSY SIGN HE IS ALSO TO ADOPT IN THE CASE OF THE CUTTING OFF OF HIS HAIR.[1]

MISHNAH 5. A MAN MAY EXAMINE ALL LEPROSY SIGNS[2] EXCEPT HIS OWN. R. MEIR RULED: NOT EVEN THE LEPROSY SIGNS OF HIS RELATIVES.[3] A MAN[4] MAY ANNUL ALL VOWS EXCEPT HIS OWN. R. JUDAH RULED: NOT EVEN THOSE VOWS OF HIS WIFE[5] THAT AFFECT RELATIONSHIPS BETWEEN HER AND OTHERS.[6] A MAN MAY EXAMINE ALL FIRSTLINGS[7] EXCEPT HIS OWN FIRSTLINGS.

(1) Lev. XIV, 9. Concealed hair need not be cut off. (2) *Sc.* even those of his nearest relatives whose lawsuits he may not try. (3) Cf. prev. n. *mut. mut.* (4) Who possesses the required authority; a Sage. (5) May one annul. (6) But do not affect him. (7) To ascertain whether they have a permanent blemish (cf. Bek. VI, 1ff).

NEGA'IM

CHAPTER III

MISHNAH I. ALL CAN CONTRACT LEPROSY UNCLEANNESS, EXCEPT A HEATHEN AND A RESIDENT ALIEN.[1] ALL[2] ARE QUALIFIED TO INSPECT LEPROSY SIGNS, BUT ONLY A PRIEST[3] MAY DECLARE THEM UNCLEAN OR CLEAN. HE[4] IS TOLD,[5] 'SAY: UNCLEAN', AND HE REPEATS 'UNCLEAN', OR 'SAY: CLEAN', AND HE REPEATS 'CLEAN'. TWO LEPROSY SIGNS MAY NOT BE INSPECTED SIMULTANEOUSLY WHETHER IN ONE MAN OR IN TWO MEN; BUT THE ONE MUST BE INSPECTED FIRST AND SHUT UP, CERTIFIED UNCLEAN OR PRONOUNCED CLEAN, AND THEN THE SECOND IS INSPECTED. ONE WHO IS SHUT UP[6] MAY NOT[7] BE SHUT UP AGAIN[8] NOR MAY ONE WHO IS CERTIFIED UNCLEAN[6] BE CERTIFIED[7] UNCLEAN AGAIN.[8] ONE WHO IS CERTIFIED UNCLEAN[6] MAY NOT[7] BE SHUT UP[8] NOR MAY ONE WHO IS SHUT UP[6] BE CERTIFIED[7] UNCLEAN.[8] BUT IN THE BEGINNING,[9] OR AT THE END OF A WEEK,[10] HE[11] MAY SHUT UP ON ACCOUNT OF THE ONE LEPROSY SIGN AND SHUT UP ON ACCOUNT OF ANOTHER ONE ALSO;[12] THE MAN[11] WHO CERTIFIES ONE SIGN UNCLEAN MAY ALSO CERTIFY THE OTHER UNCLEAN; HE MAY SHUT UP THE ONE SIGN AND DECLARE THE OTHER CLEAN, OR CERTIFY THE ONE UNCLEAN AND DECLARE THE OTHER CLEAN.

(1) *Ger Toshab*, a heathen who acquired Palestinian citizenship on condition that he renounced idolatry and undertook to observe the seven Noachian laws (cf. G. F. Moore, *Judaism* I, 338ff). (2) Even an unlearned priest under the guidance of an Israelite scholar (v. *infra*). (3) Cf. prev. n. (4) The unlearned priest. (5) By the Israelite scholar who accompanies him. (6) On account of a leprosy sign. (7) Before the conclusion of the prescribed period. (8) On account of a second leprosy sign that appeared. (9) *Sc.* if the second leprosy sign appeared before the first had received attention. (10) During which one was shut up on account of a first leprosy sign. (11) *Sc.* the priest.

MISHNAH 2. A BRIDEGROOM ON WHOM A LEPROSY SIGN HAS APPEARED IS GRANTED EXEMPTION FROM INSPECTION DURING THE SEVEN DAYS OF THE MARRIAGE FEAST IN RESPECT OF HIS OWN PERSON; AND ALSO IN RESPECT OF HIS HOUSE AND HIS GARMENT.[1] SIMILARLY DURING A FESTIVAL, ONE[2] IS GRANTED EXEMPTION FROM INSPECTION DURING ALL THE DAYS OF THE FESTIVAL.

MISHNAH 3. THE SKIN OF THE FLESH[3] BECOMES UNCLEAN FOR TWO WEEKS[4] AND BY ONE OF THE FOLLOWING THREE TOKENS:[5] BY WHITE HAIR OR BY QUICK FLESH OR BY A SPREADING. 'BY WHITE HAIR OR BY QUICK FLESH', IN THE BEGINNING,[6] AT THE END OF THE FIRST WEEK,[7] AT THE END OF THE SECOND WEEK,[7] OR AFTER IT[8] HAD BEEN PRONOUNCED CLEAN. 'OR BY A SPREADING', AT THE END OF THE FIRST WEEK,[7] AT THE END OF THE SECOND WEEK,[7] OR AFTER IT[8] HAD BEEN PRONOUNCED CLEAN. IT BECOMES UNCLEAN FOR TWO WEEKS WHICH ARE ONLY THIRTEEN DAYS.[9]

MISHNAH 4. A BOIL OR A BURNING BECOMES UNCLEAN FOR ONE WEEK[10] AND BY ONE OF THE FOLLOWING TWO TOKENS:[5] BY WHITE HAIR OR BY A SPREADING. 'BY WHITE HAIR', IN THE BEGINNING,[6] BY THE END OF THE WEEK,[7] OR AFTER IT[8] HAS BEEN PRONOUNCED CLEAN. 'OR BY A SPREADING', AT THE END OF THE WEEK,[7] OR AFTER IT[8] HAD BEEN DECLARED CLEAN. THEY BECOME UNCLEAN FOR A WEEK WHICH REPRESENTS SEVEN DAYS.

(1) If a leprosy sign appeared on either. (2) Any person on whom a leprosy sign appeared. (3) On which there appeared a leprosy sign. (4) At least, if there was no change in the sign; since in consequence it has to be shut up for no less than two periods of seven days, making a total of two weeks. (5) Which render it unclean even earlier. (6) When the sign is first inspected. (7) During which it was shut up. (8) The leprosy sign. (9) Since the last day of the first week is counted also as the beginning of the second week. (10) Even in the absence of any token of uncleanness, since it must invariably be shut up for a week.

MISHNAH 5. SCALLS BECOME UNCLEAN FOR TWO WEEKS[1] AND BY ONE OF THE FOLLOWING TWO TOKENS:[2] BY YELLOW THIN HAIR OR BY A SPREADING. 'BY YELLOW THIN HAIR' IN THE BEGINNING,[3] AT THE END OF THE FIRST WEEK,[4] AT THE END OF THE SECOND WEEK,[4] OR AFTER THEY HAVE BEEN PRONOUNCED CLEAN. 'OR BY A SPREADING', AT THE END OF THE FIRST WEEK,[4] AT THE END OF THE SECOND WEEK[4] OR AFTER THEY HAVE BEEN PRONOUNCED CLEAN. THEY BECOME UNCLEAN FOR TWO WEEKS WHICH ARE ONLY THIRTEEN DAYS.[5]

MISHNAH 6. SCALP BALDNESS OR FOREHEAD BALDNESS BECOME UNCLEAN FOR TWO WEEKS[1] AND BY ONE OF THE FOLLOWING TOKENS:[2] BY QUICK FLESH OR BY A SPREADING. 'BY QUICK FLESH', IN THE BEGINNING,[3] AT THE END OF THE FIRST WEEK,[4] AT THE END OF THE SECOND WEEK,[4] OR AFTER THEY HAVE BEEN PRONOUNCED CLEAN. 'OR BY A SPREADING', AT THE END OF THE FIRST WEEK,[4] AT THE END OF THE SECOND WEEK,[4] OR AFTER THEY HAVE BEEN PRONOUNCED CLEAN. THEY BECOME UNCLEAN FOR TWO WEEKS WHICH ARE ONLY THIRTEEN DAYS.[5]

MISHNAH 7. GARMENTS BECOME UNCLEAN FOR TWO WEEKS[1] AND BY ONE OF THREE TOKENS:[2] BY A GREENISH COLOUR OR BY A REDDISH COLOUR OR BY A SPREADING. 'BY A GREENISH COLOUR OR BY A REDDISH COLOUR', IN THE BEGINNING,[3] AT THE END OF THE FIRST WEEK,[4] AT THE END OF THE SECOND WEEK,[4] OR AFTER THEY HAVE BEEN PRONOUNCED CLEAN. 'OR BY A SPREADING', AT THE END OF THE FIRST WEEK,[4] AT THE END OF THE SECOND WEEK,[4] OR AFTER THEY HAVE BEEN PRONOUNCED CLEAN. THEY BECOME UNCLEAN FOR TWO WEEKS WHICH ARE BUT THIRTEEN DAYS.[5]

(1) At least, if there was no change in the sign; since in consequence it has to be shut up for no less than two periods of seven days, making a total of two weeks. (2) V. p. 242, n. 5. (3) V. p. 242, n. 6. (4) V. p. 242, n. 7. (5) V. p. 242, n. 9.

MISHNAH 8. HOUSES BECOME UNCLEAN FOR THREE WEEKS[1] AND BY ONE OF THE FOLLOWING THREE TOKENS:[2] BY A GREENISH COLOUR OR BY A REDDISH COLOUR OR BY A SPREADING. 'BY A GREENISH COLOUR OR BY A REDDISH COLOUR', IN THE BEGINNING,[3] AT THE END OF THE FIRST WEEK,[4] AT THE END OF THE SECOND WEEK,[4] AT THE END OF THE THIRD WEEK,[4] OR AFTER THEY HAVE BEEN PRONOUNCED CLEAN. 'OR BY A SPREADING', AT THE END OF THE FIRST WEEK,[4] AT THE END OF THE SECOND WEEK,[4] AT THE END OF THE THIRD WEEK,[4] OR AFTER THEY HAVE BEEN PRONOUNCED CLEAN. THEY BECOME UNCLEAN FOR THREE WEEKS WHICH ARE BUT NINETEEN DAYS.[5] NONE OF THE LEPROSY SIGNS IS SHUT UP FOR LESS THAN A WEEK[6] OR FOR MORE THAN THREE WEEKS.[7]

(1) Cf. p. 243, n. 1 *mut. mut.* (2) V. p. 242, n. 5. (3) V. p. 242, n. 6. (4) V. p. 242, n. 7. (5) Cf. p. 242, n. 9 *mut. mut.* (6) The boil and the burning (7) The leprosy of houses.

NEGA'IM

CHAPTER IV

MISHNAH 1. CERTAIN RESTRICTIONS APPLY TO THE WHITE HAIR THAT DO NOT APPLY TO THE SPREADING, WHILE OTHER RESTRICTIONS APPLY TO THE SPREADING AND DO NOT APPLY TO THE WHITE HAIR. WHITE HAIR NAMELY CAUSES UNCLEANNESS AT THE BEGINNING,[1] IT CAUSES UNCLEANNESS WHATEVER THE STATE OF ITS WHITENESS,[2] AND IT IS NEVER A TOKEN OF CLEANNESS.[3] 'OTHER RESTRICTIONS APPLY TO THE SPREADING', FOR THE SPREADING CAUSES UNCLEANNESS HOWEVER SMALL ITS EXTENT,[4] IT CAUSES UNCLEANNESS IN ALL FORMS OF LEPROSY SIGNS[5] AND ALSO WHERE IT IS OUTSIDE THE SIGN,[6] WHICH RESTRICTIONS DO NOT APPLY TO THE WHITE HAIR.[7]

MISHNAH 2. CERTAIN RESTRICTIONS APPLY TO THE QUICK FLESH THAT DO NOT APPLY TO THE SPREADING, WHILE OTHER RESTRICTIONS APPLY TO THE SPREADING AND DO NOT APPLY TO THE QUICK FLESH. QUICK FLESH NAMELY CAUSES UNCLEANNESS AT THE BEGINNING,[1] IT CAUSES UNCLEANNESS WHATEVER ITS COLOUR,[8] AND IT IS NEVER A TOKEN OF CLEANNESS.[3] 'OTHER RESTRICTIONS APPLY TO THE SPREADING', FOR THE SPREADING CAUSES UNCLEANNESS HOWEVER SMALL ITS EXTENT, IT CAUSES UNCLEANNESS IN

(1) When a leprosy sign is first inspected. (2) Even if it is dimmer than any of the four principal colours. (3) A spreading, however, may be one when it extended over the whole body. (4) White hair is subject to a minimum of two hairs of a prescribed length. (5) Even in those of garments and houses. (6) White hair, however, is no token of uncleanness unless it appeared within the leprosy sign. (7) Cf. prev. nn. (8) While the spreading causes uncleanness only if it has one of the four principal colours.

ALL FORMS OF LEPROSY SIGNS[1] AND ALSO WHERE IT IS OUTSIDE THE LEPROSY SIGN,[2] WHICH RESTRICTIONS DO NOT APPLY TO THE QUICK FLESH.[3]

MISHNAH 3. CERTAIN RESTRICTIONS APPLY TO WHITE HAIR THAT DO NOT APPLY TO THE QUICK FLESH, WHILE OTHER RESTRICTIONS APPLY TO QUICK FLESH AND NOT TO WHITE HAIR. WHITE HAIR NAMELY CAUSES UNCLEANNESS IN A BOIL AND IN A BURNING, WHETHER GROWING TOGETHER OR DISPERSED,[4] AND WHETHER ENCOMPASSED[5] OR UNENCOMPASSED. 'OTHER RESTRICTIONS APPLY TO QUICK FLESH', FOR QUICK FLESH CAUSES UNCLEANNESS IN SCALP BALDNESS AND IN FOREHEAD BALDNESS, WHETHER IT WAS TURNED[6] OR WAS NOT TURNED,[7] IT[8] HINDERS THE CLEANNESS OF ONE WHO IS ALL TURNED WHITE,[9] AND CAUSES UNCLEANNESS WHATEVER ITS COLOUR, WHICH RESTRICTIONS DO NOT APPLY TO WHITE HAIR.[3]

MISHNAH 4. IF THE TWO HAIRS[10] WERE BLACK AT THE ROOT AND WHITE AT THE TIP THE MAN IS CLEAN. IF THEY WERE WHITE AT THE ROOT AND BLACK AT THE TIP THE MAN IS UNCLEAN. HOW MUCH OF WHITENESS MUST THERE BE?[11] R. MEIR RULED: ANY. R. SIMEON RULED: ENOUGH TO BE CUT WITH A PAIR OF SCISSORS. IF IT WAS SINGLE AT THE ROOT BUT SPLIT AT THE TIP, HAVING THE APPEARANCE OF TWO HAIRS, THE MAN IS CLEAN. IF A BRIGHT SPOT HAD [TWO]

(1) Quick flesh, however, causes uncleanness only if it is of the prescribed size and only on skin, flesh, scalp baldness and forehead baldness. (2) But quick flesh is a cause of uncleanness only if it appears within the leprosy sign. (3) Cf. prev. nn. (4) One hair at one side of the leprosy sign and another at the other side. (5) By the leprosy sign. (6) Cf. Lev. XIII, 13. V. foll. n. (7) *Sc.* whether the quick flesh appeared after the bright spot or whether the latter appeared after the former. In the case of white hair if it preceded the bright spot no uncleanness is caused. (8) If its size is no less than that of a lentil. (9) Cf. Ibid. XIII, 12ff. White hair in such a case causes no uncleanness. (10) In a leprosy sign. (11) On the hairs to be regarded as turned white.

WHITE HAIRS AND[1] BLACK HAIR THE MAN IS UNCLEAN. THERE IS NO NEED TO CONSIDER THE POSSIBILITY THAT THE PLACE OF THE BLACK HAIR[2] LESSENED THE SPACE OF THE BRIGHT SPOT,[3] SINCE THE FORMER[4] IS OF NO CONSEQUENCE.[5]

MISHNAH 5. IF A BRIGHT SPOT WAS OF THE SIZE OF A SPLIT BEAN AND A STREAK EXTENDED FROM IT, THE LATTER, PROVIDED IT WAS TWO HAIRS IN BREADTH, SUBJECTS IT[6] TO THE RESTRICTIONS IN RESPECT OF WHITE HAIR AND SPREADING,[7] BUT NOT TO THAT IN RESPECT OF ITS QUICK FLESH.[8] IF THERE WERE TWO BRIGHT SPOTS AND A STREAK EXTENDED FROM ONE TO THE OTHER, PROVIDED IT WAS TWO HAIRS IN BREADTH, IT COMBINES THEM;[9] OTHERWISE IT DOES NOT COMBINE THEM.

MISHNAH 6. IF A BRIGHT SPOT OF THE SIZE OF A SPLIT BEAN HAD WITHIN IT QUICK FLESH OF THE SIZE OF A LENTIL AND THERE WAS WHITE HAIR WITHIN THE QUICK FLESH, IF THE QUICK FLESH DISAPPEARED[10] THE SPOT BECOMES UNCLEAN ON ACCOUNT OF THE WHITE HAIR; IF THE WHITE HAIR DISAPPEARED[11] IT BECOMES UNCLEAN ON ACCOUNT OF THE QUICK FLESH. R. SIMEON RULES THAT[12] IT IS CLEAN, SINCE IT WAS NOT THE BRIGHT SPOT[13] THAT CAUSED THE HAIR TO TURN WHITE.[14] IF A BRIGHT SPOT TOGETHER WITH

(1) Var. lec. 'or'. (2) According to var. lec. (in previous note) add 'or the white hair'. (3) In consequence of which the bright spot may have been reduced to less than the prescribed minimum of a split bean. (4) The hair follicles whose size is almost imperceptible. (5) Lit., 'substance', 'reality'. (6) The bright spot. (7) If either of these signs appear in the streak the spot is deemed unclean. (8) Which must be encompassed by the bright spot. (9) The two bright spots. Both are in all respects regarded as one unit to make up the prescribed minimum of a split bean and to combine the two hairs if one grew on the one and the other on the other side of the spot. (10) The leprosy sign having spread over its place. (11) Having fallen off or turned black. (12) In the first case. (13) But the quick flesh from which it grew. (14) The first Tanna, however, maintains that in this respect the quick flesh is regarded as a part of the bright spot.

THE QUICK FLESH IN IT WAS OF THE SIZE OF A SPLIT BEAN AND THERE WAS WHITE HAIR WITHIN THE SPOT, IF THE QUICK FLESH DISAPPEARED[1] THE SPOT IS UNCLEAN ON ACCOUNT OF THE WHITE HAIR; IF THE WHITE HAIR DISAPPEARED IT IS UNCLEAN ON ACCOUNT OF THE QUICK FLESH. R. SIMEON RULES THAT IT[2] IS CLEAN, SINCE IT WAS NOT A BRIGHT SPOT OF THE SIZE OF A SPLIT BEAN THAT CAUSED THE HAIR TO TURN WHITE. HE AGREES, HOWEVER, THAT IT IS UNCLEAN IF IT WAS OF THE SIZE OF A SPLIT BEAN[3] WHERE THE WHITE HAIR WAS.

MISHNAH 7. WITH REGARD TO A BRIGHT SPOT[4] WITHIN WHICH WAS[5] QUICK FLESH AND A SPREADING,[6] IF THE QUICK FLESH DISAPPEARED IT IS UNCLEAN ON ACCOUNT OF THE SPREADING; IF THE SPREADING DISAPPEARED IT IS UNCLEAN ON ACCOUNT OF THE QUICK FLESH. SO ALSO IN THE CASE OF WHITE HAIR AND A SPREADING.[7] IF A LEPROSY SIGN[4] DISAPPEARED[8] AND APPEARED AGAIN AT THE END OF THE WEEK,[9] IT IS REGARDED AS THOUGH IT HAD REMAINED AS IT WAS.[10] IF IT REAPPEARED AFTER IT[11] HAD BEEN PRONOUNCED CLEAN, IT MUST BE INSPECTED AS A NEW ONE.[12] IF IT HAD BEEN BRIGHT WHITE BUT WAS NOW DULL WHITE, OR IF IT HAD BEEN DULL WHITE BUT WAS NOW BRIGHT WHITE, IT[13] IS REGARDED AS THOUGH IT HAD REMAINED AS IT WAS, PROVIDED THAT IT DOES NOT BECOME LESS WHITE THAN THE FOUR PRINCIPAL COLOURS.[14] IF IT[15] CONTRACTED AND

(1) The leprosy sign having spread over its place. (2) V. p. 247, n. 12. (3) Without the addition of the quick flesh. (4) Of the prescribed size of a split bean that had been shut up for a week. (5) At the end of the week (cf. prev. n.). (6) In consequence of which it was certified unclean. (7) If one disappeared it is still unclean on account of the other that remained. (8) During the week. (9) Or if it disappeared at the end of the week on the day of inspection and appeared again later on the same day. (10) And is to be shut up again for a second week. It is not to be treated as a new leprosy sign to be possibly shut up for two weeks. (11) Having been diminished in size. (12) Lit., 'as at the beginning'. Var lec., 'in the beginning'. (13) Since its size still conformed to the minimum prescribed. (14) Enumerated *supra* I, 1. If it did become less white it must be pronounced clean. (15) A leprosy sign of the size of a split bean.

THEN SPREAD, OR IF IT SPREAD[1] AND THEN CONTRACTED, R. AKIBA RULES THAT IT IS UNCLEAN,[2] BUT THE SAGES RULE THAT IT IS CLEAN.[3]

MISHNAH 8. IF A BRIGHT SPOT OF THE SIZE OF A SPLIT BEAN[4] SPREAD TO THE EXTENT OF HALF A SPLIT BEAN, WHILE OF THE ORIGINAL SPOT THERE DISAPPEARED AS MUCH AS HALF A SPLIT BEAN, R. AKIBA RULED: IT MUST BE INSPECTED AS A NEW ONE,[5] BUT THE SAGES RULE THAT IT IS CLEAN.[6]

MISHNAH 9. IF A BRIGHT SPOT OF THE SIZE OF A SPLIT BEAN SPREAD TO THE EXTENT OF HALF A SPLIT BEAN AND A LITTLE MORE, WHILE AS MUCH AS HALF THE SIZE OF A SPLIT BEAN DISAPPEARED FROM THE ORIGINAL SPOT, R. AKIBA RULES THAT IT IS UNCLEAN,[7] BUT THE SAGES RULE THAT IT IS CLEAN.[8] IF THE BRIGHT SPOT WAS OF THE SIZE OF A SPLIT BEAN AND IT SPREAD TO THE EXTENT OF A SPLIT BEAN AND A LITTLE MORE, WHILE THE ORIGINAL SPOT DISAPPEARED, R. AKIBA RULES THAT IS IT UNCLEAN,[9] BUT THE SAGES RULE THAT IT SHOULD BE INSPECTED AS A NEW ONE.[10]

MISHNAH 10. IF A BRIGHT SPOT OF THE SIZE OF A SPLIT BEAN SPREAD[11] TO THE EXTENT OF A SPLIT BEAN, AND IN

(1) At the end of the first or the second week. (2) In his opinion the spreading, in either case, is a mark of uncleanness. (3) The spreading, they maintain, may be disregarded, since the size of the leprosy sign is now the same as it was originally. (4) That was shut up. (5) Because, of the original, less than the prescribed minimum remained, while the remainder together with the extension conform to the prescribed minimum. (6) Since the original spot had been reduced to half the prescribed minimum it must be regarded as clean. Its clean remainder, therefore, cannot be added to the extension to constitute a new leprosy sign. (7) Because the spreading exceeded the size of half a split bean. (8) Since, owing to the disappearance of half of the original spot, the new one (only slightly bigger than half a split bean) is less than the prescribed minimum. (9) Since the spot is now bigger than it was originally. (10) Because the original spot had entirely disappeared. (11) After it had been pronounced clean.

THE SPREADING THERE APPEARED QUICK FLESH OR WHITE HAIR, WHILE THE ORIGINAL SPOT DISAPPEARED, R. AKIBA RULES THAT IT IS UNCLEAN,[1] BUT THE SAGES RULE THAT IT MUST BE INSPECTED AS A NEW ONE.[2] IF IN A BRIGHT SPOT OF THE SIZE OF HALF A SPLIT BEAN NOTHING ELSE[3] APPEARED, AND THEN THERE APPEARED[4] A BRIGHT SPOT OF THE SIZE OF HALF A SPLIT BEAN AND IN IT THERE GREW ONE HAIR, SUCH A SPOT MUST BE SHUT UP. IF A BRIGHT SPOT OF THE SIZE OF HALF A SPLIT BEAN HAD ONE HAIR AND THEN THERE APPEARED[4] ANOTHER SPOT OF THE SIZE OF HALF A SPLIT BEAN WHICH ALSO HAD ONE HAIR, SUCH A SPOT MUST BE SHUT UP.[5] IF A BRIGHT SPOT OF THE SIZE OF HALF A SPLIT BEAN HAD TWO HAIRS AND ANOTHER SPOT OF THE SIZE OF HALF A SPLIT BEAN APPEARED[4] WITH ONE HAIR,[6] SUCH A SPOT MUST BE SHUT UP.[7]

MISHNAH 11. IF IN A BRIGHT SPOT OF THE SIZE OF A SPLIT BEAN THERE WAS NOTHING ELSE, AND THEN THERE APPEARED[4] A BRIGHT SPOT OF THE SIZE OF HALF A SPLIT BEAN HAVING TWO HAIRS, SUCH MUST BE CERTIFIED UNCLEAN,[8] BECAUSE IT HAS BEEN LAID DOWN: IF THE BRIGHT SPOT PRECEDED THE WHITE HAIR THE MAN IS UNCLEAN; IF THE WHITE HAIR PRECEDED THE BRIGHT SPOT HE IS CLEAN; AND IF THIS IS A MATTER OF DOUBT HE IS UNCLEAN. R. JOSHUA REGARDS THIS AS UNSOLVABLE.[9]

(1) The spreading taking the place of the original spot. (2) Hence two sacrifices will have to be brought, one for each spot. (3) Neither quick flesh nor white hair. (4) At its side. (5) Since the first hair preceded the second half of the spot. (6) And much more so if it had no hair at all. (7) Since the full sized spot did not precede the first two hairs. (8) Provided that it is known that the second half of the spot preceded the two hairs. (9) *Aliter:* Doubtful; *aliter:* Demurred; *aliter:* Rejected, v. Nid. 19*b*.

NEGA'IM

CHAPTER V

MISHNAH 1. ANY CONDITION OF DOUBT IN LEPROSY SIGNS IS REGARDED AS CLEAN, EXCEPT THIS CASE[1] AND ONE OTHER. WHICH IS THAT? IF A MAN HAD A BRIGHT SPOT OF THE SIZE OF A SPLIT BEAN AND IT WAS SHUT UP, AND BY THE END OF THE WEEK IT WAS AS BIG AS A SELA', AND IT IS DOUBTFUL WHETHER IT IS THE ORIGINAL ONE[2] OR WHETHER ANOTHER HAS ARISEN IN ITS PLACE, THE MAN MUST BE REGARDED AS UNCLEAN.

MISHNAH 2. IF A MAN HAD BEEN CERTIFIED UNCLEAN ON ACCOUNT OF WHITE HAIR, AND THE WHITE HAIR DISAPPEARED AND OTHER WHITE HAIR APPEARED, AND SO ALSO IN THE CASE OF QUICK FLESH[3] AND A SPREADING,[3] WHETHER THIS[4] OCCURRED IN THE BEGINNING,[5] AT THE END OF THE FIRST WEEK, AT THE END OF THE SECOND WEEK, OR AFTER THE MAN HAD BEEN RELEASED FROM UNCLEANNESS, HE[6] IS REGARDED AS BEING IN THE SAME POSITION AS BEFORE.[7] IF HE HAD BEEN CERTIFIED UNCLEAN ON ACCOUNT OF QUICK FLESH, AND THE QUICK FLESH DISAPPEARED AND OTHER QUICK FLESH APPEARED, AND SO ALSO IN THE CASE OF WHITE HAIR[8] AND A SPREADING,[8] WHETHER THIS[4] OCCURRED IN THE BEGINNING,[5] AT THE END OF THE FIRST WEEK, AT THE END OF THE SECOND WEEK, OR AFTER THE MAN HAD BEEN RELEASED FROM UNCLEANNESS, HE[6] IS REGARDED AS BEING IN THE SAME POSITION AS BEFORE.[7] IF HE HAD BEEN CERTI-

(1) The last mentioned (*supra* IV, 11). (2) That had spread. (3) That appeared in the place of the white hair. (4) The certification as unclean. (5) When the first inspection took place. (6) So MS.M. Var. lec., 'it'. (7) He is unclean and there is no need again to certify his uncleanness. (8) Appearing in place of the quick flesh.

FIED UNCLEAN ON ACCOUNT OF A SPREADING, AND THE SPREADING DISAPPEARED AND ANOTHER SPREADING APPEARED, AND SO ALSO IN THE CASE OF WHITE HAIR,[1] WHETHER THIS[2] OCCURRED AT THE END OF THE FIRST WEEK, AT THE END OF THE SECOND WEEK, OR AFTER THE MAN HAD BEEN RELEASED FROM UNCLEANNESS, HE[3] IS IN THE SAME POSITION AS BEFORE.[4]

MISHNAH 3. DEPOSITED HAIR[5] AKABIAH B. MAHALALEEL HOLDS TO BE UNCLEAN, BUT THE SAGES HOLD IT TO BE CLEAN. WHAT IS 'DEPOSITED HAIR'? IF A MAN HAD A BRIGHT SPOT WITH WHITE HAIR IN IT, AND THE BRIGHT SPOT DISAPPEARED LEAVING THE WHITE HAIR IN POSITION AND THEN IT REAPPEARED, AKABIAH B. MAHALALEEL HOLDS THE MAN TO BE UNCLEAN,[6] BUT THE SAGES HOLD HIM TO BE CLEAN. R. AKIBA OBSERVED: IN THIS CASE I ADMIT THAT THE MAN IS CLEAN; BUT WHAT IS 'DEPOSITED HAIR'?[7] IF A MAN HAD A BRIGHT SPOT OF THE SIZE OF A SPLIT BEAN WITH TWO HAIRS IN IT, AND A PART THE SIZE OF A HALF SPLIT BEAN DISAPPEARED LEAVING THE WHITE HAIR IN THE PLACE OF THE WHITE SPOT AND THEN IT REAPPEARED.[8] THEY[9] SAID TO HIM: AS THEY[10] REJECTED THE RULING OF AKABIAH SO IS THERE NO VALIDITY IN YOUR RULING.[11]

MISHNAH 4. ANY CONDITION OF DOUBT IN LEPROSY SIGNS IN THE BEGINNING IS REGARDED AS CLEAN BEFORE UNCLEANNESS HAS BEEN ESTABLISHED, BUT AFTER UNCLEANNESS HAS BEEN ESTABLISHED A CONDITION OF DOUBT IS

(1) 'Quick flesh' is omitted since under certain circumstances it is a cause of cleanness. (2) V. p. 251, n. 4. (3) V. p. 251, n. 6. (4) V. p. 251, n. 7. (5) This is explained presently. (6) As the bright spot reappeared where it was originally it is regarded as the original spot which preceded the white hair and which was certified unclean. (7) That is a token of uncleanness. (8) Only in such a case is the man unclean. (9) His colleagues. (10) The Sages. (11) Since a leprosy sign that is less than half a split bean is deemed to be non-existent.

REGARDED AS UNCLEAN. IN WHAT MANNER? IF TWO MEN CAME TO THE PRIEST, ONE HAVING A BRIGHT SPOT OF THE SIZE OF A SPLIT BEAN AND THE OTHER HAVING ONE OF THE SIZE OF A SELA', AND AT THE END OF THE WEEK THAT OF EACH WAS OF THE SIZE OF A SELA', AND IT IS NOT KNOWN ON WHICH OF THEM THE SPREADING HAD OCCURRED (WHETHER THIS OCCURRED WITH ONE MAN[1] OR WITH TWO MEN), EACH ONE IS CLEAN. R. AKIBA RULED: IF ONE MAN IS INVOLVED HE IS UNCLEAN,[2] BUT IF TWO MEN ARE INVOLVED EACH IS CLEAN.

MISHNAH 5. 'BUT AFTER UNCLEANNESS HAS BEEN ESTABLISHED A CONDITION OF DOUBT IS REGARDED AS UNCLEAN'.[3] IN WHAT MANNER? IF TWO MEN CAME TO THE PRIEST, ONE HAVING A BRIGHT SPOT OF THE SIZE OF A SPLIT BEAN AND THE OTHER HAVING ONE OF THE SIZE OF A SELA', AND AT THE END OF THE WEEK THAT OF EACH WAS OF THE SIZE OF A SELA' AND A LITTLE MORE, BOTH ARE UNCLEAN; AND EVEN THOUGH BOTH RESUMED THE SIZE OF A SELA' BOTH ARE UNCLEAN, AND REMAIN SO UNLESS BOTH RESUME THE SIZE OF A SPLIT BEAN. IT IS THIS THAT WAS MEANT WHEN IT WAS LAID DOWN, 'BUT AFTER UNCLEANNESS HAS BEEN ESTABLISHED A CONDITION OF DOUBT IS REGARDED AS UNCLEAN'.

(1) Who had two bright spots. (2) Since one of the spots at least is unclean. (3) Cf. prev. Mishnah.

NEGA'IM

CHAPTER VI

MISHNAH 1. THE MINIMUM SIZE[1] OF A BRIGHT SPOT[2] MUST BE THAT OF A CILICIAN SPLIT BEAN SQUARED.[3] THE SPACE COVERED BY A SPLIT BEAN EQUALS THAT OF NINE LENTILS, THE SPACE COVERED BY A LENTIL EQUALS THAT OF FOUR HAIRS;[4] THUS THE SIZE OF A BRIGHT SPOT MUST BE NO LESS THAN THAT OF THIRTY-SIX HAIRS.

MISHNAH 2. IF A BRIGHT SPOT WAS OF THE SIZE OF A SPLIT BEAN AND IN IT THERE WAS QUICK FLESH OF THE SIZE OF A LENTIL,[5] IF THE BRIGHT SPOT GREW LARGER[6] IT IS UNCLEAN,[7] BUT IF IT GREW SMALLER IT IS CLEAN. IF THE QUICK FLESH GREW LARGER IT IS UNCLEAN,[8] AND IF IT GREW SMALLER IT IS CLEAN.

MISHNAH 3. IF A BRIGHT SPOT WAS OF THE SIZE OF A SPLIT BEAN AND IN IT THERE WAS QUICK FLESH LESS IN SIZE THAN A LENTIL, IF THE BRIGHT SPOT GREW LARGER IT IS UNCLEAN,[7] BUT IF IT GREW SMALLER IT IS CLEAN. IF THE QUICK FLESH GREW LARGER IT IS UNCLEAN, BUT IF IT GREW SMALLER,[9] R. MEIR RULES THAT IT IS UNCLEAN;[10] BUT THE SAGES RULE THAT IT IS CLEAN, SINCE A LEPROSY SIGN CANNOT BE DEEMED TO SPREAD WITHIN ITSELF.[11]

(1) Lit., 'body'. (2) That is to be pronounced unclean. (3) *Sc.* each of its four sides must be as long as a Cilician split bean. (4) Growing on the body other than the head or face. (5) Thus reducing its size to less than the prescribed minimum. (6) Extending outwards. (7) On account of the spreading. (8) Var. lec., 'clean', since the bright spot decreased where the quick flesh had spread. (9) The bright spot having spread in that direction. (10) An extension within being as unclean as one without. (11) Only an external expansion is regarded as a spreading that causes uncleanness.

MISHNAH 4. IF A BRIGHT SPOT WAS LARGER IN SIZE THAN A SPLIT BEAN AND IN IT THERE WAS QUICK FLESH LARGER IN SIZE THAN A LENTIL, IRRESPECTIVE OF WHETHER THEY INCREASED OR DECREASED, THEY ARE UNCLEAN, PROVIDED THAT THEY DO NOT DECREASE TO LESS THAN THE PRESCRIBED MINIMUM.[1]

MISHNAH 5. IF A BRIGHT SPOT WAS OF THE SIZE OF A SPLIT BEAN, QUICK FLESH OF THE SIZE OF A LENTIL ENCOMPASSING IT, AND OUTSIDE THE QUICK FLESH THERE WAS ANOTHER BRIGHT SPOT, THE INNER ONE MUST BE SHUT UP AND THE OUTER ONE MUST BE CERTIFIED UNCLEAN.[2] R. JOSE RULED: THE QUICK FLESH IS NO TOKEN OF UNCLEANNESS FOR THE OUTER ONE, SINCE THE INNER BRIGHT SPOT IS WITHIN IT.[3] IF IT[4] DECREASED OR DISAPPEARED, RABBAN GAMALIEL RULED: IF ITS DESTRUCTION WAS ON ITS INNER SIDE[5] IT IS A TOKEN OF A SPREADING OF THE INNER BRIGHT SPOT[6] WHILE THE OUTER ONE IS CLEAN,[7] BUT IF ITS DESTRUCTION WAS ON ITS OUTER SIDE,[8] THE OUTER ONE IS CLEAN[9] WHILE THE INNER ONE[10] MUST BE SHUT UP. R. AKIBA RULED: IN EITHER CASE[11] IT[12] IS CLEAN.[13]

MISHNAH 6. R. SIMEON[14] STATED: WHEN IS THIS THE

(1) Viz., quick flesh of the size of a lentil surrounded on all sides by a bright spot of the size of a lentil. (2) On account of the quick flesh within it. (3) Only quick flesh that is encompassed by a bright spot is a token of uncleanness. The quick flesh in this case is not only encompassed, but also broken up by a bright spot. (4) The quick flesh under discussion. (5) The inner bright spot having covered up the quick flesh. (6) And it must be certified as unclean. (7) Since its quick flesh disappeared or decreased to less than the prescribed minimum. (8) The outer bright spot having covered it up. (9) Because its quick flesh was destroyed and its spreading inwards is of no consequence. (10) Having retained its size. (11) Whether the reduction or disappearance was on the inner or the outer side. (12) The inner bright spot. (13) In the former case, because, as stated, the spreading of the outer one inwards is of no consequence; and in the latter case, because the spreading of the inner one into the outer spot is similarly of no consequence. (14) Referring to R. Akiba's ruling in the previous Mishnah *ad fin*.

CASE?[1] WHEN THE QUICK FLESH WAS EXACTLY THE SIZE OF A LENTIL;[2] BUT IF IT EXCEEDED THE SIZE OF A LENTIL THE EXCESS IS A TOKEN OF SPREADING OF THE INNER ONE,[3] AND THE OUTER ONE IS UNCLEAN.[4] IF THERE WAS THERE[5] A TETTER LESS IN SIZE THAN A LENTIL, IT[6] IS A TOKEN OF THE SPREADING[7] OF THE INNER BRIGHT SPOT[8] BUT IT IS NO TOKEN OF SPREADING OF THE OUTER ONE.[9]

MISHNAH 7. THERE ARE TWENTY-FOUR TIPS OF LIMBS IN THE HUMAN BODY THAT DO NOT BECOME UNCLEAN ON ACCOUNT OF QUICK FLESH:[10] THE TIPS OF THE FINGERS AND THE TOES, THE TIPS OF THE EARS, THE TIP OF THE NOSE, THE TIP OF THE MEMBRUM; AND ALSO THE NIPPLES OF A WOMAN. R. JUDAH RULED: THOSE OF A MAN ALSO. R. ELIEZER RULED: ALSO WARTS AND WENS DO NOT BECOME UNCLEAN ON ACCOUNT OF QUICK FLESH.[11]

MISHNAH 8. THE FOLLOWING PLACES IN MEN[12] DO NOT BECOME UNCLEAN ON ACCOUNT OF A BRIGHT SPOT:[13] THE INSIDE OF THE EYE, THE INSIDE OF THE EAR, THE INSIDE OF THE NOSE AND THE INSIDE OF THE MOUTH, WRINKLES,[14] WRINKLES IN THE NECK, UNDER THE BREAST[15] AND THE ARMPIT,[16] THE SOLE OF THE FOOT,[17] THE NAILS, THE HEAD

(1) That the outer one is clean. (2) Lit., 'like a lentil brought' or 'applied'. (3) If it spread over that excess. (4) On account of the quick flesh. (5) Between the inner bright spot and the quick flesh around it. (6) The extension of the inner bright spot. (7) And of uncleanness. (8) Because a tetter that is less than the prescribed minimum may be disregarded. (9) Because its quick flesh was destroyed and its spreading inwards is of no consequence. (10) Because, owing to their convexity it is usually impossible to see at once the prescribed minimum of quick flesh and the leprosy sign. (11) Cf. prev. n. (12) Which are either not included in the expression, 'skin of his flesh' (Lev. XIII, 2) or are concealed parts of the body. (13) Or any other of the four colours (*supra* I, 1). (14) In any part of the body. (15) Of a suckling woman, which is covered when the child is nursed. (16) Which is concealed when the person is in the posture of one plucking olives (cf. *supra* II, 4). (17) Its hardened part which cannot be regarded as normal skin.

AND THE BEARD;[1] AND A BOIL, A BURNING AND A BLISTER[2] THAT ARE FESTERING. ALL THESE DO NOT BECOME UNCLEAN ON ACCOUNT OF LEPROSY SIGNS NOR ARE THEY COMBINED[3] WITH OTHER LEPROSY SIGNS,[4] NOR IS A LEPROSY SIGN DEEMED TO SPREAD INTO THEM,[5] NOR DO THEY BECOME UNCLEAN ON ACCOUNT OF QUICK FLESH,[6] NOR ARE THEY[7] A HINDRANCE[8] WHERE A PERSON IS ALL TURNED[9] WHITE.[10] IF SUBSEQUENTLY A BALD SPOT AROSE IN THE HEAD OR BEARD,[11] OR IF A BOIL, A BURNING OR A BLISTER FORMED A SCAR, THEY MAY BECOME UNCLEAN BY LEPROSY SIGNS THOUGH THEY CANNOT BE COMBINED WITH OTHER LEPROSY SIGNS,[12] NOR IS A LEPROSY SIGN DEEMED TO SPREAD INTO THEM,[5] NOR DO THEY BECOME UNCLEAN ON ACCOUNT OF QUICK FLESH. THEY ARE, HOWEVER, A HINDRANCE[8] WHERE[7] A PERSON IS ALL TURNED WHITE.[10] THE HEAD AND THE BEARD BEFORE THEY HAVE GROWN HAIR, AND WENS ON THE HEAD OR THE BEARD, ARE[13] TREATED AS THE SKIN OF THE FLESH.

(1) Where the only unclean leprosy sign is the scall (cf. Lev. XIII, 29ff). (2) That was due to an external cause. (3) To make up the prescribed minimum. (4) Even though their greater part is on the normal skin. (5) *Sc.* even if there was a spreading it is no sign of uncleanness. (6) That appeared in a leprosy sign on them. (7) If they did not turn white. (8) To cleanness.. (9) Except for any of these places. (10) Which is a mark of cleanness (cf. Lev. XIII, 13). (11) Thus assuming the character of normal skin of the body. (12) E.g. one on the head with one on the beard. (13) In all respects.

NEGA'IM

CHAPTER VII

MISHNAH 1. THE FOLLOWING BRIGHT SPOTS ARE CLEAN: THOSE THAT ONE HAD BEFORE THE TORAH WAS GIVEN,[1] THOSE THAT A HEATHEN HAD WHEN HE BECAME A PROSELYTE OR A CHILD WHEN IT WAS BORN, OR THOSE THAT WERE IN A CREASE[2] AND WERE SUBSEQUENTLY LAID BARE. IF THEY WERE ON THE HEAD OR THE BEARD, ON A BOIL, A BURNING OR BLISTER THAT IS FESTERING, AND SUBSEQUENTLY THE HEAD OR THE BEARD BECAME BALD, AND THE BOIL, BURNING OR BLISTER TURNED INTO A SCAR, THEY ARE CLEAN. IF THEY WERE ON THE HEAD OR THE BEARD BEFORE THESE GREW HAIR,[3] AND THEY THEN GREW HAIR[4] AND SUBSEQUENTLY BECAME BALD,[3] OR IF THEY WERE ON THE BODY BEFORE THE BOIL, BURNING OR BLISTER WAS FORMED[5] AND THEN THESE[6] FORMED A SCAR[7] OR WERE HEALED,[3] R. ELIEZER B. JACOB RULES THAT THEY ARE UNCLEAN SINCE AT THE BEGINNING AND AT THE END THEY WERE UNCLEAN, BUT THE SAGES RULE THAT THEY ARE CLEAN.[8]

MISHNAH 2. IF THEIR COLOUR[9] CHANGED,[10] WHETHER THE CHANGE WAS A CAUSE OF LENIENCY OR ONE OF RESTRICTION—(HOW IS IT A 'CAUSE OF LENIENCY'? IF, FOR INSTANCE, A BRIGHT SPOT HAD BEEN[11] AS WHITE AS SNOW

(1) Though they continued after it was given. (2) Of the body. (3) Which, being like the normal skin of the body, would be a cause of uncleanness. (4) Normally a cause of cleanness. (5) 'A scar' is, with some texts, to be deleted. (6) The boil, burning or blister, a bright spot on which is clean. (7) A bright spot on which is unclean. (8) Because there was an interval of cleanness between the two phases of uncleanness. (9) That of the clean bright spots spoken of in the previous Mishnah. (10) During the periods of their uncleanness. (11) While the man for instance was still a heathen.

AND[1] IT BECAME WHITE AS THE LIME OF THE TEMPLE, AS WHITE WOOL OR AS THE SKIN OF AN EGG, OR IF A RISING[2] HAS ASSUMED A SECONDARY SHADE,[3] OR IF ONE AS WHITE AS SNOW HAS ASSUMED A SECONDARY SHADE.[3] HOW IS IT 'ONE OF RESTRICTION'? IF, FOR INSTANCE, ITS COLOUR WAS[4] THAT OF THE SKIN OF AN EGG AND IT ASSUMED[1] THAT OF WHITE WOOL, THE LIME OF THE TEMPLE OR SNOW)— R. ELIEZER[5] B. AZARIAH RULES THAT THEY ARE CLEAN. R. ELIEZER[5] ḤISMA RULED: IF THE CHANGE WAS A CAUSE OF LENIENCY[6] THE BRIGHT SPOT IS CLEAN, BUT IF IT WAS ONE OF RESTRICTION THE SPOT MUST BE INSPECTED AS IF IT WERE A NEW ONE. R. AKIBA RULED: WHETHER THE CHANGE WAS A CAUSE OF LENIENCY OR ONE OF RESTRICTION THE SPOT MUST BE INSPECTED AS IF IT WERE A NEW ONE.

MISHNAH 3. A BRIGHT SPOT IN WHICH[7] THERE WERE NO SIGNS OF UNCLEANNESS[8] AT THE BEGINNING,[9] OR AT THE END OF THE FIRST WEEK, MUST BE SHUT UP; AT THE END OF THE SECOND WEEK OR AFTER IT HAD BEEN PRONOUNCED CLEAN, IT MUST HENCEFORTH BE HELD TO BE CLEAN. IF WHILE THE PRIEST WAS ABOUT TO SHUT IT UP OR TO PRONOUNCE IT CLEAN TOKENS OF UNCLEANNESS[10] APPEARED IN IT, HE MUST CERTIFY IT AS UNCLEAN. A BRIGHT SPOT IN WHICH APPEARED[7] TOKENS OF UNCLEANNESS MUST BE CERTIFIED AS UNCLEAN. IF WHILE THE PRIEST WAS ABOUT TO CERTIFY IT AS UNCLEAN THE TOKENS OF UNCLEANNESS DISAPPEARED EITHER AT THE BEGINNING,[9] OR AT THE END OF THE FIRST WEEK, IT MUST BE SHUT UP; BUT IF THEY DISAPPEARED AT THE END OF THE SECOND WEEK OR AFTER THE

(1) After he became a proselyte. (2) Whose colour is white as white wool. (3) That of lime of the Temple or the skin of an egg, which is dimmer than its first colour. (4) V. p. 258, n. 11. (5) Var. lec., 'Eleazar'. (6) *Sc.* if a bright colour assumed a dimmer shade. (7) When inspected by the priest. (8) Lit., 'nothing', neither quick flesh nor white hair. (9) When it was first submitted to the priest's inspection. (10) White hair or quick flesh.

SPOT HAD BEEN PRONOUNCED CLEAN,[1] IT MUST HENCEFORTH BE HELD TO BE CLEAN.

MISHNAH 4. A MAN WHO PLUCKS OUT TOKENS OF UNCLEANNESS[2] OR CAUTERIZES QUICK FLESH TRANSGRESSES A NEGATIVE COMMANDMENT.[3] AND AS REGARDS CLEANNESS, IF THEY WERE PLUCKED OUT BEFORE THE MAN CAME TO THE PRIEST, HE IS CLEAN; BUT IF AFTER HE HAD BEEN CERTIFIED AS UNCLEAN, HE REMAINS UNCLEAN. SAID R. AKIBA: I ASKED RABBAN GAMALIEL AND R. JOSHUA WHEN THEY WERE ON THE WAY TO NADWAD,[4] 'WHAT IS THE RULING IF THE PLUCKING OCCURRED WHILE IT WAS SHUT UP?' THEY SAID TO ME, 'WE HEARD NO SUCH RULING, BUT WE HAVE HEARD THAT IF THEY WERE PLUCKED BEFORE THE MAN CAME TO THE PRIEST HE IS CLEAN, AND IF AFTER HE HAD BEEN CERTIFIED AS UNCLEAN HE REMAINS UNCLEAN'. I BEGAN TO BRING THEM PROOFS[5] TO THE EFFECT THAT, WHETHER THE MAN STANDS BEFORE THE PRIEST[6] OR WHETHER HE IS THEN[6] SHUT UP, HE IS CLEAN UNLESS THE PRIEST HAD PRONOUNCED HIM UNCLEAN. WHEN DOES HE[7] ATTAIN CLEANNESS? R. ELIEZER RULED: AFTER ANOTHER LEPROSY SIGN HAS ARISEN IN HIM AND HE HAS ATTAINED CLEANNESS AFTER IT; BUT THE SAGES RULED: ONLY AFTER ANOTHER LEPROSY SIGN HAS SPREAD OVER HIS WHOLE BODY OR AFTER HIS BRIGHT SPOT HAS BEEN REDUCED TO LESS THAN THE SIZE OF A SPLIT BEAN.

MISHNAH 5. IF A MAN HAD A BRIGHT SPOT AND IT WAS CUT OFF, HE BECOMES CLEAN; BUT IF HE CUT IT OFF INTENTIONALLY, R. ELIEZER RULED: HE BECOMES CLEAN ONLY AFTER ANOTHER LEPROSY SIGN HAS ARISEN IN HIM AND HE

(1) *Sc.* tokens of uncleanness that appeared after it had been pronounced clean disappeared before the priest had certified it as unclean. (2) E.g. white hair from a leprosy sign on a normal skin. (3) Cf. Deut. XXIV, 8. (4) Var. lec., Narwad, Nadabath. (5) These are given in Tosef. Neg. III, 4. (6) When his tokens of uncleanness were plucked out. (7) The man whose tokens of uncleanness were plucked after he had been certified unclean.

HAS ATTAINED CLEANNESS AFTER IT; BUT THE SAGES RULED: ONLY AFTER IT HAS SPREAD OVER ALL HIS BODY. IF IT[1] WAS ON THE TIP OF ONE'S FORESKIN, CIRCUMCISION[2] IS PERMITTED.[3]

(1) The spreading of the leprosy sign. (2) Even when it is performed later than the prescribed eighth day after birth. Circumcision on the eighth day, which overrides the Pentateuchal prohibition against work on the Sabbath, obviously overrides that against the removal of a leprosy sign which is but a Rabbinical prohibition. (3) Since the positive commandment of circumcision overrides the negative one of removing a token of uncleanness.

NEGA'IM

CHAPTER VIII

MISHNAH 1. IF LEPROSY BROKE OUT ABROAD[1] WHEN A MAN WAS UNCLEAN,[2] HE BECOMES CLEAN;[3] BUT IF ONLY THE ENDS OF HIS MEMBERS[4] REAPPEARED,[5] HE BECOMES UNCLEAN[6] UNTIL THE BRIGHT SPOT IS REDUCED TO LESS THAN THE SIZE OF A SPLIT BEAN. [IF IT BROKE OUT ABROAD] WHEN HE WAS [DECLARED] CLEAN,[7] HE BECOMES UNCLEAN;[8] BUT IF THE ENDS OF HIS MEMBERS REAPPEARED, HE REMAINS UNCLEAN UNTIL HIS BRIGHT SPOT RESUMES ITS FORMER SIZE.

MISHNAH 2. IF A BRIGHT SPOT OF THE SIZE OF A SPLIT BEAN IN WHICH WAS QUICK FLESH OF THE SIZE OF A LENTIL BROKE OUT ABROAD COVERING A PERSON'S ENTIRE SKIN AND THEN THE QUICK FLESH DISAPPEARED, OR IF THE QUICK FLESH DISAPPEARED AND THEN[9] THE BRIGHT SPOT BROKE OUT ABROAD COVERING ALL HIS SKIN, HE IS CLEAN.[10] IF QUICK FLESH AROSE SUBSEQUENTLY HE IS UNCLEAN.[6] IF HE GREW WHITE HAIR, R. JOSHUA RULES THAT HE IS UNCLEAN,[11] BUT THE SAGES RULE THAT HE IS CLEAN.[12]

MISHNAH 3. IF A BRIGHT SPOT IN WHICH GREW WHITE HAIR[13] BROKE OUT ABROAD COVERING A MAN'S ENTIRE SKIN,

(1) And covered all his skin. Cf. Lev. XIII, 12. (2) Either after certification or even only when shut up. (3) Ibid. 13. (4) Though quick flesh on these is no cause of uncleanness. (5) *Sc.* were freed from the leprosy. (6) Ibid. 14. (7) Either after being shut up or after the termination of a certified uncleanness, cf. *infra* p. 263. (8) As the Biblical text refers only to a case where the plague broke out abroad in one who had been declared unclean. (9) Before the priest could pronounce the man clean. (10) On the same principle as in Mishnah 1. (11) As if quick flesh arose. (12) Since the text speaks only of quick flesh. (13) And consequently had been declared unclean by the priest.

EVEN THOUGH THE WHITE HAIR REMAINED IN ITS PLACE,[1] HE IS CLEAN. IF A BRIGHT SPOT IN WHICH THERE WAS A SPREADING[2] BROKE OUT ABROAD COVERING A MAN'S ENTIRE SKIN, HE IS CLEAN. BUT IN THE CASE OF ALL THESE[3] IF THE ENDS OF THE MAN'S MEMBERS REAPPEARED,[4] THE MAN IS UNCLEAN. IF THE LEPROSY BROKE OUT ABROAD COVERING A PART[5] OF THE MAN'S SKIN HE IS UNCLEAN; IF IT BROKE OUT ABROAD COVERING ALL HIS SKIN HE IS CLEAN.

MISHNAH 4. IN ALL CASES OF BREAKING OUT ABROAD AND COVERING THE ENDS OF THE MEMBERS WHEREBY THE UNCLEAN HAVE BEEN PRONOUNCED CLEAN, IF THEY[6] REAPPEARED[7] THESE[8] BECOME UNCLEAN AGAIN. IN ALL CASES OF REAPPEARANCE OF THE ENDS OF THE MEMBERS[7] WHEREBY THE CLEAN HAVE BEEN PRONOUNCED UNCLEAN, IF THEY[6] WERE COVERED AGAIN THESE[8] BECOME CLEAN AGAIN. IF SUBSEQUENTLY THEY BECOME UNCOVERED THESE[8] ARE UNCLEAN, EVEN IF THIS OCCURS A HUNDRED TIMES.

MISHNAH 5. ANY PART [OF THE BODY] THAT CAN BE SUBJECT TO THE UNCLEANNESS OF A LEPROSY SIGN[9] OF A BRIGHT SPOT MAY[10] PREVENT THE EFFECTIVENESS[11] OF THE BREAKING OUT ABROAD, AND ANY PART THAT CANNOT BE SUBJECT TO THE UNCLEANNESS OF A LEPROSY SIGN OF THE BRIGHT SPOT DOES NOT PREVENT THE EFFECTIVENESS[11] OF THE BREAKING OUT ABROAD. FOR INSTANCE: IF IT[12] BROKE OUT ABROAD, COVERING ALL ONE'S SKIN, BUT NOT THE HEAD OR THE BEARD,[13] OR A FESTERING BOIL, BURNING OR BLISTER,[13] AND THEN THE HEAD OR THE BEARD BECAME

(1) And much more so if it fell off and the priest had not yet pronounced the man to be clean. (2) V. p. 262 n. 13. (3) That were ruled *supra* (Mishnah 2 and 3) to be clean. (4) V. p. 262 n. 5. (5) Even if it was the greater part. (6) The ends of the members. (7) After they and all the man's skin had been covered by bright spot. (8) The cases of bright spot. (9) Cf. *supra* VI, 8. (10) If any part of it remained free from leprosy. (11) *Sc.* as a cause of cleanness. (12) The bright spot. (13) Which is not subject to the uncleanness of bright spot.

BALD,[1] OR THE BOIL, BURNING OR BLISTER TURNED INTO A SCAR,[1] THE MAN IS NEVERTHELESS CLEAN.[2] IF IT BROKE OUT ABROAD, COVERING ALL ONE'S SKIN, EXCEPT A SPOT OF THE SIZE OF HALF A LENTIL[3] NEAR THE HEAD OR BEARD, OR NEAR A BOIL, BURNING OR BLISTER, AND THEN THE HEAD OR THE BEARD BECAME BALD, OR THE BOIL, BURNING OR BLISTER TURNED INTO A SCAR, EVEN THOUGH THE PLACE OF THE QUICK FLESH[4] BECAME[5] A BRIGHT SPOT, THE MAN IS UNCLEAN[6] UNLESS IT BREAKS OUT ABROAD COVERING ALL HIS BODY.

MISHNAH 6. IF THERE WERE TWO BRIGHTS SPOTS, THE ONE UNCLEAN AND THE OTHER[7] CLEAN, AND LEPROSY BROKE OUT FROM ONE TO THE OTHER, AND THEN IT BROKE OUT ABROAD COVERING ALL THE MAN'S SKIN, HE BECOMES CLEAN.[8] IF THE BRIGHT SPOTS[9] WERE RESPECTIVELY ON HIS UPPER LIP AND LOWER LIP, ON TWO OF HIS FINGERS, OR ON HIS TWO EYELIDS, EVEN THOUGH THEY CLEAVE TOGETHER AND APPEAR AS ONE,[10] HE IS CLEAN. IF IT[11] BROKE OUT ABROAD COVERING ALL HIS SKIN EXCEPT A TETTER,[12] HE IS UNCLEAN. IF[13] THE ENDS OF THE MEMBERS REAPPEARED IN THE COLOUR OF A TETTER, HE IS CLEAN.[14] IF THE ENDS OF THE MEMBERS REAPPEARED TO THE EXTENT OF LESS THAN A LENTIL, R. MEIR RULES THAT HE IS UNCLEAN, BUT THE SAGES RULE THAT A TETTER [OR SKIN],[15] LESS IN SIZE THAN A LENTIL, IS

(1) When it is subject as a rule to the uncleanness of bright spot like the normal skin of the body. (2) Because at the time the bright spot first covered the body these were not subject to its uncleanness. (3) Which was covered by quick flesh. (4) Cf. prev. n. (5) Subsequently. (6) Since the leprosy did not break out abroad, covering all parts that can be affected, either before or now. (7) Having remained unchanged for two weeks. (8) Even where the breaking out began from the clean one, since its merging with the unclean one subjects it to the same status. (9) Each being of the size of half a split bean. (10) Of the size of a split bean. (11) The leprosy. (12) *Bohaḳ*, a spot on the skin dimmer than any of the four principal colours; Lev. XIII, 39. (13) After the tetter too had been covered with the leprosy, and thus pronounced clean. (14) Since it is not '*quick flesh*'. (15) Cf. L.

A TOKEN OF UNCLEANNESS IN THE BEGINNING,[1] BUT IS NO TOKEN OF UNCLEANNESS AT THE END.[2]

MISHNAH 7. A MAN WHO CAME[3] WITH ALL HIS BODY WHITE MUST BE SHUT UP. IF SUBSEQUENTLY[4] WHITE HAIR GREW, HE MUST BE CERTIFIED UNCLEAN. IF BOTH HAIRS OR ONE OF THEM TURNED BLACK,[5] IF BOTH OR ONE OF THEM BECAME SHORT, IF A BOIL ADJOINED BOTH OR ONE OF THEM, OR IF A BOIL ENCOMPASSED BOTH OR ONE OF THEM, OR IF A BOIL, THE QUICK FLESH OF A BOIL, A BURNING, THE QUICK FLESH OF A BURNING, OR A TETTER SUNDERED THEM,[6] AND THEN[7] THERE AROSE QUICK FLESH OR WHITE HAIR, HE IS UNCLEAN; BUT IF NEITHER QUICK FLESH NOR WHITE HAIR AROSE HE IS CLEAN. IN ALL THESE CASES, HOWEVER, IF THE ENDS OF THE MEMBERS REAPPEARED THE MAN[8] REMAINS AS HE WAS BEFORE.[9] IF THE LEPROSY THEN[10] BROKE OUT ABROAD, COVERING A PART OF THEM,[11] HE IS UNCLEAN.[12] IF SUBSEQUENTLY[13] IT BROKE OUT ABROAD COVERING ALL OF THEM, HE IS CLEAN.[14]

MISHNAH 8. IF[15] LEPROSY BROKE OUT ABROAD COVERING ALL A MAN'S SKIN AT ONCE, HE IS UNCLEAN IF THIS ORIGINATED IN A CONDITION OF CLEANNESS,[16] AND CLEAN IF IT ORIGINATED IN A CONDITION OF UNCLEANNESS.[16] THE MAN

(1) These prevent the effectiveness of the breaking out abroad to make the leper clean. (2) When the small space mentioned reappeared after the entire skin had been covered. (3) To the priest, for a first inspection. (4) Having been shut up. (5) After the certification. (6) The two hairs. (7) Having in virtue of these been released from the uncleanness of the white hair. (8) Who COMES WITH ALL HIS BODY WHITE. (9) If, for instance, he was to be shut up for a week and during that time the ends of the members reappeared, he must be shut up again for a similar period. If, on the other hand, they reappeared after he had been pronounced clean he remains clean (v. L. and cf. Bert.). (10) After the ends of the members have reappeared. (11) Of the ends of the members. (12) On account of the spreading. (13) After a part had been covered and the man had become unclean. (14) Since the breaking out arose from a condition of uncleanness (cf. next Mishnah). (15) As set forth in previous Mishnah. (16) This is taken as the continuation

WHO ATTAINS CLEANNESS AFTER HE WAS SHUT UP IS EXEMPT FROM THE OBLIGATION OF LOOSENING THE HAIR AND RENDING THE CLOTHES,[1] FROM CUTTING OFF THE HAIR[2] AND FROM BRINGING THE BIRDS.[3] IF HE ATTAINS CLEANNESS AFTER HE HAD BEEN CERTIFIED UNCLEAN, HE IS LIABLE TO ALL THESE. BOTH, HOWEVER, CONVEY UNCLEANNESS[4] BY ENTERING.[5]

MISHNAH 9. IF A MAN CAME[6] WITH HIS WHOLE BODY WHITE, AND ON IT THERE WAS QUICK FLESH TO THE EXTENT OF A LENTIL,[7] AND THEN[8] THE LEPROSY BROKE OUT ABROAD COVERING ALL HIS SKIN,[9] AFTER WHICH[10] THE ENDS OF THE MEMBERS REAPPEARED, R. ISHMAEL RULED: THE LAW IN THIS CASE IS THE SAME AS WHEN THE ENDS OF THE MEMBERS REAPPEAR IN THAT OF A LARGE BRIGHT SPOT.[11] R. ELIEZER[12] B. AZARIAH RULED: AS WHEN THE ENDS OF THE MEMBERS REAPPEARED IN A SMALL BRIGHT SPOT.[13]

MISHNAH 10. SOME MAN MIGHT SHOW HIS LEPROSY SIGN TO THE PRIEST AND THEREBY GAIN ADVANTAGE, WHILE ANOTHER MIGHT SHOW HIS AND LOSE THEREBY. IN WHAT MANNER? IF A MAN WAS CERTIFIED UNCLEAN AND THE TOKENS OF HIS UNCLEANNESS DISAPPEARED, AND BEFORE HE COULD SHOW IT TO THE PRIEST THE LEPROSY BROKE OUT ABROAD COVERING ALL HIS SKIN, HE IS CLEAN; WHEREAS

of the preceding Mishnah. One comes with his whole body white and is subjected to the various regulations set forth, and then the ends of members reappear only subsequently to be again affected with leprosy.

(1) Cf. Lev. XIII, 45. (2) Cf. Ibid. XIV, 8. (3) Cf. Ibid. XIV, 4. (4) To all that is in a room. (5) The room (cf. prev. n.). (6) To the priest, for a first inspection. (7) So that, quick flesh being a token of uncleanness at a first inspection, the man should have been pronounced unclean. (8) Before the priest pronounced him unclean (cf. prev. n.). (9) As a result of which he must be shut up (cf. *supra* VII, 3). (10) Having been shut up. (11) *Sc.* it is regarded as though the whole body is still white, as in Mishnah 7. (12) Var. lec., 'Eleazar'. (13) I.e., one confined to a part of the skin and unclean as in Mishnah 3 (Bert.).

IF HE HAD SHOWN IT TO THE PRIEST[1] HE WOULD HAVE BEEN UNCLEAN.[2] IF HE HAD A BRIGHT SPOT IN WHICH THERE WAS NOTHING ELSE, AND BEFORE HE COULD SHOW IT TO THE PRIEST IT BROKE OUT ABROAD COVERING ALL HIS SKIN, HE IS UNCLEAN;[3] WHEREAS IF HE HAD SHOWN IT TO THE PRIEST[4] HE WOULD HAVE BEEN CLEAN.[5]

(1) Who would have pronounced it clean. (2) Since the breaking out would have begun in a condition of cleanness. (3) *Sc.* it must be shut up. (4) Who would have shut him up for a week. (5) Because the breaking out would have begun from a leprosy that was shut up.

NEGA'IM

CHAPTER IX

MISHNAH 1. A BOIL[1] OR A BURNING[1] MAY BECOME UNCLEAN IN A WEEK[2] AND BY TWO TOKENS, VIZ., BY WHITE HAIR OR BY A SPREADING.[3] WHAT EXACTLY IS A 'BOIL'? AN INJURY RECEIVED FROM WOOD, STONE, OLIVE PEAT, OR THE WATER OF TIBERIAS,[4] OF FROM ANY OTHER OBJECT WHOSE HEAT IS NOT DUE TO FIRE IS A BOIL. WHAT EXACTLY IS A 'BURNING'? A BURN CAUSED BY A LIVE COAL, HOT EMBERS, OR ANY OBJECT WHOSE HEAT IS DUE TO FIRE IS A BURNING.

MISHNAH 2. A BOIL AND A BURNING CANNOT BE COMBINED,[5] NOR CAN THEY EFFECTIVELY[6] SPREAD FROM ONE TO THE OTHER, FROM THEM TO THE SKIN OF THE FLESH, OR FROM THE SKIN OF THE FLESH TO THEM.[7] IF THEY FESTERED THEY ARE CLEAN.[8] IF THEY FORMED A SCALE AS THICK AS GARLIC PEEL, SUCH IS THE 'SCAR OF THE BOIL' THAT IS SPOKEN OF IN THE TORAH.[9] IF THEY WERE SUBSEQUENTLY HEALED, EVEN THOUGH THERE WAS A CICATRIX IN THEIR PLACE, THEY ARE REGARDED AS 'THE SKIN OF THE FLESH'.[10]

MISHNAH 3. R. ELIEZER WAS ASKED, 'WHAT IS THE RULING WHERE A BRIGHT SPOT OF THE SIZE OF A SELA' AROSE ON THE INSIDE OF ONE'S HAND AND COVERED UP[11] THE SCAR OF A BOIL?'[12] HE REPLIED: 'IT MUST BE SHUT UP'.

(1) V. *supra*, III, 4. (2) If there appeared a bright spot. (3) During which the sufferer is shut up. (4) Flowing from its hot springs. (5) To make up the prescribed size of a split bean. (6) To be a cause of uncleanness. (7) Only a spreading on the boil or burning itself is effective. (8) Though covered by a bright spot. (9) Lev. XIII, 23. (10) Lev. XIII, 3. (11) Lit., 'and its place'. (12) So that nothing of the scar is visible.

THEY SAID TO HIM, 'FOR WHAT PURPOSE, SEEING THAT IT IS NEITHER CAPABLE OF GROWING WHITE HAIR[1] NOR CAN IT EFFECTIVELY[2] SPREAD[3] NOR DOES QUICK FLESH[4] CAUSE IN IT ANY UNCLEANNESS?' HE REPLIED, 'IT IS POSSIBLE THAT IT WILL CONTRACT[5] AND THEN SPREAD AGAIN'.[6] THEY SAID TO HIM, 'BUT WHAT ABOUT WHEN ITS EXTENT BE ONLY THAT OF A SPLIT BEAN?'[7] 'I HAVE NOT HEARD THE REASON', HE REPLIED.[8] SAID R. JUDAH B. BATHYRA TO HIM, 'I WOULD SUBMIT AN ARGUMENT ON IT'. THE OTHER REPLIED, 'IF YOU WOULD THEREBY CONFIRM THE RULING OF THE SAGES, WELL AND GOOD'. HE SAID, 'IT IS POSSIBLE THAT ANOTHER BOIL WOULD ARISE OUTSIDE IT[9] AND THE LATTER[9] WOULD THEN SPREAD TO THE FORMER'.[10] 'YOU ARE A GREAT SAGE', THE OTHER EXCLAIMED, 'FOR YOU HAVE CONFIRMED A RULING OF THE SAGES'.

(1) Since no hair grows on the inside of a hand. (2) To be a cause of uncleanness. (3) As stated *supra* Mishnah 2. (4) Which is not one of its two tokens of uncleanness (*supra* Mishnah 1). (5) To the size of a split bean. (6) Over the scar; and thus cause uncleanness. (7) 'For what purpose should it then be shut up?' For were it to contract it would be less than the minimum size and would become altogether clean. (8) Though the ruling in the latter case also is that the sufferer is to be shut up. (9) The one already there that is to be shut up. (10) And this would, of course, be a cause of uncleanness.

NEGA'IM

CHAPTER X

MISHNAH 1. SCALLS[1] MAY BECOME UNCLEAN FOR TWO WEEKS[2] AND BY TWO TOKENS, VIZ., BY YELLOW THIN[3] HAIR OR BY A SPREADING. 'BY YELLOW THIN HAIR', MEANS SO DISEASED THAT IT IS SHORT; SO R. AKIBA. R. JOḤANAN B. NURI SAID: EVEN THOUGH IT IS LONG.[4] R. JOḤANAN B. NURI ARGUED: WHAT IS THE MEANING OF THE EXPRESSION WHEN PEOPLE SAY, 'THIS STICK IS THIN', OR 'THIS REED IS THIN'? DOES 'THIN' IMPLY THAT IT IS STUNTED[5] AND SHORT AND NOT[6] STUNTED[5] AND LONG?[7] R. AKIBA REPLIED: BEFORE WE LEARN FROM THE REED LET US LEARN FROM THE HAIR. IN 'SO AND SO'S HAIR IS THIN', 'THIN' MEANS THAT IT IS STUNTED[5] AND SHORT AND NOT STUNTED AND LONG.

MISHNAH 2. YELLOW THIN HAIR CAUSES UNCLEANNESS WHETHER IT IS CLUSTERED TOGETHER[8] OR DISPERSED, WHETHER IT IS ENCOMPASSED[9] OR UNENCOMPASSED, OR WHETHER IT CAME AFTER THE SCALL[10] OR BEFORE IT; SO R. JUDAH. R. SIMEON RULED: IT CAUSES UNCLEANNESS ONLY WHEN IT CAME AFTER THE SCALL. R. SIMEON ARGUED: THIS IS A LOGICAL INFERENCE: IF WHITE HAIR,[11] AGAINST WHICH OTHER HAIR AFFORDS NO PROTECTION,[12] CAUSES UNCLEANNESS ONLY WHEN IT COMES AFTER THE SCALL,[10] HOW MUCH

(1) Cf. Lev. XIII, 30ff. (2) During which the sufferer is shut up, and is in consequence in a condition of uncleanness even though no token of uncleanness had made its appearance. (3) *Daḳ* (Lev. XIII, 30). (4) 'Thin' (*daḳ*) referring to sparseness only. (5) In thickness. (6) Var. lec., 'or'. (7) The answer, of course, is that the latter meaning is also included. (8) *Sc.* a minimum of two yellow hairs in one place. (9) By the leprosy sign. (10) Lit., 'turned over'. (11) In a leprosy sign on the normal skin. (12) Even the presence of black hair does not nullify the effect of the white hair which are a token of uncleanness.

MORE THEN SHOULD YELLOW THIN HAIR, AGAINST WHICH OTHER HAIR DOES AFFORD PROTECTION,[1] CAUSE UNCLEANNESS ONLY WHEN IT COMES AFTER THE SCALL? R. JUDAH REPLIED: WHENEVER IT WAS NECESSARY TO SAY, 'IF IT COMES AFTER'[2] SCRIPTURE HAS SAID, 'IF IT COMES AFTER', BUT THE SCALL, SINCE ABOUT IT SCRIPTURE SAID, THERE BE IN IT NO YELLOW HAIR,[3] CAUSES UNCLEANNESS WHETHER IT CAME BEFORE OR AFTER IT.

MISHNAH 3. [BLACK HAIR][4] THAT GROWS UP[5] AFFORDS PROTECTION AGAINST YELLOW HAIR AND AGAINST A SPREADING,[6] WHETHER IT WAS CLUSTERED TOGETHER OR DISPERSED, WHETHER IT WAS ENCOMPASSED OR UNENCOMPASSED. AND THAT WHICH IS LEFT[7] AFFORDS PROTECTION AGAINST YELLOW HAIR AND AGAINST A SPREADING, WHETHER IT IS CLUSTERED TOGETHER OR DISPERSED, AND ALSO WHEN ENCOMPASSED, BUT IT AFFORDS NO PROTECTION WHERE IT IS AT THE SIDE[8] UNLESS IT IS DISTANT FROM THE STANDING HAIR BY THE PLACE OF TWO HAIRS. IF ONE HAIR[9] WAS YELLOW AND THE OTHER BLACK, OR IF ONE WAS YELLOW AND THE OTHER WHITE,[10] THEY AFFORD NO PROTECTION.

MISHNAH 4. YELLOW HAIR THAT PRECEDED A SCALL IS CLEAN. R. JUDAH RULES THAT IT IS UNCLEAN. R. ELIEZER B. JACOB EXPLAINED:[11] IT NEITHER CAUSES UNCLEANNESS NOR DOES IT AFFORD PROTECTION. R. SIMEON EXPLAINED:[11] ANY GROWTH IN A SCALL THAT IS NOT A TOKEN OF UNCLEANNESS IS IPSO FACTO A TOKEN OF CLEANNESS.

(1) Two black hairs in a scall nullify the effect of the yellow hair. (2) V. p. 270 n. 10 (3) Lev. XIII, 32. (4) No less than two hairs. (5) In a scall. (6) If, for instance, the scall was certified unclean on account of any of these tokens and then black hair grew up the man becomes clean. (7) Of the black hair which was there before the scall. (8) Of the scall. (9) That came before the scall and caused no uncleanness. (10) Two white hairs, however, like two black ones, afford protection (Elijah Wilna). (11) The ruling of the first Tanna.

MISHNAH 5. HOW IS ONE SHAVED WHO HAS A SCALL?[1] THE SPACE OUTSIDE IT IS SHAVED WHILE NEXT TO IT TWO HAIRS ARE LEFT[2] IN ORDER THAT IT MAY BE NOTICED WHETHER IT SPREADS. IF IT WAS CERTIFIED UNCLEAN ON ACCOUNT OF YELLOW HAIR, AND THEN THE YELLOW HAIR DISAPPEARED AND OTHER YELLOW HAIR APPEARED, AND SO ALSO IF THERE WAS A SPREADING,[3] IRRESPECTIVE OF WHETHER THE CERTIFICATION[4] TOOK PLACE AT THE BEGINNING,[5] AT THE END OF THE FIRST WEEK, AT THE END OF THE SECOND WEEK OR AFTER THE RELEASE FROM UNCLEANNESS, THE MAN REMAINS AS HE WAS BEFORE.[6] IF THE MAN WAS CERTIFIED UNCLEAN ON ACCOUNT OF A SPREADING, AND THE SPREADING DISAPPEARED AND THEN REAPPEARED, AND SO ALSO IF THERE WAS YELLOW HAIR,[7] IRRESPECTIVE OF WHETHER THE CERTIFICATION TOOK PLACE AT THE END OF THE FIRST WEEK, AT THE END OF THE SECOND WEEK OR AFTER RELEASE FROM UNCLEANNESS, THE MAN REMAINS AS HE WAS BEFORE.[6]

MISHNAH 6. IF THERE WERE TWO SCALLS[8] SIDE BY SIDE AND A LINE OF HAIR INTERVENED BETWEEN THEM, IF A GAP APPEARED[9] IN ONE PLACE THE MAN IS UNCLEAN,[10] BUT IF IT APPEARED IN TWO PLACES HE IS CLEAN.[11] HOW BIG SHOULD THE GAP[12] BE?[13] THE SPACE OF TWO HAIRS. IF THERE WAS A GAP IN ONE PLACE, EVEN THOUGH IT IS AS BIG AS A SPLIT BEAN, THE MAN IS UNCLEAN.[14]

MISHNAH 7. IF THERE WERE TWO SCALLS ONE WITHIN

(1) Cf. Lev. XIII, 33. (2) All round the scall, so that a circle of two hairs in depth is formed around it. (3) After the yellow hair disappeared, though no other yellow hair has made its appearance. (4) As unclean, on account of the yellow hair. (5) When the priest first inspected the scall. (6) *Sc.* unclean. (7) After the spreading had disappeared, no other spreading appearing. (8) Each of the size of a split bean. (9) In the line of hair. (10) Since the scall has spread. (11) Because black hair is now encompassed by the scall and provides protection. (12) In each place. (13) That it should be capable of offering protection. (14) Because the black hair is unencompassed.

THE OTHER AND A LINE OF HAIR INTERVENED BETWEEN THEM, IF[1] THERE APPEARED A GAP IN ONE PLACE THE INNER ONE IS UNCLEAN,[2] BUT IF IN TWO PLACES IT IS CLEAN.[3] HOW BIG MUST THE GAP[4] BE?[5] THE SPACE OF TWO HAIRS. IF THERE WAS A GAP IN ONE PLACE OF THE SIZE OF A SPLIT BEAN[6] THE MAN IS CLEAN.[7]

MISHNAH 8. A MAN WHO HAS A SCALL WITH YELLOW HAIR WITHIN IT IS UNCLEAN.[8] IF SUBSEQUENTLY BLACK HAIR GREW IN IT, HE IS CLEAN; EVEN IF THE BLACK HAIR DISAPPEARED AGAIN[9] HE REMAINS CLEAN. R. SIMEON B. JUDAH CITING R. SIMEON RULED: ANY SCALL THAT HAS ONCE BEEN PRONOUNCED CLEAN CAN NEVER AGAIN BE SUBJECTED TO UNCLEANNESS.[10] R. SIMEON RULED: ANY YELLOW HAIR THAT HAS ONCE BEEN PRONOUNCED CLEAN CAN NEVER AGAIN BE SUBJECTED TO UNCLEANNESS.[11]

MISHNAH 9. IF A MAN HAD A SCALL OF THE SIZE OF A SPLIT BEAN AND IT SPREAD[12] OVER ALL HIS HEAD[13] HE BECOMES CLEAN.[14] THE HEAD AND THE BEARD ARE NOT INTERDEPENDENT;[15] SO R. JUDAH. R. SIMEON RULED: THEY ARE INTERDEPENDENT. R. SIMEON ARGUED: IS NOT THIS A LOGICAL INFERENCE: IF THE SKIN OF THE FACE AND THE SKIN OF THE

(1) During the week it was shut up. (2) Since it spread and the black hair growing at its side is not encompassed. The outer scall, however, remains clean since black hair that is left and is encompassed affords protection (cf. Mishnah 3 *supra*). (3) Because both scalls are regarded as merged into one and the hair encompassed affords protection to both. (4) In each place. (5) That it should be capable of affording protection. (6) A gap that causes the two scalls to be regarded as one. (7) Cf. *supra* n. 3. (8) Since yellow hair is a token of uncleanness at all times. (9) Only the yellow hair remaining. (10) Even though subsequently there was a spreading or other yellow hair grew up. (11) It is unclean, however, where other yellow hair grew or a new spreading appeared after the black hair disappeared. (12) After it had been pronounced unclean on account of one of the tokens of uncleanness. (13) Or beard. (14) As a bright spot that breaks out abroad and covers all one's skin. (15) *Sc.* if the scall spread all over one and not over the other the man is nevertheless clean.

BODY, BETWEEN WHICH SOMETHING[1] INTERVENES, ARE NEVERTHELESS INTERDEPENDENT, IS THERE NOT MORE REASON TO ASSUME THAT THE HEAD AND THE BEARD, BETWEEN WHICH NOTHING INTERVENES, SHOULD BE INTERDEPENDENT? THE HEAD AND THE BEARD[2] CANNOT BE COMBINED,[3] NOR IS A SPREADING[4] FROM ONE TO THE OTHER EFFECTIVE.[5] WHAT EXACTLY COUNTS AS THE BEARD? THE HAIR FROM THE JOINT OF THE JAW[6] TO THE THYROID CARTILAGE.[7]

MISHNAH 10. SCALP BALDNESS OR FOREHEAD BALDNESS[8] MAY BECOME UNCLEAN[9] FOR TWO WEEKS[10] AND BY TWO TOKENS, VIZ., BY QUICK FLESH OR BY A SPREADING. WHAT CONSTITUTES BALDNESS? IF A MAN HAD EATEN NESHEM[11] OR SMEARED HIMSELF WITH NESHEM OR HAD A WOUND FROM WHICH HAIR CAN NO LONGER GROW. WHAT IS THE EXTENT OF SCALP BALDNESS? FROM THE CROWN SLOPING BACKWARDS TO THE PROTRUDING CARTILAGE OF THE NECK. WHAT IS THE EXTENT OF FOREHEAD BALDNESS? FROM THE CROWN SLOPING FORWARDS TO THE REGION FACING THE HAIR ABOVE.[12] SCALP BALDNESS AND FOREHEAD BALDNESS CANNOT BE COMBINED,[13] NOR IS A SPREADING FROM ONE TO THE OTHER EFFECTIVE.[5] R. JUDAH RULED: IF THERE IS HAIR BETWEEN THEM THEY CANNOT BE COMBINED,[13] BUT IF THERE IS NONE THEY MUST BE COMBINED.

(1) The hair on the chin. (2) In respect of scalls. (3) A scall on the former cannot be combined with a scall on the latter to form the prescribed size if either is less than that minimum. (4) Of a scall. (5) To be a cause of uncleanness. (6) The upper one. (7) Or (with Danby) 'the knob of the windpipe'. (8) Cf. Lev. XIII, 40ff. (9) If they have a bright spot of one of the four colours enumerated *supra* I, n. 1. (10) Cf. *supra* p. 270, n. 2. (11) A drug that causes the hair to fall out. (12) Excluding the eyebrows. (13) To constitute the prescribed minimum.

NEGA'IM

CHAPTER XI

MISHNAH 1. ALL GARMENTS[1] MAY CONTRACT THE UNCLEANNESS OF LEPROSY EXCEPT THOSE OF GENTILES.[2] IF GARMENTS [WITH LEPROSY SIGNS] ARE BOUGHT FROM GENTILES THEY[3] MUST BE INSPECTED AS IF THE SIGNS HAD THEN FIRST APPEARED. THE HIDES [OF THE ANIMALS] OF THE SEA CANNOT CONTRACT THE UNCLEANNESS OF LEPROSY. IF ONE JOINED TO THEM ANYTHING OF THAT WHICH GROWS ON LAND, EVEN IF IT IS ONLY A THREAD OR A CORD,[4] PROVIDED IT IS OF A MATERIAL THAT IS SUSCEPTIBLE TO UNCLEANNESS, THEY ALSO BECOME SUSCEPTIBLE TO UNCLEANNESS.

MISHNAH 2. CAMEL'S HAIR AND SHEEP'S WOOL THAT HAVE BEEN HACKLED TOGETHER[5] ARE NOT SUSCEPTIBLE TO LEPROSY UNCLEANNESS IF THE GREATER PART IS CAMEL'S HAIR; BUT IF THE GREATER PART IS SHEEP'S WOOL THEY ARE SUSCEPTIBLE TO LEPROSY UNCLEANNESS. IF EACH REPRESENTS A HALF[6] THEY ARE ALSO SUSCEPTIBLE TO LEPROSY UNCLEANNESS. AND THE SAME LAW APPLIES ALSO TO FLAX AND HEMP THAT HAVE BEEN HACKLED TOGETHER.[5]

MISHNAH 3. COLOURED[7] HIDES AND GARMENTS ARE NOT SUSCEPTIBLE TO LEPROSY UNCLEANNESS. HOUSES,[8] WHETHER THEY ARE COLOURED OR NOT COLOURED, ARE SUSCEPTIBLE TO LEPROSY UNCLEANNESS; SO R. MEIR. R.

(1) Cf. Lev. XIII, 47ff. (2) Cf. *supra* III, 1. (3) However old the signs. (4) Which, if not attached to the hide of a sea animal, is itself insusceptible to leprosy uncleanness unless it is of a prescribed length. (5) And used in the manufacture of a garment. (6) Of the mixture. (7) Artificially or naturally. (8) Cf. Lev. XIV, 34ff.

JUDAH RULED: HIDES ARE [SUBJECT TO THE SAME RESTRICTIONS] AS HOUSES. R. SIMEON RULED: THOSE THAT ARE NATURALLY[1] [COLOURED] ARE SUSCEPTIBLE TO UNCLEANNESS BUT THOSE THAT ARE ARTIFICIALLY[2] [DYED] ARE NOT SUSCEPTIBLE TO UNCLEANNESS.

MISHNAH 4. IN A GARMENT WHOSE WARP WAS COLOURED AND WHOSE WOOF WAS WHITE, OR WHOSE WOOF WAS COLOURED AND WHOSE WARP WAS WHITE, ALL DEPENDS ON WHAT IS THE MORE APPARENT. GARMENTS CONTRACT UNCLEANNESS IF THEY ARE AN INTENSE GREEN OR AN INTENSE RED. IF A LEPROSY SIGN WAS GREEN[3] AND IT SPREAD OUT[4] RED, OR IF IT WAS RED AND IT SPREAD OUT GREEN, IT IS UNCLEAN. IF ITS COLOUR CHANGED[4] AND THEN IT SPREAD, OR IF IT CHANGED AND IT DID NOT SPREAD, IT IS REGARDED AS IF IT HAD NOT CHANGED.[5] R. JUDAH RULED: LET IT BE INSPECTED AS IF IT THEN APPEARED FOR THE FIRST TIME.[6]

MISHNAH 5. [A LEPROSY SIGN] THAT REMAINED UNCHANGED DURING THE FIRST WEEK[7] MUST BE WASHED[8] AND SHUT UP AGAIN. ONE THAT REMAINS UNCHANGED DURING THE SECOND WEEK MUST BE BURNED. ONE THAT SPREAD DURING THE FIRST OR THE SECOND WEEK MUST BE BURNED. IF IT BECOMES DIMMER IN THE BEGINNING,[9] R. ISHMAEL RULED: IT SHOULD BE WASHED AND BE SHUT UP. BUT THE SAGES RULED: THIS IS NOT REQUIRED.[10] IF THE LEPROSY SIGN BECAME DIMMER DURING THE FIRST WEEK IT MUST BE WASHED AND SHUT UP. IF IT BECAME DIMMER DURING

(1) Lit., 'by the hands of heaven'. (2) Lit., 'by the hands of man'. (3) And of the prescribed minimum. (4) While it was shut up. (5) Hence it is burned in the former case and shut up for a second week in the latter. (6) A change, in his opinion, causes the leprosy sign to be regarded as a new one. (7) Of being shut up. (8) *Sc.* the place of the sign alone is washed with the seven substances specified in Nid. IX, 6. (9) When it was first submitted to the priest's inspection before he ordered its shutting up. (10) The garment being clean in any case.

THE SECOND WEEK IT MUST BE TORN OUT, AND THAT WHICH IS TORN OUT MUST BE BURNT, BUT IT IS NECESSARY FOR A PATCH TO BE PUT ON.[1] R. NEHEMIAH RULED: A PATCH IS NOT NECESSARY.

MISHNAH 6. IF THE LEPROSY SIGN HAS REAPPEARED ON THE GARMENT,[2] THE PATCH IS PROTECTED;[3] IF IT REAPPEARED ON THE PATCH THE GARMENT MUST BE BURNT.[4] IF FROM THE MATERIAL OF A GARMENT THAT WAS SHUT UP[5] A PATCH WAS MADE ON A CLEAN GARMENT AND THE LEPROSY SIGN REAPPEARED ON THE GARMENT,[6] THE PATCH MUST BE BURNT; BUT IF IT REAPPEARED ON THE PATCH, THE FIRST GARMENT[6] MUST BE BURNT, AND THE PATCH SERVES THE SECOND GARMENT WHILE THE TOKENS ARE UNDER OBSERVATION.[7]

MISHNAH 7. IN A SUMMER GARMENT THAT HAD COLOURED AND WHITE STRIPES[8] A LEPROSY SIGN MAY EFFECTIVELY SPREAD[9] FROM ONE OF THE LATTER TO THE OTHERS.[10] R. ELIEZER WAS ASKED: BUT SUPPOSE THERE WAS ONLY ONE WHITE STRIPE?[11] HE REPLIED: I HAVE HEARD NO RULING ON THIS QUESTION. SAID R. JUDAH B. BATHYRA TO HIM: 'I WOULD SUBMIT AN ARGUMENT ON THIS'. THE OTHER REPLIED, 'IF THIS WOULD CONFIRM THE WORDS OF THE SAGES, WELL AND

(1) Over the hole. The reason is apparent from the following Mishnah. (2) In a different spot. (3) *Sc.* it need not be burned though the garment must be burned. (4) The patch itself, if its size is of no less than three by three fingerbreadths, must be shut up again. (5) *Sc.* a garment the colour of whose leprosy sign did not become dimmer until the second week when the place of the sign is torn out and burnt. (6) That was shut up. (7) The patch is shut up together with the garment as if the leprosy sign had been on the latter. The former, however, must ultimately be burnt even where the garment attained complete cleanness. (8) Or 'checks'. (9) To be a cause of uncleanness. (10) The coloured stripes or checks forming no valid intervention. (11) Which was completely covered by a leprosy sign, the rest of the garment being coloured. Why, then, should such a garment be shut up, seeing that the leprosy sign can never effectively spread?

GOOD'. 'IT IS POSSIBLE', EXPLAINED THE FIRST, 'THAT IT WOULD REMAIN ON IT IN AN UNCHANGED CONDITION FOR TWO WEEKS, AND THAT WHICH REMAINS UNCHANGED ON GARMENTS FOR TWO WEEKS IS UNCLEAN'.[1] 'YOU ARE', THE OTHER EXCLAIMED, 'A GREAT SAGE, FOR YOU HAVE CONFIRMED THE WORDS OF THE SAGES'. A SPREADING THAT ADJOINS [A FIRST LEPROSY SIGN IS EFFECTIVE][2] HOWEVER SMALL IT MAY BE; ONE THAT IS DISTANT[3] [IS EFFECTIVE[2] ONLY] IF IT IS OF THE SIZE OF A SPLIT BEAN; AND ONE THAT REAPPEARS[4] [IS ALSO EFFECTIVE[2] IF IT IS] OF THE SIZE OF A SPLIT BEAN.[5]

MISHNAH 8. THE WARP AND THE WOOF MAY FORTHWITH[6] CONTRACT THE UNCLEANNESS OF LEPROSY SIGNS. R. JUDAH RULED: THE WARP, ONLY AFTER IT HAD BEEN BOILED; BUT THE WOOF, FORTHWITH; AND BUNDLES OF FLAX,[7] AFTER THEY HAVE BEEN BLEACHED. HOW MUCH MUST THERE BE IN A COIL[8] FOR IT TO BE CAPABLE OF CONTRACTING THE UNCLEANNESS OF LEPROSY SIGNS? AS MUCH AS TO WEAVE FROM IT A PIECE OF THREE FINGERBREADTHS SQUARE, EITHER WARP OR WOOF, THOUGH IT IS ALL WARP OR ALL WOOF. IF IT[9] CONSISTED OF BROKEN THREADS[10] IT DOES NOT CONTRACT THE UNCLEANNESS OF LEPROSY SIGNS. R. JUDAH RULED: EVEN IF THE THREAD WAS BROKEN ONLY IN ONE PLACE, THOUGH IT WAS KNOTTED TOGETHER, IT DOES NOT CONTRACT THE UNCLEANNESS OF LEPROSY SIGNS.

MISHNAH 9. IF A THREAD WAS WOUND FROM ONE COIL

(1) Cf. Lev. XIII, 55. (2) To be a cause of uncleanness. (3) From the first leprosy sign; but on the same side of the garment. (4) After a leprosy sign that became dimmer during the second week had been torn out and the garment had been washed. (5) In which case the entire garment must be burnt. (6) *Sc.* as soon as they are woven even before they have been bleached. (7) The threads of which are of the same thickness for both the warp and the woof. (8) Of thread. (9) The coil. (10) That were not knotted together.

TO ANOTHER,[1] OR FROM ONE SPOOL TO ANOTHER,[1] OR FROM THE UPPER BEAM[2] TO THE LOWER BEAM,[1] AND SO ALSO IN THE CASE OF THE TWO WINGS OF A SHIRT,[3] IF A LEPROSY SIGN APPEARED ON THE ONE, THE OTHER REMAINS CLEAN. IF IT APPEARED ON THE SHEDDED WEFT OR ON THE STANDING WARP, THESE MAY FORTHWITH CONTRACT THE UNCLEANNESS OF LEPROSY. R. SIMEON RULED: THE WARP MAY CONTRACT UNCLEANNESS ONLY IF IT IS CLOSELY ORDERED.

MISHNAH 10. [IF A LEPROSY SIGN] APPEARED ON THE STANDING WARP THE WEB REMAINS CLEAN; IF IT APPEARED ON THE WEB THE STANDING WARP REMAINS CLEAN. IF IT APPEARED ON A SHEET THE FRINGES ALSO MUST BE BURNT; IF IT APPEARED ON THE FRINGES THE SHEET REMAINS CLEAN. A SHIRT ON WHICH A LEPROSY SIGN APPEARED AFFORDS PROTECTION TO ITS HEMS,[4] EVEN THOUGH THEY ARE OF PURPLE WOOL.[5]

MISHNAH 11. ANY OBJECT THAT IS SUSCEPTIBLE TO CORPSE UNCLEANNESS, THOUGH INSUSCEPTIBLE TO MIDRAS UNCLEANNESS, MAY CONTRACT THE UNCLEANNESS OF LEPROSY SIGNS; AS, FOR INSTANCE, THE SAIL OF A SHIP, A CURTAIN, THE FOREHEAD BAND OF A HAIR-NET, THE WRAPPINGS OF SCROLLS, A GIRDLE, THE STRAPS OF A SHOE OR SANDAL; IF THESE ARE AS WIDE AS A SPLIT BEAN THEY MAY CONTRACT THE UNCLEANNESS OF LEPROSY SIGNS. A THICK CLOAK ON WHICH A LEPROSY SIGN APPEARED REMAINS CLEAN, R. ELIEZER B. JACOB RULED, UNLESS THE SIGN APPEARED ON THE TEXTURE AND ON THE SOFT WOOL.[6] A SKIN BOTTLE OR A SHEPHERD'S LEATHER WALLET ARE INSPECTED IN THE POSITION IN WHICH THEY ARE USED,[7]

(1) So that both are joined together by the threads. (2) Of the loom. (3) That are held together by a single thread. (4) *Sc.* they remain clean. (5) Much more so if they are of silk which cannot contract leprosy uncleanness. (6) The woolly hairs on the surface of the material. (7) So that a leprosy sign on parts that are joined together when in use is a cause of uncleanness

AND A LEPROSY SIGN MAY EFFECTIVELY SPREAD[1] FROM ITS INNER SIDE TO ITS OUTER SIDE AND FROM ITS OUTER SIDE TO ITS INNER SIDE.

MISHNAH 12. IF A GARMENT[2] THAT HAD BEEN SHUT UP WAS MIXED UP WITH OTHERS,[3] ALL ARE CLEAN.[4] IF IT WAS CUT UP AND MADE INTO SHREDS,[5] IT IS CLEAN, AND BENEFIT MAY BE DERIVED FROM IT; BUT IF A GARMENT THAT HAD BEEN CERTIFIED UNCLEAN WAS MIXED UP WITH OTHERS, ALL ARE UNCLEAN. IF IT WAS CUT UP AND MADE INTO SHREDS IT ALSO REMAINS UNCLEAN AND IT IS FORBIDDEN TO HAVE ANY BENEFIT FROM IT.[6]

though these parts are separated from each other when it is not in use.

(1) To be a cause of uncleanness. (2) Which, e.g., had been dyed after it had contracted leprosy so that no leprosy sign on it is now distinguishable. (3) With other coloured garments not susceptible to leprosy uncleanness, v. *supra* XI, 13. (4) Since a doubtful uncleanness is regarded as clean. (5) Each smaller than three fingerbreadths square and all hanging to each other. (6) V. Lev. XIII, 52; the phrase *'a malignant leprosy'* implying that it is forbidden for any use.

NEGA'IM

CHAPTER XII

MISHNAH 1. ALL HOUSES[1] MAY CONTRACT LEPROSY UNCLEANNESS,[2] EXCEPT THOSE OF GENTILES. IF ONE BOUGHT HOUSES FROM GENTILES,[1] ANY LEPROSY SIGNS IN THEM[3] MUST BE INSPECTED AS IF THEY HAD THEN[4] FIRST APPEARED. A ROUND HOUSE, A TRIANGULAR HOUSE, OR A HOUSE BUILT ON A SHIP,[5] ON A RAFT[5] OR ON FOUR BEAMS,[5] DOES NOT CONTRACT LEPROSY UNCLEANNESS; BUT IF IT WAS FOUR-SIDED, EVEN IF IT WAS BUILT ON FOUR PILLARS,[6] IT MAY CONTRACT UNCLEANNESS.

MISHNAH 2. A HOUSE ONE OF WHOSE WALLS IS COVERED WITH MARBLE,[7] WITH ROCK,[8] WITH BRICKS OR WITH EARTH,[9] IS NOT SUSCEPTIBLE TO LEPROSY UNCLEANNESS.[10] A HOUSE THAT HAD NOT IN IT[11] STONES, WOOD AND EARTH,[12] AND A LEPROSY SIGN APPEARED IN IT, THOUGH AFTERWARDS STONES, WOOD AND EARTH WERE INTRODUCED INTO IT, REMAINS CLEAN. SO ALSO A GARMENT IN WHICH THERE WAS NO WOVEN PART OF THREE FINGERBREADTHS SQUARE AND A LEPROSY SIGN APPEARED IN IT, THOUGH AFTERWARDS THERE WAS WOVEN INTO IT A PIECE OF THREE FINGERBREADTHS SQUARE, REMAINS CLEAN. A HOUSE DOES NOT CONTRACT LEPROSY UNCLEANNESS UNLESS THERE ARE IN IT[11] STONES, WOOD AND EARTH.[12]

MISHNAH 3. AND HOW MANY STONES MUST THERE BE

(1) In Palestine. (2) Cf. Lev. XIV, 34ff. (3) However old. (4) When they were bought. (5) Since it is not resting on the ground. (6) The walls being suspended in the air. (7) Which is not susceptible to leprosy uncleanness. (8) Primordial. (9) In lumps. (10) For each wall must be of stone, earth and wood. (11) In each of its walls. (12) Cf. Lev. XIV, 45.

IN IT?[1] R. ISHMAEL RULED: FOUR.[2] R. AKIBA RULED: EIGHT.[3] FOR R. ISHMAEL USED TO RULE: A LEPROSY SIGN IS NO CAUSE OF UNCLEANNESS UNLESS IT APPEARED IN THE SIZE OF TWO SPLIT BEANS ON TWO STONES OR ON ONE STONE.[4] R. AKIBA RULED: UNLESS IT APPEARS IN THE SIZE OF TWO SPLIT BEANS ON TWO STONES, AND NOT ON ONE STONE.[5] R. ELIEZER SON OF R. SIMEON RULED: UNLESS IT APPEARS IN THE SIZE OF TWO SPLIT BEANS, ON TWO STONES, ON TWO WALLS IN A CORNER, ITS LENGTH BEING THAT OF TWO SPLIT BEANS AND ITS BREADTH THAT OF ONE SPLIT BEAN.

MISHNAH 4. THE QUANTITY OF WOOD[6] MUST BE SUCH AS WOULD SUFFICE TO BE SET UNDER THE LINTEL. R. JUDAH RULED: IT MUST SUFFICE TO MAKE THE SUPPORT AT[7] THE BACK OF THE LINTEL.[8] THE QUANTITY OF EARTH MUST BE SUCH AS WOULD SUFFICE TO FILL UP THE SPACE BETWEEN ONE ROW OF STONES AND ANOTHER. THE WALLS OF A CATTLE-STALL OR THE WALLS OF A PARTITION[9] DO NOT CONTRACT THE UNCLEANNESS OF LEPROSY SIGNS. A HOUSE IN JERUSALEM OR IN ANY PLACE OUTSIDE THE LAND OF ISRAEL DOES NOT CONTRACT UNCLEANNESS OF LEPROSY SIGNS.[10]

MISHNAH 5. WHAT IS THE PROCEDURE IN THE INSPECTION OF A HOUSE?[11] THEN HE THAT OWNETH THE HOUSE SHALL COME AND TELL THE PRIEST, SAYING, THERE SEEMETH TO ME TO BE AS IT WERE A PLAGUE IN THE

(1) In a house that may be susceptible to leprosy uncleanness. Cf. prev. Mishnah *ad fin*. (2) One in each wall. (3) Two stones in each of the four walls. (4) Hence his ruling that four stones suffice for a house of four walls. (5) He, therefore, ruled that for a house of four walls eight stones are required. (6) In each wall of a house that may be susceptible to leprosy uncleanness. (7) Lit., 'sandal'. (8) A block of wood protecting the lintel against the knocking of the door. (9) Used merely as screens against the sun. (10) Since it is written, '*Which I give to you for a possession*', Lev. XIV, 34, excluding lands outside Palestine; and as for Jerusalem, this was not divided for possession among the tribes. (11) In which appeared a leprosy sign.

HOUSE.[1] EVEN IF HE IS A LEARNED SAGE AND KNOWS THAT IT IS DEFINITELY A LEPROSY SIGN, HE MAY NOT SPEAK WITH CERTAINTY SAYING, 'A LEPROSY SIGN HAS APPEARED TO ME IN THE HOUSE', BUT ONLY, 'THERE SEEMETH TO ME TO BE AS IT WERE A PLAGUE IN THE HOUSE'. AND THE PRIEST SHALL COMMAND THAT THEY EMPTY THE HOUSE, BEFORE THE PRIEST GO IN TO SEE THE PLAGUE, THAT ALL THAT IS IN THE HOUSE BE NOT MADE UNCLEAN; AND AFTERWARD THE PRIEST SHALL GO IN TO SEE THE HOUSE;[2] EVEN BUNDLES OF WOOD[3] AND EVEN BUNDLES OF REEDS[6] MUST BE REMOVED; SO R. JUDAH. R. SIMEON OBSERVED: THIS[4] IS A BUSINESS FOR AN IDLER ONLY.[5] SAID R. MEIR: BUT WHICH [OF HIS GOODS] COULD BECOME UNCLEAN? IF YOU WERE TO SAY, 'HIS ARTICLES OF WOOD, OF CLOTH OR OF METAL', THESE, SURELY, CAN BE IMMERSED IN A RITUAL BATH WHEN THEY BECOME CLEAN. WHAT IS IT THAT THE TORAH HAS SPARED? HIS EARTHENWARE, EVEN HIS CRUSE AND HIS EWER.[6] IF THE TORAH THUS SPARED A MAN'S HUMBLE POSSESSIONS, HOW MUCH MORE SO WOULD IT SPARE HIS CHERISHED POSSESSIONS! IF FOR HIS MATERIAL POSSESSIONS SO MUCH CONSIDERATION IS SHOWN, HOW MUCH MORE SO FOR THE LIFE OF HIS SONS AND DAUGHTERS! IF FOR THE POSSESSIONS OF A WICKED MAN[7] SUCH CARE IS EXERCISED, HOW MUCH MORE SO FOR THE POSSESSIONS OF A RIGHTEOUS ONE!

MISHNAH 6. [THE PRIEST] MUST NOT GO INTO[8] HIS OWN HOUSE TO SHUT UP,[9] NOR MAY HE STAND WITHIN THE HOUSE WHEREIN IS THE LEPROSY SIGN TO SHUT IT UP. HE MUST RATHER

(1) Cf. Lev. XIV, 35. (2) Cf. Ibid., 36. (3) V. following note. (4) The removal of the bundles mentioned which are not susceptible to uncleanness. (5) *Sc.* they need not be removed, and remain clean (Bert.). (6) Which if they remained in the house, would have become permanently unclean, as these cannot be made clean by immersion (cf. Ibid. XV, 12). (7) Leprosy is a punishment for the sin of slander. (8) Var. lec., 'stand within'. (9) *Sc.* the house with a leprosy sign in it.

STAND AT THE DOOR OF THE HOUSE WHEREIN IS THE LEPROSY SIGN, AND SHUTS IT FROM THERE;[1] FOR IT IS SAID, THEN THE PRIEST SHALL GO OUT OF THE HOUSE TO THE DOOR OF THE HOUSE, AND SHUT UP THE HOUSE SEVEN DAYS.[2] HE COMES AGAIN AT THE END OF THE WEEK AND INSPECTS THE SIGN. IF IT HAS SPREAD, THEN THE PRIEST SHALL COMMAND THAT THEY TAKE OUT THE STONES IN WHICH THE PLAGUE IS, AND CAST THEM INTO AN UNCLEAN PLACE WITHOUT THE CITY.[3] AND THEY SHALL TAKE OTHER STONES, AND PUT THEM IN THE PLACE OF THOSE STONES; AND HE SHALL TAKE OTHER MORTAR, AND SHALL PLASTER THE HOUSE.[4] HE MUST NOT TAKE STONES FROM THE ONE SIDE AND BRING THEM TO THE OTHER; NOR EARTH FROM THE ONE SIDE AND BRING IT TO THE OTHER; NOR LIME FROM ANYWHERE.[5] HE MUST NOT BRING ONE STONE TO REPLACE TWO, NOR TWO TO REPLACE ONE. HE MUST RATHER BRING TWO TO REPLACE TWO OR TO REPLACE THREE OR TO REPLACE FOUR. FROM THIS TEXT[6] IT HAS BEEN INFERRED: WOE TO THE WICKED,[7] WOE TO HIS NEIGHBOUR: BOTH[8] MUST TAKE OUT THE STONES,[3] BOTH MUST SCRAPE THE WALLS,[9] AND BOTH MUST BRING THE NEW STONES.[10] HE[11] ALONE, HOWEVER, BRINGS THE EARTH, FOR IT IS SAID, AND HE[12] SHALL TAKE OTHER EARTH,[13] AND PLASTER THE HOUSE;[10] HIS NEIGHBOUR NEED NOT JOIN WITH HIM IN IN THE PLASTERING.

MISHNAH 7. HE[14] COMES AGAIN AT THE END OF THE

(1) I.e., by means of an agent or a long rope. (2) Lev. XIV, 38. (3) Ib. 40. (4) Ib. 42. (5) Since lime is not regarded as 'earth'. (6) Ibid. XIV, 40-42, where the relevant verbs are in the plural, implying that if the wall with the leprosy sign served also the house of a neighbour the latter also must join the work (v. foll. n. but one). (7) Leprosy is a punishment for the sin of slander. (8) The owner of the leprous house and his neighbour on the other side of the wall (cf. prev. n. but one). (9) Ibid. XIV, 41. (10) Ib. 42. (11) The owner of the leprous house. (12) Sing., the owner alone. (13) E.V. *mortar.* (14) The priest.

WEEK[1] AND INSPECTS THE SIGN. IF IT HAS RETURNED, HE SHALL BREAK DOWN THE HOUSE, THE STONES OF IT, AND THE TIMBER THEREOF, AND ALL THE MORTAR OF THE HOUSE; AND HE SHALL CARRY THEM FORTH OUT OF THE CITY INTO AN UNCLEAN PLACE.[2] A SPREADING THAT IS ADJOINING[3] IS EFFECTIVE[4] HOWEVER SMALL IT MAY BE; ONE THAT IS DISTANT MUST BE[4] NO LESS THAN THE SIZE OF A SPLIT BEAN; AND A LEPROSY SIGN THAT RETURNS IN HOUSES MUST BE[4] NO LESS THAN THE SIZE OF TWO SPLIT BEANS.[5]

(1) The second week during which the house was shut up after it had been replastered. (2) Lev. XIV, 45. (3) The original leprosy sign. (4) To cause uncleanness. (5) The same minimum that is prescribed for such a leprosy sign when it appears for the first time.

NEGA'IM

CHAPTER XIII

MISHNAH 1. THERE ARE TEN [CASES OF LEPROSY IN] HOUSES: IF DURING THE FIRST WEEK A LEPROSY SIGN BECAME FAINT OR DISAPPEARED,[1] IT[2] MUST BE SCRAPED AND IS THEN CLEAN. IF DURING THE SECOND WEEK IT BECAME FAINT OR DISAPPEARED,[3] IT[2] MUST BE SCRAPED AND THE OWNER MUST BRING THE BIRDS.[4] IF IT SPREAD DURING THE FIRST WEEK, THE STONES MUST BE TAKEN OUT AND THE WALL SCRAPED AND[5] PLASTERED, AND ANOTHER WEEK MUST BE ALLOWED.[6] IF IT THEN RETURNED THE ENTIRE HOUSE MUST BE PULLED DOWN; IF IT DID NOT RETURN, THE BIRDS[4] MUST BE BROUGHT.[3] IF IT REMAINED UNCHANGED DURING THE FIRST WEEK BUT SPREAD DURING THE SECOND WEEK, THE STONES MUST BE TAKEN OUT AND THE WALL SCRAPED AND[5] PLASTERED, AND ANOTHER WEEK MUST BE ALLOWED.[6] IF IT THEN RETURNED, THE HOUSE MUST BE PULLED DOWN; IF IT DID NOT RETURN THE BIRDS[4] MUST BE BROUGHT.[3] IF IT REMAINED UNCHANGED IN BOTH WEEKS, THE STONES MUST BE TAKEN OUT, AND THE WALL SCRAPED AND[5] PLASTERED, AND A WEEK MUST BE ALLOWED.[6] IF IT THEN RETURNED THE HOUSE MUST BE PULLED DOWN; IF IT DID NOT RETURN, THE BIRDS[4] MUST BE BROUGHT.[3] IF BEFORE CLEANNESS WAS ATTAINED THROUGH THE BIRDS A NEW LEPROSY SIGN APPEARED, THE HOUSE MUST BE PULLED DOWN; BUT IF IT APPEARED AFTER CLEANNESS THROUGH THE BIRDS HAD BEEN ATTAINED, IT MUST BE INSPECTED AS IF IT HAD APPEARED FOR THE FIRST TIME.

(1) These are the first two cases. (2) The place of the sign only. (3) These represent another two cases, of the ten cases referred to above. (4) Cf. Lev. XIV, 49. (5) After other stones had been put in their place. (6) For keeping the house shut under observation.

MISHNAH 2. IN THE CASE OF A STONE IN A CORNER,[1] WHEN THE STONE IS TAKEN OUT IT MUST BE TAKEN OUT WHOLLY; BUT WHEN [THE HOUSE IS] PULLED DOWN ITS OWNER PULLS DOWN HIS OWN [PART][2] AND LEAVES THAT WHICH BELONGS TO HIS NEIGHBOUR. THUS IT FOLLOWS THAT THERE ARE GREATER RESTRICTIONS FOR TAKING OUT[3] THAN FOR PULLING DOWN.[4] R. ELIEZER RULED: IF A HOUSE IS BUILT OF ROWS OF BIG STONES[5] AND SMALL STONES,[6] AND A LEPROSY SIGN APPEARED ON A BIG STONE,[7] ALL OF IT[8] MUST BE TAKEN OUT; BUT IF IT APPEARED ON THE SMALL STONES, HE[9] TAKES OUT HIS STONES AND LEAVES THOSE OF HIS NEIGHBOUR.

MISHNAH 3. IF A HOUSE IN WHICH THERE APPEARED A LEPROSY SIGN HAD AN UPPER ROOM ABOVE IT, THE BEAMS[10] ARE ALLOWED TO THE UPPER ROOM.[11] IF THE LEPROSY SIGN APPEARED IN THE UPPER ROOM THE BEAMS[10] ARE ALLOWED TO THE LOWER ROOM.[12] IF THERE WAS NO UPPER ROOM ABOVE IT, ITS STONES AND WOOD AND EARTH MUST BE PULLED DOWN WITH IT. ONE MAY, HOWEVER, SAVE THE FRAMES[13] AND THE WINDOW LATTICES. R. JUDAH RULED: A FRAME[14] THAT IS BUILT OVER THE HOUSE MUST BE PULLED DOWN WITH IT. ITS STONES AND WOOD AND EARTH CONVEY UNCLEANNESS IF THEY ARE OF THE MINIMUM SIZE OF AN OLIVE. R. ELIEZER ḤISMA RULED: WHATEVER THEIR SIZE.

(1) Between two walls one of which has a leprosy sign and belongs to one man while the other belongs to the house of a neighbour. (2) Although it forms part of his neighbour's house. (3) A stone or stones. (4) The entire house. (5) Covering the full thickness of the walls and seen, therefore, from either side of the walls. (6) That (cf. prev. n.) can be seen from one side of the walls only. (7) In a wall between the houses of two neighbours. (8) Even the part that faces the neighbour's house. (9) Whose house is affected. (10) Of the roof of the lower room which serves also as the floor of the upper room. (11) *Sc.* they need not be dismantled when the lower room is pulled down; but may be pinned under and left in position. (12) Cf. prev. n. *mut. mut.* (13) Of the windows (or 'the tiles on the roof') if these are not built into the house. (14) For holding the beams of the roof.

MISHNAH 4. A HOUSE THAT IS SHUT UP[1] CONVEYS UNCLEANNESS[2] FROM ITS INNER SIDE;[3] AND ONE THAT HAS BEEN CERTIFIED UNCLEAN, BOTH FROM ITS INNER SIDE AND FROM ITS OUTER SIDE. BOTH,[4] HOWEVER, CONVEY UNCLEANNESS IF ONE ENTERS IN.[5]

MISHNAH 5. IF A MAN BUILDS STONES FROM A HOUSE THAT WAS SHUT UP[6] INTO A CLEAN ONE,[7] AND THE LEPROSY SIGN RETURNED TO THE [FORMER] HOUSE, THE STONES MUST BE TAKEN OUT. IF IT RETURNED TO THE STONES,[8] THE FIRST HOUSE MUST BE PULLED DOWN, AND THE STONES SERVE THE SECOND HOUSE WHILE THE TOKENS ARE UNDER OBSERVATION.[9]

MISHNAH 6. IF A HOUSE OVERSHADOWED A LEPROUS HOUSE, AND SO ALSO IF A TREE OVERSHADOWED A LEPROUS HOUSE, ANY ONE WHO ENTERS THE OUTER [OF THE TWO] REMAINS CLEAN; SO R. ELEAZAR[10] B. AZARIAH. R. ELIEZER[11] OBSERVED: IF ONE STONE OF IT[12] CAUSES UNCLEANNESS BY ENTERING,[13] SHOULD NOT THE HOUSE ITSELF CAUSE UNCLEANNESS BY ENTERING?[14]

MISHNAH 7. IF AN UNCLEAN MAN[15] STOOD UNDER A TREE AND A CLEAN MAN PASSED BY, THE LATTER BECOMES UNCLEAN. IF A CLEAN MAN STOOD UNDER A TREE AND AN UNCLEAN ONE[15] PASSED BY, THE FORMER REMAINS CLEAN. IF

(1) On account of a leprosy sign in it. (2) Even if only one limb of a person came in contact with it. (3) But not from its outer side. The affected stone alone conveys uncleanness from both its sides. (4) A house shut up as well as one that was certified unclean. (5) With entire body or with its greater part and the head (cf. *supra* n. 2). (6) For the second week, on account of a leprosy sign. (7) Cf. *supra* XI, 6. (8) While they were in the clean house. (9) The second house being treated as if a leprosy sign appeared in it for the first time. After the condition of the house is duly determined the stones must be pulled out; cf. *supra* XI, 6. (10) Var lec., Eliezer. (11) Var. lec., Eleazar. (12) A house that is otherwise clean. (13) *Sc.* the one afflicted stone causes the uncleanness of the entire house. (14) To the outer house or the tree. (15) Afflicted with leprosy.

THE LATTER STOOD STILL, THE FORMER BECOMES UNCLEAN. SIMILARLY IN THE CASE OF A LEPROUS STONE[1] HE[2] REMAINS CLEAN; BUT IF IT WAS SET DOWN[3] HE BECOMES UNCLEAN.

MISHNAH 8. IF A MAN WHO WAS CLEAN PUT HIS HEAD AND THE GREATER PART OF HIS BODY INSIDE AN UNCLEAN HOUSE,[4] HE BECOMES UNCLEAN; AND IF AN UNCLEAN MAN[4] PUT HIS HEAD AND THE GREATER PART OF HIS BODY INSIDE A CLEAN HOUSE HE CAUSES IT TO BE UNCLEAN. IF OF A CLEAN CLOAK A PART THAT WAS THREE FINGERBREADTHS SQUARE WAS PUT INSIDE AN UNCLEAN HOUSE, THE CLOAK BECOMES UNCLEAN; AND AN UNCLEAN [CLOAK], OF WHICH EVEN ONLY THE SIZE OF AN OLIVE WAS PUT INSIDE A CLEAN HOUSE, CAUSES THE LATTER TO BE UNCLEAN.

MISHNAH 9. IF A MAN ENTERED A LEPROUS HOUSE, CARRYING HIS CLOTHES UPON HIS SHOULDERS[5] AND HIS SANDALS AND RINGS IN HIS HANDS,[5] BOTH HE AND THEY BECOME UNCLEAN FORTHWITH.[6] IF, HOWEVER, HE WAS WEARING HIS CLOTHES AND HAD HIS SANDALS ON HIS FEET AND HIS RINGS ON HIS HANDS, HE BECOMES UNCLEAN FORTHWITH, BUT THEY[7] REMAIN CLEAN,[8] UNLESS HE STAYED AS MUCH TIME AS IS REQUIRED FOR THE EATING[9] OF HALF A LOAF[10] OF WHEATEN BREAD BUT NOT OF BARLEY BREAD,[11] WHILE IN A RECLINING POSTURE[12] AND EATING WITH SOME CONDIMENT.[13]

(1) That was carried by under the tree. (2) The clean person standing under the same tree. (3) Or if the man who carried it stood still. (4) V. p. 288, n. 15. (5) *Sc.* he did not wear them. (6) Since the clothes, sandals and rings were only carried by the man (and not worn) they, like himself, come under the Pentateuchal law of '*he that* goeth *into the house . . . shall be unclean*' Lev. XIV, 46. (7) Since they were worn in the usual manner. (8) They are included in the category of '*clothes*' which need only be washed (cf. Lev. XIV, 47 and the definition of '*eateth*' in foll. n.). (9) This is the definition of '*eateth*' (v. prev. n.). (10) The bulk of four eggs (Rashi) or three eggs (Maim). (11) The former is more tasteful than the latter and is eaten much quicker. (12) A position in which a man eats quicker than when he walks about (cf. prev. n.). (13) Cf. prev. n. *mut. mut.*

MISHNAH 10. IF A MAN WAS STANDING WITHIN,[1] STRETCHING HIS HANDS OUTSIDE, WITH HIS RINGS ON HIS HANDS,[2] IF HE STAYED AS MUCH TIME AS IS REQUIRED FOR THE EATING OF HALF A LOAF, THEY BECOME UNCLEAN.[3] IF HE WAS STANDING OUTSIDE, STRETCHING HIS HANDS INSIDE, WITH HIS RINGS ON HIS HANDS,[2] R. JUDAH RULES THAT THEY[4] ARE UNCLEAN FORTHWITH, BUT THE SAGES RULED: ONLY AFTER HE STAYED THERE AS MUCH TIME AS IS REQUIRED FOR THE EATING OF HALF A LOAF.[5] THEY[6] SAID TO R. JUDAH: IF WHEN ALL HIS BODY IS UNCLEAN[7] HE DOES NOT RENDER THAT WHICH IS ON HIM UNCLEAN UNLESS HE STAYED THERE LONG ENOUGH TO EAT HALF A LOAF, IS THERE NOT MORE REASON THAT, WHERE NOT ALL HIS BODY IS UNCLEAN,[8] HE SHOULD NOT RENDER THAT WHICH IS ON HIM UNCLEAN UNLESS HE STAYED THERE LONG ENOUGH TO EAT HALF A LOAF?[9]

MISHNAH 11. IF A LEPER ENTERED A HOUSE ALL VESSELS IN IT, EVEN TO THE HEIGHT OF THE ROOF BEAMS, BECOME UNCLEAN. R. SIMEON RULED: ONLY TO A HEIGHT OF FOUR CUBITS.[10] VESSELS[11] BECOME UNCLEAN FORTHWITH. R. JUDAH RULED: ONLY IF THE LEPER STAYED THERE AS MUCH TIME AS IS REQUIRED FOR THE LIGHTING OF A LAMP.

MISHNAH 12. IF HE[12] ENTERS A SYNAGOGUE, A PARTITION TEN HANDBREADTHS HIGH AND FOUR CUBITS WIDE MUST BE MADE FOR HIM.[13] HE MUST ENTER FIRST AND COME OUT

(1) Within a leprous house. (2) In the manner they are usually worn. (3) Like himself, since his main body was within the house. (4) The man's hands and rings. (5) His hands, however, even according to the Sages, become unclean forthwith. (6) The Sages. (7) In the case where the man was standing within. (8) Where he stands outside. (9) R. Judah, however, maintains that in certain cases one who is unclean is subjected to lesser restrictions than one who is clean. (10) Any vessel above this height remains clean. (11) To the height of the beams according to the first Tanna, and to the height of four cubits according to R. Simeon. (12) A leper (cf. prev. Mishnah). (13) One of smaller measurements constitutes no valid protection for the remainder of the synagogue.

LAST.[1] ANY VESSEL THAT AFFORDS PROTECTION[2] BY HAVING A TIGHTLY FITTING COVER IN THE TENT OF A CORPSE[3] AFFORDS PROTECTION BY A TIGHTLY FITTING COVER IN A LEPROUS HOUSE; AND WHATSOEVER AFFORDS PROTECTION,[4] WHEN COVERED,[5] IN THE TENT OF A CORPSE[3] AFFORDS PROTECTION WHEN COVERED IN A LEPROUS HOUSE; SO R. MEIR. R. JOSE RULED: ANY VESSEL THAT AFFORDS PROTECTION BY HAVING A TIGHTLY FITTING COVER IN THE TENT OF A CORPSE AFFORDS PROTECTION WHEN COVERED[5] IN A LEPROUS HOUSE; AND WHATSOEVER AFFORDS PROTECTION WHEN COVERED IN THE TENT OF A CORPSE REMAINS CLEAN EVEN WHEN UNCOVERED IN A LEPROUS HOUSE.

(1) Since otherwise, should he happen to stand still in his passage from the door to the partition, he would render the people in the synagogue unclean. (2) Cf. Kelim X, 1. (3) *Sc.* under a roof that overshadows a corpse. (4) Cf. Oh. V, 6. (5) Even when the cover was not tightly fitting.

NEGA'IM

CHAPTER XIV

MISHNAH 1. HOW WAS A LEPER CLEANSED?[1] A NEW EARTHENWARE FLASK WAS BROUGHT AND A QUARTER OF A LOG OF LIVING WATER[2] WAS PUT IN IT. TWO UNDOMESTICATED[3] BIRDS ARE ALSO BROUGHT. ONE OF THESE WAS SLAUGHTERED OVER THE EARTHENWARE VESSEL AND OVER THE LIVING WATER, A HOLE WAS DUG AND IT WAS BURIED IN HIS[4] PRESENCE. THEREUPON CEDARWOOD, HYSSOP AND SCARLET WOOL WERE TAKEN AND BOUND TOGETHER WITH THE PROJECTING ENDS OF THE STRIP OF WOOL.[5] NEAR TO THESE WERE BROUGHT THE TIPS OF THE WINGS AND THE TIP OF THE TAIL OF THE SECOND BIRD, AND ALL TOGETHER WERE DIPPED,[6] AND THEREWITH THE BACK OF THE LEPER'S HAND WAS SPRINKLED UPON SEVEN TIMES. SOME SAY THAT THE SPRINKLING WAS DONE UPON HIS[4] FOREHEAD. IN THE SAME MANNER ONE SPRINKLED THE LINTEL OF A HOUSE[7] FROM THE OUTSIDE.

MISHNAH 2. WHEN HE WAS ABOUT TO SET FREE THE LIVING BIRD,[8] HE DID NOT TURN HIS FACE TOWARDS THE SEA OR TOWARDS THE CITY OR TOWARDS THE WILDERNESS, FOR IT IS SAID, BUT HE SHALL LET GO THE LIVING BIRD OUT OF THE CITY INTO THE OPEN FIELD.[9] WHEN HE WAS ABOUT TO CUT OFF THE HAIR OF THE LEPER HE PASSED THE RAZOR OVER THE WHOLE OF HIS SKIN,[10] AND THE LATTER

(1) Cf. Lev. XIV, 2ff. (2) *Sc.* from an ever flowing spring. (3) Lit., 'free'. (4) The leper's. (5) The strip of scarlet wool having been longer than the cedarwood and the hyssop. (6) In the mixture of the blood and the water in the earthenware vessel. (7) That was cleansed after a leprosy. (8) Cf. Lev. XIV, 7, 53. (9) Ibid. XIV, 53. (10) Other than the concealed parts (cf. *supra* II, 4).

WASHED HIS GARMENTS AND IMMERSED HIMSELF. HE IS THEN CLEAN SO FAR AS NOT TO CONVEY UNCLEANNESS BY ENTERING IN,[1] BUT HE STILL CONVEYS UNCLEANNESS LIKE A [DEAD] CREEPING THING.[2] HE MAY ENTER WITHIN THE WALL,[3] BUT MUST KEEP AWAY FROM HIS HOUSE FOR SEVEN DAYS, AND[4] HE IS FORBIDDEN MARITAL INTERCOURSE.

MISHNAH 3. ON THE SEVENTH DAY HE CUT OFF HIS HAIR A SECOND TIME IN THE MANNER OF THE FIRST CUTTING, HE WASHED HIS GARMENTS AND IMMERSED HIMSELF, AND THEN HE WAS CLEAN IN SO FAR AS NOT TO CONVEY UNCLEANNESS AS A DEAD CREEPING THING, BUT HE WAS STILL LIKE A ṬEBUL YOM.[5] HE[6] MAY EAT SECOND TITHE; AND AFTER HE HAD AWAITED SUNSET HE MAY ALSO EAT TERUMAH. AFTER HE HAD BROUGHT[7] HIS OFFERING OF ATONEMENT, HE MAY ALSO EAT HALLOWED THINGS. THUS THERE ARE THREE GRADES IN THE PURIFICATION OF A LEPER[8] AND THREE GRADES IN THAT OF A WOMAN AFTER CHILDBIRTH.[9]

MISHNAH 4. THREE CLASSES OF PERSONS CUT OFF THEIR HAIR,[10] AND THEIR CUTTING OF IT IS A COMMANDMENT: THE NAZIRITE,[11] THE LEPER,[12] AND THE LEVITES.[13] ALL THESE, FURTHERMORE, IF THEY CUT THEIR HAIR BUT NOT WITH A RAZOR,

(1) A house; or by his bed and seat. (2) Which conveys uncleanness to a man and vessels by contact only but not by carriage (cf. Lev. XI, 31). (3) Of Jerusalem. (4) So Elijah Wilna. *Aliter:* 'viz'. (Maim. Bert. and L.). (5) Who disqualifies *terumah*. (6) Like a *ṭebul yom*. (7) On the day following. (8) Viz., after the first hair cutting he no longer conveys uncleanness by entering in; after the second hair cutting and the sunset of that day he may also eat *terumah*; and after he had brought the prescribed offering he may also eat hallowed things. (9) Cf. Lev. XII, 2ff. After seven days and fourteen days from the birth of a male and a female respectively she is clean for her husband; after immersion (forty and eighty days after the birth of a male and a female respectively) and the sunset on that day she is also clean for *terumah;* and after she had brought her prescribed offering she may also eat hallowed things (Elijah Wilna). (10) Before their full cleanness can be attained. (11) Cf. Num. VI, 18. (12) Cf. Lev. XIV, 8. (13) Cf. Num. VIII, 7.

OR IF THEY LEFT BUT TWO HAIRS, THEIR ACT IS OF NO VALIDITY.

MISHNAH 5. THE TWO BIRDS[1] MUST, ACCORDING TO THE COMMANDMENT, BE ALIKE IN APPEARANCE, IN SIZE AND IN PRICE; AND THEY MUST BE PURCHASED AT THE SAME TIME. BUT THOUGH THEY ARE NOT ALIKE THEY ARE VALID; AND IF ONE WAS PURCHASED ON ONE DAY AND THE OTHER ON THE MORROW THEY ARE ALSO VALID. IF AFTER ONE OF THE BIRDS HAD BEEN SLAUGHTERED IT WAS FOUND THAT IT WAS NOT UNDOMESTICATED, A FELLOW MUST BE PURCHASED FOR THE SECOND, AND THE FIRST MAY BE EATEN. IF AFTER IT HAD BEEN SLAUGHTERED IT WAS FOUND TO BE ṬREFAH, A FELLOW MUST BE PURCHASED FOR THE SECOND AND THE FIRST MAY BE MADE USE OF.[2] IF THE BLOOD[3] HAD BEEN POURED AWAY[4] THE BIRD THAT WAS TO BE LET GO[5] MUST BE LEFT TO DIE. IF THE ONE THAT WAS TO BE LET GO DIED, THE BLOOD[3] MUST BE POURED AWAY.

MISHNAH 6. THE PRESCRIBED MEASUREMENTS OF THE CEDARWOOD[1] ARE ONE CUBIT IN LENGTH, AND IN THICKNESS A QUARTER OF THAT OF THE LEG OF A BED, WHEN ONE LEG IS DIVIDED INTO TWO HALVES AND THESE TWO INTO FOUR.[6] THE PRESCRIBED KIND OF HYSSOP IS ONE THAT IS NEITHER THE GREEK HYSSOP NOR STIBIUM HYSSOP NOR ROMAN HYSSOP NOR WILD HYSSOP NOR ANY KIND OF HYSSOP THAT HAS A SPECIAL NAME.

MISHNAH 7. ON THE EIGHTH DAY[7] HE[8] BROUGHT THREE BEASTS: A SIN-OFFERING, A GUILT-OFFERING AND A BURNT-OFFERING; AND A POOR MAN[9] BROUGHT A SIN-OFFERING OF A BIRD AND A BURNT-OFFERING OF A BIRD.[10]

(1) Cf. Lev. XIV, 4. (2) Though it may not be eaten. (3) Of the first bird. (4) Before the sprinkling. (5) Cf. Ibid. XIV, 7. (6) *Sc.* the thickness must be exactly one quarter, neither more nor less. (7) If he had cut off his hair on the seventh (cf. Ibid. XIV, 9f.). (8) The leper. (9) Cf. Ibid. XIV, 21f. (10) For a guilt-offering, however, he also must bring a beast.

MISHNAH 8. APPROACHING THE GUILT-OFFERING HE PUT HIS TWO HANDS ON IT AND THEN SLAUGHTERED IT. TWO PRIESTS RECEIVED ITS BLOOD, THE ONE IN A VESSEL AND THE OTHER IN HIS HAND.[1] HE WHO RECEIVED IT IN THE VESSEL PROCEEDED TO SPRINKLE IT ON THE WALL OF THE ALTAR, WHILE THE OTHER WHO RECEIVED IT IN HIS HAND APPROACHED THE LEPER. THE LEPER IN THE MEANTIME HAD IMMERSED HIMSELF IN THE CHAMBER OF THE LEPERS,[2] AND CAME AND TOOK UP A POSITION AT THE NIḲANOR GATE.[3] R. JUDAH STATED: HE DID NOT REQUIRE IMMERSION.[4]

MISHNAH 9. [THE LEPER] PUT IN HIS HEAD[5] AND [THE PRIEST] APPLIED [THE BLOOD] TO THE TIP OF HIS EAR; [HE PUT IN] HIS HAND AND [THE PRIEST] APPLIED [THE BLOOD] TO THE THUMB OF HIS HAND; [HE PUT IN] HIS FOOT AND [THE PRIEST] APPLIED [THE BLOOD] TO THE GREAT TOE OF HIS FOOT. R. JUDAH STATED: HE PUT IN ALL THE THREE TOGETHER. IF HE HAD NO THUMB ON HIS HAND OR NO GREAT TOE ON HIS FOOT OR NO RIGHT EAR HE COULD NEVER ATTAIN CLEANNESS.[6] R. ELIEZER RULED: [THE BLOOD] IS APPLIED TO THE PLACE WHERE THEY[7] WERE ORIGINALLY. R. SIMEON RULED: IF IT WAS APPLIED TO THE LEFT SIDE, THE OBLIGATION HAS BEEN FULFILLED.

MISHNAH 10. [THE PRIEST] THEN TOOK SOME [OF THE CONTENTS] OF THE LOG OF OIL[8] AND POURED IT INTO HIS COLLEAGUE'S HAND;[9] BUT EVEN IF HE POURED IT INTO HIS OWN HAND, THE OBLIGATION IS FULFILLED. HE THEN DIPPED [HIS RIGHT FOREFINGER] IN THE OIL AND SPRINKLED IT SEVEN TIMES TOWARDS THE HOLY OF HOLIES, DIPPING IT

(1) The left (Elijah Wilna). (2) Cf. Mid. II, 5. (3) Cf. Mid. II, 3. (4) On the eighth day, since he had once immersed himself on the seventh. (5) From the Niḳanor Gate into the Court of the Israelites whither he was not yet allowed to enter. (6) This, however, applies only where the limb was lost after he became unclean or (according to another opinion) after he reached the stage of undergoing the ceremonial of cleansing. (7) The missing limbs. (8) Cf. Lev. XIV, 15. (9) A fellow priest's.

FOR EVERY SPRINKLING. HE THEN APPROACHED THE LEPER, AND TO THE SAME PLACES THAT HE APPLIED THE BLOOD HE NOW APPLIED THE OIL, FOR IT IS SAID, UPON THE PLACE OF THE BLOOD OF THE GUILT-OFFERING. AND THE REST OF THE OIL THAT IS IN THE PRIEST'S HAND HE SHALL PUT UPON THE HEAD OF HIM THAT IS TO BE CLEANSED TO MAKE ATONEMENT.[1] THUS IF HE 'PUT UPON', ATONEMENT IS MADE, BUT IF HE DID NOT 'PUT UPON', NO ATONEMENT IS MADE; SO R. AKIBA. R. JOḤANAN B. NURI RULED: THESE[2] ARE BUT THE RESIDUE OF THE PRECEPT[3] AND, THEREFORE, WHETHER HE 'PUT UPON' OR DID NOT 'PUT UPON', ATONEMENT IS MADE,[4] ONLY TO HIM[5] IT IS ACCOUNTED AS IF HE MADE NO ATONEMENT.[6] IF ANY OIL WAS MISSING FROM THE LOG BEFORE IT WAS POURED OUT[7] IT MAY BE FILLED UP AGAIN; IF AFTER IT WAS POURED OUT, OTHER OIL[8] MUST BE BROUGHT ANEW; SO R. AKIBA. R. SIMEON RULED: IF ANY OIL WAS MISSING FROM THE LOG BEFORE IT WAS APPLIED,[9] IT MAY BE FILLED UP; BUT IF AFTER IT HAD BEEN APPLIED, OTHER OIL[8] MUST BE BROUGHT ANEW.

MISHNAH 11. IF A LEPER BROUGHT HIS SACRIFICE AS A POOR MAN[10] AND HE BECAME RICH, OR AS A RICH MAN[11] AND HE BECAME POOR, ALL DEPENDS ON THE SIN-OFFERING;[12] SO R. SIMEON. R. JUDAH RULED: ALL DEPENDS ON THE GUILT-OFFERING.[13]

(1) Lev. XIV, 28f. (2) The applications spoken of. (3) *Sc.* they are not essentials. (4) And the leper attains cleanness. (5) The priest. (6) Since he did not carry out the commandment in all its details. (7) Into the priest's hand. (8) To make up a full *log*. (9) To the prescribed limbs of the leper. (10) A bird. Cf. Ibid. XIV, 21. (11) A beast. (12) I.e., the condition of the man when he offered his sin-offering. If he was poor at the time and brought the sin-offering of a poor man (a bird), the burnt-offering that is brought after it must also be that of a poor man (a bird) although he became rich in the meantime. If he was rich at the time and brought the sin-offering of a rich man (a ewe lamb), the burnt-offering also must be that for a rich man (a he-lamb) although he became poor in the meantime. The guilt-offering does not come under consideration since it is the same for both rich and poor (13) Which is the first to be offered. The condition of the man at that moment determines the

MISHNAH 12. A POOR LEPER WHO BROUGHT THE SACRIFICE OF A RICH MAN HAS FULFILLED HIS DUTY; BUT A RICH LEPER THAT BROUGHT THE SACRIFICE OF A POOR MAN HAS NOT FULFILLED HIS DUTY. A MAN[1] MAY BRING A POOR MAN'S SACRIFICE FOR HIS SON, HIS DAUGHTER, HIS BONDMAN OR BONDWOMAN, AND THEREBY ENABLE THEM TO EAT OF THE OFFERINGS.[2] R. JUDAH RULED:[3] FOR HIS WIFE ALSO[4] HE MUST BRING THE SACRIFICE OF A RICH MAN; AND THE SAME APPLIES TO ANY OTHER SACRIFICE TO WHICH SHE IS LIABLE.

MISHNAH 13. IF THE SACRIFICES OF TWO LEPERS WERE MIXED UP AND AFTER THE SACRIFICE OF ONE OF THEM HAD BEEN OFFERED ONE OF THE LEPERS DIED,—THIS[5] IS WHAT THE MEN OF ALEXANDRIA ASKED OF R. JOSHUA. HE ANSWERED THEM: LET HIM ASSIGN[6] HIS POSSESSIONS TO ANOTHER PERSON,[7] AND BRING THE POOR MAN'S SACRIFICE.[8]

מסכת נגעים

הדרן עלך ... והדרך עלן

תושלב"ע

תורה אור

value of the sin- and the burnt-offerings that follow it. Both R. Simeon and R. Judah derive their rulings from an interpretation of a Scriptural text.

(1) Even if rich. (2) Cf. *supra* XIV, 3. (3) With reference to the ruling *supra* that a rich leper cannot fulfil his duty by bringing the sacrifice of a poor man. (4) A wife's condition being determined by that of her husband. (5) *Sc.* what is to be done by the surviving leper that the should attain his cleanness. He cannot attain it by the offering of the live sin-offering, since it might not be his but the dead man's; and he cannot rely upon the one that was offered, since that one might have been the dead man's and not his. He cannot bring another sin-offering, since the one that was already offered might possibly have been his, and the new animal brought as a sin-offering would in consequence remain unconsecrated and, therefore, forbidden to be offered on the altar. (6) Temporarily. (7) Thus becoming poor for the time being. (8) A bird; which, unlike a beast, even if it is only an uncertain offering may be offered up on the altar, v. Nid. *69b*.

PARAH

TRANSLATED INTO ENGLISH

WITH NOTES

BY

REV. DR ISRAEL W. SLOTKI, M. A., Litt. D.

INTRODUCTION

The statute of the Red Cow laid down in Numbers XIX, 2ff is the main theme of the Tractate of *Parah.*[1]

The age of the cow and incidentally that of other animal sacrifices are discussed in CHAPTER I. Disqualifications that are due, e.g., to the internal or external condition of the cow, the character of its former owner or its place of origin, the colour of parts of its body or the manner of its birth, are the subjects of CHAPTER II.

The measures that were taken to ensure meticulous cleanness of the red cow and of all who were engaged in its preparation are described in CHAPTER III, which also deals minutely with the procedure that was to be followed from the time the cow was taken out from its stall to that of the burning of its carcass and the division of its ashes.

Disqualifications in the red cow that are due to the performance of any of its services in a manner other than the one prescribed or under a name other than its own or by a priest that did not duly wash his hands and feet or wear the proper garments are enumerated in CHAPTER IV, which also indicates the conditions when the garments of those engaged in its preparation become unclean and when other work performed by them renders the cow itself invalid.

The precautions for ensuring the cleanness of the vessel that is to be used for the mixing of the ashes of the red cow with the water for sprinkling and of the man who is to mix it; and the kind of person that is eligible and the vessel that is suitable for the purpose are discussed in CHAPTER V.

The invalidity of the water or the ashes that is due to various forms of (*a*) indirect 'putting' into the vessel or (*b*) the performance of work that has no connection with the ceremonial is the main subject of CHAPTERS VI and VII respectively.

Beginning with the case of two men keeping watch over the water intended for the mixture, CHAPTER VIII proceeds to

(1) פָּרָה 'cow', 'young cow', 'heifer'.

discuss the conditions when the water does or does not become invalid and enumerates also a series of cases where an uncleanness that cannot be conveyed directly may, paradoxically, be conveyed indirectly. This is followed by the enumeration of various kinds of water that are altogether invalid where running water has been prescribed.

The procedure to be followed where a mixture of the water and the ashes of the red cow received an admixture of some common liquid or moisture of an animal body or any coloured substance is the subject with which CHAPTER IX begins, and this is followed by a discussion of the following: Intention to drink from the mixture, its disposal when invalidated, the condition of an animal that drank from it, its transportation across a water, valid ashes that were mixed with common ashes and the uncleanness that this mixture may convey.

A series of certain clean and unclean persons and objects that convey uncleanness to the man only who was clean for the red cow-offering and only to the vessel that contained the water of the red cow-offering but not to other persons and vessels are enumerated in CHAPTER X.

Causes of disqualification of the mixture form the main discussion of CHAPTER XI, which also contains the laws on the conveyance of uncleanness begun in the previous chapter and lays down rules on the kinds of hyssop and the several parts of the plant that are valid or invalid and on the number of stalks and buds on each required for the ceremonial of sprinkling.

Further rules in connection with the ceremonial of sprinkling are described in CHAPTER XII, which deals in particular with the manner of the sprinkling; the quantity and depth of the mixture required; irregularities of procedure, sprinkling on the wrong objects; the kind of uncleanness that may be conveyed on and by the man who sprinkles as well as by and on the vessel that contains the mixture and its several parts; what composite articles are or are not regarded as single units in respect of the sprinkling and the contraction of uncleanness and, finally, the times of the sprinkling.

I. W. SLOTKI

PARAH

CHAPTER I

MISHNAH 1. R. ELIEZER RULED: THE HEIFER[1] MUST BE NO MORE THAN ONE YEAR OLD AND THE RED COW[2] NO MORE THAN TWO YEARS OLD. BUT THE SAGES RULED: THE HEIFER[1] MAY BE EVEN TWO YEARS OLD AND THE RED COW[2] EVEN THREE OR FOUR YEARS OLD. R. MEIR RULED: EVEN FIVE YEARS OLD. ONE THAT IS OLDER IS VALID, BUT THEY DID NOT WAIT WITH IT SO LONG SINCE IT MIGHT IN THE MEANTIME GROW SOME BLACK HAIRS AND [THUS] BECOME INVALID.[3] R. JOSHUA STATED: I ONLY HEARD[4] OF [A COW] THAT WAS SHELASHETH.[5] THEY SAID TO HIM: WHAT DOES THE EXPRESSION 'SHELASHETH' SIGNIFY? HE REPLIED: THUS HAVE I HEARD IT WITHOUT ANY EXPLANATION. BEN 'AZZAI SAID, I WILL EXPLAIN: IF YOU SAY SHELISHITH THE MEANING IS 'THE THIRD' IN NUMBER TO OTHERS,[6] BUT WHEN YOU SAY 'SHELASHETH' THE MEANING IS ONE THAT IS 'THREE YEARS OLD'. SIMILARLY IT WAS SPOKEN OF A VINEYARD THAT IS REBA'I. THEY SAID TO HIM: WHAT DOES THE EXPRESSION 'REBA'I' SIGNIFY? HE REPLIED: THUS HAVE I HEARD IT WITHOUT ANY EXPLANATION. BEN 'AZZAI SAID, I WILL EXPLAIN: IF YOU SAY 'REBI'I' THE MEANING IS 'THE FOURTH' IN NUMBER TO OTHERS, BUT WHEN YOU SAY 'REBA'I' THE MEANING IS ONE THAT IS 'FOUR YEARS OLD'. SIMILARLY IT WAS RULED: IF A MAN ATE[7] IN A LEPROUS HOUSE HALF A LOAF, THREE[8] OF WHICH ARE MADE OF A ḲAB, HE BECOMES UNCLEAN.[9] THEY SAID TO HIM: SAY RATHER, 'EIGHTEEN[8] OF

(1) Prescribed in Deut. XXI, 3ff. (2) The red heifer, Num. XIX, 2ff. (3) Var. lec. 'or (otherwise) became invalid'. By bearing the yoke or contracting a blemish (cf. Ibid. XIX, 2). (4) That it is valid. (5) This is explained presently. (6) One third born which was deemed specially good. (7) Or spent time enough to eat. (8) Whole loaves. (9) Cf. Neg. XIII, 9.

WHICH ARE MADE OF A SE'AH'.[1] HE REPLIED: THUS HAVE I HEARD IT WITHOUT ANY EXPLANATION. BEN 'AZZAI SAID, I WILL EXPLAIN: WHEN YOU SAY, 'THREE OF WHICH ARE MADE OF A ḲAB' THE LOAF WOULD CONTAIN NO DOUGH-OFFERING,[2] BUT IF YOU SAY, 'EIGHTEEN OF WHICH ARE MADE OF A SE'AH', THE LOAF[3] HAS BEEN REDUCED BY ITS DOUGH-OFFERING.[4]

MISHNAH 2. R. JOSE THE GALILEAN RULED: BULLOCKS[5] MUST BE NO MORE THAN TWO YEARS OLD, FOR IT IS SAID, AND THE SECOND[6] YOUNG BULLOCK SHALT THOU TAKE FOR A SIN-OFFERING.[7] BUT THE SAGES RULED: THEY MAY BE EVEN THREE YEARS OLD. R. MEIR RULED: EVEN THOSE THAT ARE FOUR OR FIVE YEARS OLD ARE VALID, BUT OLD ANIMALS ARE NOT BROUGHT[8] OUT OF RESPECT.[9]

MISHNAH 3. LAMBS[5] MUST BE NO MORE THAN ONE YEAR OLD, AND RAMS[5] NO MORE THAN TWO YEARS OLD; AND ALL THESE YEARS ARE RECKONED FROM DAY TO DAY.[10] ONE THAT IS THIRTEEN MONTHS OLD IS NOT VALID EITHER AS A RAM OR AS A LAMB. R. TARFON CALLED IT PALGAS;[11] BEN 'AZZAI CALLED IT NUḲAD;[12] R. ISHMAEL CALLED IT PARAKDIGMA.[13] IF A MAN OFFERED IT HE MUST BRING FOR IT THE DRINK-OFFERING OF A RAM,[14] BUT IT IS NOT COUNTED AS HIS OFFER-

(1) Since a se'ah contains six *ḳab*. (2) And, therefore, could wholly be eaten. Only a minimum of five quarters of a *ḳab* is liable to the dough-offering. (3) Being liable (cf. prev. n.) to the dough-offering, which must be given to the priest. (4) So that its size would be smaller than the other from which no dough-offering had been taken. (5) Prescribed as sacrifices. (6) '*Sheni*' (E.V. 'another') which is superfluous, is rendered as 'two year old'. (7) Num. VIII, 8. (8) As sacrifices. (9) For the sanctity of the altar. (10) *Sc.* from the day in one calendar year to the corresponding one in the next calendar year. (11) Composed of '*pelag*' and '*gas*', 'a half of a grown up'. *Aliter.* πάλλαξ lit., 'young person'. (12) Or *noḳed*. Lit., 'a distinct coin' (Jast.); *aliter: Noḳed*, the term used in Amos I, 1 to denote a herdsman of a special kind of sheep. (13) Or *prokadegma*. Var. lec. '*parakarigma*'. Cf. παραχάραγμα 'counterfeit coin'. (14) A third of a *hin*.

ING.[1] ONE THAT IS THIRTEEN MONTHS OLD AND A DAY IS REGARDED AS A RAM.

MISHNAH 4. THE SIN-OFFERINGS OF THE CONGREGATION[7] AND THEIR BURNT-OFFERINGS,[2] THE SIN-OFFERING OF AN INDIVIDUAL,[3] THE GUILT-OFFERING OF A NAZIRITE[4] AND THE GUILT-OFFERING OF A LEPER[5] ARE VALID FROM THE THIRTIETH DAY[6] ONWARDS, AND ALSO ON THE THIRTIETH DAY. IF, HOWEVER, THEY WERE OFFERED ON THE EIGHTH DAY[2] THEY ARE VALID. VOW-OFFERINGS AND FREEWILL-OFFERINGS, FIRSTLINGS AND THE TITHE OF CATTLE AND THE PASCHAL LAMB ARE VALID FROM THE EIGHTH DAY[2] ONWARDS, AND ALSO ON THE EIGHTH DAY.

(1) If he was under an obligation to bring either a ram or a he-lamb. (2) For new moons and festivals, for instance, which consist of lambs and young goats. (3) If it is a lamb or a goat. (4) Which is a ewe lamb (cf. Num. VI, 14). (5) A he-lamb (cf. Lev. XIV, 12). (6) Of their birth; v. ibid XXII, 27.

PARAH

CHAPTER II

MISHNAH 1. R. ELIEZER RULED: A [RED] COW FOR THE SIN-OFFERING[1] THAT IS WITH YOUNG[2] IS VALID,[3] BUT THE SAGES RULE THAT IT IS INVALID. R. ELIEZER RULED: IT[4] MAY NOT BE BOUGHT FROM IDOLATERS,[5] BUT THE SAGES RULE THAT SUCH A ONE IS VALID;[6] AND NOT ONLY THIS, BUT ALL OFFERINGS OF THE CONGREGATION OR THE INDIVIDUAL MAY BE BROUGHT FROM THE LAND OF ISRAEL AND FROM OUTSIDE THE LAND, FROM NEW PRODUCE AND FROM THE OLD; EXCEPT THE OMER[7] AND THE TWO LOAVES,[8] WHICH MAY BE BROUGHT ONLY FROM NEW PRODUCE AND FROM WITHIN THE LAND.

MISHNAH 2. IF THE HORNS OR THE HOOFS OF THE [RED] COW ARE BLACK THEY ARE CHOPPED OFF.[9] THE EYE BALL, THE TEETH AND THE TONGUE[10] CAUSE NO INVALIDITY IN THE [RED] COW.[11] ONE THAT IS DWARFLIKE IS VALID. IF THERE WAS ON IT A WEN AND THIS WAS CUT OFF, R. JUDAH RULES THAT IT IS INVALID.[12] R. SIMEON RULED: [ONLY] WHEREVER, IF REMOVED, NO RED HAIR GROWS IN ITS PLACE IS IT INVALID.

MISHNAH 3. ONE THAT IS BORN FROM THE SIDE,[13] THE

(1) A phrase whereby the red cow is designated. (2) Provided the covering was done without the owner's knowledge. (3) Though the carrying of any other burden renders it invalid. The embryo being regarded as a part of the mother's body does not come under the category of 'burden'. (4) The red cow. (5) Since they may have subjected it to improper use. (6) For reasons cf. Bert., L. and Elijah Wilna. (7) Cf. Lev. XXIII, 10ff. (8) Cf. Ibid. XXIII, 17. (9) And the red cow is then valid. (10) Though they are not red. (11) Where no other is available (Elijah Wilna). (12) As is the case with other sacrifices, v. Ibid. XXII, 22. (13) By means of the caesarean cut.

HIRE OF A HARLOT OR THE PRICE OF A DOG IS INVALID.[1] R. ELIEZER RULES THAT IT IS VALID, FOR IT IS WRITTEN, SHOU SHALT NOT BRING THE HIRE OF A HARLOT OR THE PRICE OF A DOG INTO THE HOUSE OF THE LORD THY GOD,[2] WHILE THIS[3] WAS NOT BROUGHT INTO THE HOUSE.[4] ALL BLEMISHES THAT CAUSE CONSECRATED ANIMALS TO BE INVALID[5] CAUSE ALSO THE [RED] COW TO BE INVALID. IF ONE HAD RIDDEN ON IT,[3] LEANED ON IT, HUNG ON ITS TAIL, CROSSED[6] A RIVER BY ITS HELP, DOUBLED ON ITS LEADING ROPE,[7] OR PUT ONE'S CLOAK ON IT, IT IS INVALID.[8] BUT IF ONE HAD ONLY FASTENED IT BY ITS LEADING ROPE OR MADE FOR IT A SANDAL TO PREVENT IT FROM SLIPPING OR SPREAD ONE'S CLOAK ON IT BECAUSE OF FLIES, IT REMAINS VALID. THIS IS THE GENERAL RULE: WHEREVER ANYTHING IS DONE FOR ITS OWN SAKE, IT REMAINS VALID; BUT IF FOR THE SAKE OF ANY OTHER,[9] IT BECOMES INVALID.

MISHNAH 4. IF A BIRD RESTED ON IT, IT REMAINS VALID. IF A MALE BEAST MOUNTED IT, IT BECOMES INVALID.[10] R. JUDAH RULED: IF THE MALE WAS MADE TO MOUNT, IT BECOMES INVALID; BUT IF IT DID SO OF ITSELF, IT REMAINS VALID.

MISHNAH 5. IF IT[3] HAD TWO BLACK OR WHITE HAIRS GROWING WITHIN ONE FOLLICLE,[11] IT IS INVALID. R. JUDAH SAID, 'WITHIN[12] ONE KOS'.[13] IF THEY GREW WITHIN TWO FOLLICLES THAT WERE ADJACENT TO[14] ONE ANOTHER, IT IS

(1) As a red cow, as it is invalid for any other sacrifice. (2) Deut. XXIII, 19' emphasis on *'house'*. (3) The red cow. (4) *'The house of the Lord'*. (5) As sacrifices. (6) *Aliter:* Hung ... tail and crossed. (7) Placing it on its back. (8) In accordance with Num. XIX, 2, *and upon which never came yoke*. (9) Though it was for its own sake also. (10) Because the latter is supposed to be with the approval of the owner. (11) *'Guma'* (v. next note but one). (12) 'Even', in cur. edd. is to be deleted (Bert.). (13) 'Follicle', *kos* in this context having the same meaning as *'guma'* (follicle) used by the first Tanna (cf. prev. n. but one). The difference between R. Judah and the first Tanna lies only in the Hebrew and Aramaic terms they respectively use. (14) *Aliter:* opposite.

INVALID. R. AKIBA RULED: EVEN IF THERE WERE FOUR OR EVEN FIVE BUT THEY WERE DISPERSED, THEY MAY BE PLUCKED OUT.[1] R. ELIEZER RULED: EVEN AS MANY AS FIFTY.[2] R. JOSHUA B. BATHYRA RULED: EVEN IF IT HAD BUT ONE ON ITS HEAD AND ONE ON ITS TAIL, IT IS INVALID. IF IT HAD TWO HAIRS[3] WITH THEIR ROOTS BLACK AND THEIR TIPS RED OR WITH THEIR ROOTS RED AND THEIR TIPS BLACK, ALL IS DETERMINED BY WHAT IS VISIBLE;[4] SO R. MEIR. BUT THE SAGES RULED: BY THE ROOT.[5]

(1) And the cow is valid even before they were plucked, the plucking being done only for appearance sake. (2) Or even any larger number may be plucked (cf. prev. n.). (3) In one follicle. (4) *Sc.* the tips. If they were red the cow is valid; if they were black it is invalid. (5) Cf. prev. n. *mut. mut.*

PARAH

CHAPTER III

MISHNAH 1. SEVEN DAYS BEFORE THE BURNING OF THE [RED] COW THE PRIEST WHO WAS TO BURN THE COW WAS REMOVED FROM HIS HOUSE TO A CHAMBER THAT WAS FACING THE NORTH-EASTERN CORNER OF THE BIRAH;[1] AND WHICH WAS CALLED THE STONE CHAMBER.[2] THROUGHOUT THE SEVEN DAYS[3] HE WAS SPRINKLED UPON[4] WITH [A MIXTURE[5] OF] ALL THE SIN-OFFERINGS THAT WERE THERE.[6] R. JOSE STATED: HE WAS SPRINKLED UPON ON THE THIRD AND THE SEVENTH DAYS ONLY. R. ḤANINA THE VICE-HIGH PRIEST STATED: ON THE PRIEST THAT WAS TO BURN THE COW THEY SPRINKLED ALL THE SEVEN DAYS, BUT ON THE ONE THAT WAS TO PERFORM THE SERVICE ON THE DAY OF ATONEMENT THEY SPRINKLED ON THE THIRD AND THE SEVENTH DAYS ONLY.

MISHNAH 2. COURTYARDS WERE BUILT IN JERUSALEM OVER A ROCK,[7] AND BENEATH THEM WAS A HOLLOW WHICH SERVED AS A PROTECTION AGAINST A GRAVE IN THE DEPTHS,[8] AND THEY USED TO BRING THERE PREGNANT WOMEN, AND THERE THEY GAVE BIRTH TO THEIR CHILDREN AND THERE

(1) The Temple (cf. I Chron. XXIX, 1). *Aliter:* The name of a place on the Temple mount (cf. Yoma 2*a*). (2) So named because all services in connection with the red cow had to be performed only in vessels made either of baked ordure or of earthenware or of any material which, like stone, is insusceptible to uncleanness (cf. Yoma 2*a*). (3) Except the fourth. (4) As a precaution against the possibility of having contracted corpse uncleanness. (5) So Elijah Wilna. (6) From the days of Moses, when the first red cow was prepared, to date. (7) That was primordial. (8) *Sc.* the possibility of the existence of an unknown grave under the rock, טומאת התהום. Unless there is a minimum space of a cubic handbreadth above it the uncleanness of the grave penetrates through the rock and beyond it; v. Suk. 21*a*.

THEY REARED THEM.[1] AND[2] THEY BROUGHT OXEN, UPON WHOSE BACKS WERE PLACED DOORS,[3] AND THE CHILDREN SAT UPON THEM WITH STONE CUPS[4] IN THEIR HANDS. WHEN THEY REACHED SILOAM[5] THEY ALIGHTED AND FILLED THE CUPS WITH WATER[6] AND THEN THEY ASCENDED AND SAT AGAIN ON THE DOORS.[3] R. JOSE SAID: EACH CHILD USED TO LET DOWN HIS CUP[7] AND FILL IT FROM HIS PLACE.[8]

MISHNAH 3. HAVING ARRIVED[9] AT THE TEMPLE MOUNT THEY ALIGHTED. BENEATH THE TEMPLE MOUNT AND THE COURTS[10] WAS A HOLLOW WHICH SERVED AS A PROTECTION AGAINST A GRAVE IN THE DEPTHS,[11] WHILE AT THE ENTRANCE OF THE COURT[12] THE JAR OF THE ASHES OF THE SIN-OFFERINGS[13] WAS PROVIDED. A MALE FROM AMONG THE SHEEP WAS BROUGHT AND A ROPE WAS TIED BETWEEN ITS HORNS, AND A STICK OR[14] A BUSHY TWIG WAS TIED AT THE OTHER END OF THE ROPE, AND THIS[15] WAS THROWN INTO THE JAR.[16] THE MALE [SHEEP] WAS THEN STRUCK SO THAT IT STARTED BACKWARDS[17] WHEN [A CHILD] TOOK THE ASHES AND MIXED[18] AS MUCH OF IT AS COULD BE VISIBLE ON THE WATER. R. JOSE SAID: DO NOT GIVE THE HERETICS[19] AN OPPORTUNITY TO

(1) For the service of the red cow. (2) When the water for the red cow had to be brought from Siloam. (3) Which prevented any uncleanness below from penetrating to the children. (4) Which are not susceptible to uncleanness. (5) Heb. *ha-Shilloah*, the conduit near Jerusalem the completion of which is recorded on the famous Siloam inscription. (6) In order to use them for sprinkling on the priest who was to burn the red cow. (7) Without leaving his place on the door. (8) As a precaution against the uncleanness of a possible grave in the depth near Siloam. (9) On their return journey. (10) Of the Temple. (11) Cf. *supra* p. 309, n. 8. And therefore they could safely alight. (12) Of the women, on a particular spot between it and the Rampart. (13) In which were preserved ashes of all previously burnt red cows. (14) Var. lec. 'and'. (15) The stick or the twig. (16) It is not permitted to put it there directly since the man who did it, if he were suffering from the uncleanness of a flux or the like, would, by *hesseṭ*, (v. Glos.), have conveyed uncleanness to the ashes. (17) And, as a result of his sudden movement, spilled the ashes collected on the stick. (18) With water. Lit., 'sanctified'. (19) Or 'Sadducees'.

CAVIL;[1] BUT [A CHILD] HIMSELF TOOK IT[2] AND MIXED IT.[3]

MISHNAH 4. ONE MAY NOT BRING A SIN-OFFERING[4] BY VIRTUE OF [THE PURIFICATIONS MADE FOR] ANOTHER SIN-OFFERING,[5] NOR ONE CHILD[6] BY VIRTUE OF [THE PREPARATIONS MADE FOR] ANOTHER.[7] THE CHILDREN, FURTHERMORE, HAD TO BE SPRINKLED;[8] SO R. JOSE THE GALILEAN. R. AKIBA STATED: THEY HAD NO NEED TO BE SPRINKLED.[9]

MISHNAH 5. IF THEY DID NOT FIND THE RESIDUE OF THE ASHES OF THE SEVEN [RED COWS][10] THEY PERFORMED THE SPRINKLING WITH THOSE OF SIX, OF FIVE, OF FOUR, OF THREE, OF TWO OR OF ONE. AND WHO PREPARED THESE?[11] MOSES PREPARED THE FIRST, EZRA PREPARED THE SECOND, AND FIVE WERE PREPARED SINCE EZRA; SO R. MEIR. BUT THE

(1) Or 'mock', at such excessive care and precaution. (2) The ashes from the jar. (3) With water. Lit., 'sanctified'. (4) *Sc.* a red cow for which the necessary preparations in regard to cleanness have not been made. (5) Which died or became invalid after all the necessary preparations for it have been completed. (6) Even if he was kept in conditions of cleanness. (7) Who died or became unclean after he has been duly prepared for a particular red cow for which the first mentioned child (cf. prev. n.) was not specifically prepared. It was necessary that the preparations be made solely and specifically for each particular red heifer and that a particular child also be specifically assigned for it. (8) With the ashes of the red cow, in case any of them had become unclean through a dead creeping thing. They themselves performed the sprinkling upon one another since no one could possibly be cleaner than they. Bert. on the basis of the Tosef. explains that this complicated procedure was adopted by the exiles on their return from Babylon when they were *all* unclean as a result of corpse-uncleanness and had no other means of becoming clean, save through the medium of children and the ashes of the red cows of former generations that had been left in safe keeping when they went to exile. R. Jose states that there were still among them a few individuals who had kept themselves free from corpse-uncleanness all the time and they could have made the necessary preparations. (9) They only required immersion as a precaution against the possibility of having become unclean through contact with a dead creeping thing. (10) That had been burnt since the days of Moses to that day. The sprinkling had to be done with a compound of the ashes of all the seven cows (cf. *supra* III, 1 and nn). (11) Seven cows.

SAGES STATED: SEVEN WERE PREPARED SINCE THE DAYS OF EZRA. AND WHO PREPARED THEM? SIMEON THE JUST AND JOḤANAN THE HIGH PRIEST PREPARED TWO EACH,[1] AND ELIEHOENAI THE SON OF HA-ḲOF AND ḤANAMEL THE EGYPTIAN AND ISHMAEL THE SON OF PIABI PREPARED ONE EACH.

MISHNAH 6. A CAUSEWAY WAS MADE FROM THE TEMPLE MOUNT TO THE MOUNT OF OLIVES, BEING CONSTRUCTED OF ARCHES ABOVE ARCHES, EACH ARCH PLACED DIRECTLY ABOVE EACH PIER [OF THE ARCH BELOW] AS A PROTECTION[2] AGAINST A GRAVE IN THE DEPTHS,[3] WHEREBY THE PRIEST WHO WAS TO BURN THE COW, THE COW ITSELF AND ALL WHO AIDED IN ITS PREPARATION WENT FORTH TO THE MOUNT OF OLIVES.

MISHNAH 7. IF THE COW REFUSED TO GO OUT, THEY MAY NOT TAKE OUT WITH IT A BLACK ONE LEST IT BE SAID, 'A BLACK [COW] HAS BEEN SLAIN'; NOR ANOTHER RED [COW] LEST IT BE SAID, 'TWO HAVE BEEN SLAIN'. R. JOSE STATED: IT WAS NOT FOR THIS REASON, BUT BECAUSE IT IS SAID IN SCRIPTURE, AND HE SHALL BRING HER FORTH,[4] BY HERSELF.[5] THE ELDERS OF ISRAEL USED TO PRECEDE THEM ON FOOT TO THE MOUNT OF OLIVES, WHERE THERE WAS A PLACE OF IMMERSION.[6] THE PRIEST THAT WAS TO BURN THE COW WAS [DELIBERATELY] MADE UNCLEAN ON ACCOUNT OF THE SADDUCEES: IN ORDER THAT THEY SHOULD NOT SAY,[7] 'ONLY BY THOSE ON WHOM THE SUN HAS SET[8] MUST IT BE PREPARED'.

(1) R. Meir disregards one cow of each pair since owing to invalidity it was entirely superseded by the other. (2) For those who crossed the causeway. (3) Whose corpse uncleanness would otherwise have penetrated (cf. *supra* p. 309, n. 8). (4) Num. XIX, 3, emphasis on '*her*'. (5) The practical difference between the first Tanna and R. Jose is the permissibility of taking out with it any other animal or beast. According to R. Jose even this is not permitted. (6) Also built, like the causeway, over a hollow as a protection against a corpse uncleanness in the depths. (7) Var. lec., 'because they used to say'. (8) *Sc*. those only who are in all respects clean.

MISHNAH 8. THEY LAID THEIR HANDS UPON HIM[1] AND SAID,[2] 'MY LORD THE HIGH PRIEST,[3] PERFORM IMMERSION ONCE'. HE THEREUPON WENT DOWN AND IMMERSED HIMSELF AND CAME UP AND DRIED HIMSELF. DIFFERENT KINDS OF WOOD WERE SET IN ORDER THERE: CEDAR WOOD, PINE, SPRUCE AND THE WOOD OF SMOOTH FIG TREES.[4] [THE PILE] WAS BUILT UP IN THE SHAPE OF A TOWER FURNISHED WITH AIR HOLES;[5] AND ITS FORESIDE[6] WAS TURNED TOWARDS THE WEST.[7]

MISHNAH 9. IT[8] WAS BOUND WITH A ROPE OF BAST[9] AND PLACED ON THE PILE WITH ITS HEAD TOWARDS THE SOUTH AND ITS FACE TOWARDS THE WEST.[7] THE PRIEST STOOD IN THE EAST WITH HIS FACE TOWARDS THE WEST. HE SLAUGHTERED WITH HIS RIGHT HAND AND RECEIVED THE BLOOD WITH HIS LEFT. R. JUDAH SAID: HE RECEIVED THE BLOOD WITH HIS RIGHT HAND, PUT IT ON HIS LEFT HAND AND THEN SPRINKLED WITH HIS RIGHT. SEVEN TIMES HE DIPPED HIS FINGER IN THE BLOOD AND SPRINKLED IT TOWARDS THE HOLY OF HOLIES, DIPPING ONCE AGAIN FOR EACH SPRINKLING. HAVING FINISHED THE SPRINKLING HE WIPED HIS HAND ON THE BODY OF THE COW, CAME DOWN AND KINDLED THE FIRE WITH CHIPS. R. AKIBA SAID: WITH DRY BRANCHES OF PALM-TREES.

MISHNAH 10. WHEN IT[8] BURST[10] HE TOOK UP A POSITION OUTSIDE ITS PIT[11] AND TAKING HOLD OF CEDARWOOD, HYSSOP AND SCARLET WOOL, HE SAID TO THE BYSTANDERS, 'IS THIS CEDARWOOD? IS THIS CEDARWOOD?' 'IS THIS HYSSOP? IS THIS HYSSOP' 'IS THIS SCARLET WOOL? IS THIS SCARLET

(1) The priest who was to burn the cow. (2) If he happened to be a High Priest. (3) V. *infra* IV, 1. (4) All these kinds of wood produce suitable ashes. (5) Lit., 'and they opened windows in it'. (6) The largest opening into which the fire was put. (7) Where was the Holy of Holies. (8) The red cow. (9) Which is insusceptible to uncleanness. (10) From the heat. (11) In which it was being burnt.

WOOL?' THREE TIMES HE REPEATED EACH QUESTION AND THEY ANSWERED HIM 'YEA, YEA!' — THREE TIMES TO EACH QUESTION.

MISHNAH II. HE THEN WRAPPED THEM[1] TOGETHER WITH THE ENDS OF THE STRIP OF WOOL[2] AND CAST THEM INTO THE BURNING HEAP. WHEN IT WAS BURNT UP IT WAS BEATEN WITH RODS AND THEN[3] SIFTED WITH SIEVES. R. ISHMAEL STATED: THIS WAS DONE WITH STONE HAMMERS[4] AND STONEWARE SIEVES.[4] A BLACK CINDER ON WHICH THERE WERE SOME ASHES WAS CRUSHED BUT ONE ON WHICH THERE WERE NONE WAS LEFT BEHIND. A BONE WAS CRUSHED IN EITHER CASE. IT[5] WAS THEN DIVIDED INTO THREE PARTS: ONE PART WAS DEPOSITED ON THE RAMPART, ONE ON THE MOUNT OF OLIVES, AND ONE WAS DIVIDED AMONG THE COURSES.[6]

(1) The cedarwood and the hyssop. (2) Which, being longer than the cedarwood and the hyssop, projected downwards. (3) When it has been pounded to dust. (4) Which are insusceptible to uncleanness. (5) The ashes of the red cow. (6) The twenty-four courses of the priests that took the Temple services in turn, v. Glos. s. v. *Mishmar*.

PARAH

CHAPTER IV

MISHNAH 1. IF A COW FOR THE SIN-OFFERING WAS SLAIN UNDER SOME OTHER NAME, OR IF ITS BLOOD WAS RECEIVED OR SPRINKLED UNDER SOME OTHER NAME, OR IF THIS[1] WAS DONE UNDER ITS OWN NAME AND UNDER SOME OTHER NAME, OR UNDER SOME OTHER NAME AND UNDER ITS NAME, IT IS INVALID.[2] R. ELIEZER RULES THAT IT IS VALID.[3] IF THE SERVICE[1] WAS PERFORMED BY ONE WHOSE HANDS OR FEET WERE UNWASHED,[4] IT IS INVALID; BUT R. ELIEZER RULES THAT IT IS VALID.[3] IF IT[1] WAS PERFORMED BY ONE WHO WAS NOT THE HIGH PRIEST, IT IS INVALID; BUT R. JUDAH RULES THAT IT IS VALID. IF IT WAS PERFORMED BY ONE WHO WAS NOT WEARING ALL THE PRESCRIBED GARMENTS,[5] IT IS INVALID; AND IT WAS IN WHITE GARMENTS[5] THAT IT WAS TO BE PREPARED.

MISHNAH 2. IF IT WAS BURNT OUTSIDE ITS PIT,[6] OR IN TWO PITS,[7] OR IF TWO COWS WERE BURNT IN THE SAME PIT, IT IS INVALID. IF [THE BLOOD] WAS SPRINKLED BUT NOT EXACTLY IN THE DIRECTION OF THE ENTRANCE OF THE HOLY OF HOLIES, IT IS INVALID. IF HE MADE THE SEVENTH SPRINKLING OUT OF THE SIXTH[8] AND THEN SPRINKLED

(1) The slaying, receiving or sprinkling. (2) Since Scripture described it as a '*sin-offering*' the services mentioned must in their entirety be performed under that name alone; v. Zeb. 2*a*. (3) Because, unlike other sin-offerings, the services mentioned were performed outside the Temple precincts. (4) V. Ex. XXX, 19, 20. (5) Worn by the officiating priest. (6) The cavity on the Mount of Olives opposite the Holy of Holies in which the red cows were burnt. (7) A portion in each. (8) *Sc.* having dipped his finger for the sixth sprinkling he used the same blood for both the sixth and the seventh sprinklings. *Aliter:* 'Sprinkled the seventh instead of the sixth', having made a mistake in the counting.

AGAIN A SEVENTH TIME, IT IS INVALID. IF HE SPRINKLED AN EIGHTH TIME OUT OF THE SEVENTH[1] AND THEN SPRINKLED AGAIN AN EIGHTH TIME, IT IS VALID.[2]

MISHNAH 3. IF IT WAS BURNT UP WITHOUT WOOD,[3] OR WITH ANY KIND OF WOOD,[4] AND EVEN IF ONLY WITH STRAW OR STUBBLE, IT IS VALID. IF IT WAS FLAYED AND CUT UP, IT IS VALID. IF IT WAS SLAIN WITH THE INTENTION OF EATING ITS FLESH OR DRINKING ITS BLOOD, IT IS VALID. R. ELIEZER RULED: NO [UNLAWFUL] INTENTION[5] CAUSES INVALIDITY IN THE RED COW.

MISHNAH 4. ALL WHO ARE ENGAGED IN THE PREPARATION OF THE [RED] COW, FROM THE BEGINNING UNTIL THE END, RENDER THEIR GARMENTS[6] UNCLEAN, AND THEY ALSO RENDER IT[7] INVALID BY [OTHER] WORK.[8] IF SOME INVALIDITY OCCURRED WHILE IT WAS BEING SLAIN, IT CONVEYS NO UNCLEANNESS TO GARMENTS. IF IT OCCURRED WHILE THE BLOOD WAS BEING SPRINKLED, FOR ALL WHO WERE ATTENDING TO IT BEFORE THE INVALIDITY OCCURRED, IT RENDERS GARMENTS UNCLEAN, BUT FOR THOSE WHO ATTENDED TO IT AFTER IT HAD BECOME INVALID IT DOES NOT RENDER GARMENTS UNCLEAN. THUS IT FOLLOWS THAT THE RESTRICTION[9] TURNS INTO A RELAXATION.[10] THE LAW OF SACRILEGE[11] APPLIES TO IT THROUGHOUT.[12] WOOD MAY BE ADDED TO THE FIRE.[12] ITS SERVICES[13] MUST BE PERFORMED BY DAY

(1) Cf. p. 315, n. 8 *mut. mut.* (2) The one additional sprinkling cannot invalidate the heifer after the seven prescribed sprinklings have been duly performed. (3) The fire having been set to the body of the cow itself. (4) Other than those prescribed *supra* III, 8. (5) However wrong the act intended. (6) Or any utensils with which they may come in contact. (7) The red cow. (8) Done during the time one was engaged in the preparation of the red cow. (9) Invalidity of the cow where one is engaged in other work. (10) Exemption of the man's clothes from uncleanness. (11) *Me'ilah* (v. Glos.), cf. Lev. V, 15f. (12) Until it is burnt into ashes. (13) With the exception of the collection of the ashes, the filling of the jar with water and the mixing of the water and ashes which may also be done by night and by a non-priest.

AND BY A PRIEST.[1] WORK[2] RENDERS IT INVALID UNTIL IT BECOMES ASHES, AND WORK[2] CAUSES THE WATER TO BE INVALID UNTIL THE ASHES ARE PUT INTO IT.

(1) V Yoma, 42*a*. (2) Other than that connected with the service of the cow.

PARAH

CHAPTER V

MISHNAH 1. HE WHO BRINGS THE EARTHEN VESSEL FOR THE SIN-OFFERING[1] MUST PERFORM IMMERSION,[2] AND SPEND THE NIGHT[3] BY THE FURNACE.[4] R. JUDAH RULED: HE MAY ALSO BRING IT FROM THE HOUSE[5] AND IT IS VALID,[6] FOR ALL ARE DEEMED TRUSTWORTHY IN REGARD TO THE SIN-OFFERING.[7] IN THE CASE OF TERUMAH[8] ONE MAY OPEN THE FURNACE[9] AND TAKE OUT [THE VESSEL]. R. SIMEON RULED: FROM THE SECOND ROW.[10] R. JOSE RULED: FROM THE THIRD ROW.[11]

MISHNAH 2. IF A MAN IMMERSED A VESSEL FOR THE SIN-OFFERING[12] IN WATER THAT IS NOT FIT FOR THE MIXING[13] HE MUST DRY IT;[14] IF IN WATER THAT IS FIT FOR THE MIXING

(1) In which the ashes are mixed with water for the sprinkling. (2) Cleansing himself thereby from any possible uncleanness. (3) That follows the immersion. (4) Where the earthen vessels are burnt. As vessels become susceptible to uncleanness only after their manufacture has been completed by being burnt in the furnace, he has to stand by all the time so that no unclean person may open the furnace to see whether the vessel is done, and render it unclean by contact. (5) Of the potter. (6) Even if the potter is an *'am-ha-arez* who is usually careless in matters of uncleanness. (7) This was a special provision intended to prevent the *'am ha-arez* class from preparing separate red cows for themselves. (8) *Sc.* if a vessel is required for foodstuffs of *terumah*. (9) At any time, even though no watch was kept after the vessels have been duly burnt and became susceptible to uncleanness. (10) May a vessel be taken for the purposes mentioned. It may not be taken from the first row where the *'am ha-arez* may possibly, by opening first the furnace, have caused it to shake and thus rendered it unclean. (11) Cf. prev. n. *mut. mut.* (12) *Sc.* to draw the water with it or to mix in it the ashes with the water. (13) Cf. prev. n. Only living or running water may be used. (14) After the immersion, before he fills it with suitable water.

HE NEED NOT DRY IT;[1] BUT IF [HE INTENDED][2] TO COLLECT IN IT[3] WATER THAT WAS ALREADY MIXED WITH THE ASHES, HE MUST DRY IT IN EITHER CASE.[4]

MISHNAH 3. IF A PUMPKIN SHELL[5] WAS IMMERSED[6] IN WATER THAT WAS NOT FIT FOR THE MIXTURE,[7] IT IS PERMISSIBLE[8] TO MIX IN IT THE ASHES WITH THE WATER,[9] PROVIDED IT HAD NEVER BEFORE CONTRACTED UNCLEANNESS. IF IT HAS CONTRACTED AN UNCLEANNESS, IT IS NOT PERMISSIBLE[10] TO MIX IN IT THE ASHES WITH THE WATER.[11] R. JOSHUA ARGUED: IF ONE IS ALLOWED TO MIX IN IT THE ASHES AND WATER AT THE BEGINNING,[12] ONE SHOULD ALSO[13] BE ALLOWED TO DO SO AT THE END;[14] AND IF ONE IS NOT ALLOWED[15] TO DO THIS AT THE END[14] ONE SHOULD NOT BE ALLOWED[15] TO DO IT AT THE BEGINNING.[12] IN[16] EITHER CASE[17] IT IS NOT PERMISSIBLE TO COLLECT IN IT[3] WATER THAT WAS ALREADY PREPARED.[18]

(1) Though they get mixed up with the water that he deliberately puts in subsequently for mixing it with the ashes. As he must have known in the course of the immersion that some of the water would cling to the vessel, this water may be regarded as having been put in deliberately. (2) When immersing it. (3) Var. lec. 'to add to it'. (4) *Sc.* irrespective of whether the immersion took place in water that was, cr water that was not fit for the mixing; for even in the former case the water would render invalid the water that was already mixed with the ashes (v. *infra* VI, 2.) (5) That was clean and used for drawing water. (6) As an extra precaution (cf. prev. n.). (7) Of the ashes of the red cow with the water; var. lec. 'that was fit for the mixture'. (8) After it had been dried. (9) The possibility of its giving out some of the unfit water which it had previously absorbed is disregarded owing to the insignificance of its quantity which is neutralised in the fit water. (10) Even after immersion. (11) Since the smallest drop that it might give out would convey uncleanness to all its contents. (12) *Sc.* before it contracted uncleanness. (13) Since the re-issue of absorbed liquid is disregarded. (14) After uncleanness had been contracted. (15) On account of the possible re-issue of some absorbed liquid. (16) This is a continuation of the ruling of the first Tanna. (17) Whether the pumpkin-shell had contracted uncleanness before or not. (18) Lit., 'Sanctified'. *Sc.* in which the ashes of the red cow have been mixed with the water.

MISHNAH 4. A REED PIPE THAT WAS CUT[1] [FOR USE AS A CONTAINER] FOR [THE WATER OR ASHES OF] THE SIN-OFFERING, R. ELIEZER RULED, MUST[2] BE IMMERSED FORTHWITH.[3] R. JOSHUA RULED: IT MUST FIRST BE RENDERED UNCLEAN AND THEN IT IS IMMERSED.[4] ALL ARE ELIGIBLE TO PREPARE THE MIXTURE,[5] EXCEPT A DEAF MUTE, AN IMBECILE AND A MINOR. R. JUDAH HOLDS A MINOR TO BE ELIGIBLE, BUT DISQUALIFIES A WOMAN AND A HERMAPHRODITE.

MISHNAH 5. THE MIXTURE[5] MAY BE PREPARED IN ALL KINDS OF VESSELS, EVEN IN VESSELS MADE OF CATTLE DUNG, OF STONE OR OF EARTH.[6] THE MIXTURE[5] MAY ALSO BE PREPARED IN A SHIP.[7] IT MAY NOT BE PREPARED IN THE SIDES OF VESSELS,[8] OR IN THE FLANKS OF A LADLING JAR, OR IN THE BUNG OF A JAR, OR IN ONE'S CUPPED HANDS, FOR THE WATER OF THE SIN-OFFERING MAY BE DRAWN IN, MIXED IN, AND SPRINKLED FROM A VESSEL ONLY. PROTECTION[9] BY A TIGHTLY FITTING COVER[10] CAN BE AFFORDED ONLY BY VESSELS, AS PROTECTION AGAINST AN UNCLEANNESS WITHIN AN EARTHEN VESSEL CAN BE AFFORDED ONLY BY VESSELS.[11]

MISHNAH 6. THE POTTERS' EGG[12] IS FIT [AS A VESSEL].[13] R. JOSE HOLDS THAT IT IS UNFIT. A HEN'S EGG, R. MEIR AND R. JUDAH RULE, IS FIT [AS A VESSEL]; BUT THE SAGES RULE THAT IT IS UNFIT.

(1) Directly from the ground where, as a growing plant, it was not susceptible to uncleanness. (2) Though clean. (3) And used before sunset (v. foll. n.). (4) As a demonstration against the Sadducees (cf. *supra* III, 7). According to R. Eliezer the use before sunset (cf. prev. n.) is alone a sufficient demonstration. (5) Of the ashes and water of the sin-offering. (6) *Sc.* unbaked clay. (7) Though it is not regarded as a 'vessel' in respect of susceptibility to uncleanness. (8) That were broken. (9) Against uncleanness under the same roof beneath which lay a corpse. (10) For the contents under it. Cf. Kelim X, 1. (11) Cf. Kel. VIII, 3. (12) An egg-shaped lump of clay with a cavity in it from which the pot is formed. (13) For the mixing of the ashes of the sin-offering with the water.

MISHNAH 7. IN A TROUGH THAT IS [HEWN] IN A ROCK[1] IT IS NOT PERMISSIBLE TO COLLECT THE WATER,[2] OR TO PREPARE THE MIXTURE,[3] NOR MAY THE SPRINKLING BE DONE FROM IT. IT, FURTHERMORE, NEEDS NO TIGHTLY FITTING COVER,[4] AND IT DOES NOT RENDER A RITUAL BATH[5] INVALID.[6] IF IT WAS FIRST A MOVABLE VESSEL AND IT WAS SUBSEQUENTLY JOINED TO THE GROUND WITH LIME, IT IS PERMISSIBLE TO COLLECT THE WATER[2] IN IT, TO PREPARE THE MIXTURE IN IT AND TO SPRINKLE FROM IT. IT ALSO NEEDS A TIGHTLY FITTING COVER[7] AND RENDERS A RITUAL BATH INVALID.[8] IF THERE WAS A HOLE IN IT[9] BELOW, AND IT WAS STOPPED UP WITH A RAG, THE WATER IN IT IS INVALID,[10] SINCE[11] IT IS NOT WHOLLY ENCLOSED BY THE VESSEL. IF THE HOLE WAS IN THE SIDE[12] AND IT WAS STOPPED UP WITH A RAG, THE WATER IN IT IS VALID, SINCE IT IS WHOLLY ENCLOSED BY THE VESSEL. IF THE VESSEL WAS PROVIDED WITH A BRIM OF CLAY AND THE WATER HAD RISEN TO THAT SPOT, IT[13] IS INVALID; BUT IF IT[14] WAS FIRM ENOUGH FOR THE VESSEL TO BE MOVED WITH IT,[15] THE WATER REMAINS VALID.

MISHNAH 8. IF THERE WERE TWO TROUGHS IN ONE STONE[16] AND THE MIXTURE[17] WAS PREPARED IN ONE OF THEM, THE WATER IN THE OTHER IS NOT PREPARED THEREBY.[18] IF

(1) Which was fixed to the ground. (2) For mixing it with the ashes of the red cow. (3) Because it is not considered a 'vessel'. (4) To afford protection to its contents under a roof over itself and a corpse. Having the same status as a pit or ditch any cover on it affords the same protection, v. Oh. V. 6. (5) That contained less water than the prescribed minimum. (6) If rain water that collected in it flowed into the bath. As the trough is an immovable fixture the water in it is not regarded as 'drawn water' which renders a ritual bath invalid. (7) If it is to protect its contents under a roof overshadowing it and a corpse. (8) Cf. *supra* n. 6 *mut. mut.* (9) A vessel that was fit for the preparation of the mixture of the water and ashes. (10) For mixing it with ashes of the red cow. (11) Owing to the interposition of the rag. (12) Of the vessel. (13) The water that reached the brim. (14) The brim. (15) When grasping the brim only. (16) That was movable. (17) Of the ashes of the red cow and the water. (18) And may not, therefore, be used for sprinkling.

A HOLE OF THE SIZE OF THE SPOUT OF A WATER SKIN[1] WAS PASSING FROM ONE TO THE OTHER, OR IF THE WATER OVERFLOWED BOTH,[2] EVEN IF ONLY [TO A DEPTH OF] THE THICKNESS OF GARLIC PEEL, AND THE MIXTURE[3] WAS PREPARED IN ONE OF THEM, THE WATER IN THE OTHER IS ALSO PREPARED THEREBY.[4]

MISHNAH 9. IF TWO STONES WERE PLACED CLOSE TO ONE ANOTHER AND MADE INTO A TROUGH,[5] AND SO ALSO IN THE CASE OF TWO KNEADING TROUGHS,[6] AND SO ALSO IN THE CASE OF A TROUGH THAT WAS SPLIT,[7] THE WATER BETWEEN THEM[8] IS NOT DEEMED TO BE PREPARED.[9] IF THEY WERE JOINED TOGETHER WITH LIME OR GYPSUM AND THEY CAN BE MOVED TOGETHER, THE WATER BETWEEN THEM[8] IS DEEMED TO HAVE BEEN DULY PREPARED.

(1) *Sc.* one in which the two fingers nearest the thumb can be easily turned. (2) The separating partition between them being lower than the other sides. (3) V. p. 321, n. 17. (4) Provided that the quantity of the ashes put in was sufficient to be visible in both. (5) Some gap remaining between the two stones. (6) That were placed close together to form one large receptacle leaving some gap between them. (7) Thus leaving some gap between the two halves. (8) In the gaps (cf. prev. three nn.). (9) Even where the main body of the water was duly mixed with the ashes of the red cow.

PARAHH

CHAPTER VI

MISHNAH 1. IF A MAN WAS ABOUT TO MIX THE ASHES WITH THE WATER[1] AND THE ASHES[2] FELL UPON HIS HAND OR UPON THE SIDE OF THE TROUGH[3] AND THEN FELL INTO THE TROUGH, THE MIXTURE IS INVALID.[4] IF THEY[5] FELL[6] FROM THE TUBE[7] INTO THE TROUGH, THE MIXTURE IS INVALID. IF HE TOOK THE ASHES FROM THE TUBE[7] AND THEN[8] COVERED IT,[9] OR SHUT A DOOR,[10] THE ASHES[2] REMAIN VALID BUT THE WATER BECOMES INVALID.[11] IF[8] HE PUT IT[9] UP ERECT ON THE GROUND,[12] THE WATER BECOMES INVALID;[13] IF IN HIS HAND, THE WATER IS VALID, SINCE[14] IT IS POSSIBLE PROPERLY[15] TO DO SO.[16]

MISHNAH 2. IF THE ASHES[2] FLOATED ON THE WATER, R. MEIR AND R. SIMEON RULED: ONE MAY TAKE SOME OF THEM[17] AND USE THEM IN ANOTHER PREPARATION; BUT THE SAGES RULED: WITH ANY ASHES THAT HAVE TOUCHED WATER NO OTHER MIXTURE MAY BE PREPARED. IF THE WATER[18] WAS

(1) Lit., 'sanctifying', mixing the ashes of the red cow with suitable water in a trough. (2) Lit., 'sanctification'. (3) That contained the water. (4) Since the ashes must be *put* direct (cf. Num. XIX, 17) into the vessel. They must not fall into it of their own accord. (5) The ashes. (6) Of their own accord. (7) In which they are kept. (8) Before putting the ashes into the water. (9) The tube. (10) Thus doing other 'work' while engaged in the preparation of the mixture. (11) As *supra* IV, 4 *ad fin.* (12) So as to prevent the ashes in the tube from spilling. (13) The act distracting his mind from the preparation of the mixture. (14) Being a very simple act. (15) Without distracting one's mind from the preparation of the mixture. (16) Hence it is not regarded as work. Var. lec. 'since it is impossible (to do otherwise)', if one is to prevent the ashes in the tube from spilling without covering it. (17) Of the floating ashes. (18) Of a mixture.

EMPTIED OUT AND SOME ASHES[1] WERE FOUND AT THE BOTTOM, R. MEIR AND R. SIMEON RULED: ONE MAY DRY THEM AND THEN USE THEM FOR ANOTHER PREPARATION; BUT THE SAGES RULED: WITH ANY ASHES THAT HAVE TOUCHED WATER NO OTHER MIXTURE MAY BE PREPARED.

MISHNAH 3. IF THE MIXTURE WAS PREPARED IN A TROUGH[2] WHILE A EWER WAS WITHIN IT, HOWEVER NARROW ITS NECK,[3] THE WATER IN THE LATTER IS DEEMED TO BE DULY PREPARED. IF THERE WAS A SPONGE IN THE TROUGH, THE WATER IN IT[4] IS INVALID.[5] HOW SHOULD ONE PROCEED?[6] ONE EMPTIES OUT THE WATER[7] UNTIL THE SPONGE IS REACHED.[8] IF ONE TOUCHED THE SPONGE,[9] HOWEVER MUCH THE WATER THAT WASHES OVER IT, THE WATER BECOMES INVALID.[10]

MISHNAH 4. IF A MAN PLACED HIS HAND OR HIS FOOT OR LEAVES OF VEGETABLES[11] IN SUCH A MANNER AS TO ENABLE THE WATER TO RUN INTO A JAR, THE WATER IS INVALID.[12] IF HE USED[13] LEAVES OF REEDS OR LEAVES OF NUTS[14] THE WATER IS VALID. THIS IS THE GENERAL RULE: [WATER PASSING OVER] THAT WHICH IS SUSCEPTIBLE TO UNCLEANNESS IS INVALID, BUT [WATER PASSING OVER] THAT WHICH IS NOT SUSCEPTIBLE TO UNCLEANNESS IS VALID.

MISHNAH 5. IF A WELL WAS DIVERTED INTO A WINE

(1) Lit., 'sanctification'. (2) Containing water. (3) Lit., 'mouth'. (4) The sponge. (5) Because a sponge cannot be regarded as a 'vessel.' (6) In the latter case, if all the water is not to become invalid. (7) From the trough into another vessel. (8) As the water above has not been in contact with the sponge it remains valid and may be used. (9) So that some of its absorbed contents might possibly have been squeezed out. (10) Since the water that issued from the sponge gets mixed up with that in the trough. (11) Under running water. (12) Because it has passed over an object that is susceptible to uncleanness. (13) Instead of his hand, foot or vegetable leaves. (14) Which are not susceptible to the uncleanness of food-stuffs.

VAT OR INTO CISTERNS, THE WATER[1] IS INVALID FOR ZABS[2] AND LEPERS;[3] AND ALSO FOR THE PREPARATION OF THE WATER OF THE SIN-OFFERING,[4] BECAUSE IT WAS NOT DRAWN INTO A VESSEL.[5]

(1) In the vat or cistern since it can no longer be regarded as 'running' water. (2) Whose immersion must be performed in running water (Lev. XV, 13). (3) For whose sprinkling running water is required (Lev. XIV, 5). (4) Even in the vat or cistern itself. (5) Neither vat nor cistern can be regarded as a valid 'vessel'.

PARAH

CHAPTER VII

MISHNAH 1. IF FIVE MEN FILLED[1] FIVE JARS TO PREPARE WITH THEM FIVE MIXTURES[2] [RESPECTIVELY][3] AND THEN THEY CHANGED THEIR MINDS TO PREPARE[4] ONE MIXTURE FROM ALL OF THEM, OR IF THEY FILLED THE JARS TO PREPARE WITH THEM ONE MIXTURE AND THEN THEY CHANGED THEIR MINDS TO PREPARE WITH THEM FIVE MIXTURES,[3] ALL THE WATER REMAINS VALID.[5] IF ONE MAN FILLED[1] FIVE JARS INTENDING TO PREPARE FIVE [SEPARATE] MIXTURES, EVEN THOUGH HE CHANGED HIS MIND TO PREPARE ONE MIXTURE[4] FROM ALL OF THEM, ONLY THE LAST[6] IS VALID.[7] IF HE[8] INTENDED TO PREPARE ONE MIXTURE FROM ALL OF THEM AND THEN HE CHANGED HIS MIND TO PREPARE FIVE SEPARATE MIXTURES, ONLY THE WATER IN THE ONE THAT WAS MIXED FIRST IS VALID.[9] IF HE[8] SAID[10] TO ANOTHER MAN, 'PREPARE MIXTURES[11] FROM THESE FOR YOURSELF', ONLY THE FIRST[12] IS VALID;[13] BUT IF HE SAID, 'PREPARE A MIXTURE[11] FROM THESE FOR ME', ALL ARE VALID.[14]

(1) With suitable water. (2) Of ashes of the red cow with the water. (3) Each man his own mixture with the water he drew. (4) In one vessel. (5) Since no act of extraneous work intervened between the putting of the water in each jar and the mixing of it with the ashes. (6) Between the filling of which and the mixing in it of the ashes no extraneous act of work intervened. (7) The water in all the others is invalid since an act of extraneous work (the filling of the next jar or jars) intervened between the drawing of the water and the mixing of the ashes with it. (8) The man who filled all the five jars. (9) Because, all the five jars having been filled for one mixture, there is no intervention of extraneous work between the filling of the first jar and the mixing of its contents with the ashes. The mixtures of the other jars are invalid since the mixing of the first one, which is an act of work, intervened between the filling of them with the water and the mixing of that water with the ashes. (10) After he filled the five jars intending to use them for one single mixture. (11) Each jar separately. (12) Between the filling of which and the mixing in it

MISHNAH 2. IF A MAN FILLED THE WATER WITH ONE HAND AND DID SOME OTHER WORK WITH THE OTHER HAND, OR IF HE FILLED THE WATER FOR HIMSELF AND FOR ANOTHER MAN,[1] OR IF HE FILLED TWO JARS AT THE SAME TIME,[2] THE WATER OF BOTH IS INVALID, FOR WORK[3] CAUSES INVALIDITY WHETHER ONE ACTS FOR ONESELF OR FOR ANOTHER MAN.

MISHNAH 3. IF A MAN PREPARED THE MIXTURE[4] WITH ONE HAND AND DID SOME OTHER WORK WITH THE OTHER HAND, THE MIXTURE IS INVALID[5] IF HE PREPARED IT FOR HIMSELF; BUT IF HE PREPARED IT FOR ANOTHER MAN, IT IS VALID.[6] IF THE MAN PREPARED A MIXTURE[4] BOTH FOR HIMSELF AND FOR ANOTHER MAN,[7] HIS IS INVALID AND THAT OF THE OTHER MAN IS VALID.[8] IF HE PREPARES MIXTURES FOR TWO MEN SIMULTANEOUSLY, BOTH ARE VALID.[8]

MISHNAH 4. [IF A MAN SAID TO ANOTHER,][9] 'PREPARE THE MIXTURE FOR ME AND I WILL PREPARE THE ONE FOR YOU', THE FIRST[10] IS VALID.[11] [IF HE SAID,] 'FILL IN THE WATER

of the ashes no other act of work intervened. (13) Cf. *supra* n. 9. (14) Since the first man (who filled the jar) did no work between the filling and the mixing, while the second (who prepared the mixtures) cannot cause invalidity to that which does not belong to him.

(1) At the same time. The filling for the other man being an act of extraneous work. (2) Cf. prev. n. *mut. mut.* (3) Other than that necessitated for the preparation on which one is engaged. (4) Of ashes of the red cow with the water. (5) On account of the other work that was done by him while he was engaged in the preparation. (6) Since that man did no other work. Only in the filling of the water is the act of an agent (who may be paid for his services and who derives benefit from his act) deemed to be identical with that of the owner, but in the preparation of the mixture (for which no fee may be paid) the act of the agent cannot be regarded as that of the owner. (7) At the same time. (8) Since the mixture that was not his could not be rendered invalid by his work. (9) After each of them had already drawn his water. (10) *Sc.* the mixture that was prepared first. (11) The mixture that was prepared subsequently is invalid since its owner made an interruption between the filling of the vessels with the water for it and its mixing by the act of the preparation of the first mixture which in relation to it is extraneous work.

FOR ME AND I WILL FILL THE WATER FOR YOU', THAT OF THE LATTER IS VALID.[1] [IF HE SAID,] 'PREPARE THE MIXTURE FOR ME AND I WILL DRAW THE WATER FOR YOU', BOTH MIXTURES ARE VALID.[2] [IF HE SAID,] 'FILL THE WATER FOR ME AND I WILL PREPARE THE MIXTURE[3] FOR YOU',[4] BOTH MIXTURES ARE INVALID.[5]

MISHNAH 5. IF A MAN IS DRAWING WATER FOR HIS OWN USE[6] AND FOR THE MIXTURE OF THE SIN-OFFERING, HE MUST DRAW FOR HIMSELF FIRST AND FASTEN [THE BUCKET] TO THE CARRYING YOKE AND THEN HE DRAWS THE WATER FOR THE SIN-OFFERING. IF, HOWEVER, HE DREW FIRST THE WATER FOR THE SIN-OFFERING AND THEN HE DREW THE WATER FOR HIMSELF, IT IS INVALID. HE MUST[7] PUT HIS OWN BEHIND HIM AND THAT FOR THE SIN-OFFERING BEFORE HIM,[8] AND IF HE PUT THAT FOR THE SIN-OFFERING BEHIND HIM IT IS INVALID.[8] IF BOTH WERE FOR THE SIN-OFFERING, HE MAY[7] PUT ONE BEFORE HIM AND ONE BEHIND HIM AND BOTH ARE VALID, SINCE IT IS IMPOSSIBLE TO DO OTHERWISE.[9]

MISHNAH 6. IF A MAN CARRIED THE ROPE[10] IN HIS HAND, [THE MIXTURE] IS VALID IF HE KEEPS TO HIS USUAL WAY; BUT IF HE GOES OUT OF HIS WAY, IT IS INVALID.[11] THIS QUES-

(1) Since there was no interruption by other work on the part of the owner between the filling of the vessel and the mixing of the ashes. That of the first, however, is invalid since he had done an act of extraneous work, by filling the water for the other man, between the filling of the water for his own mixture, and the preparation of it. (2) Because in neither case was there any interruption by extraneous work. (3) 'With the water which you have drawn for yourself before I asked you to draw for me'. (4) 'Before I will prepare mine'. (5) Since in the case of both mixtures there was an interruption by other work done by their respective owners. (6) For his ordinary needs. (7) When carrying the two buckets of water. (8) Because, in accordance with Scripture, it has to be carefully guarded. (9) Var. lec. 'it is possible', *sc.* it is possible in this case, since the bucket before him is for the sin-offering, to bestow equal care upon the bucket behind also. (10) Which he had borrowed for the purpose of drawing the water for mixing with the ashes and which he now returns to the lender. (11) The extra journey is regarded as 'other work' which causes invalidity.

TION WAS SENT ON TO JABNEH ON THREE FESTIVALS AND ON THE THIRD FESTIVAL[1] IT WAS RULED THAT THE MIXTURE WAS VALID, AS A TEMPORARY MEASURE.[2]

MISHNAH 7. IF A MAN COILS THE ROPE LITTLE BY LITTLE,[3] [THE MIXTURE] IS VALID;[4] BUT IF HE COILED IT AFTERWARDS,[5] IT IS INVALID.[6] R. JOSE STATED: THIS ALSO HAD BEEN RULED TO BE VALID AS A TEMPORARY MEASURE.

MISHNAH 8. IF A MAN PUT THE JAR[7] AWAY IN ORDER THAT IT SHALL NOT BE BROKEN, OR IF HE INVERTED IT IN ORDER TO DRY IT SO THAT HE MIGHT DRAW MORE WATER WITH IT,[8] [THE WATER HE HAD ALREADY DRAWN] IS VALID;[9] BUT IF HE INTENDED TO CARRY IN IT THE ASHES, IT IS INVALID.[6] IF HE CLEARED POTSHERDS FROM A TROUGH[10] IN ORDER THAT IT MAY HOLD MORE WATER, THE WATER IS VALID;[11] BUT IF IT WAS INTENDED THAT THEY SHOULD NOT HINDER HIM WHEN HE POURS OUT THE WATER,[12] IT IS INVALID.

MISHNAH 9. IF A MAN CARRYING HIS WATER ON HIS SHOULDER DECIDED A MATTER OF LAW, OR SHOWED OTHERS THE WAY, OR KILLED A SERPENT OR A SCORPION, OR TOOK FOODSTUFFS FOR STORAGE, IT IS INVALID; BUT [IF HE TOOK] FOODSTUFFS TO EAT, THEN IT IS VALID.[13] IF HE KILLED A SERPENT OR A SCORPION THAT HINDERED HIM, IT REMAINS VALID. R. JUDAH STATED: THIS IS THE GENERAL RULE: IN THE

(1) V. Ḥul. 48*a*. (2) Having regard to the exigencies of the time. (3) While drawing water from the well. (4) The coiling being regarded as part of the work of the preparations for the red cow. (5) After the water had been drawn. (6) Cf. *supra* p. 328, n. 11 *mut. mut.* (7) After emptying the water he drew with it into the vessel, but prior to the mixing of the ashes. (8) For the same mixture. (9) Since the acts mentioned are the usual procedure they cannot be regarded as 'extraneous work'. (10) Between his drawing of the water and his mixing it with the ashes. (11) Since the act is part of the services in connection with the preparation of the mixture. (12) For the sprinkling after the mixing of the ashes. (13) As this serves to fortify him in his task it is not deemed extraneous work.

CASE OF ANY ACT THAT IS IN THE NATURE OF WORK, THE MIXTURE IS INVALID WHETHER THE MAN STOPPED[1] OR NOT, BUT IF IT WAS NOT IN THE NATURE OF WORK,[2] THE MIXTURE IS INVALID IF HE STOPPED, BUT IF HE DID NOT STOP IT REMAINS VALID.

MISHNAH 10. IF A MAN ENTRUSTED[3] HIS WATER[4] TO AN UNCLEAN MAN, IT IS INVALID;[5] BUT IF TO A CLEAN ONE IT IS VALID.[6] R. ELIEZER RULED: EVEN IF IT WAS ENTRUSTED TO AN UNCLEAN MAN IT IS VALID,[7] PROVIDED THE OWNER DID NO OTHER WORK IN THE MEANTIME.

MISHNAH 11. IF TWO MEN WERE DRAWING WATER FOR THE SIN-OFFERING AND ONE ASSISTED THE OTHER TO RAISE IT, OR IF ONE PULLED OUT A THORN[8] FOR THE OTHER, IT IS VALID IF THERE IS TO BE ONLY ONE MIXTURE;[9] BUT IF THERE ARE TO BE TWO SEPARATE MIXTURES, IT IS INVALID.[10] R. JOSE RULED: EVEN IF THERE ARE TO BE TWO MIXTURES THE WATER IS VALID IF THE TWO MEN HAD MADE A MUTUAL AGREEMENT BETWEEN THEM.[11]

MISHNAH 12. IF A MAN[12] BROKE DOWN A FENCE[13] WITH

(1) When the act was done. (2) As those mentioned in this Mishnah. (3) For safe keeping and protection against uncleanness. (4) For the mixture of the ashes of the red cow. (5) Because an unclean person cannot be trusted to exercise all the necesessary care. (6) Even if the owner did some other work in the meantime. While the water is under the protection of the guardian it is deemed to be in his (and not in the owner's) possession, and only if the guardian did some other work does the water become invalid. (7) For, knowing that the guardian is unclean, the owner himself keeps his eye on it. (8) That happened to stick in his finger, in the interval between the drawing of the water and its mixing with the ashes. (9) Since the assistance afforded, which was essential for the joint effort, cannot be regarded as extraneous work. (10) Because the assistance given was not essential for the giver's mixture, it is extraneous work and causes invalidity. (11) To assist each other in all their preparations for the mixtures. As each one was entirely dependent on the other, any help rendered is deemed to be work on one's own preparation. (12) While carrying the water for the ashes of the red cow. (13) That was in his way.

THE INTENTION OF PUTTING IT UP AGAIN,[1] THE WATER REMAINS VALID;[2] BUT IF HE PUT [A FENCE] UP,[3] THE WATER BECOMES INVALID. IF[4] HE ATE[5] FIGS INTENDING[6] TO STORE SOME OF THEM, THE WATER IS VALID;[7] BUT IF HE STORED FIGS[8] IT IS INVALID. IF[4] HE WAS EATING FIGS AND, LEAVING SOME OVER, THREW WHAT WAS IN HIS HAND UNDER THE FIG TREE OR AMONG DRYING FIGS IN ORDER THAT IT SHALL NOT BE WASTED, THE WATER BECOMES INVALID.[9]

(1) And much more so if he had no intention of putting it up again. (2) Elijah Wilna: The destruction is not regarded as constructive work though it is preparatory to it. (3) On his own accord, before the water had been mixed with the ashes. According to the second interpretation (previous note), the reference is to the same fence, if he put it up. (4) During the interval between the drawing of the water and the mixing of it with the ashes of the red heifer. (5) V. Mishnah 9. (6) Under compulsion by one who, otherwise, refused to allow him to eat. (7) Even if the storing was done before the preparation of the mixture. Since the storing was an essential of his eating (cf. prev. n.) and the latter was a necessity for his drawing of the water, the storing is regarded as an act essential to the preparation. (8) V. prev. n. *mut. mut.* (9) Since the storing of foodstuffs is an act of extraneous work.

PARAH

CHAPTER VIII

MISHNAH 1. IF TWO MEN WERE KEEPING WATCH OVER THE TROUGH[1] AND ONE OF THEM CONTRACTED UNCLEANNESS, THE WATER[2] REMAINS VALID, SINCE IT IS STILL UNDER THE PROTECTION OF THE OTHER. IF THE FIRST BECAME CLEAN AND THE OTHER CONTRACTED UNCLEANNESS THE WATER IS STILL VALID SINCE IT IS UNDER THE PROTECTION OF THE FIRST. IF BOTH CONTRACTED UNCLEANNESS SIMULTANEOUSLY THE WATER BECOMES INVALID. IF ONE OF THEM DID[3] SOME WORK,[4] THE WATER REMAINS VALID SINCE IT IS UNDER THE PROTECTION OF THE OTHER. IF THE FIRST CEASED[5] AND THE OTHER DID SOME WORK,[4] THE WATER STILL REMAINS VALID SINCE IT IS UNDER THE PROTECTION OF THE FIRST. IF BOTH DID SOME WORK[4] AT THE SAME TIME THE WATER BECOMES INVALID.

MISHNAH 2. THE MAN THAT PREPARES THE MIXTURE[6] OF THE SIN-OFFERING[7] MUST NOT WEAR HIS SANDALS, FOR WERE SOME OF THE LIQUID[8] TO FALL ON A SANDAL THE LATTER WOULD BECOME UNCLEAN[9] AND THUS CONVEY UNCLEANNESS TO HIM.[10] WELL MAY HE SAY, 'THAT[11] WHICH MADE YOU UNCLEAN DID NOT MAKE ME UNCLEAN, BUT YOU HAVE MADE ME UNCLEAN'. IF SOME OF THE LIQUID FELL ON HIS

(1) That contained water for mixing with the ashes of the red cow. (2) Cf. prev. n. (3) While he was supposed to keep watch over the water. (4) That had no connection with the preparation of the mixture of the ashes and the water. (5) From his work. (6) And likewise he that sprinkles it. (7) Much more so the man who sprinkles it. (8) Of the mixture. (9) From the liquid which had become invalid the moment it dropped on the sandal and was no longer subjected to the special care prescribed for the mixture of the sin-offering. (10) As a special measure enacted in connection with the preparations of the red cow mixture. (11) The liquid.

SKIN[1] HE REMAINS CLEAN.[2] IF IT FELL ON HIS GARMENT THE LATTER BECOMES UNCLEAN AND CONVEYS UNCLEANNESS TO HIM. WELL MAY HE SAY, 'THAT[3] WHICH MADE YOU UNCLEAN DID NOT MAKE ME UNCLEAN, BUT YOU HAVE MADE ME UNCLEAN'.

MISHNAH 3. HE WHO BURNS THE RED COW[4] OR THE BULLOCKS,[5] AND HE THAT LEADS AWAY THE SCAPEGOAT,[6] RENDER GARMENTS[7] UNCLEAN.[8] THE RED COW, HOWEVER, AND THE BULLOCKS AND THE SCAPEGOAT DO NOT THEMSELVES CONVEY UNCLEANNESS TO GARMENTS.[9] WELL MAY IT[10] SAY,[11] 'THOSE[12] THAT CAUSE YOU TO BE UNCLEAN DO NOT CAUSE ME TO BE UNCLEAN, BUT YOU HAVE CAUSED ME TO BE UNCLEAN'.

MISHNAH 4. A MAN THAT EATS OF THE CARRION OF A CLEAN BIRD, WHILE IT IS YET IN HIS GULLET,[13] CAUSES GARMENTS TO BE UNCLEAN;[14] BUT THE CARRION ITSELF DOES NOT CAUSE GARMENTS TO BE UNCLEAN. WELL MAY IT[10] SAY,[11] 'THAT[15] WHICH CAUSED YOU TO BE UNCLEAN DID NOT CAUSE ME TO BE UNCLEAN, BUT YOU CAUSED ME TO BE UNCLEAN'.

MISHNAH 5. ANY DERIVED UNCLEANNESS CONVEYS NO UNCLEANNESS TO VESSELS, BUT [IT DOES CONVEY IT] TO A LIQUID. IF A LIQUID BECAME UNCLEAN IT CAN CONVEY UNCLEANNESS TO THEM.[16] WELL MAY THEY[16] SAY,[17] 'THAT[18] WHICH CAUSED YOU TO BE UNCLEAN DID NOT CAUSE ME TO BE UNCLEAN, BUT YOU CAUSED ME TO BE UNCLEAN'.

MISHNAH 6. AN EARTHEN VESSEL CANNOT CONVEY

(1) Lit., 'flesh'. (2) As laid down *infra* IX, 8. (3) The liquid. (4) Cf. Num. XIX, 8. (5) That were not burnt on the altar (cf. Lev. IV, 12, 21; XVI, 27); and the same law applies also to certain he-goats (cf. Lev. XVI, 27f). Some edd. add, 'and the he-goat'. (6) Cf. Lev. XVI, 26. (7) Which they wear or touch at the time. (8) Only men and earthen vessels do not contract uncleanness from such touch (cf. prev. n.). (9) Which they touched. (10) Each garment. (11) To the man. (12) The red cow, the bullocks and the Scapegoat. (13) Before he had swallowed it. (14) V. Toh. I, 1. (15) The carrion. (16) Vessels. (17) To the liquid. (18) A derived uncleanness.

UNCLEANNESS TO ANOTHER SUCH VESSEL, BUT [CAN CONVEY IT] TO A LIQUID; AND WHEN THE LIQUID BECOMES UNCLEAN IT CAN CONVEY UNCLEANNESS TO THE VESSEL. WELL MAY IT[1] SAY,[2] 'THAT[3] WHICH HAS CAUSED YOUR UNCLEANNESS COULD NOT CAUSE ME TO BE UNCLEAN, BUT YOU HAVE CAUSED ME TO BE UNCLEAN'.

MISHNAH 7. WHATSOEVER[4] CAUSES TERUMAH TO BE INVALID CAUSES LIQUIDS[5] TO BECOME UNCLEAN IN THE FIRST GRADE SO THAT THEY CAN CONVEY UNCLEANNESS[6] AT ONE REMOVE, AND RENDER UNFIT[7] AT ONE OTHER REMOVE,[8] EXCEPT ONLY A ṬEBUL YOM.[9] WELL MAY IT[10] SAY,[11] 'WHAT[12] HAD CAUSED YOU TO BE UNCLEAN COULD NOT CAUSE ME TO BE UNCLEAN, BUT YOU HAVE CAUSED ME TO BE UNCLEAN'.

MISHNAH 8. ALL SEAS ARE[13] ON A PAR WITH A RITUAL BATH,[14] FOR IT IS SAID, AND THE GATHERING OF THE WATERS CALLED HE SEAS;[15] SO R. MEIR. R. JUDAH RULED: ONLY THE GREAT SEA[16] IS ON A PAR WITH A RITUAL BATH,[17] 'SEAS'[18] HAVING BEEN STATED[15] ONLY BECAUSE THERE ARE IN IT[16] MANY KINDS OF SEAS. R. JOSE RULED: ALL SEAS[19] AFFORD CLEANNESS WHEN RUNNING,[20] AND YET THEY ARE UNFIT[21] FOR ZABS AND LEPERS AND FOR THE PREPARATION OF THE WATER OF THE SIN-OFFERING.[22]

(1) The second vessel. (2) To the liquid. (3) The first vessel. (4) E.g. a second grade of uncleanness. (5) As a preventive measure. (6) To foodstuffs even if they are common *ḥullin* (v. Glos.). (7) To *terumah*, but not to common foodstuffs. To become 'unfit' denotes to contract an uncleanness without being able to convey it further. (8) But no more. (9) V. Glos. Though a *ṭebul yom* renders *terumah* unfit, he cannot cause liquids, even if they are *terumah*, to become a first grade of uncleanness. (10) A foodstuff (cf. *supra* n. 6). (11) To the liquids. (12) The second grade of uncleanness. (13) In respect of ritual immersion. (14) Lit., 'a gathering (of water)'. They are not like a spring. They are consequently unfit for the immersion of a *zab* and a leper and for mixing with the ashes of the red heifer, and do not cleanse when running. (15) Gen. I, 10. (16) The Mediterranean. (17) Not the smaller inland seas. (18) The plural instead of the singular. (19) Including the Great Sea. (20) Like springs. (21) Like gathered water. (22) All of which require spring water.

MISHNAH 9. AFFECTED[1] WATERS ARE UNFIT.[2] THE FOLLOWING ARE AFFECTED[1] WATERS: THOSE THAT ARE SALTY OR LUKEWARM. WATERS THAT FAIL ARE UNFIT.[2] THE FOLLOWING ARE WATERS THAT FAIL: THOSE THAT FAIL EVEN ONCE IN A SEPTENNIAL CYCLE. THOSE THAT FAIL ONLY IN TIMES OF WAR[3] OR IN YEARS OF DROUGHT ARE FIT.[2] R. JUDAH RULED: THEY ARE UNFIT.[2]

MISHNAH 10. THE WATERS OF THE KERAMIYON AND THE WATERS OF PUGAH[4] ARE UNFIT,[2] BECAUSE THEY ARE MARSH WATERS.[5] THE WATERS OF THE JORDAN AND THE WATERS OF THE YARMUK[6] ARE UNFIT,[2] BECAUSE THEY ARE MIXED WATERS.[7] AND THE FOLLOWING ARE MIXED WATERS: A FIT KIND AND AN UNFIT KIND THAT WERE MIXED TOGETHER. IF TWO KINDS THAT ARE FIT WERE MIXED TOGETHER BOTH REMAIN FIT: R. JUDAH RULES THAT THEY ARE UNFIT.[8]

MISHNAH 11. AHAB'S WELL AND THE POOL IN THE CAVE OF PAMIAS[9] ARE FIT.[2] WATER THAT HAS CHANGED ITS COLOUR AND THE CHANGE AROSE FROM ITSELF, REMAINS FIT. A WATER CHANNEL THAT COMES FROM A DISTANCE[10] IS FIT, PROVIDED ONLY THAT IT IS WATCHED SO THAT NO ONE CUTS IT OFF.[11] R. JUDAH RULED: THE PRESUMPTION ALWAYS[12] IS THAT IT IS IN A PERMITTED STATE. IF THERE FELL INTO A WELL SOME CLAY OR EARTH, ONE MUST WAIT[13] UNTIL IT BECOMES CLEAR; SO R. ISHMAEL. R. AKIBA RULED: IT IS NOT NECESSARY TO WAIT.

(1) Or 'harmful'. Lit., 'smitten'. (2) For use where running water is required. (3) When the passing troops consume much water. (4) Var. lec., Pigah. (5) V. B.B., Sonc. ed., p. 298, n. 10. (6) The great eastern tributary of the Jordan. (7) These rivers being fed by tributaries whose waters 'fail' or 'are affected'. (8) As a preventive measure against the possibility of using a mixture of two kinds of water one of which was unfit. (9) Or 'Banias', one of the sources of the Jordan. (10) Having its source in a spring. (11) From its source. Should it be cut off, it can no longer be regarded as spring water. (12) Even if it was not kept under watch. (13) Before the water may be used.

PARAH

CHAPTER IX

MISHNAH 1. IF A DROP[1] OF WATER FELL INTO A FLASK,[2] R. ELIEZER RULED, THE SPRINKLING MUST BE DONE TWICE;[3] BUT THE SAGES RULE THAT THE MIXTURE IS INVALID.[4] IF DEW DROPPED INTO IT,[5] R. ELIEZER RULED: LET IT[5] BE PUT OUT IN THE SUN AND THE DEW WILL RISE;[6] BUT THE SAGES RULE THAT THE MIXTURE IS INVALID. IF A LIQUID OR FRUIT JUICE FELL INTO IT,[5] ALL THE CONTENTS MUST BE POURED AWAY AND IT IS ALSO NECESSARY TO DRY THE FLASK.[7] IF ONLY INK, GUM OR COPPERAS, OR ANYTHING THAT LEAVES A MARK, FELL INTO IT,[5] THE CONTENTS MUST BE POURED AWAY BUT IT IS NOT NECESSARY TO DRY THE FLASK.[8]

MISHNAH 2. IF INSECTS OR CREEPING THINGS FELL INTO IT,[5] AND THEY BURST ASUNDER[9] OR THE COLOUR OF THE WATER CHANGED, THE CONTENTS BECOME INVALID. A BEETLE[10] CAUSES INVALIDITY IN ANY CASE,[11] BECAUSE IT IS LIKE A TUBE.[12] R. SIMEON AND R. ELIEZER B. JACOB RULED: A MAGGOT OR A WEEVIL OF THE CORN[10] CAUSES NO INVALIDITY, BECAUSE IT CONTAINS NO MOISTURE.

MISHNAH 3. IF A BEAST OR A WILD ANIMAL DRANK

(1) Lit., 'any soever'. (2) *Ẓeloḥith*, the vessel containing the mixture of the ashes of the red cow and the water, duly prepared for sprinkling. (3) Thus making sure that one drop at least was valid water. (4) V. Zeb. 80*a*. (5) The flask. (6) Leaving the mixture free from all dew. (7) Before it can be used again for a valid mixture. (8) For, had any of the foreign substance remained, a mark would have been left in the flask. (9) The water penetrating them and carrying back some of the moisture of their body into the mixture. (10) If it fell into the mixture. (11) Whether it burst asunder or not and whether or not the colour of the water changed. (12) Through which the water of the mixture passes and absorbs moisture from its body.

FROM IT,[1] IT BECOMES INVALID.[2] ALL BIRDS[3] CAUSE INVALIDITY, EXCEPT THE DOVE SINCE IT ONLY SUCKS UP THE WATER.[4] ALL CREEPING THINGS CAUSE NO INVALIDITY, EXCEPT THE WEASEL SINCE IT LAPS UP THE WATER. R. GAMALIEL RULED: THE SERPENT ALSO[5] BECAUSE IT VOMITS. R. ELIEZER RULED: THE MOUSE ALSO.[5]

MISHNAH 4. IF ONE INTENDED[6] TO DRINK THE WATER OF THE SIN-OFFERING, R. ELIEZER RULED: IT BECOMES INVALID. R. JOSHUA RULED: ONLY WHEN ONE TIPS THE FLASK.[7] R. JOSE STATED: THIS[8] APPLIES ONLY TO WATER THAT HAD NOT YET BEEN PREPARED,[9] BUT IN THE CASE OF WATER THAT HAD BEEN PREPARED,[10] R. ELIEZER RULED: IT BECOMES INVALID [ONLY] WHEN ONE TIPS THE FLASK;[7] AND R. JOSHUA RULED: [ONLY] WHEN ONE DRINKS.[11] AND IF IT WAS POURED DIRECT INTO ONE'S THROAT,[12] IT REMAINS VALID.

MISHNAH 5. IF THE WATER OF THE SIN-OFFERING[13] BECAME INVALID IT MAY NOT BE STAMPED INTO THE MUD SINCE IT MIGHT BECOME A SNARE FOR OTHERS.[14] R. JUDAH RULED: IT[15] BECOMES NEUTRALISED.[16] IF A COW DRANK OF THE WATER OF THE SIN-OFFERING, ITS FLESH[17] BECOMES UNCLEAN FOR TWENTY-FOUR HOURS.[18] R. JUDAH RULED: IT BECOMES NEUTRALISED IN ITS BOWELS.[19]

(1) The contents of the flask (cf. *supra* p. 336 n. 10). (2) Since spittle mixes with the water. (3) If they drank from the mixture. (4) Cf. *supra* n. 2 *mut. mut.* (5) Causes invalidity if it drank from the mixture. (6) Expressing his intention. (7) To drink out of it. Intention alone does not suffice to cause invalidity. (8) The ruling of R. Eliezer as well as that of R. Joshua just cited. (9) By the mixture of the ashes. (10) When it is evident that the water had been drawn only for that purpose. (11) From the flask. (12) So that no spittle could possibly have been mixed up with the contents that remained. (13) The prepared mixture of the water and the ashes of the red cow. (14) Who, unsuspecting the existence of the water in the mud, would touch the latter and contract uncleanness without being aware of it. (15) On being mixed up with the mud. (16) And no longer conveys any uncleanness. (17) If the cow has been slain. (18) From the time of drinking. (19) And no longer conveys any uncleanness.

MISHNAH 6. NO MAN MAY CARRY WATER OF THE SIN-OFFERING[1] OR THE ASHES OF THE SIN-OFFERING[2] ACROSS A RIVER ON BOARD A SHIP,[3] NOR MAY ONE FLOAT THEM UPON THE WATER,[4] NOR MAY ONE STAND ON THE BANK ON ONE SIDE AND THROW THEM ACROSS TO THE OTHER SIDE.[4] A MAN[5] MAY, HOWEVER, CROSS OVER[6] WITH THE WATER UP TO HIS NECK. HE THAT IS CLEAN FOR THE SIN-OFFERING[1] MAY CROSS [A RIVER][7] CARRYING IN HIS HANDS AN EMPTY VESSEL THAT IS CLEAN FOR THE SIN-OFFERING[1] OR WATER THAT HAS NOT YET BEEN DULY PREPARED.[8]

MISHNAH 7. IF VALID ASHES[9] WERE MIXED UP WITH WOOD ASHES,[10] ONE IS GUIDED BY THE GREATER QUANTITY IN RESPECT OF THE CONVEYANCE OF UNCLEANNESS,[11] BUT [THE MIXTURE][12] MAY NOT BE PREPARED WITH IT.[13] R. ELIEZER RULED: THE MIXTURE[12] MAY BE PREPARED WITH ALL OF THEM.[14]

MISHNAH 8. WATER OF THE SIN-OFFERING, EVEN IF IT IS INVALID,[15] CONVEYS UNCLEANNESS[16] TO A MAN WHO IS CLEAN FOR TERUMAH[17] [BY CONTACT] WITH HIS HANDS OR

(1) The prepared mixture of the water and the ashes of the red cow. (2) Even if it was not mixed with the water. (3) As a preventive measure. It once happened that a piece of a corpse was found stuck in the deck of a ship on board of which the mixture of the water and ashes of the red heifer was carried, v. Ḥag. 28*a*. (4) Since this is similar to carrying them on board a ship. (5) Carrying the mixture or the ashes. (6) On foot. (7) Even in a ship. (8) By the mixture of the ashes, having only been drawn for the purpose. (9) Of the red cow. (10) That are unfit for sprinkling. (11) By touch. If the valid ashes constitute the greater quantity, one who touched it is unclean; and if the wood ashes constitute the greater quantity no uncleanness is conveyed. (12) Of the ashes with water. (13) Even where the greater quantity was valid ashes. (14) With both kinds of ashes whether the greater part was wood ashes or valid ashes. As no minimum quantity of ashes was prescribed for the sprinkling, and as each application would contain at least some fraction of the valid ashes, the entire mixture may be regarded as valid and used for the purpose. (15) Owing, for instance, to a change in colour that was due to an external cause. (16) Rabbinically. (17) But not to one who is only

WITH HIS BODY; AND TO A MAN WHO IS CLEAN FOR THE SIN-OFFERING IT CONVEYS UNCLEANNESS NEITHER [BY CONTACT] WITH HIS HANDS NOR [BY CONTACT] WITH HIS BODY.[1] IF IT[2] BECAME UNCLEAN, IT CONVEYS UNCLEANNESS TO A MAN WHO IS CLEAN FOR TERUMAH [BY CONTACT EITHER] WITH HIS HANDS OR WITH HIS BODY, AND TO THE MAN WHO IS CLEAN FOR THE SIN-OFFERING IT CONVEYS UNCLEANNESS [BY CONTACT] WITH HIS HANDS BUT NOT [BY CONTACT] WITH HIS BODY.[3]

MISHNAH 9. IF VALID ASHES WERE PUT ON WATER THAT WAS UNFIT FOR THE PREPARATION,[4] [THE LATTER] CONVEYS UNCLEANNESS TO HIM THAT IS CLEAN FOR TERUMAH [BY CONTACT] WITH HIS HANDS OR WITH HIS BODY, BUT TO HIM WHO IS CLEAN[5] FOR THE SIN-OFFERING IT CONVEYS UNCLEANNESS NEITHER [BY CONTACT] WITH HIS HANDS NOR WITH HIS BODY.

clean for common food; for, owing to the invalidity of the water it is no longer subject to Pentateuchal uncleanness.

(1) So that, though he becomes unclean in certain other respects, he remains clean to draw the water, to mix it with the ashes of the red cow (the sin-offering), and to sprinkle it. (2) The water of the sin-offering. (3) Liquid uncleanness can generally be conveyed only by contact with the hands. (4) Which are thus on a par with water that became invalid. (5) Var. lec., 'the hands of him who is clean for *terumah* and the hands of him who is clean'.

PARAH

CHAPTER X

MISHNAH 1. ANY OBJECT THAT IS SUSCEPTIBLE TO MIDRAS UNCLEANNESS[1] IS FOR THE PURPOSE OF THE WATER OF THE SIN-OFFERING DEEMED TO BE UNCLEAN OF MIDDAF,[2] WHETHER IT WAS OTHERWISE UNCLEAN OR CLEAN.[3] A MAN TOO[4] IS SUBJECT TO THE SAME RESTRICTION.[5] ANY OBJECT THAT IS SUSCEPTIBLE TO CORPSE UNCLEANNESS,[6] WHETHER IT IS OTHERWISE UNCLEAN OR CLEAN, R. ELIEZER RULED, IS NOT DEEMED TO BE UNCLEAN OF MIDDAF;[7] R. JOSHUA RULED: IT IS DEEMED TO BE UNCLEAN OF MIDDAF;[8] AND THE SAGES RULED: THAT WHICH WAS UNCLEAN IS DEEMED TO BE UNCLEAN OF MIDDAF,[3] AND THAT WHICH WAS CLEAN IS NOT DEEMED TO BE UNCLEAN OF MIDDAF.[7]

MISHNAH 2. IF A MAN WHO WAS CLEAN FOR THE WATER OF THE SIN-OFFERING TOUCHED WHAT WAS UNCLEAN OF MIDDAF,[9] HE[10] BECOMES UNCLEAN.[11] IF A FLAGON THAT WAS

(1) *Sc.* one that is appointed for use as a couch or a seat, v. Glos. s.v. (2) A form of a minor or indirect uncleanness imposed Rabbinically (v. Glos. s.v.). (3) Hence if a man who is clean for the purposes of the sin-offering shifted (*hesseṭ*) any such object (unless it had been specially guarded for the purposes of the sin-offering) he becomes unclean and unfit for the services of the mixing or sprinkling of the water and ashes of the red cow as if he had shifted an actual *midras* uncleanness. (4) Even if he was clean for holy things but not specially cleansed for the purposes of the sin-offering. (5) As the objects mentioned. Hence if the man who is clean for the sin-offering water touched him he becomes equally unclean and unfit (cf. prev. n. but one). (6) But not to *midras*. (7) Hence a man who is clean for the water of the sin-offering does not become unclean by shifting it as when he shifted that which is subject to *midras* uncleanness. (8) Even if the object shifted was clean. (9) *Sc.* the coverlet of a *zab* that was not in direct contact with the *zab*, (other coverlets having intervened) which is Rabbinically unclean as *middaf*. (10) Even if he did not touch it with his hand but only with his body. (11) Much

APPOINTED FOR THE WATER OF THE SIN-OFFERING TOUCHED A MIDDAF UNCLEANNESS,[1] IT BECOMES UNCLEAN. IF A MAN WHO WAS CLEAN FOR THE WATER OF THE SIN-OFFERING TOUCHED FOODSTUFFS OR LIQUIDS[2] WITH HIS HAND, HE BECOMES UNCLEAN, BUT IF HE DID IT WITH HIS FOOT HE REMAINS CLEAN. IF HE SHIFTED THEM WITH HIS HAND,[3] R. JOSHUA RULES THAT HE BECOMES UNCLEAN, AND THE SAGES RULE THAT HE REMAINS CLEAN.

MISHNAH 3. AN [EARTHEN] JAR OF THE WATER OF THE SIN-OFFERING THAT TOUCHED A [DEAD] CREEPING THING, REMAINS CLEAN.[4] IF THE JAR WAS PUT ON IT,[5] R. ELIEZER RULES THAT IT REMAINS CLEAN, AND THE SAGES RULE[6] THAT IT BECOMES UNCLEAN. IF THE JAR TOUCHED FOODSTUFFS OR LIQUIDS[7] OR THE HOLY SCRIPTURES,[8] IT REMAINS CLEAN.[4] IF IT WAS PUT ON THEM, R. JOSE RULES THAT IT REMAINS CLEAN,[9] AND THE SAGES RULE THAT IT BECOMES UNCLEAN.[10]

MISHNAH 4. A MAN WHO WAS CLEAN FOR THE WATER OF THE SIN-OFFERING THAT TOUCHED AN OVEN[11] WITH HIS HAND BECOMES UNCLEAN,[12] BUT IF HE DID IT WITH HIS FOOT HE REMAINS CLEAN.[12] IF HE STOOD ON AN OVEN AND PUT OUT HIS HAND BEYOND THE OVEN WITH THE FLAGON[13] IN

more so if he touched the bedding under the *zab*, which is Pentateuchally a 'father of uncleanness'.

(1) Cf. *supra* n. 2. (2) That were clean in regard to *terumah* and consecrated things, but not in regard to the water of the sin-offering. (3) Without touching them. (4) Since earthenware do not contract uncleanness from their outer sides. (5) The dead creeping thing. (6) On the strength of a deduction from Num. XIX, 9 according to which the container of the water of the sin-offering must be set in '*a clean place*'. (7) That were unclean. (8) Which Rabbinically convey uncleanness to the hands or foodstuffs that touch them (cf. Yad. IV, 6). (9) Since it did not rest on a 'father of uncleanness'. (10) Because, in their view, it must rest in a place which is clean in all respects (cf. *supra* n. 6). (11) Even one that was clean for holy things. (12) As in the case of foodstuffs (*supra* X, 2). (13) For the water of the sin-offering.

HIS HAND, AND SO ALSO IN THE CASE OF A CARRYING-YOKE WHICH WAS PLACED OVER THE OVEN AND FROM WHICH TWO JARS WERE SUSPENDED ONE AT EITHER END,[1] R. AKIBA RULES THAT THEY REMAIN CLEAN,[2] BUT THE SAGES RULE THAT THEY ARE UNCLEAN.[3]

MISHNAH 5. IF HE WAS STANDING OUTSIDE AN OVEN AND HE STRETCHED FORTH HIS HAND TO A WINDOW WHEREFROM HE TOOK A FLAGON AND PASSED IT OVER THE OVEN, R. AKIBA RULES THAT IT IS UNCLEAN,[4] AND THE SAGES RULE THAT IT IS CLEAN. HE, HOWEVER, WHO WAS CLEAN FOR THE WATER OF THE SIN-OFFERING MAY STAND OVER AN OVEN WHILE HOLDING IN HIS HAND AN EMPTY VESSEL THAT IS CLEAN FOR THE WATER OF THE SIN-OFFERING OR ONE FILLED WITH WATER THAT HAS NOT YET BEEN MIXED WITH THE ASHES OF THE RED COW.

MISHNAH 6. IF A FLAGON CONTAINING THE WATER OF THE SIN-OFFERING TOUCHED A VESSEL CONTAINING CONSECRATED FOOD OR TERUMAH, THAT CONTAINING THE WATER OF THE SIN-OFFERING BECOMES UNCLEAN,[5] BUT THE ONE CONTAINING THE CONSECRATED FOOD OR THE TERUMAH REMAINS CLEAN.[6] IF HE HELD THE TWO VESSELS[7] ONE IN EACH OF HIS TWO HANDS, BOTH BECOME UNCLEAN.[8] IF THEY

(1) Outside the oven. (2) Being outside and beyond the oven they may be regarded as resting on a clean place. (3) Since they are supported by the man, or the yoke that rests on the oven, they also are deemed to rest on a place that is unclean. (4) Passing in the air-space above the oven is in his opinion regarded as on a par with passing through the interior of the oven. (5) Even for common food. The flagon that contracted uncleanness from the vessel of the *terumah* conveys uncleanness to the water of the sin-offering within it, and this unclean water then renders the flagon itself unclean in the first degree. (6) Since it only touched an uncleanness of the first degree which cannot convey any uncleanness to vessels. (7) That of the water of the sin-offering and that of the consecrated food or *terumah*. (8) That of the sin-offering becomes unclean on account of its contact with the man's hand which has become unclean like all his body, when he touched that of the

WERE BOTH WRAPPED IN SEPARATE PAPERS, THEY REMAIN CLEAN.[1] IF THE VESSEL OF THE WATER OF THE SIN-OFFERING WAS WRAPPED IN A PAPER WHILE THAT OF THE TERUMAH WAS HELD IN HIS HAND,[2] BOTH BECOME UNCLEAN.[3] IF THE ONE CONTAINING THE TERUMAH WAS HELD IN HIS HAND WRAPPED UP IN PAPER WHILE THAT CONTAINING THE WATER OF THE SIN-OFFERING WAS HELD IN HIS HAND, BOTH REMAIN CLEAN.[4] R. JOSHUA RULED: THAT CONTAINING THE WATER OF THE SIN-OFFERING BECOMES UNCLEAN. IF BOTH WERE PLACED ON THE GROUND AND A MAN TOUCHED THEM,[5] THAT OF THE SIN-OFFERING BECOMES UNCLEAN[6] BUT THAT OF THE CONSECRATED FOOD OR TERUMAH REMAINS CLEAN.[7] IF HE ONLY SHIFTED IT,[8] R. JOSHUA RULES THAT IT IS UNCLEAN, AND THE SAGES RULE THAT IT IS CLEAN.

terumah, while the vessel of *terumah* or consecrated food becomes unclean by contact with the man who was carrying the water of the sin-offering.

(1) Because, though a vessel of paper (papyrus) may contract uncleanness, a scrap of paper does not, and it, therefore, forms an intervention between the uncleanness and the man. (2) With no paper wrapper around it. (3) Because, when the man had touched with his hand the vessel of the *terumah*, that of the sin-offering becomes unclean since the paper in this case constitutes no interposition. The man who becomes unclean because of his carrying of the invalid water of the sin-offering conveys uncleanness to the vessel of the *terumah* which he had touched with his hand. (4) That of the *terumah* remains clean because the paper constitutes an interposition between the hand and the other vessel, and that of the water of the sin-offering remains clean since the uncleanness of the man, which was caused by this water, cannot be retransmitted to the water that caused it. (5) Simultaneously. (6) Since the man who became unclean by touching the flagon of the *terumah* conveys uncleanness to the water of the sin-offering which, in turn conveys uncleanness to the flagon that contains them. (7) Since the man did not carry the invalid water but only touched its container which, being but a first grade of uncleanness, cannot convey any uncleanness to the man who is only susceptible to the uncleanness imparted by a 'father of uncleanness'. (8) But did not directly touch it.

PARAH

CHAPTER XI

MISHNAH 1. A FLASK[1] THAT ONE HAS LEFT UNCOVERED AND ON RETURNING FOUND IT TO BE COVERED, IS INVALID.[2] IF ONE LEFT IT COVERED AND ON RETURNING FOUND IT TO BE UNCOVERED, IT IS INVALID IF A WEASEL[3] COULD HAVE DRUNK FROM IT[4] OR, ACCORDING TO THE RULING OF RABBAN GAMALIEL,[5] A SERPENT, OR IF IT WAS POSSIBLE FOR DEW TO FALL INTO IT IN THE NIGHT.[6] THE WATER OF THE SIN-OFFERING[7] IS NOT PROTECTED[8] BY A TIGHTLY FITTING COVER;[9] BUT WATER THAT HAD NOT YET BEEN MIXED WITH THE ASHES IS PROTECTED BY A TIGHTLY FITTING COVER.[10]

MISHNAH 2. ANY CONDITION OF DOUBT THAT IS REGARDED AS CLEAN IN THE CASE OF TERUMAH IS ALSO REGARDED AS CLEAN IN THE CASE OF THE WATER OF THE SIN-OFFERING. IN ANY CONDITION OF SUSPENSE WHERE TERUMAH IS CONCERNED[11] THE WATER OF THE SIN-OFFERING IS POURED AWAY. IF CLEAN THINGS WERE HANDLED[12] ON

(1) *Ẓeloḥith* (cf. relevant n. *supra* IX, 1) containing the water and the ashes of the red cow for sprinkling. (2) Since it is obvious that someone had handled it and this one might have been unclean for the sin-offering, who thus conveyed uncleanness to it. (3) Which vomits when it drinks. (4) Because its spittle, mingling with the water, causes invalidity. (5) *Supra* IX, 3. (6) Otherwise it is valid, since no man would be likely to uncover it (cf. *supra* n. 2). (7) That was already mixed with the ashes; and the same applies to the ashes alone. (8) From uncleanness, if it is with a corpse under the same roof. (9) Though other objects are thereby protected (cf. Num. XIX, 15). The protection cannot be extended to the water of the sin-offering since under the same roof as the corpse it cannot be said to be set in *a clean place* (cf. Num. XIX, 9). (10) Since the requirement to set in '*a clean place*' (cf. prev. n.) does not apply, to the water alone. (11) *Sc.* when it is neither eaten nor burned. (12) By a person who became clean (v. foll. n.).

ACCOUNT OF IT,[1] THEY MUST BE HELD IN SUSPENSE.[2] WOODEN LATTICE WORK[3] IS CLEAN IN RESPECT OF HOLY FOOD, TERUMAH, AND THE WATER OF THE SIN-OFFERING. R. ELIEZER RULED: LOOSELY FASTENED BOARDS[4] ARE UNCLEAN[5] IN THE CASE OF THE WATER OF THE SIN-OFFERING.[6]

MISHNAH 3. IF PRESSED FIGS OF TERUMAH FELL INTO THE WATER OF THE SIN-OFFERING AND WERE TAKEN OUT AND EATEN, THE WATER BECOMES UNCLEAN,[7] AND HE WHO EATS OF THE FIGS INCURS DEATH[8] IF THEIR BULK WAS NO LESS THAN THE SIZE OF AN EGG,[9] IRRESPECTIVE OF WHETHER THEY WERE UNCLEAN OR CLEAN. IF[10] THEIR BULK WAS LESS THAN THE SIZE OF AN EGG, THE WATER REMAINS CLEAN BUT[11] HE WHO EATS OF THEM INCURS DEATH. R. JOSE RULED: IF THEY[12] WERE CLEAN THE WATER REMAINS CLEAN.[13] IF A MAN WHO WAS CLEAN FOR THE WATER OF THE SIN-OFFERING PUT IN HIS HEAD AND THE GREATER PART OF HIS BODY INTO THE WATER OF THE SIN-OFFERING, HE BECOMES UNCLEAN.[14]

MISHNAH 4. ALL[15] THAT[16] REQUIRE IMMERSION IN WATER

(1) *Sc.* after the water that had to be poured away was sprinkled upon him. (2) Cf. *supra* p. 344, n. 11. (3) Which is not susceptible to *midras* or corpse uncleanness. (4) *Hare'adoth*, 'which shake' when one leans on them. (5) As *middaf*. (6) Since they might be used to sit or lie upon and thus are susceptible to *midras* uncleanness, v. *supra* X, 1. (7) On account of its contact with the figs of *terumah* whose grade of cleanness is deemed to be an uncleanness in respect of the water of the sin-offering. (8) *Sc.* by the hands of Heaven; for eating *terumah* while his body is unclean on account of the water on it. (9) The minimum of foodstuffs required for conveying uncleanness. (10) Some edd. omit this sentence to 'death'. (11) 'But . . . death' is omitted in some edd. and by Elijah Wilna. (12) The pressed figs. (13) In his opinion the grade of uncleanness required for *terumah* is not regarded as unclean in respect of the water of the sin-offering. (14) From the water in the vessel which being 'drawn' has a defiling effect, v. Zab. V, 1. This water in turn, being sin-offering water, coming in contact with him is rendered unclean and assumes the restrictions of a 'father of uncleanness' which causes him in turn to be unclean in the first grade. (15) Men and vessels. (16) Having contracted uncleanness from a 'father of uncleanness' and became a first grade of uncleanness.

ACCORDING TO THE RULINGS OF THE TORAH CONVEY UNCLEANNESS TO CONSECRATED THINGS, TO TERUMAH, TO COMMON FOOD,[1] AND TO SECOND TITHE; AND[2] IS FORBIDDEN TO ENTER THE SANCTUARY. AFTER IMMERSION[3] ONE[2] CONVEYS UNCLEANNESS TO HOLY THINGS AND CAUSES TERUMAH TO BE UNFIT; SO R. MEIR. BUT THE SAGES RULED: HE[2] CAUSES CONSECRATED THINGS AND TERUMAH TO BE INVALID,[4] BUT IS PERMITTED UNCONSECRATED FOOD AND SECOND TITHE; AND IF HE ENTERED THE SANCTUARY,[5] WHETHER BEFORE OR AFTER HIS IMMERSION, HE INCURS GUILT.[6]

MISHNAH 5. ALL[7] THAT REQUIRE IMMERSION IN WATER IN ACCORDANCE WITH THE WORDS OF THE SCRIBES CONVEY UNCLEANNESS TO CONSECRATED THINGS AND CAUSE TERUMAH TO BE UNFIT, BUT[2] ARE PERMITTED UNCONSECRATED FOOD AND SECOND TITHE; SO R. MEIR. BUT THE SAGES FORBID[2] SECOND TITHE. AFTER IMMERSION[8] A MAN IS PERMITTED ALL THESE, AND IF HE ENTERED THE SANCTUARY, WHETHER BEFORE OR AFTER HIS IMMERSION, HE INCURS NO GUILT.

MISHNAH 6. ALL THAT REQUIRE IMMERSION IN WATER, WHETHER ACCORDING TO THE WORDS OF THE TORAH OR ACCORDING TO THE WORDS OF THE SCRIBES, CAUSE[9] WATER OF THE SIN-OFFERING, THE ASHES OF THE SIN-OFFERING, AND HIM WHO SPRINKLED THE WATER OF THE SIN-OFFERING,[10]

(1) Since a first grade of uncleanness causes even ordinary food to become a second grade of uncleanness. (2) In the case of a man. According to Maim. this applies equally to vessels. (3) Before the sun had set over him when as a *ṭebul yom* he is still subject to a second grade of uncleanness. (4) *Sc.* even consecrated things do not become unclean (and thus capable of conveying uncleanness) but unfit only. (5) The Court of the Israelites. (6) No guilt, however, is incurred for entering the Court of the Women, though entry into it is forbidden. (7) Such as men who ate or drank what is unclean, or vessels that have touched unclean liquids. (8) Even before sunset. (9) Even after an immersion that was not intended as a preparation for the services of the sin-offering. (10) *Sc.* all who are clean for the sin-offering.

TO BECOME UNCLEAN EITHER THROUGH CONTACT OR THROUGH CARRYING; AND ALSO CAUSE THE HYSSOP THAT HAS BEEN RENDERED SUSCEPTIBLE TO UNCLEANNESS, THE WATER THAT HAD NOT YET BEEN PREPARED,[1] AND AN EMPTY VESSEL THAT IS CLEAN FOR THE SIN-OFFERING TO BECOME UNCLEAN THROUGH CONTACT AND CARRYING; SO R. MEIR. BUT THE SAGES RULED: ONLY BY CONTACT[2] BUT NOT BY CARRYING.

MISHNAH 7. ANY HYSSOP THAT BEARS A SPECIAL NAME IS INVALID.[3] ORDINARY[4] HYSSOP IS VALID. GREEK HYSSOP, STIBIUM HYSSOP, ROMAN HYSSOP OR WILD HYSSOP IS INVALID. THAT OF UNCLEAN *TERUMAH*[5] IS INVALID; BUT THAT OF CLEAN *TERUMAH*[6] SHOULD NOT BE USED FOR SPRINKLING,[7] THOUGH IF ONE HAD USED IT FOR SPRINKLING IT IS VALID. THE SPRINKLING MUST NOT BE DONE EITHER WITH THE YOUNG SHOOTS OR WITH THE BERRIES.[8] NO GUILT IS INCURRED [AFTER THE SPRINKLING HAD BEEN DONE] WITH YOUNG SHOOTS FOR ENTERING THE SANCTUARY. R. ELIEZER RULED: NOR IF IT WAS DONE WITH THE BERRIES. THE FOLLOWING ARE REGARDED AS YOUNG SHOOTS: THE STALKS BEFORE THE BUDS HAVE RIPENED.

MISHNAH 8. THE HYSSOP THAT WAS USED FOR SPRINKLING [THE WATER OF THE SIN-OFFERING] IS ALSO FIT FOR CLEANSING THE LEPER.[9] IF IT[10] WAS GATHERED FOR FIREWOOD, AND LIQUID[11] FELL UPON IT, IT MAY BE DRIED AND IT BECOMES FIT.[12] IF IT[10] WAS GATHERED FOR FOOD, AND

(1) By mixing it with the ashes of the red cow. (2) Do these become unclean. (3) For the sprinkling of the water of the sin-offering. (4) Lit., 'this'. (5) Though it was less in bulk than the size of an egg which, in regard to the water of the sin-offering, is insusceptible to uncleanness. (6) That was duly prepared for the water of the sin-offering. (7) In case the water of the sin-offering might become invalid and thus convey uncleanness to the *terumah*. (8) Of the hyssop. (9) Cf. Lev. XIV, 4ff. (10) The hyssop. (11) That was unfit for the water of the sin-offering. (12) For use in the sprinkling of the water of the

LIQUID[1] FELL UPON IT, EVEN THOUGH IT WAS DRIED, IT IS INVALID.[2] IF IT[3] WAS GATHERED FOR [THE SPRINKLING OF THE WATER OF] THE SIN-OFFERING, IT IS SUBJECT TO THE SAME LAW AS IF IT WERE GATHERED FOR FOOD. SO R. MEIR. R. JUDAH, R. JOSE AND R. SIMEON RULED: AS IF IT WERE GATHERED FOR FIREWOOD.

MISHNAH 9. THE PRESCRIBED RITE OF THE HYSSOP IS [THAT THE BUNCH[4] SHALL CONTAIN] THREE STALKS BEARING THREE BUDS.[5] R. JUDAH RULED: STALKS BEARING THREE BUDS EACH. HYSSOP THAT CONSISTS OF A GROWTH OF THREE STALKS[6] SHOULD BE CUT UP[7] AND THEN BOUND TOGETHER. IF THE STALKS WERE SEVERED BUT WERE NOT BOUND TOGETHER, OR IF THEY WERE BOUND TOGETHER BUT WERE NOT SEVERED, OR IF THEY WERE NEITHER SEVERED NOR BOUND TOGETHER, THEY ARE NEVERTHELESS VALID. R. JOSE RULED: THE PRESCRIBED RITE OF THE HYSSOP IS THAT THE BUNCH SHALL CONTAIN THREE[8] BUDS, BUT ITS REMNANTS[9] NEED ONLY HAVE TWO, WHILE ITS STUMPS[10] MAY BE[11] OF THE SMALLEST SIZE.

sin-offering. Such use is forbidden while the liquid is upon it since the invalid liquid would cause invalidity to water of the sin-offering with which it mingles.

(1) V. p. 347, n. 11. (2) Because the liquid caused the hyssop to be susceptible to uncleanness and at the same time (since it was unfit for the sin-offering) conveyed uncleanness to it. (3) V. p. 347, n. 10. (4) With which the sprinkling is done. (5) One bud on each stalk. (6) Growing from one root. (7) Into three separate stalks. (8) Some edd. insert 'stalks having three'. (9) If one was lost in the course of sprinkling. (10) Which must originally be a handbreadth in length. (11) If the bunch was worn away from use.

PARAH

CHAPTER XII

MISHNAH 1. HYSSOP THAT IS TOO SHORT[1] MAY BE MADE TO SUFFICE[1] WITH A THREAD AND A SPINDLE-REED. IT[2] IS THEN DIPPED AND BROUGHT UP AGAIN, WHEN ONE GRASPS THE HYSSOP ITSELF AND SPRINKLES WITH IT. R. JUDAH AND R. SIMEON RULED: AS THE SPRINKLING MUST BE DONE WITH THE HYSSOP ITSELF SO MUST THE DIPPING ALSO BE DONE WITH THE HYSSOP ITSELF.

MISHNAH 2. IF A MAN SPRINKLED[3] AND IT IS DOUBTFUL WHETHER THE WATER CAME FROM THE THREAD OR THE SPINDLE-REED OR THE BUDS, THE SPRINKLING IS INVALID.[4] IF HE SPRINKLED UPON TWO VESSELS AND IT IS DOUBTFUL WHETHER HE SPRINKLED ON BOTH OR WHETHER SOME WATER FROM THE ONE HAD DRIPPED ON TO THE OTHER, IT IS INVALID. IF A NEEDLE WAS FIXED TO AN EARTHENWARE AND THE MAN SPRINKLED UPON IT, AND IT IS DOUBTFUL WHETHER HE SPRINKLED ON THE NEEDLE OR WHETHER SOME WATER DRIPPED ON IT FROM THE EARTHENWARE, HIS SPRINKLING IS INVALID. IF THE FLASK[5] HAS A NARROW MOUTH, ONE MAY DIP IN[6] AND DRAW OUT IN THE USUAL WAY.[7] R. JUDAH RULED: THIS MAY BE DONE ONLY FOR THE FIRST SPRINKLING.[8] IF THE WATER OF THE SIN-OFFERING WAS DIMINISHED,[9]

(1) To reach the water of the sin-offering in the flask. (2) Being held by the spindle. (3) The water of the sin-offering. (4) Since the man is under presumptive uncleanness. Only when it is certain that the water came from the hyssop is the sprinkling valid. (5) Containing the water and the ashes of the red cow. (6) The hyssop in the water. (7) One need have no scruples lest the water on the hyssop would be squeezed out in its passage through the narrow neck. (8) But not for a subsequent one when any water that would have been squeezed out from the first might have returned to the flask and rendered its contents invalid. (9) Being insufficient for the proper dipping of the hyssop into it.

ONE MAY DIP ONLY THE TIPS OF THE BUDS AND SPRINKLE, PROVIDED THE HYSSOP DOES NOT ABSORB [ANY OF THE MOISTURE ON THE SIDES OF THE FLASK].[1] IF A MAN INTENDED TO SPRINKLE IN FRONT OF HIM AND HE SPRINKLED BEHIND HIM, OR BEHIND HIM AND HE SPRINKLED IN FRONT OF HIM, HIS SPRINKLING IS INVALID. IF HE INTENDED TO SPRINKLE IN FRONT OF HIM AND HE SPRINKLED TO THE SIDES IN FRONT OF HIM, HIS SPRINKLING IS VALID. IT IS PERMITTED TO SPRINKLE UPON A MAN WITH HIS KNOWLEDGE OR WITHOUT HIS KNOWLEDGE, AND IT IS PERMITTED TO SPRINKLE UPON A MAN AND VESSELS[2] EVEN THOUGH THERE ARE A HUNDRED OF THEM.

MISHNAH 3. IF A MAN INTENDED TO SPRINKLE UPON A THING THAT IS SUSCEPTIBLE TO UNCLEANNESS AND HE SPRINKLED UPON ONE THAT WAS NOT SUSCEPTIBLE TO UNCLEANNESS,[3] THERE IS NO NEED TO DIP AGAIN IF ANY OF THE WATER[4] STILL REMAINED ON THE HYSSOP.[5] [IF HE INTENDED TO SPRINKLE] UPON A THING THAT IS NOT SUSCEPTIBLE TO UNCLEANNESS AND HE SPRINKLED ON THAT WHICH IS SUSCEPTIBLE TO UNCLEANNESS, EVEN THOUGH THERE WAS STILL SOME WATER[4] ON THE HYSSOP, HE MUST DIP AGAIN.[6] [IF HE INTENDED TO SPRINKLE] UPON A MAN AND HE SPRINKLED UPON A BEAST, HE NEED NOT DIP[6] AGAIN IF ANY OF THE WATER[4] REMAINED ON THE HYSSOP; BUT [IF HE INTENDED TO SPRINKLE] UPON A BEAST AND HE SPRINKLED UPON A MAN, EVEN THOUGH THERE WAS STILL SOME WATER[4] ON THE HYSSOP, HE MUST DIP AGAIN. THE WATER THAT DRIPS OFF[7] IS VALID,[8] AND THEREFORE IT CONVEYS UNCLEANNESS AS THE USUAL WATER OF THE SIN-OFFERING.

(1) The requirement being to dip into the water. (2) Simultaneously, by one movement. (3) This is explained presently. (4) Of the sin-offering. (5) From the first dip. (6) The hyssop in the water. (7) Into the flask from the hyssop that was dipped with the intention of sprinkling upon a thing that is insusceptible to uncleanness. (8) For sprinkling.

MISHNAH 4. IF ONE WAS SPRINKLING[1] FROM A WALL-NICHE[2] IN A PUBLIC DOMAIN AND [A MAN WHO WAS SO SPRINKLED UPON][3] ENTERED THE SANCTUARY,[4] AND THE WATER WAS FOUND TO BE INVALID, HE IS BLAMELESS;[5] BUT IF THE SPRINKLING WAS DONE FROM A PRIVATE WALL-NICHE AND [A MAN WHO WAS SO SPRINKLED UPON][3] ENTERED THE SANCTUARY,[4] AND THE WATER WAS FOUND TO BE INVALID, HE INCURS THE PENALTY.[6] A HIGH PRIEST, HOWEVER, IS EXEMPT,[7] WHETHER THE SPRINKLING UPON HIM WAS DONE FROM A PRIVATE WALL-NICHE OR FROM ONE IN A PUBLIC DOMAIN, FOR A HIGH PRIEST NEVER INCURS A PENALTY FOR ENTERING THE SANCTUARY. [THE PEOPLE] USED TO SLIP BEFORE A CERTAIN WALL-NICHE IN A PUBLIC DOMAIN,[8] AND MOREOVER[9] THEY TROD[10] [ON THAT SPOT] AND DID NOT REFRAIN [FROM ENTERING THE SANCTUARY], BECAUSE IT WAS LAID DOWN THAT WATER OF THE SIN-OFFERING THAT SERVED ITS PURPOSE[11] CONVEYED NO UNCLEANNESS.

MISHNAH 5. A CLEAN PERSON MAY HOLD IN HIS SKIRT AN UNCLEAN AXE[12] AND SPRINKLE UPON IT;[13] AND ALTHOUGH THERE IS ON IT[14] SUFFICIENT WATER FOR A SPRINKLING HE

(1) The water with the ashes of the red cow. (2) A special niche with water of sin-offering was provided for the purification of the unclean. (3) Having been unclean and requiring the performance of the rite. (4) Not ascertaining beforehand whether the water was valid. (5) Because, a doubtful condition of uncleanness in a public domain being regarded as clean, he was under no obligation to enquire after the validity of the water. (6) Of a sacrifice. As a doubtful condition of uncleanness in a private domain is deemed to be unclean it was his duty to enquire after the validity of the water before he entered the Sanctuary. (7) If he entered the Sanctuary after he had been sprinkled upon with water that was found to be invalid. (8) On account of the abundance of the water of the sin-offering that was sprinkled there. (9) Though such water would be expected to convey uncleanness. (10) Intentionally. (11) Sprinkling. (12) Though it was a 'father of uncleanness'. (13) Since the skirt which, owing to contact with the axe (cf. prev. n.), becomes only a first grade of uncleanness cannot convey any uncleanness to the man to whom only a 'father of uncleanness' could convey uncleanness. (14) The axe, after the sprinkling.

REMAINS CLEAN.[1] OF WHAT QUANTITY MUST THE WATER CONSIST TO BE SUFFICIENT FOR A SPRINKLING? SUFFICIENT FOR THE TOPS OF THE BUDS TO BE DIPPED THEREIN AND FOR THE SPRINKLING TO BE PERFORMED.[2] R. JUDAH RULED: THEY[3] ARE REGARDED AS THOUGH THEY WERE ON A HYSSOP OF BRASS.[4]

MISHNAH 6. IF THE SPRINKLING WAS DONE WITH UNCLEAN HYSSOP,[5] THE WATER BECOMES INVALID, AND THE SPRINKLING IS INVALID IF IT[6] WAS OF THE BULK OF AN EGG. IF IT WAS LESS THAN THE BULK OF AN EGG,[7] THE WATER REMAINS VALID BUT THE SPRINKLING IS INVALID.[8] IT[9] ALSO CONVEYS UNCLEANNESS[10] TO OTHER HYSSOP,[11] AND THAT OTHER HYSSOP TO OTHER, EVEN IF THEY BE A HUNDRED.[12]

MISHNAH 7. IF THE HANDS[13] OF A MAN WHO WAS CLEAN FOR THE WATER OF THE SIN-OFFERING BECAME UNCLEAN, HIS BODY ALSO BECOMES UNCLEAN, AND HE CONVEYS UNCLEANNESS TO HIS FELLOW, AND HIS FELLOW TO HIS FELLOW, EVEN IF THEY BE A HUNDRED.

MISHNAH 8. SHOULD THE OUTER PART OF A FLAGON[14] BECOME UNCLEAN,[15] ITS INNER PART ALSO BECOMES UNCLEAN,[16] AND IT CONVEYS UNCLEANNESS TO ANOTHER FLAGON, AND

(1) Having served their purpose they no longer convey uncleanness. (2) *Sc.* there must be as much water as to suffice for these as well as for the quantity of water absorbed by the buds. (3) The buds. (4) Which absorbs no water. Hence the water absorbed is added to what remains on the surface and a smaller quantity (cf. *supra* n. 2) suffices. (5) *Sc.* unclean for the water of the sin-offering though clean in other respects. (6) The hyssop having been gathered for food (cf. *supra* XI, 8.) (7) The prescribed minimum for conveying uncleanness. (8) Since the hyssop was not clean for the sin-offering (cf. *supra* n. 5). (9) The unclean hyssop. (10) By contact. (11) Rendering consequently unclean him who touches it. (12) Rendering it unfit for sprinkling. Since in regard to the water of the sin-offering the conveyance of uncleanness is not limited to the third grade. (13) Or even only one hand. (14) Containing the water of the sin-offering. (15) From unclean liquids. (16) Contrary to the rule in other cases (cf. Kel. XXV, 9).

THE OTHER TO ANOTHER, EVEN IF THEY ARE A HUNDRED. A BELL AND A CLAPPER ARE REGARDED AS CONNECTED.[1] IN THE CASE OF A SPINDLE USED FOR COARSE MATERIAL, ONE MUST NOT SPRINKLE ON ITS ROD[2] OR RING,[2] YET IF IT WAS SO SPRINKLED IT IS VALID; IN A SPINDLE USED FOR FLAX THEY[3] ARE REGARDED AS CONNECTED. IF A LEATHER COVER OF A COT IS FASTENED TO ITS KNOBS, BOTH[4] ARE REGARDED AS CONNECTED.[1] THE BAṢE[5] DOES NOT CONSTITUTE A CONNECTION[6] EITHER IN RESPECT OF UNCLEANNESS[7] OR CLEANNESS.[8] ALL DRILLED HANDLES OF UTENSILS[9] ARE REGARDED AS CONNECTIVES.[10] R. JOḤANAN B. NURI RULES: ALSO THOSE[11] THAT[12] ARE WEDGED INTO HOLES IN THE UTENSILS.[13]

MISHNAH 9. THE BASKETS OF A PACK-SADDLE,[14] THE BED OF A BARROW,[15] THE IRON[16] CORNER OF A BIER, THE [DRINKING] HORNS OF TRAVELLERS,[15] A KEY CHAIN,[17] THE LOOSE STITCHES OF WASHERMEN,[18] AND A GARMENT STITCHED TOGETHER WITH KIL'AYIM ARE REGARDED AS CONNECTIVES[19] IN RESPECT OF UNCLEANNESS[20] BUT NOT IN THAT OF SPRINKLING.[8]

(1) Both as regards uncleanness and sprinkling. Contact with or sprinkling upon one equally affects the other. (2) Alone; since they are not regarded as connected. The sprinkling must be done on the spindle-hook which is the principal part of the instrument. (3) Rod and ring. (4) Cot and cover. (5) On which the cot or a bed stands. (6) With the cot or bed. (7) If only one contracted uncleanness the other remains clean. (8) If one was sprinkled upon the other still remains unclean. (9) The handle of a knife, for instance, into the hole of which the blade is inserted and secured. (10) With the utensils. (11) Handles. (12) No hole being drilled in them. (13) Are connectives with the utensils. (14) That are joined together. (15) Consisting of detachable parts. (16) And detachable. (17) Holding a number of keys. (18) Whereby garments are held together and protected against loss. (19) The baskets with each other, the parts of the barrow, the iron corner and the bier, the parts of the drinking horns, the stitches and the garments, and the garment stitched together with *kil'ayim*. (20) If one part becomes unclean the other also becomes similarly unclean.

MISHNAH 10. IF THE LID OF A KETTLE IS JOINED TO A CHAIN,[1] BETH SHAMMAI RULED: THESE[2] ARE REGARDED AS CONNECTED IN RESPECT OF UNCLEANNESS[3] BUT NOT IN RESPECT OF SPRINKLING.[4] BETH HILLEL RULED: IF THE KETTLE[5] WAS SPRINKLED UPON IT IS THE SAME AS IF THE LID[6] ALSO WAS SPRINKLED UPON; BUT IF THE LID ONLY[6] WAS SPRINKLED UPON IT IS NOT THE SAME AS IF THE KETTLE ALSO[5] WAS SPRINKLED UPON. ALL[7] ARE ELIGIBLE TO SPRINKLE, EXCEPT A ṬUMṬUM,[8] A HERMAPHRODITE, A WOMAN, AND A CHILD THAT IS WITHOUT UNDERSTANDING. A WOMAN MAY ASSIST [A MAN] WHILE HE SPRINKLES, AND HOLD THE WATER[9] FOR HIM WHILE HE DIPS AND SPRINKLES. IF SHE HELD HIS HAND, EVEN IF ONLY AT THE TIME OF SPRINKLING,[10] IT IS INVALID.[11]

MISHNAH 11. IF THE HYSSOP WAS DIPPED[12] IN THE DAYTIME AND THE SPRINKLING ALSO WAS DONE ON THE SAME DAY, IT IS VALID.[13] IF ONE DIPPED IT IN THE DAYTIME AND SPRINKLED AT NIGHT, OR DIPPED AT NIGHT AND SPRINKLED ON THE FOLLOWING DAY, (OR DIPPED IN THE DAYTIME AND SPRINKLED ON THE FOLLOWING DAY),[14] THE SPRINKLING IS INVALID.[15] [THE MAN HIMSELF], HOWEVER, MAY PERFORM IMMERSION AT NIGHT AND DO THE SPRINKLING ON THE FOLLOWING DAY, FOR SPRINKLING IS NOT ALLOWED[16] UNTIL THE SUN IS RISEN;[17] YET IF ANY OF THESE WAS DONE AS EARLY AS THE RISE OF DAWN IT IS VALID.

(1) Which is attached to the kettle. (2) The lid and the kettle. (3) V. p. 353, n. 20. (4) V. p. 353, n. 8. (5) Which is the main vessel. (6) Which is only subsidiary to the kettle. (7) Even the uncircumcised. (8) V. Glos. (9) Of the sin-offering. (10) Much more so if she held it when he was dipping. (11) Since, according to Num. XIX, 18, a 'clean *man*' must perform these services. (12) In the water of the sin-offering. (13) Though there may have been a long interval between the dipping and the sprinkling. (14) Var. lec. omits. (15) Cf. ibid. 19. (16) In the night. (17) Hence the sprinkling must be performed by day.

מסכת פרה
ת ו ש ל ב ע
הדרן עלך
והדרך עלן
תורה אור

ṬOHOROTH

TRANSLATED INTO ENGLISH

WITH NOTES

BY

Rev. Dr Israel W. SLOTKI, M. A., Litt. D.

INTRODUCTION

The Tractate Ṭohoroth[1] which bears the same name as the order that comprises it enunciates the laws of cleanness and uncleanness in relation mainly to foodstuffs and liquids, and to men engaged in their preparation or consumption and to vessels employed in the process.

CHAPTER I, beginning with thirteen rules that govern the carrion of clean birds, passes on to those relating to unclean ones and cattle, and proceeds to a discussion of the extent to which foodstuffs of major and minor grades of uncleanness may be combined to constitute the prescribed minima and under what conditions the same or different grades of uncleanness may be conveyed to a number of loaves or pieces of dough, for instance, that clung to one another.

CHAPTER II deals with uncleanness that may be conveyed to dry or wet *terumah* (v. Glos.) by the hands of a clean as well as an unclean person and with the various grades of uncleanness a person may contract from eating, and a foodstuff from contact with foodstuffs of corresponding grades of uncleanness.

CHAPTER III discusses the grades of uncleanness and minima applicable to foodstuffs that are capable of changing from a condition of fluidity to one of solidity and *vice versa*, and the uncleanness or cleanness of those whose bulk is increased or decreased by reason of weather conditions, concluding with a discussion on various forms of doubtful uncleanness.

CHAPTER IV continues the discussion of doubtful cases of uncleanness including those in which either the clean or the unclean object is on the move; those that are causes for the burning of *terumah;* and those that are invariably regarded as clean.

CHAPTERS V and VI are concerned mainly with doubtful cases of uncleanness in which (*a*) a public domain and (*b*) both a public and a private domain are respectively involved.

(1) טְהָרוֹת plural of טָהֳרָה, purification, cleansing (also euphemism for uncleanness).

Chapter VII discusses forms of doubtful uncleanness that are due to the presence of an *'am ha-areẓ* (v. Glos.) or his wife.

Chapter VIII brings to a conclusion the subject of the previous chapter and proceeds to enunciate rules on the stages when food-stuffs begin and cease respectively to be susceptible to uncleanness and on a number of cases of Rabbinical uncleanness caused through liquids.

Chapter IX discusses mainly the stages at which olives become susceptible to uncleanness.

Chapter X concludes the Tractate with the laws of cleanness and uncleanness that apply to an olive-press and a wine-press.

I. W. SLOTKI

ṬOHOROTH

CHAPTER I

MISHNAH 1. THIRTEEN RULINGS GOVERN THE CARRION OF A CLEAN BIRD: THERE MUST BE[1] INTENTION[2] BUT[3] IT NEED NOT BE RENDERED SUSCEPTIBLE;[4] IT CONVEYS FOOD UNCLEANNESS[5] IF ITS MINIMUM BULK IS THAT OF AN EGG; AND IT CONVEYS UNCLEANNESS[6] WHEN IN ONE'S GULLET[7] IF ITS MINIMUM BULK IS THAT OF AN OLIVE; HE THAT EATS OF IT MUST WAIT[8] UNTIL SUNSET;[9] GUILT IS INCURRED ON ACCOUNT OF IT FOR ENTERING THE SANCTUARY;[10] TERUMAH IS BURNT ON ACCOUNT OF IT;[11] HE WHO EATS A MEMBER OF IT WHILE IT IS ALIVE MUST SUFFER THE PENALTY OF FORTY STRIPES;[12] SLAUGHTERING IT[13] OR WRINGING ITS NECK[14] FREES IT FROM UNCLEANNESS EVEN WHEN IT IS ṬREFA.[15] SO R. MEIR.[16] R. JUDAH RULED: THEY DO NOT FREE IT FROM UNCLEANNESS. R. JOSE RULED: THE SLAUGHTERING[13] DOES FREE IT FROM THE UNCLEANNESS BUT THE WRINGING OF ITS NECK[14] DOES NOT.

MISHNAH 2. THE LARGE FEATHERS[17] AND THE DOWN[18]

(1) If it is to convey uncleanness. (2) To use it as human food. (3) Unlike other dry permitted foodstuffs. (4) To uncleanness, by purposely bringing it in contact with a liquid. (5) *Sc.* renders clean foodstuffs, which it touches, unclean in the second grade. (6) To the man who eats it who becomes a 'father of uncleanness' and in turn conveys an uncleanness of the first grade to clothes or vessels with which he is then in contact. (7) Even before it had been swallowed. (8) Before he can attain cleanness. (9) Immersion alone being insufficient. (10) After eating of it. (11) If it or the man who ate it came in contact with the *terumah*. (12) A round figure for the prescribed thirty-nine. (13) Outside the Temple. (14) In the Temple, as a sacrifice (cf. Lev. I, 15). (15) And forbidden as food. (16) Whose nine (out of the thirteen) rulings have so far been enumerated. The other four follow in the next Mishnah anonymously and are likewise the rulings of R. Meir. (17) *Aliter:* The small feathers. (18) Of a clean bird.

CONTRACT UNCLEANNESS,[1] AND[2] CONVEY UNCLEANNESS[3] BUT DO NOT COMBINE [WITH THE FLESH TO CONSTITUTE THE PRESCRIBED MINIMUM].[4] R. ISHMAEL RULED: THE DOWN DOES COMBINE [WITH THE FLESH]. THE BEAK[5] AND THE CLAWS[6] CONTRACT UNCLEANNESS[1] AND[2] CONVEY UNCLEANNESS AND ALSO COMBINE [WITH THE FLESH TO CONSTITUTE THE PRESCRIBED MINIMUM].[4] R. JOSE RULED: ALSO THE ENDS[7] OF THE WINGS AND THE END[7] OF THE TAIL COMBINE [WITH THE FLESH TO CONSTITUTE THE MINIMUM],[4] SINCE THEY ARE LEFT UNPLUCKED ON FATTENED BIRDS.[8]

MISHNAH 3. THE CARRION OF AN UNCLEAN BIRD NECESSITATES[9] INTENTION[10] AND[9] IT MUST BE RENDERED SUSCEPTIBLE;[11] IT CONVEYS FOOD UNCLEANNESS[12] IF ITS MINIMUM BULK[13] IS THAT OF AN EGG; THE CONSUMPTION OF A HALF OF HALF A LOAF'S BULK[14] OF IT[15] RENDERS ONE'S PERSON UNFIT TO EAT TERUMAH;[16] AN OLIVE'S BULK OF IT IN ONE'S GULLET CONVEYS NO UNCLEANNESS; HE WHO EATS OF IT NEED NOT WAIT FOR SUNSET;[17] NO GUILT IS INCURRED ON ACCOUNT OF IT[18] FOR ENTERING THE SANCTUARY;[19] BUT ON ACCOUNT OF IT[18] TERUMAH[20] MUST BE BURNT; HE WHO EATS A MEMBER OF IT WHILE IT IS ALIVE IS NOT SUBJECT TO THE

(1) In case the bird was not carrion and a dead creeping thing touched it. (2) If the bird was carrion. (3) To foodstuffs that touched them. (4) Of an egg or an olive (cf. *supra* I, 1 *ab init.*) to convey uncleanness. These do not act as 'protection' to the flesh to serve as correctives, v. 'Uḳ. I, 1. (5) So much of it as is covered with flesh. (6) Cf. prev. n. (7) Nearest the body. (8) Thus constituting a union with the flesh. (9) If it is to contract and convey uncleanness. (10) To use it as food. (11) To uncleanness, by purposely bringing it in contact with a liquid. (12) Renders foodstuffs that it touches unclean. (13) That touched a dead creeping thing. (14) The bulk of two eggs (Rashi) or one and a half eggs (Maim.). (15) When it was unclean. (16) Before performing immersion, though there is no need to wait for sunset. (17) But may eat *terumah* even before. (18) If a man ate the prescribed minimum after it had become unclean. (19) Since the uncleanness conveyed to the man is only Rabbinical. (20) That the man touched.

PENALTY OF FORTY STRIPES,[1] BUT SLAUGHTERING IT DOES NOT IMMEDIATELY[2] RENDER IT FIT.[3] THE LARGE FEATHERS AND THE DOWN CONTRACT UNCLEANNESS AND CONVEY UNCLEANNESS AND COMBINE WITH THE FLESH TO CONSTITUTE THE PRESCRIBED MINIMUM. THE BEAK AND THE CLAWS CONTRACT UNCLEANNESS AND CONVEY UNCLEANNESS AND COMBINE [WITH THE FLESH TO MAKE UP THE PRESCRIBED MINIMUM].

MISHNAH 4. IN THE CASE OF CATTLE, THE HIDE, GREASE, SEDIMENT, FLAYED-OFF FLESH, BONES, SINEWS, HORNS AND HOOFS COMBINE[4] [WITH THE FLESH] TO CONVEY FOOD UNCLEANNESS[5] BUT NOT TO CONVEY CARRION UNCLEANNESS.[6] SIMILARLY, IF A MAN[7] SLAUGHTERED AN UNCLEAN BEAST FOR AN IDOLATER AND IT WAS STILL JERKING ITS LIMBS,[8] IT CONVEYS FOOD UNCLEANNESS;[9] BUT IT CONVEYS NO CARRION UNCLEANNESS UNTIL IT IS DEAD OR ITS HEAD IS CHOPPED OFF.[10] [SCRIPTURE THUS] LAID DOWN MORE RESTRICTIONS IN REGARD TO THE CONVEYANCE OF FOOD UNCLEANNESS THAN IN REGARD TO THE CONVEYANCE OF CARRION UNCLEANNESS.

MISHNAH 5. A FOODSTUFF THAT CONTRACTED UNCLEANNESS FROM A 'FATHER OF UNCLEANNESS' AND ONE THAT CONTRACTED UNCLEANNESS FROM A DERIVED UN-

(1) Because the relevant prohibition does not apply to forbidden creatures (v. Ḥul. 102*a*). (2) While it is still struggling and subject to the prohibition of a 'member from the living'. (3) For a Noachite who is permitted carrion but not a 'member from the living'. (4) To make up the prescribed minimum of the bulk of an egg. (5) If the flesh had contracted uncleanness from a dead creeping thing for instance. (6) To make up the bulk of an olive, for eating, touching or carrying, which is the prescribed minimum in the case of carrion. (7) An Israelite. (8) When to a Noachite it is still forbidden as a 'member of a living animal'. (9) Because the slaughtering performed by the Israelite, which renders a clean beast fit for consumption, also causes an unclean beast to be regarded as food both in respect of contracting uncleanness and of conveying it. (10) This is derived in Ḥul. 117*b* from Lev. XI, 39.

CLEANNESS[1] MAY BE COMBINED TOGETHER[2] TO CONVEY UNCLEANNESS ACCORDING TO THE LIGHTER GRADE OF THE TWO. HOW SO? IF THE BULK OF HALF AN EGG OF FOOD OF A FIRST GRADE OF UNCLEANNESS AND THE BULK OF HALF AN EGG OF FOOD OF A SECOND GRADE OF UNCLEANNESS WERE MIXED TOGETHER, THE TWO[3] ARE REGARDED AS SUFFERING ONLY SECOND GRADE UNCLEANNESS;[4] AND IF THE BULK OF HALF AN EGG OF FOOD OF A SECOND GRADE OF UNCLEANNESS AND THE BULK OF HALF AN EGG OF FOOD OF A THIRD GRADE OF UNCLEANNESS WERE MIXED TOGETHER, THE TWO[3] ARE REGARDED AS SUFFERING ONLY THIRD GRADE OF UNCLEANNESS.[5] IF THE BULK OF AN EGG OF FOOD OF A FIRST GRADE OF UNCLEANNESS AND THE BULK OF AN EGG OF FOOD OF A SECOND GRADE OF UNCLEANNESS WERE MIXED TOGETHER, BOTH[3] ARE REGARDED[6] AS SUFFERING FIRST GRADE UNCLEANNESS;[7] BUT IF THEY WERE THEN DIVIDED, EACH PART[8] IS REGARDED AS SUFFERING ONLY A SECOND GRADE OF UNCLEANNESS.[9] IF EACH PART[10] SEPARATELY FELL ON A LOAF OF TERUMAH, THEY CAUSE IT TO BECOME UNFIT,[11] BUT IF THE TWO FELL TOGETHER THEY CAUSE IT TO SUFFER SECOND GRADE OF UNCLEANNESS.

MISHNAH 6. THE BULK OF AN EGG OF FOOD OF A SECOND GRADE OF UNCLEANNESS AND THE BULK OF AN EGG OF FOOD OF A THIRD GRADE OF UNCLEANNESS THAT WERE MIXED TOGETHER ARE[3] REGARDED AS SUFFERING SECOND

(1) So that the former is subject to a first grade, and the latter only to a second grade of uncleanness. (2) To make up the prescribed minimum of the bulk of an egg. (3) While they are together. (4) Which causes no uncleanness to unconsecrated foodstuffs and only *invalidity* to *terumah*. (5) That causes no invalidity even to *terumah*. (6) Since the mixture contains the full prescribed minimum of this grade of uncleanness. (7) Which consequently causes unconsecrated food to be unclean. (8) Which contains only a half of the prescribed minimum of each grade. (9) As *supra*. (10) Which is suffering second grade of uncleanness. (11) Since *terumah* is rendered invalid by a second grade of uncleanness. The term 'unfit' in connection with uncleanness denotes that the uncleanness contracted is not capable of being conveyed a grade further.

GRADE OF UNCLEANNESS.[1] IF THEY WERE THEN DIVIDED, EACH PART[2] IS REGARDED AS SUFFERING ONLY THIRD GRADE OF UNCLEANNESS.[3] IF EACH PART SEPARATELY FELL ON A LOAF OF TERUMAH THEY DO NOT RENDER IT INVALID,[4] BUT IF THE TWO FELL TOGETHER THEY CAUSE IT TO SUFFER THIRD GRADE OF UNCLEANNESS. THE BULK OF AN EGG OF FOOD OF A FIRST GRADE OF UNCLEANNESS AND THE BULK OF AN EGG OF FOOD OF A THIRD GRADE OF UNCLEANNESS THAT WERE MIXED TOGETHER ARE[5] REGARDED AS SUFFERING FIRST GRADE OF UNCLEANNESS,[6] BUT IF THEY WERE THEN DIVIDED, EACH PART IS REGARDED AS SUFFERING ONLY SECOND GRADE UNCLEANNESS,[1] FOR EVEN THE THIRD GRADE THAT TOUCHED THE FIRST HAS BECOME ONLY A SECOND GRADE. IF THE BULK OF TWO EGGS OF FOOD OF THE FIRST GRADE OF UNCLEANNESS AND THE BULK OF TWO EGGS OF FOOD OF THE SECOND GRADE OF UNCLEANNESS WERE MIXED TOGETHER THEY ARE REGARDED AS SUFFERING FIRST GRADE OF UNCLEANNESS. IF THEY WERE THEN DIVIDED, EACH PART IS STILL REGARDED AS SUFFERING FIRST GRADE OF UNCLEANNESS. BUT IF THEY WERE DIVIDED INTO THREE OR FOUR PARTS, EACH IS REGARDED AS SUFFERING FROM SECOND GRADE. IF THE BULK OF TWO EGGS OF FOOD OF THE SECOND GRADE OF UNCLEANNESS AND THE BULK OF TWO EGGS OF FOOD OF THE THIRD GRADE OF UNCLEANNESS WERE MIXED TOGETHER, THEY ARE REGARDED AS SUFFERING SECOND GRADE OF UNCLEANNESS. IF THEY WERE THEN DIVIDED, EACH PART IS STILL REGARDED AS SUFFERING SECOND GRADE OF UNCLEANNESS. BUT IF THEY WERE DIVIDED INTO THREE OR FOUR PARTS, EACH IS REGARDED AS SUFFERING ONLY THIRD GRADE OF UNCLEANNESS.

MISHNAH 7. IF PIECES OF DOUGH[7] CLUNG TO EACH

(1) V. p. 364, n. 4. (2) V. p. 364, n. 8. (3) V. p. 364, n. 9. (4) A third grade of uncleanness (unlike a second grade) cannot cause *terumah* to be invalid. (5) V. p. 364, n. 3. (6) V. p. 364, n. 7. (7) Of *terumah*.

OTHER[1] OR IF LOAVES ADHERED TO EACH OTHER,[2] AND ONE OF THEM CONTRACTED UNCLEANNESS FROM A [DEAD] CREEPING THING,[3] THEY ALL BECOME UNCLEAN IN THE FIRST GRADE;[4] AND IF THEY WERE THEN SEPARATED THEY ARE STILL REGARDED AS SUFFERING FIRST GRADE OF UNCLEANNESS. IF ONE OF THEM CONTRACTED UNCLEANNESS FROM A LIQUID[5] THEY ALL SUFFER SECOND GRADE OF UNCLEANNESS;[4] AND IF THEY WERE THEN SEPARATED THEY ARE STILL REGARDED AS SUFFERING SECOND GRADE OF UNCLEANNESS. IF ONE OF THEM CONTRACTED UNCLEANNESS FROM THE HANDS,[6] THEY ALL BECOME UNCLEAN IN THE THIRD GRADE; AND IF THEY WERE THEN SEPARATED THEY ARE STILL REGARDED AS SUFFERING THIRD GRADE OF UNCLEANNESS.

MISHNAH 8. IF TO A PIECE OF DOUGH[7] THAT WAS SUFFERING FIRST GRADE OF UNCLEANNESS OTHERS WERE MADE TO ADHERE,[1] THEY ALL BECOME UNCLEAN IN THE FIRST GRADE;[4] AND IF IT WAS SEPARATED, IT STILL REMAINS UNCLEAN IN THE FIRST GRADE BUT ALL THE OTHERS ARE REGARDED AS SUFFERING ONLY SECOND GRADE OF UNCLEANNESS.[8] IF TO A PIECE OF DOUGH[7] THAT WAS SUFFERING SECOND GRADE OF UNCLEANNESS OTHERS WERE MADE TO ADHERE,[1] THEY ALL BECOME UNCLEAN IN THE SECOND GRADE;[4] AND IF IT WAS SEPARATED, IT STILL REMAINS UNCLEAN IN THE SECOND GRADE BUT ALL THE OTHERS ARE ONLY UNCLEAN IN THE THIRD GRADE OF UNCLEANNESS. IF TO A PIECE[7] THAT WAS UNCLEAN IN THE THIRD GRADE OTHERS WERE MADE TO ADHERE,[1] IT REMAINS UNCLEAN IN THE THIRD

(1) To such an extent that it is impossible to separate one from the other without tearing away some dough from the one or the other. (2) Cf. prev. n. (3) Which is a 'father of uncleanness' and imparts a first grade of uncleanness. (4) Their adhesion causing them to be regarded as one. (5) Which is invariably subject to the first grade of uncleanness. (6) Which, unless especially taken care of, are always regarded as suffering second grade of uncleanness and impart third grade of uncleanness. (7) Of *terumah*. (8) Imparted to them by the piece that is first grade of uncleanness.

GRADE BUT ALL THE OTHERS REMAIN CLEAN,[1] IRRESPECTIVE OF WHETHER THEY WERE SUBSEQUENTLY SEPARATED FROM IT OR WHETHER THEY WERE NOT SEPARATED.

MISHNAH 9. IF OF HOLY LOAVES[2] IN WHOSE HOLLOWS THERE WAS HOLY WATER[3] ONE CONTRACTED UNCLEANNESS FROM A [DEAD] CREEPING THING, THEY ALL BECOME UNCLEAN.[4] IN THE CASE OF LOAVES OF TERUMAH,[5] UNCLEANNESS IS CONVEYED TO TWO LOAVES[6] AND INVALIDITY TO ONE.[7] IF THERE WAS DRIPPING LIQUID BETWEEN THEM,[8] EVEN IN THE CASE OF TERUMAH ALL[8] BECOME UNCLEAN.[9]

(1) Since there is no fourth grade of uncleanness in *terumah*. (2) E.g., Shewbread; and the loaves were touching each other. (3) I.e., water that was prepared in purity under conditions of holiness. (4) Since the first loaf that was touched by the creeping thing contracted a first grade of uncleanness; the second loaf contracted from the first one a second grade of uncleanness; the third loaf contracts from the second a third grade of uncleanness and (since in the case of holy things a third grade may cause a fourth grade of uncleanness) it also imparts uncleanness to the water on it which (in accordance with the uncleanness of liquids) becomes unclean in the first grade and causes the loaf to contract second grade of uncleanness and so impart to the next loaf third grade of uncleanness. The next loaf, for the same reason, imparts second grade of uncleanness to the one next to it, and so on *ad infinitum*. Var. lec.: If consecrated loaves lay in their hollows (i.e., the loaves were each lying in separate hollows of a board), and similarly holy water (in the hollows of a stone). (5) Which, unlike holy things, never suffers fourth grade of uncleanness. (6) First grade uncleanness is conveyed by the creeping thing to the first loaf which it touched, and second grade uncleanness is conveyed by the first loaf to the second one that touched it. (7) The third loaf that was touched by the second. Since in *terumah* a third cannot make a fourth it becomes only invalid but not unclean. As the loaf in the third grade cannot convey uncleanness, the water on it remains clean so that neither it nor the water can convey uncleanness to the next loaf that touched it, which (like the next loaf that touched it and the one that touched the next, and so on) consequently remains clean. (8) The loaves. (9) The liquid between the first loaf and a second becomes, in accordance with the law of unclean liquids, unclean in the first grade and consequently conveys uncleanness of the second grade to the second loaf that touched it. Similarly the water between the second and the third loaves becomes unclean in the first grade and causes the third loaf to be unclean in the second grade, and so on *ad infinitum*.

ṬOHOROTH

CHAPTER II

MISHNAH I. IF A WOMAN WHO[1] WAS PRESERVING VEGETABLES[2] IN A POT TOUCHED[3] A PROJECTING LEAF OUTSIDE THE POT ON A DRY SPOT,[4] EVEN THOUGH THERE WAS AN EGG'S BULK[5] IN THE LEAF,[6] IT ALONE BECOMES UNCLEAN[7] WHILE ALL THE REST[8] REMAINS CLEAN.[9] IF SHE TOUCHED IT[10] AT A WET SPOT[11] AND THERE WAS AN EGG'S BULK[5] IN THE LEAF,[6] ALL[12] BECOMES UNCLEAN.[13] IF THERE WAS NOT AN EGG'S BULK[5] IN IT,[14] IT ALONE BECOMES UNCLEAN BUT ALL THE REST REMAINS CLEAN. IF IT[15] RETURNED INTO THE POT, ALL[12] BECOMES UNCLEAN.[16] IF THE WOMAN WAS UNCLEAN[17] OWING TO CONTACT WITH ONE WHO CONTRACTED CORPSE UNCLEANNESS,[18] AND SHE TOUCHED THE LEAF EITHER AT

(1) When in a condition of cleanness. (2) Of *terumah*. (3) With her hands which, having been unwashed, are regarded as being in a state of second grade uncleanness. (4) Which, unlike the wet part of the leaf within the pot, had never come in contact with liquids and, therefore, has never been rendered susceptible to uncleanness. (5) The prescribed minimum for capability to convey uncleanness to others. (6) As a whole. (7) Strictly speaking, 'invalid'; i.e. in the third grade of uncleanness, having contracted it from the woman's hands (cf. *supra* n. 3). (8) Whose uncleanness could be derived only from contact with this leaf. (9) Because a third grade of uncleanness in *terumah* cannot convey uncleanness to others. (10) The leaf under discussion. (11) So that her hands (in accordance with the laws of uncleanness governing liquids) conveyed to the liquid a first grade of uncleanness. (12) The pot itself as well as its contents. (13) Because the water (cf. prev. n. but one) imparts to the leaf a second grade of uncleanness which in turn conveys to the water in the pot a first grade of uncleanness which conveys to the pot and its contents a second grade of uncleanness. (14) From 'ALL BECOMES UNCLEAN' to 'IT' is omitted from some edd. (14) The wet part of the leaf touched. (16) Even if the bulk of the leaf was less than that of an egg, because the smallest quantity of liquid on the leaf conveys uncleanness. (17) In the first grade. (18) The corpse being a 'father of the fathers of uncleanness'.

A WET SPOT OR AT A DRY SPOT, ALL[1] BECOMES UNCLEAN IF THERE WAS AN EGG'S BULK IN THE LEAF;[2] BUT IF THERE WAS NOT AN EGG'S BULK[3] IN IT, IT ALONE BECOMES UNCLEAN AND ALL THE REST REMAINS CLEAN. IF A WOMAN WHO WAS A ṬEBULATH YOM[4] EMPTIED OUT THE POT WITH UNWASHED[5] HANDS,[6] AND SHE OBSERVED SOME LIQUID ON HER HANDS, AND IT IS UNCERTAIN WHETHER IT WAS SPLASHED FROM THE POT OR WHETHER A STALK[7] HAD TOUCHED HER HANDS, THE VEGETABLES ARE INVALID[8] BUT THE POT REMAINS CLEAN.[9]

MISHNAH 2. R. ELIEZER RULED: HE WHO EATS FOOD OF FIRST [GRADE UNCLEANNESS[10] CONTRACTS] FIRST [GRADE UNCLEANNESS]; [HE WHO EATS FOOD OF] SECOND [GRADE UNCLEANNESS[10] CONTRACTS] SECOND [GRADE UNCLEANNESS]; [IF IT WAS] THIRD [GRADE UNCLEANNESS HE CONTRACTS] THIRD [GRADE UNCLEANNESS]. R. JOSHUA RULED: HE WHO EATS FOOD OF FIRST [GRADE] OR OF SECOND [GRADE UNCLEANNESS CONTRACTS] SECOND [GRADE UNCLEANNESS]; [IF IT WAS] THIRD [GRADE UNCLEANNESS, HE CONTRACTS] SECOND [GRADE UNCLEANNESS] IN REGARD TO HOLY

the man who came in contact with it is a 'father of uncleanness', and imparts to the woman first grade uncleanness.

(1) The pot as well as its contents. (2) Since the leaf which, owing to the moisture on it was susceptible to uncleanness, conveys an uncleanness of the first grade to the liquid in the pot and this in turn causes the pot and its contents to contract second grade uncleanness. (3) The prescribed minimum for capability to convey uncleanness to others. (4) Fem. of *ṭebul yom;* a *ṭebul yom* continues until sunset unclean in the second degree. (5) Lit., 'soiled'. (6) Which are regarded as suffering second grade uncleanness. (7) Of the wet vegetable. (8) As the uncleanness of a *ṭebul yom* is Pentateuchal any condition of doubt must be decided restrictively as certain uncleanness. (9) Since a *ṭebul yom* does not render liquids unclean in the first grade (cf. Parah VIII, 7) and the hands (whose uncleanness is but Rabbinical) are in this matter of doubt regarded as clean, there is nothing that could impart uncleanness to the pot. (10) A minimum of the bulk of two eggs (Rashi) or of one and a half eggs (Maim.).

THINGS[1] BUT NOT IN REGARD TO TERUMAH.[2] ALL THIS APPLIES TO COMMON FOODSTUFFS THAT WERE PREPARED IN CONDITION OF CLEANNESS THAT ARE APPROPRIATE FOR TERUMAH.[3]

MISHNAH 3. FIRST [GRADE UNCLEANNESS] IN COMMON FOOD IS UNCLEAN AND CONVEYS UNCLEANNESS;[4] SECOND [GRADE UNCLEANNESS[5]] CONVEYS INVALIDITY[6] BUT DOES NOT CONVEY UNCLEANNESS;[7] AND THIRD [GRADE UNCLEANNESS][8] MAY BE EATEN IN A DISH MIXED WITH TERUMAH.[9]

MISHNAH 4. FIRST [GRADE] AND SECOND [GRADE UNCLEANNESS] IN TERUMAH ARE UNCLEAN AND CONVEY UNCLEANNESS;[10] THIRD [GRADE UNCLEANNESS][11] CAUSES INVALIDITY[12] BUT CONVEYS NO UNCLEANNESS; AND THE FOURTH [GRADE UNCLEANNESS][13] MAY BE EATEN IN A DISH CONTAINING HOLY FOOD.[14]

MISHNAH 5. FIRST, SECOND AND THIRD [GRADES OF UNCLEANNESS] IN HOLY FOODSTUFFS ARE UNCLEAN AND CONVEY UNCLEANNESS;[12] THE FOURTH [GRADE OF UNCLEAN-

(1) Which may contract from it third grade uncleanness and convey to other consecrated things fourth grade of uncleanness. (2) Which he may consequently touch, though he must not eat it. (3) Otherwise common food cannot give rise to a third grade uncleanness; nor can it apply to actual *terumah* or to holy food which, if unclean, must not be eaten at all. (4) To *terumah*, which in turn can render other *terumah* 'invalid'. If it touched common food it only renders it 'invalid', but the latter can convey no uncleanness or even invalidity to other common food. (5) In common food. (6) To *terumah*. (7) *Sc.* the *terumah* it touched conveys neither uncleanness nor 'invalidity' to other *terumah* and much less so to common food. (8) Applicable to unconsecrated food that was kept under conditions of *terumah* cleanness. (9) If the mixing was accidental. *Aliter:* It may under certain conditions be intentionally mixed with it. (10) The first grade conveys uncleanness to *terumah* and the second grade conveys uncleanness to holy things only. (11) In *terumah*. (12) To holy food. (13) Applicable to *terumah* that was kept under conditions of cleanness appropriate to holy food. (14) Since in respect of *terumah* it is altogether clean.

NESS] IS INVALID[1] AND CAUSES NO UNCLEANNESS; AND THE FIFTH [GRADE OF UNCLEANNESS][2] MAY BE EATEN IN A DISH CONTAINING CONSECRATED FOOD.

MISHNAH 6. SECOND [GRADE UNCLEANNESS] IN COMMON FOOD CONVEYS UNCLEANNESS TO UNCONSECRATED LIQUIDS[3] AND CAUSES INVALIDITY TO FOODSTUFFS OF TERUMAH. THIRD [GRADE OF UNCLEANNESS] IN TERUMAH CONVEYS UNCLEANNESS TO CONSECRATED LIQUIDS[3] AND CAUSES INVALIDITY TO HOLY FOODSTUFFS IF IT[4] WAS PREPARED IN CONDITIONS OF CLEANNESS APPROPRIATE TO HOLY FOOD; BUT IF IT WAS ONLY PREPARED UNDER CONDITIONS OF CLEANNESS APPROPRIATE TO TERUMAH, IT CONVEYS UNCLEANNESS AT A FIRST AND AT A SECOND REMOVE, AND CAUSES INVALIDITY TO HOLY FOOD AT ONE ADDITIONAL REMOVE.[5]

MISHNAH 7. R. ELIEZER OBSERVED: THE THREE OF THEM[6] ARE ON A PAR IN THE FOLLOWING CASES. THE FIRST GRADE OF UNCLEANNESS IN HOLY FOOD, IN TERUMAH OR IN COMMON FOOD CONVEYS UNCLEANNESS AT TWO REMOVES[7] AND CAUSES INVALIDITY AT ONE ADDITIONAL REMOVE[5] IN THE CASE OF HOLY FOOD; IT CONVEYS UNCLEANNESS AT ONE REMOVE[8] AND CAUSES INVALIDITY AT ONE ADDITIONAL REMOVE[5] IN THE CASE OF TERUMAH; AND IN COMMON FOOD IT ONLY CAUSES INVALIDITY. THE SECOND [GRADE OF UNCLEANNESS] IN THE CASE OF ALL OF THEM[6] CONVEYS UNCLEANNESS AT ONE REMOVE[5] AND CAUSES INVALIDITY AT ONE ADDITIONAL REMOVE[9] AS REGARDS HOLY FOOD; IT CONVEYS UNCLEANNESS TO COMMON LIQUIDS[3] AND CAUSES THE INVALIDITY OF FOODSTUFFS OF TERUMAH. THE THIRD

(1) Var. lec., 'causes invalidity'. (2) In the case of holy foodstuffs that were kept under conditions of cleanness proper to the ashes of the red heifer. (3) Rendering them unclean in the first grade. (4) The *terumah*. (5) A third. (6) Holy food, *terumah* and common food. (7) Second and third. (8) A second. (9) A fourth.

GRADE [OF UNCLEANNESS] IN THE CASE OF ALL THESE[1] CONVEYS UNCLEANNESS TO HOLY LIQUIDS[2] AND CAUSES INVALIDITY TO HOLY FOODSTUFFS.

MISHNAH 8. IF A MAN EATS FOOD OF A SECOND [GRADE OF UNCLEANNESS] HE MUST NOT WORK IN AN OLIVE-PRESS.[3] COMMON FOODSTUFFS THAT WERE PREPARED UNDER CONDITIONS PROPER TO THE CLEANNESS OF CONSECRATED FOOD ARE STILL REGARDED AS COMMON FOOD.[4] R. ELIEZER SON OF R. ZADOK RULED: THEY ARE REGARDED AS TERUMAH TO CONVEY UNCLEANNESS AT TWO REMOVES[5] AND TO RENDER TERUMAH INVALID AT ONE ADDITIONAL REMOVE.[6]

(1) V. p. 371, n. 6. (2) V. p. 371, n. 3. (3) Where any oil of *terumah* would become invalid through contact with it. (4) Which cannot contract a third grade of uncleanness. The one particular man's fancy in treating them as consecrated food is disregarded in view of the common practice to treat them as common food. (5) First and second. (6) V. p. 371, n. 5.

ṬOHOROTH

CHAPTER III

MISHNAH 1. GREASE, BEAN-MASH AND MILK,[1] WHEN IN A CONDITION OF FLUIDITY,[2] ARE[3] UNCLEAN IN THE FIRST GRADE. IF[4] THEY TURNED SOLID THEY[5] BECOME UNCLEAN IN THE SECOND GRADE. IF THEY AGAIN TURNED INTO FLUIDITY THEY ARE CLEAN IF THEIR BULK WAS EXACTLY THAT OF AN EGG;[6] BUT IF IT WAS MORE THAN THE BULK OF AN EGG THEY REMAIN UNCLEAN, FOR AS SOON AS THE FIRST DROP ISSUED FORTH IT BECAME UNCLEAN BY CONTACT WITH AN EGG'S BULK.[7]

MISHNAH 2. R. MEIR RULED: OIL[1] ALWAYS[8] REMAINS UNCLEAN IN THE FIRST GRADE;[9] AND THE SAGES RULED: HONEY ALSO.[9] R. SIMEON OF SHEZUR RULED: ALSO WINE.[9] IF A MASS OF OLIVES[1] FELL INTO AN OVEN THAT WAS HEATED[10] THE LATTER REMAINS CLEAN IF THE BULK OF THE OLIVES WAS EXACTLY THAT OF AN EGG;[11] BUT IF IT WAS MORE THAN THAT OF AN EGG THE OVEN BECOMES UNCLEAN,[12] FOR SO SOON AS THE FIRST DROP ISSUED FORTH IT BECAME UNCLEAN

(1) That contracted any uncleanness. (2) Capable also of moistening other foodstuffs. (3) As is the rule of unclean liquids. (4) After contracting uncleanness. (5) Having been in contact, so to speak, with a liquid (their former shape) of the first grade of uncleanness. (6) Because, when the first drop was formed, the solid part was thereby reduced to less than an egg's bulk and, therefore, became incapable of conveying any uncleanness to that drop (and much less to any subsequent drop) which, having assumed a new form of existence, has also passed into a state of cleanness. (7) Of the remaining solid. The rest of the liquified matter then contracts uncleanness from that drop since any quantity of liquid is capable of conveying uncleanness. (8) Even when congealed. (9) Like liquids, since it never changes into a proper solid. (10) The heat causing some liquid to flow out from the solid olives. (11) V. *supra* n. 6. (12) From contact with the liquid.

BY CONTACT WITH AN EGG'S BULK. IF THE OLIVES WERE SEPARATED THE OVEN REMAINS CLEAN EVEN IF THERE WAS A SE'AH OF THEM.[1]

MISHNAH 3. IF A MAN WHO CONTRACTED CORPSE UNCLEANNESS PRESSED OUT[2] THE JUICE OF OLIVES OR GRAPES[3] WHOSE BULK WAS EXACTLY THAT OF AN EGG, THE JUICE REMAINS CLEAN[4] PROVIDED HE DOES NOT TOUCH THE PLACE ON WHICH THE LIQUID IS; BUT [IF THE BULK WAS] MORE THAN THAT OF AN EGG, THE JUICE BECOMES UNCLEAN,[5] FOR SO SOON AS THE FIRST DROP ISSUED FORTH IT BECAME UNCLEAN BY CONTACT WITH AN EGG'S BULK. IF THE PERSON[6] WAS A ZAB OR A ZABAH [THE JUICE] BECOMES UNCLEAN EVEN IF ONLY ONE BERRY [WAS PRESSED OUT], FOR SO SOON AS THE FIRST DROP ISSUED FORTH IT[7] BECAME UNCLEAN[8] BY CARRYING.[9] IF A ZAB MILKED A GOAT, THE MILK BECOMES UNCLEAN, FOR SO SOON AS THE FIRST DROP COMES FORTH IT[7] BECOMES UNCLEAN[8] BY CARRYING.[9]

MISHNAH 4. IF AN EGG'S BULK[10] OF FOODSTUFFS[11] WAS LEFT IN THE SUN AND IT SHRANK,[12] AND SO ALSO IN THE CASE OF AN OLIVE'S BULK OF CORPSE,[3] AN OLIVE'S[10] BULK OF CARRION,[13] A LENTIL'S BULK[10] OF A DEAD CREEPING THING,[13] AN OLIVE'S[10] BULK OF PIGGUL,[14] AN OLIVE'S BULK[10] OF NOTHAR,[14] OR AN OLIVE'S BULK[10] OF FORBIDDEN FAT[13] THEY BECOME CLEAN; NOR DOES ONE INCUR GUILT ON ACCOUNT OF THESE FOR TRANSGRESSING THE LAW OF PIGGUL, NOTHAR OR UNCLEANNESS.[15] IF THEY WERE THEN

(1) Since each olive is less than an egg's bulk. (2) In a container that was insusceptible to uncleanness. (3) Which he had touched before he pressed them. (4) V. p. 373, n. 6. (5) From contact with the unclean olives or grapes. (6) Who pressed out the juice. (7) Whatever its quantity. (8) In the first grade. (9) Or 'shaking' (*hesseṭ*) on the part of the *zab*, even if there was no direct contact. (10) The minimum that can convey uncleanness. (11) That contracted uncleanness. (12) So that less than the prescribed minimum (cf. prev. n. but one) remained. (13) That shrank (cf. prev. n.). (14) V. Glos. (15) Var. lec. 'and forbidden fat'.

LEFT OUT IN THE RAIN AND THEY SWELLED, THEY[1] BECOME UNCLEAN AND GUILT IS INCURRED ON ACCOUNT OF THEM FOR TRANSGRESSING THE LAW OF PIGGUL, NOTHAR OR UNCLEANNESS.

MISHNAH 5. ALL DOUBTFUL CASES OF UNCLEANNESS ARE DETERMINED ACCORDING TO THEIR APPEARANCE AT THE TIME THEY ARE FOUND: IF THEY WERE THEN[2] UNCLEAN THEY ARE ASSUMED TO HAVE BEEN UNCLEAN [ALL THE TIME][3] AND IF CLEAN[2] THEY ARE ASSUMED TO HAVE BEEN CLEAN [ALL THE TIME]; IF THEY WERE THEN[2] COVERED[4] THEY ARE ASSUMED TO HAVE BEEN COVERED [ALL THE TIME] AND IF UNCOVERED[2] THEY ARE ASSUMED TO HAVE BEEN UNCOVERED [ALL THE TIME]; IF A NEEDLE WAS FOUND FULL OF RUST[5] OR BROKEN,[5] IT IS CLEAN,[6] FOR ALL DOUBTFUL CASES OF UNCLEANNESS ARE DETERMINED ACCORDING TO THEIR APPEARANCE AT THE TIME THEY ARE FOUND.

MISHNAH 6. IF A DEAF-MUTE, AN IMBECILE OR A MINOR WAS FOUND IN AN ALLEY WAY[7] THAT CONTAINED AN UNCLEANNESS, HE IS PRESUMED TO BE CLEAN;[8] BUT ANY ONE OF SOUND SENSES[9] IS PRESUMED TO BE UNCLEAN.[10] FURTHER-

(1) Consisting now of the prescribed minimum. (2) When found. (3) If, for instance, a body was touched in the dark, and it is unknown whether it was that of a live or of a dead person, but later in the daylight it was found to be a corpse, it is assumed that death had occurred by the time it was touched, and the man that touched it is, therefore, unclean. (4) In cases where such covering affords protection against uncleanness. (5) A condition in which uncleanness ceases. (6) Even after the rust is removed or the needle is repaired, it being assumed that it was already in a rusty or broken condition at the time contact with the unclean object had taken place. (7) Which has the status of a private domain where doubtful cases of uncleanness are deemed to be unclean. (8) Because, as stated *infra*, one who is incapable of giving sensible information in reply to an enquiry is, in cases of doubtful uncleanness, deemed to be clean even in a private domain. (9) About whom there is doubt whether he did or did not touch an uncleanness. (10) In a private domain. In a public domain doubtful cases of uncleanness are always presumed to be clean.

MORE, WHATSOEVER LACKS UNDERSTANDING[1] TO BE INQUIRED OF IS IN A CASE OF DOUBTFUL UNCLEANNESS PRESUMED TO BE CLEAN.

MISHNAH 7. IF A CHILD[2] WAS FOUND AT THE SIDE OF A GRAVEYARD WITH LILIES IN HIS HAND, AND THE LILIES GREW ONLY IN A PLACE OF UNCLEANNESS, HE IS NEVERTHELESS CLEAN, FOR IT MAY BE ASSUMED THAT ANOTHER PERSON GATHERED THEM AND GAVE THEM TO HIM.[3] SO ALSO WHERE AN ASS WAS AMONG THE GRAVES[4] HIS HARNESS REMAINS CLEAN.[5]

MISHNAH 8. IF A CHILD[6] WAS FOUND[7] BESIDE DOUGH[8] WITH A PIECE OF DOUGH IN HIS HAND, R. MEIR RULES THAT THE DOUGH[9] IS CLEAN;[10] BUT THE SAGES RULE THAT IT IS UNCLEAN, SINCE IT IS THE NATURE OF A CHILD TO SLAP DOUGH.[11] IF A DOUGH[12] BORE TRACES OF HENS' PICKINGS AND THERE WAS UNCLEAN LIQUID IN THE SAME HOUSE, THE LOAVES[13] ARE DEEMED TO BE CLEAN IF THERE WAS DISTANCE ENOUGH BETWEEN THE LIQUID AND THE LOAVES FOR THE HENS TO DRY THEIR MOUTHS ON THE GROUND;[14] AND, IN THE

(1) Not only the categories of person mentioned but also cattle and utensils. (2) Who 'lacks understanding to be inquired of' (cf. prev. Mishnah); v. Soṭ. 28*a*ff. (3) Since the child accordingly was not in the graveyard, and since the lilies which suffered first grade uncleanness only cannot convey uncleanness to a human being, the child remains clean. (4) So that it is doubtful whether he did or did not overshadow a grave. (5) It being presumed that there was no overshadowing. (6) Who was unclean. (7) In a private domain. (8) That was clean. (9) At the side of which he was found. (10) Since some children (a minority) have not the habit of slapping dough and since the dough was in a presumptive state of cleanness the child in question (on the principle of minority plus presumption) may be assumed to belong to the class of children who do not slap dough, and the piece of dough in his hand may be presumed to have been given to him by some clean person. (11) As the majority of children do slap dough, the child in question must be presumed to be one of that class, and the dough that has presumably been touched by him must, therefore, be regarded as unclean. (12) Made into loaves. (13) Cf. prev. n. (14) After drinking of the unclean liquid, as is their nature after a drink.

CASE OF A COW OR A DOG, IF THERE WAS DISTANCE ENOUGH[1] FOR IT TO LICK ITS TONGUE;[2] AND, IN THE CASE OF ALL OTHER BEASTS, IF THERE WAS DISTANCE ENOUGH[1] FOR THEIR TONGUE TO DRY. R. ELIEZER B. JACOB HOLDS THE DOUGH TO BE CLEAN IN THE CASE OF A DOG WHO IS SAGACIOUS; FOR IT IS NOT ITS HABIT TO LEAVE FOOD[3] AND GO AFTER THE WATER.[4]

(1) Between the liquid and the dough. (2) Cf. p. 376, n. 14. (3) The dough, which is not easily procurable. (4) Which he can get much more easily. Hence it may well be presumed that before drinking the water he had well finished with the dough.

ṬOHOROTH

CHAPTER IV

MISHNAH 1. IF AN UNCLEAN[1] OBJECT WAS THROWN FROM ONE PLACE TO ANOTHER:[2] A LOAF[3] AMONG KEYS[4] OR A KEY[5] AMONG LOAVES,[6] [THAT WHICH WAS CLEAN REMAINS] CLEAN.[7] R. JUDAH[8] RULED: IF A LOAF[3] WAS THROWN AMONG KEYS[4] THE FORMER BECOMES UNCLEAN, BUT IF A KEY[5] WAS THROWN AMONG LOAVES[6] THE LATTER REMAIN CLEAN.

MISHNAH 2. IF A DEAD CREEPING THING WAS HELD IN THE MOUTH OF A WEASEL THAT WAS PASSING OVER LOAVES OF TERUMAH AND IT IS DOUBTFUL WHETHER THE CREEPING THING DID OR DID NOT TOUCH THEM, SUCH CONDITION OF DOUBT IS DEEMED CLEAN.[9]

MISHNAH 3. IF A WEASEL HELD IN ITS MOUTH A [DEAD] CREEPING THING OR IF A DOG HAD CARRION IN ITS MOUTH AND THEY PASSED BETWEEN CLEAN [PERSONS] OR IF CLEAN PERSONS PASSED BETWEEN THEM,[10] THEIR CONDITION OF DOUBT IS DEEMED CLEAN, SINCE THE UNCLEANNESS[11] HAD NO RESTING PLACE.[12] IF THEY[13] WERE PICKING AT THEM[14]

(1) Or clean (cf. foll. n.). (2) So that a doubt arose whether it touched anything clean or whether the clean object (cf. prev. n.) touched anything unclean. (3) That was clean (cf. prev. n. but one). (4) That were unclean. (5) That was unclean. (6) That were clean. (7) The assumption being that there was no contact after the haphazard throw between the clean and the unclean objects, and furthermore because the clean object under consideration lacks understanding, v. *supra* III, 6. (8) Drawing a distinction between an uncleanness at rest and one on the move. (9) Because the uncleanness was on the move, and because the bread lacks understanding, v. Sheḳ. II, 7. (10) It being doubtful whether there was contact between the clean and the unclean. (11) Which was on the move. (12) This principle applying even to persons, though these do not lack understanding. (13) Sc. the weasel or the dog. (14) The creeping thing or the carrion.

WHILE THESE[1] LAY ON THE GROUND,[2] AND A PERSON STATED, 'I WENT TO THAT PLACE BUT I DO NOT KNOW WHETHER I DID OR DID NOT TOUCH IT',[1] HIS CONDITION OF DOUBT IS DEEMED UNCLEAN, SINCE THE UNCLEANNESS HAD A RESTING PLACE.

MISHNAH 4. IF AN OLIVE'S BULK OF CORPSE WAS HELD IN A RAVEN'S MOUTH AND IT IS DOUBTFUL WHETHER IT OVERSHADOWED A MAN OR VESSELS IN A PRIVATE DOMAIN, THE MAN'S CONDITION OF DOUBT IS DEEMED TO BE UNCLEAN[3] BUT THE VESSELS' CONDITION OF DOUBT IS DEEMED CLEAN.[4] IF A MAN DREW WATER IN TEN BUCKETS[5] AND A DEAD CREEPING THING WAS FOUND IN ONE OF THEM,[6] IT ALONE IS DEEMED UNCLEAN BUT ALL THE OTHERS REMAIN CLEAN.[7] IF ONE POURED OUT FROM ONE VESSEL INTO ANOTHER AND A DEAD CREEPING THING WAS FOUND IN THE LOWER VESSEL, THE UPPER ONE REMAINS CLEAN.[8]

MISHNAH 5. ON ACCOUNT OF SIX DOUBTFUL CASES OF UNCLEANNESS IS TERUMAH BURNT:[9] ON ACCOUNT OF THE DOUBT OF A BETH HA-PERAS [GRAVE AREA],[10] ON ACCOUNT OF EARTH[11] ABOUT WHICH THERE IS DOUBT WHETHER IT CAME FROM THE LAND OF THE GENTILES,[12] ON ACCOUNT OF A DOUBT ABOUT THE GARMENTS OF AN 'AM HA-AREẒ,[13] ON

(1) V. p. 378, n. 14. (2) In a private domain. (3) For overshadowing, which reaches to the ground, is on a par with a resting uncleanness, and the man affected is capable of answering an enquiry (cf. *supra* III, 6). (4) Since vessels are not capable of answering an enquiry (cf. prev. n.). (5) One after the other. (6) A doubt thus arising whether the creeping thing was in the well and thus conveyed uncleanness to all the buckets. (7) It being assumed that where the uncleanness was found there it was all the time; and, though it came in contact with the water in the well, it conveyed no uncleanness to it, since the latter is regarded as attached to the ground which is not susceptible to uncleanness. (8) It is not assumed that the creeping thing was first in the upper vessel from which it subsequently dropped into the lower one. (9) In all other cases of doubtful uncleanness *terumah* may not be burnt. (10) Into which *terumah* was carried; on Beth ha-Peras, v. Glos. (11) Which came in contact with *terumah*. (12) In which case it would be unclean. (13) It being uncertain

ACCOUNT OF A DOUBT ABOUT VESSELS FOUND BY CHANCE,[1] ON ACCOUNT OF SPITTLE ENCOUNTERED BY CHANCE,[2] ON ACCOUNT OF A DOUBT ABOUT HUMAN URINE[2] THAT WAS NEAR THE URINE OF A BEAST.[3] ON ACCOUNT OF A CERTAINTY OF HAVING TOUCHED THESE, WHICH GIVES RISE TO THE DOUBTFUL UNCLEANNESS,[4] TERUMAH IS BURNT. R. JOSE RULED: ALSO ON ACCOUNT OF THEIR DOUBTFUL CONTACT[5] IN A PRIVATE DOMAIN;[6] BUT THE SAGES RULED: IN A PRIVATE DOMAIN THE TERUMAH IS ONLY HELD IN SUSPENSE[7] AND IN A PUBLIC DOMAIN IT IS DEEMED CLEAN.[8]

MISHNAH 6. IN THE CASE OF TWO KINDS OF SPITTLE, ONE OF WHICH WAS [POSSIBLY] UNCLEAN[9] AND THE OTHER WAS DECIDEDLY CLEAN, [ANY TERUMAH] IS TO BE HELD IN SUSPENSE IF [TOUCHED BY ONE WHO] TOUCHED OR CARRIED OR SHIFTED [ONE OF THE TWO KINDS OF SPITTLE] WHILE THEY WERE IN A PRIVATE DOMAIN, OR, WHO TOUCHED ONE OF THEM IN A PUBLIC DOMAIN WHILE IT WAS STILL MOIST, OR WHO CARRIED IT IRRESPECTIVE OF WHETHER IT WAS MOIST OR DRY. IF THERE WAS BUT ONE [KIND OF POSSIBLY] UNCLEAN SPITTLE AND A MAN TOUCHED, CARRIED OR SHIFTED IT IN A PUBLIC DOMAIN, TERUMAH[10] IS BURNT ON ACCOUNT OF IT; AND IT IS STILL MORE EVIDENT THAT THIS IS THE CASE IF IT WAS[11] IN A PRIVATE DOMAIN.

whether he did or did not touch them. If he did, uncleanness would have been conveyed to them.

(1) Which might possibly be unclean ones. (2) Which might be that of a *zab* or a menstruant and which would, therefore, convey uncleanness. (3) And thus distinguishable from it. If one kind alone is encountered a double doubt arises: Whether (*a*) it is that of a man or a beast and, if it is that of a man, whether (*b*) that man was unclean or clean. (4) Owing, as stated *supra*, to the doubtful nature of their uncleanness. (5) With *terumah;* though in such a case a double doubt arises. (6) Is *terumah* burnt. (7) Owing to the double doubt involved (cf. prev. n. but one). (8) For further notes on this Mishnah v. Shab. (Sonc. ed.) p. 156 notes. (9) In the case of certain uncleanness the *terumah*, touched in a private domain by one who came in contact with the spittle, would have had to be definitely burnt. (10) That the man subsequently touched. (11) Lit., 'and there is no need to say' that the *terumah* is to be burnt.

MISHNAH 7. THE FOLLOWING CASES OF DOUBTFUL UNCLEANNESS THE SAGES DECLARED TO BE CLEAN:[1] A CONDITION OF DOUBT CONCERNING DRAWN WATER IN RESPECT OF A RITUAL BATH,[2] AND A CONDITION OF DOUBT CONCERNING AN OBJECT OF UNCLEANNESS THAT FLOATED UPON THE WATER.[3] IN THE CASE OF A CONDITION OF DOUBT CONCERNING LIQUIDS AS TO WHETHER THEY HAVE CONTRACTED UNCLEANNESS IT IS DEEMED UNCLEAN, BUT IF IT WAS WHETHER UNCLEANNESS HAS BEEN CONVEYED IT IS DEEMED CLEAN. IF THERE IS DOUBT CONCERNING THE HANDS AS TO WHETHER THEY HAVE CONTRACTED UNCLEANNESS, HAVE CONVEYED UNCLEANNESS OR[4] HAVE ATTAINED CLEANNESS, THEY ARE DEEMED CLEAN. [THE SAGES, MOREOVER, DECLARED AS CLEAN] A CONDITION OF DOUBT THAT AROSE IN A PUBLIC DOMAIN;[5] A CONDITION OF DOUBT CONCERNING AN ORDINANCE OF THE SCRIBES; A CONDITION OF DOUBT CONCERNING COMMON FOODSTUFFS;[3] A CONDITION OF DOUBT CONCERNING CREEPING THINGS; A CONDITION OF DOUBT CONCERNING LEPROSY SIGNS; A CONDITION OF DOUBT CONCERNING A NAZIRITE VOW; A CONDITION OF DOUBT CONCERNING FIRSTLINGS; AND A CONDITION OF DOUBT CONCERNING SACRIFICES.

MISHNAH 8. 'A CONDITION OF DOUBT CONCERNING AN OBJECT OF UNCLEANNESS THAT FLOATED UPON THE WATER'[6] [IS DEEMED CLEAN] WHETHER[7] THE WATER WAS IN VESSELS OR IN THE GROUND. R. SIMEON RULED: IF IN VESSELS IT IS DEEMED UNCLEAN[8] BUT IF IN THE GROUND IT IS DEEMED

(1) Irrespective of whether they occurred in a private or in a public domain. (2) It being doubtful whether the drawn water had fallen into the ritual bath that contained less than the prescribed minimum of valid water or, if it was certain that it fell into it, whether its quantity was as much as three *logs* which constitute the minimum for invalidating a ritual bath. (3) This and the following cases are explained *infra*. (4) Having been unclean. (5) Even concerning a Pentateuchally ordained uncleanness. (6) Cf. prev. Mishnah. (7) It being uncertain whether a man had touched the uncleanness. (8) *Sc.* the man concerning whom a doubt arose as to whether he touched the unclean object is deemed unclean.

CLEAN.[1] R. JUDAH RULED: IF THE DOUBT[2] AROSE WHEN THE MAN WENT DOWN INTO THE WATER HE IS DEEMED UNCLEAN,[3] BUT IF WHEN HE CAME UP[4] HE IS DEEMED CLEAN. R. JOSE RULED: EVEN IF THE ROOM AVAILABLE[5] WAS NO MORE THAN WHAT SUFFICED FOR THE MAN AND THE UNCLEANNESS THE FORMER REMAINS CLEAN.

MISHNAH 9. 'IN THE CASE OF A CONDITION OF DOUBT CONCERNING LIQUIDS AS TO WHETHER THEY HAVE CONTRACTED UNCLEANNESS IT IS DEEMED UNCLEAN'.[6] IN WHAT CIRCUMSTANCES? IF AN UNCLEAN PERSON STRETCHED HIS FOOT BETWEEN CLEAN LIQUIDS AND THERE IS DOUBT WHETHER HE TOUCHED THEM OR NOT, SUCH A CONDITION OF DOUBT IS DEEMED TO BE UNCLEAN. IF A MAN HAD AN UNCLEAN LOAF IN HIS HAND AND HE STRETCHED IT OUT[7] BETWEEN CLEAN LIQUIDS, AND THERE IS DOUBT WHETHER IT TOUCHED THEM OR NOT, SUCH A CONDITION OF DOUBT IS DEEMED TO BE UNCLEAN. 'BUT IF IT WAS WHETHER UNCLEANNESS HAS BEEN CONVEYED, IT IS DEEMED CLEAN'.[6] IN WHAT CIRCUMSTANCE? IF A MAN HAD IN HIS HAND A STICK ON THE END OF WHICH THERE WAS AN UNCLEAN LIQUID AND HE THREW IT AMONG CLEAN LOAVES AND THERE IS DOUBT WHETHER IT TOUCHED THEM[8] OR NOT, SUCH A CONDITION OF DOUBT IS DEEMED CLEAN.

MISHNAH 10. R. JOSE RULED: A CONDITION OF DOUBT[9] IN THE CASE OF LIQUIDS IS DEEMED UNCLEAN IN RESPECT OF FOODSTUFFS[10] AND CLEAN IN RESPECT OF VESSELS.[11] HOW SO? IF THERE WERE TWO JARS,[12] THE ONE UNCLEAN

(1) Cf. p. 381, n. 8 *mut. mut.* (2) Whether the man has touched the unclean object. (3) Since it is in the nature of a floating object to be drawn towards one descending into the water. (4) When the floating object naturally recedes from him. (5) In the water. (6) *Supra* IV, 7. (7) Var. lec. 'threw it' (cf. foll. n.). (8) After it had come to a rest. (9) As to their uncleanness. (10) Because, in his opinion, liquids convey uncleanness to foodstuffs according to a Pentateuchal law. (11) Whose contraction of uncleanness from liquids is but a Rabbinical ordinance. (12) Containing water.

AND THE OTHER CLEAN, AND A DOUGH WAS PREPARED WITH THE CONTENTS OF ONE OF THEM AND A DOUBT AROSE AS TO WHETHER IT WAS PREPARED WITH THE CONTENTS OF THE UNCLEAN, OR OF THE CLEAN ONE, SUCH IS 'A CONDITION OF DOUBT IN THE CASE OF LIQUIDS [WHICH] IS DEEMED UNCLEAN IN RESPECT OF FOODSTUFFS AND CLEAN IN RESPECT OF VESSELS'.

MISHNAH 11. 'IF THERE IS DOUBT CONCERNING THE HANDS AS TO WHETHER THEY HAVE CONTRACTED UNCLEANNESS,[1] HAVE CONVEYED UNCLEANNESS[2] OR HAVE ATTAINED CLEANNESS, THEY ARE DEEMED CLEAN'.[3] 'ANY CONDITION OF DOUBT[4] THAT AROSE IN A PUBLIC DOMAIN'[3] IS DEEMED CLEAN' 'A CONDITION OF DOUBT CONCERNING AN ORDINANCE OF THE SCRIBES'[3] [NAMELY, IF A MAN IS UNCERTAIN WHETHER] HE ATE UNCLEAN FOODSTUFFS OR DRANK UNCLEAN LIQUIDS, WHETHER HE IMMERSED HIS HEAD AND THE GREATER PART OF HIS BODY IN DRAWN WATER,[5] OR WHETHER THERE FELL ON HIS HEAD AND THE GREATER PART OF HIS BODY THREE LOG OF DRAWN WATER,[6] SUCH A CONDITION OF DOUBT[7] IS DEEMED CLEAN. IF, HOWEVER, A CONDITION OF DOUBT AROSE CONCERNING A 'FATHER OF UNCLEANNESS' EVEN THOUGH IT WAS ONLY RABBINICAL, IT IS IS DEEMED UNCLEAN.

MISHNAH 12. 'A CONDITION OF DOUBT CONCERNING COMMON FOODSTUFFS'[3] REFERS TO THE CLEANNESS PRACTISED BY PHARISEES.[8] 'A CONDITION OF DOUBT CONCERNING

(1) From unclean foodstuffs or liquids. (2) To foodstuffs. (3) *Supra* IV, 7. (4) Of uncleanness. (5) Which renders the immersion invalid. (6) Which cause a clean person to become unclean. (7) As to whether he subsequently performed immersion and much more so if there is doubt as to whether uncleanness had at all been contracted. (8) Lit., 'the cleanness of separation'. To keep away from the clothes of those who are not so meticulous as oneself in the observance of the laws of cleanness and uncleanness. If a Pharisee is in doubt whether he came in contact with such clothes he may regard himself as clean and continue to eat his usual food that he keeps under conditions of cleanness.

CREEPING THINGS'[1]—[THIS IS DETERMINED] ACCORDING [TO THEIR CONDITION AT] THE TIME THEY ARE FOUND.[2] 'A CONDITION OF DOUBT CONCERNING LEPROSY SIGNS'[1]—[A LEPROSY SIGN][3] IS DEEMED CLEAN IN THE BEGINNING BEFORE IT HAD BEEN DETERMINED TO BE UNCLEAN, BUT AFTER IT HAD BEEN DETERMINED TO BE UNCLEAN, A CONDITION OF DOUBT[4] IS DEEMED UNCLEAN. 'A CONDITION OF DOUBT CONCERNING A NAZIRITE VOW'[1]—[IN SUCH A CONDITION OF DOUBT[5] THE MAN] IS PERMITTED [ALL THAT IS FORBIDDEN TO A NAZIRITE].[6] 'A CONDITION OF DOUBT CONCERNING FIRSTLINGS'[3]—[IN SUCH A CASE ONE IS EXEMPT FROM GIVING THE FIRSTLINGS TO THE PRIEST] IRRESPECTIVE OF WHETHER THEY ARE FIRSTBORN OF MEN[7] OR FIRSTLINGS OF CATTLE,[8] WHETHER THE FIRSTLINGS OF AN UNCLEAN BEAST[9] OR A CLEAN ONE, FOR IT IS THE MAN WHO ADVANCES THE CLAIM[10] AGAINST HIS FELLOW THAT MUST PRODUCE THE PROOF.[11]

MISHNAH 13. 'AND A CONDITION OF DOUBT CONCERNING SACRIFICES'[1]—IF A WOMAN HAS EXPERIENCED FIVE DOUBTFUL CASES OF MISCARRIAGE OR FIVE DISCHARGES OF DOUBTFUL ZIBAH SHE BRINGS ONLY ONE SACRIFICE[12] AND MAY THEN EAT OF THE SLAIN SACRIFICES, SHE BEING UNDER NO OBLIGATION TO BRING THE REMAINDER.[13]

(1) *Supra* IV, 7. (2) *Sc.* if a creeping thing was thrown among clean foodstuffs but was not found touching any of them, they are deemed to be clean. It is not assumed that before it came to rest it touched them. (3) Concerning which there is doubt whether it increased in size. (4) *Sc.* whether it had diminished in size. (5) Where, for instance, a man made his vow dependent on an assertion that a heap of wheat contained a certain number of measures, and the heap was lost before the assertion could be checked. (6) The drinking of wine and shaving for instance. (7) Who are redeemed with five shekels which are given to the priest. (8) Which are the priest's due. (9) An ass. (10) The priest who claims the firstling or the redemption of the firstborn. (11) As there is doubt no proof is possible, and the father of the firstborn and the owner of the firstling are exempt. (12) A sin-offering of a bird, brought as doubtful offering. (13) V. Ker. 8*a*.

ṬOHOROTH

CHAPTER V

MISHNAH 1. IF IN A PUBLIC DOMAIN THERE WAS A [DEAD] CREEPING THING[1] AND A FROG,[2] AND SO ALSO [IF THERE WAS THERE] AN OLIVE'S BULK OF A CORPSE[3] AND AN OLIVE'S BULK OF CARRION,[4] A BONE OF A CORPSE[5] AND A BONE OF CARRION,[2] A CLOD OF CLEAN EARTH[2] AND A CLOD FROM A GRAVE AREA[6] OR A CLOD OF CLEAN EARTH[2] AND A CLOD FROM THE LAND OF THE GENTILES,[4] OR IF THERE WERE TWO PATHS, THE ONE UNCLEAN[7] AND THE OTHER CLEAN, AND A MAN WALKED THROUGH ONE OF THEM BUT IT IS NOT KNOWN WHICH,[8] OR OVERSHADOWED ONE OF THEM BUT IT IS NOT KNOWN WHICH,[9] OR HE SHIFTED[10] ONE OF THEM BUT IT IS NOT KNOWN WHICH,[11] R. AKIBA RULED THAT HE IS UNCLEAN,[12] BUT THE SAGES RULE THAT HE IS CLEAN.[13]

MISHNAH 2. WHETHER[14] THE MAN SAID,[15] 'I TOUCHED

(1) One of the eight enumerated in Lev. XI, 29, which are 'fathers of uncleanness' and convey uncleanness by contact. (2) Which conveys no uncleanness whatsoever. (3) Which conveys uncleanness (cf. prev. n. but one) by overshadowing also. (4) That conveys uncleanness by contact and carrying only. (5) Which conveys uncleanness by *hesseṭ* (v. Glos.). (6) *Beth ha-Peras* (v. Glos.). This conveys uncleanness by contact and carrying only. (7) There having been a grave across its breadth which any one going through the path must pass over and thus overshadow it and contract uncleanness. (8) Of the two paths. (9) Whether the olive's bulk of corpse or that of the carrion. (10) Or carried. (11) Whether it was the bone of the corpse or that of the carrion. (12) Because, in his opinion, only food which, if once unclean, cannot any more be rendered clean, is deemed to be clean in a case of doubt in a public domain, but not men and vessels which may attain cleanness through immersion and sprinkling. *Aliter:* A doubtful case of uncleanness is deemed clean, according to R. Akiba, in a public domain only when a number of people are involved but not, as in this case, where only an individual is concerned (Wilna Gaon). (13) Cf. prev. n. *mut. mut.* (14) This is a continuation of the previous rulings. (15) In

AN OBJECT ON THIS SPOT BUT I DO NOT KNOW[1] WHETHER IT WAS UNCLEAN OR CLEAN', OR 'I TOUCHED ONE BUT I DO NOT KNOW WHICH OF THE TWO I TOUCHED', R. AKIBA RULES THAT HE IS UNCLEAN,[2] BUT THE SAGES RULE THAT HE IS CLEAN.[3] R. JOSE RULES THAT HE IS UNCLEAN IN EVERY CASE[4] AND CLEAN ONLY IN THAT OF THE PATH,[5] SINCE IT IS THE USUAL PRACTICE FOR MEN TO GO[6] BUT IT IS NOT THEIR USUAL PRACTICE TO TOUCH.[7]

MISHNAH 3. IF THERE WERE TWO PATHS,[8] THE ONE UNCLEAN[9] AND THE OTHER CLEAN,[10] AND A MAN WALKED BY ONE OF THEM AND THEN PREPARED CLEAN FOODSTUFFS[11] WHICH WERE SUBSEQUENTLY CONSUMED AND, HAVING BEEN SPRINKLED UPON ONCE AND A SECOND TIME[12] AND HAVING PERFORMED IMMERSION AND ATTAINED CLEANNESS, HE WALKED BY THE SECOND PATH AND THEN PREPARED CLEAN FOODSTUFFS,[11] THE LATTER ARE DEEMED CLEAN.[13] IF THE FIRST FOODSTUFFS WERE STILL IN EXISTENCE BOTH MUST BE HELD IN SUSPENSE.[14] IF HE HAD NOT ATTAINED CLEANNESS IN THE MEANTIME,[15] THE FIRST ARE HELD IN SUSPENSE[16] AND THE SECOND MUST BE BURNT.[17]

MISHNAH 4. IF THERE WAS A DEAD CREEPING THING AND A FROG IN A PUBLIC DOMAIN AND A MAN TOUCHED ONE

the case where there was in the public domain a creeping thing and a frog.

(1) Owing to the similarity of the frog and the creeping thing. (2) V. p. 385, n. 12. (3) V. p. 385, n. 13. (4) Enumerated in this and in the preceding Mishnah. (5) *Supra* V, 1. (6) And the imposition of uncleanness in such a case would involve undue hardship. Hence the relaxation of the restriction. (7) As uncleanness could, therefore, be avoided the restriction could well be maintained. (8) In a public domain. (9) V. *supra* p. 385, n. 7. (10) But it was not known which was which. (11) Of *terumah* which must be kept in conditions of cleanness. (12) On the third and the seventh day respectively. (13) Because the doubt occurred in a public domain. (14) Since both have to be considered simultaneously and one at least is obviously unclean. (15) Between the preparation of the first and the second foodstuffs. (16) Neither eaten nor burnt. Var. lec., 'are clean'. (17) Since they are unclean in any case.

OF THEM[1] AND THEN PREPARED CLEAN FOODSTUFFS[2] WHICH WERE SUBSEQUENTLY CONSUMED; AND THEN HE PERFORMED IMMERSION, TOUCHED THE OTHER AND THEN PREPARED CLEAN FOODSTUFFS,[2] THE LATTER ARE DEEMED CLEAN.[3] IF THE FIRST FOODSTUFFS WERE STILL IN EXISTENCE BOTH MUST BE HELD IN SUSPENSE.[4] IF HE DID NOT PERFORM IMMERSION IN THE MEANTIME,[5] THE FIRST ARE HELD IN SUSPENSE[6] AND THE SECOND MUST BE BURNT[7].

MISHNAH 5. IF THERE WERE TWO PATHS, THE ONE UNCLEAN AND THE OTHER CLEAN, AND A MAN WALKED BY ONE OF THEM AND THEN PREPARED CLEAN FOODSTUFFS,[2] AND SUBSEQUENTLY ANOTHER MAN CAME AND WALKED BY THE SECOND PATH AND THEN PREPARED CLEAN FOODSTUFFS,[2] R. JUDAH RULED: IF EACH BY HIMSELF ASKED FOR A RULING THEY ARE BOTH TO BE DECLARED CLEAN;[8] BUT IF THEY ASKED FOR A RULING SIMULTANEOUSLY,[9] BOTH ARE TO BE DECLARED UNCLEAN. R. JOSE RULED: IN EITHER CASE THEY ARE BOTH UNCLEAN.

MISHNAH 6. IF THERE WERE TWO LOAVES, THE ONE UNCLEAN AND THE OTHER CLEAN, AND A MAN ATE ONE OF THEM AND THEN PREPARED CLEAN FOODSTUFFS, AND AFTERWARDS ANOTHER MAN CAME AND ATE THE SECOND LOAF AND THEN PREPARED CLEAN FOODSTUFFS, R. JUDAH RULED: IF EACH BY HIMSELF ASKED FOR A RULING THEY ARE BOTH TO BE DECLARED CLEAN,[8] BUT IF THEY ASKED FOR ONE SIMULTANEOUSLY[9] BOTH ARE TO BE DECLARED UNCLEAN.

(1) But did not know whether it was the clean or the unclean. (2) Of *terumah* which must be kept in conditions of cleanness. (3) Because the doubt occurred in a public domain. (4) Since both have to be considered simultaneously and one at least is obviously unclean. (5) Between the preparation of the first and the second foodstuffs. (6) Neither eaten nor burnt. Var. lec., 'are clean'. (7) Being unclean in any case. (8) Since neither can be declared unclean when his uncleanness is only a matter of doubt in a public domain. (9) When it is impossible to declare them both clean since one at least must be unclean.

R. JOSE RULED: IN EITHER CASE THEY ARE BOTH UNCLEAN.

MISHNAH 7. IF A MAN SAT IN A PUBLIC DOMAIN AND SOMEONE[1] CAME AND TROD ON HIS CLOTHES, OR SPAT AND THE FORMER TOUCHED THE SPITTLE, ON ACCOUNT OF THE SPITTLE TERUMAH[2] MUST BE BURNT,[3] BUT ON ACCOUNT OF THE CLOTHES THE MAJORITY PRINCIPLE IS FOLLOWED.[4] IF A MAN SLEPT IN THE PUBLIC DOMAIN, WHEN HE RISES HIS GARMENTS SUFFER MIDRAS UNCLEANNESS;[5] SO R. MEIR. BUT THE SAGES[6] RULE THAT THEY ARE CLEAN. IF A MAN TOUCHED SOMEONE IN THE NIGHT AND IT IS NOT KNOWN WHETHER IT WAS ONE WHO WAS ALIVE OR DEAD, BUT IN THE MORNING WHEN HE GOT UP HE FOUND HIM TO BE DEAD, R. MEIR RULES THAT HE[7] IS CLEAN, BUT THE SAGES RULE THAT HE IS UNCLEAN,[8] SINCE ALL DOUBTFUL CONDITIONS OF UNCLEANNESS ARE [DETERMINED] IN ACCORDANCE WITH [THEIR APPEARANCE AT] THE TIME THEY ARE DISCOVERED.

MISHNAH 8. IF THERE WAS IN THE TOWN AN IMBECILE, A HEATHEN, OR A SAMARITAN WOMAN, ALL SPITTLE ENCOUNTERED IN THE TOWN IS DEEMED UNCLEAN.[9] IF A WOMAN TROD ON A MAN'S CLOTHES OR SAT WITH HIM IN A BOAT,[10] HIS CLOTHES REMAIN CLEAN IF SHE KNEW HIM TO BE EATING TERUMAH;[11] BUT IF NOT, HE MUST ASK HER.

(1) Who could possibly be suspected of uncleanness. (2) Which the first man touched. (3) As a preventive measure against contact with spittle that was known to be unclean. (4) *Sc.* only if the greater number of people in the place were *zabs* is *midras* uncleanness (v. Glos.) imposed. (5) Since it is possible that most of the people have trodden on them and that among these was a *zab*. (6) Holding that even in a case like this a condition of doubt in a public domain is deemed clean. (7) The live man. (8) Provided the dead man was not seen alive in the previous evening. (9) Since the class of women mentioned do not exercise the necessary care when they are in their menstruation periods. (10) Where, if she was a menstruant, she would convey to him *midras* uncleanness (cf. Zab. III, 1). (11) Since in that case she would keep away from his clothes and would not enter the same boat when in her menstruation.

MISHNAH 9. IF A WITNESS SAYS,[1] 'YOU HAVE CONTRACTED UNCLEANNESS', BUT HE SAYS, 'I HAVE NOT CONTRACTED ANY UNCLEANNESS', HE IS REGARDED AS CLEAN. IF TWO WITNESSES SAY,[1] 'YOU HAVE CONTRACTED UNCLEANNESS', AND HE SAYS, 'I HAVE NOT CONTRACTED ANY UNCLEANNESS', R. MEIR RULES THAT HE IS UNCLEAN,[2] BUT THE SAGES RULE: HE MAY BE BELIEVED ON HIS OWN EVIDENCE.[3] IF A WITNESS SAYS,[1] 'YOU HAVE CONTRACTED UNCLEANNESS', BUT TWO WITNESSES SAY, 'HE HAS NOT CONTRACTED ANY UNCLEANNESS', WHETHER IN A PRIVATE DOMAIN OR IN A PUBLIC DOMAIN, HE IS REGARDED AS CLEAN. IF TWO WITNESSES SAY, 'HE HAS CONTRACTED UNCLEANNESS', AND ONE WITNESS SAYS, 'HE HAS NOT CONTRACTED ANY UNCLEANNESS', WHETHER IN A PRIVATE DOMAIN OR IN A PUBLIC DOMAIN, HE IS REGARDED AS UNCLEAN. IF ONE WITNESS SAYS, 'HE HAS CONTRACTED UNCLEANNESS', AND ANOTHER SAYS, 'HE HAS NOT CONTRACTED ANY UNCLEANNESS', OR IF ONE WOMAN SAYS, 'HE HAS CONTRACTED UNCLEANNESS', AND ANOTHER WOMAN SAYS, 'HE HAS NOT CONTRACTED ANY UNCLEANNESS', HE IS REGARDED AS UNCLEAN IF THE EVIDENCE RELATES TO A PRIVATE DOMAIN,[4] BUT IF IT RELATED TO A PUBLIC DOMAIN HE IS REGARDED AS CLEAN.[5]

(1) To any man. (2) Since two witnesses on whose evidence a man may be sent to death may well be relied upon in subjecting one to uncleanness which involves no greater liability than that of a sacrifice for entering the Sanctuary in an unclean state. (3) Because he could well claim, even if the witnesses' evidence is accepted, that he has subsequently attained cleanness through immersion. (4) As is the rule with any condition of doubtful uncleanness in such a domain. (5) Cf. prev. n. *mut. mut.*

ṬOHOROTH

CHAPTER VI

MISHNAH 1. IF A PLACE THAT WAS A PRIVATE DOMAIN HAS BECOME A PUBLIC DOMAIN[1] AND THEN WAS TURNED AGAIN INTO A PRIVATE DOMAIN, WHILE IT IS A PRIVATE DOMAIN ANY CONDITION OF DOUBT ARISING IN IT IS DEEMED UNCLEAN BUT WHILE IT IS A PUBLIC DOMAIN ANY CONDITION OF DOUBT ARISING IN IT IS DEEMED CLEAN. IF A MAN WHO WAS DANGEROUSLY ILL IN A PRIVATE DOMAIN WAS TAKEN OUT INTO A PUBLIC DOMAIN AND THEN BROUGHT BACK INTO A PRIVATE DOMAIN,[2] WHILE HE IS IN THE PRIVATE DOMAIN ANY CONDITION OF DOUBT ARISING THROUGH HIM[3] IS DEEMED UNCLEAN[4] BUT WHILE HE IS IN THE PUBLIC DOMAIN ANY CONDITION OF DOUBT ARISING THROUGH HIM[3] IS DEEMED CLEAN.[5] R. SIMEON RULED: THE PUBLIC DOMAIN CAUSES A BREAK.[6]

MISHNAH 2. FOUR CASES OF DOUBT, R. JOSHUA RULED, ARE DEEMED UNCLEAN AND THE SAGES RULE THAT THEY

(1) A valley, for instance, is a private domain in the winter when on account of the growing crops people are kept out of it, and a public domain in the summer when many labourers carry on in it the various activities associated with the harvest. (2) Where he was found to be dead. (3) *Sc.* if there is doubt whether a person had touched him while he was still alive or when he was already dead. (4) It being assumed that he was dead in the private domain before he was taken out into the public domain. Hence the man who touched him in the private domain, whether before or after he had been taken into the public domain, is deemed unclean. (5) And any one who touched him in the public domain before he was brought back into the private domain remains clean. (6) Between the first and the second presence in the private domain; *sc.* since the dead man is deemed to have been alive while he was in the public domain he cannot possibly have been dead prior to that. Hence any condition of doubt during his first presence in the private domain must be deemed clean.

ARE DEEMED CLEAN. FOR INSTANCE? IF AN UNCLEAN MAN[1] STOOD[2] AND A CLEAN MAN PASSED BY[3] OR THE CLEAN MAN STOOD AND THE UNCLEAN ONE PASSED BY;[3] OR IF AN UNCLEAN OBJECT WAS IN A PRIVATE DOMAIN AND A CLEAN ONE IN THE PUBLIC DOMAIN OR THE CLEAN OBJECT WAS IN THE PRIVATE DOMAIN AND THE UNCLEAN ONE IN THE PUBLIC DOMAIN, AND THERE IS DOUBT WHETHER THERE WAS CONTACT[4] OR NOT, OR WHETHER THERE WAS OVERSHADOWING[4] OR NOT, OR WHETHER THERE WAS SHIFTING[5] OR NOT, R. JOSHUA RULES THAT THE CLEAN BECOMES UNCLEAN,[6] BUT THE SAGES RULE THAT THE CLEAN REMAINS CLEAN.

MISHNAH 3. IF A TREE STANDING IN A PUBLIC DOMAIN HAD WITHIN IT AN OBJECT OF UNCLEANNESS AND A MAN CLIMBED TO THE TOP OF IT, AND THE DOUBT AROSE AS TO WHETHER HE DID OR DID NOT TOUCH THE OBJECT OF UNCLEANNESS, SUCH A CONDITION OF DOUBT IS DEEMED UNCLEAN.[7] IF A MAN[8] PUT HIS HAND INTO A HOLE IN WHICH THERE WAS AN OBJECT OF UNCLEANNESS AND THERE IS DOUBT WHETHER HE DID OR DID NOT TOUCH IT, SUCH A CONDITION OF DOUBT IS DEEMED UNCLEAN.[7] IF A SHOP THAT WAS UNCLEAN WAS OPEN TOWARD A PUBLIC DOMAIN AND THERE IS DOUBT WHETHER A MAN DID OR DID NOT ENTER IT, SUCH A CONDITION OF DOUBT IS DEEMED CLEAN.[9]

(1) A leper. (2) Under any form of roof. (3) The doubt arising whether (*a*) there was contact between the two or (*b*) the man that walked remained stationary for a moment while under the roof (cf. prev. n.) and the clean man thus contracted uncleanness by overshadowing. (4) Cf. prev. n. (5) Of the unclean by the clean. (6) In his opinion a doubt involving both a private and a public domain is to be regarded as involving the former alone. (7) Because though, in respect of the Sabbath laws, a tree or a hole in a public domain is regarded as a public domain, in respect of uncleanness it is treated as a private domain. (8) While standing in the public domain. (9) The unclean shop in the public domain is on a par with a dead creeping thing lying in a public domain, and the doubt concerning entry into it is on a par with the doubt concerning the touching of the creeping thing; the former, therefore, like the latter are deemed clean (cf. *supra* V, lf).

IF THERE IS DOUBT WHETHER HE DID OR DID NOT TOUCH ANYTHING, SUCH A CONDITION OF DOUBT IS DEEMED CLEAN.[1] IF THERE WERE TWO SHOPS, THE ONE UNCLEAN AND THE OTHER CLEAN, AND A MAN ENTERED INTO ONE OF THEM, AND A DOUBT AROSE AS TO WHETHER HE ENTERED THE UNCLEAN, OR THE CLEAN ONE, SUCH A CONDITION OF DOUBT IS DEEMED UNCLEAN.[2]

MISHNAH 4. HOWEVER MANY THE DOUBTS AND THE DOUBTS ABOUT DOUBTS THAT ONE CAN MULTIPLY, A CONDITION OF DOUBT IN A PRIVATE DOMAIN IS DEEMED UNCLEAN, AND IN A PUBLIC DOMAIN IT IS DEEMED CLEAN. FOR INSTANCE? IF A MAN ENTERED AN ALLEY[3] AND AN UNCLEAN OBJECT WAS IN THE COURTYARD, AND A DOUBT AROSE AS TO WHETHER THE MAN DID OR DID NOT ENTER IT;[4] OR IF AN OBJECT OF UNCLEANNESS WAS IN A HOUSE AND THERE IS DOUBT WHETHER A MAN ENTERED OR NOT; OR EVEN WHERE HE ENTERED, THERE IS DOUBT WHETHER THE UNCLEANNESS WAS THERE OR NOT; OR EVEN WHERE IT WAS THERE THERE IS DOUBT WHETHER IT CONSISTED OF THE PRESCRIBED MINIMUM OR NOT; OR EVEN WHERE IT CONSISTED OF THE PRESCRIBED MINIMUM, THERE IS DOUBT WHETHER IT WAS UNCLEAN OR CLEAN; OR, EVEN WHERE IT WAS UNCLEAN, THERE IS DOUBT WHETHER THE MAN HAD TOUCHED IT OR NOT, ANY SUCH CONDITION OF DOUBT IS DEEMED UNCLEAN. R. ELIEZER[5] RULED: ANY CONDITION OF DOUBT IN REGARD TO ENTERING IS DEEMED CLEAN, BUT ANY CONDITION OF DOUBT IN REGARD TO CONTACT WITH THE UNCLEANNESS IS DEEMED UNCLEAN.[6]

MISHNAH 5. IF A MAN ENTERED A VALLEY[7] IN THE RAINY SEASON[8] AND THERE WAS AN UNCLEANNESS IN A

(1) Cf. prev. n. (2) Since there is no doubt that he entered one private domain at least. (3) Which in this respect is like a private domain. (4) The courtyard. (5) Var. lec. Eleazar. (6) This is derived by analogy from the conditions governing a *soṭah*, (v. Glos). (7) Comprising many fields. (8) When the fields are sown and, therefore, regarded as a private domain.

CERTAIN FIELD, AND HE STATED, 'I WENT INTO THAT PLACE[1] BUT I DO NOT KNOW WHETHER I ENTERED THAT FIELD[2] OR NOT', R. ELIEZER RULES THAT HE IS CLEAN,[3] BUT THE SAGES RULE THAT HE IS UNCLEAN.[4]

MISHNAH 6. A CONDITION OF DOUBT OCCURRING IN A PRIVATE DOMAIN IS DEEMED UNCLEAN UNLESS THE MAN CONCERNED CAN SAY, 'I DID NOT TOUCH THE UNCLEAN THING'. A CONDITION OF DOUBT IN A PUBLIC DOMAIN IS DEEMED CLEAN UNLESS THE MAN CONCERNED CAN SAY, 'I DID TOUCH THE UNCLEAN THING'. WHAT IS REGARDED AS A PUBLIC DOMAIN? THE PATHS OF BETH GILGUL[5] AND SIMILAR PLACES ARE REGARDED AS A PRIVATE DOMAIN[6] IN RESPECT OF THE LAWS OF THE SABBATH, AND A PUBLIC DOMAIN IN RESPECT OF THOSE OF UNCLEANNESS.[7] R. ELIEZER[8] STATED: THE PATHS OF BETH GILGUL WERE MENTIONED ONLY BECAUSE THEY ARE REGARDED AS A PRIVATE DOMAIN IN BOTH RESPECTS.[9] PATHS THAT OPEN OUT TOWARDS CISTERNS, PITS, CAVERNS OR WINE-PRESSES ARE REGARDED AS A PRIVATE DOMAIN IN RESPECT OF THE LAWS OF THE SABBATH AND AS A PUBLIC DOMAIN IN RESPECT OF THOSE OF UNCLEANNESS.

MISHNAH 7. A VALLEY IN SUMMER TIME[10] IS REGARDED AS A PRIVATE DOMAIN IN RESPECT OF THE LAWS OF THE SABBATH, BUT AS A PUBLIC DOMAIN IN RESPECT OF THOSE

(1) The valley. (2) Which contained the uncleanness. (3) Since the fields are separated from each other the condition of doubt is one relating to entry which is deemed clean. (4) Because the valley unites all the fields into one unit. (5) Which are not frequented by many people. On Beth Gilgul v. *MGWJ* 1921, p. 88 and 320. (6) *Sc.* not a public domain. They are in fact a *karmelith* (v. Glos). (7) Even if less than three men were present when the doubt arose. Where three men are present even a private domain proper is treated as a public domain in respect of the laws of uncleanness. (8) Var. lec. Eleazar. (9) The laws of the Sabbath and the laws of uncleanness. (10) When it is frequented by the labourers engaged in it in various harvesting activities.

OF UNCLEANNESS; AND IN THE RAINY SEASON[1] IT IS REGARDED AS A PRIVATE DOMAIN IN BOTH RESPECTS.[2]

MISHNAH 8. A BASILICA[3] IS REGARDED AS A PRIVATE DOMAIN IN RESPECT OF THE LAWS OF THE SABBATH BUT AS A PUBLIC DOMAIN IN RESPECT OF THOSE OF UNCLEANNESS. R. JUDAH RULED: IF A MAN STANDING AT ONE DOOR CAN SEE THOSE THAT ENTER AND LEAVE AT THE OTHER DOOR, IT IS REGARDED AS A PRIVATE DOMAIN IN BOTH RESPECTS; OTHERWISE IT IS REGARDED AS A PRIVATE DOMAIN IN RESPECT OF THE SABBATH AND AS A PUBLIC DOMAIN IN RESPECT OF UNCLEANNESS.

MISHNAH 9. A FORUM[4] IS REGARDED AS A PRIVATE DOMAIN IN RESPECT OF THE SABBATH LAWS AND AS A PUBLIC DOMAIN IN RESPECT OF THE LAWS OF UNCLEANNESS; AND THE SAME APPLIES TO ITS SIDES.[5] R. MEIR RULED: THE SIDES ARE REGARDED AS A PRIVATE DOMAIN IN BOTH RESPECTS.[6]

MISHNAH 10. COLONNADES[7] ARE REGARDED AS A PRIVATE DOMAIN IN RESPECT OF THE SABBATH LAWS AND AS A PUBLIC DOMAIN IN RESPECT OF THE LAWS OF UNCLEANNESS. A COURTYARD INTO WHICH MANY PEOPLE ENTER BY ONE DOOR AND LEAVE BY ANOTHER,[8] IS REGARDED AS A PRIVATE DOMAIN IN RESPECT OF THE SABBATH LAWS AND AS A PUBLIC DOMAIN IN RESPECT OF THE LAWS OF CLEANNESS.

(1) When it is deserted. (2) V. p. 393, n. 9. (3) A large hall with doors opening in all directions, used as a public meeting place but not as a thoroughfare. (4) *Faron*, a building in the style of a basilica whose doors are directly opposite one another. *Aliter:* A house in the heart of a public domain. (5) On either side of the passage from one door to the other. (6) The laws of the Sabbath and the laws of uncleanness. (7) In front of shops, having behind them raised benches on which the traders sit or display their wares. (8) Though the doors are not directly opposite one another.

ṬOHOROTH

CHAPTER VII

MISHNAH 1. IF A POTTER[1] LEFT HIS POTS[2] AND WENT DOWN TO DRINK,[3] THE INNERMOST POTS REMAIN CLEAN[4] BUT THE OUTER ONES ARE DEEMED UNCLEAN.[5] R. JOSE RULED: THIS APPLIES ONLY WHERE THEY ARE NOT TIED TOGETHER, BUT WHERE THEY ARE TIED TOGETHER, ALL THE POTS[6] ARE DEEMED CLEAN.[7] IF A MAN ENTRUSTED HIS KEY TO AN 'AM HA-AREẒ THE HOUSE REMAINS CLEAN, SINCE HE ENTRUSTED HIM ONLY WITH THE GUARDING OF THE KEY.[8]

MISHNAH 2. IF A MAN LEFT AN 'AM HA-AREẒ IN HIS HOUSE AWAKE AND[9] FOUND HIM AWAKE, OR ASLEEP AND[9] FOUND HIM ASLEEP, OR AWAKE AND[9] FOUND HIM ASLEEP, THE HOUSE REMAINS CLEAN.[10] IF HE LEFT HIM ASLEEP AND FOUND HIM AWAKE, THE HOUSE IS DEEMED UNCLEAN;[11] SO

(1) Who was a *ḥaber* (v. Glos). (2) In a public domain, and thereby caused obstruction on the road. (3) Thus losing sight of his wares which, in his absence, might be rendered unclean, v. n. 5. (4) V. next note. (5) Because the skirts of an *'am ha-areẓ* might have been caught in the interior (air-space) of the pots. This is, however, not likely to happen with the inner pots, v. Keth. 24*b*. (6) Even the inner ones (cf. foll. n.). (7) Even the outer ones are clean, because when they are tied to the others the mouths of the pots are not sufficiently exposed upwards to catch in their interior the skirts of passers-by. Maim. reads: Unclean, because by moving the outer ones the *'am ha-areẓ* might indirectly have moved the inner ones also to which they are tied. (8) The *'am ha-areẓ* would not, therefore, venture to enter the house which was not placed under his care. (9) On returning. (10) For, having been left awake the *'am ha-areẓ* would not dare to touch anything for fear that the master would return any moment. When he is left asleep and found asleep there is no need to suspect that he awoke in the meantime. (11) Since the *'am ha-areẓ* is not afraid to move about the house touching its contents because he assumes that the owner who left him asleep would be in no hurry to return.

R. MEIR. BUT THE SAGES RULED: ONLY THAT PART IS UNCLEAN TO WHICH HE CAN STRETCH OUT HIS HAND AND TOUCH IT.[1]

MISHNAH 3. IF ONE LEFT CRAFTSMEN IN HIS HOUSE, THE HOUSE IS DEEMED UNCLEAN; SO R. MEIR. BUT THE SAGES RULED: ONLY THAT PART IS UNCLEAN TO WHICH THEY CAN STRETCH OUT THEIR HANDS AND TOUCH IT.[2]

MISHNAH 4. IF THE WIFE OF A ḤABER[3] LEFT THE WIFE OF AN 'AM HA-AREẒ GRINDING CORN IN HER HOUSE, THE HOUSE IS DEEMED UNCLEAN IF SHE CEASED FROM TURNING THE HANDMILL,[4] BUT IF SHE DID NOT CEASE FROM TURNING THE HANDMILL, ONLY THAT PART OF THE HOUSE IS DEEMED UNCLEAN TO WHICH SHE CAN STRETCH OUT HER HAND AND TOUCH IT. IF THERE WERE TWO WOMEN,[5] THE HOUSE IS UNCLEAN IN EITHER CASE,[6] SINCE, WHILE THE ONE IS GRINDING, THE OTHER CAN GO ABOUT TOUCHING; SO R. MEIR. BUT THE SAGES RULED: ONLY THAT PART OF THE HOUSE IS UNCLEAN TO WHICH THEY CAN STRETCH OUT THEIR HANDS AND TOUCH IT.

MISHNAH 5. IF A MAN LEFT AN 'AM HA-AREẒ IN HIS HOUSE TO GUARD IT, WHENEVER HE[7] CAN SEE THOSE THAT ENTER AND LEAVE,[8] ONLY FOODSTUFFS AND LIQUIDS AND UNCOVERED EARTHENWARE ARE DEEMED UNCLEAN,[9] BUT COUCHES AND SEATS AND EARTHENWARE THAT HAVE TIGHTLY FITTING COVERS REMAIN CLEAN; AND WHENEVER HE[7] CANNOT SEE EITHER THOSE WHO ENTER OR THOSE WHO LEAVE,[8] EVEN THOUGH THE 'AM HA-AREẒ[10] HAS TO BE LED AND

(1) From where he lay, that is where the master found him on that same spot. (2) Without having to ascend or descend. (3) Who is trusted as much as the *ḥaber* himself. (4) Before the *ḥaber's* wife returned; since this would give her time to walk about the house and touch things. (5) Grinding the corn, each being the wife of an *'am ha-areẓ*. (6) Whether grinding did or did not cease before the *ḥaber's* wife returned. (7) The householder. (8) The house. (9) Since the *'am ha-areẓ* might have touched them. (10) Being incapable of walking.

EVEN THOUGH HE WAS BOUND, ALL IS DEEMED UNCLEAN.[1]

MISHNAH 6. IF TAX COLLECTORS[2] ENTERED A HOUSE,[3] THE HOUSE[4] IS DEEMED UNCLEAN.[5] EVEN THOUGH AN IDOLATER WAS WITH THEM[6] THEY ARE BELIEVED IF THEY SAY,[7] 'WE HAVE ENTERED BUT TOUCHED NOTHING'.[8] IF[9] THIEVES ENTERED A HOUSE, ONLY THAT PART IN WHICH THE FEET OF THE THIEVES HAVE TRODDEN IS DEEMED UNCLEAN.[8] AND WHAT DO THEY CAUSE TO BE UNCLEAN? FOODSTUFFS AND LIQUIDS AND OPEN EARTHENWARE ONLY, BUT COUCHES AND SEATS AND EARTHENWARE THAT HAVE TIGHTLY FITTING COVERS REMAIN CLEAN. IF AN IDOLATER[10] OR A WOMAN[11] WAS WITH THEM, ALL IS DEEMED UNCLEAN.[12]

MISHNAH 7. IF A MAN LEFT HIS CLOTHES IN A WALL-NICHE OF A BATH-HOUSE,[13] R. ELEAZAR B. AZARIAH RULES THAT THEY ARE DEEMED CLEAN,[14] BUT THE SAGES RULED: THEY CANNOT BE REGARDED AS CLEAN UNLESS HE GIVES HIM[15] THE KEY[16] OR THE SEAL[16] OR UNLESS HE LEFT SOME SIGN ON THEM. IF A MAN[17] LEFT[18] HIS CLOTHES[19] FROM ONE VINTAGE TO THE NEXT,

(1) Since another person, capable of conveying uncleanness to these objects, may have visited the house and touched them. (2) Of the *'am ha-areẓ* class. (3) To seize a pledge for unpaid taxes. (4) *Sc.* all the articles in it. (5) Because, when searching the house for a pledge, they may have touched the various objects in it. (6) In which case it might have been assumed that out of fear of him they would make a thorough search and, therefore, touch every article in the house. (7) Var. lec. inserts, 'we did not enter; but they are not believed if they say'. (8) V. Ḥag. 26*a*. (9) Var. lec., 'and so if'. (10) Who is considered as a *zab*. (11) Who might well have been a menstruant. (12) Since he or she may have touched all the objects in the house. (13) *Odiarin; Aliter:* A bath-attendant, Heb. *Odiarin*. (Var. lec., *oriarin*), cf. Lat. *olearius*. (14) Since no one would put his hands on them for fear of being suspected of stealing. (15) The bath-attendant or the bath-keeper (cf. prev. n. but one) to the owner of the clothes. *Aliter:* The owner of the clothes to the bath-attendant or bath-keeper. (16) Of the locker in which the clothes are kept. (17) An Israelite who was engaged in the vintage of an idolater's vineyard to prepare wine under conditions of purity. (18) With the idolater. (19) That were clean.

HIS[1] CLOTHES REMAIN CLEAN;[2] BUT IF HE LEFT THEM WITH AN ISRAELITE[3] THE CLOTHES ARE DEEMED UNCLEAN UNLESS HE[4] DECLARES, 'I HAVE TAKEN GOOD CARE[5] TO GUARD THEM'.

MISHNAH 8. IF ONE[6] WHO WAS CLEAN HAD GIVEN UP THE THOUGHT OF EATING [HIS TERUMAH], R. JUDAH RULES THAT IT[7] STILL[8] REMAINS CLEAN, SINCE IT IS USUAL FOR UNCLEAN PERSONS TO KEEP AWAY FROM IT.[9] BUT THE SAGES RULE THAT IT[10] IS DEEMED UNCLEAN.[11] IF HIS HANDS WERE CLEAN AND HE HAD GIVEN UP THE THOUGHT OF EATING TERUMAH, EVEN[12] THOUGH HE SAYS, 'I KNEW THAT MY HANDS HAVE CONTRACTED NO UNCLEANNESS', HIS HANDS ARE DEEMED UNCLEAN, SINCE THE HANDS ARE ALWAYS BUSY.[13]

MISHNAH 9. IF A WOMAN WHO ENTERED HER HOUSE TO BRING OUT SOME BREAD FOR A POOR MAN AND, WHEN SHE CAME OUT, FOUND HIM STANDING AT THE SIDE OF LOAVES OF TERUMAH, AND SIMILARLY IF A WOMAN WHO WENT OUT FOUND HER NEIGHBOUR RAKING OUT COALS UNDER A COOKING POT OF TERUMAH, R. AKIBA RULES THAT THEY[14] ARE UNCLEAN, BUT THE SAGES RULE THAT THEY ARE CLEAN. SAID R. ELIEZER B. PILA:[15] BUT WHY DOES R. AKIBA RULE THAT THEY ARE UNCLEAN AND THE SAGES RULE THAT THEY ARE CLEAN? ONLY FOR THIS REASON: THAT WOMEN ARE GLUTTONOUS AND EACH MAY BE SUSPECTED OF UNCOVERING HER NEIGHBOUR'S COOKING POT TO GET TO KNOW WHAT SHE IS COOKING.[16]

(1) Some edd. read, 'with an idolater, his'. (2) Since the idolater would not dare to touch them for fear of spoiling his vintage. (3) Who was an *'am ha-areẓ* and who is not so conscientious in this respect. (4) The *'am ha-areẓ*. (5) Lit., 'there was in my heart'. (6) A priest. (7) The *terumah*. *Aliter:* He (the priest). (8) Despite the priest's lack of interest in it. *Aliter:* Despite his decision not to eat *terumah*. (9) The *terumah*. *Aliter:* Him (the priest). (10) *Aliter*. he. (11) Cf. prev. n. but one *mut. mut.* (12) Var. lec. 'R. Judah rules even'. (13) And consequently might have touched an unclean object without the man's awareness of it. (14) The loaves and the contents of the pot. (15) I.e, Philo. Var. lec. Piabi. (16) In the case of the poor man, however, R. Akiba agrees with the Sages.

ṬOHOROTH

CHAPTER VIII

MISHNAH 1. IF A MAN WHO DWELT IN THE SAME COURTYARD WITH AN 'AM HA-AREẒ FORGOT SOME VESSELS IN THE COURTYARD, EVEN THOUGH THEY WERE JARS WITH TIGHTLY FITTING COVERS, OR AN OVEN WITH A TIGHTLY FITTING COVER, THEY ARE DEEMED UNCLEAN.[1] R. JUDAH RULES THAT AN OVEN[2] IS CLEAN WHENEVER IT HAS A TIGHTLY FITTING COVER. R. JOSE RULED: AN OVEN ALSO IS DEEMED UNCLEAN UNLESS IT WAS PROVIDED WITH A SCREEN TEN HANDBREADTHS HIGH.[3]

MISHNAH 2. IF A MAN DEPOSITED VESSELS WITH AN 'AM HA-AREẒ THEY ARE DEEMED TO BE UNCLEAN WITH CORPSE UNCLEANNESS[4] AND WITH MIDRAS UNCLEANNESS.[5] IF THE LATTER KNEW HIM[6] TO BE A CONSUMER OF TERUMAH,[7] THEY ARE FREE FROM CORPSE UNCLEANNESS[8] BUT[9] ARE UNCLEAN WITH MIDRAS UNCLEANNESS.[10] R. JOSE RULED: IF THE MAN[6] ENTRUSTED HIM[11] WITH A CHEST FULL OF CLOTHES, THEY ARE DEEMED TO BE UNCLEAN WITH MIDRAS

(1) Since the jars may have been shifted by his menstruant wife (v. Glos. s. v. *hesseṭ*). The oven, even if attached to the ground, is deemed unclean as a preventive measure against confusing what is detached from the ground (which is unclean) with what is attached. (2) Which is attached to the ground (cf. prev. n.) and is consequently immovable. (3) Which could serve as a reminder to the household of the *'am ha-areẓ* to keep away from it. (4) Requiring sprinkling with the ashes of the red heifer on the third and the seventh day. (5) So that any man that carried them or was carried on them becomes unclean. (6) The depositor. (7) I.e., a priest. (8) It is assumed that the *'am ha-areẓ* will keep away from the *terumah* if he suffers from corpse uncleanness. (9) If the vessels are suitable for *midras*. (10) For, though the man might take care to keep them in a condition of cleanness in respect of corpse uncleanness, he cannot be sure that his wife did not sit on them during her menstruation uncleanness. (11) The *'am ha-areẓ*.

WHEN THEY ARE TIGHTLY PACKED,[1] BUT IF THEY ARE NOT TIGHTLY PACKED THEY ARE ONLY DEEMED TO BE UNCLEAN WITH MIDDAF,[2] EVEN THOUGH THE KEY IS IN THE POSSESSION OF THE OWNER.[3]

MISHNAH 3. IF AN ARTICLE WAS LOST DURING THE DAY AND WAS FOUND ON THE SAME DAY IT REMAINS CLEAN.[4] IF IT WAS LOST DURING DAYTIME AND FOUND IN THE NIGHT, OR IF IT WAS LOST IN THE NIGHT AND FOUND DURING THE DAY[5] OR IF IT WAS LOST ON ONE DAY AND FOUND ON THE NEXT DAY, IT IS DEEMED TO BE UNCLEAN.[6] THIS IS THE GENERAL RULE: PROVIDED A NIGHT OR PART OF A NIGHT HAS PASSED OVER IT IT IS DEEMED UNCLEAN. IF CLOTHES HAVE BEEN SPREAD OUT[7] IN A PUBLIC DOMAIN, THEY REMAIN CLEAN;[8] BUT IF IN A PRIVATE DOMAIN THEY ARE DEEMED UNCLEAN.[9] IF, HOWEVER, ONE KEPT WATCH OVER THEM, THEY REMAIN CLEAN.[10] IF THEY FELL DOWN AND HE[11] WENT TO BRING THEM, THEY ARE DEEMED UNCLEAN.[12] IF A MAN'S BUCKET FELL INTO THE CISTERN OF AN 'AM HA-AREẒ AND HE WENT TO BRING SOMETHING WHEREWITH TO DRAW IT UP, IT IS DEEMED UNCLEAN, SINCE IT WAS LEFT FOR A TIME IN THE DOMAIN OF AN 'AM HA-AREẒ.

MISHNAH 4. IF A MAN LEFT HIS HOUSE OPEN AND FOUND

(1) Since one sitting on the lid would exercise pressure on all the clothes. (2) A minor grade of uncleanness that can be conveyed to foodstuffs and liquids only. (3) Since shifting (*hesseṭ*) is possible in a closed chest also. (4) Had any man touched it he would also have picked it up. (5) *Sc.* on the next day. (6) With *midras*. In the darkness of the night a menstruant or an idolater may have trodden on the lost article without being aware of it. (7) To dry. (8) As any other condition of doubt in a public domain which is deemed clean. There is no need to provide, as is the case with a lost article, against the possibility of *midras*, since people as a rule do not tread on clothes that are spread out to dry. (9) As is the rule with a condition of doubt in such a domain. (10) Even in a private domain. There is no need to consider the possibility of an occasional lapse. (11) Having lost sight of them. (12) They might have contracted an uncleanness while they were out of sight.

IT OPEN,[1] OR CLOSED AND FOUND IT CLOSED,[2] OR OPEN AND FOUND IT CLOSED, IT REMAINS CLEAN;[3] BUT IF HE LEFT IT CLOSED AND FOUND IT OPEN, R. MEIR RULES THAT IT IS DEEMED UNCLEAN,[4] AND THE SAGES RULE THAT IT REMAINS CLEAN,[5] SINCE, THOUGH THIEVES HAD BEEN THERE, THEY MAY HAVE CHANGED THEIR MIND[6] AND GONE AWAY.

MISHNAH 5. IF THE WIFE OF AN 'AM HA-AREẒ ENTERED A ḤABER'S HOUSE[7] TO TAKE OUT HIS SON OR HIS DAUGHTER OR HIS CATTLE, THE HOUSE REMAINS CLEAN, SINCE SHE HAD ENTERED IT WITHOUT PERMISSION.[8]

MISHNAH 6. A GENERAL RULE HAS BEEN LAID DOWN CONCERNING CLEAN FOODSTUFFS: WHATEVER IS DESIGNATED AS FOOD FOR HUMAN CONSUMPTION IS SUSCEPTIBLE TO UNCLEANNESS UNLESS IT IS RENDERED UNFIT TO BE FOOD FOR A DOG; AND WHATEVER IS NOT DESIGNATED AS FOOD FOR HUMAN CONSUMPTION IS NOT SUSCEPTIBLE TO UNCLEANNESS UNLESS IT IS DESIGNATED FOR HUMAN CONSUMPTION. FOR INSTANCE? IF[9] A PIGEON FELL INTO A WINEPRESS[10] AND ONE INTENDED TO PICK IT OUT FOR AN IDOLATER,[11] IT BECOMES SUSCEPTIBLE TO UNCLEANNESS; BUT IF HE INTENDED IT FOR A DOG IT IS NOT SUSCEPTIBLE TO UNCLEANNESS. R. JOḤANAN B. NURI RULES THAT IT IS SUSCEPTIBLE TO UNCLEANNESS. IF A DEAF MUTE, AN IMBECILE OR A MINOR INTENDED IT AS FOOD,[12] IT REMAINS INSUSCEPTIBLE; BUT IF THEY PICKED IT UP[12]

(1) Finding it open, a thief would be afraid to enter, knowing as he does that the owner might at any moment return. (2) In which case it is unlikely that a thief has dared and managed to open it, to touch the objects within, and also to close it. (3) Cf. prev. two notes. (4) A thief having apparently been there. (5) If nothing had been stolen. (6) Before they touched anything in the house. (7) Without his permission. (8) Though it was for the owner's benefit, she is afraid to remain in it long enough to touch its contents. (9) With reference to the last clause. (10) Where it died and deteriorated and thus became unfit for human consumption. (11) Who does not mind eating the bird even in its deteriorated condition. (12) For an idolater's consumption.

IT BECOMES SUSCEPTIBLE; SINCE ONLY AN ACT OF THEIRS[1] IS EFFECTIVE WHILE THEIR INTENTION IS OF NO CONSEQUENCE.

MISHNAH 7. THE OUTER PARTS OF VESSELS THAT HAVE CONTRACTED UNCLEANNESS FROM LIQUIDS, R. ELIEZER RULED, CONVEY UNCLEANNESS TO LIQUIDS[2] BUT[3] DO NOT RENDER FOODSTUFFS UNFIT.[4] R. JOSHUA RULED: THEY CONVEY UNCLEANNESS TO LIQUIDS[2] AND ALSO RENDER FOODSTUFFS[5] UNFIT. SIMEON THE BROTHER OF AZARIAH[6] RULED: THEY DO NEITHER THE ONE NOT THE OTHER,[7] BUT LIQUIDS THAT CONTRACTED UNCLEANNESS FROM THE OUTER PARTS OF VESSELS CONVEY UNCLEANNESS[8] AT ONE REMOVE AND CAUSE UNFITNESS AT A SECOND REMOVE.[9] IT[10] MAY THUS SAY,[11] 'THEY[12] THAT RENDERED YOU UNCLEAN DID NOT RENDER ME UNCLEAN BUT YOU HAVE RENDERED ME UNCLEAN'.

MISHNAH 8. IF A KNEADING TROUGH WAS SLOPING DOWNWARDS AND THERE WAS DOUGH[13] IN THE HIGHER PART AND DRIPPING MOISTURE IN THE LOWER PART, THEN THREE PIECES[14] THAT JOINTLY MAKE UP THE BULK OF AN EGG[15] CANNOT[16] BE COMBINED TOGETHER,[17] BUT TWO[18] ARE COM-

(1) In this case the picking out. (2) Even if the latter are unconsecrated. (3) Since their uncleanness is only Rabbinical. (4) Even if they were *terumah*. (5) Of *terumah*. (6) V. Zeb. 2a. (7) *Sc.* they neither convey uncleanness to unconsecrated liquids nor to foodstuffs or *terumah*. (8) To *terumah*. (9) If the *terumah* they have rendered unclean touched other *terumah*. (10) The *terumah*. (11) To the liquids from which it contracted the uncleanness. (12) The outer parts of the vessels. (13) That was unclean. (14) Two of which are on the dry part of the trough and one within the liquid, the middle one touching the upper piece and the lower piece while separating them from each other. (15) The prescribed minimum for conveying uncleanness. (16) On account of the two pieces that do not directly touch each other (cf. prev. n. but one). (17) To convey uncleanness to the liquid which in turn would have conveyed uncleanness to the trough. (18) *Sc.* the middle one and the one below it in the liquid, if together they make up the bulk of an egg.

BINED.[1] R. JOSE RULED: THE TWO ALSO CANNOT BE COMBINED UNLESS THEY COMPRESS LIQUID BETWEEN THEM.[2] IF THE LIQUID, HOWEVER, WAS LEVEL,[3] EVEN THOUGH THE PIECE RESEMBLED MUSTARD SEED[4] THEY[5] ARE COMBINED TOGETHER.[1] R. DOSA RULED: CRUMBLED FOOD CANNOT BE COMBINED TOGETHER.[1]

MISHNAH 9. IF A STICK IS COMPLETELY COVERED WITH UNCLEAN LIQUID[6] IT BECOMES CLEAN AS SOON AS IT[7] HAS TOUCHED THE [WATER IN THE] RITUAL BATH;[8] SO R. JOSHUA. BUT THE SAGES RULED: ONLY WHEN THE WHOLE OF IT[9] IS IMMERSED.[10] A JET,[11] A SLOPE[12] OR DRIPPING MOISTURE[13] DOES NOT SERVE AS A CONNECTIVE[14] EITHER FOR UNCLEANNESS[15] OR FOR CLEANNESS.[16] A POOL OF WATER,[17] HOWEVER, SERVES AS A CONNECTIVE IN RESPECT BOTH OF UNCLEANNESS AND CLEANNESS.

(1) To constitute the prescribed minimum. (2) *Sc.* they are so close to each other that the liquid between them seems to be compressed. (3) Lit., 'standing', the trough lying level and the pieces of unclean dough floating in the liquid. (4) Small and numerous but together making up the bulk of an egg. (5) On account of the liquid that forms a connecting link. (6) Water. The ruling does not apply to any other liquids. (7) *Sc.* only one end of it. (8) Though the remainder of the stick was outside the water. The water on the stick, which forms a slope, serves as a connective. (9) The stick. (10) Only then does the water on the stick become clean. (11) Of water. (11) Water running down an incline. (31) With which one touching it could not moisten another object. (14) Between the clean vessel from which it comes and the unclean one into which it descends. (15) If the jet of water, for instance, came from a clean vessel, that vessel remains clean thôugh the jet descended into an unclean vessel. (16) As, for instance, in the case of the stick, if the lower end alone touched the ritual bath the stick remains unclean. (17) Lit., 'a marsh', a collection of standing water.

ṬOHOROTH

CHAPTER IX

MISHNAH 1. AT WHAT STAGE DO OLIVES[1] BECOME SUSCEPTIBLE TO UNCLEANNESS?[2] WHEN THEY EXUDE THE MOISTURE [PRODUCED] BY [THEIR LYING IN] THE VAT[3] BUT NOT THE ONE [PRODUCED WHILE THEY ARE STILL] IN THE BASKET.[4] THIS IS ACCORDING TO THE VIEW OF BETH SHAMMAI. R. SIMEON RULED: THE MINIMUM TIME PRESCRIBED FOR PROPER EXUDATION[5] IS THREE DAYS.[6] BETH HILLEL RULED: AS SOON AS THREE OLIVES STICK TOGETHER.[7] R. GAMALIEL RULED: AS SOON AS THEIR PREPARATION[8] IS FINISHED;[9] AND THE SAGES AGREE WITH HIS VIEW.

MISHNAH 2. IF A MAN HAD FINISHED THE GATHERING[10] BUT INTENDED TO BUY SOME MORE,[11] OR IF HE HAD FINISHED

(1) That are intended for the manufacture of oil. (2) On account of the moisture they exude. (3) This liquid being desired and welcomed by the owner is, like all liquids that are deliberately put on foodstuffs or whose presence on the food is desired, capable of rendering the olives susceptible to uncleanness, v. Maksh. I, 1. (4) In which the olives are gathered and the moisture in which runs to waste through its holes. Such moisture is useless to the owner and, therefore, undesired by him (cf. prev. n.). (5) Before which time the moisture cannot be regarded as valid oil. (6) Only after the third day can the moisture be regarded as oil and thus render the olives susceptible to uncleanness. Seven kinds of liquids, of which oil is one, are capable of imparting such susceptibility to foodstuffs. (7) In the vat, owing to the moisture exuded. (8) Lit., 'their work'. (9) *Sc.* when no more olives are to be added to the batch of olives finally harvested and ready to be placed in the vat. It is then that exudation is desired and it is, therefore, then that the liquid is capable of rendering the olives susceptible to uncleanness. (10) Of his olives, from the tree. (11) To add to those in the vat; in consequence of which the exudation of the first batch is unwelcome, since by the time the second batch would begin to exude the first would be too soft and spoilt.

BUYING BUT INTENDED TO BORROW[1] SOME MORE, OR IF[2] A TIME OF MOURNING, A WEDDING FEAST OR SOME OTHER HINDRANCE BEFELL HIM[3] THEN EVEN IF ZABS AND ZABAHS WALKED OVER THEM[4] THEY[4] REMAIN CLEAN.[5] IF ANY UNCLEAN LIQUIDS FELL UPON THEM,[4] ONLY THE PLACE WHERE IT TOUCHED THEM BECOMES UNCLEAN,[6] AND ANY SAP THAT ISSUES FORTH FROM THEM[7] IS[8] CLEAN.[9]

MISHNAH 3. WHEN THEIR PREPARATION IS FINISHED THEY[4] BECOME SUSCEPTIBLE TO UNCLEANNESS. IF AN UNCLEAN LIQUID FELL UPON THEM THEY[10] BECOME UNCLEAN.[11] THE SAP THAT ISSUES FROM THEM[12] R. ELIEZER RULES IS CLEAN,[9] BUT THE SAGES[13] RULE THAT IT IS UNCLEAN. R. SIMEON STATED: THEY DID NOT DISPUTE THE RULING THAT SAP THAT ISSUES FROM OLIVES IS CLEAN; BUT ABOUT WHAT DID THEY DIFFER? ABOUT THAT WHICH COMES FROM THE VAT,[14] WHICH R. ELIEZER REGARDS AS CLEAN AND THE SAGES REGARD AS UNCLEAN.[15]

MISHNAH 4. IF A MAN[16] HAD FINISHED [THE GATHERING

(1) Var. lec. 'to gather'. Cf. prev. n. (2) Before he completed the packing of the vat. (3) So that he is compelled to complete the packing later, and the exudation of the first batch is consequently unwelcome to him (cf. prev. n. but two). (4) The olives. (5) Since the liquid, as stated *supra*, was undesired and, therefore, incapable of rendering the olives susceptible. (6) Because only that place that has been touched by the liquid has been rendered by it susceptible to uncleanness as well as unclean simultaneously. (7) Before the packing has been completed. (8) Since it is unwelcome. (9) *Sc.* it neither causes the olives to be susceptible to uncleanness nor does it itself contract any uncleanness. (10) Even the olives that have not been directly touched by the liquid. (11) Since the unclean liquid is mixed up with their sap. (12) Which, according to R. Eliezer, is no proper oil and cannot, therefore, be classed among the seven liquids that render foodstuffs susceptible to uncleanness. (13) Regarding the sap as one of the liquids that may cause susceptibility to the uncleanness of foodstuffs. (14) After the good oil had been removed. (15) Since some particles of good oil must remain in it. (16) Who was an *'am ha-areẓ* and who, after the season

OF HIS OLIVES] AND[1] PUT[2] ASIDE[3] ONE BASKETFUL, LET[4] HIM GIVE IT TO A POOR[5] PRIEST;[6] SO R. MEIR. R. JUDAH RULED: HE[7] MUST HAND HIM[8] OVER THE KEY FORTHWITH.[9] R. SIMEON RULED:[10] WITHIN TWENTY-FOUR HOURS.

MISHNAH 5. IF A MAN PUT HIS OLIVES IN A BASKET[11] THAT THEY MIGHT BE SOFTENED SO THAT THEY BE EASY TO PRESS, THEY BECOME SUSCEPTIBLE TO UNCLEANNESS;[12] BUT IF TO BE SOFTENED SO THAT THEY MAY BE SALTED[13] BETH SHAMMAI RULED: THEY BECOME SUSCEPTIBLE. BETH HILLEL RULED: THEY DO NOT BECOME SUSCEPTIBLE.[14] IF A MAN CRUSHED OLIVES[15] WITH UNWASHED[16] HANDS[17] HE CAUSES THEM TO BE UNCLEAN.[18]

MISHNAH 6. IF A MAN PUT HIS OLIVES ON A ROOF TO DRY, EVEN THOUGH THEY ARE PILED UP TO THE HEIGHT OF

of gathering, is not trusted to keep his olives in conditions of cleanness.

(1) In order that it may not become susceptible to uncleanness like the others. (2) Var. lec. 'let him put'. (3) To keep it in conditions of cleanness so that *terumah* for the priest may be taken from it. (4) Var. lec., 'and let'. (5) Var. lec., 'in the presence of a'. The reading 'poor' does not exclude a wealthy priest; but the scanty *terumah* given after the season is usually allotted to a poor priest. (6) Who must himself press out the oil and take off the *terumah* under conditions of certain cleanness. (7) Who was an *'am ha-areẓ* and who, after the season of gathering, is not trusted to keep his olives in conditions of cleanness. (8) The priest. (9) *Sc.* the same day on which the gathering of his olives had been finished; thus making sure that no uncleanness whatsoever could be conveyed to them. (10) With reference to the time within which the key must be given to the priest. (11) Var. lec. 'press'. (12) Owing to the exuding moisture which was welcomed by him. (13) And eaten in that condition. (14) Since the exuding moisture is not welcomed, the owner preferring it to remain in the olives. (15) Of *terumah*. (16) Lit., 'unclean'. (17) Which, unless washed, are always deemed to be unclean in the second grade and to convey invalidity to *terumah* and first grade uncleanness to liquids. (18) As the exuding moisture is welcomed by him it renders the olives susceptible to uncleanness and also unclean in the second grade, since the moisture that becomes unclean in the first grade conveys to the olives an uncleanness of the second grade.

A CUBIT,[1] THEY DO NOT BECOME[2] SUSCEPTIBLE TO UNCLEANNESS.[3] IF HE PUT THEM IN THE HOUSE TO PUTRIFY, THOUGH HE INTENDS TO TAKE THEM UP ON THE ROOF,[4] OR IF HE PUT THEM ON THE ROOF THAT THEY MIGHT OPEN SO THAT THEY COULD BE SALTED,[5] THEY BECOME SUSCEPTIBLE TO UNCLEANNESS. IF HE PUT THEM IN THE HOUSE WHILE HE SECURED[6] HIS ROOF[7] OR UNTIL HE COULD TAKE THEM ELSEWHERE,[8] THEY DO NOT BECOME SUSCEPTIBLE TO UNCLEANNESS.[3]

MISHNAH 7. IF THE MAN DESIRED TO TAKE FROM THEM[9] [A QUANTITY SUFFICIENT FOR] ONE PRESSING OR FOR TWO PRESSINGS,[10] BETH SHAMMAI RULED: HE MAY TAKE OFF [WHAT HE REQUIRES] IN A CONDITION OF UNCLEANNESS[11] BUT MUST COVER UP [WHAT HE TAKES] IN A CONDITION OF CLEANNESS.[12] BETH HILLEL RULED: HE MAY ALSO COVER IT UP IN A CONDITION OF UNCLEANNESS.[13] R. JOSE RULED: HE MAY[14] DIG OUT [WHAT HE REQUIRES] WITH METAL AXES[15] AND CARRY IT TO THE PRESS IN A CONDITION OF UNCLEANNESS.[16]

MISHNAH 8. IF A [DEAD] CREEPING THING WAS FOUND

(1) So that the weight of the upper olives inevitably presses down on the lower ones and causes exudation. (2) Var. lec., 'behold they are'. (3) Since the exuding moisture is not welcomed, the owner preferring it to remain in the olives. (4) To dry. (5) Var. lec., 'that they might putrify or open'. (6) *Aliter:* While he prepares a watchman's hut on. (7) Where they are subsequently to be taken to dry. (8) Cf. prev. n. (9) The mass of olives that are not yet susceptible to uncleanness. (10) *Sc.* he is not taking the entire batch to which he intends to add some more olives. (11) And it nevertheless remains clean, since the olives are still insusceptible to uncleanness. (12) Since its separation from the mass constitutes the completion of its preparation for the olive-press and the exuding moisture renders it susceptible to uncleanness. (13) So long as the greater part of the mass remains in the basket incomplete. (14) Even when moving the entire mass. (15) Though such axes are subject to many restrictions of uncleanness. (16) In his opinion the olives remain insusceptible to uncleanness until the actual pressing had begun.

IN THE MILLING STONES,[1] ONLY THE PLACE THAT IT HAS TOUCHED BECOMES UNCLEAN; BUT IF THE MOISTURE WAS RUNNING,[2] ALL BECOMES UNCLEAN.[3] IF IT[4] WAS FOUND ON THE LEAVES,[5] THE OLIVE-PRESS MEN[6] SHALL BE ASKED[7] WHETHER THEY CAN SAY, 'WE DID NOT TOUCH IT'. IF IT[4] TOUCHED THE MASS [OF OLIVES], EVEN BY AS LITTLE AS THE BULK OF A BARLEY GRAIN, [THE MASS BECOMES] UNCLEAN.

MISHNAH 9. IF IT[4] WAS FOUND ON BROKEN OFF PIECES[8] BUT IT TOUCHED AS MUCH AS AN EGG'S BULK,[9] [THE ENTIRE MASS] BECOMES UNCLEAN.[10] IF IT WAS FOUND ON SEVERED PIECES THAT LAY UPON OTHER SEVERED PIECES,[11] EVEN THOUGH IT TOUCHED[12] AS MUCH AS AN EGG'S BULK[9] ONLY THE PLACE[12] IT TOUCHED BECOMES UNCLEAN.[13] IF IT[4] WAS FOUND BETWEEN THE WALL AND THE OLIVES, THE LATTER REMAIN CLEAN.[14] IF IT WAS FOUND [ON OLIVES[15] THAT WERE LYING] ON THE ROOF [OF THE VAT],[16] [THE OLIVES IN] THE VAT REMAIN CLEAN.[14] IF IT[4] WAS FOUND IN THE VAT, [THE OLIVES ON] THE ROOF[15] ARE [ALSO] REGARDED AS UNCLEAN.[17] IF IT[4] WAS FOUND BURNT[18] UPON THE OLIVES, AND SO ALSO

(1) Of olives. (2) Thus connecting the creeping thing with the mass of olives. (3) From contact with the moisture that contracted uncleanness from the creeping thing. (4) The creeping thing. (5) That cover up the olives, and that are insusceptible to uncleanness. (6) Though they belong to the class of the *'am ha-areẓ*. (7) Since in this matter even the word of an *'am ha-areẓ* may be relied upon. (8) Of the main mass of olives, each piece being less than egg's bulk and lying on the main mass. (9) Made up of the broken off pieces. (10) On account of its contact with the egg's bulk of the small pieces that contracted uncleanness from the creeping thing. (11) The former being separated from the main mass by the latter. (12) Of the upper pieces. (13) The lower pieces remain clean since each in turn only touched an unclean piece above it that was smaller than the prescribed minimum. The pieces are not combined to constitute the required bulk. (14) It being assumed that it had never touched them. (15) Taken from the vat. (16) To dry. (17) As these olives were once in the vat it is assumed that the creeping thing was there with them before they were taken up to the roof. (18) When it no longer conveys any uncleanness.

IN THE CASE OF A RAG[1] THAT WAS SCORCHED,[2] [THE OLIVES REMAIN] CLEAN, BECAUSE ALL CASES OF UNCLEANNESS ARE DETERMINED IN ACCORDANCE WITH THEIR APPEARANCE AT THE TIME THEY ARE FOUND.[3]

(1) Of a *zab*. (2) V. p. 408, n. 18. (3) Hence it is assumed that the creeping thing or the scorched rag was in that condition during all the time that it lay on the olives.

ṬOHOROTH

CHAPTER X

MISHNAH I. IF A MAN LOCKED IN THE LABOURERS[1] IN THE OLIVE-PRESS[2] AND THERE WERE OBJECTS THEREIN SUFFERING MIDRAS UNCLEANNESS, R. MEIR RULED: THE OLIVE-PRESS IS DEEMED TO BE UNCLEAN.[3] R. JUDAH RULED: THE OLIVE-PRESS REMAINS CLEAN.[4] R. SIMEON RULED: IF THEY[5] REGARD THEM[6] AS CLEAN, THE OLIVE-PRESS IS DEEMED UNCLEAN;[7] BUT IF THEY REGARD THEM AS UNCLEAN,[8] THE OLIVE-PRESS REMAINS CLEAN. SAID R. JOSE: WHY INDEED IS UNCLEANNESS IMPOSED?[9] ONLY BECAUSE THE 'AM HA-AREẒ CLASS[10] ARE NOT VERSED IN THE LAWS OF HESSEṬ.[11]

MISHNAH 2. IF THE LABOURERS IN AN OLIVE-PRESS[12] WENT IN AND OUT,[13] AND IN THE OLIVE-PRESS[14] THERE WAS UNCLEAN LIQUID, THE LABOURERS REMAIN CLEAN IF THERE IS SPACE ENOUGH BETWEEN THE LIQUID AND THE OLIVES

(1) Who belonged to the *'am ha-areẓ* class and who are usually careless in the observance of the laws of cleanness and uncleanness but for whose cleansing he had especially arranged. (2) Thus making sure that they would not come out and contract any uncleanness from without and that no unclean person would get in and convey uncleanness. (3) The *'am ha-areẓ*, in his opinion, cannot be trusted to keep away from the unclean objects even in such circumstances. (4) Having been made clean for the purpose the labourers may be relied upon to keep away from all possible uncleanness. (5) The labourers. (6) The unclean objects in the olive-press. (7) Since they would not mind handling those objects and thus contract and convey uncleanness. (8) In which case they would avoid them. (9) In the case under discussion. (10) Who, contrary to the view of R. Meir, are not suspected of being so careless as actually to touch an unclean object. (11) V. Glos. And, shifting one of the objects even without directly touching it, would unknowingly contract and convey uncleanness. (12) Who were free from uncleanness. (13) Walking with their bare feet on the ground. (14) On the floor.

FOR THEIR FEET TO BE DRIED[1] ON THE GROUND.[2] IF AN UNCLEANNESS WAS FOUND IN A FRONT OF LABOURERS[3] IN THE OLIVE-PRESS OR GRAPE HARVESTERS,[3] THEY ARE BELIEVED IF THEY DECLARE, 'WE HAVE NOT TOUCHED IT'; AND THE SAME LAW APPLIES ALSO TO THE YOUNG CHILDREN[4] AMONG THEM.[5] THEY[6] MAY, FURTHERMORE, GO OUTSIDE THE DOOR OF THE OLIVE-PRESS AND RELIEVE THEMSELVES BEHIND THE WALL, AND STILL BE DEEMED CLEAN. HOW FAR MAY THEY GO AND STILL BE DEEMED CLEAN? AS FAR AS THEY CAN BE SEEN.[7]

MISHNAH 3. IF THE LABOURERS IN THE OLIVE-PRESS OR THE GRAPE HARVESTERS WERE ONLY BROUGHT WITHIN THE PRECINCTS OF THE CAVERN[8] IT SUFFICES;[9] SO R. MEIR. R. JOSE RULED: IT IS NECESSARY THAT ONE[10] SHOULD STAND OVER THEM UNTIL IMMERSION IS PERFORMED.[11] R. SIMEON RULED: IF THEY REGARD THE VESSELS AS CLEAN, ONE MUST STAND OVER THEM UNTIL THEIR IMMERSION IS PERFORMED; BUT IF THEY REGARD THEM AS UNCLEAN, IT IS NOT NECESSARY FOR ONE TO STAND OVER THEM UNTIL IMMERSION IS PERFORMED.

MISHNAH 4. IF A MAN DESIRES TO PUT GRAPES [INTO THE WINE-PRESS] FROM THE BASKETS OR FROM WHAT WAS

(1) Before they reached the olives. (2) In such a case the liquid which, having dried up, does not come in contact with the olives, cannot possibly convey any uncleanness to them, while the labourers themselves are not affected by the liquid which conveys no uncleanness to men. (3) V. p. 410, n. 12. (4) Who are presumed to be unclean on account of their contact with menstruants who do not refrain from embracing them. (5) *Sc.* they are believed if they declare that they have not touched the children. (6) Who belonged to the *'am ha-areẓ* class and who are usually careless in the observance of the laws of uncleanness and cleanness but for whose cleansing one had especially arranged. (7) By the owner, from his position at the press. (8) Containing the ritual bath for their immersion or that of the vessels which they are going to use. (9) To regard them as clean, even if the owner did not witness the actual immersion. (10) Who is versed in the laws of immersion. (11) Since they themselves are not familiar with these laws.

SPREAD OUT ON THE GROUND, BETH SHAMMAI RULED: HE MUST PUT THEM IN WITH CLEAN HANDS, FOR IF HE PUTS THEM IN WITH UNCLEAN HANDS HE RENDERS THEM UNCLEAN.[1] BETH HILLEL RULED: HE MAY PUT THEM IN WITH UNCLEAN HANDS AND YET HE MAY SET ASIDE HIS TERUMAH IN A CONDITION OF CLEANNESS.[2] [IF THEY ARE TAKEN] FROM THE GRAPE-BASKET[3] OR FROM WHAT WAS SPREAD OUT ON LEAVES,[4] ALL AGREE THAT THEY MUST BE PUT IN WITH CLEAN HANDS, FOR IF THEY ARE PUT IN WITH UNCLEAN HANDS THEY BECOME UNCLEAN.

MISHNAH 5. IF A MAN EATS GRAPES OUT OF THE BASKETS OR FROM WHAT IS SPREAD OUT ON THE GROUND, EVEN THOUGH THEY WERE BURST AND DRIPPED INTO THE WINE-PRESS, THE WINE-PRESS REMAINS CLEAN.[2] IF HE EATS THE GRAPES OUT OF THE GRAPE-BASKET[3] OR FROM WHAT WAS SPREAD OUT ON LEAVES, AND A SINGLE BERRY DROPPED INTO THE VAT, IF IT HAS A SEAL[5] ALL IN THE VAT REMAINS CLEAN;[6] BUT IF IT HAS NO SEAL, ALL IN THE VAT BECOMES UNCLEAN.[7] IF HE DROPPED[8] SOME OF THE GRAPES[9] AND TROD

(1) Since unclean hands convey uncleanness to exuding liquid and the liquid in turn conveys uncleanness to the grapes. (2) The exuding liquid, in their opinion, does not render the grapes susceptible to uncleanness since in a basket or on the ground it runs to waste and is, therefore, undesired and unwelcomed. (3) Lined with pitch to prevent the waste of any liquid. (4) In which cases the liquid is not wasted and, therefore, welcomed. (5) *Sc.* its stalk was still on it sealing it up, so that no liquid would come forth. (6) For, though the berry became susceptible to uncleanness when it was cut with the intention of putting it in the wine-press and, in consequence, contracted uncleanness from the man's hands, it nevertheless cannot convey uncleanness to the contents of the vat since (*a*) a foodstuff cannot convey uncleanness to another foodstuff and (*b*) it is smaller than the prescribed minimum. (7) Since the liquid in the berry contracted uncleanness from the man's hands and, there being no prescribed minimum for liquids, it conveys uncleanness to the contents of the wine-press. (8) Into the wine-press. (9) Of those whose stalks were still on them, that were cut with the intention of being put into the wine-press, and that in consequence became susceptible to uncleanness and then contracted uncleanness from the hands.

THEM[1] IN AN EMPTY PART OF THE WINE-PRESS,[2] THE CONTENTS OF THE LATTER REMAIN CLEAN IF THE BULK OF THE GRAPES WAS EXACTLY THAT OF AN EGG;[3] BUT IF IT WAS MORE THAN THE BULK OF AN EGG, THE CONTENTS BECOME UNCLEAN, FOR SO SOON AS THE FIRST DROP ISSUED IT CONTRACTED UNCLEANNESS FROM THE REMAINDER WHOSE BULK IS THAT OF AN EGG.

MISHNAH 6. IF A MAN[4] WAS STANDING AND SPEAKING BY THE EDGE OF THE CISTERN[5] AND SOME SPITTLE[6] SPIRTED FROM HIS MOUTH, AND THERE ARISES THE DOUBT WHETHER IT REACHED THE CISTERN OR NOT, THE CONDITION OF DOUBT IS REGARDED AS CLEAN.[7]

MISHNAH 7. IF THE CISTERN[5] IS EMPTIED OUT[8] AND A [DEAD] CREEPING THING WAS FOUND IN THE FIRST JAR, ALL THE OTHER JARS ARE DEEMED UNCLEAN;[9] BUT IF IT WAS FOUND IN THE LAST, ONLY THAT ONE IS UNCLEAN BUT ALL THE OTHERS[10] REMAIN CLEAN.[11] WHEN DOES THIS APPLY? ONLY WHEN THE WINE IS DRAWN DIRECTLY WITH EACH JAR, BUT IF IT WAS DRAWN WITH A LADLING-JAR[12] AND A [DEAD] CREEPING THING WAS FOUND IN ONE OF THE JARS, IT ALONE[10] IS UNCLEAN.[11] WHEN DOES THIS APPLY? ONLY

(1) To press the wine out. (2) *Sc.* one on which there was no liquid. (3) For, as soon as the first drop exudes, there remains less than the minimum prescribed for the conveyance of uncleanness. (4) An *'am ha-areẓ*. (5) In which the wine is gathered. (6) Which is deemed unclean and, in accordance with a Rabbinical law, conveys uncleanness to foodstuffs and liquids. (7) As is the case with any other unclean object that is thrown through space. (8) With a number of jars in succession. (9) It being assumed, since an uncleanness at one time may be presumed to have existed at an earlier time, that the unclean object was in the jar all the time and that it conveyed uncleanness to all the contents of the cistern when that jar was lowered into the water. (10) Since it is not presumed that an uncleanness found in one place was first present in another place. (11) The assumption being that the unclean object in the jar was never in the cistern. (12) Which draws the wine from the cistern and then empties it into the jar.

WHEN THE MAN EXAMINED [THE JAR AND THE LADLING-JAR][1] BUT DID NOT[2] COVER UP [THE CISTERN AND THE JAR],[3] OR COVERED THEM UP BUT DID NOT EXAMINE THEM;[4] BUT IF HE BOTH EXAMINED THEM AND COVERED THEM UP AND A [DEAD] CREEPING THING WAS FOUND IN ONE JAR, ALL THE CONTENTS OF THE CISTERN[5] ARE DEEMED UNCLEAN; IF IT WAS FOUND IN THE CISTERN, ALL ITS CONTENTS ARE DEEMED UNCLEAN AND IF IT WAS FOUND IN THE LADLING-JAR AL THE CONTENTS OF THE CISTERN[5] ARE DEEMED UNCLEAN.

MISHNAH 8. [THE SPACE] BETWEEN THE ROLLERS[6] AND [THE PILE OF] GRAPE SKINS IS REGARDED[7] AS A PUBLIC DOMAIN.[8] A VINEYARD IN FRONT OF THE GRAPE HARVESTERS[9] IS DEEMED[7] TO BE A PRIVATE DOMAIN[10] AND THAT WHICH IS BEHIND THE HARVESTERS[11] IS DEEMED[7] TO BE A PUBLIC DOMAIN.[12] WHEN DOES THIS LAW[13] APPLY? ONLY WHEN THE PUBLIC ENTER AT ONE END AND GO OUT AT THE OTHER.[14] THE IMPLEMENTS OF THE OLIVE-PRESS, THE WINE-PRESS AND THE BASKET-PRESS,[15] IF THEY ARE OF WOOD, NEED ONLY BE DRIED[16] WHEN[17] THEY BECOME CLEAN; BUT IF THEY ARE

(1) Before using them. (2) After each drawing of the wine. (3) To prevent any unclean object from falling into them. In such a case it may well be assumed that it was only then that the unclean object had fallen in. (4) So that it may well be presumed that the unclean object was in the jar all the time. (5) In which it must obviously have been first. (6) Beams kept for the purpose of placing upon the grape skins (after the main part of the juice had been pressed out) in order to squeeze out any possible juice that still remained in them. (7) In respect of conditions of doubtful uncleanness which are deemed clean in public, and unclean in a private domain. (8) Since many men are required for the lifting up and the carrying of the beams from their position to the pile of grape-skins. (9) *Sc.* a vineyard or a part of it that had not yet been harvested. (10) Since the public are kept out of it. (11) *Sc.* the part that had already been harvested. (12) Since the public freely use it. (13) The last mentioned. (14) Otherwise it must still be regarded as a private domain. (15) *'Iḳal* or *'Eḳel,* a basket or bale of some loose texture into which the pressed out olives are packed to undergo a further process of pressing. (16) After being washed with a mixture of ashes and water. (17) After due ritual immersion.

OF REED GRASS[1] THEY MUST BE LEFT UNUSED[2] FOR TWELVE MONTHS, OR THEY MUST BE SCALDED IN HOT WATER.[3] R. JOSE RULED: IT SUFFICES IF THEY ARE IMMERSED[4] IN THE CURRENT OF THE RIVER.[5]

(1) Which has a greater capacity for absorption. (2) Lit., 'he causes them to grow old'. (3) After which due ritual immersion restores them to cleanness. (4) For twelve hours. (5) Where the rapidity of the water-current expels the absorbed moisture.

MIḲWAOTH

TRANSLATED INTO ENGLISH

WITH NOTES

BY

RABBI M. H. SEGAL, M. A.

INTRODUCTION

The name of our Tractate, Miḳwaoth (מקואות), is an irregular[1] plural form with the feminine ending of the masculine noun *miḳweh* (מקוה). In biblical Hebrew *miḳweh* means 'a gathering' from the root *ḳwh* (קוה), 'to gather', especially 'a gathering of water' (cf. Gen. I, 10; Ex. VII, 19; Lev. XI, 36). In Mishnaic Hebrew the noun *miḳweh* assumed a special technical connotation in the sense of 'a gathering of water which serves for the purification from a defilement', a ritual bathing-pool.

PRINCIPAL RULES OF THE MIḲWEH

Our Tractate deals with the various kinds of such bathing-pools, their making and their use, and the numerous problems arising therefrom. It may facilitate the understanding of the discussions of our Tractate if we give here a brief summary of the leading rules governing the making and use of the *miḳweh*.

The Torah often speaks of washing or bathing for the purpose of purification (Lev. XI, 32, 40; XIV, 8, 9, 47; XV, 5 ff.; XVI, 26, 28; Num. XIX, 7, 8, 19, etc.). According to Jewish tradition this washing or bathing means total immersion in a special natural pool of water, or a *miḳweh*. The *miḳweh* must contain no less than 40 *se'ahs*[2] of water, which is the minimum quantity required for covering completely the body of an adult person of average size. But this applies only to a *miḳweh* formed by a gathering of rain water. If the water came from under the ground, as in a spring or well, it can purify even if its contents are less than 40 *se'ahs*, provided it affords complete immersion of the body (cf. *infra* I, 7, n. 2).

(1) Cf. M. H. Segal, *A Grammar of Mishnaic Hebrew* (Oxford 1927, § 287; דקדוק לשון המשנה (Tel Aviv, 5696), § 150. Palestinian texts, such as *The Mishnah of the Palestinian Talmud*, edited by W. H. Lowe (Cambridge 1883), always give the regular feminine form *Miḳwoth* (מקוות). (2) סאים, plural of סאה, *se'ah*. The *se'ah* contained six *ḳabs*, the *ḳab* contained four *logs*. The capacity of the *se'ah* was a little over 12 litres, or over $2^1/_2$ gallons.

The 40 *se'ahs* of rain water in the *miḳweh* must have flowed into it in a natural manner, and must not have been poured into the *miḳweh* out of a receptacle. If a *miḳweh* contains less than 40 *se'ahs,* and a quantity of three *logs* of water was drawn into a vessel and poured into the *miḳweh,* this 'drawn water' (מים שאובים) renders the *miḳweh* invalid (cf. *infra* II, 4, nn. 3 and 4). But once a *miḳweh* was filled in the prescribed manner with forty *se'ahs* of rain water, any quantity of drawn water may then be added to it without affecting its validity.

Finally, the immersion must be such as will allow the water in the *miḳweh* to cover freely the whole of the body immersed without anything interposing between the body and the water (cf. VIII, 5 ff.).

CONTENTS OF THE TRACTATE

Chapter I. Six different kinds of *miḳweh;* rules concerning uncleanness in the water of pits and in a pool of rain drippings (1—6); four other kinds of *miḳweh* (7—8).

Chapter II. Cases of doubt respecting a *miḳweh* (1—3); rules concerning drawn water in a *miḳweh* (4—8); concerning mud in a *miḳweh* (9).

Chapter III. Further rules concerning drawn water.

Chapter IV. Concerning water flowing through receptacles into a *miḳweh* (1—3); concerning a mixture of rain water and drawn water (4); on troughs (5)

Chapter V. Concerning fountains (1—3), seas (4), and other flowing water (5—6).

Chapter VI. Concerning the mingling of the water of one *miḳweh* with the water of another *miḳweh* or with the water in a receptacle (1—3); concerning water in a receptacle inside a *miḳweh* (4—6); the combination of adjoining *miḳwehs* (7—9); concerning a bath-basin and its appurtenance (10—11).

Chapter VII. Concerning substances which serve to complete the prescribed contents of the *miḳweh*, or to render it invalid (1—2); concerning wine or oil which fell into a *miḳweh* (3—5); concerning immersion in a *miḳweh* which contains exactly forty *se'ahs* (6–7).

Chapter VIII. Concerning *miḳwehs* in the Holy Land and abroad (1); concerning seminal issue and its purification in a *miḳweh* (2–4); on the immersion of a menstruant woman, and of articles held by the hand (5).

Chapter IX. What forms an interposition between the water of the *miḳweh* and the human body (1–4), between the water of the *miḳweh* and utensils and other articles (5–7).

Chapter X. On the immersion of vessels with handles, of closed articles, and of utensils with knots and other appendages (1–5); concerning the immersion of water and of vessels containing other liquids (6); concerning foods which convey uncleanness, and the uncleanness of things which are swallowed and vomited again (7–8).[1]

M. H. SEGAL

(1) My thanks are due to Prof. H. Danby for valuable help in the preparation of this work.

MIḲWAOTH

CHAPTER I

MISHNAH 1. THERE ARE SIX DEGREES OF GATHERINGS OF WATER,[1] EACH SUPERIOR TO THE OTHER.[2] THE WATER OF PITS[3]—IF AN UNCLEAN PERSON DRANK OF IT AND THEN A CLEAN PERSON DRANK OF IT, HE BECOMES UNCLEAN;[4] IF AN UNCLEAN PERSON DRANK OF IT AND WATER WAS THEN DRAWN FROM IT IN A CLEAN VESSEL, [THE VESSEL] BECOMES UNCLEAN;[4] IF AN UNCLEAN PERSON DRANK OF IT AND THEN A LOAF OF TERUMAH[5] FELL IN AND WAS WASHED IN IT, IT BECOMES UNCLEAN; BUT IF IT WAS NOT WASHED IN IT, IT CONTINUES CLEAN.[6]

MISHNAH 2. IF ONE DREW WATER FROM IT IN AN UN-

(1) במקואות, here used in the ordinary and more original sense of an assemblage of water, as in biblical Hebrew (e.g., Gen. I, 10), and not in the later technical sense of a ritual bathing-pool; cf. Introduction. The six degrees are: I, water of pits (§ 1); II, water of rain drippings (§ 6); III, the *miḳweh;* IV, the fountain (§ 7); V, smitten water; VI, living water (§ 8). (2) In their power of imparting and removing uncleanness. (3) גבאים, cf. Isa. XXX, 14. The contents are less than 40 *se'ahs*. If the pit contains 40 *se'ahs* or more, it becomes a *miḳweh*. (4) The water taken up by the drinker in his mouth having become unclean, it may be feared that a drop of it fell from his mouth back into the water of the pit, and was afterwards drunk by the clean person, or was taken up in the clean vessel. (5) Heave-offering which, by reason of its sanctity, is susceptible to uncleanness more than ordinary food; cf. Zabim V, 12; Shab. 14*a*. (6) The water in the pit is considered as joined to the ground, and as such is incapable of becoming unclean or of conveying uncleanness (cf Lev. XI, 36), until it is deliberately removed from the pit. Therefore, if the person did not wash the loaf, the unclean drop of water, which may have been absorbed by the loaf, was neutralized and its uncleanness rendered ineffective by the rest of the water in the pit. But when the person washed the loaf, he deliberately removed from the pit water absorbed by the loaf, which may have included the unclean drop. This drop, therefore, was not neutralized, but imparted its uncleanness to the loaf.

CLEAN VESSEL AND THEN A CLEAN PERSON DRANK [OUT OF THE PIT], HE BECOMES UNCLEAN;[1] IF ONE DREW WATER [FROM IT] IN AN UNCLEAN VESSEL AND THEN DREW WATER FROM IT IN A CLEAN VESSEL, IT BECOMES UNCLEAN; IF ONE DREW WATER [FROM IT] IN AN UNCLEAN VESSEL AND A LOAF OF TERUMAH FELL IN AND WAS WASHED IN IT, IT BECOMES UNCLEAN; BUT IF IT WAS NOT WASHED IN IT, IT CONTINUES CLEAN.

MISHNAH 3. IF UNCLEAN WATER[2] FELL INTO IT AND A CLEAN PERSON DRANK OF IT, HE BECOMES UNCLEAN; IF UNCLEAN WATER FELL INTO IT AND THEN WATER WAS DRAWN FROM IT IN A CLEAN VESSEL, IT BECOMES UNCLEAN; IF UNCLEAN WATER FELL INTO IT AND A LOAF OF TERUMAH FELL IN AND WAS WASHED IN IT, IT BECOMES UNCLEAN; BUT IF IT WAS NOT WASHED IN IT, IT CONTINUES CLEAN. R. SIMEON SAYS: IT BECOMES UNCLEAN[3] WHETHER IT WAS WASHED IN IT OR WHETHER IT WAS NOT WASHED IN IT.

MISHNAH 4. IF A CORPSE FELL INTO IT OR AN UNCLEAN PERSON[4] WALKED IN IT, AND A CLEAN PERSON DRANK OF IT, HE CONTINUES CLEAN. THE SAME RULE APPLIES TO THE WATER OF PITS, THE WATER OF CISTERNS,[5] THE WATER OF

(1) The same rule obtains in the case of an unclean vessel as in the case of an unclean drinker. The vessel imparts uncleanness to the water it takes up from the pit. A drop of this unclean water may have fallen back from the vessel into the pit, and may have been taken up again by the drinker in his mouth. (2) The rule applying to a drop falling back into the pit from an unclean drinker or from an unclean vessel applies also to unclean water which falls into the pit. (3) In all the three cases discussed above. He holds that even when the loaf was not washed, we may suspect that it was the clean water alone which escaped from the loaf when lifted from the pit, and that the unclean water adhered to the loaf, and rendered it unclean. (4) The corpse or the unclean person did not make the water unclean, because, as stated above p. 423, n. 6, water in a pit is considered joined to the ground, and is not susceptible to uncleanness unless it is deliberately separated from the pit. (5) They are shaped round like wells.

DITCHES,[1] THE WATER OF CAVERNS,[2] THE WATER OF RAIN DRIPPINGS[3] WHICH HAVE STOPPED,[4] AND MIḲWEHS[5] OF LESS THAN FORTY SE'AHS: THEY ARE ALL CLEAN DURING THE TIME OF RAIN;[6] WHEN THE RAIN HAS STOPPED THOSE NEAR TO A CITY OR TO A ROAD ARE UNCLEAN,[7] AND THOSE DISTANT REMAIN CLEAN UNTIL THE MAJORITY OF PEOPLE PASS [THAT WAY].[8]

MISHNAH 5. WHEN ARE THEY ACCOUNTED CLEAN AGAIN? BETH SHAMMAI SAY: WHEN THEIR CONTENTS HAVE BEEN INCREASED[9] [BY MORE THAN THE ORIGINAL QUANTITY] AND THEY OVERFLOW.[10] BETH HILLEL SAY: WHEN THEIR CONTENTS HAVE BEEN INCREASED[11] [BY MORE THAN THEIR ORIGINAL QUANTITY] ALTHOUGH THEY DO NOT OVERFLOW. R. SIMEON SAYS: WHEN THEY OVERFLOW ALTHOUGH THEIR CONTENTS HAVE NOT BEEN SO[12] INCREASED. [ALL SUCH PIT-WATER][13] IS VALID [FOR PREPARING DOUGH] FOR ḤALLAH[14] AND FOR THE WASHING OF THE HANDS.[15]

(1) Shaped long and narrow. (2) These are more or less square-shaped and roofed. (3) Pools formed by rain water running down from the hills. (4) To trickle down from the hills. If they have not stopped, they would neutralize an unclean drop falling into them. (5) Artificial pools designed for ritual immersion (cf. Introd.), somewhat rectangular in shape, but not roofed. (6) When wayfarers are few and drinking water is abundant. There is then no need to suspect that an unclean person had drunk from them, or that water had been drawn from them in an unclean vessel. And if by chance this did happen, the flowing rain water would have neutralized the unclean drop. (7) It may be suspected that an unclean wayfarer had drunk from them, or that water was drawn from them in an unclean vessel. (8) Among whom there may have been an unclean person who drank of the water, or a person who drew water in an unclean vessel. (9) By rain water. (10) So that it may be assumed that the unclean quantity had escaped. (11) The larger quantity of rain water is sufficient to neutralize the unclean quantity; cf. Maksh. II, 3. (12) Even if the new rain water was less than the original contents, but was sufficient to overfill the receptacle. (13) As defined *supra* I, n. 3. (14) I.e. dough from which *ḥallah*, or dough-offering, has to be taken; cf. Num. XV, 20; Ḥal. I. 1. (15) Before eating of common food; cf. Ḥag. II, 5.

MISHNAH 6. SUPERIOR TO SUCH [WATER] IS THE WATER OF RAIN DRIPPINGS WHICH HAVE NOT STOPPED.[1] IF AN UNCLEAN PERSON DRANK OF IT AND THEN A CLEAN PERSON DRANK OF IT, HE CONTINUES CLEAN;[2] IF AN UNCLEAN PERSON DRANK OF IT AND WATER WAS THEN DRAWN FROM IT IN A CLEAN VESSEL, IT CONTINUES CLEAN; IF AN UNCLEAN PERSON DRANK OF IT AND A LOAF OF TERUMAH FELL IN, EVEN IF IT WAS WASHED IN IT, IT CONTINUES CLEAN; IF ONE DREW WATER FROM IT IN AN UNCLEAN VESSEL AND THEN A CLEAN PERSON DRANK [OUT OF THE POOL], HE CONTINUES CLEAN; IF ONE DREW WATER FROM IT IN AN UNCLEAN VESSEL AND A LOAF OF TERUMAH FELL [INTO THE POOL], EVEN IF IT WAS WASHED IN IT, IT CONTINUES CLEAN; IF UNCLEAN WATER FELL INTO IT AND A CLEAN PERSON DRANK OF IT, HE CONTINUES CLEAN; IF UNCLEAN WATER FELL INTO IT AND ONE DREW WATER FROM IT IN A CLEAN VESSEL, IT CONTINUES CLEAN; IF UNCLEAN WATER FELL INTO IT AND A LOAF OF TERUMAH FELL IN, EVEN IF IT WAS WASHED IN IT, IT CONTINUES CLEAN. [ALL SUCH WATER] IS VALID FOR TERUMAH[3] AND FOR THE WASHING OF THE HANDS.[4]

MISHNAH 7. SUPERIOR TO SUCH [WATER] IS [THE WATER OF] THE MIKWEH CONTAINING FORTY SE'AHS,[5] FOR IN IT PERSONS MAY IMMERSE THEMSELVES[6] AND IMMERSE OTHERS.[7] SUPERIOR AGAIN IS [THE WATER OF] A FOUNTAIN WHOSE OWN WATER IS LITTLE BUT HAS BEEN INCREASED BY A GREATER QUANTITY OF DRAWN WATER; IT IS EQUIVALENT TO THE MIKWEH INASMUCH AS IT MAY RENDER CLEAN

(1) Cf. p. 425 nn. 3, 4. (2) A possible unclean drop falling back into the pool is neutralized by the fresh flow of water coming down from the hills. (3) For preparing in it food of heave-offering. (4) Even for eating *terumah*; cf. Ḥag. l.c. (5) Not filled by the hand of man; cf. Introd. (6) All persons who require purification by immersion, with the exception of persons with a running issue; cf. next Mishnah. (7) Unclean vessels and the hands before eating of the meat of sacrifices; cf. Ḥag. l.c.

BY STANDING WATER,[1] AND TO AN [ORDINARY] FOUNTAIN INASMUCH AS ONE MAY IMMERSE IN IT WHATEVER THE QUANTITY OF ITS CONTENTS.[2]

MISHNAH 8. SUPERIOR AGAIN ARE 'SMITTEN WATERS'[3] WHICH CAN RENDER CLEAN EVEN WHEN FLOWING. SUPERIOR AGAIN ARE 'LIVING WATERS'[4] WHICH SERVE FOR THE IMMERSION OF PERSONS WHO HAVE A RUNNING ISSUE[5] AND FOR THE SPRINKLING OF LEPERS,[6] AND ARE VALID FOR THE PREPARATION OF THE WATER OF PURIFICATION.[7]

(1) Whereas a fountain with its water coming from under the ground can purify also when the water is flowing. (2) It does not require to have 40 *se'ahs*, but just sufficient for the complete immersion of persons or of utensils; cf. Introd. (3) Salty water or hot water from a spring. (4) Pure and sweet spring water. (5) Cf. Lev. XV, 13. (6) Ibid. XIV, 5-7. (7) Num. XIX, 17

MIḲWAOTH

CHAPTER II

MISHNAH 1. IF AN UNCLEAN MAN WENT DOWN TO IMMERSE HIMSELF AND IT IS DOUBTFUL WHETHER HE DID IMMERSE HIMSELF OR NOT,[1] OR EVEN IF HE DID IMMERSE HIMSELF,[2] IT IS DOUBTFUL WHETHER THE MIḲWEH CONTAINED FORTY SE'AHS OR NOT, OR IF THERE WERE TWO MIḲWEHS, ONE CONTAINING FORTY SE'AHS BUT NOT THE OTHER, AND HE IMMERSED HIMSELF IN ONE OF THEM BUT HE DOES NOT KNOW IN WHICH OF THEM HE IMMERSED HIMSELF, IN SUCH A DOUBT HE IS ACCOUNTED UNCLEAN.[3]

MISHNAH 2. IF A MIḲWEH WAS MEASURED AND WAS FOUND LACKING [IN ITS PRESCRIBED QUANTITY],[4] ALL THINGS WHICH HAD BEEN PURIFIED IN IT HITHERTO,[5] WHETHER IN PRIVATE PREMISES OR IN PUBLIC PREMISES,[6] ARE ACCOUNTED UNCLEAN. TO WHAT DOES THIS RULE APPLY?[7] TO A SERIOUS UNCLEANNESS.[8] BUT IN THE CASE OF A LESSER UNCLEANNESS,[9] NAMELY IF ONE ATE UNCLEAN FOODS[10] OR DRANK UNCLEAN LIQUIDS, OR IF HIS HEAD AND THE GREATER PART OF HIS BODY ENTERED INTO DRAWN WATER,[11] OR IF

(1) Whether the immersion was carried out in accordance with the prescribed regulations. (2) He is sure the immersion was carried out properly. (3) The doubtful purification has not the power of undoing the certain state of a previous defilement. (4) 40 *se'ahs*. (5) Since the time it was known to have contained 40 *se'ahs* until it was measured. (6) Although the rule is that a doubtful defilement in public premises is deemed clean (cf. Ṭoh. IV, 7, 11; 'Ed. (Sonc. ed.) p. 11, n. 6; p. 19. n. 13.), because the doubt here is not about the defilement but about the purification of a previous certain defilement. (7) In this and in the last Mishnah. (8) Caused by a principal defilement (אב הטומאה; 'Ed. (Sonc. ed.) p. 10, n. 1), enacted by the Torah. (9) Caused by a secondary defilement enacted by rabbinic law only. (10) Of a secondary defilement of the first or second degree; cf. 'Ed. l.c. (11) Immediately after immersion in a *miḳweh*.

THREE LOGS OF DRAWN WATER FELL ON HIS HEAD AND THE GREATER PART OF HIS BODY,[1] AND HE THEN WENT DOWN TO IMMERSE HIMSELF AND HE IS IN DOUBT WHETHER HE IMMERSED HIMSELF OR NOT, OR EVEN IF HE DID IMMERSE HIMSELF THERE IS [STILL] A DOUBT WHETHER THE MIKWEH CONTAINED FORTY SE'AHS OR NOT, OR IF THERE WERE TWO MIKWEHS, ONE CONTAINING FORTY SE'AHS AND NOT THE OTHER, AND HE IMMERSED HIMSELF IN ONE OF THEM BUT DOES NOT KNOW IN WHICH OF THEM HE IMMERSED HIMSELF, IN SUCH A DOUBT HE IS ACCOUNTED CLEAN. R. JOSE CONSIDERS HIM UNCLEAN, FOR R. JOSE SAYS: ANYTHING WHICH IS PRESUMPTIVELY UNCLEAN ALWAYS REMAINS IN A CONDITION OF UNFITNESS UNTIL IT IS KNOWN THAT IT HAS BECOME CLEAN;[2] BUT IF THERE IS A DOUBT WHETHER A PERSON BECAME UNCLEAN[3] OR CAUSED UNCLEANNESS,[4] IT IS TO BE ACCOUNTED CLEAN.

MISHNAH 3. IN THE CASE OF A DOUBT ABOUT DRAWN WATER WHICH THE SAGES HAVE DECLARED CLEAN,[5] WHEN THERE IS A DOUBT WHETHER [THREE LOGS OF DRAWN WATER] FELL INTO THE MIKWEH OR NOT, OR IF, THOUGH THEY DID FALL IN, THERE IS A DOUBT WHETHER [THE MIKWEH] CONTAINED FORTY SE'AHS OR NOT, OR IF THERE WERE TWO MIKWEHS OF WHICH ONE CONTAINED FORTY SE'AHS AND THE OTHER DID NOT, AND DRAWN WATER FELL INTO ONE OF THEM AND IT IS NOT KNOWN INTO WHICH OF THEM IT FELL, IN SUCH A DOUBT IT IS ACCOUNTED CLEAN,[6] BECAUSE THERE

(1) All these acts cause secondary defilement in accordance with rabbinic law only, disqualifying the person from eating *terumah;* cf. Ṭoh. IV, 11; Zabim V, 12; Shab. 13*b*. (2) R. Jose makes no distinction between a defilement according to Mosaic law and a defilement according to rabbinic law. In either case when the defilement is certain and the purification doubtful, the defilement continues. Only when the doubt is about a defilement according to rabbinic law may it be deemed clean. (3) By any of the named secondary defilements. (4) After the person had become unclean by a secondary defilement, there arose a doubt whether he had conveyed uncleanness to *terumah* things. (5) Cf. Ṭoh. IV, 7. (6) In both cases

EXISTS [A POSSIBILITY][1] ON WHICH WE MAY DEPEND [IN DECLARING IT CLEAN]. IF THEY BOTH CONTAINED LESS THAN FORTY SE'AHS, AND [DRAWN WATER] FELL INTO ONE OF THEM AND IT IS NOT KNOWN INTO WHICH OF THEM IT FELL, IN SUCH A DOUBT IT IS ACCOUNTED UNCLEAN, BECAUSE THERE EXISTS NO [POSSIBILITY][2] ON WHICH WE MAY DEPEND [IN DECLARING IT CLEAN].

MISHNAH 4. R. ELIEZER SAYS: A QUARTER-LOG OF DRAWN WATER IN THE BEGINNING[3] MAKES THE MIḲWEH INVALID, AND THREE LOGS ON THE SURFACE OF THE WATER.[4] BUT THE SAGES SAY: BOTH IN THE BEGINNING AND AT THE END, THE MEASURE [WHICH MAKES THE MIḲWEH INVALID] IS THREE LOGS.

MISHNAH 5. IF THERE WERE THREE CAVITIES[5] IN A MIḲWEH[6] EACH HOLDING A LOG OF DRAWN WATER, IF IT IS KNOWN THAT THERE FELL THEREIN FORTY SE'AHS OF VALID WATER BEFORE REACHING THE THIRD CAVITY, [SUCH A MIḲWEH IS][7] VALID; OTHERWISE IT IS INVALID. BUT R. SIMEON DECLARES IT VALID, SINCE IT RESEMBLES A MIḲWEH ADJOINING ANOTHER MIḲWEH.[8]

MISHNAH 6. IF THE MUD[9] HAD BEEN MOVED TO THE SIDES AND THEN THREE LOGS [OF WATER] WERE DRAWN

the *miḳwehs* are valid when their contents are brought up to 40 *se'ahs*.

(1) Viz., that the three *logs* did not fall in at all, or that the *miḳweh* did contain 40 *se'ahs*, or, finally, that the three *logs* fell into the *miḳweh* containing 40 *se'ahs*. (2) Since one of the two *miḳwehs* was certainly rendered invalid, and as we do not know which of the two, both must be considered invalid. (3) Before the *miḳweh* became filled with rain water, a quarter-*log* of drawn water was put into it. (4) Poured in after the *miḳweh* had been filled with rain water, but with less than 40 *se'ahs*. (5) One above the other in the wall of the *miḳweh*. (6) Which was empty. (7) Because when the contents of the *miḳweh* reached 40 *se'ahs*, the quantity of drawn water in it was still less than three *logs*. (8) The cavities are to be considered as distinct and separate from the main *miḳweh*, and as if they were themselves *miḳwehs*. But the validity of a *miḳweh* is not affected by its contiguity with an invalid *miḳweh*. (9) In a *miḳweh* holding less than 40 *se'ahs*.

OUT FROM IT, [THE MIḲWEH IS STILL] VALID. BUT IF THE MUD HAD BEEN REMOVED AWAY[1] AND THREE LOGS WERE DRAWN FROM IT [INTO THE MIḲWEH], IT BECOMES INVALID.[2] BUT R. SIMEON PRONOUNCES IT VALID, SINCE THERE WAS NO INTENTION TO DRAW [THE WATER].[3]

MISHNAH 7. IF ONE HAD LEFT WINE-JARS ON THE ROOF TO DRY[4] AND THEY BECAME FILLED WITH WATER,[5] R. ELIEZER SAYS: IF IT WAS THE SEASON OF RAIN[6] AND[7] THERE WAS [IN THE CISTERN] A LITTLE WATER, ONE MAY BREAK THE JARS;[8] OTHERWISE ONE MAY NOT BREAK THEM.[9] R. JOSHUA SAYS: IN EITHER CASE ONE MAY BREAK THEM OR TILT THEM OVER,[10] BUT ONE MAY NOT EMPTY[11] [THEM INTO THE CISTERN].

MISHNAH 8. IF A PLASTERER FORGOT HIS LIME-TUB IN A CISTERN AND IT BECAME FILLED WITH WATER, IF WATER FLOWED ABOVE IT HOWEVER LITTLE,[12] IT MAY BE BROKEN;[13] OTHERWISE IT MAY NOT BE BROKEN.[14] THIS IS THE OPINION OF R. ELIEZER.

(1) Out of the *miḳweh*. (2) The water from the mud is considered drawn water. (3) The intention was only to remove the mud but not the water contained therein; therefore the water is deemed as still belonging to the *miḳweh*. (4) But if the intention was that they should be filled with water, the water would become equivalent to drawn water. (5) Rain water. (6) When the *miḳweh* under the roof might be expected to be filled with nearly 40 *se'ahs* of rain water. (7) Var. lec. 'or'. (8) So that their water may flow into the *miḳweh* below and make up 40 *se'ahs*. (9) If it is not the rainy season and the *miḳweh* cannot be expected to be filled with rain water, it may not, according to R. Eliezer, be filled with water from a receptacle, even though the water flows freely without human touch from the receptacle into the *miḳweh*. Again, if the cistern had no water at all, it may be feared that a quarter-*log* of water would run over from the jars into the empty *miḳweh* before the jars are broken, and this would invalidate the *miḳweh* in accordance with R. Eliezer's opinion in Mishnah 4. (10) So as to let the water flow freely from the jars into the *miḳweh* below. (11) By hand, for this would render the water in the jars drawn water. (12) Its contents are then part of the contents of the cistern. (13) And its contents allowed to mingle with the contents of the cistern which serves as a *miḳweh*. But the tub must not be lifted from the cistern and emptied into the cistern, for its contents would then become drawn water. (14) The contents of the tub are equivalent to drawn water.

BUT R. JOSHUA SAYS: IN EITHER CASE IT MAY BE BROKEN.[1]

MISHNAH 9. IF ONE HAD ARRANGED WINE-JARS IN A CISTERN[2] AND THEY BECAME FILLED WITH WATER, EVEN THOUGH THE WATER OF THE CISTERN WAS ALL SOAKED UP,[3] THEY MAY BE BROKEN.[4]

MISHNAH 10. IF A MIḲWEH CONTAINED FORTY SE'AHS OF WATER AND MUD[5] [COMBINED], R. ELIEZER SAYS: ONE MAY IMMERSE OBJECTS IN THE WATER BUT ONE MAY NOT IMMERSE THEM IN THE MUD. BUT R. JOSHUA SAYS: IN THE WATER AND ALSO IN THE MUD. IN WHAT KIND OF MUD MAY OBJECTS BE IMMERSED? MUD OVER WHICH WATER FLOATS.[6] IF THE WATER WAS ON THE ONE SIDE ONLY, R. JOSHUA ADMITS THAT OBJECTS MAY BE IMMERSED IN THE WATER BUT MAY NOT BE IMMERSED IN THE MUD.[7] OF WHAT KIND OF MUD HAVE THEY SPOKEN?[8] MUD INTO WHICH A REED WILL SINK OF ITSELF.[9] THIS IS THE OPINION OF R. MEIR. R. JUDAH SAYS: [MUD] IN WHICH[10] A MEASURING-ROD WILL NOT STAND UPRIGHT.[11] ABBA ELEAZAR B. DULA'I SAYS: [MUD] INTO WHICH A PLUMMET WILL SINK. R. ELIEZER SAYS: SUCH AS WILL GO DOWN INTO THE MOUTH OF A JAR.[12] R. SIMEON SAYS: SUCH AS WILL ENTER INTO THE TUBE OF A WATER-SKIN.[13] R. ELEAZAR B. ZADOK SAYS: SUCH AS CAN BE MEASURED IN A LOG MEASURE.[14]

(1) And let its contents flow into the cistern, because the water in the tub is not deemed drawn water. (2) Which held water, in order that the porous sides of the wine-jars might become saturated with water and not be able afterwards to soak in any wine. (3) In the soil, and there is no water left save that which is in the jars. (4) And their contents may be used for making a *miḳweh* in the cistern, because they are not deemed drawn water since it was not his intention for the water to fill the jars. (5) Thin mud; cf. *infra* VII, 1. (6) For the cavity formed by the immersed object becomes filled with water. (7) Although the mud serves to make up the 40 *se'ahs*. (8) That it may combine with water to form the 40 *se'ahs*, and that objects may be immersed in it. (9) Without being pressed down by the hand. Of the opinions that follow, each assumes a thicker mud than the preceding opinion. (10) Lit., 'a place'. (11) But must be held by the hand. (12) And so cannot serve as a stopper to the jar. (13) Even if it can stop the mouth of a jar. (14) Like a liquid.

MIḲWAOTH

CHAPTER III

MISHNAH 1. R. JOSE SAYS: IF THERE ARE TWO MIḲWEHS NEITHER OF WHICH CONTAINS FORTY SE'AHS, AND A LOG AND A HALF [OF DRAWN WATER] FELL INTO EACH, AND THEY ARE MINGLED TOGETHER, THEY REMAIN VALID, SINCE THEY HAD NEVER[1] BEEN EXPLICITLY ACCOUNTED AS INVALID; BUT IF THERE IS A MIḲWEH HOLDING LESS THAN FORTY SE'AHS, AND THREE LOGS [OF DRAWN WATER] FELL INTO IT, AND IT WAS THEN DIVIDED INTO TWO,[2] IT IS INVALID, SINCE IT HAD ALREADY BEEN EXPLICITLY ACCOUNTED AS INVALID.[3] R. JOSHUA DECLARES IT VALID; FOR R. JOSHUA USED TO SAY: ANY MIḲWEH CONTAINING LESS THAN FORTY SE'AHS INTO WHICH THREE LOGS [OF DRAWN WATER] FELL AND FROM WHICH A ḲORṬOB[4] WAS WITHDRAWN BECOMES VALID, SINCE THE THREE LOGS HAVE ALSO BEEN DIMINISHED.[5] BUT THE SAGES SAY: IT ALWAYS REMAINS INVALID UNTIL THE FORMER CONTENTS THEREOF ARE REMOVED AND A LITTLE MORE.[6]

MISHNAH 2. IN WHAT MANNER? IF THERE WAS A CISTERN[7] IN A COURTYARD AND THREE LOGS [OF DRAWN WATER] FELL INTO IT, IT WILL ALWAYS REMAIN INVALID UNTIL THE WHOLE OF IT IS REMOVED AND A LITTLE MORE, OR UNTIL [ANOTHER

(1) Before they became mingled, when the amount of drawn water which fell into each was less than three *logs*. (2) And each had its contents increased to 40 *se'ahs*. (3) Before it was divided into two. (4) The smallest liquid measure, viz., one sixty-fourth of a *log*. (5) The *ḳorṭob* which was withdrawn must have included also some portion of the drawn water. (6) To make the *miḳweh* valid a quantity of water must be withdrawn from it, which is equal to the quantity which the *miḳweh* contained when the drawn water fell into it, and a little more to reduce the drawn water in the *miḳweh* to less than three *logs*. (7) Containing less than 40 *se'ahs*.

MIKWEH CONTAINING] FORTY SE'AHS IS PLACED IN THE COURTYARD,[1] SO THAT THE HIGHER[2] MIKWEH IS RENDERED VALID BY THE LOWER.[3] R. ELIEZER B. 'AZARIAH DECLARES IT INVALID UNLESS THE [NEW MIKWEH] IS STOPPED UP.[4]

MISHNAH 3. IF THERE WAS A CISTERN FULL OF DRAWN WATER AND A CHANNEL[5] LED INTO IT AND OUT OF IT, IT CONTINUES INVALID UNTIL IT CAN BE RECKONED THAT THERE DOES NOT REMAIN IN IT THREE LOGS OF THE FORMER [WATER].[6] IF TWO MEN POURED[7] EACH A LOG AND A HALF [OF DRAWN WATER] INTO A MIKWEH, OR IF ONE WRUNG OUT HIS CLOTHES AND SO POURED IN [WATER] FROM SEVERAL PLACES,[8] OR IF ONE EMPTIED OUT A WATER-COOLER[9] AND SO POURED IN [WATER] FROM SEVERAL PLACES, R. AKIBA DECLARES IT VALID,[10] BUT THE SAGES DECLARE IT INVALID. R. AKIBA SAID: THEY[11] DID NOT SAY 'IF THEY POURED IN', BUT 'IF ONE[12] POURED IN'. BUT THEY SAID: THEY SAID NEITHER THUS NOR THUS, BUT ONLY 'IF THERE FELL THEREIN THREE LOGS[13] [OF DRAWN WATER]'.

(1) One above the other and connected. (2) Var. lec.: 'the lower'. (3) Var. lec.: 'the higher'. (4) פקק, so that one has to come first to the old *mikweh*. Var. lec.: פסק, until all its water is used up. (5) Of rain water less than 40 *se'ahs* in quantity. (6) That through the channel leading out of the cistern there flowed away the former contents of drawn water in the cistern, leaving of them less than three *logs* plus the quantity of fresh rain water which entered the cistern on the one side and flowed out on the other side. This together will be considerably more than the former contents of the cistern, required in the last Mishnah, because there the former contents of the cistern consisted of valid water which only became invalid by the addition of three *logs* of drawn water, whereas here all the former contents were invalid water. (7) Simultaneously; cf. next Mishnah. (8) To the quantity of three *logs*. (9) Containing a sievelike filter within its neck; cf. Kelim II, 8. (10) He holds that the three *logs* of water which invalidate the *mikweh* must all come from one receptacle. (11) The Sages who formulated the rule regarding drawn water in a *mikweh*. (12) Which wording implies that all the three *logs* must come from one vessel. (13) Which may imply also pouring in from more than one vessel. Cf. 'Ed. I, 3. The dispute between R. Akiba and the Sages turns on the exact wording of the traditional formula of the rule.

MISHNAH 4. [IF THE THREE LOGS OF DRAWN WATER FELL IN] FROM ONE VESSEL OR FROM TWO OR FROM THREE, THEY COMBINE TOGETHER;[1] BUT IF FROM FOUR, THEY DO NOT COMBINE TOGETHER.[2] IF A MAN WHO HAD A SEMINAL ISSUE WAS SICK AND NINE KABS OF WATER[3] FELL ON HIM, OR IF THERE FELL ON THE HEAD AND THE GREATER PART OF THE BODY OF A CLEAN PERSON THREE LOGS OF DRAWN WATER[4] FROM ONE VESSEL OR FROM TWO OR FROM THREE, THEY COMBINE TOGETHER; BUT IF FROM FOUR, THEY DO NOT COMBINE TOGETHER. IN WHAT CASE DOES THIS APPLY?[5] WHEN THE SECOND BEGAN BEFORE THE FIRST FINISHED. AND IN WHAT OTHER CASE DOES [THE OTHER STATEMENT][6] APPLY? WHEN THERE WAS NO INTENTION TO INCREASE[7] IT. BUT IF THERE WAS AN INTENTION TO INCREASE IT, IF ONLY A KORṬOB IN A WHOLE YEAR, THEY COMBINE TOGETHER TO ADD UP TO THE THREE LOGS.

(1) In accordance with the opinion of the Sages, provided each vessel contains one *log*. (2) Because one of them must contain less than one *log*. (3) Which is sufficient purification for a person with such a defilement who, owing to sickness, is unable to undergo full immersion in a *miḳweh*, provided the defilement was unintentional. If, however, the defilement was intentional, he needs complete immersion before he can occupy himself with the study of the Torah; cf. Ber. 22*b*, and *infra* VIII, 1, n. 3. (4) Which confers a defilement of the second degree, disqualifying a person from eating *terumah*; cf. Zabim V. 6; Shab. 13*b*. (5) That three *logs* of drawn water derived from two or three vessels combine to invalidate the *miḳweh*. (6) That the contents of more than three vessels are not reckoned together to invalidate the *miḳweh*. (7) To increase the quantity of water in the *miḳweh* by the addition of the drawn water.

MIḲWAOTH

CHAPTER IV

MISHNAH 1. IF ONE PUT VESSELS UNDER A WATER-SPOUT,[1] WHETHER THEY BE LARGE VESSELS[2] OR SMALL VESSELS[3] OR EVEN VESSELS OF DUNG, VESSELS OF STONE OR EARTHEN VESSELS,[4] THEY MAKE THE MIḲWEH INVALID.[5] IT IS ALL ALIKE WHETHER THEY WERE PUT THERE [PURPOSELY] OR WERE [MERELY] FORGOTTEN. THIS IS ACCORDING TO THE OPINION OF BETH SHAMMAI. BUT BETH HILLEL DECLARE IT CLEAN IN THE CASE OF ONE WHO FORGETS.[6] R. MEIR SAID: THEY VOTED AND BETH SHAMMAI HAD A MAJORITY OVER BETH HILLEL;[7] YET THEY AGREE[8] IN THE CASE OF ONE WHO FORGETS [AND LEAVES VESSELS] IN A COURTYARD[9] THAT THE MIḲWEH REMAINS CLEAN.[10] R. JOSE SAID: THE CONTROVERSY STILL REMAINS AS IT WAS.

MISHNAH 2. IF ONE PUT A BOARD UNDER A WATER-SPOUT AND IT HAD A RIM[11] TO IT, IT MAKES THE MIḲWEH INVALID; OTHERWISE IT DOES NOT MAKE THE MIḲWEH INVALID. IF HE MADE IT STAND UPRIGHT TO BE RINSED, IN NEITHER CASE DOES IT MAKE THE MIḲWEH INVALID.

(1) Conveying rain water from the roof. (2) Containing more than 40 *se'ahs*. (3) Too small to become unclean; cf. Kelim II, 2. (4) These are not susceptible to uncleanness. (5) If their contents of three *logs* are emptied into a *miḳweh* containing less than 40 *se'ahs* (so also below where this phrase occurs). For, unlike the case discussed in II, 7, these serve for the special purpose of receiving the water from the spout. (6) Because there was no intention to collect water in them. (7) And the controversy was settled in accordance with the opinion of Beth Shammai; cf. Shab. I, 4. (8) Beth Shammai. (9) Not under a water-spout. (10) Since evidently there was no intention to collect the water. (11) It is considered a receptacle, and the rain water passing from the roof along the board becomes drawn water.

MISHNAH 3. IF ONE MAKES[1] A HOLLOW IN A WATER-SPOUT TO COLLECT THE GRAVEL,[2] IT MAKES THE MIKWEH INVALID[3] IN THE CASE OF A WOODEN [SPOUT] IF IT HOLDS HOWEVER LITTLE, BUT IN THE CASE OF AN EARTHENWARE [SPOUT] IF IT WILL HOLD A QUARTER-LOG.[4] R. JOSE SAYS: ALSO IN THE CASE OF AN EARTHENWARE [SPOUT] IF IT HOLDS HOWEVER LITTLE: THEY HAVE SPOKEN OF 'A QUARTER-LOG'[5] ONLY IN THE CASE OF BROKEN SHERDS OF AN EARTHENWARE UTENSIL. IF THE PIECES OF GRAVEL MOVED ABOUT INSIDE [THE HOLLOW], IT MAKES THE MIKWEH INVALID.[6] IF EARTH CAME DOWN INTO IT AND WAS PRESSED DOWN,[7] [THE MIKWEH CONTINUES] VALID. IF THE SPOUT WAS NARROW AT EACH END AND WIDE IN THE MIDDLE, IT DOES NOT MAKE [THE MIKWEH] INVALID, BECAUSE IT[8] HAD NOT BEEN FASHIONED FOR GATHERING [ANYTHING IN IT].[9]

MISHNAH 4. IF DRAWN WATER AND RAIN WATER WERE MINGLED TOGETHER IN A COURTYARD OR IN A CAVITY OR ON THE STEPS OF A CAVE,[10] IF THE GREATER PART WAS VALID,[11] THE WHOLE IS VALID; AND IF THE GREATER PART WAS INVALID,[12] THE WHOLE IS INVALID. IF THEY WERE EQUAL IN QUANTITY, THE WHOLE IS INVALID. WHEN [DOES THIS APPLY]?[13] WHEN THEY WERE MINGLED TOGETHER BEFORE THEY ARRIVED AT THE MIKWEH. BUT IF THEY FLOWED [EACH ONE DIRECT] INTO THE WATER [OF THE MIKWEH],[14] IF IT WAS KNOWN THAT THERE FELL IN FORTY SE'AHS OF VALID WATER

(1) Before fixing the spout to the roof. (2) Coming down in the rain water. (3) The cavity becomes a receptacle for the water that passes through it into the *mikweh*. The spout itself is not deemed a receptacle, because it is open at both ends. (4) If it holds less than a quarter-*log*, it is not considered a vessel; cf. Kelim II, 2. (5) As the minimum capacity of a vessel. (6) Though the gravel fills the cavity. (7) Filling the cavity. (8) The wide part in the middle. (9) But only for facilitating the flow of the water. (10) Containing a *mikweh*. (11) The rain water exceeds in quantity the drawn water. (12) Consisting of drawn water. (13) That the *mikweh* is valid when rain water makes up the greater part of the mixture. (14) I.e., the drawn water flowed directly from the vessel into the *mikweh*.

BEFORE THERE CAME DOWN THREE LOGS OF DRAWN WATER, [THE MIḲWEH IS] VALID; OTHERWISE IT IS INVALID.

MISHNAH 5. IN THE CASE OF A TROUGH[1] IN THE ROCK,[2] WATER MAY NOT BE GATHERED IN IT,[3] NOR MAY THE WATER OF PURIFICATION BE CONSECRATED[4] THEREIN, NOR MAY ONE SPRINKLE[5] THEREFROM; AND IT DOES NOT REQUIRE A TIGHTLY STOPPED-UP COVERING,[6] AND IT DOES NOT MAKE THE MIḲWEH INVALID.[7] IF IT WAS A [MOVABLE] VESSEL[8] AND HAD BEEN JOINED TO THE GROUND WITH LIME, WATER MAY BE GATHERED IN IT, AND THE WATER OF PURIFICATION MAY BE CONSECRATED THEREIN, AND ONE MAY SPRINKLE THEREFROM, AND IT REQUIRES A TIGHTLY STOPPED-UP COVERING, AND IT MAKES THE MIḲWEH INVALID. IF A HOLE WAS MADE IN IT BELOW OR AT THE SIDE SO THAT IT COULD NOT CONTAIN WATER IN HOWEVER SMALL A QUANTITY,[9] IT IS VALID.[10] AND HOW GREAT SHOULD BE THE HOLE? LIKE THE TUBE OF A WATER-SKIN. R. JUDAH B. BATHYRA SAID: IT HAPPENED IN THE CASE OF THE TROUGH OF JEHU[11] IN JERUSALEM THAT THERE WAS A HOLE IN IT LIKE THE TUBE OF A WATER-SKIN, AND IT WAS USED FOR ALL THINGS IN JERUSALEM WHICH NEEDED A STATE OF PURITY. BUT BETH SHAMMAI SENT AND BROKE IT DOWN, FOR BETH SHAMMAI SAY: [IT REMAINS A VESSEL] UNLESS THE GREATER PART OF IT IS BROKEN DOWN.

(1) Cf. Parah V, 7. (2) If filled with water from a fountain. Being naturally joined to the ground, it cannot be considered a vessel; cf. *supra* I, 1, n. 6. (3) For the Water of Purification, for which a vessel is required; cf. Num. XIX, 17. (4) By mixing in it the ashes of the Red Heifer. (5) If properly prepared Water of Purification is put on to it; ibid. XIX, 18. (6) Ibid. XIX, 15. It protects its contents against defilement from a corpse even if it has only an ordinary covering; cf. Ohol. V, 6. (7) If three *logs* of rain water flow from it into a *miḳweh* containing less than 40 *se'ahs*. (8) The trough had been hollowed out in a movable stone. (9) It loses the character of a vessel and becomes like a channel. (10) The water which flows from it does not render the *miḳweh* invalid. (11) The site of this trough is not known. The name Jehu occurs in Judah, I Chron. II, 38. etc. S. Klein conjectures that the trough belonged to a family which traced its descent from Jehu, King of Israel; cf. the Well of Ahab, Parah VIII, 11; v. ציון, IV (Jerusalem, 1938), p. 40f.

MIḲWAOTH

CHAPTER V

MISHNAH 1. [WATER FROM] A FOUNTAIN WHICH IS MADE TO PASS OVER INTO A TROUGH[1] BECOMES INVALID;[2] IF IT WAS MADE TO PASS OVER THE EDGE IN ANY QUANTITY, [WHAT IS] OUTSIDE [THE TROUGH] IS VALID,[3] FOR [THE WATER OF] A FOUNTAIN PURIFIES HOWEVER LITTLE ITS QUANTITY.[4] IF IT IS MADE TO PASS OVER INTO A POOL AND THEN IS STOPPED, THE POOL COUNTS AS A MIḲWEH;[5] IF IT IS MADE TO FLOW AGAIN,[6] IT IS STILL INVALID FOR PERSONS WITH A RUNNING ISSUE AND FOR LEPERS AND FOR THE PREPARATION OF THE WATER OF PURIFICATION[7] UNTIL IT IS KNOWN THAT THE FORMER [WATER] IS GONE.

MISHNAH 2. IF IT WAS MADE TO PASS OVER THE OUTSIDE OF VESSELS OR OVER A BENCH, R. JUDAH SAYS: LO, IT REMAINS AS IT WAS BEFORE.[8] R. JOSE SAYS: LO, IT IS LIKE A MIḲWEH,[9] EXCEPT THAT ONE MAY NOT IMMERSE ANYTHING ABOVE THE BENCH.[10]

MISHNAH 3. IF [WATER FROM] A FOUNTAIN THAT FLOWS INTO MANY CHANNELS[11] WAS INCREASED[12] IN QUANTITY SO

(1) Which had been hollowed out in a movable stone and then fixed to the ground; cf. *supra* IV, 5. (2) For immersion either in the trough itself or in the water that passes out of the trough, for since the trough is like a vessel, this water becomes drawn water. (3) For immersion. (4) Cf. *supra* I, 7. (5) And requires 40 *se'ahs* of standing water; cf. *supra* I, 7. (6) The flow from the fountain into the pool was restored. It then becomes valid for immersion even if its quantity is less than 40 *se'ahs*, but not for those who require for their purification 'living water'. (7) Cf. *supra* I, 8, and notes 5-7. (8) With the efficacy of a fountain. (9) And requires 40 *se'ahs* of standing water. (10) Or above the backs of the vessels, lest one may be led to immerse things in vessels. (11) Lit., 'is drawn out like a centipede'. (12) By pouring into it drawn water.

THAT IT WAS MADE TO FLOW IN ABUNDANCE, IT REMAINS AS IT WAS BEFORE.[1] IF IT WAS A STANDING FOUNTAIN[2] AND ITS QUANTITY WAS INCREASED[3] SO THAT IT WAS MADE TO FLOW, IT BECOMES EQUAL TO A MIKWEH IN THAT IT CAN PURIFY IN STANDING WATER,[4] AND TO A FOUNTAIN IN THAT ONE MAY IMMERSE [OBJECTS] THEREIN HOWEVER SMALL ITS QUANTITY.

MISHNAH 4. ALL SEAS[5] ARE DEEMED VALID AS A MIKWEH,[6] FOR IT IS WRITTEN, 'AND THE MIKWEH[7] OF THE WATERS CALLED HE SEAS'.[8] THIS IS THE OPINION OF R. MEIR. R. JUDAH SAYS: THE GREAT SEA[9] ALONE IS A VALID MIKWEH, FOR THE REASON THAT SCRIPTURE SAYS 'SEAS' IS BECAUSE IN IT ARE MANY KINDS OF SEAS.[10] R. JOSE SAYS: ALL SEAS PURIFY AS FLOWING WATERS,[11] BUT THEY ARE INVALID FOR PERSONS WITH A RUNNING ISSUE AND FOR LEPERS AND FOR THE PREPARATION OF THE WATER OF PURIFICATION.[12]

MISHNAH 5. FLOWING WATER[13] IS AS WATER OF A FOUNTAIN AND DRIPPING WATER[14] IS AS A MIKWEH. R. ZADOK[15] TESTIFIED THAT IF FLOWING WATER EXCEEDED DRIPPING WATER [WITH WHICH IT WAS MIXED] IT WAS VALID [AS FLOWING WATER].[16] IF DRIPPING WATER BECAME FLOWING WATER, ITS FLOW MAY BE BLOCKED[17] BY A STICK OR BY A REED OR EVEN BY A MAN OR A WOMAN WHO HAS A RUNNING ISSUE, AND THEN ONE MAY GO DOWN AND IMMERSE ONESELF

(1) It retains the characteristics of a fountain. (2) I.e., a well or a lake. (3) By the addition of drawn water. (4) But not in its flowing water, since this is derived from drawn water. (5) Parah VIII, 8. (6) And require 40 *se'ahs* of standing water, and are invalid for those who need 'living water'. (7) 'The gathering together'; cf. Introd. (8) Gen. I, 10. (9) The Mediterranean, and likewise the oceans, to the exclusion of inland seas and lakes. (10) It gathers water from numerous sources. (11) Like fountains. (12) Because these require 'living water', and sea water being salty is 'smitten water', cf. *supra* I, 8. (13) Streams and rivers. (14) Rain water. (15) Cf. 'Ed. VII, 3. (Sonc. ed.) p. 42, and notes. (16) And is treated as a fountain. (17) So as to make it standing water, as required in a *mikweh*.

THEREIN. THIS IS THE OPINION OF R. JUDAH. R. JOSE SAYS: ONE MAY NOT STOP THE FLOW OF WATER[1] WITH ANYTHING WHICH IS LIABLE TO UNCLEANNESS.

MISHNAH 6. IF A WAVE WAS SEPARATED [FROM THE SEA] AND COMPRISED FORTY SE'AHS, AND IT FELL ON A MAN OR ON VESSELS,[2] THEY BECOME CLEAN. ANY PLACE CONTAINING FORTY SE'AHS IS VALID FOR IMMERSING ONE-SELF AND FOR IMMERSING OTHERS.[3] ONE MAY IMMERSE IN TRENCHES[4] OR IN DITCHES[5] OR EVEN IN A DONKEY-TRACK[6] THE WATER OF WHICH IS JOINED[7] [WITH A VALID MIḲWEH] IN A VALLEY. BETH SHAMMAI[8] SAY: ONE MAY IMMERSE IN A RAIN TORRENT.[9] BUT BETH HILLEL SAY: ONE MAY NOT IM-MERSE.[10] THEY[11] ADMIT, HOWEVER, THAT ONE MAY BLOCK ITS FLOW WITH VESSELS[12] AND IMMERSE ONESELF THEREIN, BUT THE VESSELS WITH WHICH THE FLOW IS BLOCKED ARE NOT THEREBY [VALIDLY] IMMERSED.[13]

(1) So most commentators explain the reading in the editions מזחילין, which being in the causative stem (*hiph'il*) should rather be rendered 'one may not cause to flow'. However, the Cambridge text (cf. Introd. n. 1), and MS.M. read מזחלים, which may be interpreted as a privative *pi'el*, to prevent or stay the flow. (2) Who were unclean, immersing them accidentally. (3) Vessels and the hands before eating sacrificial meat; cf. I, 7, n. 7. (4) Square-shaped like caverns, but not roofed over; cf. I, 4, n. 2. (5) Narrow at the top and wide at the bottom; cf. B.Ḳ. 50*b*. (6) Or holes made by the feet of other animals. (7) Through a hole of the size prescribed *infra* VI, 1. (8) 'Ed. V, 2. (9) In the running water, though the whole stream contains no more than 40 *se'ahs*. (10) Except when the stream forms a pool of 40 *se'ahs* of standing water. (11) Beth Hillel. (12) So as to form standing water. (13) Because only one of their sides is immersed in standing water.

MIḲWAOTH

CHAPTER VI

MISHNAH 1. ANY [GATHERING OF WATER] WHICH IS JOINED WITH [THE WATER OF] A MIḲWEH IS AS VALID AS THE MIḲWEH[1] [ITSELF]. ONE MAY IMMERSE IN HOLES OF A CAVERN[2] AND IN CREVICES OF A CAVERN[2] JUST AS THEY ARE;[3] BUT ONE MAY NOT IMMERSE IN THE PIT[4] OF A CAVERN EXCEPT IT HAD A HOLE AS BIG AS THE TUBE OF A WATER-SKIN. R. JUDAH SAID: WHEN [IS THIS THE CASE]? WHEN IT STANDS BY ITSELF;[5] BUT IF IT DOES NOT STAND BY ITSELF, ONE MAY IMMERSE THEREIN JUST AS IT IS.[6]

MISHNAH 2. IF A BUCKET WAS FULL OF UTENSILS AND THEY WERE[7] IMMERSED, LO, THEY BECOME CLEAN; BUT IF [THE BUCKET] WAS NOT IMMERSED [FOR ITS OWN SAKE][8], THE WATER IN THE BUCKET IS NOT RECKONED AS JOINED[9] [WITH THE WATER OF THE MIḲWEH] UNLESS IT BE JOINED [BY MEANS OF THE NECK OF THE BUCKET WHICH IS AS BIG] AS THE TUBE OF A WATER-SKIN.

MISHNAH 3. IF THERE WERE THREE MIḲWEHS, TWO OF WHICH HELD TWENTY SE'AHS [OF VALID WATER] AND THE

(1) It becomes part of the *miḳweh*. One may immerse in it though it contains less than 40 *se'ahs*, and it may serve to make up 40 *se'ahs* in the *miḳweh* itself. (2) Forming a *miḳweh*. (3) Their water need not be joined by a hole to the water in the cavern. (4) As explained by R. Judah in the following. (5) It forms an independent pool separated by a wall from the pool in the cavern. (6) It is part of the pool in the cavern, and need not have 40 *se'ahs*, nor be connected with the pool by a hole. (7) Var. lec.: 'it was'. The bucket as well as the utensils needed immersion. (8) Lit., 'if one did not immerse', i.e., the bucket itself was clean, and needed no immersion; cf. Ḥag. 22*a*. (9) For the purpose of purifying the utensils. The text is very doubtful. Ḥag. *l.c.* and some commentators omit 'not'.

THIRD HELD TWENTY SE'AHS OF DRAWN WATER, AND THAT HOLDING DRAWN WATER WAS AT THE SIDE, IF THREE PERSONS WENT DOWN[1] AND IMMERSED THEMSELVES THEREIN AND [THE WATER OF THE THREE MIḲWEHS] JOINED,[2] THE MIḲWEHS ARE CLEAN[3] AND THEY THAT IMMERSED THEMSELVES BECOME CLEAN. IF THE ONE HOLDING THE DRAWN WATER WAS IN THE MIDDLE[4] AND THREE PERSONS WENT DOWN AND IMMERSED THEMSELVES THEREIN AND [THE WATER OF THE THREE MIḲWEHS] JOINED, THE MIḲWEHS CONTINUE AS THEY WERE BEFORE[5] AND THEY THAT IMMERSED THEMSELVES ARE AS THEY WERE BEFORE.[6]

MISHNAH 4. IF A SPONGE OR A BUCKET CONTAINING THREE LOGS OF WATER FELL INTO A MIḲWEH,[7] THEY DO NOT MAKE IT INVALID, BECAUSE THEY HAVE ONLY SAID:[8] 'IF THREE LOGS FELL IN'.[9]

MISHNAH 5. ONE MAY NOT IMMERSE IN A COFFER OR IN A BOX[10] WHICH IS IN THE SEA EXCEPT IT HAS A HOLE[11] AS LARGE AS THE TUBE OF A WATER-SKIN. R. JUDAH SAYS: IN THE CASE OF A LARGE VESSEL[12] [THE HOLE SHOULD BE] FOUR HANDBREADTHS, AND IN A SMALL ONE [THE HOLE SHOULD BE AS LARGE AS] THE GREATER PART OF IT. IF THERE IS IN THE SEA A SACK OR A BASKET, ONE MAY IMMERSE THEREIN AS IT IS, SINCE THE WATER [IN THE SEA AND IN THE SACK OR BASKET] IS JOINED TOGETHER.[13] IF THEY ARE PLACED

(1) Simultaneously. (2) By overflowing through the immersion of the three persons. (3) All the three *miḳwehs* become valid. They are now considered as one *miḳweh* containing 40 *se'ahs* of valid water to which were added 20 *se'ahs* of drawn water. (4) Thus preventing the junction of the two with the valid water. (5) They remain three separate *miḳwehs*, two with valid water but of insufficient quantity, and one with invalid water. (6) Unclean. (7) Containing less than 40 *se'ahs*. (8) Cf. *supra* III, 3, n. 13. (9) Whereas here some portion of the three *logs* remained in the pores of the sponge or in the folds of the bucket. (10) Even though they contain 40 *se'ahs*. (11) Which joins their water to the water in the sea. (12) Some nine handbreadths in height. (13) Through their holes.

UNDER A WATER-SPOUT, THEY DO NOT MAKE THE MIḲWEH INVALID,[1] AND THEY MAY BE IMMERSED AND BROUGHT OUT IN THE ORDINARY WAY.[2]

MISHNAH 6. IF THERE WAS A DEFECTIVE [EARTHENWARE] VESSEL IN THE MIḲWEH AND UTENSILS WERE IMMERSED THEREIN, THEY BECOME CLEAN FROM THEIR [FORMER] UNCLEANNESS[3] BUT ARE AGAIN RENDERED UNCLEAN BECAUSE OF THE EARTHENWARE VESSEL;[4] BUT IF WATER FLOWED ABOVE IT IN ANY QUANTITY, THEY WILL REMAIN CLEAN.[5] IF [WATER OF] A FOUNTAIN ISSUED FROM AN OVEN[6] AND A MAN WENT DOWN AND IMMERSED HIMSELF, HE IS CLEAN[7] BUT HIS HANDS BECOME UNCLEAN;[8] BUT IF [THE WATER WAS AS] HIGH ABOVE THE OVEN AS THE HEIGHT OF HIS HANDS,[9] HIS HANDS ALSO ARE CLEAN.

MISHNAH 7. MIḲWEHS CAN BE JOINED TOGETHER [AS ONE IF THEIR CONNECTION IS AS BIG] AS THE TUBE OF A WATER-SKIN IN THICKNESS AND IN CAPACITY, IN WHICH TWO FINGERS[10] CAN BE TURNED ROUND IN FULL. IF THERE IS A DOUBT [WHETHER IT IS AS BIG] AS THE TUBE OF A WATER-

(1) The rain water from the spout flowing through them into the *miḳweh* is not deemed drawn water as in *supra* IV, 1, n. 5. (2) And not bottom upwards as prescribed for a bolster or a cushion of leather, v. *infra* VII, 6. (3) Because the water in the defective or broken earthenware vessel is considered as joined to the water in the *miḳweh* through the breakage in the vessel. (4) If it is unclean. For an earthenware vessel is not rendered clean by immersion in a *miḳweh* (Lev. XI, 33), and though the water in it, as part of the *miḳweh*, is clean, yet uncleanness remains in the air-space of the vessel above the water. Hence when utensils are immersed in such an earthenware vessel, the water which adheres to them renders them unclean as they are raised into the air-space of the earthenware vessel. (5) Because the air-space of the unclean earthenware vessel is all covered by the clean water. (6) Of earthenware, fixed to the ground and open at the top, and large enough to hold a man. The oven is unclean. (7) Because a man's body is not rendered unclean by the air-space of an unclean vessel. (8) Hands do become unclean by the air-space; cf. Yad, III, 1. (9) The surface of the water covered his hands. (10) Those near the thumb.

SKIN OR NOT, IT IS INVALID, BECAUSE [THE RULE CONCERNING IMMERSION] IS A COMMAND OF THE TORAH.[1] THE SAME APPLIES ALSO TO THE OLIVE'S BULK OF A CORPSE AND THE OLIVE'S BULK OF CARRION AND THE LENTIL'S BULK OF A CREEPING THING.[2] ANYTHING WHICH REMAINS[3] IN [THE SPACE MEASURING] THE TUBE OF A WATER-SKIN LESSENS [ITS MEASURE].[4] RABBAN SIMEON B. GAMALIEL SAYS: IF IT IS ANY WATER CREATURE[5] WHATSOEVER, [THE MIḲWEHS] REMAIN CLEAN.

MISHNAH 8. MIḲWEHS MAY BE MADE CLEAN [BY JOINING DRAWN WATER FROM] A HIGHER [MIḲWEH TO VALID WATER] FROM A LOWER [MIḲWEH OR DRAWN WATER FROM] A DISTANT [MIḲWEH TO VALID WATER] IN A [MIḲWEH] NEAR AT HAND. IN WHAT MANNER? ONE BRINGS A TUBE OF EARTHENWARE OR OF LEAD[6] AND PUTS HIS HAND BENEATH IT[7] TILL IT IS FILLED WITH WATER; THEN HE DRAWS IT ALONG TILL [THE TWO WATERS] TOUCH—EVEN IF IT BE BY A HAIR'S BREADTH IT IS SUFFICIENT. IF IN THE HIGHER [MIḲWEH] THERE WERE FORTY SE'AHS AND NOTHING IN THE LOWER, ONE MAY DRAW WATER AND CARRY IT ON THE SHOULDER[8] AND PLACE IT IN THE HIGHER [MIḲWEH] TILL FORTY SE'AHS HAVE FLOWED DOWN INTO THE LOWER [MIḲWEH].

MISHNAH 9. IF A WALL BETWEEN TWO MIḲWEHS[9] HAD A

(1) And in the case of a doubt respecting the fulfilment of a Mosaic law we must abide by the more stringent alternative. (2) These are the minimum quantities which cause defilement, and if there is a doubt whether they were of the required quantity or not, we must assume that they were, and that they did cause defilement. (3) And not carried off by the water flowing through the opening which joins the two *miḳwehs*. (4) And the two *miḳwehs* remain separate. (5) It is considered part of the water. (6) Or of any other metal. (7) To shut the lower end of the tube. (8) I.e., fill the lower *miḳweh* with drawn water through the higher one. For since the two *miḳwehs* are reckoned as one, and the upper one has 40 *se'ahs* of valid water, no amount of drawn water can render either of them invalid. (9) One of which had less than 40 *se'ahs*.

PERPENDICULAR CRACK, [THEIR WATERS] MAY BE RECKONED TOGETHER [TO MAKE UP THE REQUIRED QUANTITY]; [IF IT WAS CRACKED] LENGTHWISE, THEY CANNOT BE RECKONED TOGETHER, UNLESS THERE IS AT ONE PLACE [A HOLE AS BIG] AS THE TUBE OF A WATER-SKIN. R. JUDAH SAYS: THE RULE IS JUST THE REVERSE. IF THERE IS A BREACH[1] [ON THE TOP OF THE WALL] FROM ONE [MIKWEH] TO THE OTHER, [THEY CAN BE RECKONED TOGETHER] IF THE HEIGHT IS AS [THE THICKNESS OF] THE SKIN OF GARLIC AND THE BREADTH LIKE THE TUBE OF A WATER-SKIN.

MISHNAH 10. THE OUTLET[2] OF A BATH, IF IT IS IN THE CENTRE, RENDERS [THE BATH] INVALID[3] [AS A MIKWEH]; BUT IF IT IS AT THE SIDE, IT DOES NOT RENDER IT INVALID, BECAUSE THEN IT IS LIKE ONE MIKWEH ADJOINING ANOTHER MIKWEH. THIS IS THE OPINION OF R. MEIR. BUT THE SAGES SAY: IF THE BATH-BASIN CAN CONTAIN A QUARTER-LOG BEFORE [THE WATER] REACHES THE OUTLET,[4] IT IS VALID; BUT IF NOT, IT IS NOT VALID.[5] R. ELEAZAR B. ZADOK SAYS: IF THE OUTLET CAN CONTAIN [WATER], IT IS INVALID IN ANY POSITION WHATEVER.

MISHNAH 11. IF IN THE BATH'S 'PURIFIER'[6] THE BOTTOM [PIPE] WAS FULL OF DRAWN [WATER] AND THE TOP [PIPE] FULL OF VALID[7] [WATER], IF [THE SPACE] IN FRONT OF THE HOLE CAN CONTAIN THREE LOGS IT IS INVALID[8] [AS A

(1) Which forms a connecting channel between the two *mikwehs*. (2) In the shape of a receptacle, having a hole for the discharge of foul water with a stopper. (3) Because the outlet is then regarded as a receptacle and water which is made to flow over vessels is thus invalid. (4) The outlet is higher than the bottom of the bath-basin, so that water gathers in the bath-basin before any water reaches the outlet. (5) Even if the outlet is at the side. (6) An arrangement for a cold-water douche after a hot bath, consisting of two pipes one above the other with a hole in the upper pipe communicating with the lower one. (7) Less than 40 *se'ahs*. (8) The three *logs* of drawn water at the hole in the lower pipe render the water in the upper-pipe invalid. It goes without saying that such would be the case also if the

MIKWEH]. HOW LARGE NEED THE HOLE BE TO CONTAIN THREE LOGS? A THREE-HUNDRED-AND-TWENTIETH PART[1] OF THE POOL. THIS IS THE OPINION OF R. JOSE. BUT R. ELEAZAR SAYS: EVEN THOUGH THE BOTTOM [PIPE] WERE FULL OF VALID [WATER] AND THE TOP [PIPE] FULL OF DRAWN [WATER] AND BY THE HOLE'S SIDE WERE THREE LOGS, [THE BATH IS] VALID, FOR THEY HAVE ONLY SAID: 'IF THREE LOGS FELL IN'.[2]

upper pipe contained drawn water and the lower pipe contained valid water.

(1) This is the proportion of three *logs* to 40 *se'ahs*, since a *se'ah* consists of 24 *logs;* cf. Introd., n. 2. (2) But here the drawn water does not fall into the valid water, but both, the valid water of one pipe and the drawn water of the other pipe, are mixed together in the *mikweh;* and since the valid water is more in quantity than the drawn water, the *mikweh* is valid as in the case discussed above, IV, 4.

MIḲWAOTH

CHAPTER VII

MISHNAH 1. SOME MATERIALS MAKE UP THE MIḲWEH [TO THE REQUIRED QUANTITY][1] AND DO NOT MAKE IT INVALID;[2] SOME MAKE IT INVALID AND DO NOT MAKE UP [THE REQUIRED QUANTITY]; AND SOME NEITHER MAKE UP [THE REQUIRED QUANTITY] NOR MAKE IT INVALID. THESE MAKE UP THE REQUIRED QUANTITY AND DO NOT MAKE THE MIḲWEH INVALID: SNOW, HAIL, HOARFROST, ICE, SALT, AND THIN[3] MUD. R. AKIBA SAID: R. ISHMAEL ONCE ARGUED AGAINST ME SAYING: SNOW DOES NOT MAKE UP THE MIḲWEH [TO ITS REQUIRED QUANTITY]. BUT THE MEN OF MADEBA[4] TESTIFIED IN HIS NAME THAT HE HAD ONCE TOLD THEM: GO AND BRING SNOW AND WITH IT FROM THE FIRST[5] PREPARE A MIḲWEH. R. JOḤANAN B. NURI SAYS: HAILSTONES ARE LIKE DRAWN WATER. IN WHAT MANNER DO THEY MAKE UP [THE REQUIRED QUANTITY] AND DO NOT RENDER IT INVALID? IF THE MIḲWEH CONTAINED FORTY SE'AHS LESS ONE, AND A SE'AH[6] OF THEM[7] FELL IN AND MADE UP [THE REQUIRED QUANTITY], THEY THUS MAKE UP [THE REQUIRED QUANTITY] BUT DO NOT RENDER IT INVALID.

MISHNAH 2. THESE RENDER THE MIḲWEH INVALID AND DO NOT MAKE UP [THE REQUIRED QUANTITY]: DRAWN WATER, WHETHER CLEAN OR UNCLEAN, WATER THAT HAS BEEN USED FOR PICKLING OR FOR SEETHING, AND GRAPE-SKIN[8]

(1) If they enter a *miḳweh* containing less than 40 *se'ahs*. (2) If three *logs* of them fall into a *miḳweh* of less than 40 *se'ahs*. (3) Lit., 'like spittle'. (4) East of the Jordan, cf. Num. XXI, 30. (5) To make a new *miḳweh*. (6) A quantity which when melted was equal to a *se'ah*. (7) Of the materials in the above list. (8) 'Tamed', an inferior wine made by steeping in water husks and stones of pressed grapes; cf. Ma'as. Sh. I, 3.

WINE STILL UNFERMENTED.[1] IN WHAT MANNER DO THEY MAKE THE MIḲWEH INVALID AND DO NOT MAKE UP [THE REQUIRED QUANTITY]? IF A MIḲWEH CONTAINED FORTY SE'AHS LESS A ḲORṬOB,[2] AND A ḲORṬOB OF THESE FELL INTO IT, IT DOES NOT MAKE UP [THE REQUIRED QUANTITY]; AND IF THERE WERE THREE LOGS OF ANY OF THESE, THEY WOULD RENDER THE MIḲWEH INVALID. BUT THE OTHER LIQUIDS,[3] AND THE JUICE OF FRUITS, BRINE, AND LIQUID IN WHICH FISH HAS BEEN PICKLED, AND GRAPE-SKIN WINE THAT HAS FERMENTED AT TIMES MAKE UP [THE REQUIRED QUANTITY] AND AT TIMES DO NOT MAKE IT UP.[4] HOW IS THIS? IF A MIḲWEH CONTAINED FORTY SE'AHS LESS ONE, AND A SE'AH OF ANY OF THESE FELL IN IT, THIS DOES NOT MAKE UP[5] [THE REQUIRED QUANTITY]. BUT IF THE MIḲWEH CONTAINED FORTY SE'AHS AND A SE'AH OF ANY OF THESE WAS PUT IN AND ONE SE'AH WAS REMOVED, LO, THE MIḲWEH IS STILL VALID.[6]

MISHNAH 3. IF BASKETS OF OLIVES OR BASKETS OF GRAPES WERE WASHED IN THE MIḲWEH AND THEY CHANGED ITS COLOUR, IT CONTINUES VALID. R. JOSE SAYS: DYE-WATER RENDERS IT INVALID BY A QUANTITY OF THREE LOGS,[7] BUT NOT THROUGH CHANGING ITS COLOUR.[8] IF WINE OR THE SAP OF OLIVES FELL INTO IT AND CHANGED ITS COLOUR, IT BECOMES INVALID.[9] WHAT SHOULD ONE DO [TO MAKE IT

(1) It is still considered water. (2) V. *supra* III, 1, n. 4. (3) The seven liquids enumerated in Maksh. VI, 4, including wine, oil, milk, etc. (4) Neither do these liquids render the *miḳweh* invalid if they fall into it and do not change the colour of the water. These liquids thus form the third class of materials which neither make up the required quantity of the *miḳweh*, nor render it invalid. (5) But neither does it render the water in the *miḳweh* invalid. (6) Although the greater portion of the *se'ah* removed must have consisted of the valid water, so that now the *miḳweh* must contain less than 40 *se'ahs* of its original water. (7) Like ordinary drawn water. (8) Because the dye is an artificial addition to the water. (9) Because the colour of wine or olives is natural to them and inseparable from them. A *miḳweh* so coloured would appear to be not a *miḳweh* of water, as prescribed by the Torah, but a *miḳweh* filled with wine or with the sap of olives.

VALID AGAIN]?[1] ONE SHOULD WAIT WITH IT TILL THE RAIN FALLS AND THE COLOUR REVERTS TO THE COLOUR OF WATER. IF IT CONTAINED FORTY SE'AHS,[2] WATER MAY BE DRAWN AND CARRIED ON THE SHOULDER AND PUT THEREIN UNTIL THE COLOUR REVERTS TO THAT OF WATER.

MISHNAH 4. IF WINE OR THE SAP OF OLIVES FELL INTO THE MIKWEH[3] AND CHANGED THE COLOUR OF A PORTION OF THE WATER,[4] ONE MAY NOT IMMERSE ONESELF THEREIN IF IT HAS NOT FORTY SE'AHS WITH THE COLOUR OF WATER.

MISHNAH 5. IF A KORTOB OF WINE FELL INTO THREE LOGS OF WATER AND ITS COLOUR BECAME LIKE THAT OF WINE, AND THE WATER THEN FELL INTO A MIKWEH,[5] IT DOES NOT RENDER IT INVALID.[6] IF THERE WERE THREE LOGS OF WATER LESS A KORTOB INTO WHICH A KORTOB OF MILK FELL, AND THEIR COLOUR REMAINED LIKE THE COLOUR OF WATER, AND THEN THEY FELL INTO A MIKWEH, THEY DO NOT RENDER IT INVALID.[7] R. JOHANAN B. NURI SAYS: ALL GOES BY THE COLOUR.[8]

MISHNAH 6. IF A MIKWEH CONTAINED FORTY SE'AHS EXACTLY AND TWO PERSONS WENT DOWN AND IMMERSED THEMSELVES ONE AFTER THE OTHER, THE FIRST BECOMES CLEAN BUT THE SECOND REMAINS UNCLEAN.[9] R. JUDAH SAYS: IF THE FEET OF THE FIRST WERE STILL TOUCHING

(1) In the case of a *mikweh* containing less than 40 *se'ahs* which may not be increased by drawn water. (2) Which does not become invalid by the addition of any quantity of drawn water. (3) Holding less than 40 *se'ahs*. (4) At one side of the *mikweh*. That portion can no longer be reckoned as part of the *mikweh*. (5) Holding less than 40 *se'ahs*, and the colour of which was not changed. (6) Because the three *logs* are no longer considered as water. (7) Because milk cannot make up the required quantity of the three *logs* of water. (8) And if the milk did not change the colour of the water, it combines with the water to make up three *logs*, and so renders the *mikweh* invalid. (9) Because some water must have adhered to the body of the first person, thus reducing the quantity of the *mikweh* to less than 40 *se'ahs*.

THE WATER,[1] THE SECOND ALSO BECOMES CLEAN. IF ONE IMMERSED A THICK CLOAK[2] AND WHEN HE DREW IT OUT A PART WAS STILL IN CONTACT WITH THE WATER [AND THEN ANOTHER PERSON IMMERSED HIMSELF IN THE MIKWEH], HE BECOMES CLEAN.[3] IF A BOLSTER OR A CUSHION OF LEATHER WAS IMMERSED, AS SOON AS IT IS TAKEN OUT OF THE WATER BY ITS OPEN ENDS THE WATER WHICH STILL REMAINS IN IT IS DRAWN WATER.[4] HOW SHOULD ONE DO IT? ONE SHOULD IMMERSE THEM AND DRAW THEM UP BY THEIR LOWER EDGES.[5]

MISHNAH 7. IF A BED WAS IMMERSED THEREIN,[6] ALTHOUGH ITS FEET SINK INTO THE THICK MUD, IT STILL BECOMES CLEAN BECAUSE THE WATER TOUCHED THEM BEFORE [THE MUD].[7] IF THE WATER OF A MIKWEH[8] IS TOO SHALLOW,[9] ONE MAY PRESS DOWN EVEN BUNDLES OF STICKS, EVEN BUNDLES OF REEDS, SO THAT THE LEVEL OF THE WATER MAY RISE,[10] AND THEN GO DOWN AND IMMERSE ONESELF. IF AN [UNCLEAN] NEEDLE IS PLACED ON THE STEP[11] [LEADING DOWN TO A MIKWEH] IN A CAVERN, AND THE WATER IS PUT IN MOTION, ONCE A WAVE HAS PASSED OVER IT, [THE NEEDLE] BECOMES CLEAN.

(1) When the second person immersed himself, the whole of the body of the first person may thus be considered as if still in the water. (2) In a *mikweh* containing 40 *se'ahs* exactly. (3) The water absorbed by the cloak is considered as if still in the *mikweh*. (4) They form a receptacle, and if immersed in a *mikweh* of 40 *se'ahs* exactly, the water running down from them into the *mikweh*, if three *logs* in quantity, will render the *mikweh* invalid. (5) So that no water will be held inside them. (6) In a *mikweh* containing 40 *se'ahs* exactly. (7) Or, according to some commentators, because the water fills the holes in the mud before the feet of the bed sink in them. (8) Containing more than 40 *se'ahs*. (9) For the body to be completely covered by it. (10) Lit., 'swell up'. (11) The owner will not immerse the needle in the cavern for fear of its being lost.

MIḲWAOTH

CHAPTER VIII

MISHNAH 1. THE LAND OF ISRAEL IS CLEAN[1] AND ITS MIḲWEHS ARE CLEAN.[2] THE MIḲWEHS OF THE NATIONS OUTSIDE THE LAND ARE VALID FOR THOSE WHO HAD A SEMINAL ISSUE[3] EVEN THOUGH THEY ARE FILLED WITH A SWIPE-BEAM;[4] THOSE IN THE LAND OF ISRAEL WHEN OUTSIDE THE ENTRANCE [TO THE CITY][5] ARE VALID ALSO FOR MENSTRUANTS,[6] AND THOSE WITHIN THE ENTRANCE [TO THE CITY] ARE VALID FOR THOSE WHO HAD A SEMINAL ISSUE BUT INVALID FOR ALL [OTHERS] WHO ARE UNCLEAN.[7] R. ELIEZER SAYS: THOSE WHICH ARE NEAR TO A CITY OR TO A ROAD ARE UNCLEAN BECAUSE OF THE WASHING [OF CLOTHES[8] THEREIN]; BUT THOSE AT A DISTANCE ARE CLEAN.

MISHNAH 2. THESE ARE THE PERSONS THAT HAD A SEMINAL ISSUE WHO REQUIRE IMMERSION: IF HE NOTICED THAT HIS URINE ISSUED IN DROPS OR WAS MUDDY, AT THE BEGINNING[9] HE IS CLEAN;[10] IN THE MIDDLE AND AT THE END, HE IS UNCLEAN;[11] FROM THE BEGINNING TO THE END, HE IS CLEAN.[10] IF IT WAS WHITE AND VISCOUS, HE IS UN-

(1) Even localities occupied by non-Jews. (2) They are not suspected of having become invalid by drawn water. (3) To purify them for the study of the Torah; cf. *supra* III, 4, n. 3. Such a defilement can be removed by immersion even in a *miḳweh* with drawn water. (4) Carrying drawn water. (5) Where few people come, and one need not suspect the presence of drawn water in a *miḳweh*. (6) Even for such a severe defilement as that of menstruation; cf. Lev. XX, 18. (7) Because such *miḳwehs* are used for ordinary bathing and for washing clothes, and may be suspected of having been filled with drawn water. (8) Even though they are filled with rain water, they may yet be suspected of having received three *logs* of water wrung out of the clothes washed in them and thus rendered drawn before they had 40 *se'ahs* of rain water. (9) Of his urination. (10) It is not semen. (11) It is semen.

CLEAN.[1] R. JOSE SAYS: WHAT IS WHITE COUNTS LIKE WHAT IS MUDDY.[2]

MISHNAH 3. IF HE EMITTED THICK DROPS FROM THE MEMBER, HE IS UNCLEAN.[1] THIS IS THE OPINION OF R. ELEAZAR ḤISMA. IF ONE HAD IMPURE DREAMS IN THE NIGHT AND AROSE AND FOUND HIS FLESH[3] HEATED, HE IS UNCLEAN.[4] IF A WOMAN[5] DISCHARGED SEMEN ON THE THIRD DAY,[6] SHE IS CLEAN.[7] THIS IS THE OPINION OF R. ELEAZAR B. 'AZARIAH. R. ISHMAEL SAYS: SOMETIMES THERE ARE FOUR 'ONAHS,[8] AND SOMETIMES FIVE, AND SOMETIMES SIX. R. AKIBA SAYS: THERE ARE ALWAYS FIVE.

MISHNAH 4. IF A GENTILE WOMAN DISCHARGED SEMEN FROM AN ISRAELITE, IT IS UNCLEAN. IF AN ISRAELITE WOMAN DISCHARGED SEMEN FROM A GENTILE, IT IS CLEAN. IF A WOMAN HAD INTERCOURSE AND THEN WENT DOWN AND IMMERSED HERSELF BUT DID NOT[9] SWEEP OUT THE HOUSE,[10] IT IS AS THOUGH SHE HAD NOT IMMERSED HERSELF.[11] IF A MAN WHO HAD A SEMINAL ISSUE IMMERSED HIMSELF BUT DID NOT FIRST PASS URINE, HE AGAIN BECOMES UNCLEAN

(1) V. p. 452, n. 11. (2) And it differs according as it is discharged at the beginning or in the middle and at the end. (3) A euphemism for the male member; cf. Lev. XV, 2, etc. (4) Even though he did not perceive a discharge. (5) Cf. Shab. IX, 3. (6) After intercourse. The number of days is derived from Ex. XIX, 15. (7) After such a time the semen loses its efficacy. (8) During which the discharge remains unclean. An *'onah* (lit., 'period') is a day or a night, half an astronomical day. R. Ishmael holds that two full astronomical days (viz., a complete night and the day following it) must elapse to render the discharge clean. Thus if intercourse took place at the end of the first day and the discharge at the beginning of the fourth day, two complete days or four *'onahs* intervening, it is clean. But if intercourse took place in the morning of the first day, the discharge will still not be clean till the beginning of the fourth day, a lapse of five *'onahs*. Likewise, if intercourse took place in the evening (preceding) the first day, the discharge is not clean till the beginning of the fourth day, a lapse of six *'onahs*. (9) Previous to immersion. (10) A euphemism; did not clean her private parts from any trace of semen. (11) Because she may have a discharge after her immersion.

WHEN HE PASSES URINE.[1] R. JOSE SAYS: IF HE WAS SICK OR OLD HE IS UNCLEAN, BUT IF HE WAS YOUNG AND HEALTHY HE REMAINS CLEAN.[2]

MISHNAH 5. IF A MENSTRUANT PLACED COINS IN HER MOUTH AND WENT DOWN AND IMMERSED HERSELF, SHE BECOMES CLEAN FROM HER [FORMER] UNCLEANNESS,[3] BUT SHE BECOMES UNCLEAN ON ACCOUNT OF HER SPITTLE.[4] IF SHE PUT HER HAIR IN HER MOUTH[5] OR CLOSED HER HAND[5] OR PRESSED HER LIPS TIGHTLY,[5] IT IS AS THOUGH SHE HAD NOT IMMERSED HERSELF.[6] IF A PERSON HELD ON TO ANOTHER MAN OR TO VESSELS AND IMMERSED THEM, THEY REMAIN UNCLEAN;[7] BUT IF HE HAD WASHED HIS HAND BEFORE IN THE WATER, THEY BECOME CLEAN.[8] R. SIMEON SAYS: HE SHOULD HOLD THEM LOOSELY THAT WATER MAY ENTER INTO THEM. THE SECRET[9] AND WRINKLED PARTS OF THE BODY DO NOT NEED THAT WATER SHOULD ENTER INTO THEM.[10]

(1) The urine may carry a discharge of semen. (2) The original discharge must have been complete, leaving nothing behind for an additional discharge in the urine. (3) For fresh intercourse. (4) Before the immersion some spittle may have come on the coin in her mouth. This spittle does not become clean by the immersion like the rest of the spittle in her mouth, and conveys uncleanness to the woman. (5) Preventing their contact with the water. (6) Because the immersion was not complete. (7) The water in the *miḳweh* did not cover the place held by the hand. (8) The water adhering still to his hand combines with the water of the *miḳweh* to serve as immersion for the place held by the hand. (9) The inside of the mouth, ears, and nose. (10) But they must be left free for contact with the water.

MIḲWAOTH

CHAPTER IX

MISHNAH 1. THE FOLLOWING INTERPOSE[1] IN THE CASE OF A PERSON: THREADS OF WOOL AND THREADS OF FLAX AND THE RIBBONS ON THE HEADS OF GIRLS.[2] R. JUDAH SAYS: THOSE OF WOOL OR OF HAIR DO NOT INTERPOSE, BECAUSE WATER ENTERS THROUGH THEM.

MISHNAH 2. THE MATTED HAIR ON THE HEART AND ON THE BEARD AND ON A WOMAN'S[3] SECRET PARTS; PUS OUTSIDE THE EYE, HARDENED PUS OUTSIDE A WOUND AND THE PLASTER OVER IT, DRIED-UP JUICE, CLOTS OF EXCREMENT ON THE BODY, DOUGH UNDER THE FINGER NAIL, SWEAT-CRUMBS, MIRY CLAY, POTTER'S CLAY, AND ROAD-CLAY. WHAT IS MEANT BY 'MIRY CLAY'? THIS MEANS THE CLAY IN PITS, FOR IT IS WRITTEN: 'HE BROUGHT ME UP OUT OF A HORRIBLE PIT, OUT OF THE MIRY CLAY'.[4] 'POTTER'S CLAY' IS ACCORDING TO ITS LITERAL SENSE. R. JOSE DECLARES POTTER'S CLAY CLEAN,[5] BUT CLAY FOR PUTTY UNCLEAN. 'ROAD-CLAY'[6] IS CLAY WHICH BECOMES LIKE ROAD-SIDE PEGS.[7] IN THESE [KINDS OF CLAY][8] ONE MAY NOT IMMERSE ONESELF NOR IMMERSE WITH THEM;[9] BUT IN ALL OTHER CLAY ONE MAY IMMERSE WHEN IT IS WET. ONE MAY NOT IMMERSE ONESELF WITH DUST [STILL] ON ONE'S FEET.[10] ONE MAY NOT IMMERSE A

(1) Between the body and the water of the *miḳweh* to render the immersion void if they are worn on the body while immersing; cf. *supra* VIII, 5, nn. 5-7, and Introd. (2) If tied tightly or interlaced. (3) A married woman only, who finds such hair annoying in intercourse with her husband. (4) Psalms XL, 3. This shows that miry clay (טיט היון) is found in pits. (5) Water can penetrate through this clay, but not through putty. (6) גין יוני, of uncertain meaning and pointing (?יְוָנִי); cf. Kohut, *'Aruch*, II, p. 341. (7) When it becomes dry and hard; cf. B.Ḳ. 81*a*. (8) If any such clay is in the *miḳweh*. (9) If any such clay is sticking to the body. (10) The dust may turn in the water into clay.

KETTLE WITH SOOT [ON IT] EXCEPT IT HAS BEEN SCRAPED.

MISHNAH 3. THE FOLLOWING DO NOT INTERPOSE: THE MATTED HAIR OF THE HEAD AND OF THE ARMPITS AND OF A MAN'S SECRET PARTS. R. ELIEZER SAYS: IT IS THE SAME WITH A MAN OR A WOMAN: IF IT IS SOMETHING WHICH ONE FINDS ANNOYING, IT INTERPOSES; BUT IF IT IS SOMETHING WHICH ONE DOES NOT FIND ANNOYING, IT DOES NOT INTERPOSE.

MISHNAH 4. PUS WITHIN THE EYE, HARDENED PUS WITHIN A WOUND, JUICE THAT IS MOIST, MOIST EXCREMENT ON THE BODY, EXCREMENT INSIDE THE FINGER NAIL, AND A DANGLING FINGER NAIL.[1] THE DOWNY HAIR OF A CHILD IS NOT LIABLE TO UNCLEANNESS[2] AND DOES NOT CAUSE UNCLEANNESS. THE SKIN WHICH FORMS OVER A WOUND IS LIABLE TO UNCLEANNESS AND CAUSES UNCLEANNESS.

MISHNAH 5. IN THE CASE OF ARTICLES THE FOLLOWING INTERPOSE: PITCH AND MYRRH[3] IN THE CASE OF GLASS VESSELS, WHETHER INSIDE OR OUTSIDE; THEY INTERPOSE [WHEN FOUND] ON A TABLE OR ON A BOARD OR ON A COUCH THAT ARE [USUALLY] KEPT CLEAN,[4] BUT THEY DO NOT INTERPOSE [WHEN FOUND] ON THESE ARTICLES IF ALLOWED TO REMAIN DIRTY. THEY INTERPOSE IN THE CASE OF BEDS BELONGING TO HOUSEHOLDERS,[5] BUT THEY DO NOT INTERPOSE ON BEDS BELONGING TO A POOR PERSON. THEY INTERPOSE ON THE SADDLE OF A HOUSE-HOLDER, BUT THEY DO NOT INTERPOSE ON THE SADDLE OF A DEALER IN WATER-SKINS. THEY INTERPOSE IN THE CASE OF A PACK-SADDLE.[6] RABBAN SIMEON B. GAMALIEL SAYS: [ONLY IF THE STAIN IS AS BIG] AS AN ITALIAN ISSAR.[7]

(1) This concludes the list of things which do not interpose. (2) If it comes in contact with a defilement. (3) והמור. Var. lec.: וחמר, 'and bitumen'. (4) And the stain causes annoyance. (5) A rich person who is fastidious about the cleanliness of his furniture. (6) Some texts omit this sentence. (7) The Roman *As*, a coin which was equal to 1/24 of a *denar*.

MISHNAH 6. THEY DO NOT INTERPOSE [IF FOUND] ON CLOTHING ON ONE SIDE [ONLY], BUT [IF FOUND] ON TWO SIDES[1] THEY INTERPOSE. R. JUDAH SAYS IN THE NAME OF R. ISHMAEL: ON ONE SIDE ALSO. R. JOSE SAYS: IN THE CASE OF BANNA'IM[2] THEY INTERPOSE ALSO IF ON ONE SIDE, BUT IN THE CASE OF THE UNCULTURED ONLY IF ON BOTH SIDES.

MISHNAH 7. THEY DO NOT INTERPOSE IN THE CASE OF APRONS BELONGING TO WORKERS IN PITCH, POTTERS, OR TRIMMERS OF TREES. R. JUDAH SAYS: THE SAME APPLIES ALSO TO SUMMER FRUIT-DRIERS. THIS IS THE GENERAL RULE: IF IT IS SOMETHING WHICH CAUSES ANNOYANCE, IT INTERPOSES; BUT IF IT IS SOMETHING WHICH DOES NOT CAUSE ANNOYANCE, IT DOES NOT INTERPOSE.

(1) When a stain causes annoyance. (2) בנאים, 'builders' explained in Shab. 114a as scholars learned in the law who build up the world (cf. Ber. 64*a*). Another explanation given there is 'bath-attendants' (בלנאים or בלנים), but this does not correspond to the following 'uncultured' (בור).

MIḲWAOTH

CHAPTER X

MISHNAH 1. ANY HANDLES OF VESSELS WHICH HAVE BEEN FIXED NOT IN THEIR CUSTOMARY MANNER, OR, IF FIXED IN THEIR CUSTOMARY MANNER, HAVE NOT BEEN FIXED FIRMLY, OR, IF FIXED FIRMLY, HAVE BEEN BROKEN,[1] LO, THEY INTERPOSE.[2] IF A VESSEL IS IMMERSED WITH ITS MOUTH DOWNWARDS, IT IS AS THOUGH IT HAD NOT BEEN IMMERSED.[3] IF IMMERSED IN THE REGULAR MANNER BUT WITHOUT THE ATTACHMENT,[4] [IT BECOMES CLEAN] ONLY IF TURNED ON ITS SIDE.[5] IF A VESSEL IS NARROW AT EACH END AND BROAD IN THE CENTRE, IT BECOMES CLEAN ONLY IF TURNED ON ITS SIDE.[5] A FLASK WHICH HAS ITS MOUTH TURNED INWARDS[6] BECOMES CLEAN ONLY IF A HOLE IS MADE AT THE SIDE.[5] AN INKPOT OF LAYMEN[7] BECOMES CLEAN ONLY IF A HOLE IS MADE AT THE SIDE. THE INKPOT OF JOSEPH THE PRIEST HAD A HOLE AT ITS SIDE.[8]

MISHNAH 2. IN THE CASE OF A BOLSTER AND A CUSHION OF LEATHER IT IS NECESSARY THAT THE WATER ENTER INSIDE THEM;[9] BUT IN THE CASE OF A ROUND CUSHION OR

(1) In all these cases the handle cannot be considered a permanent or an essential part of the vessel. (2) They prevent the water from covering that part of the vessel where the handle is attached. (3) Because air remains in the vessel and prevents the water from filling it. (4) The reading and meaning of this word are very doubtful. It is variously explained as an additional opening, or handle, or long neck, or saucer-like bottom. (5) To enable the water to fill it completely. (6) In order to prevent the escape of the liquid when the flask is turned upside down. (7) Or 'private persons' who are not professional scribes. The inkpot was made in the same fashion with the rim of its mouth turned inwards. The Cambridge text (cf. Introd. n. 1.) omits 'of laymen'. (8) In accordance with this rule. (9) Because they are sometimes opened for a change of their filling.

A BALL OR A BOOTMAKER'S LAST OR AN AMULET OR A PHYLACTERY,[1] IT IS NOT NECESSARY THAT THE WATER ENTER INSIDE THEM. THIS IS THE GENERAL RULE: ANY ARTICLE THE FILLING OF WHICH IS NOT HABITUALLY TAKEN OUT AND PUT IN MAY BE IMMERSED UNOPENED.

MISHNAH 3. THE FOLLOWING DO NOT REQUIRE THAT THE WATER SHALL ENTER INSIDE THEM: KNOTS [IN THE CLOTHES] OF A POOR MAN,[2] OR IN TASSELS, OR IN THE THONG OF A SANDAL, OR IN A HEAD-PHYLACTERY[3] IF IT IS FASTENED TIGHTLY, OR IN AN ARM-PHYLACTERY[3] IF IT DOES NOT MOVE UP OR DOWN, OR IN THE HANDLES OF A WATER-SKIN, OR IN THE HANDLES OF A WALLET.[4]

MISHNAH 4. THE FOLLOWING REQUIRE THAT WATER SHALL ENTER INSIDE THEM: THE KNOT IN AN UNDERGARMENT[5] WHICH IS TIED TO THE SHOULDER, (LIKEWISE THE HEM OF A SHEET[6] MUST BE STRETCHED OUT), AND THE KNOT OF A HEAD-PHYLACTERY IF IT IS NOT FASTENED TIGHTLY, OR OF THE ARM-PHYLACTERY IF IT MOVES UP AND DOWN, AND THE LACES OF A SANDAL. CLOTHES WHICH ARE IMMERSED WHEN THEY HAVE JUST BEEN WASHED[7] MUST BE KEPT IMMERSED UNTIL THEY THROW UP BUBBLES,[8] BUT IF THEY ARE IMMERSED WHEN ALREADY DRY, THEY MUST BE KEPT IMMERSED UNTIL THEY THROW UP BUBBLES AND THEN CEASE TO THROW UP BUBBLES.[9]

MISHNAH 5. ANY HANDLES OF VESSELS WHICH ARE TOO

(1) These are not usually opened. (2) To tie up rents. (3) Cf. Deut. VI, 8. (4) They are permanent knots. (5) It has a wide opening at the neck, which is drawn in and tied to the shoulder. (6) Which serves as a curtain with folds at the top hem. (7) And are full of folds and wrinkles. (8) The bubbles show that the water still adhering to the clothes has mingled with the water of the *miḳweh*, and has thus become part of the water of the *miḳweh*. It is not necessary then for the water of the *miḳweh* to penetrate into all the folds of the clothes. (9) When we may be sure that the water of the *miḳweh* has penetrated into all the folds and wrinkles of the clothes.

LONG AND WHICH WILL BE CUT SHORT, NEED ONLY BE IMMERSED UP TO THE POINT OF THEIR PROPER MEASURE.[1] R. JUDAH SAYS: [THEY ARE UNCLEAN] UNTIL THE WHOLE OF THEM IS IMMERSED. AS FOR THE CHAIN OF A LARGE BUCKET, TO THE LENGTH OF FOUR HANDBREADTHS, AND A SMALL BUCKET, TO THE LENGTH OF TEN HANDBREADTHS; AND THEY NEED ONLY BE IMMERSED UP TO THE POINT OF THEIR PROPER MEASURE.[2] R. TARFON SAYS: IT IS NOT CLEAN UNLESS THE WHOLE OF THE RING[3] IS IMMERSED. THE ROPE BOUND TO A BASKET IS NOT COUNTED AS A CONNECTION UNLESS IT HAS BEEN SEWN ON.[4]

MISHNAH 6. BETH SHAMMAI SAY: HOT WATER[5] MAY NOT BE IMMERSED IN COLD, OR COLD IN HOT, FOUL IN FRESH OR FRESH IN FOUL.[6] BUT BETH HILLEL SAY: IT MAY BE IMMERSED. IF ONE IMMERSED A VESSEL FULL OF LIQUIDS,[7] IT IS AS THOUGH IT HAD NOT BEEN IMMERSED;[8] IF IT WAS FULL OF URINE, THIS IS RECKONED AS WATER; IF IT CONTAINED WATER OF PURIFICATION,[9] [IT IS UNCLEAN] UNLESS THE WATER [OF THE MIKWEH WHICH ENTERS THE VESSEL] EXCEEDS THE WATER OF PURIFICATION. R. JOSE SAYS: EVEN IF A VESSEL WITH THE CAPACITY OF A KOR[10] CONTAINS BUT A QUARTER-LOG,[11] IT IS AS THOUGH IT HAD NOT BEEN IMMERSED.

(1) As given in Kelim XXIX. The rest is not considered as belonging to the vessel. (2) Even if this ends in the middle of a ring. Cf. Kelim XIV, 3. (3) If the appointed measure ends in the middle of the ring. (4) Therefore when not sewn on, it must be undone before the basket is immersed. (5) Water can be rendered clean by filling it in a vessel in which it is immersed to the rim, when the water in the vessel establishes contact with the water of the *mikweh*. (6) The water to be immersed must be of the same kind as the water of the *mikweh*. (7) Other than water; cf. *supra* VII, 2, p. 449 n. 3. (8) These liquids do not mingle with the water of the *mikweh*, and therefore they interpose between the inside of the vessel and the water of the *mikweh*. (9) This water, on account of its importance, cannot be considered as mingled with the water of the *mikweh*, unless the latter exceeds it in quantity. (10) Cf. Ezek. XLV, 14. It is equal to thirty *se'ahs*. (11) Of liquid other than water or of Water of Purification.

MISHNAH 7. ALL FOODS[1] COMBINE TOGETHER[2] TO MAKE UP THE HALF OF A HALF-LOAF[3] WHICH MAKES THE BODY UNFIT. ALL LIQUIDS COMBINE TOGETHER[4] TO MAKE UP THE QUARTER-LOG WHICH MAKES THE BODY UNFIT. THIS FORMS A RULE OF GREATER STRINGENCY IN THE CASE OF ONE WHO DRINKS UNCLEAN LIQUIDS THAN IN THE CASE OF THE MIḲWEH, FOR IN HIS CASE THEY HAVE MADE ALL OTHER LIQUIDS LIKE WATER.[5]

MISHNAH 8. IF ONE ATE UNCLEAN FOODS OR DRANK UNCLEAN LIQUIDS, AND HE IMMERSED HIMSELF AND THEN VOMITED THEM UP,[6] THEY ARE STILL UNCLEAN BECAUSE THEY DID NOT BECOME CLEAN IN THE BODY.[7] IF ONE DRANK UNCLEAN WATER AND IMMERSED HIMSELF AND THEN VOMITED IT UP, IT IS CLEAN BECAUSE IT BECAME CLEAN IN THE BODY.[8] IF ONE SWALLOWED A CLEAN RING AND THEN WENT INTO THE TENT OF A CORPSE,[9] IF HE SPRINKLED HIMSELF ONCE AND TWICE[10] AND IMMERSED HIMSELF AND THEN VOMITED IT UP, LO, IT REMAINS AS IT WAS BEFORE.[11] IF ONE SWALLOWED AN UNCLEAN RING, HE MAY IMMERSE HIMSELF AND EAT TERUMAH;[12] IF HE VOMITED IT UP, IT IS UNCLEAN[13]

(1) Cf. Me'ilah IV, 5. (2) If a man ate small quantities of unclean foods of different kinds, these quantities may be reckoned together to make up the minimum quantity of unclean food which renders a person unfit for eating *terumah*. (3) A bulk of two eggs, (Rashi), or of an egg and a half, according to Maimonides. (4) If a person drank small quantities of unclean liquids of different kinds. (5) To combine with water in order to make up the required quantity, whereas in the case of the *miḳweh* other liquids do not combine with water. (6) Before they had remained in the stomach sufficiently long for digestion. (7) Unclean foods and liquids except water cannot be purified by immersion. (8) Unclean water can be purified by immersion, cf. p. 460, n. 5. (9) Or any other premises with remains of a dead human body. (10) With Water of Purification, in accordance with the law in Num. XIX, 19. (11) The ring remains clean, because a swallowed article is not affected by the defilement of the person after swallowing it. (12) The ring had a principal defilement (אב הטומאה), and by coming in contact with it before swallowing it, the person received a secondary defilement of the first degree, and requires immersion for eating *terumah*. (13) It did not become clean by the person's immersion.

AND IT RENDERS HIM UNCLEAN.[1] **IF AN ARROW WAS STUCK INTO A MAN, IT INTERPOSES SO LONG AS IT IS VISIBLE;**[2] **BUT IF IT IS NOT VISIBLE, HE MAY IMMERSE HIMSELF AND EAT TERUMAH.**[3]

מסכת מקואות
הדרן עלך
והדרך עלן
תורה אור

(1) By coming in contact with the ring in the act of vomiting it out. (2) It sticks out of the body. (3) Even if the arrow is unclean, because an object enclosed in the body cannot convey uncleanness.

MAKSHIRIM

TRANSLATED INTO ENGLISH

WITH NOTES

BY

RABBI M. H. SEGAL, M. A.

INTRODUCTION

The name Makshirin or Makshirim (מכשירים, מכשירין) is the plural masculine of the participle of the causative stem of the late Hebrew verb *kasher*[1] (כשר, to be fit, be proper, be suitable or capable). It means 'things which render fit or capable', which endow with a quality or with a capacity for something. In our Tractate the causative stem of this verb is used in a technical sense of liquids which render foods capable of contracting an impurity.

The subject of the Tractate is based upon the principle laid down in Lev. XI, 34, 37, 38, that no food or produce of the soil can contract an impurity, unless at some time or another it had been moistened by water. *Of all meat which may be eaten, that on which water cometh shall be unclean; and all drink that may be drunk in every vessel shall be unclean. And if any part of their carcass fall upon any sowing seed which is to be sown, it shall be clean. But if any water be put upon the seed, and any part of their carcass fall thereon, it shall be unclean unto you.* The term '*water*' in this passage is interpreted by Jewish tradition to include all the other natural liquids. Furthermore, from the expression '*in every vessel*' it is inferred that the liquid must be removed from its natural place, and be put upon the food. Food moistened by the water of a river or a pool cannot become capable of contracting an impurity, unless the water had been separated from the surface of the sheet of water on the ground.

Finally, from the fact that the verb יֻתַּן '*will be put*' [v. 38], which is the passive of נתן, 'to give' or 'to put', may also be pointed as an active יִתֵּן,[2] 'he will put', it is inferred that in the act of moistening the food by the liquid the passive and active elements must be combined; that though the liquid need not be put upon the food by a direct human act, it is yet necessary that the moistening of the food shall take place through the intention of the owner, or shall satisfy his desire or his needs.

(1) Cf. Esther VIII, 5; Eccl. XI, 6 and in the causative stem, Eccl. X, 10.
(2) Cf. Ḳid. 59*b*; B.M. 22*b*.

Accordingly, the discussions of our Tractate turn mainly on these two chief topics: the moistening of food about which a doubt may arise whether it was done with the intention or to the satisfaction of the owner, and which other liquids beside water can endow food with the capacity for contracting an impurity. These discussions lead also to the consideration of a number of other problems connected chiefly with the rules of purity and impurity.

CONTENTS OF THE TRACTATE

Chapter I. Concerning the owner's satisfaction with the moistening of the produce (1); various cases of moistening by rain water dropping from trees, from vegetables or from the human body (2—5); moistening of produce by spittle and without intention (6).

Chapter II. Moistening by human perspiration, by the exudation from walls caused by the presence of water (1—2); various cases of mixtures and similar problems which must be decided by the character of the larger constituent, or, when the constituents are equal, according to the more stringent alternative (3—11).

Chapter III. Moistening by the absorption of water or other liquid in the vicinity of the produce (1—5); the action of rain or dew in imparting moisture; accidental moistening which causes satisfaction to the owner (5—7); damping of wooden articles and wetting of an animal while drinking (8).

Chapter IV. Wetting of the human body while drinking; spilling while drawing water in a jar (1); rain water on a human body (2); rain running down a wall (3); dripping of rain through a leakage in a roof (4—5); moistening caused by water coming from a *miḳweh* or other standing water (5—9); liquid on wood or absorbed by wood (10).

Chapter V. Moisture by water derived from a river through immersion or swimming, or from a cistern through measuring or testing its contents (1—5), or through cleaning a hide in a pool (6); water in a boat; rain water on a hot iron nail or a burning firebrand; water on a table cover or a matting (7—8); concerning a stream of liquid poured over from a clean vessel into an unclean vessel (9–10); perspiration caused by stirring a hot pot; sap of grapes weighed in scales (11).

Chapter VI. Moisture of dew (1–2); purity of vegetables, grain and fish in markets (2–3); list of liquids other than water which render produce susceptible to uncleanness and which also convey impurity (4–8).

M. H. SEGAL

MAKSHIRIN

CHAPTER I

MISHNAH 1. ANY LIQUID[1] WHICH WAS DESIRED AT THE BEGINNING[2] THOUGH IT WAS NOT DESIRED AT THE END, OR WHICH WAS DESIRED AT THE END THOUGH IT WAS NOT DESIRED AT THE BEGINNING, COMES UNDER THE LAW OF 'IF WATER BE PUT'.[3] UNCLEAN LIQUIDS RENDER UNCLEAN[4] WHETHER [THEIR ACTION] IS DESIRED OR IS NOT DESIRED.

MISHNAH 2. IF ONE SHOOK A TREE IN ORDER TO CAUSE FOOD OR AN UNCLEAN THING[5] TO DROP DOWN FROM IT, [THE RAIN WATER DROPPING DOWN FROM IT] DOES NOT COME[6] UNDER THE LAW OF 'IF WATER BE PUT'. IF [HE SHOOK THE TREE] IN ORDER TO CAUSE LIQUIDS TO DROP DOWN FROM IT, BETH SHAMMAI SAY: BOTH [THE LIQUIDS] THAT DROP DOWN AND [THE LIQUIDS] THAT REMAIN[7] [ON THE TREE] COME UNDER THE LAW OF 'IF WATER BE PUT'. BUT BETH HILLEL SAY: [THE LIQUIDS] THAT DROP DOWN COME UNDER THE LAW OF 'IF WATER BE PUT', BUT [THE LIQUIDS]

(1) Any one in the list given *infra* VI, 4-5. (2) The moistening of the produce by the liquid first pleased the owner, but afterwards displeased him; or, on the contrary, it first displeased him and then pleased him. According to other commentators the meaning is that the owner was pleased with the beginning of the flow of the liquid for some other purpose, but was displeased when in the end the liquid settled on the produce, or the reverse. (3) Lev. XI, 38; i.e., such a liquid when it has moistened the produce renders it capable of contracting an uncleanness by the touch of an unclean thing; cf. Introduction. (4) When they moisten produce, they render it susceptible to uncleanness and at the same time make it unclean by their touch. (5) Such as a piece from a dead creature left in the branches by a bird. (6) If the rain water fell on produce, it does not render it capable of contracting an impurity, because he did not intend to shake down the rain water. (7) If what remains in the tree afterwards falls on produce. His intention to bring down the rain water extends also to what remains in the tree.

THAT REMAIN [ON THE TREE] DO NOT COME UNDER THE LAW OF 'IF WATER BE PUT', BECAUSE HIS INTENTION WAS THAT [THE LIQUIDS] SHOULD DROP DOWN FROM ALL THE TREE.[1]

MISHNAH 3. IF ONE SHOOK A TREE[2] AND IT FELL[3] ON ANOTHER TREE, OR A BRANCH AND IT FELL ON ANOTHER BRANCH, AND UNDER THEM WERE SEEDS OR VEGETABLES [STILL] JOINED TO THE GROUND, BETH SHAMMAI SAY: THIS COMES UNDER THE LAW OF 'IF WATER BE PUT'. BUT BETH HILLEL SAY: THIS DOES NOT COME[4] UNDER THE LAW OF 'IF WATER BE PUT'. R. JOSHUA SAID[5] IN THE NAME OF ABBA JOSE CHOLIKOFRI,[6] A CITIZEN OF TIBEON:[7] MARVEL AT THYSELF IF THERE IS ANYTHING IN THE TORAH ABOUT A LIQUID CAUSING SUSCEPTIBILITY TO UNCLEANNESS EXCEPT ONE PUT IT ON WITH INTENTION, FOR IT IS SAID: 'IF WATER BE PUT UPON THE SEED'.[8]

MISHNAH 4. IF ONE SHOOK[9] A BUNDLE OF VEGETABLES AND [WATER] DROPPED DOWN FROM THE UPPER [SIDE] TO THE LOWER [SIDE], BETH SHAMMAI SAY: THIS COMES[10] UNDER THE LAW OF 'IF WATER BE PUT'. BUT BETH HILLEL SAY: THIS DOES NOT COME[11] UNDER THE LAW OF 'IF WATER BE PUT'. BETH HILLEL SAID TO BETH SHAMMAI: IF ONE SHAKES A STALK, DO WE APPREHEND LEST WATER DROPS FROM ONE LEAF ON THE OTHER LEAF?[12] BETH SHAMMAI SAID TO THEM:

(1) And since he left some behind in the tree, it follows that he did not attach any value to this remainder. (2) To bring down its fruit. (3) And the fruit fell from the second tree or from the second branch on to the ground into seed or vegetables which had water on them. (4) Because he did not intend them to fall on the other tree or on the other branch. The text and the interpretation of this passage are very uncertain. The explanation given here follows Maimonides and Bertinoro. (5) In support of Beth Hillel's opinion. (6) So named after some unknown locality. (7) A town in lower Galilee. (8) And since in this case it was not put on with intention, it cannot render susceptible. (9) To shake off some water. (10) Because the water fell on the lower side by the owner's deliberate act. (11) His intention was to shake off the water altogether, and not to wet the lower side. (12) And render it susceptible to uncleanness. But if no susceptibility is caused in the case of a stalk, why should it be caused in the case of a bundle?

A STALK IS ONLY ONE, BUT A BUNDLE HAS MANY STALKS.[1] BETH HILLEL SAID TO THEM: LO, IF ONE LIFTED[2] A SACK FULL OF FRUIT AND PUT IT BESIDE THE RIVER,[3] DO WE APPREHEND LEST WATER DROPS FROM THE UPPER [SIDE] TO THE LOWER [SIDE]?[4] IF, HOWEVER, HE LIFTED TWO SACKS AND PLACED THEM ONE UPON THE OTHER, THE LOWER [SACK] COMES[5] UNDER THE LAW OF 'IF WATER BE PUT'. R. JOSE SAYS: THE LOWER [SACK] ALSO REMAINS INSUSCEPTIBLE TO UNCLEANNESS.

MISHNAH 5. IF ONE RUBBED[6] A LEAK OR PRESSED HIS HAIR[7] WITH HIS GARMENT, R. JOSE SAYS: THE LIQUID WHICH CAME OUT COMES[8] UNDER THE LAW OF 'IF WATER BE PUT', BUT THE LIQUID THAT REMAINED DOES NOT COME UNDER THE LAW OF 'IF WATER BE PUT', BECAUSE HIS INTENTION WAS THAT THE LIQUID SHOULD COME OUT OF ALL OF IT.[9]

MISHNAH 6. IF ONE BLEW ON LENTILS IN ORDER TO TRY WHETHER THEY WERE GOOD,[10] R. SIMEON SAYS: THIS DOES NOT COME[11] UNDER THE LAW OF 'IF WATER BE PUT'. BUT[12] THE SAGES SAY: THIS DOES COME[13] UNDER THE LAW OF 'IF WATER BE PUT'. IF ONE ATE SESAME WITH HIS FINGER[14]

(1) Therefore in the case of a bundle it is like dropping liquid from one fruit to another fruit. (2) From the river in which it had fallen accidentally. (3) To let the water run out of the sack. (4) No, because the fruit in the lower side of the sack does not become susceptible. Similarly, the lower stalk in a bundle of vegetables should not become susceptible by the water coming down upon it from the upper stalks of the same bundle. (5) Because by placing one sack upon the other he must have intended that water should flow from the upper sack upon the lower sack. (6) To remove its moisture. (7) Which had become wet by rain. (8) It renders produce susceptible to uncleanness, because it came out by his deliberate act. (9) In accordance with the opinion of Beth Hillel, *supra* p. 470, n. 1. (10) And his spittle fell upon the lentils and moistened them. (11) The moistening was done without intention. (12) Some texts omit this sentence. (13) His blowing was done with intention, and the moistening is the direct act of the blowing. (14) By wetting his finger so as to pick up easily the grains of the sesame, and thus transferring moisture to the sesames on the palm of his hand.

AND LIQUID CAME ON HIS HAND, R. SIMEON SAYS: THIS DOES NOT COME[1] UNDER THE LAW OF 'IF WATER BE PUT'. BUT THE SAGES SAY: THIS DOES COME[2] UNDER THE LAW OF 'IF WATER BE PUT'. IF ONE HID HIS FRUIT IN WATER FROM THIEVES, IT DOES NOT COME[3] UNDER THE LAW OF 'IF WATER BE PUT'. ONCE IT HAPPENED THAT THE MEN OF JERUSALEM HID THEIR FIG CAKES IN WATER FROM THE ROBBERS,[4] AND THE SAGES DECLARED THAT THEY WERE NOT SUSCEPTIBLE TO UNCLEANNESS. IF ONE PUT HIS FRUIT IN THE STREAM OF A RIVER TO MAKE IT COME DOWN WITH HIM, IT DOES NOT COME UNDER THE LAW OF 'IF WATER BE PUT'.

(1) His intention was only to wet his finger but not the palm. (2) The moisture on the palm is a direct consequence of his wetting the finger. (3) It was not his intention to moisten the fruit. (4) סיקרין, Latin *sicarii*, armed terrorists who infested Jerusalem in the last days of the Second Temple. Another reading is סיקריקין, confiscators of property; cf. Bik. I, 2; II, 3; Giṭ. 55*b*.

MAKSHIRIN

CHAPTER II

MISHNAH 1. THE EXUDATION OF HOUSES, OF CISTERNS, OF DITCHES AND CAVERNS[1] DOES NOT CAUSE[2] SUSCEPTIBILITY TO UNCLEANNESS. A MAN'S PERSPIRATION DOES NOT CAUSE SUSCEPTIBILITY TO UNCLEANNESS. IF A MAN DRANK UNCLEAN WATER AND PERSPIRED, HIS PERSPIRATION DOES NOT CAUSE[3] SUSCEPTIBILITY TO UNCLEANNESS. IF HE ENTERED[4] INTO DRAWN WATER AND PERSPIRED, HIS PERSPIRATION CAUSES[5] SUSCEPTIBILITY TO UNCLEANNESS. IF HE DRIED HIMSELF AND THEN PERSPIRED, HIS PERSPIRATION DOES NOT CAUSE SUSCEPTIBILITY TO UNCLEANNESS.

MISHNAH 2. THE EXUDATION OF AN UNCLEAN BATH[6] IS UNCLEAN,[7] BUT THAT OF A CLEAN BATH[8] COMES[9] UNDER THE LAW OF 'IF WATER BE PUT'. IF THERE WAS A POOL IN A HOUSE WHICH CAUSED THE HOUSE TO EXUDE AND THE POOL WAS UNCLEAN, THE EXUDATION OF ALL THE HOUSE WHICH WAS CAUSED BY THE POOL[10] IS UNCLEAN.

(1) From their walls. Cf. Miḳ. I, 4. (2) Exudation and perspiration do not come within the category of liquids enumerated *infra* VI, 4ff; cf. ibid. 7. (3) The water he drank was digested, and the perspiration is not the same as the water. (4) Even without intention. (5) Because the perspiration mingled with the water which adhered to his body, and which was drawn by a deliberate human act. But if he had entered without intention into a pool of water which had been filled automatically without human agency and perspired, his perspiration would not cause susceptibility, because there was no deliberate human act in connection with that water. (6) A bath containing unclean drawn water; cf. Miḳ. Introduction. (7) When it touches food it renders it both susceptible and unclean. (8) Consisting of a spring or a pool of rain water. (9) It renders produce susceptible if, namely, the exudation is acceptable to the owner. (10) But what is not caused by the pool is like the exudation of houses spoken of in Mishnah 1.

MISHNAH 3. IF THERE WERE TWO POOLS, THE ONE CLEAN AND THE OTHER UNCLEAN, WHAT EXUDES NEAR THE UNCLEAN POOL IS UNCLEAN, AND WHAT EXUDES NEAR THE CLEAN POOL IS CLEAN, AND WHAT IS AT EQUAL DISTANCE [FROM BOTH POOLS] IS UNCLEAN.[1] IF[2] UNCLEAN IRON[3] WAS SMELTED WITH CLEAN IRON AND THE GREATER PART [CAME] FROM THE UNCLEAN IRON, IT IS UNCLEAN; IF THE GREATER PART [CAME] FROM THE CLEAN IRON, IT IS CLEAN; BUT IF THERE WAS HALF OF EACH, IT IS UNCLEAN. IF IN POTS WHICH ISRAELITES AND HEATHENS USED FOR PASSING WATER THE GREATER PART [OF THE CONTENTS CONSISTED] OF UNCLEAN [URINE],[4] IT IS UNCLEAN; IF THE GREATER PART [OF THE CONTENTS CONSISTED] OF CLEAN [URINE],[5] IT IS CLEAN; BUT IF THERE WAS HALF OF EACH, IT IS UNCLEAN. IF IN SLOP-WATER, IN WHICH RAIN HAD FALLEN, THE GREATER PART CONSISTED OF THE UNCLEAN WATER,[6] IT IS UNCLEAN; IF THE GREATER PART CONSISTED OF CLEAN WATER,[7] IT IS CLEAN; BUT IF THERE WAS HALF OF EACH, IT IS UNCLEAN. WHEN [IS THIS THE CASE]?[8] WHEN THE SLOP-WATER CAME FIRST; BUT IF THE RAIN WATER CAME BEFORE [THE SLOP-WATER], IT IS UNCLEAN[9] WHATEVER THE QUANTITY [OF THE RAIN WATER].

MISHNAH 4. IF ONE SECURED HIS ROOF OR WASHED HIS GARMENT[10] AND RAIN CAME DOWN UPON IT,[11] IF THE GREATER PART[12] CONSISTED OF THE UNCLEAN WATER, IT IS

(1) There being a doubt whether it came from the clean pool or from the unclean pool, we must adopt the stringent alternative. (2) Cf. Kelim XI, 4. From here to the end of the chapter a series of cases is given to illustrate the principle that where is a doubt we must adopt the more stringent alternative. (3) Derived from broken vessels which were unclean. (4) Viz., of the heathens, whose urine is unclean according to a rabbinic enactment, like the urine of persons with a running issue (זב); cf. Shab. 17*b*. (5) Of the Israelites. (6) The presumption is that the slops are unclean. (7) The rain water. (8) That the slop-water is neutralized by the larger quantity of rain water. (9) The unclean slop-water when poured into rain water rendered it unclean. (10) With unclean slop-water. (11) On the dripping roof or on the dripping garment. (12) Of the mixture of dripping water.

UNCLEAN; IF THE GREATER PART CONSISTED OF THE CLEAN WATER, IT IS CLEAN; BUT IF THERE WAS HALF OF EACH, IT IS UNCLEAN. R. JUDAH SAYS: IF THE DRIPPING INCREASED,[1] [IT IS CLEAN].

MISHNAH 5. IF IN A CITY IN WHICH ISRAELITES AND HEATHENS DWELT TOGETHER THERE WAS A BATH WORKING[2] ON THE SABBATH, IF THE MAJORITY [OF THE INHABITANTS] WERE HEATHENS, ONE MAY BATHE THEREIN IMMEDIATELY[3] [AFTER THE CONCLUSION OF THE SABBATH]; IF THE MAJORITY WERE ISRAELITES, ONE MUST WAIT UNTIL THE WATER CAN BE HEATED;[4] IF THEY WERE HALF AND HALF, ONE MUST [ALSO] WAIT UNTIL THE WATER CAN BE HEATED. R. JUDAH SAYS: IF THE BATH-BASIN WAS SMALL AND THERE WAS THERE A [HEATHEN] AUTHORITY, ONE MAY BATHE THEREIN IMMEDIATELY[5] [AFTER THE CONCLUSION OF THE SABBATH].

MISHNAH 6. IF ONE FOUND VEGETABLES SOLD THEREIN [ON THE SABBATH], IF THE MAJORITY [OF THE INHABITANTS] WERE HEATHENS, ONE MAY BUY THEREOF IMMEDIATELY[6] [AFTER THE CONCLUSION OF THE SABBATH]; IF THE MAJORITY WERE ISRAELITES, ONE MUST WAIT UNTIL [VEGETABLES] CAN ARRIVE FROM THE NEAREST PLACE;[7] IF THEY WERE HALF AND HALF, ONE MUST [ALSO] WAIT UNTIL [VEGETABLES] CAN ARRIVE FROM THE NEAREST PLACE; BUT IF THERE WAS THERE A [HEATHEN] AUTHORITY, ONE MAY BUY IMMEDIATELY [AFTER THE CONCLUSION OF THE SABBATH].

(1) In frequency, though not in volume. The increased frequency proves that the rain water is more than the dirty water. (2) And heated on the Sabbath for bathing. It is forbidden to make use of the work done on the Sabbath by a non-Jew for a Jew. (3) The bath was heated on the Sabbath for the majority who are non-Jews. (4) After the conclusion of the Sabbath, when one may presume that the bath was not heated for the Jews on the Sabbath. (5) It is assumed that it was heated on the Sabbath for the non-Jewish authority for whom a bath must ever be ready. (6) They were cut and brought into the city on the Sabbath for the non-Jewish majority. (7) Where vegetables are grown for the market.

MISHNAH 7. IF AN ABANDONED CHILD WAS FOUND THERE, IF THE MAJORITY [OF THE INHABITANTS] WERE HEATHENS, IT MAY BE DEEMED A HEATHEN;[1] IF THE MAJORITY WERE ISRAELITES, IT MUST BE DEEMED AN ISRAELITE; IF THEY WERE HALF AND HALF, IT MUST [ALSO] BE DEEMED AN ISRAELITE. R. JUDAH SAYS: WE MUST CONSIDER WHO FORM THE MAJORITY OF THOSE WHO ABANDON THEIR CHILDREN.[2]

MISHNAH 8. IF ONE FOUND THERE LOST PROPERTY, IF THE MAJORITY [OF THE INHABITANTS] WERE HEATHENS, HE NEED NOT PROCLAIM[3] IT; IF THE MAJORITY WERE ISRAELITES, HE MUST PROCLAIM IT; IF THEY WERE HALF AND HALF, HE MUST [ALSO] PROCLAIM IT. IF ONE FOUND BREAD THERE, WE MUST CONSIDER WHO FORM THE MAJORITY OF THE BAKERS.[4] IF IT WAS BREAD OF PURE FLOUR,[5] WE MUST CONSIDER WHO FORM THE MAJORITY OF THOSE WHO EAT BREAD OF PURE FLOUR. R. JUDAH SAYS: IF IT WAS COARSE BREAD, WE MUST CONSIDER WHO FORM THE MAJORITY OF THOSE WHO EAT COARSE BREAD.[6]

MISHNAH 9. IF ONE FOUND MEAT THERE, WE MUST CONSIDER WHO FORM THE MAJORITY OF THE BUTCHERS. IF IT WAS COOKED MEAT, WE MUST CONSIDER WHO FORM THE MAJORITY OF THOSE WHO EAT COOKED MEAT.

MISHNAH 10. IF ONE FOUND FRUIT BY THE WAYSIDE,[7] IF THE MAJORITY [OF THE INHABITANTS] GATHERED FRUIT

(1) And may be given food forbidden to an Israelite. (2) And these as a rule are non-Jews. (3) So that the owner may report himself and recover his lost property; cf. B.M. II, 1. In the case of the lost property of a heathen one is not bound to make an effort to trace its owner, because heathens do not restore lost property to its owner. (4) If the majority are heathens, the bread is forbidden by a rabbinic enactment; cf. Shab. 17*b*. (5) Lit., 'of dough'. (6) This was the kind of bread generally in use in the place of R. Judah (Tosaf. Yom Ṭob). (7) On the way from the field to the city.

FOR THEIR HOMES,[1] HE IS ABSOLVED [FROM TITHES];[2] IF [THE MAJORITY GATHERED IT] FOR SELLING IN THE MARKET,[3] HE IS LIABLE [TO TITHES]; BUT IF THEY WERE HALF AND HALF, THE FRUIT IS DEMAI.[4] IF THERE WAS A GRANARY INTO WHICH BOTH ISRAELITES AND HEATHENS LAID IN THEIR PRODUCE, IF THE MAJORITY WERE HEATHENS, [THE PRODUCE MUST BE CONSIDERED] CERTAINLY UNTITHED;[5] IF THE MAJORITY WERE ISRAELITES, [IT MUST BE CONSIDERED] DEMAI;[6] IF THEY WERE HALF AND HALF, [IT MUST BE CONSIDERED] CERTAINLY UNTITHED. THIS IS THE OPINION OF R. MEIR. BUT THE SAGES SAY: EVEN IF THEY WERE ALL HEATHENS, AND ONLY ONE ISRAELITE LAID HIS PRODUCE INTO THE GRANARY, [IT MUST BE CONSIDERED] DEMAI.[7]

MISHNAH 11. IF THE FRUIT OF THE SECOND YEAR[8] EXCEEDED IN QUANTITY THE FRUIT OF THE THIRD YEAR, OR THE FRUIT OF THE THIRD YEAR EXCEEDED THE FRUIT

(1) In such a case the fruit does not become liable to tithes till it is brought into the house. (2) And also from setting apart the priestly *terumah*. But only if he wants to make of the fruit a light meal; cf. Ma'as. I, 5. (3) In such a case the produce becomes liable to tithes and *terumah* as soon as it is gathered in the field. (4) 'Doubtful', like the produce of an *'am ha-areẓ'*, who is suspected of failing to tithe his produce; cf. Demai, Introduction. In such a case the produce is liable to tithes only, but not to *terumah*. (5) This Tanna being of the opinion that the produce grown on the soil of a heathen is liable to tithes. (6) Subject only to the rules regulating the produce of an *'am ha-areẓ*, because it is assumed that there is an *'am ha-areẓ* among the Israelites who stores his produce in the granary. (7) The Sages hold that the produce grown on the soil of a heathen is exempt from tithes and consequently, unless the granary is used also by at least one Israelite, there is no liability to tithes. (8) Of the Sabbatical cycle (שמיטה); cf. Lev. XXV, 2ff. In the first, second, fourth and fifth years of the cycle, produce was liable to the First Tithe given to the Levite, and to the Second Tithe which had to be consumed, itself or its value, in Jerusalem (cf. Deut. XIV, 23ff). In the third and sixth years of the cycle, produce was liable to the First Tithe of the Levite and to the Third Tithe which was given to the poor; cf. Demai, Introduction § 2 (3). In the case of a mixture of the produce of the different years enumerated in the text, the question arises whether the mixture is liable, beside to the First Tithe, also to the Second Tithe or to the Third Tithe or to both.

OF THE FOURTH YEAR, OR THE FRUIT OF THE FOURTH YEAR EXCEEDED THE FRUIT OF THE FIFTH YEAR,[1] OR THE FRUIT OF THE FIFTH YEAR EXCEEDED THE FRUIT OF THE SIXTH YEAR, OR THE FRUIT OF THE SIXTH YEAR EXCEEDED THE FRUIT OF THE SEVENTH YEAR,[2] OR THE FRUIT OF THE SEVENTH YEAR EXCEEDED THE FRUIT OF THE YEAR AFTER THE CONCLUSION OF THE SEVENTH YEAR,[3] WE MUST CONSIDER WHAT FORMS THE GREATER PART; IF THEY ARE HALF AND HALF, WE MUST DECIDE ACCORDING TO THE MORE STRINGENT ALTERNATIVE.[4]

(1) Some texts omit this clause, since the fourth and fifth years are alike in their obligation respecting tithes. (2) The Sabbatical year, when produce was subject to the special regulations set out in Tractate Shebi'ith. Seventh year produce was exempt from all tithes. (3) Viz., the first year of the new Sabbatical cycle. (4) Viz., according to the rules governing both years. In the case of a mixture of the produce of the second and third years and of the fifth and sixth years, beside First Tithe, Second Tithe must be separated and its value given to the poor to be consumed in Jerusalem. In the case of a mixture of produce of the sixth and seventh years, First and Third Tithes must be given, and in a mixture of the seventh and first years, First and Second Tithes must be given, and in both these cases the regulations of seventh year produce must be observed.

MAKSHIRIN

CHAPTER III

MISHNAH 1. IF A SACK FULL OF FRUIT WAS PUT BY THE SIDE OF A RIVER OR BY THE SIDE OF THE MOUTH OF A CISTERN[1] OR ON THE STEPS OF A CAVERN, AND [THE FRUIT] ABSORBED WATER, ALL [THE FRUIT] WHICH ABSORBED THE WATER COMES[2] UNDER THE LAW OF 'IF WATER BE PUT'. R. JUDAH SAYS: ALL [THE FRUIT] WHICH FACED[3] THE WATER COMES UNDER THE LAW OF 'IF WATER BE PUT', BUT ALL [THE FRUIT] WHICH DID NOT FACE THE WATER DOES NOT COME UNDER THE LAW OF 'IF WATER BE PUT'.

MISHNAH 2. IF A JAR[4] FULL OF FRUIT WAS PUT INTO LIQUIDS, OR IF A JAR FULL OF LIQUIDS WAS PUT INTO FRUIT AND [THE FRUIT] ABSORBED WATER, ALL [THE FRUIT] WHICH ABSORBED THE WATER COMES UNDER THE LAW OF 'IF WATER BE PUT'. OF WHAT LIQUIDS HAVE THEY SAID IT? OF WATER, WINE AND VINEGAR;[5] BUT ALL THE OTHER LIQUIDS[6] DO NOT CAUSE SUSCEPTIBILITY TO UNCLEANNESS. R. NEHEMIAH DECLARES PULSE INSUSCEPTIBLE,[7] BECAUSE PULSE DOES NOT ABSORB [LIQUIDS].

MISHNAH 3. IF[8] ONE DREW OFF[9] HOT BREAD[10] AND PUT IT UPON THE MOUTH OF A JAR OF WINE, R. MEIR DECLARES

(1) Containing a pool of water. (2) It becomes susceptible to uncleanness, because it is the owner's wish that the fruit should become fuller and heavier by the absorption of moisture. (3) And thus absorbed moisture direct from the water. (4) Of porous material like earthenware which absorbs water. (5) These are capable of being absorbed. (6) Of the list *infra* VI, 4. (7) Even if moistened by water, wine or vinegar. (8) Cf. Ter. X, 3. (9) From the sides of the baking-oven. (10) Which was kneaded in fruit juice. Bread kneaded in water becomes susceptible by the water before it is baked.

IT SUSCEPTIBLE TO UNCLEANNESS;[1] BUT R. JUDAH DECLARES IT INSUSCEPTIBLE.[1] R. JOSE DECLARES IT INSUSCEPTIBLE[1] IN THE CASE OF WHEATEN BREAD AND SUSCEPTIBLE IN THE CASE OF BARLEY BREAD, BECAUSE BARLEY ABSORBS [LIQUIDS].

MISHNAH 4. IF ONE SPRINKLED HIS HOUSE[2] [WITH WATER] AND PUT WHEAT THEREIN AND IT BECAME MOIST, IF [THE MOISTURE CAME] FROM THE WATER, IT COMES UNDER THE LAW OF 'IF WATER BE PUT'; BUT IF [THE MOISTURE CAME] FROM THE STONY FLOOR, IT DOES NOT COME[3] UNDER THE LAW OF 'IF WATER BE PUT'. IF ONE WASHED HIS GARMENT IN A TUB AND PUT WHEAT THEREIN[4] AND IT BECAME MOIST, IF [THE MOISTURE CAME] FROM THE WATER,[5] IT COMES UNDER THE LAW OF 'IF WATER BE PUT'; BUT IF [THE MOISTURE CAME] OF ITSELF,[6] IT DOES NOT COME UNDER THE LAW OF 'IF WATER BE PUT'. IF ONE MOISTENED [PRODUCE] WITH SAND, THIS COMES[7] UNDER THE LAW OF 'IF WATER BE PUT'. IT HAPPENED WITH THE MEN OF MAḤOZ[8] THAT THEY USED TO MOISTEN [THEIR PRODUCE] WITH SAND, AND THE SAGES SAID TO THEM: IF YOU HAVE ALWAYS DONE THUS,[9] YOU HAVE NEVER PREPARED YOUR FOOD IN PURITY.[10]

MISHNAH 5. IF ONE MOISTENED [PRODUCE] WITH DRYING CLAY, R. SIMEON SAYS: IF THERE WAS STILL IN IT DRIPPING LIQUID, IT COMES UNDER THE LAW OF 'IF WATER BE PUT';

(1) Or, according to another interpretation, unclean, clean. The bread had been kneaded in water, and was thus already susceptible before it was baked. But the wine was unclean, and the controversy turns on whether the exudation of the wine absorbed by the hot bread can render the bread unclean. (2) The floor to lay the dust. (3) Like the exudation of houses, supra II, 1. (4) After emptying the tub. (5) Which may have adhered to the inside of the tub. (6) From dampness in the air, or the like. (7) The sand contained some moisture. (8) Which was rich in sand dunes; cf. 'Ar. III, 2. It was probably situated near Jabneh. (9) Under the impression that the produce did not become susceptible. (10) It had become susceptible by the sand, and then may have contracted an impurity.

BUT IF THERE WAS NOT, IT DOES NOT COME UNDER THE LAW OF 'IF WATER BE PUT'. IF ONE SPRINKLED[1] HIS THRESHING-FLOOR WITH WATER, HE NEED NOT APPREHEND LEST WHEAT BE PUT THERE AND IT BECOME MOIST.[2] IF ONE GATHERED GRASS WITH THE DEW STILL ON IT IN ORDER TO MOISTEN WHEAT THEREWITH,[3] IT DOES NOT COME UNDER THE LAW OF 'IF WATER BE PUT'; BUT IF HIS INTENTION WAS FOR THIS PURPOSE,[4] IT DOES COME UNDER THE LAW OF 'IF WATER BE PUT'. IF ONE CARRIED WHEAT TO BE MILLED AND RAIN CAME DOWN UPON IT AND HE WAS GLAD OF IT, IT COMES UNDER THE LAW OF 'IF WATER BE PUT'. R. JUDAH SAID: ONE CANNOT HELP BEING GLAD OF IT;[5] NAY, [IT COMES UNDER THE LAW] ONLY IF HE STOPPED [ON HIS WAY].[6]

MISHNAH 6. IF HIS OLIVES WERE PUT ON THE ROOF AND RAIN CAME DOWN UPON THEM AND HE WAS GLAD OF IT, IT COMES UNDER THE LAW OF 'IF WATER BE PUT'. R. JUDAH SAYS: ONE CANNOT HELP BEING GLAD; NAY, [IT COMES UNDER THE LAW] ONLY IF HE STOPPED UP THE RAIN-PIPE[7] OR IF HE SHOOK [THE OLIVES] THEREIN.

MISHNAH 7. IF ASS-DRIVERS WERE CROSSING A RIVER AND THEIR SACKS [FILLED WITH PRODUCE] FELL INTO THE WATER AND THEY WERE GLAD OF IT, IT COMES UNDER THE LAW OF 'IF WATER BE PUT'. R. JUDAH SAYS: ONE CANNOT HELP BEING GLAD OF IT; NAY, [IT COMES UNDER THE LAW] ONLY IF THEY TURNED OVER [THE SACKS].[8] IF ONE'S FEET WERE FULL OF CLAY (LIKEWISE, TOO, THE FEET OF HIS BEAST) AND HE CROSSED A RIVER AND HE WAS GLAD OF IT,[9] THIS

(1) To lay the dust on it. (2) The floor is sure to get dry before the wheat is put there. (3) In the grass itself. (4) To use the moisture of the dew. (5) And on your view, the law should apply in any case. (6) To let the wheat get wet by the rain, thus showing by his action that he desired it. Mere intention without an attendant action does not impart, on the view of R. Judah, susceptibility to uncleanness (Bert.). (7) That the water should not escape from the roof. (8) To let them get wet on all sides. (9) That the water of the river had washed off the mud of his feet.

COMES UNDER THE LAW OF 'IF WATER BE PUT'.[1] R. JUDAH SAYS: ONE CANNOT HELP BEING GLAD OF IT; NAY, [IT COMES UNDER THE LAW] ONLY IF HE STOPPED AND RINSED[2] [THE FEET]. BUT IN THE CASE OF A MAN[3] OR AN UNCLEAN BEAST[4] IT ALWAYS CAUSES[5] SUSCEPTIBILITY TO UNCLEANNESS.

MISHNAH 8. IF ONE LOWERED INTO WATER WHEELS OR GEAR OF OXEN AT THE TIME OF THE EAST WIND[6] IN ORDER THAT THEY MIGHT BECOME TIGHTENED, THIS COMES[7] UNDER THE LAW OF 'IF WATER BE PUT'. IF ONE TOOK DOWN A BEAST TO DRINK, THE WATER WHICH CAME UP ON ITS MOUTH COMES[8] UNDER THE LAW OF 'IF WATER BE PUT', BUT THAT WHICH CAME UP ON ITS FEET DOES NOT COME[9] UNDER THE LAW OF 'IF WATER BE PUT'. IF, HOWEVER, HE INTENDED THAT ITS FEET SHOULD BE WASHED, ALSO THE WATER THAT CAME UP ON ITS FEET COMES UNDER THE LAW OF 'IF WATER BE PUT'. AT THE TIME OF FOOTSORENESS OR OF THRESHING[10] IT ALWAYS CAUSES SUSCEPTIBILITY TO UNCLEANNESS. IF A

(1) The water on the feet causes susceptibility to uncleanness. (2) The feet of a domestic animal like an ox which is used for rough work, and its owner is indifferent about the cleanliness of its feet. Therefore, water on its feet cannot be considered as desired by the owner, unless he stopped and rinsed its feet. (3) Who is fastidious about the cleanliness of his feet. (4) A domestic animal, the flesh of which is forbidden for food (Lev. XI, 2ff.; Deut. XIV, 4ff.), like a horse or an ass, which is used only for riding. The owner is anxious that the feet of a riding-animal should be clean. (5) One is particularly pleased when the feet of a man or of a riding-animal are washed in the river, therefore even R. Judah admits that the water falling from their feet after crossing a river can render produce susceptible to uncleanness. (6) Which causes wooden articles to crack by its dry heat; cf. Kelim XX, 2. (7) Water dripping from them causes produce to become susceptible, because the water came on these articles by the wish of the owner. (8) Because it is usual for its mouth to get wet, and is therefore considered as if intended by the owner. (9) Because it is not necessary that its feet should become wet when drinking, and is therefore not considered as if it was desired by the owner. (10) Because then the wetting of the feet is desired by the owner for the sake of the health of the animal, or for the cleanliness of the corn.

DEAF-MUTE OR AN IDIOT OR A MINOR TOOK IT DOWN, EVEN THOUGH HIS INTENTION WAS THAT ITS FEET SHOULD BE WASHED, IT DOES NOT COME UNDER THE LAW OF 'IF WATER BE PUT', BECAUSE WITH THESE THE ACT ALONE COUNTS, BUT NOT THE INTENTION.[1]

(1) Cf. *infra* VI, 1; Ṭoh. VIII, 6; Kelim XVII, 15.

MAKSHIRIN

CHAPTER IV

MISHNAH 1. IF ONE STOOPED DOWN TO DRINK,[1] THE WATER WHICH CAME UP ON HIS MOUTH OR ON HIS MOUSTACHE COMES UNDER THE LAW OF 'IF WATER BE PUT';[2] BUT [WHAT CAME UP] ON HIS NOSE OR ON HIS HEAD OR ON HIS BEARD[3] DOES NOT COME UNDER THE LAW OF 'IF WATER BE PUT'. IF ONE DREW WATER WITH A JAR, THE WATER WHICH CAME UP ON THE BACK THEREOF, OR ON THE ROPE WHICH WAS WOUND ROUND ITS NECK, OR ON THE ROPE WHICH WAS NEEDED FOR ITS USE,[4] COMES UNDER THE LAW OF 'IF WATER BE PUT'. HOW MUCH ROPE IS NEEDED FOR ITS USE? R. SIMEON B. ELEAZAR SAYS: A HANDBREADTH. IF HE PUT THE JAR UNDER THE RAIN-PIPE, IT[5] DOES NOT COME UNDER THE LAW OF 'IF WATER BE PUT'.

MISHNAH 2. IF RAIN CAME DOWN UPON A PERSON,[6] EVEN IF HE WAS UNCLEAN WITH A PRINCIPAL DEFILEMENT,[7] IT DOES NOT COME[8] UNDER THE LAW OF 'IF WATER BE PUT'; BUT IF HE SHOOK IT OFF, IT[9] DOES COME UNDER THE LAW OF 'IF WATER BE PUT'. IF ONE STOOD UNDER A RAIN-PIPE

(1) From a river. (2) Since the mouth and the moustache necessarily get wet when one is drinking, the water on them may be considered as desired by the drinker. (3) These need not get wet, and therefore the water on them cannot be considered as desired by the drinker; cf. *supra* III, 8, nn. 8, 9. (4) These necessarily get wet. (5) Any water on the back of the jar or on its rope, since in this case they need not get wet. (6) Accidentally. (7) Cf. Kelim I, 1; 'Ed. (Sonc. ed.) p. 9, n. 4. (8) Since the rain water fell on the unclean person without his wish, it does not become unclean (cf. *infra* VI, 8), and therefore does not come within the category of unclean liquids which render unclean and cause susceptibility even when not desired (*supra* I, 1, n. 4). (9) The water that fell off, in accordance with the opinion of Beth Hillel, *supra* I, 2.

TO COOL HIMSELF OR TO WASH HIMSELF, [THE WATER FALLING ON HIM] IS UNCLEAN[1] IF HE IS UNCLEAN; BUT IF HE IS CLEAN, IT [ONLY] COMES UNDER THE LAW OF 'IF WATER BE PUT'.

MISHNAH 3. IF ONE INCLINED A DISH AGAINST A WALL THAT IT MIGHT BE RINSED,[2] IT COMES UNDER THE LAW OF 'IF WATER BE PUT'; BUT IF IN ORDER THAT THE WALL MIGHT NOT BE DAMAGED,[3] IT DOES NOT COME UNDER THE LAW OF 'IF WATER BE PUT'.

MISHNAH 4. IF DRIPPINGS [FROM A ROOF] FELL[4] INTO A JAR,[5] BETH SHAMMAI SAY: IT SHOULD BE BROKEN.[6] BUT BETH HILLEL SAY: IT MAY BE EMPTIED OUT.[7] BUT THEY[8] AGREE THAT ONE MAY PUT OUT HIS HAND AND TAKE FRUIT THEREFROM AND LEAVE IT INSUSCEPTIBLE TO UNCLEANNESS.[9]

MISHNAH 5. IF DRIPPINGS [FROM A ROOF] FELL[4] INTO A TUB, THE WATER WHICH SPLASHED OUT OR RAN OVER DOES NOT COME UNDER THE LAW OF 'IF WATER BE PUT'. IF ONE MOVED THE TUB IN ORDER TO POUR OUT THE WATER, BETH SHAMMAI SAY: IT COMES[10] UNDER THE LAW OF 'IF WATER BE PUT'. BUT BETH HILLEL SAY: IT DOES NOT COME[11] UNDER THE LAW OF 'IF WATER BE PUT'. IF ONE PLACED THE TUB

(1) And renders produce susceptible and unclean at the same time; cf. *supra* I, 1 n. 4. (2) In the rain water coming down the wall. (3) By the rain water, which is not wanted. (4) Against one's wishes. (5) Containing produce. (6) In order to get out the produce inside it; for if he tilts the jar over to empty it, the water running out together with the falling produce will render the produce susceptible. (7) By tilting over the jar, since he only wishes to empty the produce and not the water. (8) Beth Shammai. (9) Even though his hand may cause the water to come on the produce. (10) Since he poured the water away only when the tub was moved to another place, it may be said that he did not object to the water when the tub was in its original place. (11) His pouring away showed that he did not want the water even in the tub's original place.

IN ORDER THAT THE DRIPPINGS [FROM THE ROOF] SHOULD FALL INTO IT,[1] BETH SHAMMAI SAY: THE WATER THAT SPLASHES OUT OR RUNS OVER[2] COMES UNDER THE LAW OF 'IF WATER BE PUT', BUT BETH HILLEL SAY: IT[3] DOES NOT COME UNDER THE LAW OF 'IF WATER BE PUT'. IF ONE MOVED THE TUB IN ORDER TO POUR OUT THE WATER, BOTH AGREE THAT IT[4] COMES UNDER THE LAW OF 'IF WATER BE PUT'. IF ONE IMMERSED VESSELS OR WASHED HIS GARMENT IN A CAVERN,[5] THE WATER THAT CAME UP ON HIS HANDS[6] COMES UNDER THE LAW OF 'IF WATER BE PUT'; BUT WHAT CAME UP ON HIS FEET[7] DOES NOT COME UNDER THE LAW OF 'IF WATER BE PUT'. R. ELIEZER SAYS: IF IT WAS NOT POSSIBLE FOR HIM TO GO DOWN INTO THE CAVERN WITHOUT SOILING HIS FEET, WHAT CAME UP ON HIS FEET ALSO COMES[8] UNDER THE LAW OF 'IF WATER BE PUT'.

MISHNAH 6. IF A BASKET FULL OP LUPINES WAS PLACED IN A MIḲWEH,[9] ONE MAY PUT[10] OUT HIS HAND AND TAKE LUPINES THEREFROM AND LEAVE THEM CLEAN.[11] BUT IF HE LIFTED THEM[12] OUT OF THE WATER, THOSE THAT TOUCH THE BASKET ARE UNCLEAN,[13] BUT THE REST OF THE LUPINES ARE CLEAN.[14] IF THERE WAS A RADISH IN A CAVERN,[15] A MEN-

(1) And not in the courtyard. (2) And all the more so the water inside the tub. (3) Only what splashed out and what ran over, but not what is inside. (4) Even what splashed out and what ran over. (5) Containing a pool of water. (6) He is satisfied with this water. (7) This is against his wish. (8) Because he wishes his feet to be cleaned by the water. (9) A pool for the purification of a defilement by immersion; cf. Miḳwaoth Introduction. (10) Even a person affected with a principal defilement; cf. *supra* 2, n. 7. (11) The water in the *miḳweh* being joined to the ground cannot cause susceptibility to uncleanness; cf. Introduction. (12) The lupines together with the basket. (13) The basket becomes unclean with a secondary defilement of the first degree (ראשון לטומאה), and the lupines, having become susceptible by the water which adhered to them when lifted, contract a secondary defilement of the second degree (שני לטומאה); cf. 'Ed. (Sonc. ed.) p. 9, n. 4. (14) In spite of their contact with the unclean lupines of the second degree, for a second degree defilement cannot convey uncleanness to produce of a common character (חולין), like these lupines, but only to produce of priestly heave-offering (תרומה). (15) In a pool of water.

TRUANT WOMAN MAY RINSE IT AND LEAVE IT CLEAN.[1] BUT IF SHE LIFTED IT, HOWEVER LITTLE, OUT OF THE WATER, IT BECOMES UNCLEAN.[2]

MISHNAH 7. IF FRUIT FELL INTO A CHANNEL OF WATER,[3] AND ONE WHOSE HANDS WERE UNCLEAN PUT OUT HIS HANDS AND TOOK IT, HIS HANDS BECOME CLEAN[4] AND THE FRUIT [ALSO] REMAINS CLEAN.[5] BUT IF HIS INTENTION WAS THAT HIS HANDS SHOULD BE RINSED, HIS HANDS BECOME CLEAN AND THE FRUIT COMES[6] UNDER THE LAW OF 'IF WATER BE PUT'.

MISHNAH 8. IF A POT[7] FULL OF WATER WAS PLACED IN A MIKWEH, AND A MAN WHO WAS UNCLEAN WITH A PRINCIPAL DEFILEMENT PUT HIS HAND INTO THE POT, IT BECOMES UNCLEAN.[8] BUT IF [HE WAS UNCLEAN] BY THE TOUCH OF A DEFILEMENT,[9] THE POT REMAINS CLEAN,[10] BUT ANY OF THE OTHER LIQUIDS[11] [CONTAINED IN THE POT] BECOMES UNCLEAN, FOR WATER CANNOT PURIFY THE OTHER LIQUIDS.[12]

MISHNAH 9. IF ONE DREW WATER THROUGH A CHANNEL,[13]

(1) V. p. 486, n. 4. (2) The water on it when lifted makes it susceptible to contract uncleanness from the touch of the menstruant woman. (3) Joined to a valid *miḳweh*. (4) Although this washing of the hands was unintentional, it suffices for handling produce of a common character. (5) Since it fell in accidentally, it did not become susceptible. (6) It becomes susceptible by the water on his hands. (7) Of earthenware. (8) An earthenware vessel becomes unclean by the entry into its air-space of a principal defilement, but cannot be made clean by the water of a *miḳweh*; cf. Lev. XI, 33; Miḳ, (Sonc. ed.) VI, 6, n. 4. (9) He was unclean by a secondary defilement of the first degree after he had touched a principal defilement; cf. *supra* 6, nn. 13, 14. (10) An earthenware vessel cannot be rendered unclean except by a principal defilement. The water in the pot is also clean, by coming in contact with the water of the *miḳweh*; v. Miḳ. (Sonc. ed.) X, 6, n. 5. (11) Enumerated *infra* VI, 4, 5. (12) Because they cannot mingle with the water of the *miḳweh*; cf. Miḳ. (Sonc. ed.) X, 6, n. 8. (13) קילון, κήλων. Maimonides and others explain it as a swape-pipe or bucket; cf. Miḳ. VIII, 1.

IT CAUSES[1] SUSCEPTIBILITY TO UNCLEANNESS FOR THREE DAYS. R. AKIBA SAYS: IF THE CHANNEL WAS DRIED, IT AT ONCE DOES NOT CAUSE[2] SUSCEPTIBILITY TO UNCLEANNESS; BUT IF IT WAS NOT DRIED, IT CAUSES SUSCEPTIBILITY EVEN FOR THIRTY DAYS.

MISHNAH 10. IF UNCLEAN LIQUIDS FELL UPON WOOD AND RAIN CAME DOWN UPON IT[3] AND [THE RAIN WATER] EXCEEDED [THE LIQUIDS] IN QUANTITY, THEY BECOME CLEAN;[4] BUT IF THE WOOD HAD BEEN TAKEN OUTSIDE IN ORDER THAT RAIN SHOULD COME DOWN UPON IT, THEY ARE UNCLEAN[5] EVEN THOUGH [THE RAIN WATER] EXCEEDED IN QUANTITY. IF [THE WOOD] HAD ABSORBED UNCLEAN LIQUIDS,[6] THEY BECOME CLEAN EVEN THOUGH THE WOOD HAD BEEN CARRIED OUTSIDE IN ORDER THAT RAIN SHOULD COME DOWN UPON IT.[7] BUT ONE MAY NOT LIGHT THE WOOD IN AN OVEN EXCEPT WITH CLEAN HANDS.[8] R. SIMEON SAYS: IF THE WOOD WAS FRESHLY-CUT WHEN IT WAS LIGHTED, AND THE LIQUIDS THAT CAME OUT OF IT[9] EXCEEDED IN QUANTITY THE LIQUIDS WHICH IT HAD ABSORBED, THEY BECOME CLEAN.[10]

(1) Any moisture in the channel. (2) The moisture cannot be from the water which had passed through the channel. (3) Unexpectedly. (4) The rain water neutralizes the unclean liquid. (5) Because the rain water, being expected and desired, becomes itself unclean by the liquid. (6) And the liquid disappeared from the surface of the wood. (7) Because there is no contact between the unclean liquid and the rain water. (8) The hands may render the rain water on the wood unclean, and this may convey uncleanness to the oven. (9) The natural sap of the wood. (10) The unclean liquid is neutralized by the sap.

MAKSHIRIN

CHAPTER V

MISHNAH 1. IF A MAN IMMERSED HIMSELF IN A RIVER[1] AND THERE WAS IN FRONT OF HIM ANOTHER RIVER AND HE CROSSED IT,[2] THE SECOND [WATER] PURIFIES[3] THE FIRST [WATER]. IF HIS FELLOW WHO WAS INTOXICATED PUSHED HIM IN OR HIS BEAST,[4] THE SECOND [WATER] PURIFIES THE FIRST [WATER]; BUT IF [HE DID IT] OUT OF PLAYFULNESS, IT COMES[5] UNDER THE LAW OF 'IF WATER BE PUT'.

MISHNAH 2. IF A MAN SWAM IN WATER, THE WATER THAT SPLASHED OUT[6] DOES NOT COME UNDER THE LAW OF 'IF WATER BE PUT'; BUT IF IT WAS HIS INTENTION TO SPLASH HIS FELLOW, THIS COMES UNDER THE LAW OF 'IF WATER BE PUT'. IF ONE MADE A 'BIRD'[7] IN THE WATER, NEITHER [THE WATER] THAT SPLASHED OUT[8] NOR WHAT REMAINED IN IT[9] COMES UNDER THE LAW OF 'IF WATER BE PUT'.

MISHNAH 3. IF DRIPPINGS [FROM A ROOF] CAME DOWN INTO FRUIT AND IT WAS MIXED UP IN ORDER THAT IT MIGHT BECOME DRY[10] [QUICKLY], R. SIMEON SAYS: IT COMES[11] UNDER THE LAW OF 'IF WATER BE PUT'. BUT THE SAGES SAY: IT

(1) The water of this river which was still on his body could render produce susceptible, because he wished it to come on his body (2) Against his wish. (3) I.e., neutralizes it, so that neither the water from the first river nor from the second river can cause susceptibility. (4) Into a river after they had become wet with intention. (5) The second water was also acceptable. (6) Without the intention of the swimmer. (7) A game for blowing bubbles by means of a tube placed in water; var. lec. 'a tube'. (8) Without intention. (9) In the tube. (10) The owner mixed up the wet fruit with the dry fruit, so as to accelerate the drying of the moisture by spreading it over a wider space. (11) The dry fruit was deliberately moistened by the owner's act.

DOES NOT COME[1] UNDER THE LAW OF 'IF WATER BE PUT'.

MISHNAH 4. IF A CISTERN WAS MEASURED WHETHER FOR ITS DEPTH OF FOR ITS BREADTH, IT COMES[2] UNDER THE LAW OF 'IF WATER BE PUT'. THIS IS THE OPINION OF R. TARFON. BUT R. AKIBA SAYS: IF [IT WAS MEASURED] FOR ITS DEPTH,[3] IT COMES UNDER THE LAW OF 'IF WATER BE PUT'; BUT IF FOR ITS BREADTH, IT DOES NOT COME[4] UNDER THE LAW OF 'IF WATER BE PUT'.

MISHNAH 5. IF ONE PUT HIS HAND OR HIS FOOT OR A REED INTO A CISTERN IN ORDER TO ASCERTAIN WHETHER IT HAD ANY WATER, IT DOES NOT COME[5] UNDER THE LAW OF 'IF WATER BE PUT'; BUT IF TO ASCERTAIN HOW MUCH WATER IT HAD, THIS COMES[6] UNDER THE LAW OF 'IF WATER BE PUT'. IF ONE THREW A STONE INTO A CISTERN TO ASCERTAIN WHETHER IT HAD ANY WATER, [THE WATER] THAT WAS SPLASHED DOES NOT COME UNDER THE LAW OF 'IF WATER BE PUT', AND ALSO [THE WATER] THAT IS ON THE STONE[7] IS CLEAN.[8]

MISHNAH 6. IF ONE BEAT UPON A HIDE[9] OUTSIDE THE WATER, IT COMES[10] UNDER THE LAW OF 'IF WATER BE PUT';

(1) His intention was not to moisten any of the fruit, but to remove the moisture from the whole fruit as quickly as possible. (2) The water of the measuring-rod. (3) When the water on the measuring-rod is necessary, in order to indicate by its mark on the rod the exact depth of the water. (4) In measuring the breadth the water on the measuring-rod is immaterial for ascertaining the extent of the cistern. (5) The water on the hand or on the foot or on the rod is not wanted. (6) The water on the hand or on the foot or on the rod is wanted, in order to show by its mark the exact quantity of water in the cistern. (7) Even on the part of the stone above the surface of the water in the cistern. (8) It cannot contract an uncleanness nor can it cause susceptibility to uncleanness. (9) To remove the moisture after washing the hide in a pool. (10) The moisture coming out of the hide causes susceptibility, because there is here the intention of removing the moisture, as in the case of a tree which is shaken in order to drop the rain water from its branches, *supra* I, 2.

BUT IF [HE BEAT IT] INSIDE THE WATER,[1] IT DOES NOT COME[2] UNDER THE LAW OF 'IF WATER BE PUT'. R. JOSE SAYS: IT COMES UNDER THE LAW OF 'IF WATER BE PUT' ALSO IF [HE BEAT IT] INSIDE THE WATER, BECAUSE HIS INTENTION WAS THAT THE WATER SHOULD COME OFF TOGETHER WITH THE FILTH.[3]

MISHNAH 7. THE WATER THAT COMES UP INTO A SHIP OR INTO THE BILGE OR ON THE OARS DOES NOT COME[4] UNDER THE LAW OF 'IF WATER BE PUT'. THE WATER THAT COMES UP IN SNARES, NETS, OR GINS, DOES NOT COME[4] UNDER THE LAW OF 'IF WATER BE PUT'; BUT IF THEY WERE SHAKEN,[5] IT DOES COME[6] UNDER THE LAW OF 'IF WATER BE PUT'. IF A SHIP WAS LED OUT INTO THE GREAT SEA[7] IN ORDER TO TIGHTEN IT,[8] OR IF A NAIL[9] WAS TAKEN OUT INTO THE RAIN IN ORDER TO TEMPER IT, OR IF A BRAND WAS LEFT IN THE RAIN IN ORDER TO EXTINGUISH IT, THIS COMES[10] UNDER THE LAW OF 'IF WATER BE PUT'.

MISHNAH 8. [WATER ON] THE COVERING OF TABLES OR ON THE MATTING OF BRICKS DOES NOT COME[11] UNDER THE LAW OF 'IF WATER BE PUT'; BUT IF THEY WERE SHAKEN, IT DOES COME[12] UNDER THE LAW OF 'IT WATER BE PUT'.

MISHNAH 9. ANY UNINTERRUPTED FLOW OF LIQUID[13] IS CLEAN,[14] EXCEPT [THE FLOW] OF HONEY OF ZIPHIM[15] AND

(1) The hide is beaten while inside the pool in order to remove its hair and its filth. (2) There can be no intention here of removing moisture, since the hide still remains in the water. (3) In order to get on it fresh clean water and complete its cleansing. (4) One is indifferent to such water. (5) To remove the water. (6) The removal was done by intention, as in p. 490, n. 10. (7) The Mediterranean, or into any other sea. (8) To tighten the wooden planks which had become loose while the boat was ashore. (9) Hot from the fire. (10) In all these cases the water is desired. (11) The water is not wanted. (12) Cf. p. 490, n. 10. (13) Poured from a clean vessel into an unclean vessel. (14) In the upper vessel; cf. Ṭoh. VIII, 9; Yad. IV, 7. (15) According to an explanation in Soṭ. 58*b* the honey is so named after Ziph in the south of Judah; cf. Joshua XV, 55; Ps. LIV, 2.

OF BATTER.[1] BETH SHAMMAI SAY: ALSO [THE FLOW OF] THICK POTTAGE OF GRITS, OR OF BEANS, BECAUSE IT BOUNDS BACKWARDS.

MISHNAH 10. [THE FLOW] OF HOT WATER POURED[2] INTO HOT WATER, OF COLD WATER [POURED] INTO COLD WATER, OF HOT WATER [POURED] INTO COLD WATER REMAINS CLEAN; BUT [THE FLOW] OF COLD WATER [POURED] INTO HOT WATER BECOMES UNCLEAN.[3] R. SIMEON SAYS: ALSO [THE FLOW] OF HOT WATER POURED INTO HOT WATER BECOMES UNCLEAN IF THE STRENGTH OF THE HEAT OF THE LOWER [WATER] IS GREATER THAN THAT OF THE UPPER [WATER].[4]

MISHNAH 11. IF A WOMAN WHOSE HANDS WERE CLEAN STIRRED[5] AN UNCLEAN POT AND HER HANDS PERSPIRED, THEY BECOME UNCLEAN.[6] IF HER HANDS WERE UNCLEAN AND SHE STIRRED A CLEAN POT AND HER HANDS PERSPIRED, THE POT BECOMES UNCLEAN.[7] R. JOSE SAYS: ONLY IF HER HANDS DRIPPED.[8] IF GRAPES WERE WEIGHED IN THE SCALE OF A BALANCE, THE WINE[9] IN THE SCALE IS CLEAN[10] UNTIL IT IS POURED INTO A VESSEL.[11] LO, THIS IS LIKE BASKETS OF OLIVES AND GRAPES WHEN THEY ARE DRIPPING [WITH SAP].[12]

(1) צפחת. The meaning of this word is uncertain. It is usually taken as צפיחית, Ex. XVI 31. Maim. explains it as honey from a place called Ẓappaḥath. These are thick liquids, and when the flow stops suddenly, it is likely to bound back from the unclean vessel into the clean vessel, and thus render it unclean. (2) From a clean vessel into an unclean vessel. (3) The hot water in the unclean vessel causes steam to rise which mixes with the water in the clean vessel and renders it unclean. (4) Thus forming steam in the lower unclean vessel, which rises into the cooler clean vessel. (5) With a ladle. (6) The perspiration caused by the steam of the unclean pot renders her hands unclean. (7) By the perspiration of her unclean hands. (8) But not by the steam of the hot sweat. (9) The sap that escapes from the grapes. (10) Nor can it cause susceptibility to uncleanness. (11) Only then can it be considered a liquid. (12) Which likewise is not considered a liquid until it is poured into a vessel; cf. *infra* VI, 8.

MAKSHIRIN

CHAPTER VI

MISHNAH 1. IF ONE CARRIED UP HIS FRUIT TO THE ROOF BECAUSE OF MAGGOTS,[1] AND DEW CAME DOWN UPON IT, IT DOES NOT COME UNDER THE LAW OF 'IF WATER BE PUT'; BUT IF HIS INTENTION WAS FOR THIS PURPOSE,[2] IT COMES UNDER THE LAW OF 'IF WATER BE PUT'. IF A DEAF-MUTE, OR AN IDIOT, OR A MINOR CARRIED IT UP, ALTHOUGH HE EXPECTED THAT DEW SHOULD COME DOWN UPON IT, IT DOES NOT COME UNDER THE LAW OF 'IF WATER BE PUT', BECAUSE WITH THESE THE ACT ALONE COUNTS, BUT NOT THE INTENTION.[3]

MISHNAH 2. IF ONE CARRIED UP TO THE ROOF BUNDLES [OF VEGETABLES] OR CAKES OF FIGS OR GARLIC SO AS TO KEEP THEM FRESH, IT DOES NOT COME[4] UNDER THE LAW OF 'IF WATER BE PUT'. ALL BUNDLES [OF VEGETABLES] IN THE MARKET PLACES ARE UNCLEAN.[5] R. JUDAH DECLARES THEM CLEAN IF THEY ARE FRESH.[6] R. MEIR SAID: WHEREFORE HAVE THEY DECLARED THEM UNCLEAN? ONLY BECAUSE OF LIQUID FROM THE MOUTH.[7] ALL COARSE AND FINE FLOURS

(1) To prevent the fruit from becoming wormy. (2) To get the fruit damp by the dew. (3) Cf. *supra* III, 8. (4) If dew fell on the vegetables. (5) Because the dealers are wont to sprinkle them with water to keep them fresh, thus rendering them susceptible to uncleanness, and then they are handled by unclean hands. (6) Fresh vegetables are not sprinkled by the dealers, and thus have not become susceptible to uncleannes from unclean hands. (7) R. Meir holds that the reason why vegetables in the market have been declared unclean is not because they are handled by unclean hands, but because the dealers, who may be affected by a running issue (cf. *infra* 6), undo the bundles with their teeth, and thus cause unclean spittle from their mouth to come upon the vegetables. Therefore there is no difference whether the vegetables are fresh or not.

OF THE MARKET PLACES ARE UNCLEAN.[1] CRUSHED WHEAT, GROATS, AND PEARL-BARLEY[2] ARE UNCLEAN EVERYWHERE.[3]

MISHNAH 3. ALL EGGS MAY BE PRESUMED CLEAN EXCEPT THOSE OF DEALERS IN LIQUIDS;[4] BUT IF THEY SOLD WITH THEM DRY FRUIT, THEY ARE CLEAN.[5] ALL FISH MAY BE PRESUMED UNCLEAN.[6] R. JUDAH SAYS: PIECES OF ILTITH,[7] EGYPTIAN FISH WHICH ARRIVES IN A BASKET, AND SPANISH TUNNY, THESE MAY BE PRESUMED CLEAN.[8] ALL KINDS OF BRINE MAY BE PRESUMED UNCLEAN. CONCERNING ALL THESE[9] AN 'AM HA-AREẒ[10] MAY BE TRUSTED WHEN HE DECLARES THEM TO BE CLEAN, EXCEPT IN THE CASE OF FISH,[11] SINCE THEY[12] ARE USUALLY STORED WITH ANY 'AM HA-AREẒ.[13] R. ELIEZER B. JACOB SAYS: CLEAN BRINE INTO WHICH WATER FELL IN ANY QUANTITY MUST BE DEEMED UNCLEAN.[14]

MISHNAH 4. THERE ARE SEVEN LIQUIDS:[15] DEW, WATER, WINE, OIL, BLOOD,[16] MILK AND BEES' HONEY. HORNETS'

(1) Because the wheat is damped before milling, and thus the flour has become susceptible to uncleanness by the contact of those who handle it. (2) For the exact meaning of these kinds of grain, cf. M.Ḳ. 13*b*. (3) Even not in the market place, because they are damped in the process of crushing, and are then handled by unclean hands. (4) Who handle the eggs with liquid dripping from their hands and thus render them susceptible to become unclean by those who handle them. (5) Because they are careful to keep their hands dry. (6) Cf. 'Uḳ. III, 8. They have been rendered susceptible by the water shaken off from the nets. (7) A species of large fish. (8) These are spoilt by water, and have therefore been kept dry. (9) Eggs, fruit and brine. (10) עם הארץ. Lit., 'the people of the land', the untutored peasant, or any other person who is lax about the observance of the laws of purity and the laws of tithing produce, as distinguished from the learned חבר, or associate of those who are scrupulous about these laws. Cf. *supra* II, 10. n. 4; Demai, Introduction § 3; 'Ed. I, 14 (Sonc. ed.) p. 8, n. 1. (11) According to some commentators 'the brine of fish'. The *'am ha-areẓ* is not to be trusted when he declares that fish (or the brine of fish) has not become susceptible. (12) Var. lec. 'it', viz., fish. (13) Which proves that he can be trusted. (14) Water renders it susceptible, and it then becomes unclean by handling. (15) Which render produce susceptible to uncleanness. (16) Human blood, v. next Mishnah.

HONEY DOES NOT CAUSE SUSCEPTIBILITY TO UNCLEANNESS AND MAY BE EATEN.

MISHNAH 5. A SUB-SPECIES OF WATER[1] ARE THE LIQUIDS THAT COME FORTH FROM THE EYE, FROM THE EAR, FROM THE NOSE AND FROM THE MOUTH, AND URINE, WHETHER OF ADULTS OR OF CHILDREN,[2] WHETHER [ITS FLOW IS] CONSCIOUS OR UNCONSCIOUS. A SUB-SPECIES OF BLOOD ARE BLOOD FROM THE SLAUGHTERING OF CATTLE AND WILD ANIMALS AND BIRDS THAT ARE CLEAN, AND BLOOD FROM BLOODLETTING FOR DRINKING.[3] WHEY IS DEEMED LIKE MILK, AND THE SAP OF OLIVES IS DEEMED LIKE OIL, SINCE IT IS NEVER FREE FROM OIL.[4] THIS IS THE OPINION OF R. SIMEON. R. MEIR SAYS: EVEN THOUGH IT CONTAINS NO OIL. THE BLOOD OF A CREEPING THING IS DEEMED LIKE ITS FLESH,[5] IT CAUSES UNCLEANNESS BUT DOES NOT CAUSE SUSCEPTIBILITY TO UNCLEANNESS, AND WE HAVE NOTHING LIKE IT.[6]

MISHNAH 6. THE FOLLOWING CAUSE UNCLEANNESS AND ALSO SUSCEPTIBILITY[7] [TO UNCLEANNESS]; THE ISSUE[8] OF A PERSON WHO HAS A RUNNING ISSUE, HIS SPITTLE, HIS SEMEN AND HIS URINE, A QUARTER-LOG FROM A CORPSE, AND THE BLOOD OF A MENSTRUANT WOMAN. R. ELIEZER SAYS: SEMEN DOES NOT CAUSE SUSCEPTIBILITY. R. ELEAZAR B. 'AZARIAH SAYS: THE BLOOD OF A MENSTRUANT WOMAN DOES NOT CAUSE SUSCEPTIBILITY. R. SIMEON SAYS: THE BLOOD OF A CORPSE DOES NOT CAUSE SUSCEPTIBILITY, AND IF IT FELL ON A GOURD, IT SHOULD BE SCRAPED OFF,[9] AND IT REMAINS CLEAN.

MISHNAH 7. THE FOLLOWING CAUSE NEITHER UNCLEAN-

(1) That causes susceptibility under the heading of water. (2) According to other commentators: 'Whether liquid excrement or real urine'. (3) Its flow is desired. (4) It contains a proportion of oil. (5) It can be added to the flesh to make up a lentil's bulk which is the minimum quantity of a creeping thing to convey uncleanness; cf. Me'il. IV, 3. (6) That blood should be accounted as flesh. (7) Simultaneously. (8) Cf. Kelim I, 3. (9) Because blood is forbidden to be eaten.

NESS NOR SUSCEPTIBILITY TO UNCLEANNESS: SWEAT,[1] ILL-SMELLING SECRETION, EXCREMENT, BLOOD ISSUING WITH ANY OF THESE, LIQUID[2] [ISSUING FROM A STILL-BORN CHILD] OF EIGHT MONTHS (R. JOSE SAYS: EXCEPT ITS BLOOD),[3] [THE DISCHARGE FROM THE BOWELS OF] ONE WHO DRINKS THE WATER OF TIBERIAS[4] EVEN THOUGH IT COMES OUT CLEAN, BLOOD FROM THE SLAUGHTERING OF CATTLE AND WILD ANIMALS AND BIRDS THAT ARE UNCLEAN, AND BLOOD FROM BLOODLETTING FOR HEALING.[5] R. ELIEZER DECLARES THESE[6] UNCLEAN. R. SIMEON B. ELEAZAR SAYS: THE MILK OF A MALE IS CLEAN.[7]

MISHNAH 8. A WOMAN'S MILK RENDERS UNCLEAN WHETHER [ITS FLOW IS] DESIRED OR IS NOT DESIRED,[8] BUT THE MILK OF CATTLE RENDERS UNCLEAN ONLY IF [ITS FLOW IS] DESIRED. R. AKIBA SAID: THE MATTER CAN BE PROVED BY AN INFERENCE FROM MINOR TO MAJOR: IF A WOMAN'S MILK, THE USE OF WHICH IS CONFINED TO INFANTS, CAN RENDER UNCLEAN WHETHER [ITS FLOW IS] DESIRED OR IS NOT DESIRED, ALL THE MORE SHOULD THE MILK OF CATTLE, THE USE OF WHICH IS COMMON TO INFANTS AND TO ADULTS, RENDER UNCLEAN BOTH WHEN [ITS FLOW IS] DESIRED AND WHEN IT IS NOT DESIRED. BUT THEY[9] SAID TO HIM: NO; A WOMAN'S MILK RENDERS UNCLEAN WHEN [ITS FLOW IS] NOT DESIRED, BECAUSE THE BLOOD ISSUING FROM HER WOUND IS UNCLEAN;[10] BUT HOW COULD THE MILK OF CATTLE RENDER UNCLEAN WHEN [ITS FLOW IS] NOT DESIRED, SEEING THAT THE BLOOD ISSUING FROM ITS WOUND IS CLEAN? HE SAID TO THEM: I ADOPT A MORE RIGOROUS RULING IN THE CASE OF MILK THAN IN THE CASE OF BLOOD, FOR IF ONE MILKS

(1) Cf. *supra* II, 1. (2) Such as blood, urine, etc. (3) Its blood conveys impurity. (4) Which acts as a purgative. (5) Its flow is not desired. (6) The last two kinds of blood. (7) Like mere perspiration. (8) If it dripped from the breast automatically; cf. Kelim VIII, 11. (9) The Sages holding the opinion as given in the beginning of the Mishnah. (10) Like the blood of a corpse, and this blood flows from the wound automatically.

FOR HEALING,[1] [THE MILK] IS UNCLEAN,[2] WHEREAS IF ONE LETS BLOOD FOR HEALING, [THE BLOOD] IS CLEAN.[3] THEY SAID TO HIM: LET BASKETS OF OLIVES AND GRAPES PROVE[4] IT; FOR LIQUIDS FLOWING FROM THEM ARE UNCLEAN ONLY WHEN [THE FLOW IS] DESIRED, BUT WHEN [THE FLOW IS] NOT DESIRED THEY ARE CLEAN.[5] HE SAID TO THEM: NO; IF YOU SAY [THUS] OF BASKETS OF OLIVES AND GRAPES WHICH ARE AT FIRST A SOLID FOOD AND AT THE END BECOME A LIQUID, COULD YOU SAY [THE SAME] OF MILK WHICH REMAINS A LIQUID FROM BEGINNING TO END?[6] THUS FAR WAS THE ARGUMENT.[7] R. SIMEON SAID: FROM THENCEFORWARD WE[8] USED TO ARGUE BEFORE HIM: LET RAIN WATER PROVE IT, FOR IT REMAINS A LIQUID FROM BEGINNING TO END, AND RENDERS UNCLEAN ONLY WHEN [ITS FLOW IS] DESIRED. BUT HE SAID TO US: NO; IF YOU SAY [THUS] OF RAIN WATER, IT IS BECAUSE MOST OF IT IS INTENDED NOT FOR MAN[9] BUT FOR THE SOIL AND FOR TREES, WHEREAS MOST MILK IS INTENDED FOR MAN.

מסכת מכשירין

(1) An animal to relieve its pain. (2) It is capable of becoming unclean, since its flow is desired. (3) As stated in the last Mishnah. (4) Animal's milk may be compared to the juice flowing from such baskets, since both serve as human food. (5) Cf. *supra* V, 11, n. 11. (6) Milk is more of a liquid than fruit juice. (7) Between R. Akiba and his colleagues. (8) R. Akiba's disciples. (9) The use of rain for man is limited, therefore rain cannot render human food susceptible to uncleanness unless a man desires its flow upon his food.

ZABIM

TRANSLATED INTO ENGLISH

WITH NOTES

BY

RABBI DR S. M. LEHRMAN, M.A., PH. D.

INTRODUCTION

The Tractate Zabim ('they that suffer a flux'), comprising five chapters, is a detailed commentary of the Biblical Law concerning a man who has suffered a flux and a woman who has had a blood-issue outside her regular menstruation period. The text of the discussion is Lev. XV, 1–15, 25–30; and in accordance with the Rabbinic principle 'to erect a fence round the law', many precautions were added to those of the Bible. Thus any object on which they sat, rode or lay was defiled, as were those things that were directly or indirectly moved by, or bore the bulk of the pressure of the affected person. They even convey uncleanness to objects with which they, in turn, come into contact. To become a real *zab*, three issues on the same day or on consecutive days had to be experienced, after which the *zab* had to count seven 'clean' days, change all his clothes, and obtain immersion in running water. On the eighth day he had to bring two turtle-doves, or two young pigeons, for the priest to offer up; one as a sin-offering and the other as a burnt-offering.

Cleanliness, in Judaism, was regarded not only as next to godliness, but godliness itself. Neglect of one's health was regarded as a serious offence against God, in whose image man was shaped. This Tractate, discussing in elaborate detail a particular Biblical Law relating to bodily purity, has no greater aim than to emphasize once again that the entire system of Jewish Law has the hallowing of life as its goal; for it is holiness alone which suffuses life with a warm and noble glow. For if the body suffers ailments, the soul, too, will be tarnished. With spiritual cure, would inevitably come the bodily cure.

S. M. LEHRMAN

ZABIM

CHAPTER I

MISHNAH 1. IF A MAN HAS SEEN ONE ISSUE OF THE FLUX,[1] BETH SHAMMAI SAY: HE IS TO BE COMPARED TO [A WOMAN] WHO AWAITS DAY AGAINST DAY;[2] BUT BETH HILLEL SAY: HE IS TO BE COMPARED TO ONE WHO HAS SUFFERED [NOCTURNAL] POLLUTION.[3] SHOULD HE SEE AN ISSUE [ONE DAY], AND ON THE SECOND IT STOPPED, AND ON THE THIRD DAY HE SAW TWO [ISSUES], OR ONE [ISSUE] THAT WAS AS COPIOUS AS TWO,[4] BETH SHAMMAI SAY: HE IS A REAL ZAB;[5] BUT BETH HILLEL SAY: HE DEFILES THOSE OBJECTS ON WHICH HE SITS OR LIES, AND MUST ALSO OBTAIN IMMERSION IN RUNNING WATER, BUT HE IS EXEMPT FROM THE OFFERING.[6] R. ELEAZAR B. JUDAH SAID: BETH SHAMMAI CONCUR THAT IN SUCH A CASE HE CANNOT BE DEEMED A REAL ZAB;[7] WHERE

(1) A *zab* is one who is afflicted with gonorrhoea as distinct from a semen discharge. (2) Who, though not treated as a real *zabah* until she has had three issues (as defined), nevertheless defiles objects on which she sits or lies after the first issue; cf. Nid. 39*a*. Cf., however, ibid. 72*b*. (3) Cf. Lev. XV, 16ff. Such a one does not convey uncleanness to objects lain or sat upon; neither does it defile by carriage but only by contact. (4) I.e., the issue lasted as long as he could traverse during its duration a distance of fifty cubits. The measure of time usually employed is the time taken by man to immerse and dry himself. (5) Subject to all laws enumerated in Lev. XV, 11-15. When one has seen two issues on one day, or on two consecutive days, he must begin to count seven clean days, but is exempt from bringing a sacrifice; but if he has suffered three issues on one day, or on three consecutive days, he becomes a real *zab* and he must count seven clean days and bring a sacrifice (Lev. XV, 2-3). In the case of a woman, however, these three issues had to occur on three consecutive days. (6) The differentiating points of view between the two rival schools are these: Beth Shammai say a real *zab* is one who has beheld three issues, even if there was an interval of a fluxless day between the first and third, but according to Beth Hillel, the fluxless second day neutralizes the issue of the first. (7) Since the fluxless second day neutralizes the issue beheld on the previous day.

THEY DO DISPUTE IS IN THE CASE OF ONE WHO HAD SUFFERED TWO [ISSUES], OR ONE [ISSUE] THAT WAS AS COPIOUS AS TWO [ON ONE DAY], AND STOPPED ON THE SECOND DAY, AND ON THE THIRD DAY HE SAW ANOTHER [ISSUE]. IN SUCH A CASE BETH SHAMMAI SAY: HE IS A REAL ZAB;[1] BUT BETH HILLEL SAY: HE ONLY DEFILES THOSE OBJECTS ON WHICH HE SITS OR LIES, AND MUST OBTAIN IMMERSION IN RUNNING WATER, BUT IS EXEMPT FROM THE OFFERING.[2]

MISHNAH 2. IF ONE SUFFERS AN ISSUE OF SEMEN ON THE THIRD DAY OF COUNTING AFTER HIS FLUX,[3] BETH SHAMMAI SAY: IT RENDERS VOID THE TWO CLEAN DAYS THAT HAVE PRECEDED;[4] BUT BETH HILLEL SAY: IT RENDERS VOID ONLY THAT DAY.[5] R. ISHMAEL SAYS: IF HE SUFFERED IT ON THE SECOND DAY,[6] IT RENDERS VOID THE PRECEDING DAY;[7] BUT R. AKIBA SAYS: IT MATTERS NOT WHETHER HE SUFFERED IT ON THE SECOND OR THIRD DAY[8]—[IN EITHER CASE] BETH SHAMMAI SAY, IT RENDERS VOID THE TWO PRECEDING DAYS, AND BETH HILLEL SAY, IT RENDERS VOID ONLY THAT DAY ITSELF. BUT THEY[9] CONCUR THAT IF HE SUFFERED IT ON THE FOURTH DAY [OF COUNTING] IT RENDERS VOID ONLY THAT DAY [OF THE COUNTING],[10] PROVIDED IT WAS A DISCHARGE OF SEMEN; BUT IF IT HAD BEEN AN ISSUE OF FLUX, THEN EVEN IF THIS HAD OCCURRED ON THE SEVENTH DAY,

(1) Maintaining that since the counting of seven clean days has begun with the appearance of two issues on the first day, the fluxless second day is of no account, and it is as if he had beheld three issues; accordingly a sacrifice must be brought. (2) Due to the absence of issue on the second day, he cannot be pronounced as a real *zab*; hence no offering is brought. (3) Having suffered two issues of flux and thereupon commenced the counting of seven clean days. (4) And another counting of seven days must commence; Nid. 22*a*. (5) On which he suffered an issue of semen, and only five further days are to be counted; the first two being included in the total of seven. (6) I.e., he had counted one clean day and had beheld an issue of semen on the second day. (7) Even Beth Hillel agree that in such a case the preceding day is rendered void. (8) Maintaining that in such an instance the dispute holds good. (9) Beth Shammai. (10) Since three clean days had transpired.

IT RENDERS VOID ALL THE DAYS THAT HAD PRECEDED.[1]

MISHNAH 3. IF HE SAW ONE ISSUE ON ONE DAY AND TWO ON THE NEXT DAY, OR TWO ON ONE DAY AND ONE ON THE MORROW, OR THREE ON THREE [CONSECUTIVE] DAYS, OR THREE NIGHTS, HE IS DEEMED A REAL ZAB.[2]

MISHNAH 4. IF HE SAW ONE [ISSUE] AND A PAUSE TOOK PLACE OF SUFFICIENT DURATION TO ALLOW AN IMMERSION AND A DRYING,[3] AND AFTER THAT HE SAW TWO ISSUES, OR ONE AS COPIOUS AS TWO,[4] OR IF HE SAW TWO [ISSUES] OR ONE AS COPIOUS AS TWO, AND AN INTERVAL TOOK PLACE OF SUFFICIENT DURATION TO ALLOW AN IMMERSION AND A DRYING, AND AFTER THAT HE AGAIN SAW AN ISSUE, HE IS A REAL ZAB.

MISHNAH 5. IF HE SAW ONE ISSUE WHICH WAS AS COPIOUS AS THREE, LASTING AS LONG [AS IT TAKES TO GO] FROM GAD-YAWAN[5] TO SILOAH,[6] IN WHICH TIME ONE CAN BATHE AND DRY TWICE,[7] HE BECOMES A REAL ZAB. IF HE SAW ONE ISSUE WHICH WAS AS COPIOUS AS TWO, HE DEFILES [OBJECTS] ON WHICH HE LIES OR SITS AND MUST OBTAIN IMMERSION IN RUNNING WATER, BUT IS EXEMPT FROM BRINGING A SACRIFICE. R. JOSE SAID: THEY HAVE NOT SPOKEN OF ONE ISSUE AS COPIOUS UNLESS THERE WAS SUFFICIENT THEREIN TO MAKE UP THREE.[8]

(1) For the Bible lays emphasis on seven clean days; viz., until all the seven consecutive days are free from flux; v. Nid. 33*b*. (2) V. *supra* I, 2. (3) Less than this time is not accounted an interval, and the second flux is included with the first. To count it as two distinct issues, this lapse of time must ensue. (4) I.e., there is sufficient time between the commencement and conclusion of the flux for immersion and drying the body. (5) Gad (the God of Fortune) of the Greeks, cf. Isa. LXV, 11. Probably the name of a pool connected with Siloah, near Jerusalem; cf. Sanh. 63*b*. V. 'Er. 22*b*; Ṭoh. VI, 6. *Aliter:* the shrine of a pagan idol (Bert.). (6) Siloam; Isa. VIII, 6. (7) I.e., in which a distance of one hundred cubits can be traversed. (8) Only then was the sacrifice obligatory. According to R. Jose, no issue, copious as it was, could be deemed as more than one, unless quantitatively it contained the amount of three separate issues.

MISHNAH 6. IF HE BEHELD ONE ISSUE AT DAY-TIME AND ANOTHER AT TWILIGHT, OR ONE AT TWILIGHT AND THE OTHER ON THE MORROW, THEN IF IT WERE KNOWN[1] THAT PART OF THE ISSUE[2] OCCURRED AT DAY-TIME AND PART THEREOF ON THE MORROW,[3] HIS STATUS IS CERTAIN IN RESPECT OF A SACRIFICE AND UNCLEANNESS;[4] BUT IF IT IS IN DOUBT WHETHER PART [OF THE ISSUE] OCCURRED DURING THE DAY AND PART THEREOF [ON WHAT IS] THE DAY FOLLOWING,[5] HE IS IN A STATUS OF CERTAINTY IN RESPECT OF DEFILEMENT,[6] BUT IN ONE OF DOUBT IN RESPECT OF A SACRIFICE.[7] IF HE HAD SEEN ISSUES ON TWO SEPARATE DAYS AT TWILIGHT,[8] HIS STATUS IS IN DOUBT BOTH IN RESPECT OF DEFILEMENT[9] AND IN RESPECT OF A SACRIFICE.[10] IF [HE HAD SEEN ONLY] ONE ISSUE AT TWILIGHT, THERE IS A DOUBT [ALSO] IN RESPECT OF [HIS] DEFILEMENT.[11]

(1) I.e., theoretically, as in point of fact this cannot be ascertained. (2) Which was seen at twilight. (3) Even if there be not the stipulated time of immersion and drying between; the reason being that twilight is at the parting of two distinct days — a day dying and a day awaiting birth. (4) Having witnessed three issues; for the one at twilight, being at the parting of two days, is deemed as two. (5) For the issue may have terminated while it was yet day, or commenced only after nightfall. (6) Having at least beheld two issues. (7) Since it is questionable whether the issue at twilight is to be deemed one or two. (8) The first issue was when twilight commenced, and the second when twilight ended. An illustration: If he had seen an issue on Friday eve, with the appearance of twilight, and the second issue at the termination of the Sabbath — the Sabbath Day itself being issue-less — accordingly, he had not experienced two issues on two consecutive days. If, however, twilight is reckoned either as belonging to the day or night, there are two issues on two consecutive days, and the counting of seven clean days must commence, though no sacrifice is brought. On the other hand, if twilight be divided as partly belonging to day and partly to night, then the issue beheld is deemed as two, and together with the one witnessed in that day, constitute three issues, and sacrifice must be brought, though he must not eat thereof on account of doubt of its liability (Bert.). (9) Lest one clear day had elapsed between the two issues. (10) Since the twilight's issue may have been *bipartite*, belonging both to this day and the day following. (11) Lest it be only of sufficiency for one issue.

ZABIM

CHAPTER II

MISHNAH 1. ALL PERSONS[1] BECOME UNCLEAN THROUGH A FLUX, ALSO PROSELYTES AND SLAVES WHETHER FREED OR NOT, A DEAF-MUTE, AN IMBECILE OR MINOR, A EUNUCH WHETHER [HE HAD BEEN EMASCULATED] BY MAN, OR WAS A EUNUCH FROM [THE TIME OF SEEING] THE SUN.[2] UPON ONE WHOSE SEX WAS UNKNOWN, OR UPON A HERMAPHRODITE,[3] THE STRINGENCIES APPERTAINING TO BOTH MAN AND WOMAN ARE IMPOSED: THEY DEFILE THROUGH BLOOD LIKE A WOMAN, AND THROUGH FLUX[4] LIKE A MAN. THEIR UNCLEANNESS, HOWEVER, STILL REMAINS IN DOUBT.[5]

MISHNAH 2. ALONG [THE FOLLOWING] SEVEN LINES IS A ZAB EXAMINED AS LONG AS HE HAD NOT ENTERED THE BOUNDS OF ZIBAH:[6] [ENQUIRIES] AS TO [WHAT WAS] HIS FOOD,[7] DRINK,[8] AS [TO WHAT] HE HAD BORNE, WHETHER HE HAD JUMPED, WHETHER HE HAD BEEN ILL, WHAT HE HAD SEEN,[9] OR [WHETHER HE HAD] OBSCENE REFLECTIONS. [IT DIFFERED LITTLE] WHETHER HE HAD REFLECTED [OBSCENELY] PRIOR TO SEEING [A WOMAN], OR WHETHER HE HAD SEEN

(1) The term *'all'* is always inclusive in sense; here it serves to include even a child of a day old. (2) I.e., a eunuch by nature, v. Yeb. VIII, 4. (3) Cf. Bik. IV. (4) Lit., 'white'. (5) As a man he should be clean on experiencing a flow of blood; as a woman he should be clean on suffering a discharge of flux. If, however, he experienced a flow of both (blood and flux) then he is certainly unclean; and if he had touched *terumah* it has to be burnt. (6) If he had not yet suffered two issues that make it necessary for him to begin the seven days' counting, he is examined as to whether that second issue was not due to some accidental external cause, and hence treated like semen. (7) Solid meals of oily foods often precipitated a discharge of semen. (8) So did excessive drinking, and the carrying of heavy burdens. (9) The mere sight of a very attractive woman would also often be a cause.

[A WOMAN] PRIOR TO HIS [OBSCENE] REFLECTIONS.[1] R. JUDAH ADDS: EVEN IF HE HAD WATCHED BEASTS, WILD ANIMALS OR BIRDS HAVING INTERCOURSE WITH EACH OTHER, AND EVEN WHEN HE HAD SEEN A WOMAN'S DYED GARMENTS. R. AKIBA ADDED: EVEN IF HE HAD EATEN ANY KIND OF FOOD, BE IT GOOD OR BAD, OR HAD DRUNK ANY KIND OF LIQUID.[2] WHEREUPON THEY EXCLAIMED TO HIM: ['ACCORDING TO YOUR VIEW] THERE WILL BE NO ZABIM IN THE WORLD HENCEFORTH!'[3] HIS RETORT TO THEM WAS: 'YOU ARE NOT HELD RESPONSIBLE FOR THE EXISTENCE OF ZABIM!'[4] AS SOON, HOWEVER, AS IT HAD ENTERED THE BOUNDS OF ZIBAH,[5] NO FURTHER EXAMINATION TOOK PLACE.[6] [HIS FLUX] RESULTING[7] FROM AN ACCIDENT, OR THAT WAS AT ALL DOUBTFUL,[8] OR AN ISSUE OF SEMEN, THESE ARE UNCLEAN,[9] SINCE THERE IS WHEREON TO RELY.[10] IF HE BEHELD A FIRST [ISSUE] HE IS EXAMINED; ON THE SECOND [ISSUE] HE IS EXAMINED,[11] BUT ON THE THIRD [ISSUE] NO EXAMINATION TAKES PLACE.[12] R. ELIEZER SAYS: ALSO ON THE THIRD [ISSUE] HE IS EXAMINED TO ASCERTAIN HIS LIABILITY TO A SACRIFICE.

MISHNAH 3. IF ONE SUFFERED [A DISCHARGE OF] SEMEN

(1) For each independently could have been a cause of semen, and consequently it is not treated as flux. (2) Even such that do not usually suffuse the body with a glow of warmth. (3) Since few, if any, would as a result be declared as *zabim*. (4) Who says there must be *zabim* in the world! (5) I.e, after he had beheld two issues not accidentally. (6) Even if the third issue resulted from accidental causes he has to bring the prescribed sacrifice on becoming clean. Similarly, if during the counting of the seven clean days he had beheld a flux, though accidental, the counting must commence anew. (7) As enumerated above. (8) Whether it was semen or a flux. V. Nazir *66a*. (9) Defiling also by contact, v. Kel. I, 3. (10) Lit., 'the matter has feet (to stand on)'. No further evidence is necessary since we have already established the fact that he is a *zab*. (11) Whether or not it was accidental and thereby determine his obligation to bring a sacrifice should he have two more issues. Even if the first issue was pronounced as a result of accidental causes, but the second was natural, he defiles objects on which he sits or lies, requires immersion in running water, and the counting of seven clean days. (12) Neither for uncleanness nor for sacrifice.

HE DOES NOT CONVEY UNCLEANNESS BY REASON OF A FLUX[1] FOR TWENTY-FOUR HOURS.[2] R. JOSE SAYS: [ONLY] THAT DAY. IF A GENTILE EXPERIENCED A DISCHARGE OF SEMEN, AND HE BECAME A PROSELYTE, HE BECOMES IMMEDIATELY UNCLEAN BY REASON OF A FLUX.[3] IF [A WOMAN] HAD [AN ISSUE] OF BLOOD,[4] OR HAD EXPERIENCED DIFFICULTY [IN CHILDBIRTH],[5] [THE TIME PRESCRIBED] IS TWENTY-FOUR HOURS.[6] IF ONE SMITES HIS SERVANT, THE 'DAY OR TWO'[7] IS TWENTY-FOUR HOURS. IF A DOG ATE A CORPSE'S FLESH, THE THREE DAYS [DURING WHICH IT CONTINUES WITHIN] IN A NATURAL STATE ARE OF TWENTY-FOUR HOURS.[8]

MISHNAH 4. A ZAB[9] DEFILES THOSE OBJECTS ON WHICH HE LIES[10] BY FIVE WAYS, WITH THE RESULT THAT THEY [IN TURN] DEFILE MEN AND GARMENTS.[11] [THESE ARE:] BY STANDING, SITTING, LYING, LOUNGING OR LEANING. WHAT HE LIES UPON DEFILES MAN BY SEVEN WAYS, SO THAT HE [IN TURN] DEFILES GARMENTS.[11] [THESE ARE:] BY STANDING, SITTING, LYING, LOUNGING, OR LEANING UPON IT, OR BY TOUCHING OR CARRYING IT.[12]

(1) On the second issue. (2) Attributing the flux to some external cause, as in Mishnah 2. (3) A proselyte assumes the legal status of a newly-born child. Accordingly the flux beheld now that he is an Israelite has no connection with that experienced prior to his conversion. (4) The following instances are not germane to our theme, but are cited here to include these instances in which twenty-four hours is a criterion. (5) Outside the period of menstruation such blood-issue is not unclean. (6) For the former case v. Nid. *2a*, and for the latter, ibid *36b*. (7) Ex. XXI, 21. (8) V. Ohol. XI, 7. The examples above by no means exhaust all cases of twenty-four hours. (9) The *zab* is cited but it refers to a menstruant, a leper, or one who has given birth to a child. (10) Or sits upon. (11) I.e., the men in turn defiling the garments which they touched while still in contact with the unclean object. (12) Viz., the object which the *zab* had used as a couch.

ZABIM

CHAPTER III

MISHNAH 1. IF A ZAB AND ONE THAT WAS CLEAN SAT TOGETHER IN A BOAT, OR ON A RAFT, OR RODE TOGETHER ON A BEAST, THEY,[1] THOUGH THEIR GARMENTS HAD NOT ACTUALLY TOUCHED,[2] SUFFER MIDRAS[3] UNCLEANNESS. IF THEY SAT TOGETHER ON A PLANK, A BENCH OR A BEDFRAME,[4] OR ON A BEAM, WHEN THESE WERE NOT FIXED TIGHTLY,[5] [OR] IF THEY HAD BOTH CLIMBED A TREE OF INFERIOR STRENGTH,[6] OR [WERE SWAYING] ON A BRANCH OF INFERIOR STRENGTH[7] OF A FIRM TREE; OR IF THEY WERE BOTH [CLIMBING] ON AN EGYPTIAN LADDER,[8] NOT SECURED BY A NAIL,[9] OR IF THEY SAT TOGETHER ON A BRIDGE, RAFTER OR DOOR, NOT SECURED BY CLAY, THEY[10] ARE UNCLEAN. ACCORDING TO R. JUDAH THEY ARE CLEAN.

MISHNAH 2. IF THEY WERE BOTH[11] CLOSING OR OPENING [A DOOR], [HE THAT WAS CLEAN AND HIS GARMENTS BECOME UNCLEAN]. BUT THE SAGES SAY: [UNCLEANNESS IS NOT CONVEYED][12] UNLESS ONE WAS SHUTTING AND THE OTHER OPENING [IT].[13] IF ONE WAS LIFTING THE OTHER OUT OF A PIT [UN-

(1) The clean man and his garments. (2) The clean person, by his weight, causes the boat, raft or beast to sink to one side and rise at the other, thereby causing the *zab* to be lifted up or suspended by him. (3) V. Glos. (4) A frame on which a couch is spread; it used to be placed in a little bed-chamber and taken apart; or it was placed against the wall in day-time. *Aliter:* boards placed under a bed to prevent its rotting owing to the humidity of the ground below. (5) With the result that they both swayed and each leaned against the other. (6) The tree's strength was determined by ability to hollow out of its stem the size of a quarter of a *ḳab* (Bert.). (7) Which could be hidden in the palm of a man's hand; B.M. 105*a*. (8) Of the small variety; B.B. III, 6. (9) With the result that it bent. (10) The man that was clean and his garments. (11) The *zab* and the clean person. (12) From the *zab* to the clean man. (13) At the same time. The clean person thus bearing the counter-weight of the *zab*.

CLEANNESS IS CONVEYED]. BUT R. JUDAH SAID, ONLY IF HE THAT WAS CLEAN WAS PULLING OUT HIM THAT WAS UNCLEAN.[1] IF THEY WERE TWISTING ROPES TOGETHER [UNCLEANNESS IS CONVEYED]. BUT THE SAGES SAY, UNLESS THE ONE PULLED ONE WAY AND THE OTHER PULLED THE OTHER WAY. IF THEY WERE BOTH WEAVING TOGETHER, WHETHER THEY WERE STANDING OR SITTING, OR GRINDING WHEAT, [UNCLEANNESS IS CONVEYED]. R. SIMEON DECLARES [THE CLEAN MAN] IN EVERY CASE UNDEFILED, EXCEPT WHERE THEY [BOTH] WERE GRINDING WITH A HAND-MILL. IF THEY [BOTH] WERE UNLOADING OR LOADING AN ASS, THEY[2] ARE UNCLEAN IF THE LOAD WAS HEAVY, BUT CLEAN IF THE LOAD WAS LIGHT. IN BOTH CASES,[3] HOWEVER, THEY ARE CLEAN FOR MEMBERS OF THE SYNAGOGUE,[4] BUT ARE UNCLEAN FOR HEAVE-OFFERING.[5]

MISHNAH 3. IF THE ZAB AND THE CLEAN PERSON SAT TOGETHER IN A LARGE BOAT (WHAT IS A LARGE BOAT? R. JUDAH SAID: ONE THAT DOES NOT SWAY WITH A MAN'S WEIGHT), OR IF THEY SAT ON A PLANK, BENCH, BED-FRAME, OR BEAM WHEN THESE WERE FIRMLY SECURED;[6] OR IF THEY BOTH CLIMBED A STRONG TREE, A FIRM BRANCH, OR A TYRIAN[7] LADDER, OR AN EGYPTIAN LADDER FIXED BY A NAIL; OR IF THEY SAT ON A BRIDGE, RAFTER OR DOOR, WHEN THESE WERE FASTENED WITH CLAY, IF ONLY AT ONE END, THEY REMAIN CLEAN. IF THE CLEAN MAN STRUCK THE UNCLEAN, HE STILL REMAINS CLEAN;[8] BUT IF THE UNCLEAN STRUCK HIM THAT WAS CLEAN, HE BECOMES DEFILED; FOR [IN THAT CASE] IF HE THAT WAS CLEAN DREW BACK, THE UNCLEAN WOULD HAVE FALLEN.[9]

(1) In that case, the clean person is bearing the weight of the *zab*. This would not be so if the reverse was the case. (2) The man who was clean and his garments. (3) Be the load heavy or light. (4) Who eat *ḥullin* in purity, since doubt is attached if the clean person actually bore the weight of the *zab*. (5) This being a Rabbinic injunction even in the case of uncertain defilement. (6) Cf. *supra* III, 1. (7) Of a larger variety than the Egyptian ladder; v. B.B. III, 6. (8) From *midras* uncleanness, since he does not bear the weight of the *zab*. He and his garments do suffer *hesseṭ* uncleanness, having been 'shifted' by the *zab*; v. *infra* V, 1. (9) In his attempt to strike, hence it is as if the *zab* had actually leaned against him.

ZABIM

CHAPTER IV

MISHNAH 1. R. JOSHUA SAID: IF A MENSTRUANT[1] SAT IN ONE BED WITH ONE THAT WAS CLEAN, [EVEN] THE CAP ON HER[2] HEAD SUFFERS MIDRAS UNCLEANNESS; AND IF SHE SAT IN A BOAT, THE VESSELS ON THE TOP OF THE MAST [ALSO] CONTRACT MIDRAS UNCLEANNESS.[3] IF SHE TOOK A TUB FULL OF CLOTHES AND THEIR WEIGHT WAS HEAVY, THEY BECOME UNCLEAN,[4] BUT IF THEIR WEIGHT WAS LIGHT, THEY REMAIN CLEAN. IF A ZAB KNOCKED AGAINST A BALCONY AND THEREBY CAUSED A LOAF OF TERUMAH TO FALL DOWN, IT REMAINS CLEAN.[5]

MISHNAH 2. IF HE KNOCKED AGAINST A JOIST, A RAFTER-FRAME, WATER-SPOUT, OR SHELF, THOUGH FIXED WITH ROPES,[6] OR IF [HE KNOCKED AGAINST] AN OVEN, OR A FLOUR CONTAINER,[7] OR THE LOWER MILL-STONE, OR THE JACK[8] OF A HAND-MILL, OR THE SE'AH MEASURE[9] OF AN OLIVE-GRINDER, [THE LOAF REMAINS CLEAN].[10] R. JOSE ADDS: ALSO [IF HE KNOCKS] AGAINST THE BEAM OF THE BATH-KEEPER,[11] IT REMAINS CLEAN.

MISHNAH 3. IF HE KNOCKED AGAINST A DOOR, DOOR-

(1) Applies also to the *zab* and the clean person. (2) The clean person. (3) Defilement is contracted, though it be impossible for unclean persons to tread there. (4) Cf. *supra* III, 2. (5) Since its fall was not actually due to direct pressure of the *zab*, but to his vibration. (6) I.e., not with nails, as is usually done, to secure more firmness. (7) To collect the flour when wheat is ground. (8) The receptacle which harbours the hand-mill. (9) A large measure fixed in the ground. (10) Being considered firm enough to withstand the knocking of the unclean person; and since the falling of the loaf is only due to vibration, no defilement takes place. (11) On which he sits.

BOLT,[1] LOCK, OAR,[2] MILL-STONE FRAME,[3] OR AGAINST A WEAK TREE, OR WEAK BRANCH OF A STRONG TREE, OR AGAINST AN EGYPTIAN LADDER UNSECURED BY NAILS, OR AGAINST A BRIDGE, BEAM OR DOOR, NOT MADE SECURE WITH CLAY, THEY BECOME UNCLEAN.[4] [IF HE KNOCKED] AGAINST A CHEST,[5] BOX OR CUPBOARD, THEY BECOME UNCLEAN. R. NEHEMIAH AND R. SIMEON, HOWEVER, PRONOUNCE THEM CLEAN IN SUCH CASES.[6]

MISHNAH 4. A ZAB WHO LAY LENGTHWISE ACROSS FIVE BENCHES, OR FIVE MONEY-BAGS, [MAKES THEM] UNCLEAN,[7] BUT [IF HE LAY ACROSS] THEIR BREADTH, THEY ARE CLEAN.[8] IF HE SLEPT [ON THEM],[9] AND IT WAS FEARED LEST HE HAD TURNED HIMSELF ABOUT[10] ON THEM, THEY ARE UNCLEAN. IF HE WAS LYING ON SIX SEATS, WITH TWO HANDS ON TWO [SEATS], TWO FEET ON ANOTHER TWO, HIS HEAD ON ONE, WITH HIS BODY ON ANOTHER ONE, ONLY THAT ONE ON WHICH HIS BODY LAY[11] IS RENDERED UNCLEAN. IF [A ZAB] STOOD ON TWO SEATS, R. SIMEON SAYS: IF THESE WERE DISTANT ONE FROM THE OTHER, THEY REMAIN CLEAN.[12]

MISHNAH 5. IF THERE WERE PILED TEN CLOAKS ONE ON TOP OF THE OTHER AND HE SAT ON THE UPPERMOST ONE, ALL ARE UNCLEAN.[13] IF THE ZAB WAS IN ONE SCALE OF THE BALANCE AND IN THE OTHER SCALE OPPOSITE THERE WERE

(1) A door-pin fitting into sockets top and bottom. (2) Cf. Ezek. XXVII, 29. (3) A hopper to receive the flour dust. It was of a portable nature. (4) Being unsteady they bore the full weight of the *zab*. (5) A strong box; v. Git. 68*a*. (6) Referring to the last three objects, on account of their massive character. (7) Since the greater part of each had borne his weight as he lay on his back or stomach. (8) In this position his weight was not felt on each. (9) Across their breadth. (10) Lengthwise. (11) And which had borne his weight. The other seats also suffer minor uncleanness for having touched the *zab*, but they do not carry uncleanness to man and object. (12) For none had borne his full weight. (13) Not necessarily ten cloaks; for even if the *zab* sits on a large stone on top of one hundred cloaks, all the cloaks below become unclean, as objects on which the *zab* had sat.

OBJECTS FIT TO SIT OR LIE UPON, AND THE ZAB OVERWEIGHED, THEY ARE CLEAN;[1] BUT IF THEY OVERWEIGHED, THEY ARE UNCLEAN. R. SIMEON SAYS:[2] IF THERE WAS BUT ONE [PLACE][3] IT BECOMES UNCLEAN;[4] BUT IF THERE WERE MANY[5] THEY REMAIN CLEAN, SINCE NONE OF THEM HAD BORNE THE GREATER PART [OF THE ZAB'S WEIGHT].[6]

MISHNAH 6. IF A ZAB [SAT] IN ONE SCALE OF THE BALANCE, WHILST FOOD AND LIQUIDS WERE IN THE OTHER SCALE, [THE LATTER BECOME] UNCLEAN;[7] IN THE CASE OF A CORPSE,[8] HOWEVER, EVERYTHING[9] REMAINS CLEAN,[10] SAVE A MAN.[11] THIS IS [AN EXAMPLE OF] THE GREATER STRINGENCY APPLYING TO A ZAB THAN TO A CORPSE; AND THERE IS ALSO ANOTHER INSTANCE OF GREATER STRINGENCY IN THE CASE OF A ZAB THAN A CORPSE.[12] FOR WHEREAS THE ZAB DEFILES ALL OBJECTS ON WHICH HE SITS OR LIES UPON, SO THAT THESE LIKEWISE CONVEY UNCLEANNESS TO MEN AND GARMENTS,[13] AND CONVEY, MOREOVER, TO WHAT IS ABOVE HIM A MIDDAF UNCLEANNESS,[14] SO THAT THESE IN TURN DEFILE FOOD AND LIQUIDS, IN THE CASE OF A CORPSE NO SUCH UNCLEANNESS TAKES PLACE.[15] GREATER STRINGENCY IS ALSO

(1) I.e., from *midras* uncleanness, due to the absence of direct pressure from the *zab;* but they do contract minor uncleanness, *middaf* uncleanness (v. Glos.). (2) Following his view in Mishnah 4. (3) At the opposite end of the scale to sit or lie upon. (4) If that end went down the scales; in that case it bears the *zab's* full pressure. (5) Places opposite the *zab* fit to sit or lie upon. (6) Each of the places bearing only a minor part of his full weight. (7) Through pressure (*hesseṭ*), regardless of the fact which overweighed the other, as above. (8) I.e., if a corpse was in one of the scales. (9) In the other scale, whether food, liquids, or objects serving as seats or couches. (10) A corpse does not defile through pressure. (11) Who is defiled when he overweighs a corpse at the other end of the scale; cf. Nid. 69*a*. (12) Var. lec.: 'and there is greater stringency in the case of a corpse than a *zab*'. (13) V. *supra* II, 4. (14) Heb. מדף ('driving', 'breathing'). Hence slight or indirect contact. *Middaf* is not a 'father of uncleanness' but a minor grade, infecting only foods and liquids, but not men and vessels. Maimonides explains *middaf* as the stench arising from the corpse, thereby contaminating all surrounding objects. (15) The objects beneath the corpse do not defile man so that he should defile garments.

FOUND IN THE CASE OF A CORPSE, SINCE IT CAN CONVEY UNCLEANNESS BY OVERSHADOWING,[1] AND IMPOSES SEVEN DAYS' DEFILEMENT, WHEREAS IN THE CASE OF A ZAB NO SUCH UNCLEANNESS IS CONVEYED.

MISHNAH 7. IF HE SAT ON A BED AND THERE WERE FOUR CLOAKS UNDER THE FOUR LEGS OF THE BED, ALL BECOME UNCLEAN, SINCE THE BED CANNOT STAND ON THREE LEGS;[2] BUT R. SIMEON DECLARES THEM CLEAN.[3] IF HE RODE ON A BEAST[4] AND THERE WERE FOUR CLOAKS UNDER THE LEGS OF THE BEAST, THEY ARE CLEAN, SINCE THE BEAST CAN STAND UP ON THREE LEGS.[5] IF THERE WAS ONE CLOAK UNDER ITS TWO FORELEGS OR ITS TWO HINDLEGS, OR UNDER A FORELEG AND A HINDLEG, IT BECOMES UNCLEAN.[6] R. JOSE SAYS: A HORSE CONVEYS UNCLEANNESS THROUGH ITS HINDLEGS, BUT AN ASS THROUGH ITS FORELEGS, SINCE A HORSE LEANS UPON ITS HINDLEGS AND AN ASS UPON ITS FORELEGS. IF HE[7] SAT ON A BEAM OF AN OLIVE-PRESS, THE VESSELS IN THE OLIVE-PRESS[8] ARE UNCLEAN; BUT IF HE SAT ON A FULLER'S PRESS, THE GARMENTS BENEATH IT ARE CLEAN;[9] R. NEHEMIAH, HOWEVER, DECLARES THEM UNCLEAN.[10]

(1) Levitical uncleanness arising from being under the same roof with, or forming a shelter over, a corpse. (2) Each leg, therefore, can be said to support the whole weight of the *zab*. (3) Cf. *supra* IV, 5. (4) The beast remaining at a standstill; for were it trotting along, the cloaks would become unclean. For the animal always has in trotting one leg up, and really stands on three legs. (5) Each foot being regarded only as a help, but not as essential to bear the full weight of the *zab*. (6) Since an animal cannot remain standing on two legs, the cloak bore at one time the full weight of the *zab*. (7) The *zab*. (8) עקל is variously explained as a rope-basket in which olives are kept during the pressing process (Bert.); or a basket into which the pressed olives are thrown (so Maim.); cf. Meg. I, 7; Ṭoh. X, 8. (9) By sitting on a corner of the press, the garments that are being creased within do not bear his full weight (v. Bert.). (10) For it is impossible that some of the garments should not bear his full weight.

ZABIM

CHAPTER V

MISHNAH 1. HE WHO TOUCHES A ZAB, OR WHOM A ZAB TOUCHES, WHO MOVES[1] OR WHOM A ZAB MOVES, DEFILES FOOD AND LIQUIDS AND VESSELS THAT ARE RINSED[2] BY TOUCH, BUT NOT BY CARRIAGE.[3] THIS WAS THE GENERAL PRINCIPLE WHICH R. JOSHUA FORMULATED: ALL THOSE THAT DEFILE GARMENTS[4] WHILE STILL IN CONTACT [WITH THEIR SOURCE OF UNCLEANNESS] ALSO DEFILE FOODS AND LIQUIDS SO AS TO BECOME [UNCLEAN] IN THE FIRST GRADE, AND THE HANDS[5] SO THAT THEY BECOME [UNCLEAN] IN THE SECOND GRADE; BUT THEY DO NOT DEFILE MEN OR EARTHENWARE VESSELS. ONCE, HOWEVER, THEY HAVE BEEN SEPARATED FROM THEIR SOURCE OF UNCLEANNESS THEY DEFILE LIQUIDS SO AS TO BECOME [UNCLEAN] IN THE FIRST GRADE,[6] AND AND FOOD AND THE HANDS SO THAT THEY BECOME [UNCLEAN] IN THE SECOND GRADE,[7] BUT THEY DO NOT DEFILE GARMENTS.

MISHNAH 2. YET ANOTHER GENERAL PRINCIPLE DID THEY FORMULATE: ALL THAT IS CARRIED ABOVE A ZAB BECOMES DEFILED,[8] BUT ALL THOSE THINGS ABOVE WHICH

(1) By causing the board on which the *zab* stands to shake. (2) Which need only to be rinsed (immersed) in order to regain levitical purity. Made usually of wood or metal; those of earthenware must be broken when defiled; Lev. XV, 12. (3) If at the time of his contact with the *zab* he was carrying garments which had not been touched, they are clean. (4) Viz., those that are in contact with a *zab* or *zabah*. (5) Sc. of a clean person not touched by the *zab*. (6) Liquids suffer first-grade uncleanness even when touched not by those who are 'fathers', on account of their susceptibility to defilement, unlike foodstuffs which require special preparation to render them susceptible. (7) On account of their separation from the source. (8) Including such things not usually borne above a *zab*, and even if there were many things blocking the way between them.

HE IS CARRIED ARE CLEAN;[1] EXCLUDING SUCH OBJECTS ON WHICH HE CAN SIT OR LIE UPON,[2] AND A MAN. HOW SO? IF A ZAB HAD HIS FINGER[3] BENEATH A LAYER OF STONES AND ONE THAT WAS CLEAN WAS ABOVE,[4] HE CONVEYS UNCLEANNESS AT TWO [REMOVES], AND RENDERS UNFIT [TERUMAH] AT ONE [FURTHER REMOVE]. IF HE SEPARATED [FROM THE SOURCE OF UNCLEANNESS],[5] HE STILL DEFILES WITH FIRST-GRADE UNCLEANNESS AND RENDERS [TERUMAH] UNFIT AT YET ONE [FURTHER REMOVE]. IF THE UNCLEAN WAS ABOVE, AND THE CLEAN PERSON BELOW,[6] HE CONVEYS UNCLEANNESS AT TWO [REMOVES],[7] AND RENDERS [TERUMAH] UNFIT AT YET ONE [FURTHER REMOVE]. IF HE SEPARATED [FROM THE SOURCE OF UNCLEANNESS], HE DEFILES AT ONE [REMOVE] AND RENDERS [TERUMAH] UNFIT AT YET ONE [MORE REMOVE]. IF FOODS OR LIQUIDS, OR OBJECTS ON WHICH HE COULD SIT OR LIE UPON OR OTHER ARTICLES[8] WERE ABOVE,[9] THEY DEFILE AT THE TWO REMOVES,[10] AND RENDER [TERUMAH] UNFIT AT ONE [FURTHER REMOVE]. IF THEY HAD BECOME SEPARATED [FROM THE SOURCE OF UNCLEANNESS], THEY DEFILE AT ONE [REMOVE] AND RENDER [TERUMAH] UNFIT AT ONE [MORE REMOVE]. ALL OBJECTS FIT TO SIT OR LIE UPON THAT WERE BELOW[11] DEFILE AT TWO [REMOVES], AND RENDER [TERUMAH] UNFIT AT ONE [MORE

(1) Provided they are untouched. (2) Specially designated for this purpose. Also objects on which he can ride. (3) The bulk of the *zab's* body pressure being required only when he lies upon an object. (4) With such a layer thickness, the clean person cannot be said to be exerting pressure on the *zab;* yet he is here deemed to be carried by the *zab* and becomes a 'father of uncleanness'. (5) Either by removal of the *zab's* finger from beneath the layer of stones, or by the departure of the clean person from his stone seat. His uncleanness is then only of the first grade. (6) Having only his finger beneath the layer. (7) Since the *zab* is, as it were, carried by him. (8) Heb. *middaf,* i.e., the uncleanness of objects arising from their indirect contact with sources of impurity; such uncleanness was deemed to be only of a minor degree. Hence other articles not fit for sitting or lying on. (9) I.e., above the layer of stones beneath which was the *zab's* finger. (10) Objects on which he sits or lies upon always being deemed 'fathers of uncleanness'. (11) And that bore the brunt of the *zab's* pressure above.

REMOVE]. FOODS AND LIQUIDS AND OTHER ARTICLES[1] THAT ARE BELOW, REMAIN CLEAN.[2]

MISHNAH 3. SINCE IT WAS SAID[3] THAT WHATSOEVER CARRIES OR IS CARRIED BY OBJECTS ON WHICH ONE SITS OR LIES UPON REMAIN CLEAN, EXCLUDING THE CASE OF A MAN;[4] WHATSOEVER CARRIES OR IS CARRIED BY CARRION IS CLEAN,[5] SAVE HIM THAT MOVES IT.[6] R. ELIEZER ADDS: ALSO HE THAT CARRIES IT.[7] HE WHO CARRIES OR IS CARRIED UPON A CORPSE REMAINS CLEAN, SAVE WHEN OVERSHADOWING TAKES PLACE,[8] OR A MAN WHEN HE MOVES IT.[9]

MISHNAH 4. IF PART OF AN UNCLEAN PERSON[10] RESTS UPON A CLEAN PERSON, OR PART OF A CLEAN PERSON RESTS UPON AN UNCLEAN PERSON, OR IF THE CONNECTIVES[11] OF AN UNCLEAN PERSON REST UPON A CLEAN PERSON, OR THE CONNECTIVES OF A CLEAN PERSON UPON ONE UNCLEAN, HE[12] BECOMES UNCLEAN. R. SIMEON SAYS: IF PART OF AN UNCLEAN PERSON IS UPON A CLEAN PERSON, HE IS UNCLEAN;[13]

(1) V. p. 517, n. 8. (2) In accordance with the principle enunciated above which declared objects above which a zab was borne clean, save those things on which a man sits or lies. (3) This Mishnah explains the rule laid down in the one preceding, and gives a reason for proclaiming clean the foods and liquids below the layer of stones under which the *zab* had his finger. Var. lec. delete the words SINCE IT WAS SAID. (4) Who becomes defiled by carrying objects used for sitting purposes, even without touching or moving them. (5) Even if it were a man who was the carrier. (6) He becomes defiled. (7) Cf. Hul. 124*b* where this is emended to read: 'that is, if he carries it', and not just by moving it. (8) There can be a case of carrying without overshadowing, i.e., if there is a top storey intervening in which there are vessels weighing down boards of the ceiling of a room in which there is a corpse. (9) But if the corpse is not moved from its place, he is clean. (10) I.e., a *zab*, whose very finger defiles by the touch. (11) These are hair, nails or teeth. (12) Namely, the person that was clean. The point re-emphasized is that the full pressure of the bulk of the *zab's* body is required only when he is lying on an object. (13) Maintaining that even in this case it is essential for the bulk of a *zab's* body to be upon the clean person, if defilement was to be the result.

BUT IF PART OF A CLEAN PERSON IS UPON ONE THAT IS UNCLEAN, HE IS CLEAN.

MISHNAH 5. IF AN UNCLEAN PERSON[1] RESTS UPON PART OF AN OBJECT FIT TO LIE UPON, OR A CLEAN PERSON[1] RESTS UPON PART OF AN OBJECT FIT TO LIE UPON,[2] IT BECOMES UNCLEAN.[3] IF PART OF AN UNCLEAN PERSON RESTS ON AN OBJECT FIT TO LIE UPON, OR PART OF A CLEAN PERSON RESTS UPON SUCH AN OBJECT,[2] IT REMAINS CLEAN.[4] THUS WE FIND THAT UNCLEANNESS IS CONTRACTED AND CONVEYED BY THE LESSER PART THEREOF.[5] SIMILARLY,[6] IF A LOAF OF TERUMAH WAS PLACED UPON AN OBJECT FIT TO LIE UPON [THAT WAS UNCLEAN], AND THERE WAS A LAYER OF PAPER BETWEEN, WHETHER IT[7] WAS ABOVE OR BELOW, IT REMAINS CLEAN. SIMILARLY, IN THE CASE OF A STONE SMITTEN WITH LEPROSY[8] IT[9] REMAINS CLEAN;[10] BUT R. SIMEON PRONOUNCED SUCH A CASE UNCLEAN.[11]

MISHNAH 6. HE WHO TOUCHES A ZAB, OR A ZABAH, A MENSTRUANT, OR A WOMAN AFTER CHILDBIRTH, OR A LEPER, OR ANY OBJECT ON WHICH THESE HAD BEEN SITTING OR LYING, CONVEYS UNCLEANNESS AT TWO [REMOVES], AND RENDERS [TERUMAH] UNFIT AT ONE [FURTHER REMOVE].[12] IF HE HAD BECOME SEPARATED,[13] HE STILL CONVEYS UNCLEANNESS AT ONE [REMOVE], AND RENDERS [TERUMAH] UNFIT AT ONE [FURTHER REMOVE]. THIS IS THE CASE WHETHER HE

(1) Viz., the greater part of him. (2) Which was unclean. (3) Namely, that which had been clean. (4) Viz., the person or object hitherto clean. (5) Of what is fit to lie on. (6) In illustration of the first ruling in Mishnah 3. (7) I.e., the source of defilement. (8) Either below or above the loaf of bread separated by a piece of paper. (9) The loaf. (10) The leprous stone does convey uncleanness through overshadowing only to objects that are under the same roofing as itself. (11) Maintaining that a leprous stone defiles through overshadowing in the same way as a corpse. (12) The five sources of uncleanness enumerated are of so rigid a nature that their mere touch is sufficient to cause the defilement of garments and vessels. They are all 'fathers of uncleanness'. (13) From the original course of uncleanness.

HAD TOUCHED, OR HAD MOVED, OR HAD CARRIED, OR WAS CARRIED.[1]

MISHNAH 7. IF ONE TOUCHES THE FLUX OF A ZAB, HIS SPITTLE, SEMEN OR URINE, OR THE BLOOD OF A MENSTRUANT, HE CONVEYS UNCLEANNESS AT TWO [REMOVES], AND RENDERS [TERUMAH] UNFIT AT ONE [MORE REMOVE]; BUT IF HE BECAME SEPARATED,[2] HE DEFILES AT ONE [REMOVE] AND RENDERS [TERUMAH] UNFIT AT ONE [MORE REMOVE]. THIS IS THE CASE WHETHER HE HAD TOUCHED OR MOVED IT.[3] R. ELIEZER SAID: ALSO IF HE HAD LIFTED IT.[4]

MISHNAH 8. IF HE CARRIED THAT WHICH WAS RIDDEN UPON,[5] OR IF HE WAS CARRIED THEREON, OR HAD MOVED IT, HE DEFILES AT TWO [REMOVES], AND RENDERS [TERUMAH] UNFIT AT ONE [MORE REMOVE]; BUT IF HE BECAME SEPARATED [FROM THE UNCLEANNESS], HE DEFILES AT ONE [REMOVE] AND RENDERS [TERUMAH] UNFIT AT ONE [MORE REMOVE]. IF HE CARRIES CARRION, OR THE WATER OF THE SIN-OFFERING OF WHICH THERE WAS SUFFICIENT FOR A SPRINKLING,[6] HE DEFILES AT TWO [REMOVES], AND RENDERS [TERUMAH] UNFIT AT ONE [MORE REMOVE]; BUT IF HE BECAME SEPARATED,[2] HE DEFILES AT ONE [REMOVE] AND RENDERS [TERUMAH] UNFIT AT ONE [MORE REMOVE].

MISHNAH 9. HE WHO ATE OF THE CARRION OF A CLEAN BIRD, AND IT STILL IS IN HIS GULLET,[7] HE DEFILES AT TWO [REMOVES], AND RENDERS [TERUMAH] UNFIT AT ONE [MORE REMOVE]. IF HE PUT HIS HEAD WITHIN THE AIR-SPACE

(1) Even without touching; a law derived by the Rabbis from the Bible; cf. Pes. 67*b*, Shab. 3*b*. (2) From the source of uncleanness. (3) V. Mishnah 3, n. 5. (4) Bert. renders R. Eliezer's meaning thus: 'provided he had lifted it', maintaining that touching and moving alone are insufficient. The *halachah* does not concur with his point of view. (5) By the unclean enumerated in Mishnah 6. (6) This water defiles garments by carrying, but not by touch. If it is of insufficient quantity, it defiles by contact and not by mere carrying. (7) I.e., as long as it remains in his gullet he is regarded as a 'father of uncleanness'; V. Ṭoh. I. 1.

OF AN OVEN,[1] BOTH HE AND THE OVEN ARE CLEAN;[2] BUT IF HE VOMITED OR SWALLOWED IT, HE DEFILES AT ONE [REMOVE] AND RENDERS [TERUMAH] UNFIT AT ONE [MORE REMOVE].[3] BUT AS LONG AS IT IS STILL IN HIS MOUTH, THAT IS PRIOR TO SWALLOWING IT, HE REMAINS CLEAN.[4]

MISHNAH 10. HE WHO TOUCHES A DEAD REPTILE, OR SEMEN, OR HIM THAT HAS SUFFERED CORPSE UNCLEANNESS, OR A LEPER DURING HIS DAYS OF COUNTING,[5] OR WATER OF SIN-OFFERING OF INSUFFICIENT QUANTITY WITH WHICH TO PERFORM THE SPRINKLING,[6] OR CARRION, OR AN OBJECT RIDDEN UPON,[7] DEFILES AT ONE [REMOVE] AND RENDERS [TERUMAH] UNFIT AT ONE [MORE REMOVE].[8] THIS IS THE GENERAL PRINCIPLE: ALL WHO TOUCH ANY OBJECT REGARDED BY THE TORAH AS A 'FATHER OF UNCLEANNESS'[9] DEFILE AT ONE [REMOVE] AND RENDER [TERUMAH] UNFIT AT ONE [MORE REMOVE], WITH THE EXCLUSION [OF THE CORPSE] OF A MAN.[10] IF HE[11] HAD BECOME SEPARATED,[12] HE DEFILES AT ONE [REMOVE] AND RENDERS [TERUMAH] UNFIT AT ONE [MORE REMOVE].

MISHNAH 11. HE WHO HAS SUFFERED A [NOCTURNAL] POLLUTION IS LIKE ONE WHO HAS TOUCHED A DEAD REPTILE,[13] AND HE THAT HAS HAD CONNECTION WITH A MENSTRUANT

(1) And the carrion is still in his gullet. (2) Though he defiles garments, he cannot contaminate man or earthenware vessels. (3) Since he is no longer a 'father of uncleanness'; cf. Shebu. *9b*. (4) And not even the slightest uncleanness attaches to him; for the Bible makes the actual 'eating' the criterion; V. Lev. XXII, 8. (5) I.e., during the seven intermediate days between his first and second shaving. (6) Cf. Mishnah 8, n. 6. (7) By a *zab*. (8) All the things hitherto enumerated defile garments only with carrying, but not by touch; hence he who touches them, though still connected with the source of uncleanness, is not a 'father of uncleanness'. (9) I.e., a *zab*, menstruant, woman after childbirth, one who has suffered corpse-uncleanness and others not enumerated in the Mishnahs above. (10) He who touches it becomes a 'father of uncleanness' and remains so even after he had separated from the corpse, and consequently defiles at two removes, etc. (11) *Sc.* who touched a dead reptile etc. (12) From the source of defilement. (13) Who does not become a 'father of uncleanness' but suffers first-grade uncleanness only.

IS LIKE ONE WHO HAS SUFFERED CORPSE UNCLEANNESS.[1] HE WHO HAS HAD CONNECTION WITH A MENSTRUANT, HOWEVER, HAS THE MORE STRINGENT IMPOSITION IN THAT HE CONVEYS MINOR GRADES OF UNCLEANNESS TO WHAT HE LIES OR SITS UPON, SO AS TO MAKE FOODS AND LIQUIDS UNCLEAN.[2]

MISHNAH 12. THE FOLLOWING RENDER TERUMAH UNFIT:[3] ONE WHO EATS FOODS OF FIRST OR SECOND GRADE UNCLEANNESS, AND WHO DRINKS UNCLEAN LIQUIDS,[4] AND THE ONE WHO HAS IMMERSED HIS HEAD AND THE GREATER PART OF HIM IN WATER WHICH HAD BEEN DRAWN,[5] AND A CLEAN PERSON UPON WHOSE HEAD AND GREATER PART OF HIM THERE FELL THREE LOGS OF DRAWN WATER,[6] AND A SCROLL [OF SCRIPTURES],[7] AND [UNWASHED] HANDS,[8] AND ONE THAT HAS HAD IMMERSION THAT SAME DAY,[9] AND FOODS AND VESSELS WHICH HAVE BECOME DEFILED BY LIQUIDS.[10]

(1) Who is a 'father of uncleanness' suffering seven days' defilement. (2) Unlike the case of one who suffers corpse-defilement. V. Lev. XV, 7 with its insistence that only the *zab* renders vessels which serve as a seat or couch unclean; cf. Kel. I, 3. (3) V. Shab. 13*b* ff. (4) In these three instances second-grade uncleanness is contracted. The Rabbinic precaution was lest he eat of the *terumah* whilst these things are still in his mouth. (5) A further precaution lest the law of the ritual bath (*mikweh*) be forgotten from Israel. (6) For until he has obtained complete immersion his touch invalidates *terumah*. (7) Cf. Ṭoh. XV, 6; Yad. III, 2. (8) A precautionary measure in favour of *terumah*, v. Shab. 14*a*. (9) He must await sunset to be wholly pronounced clean. If in the meantime he touches *terumah* it must be burnt. (10) Being more susceptible to contract uncleanness they became impure at a first remove.

ṬEBUL YOM

TRANSLATED INTO ENGLISH

WITH NOTES

BY

RABBI DR S. M. LEHRMAN, M.A., PH.D.

INTRODUCTION

This little treatise is based on Lev. XXII, 7, and its four chapters comprising twenty-six paragraphs define the uncleanness still attaching to a *ṭebul yom*. This term connotes 'one who had immersed himself that day', that is, one who has incurred any uncleanness for which the Bible prescribed impurity 'until evening', though immersion had taken place during the day. The degree of uncleanness, however, in such a case is slight, being only of second grade, and affecting only *terumah* and holy things, on account of its greater sanctity and the stringency of the rules by which it is encircled. *Ḥullin* and other unsanctified objects may be touched by him without imparting to them any uncleanness. Another restriction on the *ṭebul yom* was that he was disallowed to enter the Temple beyond the Court of the Gentiles (Kel. I, 8).

The contents of this little book—to which there is no Talmud either in the Babylonian or Palestinian Talmud—are soon told. We are given instances where defilement is imparted to the entire object, of which only a part came into direct contact with the *ṭebul yom*. This leads to an important discussion as to what things can be described as 'connectives'. Liquids that became defiled by his touch are then reviewed, and finally an enumeration of those utensils that become likewise affected is given. Interesting also is the reference to those *halachic* rules which have undergone change in the process of time, and of those which were introduced by the *Soferim*, for which R. Joshua could give no adequate reason.

Characteristic of the Rabbinic consideration for the property and rights of the Israelite, the treatise ends with the protection provided by the Rabbinic Court in the case of an omission on the part of the individual to make important reservation as to his liability to *terumah*. With the laws of the *Prozbul* (v. Glos.), the *'erub* for the Sabbath Day, the concessions made in the case of the *'Agunah*, and other instances where measures were introduced to meet special exigencies, this further provision with which this volume closes is proof positive of the supreme solicitude Judaism shows for the needs of daily life.

S. M. LEHRMAN

ṬEBUL YOM

CHAPTER I

MISHNAH 1. IF ONE[1] HAD COLLECTED DOUGH-OFFERING[2] [PORTIONS] WITH THE INTENTION OF SEGREGATING THEM AFTERWARDS AGAIN, BUT IN THE MEANTIME THEY HAD BECOME STUCK TOGETHER,[3] BETH SHAMMAI SAY: THEY SERVE AS CONNECTIVES[4] IN THE CASE OF A ṬEBUL YOM. BUT BETH HILLEL SAY: THEY DO NOT SERVE AS CONNECTIVES. PIECES OF DOUGH[5] THAT HAD BECOME STUCK TOGETHER, OR LOAVES[5] THAT HAD BECOME JOINED, OR A BATTER-CAKE THAT HAD BEEN BAKED ON TOP OF ANOTHER BATTER-CAKE BEFORE IT COULD FORM A CRUST IN THE OVEN, OR IF THERE WAS FROTH[6] ON THE WATER THAT WAS BUBBLING, OR THE FIRST SCUM[7] THAT RISES WHEN BOILING GROATS OF BEANS, OR THE SCUM OF NEW WINE (R. JUDAH SAYS: ALSO THAT OF RICE) BETH SHAMMAI SAY: ALL SERVE AS CONNECTIVES IN THE CASE OF THE ṬEBUL YOM. BUT BETH HILLEL SAY: THEY DO NOT SERVE AS CONNECTIVES.[8] THEY[9] CONCUR, HOWEVER,

(1) The priest made a house-to-house collection and piled the pieces of dough on top of each other. (2) V. Num. XV, 18-21; v. Glos., s. v. *Ḥallah*. (3) Lit., 'and they bit'. (4) To *ḥallah* is attributed the same sanctity and the same degree of susceptibility to uncleanness as to *terumah*, and hence it becomes '*pasul*' (unfit) if touched by the *ṭebul yom*. Even if only part were touched the whole becomes unclean; for it is regarded as one inseparable mass. (5) Of *terumah*, and so in all that follows we are concerned with *terumah*. (6) קולית 'something hollow or round'; a hollow ball of water, bubble. The water needed for *terumah* shares its stringencies; hence if a *ṭebul yom* touches the froth or first scum, he conveys uncleanness to the whole, according to Beth Shammai. (7) The first scum does not yet render the beans into one solid mass, yet Beth Shammai already regard it as a connective. (8) The distinction between *ḥallah* and *terumah* is that whereas the former comprises only a Rabbinical injunction in these times, the latter even now enjoys the rank of a Biblical command, hence both cases had to be stated (L.). (9) Beth Hillel. They dispute only in the case of a *ṭebul yom*, since he lacks only sunset to be wholly clean.

[THAT THEY SERVE AS CONNECTIVES] IF THEY COME INTO CONTACT WITH OTHER KINDS OF UNCLEANNESS, WHETHER THEY BE OF MINOR[1] OR MAJOR GRADES.[2]

MISHNAH 2. IF ONE HAD COLLECTED PIECES OF DOUGH-OFFERING NOT WITH THE INTENTION OF SEGREGATING THEM AFTERWARDS, OR A BATTER-CAKE THAT HAD BEEN BAKED ON ANOTHER AFTER A CRUST HAD FORMED IN THE OVEN,[3] OR A FROTH HAD APPEARED IN THE WATER PRIOR TO ITS BUBBLING UP, OR THE SECOND SCUM THAT APPEARED IN THE BOILING OF GROATS OF BEANS, OR THE SCUM OF OLD WINE, OR THAT OF OIL OF ALL KINDS,[4] OR OF LENTILS (R. JUDAH SAYS: ALSO THAT OF BEANS[5])—ALL THESE ARE RENDERED UNCLEAN[6] WHEN TOUCHED BY A ṬEBUL YOM. AND NEEDLESS TO SAY, [THIS IS THE CASE IF TOUCHED] BY OTHER SOURCES OF UNCLEANNESS.

MISHNAH 3. THE KNOB[7] ON THE BACK OF THE LOAF, OR THE SMALL GLOBULE OF SALT,[8] OR THE BURNT CRUST LESS THAN A FINGER'S BREADTH—R. JOSE SAYS: WHATSOEVER IS EATEN WITH THE LOAF BECOMES UNCLEAN [WHEN TOUCHED BY THE ṬEBUL YOM].[9] AND NEEDLESS TO SAY, THIS IS SO [WHEN TOUCHED] BY OTHER UNCLEAN THINGS.

MISHNAH 4. A PEBBLE IN A LOAF OR A LARGE GLOBULE OF SALT, OR A LUPINE,[10] OR A BURNT CRUST LARGER THAN A FINGER'S BREADTH,[11] [DO NOT SERVE AS CONNECTIVES]. BUT

(1) Derived uncleanness. (2) A 'father of uncleanness' (3) For once a crust has formed it is hard to separate them, and the two cakes are considered as one. (4) Lit., 'always'; i.e., both old or new oil. (5) Or 'vetchlings'. (6) If of *terumah*. (7) The peg-shaped attachment to a loaf supposed to serve as a trade mark. (8) That had become stuck to the loaf and baked with it. (9) And since they are occasionally eaten with the loaf, they serve as connectives. (10) On account of their extreme hardness lupines had to be cooked at least six times before they were fit to be eaten. (11) These things served either as trade marks or marked the grades of the loaf. As such they were 'never eaten, and hence could not be deemed as connect-

R. JOSE SAYS: [ONLY] WHATSOEVER THAT IS NOT EATEN WITH THE LOAF REMAINS CLEAN EVEN WHEN TOUCHED BY A 'FATHER OF UNCLEANNESS';[1] AND NEEDLESS TO SAY [IS THIS SO WHEN TOUCHED] BY A ṬEBUL YOM.

MISHNAH 5. UNSHELLED[2] BARLEY OR SPELT, ROOT OF CROWFOOT,[3] ASAFOETIDA,[4] SILPHIUM[5] (R. JUDAH SAYS: BLACK BEANS)[6] REMAIN CLEAN[7] EVEN [WHEN COMING INTO CONTACT] WITH A 'FATHER OF UNCLEANNESS', LET ALONE [IF TOUCHED] BY A ṬEBUL YOM. SO R. MEIR: BUT THE SAGES SAY: THEY ARE CLEAN IF TOUCHED BY A ṬEBUL YOM, BUT UNCLEAN [WHEN TOUCHED] BY OTHER SOURCES OF DEFILEMENT. IN THE CASE OF SHELLED BARLEY OR SPELT, OR WHEAT EITHER WITH THE HUSK ON OR WITHOUT IT, OR BLACK CUMMIN, OR SESAME OR PEPPER (R. JUDAH SAYS: ALSO WHITE BEANS), THEY BECOME UNCLEAN EVEN WHEN TOUCHED BY A ṬEBUL YOM,[8] LET ALONE [WHEN THEY HAVE COME INTO CONTACT] WITH OTHER SOURCES OF UNCLEANNESS.

ives for the bread, even when touched by a 'father of uncleanness' itself.

(1) Where they are eaten with the loaf even these serve as connectives. (2) A state unfit for human consumption, accordingly not susceptible to uncleanness. (3) Used as a spice, but considered noxious for beasts. (4) An umbelliferous plant used as a resin, or in leaves, for a spice, or for medicinal purposes; cf. Shab. 14*a*, Ḥul. 58*b*. (5) A mucilaginous plant; Lat. '*Alum*', of the same species as asafoetida. (6) Which were used specifically for medicinal purposes. (7) Since only the smallest portion was placed in the food, they cannot be regarded as food and susceptible to uncleanness. (8) Since they are all regular food ingredients.

ṬEBUL YOM

CHAPTER II

MISHNAH 1. LIQUIDS THAT ISSUE[1] FROM A ṬEBUL YOM ARE LIKE THOSE[2] WHICH HE HAS TOUCHED: NEITHER OF THEM HAS POWER TO DEFILE.[3] WITH REGARD TO ALL OTHERS THAT ARE UNCLEAN, BE THEY OF MINOR[4] OR MAJOR[5] [DEGREE], THE LIQUIDS ISSUING FROM THEM ARE LIKE THOSE THEY TOUCH; BOTH ARE CONSIDERED OF FIRST GRADE UNCLEANNESS.[6] THE SOLE EXCEPTION BEING SUCH LIQUID THAT IS IN ITSELF A 'FATHER OF UNCLEANNESS'.[7]

MISHNAH 2. IF A POT WAS FULL OF LIQUID AND A ṬEBUL YOM TOUCHED IT, THE LIQUID BECOMES UNFIT IF IT IS TERUMAH, BUT THE POT IS CLEAN.[8] BUT IF THE LIQUID IS COMMON FOOD [ḤULLIN] THEN ALL REMAINS CLEAN.[9] IF HIS HANDS WERE SOILED, ALL BECOMES UNCLEAN.[10] HERE GREATER STRINGENCY IS APPLIED TO SOILED HANDS THAN TO A ṬEBUL YOM; BUT GREATER STRINGENCY IS APPLIED TO A ṬEBUL YOM THAN TO SOILED HANDS, SINCE ANY DOUBT RESPECTING THE ṬEBUL YOM RENDERS TERUMAH UNFIT, BUT ANY DOUBT CONCERNING [SOILED] HANDS IS DEEMED CLEAN.[11]

(1) Such as spittle, urine, tears, blood of a wound and milk from a woman (Bert.). (2) Of *terumah*. (3) Suffering only third grade uncleanness. (4) When touched by a dead reptile. (5) When coming into contact with a *zab*. (6) Bestowing second and third grade respectively. (7) As, for instance, the issue of a person with a flux, a *zab*. (8) For it is only *terumah*, on account of its great sanctity that even a *ṭebul yom* can invalidate. *Terumah* that becomes unfit cannot in its turn convey uncleanness. (9) Since a *ṭebul yom* cannot render unclean *ḥullin* or tithe-offerings. (10) Soiled hands defile liquids (v. Parah VIII, 7); when liquids are thus defiled they become first grade uncleanness, making vessels second grade. (11) Such as a doubt arising as to which of the two loaves of *terumah* lying before him the *ṭebul yom* has touched, when we

MISHNAH 3. IF THE PORRIDGE WAS OF TERUMAH AND THE GARLIC OR OIL [IT CONTAINED] WAS OF ḤULLIN, AND A ṬEBUL YOM TOUCHED PART OF THEM, THEN THE WHOLE BECOMES UNFIT;[1] BUT IF THE PORRIDGE WAS OF ḤULLIN AND THE GARLIC OR OIL IT CONTAINED WAS OF TERUMAH, AND A ṬEBUL YOM TOUCHED PART OF THEM, HE RENDERS UNFIT ONLY THE PART HE HAS TOUCHED.[2] IF THE GREATER PART WAS GARLIC THEN THEY GO AFTER THE MAJORITY.[3] WHEN IS IT SO?[4] SAID R. JUDAH: WHEN IT[5] FORMED ONE COHESIVE MASS IN THE POT, BUT IF IT WAS SCATTERED SMALL IN THE MORTAR, THEN IT IS CLEAN, SINCE IT IS HIS WISH THAT IT SHOULD BE SO SCATTERED.[6] [SIMILARLY] WITH ALL OTHER MASHED FOODS WHICH WERE MASHED WITH LIQUIDS;[7] THOSE, HOWEVER, WHICH ARE USUALLY MASHED[8] WITH LIQUIDS AND YET WERE MASHED WITHOUT LIQUIDS, THOUGH[9] THEY FORMED ONE COHESIVE MASS IN THE POT, ARE REGARDED AS A CAKE OF PRESERVED FIGS.[10]

MISHNAH 4. IF THE PORRIDGE AND BATTER-CAKE[11] WERE OF ḤULLIN AND THE OIL OF TERUMAH WAS FLOATING ABOVE THEM, AND A ṬEBUL YOM TOUCHED THE OIL, HE RENDERS UNFIT ONLY THE OIL. IF, HOWEVER, HE STIRRED IT ALTOGETHER, ALL THE PLACES WHITHER THE OIL GOES BECOME UNFIT.[12]

pronounce both to be unclean. In the case, however, of soiled hands the loaves are clean; cf. Yad. II, 4.

(1) Even if he touched merely the oil and garlic, these as ingredients serve as connectives to the porridge. (2) The porridge cannot serve as a connective to the garlic and oil. (3) The porridge in this case can serve as a connective. (4) That if he touches the garlic the whole porridge is rendered unclean. (5) The garlic. (6) To be used in small portions as ingredients; in which case it cannot be regarded as a connective for the other contents in the mortar. (7) A distinction is made as to whether they are served whole in the pot or whether they are mashed in the mortar. (8) Var. lec.: But with all other mashed . . . . with liquids or that are usually mashed etc. (9) V. L. (10) In which case we do not say that if part thereof is touched, all becomes unclean; single figs are not regarded as connectives. (11) This is the wafer that used to be placed into the jelly or porridge. (12) Being impossible to separate oil.

MISHNAH 5. IF A FILM OF JELLY[1] HAD FORMED OVER THE FLESH OF HALLOWED THINGS, AND A ṬEBUL YOM HAD TOUCHED THE JELLY, THE SLICES [OF FLESH] ARE CLEAN;[2] BUT IF HE TOUCHED ONE OF THE SLICES, THAT SLICE AND ALL [THE JELLY] THAT COMES UP WITH IT[3] FORM A CONNECTIVE THE ONE WITH THE OTHER. R. JOḤANAN B. NURI SAYS: THE TWO OF THEM SERVE AS CONNECTIVES TO EACH OTHER.[4] SIMILARLY, WITH [COOKED] BEANS THAT HAVE FORMED A LAYER OVER PIECES OF BREAD.[5] BEANS COOKED IN A POT, AS LONG AS THEY ARE STILL SEPARATE, DO NOT SERVE AS CONNECTIVES; BUT WHEN THEY BECOME A SOLID PULP,[6] THEY DO ACT AS CONNECTIVES. IF THEY FORMED SEVERAL SOLID PULPS,[7] THEY ARE TO BE COUNTED.[8] IF OIL FLOATS ON WINE AND A ṬEBUL YOM TOUCHED THE OIL, ONLY THE OIL IS RENDERED UNFIT; BUT R. JOḤANAN B. NURI SAYS: EACH SERVES AS A CONNECTIVE WITH THE OTHER.[9]

MISHNAH 6. IF A JAR[10] HAD SUNK INTO A CISTERN CONTAINING WINE,[11] AND A ṬEBUL YOM TOUCHED IT, AND [HE TOUCHED IT] WITHIN THE RIM,[12] IT SERVES AS A CONNECTIVE;[13] BUT IF OUTSIDE THE RIM,[14] IT DOES NOT ACT AS A CONNECTIVE. R. JOḤANAN B. NURI, HOWEVER, SAYS: EVEN THOUGH [THE LEVEL OF WINE IN THE CISTERN] IS THE HEIGHT OF A

(1) This jelly comprises all the pot ingredients which had become congealed. (2) Not regarding the jelly as a connective. (3) But the other jelly does not serve as a connective. (4) Hence, even if he touches the film of the jelly, the slices of flesh become unclean. (5) Which were usually spread with beans. (6) The process of cooking first splits them, then forms them into a solid pulp. (7) And then came into contact with a dead reptile. (8) If the separate pulps touched each other. That touched by a dead reptile becomes first grade unclean; the piece that touches that which is 'first grade' becomes second grade unclean. (9) So that if the *ṭebul yom* touched the oil, the wine also is rendered unfit. (10) Containing wine of *terumah*. (11) Of *ḥullin;* and this wine flowing into the jar floats on the surface, forcing the *terumah* wine to the bottom of the jar. (12) Touching the *ḥullin* wine floating on top. (13) Though he did not come into contact with the *terumah*. (14) I.e., he does not touch the wine inside the jar, but only the *ḥullin* wine floating round the jar.

MAN[1] [ABOVE THE SUNKEN JAR], AND HE TOUCHED [THE WINE] DIRECTLY ABOVE THE MOUTH OF THE JAR, IT SERVES AS A CONNECTIVE.

MISHNAH 7. IF A JAR[2] HAD A HOLE EITHER AT ITS NECK,[3] BOTTOM OR SIDES, AND A ṬEBUL YOM TOUCHED IT [AT THE HOLE], IT BECOMES UNCLEAN.[4] R. JUDAH SAYS: ONLY IF THE HOLE IS AT ITS NECK OR BOTTOM IT BECOMES UNCLEAN; BUT IF ON ITS SIDES, ON THIS SIDE OR ON THAT, IT REMAINS CLEAN.[5] IF ONE POURED [LIQUID] FROM ONE VESSEL INTO ANOTHER, AND A ṬEBUL YOM TOUCHED THE STREAM, AND THERE WAS SOMETHING WITHIN THE VESSEL, THEN [WHATSOEVER HE TOUCHES] IS NEUTRALIZED IN A HUNDRED AND ONE.[6]

MISHNAH 8. IF A BUBBLE[7] OF A JUG WAS PIERCED WITH HOLES ON ITS INNER SIDE AND ON ITS OUTER SIDE, WHETHER ABOVE OR BELOW,[8] [AND THE HOLES ARE] OPPOSITE ONE ANOTHER, IT BECOMES UNCLEAN [IF TOUCHED] BY A 'FATHER OF UNCLEANNESS';[9] AND IT [LIKEWISE] BECOMES UNCLEAN

(1) Even if the wine in the cistern rises above the sunken jar up to a man's height, and he touches the wine directly above the mouth of the jar, it serves as a connective and the whole jar's contents become unclean. (2) Containing wine of *terumah*. (3) Var. lec. omit. (4) Since the hole causes the wine to flow into it, the part touched serves as a connective. (5) His view-point being that only when the hole is at the neck or bottom may all the wine pass through it; but when it is at its sides, only a small portion of the wine will pass through. The portion he touches, which alone is invalidated, becomes neutralized in one hundred and one times the quantity; cf. Ter. V, 4. (6) I.e., if the wine in the receiving vessel is a hundred times the quantity of that he had touched, maintaining that only the stream of liquid is defiled, and does not act as a connective. It is like a case of unclean *terumah* getting mixed with clean *terumah*, where neutralization is 1 : 101. In the case of major sources of uncleanness, the stream of liquid serves as a connective and defiles all the liquid in both vessels. (7) An imperfection found in a clay jar formed while it was being baked. If pierced on the inner and outer side when the jar is filled the liquid penetrates the bubble through the inner hole and in its attempt to seek exit surges through the outer one. (8) I.e., on top or at the bottom of the jar. (9) And if he touched the hole on the outer side, all the wine in the jar becomes unclean.

IF IT IS IN A TENT WHEREIN LIES A CORPSE.[1] IF THE INNER HOLE IS BELOW AND THE OUTER ABOVE, IT BECOMES UNCLEAN [IF TOUCHED] BY A 'FATHER OF UNCLEANNESS', AND IT BECOMES UNCLEAN IN A TENT WHEREIN THERE IS A CORPSE; IF THE INNER HOLE IS ABOVE AND THE OUTER BELOW, IT REMAINS CLEAN IF TOUCHED BY A 'FATHER OF UNCLEANNESS',[2] BUT IT BECOMES UNCLEAN IN A TENT WHEREIN THERE IS A CORPSE.[3]

(1) And even if the mouth of the jar was sealed with 'a tightly stopped-up cover'; cf. Kel. X, 2. (2) A stream of liquid can serve as a connective only with what is below but not with what is above. (3) The holes serving as a door for the uncleanness to penetrate into the vessel.

ṬEBUL YOM

CHAPTER III

MISHNAH 1. ALL [STALKS THAT SERVE AS] HANDLES TO FRUITS, WHICH COUNT AS CONNECTIVES WHEN TOUCHED BY A 'FATHER OF UNCLEANNESS', ALSO COUNT AS CONNECTIVES WHEN TOUCHED BY A ṬEBUL YOM. IF A FOODSTUFF WAS SEVERED YET A SMALL PART WAS STILL ATTACHED, R. MEIR SAYS: IF ONE TAKES HOLD OF THE LARGER PART AND THE SMALLER PART IS PULLED AWAY WITH IT, THEN THE LATTER IS REGARDED AS THE FORMER.[1] R. JUDAH, HOWEVER, SAYS: IF ONE TAKES HOLD OF THE SMALLER PART AND THE GREATER IS ALSO PULLED AWAY WITH IT, THEN THE LATTER IS LIKE THE FORMER. R. NEHEMIAH SAYS: [THIS REFERS ONLY] TO THE CASE OF THE CLEAN PORTION,[2] BUT THE SAGES SAY: [IT REFERS ONLY] TO THE UNCLEAN PORTION.[3] IN THE CASE OF ALL OTHER FRUITS,[4] THOSE USUALLY HELD BY THE LEAF SHOULD BE TAKEN BY THE LEAF, AND THOSE USUALLY HELD BY THE STALK SHOULD BE TAKEN BY THE STALK.[5]

MISHNAH 2. IF A BEATEN EGG WAS ON TOP OF VEGETABLES OF TERUMAH,[6] AND A ṬEBUL YOM TOUCHES THE EGG, THEN HE RENDERS UNFIT ONLY THAT STALK [OF THE VEGE-

(1) Serving as a connective, so that if the *ṭebul yom* touches one portion, the other, too, is affected. (2) I.e., this estimation is only made of the part untouched by the *ṭebul yom*, and if it is pulled away with the part touched, whether it be larger or smaller, it becomes unclean; v. Ḥul. 127*b*. (3) According to the Sages this estimation is only made of the part that had become unclean, and if it was pulled away with the clean part it becomes unclean. (4) Vegetables. (5) And if the whole becomes severed then each part serves as a connective. It is obvious that if the bigger portion is pulled away together with the smaller, it serves as a connective to the smaller. (6) Within a pot. Were the egg whole, it would not have served as a connective.

TABLES] THAT IS OPPOSITE THE PART [OF THE EGG] HE TOUCHED.[1] R. JOSE, HOWEVER, SAYS: IT AFFECTS THE WHOLE OF THE UPPER LAYER;[2] AND IF IT WAS ARRANGED LIKE A CAP[3] IT DOES NOT SERVE AS A CONNECTIVE.

MISHNAH 3. THE STREAK OF AN EGG[4] THAT HAD BECOME CONGEALED ON THE SIDE OF A PAN THAT HAD BEEN TOUCHED BY A ṬEBUL YOM WITHIN THE RIM [OF THE PAN], SERVES AS A CONNECTIVE;[5] BUT IF OUTSIDE THE RIM, IT DOES NOT SERVE AS A CONNECTIVE. R. JOSE MAINTAINS THAT ONLY THE STREAK AND THE PART THAT CAN BE PEELED AWAY WITH IT [SERVES AS A CONNECTIVE].[6] THE SAME APPLIES TO BEANS THAT HAD FORMED A LAYER OF JELLY ON THE RIM OF THE POT.[7]

MISHNAH 4. DOUGH[8] THAT HAD BEEN MIXED [WITH DOUGH OF TERUMAH], OR THAT HAD BEEN LEAVENED WITH YEAST OF TERUMAH, IS NOT RENDERED UNFIT BY [THE TOUCH OF] A ṬEBUL YOM;[9] R. JOSE AND R. SIMEON, HOWEVER, PRONOUNCE IT UNFIT. DOUGH[10] THAT HAD BECOME SUSCEPTIBLE [TO UNCLEANNESS] BY A LIQUID,[11] AND IT WAS KNEADED

(1) Though the egg is *ḥullin*, which cannot be defiled by a *ṭebul yom*, yet those vegetables exactly opposite the part of the egg touched are rendered unclean. (2) Viz., the whole top layer of the stalk on which the egg lies is affected. (3) In cooking the eggs get blown up, forming a helmet-shape over the vegetables with vacant space between it and the vegetables below. Since the egg does not, therefore, actually touch the vegetables, it cannot be counted among the connectives. (4) Boiled with *terumah* that is liable to be invalidated by a *ṭebul yom*. (5) Rendering all the contents unclean. (6) Even if the streak of the egg is without the pan. (7) Having the same ruling as eggs. (8) Of *ḥullin*; cf. Ḥal. I, 4. (9) Since the *ṭebul yom* cannot defile the *ḥullin* in the dough. Though the mixture is forbidden to non-priests it is not deemed in this respect of the rank of *terumah* because the prohibition of the mixture is only due to Rabbinical injunction; for according to Biblical ruling it is neutralized in the proportion of 1 : 2; v. 'Orlah II, 6. (10) Of *terumah*. (11) V. Lev. XI, 38. Edibles coming into contact with liquids become susceptible provided that such liquid was applied purposively, or whose presence on the food was at least acceptable.

WITH FRUIT JUICE,[1] AND LATER TOUCHED BY A ṬEBUL YOM, R. ELEAZAR B. JUDAH OF BARTHOTHA SAYS IN THE NAME OF R. JOSHUA: IT BECOMES TOTALLY UNFIT.[2] R. AKIBA, HOWEVER, SAYS IN HIS NAME: HE RENDERS UNFIT ONLY THE PART THAT HE TOUCHED.[3]

MISHNAH 5. IF VEGETABLES OF ḤULLIN WERE COOKED WITH OIL OF TERUMAH AND A ṬEBUL YOM TOUCHED IT, R. ELEAZAR B. JUDAH OF BARTHOTHA SAYS IN THE NAME OF R. JOSHUA: IT BECOMES TOTALLY UNFIT.[4] R. AKIBA, HOWEVER, SAYS IN HIS NAME: HE RENDERS UNFIT ONLY THE PART THAT HE TOUCHED.[5]

MISHNAH 6. IF A CLEAN PERSON CHEWED FOOD AND IT FELL ON HIS GARMENTS AND ON A LOAF OF TERUMAH, IT[6] IS NOT RENDERED SUSCEPTIBLE TO UNCLEANNESS.[7] IF HE ATE CRUSHED OLIVES OR MOIST DATES WITH THE INTENTION OF SUCKING THE STONE THEREOF, AND IT FELL ON HIS GARMENTS AND ON A LOAF OF TERUMAH, [THE LATTER] BECOMES SUSCEPTIBLE TO UNCLEANNESS.[8]. IF, HOWEVER, HE ATE DRIED OLIVES, OR DRIED FIGS WITHOUT THE INTENTION OF SUCKING THE STONE THEREOF, AND THEY FELL ON HIS GARMENTS AND ON A LOAF OF TERUMAH, THE LATTER IS NOT RENDERED SUSCEPTIBLE TO UNCLEANNESS.[9] THIS IS THE CASE IRRESPECTIVE OF THE FACT WHETHER IT WAS A

(1) Which was not one of the seven liquids enumerated in Maksh. VI, 4 that rendered foods susceptible. If the dough had not received water before, the fruit juice now does not make it susceptible. (2) Contending that the fruit juice serves the dough as a connective. (3) Maintaining that since fruit juice does not make the dough susceptible, it is deemed non-existent. (4) Being of the opinion that oil renders susceptible and acts as a connective. (5) Being of the opinion that fruit juice, even which renders susceptible, such as oil, does not serve as a connective with the dough to defile it, since the dough is *ḥullin*. (6) The loaf. (7) Lit., 'is clean'. Since this liquid was not dropped on purpose (Maim.). (8) Since his intention was to extract juice, he should have known that some would fall on the loaf. (9) For on no account could the moisture have been said to have been applied on purpose.

CLEAN MAN OR A ṬEBUL YOM [WHO WAS EATING]. R. MEIR SAYS: IN EITHER CASE IT BECOMES SUSCEPTIBLE TO UNCLEANNESS IN THE CASE OF A ṬEBUL YOM, SINCE LIQUIDS ISSUING FROM UNCLEAN PERSONS RENDER ANYTHING SUSCEPTIBLE REGARDLESS OF THE ACCEPTABILITY OF THEIR PRESENCE OR NOT. BUT THE SAGES SAY: A ṬEBUL YOM IS NOT REGARDED AS AN UNCLEAN PERSON.[1]

(1) Accordingly, he cannot make all liquids, whether acceptable or not, predisposed to uncleanness. Cf. Maksh. I.

ṬEBUL YOM

CHAPTER IV

MISHNAH 1. IF FOOD THAT WAS TITHE-OFFERING HAD BEEN RENDERED SUSCEPTIBLE BY A LIQUID, AND A ṬEBUL YOM OR UNWASHED HANDS[1] TOUCHED IT, TERUMAH OF TITHE[2] MAY STILL BE SET APART FROM IT IN PURITY, SINCE IT ONLY SUFFERED THIRD GRADE UNCLEANNESS, AND THIRD GRADE UNCLEANNESS COUNTS AS CLEAN IN ḤULLIN.

MISHNAH 2. A WOMAN THAT HAD IMMERSED HERSELF THE SAME DAY MAY KNEAD DOUGH, CUT OFF THE DOUGH-OFFERING,[3] AND SET IT APART, BUT MUST PLACE IT ON AN INVERTED BASKET OF TWIGS,[4] OR ON A TRAY[5], AND THEN BRING IT NEAR[6] AND DECLARE IT BY ITS NAME.[7] FOR IT[8] SUFFERED ONLY THIRD GRADE UNCLEANNESS,[9] AND THIRD GRADE UNCLEANNESS IS DEEMED AS CLEAN IN ḤULLIN.

MISHNAH 3. IN A TROUGH WHICH HAD BEEN IMMERSED THAT VERY DAY, ONE MAY KNEAD DOUGH AND CUT OFF THE PORTION FOR ḤALLAH AND BRING IT NEAR AND EVEN PRO-

(1) Both possessing second grade impurity only. (2) Given to the priest by the Levite from the tithe received from the Israelites (Num. XVIII, 25*ff*.); this was regarded as *ḥullin*, which a *ṭebul yom* could not defile. Accordingly, this additional tithe could be taken therefrom. (3) But without designating it as such; for once this is done it is no longer *ḥullin*. (4) Not susceptible to uncleanness. This was stipulated in order that she may no longer touch the dough-offering. (5) Which does not possess distinct receptacles and consequently is not susceptible to uncleanness. Neither of these two vessels is 'susceptible'. (6) To the rest of the dough, of which it is to constitute a portion dedicated as *ḥallah*. For this requirement v. Ḥal I, 9. (7) *Ḥallah*. (8) I.e., the dough she had touched. (9) Since the *ṭebul yom* possesses only second grade uncleanness.

NOUNCE IT BY NAME [AS ḤALLAH];[1] FOR IT[2] SUFFERS ONLY THIRD GRADE UNCLEANNESS AND A THIRD GRADE COUNTS AS CLEAN IN ḤULLIN.

MISHNAH 4. IF A FLAGON THAT HAD BEEN IMMERSED THE SAME DAY AND HAD BEEN FILLED OUT OF A CASK CONTAINING TITHES FROM WHICH THE HEAVE-OFFERING[3] HAD NOT YET BEEN TAKEN, AND ONE SAID, LET THIS BE HEAVE-OFFERING OF TITHE AFTER NIGHTFALL,[4] IT BECOMES HEAVE-OFFERING OF TITHE. BUT IF HE SAID: LET THIS BE THE FOOD FOR THE [SABBATH] 'ERUB,[5] HIS REMARKS ARE NOT VALID AT ALL.[6] IF THE CASK WAS BROKEN,[7] THE CONTENTS OF THE FLAGON STILL REMAIN TITHE FROM WHICH HEAVE-OFFERING HAD NOT YET BEEN TAKEN;[8] IF THE FLAGON IS BROKEN,[9] THEN WHAT IS IN THE CASK STILL REMAINS TITHE FROM WHICH HEAVE-OFFERING HAD NOT YET BEEN TAKEN.[10]

MISHNAH 5. FORMERLY THEY USED TO SAY: ONE MAY

(1) On account of an uncleanness it had contracted. From the *ṭebul yom* the Mishnah now turns to a vessel that had been immersed that very day. The point stressed is that we are not afraid lest it be exchanged for anything unclean. (2) I.e., the dough which has touched the kneading-trough. (3) The tithe which the Levite has to give to the priest from the tithe he receives. (4) I.e., when the flagon becomes completely clean. (5) Lit., 'mixture'. According to Sabbath law, the movements of people in a town are restricted on a Sabbath to two thousand cubits from the boundaries of a town. But if enough food for his meals is despatched in an accessible place on the eve of Sabbath, at the prescribed two thousand cubits' distance, this spot counts as a man's temporary abode, thereby allowing him a range of two thousand cubits beyond the common Sabbath limit. Similarly, an '*erub* may be arranged as between various domiciles within a courtyard; for if all the occupants have a share in the deposit of food placed in a known place in the courtyard, they are all thereby given unrestricted access to the premises of the other occupants. (6) Because an '*erub* can only be made of such food that is ready to be eaten before sunset; but here nightfall is still needed to make it permissible for common use. (7) Before nightfall. (8) For when heave-offering could at last be taken therefrom, it was already non-existent. (9) While yet day. (10) Cf. n. 6.

REDEEM[1] FOR THE PRODUCE OF AN 'AM HA-AREẒ.[2] LATER THEY RECONSIDERED AND SAID: ALSO FOR MONEY OF HIS.[3] FORMERLY THEY USED TO SAY: IF A MAN IS LED OUT IN CHAINS[4] AND COMMANDS: 'WRITE A BILL OF DIVORCE FOR MY WIFE', IT HAD TO BE WRITTEN AND DELIVERED;[5] BUT AFTER CONSIDERATION THEY ADDED THE CASE OF A MAN UNDERTAKING A SEA VOYAGE, OR SETTING OUT WITH A CARAVAN.[6] R. SIMEON OF SHEZUR ADDED THE CASE OF ONE WHO WAS AT THE POINT OF DEATH.[7]

MISHNAH 6. ASHKELON LEVERS[8] THAT HAD BECOME BROKEN, ONLY THEIR HOOKS STILL REMAINING, ARE SUSCEPTIBLE TO UNCLEANNESS.[9] A PITCH-FORK, WINNOWING-FAN, RAKE[10] [SO, TOO, A HAIR COMB], WHICH HAD LOST ONE OF ITS TEETH, AND ANOTHER OF METAL WAS CONSTRUCTED FOR IT, ARE ALL SUSCEPTIBLE TO UNCLEANNESS.[11] CONCERNING ALL THESE,[12] R. JOSHUA SAID: THIS IS A NEW THING WHICH

(1) Second-tithe money in Jerusalem; Deut. XIV, 22*ff*. The owner had to take his money to Jerusalem, there to spend it, or else he had to 'redeem' it by putting aside coins of value (plus one fifth) in order to make that produce free for use as *hullin;* the coins themselves then count as second-tithe money, to which their sanctity is transferred, or to other coins for which they, in turn, may be exchanged. These coins were taken to Jerusalem, there to be exchanged for food, or peace-offerings, and consumed in purity. (2) Though one tithe could not be used in exchange for another, we do not suspect the *'am ha-areẓ* of tithing his produce (Bert.). (3) Without fearing that this money itself may be of second-tithe products (Bert.). (4) As a prisoner; Giṭ. VI, 5. (5) Although he did not say 'deliver it', we surmise that his omission is due to the perturbed state of his mind. (6) These expeditions in olden times used to be fraught with serious danger. (7) There could be no greater perturbation of mind than this; moreover, in this state, breath is scarce and words must be used economically. (Though the last statement of the Mishnah is somewhat irrelevant to the main issue, yet the Mishnah follows the usual practice of citing other similar statements). (8) With which pitchers used to be hooked out of the wells. *Aliter:* 'pitched stands' or 'water coolers'; Kel. XIII, 7. (9) Since they can still serve their purpose they are still regarded as vessels. (10) An agricultural implement with many teeth, forming a sort of sieve whereby to separate the grain from the chaff; Kel. ibid. (11) As metal utensils. (12) Some opine that 'all these' refer to *supra* IV, 2.

THE SCRIBES HAVE MADE AND I HAVE NOTHING TO REPLY.[1]

MISHNAH 7. IF ONE WAS TAKING TERUMAH[2] FROM A CISTERN AND SAID: 'LET THIS BE TERUMAH PROVIDED IT COMES UP SAFELY', [IT IS IMPLIED THAT HE MEANT] SAFELY FROM BEING BROKEN OR SPILLED,[3] BUT NOT FROM CONTRACTING UNCLEANNESS;[4] BUT R. SIMEON DECLARES: ALSO FROM UNCLEANNESS.[5] IF IT WERE BROKEN,[6] IT DOES NOT RENDER [THE CONTENTS OF THE CISTERN] SUBJECT TO THE RESTRICTIONS OF TERUMAH. HOW FAR AWAY[7] CAN IT BE BROKEN AND STILL NOT MAKE IT SUBJECT TO TERUMAH RESTRICTIONS? ONLY SO FAR THAT IF IT ROLLS BACK, IT CAN REACH THE CISTERN.[8] R. JOSE ADDS: EVEN IF ONE HAD THE INTENTION OF MAKING SUCH A STIPULATION, BUT DID NOT DO SO, AND IT GOT BROKEN, IT DOES NOT NEVERTHELESS MAKE IT SUBJECT TO TERUMAH RESTRICTIONS, FOR THIS IS A STIPULATION LAID DOWN BY THE BETH DIN.[9]

(1) 'To those who would question their ruling'. Perhaps he was inclined himself to agree with the critics. (2) Of wine or oil. (3) A common fear; and if the wine or oil is spilled in the cistern, no *terumah* was taken. (4) Accordingly, even if it becomes unclean it is still regarded as *terumah*. (5) Being assumed that he meant also safe from contamination. The significance of his stipulation is the object of discussion. (6) And the wine fell back into the cistern. (7) From the cistern. (8) For such a short distance is included in his stipulation. (9) The Beth din took for granted that each person desires to make such stipulations, only is deterred from so doing by forgetfulness.

YADAYIM

TRANSLATED INTO ENGLISH

WITH NOTES

BY

DR ISIDORE FISHMAN, PH. D., M. A.

INTRODUCTION

The Tractate Yadayim ('Hands') deals mainly with the ritual uncleanness of the hands and with the *Halachic* rules governing their cleansing.

The necessity for the ritual cleansing of the hands is nowhere stated in the Bible. The Rabbis found some support for this institution in Lev. XV, 11, *And whomsoever he that hath the issue toucheth, without having rinsed his hands in water* (Ḥul. 106*a*). The development of this rite can, however, be traced through its various stages. Solomon is said to have enacted that the hands must be cleansed before touching food (Shab. 15*a*). By the beginning of the first century, the rite was well established as it is included among the eighteen decrees of Beth Shammai which prevailed against the views of Beth Hillel, namely, that the hands be cleansed before touching *terumah*, the underlying reason being that hands are constantly in use and become dirty very quickly (Shab. 15*a*). To ensure the observance of this decree it was further laid down that hands are at all times in the second degree of uncleanness and therefore if they touched *terumah* without having been cleansed first, would render it 'unfit' (Yad. III, 2 and notes *infra*).

Finally the rite was extended to the eating of common food, *ḥullin* (Ḥag. II, 4 and 18*b*). This was introduced in order to accustom a person to cleanse his hands at all times before handling food, and thus ensure that *terumah* would not be touched by unclean hands (Ḥul. 106*a*). The hygienic reason is, of course, obvious (cf. Tosaf. Ḥul. 106*a* s.v. מצוה).

This final extension of the rite must have taken place by the early part of the first century, as it formed one of the chief breaches between Jesus and the Pharisees.[1] It was certainly widespread among the people in the time of the Amoraim, who laid great stress on the importance of the cleansing of the hands. For example,

(1) V. Büchler, A, *Der Galiläische 'Am ha-areẓ des Zweiten Jahrhunderts*, (1906) pp. 114, 126-130; Klausner, J., *Jesus of Nazareth* (1925) pp. 288*ff*; and Allon, G., Tarbiz IX (1938) pp. 186*ff*.

the neglect of washing the hands is stated to be one of the three things which bring a man to poverty (Shab. 62*b*). And according to R. Abbahu, anyone who eats bread with unwashed hands is as though eating unclean bread (Soṭ. 4*b*).

CONTENTS

ISIDORE FISHMAN

YADAYIM

CHAPTER I

MISHNAH I. [A MINIMUM OF] A QUARTER [OF A LOG][1] OF WATER MUST BE POURED[2] OVER THE HANDS[3] [TO BE SUFFICIENT] FOR ONE [PERSON] AND IS EVEN [SUFFICIENT] FOR TWO;[4] A MINIMUM OF HALF[5] A LOG MUST BE POURED OVER THE HANDS [TO BE SUFFICIENT] FOR THREE OR FOUR PERSONS;[6] ONE LOG OR MORE [IS SUFFICIENT] FOR FIVE, TEN, OR ONE HUNDRED PERSONS.[7] R. JOSE SAYS: BUT PROVIDED ONLY THERE IS NOT LESS THAN A QUARTER OF A LOG LEFT FOR THE LAST PERSON AMONG THEM. MORE [WATER] MAY BE ADDED TO THE SECOND WATER,[8] BUT MORE MAY NOT BE ADDED TO THE FIRST WATER.[9]

(1) A *log* is a liquid measure equal in quantity to the liquid contents of six eggs. Cf. B.B. 90*a*. (2) Lit., 'they put (water) upon the hands'. (3) I.e., in order to cleanse them. (4) Even though there may not be as much as a quarter of a *log* of water remaining to be poured over the hands of the second person, it is nevertheless valid, as it originally formed part of the requisite quantity necessary to produce a condition of cleanness. Cf. Ḥul. 107*a*. (5) Var. lec.: 'a half *log* or more'. (6) According to calculation, the minimum for three should be $^3/_8$, nevertheless half a *log* was required for fear that each person in concern for those that follow him would economize in the use of water and not wash his hands properly (Bert.). (7) Not to be taken literally but meaning that a minimum of a *log* of water will suffice for any number as long as there is enough water remaining to be poured over the hands of the last person in the manner prescribed. Cf. Asheri *ad loc.* Maim. is of the opinion that this Mishnah refers to the water poured over the hands the second time and that a minimum of a quarter of a *log* must be poured over the hands of each person the first time. Cf. next note and *infra* II, 1. (8) Water must be poured over the hands twice to ensure that they become absolutely clean. Maim. explains that after water has been poured over the hands the first time the water becomes unclean through the hands, hence a second cleansing is necessary. The first pouring is designated the first water, the second, the second water. (9) The water must cover the hands as far as the wrist both times, hence if at the first pouring out the amount of water is insufficient to cover

MISHNAH 2. WATER MAY BE POURED OVER THE HANDS OUT OF ANY KIND OF VESSEL, EVEN OUT OF VESSELS MADE OF ANIMAL ORDURE,[1] OUT OF VESSELS MADE OF STONE[1] OR OUT OF VESSELS MADE OF CLAY.[1] WATER MAY NOT BE POURED FROM THE SIDES OF [BROKEN] VESSELS[2] OR FROM THE BOTTOM OF A LADLE[2] OR FROM THE BUNG OF A BARREL.[3] NOR MAY ANYONE POUR [WATER] OVER THE HANDS OF HIS FELLOW OUT OF HIS CUPPED HANDS BECAUSE ONE MAY NOT DRAW, NOR SANCTIFY,[4] NOR SPRINKLE[5] THE WATER OF PURIFICATION,[6] NOR POUR WATER OVER THE HANDS EXCEPT IN A VESSEL. AND ONLY VESSELS CLOSELY COVERED WITH A LID PROTECT [THEIR CONTENTS FROM UNCLEANNESS][7] AND[8] ONLY VESSELS PROTECT [THEIR CONTENTS FROM UNCLEANNESS] FROM EARTHENWARE VESSELS.[9]

MISHNAH 3. IF WATER HAS BECOME SO UNFIT[10] THAT IT CANNOT BE DRUNK BY CATTLE, IF IT WAS IN A VESSEL IT

the hands as far as the wrist, they still remain unclean, and therefore the water may not be added to, but a fresh quantity of water must be used after first drying the hands.

(1) Though vessels made of these materials are not susceptible to uncleanness (cf. Par. V, 5), they are nevertheless considered 'vessels' for the purpose of washing the hands. (2) Because they are not whole vessels but broken parts of a vessel. (3) A bung cannot itself be used as a vessel. But if it were shaped into a vessel it could be used to pour water over the hands. Cf. Tosef. *ad loc.* and Ḥul. 107*a*. (4) By mixing the ashes of the Red Heifer with the water. (5) By dipping hyssop into the water containing the ashes and sprinkling it over the unclean object. Cf. Num. XIX, 18. (6) The reference here is to the Red Heifer the ashes of which were mixed with running water in a vessel and sprinkled over the person or vessel which had become unclean through contact with a dead body or through being present in the tent where the dead body lay; cf. Num. XIX, 17. (7) In the tent where the dead body lay. *Every open vessel which hath no covering close-bound upon it is unclean* (Num. XIX, 15). Thus only whole vessels and not broken parts of a vessel protect their contents from contracting uncleanness in the Tent, when closely covered with a lid. (8) שאין equivalent to ואין. Cf. parallel passage in Par. V, 5. (9) For notes v. Par. (Sonc. ed.) V, 5. (10) I.e., unfit by reason of stench and putridity; cf. Zeb. 22*a*.

IS INVALID,[1] BUT IF IT WAS IN THE GROUND[2] IT IS VALID. IF THERE FELL INTO IT INK, RESIN,[3] OR VITRIOL[4] AND ITS COLOUR CHANGED, IT IS INVALID.[5] IF A PERSON DID ANY WORK WITH IT[6] OR SOAKED HIS BREAD THEREIN, IT IS INVALID.[5] SIMEON OF TEMAN SAYS: EVEN IF HE INTENDED TO SOAK HIS BREAD IN ONE WATER AND IT FELL IN ANOTHER WATER [DO YOU STILL CONSIDER THE OTHER WATER TO BE INVALID? IN SUCH A CASE I CONSIDER THAT THE OTHER WATER] IS VALID.[7]

MISHNAH 4. IF HE CLEANSED VESSELS THEREIN OR SCRUBBED[8] MEASURES THEREIN, [THE WATER] IS INVALID; IF HE RINSED THEREIN VESSELS WHICH HAD ALREADY BEEN RINSED OR NEW VESSELS, IT IS VALID. R. JOSE DECLARES IT TO BE INVALID IF THEY WERE NEW VESSELS.[9]

MISHNAH 5. WATER IN WHICH THE BAKER DIPS GELUSḲIN[10] IS INVALID;[11] BUT IF HE [MERELY] MOISTENED HIS HANDS THEREIN[12] IT IS VALID. ALL ARE FIT TO POUR WATER OVER THE HANDS, EVEN A DEAF-MUTE, AN IMBECILE, OR A MINOR. A PERSON MAY PLACE THE BARREL BETWEEN HIS KNEES AND

(1) I.e., invalid to be used for pouring over the hands. (2) The water in the ground forms a ritual bath and is valid for the purpose of immersing the hands therein; cf. Tosef. *ad loc.* and Ḥul. 106*a.* (3) קומוס, gum, resin, especially ink prepared with gum. (4) קנקנתום sometimes קלקנתום, vitriol, used as an ingredient of shoe-black and of ink. (5) Since the water is no longer in its natural state. (6) E.g., if he cooled wine in it (Asheri). (7) So Bert. *Aliter:* If he intended to soak his bread in one water and it fell in another it is invalid. *Aliter:* 'Even if he intended to soak his bread in one water and it fell in another it is valid', and needless to say, where there was no intention at all to soak the bread. (8) To remove the traces of anything which had adhered to the measure. (9) Because although they are clean it is customary to rinse them first before using them. (10) Round bread of fine meal. The reference here is to the dough before it is baked. (11) As he had done work with it. Cf. *supra* I, 3. (12) And then moistened the bread with his wet hands, it is valid because no work has been done with the actual water in the vessel.

POUR OUT THE WATER[1] OR HE MAY TURN THE BARREL ON ITS SIDE AND POUR IT OUT.[2] AN APE[3] MAY POUR WATER OVER THE HANDS. R. JOSE DECLARES THESE [LATTER] TWO CASES INVALID.[4]

(1) The water must be poured out through human action, כח גברא (cf. Ḥul. 107*a*). By placing the barrel between his knees this requirement is considered fulfilled. (2) Once he has turned the barrel on to its side and the water is flowing he may even leave it and it is still considered valid as satisfying the above requirement. (3) This Tanna considers כח גברא to mean that the water must be poured out through someone's effort but not necessarily through *human* action. (4) R. Jose is of the opinion that '*human* action' is essential and therefore an ape may not pour out the water. Furthermore he considers that no human action comes into force on the actual washing of the hands if he merely turns the barrel on its side.

YADAYIM

CHAPTER II

MISHNAH 1. IF A PERSON POURS[1] WATER OVER ONE OF HIS HANDS WITH A SINGLE RINSING HIS HAND BECOMES CLEAN.[2] IF OVER BOTH HIS HANDS WITH A SINGLE RINSING, R. MEIR DECLARES THEM TO BE UNCLEAN UNTIL HE POURS A MINIMUM OF A QUARTER OF A LOG OF WATER OVER THEM.[3] IF A LOAF OF TERUMAH[4] FELL ON THE WATER THE LOAF IS CLEAN.[5] R. JOSE DECLARES IT TO BE UNCLEAN.[6]

MISHNAH 2. IF HE POURED THE FIRST WATER[7] OVER

(1) נטל an elliptical expression for נטל מים על ידיו cf. Levy *op. cit.* According to Strack, *Einleitung in Talmud und Midrash*, elliptic for נטילת כלי לתן על הידים i.e., lifting the vessel in order to pour water over the hands. Some derive it from נטלא, the name for the vessel used for pouring out the water. Cf. Frankel, *Aramäische Fremdwörter in Arabischen*, p. 65. The root נטל however, occurs in Biblical Hebrew. Cf. B.D.B. p. 642, with the meaning, to lift; and cf. note to *supra* I, 1 נוטלין לידים. (2) Even if there be less than a quarter of a *log* of water in the vessel. This is the case when he is not the first person to wash his hands from the water but washes them from the 'residue of the requisite quantity' necessary. Cf. *supra* I, 1. The one hand nevertheless becomes clean with a single rinsing and a second pouring out is unnecessary. But if he pours out the water over *both* his hands with a single rinsing, even though the water be the residue of the requisite quantity it is not sufficient and he must pour the water over his hands a second time as far as the wrist. (3) R. Meir is of the opinion that a second pouring of water over the hands is only necessary if there was less than a quarter of a *log* of water poured out on the first occasion. Cf. Asheri *ad loc.* (4) V. Glos. (5) I.e., if he has poured out a quarter of a *log* over his hands the first time and the loaf of *terumah* fell in the water as it lay on the ground, or if he touched it whilst his hands were still wet, or before he poured the second water over his hands, the loaf is nevertheless clean since his hands have been cleansed by the first water which was a quarter of a *log* in quantity. (6) Since the water itself is unclean. (7) Being less than a quarter of a *log* in quantity. This is the case when the water is the residue of the 'requisite quantity', v. *supra* I, 2. If it were more than a

HIS HANDS [WHILST STANDING] IN ONE PLACE, AND THE SECOND WATER OVER HIS HANDS [WHILST STANDING] IN ANOTHER PLACE, AND A LOAF OF TERUMAH FELL ON THE FIRST WATER,[1] THE LOAF BECOMES UNCLEAN. BUT IF IT FELL ON THE SECOND WATER IT REMAINS CLEAN.[2] IF HE POURED THE FIRST AND THE SECOND WATER [WHILST STANDING] IN ONE PLACE, AND A LOAF OF TERUMAH FELL THEREON, THE LOAF BECOMES UNCLEAN.[3] IF HE POURED THE FIRST WATER OVER HIS HANDS AND A SPLINTER OR A PIECE OF GRAVEL IS FOUND ON HIS HANDS, THEY REMAIN UNCLEAN,[4] BECAUSE THE LATTER WATER ONLY MAKES THE FIRST WATER ON THE HANDS CLEAN. R. SIMEON B. GAMALIEL SAYS: IF ANY WATER-CREATURE [FALLS ON THE HANDS WHILST THEY ARE BEING CLEANED] THEY NEVERTHELESS BECOME CLEAN.[5]

MISHNAH 3. HANDS BECOME UNCLEAN AND ARE MADE CLEAN AS FAR AS THE WRIST. HOW SO? IF HE POURED THE FIRST WATER OVER THE HANDS AS FAR AS THE WRIST AND POURED THE SECOND WATER OVER THE HANDS BEYOND THE WRIST AND THE LATTER FLOWED BACK TO THE HANDS, THE HANDS NEVERTHELESS BECOME CLEAN.[6] IF HE POURED THE

quarter of a *log* in quantity, the loaf of *terumah* would remain clean if it touched the first water. Cf. *supra* II, 1.

(1) I.e., it fell on the spot where the first water had fallen. (2) Because the second water is clean. (3) Because the second water only makes the first water on the *hands* clean but not the water on the ground. V. *infra*. (4) They are unclean even if he pours the second water over them, because the water on the splinter or on the piece of gravel becomes unclean by being in contact with the hands, and the second water only makes the *first* water clean and not the water on the splinter or on the piece of gravel, which consequently makes his hands unclean. Maim: The splinter or gravel forms an interposition and consequently the second water does not cleanse his hands. (5) Water-creatures such as, for example, water-gnats are treated as water. (6) All the regulations relating to the uncleanness of hands apply up to the wrist. Consequently in this case the second water makes the first water on the hands clean as far as the wrist only, and as the first water did not flow beyond the wrist the part of the second water beyond the wrist does not come into contact with it, nor does it become unclean by coming into contact with that

FIRST AND THE SECOND WATER OVER THE HANDS BEYOND THE WRIST AND THEY FLOWED BACK TO THE HANDS, THE HANDS REMAIN UNCLEAN.[1] IF HE POURED THE FIRST WATER OVER ONE OF HIS HANDS AND THEN CHANGED HIS MIND AND POURED THE SECOND WATER OVER BOTH HIS HANDS, THEY REMAIN UNCLEAN.[2] IF HE POURED THE FIRST WATER OVER BOTH HIS HANDS AND THEN CHANGED HIS MIND AND POURED THE SECOND WATER OVER ONE OF HIS HANDS, HIS ONE HAND BECOMES CLEAN. IF HE POURED WATER OVER ONE OF HIS HANDS AND RUBBED IT ON THE OTHER HAND IT REMAINS UNCLEAN.[3] IF HE RUBBED IT ON HIS HEAD OR ON THE WALL[4] IT BECOMES CLEAN. WATER MAY BE POURED OVER THE HANDS OF FOUR OR FIVE PERSONS, EACH HAND BEING BY THE SIDE OF THE OTHER, OR BEING ONE ABOVE THE OTHER, PROVIDED THAT THE HANDS ARE HELD LOOSELY SO THAT THE WATER FLOWS BETWEEN THEM.

MISHNAH 4. IF THERE WAS A DOUBT WHETHER ANY WORK HAS BEEN DONE WITH THE WATER OR NOT,[5] OR WHETHER THE WATER CONTAINS THE REQUISITE QUANTITY OR NOT, OR WHETHER IT IS UNCLEAN[6] OR CLEAN, THEN WHERE THERE IS SUCH A DOUBT THE WATER IS CONSIDERED TO BE

part of the hand beyond the wrist, and therefore the hands become clean.

(1) Beyond the wrist the second water cannot cleanse the first water, and since the second water comes there into contact with the first water, the hands remain unclean; cf. Soṭ. 4*b*. (2) I.e., if he poured the first water over each hand separately and then poured the second water over both hands held together. The first water on each hand becomes unclean on coming into contact with the unclean water on the other hand, and so conveys uncleanness to each hand. The second water therefore does not cleanse them since each hand is still unclean. Maim. *ad loc.* explains that he poured the first water on one hand only and poured the second water over both hands held together. The second water becomes unclean on being poured over the other unclean hand, and therefore does not cleanse the hands. (3) Since the other hand is unclean and therefore conveys uncleanness to the water on the hand when he touches it. (4) In order to dry the hands. (5) Cf. *supra* I, 3. (6) I.e., unclean for the purpose of pouring the water over the hands.

CLEAN. BECAUSE THEY[1] HAVE SAID IN A CASE OF DOUBT CONCERNING HANDS AS TO WHETHER THEY HAVE BECOME UNCLEAN OR HAVE CONVEYED UNCLEANNESS OR HAVE BECOME CLEAN, THEY ARE CONSIDERED TO BE CLEAN. R. JOSE SAYS: IN A CASE [OF DOUBT AS TO] WHETHER THEY HAVE BECOME CLEAN THEY ARE CONSIDERED TO BE UNCLEAN. HOW SO? IF HIS HANDS WERE CLEAN AND THERE WERE TWO UNCLEAN LOAVES BEFORE HIM AND THERE WAS A DOUBT WHETHER HE TOUCHED THEM OR NOT;[2] OR IF HIS HANDS WERE UNCLEAN AND THERE WERE TWO CLEAN LOAVES[3] BEFORE HIM AND THERE WAS A DOUBT WHETHER HE TOUCHED THEM OR NOT; OR IF ONE OF HIS HANDS WAS UNCLEAN AND THE OTHER CLEAN AND THERE WERE TWO CLEAN LOAVES[3] BEFORE HIM AND HE TOUCHED ONE OF THEM AND THERE WAS A DOUBT WHETHER HE TOUCHED IT WITH THE UNCLEAN HAND OR WITH THE CLEAN HAND; OR IF HIS HANDS WERE CLEAN AND THERE WERE TWO LOAVES BEFORE HIM ONE OF WHICH WAS UNCLEAN AND THE OTHER CLEAN AND HE TOUCHED ONE OF THEM AND THERE WAS A DOUBT WHETHER HE TOUCHED THE UNCLEAN ONE OR THE CLEAN ONE; OR IF ONE OF HIS HANDS WAS UNCLEAN AND THE OTHER CLEAN AND THERE WERE TWO LOAVES BEFORE HIM ONE OF WHICH WAS UNCLEAN AND THE OTHER CLEAN, AND HE TOUCHED BOTH OF THEM, AND THERE IS A DOUBT WHETHER THE UNCLEAN HAND TOUCHED THE UNCLEAN LOAF OR WHETHER THE CLEAN HAND TOUCHED THE CLEAN LOAF OR WHETHER THE CLEAN HAND TOUCHED THE UNCLEAN LOAF OR WHETHER THE UNCLEAN HAND TOUCHED THE CLEAN LOAF, THE HANDS REMAIN IN THE SAME STATE AS THEY WERE BEFORE AND THE LOAVES REMAIN IN THE SAME STATE AS THEY WERE BEFORE.

(1) I.e., the Sages; cf. Ṭoh. IV, 7. (2) Unclean food conveys uncleanness to the hands. Cf. *infra* III, 2. (3) I.e., loaves of *terumah* which are rendered unfit if touched by the hands. Cf. *infra* III, 1.

YADAYIM

CHAPTER III

MISHNAH 1. IF A PERSON PUTS HIS HANDS INSIDE A HOUSE SMITTEN WITH LEPROSY,[1] HIS HANDS BECOME UNCLEAN IN THE FIRST DEGREE.[2] [THESE ARE] THE WORDS OF R. AKIBA. BUT THE SAGES SAY: HIS HANDS BECOME UNCLEAN IN THE SECOND DEGREE. WHOEVER CONVEYS UNCLEANNESS TO THE GARMENTS AT THE TIME WHEN HE TOUCHES [THE UNCLEANNESS][3] CONVEYS A FIRST DEGREE OF UNCLEANNESS TO THE HANDS.[4] [THESE] ARE THE WORDS OF R. AKIBA. BUT THE SAGES SAY: IN SUCH A CASE HE CONVEYS A SECOND DEGREE OF UNCLEANNESS. THEY SAID TO R. AKIBA: WHERE DO WE FIND ANYWHERE THAT THE HANDS BECOME UNCLEAN IN THE FIRST DEGREE? HE SAID TO THEM: BUT HOW IS IT POSSIBLE FOR THEM TO BECOME UNCLEAN IN THE FIRST DEGREE WITHOUT HIS WHOLE BODY BECOMING UNCLEAN,[5] SAVE ONLY IN THESE CASES?[6] FOODSTUFFS AND VESSELS WHICH HAVE BEEN RENDERED UNCLEAN BY LIQUIDS CONVEY A SECOND DEGREE OF UNCLEANNESS TO THE HANDS. [THESE ARE] THE WORDS OF R. JOSHUA. BUT THE SAGES SAY: THAT WHICH HAS BEEN RENDERED UNCLEAN BY A 'FATHER OF UNCLEANNESS' CONVEYS UNCLEANNESS TO THE HANDS, BUT THAT WHICH HAS BEEN RENDERED UNCLEAN BY AN 'OFFSPRING OF UNCLEANNESS'[7] DOES NOT CONVEY UNCLEAN-

(1) V. Neg. XII-XIII. (2) The house smitten with leprosy is a 'father of uncleanness' and therefore according to R. Akiba conveys uncleanness of the first degree to the hands. (3) I.e., where one touches any of the uncleannesses specified in Zab. V, 7; e.g., the spittle of a *zab*. (4) Although he who had come into contact with such uncleanness does not convey further uncleannesses to a man. (5) For to suffer firstgrade uncleanness one must have contracted it from a 'father of uncleanness'; but if the hands had come into contact with such a grade of uncleanness the whole body becomes unclean. (6) Which are exceptions. (7) Liquids are 'offsprings of uncleanness'.

NESS TO THE HANDS. R. SIMEON B. GAMALIEL SAID: A PRACTICAL INSTANCE OCCURRED WHEN A CERTAIN WOMAN CAME BEFORE MY FATHER AND SAID TO HIM, MY HANDS PROTRUDED INTO THE AIR-SPACE INSIDE AN EARTHENWARE VESSEL.[1] HE SAID TO HER: MY DAUGHTER, WHAT WAS THE CAUSE OF ITS UNCLEANNESS?[2] BUT I DID NOT HEAR WHAT SHE SAID TO HIM. THE SAGES SAID: THE MATTER IS CLEAR. THAT WHICH HAS BEEN RENDERED UNCLEAN BY A 'FATHER OF UNCLEANNESS' CONVEYS UNCLEANNESS TO THE HANDS, BUT IF BY AN 'OFFSPRING OF UNCLEANNESS' IT DOES NOT CONVEY UNCLEANNESS TO THE HANDS.

MISHNAH 2. EVERYTHING WHICH RENDERS TERUMAH UNFIT[3] CONVEYS A SECOND DEGREE OF UNCLEANNESS TO THE HANDS.[4] ONE [UNWASHED] HAND CAN CONVEY UNCLEANNESS TO THE OTHER HAND. [THESE[4] ARE] THE WORDS OF R. JOSHUA.[4] BUT THE SAGES SAY: THAT WHICH IS IN THE SECOND DEGREE OF UNCLEANNESS CANNOT CONVEY A SECOND DEGREE OF UNCLEANNESS. HE SAID TO THEM: BUT DO NOT THE HOLY SCRIPTURES WHICH ARE IN THE SECOND DEGREE OF UNCLEANNESS[5] RENDER UNCLEAN THE HANDS?[6] THEY SAID TO HIM: THE LAWS OF THE TORAH MAY NOT BE ARGUED

(1) Which had been rendered unclean. (2) Was it rendered unclean by a 'father of uncleanness' or by an 'offspring of uncleanness', such as a liquid? (3) *Terumah* is rendered unfit by anything which is in the second degree of uncleanness. Cf. Zab. V, 12 and *supra* III, 1, n. 2. They are enumerated in the eighteen decrees of Beth Shammai. Cf. Shab. 14*a*. (4) Both statements are by R. Joshua. (5) Among the eighteen decrees enacted by Beth Shammai was that the Holy Scriptures rendered *terumah* unfit on coming into contact with it; the reason being that the priests stored the *terumah* side by side with the Scrolls of the Holy Scriptures with the result that the mice which gnawed the *terumah* nibbled also at the Scrolls. The object of this decree was to prevent this desecration. Cf. Shab. 14*a* and Rashi *loc. cit.* Holy Scriptures were thus declared to be in the second degree of uncleanness so as to render *terumah* unfit. (6) In order to ensure that the Holy Scriptures would not be touched by the bare hands, it was further enacted that hands which touched a Scroll of the Scriptures became unclean in the second degree and therefore rendered *terumah* unfit. Cf. Shab. 14*a* and Tosaf. s. v. האוחז.

FROM THE LAWS OF THE SCRIBES, NOR MAY THE LAWS OF THE SCRIBES BE ARGUED FROM THE LAWS OF THE TORAH, NOR MAY THE LAWS OF THE SCRIBES BE ARGUED FROM [OTHER] LAWS OF THE SCRIBES.[1]

MISHNAH 3. THE STRAPS OF THE TEFILLIN[2] [WHEN CONNECTED] WITH THE TEFILLIN RENDER UNCLEAN THE HANDS.[3] R. SIMEON SAYS: THE STRAPS OF THE TEFILLIN DO NOT RENDER UNCLEAN THE HANDS.

MISHNAH 4. THE MARGIN ON A SCROLL[4] WHICH IS ABOVE[5] OR BELOW OR AT THE BEGINNING[6] OR AT THE END RENDERS UNCLEAN THE HANDS. R. JUDAH SAYS: THE MARGIN AT THE END DOES NOT RENDER UNCLEAN [THE HANDS] UNTIL A HANDLE IS FASTENED TO IT.[7]

MISHNAH 5. A SCROLL[8] ON WHICH THE WRITING HAS BECOME ERASED AND EIGHTY-FIVE LETTERS REMAIN THEREON, AS MANY AS ARE IN THE SECTION BEGINNING, 'AND IT CAME TO PASS WHEN THE ARK SET FORWARD', ETC.[9] RENDERS

(1) The Scribes, i.e., Solomon, enacted that hands must be cleansed since they convey uncleanness, v. Introduction. The Scribes, i.e., the Rabbis, enacted that the Holy Scriptures convey uncleanness. Hence one cannot deduce that just as in the case of the Holy Scriptures a second degree of uncleanness conveys a second degree of uncleanness, so in the case of other defilements, a second degree of uncleanness conveys a second degree. (2) V. Glos. (3) The *tefillin* contain four sections of the Pentateuch. The Sages thus extend the principle that hands which have touched the Holy Scriptures render *terumah* unfit. (4) I.e., a scroll of a Book of the Holy Scriptures. (5) I.e., above the writing on the scroll. The width of the margin above must be three fingerbreadths and the width of that below must be one span. Cf. Men. 30a. (6) At the beginning of the scroll there must be a margin sufficient in width for winding round the cylinder, and at the end there must be a margin sufficient for winding round the whole circumference of the scroll when it is rolled up; cf. B.B. 13*a*. (7) R. Judah is of the opinion that until a handle is fastened to the scroll the margin at the end has no holiness attached to it, as it can be cut away if desired. (8) Sc. of the Pentateuch. (9) Num. X, 35-36. These two verses were considered to constitute a separate Book; cf. Shab. 116*a*.

UNCLEAN THE HANDS. A SINGLE SHEET[1] ON WHICH THERE ARE WRITTEN EIGHTY-FIVE LETTERS, AS MANY AS ARE IN THE SECTION BEGINNING, 'AND IT CAME TO PASS WHEN THE ARK SET FORWARD', RENDERS UNCLEAN THE HANDS. ALL THE HOLY WRITINGS[2] RENDER UNCLEAN THE HANDS. THE SONG OF SONGS AND ECCLESIASTES RENDER UNCLEAN THE HANDS.[3] R. JUDAH SAYS: THE SONG OF SONGS RENDERS UNCLEAN THE HANDS, BUT THERE IS A DISPUTE ABOUT ECCLESIASTES.[4] R. JOSE SAYS: ECCLESIASTES DOES NOT RENDER UNCLEAN THE HANDS, BUT THERE IS A DISPUTE ABOUT THE SONG OF SONGS. R. SIMEON SAYS: [THE RULING ABOUT] ECCLESIASTES IS ONE OF THE LENIENCIES OF BETH SHAMMAI AND ONE OF THE STRINGENCIES OF BETH HILLEL.[4] R. SIMEON B. 'AZZAI SAID: I RECEIVED A TRADITION FROM THE SEVENTY-TWO[5] ELDERS

(1) One of the sheets of a Pentateuch scroll. Lit., 'a scroll'. (2) I.e., not only the Books of the Pentateuch but also the Prophetical Books and the Hagiographa. (3) Since they are part of the Holy Scriptures. (4) The earliest discussion as to whether Ecclesiastes should be regarded as a sacred book took place between Beth Shammai and Beth Hillel. According to the former, Ecclesiastes did not convey uncleanness to the hands, i.e., was not to be regarded as a sacred work and therefore not to be included in the Canon, but according to Beth Hillel it did convey uncleanness to the hands and therefore was to be included in the Canon; cf. 'Ed. V, 3. The basis of Beth Shammai's contention was evidently that recorded in Shab. 30*b* where it is stated that the Sages did not intend to include Ecclesiastes in the Canon of the Bible, because its statements seemed to contradict one another. They finally decided to include it because it begins and ends with words which indicate its sacred character. A further reason which supports the view of Beth Shammai is given by R. Simeon b. Menasyah who expressed the view that the Song of Songs conveyed uncleanness to the hands because it was inspired by the Holy Spirit, whereas Ecclesiastes was inspired solely by the Wisdom of Solomon himself. Cf. Tosef. *ad loc.* and Meg. 7*a*. (5) The Greater Sanhedrin consisted of seventy-one members; cf. Sanh. I, 6. Various suggestions have been made to account for the additional one member referred to in this Mishnah. According to Tosaf. Sanh. 16*b* s. v. אחד there was an additional member of the Sanhedrin known as the *Mufla*, i.e., the distinguished member of the Sanhedrin who was first in authority. Lauterbach suggests that the number seventy-two included both Rabban Gamaliel and R. Eleazar b. 'Azariah. Cf. *J. E.* s. v. Sanhedrin and Ber. 28*a*.

ON THE DAY WHEN THEY APPOINTED R. ELEAZAR B. 'AZARIAH HEAD OF THE ACADEMY[1] THAT THE SONG OF SONGS AND ECCLESIASTES RENDER UNCLEAN THE HANDS. R. AKIBA SAID: FAR BE IT! NO MAN IN ISRAEL DISPUTED ABOUT THE SONG OF SONGS [BY SAYING] THAT IT DOES NOT RENDER UNCLEAN THE HANDS. FOR THE WHOLE WORLD IS NOT AS WORTHY AS THE DAY ON WHICH THE SONG OF SONGS WAS GIVEN TO ISRAEL; FOR ALL THE WRITINGS ARE HOLY BUT THE SONG OF SONGS IS THE HOLY OF HOLIES. SO THAT IF THEY HAD A DISPUTE, THEY HAD A DISPUTE ONLY ABOUT ECCLESIASTES. R. JOḤANAN B. JOSHUA THE SON OF THE FATHER-IN-LAW OF R. AKIBA SAID: IN ACCORDANCE WITH THE WORDS OF BEN 'AZZAI SO THEY DISPUTED,[2] AND SO THEY REACHED A DECISION.[3]

(1) V. Ber. 27*b*. (2) About both the Song of Songs and Ecclesiastes. (3) That both render unclean the hands.

YADAYIM

CHAPTER IV

MISHNAH I. ON THAT DAY[1] THE VOTES WERE COUNTED AND THEY DECIDED THAT A FOOTBATH HOLDING FROM TWO LOGS TO NINE ḲABS[2] WHICH WAS CRACKED COULD CONTRACT MIDRAS[3] UNCLEANNESS. BECAUSE R. AKIBA SAID A FOOTBATH [MUST BE CONSIDERED] ACCORDING TO ITS DESIGNATION.[4]

MISHNAH 2. ON THAT DAY THEY SAID: ALL ANIMAL SACRIFICES[5] WHICH HAVE BEEN SACRIFICED UNDER THE NAME OF SOME OTHER OFFERING[6] ARE [NEVERTHELESS] VALID,[7] BUT THEY ARE NOT ACCOUNTED TO THEIR OWNERS AS A FULFILMENT OF THEIR OBLIGATIONS,[8] WITH THE EXCEPTION OF THE PASCHAL-OFFERING[9] AND THE SIN-OFFERING.[9] [THIS APPLIES TO] THE PASCHAL-OFFERING IN ITS DUE TIME[10] AND TO

(1) I.e., on the day when they appointed R. Eleazar b. 'Azariah head of the Academy after Rabban Gamaliel had been deposed. V. *supra* III, 4. Wherever the words בו ביום occur, this day is meant. V. 'Ed. (Sonc. ed.) Introduction. (2) A *ḳab* is a measure of capacity equal in quantity to four *logs*. (3) V. Glos. A footbath which was cracked and therefore could no longer hold any water was used for sitting on. Cf. Maim. on Kel. XX, 5. It therefore comes within the category of a 'utensil' and is thus liable to contract *midras* uncleanness. Cf. Lev. XV, 4. (4) I.e., as a footbath only and does not come within the category of a 'utensil', and thus does not contract *midras* uncleanness. (5) Cf. Zeb. I. 1. (6) E.g., if an animal brought as a burnt-offering is offered as a peace-offering. (7) I.e., the blood must nevertheless be sprinkled on the altar and the relevant portions burnt on the altar or eaten. (8) He must still bring the offering which he vowed to offer; cf. Deut. XXIII, 24, *That which is gone out of thy lips thou shalt observe and do*. V. Zeb. 2*a*. (9) Which if sacrificed under the name of another offering are invalid; v. Zeb. 7*b*. (10) I.e., if the Paschal-offering is sacrificed on the eve of Passover under the name of another offering it is invalid; but if it be offered up before mid-day of the fourteenth of Nisan or after the eve of Passover it is considered a peace-offering and all the laws appertaining to peace-offerings apply. Cf. Zeb. 8*a*.

THE SIN-OFFERING AT ANY TIME. R. ELIEZER SAYS: [WITH THE EXCEPTION] ALSO OF THE GUILT-OFFERING.[1] [SO THAT THIS APPLIES TO] THE PASCHAL-OFFERING IN ITS DUE TIME AND TO THE SIN- AND GUILT-OFFERINGS AT ANY TIME. R. SIMEON B. 'AZZAI SAID: I RECEIVED A TRADITION FROM THE SEVENTY-TWO ELDERS ON THE DAY WHEN THEY APPOINTED R. ELEAZAR B. 'AZARIAH HEAD OF THE COLLEGE THAT ALL ANIMAL SACRIFICES WHICH ARE EATEN AND WHICH HAVE NOT BEEN SACRIFICED UNDER THEIR OWN NAME ARE NEVERTHELESS VALID, BUT THEY ARE NOT ACCOUNTED TO THEIR OWNERS AS A FULFILMENT OF THEIR OBLIGATIONS, WITH THE EXCEPTION OF THE PASCHAL-OFFERING AND THE SIN-OFFERING. BEN 'AZZAI ONLY ADDED [TO THESE EXCEPTIONS] THE BURNT-OFFERING, BUT THE SAGES DID NOT AGREE WITH HIM.

MISHNAH 3. ON THAT DAY THEY SAID: WHAT IS THE LAW APPLYING TO AMMON AND MOAB IN THE SEVENTH YEAR?[2] R. TARFON DECREED TITHE FOR THE POOR;[3] AND R. ELEAZAR B. 'AZARIAH DECREED SECOND TITHE.[4] R. ISHMAEL SAID: ELEAZAR B. 'AZARIAH, THE ONUS IS UPON YOU TO PRODUCE YOUR PROOF BECAUSE YOU ARE EXPRESSING THE STRICTER VIEW;[5] FOR THE ONUS IS UPON THE PERSON WHO EXPRESSES A STRICTER VIEW TO PRODUCE THE PROOF. R. ELEAZAR B. 'AZARIAH SAID TO HIM: ISHMAEL, MY BROTHER, I HAVE NOT

(1) Cf. Lev. VII, 1. (2) I.e., which tithe must Israelites living in these countries give in the Sabbatical year? Tithe is payable from harvest reaped in the seventh year in countries outside the Land of Israel. Cf. Sheb. VI, 1. In the Land of Israel itself no harvest was permitted to be reaped in the seventh year (cf. Lev. XXV, 4*ff.*) and therefore no tithe was payable. (3) Tithe given to the poor every third and sixth year of a cycle of seven years. Cf. Deut. XIV, 28*ff.* (4) Tithe given every first, second, fourth and fifth year of a cycle of seven years. Second tithe had to be consumed in Jerusalem, (Deut. XIV, 22*ff.*) or redeemed by its equivalent in money plus one-fifth of its value (Lev. XXVII, 30*f*). The latter sum had to be spent on food and drink in Jerusalem (Deut. XIV, 26). (5) Since second tithe is consecrated, being eaten only in Jerusalem, but tithe for the poor is unconsecrated. Cf. Maim. *ad loc.*

DEVIATED FROM THE SEQUENCE OF YEARS,[1] TARFON, MY BROTHER, HAS DEVIATED THEREFROM AND THE ONUS IS UPON HIM TO PRODUCE THE PROOF. R. TARFON ANSWERED: EGYPT IS OUTSIDE THE LAND OF ISRAEL, AMMON AND MOAB ARE OUTSIDE THE LAND OF ISRAEL: JUST AS EGYPT MUST GIVE TITHE FOR THE POOR IN THE SEVENTH YEAR,[2] SO MUST AMMON AND MOAB GIVE TITHE FOR THE POOR IN THE SEVENTH YEAR. R. ELEAZAR B. 'AZARIAH ANSWERED: BABYLON IS OUTSIDE THE LAND OF ISRAEL, AMMON AND MOAB ARE OUTSIDE THE LAND OF ISRAEL: JUST AS BABYLON MUST GIVE SECOND TITHE IN THE SEVENTH YEAR,[3] SO MUST AMMON AND MOAB GIVE SECOND TITHE IN THE SEVENTH YEAR. R. TARFON SAID: ON EGYPT WHICH IS NEAR, THEY IMPOSED TITHE FOR THE POOR SO THAT THE POOR OF ISRAEL MIGHT BE SUPPORTED THEREBY DURING THE SEVENTH YEAR; SO ON AMMON AND MOAB WHICH ARE NEAR, WE SHOULD IMPOSE TITHE FOR THE POOR SO THAT THE POOR OF ISRAEL MAY BE SUPPORTED THEREBY DURING THE SEVENTH YEAR. R. ELEAZAR B. 'AZARIAH SAID TO HIM: BEHOLD, THOU ART LIKE A PERSON WHO WOULD BENEFIT THEM WITH GAIN, YET THOU ART REALLY AS ONE WHO CAUSES SOULS TO PERISH. WOULDST THOU ROB THE HEAVENS SO THAT DEW OR RAIN SHOULD NOT DESCEND?[4] AS IT IS SAID, WILL A MAN ROB GOD? YET YE ROB ME. BUT YE SAY WHEREIN HAVE WE ROBBED THEE? IN TITHES AND HEAVE-OFFERINGS.[5] R. JOSHUA SAID: BEHOLD, I SHALL BE AS ONE WHO REPLIES ON BEHALF OF TARFON, MY BROTHER, BUT NOT IN ACCORDANCE WITH THE SUBJECT MATTER OF HIS ARGUMENTS. THE LAW REGARDING EGYPT IS A NEW ACT AND THE LAW REGARDING BABYLON IS AN OLD ACT, AND THE LAW WHICH IS BEING ARGUED BEFORE US IS A NEW ACT. A NEW ACT SHOULD BE

(1) Second tithe is ordinarily given in the year following that in which tithe for the poor is given. Since tithe for the poor is given in the sixth year of the seven years' cycle, it follows that in countries outside the Land of Israel second tithe should be given in the seventh year. (2) An ordinance of the Elders who lived after the time of Ezra. (3) An ordinance of the Prophets. (4) Cf. Mal. III, 10. (5) Ibid. III, 8.

ARGUED FROM [ANOTHER] NEW ACT, BUT A NEW ACT SHOULD NOT BE ARGUED FROM AN OLD ACT. THE LAW REGARDING EGYPT IS THE ACT OF THE ELDERS AND THE LAW REGARDING BABYLON IS THE ACT OF THE PROPHETS, AND THE LAW WHICH IS BEING ARGUED BEFORE US[1] IS THE ACT OF THE ELDERS. LET ONE ACT OF THE ELDERS BE ARGUED FROM [ANOTHER] ACT OF THE ELDERS, BUT LET NOT AN ACT OF THE ELDERS BE ARGUED FROM AN ACT OF THE PROPHETS. THE VOTES WERE COUNTED AND THEY DECIDED THAT AMMON AND MOAB SHOULD GIVE TITHE FOR THE POOR IN THE SEVENTH YEAR. AND WHEN R. JOSE B. DURMAS̱KITH[2] VISITED R. ELIEZER[3] IN LYDDA HE SAID TO HIM: WHAT NEW THING DID YOU HAVE IN THE HOUSE OF STUDY TO-DAY? HE SAID TO HIM: THEIR VOTES WERE COUNTED AND THEY DECIDED THAT AMMON AND MOAB MUST GIVE TITHE FOR THE POOR IN THE SEVENTH YEAR. R. ELIEZER WEPT AND SAID: THE COUNSEL OF THE LORD IS WITH THEM THAT FEAR HIM: AND HIS COVENANT, TO MAKE THEM KNOW IT.[4] GO AND TELL THEM: DO NOT HAVE ANY APPREHENSION ON ACCOUNT OF YOUR VOTING. I RECEIVED A TRADITION FROM R. JOḤANAN B. ZAKKAI WHO HEARD IT FROM HIS TEACHER, AND HIS TEACHER FROM HIS TEACHER, AND SO BACK TO AN HALACHAH GIVEN TO MOSES FROM SINAI,[5] THAT AMMON AND MOAB MUST GIVE TITHE FOR THE POOR IN THE SEVENTH YEAR.

MISHNAH 4. ON THAT DAY JUDAH, AN AMMONITE PROSELYTE, CAME AND STOOD BEFORE THEM IN THE HOUSE OF STUDY. HE SAID TO THEM: HAVE I THE RIGHT TO ENTER INTO THE ASSEMBLY?[6] RABBAN GAMALIEL SAID TO HIM: THOU ART FORBIDDEN. R. JOSHUA SAID TO HIM: THOU ART PERMITTED. RABBAN GAMALIEL SAID TO HIM: THE SCRIPTURAL VERSE SAYS, AN AMMONITE OR A MOABITE SHALL NOT ENTER INTO

(1) That of Ammon and Moab. (2) I.e., of Damascus. Cf. A.T. 393*ff*. (3) R. Eliezer had been placed under the ban (cf. B.M. 59*b*). He was thus unable to participate in the discussions which took place in the House of Study. (4) Ps. XXV, 14. (5) I.e., an ancient ordinance. (6) I.e., can I marry an Israelite woman? Cf. Yeb. VIII, 3.

THE ASSEMBLY OF THE LORD: EVEN TO THE TENTH GENERATION, ETC.[1] R. JOSHUA SAID TO HIM: BUT ARE THE AMMONITES AND MOABITES STILL IN THEIR OWN TERRITORY? SENNACHERIB, THE KING OF ASSYRIA, HAS LONG SINCE COME UP AND MINGLED ALL THE NATIONS, AS IT IS SAID: IN THAT I HAVE REMOVED THE BOUNDS OF THE PEOPLES, AND HAVE ROBBED THEIR TREASURES, AND HAVE BROUGHT DOWN AS ONE MIGHTY THE INHABITANTS.[2] RABBAN GAMALIEL SAID TO HIM: THE SCRIPTURAL VERSE SAYS, BUT AFTERWARD I WILL BRING BACK THE CAPTIVITY OF THE CHILDREN OF AMMON,[3] SO THAT THEY HAVE ALREADY RETURNED. R. JOSHUA SAID TO HIM: THE SCRIPTURAL VERSE SAYS, I WILL TURN THE CAPTIVITY OF MY PEOPLE ISRAEL AND JUDAH,[4] YET THEY HAVE NOT ALREADY RETURNED. SO THEY PERMITTED HIM TO ENTER THE ASSEMBLY.

MISHNAH 5. THE ARAMAIC SECTIONS IN EZRA AND DANIEL RENDER UNCLEAN THE HANDS.[5] IF AN ARAMAIC SECTION WAS WRITTEN[6] IN HEBREW, OR A HEBREW SECTION WAS WRITTEN[6] IN ARAMAIC, OR HEBREW SCRIPT,[7] IT[8] DOES NOT RENDER UNCLEAN THE HANDS. IT NEVER RENDERS UNCLEAN THE HANDS UNTIL IT IS WRITTEN IN THE ASSYRIAN SCRIPT,[9] ON HIDE, AND IN INK.

MISHNAH 6. THE SADDUCEES SAY: WE COMPLAIN

(1) Deut. XXIII, 4. (2) Isa. X, 13; said by the boastful king of Assyria. It can therefore no longer be said that anyone born in Ammon is a real Ammonite, as he is a descendant of mixed races. (3) Jer. XLIX, 6. (4) Jer. XXX, 3. (5) Since they are part of the Holy Scriptures. (6) I.e., translated. (7) כתב עברי Hebrew Script. This is the name given to the older form of the Hebrew alphabet which was used by the Hebrews, Moabites, and Phoenicians. It was angular in shape, and can be seen on the Moabite stone and on various Hebrew inscriptions discovered in Samaria, Gezer and Siloam. The 'Hebrew Script' was replaced by the 'Assyrian Script' i.e., the square alphabet now in use. This was introduced by Ezra, and was so called because (*a*) it was brought back from Assyria, or (*b*) because its characters are straight in form, שמאושרות בכתב. Cf. Sanh. 21*b* and 22*a* and notes in Sonc. ed. *a. l.* (8) I.e., a book of the Holy Scriptures. (9) I.e., the square characters.

AGAINST YOU, O YE PHARISEES, BECAUSE YOU SAY THAT THE HOLY SCRIPTURES RENDER UNCLEAN THE HANDS,[1] BUT THE BOOKS OF HAMIRAM[2] DO NOT CONVEY UNCLEANNESS TO THE HANDS. R. JOḤANAN B. ZAKKAI SAID: HAVE WE NOTHING AGAINST THE PHARISEES EXCEPTING THIS?[3] BEHOLD THEY SAY THAT THE BONES OF AN ASS ARE CLEAN, YET THE BONES OF JOḤANAN[4] THE HIGH PRIEST ARE UNCLEAN.[5] THEY SAID TO HIM: PROPORTIONATE TO THE LOVE FOR THEM, SO IS THEIR UNCLEANNESS, SO THAT NOBODY SHOULD MAKE SPOONS OUT OF THE BONES OF HIS FATHER OR MOTHER. HE SAID TO THEM: SO ALSO THE HOLY SCRIPTURES; PROPORTIONATE TO THE LOVE FOR THEM, SO IS THEIR UNCLEANNESS. THE BOOKS OF HAMIRAM WHICH ARE NOT PRECIOUS DO NOT CONVEY UNCLEANNESS TO THE HANDS.[6]

MISHNAH 7. THE SADDUCEES SAY: WE COMPLAIN AGAINST YOU, O YE PHARISEES, THAT YOU DECLARE AN UNINTERRUPTED FLOW OF A LIQUID TO BE CLEAN.[7] THE PHARISEES SAY: [DO] WE COMPLAIN AGAINST YOU, O YE SADDUCEES, THAT YOU DECLARE A STREAM OF WATER WHICH FLOWS FROM THE BURIAL-GROUND TO BE CLEAN?[8] THE

(1) Cf. *supra* II, 2. (2) The meaning of this word is obscure. The Mishnah is evidently referring to a well known example of secular writings. *Aruch* offers three explanations s. v. מרום viz., (*a*) heretical books, from מור to change: (*b*) the books of מרום the name of a heretic (so also Maim. and Rosh reading מירם): (*c*) books of Greek wisdom called in Greek, Homeros. Many scholars have suggested that it refers to the works of Homer. Kohut in the *J. Q. R.* Vol. III 546-548, who collects all the various conjectures, himself suggests pleasure, entertainment, i.e., books of entertainment. (3) Speaking ironically. (4) Evidently the Joḥanan referred to in Ber. 29*a* as having become a Sadducee after eighty years' service as High Priest. (5) The Sadducees accepted the principle that the bones of an ass are clean whereas those of the human being are unclean. (6) R. Joḥanan answered the Sadducees by using the principle which they themselves accepted. (7) Cf. Maksh. V, 9. If a liquid is poured from a clean vessel into an unclean vessel, the liquid remaining in the former vessel remains clean, as the uninterrupted flow does not form a connective. (8) Cf. Miḳ. I. 4. The Sadducees agreed that this was the case. On this controversy v. Finkelstein, *The Pharisees* II, p. 638.

SADDUCEES SAY: WE COMPLAIN AGAINST YOU, O YE PHARISEES, IN THAT YOU SAY, 'MY OX OR ASS WHICH HAS DONE INJURY IS LIABLE,[1] YET MY MANSERVANT OR MAIDSERVANT WHO HAS DONE INJURY IS NOT LIABLE'.[2] NOW IF IN THE CASE OF 'MY OX OR MY ASS' FOR WHICH I AM NOT RESPONSIBLE IF THEY DO NOT FULFIL RELIGIOUS DUTIES,[3] YET I AM RESPONSIBLE FOR THEIR DAMAGE, IN THE CASE OF 'MY MANSERVANT OR MAIDSERVANT' FOR WHOM I AM RESPONSIBLE TO SEE THAT THEY FULFIL RELIGIOUS DUTIES,[4] HOW MUCH MORE SO THAT I SHOULD BE RESPONSIBLE FOR THEIR DAMAGE? THEY SAID TO THEM: NO, IF YOU ARGUE ABOUT 'MY OX OR MY ASS' WHICH HAVE NO UNDERSTANDING, CAN YOU DEDUCE ANYTHING THEREFROM CONCERNING 'MY MANSERVANT OR MAIDSERVANT' WHO HAVE UNDERSTANDING? SO THAT IF I WERE TO ANGER EITHER OF THEM THEY WOULD GO AND BURN ANOTHER PERSON'S STACK AND I SHOULD BE LIABLE TO MAKE RESTITUTION?[5]

MISHNAH 8. A GALILEAN SADDUCEE[6] SAID: I COMPLAIN AGAINST YOU, O YE PHARISEES, THAT YOU WRITE THE NAME OF THE RULER AND THE NAME OF MOSES TOGETHER ON A BILL OF DIVORCEMENT.[7] THE PHARISEES SAID: [DO] WE COMPLAIN AGAINST YOU, O GALILEAN SADUCEE, THAT YOU WRITE THE NAME OF THE RULER TOGETHER WITH THE DIVINE

(1) I.e., I am responsible for the damage they do. Cf. Ex. XXI, 35. The Sadducees did not dispute this, as it is expressly stated in the Torah. (2) Cf. B.Ḳ. VIII, 4. Not being expressly stated in the Torah, the Sadducees did not accept this. (3) Since the Torah does not enjoin religious duties on animals. (4) E.g., to see that they do not work on the Sabbath. (5) Hence the law provides that I should not be liable for the damage they do. On this controversy v. Finkelstein L. *op. cit.* II, p. 684. (6) Var. lec. a Galilean *min* (v. Glos.). Finkelstein (*op. cit.* p. 645) holds the heretic involved to have been a Galilean Nationalist who opposed the recognition of the non-Davidic and of the Roman rulers in Jewish ceremonial. (7) The bill of divorcement began with the date which stated the year of the rule of the reigning king. It ended with the words, 'in accordance with the religion of Moses and of Israel'. According to this Sadducee, the mention of both names on the one document was derogatory to Moses.

NAME ON A SINGLE PAGE? AND FURTHERMORE THAT YOU WRITE THE NAME OF THE RULER ABOVE AND THE DIVINE NAME BELOW? AS IT IS SAID, AND PHAROAH SAID, WHO IS THE LORD THAT I SHOULD HEARKEN UNTO HIS VOICE TO LET ISRAEL GO?[1] BUT WHEN HE WAS SMITTEN WHAT DID HE SAY? THE LORD IS RIGHTEOUS.[2]

(1) Ex. V, 2. I.e., it is not in the least derogatory since in the Scriptures the name of the ruler is mentioned even before the Divine name. (2) Ex. IX, 27. This is added so as to avoid ending the Tractate with the previous verse which expresses defiance of God.

ʽUḲẒIN

TRANSLATED INTO ENGLISH

WITH NOTES

BY

RABBI DR S. M. LEHRMAN, M.A., PH.D.

INTRODUCTION

With Tractate 'Uḳẓin ('stalks'), which enjoys the reputation of being one of the most difficult of the sixty-three tractates which comprise the entire Talmud,[1] R. Judah Hannasi brought his monumental task to a close. In our edition it forms the last and twelfth tractate of Seder Ṭohoroth, being placed after Yadayim. More logical, however, is the sequence of the Tosefta where it immediately follows Ṭebul Yom, in which we are taught the laws of the 'handles' of vessels which are susceptible to uncleanness, and which serve as 'connectives', so that if such part suffers uncleanness, this is imparted to the rest.

The tractate, as is indicated by its name, deals mainly with the imparting of ritual impurity by means of roots, stalks and husks of plants. For this law there is no foundation in the Bible, being based solely on Rabbinic dialectics. According to Maimonides, this is the reason why it has been placed very last in the Mishnah.[2]

The contents of its twenty-seven paragraphs, divided into three chapters, are soon told. The first two chapters discuss the uncleanness of roots, stalks and husks, the instance of olives that have been preserved with their leaves, of pomegranates and melons partly crushed and of plants growing in vases or pots. The last chapter discusses those objects that need contact with water to make them 'susceptible', the conditions under which spices, pepper and fish receive uncleanness, and the things which require, or do not require 'intention' or to be rendered susceptible to uncleanness. As a fitting close to the Mishnah, setting the seal to that passionate ideal which has stirred Talmudic Sages in all their disputations and discussions arising from a minute study of the Bible, and expressive at the same time of Israel's yearning at all times, is the last paragraph with its grand assurance of peace.[3]

S. M. LEHRMAN

(1) V. Ber. 20a; 'Er. 53a; Hor. 13b. (2) V. his *Introduction to Zera'im.* (3) V III, 12.

'UḲẒIN

CHAPTER I

MISHNAH 1. THAT WHICH SERVES AS A HANDLE,[1] THOUGH NOT ACTUALLY AS A PROTECTION,[2] BOTH CONTRACTS UNCLEANNESS[3] AND CONVEYS UNCLEANNESS;[4] BUT IT IS NOT INCLUDED.[5] IF IT SERVES AS A PROTECTION THOUGH NOT AS A HANDLE,[6] IT CONTRACTS AND CONVEYS UNCLEANNESS AND IS INCLUDED.[7] IF IT SERVES NEITHER AS A PROTECTION NOR AS A HANDLE,[8] IT NEITHER CONTRACTS NOR CONVEYS UNCLEANNESS.[9]

MISHNAH 2. ROOTS OF GARLIC, ONIONS OR LEEKS[10] THAT ARE YET MOIST, OR THEIR TOP-PARTS,[11] BE THEY MOIST OR DRY, ALSO THE SCAPE THAT IS WITHIN THE EDIBLE PART,[12] THE ROOTS OF THE LETTUCE, THE RADISH AND THE TURNIP,[13]

(1) To fruit or plants, like the stalks of apples, grapes, plums, or a marrowless bone held in the hand in order to enjoy the meat thereon. (2) Thus excluding that part of the stalk actually touching the fruit and attached to the kernel. (3) For though the handle itself is not edible, but since it serves as a connective to the fruit, it is rendered unclean when the edible part suffers uncleanness. (4) If the handle suffers uncleanness the edible part becomes also unclean. Derived from Lev. XI, 37 (v. Bert.). (5) With the rest of the food to complete the egg's bulk necessary for the transmission of uncleanness. (6) I.e., the husk of plant or fruit protecting it, which men do not grip hold of when eating; accordingly, it is regarded as part of the fruit itself. (7) Which includes such things as wheat and barley in their husks used for the purpose of sowing. This is inferred from Lev. XI, 37, for were it to refer merely to the contraction and imparting of uncleanness, it would have been too obvious. (8) Like the fibrous substance of fruits or vegetables. (9) And, of course, cannot be included. (10) With heads to them. (11) The protuberance on blossom-end of fruits, having the appearance of a pestle seated in a mortar; hence the upper portion of fruit. (12) I.e., the radical stem, bearing fructification, but no leaves. The scape is the central stalk of the onion, as far as it is surrounded by the edible part (v. L.). (13) נפוס, a kind of radish resembling the carrot as to foliage, and the radish as to taste, cf. Kil. I, 3, 5.

[ARE INCLUDED]. SO R. MEIR. R. JUDAH SAYS: ONLY THE LARGE ROOTS OF THE RADISH ARE SO INCLUDED, BUT ITS FIBROUS ROOTS ARE NOT INCLUDED. THE ROOTS OF THE MINT, RUE,[1] WILD HERBS AND GARDEN HERBS THAT HAVE BEEN UPROOTED IN ORDER TO BE PLANTED ELSEWHERE,[2] AND THE SPINAL CORD OF AN EAR OF CORN TOGETHER WITH ITS HUSK,[3] (R. ELEAZAR SAYS: ALSO THE COBWEB-LIKE COVERING OF FRUITS)[4] ALL THESE THINGS CONTRACT AND CONVEY UNCLEANNESS[5] AND ARE INCLUDED.[6]

MISHNAH 3. THE FOLLOWING BOTH CONTRACT AND IMPART UNCLEANNESS, BUT ARE NOT INCLUDED [TOGETHER WITH THE REST]: ROOTS OF GARLIC,[7] ONIONS OR LEEKS WHEN THEY ARE DRY, THE SCAPE THAT IS NOT WITHIN THE EDIBLE PART,[8] THE TWIG OF A VINE,[9] A HANDBREADTH LONG ON EITHER SIDE,[10] THE STEM OF THE CLUSTER, WHATSOEVER BE ITS LENGTH,[11] THE TAIL OF THE CLUSTER BEREFT OF GRAPES,[12] THE STEM OF THE 'BROOM'[13] OF THE PALM-TREE TO A LENGTH OF FOUR HANDBREADTHS,[14] THE STALK OF THE EAR [OF CORN] TO A LENGTH OF THREE HANDBREADTHS, AND THE STALK OF ALL THINGS THAT ARE CUT, TO THE LENGTH OF THREE HANDBREADTHS.[15] IN THE CASE OF THOSE THINGS NOT USU-

(1) Cf. Kil. I, 8: 'You must not graft rue on white cassia because it would be a combination of a herb with a tree'. (2) With the result that he takes good care to see that the roots are plucked up with herbs, to which they serve as a protection. (3) Which serves as a protection to the ear of corn. (4) The downy growth on the tops of vegetables, resembling almost a spider's web, a view with which the *halachah* does not concur. (5) As protection. (6) To make up the required egg's bulk to impart uncleanness. (7) Being dried up, they no longer serve as 'protection', but solely as 'handles'. (8) V. p. 573 n. 12. (9) From which a grape-cluster hangs. (10) Were the branch less, it could not be called 'handle', being too slender to support a heavy cluster of grapes, and not of sufficient size of which to take a grip (L.). (11) Even if this be very great. So Bert. According to L., however, even if it be smaller than a handbreadth. (12) After the grapes had fallen off, the tail of the cluster need not be of the stipulated handbreadth. (13) The fan-shaped twig of the palm-tree which resembles a broom, with which it is possible to sweep the house; cf. Suk. 40*a*. (14) But not more. (15) The three

ALLY CUT, THEIR STALKS AND ROOTS OF ANY SIZE WHATSOEVER.[1] AS FOR THE OUTER HUSKS OF GRAINS,[2] THEY BOTH CONTRACT AND IMPART UNCLEANNESS,[3] BUT ARE NOT INCLUDED.[4]

MISHNAH 4. THE FOLLOWING, HOWEVER, NEITHER CONTRACT NOR IMPART UNCLEANNESS, AND ARE NOT INCLUDED:[4] THE ROOTS OF CABBAGE-STALKS,[5] YOUNG SHOOTS OF BEET GROWING OUT OF THE ROOT,[6] AND SUCH TURNIP-HEADS THAT ARE ORDINARILY CUT OFF BUT IN THIS CASE WERE PULLED UP [WITH THEIR ROOTS].[7] R. JOSE DECLARES THEM ALL SUSCEPTIBLE TO CONTRACT UNCLEANNESS,[8] BUT HE DECLARES INSUSCEPTIBLE CABBAGE-STALKS AND TURNIP-HEADS.[9]

MISHNAH 5. STALKS OF ALL EDIBLES THAT HAVE BEEN THRESHED IN THE THRESHING-FLOOR ARE CLEAN;[10] BUT R. JOSE PRONOUNCES THEM UNCLEAN.[11] A SPRIG OF A VINE WHEN STRIPPED OF ITS GRAPES IS CLEAN,[10] BUT IF ONE GRAPE ALONE IS LEFT THEREON, IT IS UNCLEAN.[12] A TWIG OF A DATE-TREE STRIPPED OF ITS DATES IS CLEAN,[13] BUT IF ONE DATE REMAINS

handbreadths are thus explained: one of which the reaper takes hold, one that is left near the ears of corn, and one below, so that his hand does not receive a cut from the sickle.

(1) I.e., long or short, for once they have been uprooted he does not mind how much is left of the ear of corn. (2) The glumes of the ears of corn; Ḥul. 119*b*. (3) Since all are stalks whereby the fruit is held. (4) Together with the rest to constitute the egg's bulk. (5) On top of the cabbage are leaves of helmet shape. These are usually thrown away. (6) Left in the soil when the beets are cut for others to grow. (7) All these serve neither as 'handles' nor as 'protection'. (8) Regarding them all as 'handles' to the food. (9) Which he agrees are of no purpose whatsoever. (10) Viz., not susceptible to defilement. Threshing used to be done with the aid of animals or sticks, thus rendering the stalks too weak to be considered after this as handles; Ḥul. 118*a*. (11) Namely susceptible to uncleanness; his contention being that they are liable to be upturned with the pitchfork together with the grain, hence they serve as handles; cf. Suk. 14*a*. (12) This one grape causes the sprig to be considered as a handle. (13) Not regarding this twig as a handle to the stalk of the broom.

THEREON, IT IS SUSCEPTIBLE. SIMILARLY, WITH PULSE:[1] IF THE PODS WERE STRIPPED FROM THE STEM IT IS CLEAN, BUT IF EVEN ONE POD ALONE REMAINS, IT IS UNCLEAN. R. ELEAZAR B. 'AZARIAH DECLARES [THE STALK] OF THE BEAN CLEAN,[2] BUT DECLARES UNCLEAN THE STALK OF OTHER PULSE,[3] SINCE IT IS OF USE[4] WHEN [THE PULSE] IS HANDLED.[5]

MISHNAH 6. STALKS OF FIGS AND DRIED FIGS, KELUSIM FIGS,[6] AND CAROBS BOTH CONTRACT AND IMPART UNCLEANNESS, AND ARE INCLUDED.[7] R. JOSE SAYS: ALSO THE STALKS OF THE GOURD,[8] OF PEARS AND PIPPINS,[9] QUINCES,[10] AND CRAB-APPLES.[11] THE STALKS OF THE GOURD[12] AND THE ARTICHOKE [TO THE LENGTH OF] ONE HANDBREADTH (R. ELEAZAR SON OF R. ZADOK SAYS: TWO HANDBREADTHS)—[ALL] THESE CONTRACT AND IMPART UNCLEANNESS; BUT ARE NOT INCLUDED.[13] AS FOR THE STALKS OF ALL OTHER FRUITS, THEY NEITHER CONTRACT NOR IMPART UNCLEANNESS.[14]

(1) Others render 'summer-fruits'. (2) Being of the large kind, they do not need the protection of the twig. (3) Being small, the twig of necessity acts as a kind of protection to them. (4) Lit., 'he desires'. (5) Accordingly, he wishes them to be attached to the sprig, which thus acts as a handle to them; Ḥul. 119*a*. (6) A species of dried figs, so Maim.; according to Rashi: a kind of pea or bean. *Aliter*: the fruit of the Judas tree. These were used for cooking purposes; Ned. 50*a*. *Aliter:* acorns. (7) To constitute the required egg's bulk, for occasionally they are eaten with the fruit. (8) A general name for cucumbers and pumpkins. These gourd-stalks are sometimes cooked together with the edible parts. (9) *Kerustemilin*. According to L., a kind of crab-apple; cf. Ma'as. I, 3 where it refers to the 'crustumenian pear'. (10) *Perishin* (lit., 'set aside, excellent'); they are so called because there is no species of fruit so well adapted for cooking as this (J. Kil. I, 27*a*); cf. Suk. 31*a*. (11) Medlars, a small and shrunken fruit. (12) Bert. stresses that the Mishnah only refers to the Greek species of gourd; for the stalks of others are very tiny. (13) With the food to constitute the required amount to convey uncleanness. (14) Needless to say, they are not included with the rest to constitute the egg's bulk.

'UḲẒIN

CHAPTER II

MISHNAH 1. LEAVES OF OLIVES PICKLED[1] TOGETHER WITH THE OLIVES REMAIN CLEAN,[2] FOR THEIR PICKLING WAS ONLY FOR THE SAKE OF APPEARANCES.[3] THE FIBROUS SUBSTANCE[4] ON A CUCUMBER AND THE FLOWER-LIKE SUBSTANCE THEREIN ARE CLEAN;[5] BUT R. JUDAH IS OF THE OPINION THAT AS LONG AS IT IS STILL LYING BEFORE THE MERCHANT, IT IS UNCLEAN.[6]

MISHNAH 2. ALL KINDS OF FRUIT-STONES BECOME UNCLEAN AND IMPART UNCLEANNESS BUT ARE NOT INCLUDED;[7] BUT THE STONES OF FRESH DATES,[8] EVEN WHEN DETACHED [FROM THE EDIBLE PART], ARE INCLUDED,[9] BUT THOSE OF DRIED DATES ARE NOT INCLUDED. ACCORDINGLY, THE PERICARP[10] OF DRIED DATES IS INCLUDED,[11] BUT THAT OF FRESH

(1) In wine or vinegar, or other preservative liquids. (2) I.e., they are insusceptible to uncleanness, as they are regarded neither as handle nor protection to the olives. (3) For when the leaves are still attached, the olives lend the appearance of having just been plucked, and serve as a guarantee for freshness. Thus his intention never was to eat the olive leaves, or to preserve the olives from getting spoiled. (4) A parasitic growth on shrubs. (5) Being neither handle nor protection. (6) While still unsold, this fibrous substance gives the cucumber the appearance of having been just plucked and proves more attractive to the purchaser. Accordingly, they may be regarded as a kind of protection to the fruit. In addition, they prevent the cucumber from being soiled by the fingers of intending purchasers whose custom it is to feel the fruit before buying. In this wise, they differ from the case first cited in our Mishnah concerning the leaves of the olives, with the ruling on which R. Judah agrees. (7) To constitute the required egg's bulk; these stones being considered as handles but not as protection. (8) Containing sap, they can be sucked in the mouth. (9) With the edible part, since their juice is acceptable. (10) The membraneous enclosure separating the stone of the date from the flesh. (11) With the edible part. In dry dates, the skin is thin and can be eaten with the fruit.

DATES IS NOT INCLUDED.[1] IF ONLY PART OF A FRUIT-STONE IS DETACHED, THEN ONLY THAT PART NEAR THE EDIBLE PORTION IS INCLUDED.[2] [SIMILARLY] WITH A BONE ON WHICH THERE IS FLESH, ONLY THAT PART THAT IS CLOSE TO THE EDIBLE PART IS INCLUDED. [IF THE BONE] HAS FLESH ONLY UPON ONE SIDE THEREOF, R. ISHMAEL SAYS: WE TAKE IT AS THOUGH [THE FLESH] ENCOMPASSES IT LIKE A RING;[3] BUT THE SAGES SAY: [ONLY] THAT PART CLOSE TO THE EDIBLE PART IS INCLUDED [AS IS THE CASE] FOR EXAMPLE WITH SAVORY,[4] HYSSOP AND THYME.[5]

MISHNAH 3. IF A POMEGRANATE OR MELON HAS ROTTED IN PART, [WHAT IS ROTTEN] IS NOT INCLUDED;[6] AND IF [THE FRUIT] IS SOUND AT EITHER END BUT HAS ROTTED IN THE MIDDLE, [WHAT IS ROTTEN] IS NOT INCLUDED.[7] THE NIPPLE OF A POMEGRANATE IS INCLUDED, BUT THE FIBROUS SUBSTANCE THEREOF IS NOT INCLUDED. R. ELEAZAR SAYS: ALSO THE COMB[8] [THEREOF] IS NOT SUSCEPTIBLE TO UNCLEANNESS.[9]

MISHNAH 4. ALL KINDS OF HUSKS CONTRACT AND IMPART UNCLEANNESS, AND ARE INCLUDED.[10] R. JUDAH SAYS: AN ONION HAS THREE SKINS: THE INNERMOST ONE WHETHER

(1) Being bitter, the husk is usually cast aside. (2) Part of the fresh fig was left with the fruit-stone, and the part near the edible portion was regarded as a protection. (3) And all that part which could be then encompassed is included. (4) A plant classified with the hyssop; Ma'as. III, 9; Sheb. VIII, 1. (5) The stalks close to the edible parts of these plants are included (Asheri). (6) To form the egg's bulk, since the rotted part must be cast away. (7) Since the rotted centre can in no wise be included as edible. V. L. for the necessity of adding this statement. (8) The sprouting hairs on the nipple of the pomegranate bear a striking resemblance to a comb. (9) For even when they are lopped off from the fruit, the fruit-stones are not revealed; hence, they cannot be regarded as a protection. In the case of the nipple, however, the fruit-stones are laid bare when that is cut off, and the fruit does suffer as a consequence. (10) To form the required bulk. Bert. excludes from this general statement the moist outward shells of nuts at the time of their gathering, for these also are not a protection; cf. Ḥul. 119*b* on the subject.

IT IS IN ITS ENTIRE STATE OR WHETHER IT BE PIERCED WITH HOLES[1] IS INCLUDED; THE MIDDLE ONE WHEN IT IS IN A WHOLE STATE IS INCLUDED, BUT WHEN IT IS PIERCED WITH HOLES IT IS NOT INCLUDED;[2] THE OUTERMOST SKIN IS IN EITHER CASE REGARDED AS INSUSCEPTIBLE TO UNCLEANNESS.[3]

MISHNAH 5. IF ONE CHOPS UP [FRUIT] FOR COOKING PURPOSES, EVEN IF [THE CHOPPING HAD] NOT BEEN COMPLETELY FINISHED,[4] IT IS NOT REGARDED AS CONNECTED. IF HIS INTENTION, HOWEVER, HAD BEEN TO PICKLE[5] OR TO BOIL IT,[6] OR TO SET IT ON THE TABLE,[7] THEN IT IS REGARDED AS CONNECTED.[8] IF HE BEGAN TO TAKE [THE PIECES] APART, [ONLY] THAT PART OF THE FOOD WHICH HE BEGAN TO TAKE APART IS NOT CONSIDERED A CONNECTIVE.[9] NUTS THAT HAD BEEN STRUNG TOGETHER,[10] OR ONIONS THAT HAD BEEN PILED TOGETHER, COUNT AS CONNECTIVES.[11] IF HE BEGAN TO TAKE THE NUTS APART,[12] OR TO STRIP THE ONIONS, ONLY THAT [ON WHICH HE BEGAN] IS NOT DEEMED AS CONNECTIVE.[13]

(1) Though such a state can scarcely be regarded as a protection to the edible part of the onion. (2) For unlike the innermost skin, it is not eaten. (3) Regardless of the fact whether it is whole or pierced. This skin is very thin and peels off when only touched by the hand; accordingly it can be regarded neither as handle nor as protection. (4) I.e., some of the pieces are still attached. Since in the process of cooking they will eventually become detached, they are already considered apart. (5) In vinegar or pungent salt water. (6) Lit., 'to seethe them'; i.e., to overboil them. For שליקה is a more intensive process than plain cooking, בישול. In the case of pickling and boiling intensively, they become hard again and do not fall apart as in the case of plain cooking. (7) Without chopping them up, separating them just sufficiently to enable his guests to take up separate portions, being content that they should be attached until such time as required. (8) Each one serving as a handle to the other, and because they are considered as one pile, since the cutting has not been complete. (9) And we do not surmise that since he began to separate some of them his intention was to do so to all. (10) On a thread to dry whilst they are still in a tender state. (11) Being considered as one pile. (12) A few nuts began to break, leaving a portion still attached. (13) For the others will soon follow suit.

[SHELLS OF] NUTS AND ALMONDS ARE CONSIDERED AS CONNECTIVES [WITH THE EDIBLE PART] UNTIL THEY ARE CRUSHED.[1]

MISHNAH 6. [THE SHELL OF] A ROASTED EGG[2] [IS CONSIDERED A CONNECTIVE][3] UNTIL IT IS CRACKED;[4] THAT OF A HARD-BOILED EGG [IS CONSIDERED A CONNECTIVE] UNTIL IT IS ENTIRELY BROKEN UP.[5] A MARROW-BONE SERVES AS A CONNECTIVE[6] UNTIL IT IS WHOLLY CRUSHED;[7] AND [THE RIND OF] A POMEGRANATE THAT HAS BEEN DIVIDED INTO HALVES SERVES AS CONNECTIVE UNTIL IT HAS BEEN KNOCKED WITH A STICK.[8] SIMILARLY, LOOSE STITCHES OF LAUNDRYMEN[9] OR A GARMENT THAT HAD BEEN STITCHED TOGETHER WITH THREADS OF MIXED STUFF,[10] SERVE AS CONNECTIVES UNTIL ONE BEGINS TO LOOSEN THEM.[11]

MISHNAH 7. THE [OUTER] LEAVES OF VEGETABLES IF THEY ARE GREEN[12] ARE INCLUDED,[13] BUT IF THEY HAVE WHITENED[14] THEY ARE NOT INCLUDED. R. ELEAZAR B. ZADOK SAYS: THE WHITE LEAVES OF CABBAGE ARE INCLUDED BECAUSE THEY ARE EDIBLE. SO ALSO THOSE OF LETTUCES,[15] BECAUSE THEY PRESERVE THE EDIBLE PART.

(1) For the shells, even when cracked, still serve as a protection to the nuts. (2) Or, 'lightly-boiled'. (3) For the smallest hole therein enables one to sip the contents of the egg still in a liquid state. (4) Cf. Ḥul. 92*b*. Once a crack has occurred, the liquid will find a way out through the hole, and the shell will no longer act as a protection. (5) For the egg will still remain within the shell, even if the latter suffers a severe crack. It is, therefore, a protection until completely broken. (6) With the marrow. (7) When it cannot serve as protection to the marrow. (8) To extract its edible seeds. (9) It was their custom loosely to sew the garments together so that they should not get lost, and then to separate them. (10) Cf. Par. XII, 9. His avowed intention was to unloose them later, for *kil'ayim* is forbidden in the Torah, but as long as they are sewn together they are counted as connectives. (11) Hence should one of the garments contract uncleanness, the other also is affected. Once he begins to loosen the stitches which bind them together, they can no longer be deemed as one garment. (12) When they are eaten. (13) With the edible parts. (14) I.e., when they have withered, a condition which renders them inedible. (15) Which though not eaten still serve as a protection.

MISHNAH 8. WITH REGARD TO THE LEEK-LIKE SPROUTS OR THE CENTRE SPROUTS OF ONIONS, IF THERE IS SAP IN THEM THEY ARE TO BE MEASURED AS THEY ARE;[1] IF THERE IS A VACUUM WITHIN THEM, IT MUST BE SQUEEZED TIGHTLY TOGETHER.[2] SPONGY BREAD[3] IS MEASURED AS IT IS,[1] BUT IF THERE IS A VACUUM WITHIN IT, IT MUST BE PRESSED FIRMLY. THE FLESH OF A CALF WHICH HAD SWOLLEN,[4] OR THE FLESH OF AN OLD [BEAST] THAT HAS SHRUNKEN IN SIZE, ARE MEASURED IN THE CONDITION THEY ARE IN.[5]

MISHNAH 9. A CUCUMBER PLANTED IN A POT[6] WHICH SO GREW TILL IT REACHED OUT OF THE POT IS NOT DEEMED SUSCEPTIBLE.[7] R. SIMEON SAID: WHAT IS THEREIN TO MAKE IT CLEAN?[8] NO;[9] THAT WHICH HAS ALREADY BECOME UNCLEAN CONTINUES IN ITS UNCLEANNESS,[10] AND ONLY THAT WHICH IS INSUSCEPTIBLE[11] CAN BE EATEN.

MISHNAH 10. VESSELS MADE OF CATTLE DUNG OR OF EARTH[12] THROUGH WHICH THE ROOTS CAN PENE-

(1) Viz., without squeezing the core as in the case of the vacuum. (2) In order to include the sap so as to obtain the egg's bulk necessary to impart uncleanness. (3) I.e., bread blown up like a sponge. (4) In the process of cooking, the flesh of the calf swells in dimension, whereas that of an old beast shrinks. (5) Though the calf's flesh may have been less than the size of an egg prior to the cooking, or the flesh of an old beast more, still we estimate them in their present condition; cf. Ṭoh. V, 7. (6) Which has no hole beneath, with the result that the cucumber has not the legal ruling applied to things growing directly out of the soil (v. next Mishnah). Our Mishnah deals with a case where the cucumber had already received contact with liquid. (7) Since the cucumber now reaches outside the pot, and only air separates it from the soil, even if that part of the cucumber within the pot had come into contact with defilement prior to its replanting, it now becomes clean, as is the law of all unclean seedlings that have been planted; v. Ter. IX, 7 (Bert.). (8) Why should that part within the pot which had become unclean now be declared clean? Is it not enough to pronounce just that part outside the pot clean, but that within as unclean, since the pot has no hole beneath? (9) R. Simeon is continuing his argument. (10) Viz., that part within the pot. (11) The part without the pot. (12) Unbaked clay. There are three utensils which do not contract uncleanness neither according to

TRATE,[1] DO NOT RENDER THE SEEDS SUSCEPTIBLE.[2] A PERFORATED PLANT-POT DOES NOT RENDER SEEDS SUSCEPTIBLE;[3] BUT IF IT HAS NO HOLE, THE SEEDS DO BECOME SUSCEPTIBLE.[4] WHAT SHOULD BE THE HOLE'S DIMENSION? SUCH THAT A SMALL ROOT CAN PUSH ITS WAY THROUGH. IF IT WAS FILLED WITH EARTH TO ITS BRIM,[5] IT IS DEEMED AS A BOARD WITHOUT AN EDGE.[6]

Biblical nor Rabbinical injunction: vessels of stone, cattle-dung or unbaked clay.

(1) Though the vessels themselves are not actually perforated, yet their sides are so thin that their roots within can force their way out. Hence does the Mishnah omit stone vessels, the sides of which can obviously resist the drive of the roots outwards. (2) For such vessels are accounted as if they had been part of the soil; hence the objects within are insusceptible to uncleanness. (3) Being considered as if growing directly out of the soil. Having a hole, which connects the plant directly with the soil beneath, the pot loses the status of a vessel. (4) For then it is regarded as a vessel, and the plants therein have the same ruling as those that have already been plucked from the soil. (5) The unperforated plant pot was filled with earth, and thus not accounted at all as a vessel. (6) I.e., an edge, by which a flat utensil is made into a vessel-like receptacle. Because it has no such receptacle it cannot be considered susceptible, and is regarded as the soil itself from which it is separated on the four sides thereof only by air; cf. Kel. II, 3 where the general principle is laid down that 'those earthenware vessels which have no inner part, no regard is paid to their outward part'.

'UḲẒIN

CHAPTER III

MISHNAH 1. SOME THINGS NEED TO BE RENDERED SUSCEPTIBLE [TO UNCLEANNESS],[1] BUT THEY DO NOT NEED INTENTION,[2] [WHILST OTHERS NEED] INTENTION AND TO BE RENDERED SUSCEPTIBLE. [STILL OTHERS THERE ARE THAT] NEED INTENTION, BUT DO NOT NEED TO BE RENDERED SUSCEPTIBLE, [WHILST OTHERS THAT] NEED NEITHER TO BE RENDERED SUSCEPTIBLE NOR INTENTION. SUCH EDIBLES THAT ARE DESIGNATED AS HUMAN FOOD NEED TO BE RENDERED SUSCEPTIBLE, BUT DO NOT NEED INTENTION.[3]

MISHNAH 2. THAT WHICH HAS BEEN SEVERED FROM A MAN,[4] BEAST, WILD ANIMAL, BIRD, OR FROM THE CARRION OF AN UNCLEAN BIRD,[5] AND THE FAT IN VILLAGES,[6] AND (ALL KINDS OF WILD VEGETABLES,[7] SAVE TRUFFLES[8] OR

(1) By coming in contact with any one of the seven liquids enumerated in Maksh. VI, 4. (2) To be used as food so as to make them subject to rules of food uncleanness. (3) Since they will eventually be used for food, though not set aside for the purpose now. Even if such fruit had not been specifically plucked for human consumption, but had fallen of its own accord, it becomes unclean after having been rendered susceptible. (4) Only the entire limb from a living being makes objects unclean, but not the flesh. Hence both contact with liquid and intention are required. If the flesh had been cut off to throw to a dog to eat, it is deemed sufficient intention; cf. Ker. 21*a*. (5) For though dead, no major defilement attaches to it; Ṭoh. I, 3. Accordingly it requires to be rendered susceptible both in town and village. (6) Where it is not usual for fat to be eaten, hence intention is required. In towns, however, where among the large throngs there are sure to be those who also eat fat, no specific intention is required; but in both places it needs to be rendered susceptible. (V. discussion in L.). (7) Growing of their own accord without having been sown; hence not specified for human food. (8) Heb. *shemarḳa'im*, 'a species of very acrid onions' (Maim.).

FUNGUS[1]—R. JUDAH SAYS, SAVE FIELD-LEEKS,[2] PURSLANE[3] AND THE ASPHODEL.[4] AND R. SIMEON SAYS, SAVE CARDOON,[5] AND R. JOSE SAYS, SAVE ACORNS[6]—BEHOLD ALL THESE[7] NEED BOTH INTENTION AND TO BE RENDERED SUSCEPTIBLE [TO UNCLEANNESS].[8]

MISHNAH 3. THE CARRION OF AN UNCLEAN BEAST AT ALL PLACES,[9] AND OF A CLEAN BIRD IN VILLAGES, NEED INTENTION[10] BUT DO NOT NEED TO BE RENDERED SUSCEPTIBLE.[11] THE CARRION OF A CLEAN BEAST IN ALL PLACES,[12] AND THAT OF A CLEAN BIRD, AND ALSO FAT[13] IN THE MARKET PLACES, REQUIRE NEITHER INTENTION[14] NOR TO BE RENDERED SUSCEPTIBLE.[15] R. SIMEON SAYS, ALSO[16] [THE CARRION OF] THE CAMEL, RABBIT, CONEY OR PIG.

(1) Though these two plants likewise grow wild, yet on account of their being occasionally served as human food, require contact with liquids, but no specific intention. (2) As also not requiring intention. (3) A low, succulent herb used in salads. (4) A genus of liliaceous plants. (5) A composite kitchen garden plant allied to the artichoke; a species of edible thistles. (6) Heb. *balosin*. Jast. emends to *bulbus*, and renders 'a bulbous root, a delicious kind of onion'; (7) I.e., all enumerated things apart from those excepted by the three Rabbis, whose contention was that since they are sometimes eaten, no specific intention is required. (8) This intention must precede the contact with the liquid (v. L.). (9) For they are not usually eaten, even in towns. (10) To convey food uncleanness even where it is less than an olive's bulk, provided it was combined with some foodstuff of less than an egg's bulk, v. Ker. 21*a*. (11) Being already unclean *per se;* v. *infra* 9, n. 7. For the purpose of elucidation, this Rabbinic ruling must be cited: carrion, whether of wild animals, clean or unclean cattle, imparts uncleanness by contact and carrying. The carrion of a clean bird has but the one uncleanness—that when there is an olive's bulk thereof in the eater's gullet (v. Ṭoh. I, 1). The carrion of an unclean bird, of fish, clean and unclean, and of locusts, have no uncleanness at all. (12) Being regarded as food. (13) Sc. carrion fat of an unclean beast which defiles as the flesh does; v. however Rashi, Ker. 21*a*. (14) Since there are bound to be some people who occasionally eat such food. (15) Since it will later be the cause of major defilement (gullet uncleanness), contact with liquids is non-essential. (16) As not requiring intention in the towns, since there are bound to be some therein who eat even these things. Specific intention is only required

MISHNAH 4. THE DILL[1] STALK AFTER HAVING GIVEN ITS TASTE TO A DISH IS NO LONGER SUBJECT TO THE LAWS OF TERUMAH,[2] AND ALSO NO LONGER IMPARTS FOOD UNCLEANNESS.[3] THE YOUNG SPROUTS OF THE SERVICE-TREE,[4] OF GARDEN CRESS,[5] OR LEAVES OF THE WILD ARUM,[6] DO NOT IMPART FOOD UNCLEANNESS UNTIL THEY ARE SWEETENED.[7] R. SIMEON SAYS: ALSO [THE LEAVES OF] THE COLOCYNTH ARE LIKE THEM.

MISHNAH 5. COSTUS,[8] AMOMUM,[9] PRINCIPAL SPICES, [ROOTS OF] CROWFOOT,[10] ASAFOETIDA,[11] PEPPER AND LOZENGES MADE OF SAFFRON[12] MAY BE BOUGHT WITH TITHE MONEY,[13] BUT THEY DO NOT CONVEY FOOD UNCLEANNESS.[14] SO R. AKIBA. SAID R. JOḤANAN B. NURI TO HIM: IF THEY MAY BE BOUGHT WITH [SECOND] TITHE MONEY, THEN WHY SHOULD THEY NOT IMPART FOOD UNCLEANNESS? AND IF THEY DO NOT IMPART FOOD UNCLEANNESS, THEN THEY

in such cases where the food is not used for human consumption whatsoever. R. Simeon differs from the Tanna of our Mishnah who generalized that: 'the carrion of unclean beasts anywhere requires attention'.

(1) Of *terumah*. An umbelliferous annual yellow-flowered herb; cf. Shab. 126*b*; M. Ḳ. 3*a*. (2) And, accordingly, a non-priest eating thereof is not deemed culpable. (3) For once it had been cooked all its taste departs and it becomes uneatable. (4) The interior of which is eaten as a relish, after they have been pickled. (5) *Aliter:* 'candy-tuft', a plant with white, pink or purple flowers in flat tufts. (6) A plant similar to colocasia, with edible leaves and not bearing beans; usually classified with onions and garlic. (7) And then they become edible. (8) The name of a fragrant root or shrub, forming one of the ingredients of frankincense. (9) An Indian spice; cf. Gen. R. XLV, where amomum is prescribed as a medicine for sterility. (10) Used as a spice, but considered poisonous for beasts. (11) An umbelliferous plant used as a resin, or in leaves for a spice and for medicinal purposes. (12) Or 'safflower', a thistle-like plant yielding red dye, used especially for rouge. (13) Refers to the second tithe, which the owner had to take to Jerusalem there to consume; or else he must redeem it by putting aside coins equivalent to their value plus one-fifth, after which that produce becomes free for ordinary use. The coins themselves assume the sanctity of the tithe and must also be taken to Jerusalem to buy therewith food or peace-offerings, and there to be consumed in cleanness. (14) Since they are not used for food but only for flavouring,

SHOULD ALSO NOT BE BOUGHT WITH [SECOND] TITHE MONEY.[1]

MISHNAH 6. UNRIPE FIGS OR GRAPES, R. AKIBA SAYS, CONVEY FOOD UNCLEANNESS; BUT R. JOḤANAN B. NURI SAYS: [THIS IS ONLY] WHEN THEY HAVE REACHED THE SEASON WHEN THEY ARE LIABLE TO TITHES.[2] OLIVES AND GRAPES THAT HAVE HARDENED,[3] BETH SHAMMAI SAY, BECOME SUSCEPTIBLE TO UNCLEANNESS,[4] WHEREAS BETH HILLEL SAY: THEY ARE INSUSCEPTIBLE.[5] BLACK CUMMIN, BETH SHAMMAI SAY, IS NOT SUSCEPTIBLE, BUT BETH HILLEL SAY: IT IS SUSCEPTIBLE.[6] [THEIR DISPUTE ALSO EXTENDS] TO [THEIR LIABILITY TO] TITHES.[7]

MISHNAH 7. THE TERMINAL BUD OF A PALM[8] IS LIKE WOOD IN EVERY RESPECT,[9] SAVE THAT IT MAY BE BOUGHT FOR [SECOND] TITHE MONEY.[10] UNRIPENED DATES[11] ARE CONSIDERED FOOD,[12] BUT ARE EXEMPT FROM TITHES.[13]

MISHNAH 8. WHEN DO FISH BECOME SUSCEPTIBLE TO UNCLEANNESS?[14] BETH SHAMMAI SAY: AFTER THEY HAVE

(1) His argument being that since Deut. XIV, 26 stresses: '*And thou shalt bestow thy money . . . . and thou shalt eat*', the obvious implication is that only such things that can be eaten in their natural condition may be bought for the money. (2) Each fruit has a different season for tithing purposes; Ma'as. I, 1*ff*. (3) Prior to their ripening. (4) Still being regarded as food on account of the oil therein. (5) Not considered as food, since none will take the trouble of extracting the oil therefrom. (6) Cf. Ber. 40*a*. (7) According to Beth Shammai it will not be liable to tithes, since it is not susceptible to uncleanness, not being regarded as food. (8) *Ḳor* is the marrow or white heart of a palm or cabbage-tree. During the summer months it is soft and edible, but during the winter it hardens exceedingly. (9) V. 'Er. 28*b*; hence it is not susceptible to food uncleanness. (10) Being considered as food that had received its growth directly from the soil. (11) *Kofniyoth* is the inflorescense of palms, a date-berry in its early stages; cf. M. Sh. I, 14 where they are considered fruit in every respect. (12) For the purpose of imparting uncleanness. (13) Because the fruit has not yet ripened. (14) For as long as they are still alive they are not susceptible to, and cannot impart, uncleanness.

BEEN CAUGHT.[1] BETH HILLEL SAY: ONLY AFTER THEY ARE DEAD.[2] R. AKIBA SAYS: [IT ALL DEPENDS] IF THEY CAN STILL LIVE.[3] IF A BRANCH OF A FIG TREE WAS BROKEN OFF, BUT IT WAS STILL ATTACHED BY ITS BARK,[4] R. JUDAH SAYS: [THE FRUIT THEREON] IS STILL NOT SUSCEPTIBLE TO UNCLEANNESS; BUT THE SAGES SAY: [IT ALL DEPENDS] WHETHER THEY COULD STILL LIVE.[5] GRAIN THAT HAD BEEN UPROOTED, EVEN THOUGH IT BE ATTACHED TO THE SOIL BY THE SMALLEST OF ROOTS, IS NOT SUSCEPTIBLE TO UNCLEANNESS.[6]

MISHNAH 9. THE FAT [OF THE CARCASE] OF A CLEAN BEAST IS NOT REGARDED AS UNCLEAN WITH CARRION UNCLEANNESS;[7] FOR THIS REASON IT MUST FIRST BE MADE SUSCEPTIBLE. THE FAT OF AN UNCLEAN BEAST, HOWEVER, IS REGARDED AS UNCLEAN WITH CARRION UNCLEANNESS;[8] FOR THIS REASON IT NEED NOT BE MADE AT FIRST SUSCEPTIBLE.[9] AS FOR UNCLEAN FISH AND UNCLEAN LOCUSTS,[10] INTENTION IS REQUIRED IN VILLAGES.[11]

(1) When they are already counted as dead, though still struggling in their nets. As fish do not require ritual slaughter, their death is only a matter of course. (2) Since nobody eats live fish, they can only be considered susceptible after they are dead. (3) I.e., if they can still survive after they have been taken out of the net and cast back into the sea, then they are not susceptible. (4) Thus the figs on the branch are still connected with the tree and regarded as rooted to the soil; cf. Ḥul. 126*b*. The same applies to other fruits, but the bark of the fig is mentioned on account of its thickness, and even when the bough is broken it still remains attached to the tree. (5) I.e., whether the fruit would grow again if fastened to the tree. (6) Maintaining that this is sufficient to make the grain sprout afresh. (7) This Mishnah is an explanation of *supra* III, 3. The guiding principle is that if eventually it will become a source of major defilement (so as to convey uncleanness to men and vessels), no preliminary contact with one of the seven liquids is required. (8) Provided, of course, it has the required egg's bulk. The Bible declared clean only the fat of the clean beast that afterwards became carrion (v. Lev. VII, 25), but the fat of an unclean beast defiles together with the flesh thereof. (9) Before it imparts food uncleanness; but there must be intention since it is not usually eaten; v. Mishnah 3, n. 11. (10) That are dead. (11) But not in the towns. Contact with liquids they must have everywhere, seeing that they do not carry with them any major defilement.

MISHNAH 10. A BEE-HIVE,[1] SAYS R. ELIEZER, IS TREATED AS IF IT WERE IMMOVABLE PROPERTY;[2] HENCE A PROZBUL[3] MAY BE WRITTEN ON ITS SECURITY; IT IS ALSO NOT SUSCEPTIBLE TO UNCLEANNESS AS LONG AS IT REMAINS IN ITS OWN PLACE.[4] THE ONE WHO SCRAPES HONEY THEREFROM ON A SABBATH DAY BECOMES LIABLE TO A SIN-OFFERING.[5] BUT THE SAGES SAY: IT IS NOT TO BE TREATED AS IF IT WERE IMMOVABLE PROPERTY, AND HENCE NO PROZBUL MAY BE WRITTEN ON ITS SECURITY; IT IS SUSCEPTIBLE EVEN IF IT REMAINS IN ITS OWN PLACE; AND THE ONE WHO SCRAPES HONEY THEREFROM ON THE SABBATH IS EXEMPT [FROM A SIN-OFFERING].[6]

MISHNAH 11. WHEN DO HONEYCOMBS BECOME SUSCEPTIBLE TO UNCLEANNESS ON ACCOUNT OF THEIR BEING REGARDED AS LIQUIDS?[7] BETH SHAMMAI SAY: FROM THE MOMENT HE BEGINS TO SMOKE[8] THE BEES OUT; BUT BETH HILLEL SAY: FROM THE TIME AFTER [THE HONEYCOMB] HAS BEEN BROKEN.[9]

MISHNAH 12. R. JOSHUA B. LEVI SAID: IN THE WORLD TO COME[10] THE HOLY ONE, BLESSED BE HE, WILL MAKE EACH

(1) Cf. Shebi, X, 7. (2) And can, therefore, be acquired with the three legal procedures of money, document and usucaption. (3) Cf. Shebi. X, 6; Giṭ. 37*a*; v. Glos. (4) Being then treated as if it were actually attached to the soil. (5) As in the case of plucking anything rooted to the soil on the Sabbath. (6) Thus regarding the bee-hive in every respect as something entirely detached from the soil. The reference is to a hive which is just lying on the ground, uncemented to the soil with lime. (7) For as long as the honey is in the hive it is regarded as food (v. previous Mishnah), and subject to the regulations of food uncleanness. As a liquid, however, it contracts first grade uncleanness if touched by anything unclean, v. Par. VIII, 7. (8) He sets twigs on fire to drive out bees from the hive. Maim.: 'He heats the honeycomb in order to make its honey sweeter'. *Aliter*: 'When he stirs up strife with the bees to drive them out'. *Aliter:* 'When he contemplates scraping out the honey'. (9) When he is about to scrape the honey out of the hive, he cuts it with a knife and extracts therefrom the honeycomb. This act is described as a breaking of the honeycomb. (10) Since this Mishnah sets the

RIGHTEOUS PERSON TO INHERIT THREE HUNDRED AND TEN WORLDS, FOR IT IS WRITTEN: 'THAT I MAY CAUSE THOSE THAT LOVE ME TO INHERIT YESH;[1] AND THAT I MAY FILL THEIR TREASURIES'.[2] R. SIMEON B. ḤALAFTA SAID: THE HOLY ONE, BLESSED BE HE, FOUND NO VESSEL THAT COULD CONTAIN BLESSING FOR ISRAEL SAVE THAT OF PEACE, AS IT IS WRITTEN: 'THE LORD WILL GIVE STRENGTH UNTO HIS PEOPLE; THE LORD WILL BLESS HIS PEOPLE WITH PEACE'.[3]

seal on the entire Talmud, it was thought appropriate to indicate the heavenly blessing to be meted out in the world to come as a reward of its long and arduous study. In some editions this last Mishnah is omitted.

(1) יש, (E. V. '*substance*') numerically equivalent to 310. This is a recognized Rabbinic exegetic device called *Gematria;* cf. Aboth III, 19. The pleasure awaiting him who has made the study of the Torah his '*chief delight*' and his '*meditation day and night*' will be 310 times greater than any kind of earthly pleasure. (2) Prov. VIII, 21. The entire chapter is devoted to the importance of a study of the Torah. (3) Ps. XXIX, 11.

GLOSSARY

INDEX OF SCRIPTURAL REFERENCES

GENERAL INDEX

TRANSLITERATION OF HEBREW LETTERS

ABBREVIATIONS

GLOSSARY

AGGADAH (Lit., 'tale', 'lesson'); the name given to those sections of Rabbinic literature which contain homilectic expositions of the Bible, stories, legends, folk-lore, anecdotes or maxims. Opposed to *halachah*, q.v.

'AM HA-AREẒ pl. *'amme ha-areẓ*, (lit., 'people of the land', 'country people'); the name given in Rabbinic literature to (*a*) a person who through ignorance was careless in the observance of the laws of Levitical purity and of those relating to the priestly and Levitical gifts. In this sense opposed to *ḥaber*, q.v.; (*b*) an illiterate or uncultured man, as opposed to *talmid ḥakam*, q.v.

BARAITHA (Lit., 'outside'); a teaching or a tradition of the Tannaim that has been excluded from the Mishnah and incorporated in a later collection compiled by R. Ḥiyya and R. Oshaiah, generally introduced by 'Our Rabbis taught', or, 'It has been taught'.

BETH PERAS. An area (of a square *peras* = half the length of a furrow) regarded as unclean owing to crushed bones scattered in it from a ploughed grave.

BOGERETH. A girl from the age of twelve and a half years plus one day onwards.

DENAR. *Denarius*, a silver or gold coin, the former being worth one twenty-fourth (according to others one twenty-fifth) of the latter.

'ERUB (Lit., 'mixture'); a quantity of food, enough for two meals, placed (*a*) 2000 cubits from the town boundary, so as to extend the Sabbath limit by that distance; (*b*) in a room or in a court-yard to enable all the residents to carry to and fro in the court-yard on Sabbath.

GEMARA (Lit., 'completion' or 'learning'). The traditions, discussions and rulings of the Amoras, based mainly on the Mishnah and forming (*a*) the Babylonian Talmud and (*b*) the Palestinian Talmud.

ḤABER. 'Fellow', 'associate', opp. to *'am ha-areẓ* (q.v.); one scrupulous in the observance of the law, particularly in relation to ritual cleanness and the separation of the priestly and Levitical dues.

HALACHAH (Lit., 'step', 'guidance') (*a*) the final decision of the Rabbis, whether based on tradition or argument, on disputed rules of conduct; (*b*) those sections of Rabbinic literature which deal with legal questions, as opposed to the *Aggadah*.

ḤALIẒAH (Lit., 'drawing off'); the ceremony of taking off the shoe of the brother of a husband who has died childless. (V. Deut. XXV, 5-9.)

ḤALLAH. The portion of the dough which belongs to the priest (v. Num. XV, 20f); in the Diaspora this is not given to the priest but burnt.

HEḲDESH. Any object consecrated to the Sanctuary.

HESSEṬ (Lit., 'shaking'); levitical uncleanness caused through the vibration of an unclean object.

HIN. Measure of capacity equal to three *ḳabs* or twelve *logs*.

ḤULLIN (Lit., 'profane'); ordinary unhallowed food, as opposed to *terumah*, q.v.; unconsecrated animals, as opposed to *heḳdesh*, q.v.

ḲAB. Measure of capacity equal to four *logs* or one sixth of a *se'ah*.

KARMELITH. An area which is neither a public nor a private domain, and which is subject to special laws in respect of the Sabbath and the legal acquisition of objects that happen to be within its limits.

KOR. A measure of capacity = thirty *se'ahs* (q.v.).

LOG. A liquid messure equal to a quarter of a *ḳab* (q.v.), or the space occupied by six eggs, c. 549 cubic centimetres.

ME'ILAH. Illegal or improper use of consecrated objects (v. Lev. V, 15ff).

MIDRAS (Lit., 'treading', 'place of treading'). It denotes uncleanness of the first degree ('Father of uncleanness') contracted by an object on which a gonorrhoeist (more exactly those mentioned in Lev. XII, 2; XV, 2, 25) sits, lies, rides or leans against. Any object fit for, and usually used as a seat, cover, etc. is susceptible to *midras*-uncleanness.

MIḲWEH (Lit., 'a gathering [of water]'); a ritual bath containing not less than forty *se'ahs* of water.

MIN pl. *minim*, (lit., 'kind', 'species'); (*a*) a heretic, esp. (*b*) a member of the sect of the early Jewish Christians.

MISHMAR (rt. SHaMaR, 'to keep'), a guard of priests and Levites representing one of the eight divisions which carried on the Temple services in rotation. The *mishmar* again was subdivided into smaller groups each being designated *beth ab*, q.v.

MISHNAH (rt. SHaNaH, 'to learn', 'to repeat'), (*a*) the collection of the statements, discussions and Biblical interpretations of the Tannaim in the form edited by R. Judah the Patriarch c. 200; (*b*) similar minor collections by previous editors; (*c*) a single clause or paragraph the author of which was a Tanna.

NOTHAR ('left over'); portions of sacrifices left over after the prescribed time within which they must be eaten.

OHEL (Lit., 'tent'); technical name for the uncleanness conveyed by a dead human body, or part of it, to men or utensils which are under the same tent or roof.

PROSBUL. Perhaps from προσβολή, or an abbreviation of πρὸς βουλή or βουλευτῶν; a form of declaration before the Beth din by means of which a creditor, provided he possessed some landed property, could secure exemption from the laws of Sabbatical release (v. Deut. XV, 2) and thus retain his right to the collection of his debts after the Sabbatical year had elapsed.

SE'AH. Measure of capacity, equal to six *ḳabs*.

SEGAN. The title given to the Deputy High Priest.

SOṬAH. A married woman suspected of infidelity who has been formally warned by her husband.

TALMID ḤAKAM (Lit., 'disciple of the wise'); scholar, student of the Torah.

TALMUD (Lit., 'teaching', 'learning') applies (*a*) to the Gemara (q.v.) or (*b*) generally to the Mishnah and Gemara combined.

ṬEBUL YOM (Lit., 'bathed during the day'); a person who has bathed to cleanse himself at the end of the period of his defilement, but who must wait until sunset to regain his ritual purity (Lev. XXII, 7).

TEFILIN. Phylacteries; small cases containing passages from the Scripture and affixed to the forehead and arm during the recital of morning prayers, in accordance with Deut. VI, 8.

TERUMAH. 'That which is lifted or separated'; the heave-offering given from the yields of the yearly harvests, from certain sacrifices, and from the *shekels* collected in a special chamber in the Temple (*terumath ha-lishkah*). *Terumah gedolah* (great offering): the first levy on the produce of the year given to the priest (v. Num. XVIII, 8ff). Its quantity varied according to the generosity of the owner, who could give one-fortieth, one fiftieth, or one-sixtieth of his harvest. *Terumath ma'aser* (heave-offering of the tithe): the heave-offering given to the priest by the Levite from the tithes he receives (v. Num. XVIII, 25ff).

ṬREFA or ṬEREFA (Lit., 'torn'); (*a*) an animal torn by a wild beast; (*b*) any animal suffering from a serious organic disease, whose meat is forbidden even if it has been ritually slaughtered.

ZAB. (fem. ZABAH). The biblical term for a person who has experienced seminal emission (Lev. XV, 2).

SCRIPTURAL REFERENCES

GENESIS

EXODUS

LEVITICUS

GENERAL INDEX*

A

B

* An Index of Rabbinical Names will be provided in the special Index Volume to be published on completion of the translation of the entire Talmud.

I

J

K

L

M

P

Q

R

S

T

TRANSLITERATION OF HEBREW LETTERS

א (in middle of word)	=	'
ב	=	b
ו	=	w
ח	=	ḥ
ט	=	ṭ
כ	=	k
ע	=	'
פ	=	f
צ	=	ẓ
ק	=	ḳ
ת	=	th

Full particulars regarding the method and scope of the translation are given in the Editor's Introduction.

ABBREVIATIONS

Alfasi	R. Isaac b. Jacob Alfasi (1013-1103).
Aruk	Talmudic Dictionary by R. Nathan b. Jehiel of Rome (d. 1106).
Asheri	R. Asher b. Jeḥiel (1250-1327).
A.Z.	'Abodah Zarah.
b.	ben, bar: son of.
B.B.	Baba Bathra.
BaḤ.	Bayith Ḥadash, Glosses by R. Joel b. Samuel Sirkes (1561-1640).
Beḳ.	Beḳoroth.
Ber.	Berakoth.
B.Ḳ.	Baba Ḳamma.
B.M.	Baba Meẓi'a.
Cur. ed(d).	Current edition(s).
D.S.	*Dikduke Soferim* by R. Rabbinowicz.
'Ed.	'Eduyyoth.
E.J.	*Encyclopaedia Judaica.*
'Er.	'Erubin.
E. V.	English Version.
Giṭ.	Giṭṭin.
Glos.	Glossary.
Ḥag.	Ḥagigah.
Hor.	Horayoth.
Ḥul.	Ḥullin.
J.E.	*Jewish Encyclopedia.*
J.T.	Jerusalem Talmud.
Jast.	M. Jastrow's Dictionary of the Targumim, the Talmud Bible and Yerushalmi, and the Midrashic Literature.
Keth.	Kethuboth.
Ḳid.	Ḳiddushin.
Ma'as.	Ma'asroth.
Mak.	Makkoth.
Meg.	Megillah.
Men.	Menaḥoth.
MGWJ.	*Monatsschrift für Geschichte und Wissenschaft des Judentums.*
M.Sh.	Ma'aser Sheni.
MS.M.	Munich Codex of the Talmud.
Naz.	Nazir.
Ned.	Nedarim.
Nid.	Niddah.
Obermeyer	Obermeyer J., *Die Landschaft Babylonien.*
P.B.	*The authorized Daily Prayer Book,* S. Singer.

Pes.	Pesaḥim.
R.	Rab, Rabban, Rabbenu, Rabbi.
Rashal	Notes and Glosses on the Talmud by R. Solomon Luria (d. 1573).
Rashi	Commentary of R. Isaac Yiẓḥaḳi (d. 1105).
R.H.	Rosh Hashannah.
R.V.	Revised version of the Bible.
Sanh.	Sanhedrin.
Shab.	Shabbath.
Sheḳ.	Sheḳalim.
Sonc. ed.	English Translation of the Babylonian Talmud, Soncino Press, London.
Soṭ.	Soṭah.
Suk.	Sukkah.
TA.	*Talmudische Archäologie*, by S. Krauss.
Ta'an.	Ta'anith.
Ter.	Terumoth.
Tosaf.	Tosafoth.
Tosef.	Tosefta.
Wilna Gaon	Notes by Elijah of Wilna (1720-1797) in the Wilna editions of the Talmud.
Yeb.	Yebamoth.
Zeb.	Zebaḥim.